ISBN 978-0-282-93557-3
PIBN 10873896

BOOK VI.

THE ASHTÁDHYÁYÍ OF PÁṆINI.

TRANSLATED INTO ENGLISH

BY

SRISA CHANDRA VASU, B. A.,

Provincial Civil Service, N. W. P.

Vol. II

Benares:

PUBLISHED BY SINDHU CHARAN BOSE,

at the Panini Office,

1897.

TO

Hon'ble Sir John Edge, Kt. Q. C.,

CHIEF JUSTICE OF THE NORTH-WESTERN PROVINCES,

THIS WORK

IS,

WITH HIS LORDSHIP'S PERMISSION,

AND IN RESPECTFUL APPRECIATION OF HIS LORDSHIP'S SERVICES TO THE CAUSE OF ADMINISTRATION OF JUSTICE AND OF EDUCATION

IN

THESE PROVINCES,

Dedicated

BY HIS LORDSHIP'S HUMBLE SERVANT

THE TRANSLATOR.

ओ३म् ।

अथ षष्ठाध्यायस्य प्रथमः पादः ।

BOOK SIXTH.

CHAPTER FIRST.

एकाचो द्वे प्रथमस्य ॥ १ ॥ पदानि ॥ एक, अचः, द्वे, प्रथमस्य, ॥

वृत्तिः ॥ अधिकारो ऽयम् । एकाच इति च द्वे इति च प्रथमस्येति च त्रितयमधिकृतं वेदितव्यम । इत उत्तरं यद्वक्ष्यामः प्राक्संप्रसारणविधानात् तत्रैकाचः प्रथमस्य द्वे भवत इत्येवं तद्वेदितव्यम् । वक्ष्यति लिटि धातोरनभ्यासस्येति । तत्र धातोरवयवस्यानभ्यासस्य प्रथमस्यैकाचो द्वे भवतः ॥

1. In the room of the first portion, containing a single vowel, there are two.

Upto Sûtra VI. I. 12 inclusive it is to be understood that for the first syllable two are to be made, i. e, the first syllable is to be reduplicated. This is an adhikâra sûtra: all the three words viz एकाचः, and द्वे and प्रथमस्य are to be read in the subsequent sûtras upto VI. I. 12, before the rule of Samprasârana begins. Thus Sûtra VI. I. 8 says "when लिट् follows, of an unreduplicated verbal root". The sense of this sûtra is incomplete, unless we supply the three words of this sûtra, when it will read thus: "when लिट् follows, there are two in the room of the first portion, containing a single vowel of an unreduplicated verbal root". Thus from जागृ:—जजागार (जागृ + णल् IV. 3. 82 = जा + जागृ + अ = ज + जागर् + अ VII. 4. 59 = जजागार "he awoke"). So also पपाच्, इयाय, आर from the roots पच्, इ and ऋ ॥ The reduplication takes place through the force of the affix that follows. Thus the affixes of the Perfect Tense (लिट्), the Desiderative (सन्), the Intensive (यङ्), the श्लु vikaraṇa, the Aorist in चङ्; all cause reduplication.

The word एकाच means that which consists of one vowel (अच्) ॥ When a stem or root consists of more than one vowel (is a dissyllabic or polysyllabic root), then the एकाच् प्रथमः will be the *first syllable:* as in जागृ the portion जा is the प्रथम एकाच् 'the first portion consisting of one vowel'. When a root consists of a single vowel, as इ 'to go', then strictly speaking there cannot be any portion which may be called first (प्रथम) or ekâch consisting of a single vowel). Here, however, will this rule be applied and इ will be reduplicated, according to the maxim "व्यपदेशिवदेकस्मिन्"—"An operation which affects something on account of some special designation which for certain reasons attaches to the latter, affects likewise that which stands alone and to which therefore, just because the reasons for it do not exist, that special designation does not attach". So also in पच् there is no *first* syllable strictly speaking, but still the rule will apply under the above maxim. In making Reduplications the Rule I. 1. 59 should always be borne in mind. Thus पच्+अ (णल् of लिट्) =पाच् पाच्+अ=प पाच्+अ (VII. 4. 59 and 60)=पपाच ॥

The word द्वि in the sûtra indicates that the very word-form is to be doubled or pronounced-twice, and not that another word of similar meaning is substituted. In fact this is not a rule ordaining *substitution* of two, in the room of one; but of the *repetition* of the one. Compare VIII. 1. 1.

अजादेर्द्वितीयस्य ॥ २ ॥ पदानि ॥ अच्, आदेः, द्वितीयस्य ॥

वृत्तिः ॥ प्रथमद्विर्वचनापवादो ऽयम् । अजादेर्द्वितीयस्यैकाचो द्विर्वचनमधिक्रियते । अच् आदिर्यस्य धातो-स्तदवयवस्य द्वितीयस्यैकाचो द्वे भवतः ॥

2. Of that whose first syllable begins with a vowel, there are two in the room of the second portion containing a single vowel.

This debars the reduplication of the *first* syllable. In a verbal root beginning with a vowel, and consisting of more than one syllable, the *second* syllable is to be reduplicated and not the first. Thus the सनन्त root अटिष, (अट्+सन्=अट्+इट्+सन् VII. 2. 35=अटिष), reduplicates the second syllable टिष् and the 3rd per. sing is अटि टिषति, the ष् being elided by VII. 4. 60: and स changed to ष by VIII. 3. 59. So also अशिशिषति, अरिरिषति ॥ The last form is thus evolved, ऋ+सन्=ऋ+इट्+सन् (VII. 2. 74)=अर+इ+स (VII. 3. 84, and VI. 1. 51). Here now we have to make reduplication, and if I. 1. 59 be applied, then since a vowel affix इ follows, the reduplication of अर should take place i. e. the ऋ the sthânî should be reduplicated. But we have explained the sûtra द्विर्वचनेऽचि I. 1. 59, by the phrase द्विर्वचननिमित्तेऽचि, i. e. the vowel-affix causing reduplication. Here the vowel-affix इट् does not cause reduplication, but the consonant-affix सन् that does so. Therefore rule I. 1. 59 does not apply, for इट् itself is a कार्यी, and the maxim applies कार्यमनुभवन्हि कार्यी निमित्ततया नाश्रीयते "surely that which undergoes an operation can, so for as it undergoes that operation, not be made the cause of the application of a grammatical rule". Thus from the root शीङ् is formed शयिता ; here the root शी is guṇated before the augment इट्. Rule I. 1. 5 declaring the prohibition of guṇation with regard to किन् or ङित् words does not apply here. For though शीङ् has an indicatory ङ, yet as it undergoes an operation itself, it cannot be the cause of the application of another rule.

Some persons explain the word अजादेः as the Ablative singular (and not Genitive Singular) of अजादिः and they consider the word as a Karma-dhâraya compound and not a Bahuvrihi compound. According to them the word means:—"The syllable *following* the *initial vowel* is reduplicated". (अच्चासावादिश्चेत्यजादिः, अजादेरुत्तरस्यएकाचो द्वे भवतः) ॥ According to this interpretation, the word द्वितीयस्य is merely explanatory.

न न्द्राः संयोगादयः ॥ ३ ॥ पदानि ॥ न, न्द्राः, संयोगादयः ॥

वृत्तिः ॥ द्वितीयस्येति वर्तते । द्वितीयस्यैकाचो ऽवयवभूतानां न्द्राणां तदन्तर्भावात् प्राप्तं द्विर्वचनं प्रतिषिध्यते । नकारदकाररेफा द्वितीयैकाचो ऽवयवभूताः संयोगादयो न द्विरुच्यन्ते ॥

वार्त्तिकम् ॥ बकारस्याप्ययं प्रतिषेधो वक्तव्यः ॥
वा० ॥ दकारोपधोपदेशे तु न वक्तव्यः ॥ वा० ॥ यकारपरस्य रेफस्य प्रतिषेधो न भवतीति वक्तव्यम् ॥
वा० ॥ ईर्ष्यतेस्तृतीय द्वे भवत इति वक्तव्यम् ॥ वा० ॥ कण्ड्वादीनां तृतीयस्यैकाचो द्वे भवत इति वक्तव्यम् ॥
वा० ॥ नामधातूनां तृतीयस्यैकाचो द्वे भवत इति वक्तव्यम् ॥ वा० ॥ यथेष्टं नामधातुष्विति वक्तव्यम् ॥

3. The letters न्, द् and र् being the first letter of a compound consonant and being part of the second syllable, are not reduplicated.

The word dvitîyasya "of the second syllable", is understood here. This sûtra debars the doubling of the consonants n, d, and r when forming parts of the second syllable, provided these letters occur in the beginning of a conjunct (saṅyoga) letter. Thus the Desiderative root of उन्द् is उन्दिष, formed by adding सन् and इट् ॥ The second syllable here is न्दिष् which is to be reduplicated by the last rule. But in doing so, न् will not be doubled. Thus we get the form उन्दिदिषति; so also from अड्ड् and अर्च् we have अड्डिडिषति, and अर्चिचिषति ॥

Why do we say "when न्, द् and र् are the letters"? Observe ईचिक्षिषते from ईक्ष् in which क् is the initial letter and has been reduplicated in to च् ॥ Why do we say "being the first letter in a conjunct consonant"? Observe प्राणिणिषति from the root अन् 'to breathe', the न् being changed into ण् by VIII. 4. 19 and 21. The phrase अजादेः of the last sûtra is understood in this sûtra also. Thus दरिद्रासति ॥ Some explain the word अजादेः understood in this sûtra in the same way as in the last, namely as a karmadhâraya compound in the Ablative singular. They do so, in order to explain the form इन्दिद्रीयिषति, which is thus evolved इन्द्रमिच्छति = इन्द्र + क्यच् III. 1. 8 = इन्द्रीय ॥ Then इन्द्रीयितुमिच्छति = इन्द्रीय + सन् ॥ Here though the second syllable consists of n, d and r, yet न् alone is rejected in reduplication and not द and र also, as द and रि are not immediately *after* the *initial vowel* (अजादि) इ in this case.

Vârt:—This prohibition should be stated with regard to the letter ब् also. As उब्ज्—उब्जिजिषति ॥ This prohibition applies when the word is taught primarily as having a penultimate ब् ॥ But when it is taught as primarily having a penultmate ह्, then the rule does not apply: the व should then be ordained as a substitute of ह्॥ See Tudadi root 20.

Vârt:—There is no prohibition of the र when it is followed by य॥ Thus अरार्यते॥ This is the Intensive form of the verb ऋ, and is thus evolved: ऋ+यङ् (III. 1. 22. Vârt)=अर्+य (VII. 4. 30)=अर्य, then follows reduplication by the rules of this sûtra. The second syllable र्य has an initial र which is not however rejected in reduplication.

Vârt:—In the case of the verb ईर्ष्यति the third should be reduplicated, "Third of what"? Some say the third of the consonants, and according to them the form is ईर्ष्यियिषति॥ Some say the third syllable, therefore of the root ईर्ष्यिष (ईर्ष्य+इट्+सन्), the third syllable ष is reduplicated: Thus ईर्ष्यिषष, ईर्ष्यिषिष (VII. 4. 79) the अ of ष is changed into short इ by VII. 4. 79.=ईर्ष्यिषिषति॥

Vârt:—The third syllable of the verbs कण्डूय &c. is to be reduplicated. Thus कण्डूय+इट्+सन्=कण्डूयिष=कण्डूयियिषति; so also असूयियिषति &c.

Vârt:—The third syllable of verbs derived from nouns is optionally reduplicated. Thus अश्वीयियिषति or अशिश्वीयिषति॥

Vârt:—Others say, any syllable of a नामधातु (verbs derived from nouns) may be reduplicated, Thus from the noun पुत्र is derived the root पुत्रीय, the desiderative root of which is पुत्रीयिष, which requires reduplication. Here any syllable may be reduplicated: as. 1, पुपुत्रीयिषति, 2. पुतित्रीयिषति, 3. पुत्रीयियिषति, 4. पुत्रीयिषिषति॥ Or there may be double and treble reduplication simultaneously as. पुपुतित्रीयियिषति॥

पूर्वोऽभ्यासः॥ ४॥ पदानि॥ पूर्वः, अभ्यासः॥

वृत्तिः॥ द्वे इति प्रथमान्तं यदनुवर्त्तते तदर्थादिह षष्ठ्यन्तं ज्ञायते। तत्र प्रत्यासत्तेरस्मिन्प्रकरणे ये द्वे विहिते तयोर्यः पूर्वो ऽवयवः सो ऽभ्याससंज्ञो भवति॥

4. The first of the two is called the Abhyâsa or the Reduplicate.

The word द्वे in the nominative case is understood here, but for the purposes of this sûtra it is taken in the Genitive case i. e. द्वयोर्यः पूर्वः "the first of the two" ordained above. The word Abhyâsa occurs in sûtras III. 1. 6, VI. 1. 7 &c.

उभे अभ्यस्तम्॥ ५॥ पदानि॥ उभे, अभ्यस्तम्॥

वृत्तिः॥ द्वे इति वर्त्तमाने उभेग्रहणं समुदायसंज्ञाप्रतिपत्त्यर्थम्। ये द्वे विहिते ते उभे अपि समुदित अभ्यस्तसंज्ञे भवतः॥

5. The both are collectively called Abhyasta.

Though the word द्वे was understood in the sûtra, the use of the word उभे 'both' indicates that the word Abhyasta applies to the two taken together and not to any one of them separately. The word abhyasta occurs in sûtras III. 4. 109, VI. 1. 32 &c, Thus sûtra VI, 1, 189 declares "the first vowel of an Abhyasta gets the udâtta accent". The Abhyasta being the collective name of the both, the accent will fall on the first and not on the second, as in ददाति dádati, the accent is on the first अ ॥ So also by VII. 1. 4 अत् takes the place of झ after an Abhyasta, therefore, दद + झि = दद + अति = ददति ॥ So also ददत् (VI. 4. 112).

जक्षित्यादयः षट् ॥ ६ ॥ पदानि ॥ जक्ष, इत्यादयः, षट् ॥

वृत्तिः ॥ अभ्यस्तमिति वर्त्तते । जक्ष इत्ययं धातुरित्यादयश्चान्ये षट् धातवो ऽभ्यस्तसंज्ञा भवन्ति । सेयं सप्तानां धातूनामभ्यस्तसंज्ञाविधीयते ॥ जक्षभक्षहसनयोरित्यतः प्रभृति वेवीङ् वेतिना तुल्यइति यावत् ॥

6. So also the six roots beginning with jakshi are called abhyasta.

The word abhyasta is understood here. The verb jakshi and the six verbs that follow it in the Dhâtupâṭha, in all seven verbs, get this designation. These are जक्ष, जागृ, दरिद्रा, चकास्, शास्, दीधी, and वेवी ॥ Pânini has overlooked वेवी and mentions only the first six. By getting the designation of Abhyasta these verbs get acute accent on the first syllable when followed by a sârvadhâtuka Tense-affix not having the intermediate इट् and beginning with a vowel. Thus जाग्रति já-grati, जक्षति jákshati, दरिद्रति dáridrati, चकासति chákâsati, शासति śâśati, दीध्यते dìdhyate, and वेव्यते vevyate. The present participle दीध्यत् is irregularly formed by adding the affix शतृ (अत्) and when so formed it does not take the augment नुम् by VII. 1, 78.

तुजादीनां दीर्घो ऽभ्यासस्य ॥ ७ ॥ पदानि ॥ तुज, आदीनाम्, दीर्घः, अभ्यासस्य ॥

वृत्तिः ॥ तुजादीनामितिप्रकारेआदिशब्दः । कश्च प्रकारः । तुजेर्दीर्घोभ्यासस्य न विहितः, दृश्यते च, ये तथाभूतास्ते तुजादयस्तेषामभ्यासस्य दीर्घः साधुर्भवति ॥

7. In the room of a short vowel of the Reduplicate of the roots तुज् &c, a long is substituted.

There is no list of तुजादि verbs given any where. The word आदि in तुजादि therefore should be construed as "verbs *like* tuj". So that wherever we may find a word having a long vowel in the Reduplicate, we should consider it a valid form, Thus तूतुजानः (तुज् + कानच् III. 2. 106 = तूतुजानः Rig. I. 3. 6), मामहानः, अनड्वान् दाधार, स्वधां मीमाय, स तूताव ॥ This lengthening only takes place in the Vedas before some special affixes, and not every where or in secular literature. As तुताज शबलान् हरीन् ॥

लिटि धातोरनभ्यासस्य ॥ ८ ॥ पदानि ॥ लिटि, धातोः, अनभ्यासस्य ॥

वृत्तिः ॥ लिटि परतो ऽनभ्यासस्य धातोरवयवस्य प्रथमस्यैकाचोः द्वितीयस्य वा यथायोगं द्वे भवतः ॥ वार्त्तिकम् ॥ द्विर्वचनप्रकरणे छन्दसि वेति वक्तव्यम् ॥ वा० ॥ लिटि द्विर्वचने जागर्तेर्वेति वक्तव्यम् ॥

8. When the tense-affixes of the Perfect follow, there is reduplication of the root, which is not already reduplicated.

The reduplication is either of the first syllable or of the second syllable according as the root begins with a consonant or a vowel. Thus पच् + णल् = पच् पच् + णल् = पपाच ॥ So also पपाठ, प्रोर्णुनाव ॥ In the case of ऊर्णु, Rule III. 1. 36 does not apply, so the Perfect of this word is not formed by adding आम् and the auxiliary verbs कृ, भू and अस्; but regularly. In fact ऊर्णु is regarded as if it was नु ॥ See sûtra III. 1. 36 Vârt. वाच्य ऊर्णोर्णुवद् भावो यङ् प्रसिद्धिः प्रयोजनं, आमश्च प्रतिषेधार्थमेकाचश्चेडुपग्रहात् ॥

Why do we say when लिट् follows? Observe कर्त्ता, हर्त्ता ॥ Why do we say "of a Dhâtu"? Observe सुसूवांसो विभृण्विरे, सोमिन्द्रायसुन्दिरे ॥ The question arises from the fact that the root (dhâtu) always directly precedes the affixes of the Perfect, no vikaraṇa intervenes as in the case of other tenses. So there was no necessity of using the word dhâtu in the sûtra. To this it is replied that by III. 4. 117, sometimes लिट् is treated as sârvadhâtuka, and then it takes vikaraṇa. As भृ taking the vikarana श्नु becomes भृणु; (III. 1. 74) this whole *base* is not a dhâtu, therefore when the affixes of Perfect are added there is no reduplication, and we have भृण्विरे ॥ See III. 4. 117.

Why do we say 'of a non-reduplicate'? Observe कृष्णो नोनाव वृषभो यदीदम् । नोनूयतेर्नोनाव, i. e. it is the Perfect Tense of the Intensive verb नोनूय, and is not reduplicated again, यङ् having already caused reduplication. So also संमान्या मरुतः समिमिक्षुः ending in the उस् of the Perfect.

Vârt:—In the Chhandas there is optionally reduplication of the root in the Perfect and other tenses. As आदित्यान् याचिषामहे or यियाचिषामहे; देवतानो दाति प्रियाणि or ददाति प्रियाणि ॥ मघवा दातु or ददातु, नस्तुतो वीरवद् धातु or दधातु ॥

Vârt:—The root जागृ is optionally reduplicated in the Perfect. As, यो जागार (or जजागार) तमृचः कामयन्ते ॥

सन्यङोः ॥ ९ ॥ पदानि ॥ सन् यङोः, ॥

वृत्तिः ॥ धातोरनभ्यासस्येति वर्त्तते । सन्यङोरिति च षष्ठ्यन्तमेतत् । सन्नन्तस्य यङन्तस्य चानभ्यासस्य धातोरवयवस्य प्रथमस्यैकाचो द्वितीयस्य वा यथायोगं द्वे भवतः ॥

9. Of a non-reduplicate root ending in सन् (Desiderative) or यङ (Intensive) affixes, there is reduplication.

The word सन् यङोः should be construed as genitive dual and not as Locative dual. In the latter case, the meaning would be "when the affixes सन् and यङ् follow, a non-reduplicate root is reduplicated". The difficulty would be that while the root alone would be reduplicated, the augment इट् would not, as in अटिटिषति, अशिशिषति ॥

The phrase धातोरनभ्यासस्य is understood here also. The reduplication is of the first or second syllable, according as the root has an initial consonant or vowel. Thus पच् + सन् (III. 1. 7) पक्ष, reduplicate पिपक्षति (VII. 4. 79). So पत्

पिपतिषति, ऋ—अरिरिषति, उन्द—उन्दिदिषति ॥ So also of यङन्तः—as, पापच्यते (VII. 4. 83), अटाट्यते, आशश्यते, अरार्यते, प्रोर्णोनूयते ॥ If a root is already a reduplicated one, there is no reduplication: as जुगुप्सिषते, लोलूयिषते being the Desiderative forms of जुगुप्स (already formed by svârthika सन् III. 1. 5), and of लोलूय (the Intensive form of लू) ॥ See III. 1. 22.

श्लौ ॥ १० ॥ पदानि ॥ श्लौ ॥

वृत्तिः ॥ श्लौ परतो ऽनभ्यासस्य धातोरवयवस्य प्रथमस्यैकाचो द्वितीयस्य वा यथायोगं द्वे भवतः ॥

10. Of a non-reduplicate root there is reduplication when the vikaraṇa ślu (श्लु) follows.

The श्लु is the characteristic sign of the roots of the third class, and causes the elision of the vikaraṇa शप् ॥ The reduplication is of the first or second syllable, according as the root has an initial consonant or a vowel. Thus जुहोति (from हु), बिभेति, जिह्रेति ॥

चङि ॥ ११ ॥ पदानि ॥ चङि ॥

वृत्तिः ॥ चङि परतो ऽनभ्यासस्य धातोरवयवस्य प्रथमस्यैकाचो द्वितीयस्य वा यथायोगं द्वे भवतः ॥

11. Of a non-reduplicate root there is reduplication when the affix चङ् of the Aorist follows.

The reduplication is of the first or second syllable according as the root begins with a consonant or a vowel. Thus अपीपचत्, अपीपठत्, (VII. 4. 93 and 94). So also आटिटत्, आशिशत्, आर्दिदत् ॥ These are aorists of the causative roots पाचि &c.

When the Reduplicated Aorist of the Causative (ण्यन्त) verbs पच् &c is to be formed, as here, we should first elide the causative sign णि, then shorten the penultimate vowel, and then reduplicate. Then by VII. 4. 93 the effect would be like as if सन् had followed, and this would not be prohibited by the short vowel being consdered sthânivat. For rule VII.4.93 says "Let the effect be as if सन् had followed, on the reduplicate, if followed by a light vowel, of an inflective base to which णि followed by चङ् is affixed; provided there is not the elision of any letter in the pratyâhâra अक् occasioned by the affixing of णि ॥" One of the conditions for the application of this rule is that the reduplicate must be followed by a *light* vowel. We have said above that the long penultimate is to be shortened before चङ् ॥ Now arises the difficulty. Should this light vowel coming in the room of a heavy vowel be considered like the heavy vowel by the rule of sthânivat âdeśa (I. 1. 56), or not? It should not be considered so, for the reasons given in I. 1. 57. For it was established there that the sthânivadbhâva will arise then only when some operation is to be done to a thing *anterior* to the non-substituted i. e. original vowel. Here no operation is to be applied to something *anterior* to such original (अनादिष्ट) vowel, but to a form consisting of such substituted (आदिष्ट) vowel. Therefore, the light vowel is not considered non-existent for the purposes of सन्वद्भाव ॥ If this order of operation is not followed, there would arise incongruities. The order must be this: 1st the elision of णि (VI. 4. 51) 2nd the shortening of the penultimate (VII 4. 4) 3rd the reduplication. If the reduplication take place first and the vowel be shortened, then the reduplication having taken place before the substitution of the vowel had taken place, such substitute will now be considered as sthânivad: the *light* vowel being considered as still *heavy*, will prevent the application of सन्वद्भाव ॥ The difficulty will be in the form of आशीशमत्, where the short is ordained after the णि ॥ If this be the order of operations, there will not be the reduplication of the second syllable टि in the word अटिटत्? This is, howwer, done by I. 1. 59. which see.

दाश्वान् साह्वान् मीढ्वांश्च ॥ १२ ॥ पदानि ॥ दाश्वान्, साह्वान्, मीढ्वान्, च ॥

वृत्तिः ॥ दाश्वान् साह्वान् मीढ्वानित्येते शब्दाश्छन्दसि भाषायां चाविशेषेण निपात्यन्ते ॥

वार्त्तिकम् ॥ कृञादीनां के द्वे भवत इति वक्तव्यम् ॥ वा० ॥ चरिचलिपतिवदीनां द्वित्वमच्यक्चाभ्यासस्य ॥ वा० ॥ वेति वक्तव्यम् ॥ वा० ॥ हन्तेर्घत्वं च ॥ वा० ॥ पाटेर्णिलुक् चोक् च दीर्घश्चाभ्यासस्य ॥

12. The participles dâśvân, sâhvân and mîḍhvân are irregularly formed without reduplication.

The word दाश्वान् is from the root दाश् 'to give' with the affix क्वसु (III. 2. 107), here the reduplication and the augment इट् are prohibited irregularly. As दाश्वांसो दाशुषः सुतम् (Rig I. 3, 7). The word साह्वान् is derived from the root सह् 'to endure', by adding the affix क्वसु (III. 2. 107), the irregularity being in lengthening the penultimate, not allowing the augment इट् and the reduplication. Thus साह्वान् बलाहकः ॥ So also मीढ्वान् comes from मिह् 'to sprinkle' with the affix क्वसु (III. 2. 107) the irregularity consisting in non-reduplication, non-application of इट्, the lenthening of the penultimate vowel, and the change of ह into ढ ॥ As मीढ्वस्तोकाय तनयाय मृडय ॥ It is not necessary that these words should be in the singular always, in their plural forms also they do not reduplicate.

Vârt:—Reduplication takes place when कृञ् &c, are followed by the affix क ॥ Thus क्रियते अनेन = कृ + क = चक्रम्, क्लिद् + क = चिक्लिदम् ॥ The affix क comes after कृञ् and क्लिद् with the force of the affix घञ् ॥

Vârt:—The roots चर्, चल्, पत्, and वद् take reduplication when followed by the affix अच् (III. 1. 134) and the reduplicate (abhyâsa) takes the augment आक् ॥ The final consonants of the Abhyâsa (reduplicate) are not elided in these verbs, in order to give scope to the augment, for if the final consonants be elided by VII. 4. 60, then the addition of the augment becomes unnecessary; as there is no difference between the augment and the âdesa (shortening of the vowel) taught in VII. 4. 59. Thus चराचरः, चलाचल, पतापतः, वदावदः ॥

Vârt:—The above vârtika is optional, so we have the forms चरः पुरुषः, चलो रथः, वशो मनुष्यः &c.

Vârt:—The root हन् is reduplicated before the affix अच्, and the augment आक् comes after the Abhyâsa, and घ is the substitute of ह of the Abhyâsa. Thus हन्+अच्=घन्+आक्+हन्+अच्=घनाघनः (The second ह is changed into घ by VII. 3. 55), as in the phrase घनाघनः क्षोभनश्चर्षणीनाम् ॥

Vârt:—The causative root पाटि is reduplicated before the affix अच्, there is elision of णि (sign of the causative), and उक् is the augment of the Abhyâsa, and it is lengthened. Thus पाटि+अच्=पाटूपटः ॥

ष्यङः संप्रसारणं पुत्रपत्योस्तत्पुरुषे ॥ १३ ॥ पदानि ॥ ष्यङः, संप्रसारणम्, पुत्र, पत्योः, तत्पुरुषे ॥

वृत्तिः ॥ पुत्त्र पति इत्येतयोरुत्तरपदयोस्तत्पुरुषे समासे ष्यङः संप्रसारणं भवति ॥

वार्त्तिकम् ॥ ष्यङः सम्प्रसारणे गौकाक्षायाः प्रतिषेधः ॥

13. There is vocalisation of the semivowel य् of the affix ष्यङ् (IV. 1. 78) when followed in a Tatpurusha compound, by the words पुत्र and पति ॥

When the words पुत्र and पति are the second members, forming a Tatpurusha compound, there is samprasâraṇa (vocalising the semi-vowels) of the affix ष्यङ् of the preceding. That is य् is changed into इ ॥ Thus करीषस्येव गन्धोऽस्य=करीषगन्धिः (a Bahuvrihi compound taking the samâsanta affix or rather substitute इ by V. 4. 137) करीषगन्धेरपत्यम्=करीषगन्धि+अण् (IV. 1. 92)=कारीषगन्धः ॥ The feminine of this will be formed by adding ष्यङ् (IV. 1. 78). Thus we have कारीषगन्ध्या (see IV. 1. 78). Now in forming the Tatpurusha compound of this word with पुत्र or पति, the final य will be changed into इ and we have कारीषगन्धीपुत्रः, कारीषगन्धीपतिः ॥ The आ of या becomes merged into इ (VI. 1. 108), and the short इ is lengthened (VI. 3. 139). So also कौमुदगन्धीपुत्रः ० कौमुदगन्धीपतिः ॥

Why do we say "of the affix ष्यङ्"? Observe इभ्यापुत्रः, क्षत्रियापुत्रः ॥

Why do we say "when followed by पुत्र or पति"? Observe कारीषगन्ध्याकुलम्, कौमुदगन्ध्याकुलम् ॥

Why do we say "when forming a Tatpurusha compound"? Observe कारीषगन्ध्यापतिरस्य ग्रामस्य=कारीषगन्ध्यापतिरयं ग्रामः ॥ It is a Bahuvrihi compound.

The affix ष्यङ् is here the feminine affix ष followed by चाप् (आ) (see IV. 1. 77 and 74).

A general maxim relating to all affixes is "an affix denotes whenever it is employed in Grammar, a word-form which begins with that to which that affix has been added, and ends with the affix itself: प्रत्ययग्रहणे यस्मात् स विहितस्तदादेस्तदन्तस्य ग्रहणम्" ॥ This maxim, however, does not apply in case of feminine affixes, where we have this rule "a feminine affix denotes whenever it is employed in a rule, a word-form which ends with that affix, but which need not necessarily begin with that to which the affix has been added, but where the word form is subordinate : स्त्रीप्रत्यये चानुपसर्जने न" ॥ Thus we have परमकारीषगन्ध्यायाः पुत्रः = परमकारीषगन्धीपुत्रः and so also परमकारीषगन्धीपतिः ॥ Not so when the word is an upasarjana or subordinate in a compound. As अतिक्रान्ता कारीषगन्ध्याम् = अतिकारीषगन्ध्या, तस्यपुत्रः = अतिकारीषगन्ध्यापुत्रः, अतिकारीषगन्ध्यापतिः ॥

This vocalisation takes place when पुत्र and पति alone, not compounded with any other word, stand at the end : not so when a word beginning or ending with these words follows. Thus कारीषगन्ध्यापुत्रकुलं, कारीषगन्ध्यापरमपुत्रः &c.

Though a word ending in ष्यङ् may have may semi-vowels, yet the vocalisation takes place of the affix य (ष्यङ्) only, according to the maxim निर्दिश्यमानस्यादेशा भवन्ति "substitutes take the place of that which is actually enunciated ".

The word संप्रसारण has regulating influence upto VI. 1. 44 inclusive. The rules of vocalisation (change of semi-vowels into vowels) is contained in these sûtras.

Vârt:—Prohibition must be stated when पति and पुत्र follow the word गौकाक्ष्य ॥ As गौकाक्ष्यापुत्रः, गौकाक्ष्यायातः instead of गौकाक्षिपुत्रः &c.

बन्धुनि बहुव्रीहौ ॥ १४ ॥ पदानि ॥ बन्धुनि, बहुव्रीहौ ॥

वृत्तिः ॥ ष्यङः संप्रसारणमित्यनुवर्त्तते । बन्धुशब्दउत्तरपदे बहुव्रीहौ समासे ष्यङः संप्रसारणं भवति ॥
वा० ॥ मातच्मातृकमातृषु ॥

14. There is vocalisation of the affix ष्यङ् when the word बन्धु follows in a Bahuvrîhi compound.

Thus कारीषगन्ध्याबन्धुरस्य = कारीषगन्धीबन्धुः ॥ So also कौमुदगन्धीबन्धुः ॥

Why do we say "when the compound is a Bahuvrihi"? Observe कारीषगन्ध्याया बन्धुः = कारीषगन्ध्याबन्धुः, which is a Tatpurusha compound. Like the last sûtra, we have here also परमकारीषगन्धिबन्धुः, but अतिकारीषगन्ध्याबन्धुः, कारीषगन्ध्याबन्धुधनः, कारीषगन्ध्यापरमबन्धुः ॥

Though the word बन्धुनि is exhibited in the sûtra in the neuter gender, it is in fact a masculine word.

Vârt :—There is vocalisation of ष्यङ् in a Bahuvrihi compound with मातच्, मातृक and मात optionally: as कारीषगन्धीमातः or कारीषगन्ध्यामातः, कारीषगन्धिमातृकः or कारीषगन्ध्यामातृकः, कारीषगन्धिमाता, कारीषगन्ध्यामाता ॥ The indicatory च of मातच् makes the word take the udâtta on the last syllable (VI. 1. 163), thus debarring the especial accent of the Bahuvrîhi (VI. 2. 1). All Bahuvrîhi compounds ending in ऋ take the samâsânta affix कप्, so मातृ would have become मातृक by force of V. 4. 153, so the separate enumeration of मातृ and मातृक here shows that कप् is also optional.

वचिस्वपियजादीनां किति ॥ १५ ॥ पदानि ॥ वचि, स्वपि, यजादीनाम्, किति ॥

वृत्तिः ॥ संप्रसारणमिति वर्त्तते । ष्यङ इति निवृत्तम् । वचि । वच परिभाषणे । ब्रुवो वचिरिति च । स्वपि ॥ ञिष्वप् शये । यजादयो, यज देवपूजासंगतिकरणदानेष्वित्यतःप्रभृति आ गणान्तात् । तेषां वचिस्वपियजादीनां किति प्रत्यये परतः संप्रसारणं भवति ॥

15. The semivowels of the roots वच्, स्वप् and यजादि verbs are vocalised when followed by an affix having an indicatory क ॥

The anuvritti of ष्यङ् does not run into this sûtra. The root वच includes the वच परिभाषणे of the Adâdi class (II. 54) and the वच् substitute of ब्रू (II. 4. 53) स्वप् is the root ञिष्वप् शये of the Adâdi class (II 59). The यजादि verbs are the last nine roots of the Bhvâdi class viz. यज्, वप्, वह, वस्, वेञ्, व्येञ्, ह्वेञ्, वद् and श्वि ॥ The semivowels of these eleven verbs are changed into the corresponding vowel, when an affix having an indicatory क is added to them. Thus with the Past Participle affixes क्त and क्तवतु we have the following forms:— 1. वच्—उक्तः, उक्तवान्, (VIII. 2. 30). 2 स्वप्—सुप्तः, सुप्तवान् 3 यज्—इष्टः, इष्टवान्. (VIII. 2. 36) 4 वप्—उप्तः, उप्तवान्, 5 वह्—ऊढः, ऊढवान् (VIII. 2. 31, 40, VIII. 3. 13 and VI. 3. 111) 6 वस्—उषितः उषितवान्, (VII. 2. 56 VIII. 3. 60) 7 वेञ् —उतः, उतवान्, 8 व्येञ्—संवीतः, संवीतवान्, 9 ह्वेञ्—हूतः, हूतवान्, 10 वद्—उदितः, उदितवान्, 11 टुओश्वि—शूनः, शूनवान् ॥

धातोः स्वरूपग्रहणे तत्प्रत्यय कार्यं विज्ञायते:—When in a Grammatical rule, an operation (dependant on an affix) is taught with regard to a root (dhâtu) by mentioning particular verbs (dhâtu) specifically, and not by using the word "dhâtu", generally, then the operation takes place only when the root is followed by such an affix as can be added to roots by emunciating the word धातोः ॥ The existence of this maxim is inferred in the formation of the word भ्रौणहत्यम् in VI. 4. 174, which see. Therefore, there is no vocalisation of वच् in the following वाच्यति, वाचिकः ॥ Here वाच्यति is formed by adding क्यच् to वाच् (वाचमिच्छति) ॥ वाच् is formed by क्विप् added to वच्, the vowel being lengthened and samprasârana being expressly prevented by Unâdi II. 57. Now, it is a general rule that a root taking the affix क्विप्, विट्, or विच् does not lose its character of a dhâtu. Therefore वाच् is a root (धातु), and it ought to take vocalisation before the affix क्यच् ॥ But क्यच् is not enunciated to come after a dhâtu, but after a सुबन्त (सुप आत्मनः क्यच् III. 1. 8) in the rule ordaining its affixing. So also वाचिकः formed by adding ठक् to वाच् (See Vârt. V. 3. 83).

ग्रहिज्यावयिव्यधिवष्टिविचतिवृश्चतिपृच्छतिभृज्जतीनां ङिति च ॥१६॥ पदानि ॥ ग्रहि, ज्या, वयि, व्यधि, वष्टि, विचति; वृश्चति, पृच्छति, भृज्जतीनाम्, ङिति, च ॥

वृत्तिः ॥ ग्रह उपादाने, ज्या वयोहानौ, वेञो वयिः, व्यध ताडने, वश कान्तौ, व्यचँ व्याजीकरणे, ओव्रश्चू छेदने, प्रच्छ ज्ञीप्सायां, भ्रस्ज पाके, इत्येतेषां धातूनां ङिति प्रत्यये परतश्चकारात्किति च संप्रसारणं भवति ।

परिभाषा ॥ निष्ठादेशः षत्वस्वरप्रत्ययविधीड्विधिषु सिद्धो वक्तव्यः ॥

16. There is vocalisation of the semi-vowels of the following verbs, when an affix having an indicatory क् or ङ् follows:—ग्रह 'to take', ज्या 'to become old', वेञ् 'to weave', व्यध 'to strike', वश 'to shine', व्यच 'to deceive', व्रश्च 'to cut', प्रच्छ 'to ask', and भ्रस्ज 'to cook, to fry'.

By force of the word 'च' 'and', the anuvritti of क्ङिति is read into this sûtra. Thus 1. ग्रह—गृहीतः, गृहीतवान् (by क्त and क्तवतु), गृह्णाति (I. 2. 4), जरीगृह्यते (by यङ of the Intensive). 2. ज्या—जीनः, जीनवान् (VIII. 2. 44 त changed to न); जिनाति (I. 2. 4), the short इ is lengthened by VI. 4. 2 and is shortened again by VII. 3. 80. जेजीयते (यङ्), 3. वयि—The root वेञ् is replaced by वय when लिट् follows (II. 4. 41). This वयि can have no ङित् affix after it, it takes only लिट् terminations, which as we know are कित् (I. 2. 5). The examples, therefore given will be of कित् affixes only. Thus ऊयतुः, ऊयुः ॥ Now arises this question 'why do you enumerate वयि, for is not वेञ् (for which वयि is substituted) already included in यजादि class of verbs given in the last sûtra, and by force of that sûtra, वयि will get samprasârana before कित् affixes", The reply is "वयि is numerated here in order to show that the prohibition of samprasârana with regard to वेञ् as taught in VI. 1. 40, does not apply to its substitute वयि in the Perfect Tense". Thus while the Perfect of वेञ् is ववौ, ववतुः, ववुः, the Perfect of its substitute वयि is उवाय, ऊयतुः and ऊयुः ॥ More over VI. 1. 38 teaches that the य of वय is not vocalised in लिट् affixes, which therefore, implies (jñâpaka) that the other semivowel i. e. व of वय will be vocalised. 4. व्यध—विद्धः, विद्धवान्, and with ङित् affixes विध्यति, वेविध्यते ॥ 5. वश—उशितः, उशितवान्, and with ङित् affixes उष्टः, उशन्ति ॥ 6. व्यच—विचितः, विचितवान् विचति, वेविच्यते ॥ By a Vârtika under I. 2. 1, the word व्यच is considered to belong to कुटादि class, and therefore all affixes after it, other than those having an indicatory ञ्, ण् or the affix अस्, are considered as ङित्, and therefore, there will be samprasârana before these affixes: as, उद्विचिता, उद्विचितुम्, उद्विचितव्यम् ॥ 7. व्रश्च—वृक्णः, वृक्णवान् ॥ How is the final च of व्रश्च changed into क, for by VIII. 2. 36 च ought to have been changed into ष before the झलादि affix क्त? To this we reply the affix क्त is replaced by न (VII. 2. 42) and as this न is not a झलादि affix, Rule VIII. 2. 36 does not apply. This is done on the following maxim: "The substitute of the Nishthâ should be considered to be siddha or effective when applying the rules relating to the change of a letter into ष, to accent, to affix, and to the addition of the augment इट्". But when च is to be changed into क, the substitute is considered asiddha (not to have taken place). Thus we have the forms वृक्णः &c. Before ङित् affixes we have वृश्चति, वरीवृश्च्यते ॥ 8. प्रच्छ—पृष्टः (VIII. 2. 36), पृष्टवान्, ङित्—पृच्छति, परीपृच्छ्यते ॥ The forms पप्रच्छ and बभ्रज्ज would have been evolved by the simple rules of Reduplication even, without the application of this rule. But प्रच्छ+नङ् (III. 3. 90)=प्रश्नः ॥ Here there is no vocalisation, because Pânini himself uses the word प्रश्नः in sûtra III. 2. 117 showing that this is the proper form though irregular. 9. भ्रस्ज—भृष्टः (VIII. 2. 36), भृष्टवान्, ङित्—भृज्जति, क्ङी भृज्ज्यते ॥ The स of भ्रस्ज is changed first into द by झलां जश् झशि (VIII. 4. 53), and then द is changed into ज by स्तोः श्चुना श्चुः (VIII. 4. 40).

लिट्यभ्यासस्योभयेषाम् ॥ १७ ॥ पदानि ॥ लिटि, अभ्यासस्य, उभयेषाम्, (संप्रसारणम्) ॥

वृत्तिः ॥ उभयेषां वाच्यादीनां ग्रहादीनां च लिटि परतो ऽभ्यासस्य संप्रसारणं भवति ॥

17. There takes place vocalisation of the semi-vowel of the reduplicate (abhyâsa) of both vachyâdi (VI. 1. 15) and grahâdi (VI. 1. 16) words, when the affixes of लिट् follow.

Thus वच—उवाच; उवाचिथ, स्वप्—सुष्वाप, सुष्वपिथ, यज—इयाज, इयजिथ, डुवप्—उवाप, उवपिथ ॥ As regards ग्रहादि verbs; ग्रह—जग्राह, जग्रहिथ (there is no speciality in case of this verb, as these forms would have been evolved without even this rule). ज्या—जिज्यौ, जिज्यिथ, वयि—उवाय, and उवयिथ ; व्यध—विव्याध, विव्यधिथ, वश—उवाश, उवशिथ, व्यच्—विव्याच, विव्यचिथ, व्रश्च—वव्रश्च and वव्रश्चिथ ॥ Some say that with regard to व्रश्च, it is equal whether there existed this present rule or not. For they argue thus, व्रश्च+णल्=व्रश्च्+व्रश्च्+अ=व+व्रश्च्+अ (हलादि शेषः VII. 4. 60)=वव्रश्च ॥ To this we reply, this form would be evolved no doubt had this rule not existed. But when this rule is applied, and you make reduplication without first vocalising the र, then you will have to vocalise व by force of this rule. Hence the necessity of this rule with regard to व्रश्च also, for having changed र into ऋ, we have वृव्रश्च् and then change ऋ into अ by VII. 4. 66. Then this अ substitute becomes sthânivat to ऋ (I. 1. 59), and therefore there is no vocalisasion of this व, for rule VI. 1. 37, prevents the vocalisation of a letter standing before one which has already been vocalised. There is no speciality with regards to प्रच्छ and भ्रस्ज verbs.

This vocalisation of the reduplicate is taught with regard to those affixes which are not कित् ॥ With regard to कित् affixes, the Rule VI. 1. 15 will apply. And as the rule of vocalisation is subsequent to that of reduplication in order, therefore by the maxim of परत्व I. 4. 2, vocalisation will take place first and then reduplication, according to the maxim पुनः प्रसङ्ग विज्ञानात्सिद्धम् "occasionally the formation of a particular form is accounted for by the fact that a preceding rule is allowed to apply again, after it had previously been superseded by a subsequent rule". Thus वच्+अतुः (which is कित् I. 2. 5)=उच्+अतुः=उच्+उच्+अतुः=ऊचतुः, ऊचुः ॥

Though the phrase इभवयाम् could have been supplied into this sûtra by the context and the governing scope of the preceding sûtras, its express mention in this sûtra is for the sake of indicating, that the rule of vocalisation supersedes even the rule of हलादिः शेषः VII. 4. 60, the vocalisation must take place at all events. Thus व्यध + णल् = व्य + व्यध + अ ॥ Here by VII. 4. 60, the second consonant य of व्य ought to have been elided, and the equation would have stood व + व्यध् + अ, and there would have been vocalisation of व by this rule. But that is not intended; there is vocalisation of य and we have विव्याध ॥ In fact, the universal maxim of vocalisation is —"The samprasârana and the operations dependent on it possess greater force than other operations which are simultaneously applicable". संप्रसारणं तदाश्रयं च कार्यम् बलवत् ॥

स्वापेश्चङि ॥ १८ ॥ पदानि ॥ स्वापेः, चङि, (सम्प्रसारणम्) ॥

वृत्तिः ॥ स्वापेरिति स्वपेर्ण्यन्तस्य ग्रहणं तस्य चङि परतः संप्रसारणं भवति ॥

18. Of the causative verb स्वापि "to cause one to sleep", there is vocalisation of the semivowel, when the affix चङ् of the Reduplicated Aorist follows.

Thus the Aorist of स्वापि is असूषुपत्, असूषुपताम्, असूषुपन् ॥ The vocalisation takes place before reduplication, then there is guṇa of the penultimate short vowel, then this is again shortened by VII. 4. 1, then there is reduplication, and then lengthening of the vowel of the reduplicate by VII. 4. 94. Thus स्वापि + चङ् = सुपि + चङ् = सुप् (VI. 4. 51) + चङ् (VII. 3. 86) = सोप् + चङ् = सुप् + चङ् (VII. 4. 1) = सु + सुप् + चङ् (VI. 1. 11) = सूषुपत् (VII. 4. 94) which with the augment अ becomes असूषुपत् ॥

Why do we say 'when चङ् follows'? Observe स्वाप्यते, स्वापितः ॥ The anuvritti of किति has ceased, that of ङिति however is here.

स्वपिस्यमिव्येञां यङि ॥१९॥ पदानि ॥ स्वपि, स्यमि, व्येञाम्, यङि,(संप्रसारणम्)॥

वृत्तिः ॥ ञिष्वप् शये स्यमु स्वन ध्वन शब्दे, व्येञ् संवरणे, इत्येतेषां धातूनां यङि परतः संप्रसारणं भवति ॥

19. There is vocalisation of the semivowel of the verbs स्वप् 'to sleep', स्यम् 'to shout', and व्ये 'to cover', when followed by the affix यङ् of the Intensive.

Thus सोषुप्यते, सेसिम्यते, वेवीयते (VII. 4. 25 the short इ is lengthened). Why do we say 'when यङ् follows'? Observe स्वप्नक् formed by नजिङ् III. 2. 172.

न वशः ॥ २० ॥

वृत्तिः ॥ यङीति वर्त्तते । वशेर्धातोर्यङि परतः सम्प्रसारणं न भवति ॥

20. There is not vocalisation of the semi-vowel of वश, when the affix यङ् follows.

The word यङि is understood here. As वावश्यते, वावश्येते, वावश्यन्ते ॥ Why do we say "when यङ् follows"? Observe उष्टः, उशन्ति ॥ See VI. 1. 16 to which this rule is an exception.

चायः की ॥ २१ ॥ पदानि ॥ चायः, की ॥

वृत्तिः ॥ यङीति वर्त्तते । चायि पूजानिशामनयोरित्येतस्य धातोर्यङि परतः कीत्ययमादेशो भवति ॥

21. The verb की is substituted for the verb चायृ 'to worship, to observe', when the Intensive affix यङ् follows.

The phrase यङि is understood here. Thus चेकीयते, चेकीयेते, चेकीयन्ते ॥ The exhibition of की in the sûtra with a long ई indicates that there is long vowel even in tenses where यङ् is elided, as चेकीतः ॥ For if the sûtra had enunciated कि with a short इ as the substitute of चायृ, the forms चेकीयते &c would have been still valid. Thus कि + यङ् = चि + कि + य = चे + कि + य = चे + की + य (VII. 4. 25 causing the lengthening of the short इ). But then the Nishṭhâ would have been चेकितः which is wrong.

स्फायः स्फी निष्ठायाम् ॥ २२ ॥ पदानि ॥ स्फायः, स्फी, निष्ठायाम् ॥

वृत्तिः ॥ स्फायी ओप्यायी वृद्धावित्यस्य धातोर्निष्ठायां परतः स्फीत्ययमादेशो भवति ॥

22. The स्फी is the substitute of स्फाय 'to swell', when the Nishṭhâ affixes follow.

Thus स्फीतः, स्फीतवान् ॥ Why do we say "when the Nishṭha affixes follow"? Observe स्फातिः formed by क्तिन् ॥ In the phrase स्फाती भवति, the word स्फाती is the feminine of the word स्फाति formed by क्तिन् ॥ The phrase निष्ठायाम् "when the Nishtha follows" governs all the subsequent sûtras up to VI. 1. 29.

स्त्यः प्रपूर्वस्य ॥ २३ ॥ पदानि ॥ स्त्यः, प्र, पूर्वस्य, (सम्प्रसारणम्) ॥

वृत्तिः ॥ निष्ठायामिति वर्त्तते सम्प्रसारणमिति च । स्त्या इत्येतन्न स्वर्यते । स्त्यै ष्ट्यै शब्दसंघातयोर्द्वयोरप्येतयो र्द्वयोः स्त्यारूपमापन्नयोः सामान्येन ग्रहणम् । स्त्या इत्येतस्य प्रपूर्वस्य धातोर्निष्ठायां परतः संप्रसारणं भवति ॥

23. The verb स्त्या (स्त्यै and ष्ट्यै) when preceded by प्र changes its semivowel to a vowel, when a Nishṭhâ affix follows.

The phrases "when the nishthâ follows", and "there is vocalisation" are understood here. The anuvritti of स्फी does not run here. The roots स्त्यै and ष्ट्यै both assume the form स्त्या and are included here. Thus प्र + स्त्या + क्त = प्र + स्ति + त (VI. 1. 108) = प्रस्तीतः (VI. 4. 2), and प्रस्तीतवान् ॥ The त of nishṭhâ affix would have been changed into न् by VIII. 2. 43 in as much as the root स्त्या has a semivowel and ends in long आ ॥ But by the vocalisation of य, the condition of यण्वत् for the application of VIII. 2. 43, no longer existing, the affix त is not changed to न ॥ But त is optionally changed to म by VIII. 2. 54 as प्रस्तीमः and प्रस्तीमवान् ॥

Why do we say "when preceded by प्र?" Observe संस्त्यानः (VIII. 2 43), संस्त्यानवान् ॥ If it was intended that vocalisation should take place when प्र

singly stood before, then the sûtra could well have run thus प्रस्थः ॥ The use of the word पूर्वस्य implies that the rule applies when प्र stands first, though other upasargas may intervene between it and the root. Thus प्रसंस्तीतः, प्रसंस्तीतवान् ॥ The compound प्रपूर्वस्य should be explained as a Bahuvrîhi = प्रः पूर्वो यस्य धातूपसर्गसमुदायस्य स प्रपूर्व (that which consisting of root and upasarga is preceded by प्र is called प्रपूर्व). Therefore the rule is made applicable to प्रसंस्तीतः &c.

द्रवमूर्त्तिस्पर्शयोः श्यः ॥ २४ ॥ पदानि ॥ द्रवमूर्त्ति, स्पर्शयोः, श्यः ॥

वृत्तिः ॥ द्रवमूर्त्तौ द्रवकाठिन्ये स्पर्शे वर्त्तमानस्य श्यैङ् गतावित्यस्य धातोर्निष्ठायां परतः संप्रसारणं भवति ॥

24. There is vocalisation of the semivowel of the root श्या (श्यै) 'to go' when the nishṭhâ affixes follow, when the sense is "coagulation" or "cold to touch".

The word द्रवमूर्त्ति means hardening of a fluid, by coagulation &c. Thus शीनं घृतं, शीना वसा, शीनं मेदः "a coagulated butter, grease &c". The त of nishṭhâ is changed to न by VIII. 2. 47. But when the sense is that of 'cold', the त is not changed; as शीतं वर्त्तते, शीतो वायुः, शीतमुदकम् ॥ The word शीत is here used both as a noun meaning 'cold weather &c', and an adjective denoting 'cold'. There is no vocalisation when the sense is not that of 'coagulation' or 'cold', as संश्यानो वृश्चिकः 'the rolled up scorpion'. The short इ is lengthened in शीन &c, by VI. 4. 2.

प्रतेश्च ॥ २५ ॥ पदानि ॥ प्रतेः, च, (संप्रसारणम्) ॥

वृत्तिः ॥ श्य इति वर्त्तते । प्रतेरुत्तरस्य श्यायतेर्निष्ठायां परतः संप्रसारणं भवति ॥

25. There is vocalisation of श्या preceded by the upasarga प्रति, when the nishṭhâ affixes follow.

Thus प्रतिशीनः प्रतिशीनवान् ॥ This sûtra applies to cases where the words need not have the meaning of "coagulation" or "cold".

विभाषाऽभ्यवपूर्वस्य ॥२६॥ पदानि ॥ विभाषा, अभि, अव, पूर्वस्य, (संप्रसारणम्) ॥

वृत्तिः ॥ श्य इति वर्त्तते । अभि अव इत्येवंपूर्वस्य श्यायतेर्निष्ठायां विभाषा संप्रसारणं भवति ॥

26. There is optionally the vocalisation of श्या followed by the Nishṭhâ affixes, when the upasargas अभि and अव precede it.

Thus अभिशीनम् or अभिश्यानम् घृतं, अवशीनम् or अवश्यानम् वृश्चिकः ॥ This option applies even when the word means "coagulation" and "cold". As अवशीनं or अवश्यानं घृतं, मेदः ॥ अवशीतो or अवश्यानो वायुः, &c. अवशीतं or अवश्यानमुदकं ॥

The पूर्व in this sûtra serves the same purpose as in VI. 1. 23. Thus अभिसंशीनं or अभिसंश्यानं, अवसंशीनं, अवसंश्यानं ॥ According to the author of Siddhânta Kaumudi, the word पूर्व shows that it is a vyavasthita vibhâshâ, hence there is no option allowed when अभि and अव are in the middle, as, समभिश्यानं, समवश्यानं ॥ Here we cannot have the alternative forms समभिशीनं &c.

शृतं पाके ॥ २७ ॥ पदानि ॥ शृतम्, पाके, ॥

वृत्तिः ॥ विभाषेत्यनुवर्त्तते । श्रा पाके इत्येतस्य धातोर्ण्यन्तस्याण्यन्तस्य च पाके ऽभिधेये क्तप्रत्यये परतः शृभावो निपात्यते विभाषा ॥

27. Optionally शृत is formed in the sense of 'cooked', by the vocalisation of the semivowel of श्रा before the nishṭhâ affix क्त ॥

The word विभाषा is understood here. The roots श्रै 'to cook' of the Bhvadi class, and श्रा 'to cook' of the Adâdi class, and श्रा 'to cook' of the Bhvâdi sub-class Ghaṭâdi, are meant here. In all these, शृ replaces श्रा, whether causative or not. Thus शृतं क्षीरं, शृतं हविः ॥ This is a vyavasthita vivhâshâ; so that श्रा is invariably changed to शृ when referring to क्षीर and हवि, but not anywhere else. Thus श्राणा यवागूः, श्रपिता यवागूः (VII. 3. 36 and VI. 4. 92). This word does not take double causative though the sense may require it. As श्रपितं क्षीरं देवदत्तेन यज्ञदत्तेन "Devadatta through Yajñadatta has caused the milk to be cooked". The श्रा is intransitive. When the sense is that of Reflexive, or Causative, there the form शृत is to be used. As शृतं क्षीरं स्वयमेव, शृतं क्षीरं देवदत्तेन ॥

प्यायः पी ॥ २८ ॥ पदानि ॥ प्यायः, पी ॥

वृत्तिः ॥ विभाषेत्येव । ओप्यायी वृद्धावित्यस्य धातोर्निष्ठायां विभाषा पीत्ययमादेशो भवति ॥

28. पी is optionally the substitute of the root प्याय् 'to increase' before the Nishṭhâ affixes.

The root ओप्यायी वृद्धौ belongs to Bhvâdi class. The indicatory ओ shows that the affixes त and तवत् are changed into न and नवत् (VIII. 2. 45). Thus पीनं मुखम्, पीनौ बाहू, पीनमुरः ॥ The option here is also a regulated option (vyavasthita-vibhâshâ). The substitution takes place *invariably* when the root is without upasarga, and *never* when it is preceded by an upasarga. Thus प्रप्यानः, आप्यानश्चन्द्रमाः ॥ The substitution, however, must take place when the preposition आङ् precedes the root, and the words अन्धु and ऊधस् are in composition: as आपीनोऽन्धुः, आपीनमूधः ॥

लिड्यङोश्च ॥ २९ ॥ पदानि ॥ लिट्, यङोः, च, (पी) ॥

वृत्तिः ॥ विभाषेति निवृत्तम् । प्यायः पीत्येतच्चशब्देनानुकृष्यते । लिटि यङि च परतः प्यायः पीत्ययमादेशो भवति ॥

29. There is substitution of पी for प्याय् when the affixes of the Perfect (लिट्) and the Intensive (यङ्) follow.

The anuvritti of the word विभाषा ceases. The phrase प्यायः पी of the last sûtra is drawn into this by force of the word च 'and'; thus आपिप्ये, आपिप्याते, आपिप्यिरे ॥ The substitution of पी a subsequent rule, would have debarred reduplication which precedes it in order. The reduplication, however, takes place after the substitution, by force of the maxim of पुनः प्रसङ्ग &c mentioned in VI. 1. 17. Thus पी+लिट्=पि+पी+त=पि+प्य+ए (VI. 4. 82 the य being substituted)=आपिप्ये with the affix आ. So also in the Intensive, as आपेपीयते, आपेपीयेते, आपेपीयन्ते ॥

विभाषा श्वेः ॥ ३० ॥ पदानि ॥ विभाषा, श्वेः ॥

वृत्तिः ॥ लिड्यङोरिति वर्त्तते संप्रसारणमिति च । लिटि यङि च श्वयतेर्धातोर्विभाषा संप्रसारणं भवति ।

30. There is optionally the vocalisation of the semivowel of श्वि before the affixes of the Perfect and the Intensive.

The phrases लिड् यङोः and सम्प्रसारणं are to be read into this sûtra. Thus शुशावे or शिश्वाय, शुशुवतुः or शिश्वियतुः ॥ So also in the Intensive as शोशूयते or शेश्वीयते ॥ The root श्वि would not have taken vocalisation before यङ् by any previous rule, this sûtra teaches optional vocalisation. The root would have taken vocalisation before लिट्, which is a कित् affix, invariably by VI. 1. 15, this sûtra modifies that by making the substitution optional. In the alternative, when the root does become vocalised, the reduplicate is also not vocalised in spite of VI. 1. 17. This explains the form शिश्वाय, which by VI. 1. 17 would have been शुश्वाय ॥ श्वि+णल्=(श् उइ+णल् VI. 1. 30)=शु+णल् (VI. 1. 108)=शु+शु+अ (VI. 1. 8)=शुशाव ॥

णौ च संश्चङोः ॥ ३१ ॥ पदानि ॥ णौ, च, सन्, चङोः, (संप्रसारणम्,) ॥

वृत्तिः ॥ विभाषा श्वेरिति वर्त्तते । सन्परे चङ्परे च णौ परतः श्वयतेर्धातोर्विभाषा संप्रसारणं भवति ॥

31. There is optionally the vocalisation of the semivowel, in the causative of श्वि, when followed by the Desiderative सन् and the Aorist चङ् affix.

The phrase विभाषा श्वेः is understood here. In forming the Desiderative and the Reduplicated Aorist forms of the Causative of श्वि, there is optional vocalisation. Thus शुशावयिषति or शिश्वाययिषति ॥ So also in the Reduplicated Aorist चङ्, as अशूशवत् or अशिश्वयत् ॥ By the maxim संप्रसारणं संप्रसारणाश्रयं च बलीयो भवति (see sûtra VI. 1. 17), the antaranga substitution of Vriddhi &c is superseded by the samprasâraṇa and the subsidiary operations relating to it here. The vṛiddhi and the substitntion of आव take place *after* the samprasâraṇa has taken place. The sûtra VII. 4. 80 teaching the substitution of ई for the उ of the reduplicate, when सन् follows, shows by implication that the substitution caused by णि is sthânivat though it itself does not cause reduplication (I. 1. 59). Thus श्वि+णि=श्वै+इ=श्वाय्+इ=श्वायि ॥ In reduplicating श्वायि we cannot form श्वाश्वाय, but must consider the substitute equal to the original इ of श्वि and must reduplicate it. We thus get शिश्वाययिषति ॥ In the case of vocalisation, the rules of Vriddhi &c are postponed. Thus श्वि+णि+सन् (VI. I. 108)=शु+णि+सन=शौ+इ+सन्=शाव्+इ+इट्+सन्=शावे+इट्+सन्=शावयि+सन् ॥ Here we require reduplication. Here the substitute आव् in शाव् though not *caused* by सन्, is treated sthânivat under I. 1. 59 to उ, which is carried in reduplication. Similarly the Aorist: श्वि + णि + चङ् = शु + इ + अ = शु + शु + इ + अ = शु + शौ + इ + अ = शु + शाव् + इ + अ = शु + शाव् + इ ÷ अ (VII. 4. 1) = शु + शव् ÷ ० ÷ अ (VI. 4. 51) = अशूशवत् (VII. 4. 94)

ह्वः संप्रसारणम् ॥ ३२ ॥ पदानि ॥ ह्वः, संप्रसारणाम् ॥

वृत्तिः ॥ णौ च संश्चङोरिति वर्त्तते । सन्परे चङ्परे च णौ परतो ह्वः संप्रसारणं भवति ॥

32. There is the vocalisation of the semivowel of the causative of *hve* (ह्वे) before the Desiderative and the Reduplicated Aorist affixes.

The whole of the last sûtra is to be read into this sûtra. Thus जुहाव-यिषति and जुहावयिषतः, जुहावयिषन्ति; अजूहवत्, अजूहवताम् and अजूहवन् ॥ The root ह्वा does not take the augment य required by VII. 3. 37 before the affix णि, because the Samprasârana rule is stronger. The repetition of the word संप्रसारण in this sûtra, though its anuvritti was present, indicates that the force of the word विभाषा has ceased. Though this and the next sûtra could well have been made one, their separation shows that the samprasârana does not take place when another affix, not causing reduplication, intervenes. As ह्वायकामिच्छति = ह्वायकीयति; the Desiderative of this verb is जिह्वायकीयिषति ॥

अभ्यस्तस्य च ॥ ३३ ॥ पदानि ॥ अभ्यस्तस्य, च, (संप्रसारणम्) ॥

वृत्तिः ॥ ह्व इति वर्त्तते, तदभ्यस्तस्य चेत्यनेन व्यधिकरणम्, अभ्यस्तस्य या ह्वयतिः, कश्चाभ्यस्तस्य ह्वयतिः, कारणं, तेनाभ्यस्तकारणस्य ह्वयतेः प्रागेव द्विर्वचनात्संप्रसारणं भवति ॥

33. There is vocalisation of the semivowel of ह्वा in the reduplicated form, in both the syllables.

The abhyasta means the reduplicate and the reduplicated, both the syllables. The vocalisation takes place before reduplication. Thus जुहाव, जोहूयते, and जुहूषति ॥ This and the last sûtra are one, in the original of Pânini, they have been divided into two by the authority of a Vârtika.

बहुलं छन्दसि ॥ ३४ ॥ पदानि ॥ बहुलम्, छन्दसि, (संप्रसारणम्) ॥

वृत्तिः ॥ ह्व इति वर्त्तते । छन्दसि विषये ह्वयतेर्धातो र्बहुलं संप्रसारणं भवति ॥

34. In the Chhandas, the semivowel of this root is diversely vocalised.

Thus हुवे or ह्वयामि, as इन्द्राग्नी हुवे 'Invoke Indra and Agni'. देवीं सरस्वतीं हुवे ॥ The form हुवे is Atmanepada, Present tense, 1st Pers. sing. the vikarana शप् is elided, then there is vocalisation and substitution of उवङ् ॥ So also ह्वयामि मरुतः शिवान्, ह्वयामि विश्वान् देवान् ॥ So also हवः as श्रुधीहवम् (Rig I. 2. 1.) 'hear the invocation'.

चायः की ॥ ३५ ॥ पदानि ॥ चायः, की ॥

वृत्तिः ॥ बहुलं छन्दसीति वर्त्तते । चायतेर्धातोश्छन्दसि विषये बहुलं कीत्ययमादेशो भवति ॥

35. For चाय् is diversely substituted की in the Chhandas.

Thus विधुना निचिक्युः, नान्य चिक्युर्न निचिक्युरन्यम् ॥ These are forms ending in the affix उस् of the Perfect. Sometimes there is no substitution. As अग्निर्ज्योतिर्निचाय्यः ॥

अपस्पृधेथामानृचुरानृहुश्चिच्युषेतित्याजश्राताः श्रितमाशीराशीर्त्ताः ॥ ३६ ॥ पदानि ॥ अपस्पृधेथाम्, आनृचुः, आनृहुः, चिच्युषे, तित्याज, श्राताः, श्रितम्, आशीः, आशीर्ताः, ॥

वृत्तिः ॥ अपस्पृधेथाम् आनृचुः आनृहुः चिच्युषे तित्याज, श्राताः, श्रितम्, आशीः, आशीर्तः, एते निपात्यन्ते छन्दसि विषये ॥

36. In the Chhandas, the following irregular forms are met with :—अपस्पृधेथाम्, आनृचुः, आनृहुः, चिच्युषे, तित्याज, श्राताः, श्रितम्, आशीः and आशीर्तः ॥

The word छन्दसि is understood here. From the root स्पर्द्ध 'to challenge', is formed अपस्पृधेथाम् being the Imperfect (लङ्), 2nd Pers. Dual, Atmanepada: there is reduplication of the root, vocalisation of र्, and the elision of अ irregularly. As, इन्द्रश्च विष्णो यदपस्पृधेथाम् ॥ In secular language the form is अपस्पर्धेथाम् ॥ Some say, it is derived from स्पर्द्ध with the preposition अप, the vocalisation of र, the elision of अ, and the non-prefixing of the augment अट् in the Imperfect (VI. 4. 75). The counter-example of this will be अपास्पर्द्धेथाम् ॥ From अर्च and अर्ह 'to respect, to worship', are derived आनृचुः and आनृहुः in the Perfect before the 3rd per. pl. उस्, there being vocalisation of र and the elision of अ irregularly. Then there is reduplication, then ऋ changed to अ, then the lengthening of this अ, then the addition of the augment न, as : अर्च्+उस्=ऋच्+उस्=ऋ+ऋच्+उस्=अ+ऋच्+उस् (VII. 4. 66)=आ+ऋच्+उस् (VII. 4. 70)=आ+न्+ऋच्+उस् (VII. 4. 71)=आनृचुः ॥ The irregularity consists in the samprasârṇa with the elision of अ ॥ Thus यवमा अर्कमानृचुः, न वसून्यानृहुः ॥ The secular forms will be आनर्चुः, आनर्हुः ॥ The form चिच्युषे is the Perfect 2nd per. sing. of the root च्युङ् 'to go': there is vocalisation of the reduplicate, and the non-addition of the augment इट् before the affix से ॥ This is the irregularity. The regular form is चुच्युविषे ॥ The form तित्याज is the Perfect of त्यज्, the vocalisation of the reduplicate is the irregularity. The regular form is तत्याज ॥ From the root श्रीञ् 'to cook', is derived श्राता before the Nishthâ affix, श्री changed to श्रा irregularly. As श्रातास्त इन्द्रसोमाः ॥ The form श्रितं is also derived from the same root by shortening the vowel with the same affix. As सोमो गौरी अधिश्रितः, श्रिता नो गृहाः ॥ Some say the श्रा substitution of श्री takes place when the word refers to सोम, in the plural, and श्रि when it refers to other than सोम ॥ Sometimes the word श्रातः is seen in the singular, referring to objects other than सोम । Thus यदि श्रातो जुहोतन ॥ In fact, the exhibition of the word श्राताः in the plural in the sûtra is not absolutely necessary. The words आशीर् and आशीर्त्तः are from the same root श्री, with the prefix आङ् and taking the affixes क्विप् and क्त respectively. Before these श्री is replaced by शीर्, and the non-addition of न in the Nishṭhâ is irregular. As, तामाशीरा दुहन्ति आशीर्त्त ऊर्जम्, क्षीरैर्मध्यत आशीर्त्तः ॥

न संप्रसारणे संप्रसारणम् ॥ ३७ ॥ पदानि ॥ न, संप्रसारणे, सम्प्रसारणम् ॥

वृत्ति ॥ संप्रसारणे परतः पूर्वस्य यणः संप्रसारणं न भवति ।

वार्त्तिकम् ॥ ऋचि त्रेरुत्तरपदादिलोपश्छन्दसि ॥ वा० ॥ रयेर्मतौ बहुलम् ॥

37. When a semivowel hase been once vocalised, there is no vocalisation of the other semivowel that may precede it in the same word.

Thus व्यध्; has two semi-vowels व् and य्; when य् is once vocalised into इ, the preceding व will not be vocalised into उ ॥ Thus we have विद्धः ॥ From व्यच्—विचितः, व्येञ्—संवीतः ॥ Though the rule of vocalisation does not specify what particular semivowel is to be vocalised, yet according to the maxim that the operation is to be performed on the letter nearest to the operator, the second semivowel in the above cases is vocalised and the first is not, by force of this rule. Had the first semi-vowel been vocalised, then there would be no scope for this sûtra, because then no semi-vowel will be found *preceding* a vocalised letter. This sûtra is a jñapaka that the vocalisation commences with the second of the conjunct semi-vowels.

Though the anuvritti of संप्रसारण was understood here, the repetition of this word shows that the prohibition of double vocalisation in the same word applies even when the semivowels are not contiguous. Thus by VI. 1. 133 there is vocalisation of the word युवन्, the व being changed to उ, the य is not changed as यूना ॥ It might be objected that when the उ of यु, and उ the samprasâraṇa of व coalesce into one by sandhi rules, then there being the substitution of one long ऊ for the two उ's and this is sthânivat to the original, the य and व् of युवन् should be considered in fact as contiguous and not separated by an intervening letter, and therefore, the explanation given above does not hold good; we reply. The substitution of one long vowel for two vowels, is not considered sthânivat (See I. 1. 58). Even though it be considered as sthânivat, it is still a separating letter.

Vart:—There is vocalisation of the semivowel of त्रि when followed by ऋच्, and there is elision of the ऋ of ऋच्, when it refers to Metres. As तिस्र ऋचो यस्मिन्=तृचं सुक्तं ॥ तृचं साम ॥ The word तृच् takes the samâsânta affix अ by V. 4. 74. Why do we say when referring to a metre? Observe त्र्यृचं कर्म ॥

Vârt:—In the Chhandas there is diversely vocalisation of the semi-vowel of रयि followed by the affix मतुप् as रयि + मत् = रइ + मत् = र + इ + मत् = र + इ + वत् (VIII. 2. 15) = रेवत्; as, आ रेवानेतु नो विशः ॥ Sometimes it does not take place, as रयिमान् पुष्टिवर्द्धनः ॥ The म here is not changed to व as required by VIII. 2. 15.

Vârt:—There is vocalisation of कक्ष्या before मत् when a Name is meant: as कक्षीवन्तं य औशिजः ॥ This Vârtika is unnecessary. See VIII. 2. 12 where the form कक्षीवत् is given.

लिटि वयो यः ॥ ३८ ॥ पदानि ॥ लिटि, वयः, यः (संप्रसारणम् न) ॥

वृत्तिः ॥ न संप्रसारणमित्यनुवर्त्तते । लिटि परतो वयो यकारस्य संप्रसारणं न भवति ॥

38. In the substituted root वय (II. 4. 41), the य in the Perfect is not vocalised.

The phrase न सम्प्रसारणं is understood here. Thus उवाय, ऊयतुः, ऊयुः ॥ The word लिट् is employed in this aphorism for the sake of subsequent sûtras, this one could have done well without it even.

वश्चास्यान्यतरस्यां किति ॥३९॥ पदानि ॥ वः, च, अस्य, अन्यतरस्याम्, किति॥

वृत्तिः ॥ अस्य वयो यकारस्य किति लिटि परतो वकारादेशो भवत्यन्यतरस्याम् ॥

39. Before the tense-affixes of the Perfect that have an indicatory क (I. 2. 5), for the य् of वय् may optionally be substituted a व् ॥

Thus ऊयतुः or ऊवतुः, ऊवुः or ऊयुः ॥ According to Pâtanjali, the phrase वश्चास्य of this sûtra could have been dispensed with; this much would have been enough:— अन्यतरस्यां किति वेञः ॥ Thus वे + अतुस् = वा + वा + अतुस् = ववतुः and ववुः (the vocalisation being prohibited). In the alternative:—वा + अतुस् = उ + अतुस् = उ + उवङ् + अतुस् (VI. 1. 77) = ऊवतुः, ऊवुः ॥ Here there is vocalisation. In the case of वय् substitute, the य is never vocalised, so we have ऊयतुः, ऊयुः ॥ Thus all the three forms have been evolved without using वश्चास्य ॥

वेञः ॥ ४० ॥ पदानि ॥ वेञः, (संप्रसारणम्, न) ॥

वृत्तिः ॥ लिटीत्यनुवर्त्तते । वेञ् तन्तुसंतानइत्यस्य धातोर्लिटि परतः संप्रसारणं न भवति ॥

40. The semivowel of वे 'to weave' is not vocalised in the Perfect.

Thus ववौ, ववतुः, ववुः ॥ This root belongs to यजादि class and would have been vocalised before कित् affixes by VI. 1. 15; and before non-कित् affixes the Reduplicate syllable of the Perfect would have been vocalised by VI. 1. 17. Both vocalisations are prohibited here.

ल्यपि च ॥ ४१ ॥ पदानि ॥ ल्यपि, च, (संप्रसारणम्, न) ॥

वृत्तिः ॥ वेञ इत्यनुवर्त्तते । ल्यपि च परतो व्येञः संप्रसारणं न भवति ॥

41. The semivowel of वे is not vocalised when the Participial affix ल्यप् follows.

Thus प्रवाय, उपवाय ॥ The separation of this sûtra from the last, is for the sake of the subsequent sûtras, into which the anuvritti of ल्यप् only runs.

ज्यश्च ॥ ४२ ॥ पदानि ॥ ज्यः, च, (संप्रसारणम् न) ॥

वृत्तिः ॥ ल्यपीत्येव । ज्या वयोहानावित्यस्य धातोर्ल्यपि परतः संप्रसारणं न भवति ॥

42. The semivowel of ज्या 'to grow old' is not vocalised when the affix ल्यप् follows.

Thus प्रज्याय, उपज्याय ॥

व्यश्च ॥ ४३ ॥ पदानि ॥ व्यः, च, (संप्रसारणम्, न) ॥

वृत्तिः ॥ ल्यपीत्येव । व्येञ् संवरणइत्येतस्य धातोर्ल्यपि परतः संप्रसारणं न भवति ॥

43. The semivowel of व्या (व्ये) 'to cover' is not vocalised when the affix ल्यप् follows.

As प्रव्याय, उपव्याय ॥ The separation of this sûtra from the last, is for the sake of the subsequent sûtra, in which the anuvritti of व्ये runs.

विभाषा परेः ॥ ४४ ॥ पदानि ॥ विभाषा, परेः, (सम्प्रसारणम्, न) ॥

वृत्तिः ॥ ल्यपि च व्यश्चेत्यनुवर्त्तते । परेरुत्तरस्य व्येञित्येतस्य धातोर्ल्यपि परतो विभाषा संप्रसारणं न भवति ॥

44. The vocalisation may optionally take place when व्ये preceded by परि takes the affix ल्यप् ॥

Thus परिवीय यूपम् or परिव्याय ॥ The augment तुक् presented by VI. 1. 71 is debarred by VI. 4. 2. which causes the lengthening of the vowel: since VI. 4. 2 is subsequent to VI. 1. 71.

आदेच उपदेशेऽशिति ॥ ४५ ॥ पदानि ॥ आत्, एचः, उपदेशे, अशिति ॥

वृत्तिः ॥ धातो रिति वर्त्तते । एजन्तो यो धातुरुपदेशे तस्याकारादेशो भवति शिति तु प्रत्यये न भवति ॥

45. In a root, which in the system of grammatical instruction (i. e. in the Dhâtupâṭha), ends with a diphthong (ए, ऐ, ओ and औ), there is the substitution of आ for the diphthong, provided that no affix with an indicatory श् follows it.

The word धातोः is to be read into this sûtra from VI. 1. 8. Thus ग्लै—ग्लाता, ग्लातुम्, ग्लातव्यम्, शो—निशाता, निशातुम्, निशातव्यम् ॥ Why do we say ending with an एच् (diphthong)? Observe कर्त्ता from कृ, and हर्त्ता from हृ ॥ Why do we say in upadeśa or Dhâtupâtha? Observe चेता, स्तोता where चे and स्तो are not the forms taught in the first enunciation of the root in the Dhâtupâtha, but are secondary forms. Why do we say, before non-शित् affixes? Observe ग्लै-।-शप् + तिप् = ग्लायति, म्लायति ॥ Exception is, however, made in the case of the affix एश् of the Perfect: as जग्ले, मम्ले ॥ This is explained by interpreting the word शित् as शिदादि, that is the affixes having an indicatory श in the beginning: एश् has श् at the end. This is done on the maxim यस्मिन् विधिस्तदादावल् ग्रहणे "when a term which denotes a letter is exhibited in a rule in the form of the Locative case, and qualifies some thing else which likewise stands in the Locative case, that which is qualified by it must be regarded as beginning with the letter which is denoted by the term in question and not as ending whith it".

The word अशिति is an example of प्रसज्यप्रतिषेधः. a simple prohibition of a contingent case. Therefore, the substitution of आ for एच् vowels, is not caused by the affixes that follow, but must take place prior to the occasion for the application of the affixes arises. Thus III. 1. 136 ordains क after roots ending in आ; so that ग्लै and म्लै are presupposed to end in आ when applying this affix: thus सुग्लः, सुम्लः ॥ Similarly by III. 3. 128 we apply युच् to ग्लै and म्लै by presupposing it as आदन्त roots: as सुग्लानः, सुम्लानः ॥

The word आ is understood in all the subsequent sûtras upto VI. 1. 57

न व्यो लिटि ॥ ४६ ॥ पदानि ॥ न, व्यः, लिटि, (आत्) ॥

वृत्तिः ॥ व्येञ् इत्येतस्य धातोर्लिटि परत आकारादेशो न भवति ॥

46. There is not the substitution of आ for the Diphthong of the root व्ये when the affixes of the Perfect follow.

Thus संविव्याय, संविव्ययिथ ॥ The reduplicate of the Perfect is vocalised here by VI. 1. 17. The Vriddhi in संविव्याय takes place by VII. 2. 115 before the णित् affix णल् ॥

स्फुरतिस्फुलत्योर्घञि ॥ ४७ ॥ पदानि ॥ स्फुरति, स्फुलत्योः, घञि, (आत्) ॥

वृत्तिः ॥ आदेच इति वर्त्तते। स्फुर स्फुल चलनइत्येतयोर्द्धात्वोरेचः स्थाने घञि परत आकारादेशो भवति ॥

47. In the roots स्फुर् and स्फुल् 'to move', there is the substitution of the आ for the diphthong when the affix घञ् follows.

Thus विस्फारः instead of विस्फोरः, and विस्फालः instead of विस्फोलः ॥ By VIII. 3. 76, the स is optionally changed to ष after वि, as विष्फारः, and विष्फालः ॥

क्रीङ्जीनां णौ ॥ ४८ ॥ पदानि ॥ क्री, इङ्, जीनाम्, णौ, (आत्) ॥

वृत्तिः ॥ डुक्रीञ् द्रव्यविनिमये, इङ् अध्ययने, जि जये, इत्येतेषां धातूनामेचः स्थाने णौ परत आकारादेशो भवति ॥

48. The substution of आ for the diphthong takes place in the causatives of the roots क्री 'to by', इ 'to study' and जि 'to conquer.'

Thus क्रापयति, अध्यापयति and जापयति ॥ The augment पु is added by VII. 3. 36, since these roots end in long आ ॥

सिध्यतेरपारलौकिके ॥ ४९ ॥ पदानि ॥ सिध्यतेः, अपारलौकिके ॥

वृत्तिः ॥ णाविति वर्त्तते। षिधु हिंसासंराद्धयो रित्यस्य धातोरपारलौकिकेर्थे वर्त्तमानस्यैचः स्थाने णौ परत आकारादेशो भवति ॥

49. The substitution of आ takes place for the diphthong in the causative of सिध्, when it does not refer to the next life.

The word पारलौकिक is derived form परलोक 'the next world' by adding the affix ठञ् with the force of 'for the sake of' (V. I. 109). The double Vṛiddhi takes place by VII. 3. 20. The sense of the word सिध् must refer to अज्ञान or non-intelligent things for the purposes of this substitution. Thus अन्नं साधयति, ग्रामं साधयति ॥ Why do we say when not referring to the next world? See तपस्तापसं सेधयति, स्वान्येवनं कर्माणि सेधयन्ति ॥ The force of सिध् is here that of knowledge, तापसः सिद्ध्यति = ज्ञानविशेषमासादयति ॥ The ascetic acquires certain knowledge through austerities, the knowledge so acquired produces its result in the next world (परलोकं) i. e. the next life, therefore, the साधन of the ascetic is for the sake of the next life, and so there is no substitution of आ for ए ॥ Why the substitution does not take place here: अन्नं साधयति, ब्राह्मणेभ्यो दास्यामि 'he causes food to be prepared for the purpose of giving to the Brahmanas'. Here though the gift of the food produces effect in the next world, yet as that is the effect of दान and not of the verb सिध्, the substitution does take place. When the verb सिध् *directly* and not through the mediation of another action, produces pâraloukika effect, then the substitution does not take place. The verb सिध् here belongs to the Divâdi class and not to the Bhvâdi, as the form सिध्यति in the sûtra shows it.

मीनातिमिनोतिदीङां ल्यपि च ॥ ५० ॥ पदानि ॥ मीनाति, मिनोति, दीङाम्, ल्यपि, च ॥

वृत्तिः ॥ आदेच उपदेशइति वर्त्तते । मीञ् हिंसायाम्, डुमिञ् प्रक्षेपणे, दीङ् क्षये, इत्येतेषां धातूनां ल्यपि विषये चकारादेचश्च विषये उपदेशएव प्राक् प्रत्ययोत्पत्तेरलोन्त्यस्य स्थाने आकारादेशो भवति ॥

50. And there is substitution of आ for the finals of मी 'to hurt', मि 'to scatter', and दी 'to decay' when the affix ल्यप् follows, as well as before those affixes which demand this substitution for the diphthong.

By force of the word च 'and' in the sûtra, the substitution takes place of the diphthongs also of these verbs before all affixes other than ल्यप्, and this substitution takes place, before the occasion for the applying of the affixes arises (उपदेशावस्थायाम् आत्वं भवति) ॥ So that these verbs should be understood as if they were enunciated with an आ, so that all rules of affixes relating to आ will apply to them. Thus प्रमाता, प्रमातव्यम्, प्रमातुम्, प्रमाय, निमाता, निमातुम्, निमातव्यम्, निमाय, उपदाता, उपदातव्यम्, उपदातुम्, उपदाय ॥ The substitution of आ being understood to have taken place in the very उपदेश (in the dhâtupâṭha) of these roots, the affixes relating to roots ending in इ or ई do not apply to these at all. Thus उपदायो वर्त्तते, ईषदुपदानं, formed by घञ् and युच् by taking दी = दा and adding these affixes (III. 3. 128 and III. 3. 18) and not the affixes अच् (III. 3. 56) and खल् (III. 3. 126).

विभाषा लीयतेः ॥ ५१ ॥ पदानि ॥ विभाषा, लीयतेः ॥

वृत्तिः ॥ ल्यपीति वर्त्तते, आदेच उपदेशइति च । लीङ् श्लेषणइति दिवादिः ली श्लेषणइति क्र्यादिस्तयोरुभयोरपि यका निर्देशः स्मर्यते । लीयतर्द्धातोर्थापि च एचश्च विषये उपदेशएवालोन्त्यस्य स्थाने विभाषा आकारादेशो भवति ॥

वार्त्तिकम् ॥ निमीमिलियां खलचोः प्रतिषेधो वक्तव्यः ॥

51. There is optionally the substitution of आ for the final of ली 'to adhere', in the very dhâtupâṭha, when the affix ल्यप् follows or such an affix as would demand this substitution of the diphthong.

The final of ली will take guṇa substitution before णित् affixes, and will become ले, this incipient diphthong ए is changed to आ by this rule. The same is the case with all the roots subsequently taught, thus खिद् will be खेद्, and then ए changed to आ, गुर् = गोर् and ओ changed to आ &c. Therefore we have employed the anuvritti of एच् 'diphthong' in all sûtras. The words ल्याप and आदेच उपदेश are understood here. The roots ली belonging to Divâdi and Kriyâdi are both included here. Thus विलाता, विलातुम्, विलातव्यम्, विलाय, विलेता विलेतुम्, विलेतव्यम् and विलीय ॥

Vârt:—The आ substitution does not take place when the affix अच् (III. 3. 56, III. 1. 134) and खल् (III. 3. 126) come after नि, मि, मी and ली : as, ईषन्निमयः, निमयो वर्त्तते । ईषत्प्रमयः, प्रमयो वर्त्तते । ईषद् विलयः, विलयो वर्तते ॥

The ली invariably takes आ substitution when the sense is that of 'showing respect,' 'deceiving' or 'insulting'. As कस्त्वामुल्लापयते, श्येनो वर्त्तिकामुल्लापयते ॥ The option allowed by this aphorism is a restricted option (vyavasthita-vibhâshâ) The substitution of आ for the final of ई is *optional* when the sense of the root is not that of 'showing respect', 'subduing' or 'deceiving'. But when it has any one of these three senses, the substitution is *compulsory*. See I. 1. 70.

खिदेश्छन्दसि ॥ ५२ ॥ पदानि ॥ खिदेः, छन्दसि ॥

वृत्तिः ॥ विभाषेति वर्त्तते । खिद दैन्यइत्यस्य धातोरेचः स्थाने छन्दसि विषये विभाषा आकार आदेशो भवति ॥

52. There is optionally the substitution of आ in the room of the diphthong of the verb खिद् 'to suffer pain', in the Chhandas.

The word विभाषा is understood here. Thus चित्तं चिखाद or चिखेद ॥ In secular literature we have चित्तं खेदयति ॥

अपगुरो णमुलि ॥ ५३ ॥ पदानि ॥ अप, गुरः, णमुलि, (आत्) ॥

वृत्तिः ॥ गुरी उद्यमनइत्यस्य धातोरपपूर्वस्य णमुलि परत एचः स्थाने विभाषा आकार आदेशो भवति ।

53. There is optionally the substitution of आ in the room of the diphthong of the root गुर 'to exert' when preceded by the preposition अप and taking the affix णमुल् ॥

The affix णमुल् forming the Absolutive Participle is added by III. 4. 22, and the word formed by it is repeated. Thus अपगारमपगारम् or अपगोरमपगोरम् ॥ So also this affix is added by III. 4. 53: as, अस्यपगारं युध्यन्ते or अस्यपगोरं युध्यन्ते "they are fighting with raised swords'.

चिस्फुरोर्णौ ॥ ५४ ॥ पदानि ॥ चि, स्फुरोः, णौ ॥

वृत्तिः ॥ चिञ् स्फुर इत्येतयोर्धात्वोर्णौ परत एचः स्थाने विभाषा आकारादेशो भवति ॥

54. There is optionally the substitution of आ in the room of the diphthong of the roots चि and स्फुर when in the Causative.

Thus चापयति, चाययति (VII. 3. 36 for the addition of पु) so also स्फोरयति or स्फारयति ॥

प्रजने वीयतेः ॥ ५५ ॥ पदानि ॥ प्रजने, वीयतेः ॥

वृत्तिः ॥ णाविति वर्त्तते । वी गतिप्रजनकान्त्यसनखादनेषु इत्यस्य धातोः प्रजने वर्त्तमानस्य णौ परतो विभाषा आकारादेशो भवति ।

55. There is optionally the substitution of आ in the room of the diphthong of the root वी in the causative, when meaning 'to conceive an embryo'.

The root वी Adâdi 39 means 'to go, to conceive, to shine, to eat, and to desire'. The substitution takes place when it means 'to impregnate or conceive'. Thus पुरो वातो गाः प्रवापयति or प्रवाययति = गर्भं ग्राहयति ॥ The word प्रजन means the receiving of the embryo which in course of time will lead to the birth of a child.

बिभेतेर्हेतुभये ॥ ५६ ॥ पदानि ॥ बिभेतेः, हेतु भये ॥

वृत्तिः ॥ णाविति वर्त्तते विभाषेति च । हेतुरिह पारिभाषिकः स्वतन्त्रस्य प्रयोजकस्ततो यद्भयम्, स यस्य भयस्य साक्षाद्धेतुः, तद्भयं हेतुभयम् । तत्र वर्त्तमानस्य ञिभी भयइत्यस्य धातोर्णौ परतो विभाषा आकारादेशो भवति ॥

56. There is optionally the substitution of आ for the diphthong of the root भी 'to fear', in the Causative, when the fear is produced directly through the agent of the causative.

The words णौ and विभाषा are understood here. The word हेतु in the sûtra is the technical हेतु meaning स्वतन्त्रस्य प्रयोजकः (I. 4. 54 and 55). When the

Hetu Agent himself is directly the cause of the fear, that fear is called the हेतुभय "the fear caused by the Hetu". Thus मुण्डो भापयते (VII. 3. 36) or भीषयते (VII. 3. 40). So also जटिलो भापयते or भीषयते ॥ This root takes the affixes of the Atmanepada, by I. 3. 68; and the augment षु is added by VII. 3. 40, which does not come when there is आ substitution, for the भी in VII. 3. 40 is equal to भी + ई i. e. भी ending in ई; and means भी ending in ई takes the augment षु ॥

Why do we say 'when the agent of the causative is the producer of the fear'? Observe कुञ्चिकयैनं भाययति देवदत्तः ॥ Here the fear is produced from the कुञ्चिका and not from Devadatta the Agent.

नित्यं स्मयतेः ॥ ५७ ॥ पदानि ॥ नित्यं, स्मयतेः ॥

वृत्ति ॥ णाविति वर्त्तते, हेतुभय इति च । नित्यग्रहणाद्विभाषाति निवृत्तम् । स्मिङ् ईषद्धसनइत्यस्य धातोर्हेतुभयेर्थे णौ परतो नित्यमाकारादेशो भवति ॥

57. There is invariably the substitution of आ for the diphthong of the root स्मि 'to smile' in the Causative, when the astonishment is produced directly through the Agent of the Causative.

The words णौ and हेतुभय are both understood here. The word नित्य shows that the anuvritti of विभाषा ceases. Thus मुण्डोजटिलो वा विस्मापयते ॥ Otherwise we have कुञ्चिकयैनं विस्माययति ॥ The word भय here is taken to mean स्मयति i. e. 'wondering, feeling astonished'. See I. 3. 68 where also this meaning has been extended to भय by its connection with भीस्मि together; the proper word ought to have been हेतुस्मये in connection with स्मि, and हेतुभये in connection with भी ॥

सृजिदृशोर्झल्यमकिति ॥ ५८ ॥ पदानि ॥ सृजि, दृशोः, झलि, अम्, अकिति ॥

वृत्ति ॥ सृज विसर्गे, दृशिर् प्रेक्षणे, इत्येतयोर्धात्वोर्झलादावाकिति प्रत्यये परतो ऽमागमो भवति ॥

58. The augment अम् (अ) comes after the ऋ of सृज् 'to create', and दृश 'to see', when an affix beginning with a झल् letter (the Mute and the Sibilant) follows: provided that it has no indicatry क ॥

Thus सृज् + तृन् = सृ + अ + ज् + तृ = स्रष्टृ nom. sing. स्रष्टा, so also स्रष्टुम्, स्रष्टव्यम्, द्रष्टा, द्रष्टुम्, द्रष्टव्यम् ॥ This अम् augment prevents the guṇa substitute ordained by VII. 3. 86. But in अस्राक्षीत् and अद्राक्षीत् the Vṛiddhi takes place in the Aorist, after the augment अम् had taken effect.

Why do we say when beginning with a Mute or a Sibilant? Observe सर्जनम्, दर्शनम् with यु ॥ Why do we say not having an indicatory क? Observe सृष्टः, दृष्टः before the affix क्त ॥ The forms of roots being exhibited in the sûtra, the rule applies when affixes relating to verbs come after these, and not when other affixes relating to noun follow. Thus रज्जुसृड्भ्याम्, देवदृग्भ्याम् ॥ Here the words are used as nouns rather than verbs. For the maxim धातोः स्वरूपग्रहणे तत्प्रत्यये कार्यं applies here.

अनुदात्तस्य चर्दुपधस्यान्यतरस्याम् ॥ ५९ ॥ पदानि ॥ अनुदात्तस्य, च, ऋत्, उपधस्य, अन्यतरस्याम् ॥

वृत्तिः ॥ उपदेशइति वर्त्तते, झल्यमकितीति च। उपदेशे ऽनुदात्तस्य धातोर्ऋकारोपधस्य झलादावकिति प्रत्यये परतो ऽन्यतरस्याममागमो भवति ॥

59. The augment अम् comes optionally after the ऋ of those roots which are exhibited in the Dhâtupâṭha as anudâtta, when such roots end in a consonant having a ऋ as penultimate, and are followed by an affix beginning with a mute or sibilant and not having an indicatory क ॥

The word उपदेश is understood here, so also झल्यमकिति ॥ Thus त्रप्ता or तर्पिता or तर्प्ता, द्रप्ता, दर्पिता or दर्प्ता ॥ The roots तृप 'to satisfy', and दृप 'to be happy to release', belong to Divâdi class, sub-class Radhâdi, and they take the augment इट् optionally (VII, 2. 45), so we have the three forms given above: for these roots are also anudâtta in their first enunciation.

Why do we say "which are anudâtta in the Upadesá or the system of grammatical instruction"? Observe वर्ढा, वर्ढुम्, वर्ढव्यम्, from वृहू उद्यमने which is exhibited as उदात्त, and because it has an indicatory ऊ it takes इट् optionally. Why do we say 'having a penultimate ऋ letter'? Observe भेत्ता, छेत्ता ॥ Why do we say 'before an affix beginning with a mute or a sibilant'? Observe तर्पणम्, दर्पणम् ॥ Why do we say 'not having an indicatory क'? Observe तृप्तः, दृप्तः ॥ Before affixes not beginning with a झल् consonant this augment will not be inserted, as तर्पणम्, दर्पणम् ॥

शीर्षश्छन्दसि ॥ ६० ॥ पदानि ॥ शीर्षन्, छन्दसि ॥

वृत्तिः ॥ शीर्षन्निति शब्दान्तरं शिरःशब्देन समानार्थं छन्दसि विषये निपात्यते ॥

60. The word शीर्षन् is found in the Chhandas.

This word is another form of शिरः and means 'head'. This is not a substitute of शिर in the Vedas, for both forms are found therein. Thus शीर्ष्णा हि तत्र सोमं क्रीतं हरन्ति, अस्य शीर्ष्णो दीर्घाग्रम् ॥ In the secular literature there is only one form शिरः ॥

ये च तद्धिते ॥ ६१ ॥ पदानि ॥ ये, च, तद्धिते ॥

वृत्तिः ॥ शीर्षन्निति वर्त्तते । आदेशोयमिष्यते स कथं तद्धितइति हि परं निमित्तमुपादीयते स तदनुरूपां प्रकृतिं शिरःशब्दमाक्षिपति । यकारादौ तद्धिते परतः शिरःशब्दस्य शीर्षन्नादेशो भवति ॥

'वार्त्तिकम् ॥ वा केशेषु ॥

61. There is the substitution of this stem शीर्षन् for शिरस् when a Taddhita-affix beginning with य follows.

The word शीर्षन् is understood here. This rule teaches substitution. The original for which this substitution comes is not given in the sûtra, we must infer it. The appropriate original is शिरस् ॥ Thus शीर्षण्यो हि मुख्यो भवति,

शीर्षण्यः स्वरः ॥ The affix यत् is here added by IV. 3. 55. The word शीर्षण् retains its original form before this affix यत्, the final अन् not being replaced by anything else (VI. 4. 168) Wl.y do we say when 'a Taddhita-affix follows'? Observe शिर इच्छति = शिरस्यति, here य is not a Taddhita affix, and so there is no substitution.

Vârt:—The substitution is optional when meaning 'hair'. As शीर्षण्याः केशाः or शिरस्याः केशाः ॥

अचि शीर्षः ॥ ६२ ॥ पदानि ॥ अचि, शीर्षः ॥

वृत्तिः ॥ अजादौ तद्धिते शिरसः शीर्षशब्द आदेशो भवति ॥

62. There is the substitution of शीर्ष for शिरस् when a Taddhita affix beginning with a vowel follows.

Thus हस्तिशिरसोऽपत्यं = हास्तिशीर्षिः formed by adding the Patronymic affix इञ् (IV. 1. 96). So also स्थूलशिरस इदम् = स्थौलशीर्षम् ॥ Had the word been शीर्षन् (instead of शीर्ष as taught herein) then it would have retained its final न् before these affixes and would not have given the proper forms (VI. 4. 168). Again in forming the feminine of हास्तिशीर्षिः by adding ष्यङ् (IV. 1. 78), arises this difficulty :—ष्यङ् (य) is a Taddhita affix beginning with य, when this is applied to हास्तिशीर्षिः, we must apply the last rule and change the शीर्ष into शीर्षन् (for शीर्षन् being the substitute of शिरस is *prima facie* a substitute of शीर्ष also for the purposes of that rule VI. 1. 61). The form which we get will be this, हास्तिशीर्षिः + ष्यङ् = हास्तिशीर्षण् + य (VI. 1. 61) = हास्तिशीर्षण्या (VI. 4. 168). But this is a wrong form, the desired form is हास्तिशीर्ष्या ॥ How do we explain this? Thus हास्तिशीर्षि + ष्यङ् = हास्तिशीर्ष् + य (the इ is elided by VI. 4. 148 and in the room of इ we substitute a *zero* or लोपादेश) ॥ Now this âdeśa becomes sthânivat to इ, thus the affix य not being *directly* applied to शीर्ष, because this zero intervenes, शीर्ष is not replaced by शीर्षन् as required by VI. 1. 61, for it is not *followed* by an affix beginning with य but by a zero sthânivat to इञ् affix.

This sûtra is not of Pâṇini, but is really a Vârtika raised to the rank of a sûtra by later authors.

पद्दन्नोमास्हृन्निशसन्यूषन्दोषन्यकञ्छकन्नुदन्नासञ्छस्प्रभृतिषु ॥ ६३ ॥ पदानि ॥ पद्, दत्, नस्, मास्, हृत्, निश्, असन्, यूषन्, दोषन्, यकन्, शकन्, उदन्, आसन्, शस्, प्रभृतिषु ॥

वृत्ति ॥ पाद दन्त नासिका मास हृदय निशा असृज् यूष दोष यकृत् शकृत् उदक आसन इत्येतेषां शब्दानां स्थाने शस्प्रभृतिप्रत्ययेषु परतः पद् दत् नस् मास् हृत् निश् असन् यूषन् दोषन् यकन् शकन् उदन् आसन् इत्येते आदेशा यथासंख्यं भवन्ति ॥

वा० ॥ पद्यादिषु मांस्पृत्स्नूनामुपसंख्यानम् ॥ वा० ॥ नस् नासिकाया यत्तस्क्षुद्रेषु ॥

वा० ॥ यति वर्णनगरयोर्नेति वक्तव्यम् ॥

63. In the weak cases (beginning with the accusative plural) the following stems are substituted :—पद् for पाद्, दत् for दन्त, नस् for नासिका, मास् for मास, हृद् for हृदय, निश् for निशा, असन् for असृज्, यूषन् for यूष, दोषन् for दोस्, यकन् for यकृत, शकन् for शकृत, उदन् for उदक and आसन् for आस्य ॥

The Kâśikâ gives आसन् as the substitute for आसन, the Sidhânta Kaumudi gives the original as आस्य which has been adopted in the above. Some say that these substitutions take place in the Vedic Literature only, others say, they are general. Others read the word 'optionally' into this sûtra from VI. 1. 59 and hold that these substitutes are optional and not compulsory.

Examples :—1. पद्—निपद्श्चतुरो जहि, पद्ावर्तय गोदुहम् ॥ 2 दत्—या दती धावति तस्यै श्यावदन् ॥ 3 नस्—सूकरस्त्वखनन्नसा ॥ 4 मास्—मासित्वा पश्यामि चक्षुषा ॥ 5 हृद्—हृदा पूतेन मनसा जातवेदसम् । 6 निश्—अमावास्यायां निशि यजेत ॥ 7 असन्—असिक्नौ स्नावरोहति । 8 यूषन्—या पात्राणि यूष्ण आसेचनानि ॥ 9 दोषन्—यत्ते दोष्णो दौर्भाग्यम् ॥ 10 यकन्—यक्नो वद्यति ॥ 11 शकन् शक्नो वद्यति ॥ 12 उदन्—उद्नो दिव्यस्य नावा ते ॥ 13 आसन्—आसनि किं लभे मधूनि ।

Why do we say when the weak terminations शस् &c follow? Observe पादौ ते प्रतिपीड्यौ नासिके तें कृशे ॥ As examples of this substitutions in the secular literature also, the following may be given :—

व्यायामक्षुण्ण गात्रस्य पद्भ्यामुद्वर्तितस्य च ।
व्याधयो नोपसर्पन्ति वैनतेयमिवोरगाः ॥

These substitutions take place before other affixes also : as, शला दोषणी, ककुद्दोषणी याचते महादेवः ॥

Vârt:—The following substitutions also take place : मांस for मांस, पृत् for पृतना, and स्नु for सानुः as यन्नीक्षणं मांस्पचन्याः for मांसपचन्याः (Yaj. XXV. 36), पृत्सु मर्त्यम् for पृतनासुमर्त्यम्, न ते दिवो न पृथिव्या अधिस्नुषु for अधिसानुषु ॥

Vârt :—The नस् is substituted for नासिका only when the affixes यत् and तस् and the word क्षुद्र follow : as, नस्यम्, नस्तः, नस् क्षुद्र ॥ The यत् is taught in IV. 3. 55 and V. 1. 6 ; तस् is taught in V. 4. 45.

Vârt :—The substitution of नस् for नासिका before the affix यत् does not take place when it refers to 'letters', or 'cities' as: नासिक्यो वर्णः 'a nasal letter' नासिक्यं नगरम् ॥

धात्वादेः षः सः ॥ ६४ ॥ पदानि ॥ धात्वादेः, षः, सः ॥

वृत्ति ॥ धातोरादेः षकारस्य स्थाने सकारादेशो भवति ॥

वार्त्तिकम् ॥ सुब्धातुष्ठिवुष्वष्कतीनां प्रतिषेधो वक्तव्य ॥

64. There is the substitution of स in the room of the ष् being the initial of a verbal root as enunciated in the Dhâtupâṭha.

The roots exhibited in the Dhâtupâṭha with an initial ष, change it for स ॥ Thus षह—सहते, षिच्—सिचति ॥ Why do we use the word 'root'? Observe

षोडश, षडिकः, षण्डः ॥ Why do we say 'initial'? Observe—कर्षति, कृषति ॥ Why have then roots been exhibited in the Dhâtupâṭha with an initial ष, when for all practical purposes this ष is to be replaced by स, would it not have been easier to spell at once these words with a स? This appears cumbersome no doubt, but the spelling of the roots with ष is for the sake of brevity. Certain roots change their स into ष when preceded by certain letters: those roots which thus change their letter स for ष have been at once taught with an initial ष, and thus by VIII. 3. 59 their स is changed to ष ॥ Thus from षिव—instead of सिसव we have सिषव ॥ Thus root is exhibited in the Dhâtupâṭha with a ष, and thus we know that the स must be changed to ष ॥ Otherwise a list of such roots would have to be separately given. One must refer to the Dhâtupâṭha for a list of such roots. As a general rule, however, all roots beginning with a स and followed by a vowel or a dental letter have been taught in the Dhâtupâṭha as beginning with an initial ष, as well as the following roots ष्मि, ष्वद्, ष्विद्, ष्वञ्ज and ष्वप, though followed by म् or व् ॥ The following roots though followed by a vowel or a dental are not taught with an initial ष viz. सृप्, सृज्, स्तृ, स्त्या, सेक, and सृ ॥

Vârt:—Prohibition must be stated of the roots derived from nouns, and of ष्ठिव् and ष्वष्क ॥ Thus षोडीयते, षण्डीयते are roots derived from nouns, and though these roots begin with ष are not changed: so ष्ठिव्—ष्ठीवति, ष्वष्क—ष्वष्कते ॥ The word ष्ठिव contains in it two roots ष्ठिव् and ष्थिव्, one with ठ, another with थ, and thus we have two forms in the reduplication:—तेष्ठीव्यते, टेष्ठीव्यते ॥ The substitution of स for ष takes place in the case of the root that has थ ॥

णो नः ॥ ६५ ॥ पदानि ॥ णः, नः ॥

वृत्ति ॥ धातोरादेरित्यनुवर्त्तते । धातोरादेर्णकारस्य नकार आदेशो भवति ॥

65. There is the substitution of न् for the initial ण् of the root in the Dhâtupâṭha.

The phrase धात्वादेः is understood here. Thus णीञ्—नयति, णम—नमति, णह—नह्यति ॥ But not अण्—अणति ॥ This does not apply to roots derived from nouns. णकारमिच्छति = णकारीयति ॥ The roots are exibited in the Dhâtupaṭha with ण for a similar reason as they are exibited with ष ॥ By VIII. 4. 14, these roots change their न into ण when preceded by certain prepositions. All roots beginning with a न should be understood to have been so taught, with the exception of the following:—नृ, नन्दि नर्दि, नक्क, नाटि, नाधृ and नाथृ ॥

लोपो व्योर्वलि ॥ ६६ ॥ पदानि ॥ लोपः, व्योः, वलि ॥

वृत्ति ॥ धातोरिति प्रकृतं यद् तद्धात्वादेरिति पुनर्धातुग्रहणान्निवृत्तम् । तेन धातोरधातोश्च वकारयकारयोर्वलि परतो लोपो भवति ॥

66. There is lopa-substitution (elision) of the व् and य् when followed by any consonant except य् ॥.

The final व् or य् of any stem, be it a root or not, is elided by an affix &c, beginning with a वल् consonant i. e. any consonant except य ॥ Thus दिव्+वस् (III. 2. 107)=दिव्+दिव्+वस्=दिदिवस् nom. singular दिदिवान्, दिदिवांसौ, दिदिवांसः ॥ Thus ऊय्+तं=ऊतं, 'spun', क्नूय्+त=क्नूतं 'made a noise'. So also the affix ढ्रक् comes after गोधा in forming patronymic (IV. 1. 129). Of the affix ढ्रक्, ढ is replaced by एय् (VII. 1. 2). Thus गोधा+एय्+र=गौधेरः (the य of the affix being even elided before र) ॥ So also in पचेरन्, यजेरन् the य of लिङ् (III. 4. 102) is elided before रन् (III. 4. 105). So also व is elided in the following:—from जीव्—जीरदानुः (by Uṇâdi affix जीवे रदानुक्) from स्निव्—अस्रेमाणम् formed by the Uṇâdi affix मनिन् with the negative अ ॥ There being diversity in the application of Uṇâdi affixes (III. 3. 1), there is not ऊठ् substitution for व् as required by VI. 4. 19.

Why do we say "before any consonant except य?" Observe ऊय्यते, क्नूय्यते when य् is not elided. Why the word लोप is placed first? The elision of व् and य् should take place prior to the elision of the apṛikta व् taught in the next sûtra. Thus कण्डूय+क्विप्=कण्डू य् (VI. 4. 48)=कण्डू+य्=कण्डू. ॥ So लोलूय+क्विप्=लोलूः ॥ Why व् of व्रश्च is not elided before र which is a वल् consonant? It is not elided, because it is so taught. Had the elision of व् been intended, the root would have been enunciated as रश्च instead of व्रश्च ॥ If you say the व is taught for the sake of forms like वृश्चति by samprasârana. and वव्रश्च by reduplication, here also the 'lopa' would have applied, as being an Antaranga rule, while samprasâraṇa, and the elision of र् by हलादिशेषः are Bahiranga.

वेरपृक्तस्य ॥ ६७ ॥ पदानि ॥ वेः, अपृक्तस्य ॥

वृत्तिः ॥ लोप इति वर्त्तते । वेरिति क्विबादयो विशेषानुबन्धानुत्सृज्यसामान्येन गृह्यन्ते । वेरपृक्तस्य लोपो भवति ॥

67. There is elision of the affix वि when reduced to the single letter व् ॥

The affix वि includes क्विप्, क्विन्, ण्वि &c. In all these, the real affix is व्, which being an aprikta (I. 2. 41), is elided. Thus ब्रह्महा, भ्रूणहा (III. 2. 87). Here the affix क्विप् is elided. So also घृतस्पृक्, तैलस्पृक् (III. 2. 58). Here the affix क्विन् is elided. So also अर्धभाक् पादभाक्, तुरीयभाक् (III. 2. 62). Here the affix ण्वि is elided.

Why do we say "of an aprikta—an affix consisting of a single letter"? Observe दर्विः formed by the affix विन् (वि being the real affix); so also जागृविः formed क्विन्, see Uṇâdi Sûtras IV. 53. 44. No root can become a noun unless some kṛit affix is added to it (see I. 2. 45 and 46); hence the necessity of these imaginary affixes, in order to raise certain roots bodily, without any change, to the rank of nouns—from Dhâtu to a Prâtipadika the way lies only through an affix. And though these imaginary affixes are after all totally elided, yet by

I. 1. 62, they leave their characteristic mark behind, namely the derivative word becomes a nominal stem &c. Thus च्वि words are adverbs (Gati) and Indeclinables.

हल्ङ्याब्भ्यो दीर्घात्सुतिस्यपृक्तं हल् ॥ ६८ ॥ पदानि ॥ हल्, ङ्याप्भ्यः, दीर्घात्, सु, ति, सि, अपृक्तम्, हल् ॥

वृत्तिः ॥ लोप इति वर्त्तते । तदिह लौकिकेनार्थेनार्थवत कर्मसाधनं द्रष्टव्यम् । लुप्यतइति लोपः । हलन्तान् ङ्यन्तादाबन्ताच्च दीर्घात्परं सु ति सि इत्येतदपृक्तं हल् लुप्यते ॥

Kârikâ :—संयोगान्तस्य लोपे हि नलोपादिर्न सिद्ध्यति । रात्तु तेनैव लोपः स्याद्धलस्तस्माद्विधीयते ॥

68. After a consonant there is the elision of the nominative-affix स् and the tense-affix ति and सि (when reduced to the form of त् and स्) being consonants; and so also after the long vowels ई and आ of the feminine (affix ङी and आप्), there is the elision of the nominative affix स् ॥

The sûtra translated literally means:—After a word ending in a consonant, or ङी, or आप् when a long vowel, the affixes सु, ति and सि when reduced to a single consonant affix (अपृक्तं हल्) are elided. But ति and सि are elided only after a consonant and hence we have translated it as above. As examples of the elision of सु after a consonant:—राजन् + स् = राजान् (VI. 4. 8) + 0 = राजा, तक्षा, उखास्रत्, पर्णध्वत् ॥ After a ङी :—as, कुमारी, गौरी, शार्ङ्गरवी ॥ After आप् :—खट्वा, बहुराजा, कारी षगन्ध्या ॥ The elision of ति and सि takes place only after consonants:—as, अबिभर्भवान् (भृ + लङ् + तिप् = अ + भृ + श्लु + त् = अ + भृ + भृ + त् (VI. 1. 10) = अ + भर् + भृ + त् (VII. 4: 66 and I. 1. 51) = अ + भ + भृ + त् (VII. 4. 60) = अ + ब + भृ + त् (VIII. 4. 54) = अ + बि + भृ + त् (VII. 4. 76) = अ + बि + भर् + त् (VII. 3. 84) = अबिभर् + त् = अबिभर् ॥ So also अजागर् भवान् ॥ In both these cases त् of the Imperfect has been elided. The स् is elided in the following:—अभिनोऽत्र, अच्छिनोऽत्र ॥ (भिद् + लङ् + सिप् ॥ The द् is changed into र् by VIII. 2. 75 and स् is elided by this rule).

Why do we say "after a consonant, or a feminine affix ई and आ"? Observe ग्रामणीः, सेनानीः ॥ Why do we say "after a long-vowelled feminine affix"? Observe निष्कौशाम्बिः, अतिखट्वः, where the feminine affixes have been shortened. Why do we say "when followed by सु, ति and सि"? Observe अभैत्सीत् ॥ The सि being read along with ति, does not include सिच्, but refers to सिप् only. Why do we say 'when reduced to a single letter'? Observe भिनत्ति, छिनत्ति ॥ Why do we say 'the *consonant* is elided'? Observe बिभेद, चिच्छेद ॥ Here the apṛikta affix अ of the Perfect is not elided: though it being the substitute of ति is like ति, and ought to have been elided, had the word हल् not been used in the sûtra.

Why has the elision of स् (सु), त् (तप्) and स् (सिप्) been ordained after consonants, as they would of themselves have been dropped by VIII. 2. 23, being the finals of a compound consonant? Then the forms राजा, तक्षा could not be evolved. As राजन्+स्=राजान्+स् (VI. 4. 8)=राजान्स् and by eliding स् by Rule VIII. 2. 23, the form would have become राजान्, and the final न् could not have been elided by VIII. 2. 7; for it is a maxim enunciated in the very opening of the Second chapter of the 8th Book, that in the last three chapters of that Book (2nd, 3rd and 4th Books), a subsequent rule is as if it had not taken effect, so far as any preceding rule is concerned; therefore, the rule VIII. 2. 7 ordaining the elision of न्, does not find scope, since VIII. 2. 23 (ordaining elision of स्) is considered as if it had not taken effect. So also in the case of उखास्रत् and पर्णध्वत् ॥ उखा+स्रन्स्+क्विप् III. 2. 76=उखा+स्रस् (the nasal being elided by VI. 4. 24); now add सु, we have उखास्रस्+स्=उखास्रस्स्; elide the final स् not by this rule, but by VIII. 2. 23, we have उखास्रस्, here we cannot change the स् into द् by VIII. 2. 72 for स् is not *final* in a *pada*, for Rule VIII. 2. 23 is considered as not to have taken effect. So also in the case of अभिनोऽत्र ॥ The word अभिनः is 2nd. Pers. sing. of the Imperfect of भिद् of Rudhâdi class. Thus भिद्+लङ्+सिप्=अ+भिद्+श्नम्+स्=अ+भिनद्+स्=अभिनर् +स् (द् changed to र् by VIII. 2. 75)=अभिनर्स् ॥ If we elide the final स् of the cojunct by VIII. 2. 23, then in अभिनर्+अत्र, the र् would not be changed into उ to form अभिनोऽत्र by VI. 1. 113 since the ellision of स is considered as to have not taken effect when applying this rule. So also in अबिभर् भवान्, by Rule VIII. 2. 24, there would be no lopa even, for संयोगान्तलोप rule is restricted by रात्सस्य (VIII. 2. 24), i. e. स् only and no other consonant is elided after र्, therefore there will be no elision of त् in अबिभर्त् by VIII. 2. 23.

एङ्ह्रस्वात्संबुद्धेः ॥ ६९ ॥ पदानि ॥ एङ्, ह्रस्वात्, सम्बुद्धेः ॥

वृत्तिः ॥ लोप इति वर्त्तते, हलिति च । अपृक्तमिति नाधिक्रियते । तथा च पूर्वसूत्रे पुनरपृक्तग्रहणं कृतम् । एङन्तात्प्रातिपदिकाद् ह्रस्वान्ताच्च परो हल्लुप्यतेसचेत्संबुद्धेर्भवति ॥

69. The consonant of the nominative-affix (सु and its substitute अम्) is elided in the Vocative singular after a nominal-stem enidng in ए or ओ or a short vowel.

The word लोप is understood here also; as well as हल् ॥ The word अपृक्त however is not to be read here, as its repetition in VI. 1. 68 (though its anuvritti was there from the preceding sûtra) indicates. The affix of Vocative is the same as that of the nominative. By VII. 3. 108, the short vowel of the stem is replaced by a guṇa vowel when the Vocative Singular affix follows. Thus we have अग्ने and वायो for अग्नि and वायु; and by VII. 3. 107, a short vowel is substituted for the long vowel ई and ऊ of the feminine: as नदि and वधु for नदी and वधू ॥ Now applying the present sûtra, the affix स् is elided after all the above words. As हे अग्ने !, हे वायो !, हे देवदत्त!, हे नदि !, हे वधु ! The Vocative Singular of कुण्ड a Neuter noun is thus formed. By VII. 1. 24, अम replaces म् of the nominative, the अ of अम् and the final अ of कुण्ड coalesce into one अ by VI. 1. 107, which becomes कुण्डम् ॥ Here by the rule that 'consonant' only is to be elided, we elide म् only (and not अ which becomes a part of the word by VI. 1. 85, for it is considered both as the final of the word and the initial of the affix). Now म् is not an अपृक्त हल् for it is part of the affix अम्, and its elision would not have taken place had we read the anuvritti of apṛikta into this sûtra. Thus we have हे कुण्ड ! II But in हे कतरत् ! there is not the elision of the त् of the affix अत्, the substitute of सु for the affix there is अद्ड् (VII. 1. 25). This affix being डित् causes the elision of the final अ of कतर (VI. 4. 143), and we have कतर्+अत्, here we have not a prâtipadika which ends in a *short* vowel, but in a *consonant*, hence त् is not elided. See also VII. 1. 25. The word एङ् is used in the sûtra in order to indicate that the guṇa substitution is stronger than lopa. Therefore in हे अग्नि+सु, the affix is not elided first and then guṇa substituted for इ, but first there is guṇa substitution and then the affix is elided.

शेश्छन्दसि बहुलम् ॥ ७० ॥ पदानि ॥ शेः, छन्दसि, बहुलम् ॥

वृत्तिः ॥ शि इत्येतस्य बहुलं छन्दसि विषये लोपो भवति ॥

70. In the Chhandas, the elision of the case-ending इ (शि) of the nominative and accusative plural neuter, is optional.

Thus या क्षेत्रा or यानि क्षेत्राणि, या वना or यानि वनानि ॥

ह्रस्वस्य पिति कृति तुक् ॥ ७१ ॥ पदानि ॥ ह्रस्वस्य, पिति, कृति, तुक् ॥

वृत्तिः ॥ पिति कृति परतो ह्रस्वस्य तुगागमो भवति ॥

71. To a root ending in a short vowel is added the augment त् (तुक्) when a Krit-affix having an indicatory प् follows.

Thus अग्नि+चि+क्विप्=अग्निचित्, so also सोमसुत् ॥ Similarly प्रकृत्य and प्रहृत्य and उपस्तुत्य formed by the affix ल्यप् ॥ Why do we say "ending in a short vowel"? Observe ग्रामणीः, आलूय ॥ Why do we say "having an indicatory प्"? Observe कृतम्, हृतम् ॥ Why do we say "a krit affix"? Observe पटुतरः, पटुतमः, with the Taddhita-affixes तरप् and तमप् ॥ In the compound ग्रामणिकुलम्, though the root is made short, yet there is no augment तुक्, in as much as the rule by which the root has been shortened is a Bahiranga rule, and the present rule is an Antaranga one. The maxim is असिद्धं बहिरङ्गमन्तरङ्गे II "That which is Bahiranga is regarded as not having taken effect, or as not existing, when that which is Antaranga is to take effect".

संहितायाम् ॥ ७२ ॥ पदानि ॥ संहितायाम् ॥

वृत्तिः ॥ अधिकारो ऽयमनुदात्तं पदमेकवर्जमिति यावत् । प्रागेतस्मात्सूत्रादित उत्तर यद्वक्ष्यामः संहितायामित्येवं तद्वेदितव्यम् ॥

72. In the following sûtras upto VI. 1. 157 inclusive, the words संहितायाम् 'in an unbroken flow of speech', should be supplied.

This is an adhikâra or governing sûtra, exerting its influence upto VI. 1. 158. What ever we shall say in the sûtras preceding that, must be understood to apply to words which are in संहिता, that is, which are pronounced together with an uninterrupted voice. Thus दध्यत्र, मध्वत्र the इ and उ are changed to य and व when the two words are pronounced without any hiatus. Otherwise we shall have दधि अत्र, मधु अत्र ॥

छे च ॥ ७३ ॥ पदानि ॥ छे, च ॥

वृत्तिः ॥ ह्रस्वस्य तुगिति वर्त्तते । छकारे परतः संहितायां विषये ह्रस्वस्य तुगागमो भवति ॥

73. The augment त् is added to a preceding short vowel also when छ follows in an uninterrupted speech.

Thus इच्छति, गच्छति ॥ The त is changed to च by VIII. 4. 40. The short vowel itself is the आगमी (the thing to which the augment is added), and not the word ending in that short vowel. Therefore in चिच्छिदतुः, चिच्छिदुः, the augment is not to be considered as part of the Reduplicate चि, but of the short इ only; and therefore it is not elided by हलादिः शेष (VII. 4. 60) rule applying to reduplicates. This follows on the maxim नावयवावयवः समुदायावयवो भवति "the part of a part cannot be considered as a part of the whole". Here त् is a part of the abhyâsa syllable चि which is itself a part of the verbal base, therefore त् is not considered as an abhyâsa: or because त् being an augment of इ is considered as part of इ and not of चि of which इ is the part.

आङ्माङोश्च ॥ ७४ ॥ पदानि ॥ आङ्, माङोः, च ॥

वृत्तिः ॥ तुगित्यनुवर्त्तते, छइति च । आङो ङित ईषदादिषु चतुर्ष्वर्थेषु वर्त्तमानस्य माङश्च प्रतिषेधवचनस्य छकारे परतस्तुगागमो भवति ॥

74. The augment त is added to the particle आ and the prohibitive particle मा, when छ follows in a continuous text.

The Particle आ has the four senses of 1. littleness (ईषदर्थः) 2. with verbs, as a prefix (क्रियायोगः) 3. the limit inceptive (अभिविधि) and 4. the limit exclusive (मर्यादा). This sûtra ordains तुक *necessarily*, where by VI. 1. 76, it would have been optional. Thus ईषच्छाया = आच्छाया; 2. With verbs:—as आच्छादयति, 3 and 4. आच्छायायाः, आच्छायम ॥ So also the negative particle मा, as, माच्छिदत्, माच्छिदत् ॥ The ङ in आङ्

and माङ् shows that आ when used as a Gati and a Karmapravachanîya and मा when used as a negative particle are meant. Therefore, the तु is not necessary in the following :—आछाया मानयाति, प्रमाछन्दः ॥ The तुक् may be optionally added in these as आच्छाया and प्रमाच्छन्दः ॥ The आ here has the force of recollection (स्मरण); आछाया "Oh the shade". The word प्रमा is formed from the verbal root माङ् by the prefix प्र and the affix अङ् (III. 3. 106) with the feminine affix टाप्, and the word ending in टाप् has not the indicatory ङ् ॥

दीर्घात् ॥ ७५ ॥ पदानि ॥ दीर्घात्, तुक् ॥

वृत्ति ॥ छे तुगिति वर्त्तते । दीर्घात्परो यश्छकारस्तस्मिन्पूर्वस्य तस्यैव दीर्घस्य तुगागमो भवति ॥

75. The augment तु is added to a long vowel, when followed by छ in a continuous text.

Thus ह्रीच्छति, म्लेच्छति, अपचाच्छायते, विचाच्छायते ॥ The augment belongs to the long vowel and not to the whole syllable ending in that long vowel.

पदान्ताद्वा ॥ ७६ ॥ पदानि ॥ पदान्तात्, वा, तुक् ॥

वृत्ति ॥ दीर्घाच्छेतुगिति वर्त्तते । पदान्ताद्दीर्घात्परो यश्छकारस्तस्मिन्पूर्वस्य तस्यैव दीर्घस्य पूर्वेण नित्यं प्राप्तो वा तुगागमो भवति ॥

वार्त्तिकम् ॥ विश्वजनादीनां छन्दसि वा तुगागमो भवतीति वक्तव्यम् ॥

76. The augment तु, is added optionally to a long vowel final in a full word (Pada) when followed by छ ॥

This allows option where by the last it would have been compulsory to add it. The augment is of the long vowel, and not of the word ending in long vowel. Thus कुटीच्छाया or कुटीछाया, कुवलीच्छाया or कुवलीछाया ॥ The तुक् augment here is added to the *end* of a pada, and this is therefore a padânta rule and not a pada-vidhi. Therefore the two words need not be in construction for the application of this rule; (समर्थ पदविधि) not applying. Thus तिष्ठतु कुमारीच्छत्रं हर देवदत्तस्य, "let the girl stay. Take the umbrella of Devadatta". Here कुमारी and छत्रं are not in construction, but तुक् is stll added optionally.

Vârt :—The augment त is optional in the Chhandas, after the words विश्वजन &c. As, विश्वजनच्छत्रम् or विश्वजनछत्रम्, नच्छायां कुरवोपराम् or नछायां कुरवोपराम् ॥

इको यणचि ॥ ७७ ॥ पदानि ॥ इकः, यण्, अचि ॥

वृत्ति ॥ अचि परत इको यणादेशो भवति ॥

वार्त्तिकम् ॥ इकः प्लुतपूर्वस्य सवर्णदीर्घबाधनार्थं यणादेशो वक्तव्यः ॥

77. The semivowels य्, व्, र्, ल् are the substitutes of the corresponding vowels इ, उ, ऋ and ऌ (long and short), when followed by a vowel.

This sûtra is rather too wide. It must be restricted by VI. I. 101, namely the following vowel must not be of the same class as the preceding for the application of this rule. Thus दधि + अत्र = दध्यत्र, मधु + अत्र = मध्वत्र, कर्तृ + अर्थम् = कर्त्रर्थम्, हर्तृ + अर्थम् = हर्त्रर्थम्, लृ आकृति = लाकृतिः ॥

Vârt:—This semivowel substitution of vowels takes place, when preceded by a prolated vowel, even to the supersession of VI. 1. 101 requiring lengthening. Thus अग्ना ३ इ इन्द्रं = अग्ना ३ यिन्द्रम्, पटा ३ उ उदकम् = पटा ३ वुदकम्, अग्ना ३ इ आशा = अग्ना ३ याशा, पटा ३ उ आशा = पटा ३ वाशा ॥ भो ३ इ इन्द्रम् = भो ३ यिन्द्रम् ॥ The phrase 'when a vowel follows' exerts its influence upto VI. 1. 108.

एचो ऽयवायावः ॥ ७८ ॥ पदानि ॥ एचः, अय् - अव् - आय्-आवः ॥

वृत्तिः ॥ एचः स्थाने ऽचि परतो ऽय् अव् आय् आव् इत्येते आदेशा यथासंख्यं भवन्ति ॥

78. For the vowels ए, ऐ, ओ and औ are respectively substituted अय्, आय्, अव् and आव् when a vowel follows.

Thus चि + ल्युट् = चे + अन = चयनम्, लो + अन = लवनं; चै + अक = चायकः, लौ + अक = लावकः ॥ So also कयेते, व्ययेते, यावरुणद्धि, रु + युच् (III. 2. 148) = रो + अन = रवणः ॥

वान्तो यि प्रत्यये ॥ ७९ ॥ पदानि ॥ वान्तः, यि, प्रत्यये ॥

वृत्तिः ॥ योयमेचः स्थाने वान्तादेश ओकारस्य अव् औकारस्याव् स यकारादौ प्रत्यये परतो भवति ॥

वार्त्तिकम् ॥ गोर्यूतौ छन्दसि ॥ वा० ॥ अध्वपरिमाणे च ॥

79. The substitution of अव् and आव् for ओ and औ also takes place before an affix beginning with य ॥

The वान्त are those which end in व् viz. अव् and आव् ॥ Of the four substitutes taught in the preceding sûtra, those which end in व् (viz. अव् and आव्) also come when an affix with an initial य follows. It follows that the substituted letters must be ओ and औ ॥ Thus बभ्रु + यञ् = बाभ्रो + य = बाभ्रव्यः (VI. 4. 146 and IV. 1. 105). So also माण्डव्यः, शंकव्यंदारु, पिचव्यः कार्पासः, नाव्यो(IV. 4. 91) ह्रदः॥ Why do we say "अव् and आव्"? Observe रायमिच्छति = रैयति, no change of ऐ before य ॥ Why do we say "before य"? Observe गोभ्याम्, नौभ्याम् ॥ Why do we say "an affix"? Observe गोयानम्, नौयानम् ॥

Vârt:—The word गो is changed before यूति in the Vedas. As गो + यूति = गव्यूति, as आनो मित्रा वरुणा घृतैर्गव्यूतिमुक्षतम् ॥ Why do we say 'in the Vedas'? Observe गोयूतिः ॥

Vârt:—This substitution takes place when referring to the measur of a road: —as, गव्यूति मात्रमध्वानं गतः ॥ This is in the secular literature, गव्यूति meaning क्रोशयुगम् ॥

धातोस्तन्निमित्तस्यैव ॥ ८० ॥ पदानि ॥ धातोः, तन्निमित्तस्य, एव ॥

वृत्तिः ॥ एच इति वर्त्तते । वान्तो यि प्रत्यय इति च । धातोर्य एच् तन्निमित्तो यकारादिप्रत्ययनिमित्तस्तस्य यकारादौ प्रत्यये परतो वान्तादेशो भवति ॥

80. For the final diphthongs ओ and औ of a root, are substituted अव् and आव् respectively, before an affix beginning with य, then only when such diphthong has been itself first evolved by that affix.

The words एचः, वान्तो यि प्रत्यये are understood in this sûtra. The word तन्निमित्त means 'caused by that' i. e. caused or occasioned by that affix beginning with य II Thus लू forms its Future Passive Participle by यत् (III. 1. 97), this affix causes the guṇa of ऊ by VII. 3. 84: Thus लू+य=लो+य, which according to the present sûtra becomes लव्यम् ॥ So also पू—पो+य=पव्यम् ॥ लू+ण्यत्(III.1.125) =लौ+य=अवश्य लाव्यम् and अवश्य पाव्यम् ॥ Why do we say 'of a root'? This rule should not apply to a nominal stem. For then, though it may be all right in the case of बभ्रु+य=बाभ्रो+य=बाभ्रव्यः; it will not apply to cases like गो+य=गव्य, नौ+य=नाव्य, where ओ and औ are not *caused* by the affix, but are integral parts of the stem before the affixes were added. Why do we say 'caused by that affix itself'? The substitution will not take place, when the change is not caused by that affix. Thus the Passive of वे with the upasarga आ is आ+वे+यक्+ते=Here by Samprasâraṇa(VI.1.15),वे becomes उ,as आ+उ+य+ते; now by sandhi आ+उ=ओ VI. 1. 87), we have ओ+यते=ओयते II Since ओ is not caused by य, there is no अव् substitution. So also औयत, लैयमानिः, पैयमानिः (IV. 1. 95). The word एव in the aphorism has the force of limitation, with regard to roots. In the case of roots, ओ and औ before य are changed then only to अव् and आव् when य has caused the production of ओ and औ; in case of nouns there is no such limitation. Here the substitution takes place whether the य has caused the production of ओ and औ or not.

क्षय्यजय्यौ शक्यार्थे ॥ ८१ ॥ पदानि ॥ क्षय्य - जय्यौ , शक्य - अर्थे ॥

वृत्तिः ॥ क्षि जि इत्येतयोर्धात्वोर्यति प्रत्यये परतः शक्यार्थे गम्यमाने एकारस्यायादेशो निपात्यते ॥

81. In क्षय्य and जय्य there is substitution of अय् for ए only then when the sense is that of "to be possible to do".

The roots क्षि and जि before the affix यत् (III. 1. 97) assume these forms when meaning to be able to do the action denoted by the verb. As शक्यः क्षेतुं=क्षय्यः (क्षि+य=क्षे+य); so also जय्यः ॥ Why do we say when meaning "to be possible to do"? Observe क्षेयं पापं, जेयो वृषलः ॥ Here the meaning is that of 'necessity'.

क्रय्यस्तदर्थे ॥ ८२ ॥ पदानि ॥ क्रय्यः, तदर्थे ॥

वृत्तिः ॥ क्रीणातेर्धातोस्तदर्थे क्रयार्थे यत्तस्मिन्नभिधेये यति प्रत्यये परतो ऽयादेशो निपात्यते ॥

82. In क्रय्य there is substitution of अय् for ए when the sense is that of 'exposed or put out for sale, saleable'.

The word क्रय्य is derived from क्री 'to buy', with the affix यत्; the guṇa ए being changed to य ॥ The word तदर्थे means 'for the purpose of that'

i. e., for the purpose of being bought. As क्रय्या गौः, क्रय्यः कम्बलः ॥ Why do we say 'when the sense is that of saleable'? Observe क्रेयं नो धान्यं न चास्ति क्रय्यम् "we want to purchase corn, but it is not put out for sale".

भय्यप्रवय्ये च छन्दसि ॥ ८३ ॥ पदानि ॥ भय्य - प्रवय्ये , च, छन्दसि, ॥

वृत्तिः ॥ बिभेतेर्धातोः प्रपूर्वस्य च वी इत्येतस्य यति प्रत्यये परतश्छन्दसि विषये ऽयादेशो निपात्यते ॥

वार्त्तिकम् ॥ ह्रदय्या आप उपसंख्यानम् ॥

83. The forms भय्य and प्रवय्या are found in the Chhandas.

The word भय्य is derived from भी + यत्, and प्रवय्या from प्र + वी + यत् ॥ The guṇa ए is changed to अय् ॥ Thus भय्यं किलासीत् ॥ वत्सतरी प्रवय्या ॥ The यत् is added to भी with the force of Ablative by virtue of the diversity allowed by कृत्यलुटो बहुलं (III. 3. 113) ॥ Thus बिभेति अस्माद् = भय्यम् "frightening or fearable". The word प्रवय्या is always used in the feminine: in other places प्रवेयं is the proper form. Why do we say 'in the Vedas'? Observe भेयम्, प्रवेयम् in secular literature.

Vârt:—The word ह्रदय्या should also be enumerated when referring to water. As ह्रदे भवा = ह्रदय्या आपः ॥ The affix यत् is added by IV. 4. 110 (ह्रदे + य = ह्रदय् + य) ॥

एकः पूर्वपरयोः ॥ ८४ ॥ पदानि ॥ एकः, पूर्व - परयोः, ॥

वृत्तिः ॥ अधिकारोयम् । ख्यत्यात्परस्येति प्रागेतस्मात्सूत्रादित उत्तरं यद्वक्ष्यामस्तत्र पूर्वस्य परस्य द्वयोरपि स्थाने एकादेशो भवतीत्येतद्वेदितव्यम् ॥

84. From here upto VI. 1. 111 inclusive is always to be supplied the phrase "for the preceding and the following one is substituted".

This is an adhikâra sûtra. In every sûtra upto VI. 1. 112 (excluding the last), whatever we shall teach, there in the room of the two, namely, the preceding and the succeeding, it should be understood, that the substitution is one. These form the well known ru'es of *ekâdesa*, one letter or form replacing two consecutive letters &c. Thus VI. 1. 87 teaches 'There is guṇa substitution, when अ or आ is followed by a vowel'. We must supply into that sûtra the phrase एकः पूर्वपरयोः i. e. one guṇa is the substitute for the final अ or आ and the initial vowel. Thus खट्वा + इन्द्रः = खट्वेन्द्रः ॥ Here ए is the single substitute of the both preceding letter आ and the succeeding letter इ ॥ The words पूर्व पर show that the substitute operates simultaneously on both. Otherwise the substitute would have come in the place of *one* only or of each one separately. Thus in आद् गुणः (अचि) = "after अ or आ, there is guṇa, in a vowel". Here आत् is in the ablative, and by I. 1. 67 the guṇa operation would have taken place on the letter *following* it: so also अचि is in the Locative and by I. 1. 66, the guṇa operation would have taken place on the *preceding* ; so it is not clear of what letter there should be guṇa substitution, of the preceding or the succeeding. But the present rule shows it must operate on both simultaneously. The word एक 'single', shows that a separate or a different substitute does not operate: i. e. the substitute must be one, there should not be two separate substitutes one for each sthâni, such as we find in the sûtra VIII. 2. 42 (रदाभ्यां निष्ठातो नः, पूर्वस्य च दः, "न is the substitute of the त of nishṭhâ, after र् and द, and of the precediug द"). Here न् is taught as substitute both of त् and द्, and as एक is not used in the sûtra, we get *two* न, as भिद्+त=भिन्+न=भिन्नः ॥ But this is not the case here. According to Mahabhâshya the word एक is redundant.

अन्तादिवच्च ॥ ८५ ॥ पदानि ॥ अन्त - आदि - वत्, च, ॥

वृत्तिः ॥ एक इति वर्त्तते पूर्वपरयोरिति च। एकः पूर्वपरयोरिति योऽयमेकादेशो विधीयते स पूर्वस्यान्तवद्भवति, परस्यादिवद्भवति ॥

85. And this single substitute is considered as the final of the preceding (form), and the initial of the succeeding (form).

The single substitute taught in the last, is considered in the light of the final of the preceding form and the initial of the succeeding. An âdeśa is like the sthâni, but in an ekâdeśa, the sthânî is indeterminate, or rather the sthânî is the *collection* or the *sum* of the preceding and the succeeding. Hence the necessity of this sûtra. The sense of this atideśa sûtra is this: as the beginning and the end of a thing are both *included* in the thing itself, and therefore when the thing is mentioned, the beginning and the end are both taken; so is the case with this single substitute. Thus to the stem ब्रह्मबन्धु we add ऊ the feminine affix (IV. 1. 66); and now उ+ऊ=ऊ (VI. 1. 101) i. e. ब्रह्मबन्धु+ऊ=ब्रह्मबन्धू ॥ Here ब्रह्मबन्धु is a Nominal-stem (प्रातिपदिक) and the affix ऊ is a non-prâtipadika, and the single-substitute ऊ is considered as the final of the prâtipadika. So that we can apply to the form ब्रह्मबन्धू the term prâtipadika and by virtue of this designation we can add the case-endings to it by IV. 1. 1. But for this rule, we could not have added the case-endings to it, because by virtue of the feminine affix ऊ the word would have rather ceased to be a prâtipadika (I. 1. 46), because this feminine affix ऊ is not included in IV. 1. 1. Similarly for the final non-case-ending अ of वृक्ष and the case-ending औ, there comes a single substitute औ by VI. 1. 88, this ekâdeśa औ is considered both as a non-case affix and a case affix, that is, as the initial of the affix औ, and the final of वृक्ष and thus the word वृक्षौ gets the designation of Pada I. 4. 14 as it *ends* in the सुप् affix औ ॥

This अन्तादिवद्भाव does not apply in rules relating to letters i. e. to rules depending for their application on letters. Thus खट्व+आ=खट्वा ॥ Here the ekâdeśa आ is as the final अ of खट्व, but not for the purposes of the application of the rule which says that the भिस् is changed to ऐस् after a nominal-stem ending in अ, so the Instrumental plural of खट्वा will not end in ऐः, but will be खट्वाभिः ॥ So also in जुहाव ॥ It is the Perfect 3rd per. sing. of ह्वे or ह्वा (VI. 1. 45). By VI. 1. 53, the व् is changed to उ, and we have जुह्व्आ = जुहुअआ which by VI 1. 108 becomes जुहु, the उ being the single substitute of उ and आ ॥ This single-substitute उ should not be considered as आ for the application of the rule VII. 1. 34 by which the Perfect affix णल् (अ) is changed in औ after roots ending in आ ॥ Similarly in अस्यै + अश्वः = अस्या अश्वः (the य् being elided by VIII. 3. 19). अस्यै is the Dative singular of इदम् in the Feminine with आ ॥ By VII. 3. 114 स्या is added in the Dative with the shortening of the preceding आ ; as अ + स्या + ए = अस्यै ॥ Here ऐ is the single substitute for आ and ए ॥ Here for the application of VI. 1. 109 the single substitute ऐ should not be considered like ए ॥ The sthânî of the single-substitute (ekâdeśa) is the *sum* of the preceding and the sueceeding, both taken collectively is replaced by *one*, and not any one of them separately. For that which is replaced by another is called sthânî: as when भू replaces अस् the whole form अस् is called sthâni, and not अ or स् separately. The parts, may be called sthâni only inferentially, because the whole is made up of parts. The parts not being considered as sthâni, the rule of sthânîvad bhâva will not apply to an ekâdeśa with regards to the parts, and no operations dependant on such parts will be effected by such ekâdeśa. But it is intended that such operations should take place. Hence this sûtra.

षत्वतुकोरसिद्धः ॥ ८६ ॥ पदानि ॥ षत्व - तुकोः, असिद्धः ॥

वृत्तिः ॥ षत्वे तुकि च कर्तव्ये एकादेशो ऽसिद्धो भवति, सिद्धकार्यं न करोतीत्यर्थः ।
वार्त्तिकम् ॥ संप्रसारणङीट्सु प्रतिषेधो वक्तव्यः ॥

86. The substitution of a single âdeśa is to be considered as to have not taken effect, when otherwise स would have to be changed to ष, or when the augment त् (तुक्) is to be added.

The word असिद्ध means not-accomplished i. e. the operation caused by its having taken effect is not produced. The word asiddha always debars operations dependent upon the âdeśa, and gives scope to the operations dependent upon the general rule (असिद्धवचनमादेशलक्षणप्रतिषेधार्थमुत्सर्गलक्षणभावार्थं च ॥) Thus कोऽसिचत् here स is not changed to ष ॥ The equation is thus exhibited : कस् + असिचत् = कर् + असिचत् (the स changed to र by VIII. 2.66) = कउ + असिचत् (उ being substituted for र by VI. 1. 113) = को + असिचत् (अ-।-उ = ओ॰VI. 1. 87) = कोऽसिचत् (ओ-।-अ = ओ VI. 1. 109). Now applies our sûtra. By VIII. 3. 59, स coming after ओ requiredto be changed into ष, but here the single-substitute ओ is considered to be non-effective for this purpose. Similarly कोऽस्य, योऽस्य, कोऽस्मै, योऽस्मै ॥ Similarly in अधीत्य there is the addition of तु by VI. 1. 71, though actually preceded by a *long* vowel. That long vowel had resulted from the ekâdeśa of ई for इ+इ, and this ekâdeśa is considered as if non-effective for the purposes of तुक् augment. Similarly in प्र+इ+तुक्+य = प्रेत्य. Here also अ+इ = ए is considered asiddha.

Vârt:—Prohibition must be stated in the case of samprasâraṇa, the Locative singular case-ending ङि (इ), and the 1st per. sing. Atmanepada affix इट् ॥ Of vocalisation we have the following: शकहूषु = शकान् ह्वयति, then we add क्विप्, before which there is vocalisation of व्, this उ combining with in the following आ becomes उ ekâdeśa; as शकह्वा+क्विप् = शकहुआ+o (VI. 1. 15) + शकहु (VI. 1. 108). The Locative plural is formed by सु: शकहु+सु = शकहूषु (the lengthening taking place by VI. 4. 2). Here स is changed to ष the ekâdeśa उ for उ+अ not being considered asiddha. So also परिवीषु (परि + व्ये + क्विप् = परि + वइए + क्विप् = परिवि, add सु) ॥ Of the affix ङि we have:—वृक्ष+इ = वृक्षे, add छत्रम्, then the single substitute ए being considered not asiddha we have वृक्षेच्छत्रम् or वृक्षेछत्रम ॥ Of the affix इट् of 1st Pers. Atmanepada we have अपचे+छत्रम् = अपचेच्छत्रम् or अपचेछत्रम ॥ In both these cases we optionally add तुक् by VI. 1. 75-76, by considering the ekâdeśa (VI. 1. 87) as to have taken effect, and making the finals दीर्घ or long. Here the ekâdeśa is *not* asiddha and therefore तुक् is *optinal* and not compulsory.

आद्गुणः ॥ ८७ ॥ पदानि ॥ आत्, गुणः ॥

वृत्तिः ॥ अचीत्यनुवर्तते । अवर्णात्परो योऽच् अचि च पूर्वो यो ऽवर्णस्तयोः पूर्वपरयोरवर्णाचोः स्थाने एको गुण आदेशो भवति ॥

87. The guṇa is the single substitute of the final अ or आ of a preceding word and the simple vowel of the succeeding (अ or आ+a vowel = guṇa).

The word अचि is understood here. For the vowel which follows an अ or आ, and for the अ or आ which precedes a vowel, in the room of both these preceding and succeeding vowels, there is the single substitute guṇa. Thus तव + इदम् = तवेदम्, खट्वा + इन्द्रः = खट्वेन्द्रः, माला + इन्द्रः = मालेन्द्रः, तव + ईहते = तवेहते, खट्वा + ईहते = खट्वेहते, तव + उदकम् = तवोदकम्, खट्वा + उदकम् = खट्वोदकम्, तव + ऋश्यः = तवर्श्यः, खट्वा + ऋश्यः = खट्वर्श्यः, तव + लृकारः = तवल्कारः, खट्वा + लृकारः = खट्वल्कारः ॥ By analogy of I. 1. 51, the guṇa substitute of ऋ being अ is always followed by र्, as that of लृ is followed by ल् ॥ This universal rule is limited by the following aphorism.

वृद्धिरेचि ॥ ८८ ॥ पदानि ॥ वृद्धिः, एचि ॥

वृत्तिः ॥ आदिति वर्तते । अवर्णात्परो य एच् एचि च पूर्वो यो ऽवर्णस्तयोः पूर्वपरयोरवर्णैचोः स्थाने वृद्धिरेकादेशो भवति ॥

88. The Vṛiddhi is the single substitute of अ or आ of a preceding word and the initil diphthong of the succeedind (अ or आ-।-diphthong = vṛiddhi).

The word आत् is understood here. For the diphthong which follows an अ or आ, and for the अ or आ which precedes a diphthong, in the room of both these preceding and succeeding अ or आ and diphthong, there is a single substitute viz. the Vṛiddhi.- This debars guṇa taught in the last sûtra. Thus ब्रह्म + एडका = ब्रह्मैडका, खट्वा + एडका = खट्वैडका, ब्रह्म + ऐतिकायनः = ब्रह्मैतिकायनः, खट्वा + ऐतिकायनः = खट्वैतिकायनः ॥ ब्रह्म + ओदनः = ब्रह्मौदनः, खट्वा + ओदनः = खट्वौदनः, ब्रह्म + औपगवः = ब्रह्मौपगवः, खट्वा + औपगवः = खट्वौपगवः ॥

एत्येधत्यूठ्सु ॥ ८९ ॥ पदानि ॥ एति, एधति, ऊठसु ॥

वृत्तिः ॥ वृद्धिरेचीति वर्तते, आदिति च । तदेतदेज्ग्रहणमेतेरेव विशेषणं न पुनरेधतेरव्यभिचारादूठश्चासंभवात् । इण् गतावित्येतस्मिन्धातावेचि एध वृद्धावित्येतस्मिन् ऊठि च पूर्वं यदवर्णं ततश्च परो योच् तयोः पूर्वपरयोरवर्णाचोः स्थाने वृद्धिरेकादेशो भवति ॥

वार्त्तिकम् ॥ अक्षादूहिन्यां वृद्धिर्वक्तव्या ॥ वा० ॥ स्वादीरेरिण्योर्वृद्धिर्वक्तव्या ॥

वा० ॥ प्रादूहोढोढ्येषैष्येषु वृद्धिर्वक्तव्या ॥ वा० ॥ ऋते च तृतीयासमासे ऽवर्णाद् वृद्धिर्वक्तव्या ॥

वा० ॥ प्रवत्सतरकम्बलवसनानामृणे वृद्धिर्वक्तव्या ॥ वा० ॥ ऋणदशाभ्यां वृद्धिर्वक्तव्या ॥

89. The Vṛiddhi is the single substitute for the अ or आ-।-ए of एति (root इ) and एधति (root एध), and for अ or आ-।-ऊ of ऊठ् (the substitute of वा in वाह् by VI. 4. 132).

The whole of the last sûtra and आत् are understood here. The एच् of the last sûtra qualifies the root इ in एति, i. e. when the root इ assumes the form ए by internal changes, then apples this Vṛiddhi rule. The एच् does not qualify the root एध् as that root always has an initial diphthong, nor does एच् qualify ऊठ् for ऊ is not a diphthong. Thus उप + एति = उपैति, उप + एषि = उपैषि, उपैमि; उप-।-एधते = उपैधते, प्रैधते; प्रष्ठ-।-ऊहा = प्रष्ठौहा ॥ In the last example, guṇa was the substitute required by VI. 1. 87, the present sûtra ordains Vṛiddhi instead. In the case of एति and एधति, the Vṛiddhi was debarred by VI. 1. 94, this sûtra makes an exception to that rule. The present sûtra is an exception to VI. 1. 94 and not to VI. 1. 95, because the maxim is पुरस्तादपवादा अनन्तरान् विधीन् बाधन्ते नोत्तरान् "Apavâdas that precede the rules which teach operations that have to be superseded by the apavâda operations, supersede only those rules that stand nearest to them, not the subsequent rules". Therefore the present rule does not apply here, :—उप + आ-।-इत = उप + एत = उपेतः (Here though इ is changed to ए, the rule does not apply). Therefore the form उपैहि is wrong. So also उप-।-इत = उपेतः for here the root इ has not assumed the form ए, therefore the rule does not apply, the word एचि qualifies the root इ ॥

Vârt:—The Vṛiddhi is the single substitute when अक्ष is followed by ऊहिनी, as अक्षौहिणी सेना ॥

Vârt :—The Vṛiddhi is the single substitute when स्व is followed by ईर or ईरिण, or ईरिणी thus स्वैरम्, स्वैरिणी ॥ The word ईर is formed by the affix घञ् added to ईर् गतौ (Ad. 8) स्वेनाभिप्रायेण ईरणं = स्वैरम the compounding takes place by II. 1. 32. Another form is स्वैरी = स्वेनाभिप्रायेणेर ते गच्छति with the affix णिनि (III. 2. 78).

Vârt :—The Vṛiddhi is the single substitute when प्र is followed by ऊह, ऊढ, ऊढि, एष, एष्य; as प्रौहः, प्रौढः, प्रौढिः, प्रैषः, प्रैष्यः ॥ The word एष is derived from the root इषु to wish' (Tud. 59), इष् 'to go' (Div. 18), and इष् 'to repeat' (Kry. 53), by adding the affix घञ् ; and the word एष्य is derived form the same roots by adding ण्यत् ॥ This Vârtika ordains Vṛiddhi, while VI. 1. 94 would have caused पररूप: ॥ While the roots ईष् 'to glean', and ईष् 'to go' to injure, 'to show'. (Bh. 115 and 642), form ईषः and ईष्यः with the above affixes ; and with प्र, their forms will be प्रेषः and प्रेष्यः ॥

Vârt :—The Vṛiddhi is the single substitute when a word ending in अ is followed by ऋत and forms an Instrumental Tatpurusha compound: as सुखेन ऋतः = सुखार्तः, दुःखेन ऋतः = दुःखार्तः, but सुखेन इतः = सुखेतः ॥ Why in Instrumental? Observe परमर्तः ॥ Why 'Compound'? See सुखेनर्तः ॥

Vârt:—The Vṛiddhi is the single substitute when the word ऋण follows the following:—प्र, वत्सतर, कम्बल, वसन ॥ As प्रार्णम् 'principal debt', वत्सतरार्णम् 'the debt of a steer', कम्बलार्णम् 'debt of a blanket', वसनार्णम् 'debt of a cloth'.

Vârt—So also when the words ऋण and दश are followed by ऋणः—as, ऋणार्णम् and दशार्णम् ॥ The word ऋणार्ण means a debt incurred to pay off a prior debt. The Dasârṇa is the name of a river and of a country.

आटश्च ॥ ९० ॥ पदानि ॥ आटः, च ॥

वृत्तिः ॥ एचीति निवृत्तम् । अचीत्यनुवर्त्तते । आटः परो यो ऽच् अचि च पूर्वो य आट् तयोः पूर्वपरयोरचोः स्थाने वृद्धिरेकादेशो भवति ।

90. The Vṛiddhi is the single substitute when the augment आट् is followed by any vowel.

The anuvritti of एचि ceases : that of अचि however, is present. The vowel that is subsequent to the augment आट्, and the आट् which is precedent to a vowel—in the room of these two i. e. the आट् and the vowel—subsequent and precedent, the Vṛiddhi is the single substitute. The augment आट् is added to the roots beginning with a vowel, in the Imperfect, Aorist and Conditional Tenses (VI. 4. 72 &c). Thus ऐक्षिष्ट, ऐक्षत, ऐक्षिष्यत, औम्भीत्, औदुर्भीत्, औब्जीत् from roots ईक्षदर्शने (Bhu. 641), उभ उम्भ पूरणे (Tud. 32) and उ ब्ज आर्जवे (Tud. 20). According to Siddhânta Kaumudî the आट् is the augment which ङित् case-affixes take after *nadî*-words (VII. 3. 112). According to him the following are the examples :—बहुश्रेयसी-।-आट्-।-ङे = बहुश्रेयस्यै (Dative Singular). The आट् is the augment also in the Vedic Tense लेट् ॥

The च् 'and' in the sûtra shows that the पररूप rule, taught in VI. 1. 95, 96 when उस्, ओं and आङ्. follow, is superseded, when the preceding vowel is आट्॥ Thus औस्रीयत्, औकारीयत् ॥ आ-।-ऊढा = ओढा, तमिच्छत् = औढीयत् ॥

उपसर्गादृति धातौ ॥ ९१ ॥ पदानि ॥ उपसर्गात्, ऋति, धातौ ॥

वृत्तिः ॥ आदित्येव । अवर्णान्तादुपसर्गादृकारादौ धातौ परतः पूर्वपरयोः स्थाने वृद्धिरेकादेशो भवति ॥

91. The Vṛiddhi is the single substitute when the अ or आ of a preposition (upasarga) is followed by the short ऋ of a verb.

The word आत् is understood here also. When a preposition ending in अ or आ is followed by a root beginning with ऋ, the Vṛiddhi is the single substitute for the precedent अ or आ and the subsequent ऋ ॥ This debars the guṇa taught in VI. 1. 87. Thus उप + ऋच्छति = उपार्च्छति, प्रार्च्छति, उपार्ध्नोति ॥ Why do we say 'after a preposition'? Observe खट्वर्च्छति, मालर्च्छति, प्रर्च्छकोदेशः = प्रगता ऋच्छका अस्माद् देशात् ॥ Here the word प्र is not treated as an upasarga, hence this sûtra does not apply. It is a Gati here. Why do we say 'when ऋ follows'? Observe उप-। इत = उपेतः ॥ Why have we used त् after ऋ indicating that short ऋ is to be taken? Observe उप + ॠकारी यति = उपर्कारीयति ॥ No option is allowed here by the subsequent sûtra. The त् is used, in fact, for the sake of the subsequent sûtra in case of Denominative verbs, no ordinary verb can begin wirh a long ॠ ॥ Why have we employed the word धातु, when the word 'upasarga' would have caused us to infer its correlative धातु? It is used in order to prevent the application of the rule VI. 1. 129 which causes प्रकृतिभावः or non-sandhi of ऋ ॥ The repetition of 'Dhâtu' shows that the alternative prakriti bhava taught in VI. 1. 129, would not apply in the case of the ऋ of a Dhâtu.

वा सुप्यापिशलेः ॥ ९२ ॥ पदानि ॥ वा, सुपि, आपिशलेः ॥

वृत्तिः ॥ आदित्येव । उपसर्गादृति धाताविति च । सुबन्तावयवे धातावृकारादौ परतो ऽवर्णान्तादुपसर्गात्पूर्वपरयोरापिशलेराचार्यस्य मतेन वा वृद्धिरेकादेशो भवति ॥

92. According to the opinion of Âpiśali, the Vṛiddhi is optionally the single substitute, when the अ or आ of a preposition is followed by a Denominative Verb beginning with ऋ ॥

Thus उपार्षभीयति or उपर्षभीयति, उपल्कारीयति or उपाल्कारीयति ॥ The ऋ and ऌ are considered as homogenous letters, therefore the word ऋ in the last sûtra includes ऌ also. The name of the Grammarian Ápisali is mentioned for the sake of respect; the वा itself was enough to make it an optional rule.

औतो ऽम्शसोः ॥ ९३ ॥ पदानि ॥ आ, ओतः, अम् - शसोः ॥

वृत्तिः ॥ ओतो ऽमि शसि च परतः पूर्वपरयोराकार आदेशो भवति ॥

93. For ओ of a Nominal stem+अ of the Accusative case-ending अम् and अस्, the single substitute is आ ॥

The word ओतः is a compound of आ + ओतः ॥ Thus गो + अम्, = गाम्, गो + अस् = गाः ॥ Thus गां पश्य, गाः पश्य: ॥ This debars the Vriddhi of VII. 1. 90. So also द्यां or द्याः पश्य; as the word द्यो is also a nominal stem ending in ओ ॥ The Sârvanâmsthâna affixes are णित् after this word also (see VII. 1. 96) which would have caused Vriddhi, therefore, this आ debars the Vriddhi. The word अम् here means the affix of the Accusative Singular, as it is read in connection with the case-affix शस्, and as the word सुप् of the last sûtra governs this also. Therefore अम् the verbal Tense-affix of the Imperfect is not meant: thus we have अचिनवम्, असुनवम् ॥

एङि पररूपम् ॥ ९४ ॥ पदानि ॥ एङि, पररूपम् ॥

वृत्तिः ॥ आदित्येव, उपसर्गाद्धाताविति च। अवर्णान्तादुपसर्गादेङादौ धातौ पूर्वपरयोः पररूपमेकादेशो भवति॥
वार्त्तिकम् ॥ शकन्ध्वादिषु पररूपं वक्तव्यम् ॥ वा० ॥ एवे चानियोगे पररूपं वक्तव्यम् ॥
वा० ॥ ओत्वोष्ठयोः समासे वा पररूपं वक्तव्यम् ॥ वा० ॥ एमन्नादिषु छन्दसि पररूपं वक्तव्यम् ॥

94. For the अ or आ of the Preposition+ए or ओ of a verbal root, the second vowel is the single substitute.

The words आत्, उपसर्गाद्धातौ are understood here. In an upasarga ending in अ or आ followed by a root beginning with ए or ओ, the vowels coalesce and the single-substitute is the form of the second vowel (पररूप) ॥ This debars Vriddhi taught in VI. 1. 88. Thus उपेलयति, प्रेलयति, उपोषति, प्रोषति ॥ Some read into this sûtra the option allowed by VI. 1. 92, according to them the para-rûpa substitution is optional in the case of Denominative roots. Thus उपेडकीयति or उपैडकीयति, उपोस्नीयति or उपौस्नीयति ॥

Vârt:—The Para-rûpa substitution takes place in the case of शकन्धुः &c. As शक + अन्धुः = शकन्धुः, कुल + अटा = कुलटा, सीम + अन्तः = सीमन्तः 'hair'; when not referring to 'hair', the form is सीमान्तः ॥

Vârt:—The Para-rûpa substitution takes place when एव follows a word, and the sense is not that of 'appointment'. Thus इह + एव = इहेव; अद्य + एव = अद्येव ॥ When the sense is that of नियोग, the Vriddhi takes place: as इहैव भव, माऽन्यत्र गाः ॥

Vârt:—The Para-rûpa substitution takes place optionally when ओतु and ओष्ठ are compounded with another word: as स्थूल ओतुः = स्थूलौतुः or स्थूलोतुः, so also बिम्बौष्ठी or बिम्बोष्ठी ॥ When not a compound, the Vriddhi is compulsory: as तिष्ठ देवदत्तौष्ठं पश्य 'Stay Devadatta, see the lip'.

Vârt:—In the Vedas, the para-rûpa substitution takes place when एमन् &c. follow. Thus अपां त्वा एमन् = अपां त्वेमन् ॥ So also अपां त्वा ओद्मन् = अपां त्वोद्मन् ॥

ओमाङोश्च ॥ ९५ ॥ पदानि ॥ ओम् - आङोः, च ॥

वृत्तिः ॥ आदित्येव । अवर्णान्तादोमि आङि च परतः पूर्वपरयोः स्थाने पररूपमेकादेशो भवति ॥

95. For the अ or आ + ओ of ओम्, or + the vowel of the Preposition आङ्, the second vowel is the single substitute.

The आत् is understood here. Thus का-।-ओम् = कोम् ; या-।-ओम् = योम् ; as कोमित्यवोचत्, योमित्यवोचत् ; आ-।-ऊढा = ओढा, then अद्य-।-आढा = अद्योढा, कश-।-ओढा = कशोढा, तश + ओढा = तशोढा ॥ आ + ऋश्यात् = अर्श्यात्, then अद्य-।-अर्श्यात् = अद्यर्श्यात् ॥ Thus this rule supersedes both the Vṛiddhi and the lengthening (VI. 1. 88, and 101).

उस्यपदान्तात् ॥ ९६ ॥ पदानि ॥ उसि, अपदान्तात् ॥

वृत्तिः ॥ आदित्येव । अवर्णादपदान्तादसि पूर्वपरयोराद्गुणापवादः पररूपमेकादेशो भवति ॥

96. For the अ or आ (not standing at the end of a Pada or full word) + उ of उस् the Tense-affix, the second vowel is the single substitute.

The आत् is understood here. This debars the guṇa substitution taught in VI. 1. 87. Thus भिन्द्या-।-उस् = भिन्द्युः, छिन्द्या-।-उस् = छिन्द्युः ॥ अदा-।-उस् = अदुः, (लुङ् of दा) अया-।-उस् = अयुः ॥ All these are examples of लिङ् (Potential) and लङ् (Imperfect). Thus भिन्द् + यासुट् + झि (the यासुट् is added by III. 4. 103) = भिन्द् + य + उस् (जुस् replaced झि III. 4. 108) = भिन्द्युस् ॥ अदा + सिच् + झि = अदा + 0 (II. 4. 77) + जुस् (III. 4. 110) = अदा + उस् = अदुः ॥ अ + या + झि = अ + या + उस् (VI. 4. 111) = अयुः ॥ The उस् is also the substitute of झि in लिट् (Perfect) see III. 4. 82. When the preceding vowel is not अ or आ, this rule does not apply. Thus the 3rd per. pl. of the Perfect of कृ is :—चकृ-।-उस् = चक्रुः ॥ So also from भी we have अबिभे-।-उस् = अबिभयुः ॥ The word अपदान्तात् 'not being final in a pada' does strictly speaking, serve no good purpose in this sùtra. For the *affix* उस् can never be added to a Pada, it must always be added to a stem, that has not yet risen to the rank of a Pada. If उस्, however, be taken as the syllable उस् (whether an affix or part of an affix or not), then the limitation of अपदान्तात् becomes valid. Thus का + उस्रा = कोस्रा, का + उषिता = कोषिता ॥ Most likely this word has been read here for the sake of the subsequent sútra or because उस् syllable is taken here and not merely the affix उस् ॥

अतो गुणे ॥ ९७ ॥ पदानि ॥ अतः, गुणे ॥

वृत्ति ॥ अपदान्तादिति वर्त्तते । अकारादपदान्ताद्गुणे परतः पूर्वपरयोः स्थाने पररूपमेकादेशो भवति ॥

97. Also when the short अ, not being final in a Pada, is followed by a Guṇa letter, then in the room of both the precedent and the subsequent—the single subitstute is the form of the subsequent i. e. the Guṇa.

Thus पच्-।-शप्-।-अन्ति = पच-।-अन्ति = पचन्ति so also यजन्ति ॥ This debars lengthening of VI. 1. 101. पच + ए = पचे, यज + ए = यजे, here the Vṛiddhi is debarred (VI. 1. 88). Why do we say "after the short vowel अ?" Observe या-।-अन्ति = यान्ति, वान्ति ॥ Why do we say when followed by 'a Guṇa letter?' Observe

अपच-।-इ = अपचे, अयजे ॥ When final in a Pada, this rule does not apply: as दण्ड-।-अग्रं = दण्डाग्रम्, यूपाग्रम्, क्षुद्राग्रम् ॥

अव्यक्तानुकरणस्यात इतौ ॥ ९८ ॥ पदानि ॥ अव्यक्तानुकरणस्य, अतः, इतौ ॥

वृत्तिः ॥ अव्यक्तमपरिस्फुटवर्णं तदनुकरणं परिस्फुटवर्णमेव केन चित्सादृश्येन तदव्यक्तमनुकरोति तस्य यो-ऽच्छब्दस्तस्सादितौ पूर्वपरयोः स्थाने पररूपमेकादेशो भवति ॥

वार्त्तिकम् ॥ अनेकाच इति वक्तव्यम् ॥

98. The इ of इति is the single substitute for the अत् (of a word denoting imitation of an inarticulate sound)-।-इति ॥

The sound which is not distinct and clear, is called अव्यक्त; when some one utters distinctly something which has some resemblance to that sound, by some contrivance, it is called अनुकरण or imitation of that sound. Thus पटत्-।-इति = पटिति, घटत् + इति = घटिति, झटत् + इति = झटिति, छमत् + इति = छमिति ॥

Why do we say 'imitation of an inarticulate sound'? Observe जगत्-।-इति = जगदिति ॥ Why do we say "of अत्"? Observe मरद् + इति = मरदीति ॥ Why do we say when followed by इति? Observe पटत् + अत्र = पटदत्र ॥

Vârt:—This applies when the word consists of more than one syllable. Therefore it does not apply in the following:—स्रत् + इति = स्रदिति ॥ How do you. explain the form घटदिति in the following:—घटदिति गम्भीरमम्बुदैर्नदितम् ॥ Here the word is not घटत्-।-इति but घटद्-।-इति ॥

नाम्रेडितस्यान्त्यस्य तु वा ॥ ९९ ॥ पदानि ॥ न, आम्रेडितस्य, अन्त्यस्य, तु, वा ॥

वृत्तिः ॥ अव्यक्तानुकरणस्याम्रेडितस्य यो ऽच्छब्द इतौ तस्य पररूपं न भवति तस्य योन्त्यस्तकारस्तस्य वा भवति ॥

99. This substitution does not take place when a sound-imitation word is doubled, here, however, for the final त्-।-इ of इति, the single substitute is optionally इ (the second vowel).

Thus पटत्पटदिति or पटत्पटेति करोति (पटत्पटत् + इति = पटत्पट + इ + ति = पटत्पटेति) ॥ The word is doubled by VIII. 1. 4. The para-rûpa substitution will take place when the whole word so reduplicated denotes a sound imitation, thus पटत्पटेति करोति ॥ Here we apply the precedeing sûtra. The âmreḍita is the name of the second member of the doubled word (VIII. 1. 2).

नित्यमाम्रेडिते डाचि ॥ १०० ॥ पदानि ॥ नित्यम्, आम्रेडिते, डाचि ॥

वृत्तिः ॥ अव्यक्तानुकरणस्यातो ऽन्त्यस्येति चानुवर्त्तते । डाच्परं यदाम्रेडितं तस्मिन्पूर्वस्याव्यक्तानुकरणस्या-ऽच्छब्दस्य योन्त्यस्तकारस्तस्य पूर्वस्य परस्य चाद्यस्य वर्णस्य नित्यं पररूपमेकादेशो भवति ॥

100. Of such a doubled sound-imitation word, to which the affix आ is added which causes the elision of the final अत्, for the final त् of the first member and the initial

consonant of the second member, such subsequent consonant is always the single substitute.

Thus पटपटा करोति (V. 4. 57), इमइमा करोति ॥ पटत्पटत्-।-डाच् (V. 4. 57) = पटत्पटा = पटपटा (त्+प्=प्) ॥ This sûtra is really a Vârtika. When the affix डाच् (V. 4. 57) is added to पटत्, there is doubling of the word by the Vârtika under VIII. 1. 12: this doubling takes place before the final अत् is elided.

अकः सवर्णे दीर्घः ॥ १०१ ॥ पदानि ॥ अकः, सवर्णे, दीर्घः ॥

वृत्तिः ॥ अकः सवर्णे ऽचि परतः पूर्वपरयोः स्थाने दीर्घ एकादेशो भवति ॥

वार्त्तिकम् ॥ सवर्णदीर्घत्वे ऋति ऋवा वचनम ॥ वा० ॥ लृति लृ वा वचनम् ॥

101. When a simple vowel is followed by a homogenous vowel, the corresponding long vowel is the single substitute for both the precedent and the subsequent vowels.

Thus दण्ड + अग्रम् = दण्डाग्रम्, दधि + इन्द्रः = दधीन्द्रः, मधु + उद्के = मधूद्के and होतृ + ऋश्य होतृश्यः ॥ Why do we say 'an अक् or simple vowel?' Observe अग्ने-।-ए = अग्नये ॥ Why do we say 'by a homogenous vowel?' Observe दधि-।-अत्र = दध्यत्र ॥ The word अचि is understood here also. The word सवर्णे, therefore, qualifies the word अचि understood. The rule will not apply if a homogenous consonant follows. As कुमारी शेते ॥ The ई and श are homogenous, in spite of I. 1. 10: for that prohibition does not apply to the long ई and श, because the rule of classification and inclusion contained in अणुदित्सवर्णस्य चाप्रत्ययः (I. 1. 69) is not brought into operation at the time when नाज् झलौ (I. 1. 10) rule operates, because of its being a portion of सवर्ण rule. Therefore, so long as it does not come into operation it is not accomplished. Therefore first the rule of नाज् झलौ comes into play, then the rule of सवर्ण definition (I. 1. 9) and then comes the ग्रहणकवाक्यं (I. 1. 68). Therefore in नाज् झलौ those अच् only are taken which are not included in the *class* of homogenous vowels i. e. only the 9 vowels contained *directly* in अच्, and not the सवर्ण vowels which I. 1. 68 would have denoted. Therefore though *short* इ and श are not सवर्ण by I. 1. 10: the *long* ई and श would be savarṇa.

Vârt:—When ऋ short is followed by ऋ short, the long substitution is optional: so also with लृ ॥ This vârtika is necessitated because (1) the two ऋ or लृ—the precedent and the subsequent—are not homogenous, because one is samvṛita and the other vivṛita, or (2) because their prosodial length is 1½ and so the word दीर्घ cannot be applied with consistency in their case (ऋकार &c). Thus होतृऋकारः = होतॄकारः or होतृकारः, so also होतृ-।-लृकारः = होतॄकारः or होत्लृकारः ॥ The दीर्घ of लृ is ॠ ॥

प्रथमयोः पूर्वसवर्णः ॥ १०२ ॥ पदानि ॥ प्रथमयोः, पूर्व - सवर्णः, ॥

वृत्तिः ॥ अक इति दीर्घ इति वर्तते । प्रथमाशब्दो विभक्तिविशेषे रूढस्तत्साहचर्यात् द्वितीयापि प्रथमेत्युक्ता । तस्यां प्रथमायां द्वितीयायां च विभक्तावचि अकः पूर्वपरयोः स्थाने पूर्वसवर्णदीर्घ एकादेशो भवति ॥

102. For the simple vowel of a nominal-stem and for the vowel of the case-affixes of the Nominative and the Accusative in all numbers, there is the single substitution of a long vowel corresponding to the first vowel.

The words अकः and दाघः are both understood here. The word प्रथमा here means the प्रथमा विभक्ति i. e. the 1st case or the Nominative, and includes here the द्वितीया विभक्ति also. This sûtra teaches the substitution of a पूर्वरूप or a homogenous long vowel corresponding to the first vowel. Thus अग्नि+औ =अग्नी ; वायु+औ=वायू ; वृक्ष+अस्=वृक्षाः, so also प्लक्षाः, वृक्षान्, प्लक्षान् ॥ In the case of these last four examples (वृक्ष+अस् &c) the rule VI. 1. 97 would have caused para-rûpa substitution i. e. would have given the form वृक्ष+अस्=वृक्षः, and that rule would have debarred the lengthening rule VI. 1. 101 on the maxim "apavâdas that precede the rules which teach operations that have to be superseded by the apavâda operations, supersede those rules that stand nearest to them :" but not this पूर्वसवर्ण lengthening rule as it does not stand nearest. The word अचि 'when a vowel follows' is understood here also. Thus वृक्ष+स्=वृक्षः, प्लक्षः ॥ The word अक् 'the simple vowel' is understood here also. Thus नौ+औ=नावौ ॥ Why do we say 'a vowel homogenous to the antecedent?' The substitute will not be one homogenous to the second or the subsequent vowel. The दीर्घ or 'long' is used in order to debar the substitution of pluta vowel having 3 measures for a pluta vowel.

तस्माच्छसो नः पुंसि ॥ १०३ ॥ पदानि ॥ तस्मात्, शसः, नः, पुंसि ॥

वृत्तिः ॥ तस्मात्पूर्वसवर्णदीर्घादुत्तरस्य शसो ऽवयवस्य सकारस्य पुंसि नकारादेशो भवति ॥

103. After such a long vowel homogenous with the first, न् is substituted for the स् of the Accusative case affix शस् in the masculine.

Thus वृक्ष+शस्=वृक्ष+अन्=वृक्षान् ॥ So also अग्नीन्, वायून, कर्तॄन्, होतॄन्, पण्डकान् स्थूरान्, अरकान्, पश्य &c. All these are masculine nouns. Now the word चञ्चा formed by the elision of कन् meaning a figure like a चञ्चा (V. 3. 98), may refer to both the males and females. It will however retain its feminine form though referring to a male being (See लुपि युक्तवद् व्यक्ति वचने I. 2. 51). In forming the accusative plural of चञ्चा, the स् will not be changed into न् ॥ Thus चञ्चाः पश्य, वध्रिकाः पश्य ॥ Why do we say 'after *such* a long vowel homogenous with the first'? The rule will not apply if the long vowel has resulted by being a single substitute for the antecedent and the subsequent. Thus आ is substituted for ओ+अ by VI. 1. 93. Here स् will not be replaced by न् as गाः पश्य ॥ Why do we say 'of the Accusative plural'? Observe वृक्षाः, प्लक्षाः endings in जस् Nom Pl. Why do we say "in the masculine?" Observe, धेनुः, बह्वीः, कुमारीः ॥

नादिचि ॥ १०४ ॥ पदानि ॥ न, आत्, इचि ॥

वृत्तिः ॥ अवर्णादिचि पूर्वसवर्णदीर्घो न भवति ॥

104. The substitution of a long vowel homogenous with the first, does not take place when अ or आ is followed by a vowel (other than अ) of the case-affixes of the Nominative and the Accusative.

Thus वृक्षौ, प्लक्षौ, खट्वे, कुण्डे ॥ Here Rules VI. 1. 87 &c. apply. Why do we say "after अ or आ?" Observe अग्नी ॥ Why do we say "followed by an इच् (a vowel other than अ)"? Observe वृक्षाः here VI. 1. 102 applies.

दीर्घाज्जसि च ॥ १०५ ॥ पदानि ॥ दीर्घात्, जसि, च ॥

वृत्तिः ॥ दीर्घाज्जसि इचि च परतः पूर्वसवर्णदीर्घो न भवति ॥

105. The substitution of a long vowel homogenous with the first, does not take place when a long vowel is followed by a nominative or accusative case-affix beginning with a vowel (other than अ) or by the Nom. Pl. affix अस् ॥

Thus कुमार्यौ, कुमार्य, ब्रह्मबन्ध्वौ, ब्रह्मबन्ध्वः ॥

वा छन्दसि ॥ १०६ ॥ पदानि ॥ वा, छन्दसि ॥

वृत्तिः ॥ दीर्घाच्छन्दसि विषये जसि च इचि च परतो वा पूर्वसवर्णदीर्घो न भवति ॥

106. In the Vedas, the long vowel may optionally be the single substitute of both vowels in these cases last mentioned.

Thus मारुतीः or मारुत्यः, पिण्डीः or पिण्ड्यः, वाराही or वाराह्यौ; उपानही or उपानह्यौ ॥

अमि पूर्वः ॥ १०७ ॥ पदानि ॥ अमि, पूर्वः ॥

वृत्तिः ॥ अक इत्येव । अमि परतो ऽकः पूर्वपरयोः स्थाने पूर्व एकादेशो भवति ॥

107. There is the single substitution of the first vowel, when a simple vowel is followed by the अ of the case ending अम् ॥

The word अकः is understood here. Thus वृक्ष+अम्=वृक्षम् (VII. 1. 24) प्लक्षम्, अग्नि+अम्=अग्निम्, वायुम् ॥ The word पूर्व 'antecedent, first' in the sûtra shows that the first vowel itself is substituted and not any of its homogenous vowels. Otherwise in कुमारी+अम्=कुमारीम् the ई would have been of three mâtrâs or measures, as it comes in the room of ई+अ, the aggregate mâtrâs of which are three.

In the Vedas, there is option, as शमीं or शम्यं, गौरीं or गौर्यम् ॥ अम् is the ending of the Accusative singular of all genders and also of the nominative singular in the Neuter in certain cases. (See VII. I. 23, 24 and 28).

संप्रसारणाच्च ॥ १०८ ॥ पदानि ॥ सम्प्रसारणात्, च ॥

वृत्तिः ॥ पूर्व इत्येव । संप्रसारणादचि परतः पूर्वपरयोः स्थाने पूर्व एकादेशो भवति ॥

108. There is the single substitution of the first vowel for the vocalised semivowel and the subsequent vowel.

The word पूर्वः is understood here. When a vocalised semi-vowel is followed by a vowel, the vocalised vowel is alone substituted, the subsequent vowel merging in it. Thus यज्+क्त = इअज्+क्त (VI. I. 15) = इष्टम् (इ+अ = इ); so उप्तम् (वप्+क्त = उ अप्+त), ग्रह्+इत = गृ अह्+इत = गृहीतं ॥ Had there not been this merging, the vocalisation would become either useless or the two vowels would have been heard separately without sandhi. Thus in वप्+त = उअप्+त, if the अ did not merge in उ, then it would cause sandhi, and उ would be changed to व् by इकोयणचि and the word would again assume the form वप् ॥ But this यणादेश would caues samprasarâṇa rule non-effective, hence it follows that but for the present rule, the two vowels would have been heard separately as उ अप्त ॥

The rule of option in the Chhandas (VI. I. 106) applies here also. Thus we have यज्यमानौ मित्रावरुणौ or इज्यमानौ ॥ "When you have just said that the two vowels will remain separate and there will be no यणादेश when there is no purvavad-bhâva we do you form यज्यमान् ; it ought to be इ अज्यमान्" ? We have only said that vocalisation rule becomes useless if there was not this rule of merging of the subsquent vowel; but where there is this rule of purva-vad-bhâva, and only an *option* is allowed, then the rule of vocalisation does not become totally useless because it finds its scope in cases like इष्टः &c, therefore when in the *alternative* it is not applied, there यणादेश will take place naturally, and the ordinary rules of sandhi will apply. The merging, moreover, refers to the vowel which is in the same aṅga or base with the samprasâraṇa. Thus शकान् ह्वयति = शकह्वा + क्विप् = शकह् उ आ = शकहू ॥ Here आ which is in the same अङ्ग with हु merges in to उ ॥But in forming the dual, we have शकहू + औ ॥ Here औ coming after the samprasâṛana ऊ does not merge therein, and we have शकह्वौ ॥ Similarly शकहू + अर्थं = शकह्वर्थम् ॥ In fact when *once* the para-purvatva has taken effect, then subsequent vowels will produce their effect because in the antaranga operation इ अ ष्ट into इष्ट, the purva-rupa is ordained to save the samprasâraṇa from modification, but there is no such necessity, when a Bahiranga operation is to be applied.

एङः पदान्तादति ॥ १०९ ॥ पदानि ॥ एङः, पदान्तात्, अति ॥

वृत्तिः ॥ एङ् यः पदान्तस्तस्मादति परतः पूर्वपरयोः स्थाने पूर्वरूपमेकादेशो भवति ॥

109. In the room of ए or ओ final in a Pada, and the short अ, which follows it, is substituted the single vowel of the form of the first (ए or ओ) ॥

Thus अग्ने-।-अत्र = अग्नेऽत्र, वायो-।-अत्र = वायोऽत्र ॥ This supersedes the substitutes अय् and अव् ॥ Why do we say 'of ए or ओ'? Observe दध्यत्र, मध्वत्र ॥ Why do we say 'final in a Pada'? Observe चे-।-अन = चयनम्, लो-।-अन = लवनम् ॥ Here the ए or ओ are in the body of the word, and not at the end of a word. Why do we say "when followed by a short अ'? Observe वायो-।-इति = वायविति, भानो-।-इति = भानविति ॥ Why do we say 'short'? Observe वायो आयाहि = वायवायाहि ॥

ङसिङसोश्च ॥ ११० ॥ पदानि ॥ ङसिङसोः, च ॥

वृत्तिः ॥ एङ इति वर्त्तते, अतीति च । एङ उत्तरयोर्ङसिङसोरति परतः पूर्वपरयोः स्थाने पूर्वं एकादेशो भवति ॥

110. In the room of ए or ओ (in the body of a word),-।-अ of the case-affix अस् of the Ablative and Genitive Singular, the single substitute is the form of the precedent.

Thus अग्ने-।-अस् = अग्नेः, वायोः ॥ The इ and उ of अग्नि and वायु are guṇated by VII. 3. 111. This sûtra applies when the ए or ओ are in the middle of a word and not padânta, as in the last. Thus अग्नेरागच्छति, वायोरागच्छति, अग्नेः स्वम्' वायोः स्वम् ॥

ऋत उत् ॥ १११ ॥ पदानि ॥ ऋतः, उत् ॥

वृत्तिः ॥ ङसिङसोरित्येव ऋकारान्तादुत्तरयोर्ङसिङसोरति पूर्वपरयोरुकार एकादेशो भवति ॥

111. In the room of ऋ-।-अ of the case-affix अस् of the Ablative and Genitive singular, the single substitute is the letter short उ ॥

Thus होतृ-।-अस् = होतुर्स् (The उ must always be followed by र् I. 1. 51 though this उ is not the substitute of ऋ only, but of ऋ + अ conjointly: on the maxim that a substitute which replaces *two*, both shown in the genitive case, as ऋतः and अकारस्य in this sûtra, gets the attributes of every one of these separately as the son C of a father A and mother B (though both conjointly produce him) may be called indifferently the son of A or the son of B. So the उ may be called the substitute of ऋ or अ) ॥ The final स् is then elided by VIII. 2. 24 and we have होतुर् = होतुः ॥ Thus होतुरागच्छति, होतुः स्वम् ॥

ख्यत्यात्परस्य ॥ ११२ ॥ पदानि ॥ ख्य - त्यात्-, परस्य ॥

वृत्तिः ॥ ङसिङसोरिति वर्त्तते उदिति च । ख्यत्यादिति खिशब्दखीशब्दयोस्तिशब्दतीशब्दयोश्चकृतयणादेशयोरिदंग्रहणं, ताभ्यां परस्य ङसि ङसोरत उकारादेशो भवति ॥

112. There is the substitution of उ for the अ of

अस् of the Ablative and Genitive singular, after सखि and पति, when for the इ of those two stems य् is substituted.

The phrase ङसिङसोः and उत् are understood here also. The ख्य means and includes खि and खी when the ई is changed to य, and त्य denotes ति and ती, the इ being changed to य ॥ Thus सखि-।-अस् = सख्युः as सख्युरागच्छति, सख्युः स्वम् ॥ So also पत्युरागच्छति, पत्युः स्वम् ॥ The illustration of खी is सखी which is derived from the Denominative Verb thus : सहखेन वर्तते = सखः, सखमिच्छति = सख-।-क्यच् (III. 1. 8) = सखीय (VII. 4. 3). Now by adding क्विप् to the denominative root सखीय we get सखीः 'one who wishes for a friend'. The Ablative and Genitive Singular of this word will be सखी-।-अस् = सख्युः also. Of ती we have the following example. लूनमिच्छति = लूनीय, add क्विप् = लूनीः, the Ablative and Genitive singular of which is also लून्युः, the न् of लूनी being the substitute of त् of Nishṭhâ, is considered like त् (VIII. 2. 1). The peculiar exhibition of ख्य and त्य in the sûtra, instead of saying directly सखिपतिभ्यां indicates that the rule does not apply to words like अतिसखि &c : where we have अतिसखेः, सेनापतेः ॥ The word अतिसखि is घि in spite of the prohibition (I. 4. 7), for that prohibition applies only to सखि and not to a compound which ends in it, on the maxim ग्रहणवता प्रातिपदिकेन तदन्तविधिर्नास्ति ॥ "That which cannot possibly be anything but a Prâtipadika does (contrary to I. 1. 72) not denote that which ends with it, but it denotes only itself". According to Dr. Ballantyne this rule applies to all खी and ती, such as सुखीः one who loves pleasure' (सुखमिच्छति = सुखीय-।-क्विप्). and सुतीः 'one who wishes a son' (सुतमिच्छति = सुतीय-।-क्विप्) : Thus सुख्युः, सुत्युः &c.

अतो रोरप्लुतादप्लुते ॥ ११३ ॥ पदानि ॥ अतः, रोः, अप्लुतात्, अप्लुते, ॥

वृत्तिः ॥ अति, उदिति वर्त्तते । अकारादप्लुतादुत्तरस्य रोरेफस्य उकारानुबन्धविशिष्टस्य अकारे ऽप्लुते परत उकारादेशो भवति ॥

113. The उ is the substitute of रु (the र् substitute of a final स् VIII. 2. 66) when an अ, which is not a *pluta*, both precedes and follows it.

The phrase उत् is understood here, as well as the word अति of VI. 1. 109, 111. Thus वृक्ष-।-सु (1st singular) = वृक्षस् = वृक्षर् (VIII. 2. 66). वृक्षर्-।-अत्र = वृक्षउ-।-अत्र = वृक्षो-।-अत्र (VI. 1. 87) = वृक्षोऽत्र (VI. 1. 109); so also प्लक्षोऽत्र ॥ This ordains उ for र्, whereby VIII. 3. 17, there would have been otherwise य ; and this उ does not become asiddha (as it depends upon रु VIII. 2. 66) for the purposes of VIII. 3. 17, as it otherwise would have been by VIII. 2. 1.

Why do we say 'after an अ'? Observe अग्निर्-।-अत्र = अग्निरत्र ॥ Why do say 'a *short* अ'? Observe वृक्षाः-।-अत्र = वृक्षा अत्र ॥ Why do we use रु with its indicatory उ, and not use the र् generally ? Observe स्वर्-।-अत्र = स्वरत्र, प्रातर्-।-अत्र प्रातरत्र ॥ Here the final र् is part of the words, and is not produced from स् ॥

The word भवि is understood here also from VI. 1. 109. The र must be *followed* by a short अ, therefore, not here: वृक्षर्+इह = वृक्ष इह ॥ The subsequent अ must be short, the rule does not apply here वृक्षर्+आश्रितः = वृक्ष आश्रितः ॥ Why do we say 'preceded by an apluta अ'? The rule will not apply if a Pluta vowel precedes it. As, सुस्रोता ३ अत्र त्वमसि (VIII. 2. 84). Why do we say "when followed by an apluta अ"? Observe तिष्ठतु पय आ३ग्निदत्त (VIII. 2. 86). Here प्लुत being held asiddha, there would have been उ substitution, had not the phrase अप्लुत been used in the aphorism.

हशि च ॥ ११४ ॥ पदानि ॥ हशि, च ॥

वृत्तिः ॥ हशि च परतो ऽत उत्तरस्य रोरुकारादेशो भवति ॥

114. The उ is the substitute of रु (the र substitute of स् VIII. 2. 66) when it is followed by a soft consonant and preceded by an apluta short अ ॥

The हश् pratyâhâra includes all sonants or soft consonants. Thus पुरुषो याति or हसति or ददाति &c.

प्रकृत्या ऽन्तःपादमव्यपरे ॥ ११५ ॥ पदानि ॥ प्रकृत्या, अन्तः-पादम्, अव्यपरे ॥

वृत्तिः ॥ एङो ऽतीत्येव । एङ इति यत्पञ्चम्यन्तमनुवर्त्तते तदर्थादिह प्रथमान्तं भवति । प्रकृतिरिति स्वभावः कारणं वा ऽभिधीयते । अन्तरित्यव्ययमधिकरणभूतं मध्यमाचष्टे । पादशब्देन च ऋक्पादस्यैव ग्रहणमिष्यते न तु श्लोकपादस्य । अवकारयकारपरे ऽति परत एङ् प्रकृत्या भवति ॥

115. The final ए or ओ and the following अ when occurring in the middle half of a foot of a Vedic verse, retain their original forms, except when the अ is followed by व् or य् ॥

The word एङः is understood here, but it should be construed here in the nominative case and not in the Ablative. The word प्रकृति means 'original nature, cause'. The word अन्तर् is an Indeclinable, used in the Locative case here and means 'in the middle'. The word पादः 'the foot of a verse' refers to the verses of the Vedas, and not to the verses of secular poetry. The word अति is also understood here. Thus ते अग्रे अश्वमायुञ्जन्; ते अस्मिन् जवमादधुः, उपप्रयन्तो अध्वरम्; शिरो अपश्यम्; सुजाते अश्वसूनृते (R. Veda. V. 79. 1); अध्वर्यो अद्रिभिः सुतम् (Rig IX. 51. 1); शुक्रं ते अन्यत् (Rig. VI. 58. 1).

Why do we say 'in the inner half of a foot of a verse?' Observe कया मती कुत एतास एते ऽर्चन्ति ॥ Why do we say "when व् or य् does not follow अ?" Observe ते ऽवदन् (Rig X. 109. 1), ते ऽयजन्त ॥ Why do we say ए or ओ? Observe अन्वग्निरुषसामग्रमख्यत् ॥ Some read this sûtra as नान्तः पादमव्यपरे ॥ According to them, this sûtra supersedes the whole rule of juxtaposition or संहिता (VI. 1. 72).

अव्यादवद्यादवक्रमुरव्रतायमवन्त्ववस्युषु च ॥ ११६ ॥ पदानि ॥ अव्यात्' अवद्यात् , अवक्रमुः, अव्रत, अयम्, अवन्तु, अवस्युषु, च ॥

वृत्तिः ॥ अव्यात् अवद्यात् अवक्रमुः अव्रत अयम् अवन्तु अवस्यु इत्येतेषु यकारवकारपरेष्वाति परतोऽन्तः पादमेङ् प्रकृत्या भवति ॥

116. The ए or ओ retain their original form in the middle of a Vedic verse, when the following words come after them (though the अ in these has a व् and य् following it) :—अव्यात्, अवद्यात्, अवक्रमुः, अव्रत, अयम, अवन्तु, अवस्यु ॥

Thus अग्निः प्रथमोवसुभिर्नो अव्यात् ॥ मित्रमहो अवद्यात् (Rig IV. 4. 15), मा शिवासो अवक्रमुः (Rig VII. 32. 27); ते नो अव्रताः (Not in the Rig Veda). Prof. Bohtlingk gives the following examples from the Rig Veda :—सीक्षन्तो अव्रतम् (VI. 14. 3), संदहन्तो अव्रतान् (IX. 73. 5), कर्ते अव्रतान् (IX. 73. 8). शतधारो अयं मणिः, ते नो अवन्तु पितरः (Not in the Rig Veda: according to Prof. Bohtlingk the अ of अवन्तु is generally elided in the Veda after ए or आ) कुशिकासो अवस्यवः (Rig III. 42. 9).

यजुष्युरः ॥ ११७ ॥ पदानि ॥ यजुषि, उरः ॥

वृत्तिः ॥ उरः शब्द एङन्तो यजुषि विषये ऽति पकृत्या भवति ॥

117. In the Yajur-Veda, the word उरस् when changed to उरो, retains its original form when followed by a short अ which is also retained.

Thus उरो अन्तरिक्षम् (Yaj. Veda Vajasan. IV. 7). Some read the sûtra as यजुष्युरोः ॥ They take the word as उरु ending in उ, which in the Vocative case assumes the form उरो ॥ They give the following example उरो अन्तरिक्षं सजूः ॥ But in the Yajur Veda VI. 11, the text reads उरोरन्तरिक्षात् सजूः ॥ In the Yajur Veda, there being no stanzas, the condition of अन्तः पादं does not apply here.

आपोजुषाणोवृष्णोवर्षिष्ठेम्बेम्बालेम्बिकेपूर्वे ॥ ११८ ॥ पदानि ॥ आपः, जुषाणः, वृष्णोः, वर्षिष्ठे, अम्बे, अम्बाले, अम्बिके, पूर्वे ॥

वृत्तिः ॥ यजुषीत्येव । आपो जुषाणो वृष्णो वर्षिष्ठ इत्येते शब्दा अम्बे अम्बाले इत्येता च यावम्बिकेशब्दात्पूर्वौ यजुषि पठितौ त आति परतः प्रकृत्या भवन्ति ॥

118. In the Yajur Veda, the short अ is retained after आपो, जुषानो, वृष्णो, वर्षिष्ठे, and also in and after अम्बे or अम्बाले when they stand before अम्बिके ॥

Thus आपो अस्मान् मातरः शुन्धयन्तु (Yaj. IV. 2). जुषाणो अप्तुराज्यस्य (Yaj. V. 35), वृष्णो अंशुभ्यां गभस्ति पूतः (Yaj. VII. 1). वर्षिष्ठे अधिनाके ॥ The Vajasaneyi Sanhita has वर्षिष्ठेऽधि (V. S I. 22): The Taittariya Sanhita has वर्षिष्ठे अधि ॥ (I. 1. 8. 1. 4, 43, 2. 5. 5. 4) अम्बे अम्बाले अम्बिके (V. S. 23. 18 where the reading is अम्बे अम्बिके ऽम्बालिके) but Tait S. VII. 4. 19. 1, and Tait Br. III. 9. 6. 3 has अम्बे अम्बाल्यम्बिके ॥ The words अम्बे &c, though in the Vocative, do not shorten their vowel by VII. 3. 107, because they have been so read here.

अङ्गइत्यादौ च ॥ ११९ ॥ पदानि ॥ अङ्गे, इति-आदौ, च ॥

वृत्तिः ॥ अङ्गशब्दे य एङ् तदादौ चाकारे यः पूर्वः स यजुषि विषये ऽति प्रकृत्या भवति ॥

119. In the Yajur Veda, when the word अङ्गे is followed by अङ्गे, the subsequent short अ is retained, as well as the preceding ए or ओ ॥

Thus ऐन्द्रः प्राणो अङ्गे अङ्गे अदाध्यत्, ऐन्द्रः प्राणो अङ्गे अङ्गे निदीध्यत्, ऐन्द्रः प्राणो अङ्गे अङ्गे निदीतः, ऐन्द्रः प्राणो अङ्गे अङ्गे अशोचिषम् (Yaj. 6. 20).

अनुदात्ते च कुधपरे ॥ १२० ॥ पदानि ॥ अनुदात्ते, च, कु-धपरे ॥

वृत्तिः ॥ यजुषीत्येव । अनुदात्ते चाति कवर्गधकारपरे परतो यजुषि विषये एङ् प्रकृत्या भवति ॥

120. In the Yajur Veda, when an anudâtta अ is followed by a Guttural or a ध, the antecedent ए or ओ retains its form, as well as this subsequent अ ॥

Thus अयं सो अग्निः (Yaj. 12. 47), अयं सो अध्वरः ॥ Why do we say when अ is gravely accented? Observe अधोऽग्रे, here अग्रे has acute accent on the first syllable. Why do we say "when followed by a Guttural (कु) or a ध"? Observe सोऽयमग्निः सहस्रियः ॥

अवपथासि च ॥ १२१ ॥ पदानि ॥ अवपथासि, च ॥

वृत्तिः ॥ यजुषीत्येव । अनुदात्तइति चशब्देनानुकृष्यते । अवपथाःशब्दे ऽनुदात्ते ऽकारादौ परतो यजुषि विषयएङ् प्रकृत्या भवति ॥

121. In the Yajur Veda, when the gravely accented अ of अवपथास् follows ए or ओ, the vowels retain their original form.

Thus त्री रुद्रेभ्यो अवपथाः ॥ The word अवपथाः is 2nd per. Singular Imperfect of वप् in the Atmanepada. Thus अ-।-वप्-।-शप्-।-थास् ॥ The अ is grave by VIII. 1. 28. When it is not gravely accented, the अ drops. As यद्रुद्रेभ्यो ऽवपथाः ॥ Here अ is not grave by virtue of VIII. 1. 30.

सर्वत्र विभाषा गोः ॥ १२२ ॥ पदानि ॥ सर्वत्र, विभाषा, गोः ॥

वृत्तिः ॥ सर्वत्र, छन्दसि भाषायां चाति परतो गोरेङ् प्रकृत्या भवति विभाषा ॥

122. After गो the subsequent अ may optionally be retained everywhere, in the Vedas as well as in the secular literature.

Thus गोऽग्रं or गो अग्रं ॥ In the Vedas also अपशवो वा अन्ये गो अश्वेभ्यः, पशवो गोऽश्वाः ॥

अवङ् स्फोटायनस्य ॥ १२३ ॥ पदानि ॥ अवङ्, स्फोटायनस्य ॥

वृत्तिः ॥ अतीति निवृत्तम् । अचीत्येतत्त्वनुवर्त्ततएव । अचि परतो गोः स्फोटायनस्याचार्यस्य मतेनावङादेशो भवति ॥

123. According to the opinion of Sphoṭâyana, there is the substitution of अवङ् for the ओ of गो when it is followed by any vowel.

The anuvritti of अति ceases, that of आर्च manifests itself. Thus गो+अग्र=गवाग्रम्, so also गवाजिनम्, गवौदनम्, गवाष्ट्रम्, or in the alternative we have गोऽग्रम्, गोऽजिनम्, गवोदनम्, गवुष्ट्रम् ॥ The substitute अवङ् is accutely accented on the first syllable, This accent will be the original accent in the Bahuvrihi compound (VI. 2. 1). Thus गावा अग्रमस्य=गैवाग्रः ॥ In other places, however, this accent will be superseded by the samâsânta Udâtta accent (VI. 1. 223) The mention of Sphoṭâyana is for the sake of respect, for the anuvritti of विभाषा was already understood in it. This is a vyavasthita vibhâshâ, hence in गवाक्षः the अवङ् substitution is compulsory and not optional.

इन्द्रे च नित्यम् ॥ १२४ ॥ पदानि ॥ इन्द्रे, च, नित्यम् ॥

वृत्तिः ॥ इन्द्रशब्दस्थे ऽचि परतो गोर्नित्यमवङादेशो भवति ॥

124. The substitution of अव for the ओ of गो is compulsory when a vowel to be found in the word इन्द्र follows it.

Thus गवेन्द्रः ॥ So also गवन्द्र यज्ञः ॥ The word नित्य is not found in some texts or in Mahâbhâshya.

प्लुतप्रगृह्या अचि ॥ १२५ ॥ पदानि ॥ प्लुतप्रगृह्या अचि, ॥

वृत्तिः ॥ प्लुताश्च प्रगृह्याश्चाचि प्रकृत्या भवन्ति ॥

125. The Pluta (VIII. 2. 82 etc.) and Pragrihya (I. 1. 11 etc.) vowels remain unaltered when followed by a vowel (so far as the operation of that vowel is concerned).

Thus देवदत्ता ३ अत्र न्वसि, यज्ञदत्ता ३ इदम् आनय ॥ These are examples of prolated vowels. The prolation of vowels is taught in the tripâdi or the last three chapters of Ashtadhyâyi ; and the tripadi are considered asiddha for the purposes of previous sûtras (VIII, 2. 1,). This is not the case here, otherwise the mention of pluta would be redundant. . Of the Excepted or Pragrihya vowels the following are the examples: अग्नी इति, वायू इति, खट्वे इति, माले इति ॥ Though the anuvritti of अचि was current in this sûtra from VI. 1. 77 : its repetition here is for the sake of ordaining प्रकृतिभाव ॥ That is, the pluta and the pragrihya retain their original forms when such a vowel follows which would have caused a substitution. Thus जानु उ अस्य, रुजति here in combining जानु+उ into जानू, the अ is no cause of lengthening, therefore, the lengthening will take place. Now since उ is a pragrihya, it follows that जानू which ends in ऊ is also a pragrihya, and therefore it should not be changed before अ of अस्य ॥ Hence we have the form जानू+अस्य=जानू अस्य ॥ There may also be the form जान्वस्य, not by इकोयणचि, but by मय उञो वो वा (VIII. 3. 33). In fact, the repetition of आच in this sûtra is necessary, in order to enable us to give this *peculiar* meaning to the sûtra. Otherwise, had the sûtra been simply प्लुतप्रगृह्याः, it would have been translated ordinaeily thus: "The Pluta and Pragrihya retain their form, when ever a vowel follows". Therefore in जानु उ अस्य, since उ is followed by a vowel, it will retain its form, and will not coalesce with the उ of जानु ॥ But this is not intended. Hence the repetition of the word अचि, and the peculiar explanation given above, namely, Pluta and Pragrihya vowels retain their form before a vowel which would otherwise have caused a substitution, but it would not prevent the operation of any other rule. Therefore in जानु उ अस्य रुजाति· the उ+उ will become lengthened, because अ is not the *cause* of lengthening; it causes the change of उ to व्, which of course is prevented. The word नित्य of the last sûtra is understood here also. These pluta and pragrihya always retain their form and are not influenced by the rule of shortening given in VI. 1. 127.

आङो ऽनुनासिकश्छन्दसि ॥ १२६ ॥ पदानि ॥ आङः, अनुनासिकः, छन्दसि ॥

वृत्तिः ॥ आङो ऽचि परतःसंहितायां छन्दसि विषये ऽनुनासिकादेशो भवति स च प्रकृत्या भवति ॥

126. For the adverb आ, is substituted in the Chhandas the nasalised आँ, when a vowel follows it, and it retains its original form.

Thus अभ्र आँ अपः (Rig V. 48. 1); गभीर आँ उग्रपुत्रे जिघांसतः (Rig VIII. 67. 11). Some read the word बहुलं into this sûtra. Hence there is coalescence here: इन्द्रो बाहुभ्यामातरत्=आ अतरत् ॥

इको ऽसवर्णे शाकल्यस्य ह्रस्वश्च ॥ १२७ ॥ पदानि ॥ इकः, असवर्णे, शाकल्यस्य, ह्रस्वः, च ॥

वृत्तिः ॥ इको ऽसवर्णे ऽचि परतः शाकल्यस्याचार्यस्य मतेन प्रकृत्या भवन्ति, ह्रस्वश्च तस्यकः स्थाने भवति ॥
वार्त्तिकम् ॥ सिन्नित्यसमासयोः शाकलप्रतिषेधो वक्तव्यः ॥
वा० ॥ ईषाअक्षादिषु छन्दसि प्रकृतिभावमात्र वक्तव्यम् ॥

127. According to the opinion of Śâkalya, the simple vowels with the exception of अ, when followed by a nonhomogenous vowel, retain their original forms; and if the vowel is long, it is shortened.

Thus दधि अत्र, मधु अत्र, कुमारि अत्र, किशोरि अत्र ॥ In the alternative we have दध्यत्र, मध्वत्र, कुमार्यत्र, किशोर्यत्र ॥ Why do we say 'the इक् vowels i. e. simple vowels with the exception of अ'? Observe खट्वेन्द्रः ॥ 'Why do we say followed by a non-homogenous vowel'? Observe कुमारीन्द्रः ॥ The name of

Sâkalya is mentioned for the sake of respect. Because the alternative nature of this sûtra is clear from its very formation.

Vart:—This rule of Sâkalya is prohibited in the case of words formed by an affix having an indicatory स् and of words which form invariable compounds (nitya samâsa):—Thus अयं ते योनिर्ऋत्वियः, प्रजां बिशम ऋत्वियाम् The word ऋत्विय is formed by a सित् affix, namely by घस् (V. 1. 106), added to ऋतु; and therefore the उ is changed to व ॥ Before a सित् affix the previous word is considered a pada (I. 4. 16) Of nitya-compounds are वैयाकरणः, सौवश्वः, व्याकरणं, कुमार्यर्थम् which are so by II. 2. 18 &c.

Vârt:—In the Vedas ईषा अक्षः &c are found uncombined. As, ईषा अक्षा, का ईमिरे पिशंगिला, यथा अङ्गदः, पथा अगमन् &c.

ऋत्यकः ॥ १२८ ॥ पदानि ॥ ऋति, अकः, (प्रकृत्याः) ॥

वृत्तिः ॥ शाकल्यस्य ह्रस्वश्चेत्येतदनुवर्त्तते । ऋकारे परतः शाकल्यस्याचार्यस्य मतेनाकः प्रकृत्या भवन्ति, ह्रस्वश्च तस्याकः स्थाने भवति ॥

128. According to the opinion of Sâkalya, the simple vowel followed by ऋ retains its original form, and if the simple vowel is long, it is shortened.

Thus खट्वा ऋश्यः, कुमारि ऋश्यः, होतृ ऋश्यः ॥ Why do we say when followed by ऋ? Observe, खट्वेन्द्रः ॥ Why do we say "the simple vowels (अकः)"? Observe वृक्षावृश्यः (वृक्षौ + ऋश्य) ॥ This rule applies even when the vowels are homogenous (which were excepted by the last rule), and it is not confined to इक् vowels as the last, but applies to अ and आ also.

अप्लुतवदुपस्थिते ॥ १२९ ॥ पदानि ॥ अ, प्लुत - वत्, उपस्थिते, ॥

वृत्तिः ॥ उपस्थितं नामानार्ष इतिकरणः समुदायादवच्छिद्य पदं येन स्वरूपे ऽवस्थाप्यते तस्मिन्परतो ऽप्लुतवद्भवति ॥ प्लुतकार्यं प्रकृति भावं न करोति ॥

129. Before the word इति in the Padapâṭha, a Pluta vowel is treated like an ordinary apluta vowel.

The word उपस्थित means the affixing of इति in non-Rishi texts; i. e. when a Vedic text is split up into its various padas or words and इति is added. That is in Padapâṭha, the Pluta is treated like an ordinary vowel, and hence there being no प्रकृतिभाव (VI. 1. 125), there is sandhi. Thus सुश्लोका३ इति = सुश्लोकेति, सुमङ्गला इति = सुमगलेति ॥ Why have we used the word वत् "like as"; instead of saying "the Pluta becomes Apluta" why do we say "Pluta is treated like apluta"? By not using वत्, the whole Pluta itself would be changed into Apluta, and would give rise to the following incongruity. There is prakriti bhâva in the case of pluta and pragrihya. A vowel which is pluta need not be pragrihya, nor a pragrihya, a pluta. But where a vowel is both a pluta and a pragrihya at one and the sametime, there will arise the difficulty. Thus in the dual अग्नी or वायू, the ई and ऊ are pragrihya. They may be made pluta also as अग्नी ३ or वायू ३ ॥ Now if before इति, the pluta *became* apluta, then we shall not hear the prolation at all in अग्नी इति वायू इति formed by अग्नी ३ + इति &c. For here the vowels will retain their form by being pragrihya by VI. 1. 125, and in additon to that they will lose their pluta, by the present rule. But this is not intended. Hence the pluta is heard in अग्नी ३ इति, वायू ३ इति ॥

ई३ चाक्रवर्मणस्य ॥ १३० ॥ पदानि ॥ ई, चाक्रवर्मणस्य ॥

वृत्तिः ॥ ई३ कारः प्लुतो ऽचि परतश्चाक्रवर्मणस्याचार्यस्य मतेनाप्लुतवद्भवति ॥

130. According to the the opinion of Châkravarmaṇa, the pluta ई ३ followed by a vowel is treated like an ordinary vowel.

Thus अस्तु हीत्यब्रवीत or अस्तु ही३ इत्यब्रवीत् ॥ चिनु हीदम् or चिनु ही३ इदम् ॥ The name of Châkravarmaṇa is used for the sake of making this an optional rule. This option applies to इति rule (VI. 1. 129) as well as to words other than इति ॥ In the case of इति it allows *sandhi* optionally, when by the last rule there would have been always sandhi. In the case of words other than इति, it ordains *prakriti bhâva* optionally, when there would have been always prakriti bhâva by VI. 1. 125. This is a case of उभयत्रविभाषा, prâpta and aprâpta both.

Ishti:—This apluta-vad-bhâva applies to pluta vowels other than ई; as वशा ३ इयम् or वशेयम् ॥

दिव उत् ॥ १३१ ॥ पदानि ॥ दिवः, उत् ॥

वृत्तिः ॥ एङः पदान्तादतीत्यतःपदग्रहणमनुवर्तते । दिव इति प्रातिपदिकं गृह्यते न धातुः, सानुबन्धकत्वात् ॥

131. For the final of the nominal-stem दिव्, there is the substitution of उ, when it is a Pada (I. 4. 14 &c).

The portion पद of the word पदान्त must be read into this sûtra from VI. 1. 109. The word दिव् is here a nominal-stem and not a verbal-root. Thus दिवि कामो यस्य = द्युकामः, द्युमान्, विमलद्यु दिनं, द्युभ्याम्, द्युभिः ॥ We have said that दिव् is here a prâtipadika and not a dhâtu, for as a dhâtu it ought to have its servile letter anubandha and should have been read as दिवु ॥ In the case of its being used as a verb, there takes place the substitution of long ऊ for व् by VI. 4. 19. In that case we shall have अक्षद्यूभ्याम्, अक्षद्यूभिः ॥ The उत् with a त् shows that short उ is meant, and debars ऊठ (VI. 4. 19). In the case of ऊठ् substitution the forms will be द्यूभ्याम्, द्यूभिः ॥ The ऊठ् also comes because it is taught in a subsequent sûtra. Why do we say 'when it is a Pada'? Observe दिवौ, दिवः ॥

एतत्तदोः सु लोपो ऽकोरनञ्समासे हलि ॥ १३२ ॥ पदानि ॥ एतत् - तदोः, सु लोपः, अकोः, अ - नञ् - समासे, हलि, ॥

वृत्तिः ॥ एतत्तदौ यावककारौ नञ्समासे न वर्त्तेते तयोर्यः सुशब्दः कश्च तयोः सुशब्दो यस्तदर्थेन संबद्धस्तस्य संहितायां विषये हलि परतो लोपो भवति ॥

132. After एतद् and तद् there is elision of the case-affix सु (of the nominative singular), when a consonant follows it, when these words are not combined with क (V. 3. 71) and have not the Negative Particle in composition.

Thus एषः + ददाति = एष ददाति, स ददाति, एषभुङ्क्ते, स भुङ्क्ते ॥ Why do we say of एतद् and तद्? Observe यो ददाति, यो भुङ्क्ते ॥ Why do say "the case affix of the Nom. singular?" Observe एतौ गावौ चरतः ॥ Why do we say 'without क'? Observe एषको ददाति, सको ददाति ॥ The words एतद् and तद् with the affix अकच्, which falls in the middle, would be considered just like एतत् and तद् without such affix, and in fact would be included in the words एतद् and तद्, hence the necessity of the prohibition. The general maxim is: तन्मध्यपतितस्तद् ग्रहणेन गृह्यते 'any term that may be employed in Grammar denotes not merely what is actually denoted by it, but it denotes also whatever word-form may result when something is inserted in that which is actually denoted by it".

Why do we say "when not compounded with the negative particle"? Observe अनेषो ददाति, असो ददाति ॥ In the compound with the negative particle नञ्, the second member is the principal and takes the case affixes. Why do we say 'when followed by a consonant'? Observe एषोऽत्र, सोऽत्र ॥

स्यश्छन्दसि बहुलम् ॥ १३३ ॥ पदानि ॥ स्यः, छन्दसि, बहुलम्, (सोः, लोपः,) ॥

वृत्तिः ॥ स्य इत्येतस्य छन्दसि हलि परतो बहुलं सोर्लोपो भवति ॥

133. In the Chhandas, the case-affix of the nominative singular is diversely elided after स्य, when a consonant follows it.

Thus उत स्य वाजी क्षिपणिं तुरण्यति ग्रीवायां बद्धो अपिकक्ष आसनि (Rig IV. 40. 4), एष स्य ते मधुमाँ इन्द्र सोमः (Rig IX. 87, 4) ॥ Sometimes it does not take place: as यत्र स्यो निपतेत् ॥ The स्य means 'he'.

सो ऽचि लोपे चेत्पादपूरणम् ॥ १३४ ॥ पदानि ॥ सः, अचि, लोपे, चेत्, पादपूरणम्, ॥

वृत्तिः ॥ स इत्येतस्याचि परतः सुलोपो भवति लोपे सति चेत्पादः पूर्यते ॥

Kârikâ सैष दाशरथी रामः, सैष राजा युधिष्ठिरः ॥
सैष कर्णो महात्यागी सैष भीमो महाबलः ॥

134. 'The case-affix of सस् 'he', is elided before a vowel, if by such elision the metre of the foot becomes complete.

Thus सेदु राजा क्षयति चर्षणीनाम् (Rig I. 32. 15) सौषधीरनुरुध्यसे (Rig VIII. 43. 9). The case-ending being elided, the Sandhi takes place. Why do we say 'when by such elision the metre of the line is completed'? Observe स इव व्याघ्रो भवेत् ॥ The word अचि in the sûtra is for the sake of distinctness: for the purposes of metre would not have been served by eliding the affix before a consonant, for then the syllables would remain the same. It is by sandhi that a syllable is lessened; and sandhi would take place only with a vowel. Some explain the word पाद as 'a foot of a Śloka' also, and according to them this rule is not confined to Vedic metres only. Thus we have:—सैष दाशरथी रामः, सैष राजा युधिष्ठिरः, सैष कर्णो महात्यागी, सैष भीमो महाबलः ॥

सुट् कात्पूर्वः ॥ १३५ ॥ पदानि ॥ सुट्, कात्, पूर्वः, ॥

वृत्तिः ॥ अधिकारोयं, पारस्करप्रभृतीनि च संज्ञायामिति यावत् । इत उत्तरं यद्वक्ष्यामस्तत्र सुडिति कात्पूर्व इति चेतदधिकृतं वेदितव्यम् ॥

135. Upto VI. 1. 157 inclusive, the following sentence is to be supplied in every aphorism:—"before क् is added स्" ॥

This is an adhikâra sûtra and extends upto VI. 1. 157. Whatever we shall teach hereafter, in all those, the phrase 'the augment सुट् is placed before the letter क्' should be supplied to complete the sense. Thus VI. 1. 137 teaches "After सम्, परि and उप when followed by the verb कृ, the sense being that of adorning". Here the above phrase should be read into the sûtra to complete the sense, i. e. "the augment स् is added before the क् of कृ when it is preceded by सम्, परि and उप, and the sense is that of adorning". Thus सम्+स् +कृ+तृ=संस्कर्ता, संस्कर्तुम्, संस्कर्तव्यम् ॥ In the succeeding aphorisms it will be seen that the augment सुट् comes only before those roots which begin with क ॥ What is then the necessity of using the phrase कात्पूर्वः in this sûtra? It is used to indicate that the स् remains unattached to कृ, though it stands before it. Thus though कृ becomes स्कृ, yet the latter should not be considered to be a verb beginning with a conjunct (sanyoga) consonant: and therefore the guṇa taught in VII. 4. 10 (the root ending in ऋ and preceded by a conjunct letter, takes guṇa before लिट्) does not apply, nor do the rules like VII. 4. 29, nor the rules ordaining the addition of intermediate इट् (VII. 2. 43) by which the इट् would come in लिङ् and सिच् (Imperfect and Aorist): as, संस्कृषीष्ट and समस्कृत; and so also VII. 4. 29, does not apply as संस्क्रियते the Passive Imperfect (यक्ि लिङि) of संस्कृ ॥ If so, then the anudâtta accent taught in VIII. 1. 28 would not take place, since the augment सुट् would intervene between the non-तिङ्-word सं and the तिङन्त word करोति, thus संस्करोति would have accent on the verb. It is a maxim स्वरविधौ व्यञ्जनमविद्यमानवत् 'in applying a rule relating to accent the intervening consonants are considered as if non-existent'; and therefore सुट् does not offer any intervention to the application of the rule VIII. 1. 28. If स् is not to be taken as attached to क, how do you explain the guṇa in the Perfect 3rd Per. Dual and Plural in संचस्करतुः and संचस्करुः which apparently is done by applying VII. 4. 10. Though that rule strictly applies to roots beginning with a conjunct consonant, it will apply also to roots like संस्कृ which have a conjunct consonant for their penultimate; and the guṇa is done also on the maxim तन्मध्यपतितस्तद् ग्रहणेन गृह्यते (See VI. 1. 132). The indicatory ट् in सुट् is for the purpose of differentiating it from सु in the Sûtra VIII. 3. 70.

अडभ्यासव्यवायेपि ॥ १३६ ॥ पदानि ॥ अट्, अभ्यास - व्यवाये, अपि ॥

वृत्तिः ॥ अड्व्यवाये ऽभ्यासव्यवाये सुट् कात्पूर्वो भवति ॥

136. The augment सुट् is placed before क even when the augment अट् (VI. 4. 71) or the Reduplicate intervenes (between the preposition and the verb).

Thus समस्करोत् (= सम् + अकरोत्), समस्कार्षीत्, संचस्कार (= सम् + चकार), परिचस्कार ॥ This sûtra is not that of Pâṇini, but is made out of two Vârtikas: अड् व्यवायउप संख्यानाम्; and अभ्यासव्यवाये च ॥ The augmented root स्कृ would have given the form चस्कार by VII. 4. 61, if स् be considered an integral part of कृ, and no rule of Antaranga and Bahiranga be taken into consideration. It might be said where is the necessity then of this sûtra? The operation relating to a Dhâtu and Upasarga is Antaranga, i. e. a root is first joined with the Upasarga, and it undergoes other operations afterwards. Therefore, first the augment सुट् is added, and then the अट् and अभ्यास operations take place. Thus संस्कृ is the form to which अट् and अभ्यास operations are to be applied. Now, we have said in the foregoing aphorism, that सुट् is considered as unattached to क; and therefore, the augment अट् may be added after this सुट्, and so also the reduplication may take place without it. Thus we may have the forms like संसकरोत् and संस्चकार ॥ But this is not desired, hence the necessity of the present sûtra teaching that even after अट् and reduplicate, the सुट् must be placed before क and no where else.

संपर्युपेभ्यः करोतौ भूषणे ॥ १३७ ॥ पदानि ॥ सम - परि - उपभ्येः, करोतौ, भूषणे ॥

वृत्तिः ॥ सम् परि उप इत्येतेभ्यो भूषणार्थे करोतौ परतः सुट् कात्पूर्वो भवति ॥

137. The augment सुट् is placed before क when सम्, परि and उप are followed by the verb कृ and the sense is that of ornamenting.

Thus संस्कर्ता, संस्कर्तुम्, संस्कर्तव्यम् ॥ The म् of सम् is changed to anusvâra by VIII. 3. 5. So also परिष्कर्ता परिष्कर्तुं परिष्कर्तव्यम् ॥ The स is changed to ष by VIII. 3. 70. So also with उप, as उपष्कर्ता, उपष्कर्तुम् उपष्कर्तव्यम् ॥ Why do we say 'when meaning to ornament'? Observe उपकरोति ॥ Sometimes सुट् comes after सम् even when the sense is not that of ornamenting: thus संस्कृतमन्नम् ॥

समवाये च ॥ १३८ ॥ पदानि ॥ समवाये, (च सुट्)

वृत्तिः ॥ समवायः समुदायस्तस्मिन्नर्थे करोतौ संपर्युपेभ्यः कात्पूर्वः सुडागमो भवति ॥

138. The augment सुट् is placed before क, when the verb कृ comes after सम्, परि and उप, the sense being that of combining.

The word समवाय means aggregation. Thus तत्र नः संस्कृतम् तत्र नः परिष्कृतम्, तत्र नः उपस्कृतम्=समुदितम् that is 'we assembled there'.

उपात्प्रतियत्नवैकृतवाक्याध्याहारेषु ॥ १३९ ॥ पदानि ॥ उपात्, प्रति, यत्न, वैकृत, वाक्य - अध्याहारेषु ॥

वृत्तिः ॥ सतो गुणान्तराधानमाधिक्याय वृद्धस्य वा तादवस्थ्याय समीहा प्रतियत्नः । विकृतमेव वैकृतम् । प्रज्ञादित्वादण् । गम्यमानार्थस्य वाक्यस्य स्वरूपेणोपादानं वाक्यस्याध्याहारः । एतेष्वर्थेषु गम्यमानेषु करोतौ धातौ परत उपात् सुट् कात्पूर्वो भवति ॥

139. The augment सुट् is placed before क, when the verb कृ comes after उप, and the sense is that of 'to take pains for something, to prepare, and to supply an ellipses in a discourse'.

To take pains in imparting a new quality to a thing in order to increase its value, or to keep it safe from deterioration is called प्रतियत्नः ॥ That which is prepared or altered is called वैकृतं ॥ The word वैकृतं is the same as विकृतं, the affix अण् being added without changing the sense, by considering it to belong to प्रज्ञादि class (V. 4. 38). To supply by distinct statement the sense of a sentence which is alluded to, is called the अध्याहार of a sentence. Thus in the sense of 'taking pains' we have एधोदकस्योपस्कुरुते (See I. 3. 32); काण्डगुणस्योपस्कुरुते ॥ In the sense of 'altering by preparing' we have: उपस्कृतं भुङ्क्ते, उपस्कृतं गच्छति ॥ In the sense of 'supplying a thesis' we have उपस्कृतं जल्पति, उपस्कृतमधीते ॥ When not having any one of the above five senses (VI. 1. 137-139) we have उपकरोति ॥

किरतौ लवने ॥ १४० ॥ पदानि ॥ किरतौ, लवने ॥

वृत्तिः ॥ उपादित्येव । उपादुत्तरस्मिन्किरतौ धातौ लवनविषये सुट् कात्पूर्वो भवति ॥

वार्त्तिकम् ॥ णमुलन्तवक्तव्यः ॥

140. The augment सुट् is placed before क, when the verb कृ comes after उप and the sense is that of 'to cut or split',

Thus उपस्कारं मद्रका लुनन्ति, उपस्कारं काश्मीरका लुनन्ति = विक्षिप्य लुनन्ति ॥

Vârt:—The above augment takes place when णमुल् is added to the verb उप-कृ, as shown in the above examples. When the meaning is not that of 'to cut', the form is उपकिरति ॥

हिंसायां प्रतेश्च ॥ १४१ ॥ पदानि ॥ हिंसायाम्, प्रतेः, च, ॥

वृत्तिः ॥ किरतावित्येव । उपात्प्रतेश्चोत्तरस्मिन्किरतौ हिंसायां विषये सुट् कात्पूर्वो भवति ॥

141. The augment सुट् is placed before क, when the verb कृ comes after उप and प्रति, and the sense is "to cause suffering".

Thus उपस्कारम् or प्रतिस्कारं हन्त ते वृषल भूयात् = तथा ते वृषल विक्षेपो भूयाद् यथा हिंसामनुबध्नात ॥

Why do we say when 'the sense is to cause pain'? Observe प्रतिकीर्णम् ॥

अपाच्चतुष्पाच्छकुनिष्वालेखने ॥ १४२ ॥ पदानि ॥ अपात्, चतुष्पात् , शकुनिषुः, आलेखने (सुट्,) ॥

वृत्तिः ॥ किरतावित्येव । अपादुत्तरस्मिन्किरतौ चतुष्पाच्छकुनिषु, यदालेखनं तस्मिन् विषये सुट् कात्पूर्वो भवति ॥

वार्त्तिकम् ॥ हर्षजीविकाकुलायकरणेष्विति वक्तव्यम् ॥

वा० ॥ हर्षजीविकाकुलायकरणेष्वेव किरतेरात्मनेपदस्योपसंख्यानम् ॥

142. The augment सुट् is placed before क, when the verb कृ comes after अप and the sense is 'the scraping of earth by four-footed animals or birds'.

Thus अपस्किरते वृषभो हृष्टः, अपस्किरते कुक्कुटो भक्ष्यार्थी ; अपस्किरते श्वा आश्रयार्थी = आलिख्य विक्षिपति ॥ Why do we say 'four-footed animals or birds'? Observe अपकिरति देवदत्तः ॥

Vârt:—This rule applies when the scraping is through pleasure, or for the sake of finding food, or making a resting place, Therefore not here:— अपकिरति श्वा ओदनपिण्डमाशितः ॥ And it is in the above senses of scraping through pleasure &c, that the root takes Âtmanepada affixes; otherwise the Parasmaipada affixes will follow. See I. 3. 21. Vârt.

कुस्तुम्बुरूणि जातिः ॥ १४३ ॥ पदानि ॥ कुस्तुम्बुरूणि, जातिः, (सुट्) ॥

वृत्तिः ॥ कुस्तुम्बुरूणीति सुट् निपात्यते जातिश्चेद्भवति ॥

143. The word कुस्तुम्बुरु is irregularly formed with the augment सुट् and means 'a species of herb'.

The कुस्तुम्बुरु is the name of coriander: i. e. धान्यकं; the seeds are also so called. The exhibition of the word in the sûtra in the Neuter gender does not however show that the word is always Neuter. When not meaning coriander, the form is कुतुम्बुरु (कुत्सितानि तुम्बुरूणि) ॥ The word तुम्बुरु here means the fruit of the ebony tree.

अपरस्पराः क्रियासातत्ये ॥ १४४ ॥ पदानि ॥ अपरस्पराः, क्रिया - सातत्ये ॥

वृत्तिः ॥ अपरस्परा इति सुट् निपात्यते क्रियासातत्ये गम्यमाने ॥

Kârikâ लुम्पेदवश्यमः कृत्ये तुंकाममनसोरपि ।
समो वा हिततततयोर्मांसस्य पचियुड्घञोः ॥

144. The word अपरस्पराः is formed by the augment सुट् when the sense is that of 'uninterrupted action'.

Thus अपरस्पराः सार्था गच्छन्ति = सन्ततमविच्छेदेन गच्छन्ति ॥ When the continuity of action is not meant, we have अपरपराः सार्था गच्छन्ति = अपरे परेच सकृदेव गच्छन्ति ॥ The सातत्य comes from सततं, by adding ष्यञ् to form the abstract noun, सततस्य भावः (V. I. 123) = सातत्यं ॥ How do you explain सततम्, it ought to be सन्ततम्? The म् of सम् is optionally elided before ततं, on the strength of the Kârika:—"The म् of अवश्यम् is elided before a word ending in a kṛitya affix, the म् of तुम् is elided before काम and मनस्, the म् of सम् is elided optionally before हित and तत, the final अ of मांस is elided before पाक or पचन ॥ As (1) अवश्यं कर्तव्यं = अवश्यकर्तव्यं, (2) भोक्तुम् कामः = भोक्तु कामः, भोतुमनः ॥ (3) समाहितं = सहितं, सम् ततं = सततं ॥ (4) मांस् पाकः, मांस् पचनम् ॥

गोष्पदं सेवितासेवितप्रमाणेषु ॥ १४५ ॥ पदानि ॥ गोः-पदम्, सेवित - असेवित - प्रमाणेषु ॥

वृत्तिः ॥ गोष्पदमिति सुट् निपात्यते तस्य च षत्वं सेविते ऽसेविते प्रमाणे च विषये ॥

145. The word गोष्पद is formed by सुट्, when meaning a locality visited or not visited by cows, or when it means a quantity.

Thus गोष्पदो देशः = गावः पद्यन्ते यस्मिन् देशे स गोभिः सेवितो देशः ॥ So also अगोष्पदान्यरण्यानि ॥ The word गोष्पद by itself does not mean 'not visited by cows'. Therefore the negative particle is added to give that sense. So also गोष्पदमात्रं क्षेत्रं, गोष्पदपूरं वृष्टो देवः ॥ Here the word has no reference to cow, but to the quantity of land and rain. When it has not the above senses, the form is गोपदम् = गोः पदम् ॥ What is the use of the word असेवित in the sûtra, the word गोष्पद will give अगोष्पद by adding the negative particle, न गोष्पद = अगोष्पद? The force of नञ् compound is that of सदृश "like that but not that". As अब्राह्मण means "a man who is a Kshatrya &c. not a Brâhmana, but does not mean a stone &c". Therefore अगोष्पद with नञ् would mean "a place like a pasture land but in which cows do not graze, but in which there is a possibility of cows grazing". But it is intended that it should refer to a place where there is no such possibility, hence असेवित is used. Therefore, deep forests where cows can never enter, are called अगोष्पद ॥

आस्पदं प्रतिष्ठायाम् ॥ १४६ ॥ पदानि ॥ आस्पदम्, प्रतिष्ठायाम्, (सुट्) ॥

वृत्तिः ॥ आत्मयापनाय स्थानं प्रतिष्ठा तस्यामास्पदमिति सुट् निपात्यते ॥

146. The word आस्पद is formed by सुट् when meaning 'a place or position'.

The word प्रतिष्ठा means 'firm place, established position, rank, dignity, authority'. Thus आस्पदम् अनेन लब्धम् ॥ Why do we say when 'meaning a place'? Observe आ पदात्=आपदम् ॥

आश्चर्यमनित्ये ॥ १४७ ॥ पदानि ॥ आश्चर्यम्, अनित्ये ॥

वृत्तिः ॥ अनित्यतया विषयभूतया ऽद्भुतत्वमिहलक्ष्यते तस्मिन्नाश्चर्यं निपात्यते । चरेराङि चागुराविति यत्प्रत्यये कृते निपातनात्सुट् ॥

147. The word आश्चर्य is formed by सुट्, when meaning something 'unusual'.

The word आश्चर्य is formed by adding the affix यत् to the verb चर् with the preposition आ, and the augment सुट् ॥ Thus आश्चर्यं यदि स भुंजीत, आश्चर्यं यदि सो ऽधीयीत ॥ When not having this sense, we have आचर्यं कर्म शोभनम् ॥

वर्चस्के ऽवस्करः ॥ १४८ ॥ पदानि ॥ वर्चस्के, अवस्करः ॥

वृत्तिः ॥ कुत्सितं वर्चो, वर्चस्कमन्नमलं, तस्मिन्नभिधेये ऽवस्कर इति निपात्यते । अवपूर्वस्य किरतेः कर्मणि ऋदोरप् इत्यप् निपातनात्सुट् ॥

148. The word अवस्कर is formed with सुट् meaning "excrement".

That which has bad lustre is called वर्चस्क (कुत्सितं) ॥ It applies to the ejected food. To the root कृ is added the affix अप् (III. 3. 57), the preposition अव and irregularly the सुट् ॥ Thus अवस्करोऽन्नमलम् ॥ The place where the excreta lie (the rectum) is also so called. When not having this sense, we have अवकरः ॥

अपस्करो रथाङ्गम् ॥ १४९ ॥ पदानि ॥ अपस्करः, रथाङ्गम् ॥

वृत्तिः ॥ अपस्कर इति निपात्यते रथाङ्गं चेद्भवति । अपपूर्वात्किरतेर्ऋदोरबित्यप्, निपातनात् सुट् ॥

149. The word अपस्कर is formed with सुट् meaning 'the part of a chariot'.

This word is also derived from कृ with the preposition अप and the affix अप् (III. 3. 57) and सुट् augment. When not having this meaning, we have अपकर. ॥

विष्करः शकुनिर्विकिरो वा ॥ १५० ॥ पदानि ॥ विष्करः, शकुनिः, विकिरः, वा ॥

वृत्तिः ॥ विकिर इति किरतेर्विपूर्वस्येगुपधज्ञाप्रीकिरः कः इति कप्रत्यये विहिते सुट् निपात्यते शकुनिश्चेद्भवति । विकिरशब्दाभिधेयो वा शकुनिर्भवति ॥

Verse सर्वे शकुनयो भक्ष्या विष्किराः कुक्कुटादते ।

150. The word विष्किर is formed with सुट् optionally when denoting a kind of bird, the other form being विकिर ॥

This word is formed by adding the affix क (III. I. 135) to कृ with the preposition वि and the augment सुट् ॥ The word विष्किर also refers to birds only, a kind of cock. The phrase शकुनिर्विकिरो वा is added from the Vârtika and is no part of the original sûtra. Thus सर्वे शकुनयो भक्ष्या विष्किराः कुक्कुटादयः ॥ Though the sûtra विष्किरोवाशकुनौ would have given the optional form विकिर, the specific mention of this form in the sûtra indicates that विकिर always means 'bird' and nothing else. Otherwise विकिर would have refferred to some thing other than a bird.

ह्रस्वाच्चन्द्रोत्तरपदे मन्त्रे ॥ १५१ ॥ पदानि ॥ ह्रस्वात्, चन्द्रोत्तरपदे, मन्त्रे ॥

वृत्तिः ॥ चन्द्रशब्दउत्तरपदे ह्रस्वात्परः सुडागमो भवति मन्त्रविषये ॥

151. In a Mantra, the सुट् is added to चन्द्र when it is second member in a compound and is preceded by a short vowel.

Thus सुश्चन्द्रो युष्मान् ॥ Why do we say after a short vowel? Observe सूर्याचन्द्रमसाविव ॥ Why do we say 'in a Mantra'? Observe, सुचन्द्रा पौर्णमासी ॥ The उत्तरपद can only be in a compound (samâsa) as it is well-known to all. and it does not mean, 'the second word', as the literal meaning might convey: Therefore the rule does not apply here शुक्रमसि चन्द्रमसि ॥

प्रतिष्कशश्च कशेः ॥ १५२ ॥ पदानि ॥ प्रतिष्कशः, च, कशेः ॥

वृत्तिः ॥ कश गतिशासनयोरित्येतस्य धातोः प्रतिपूर्वस्य पचाद्यचि कृते सुट् निपात्यते, तस्यैव षत्वम् ॥

Verse ग्राममद्य प्रवेक्ष्यामि भव मे त्वं प्रतिष्कशः ।

152. To the root कश् 'to go, to punish', is added the augment सुट्, when preceded by the preposition प्रति, the form being प्रतिष्कशः ॥

The word प्रतिष्कश is formed by adding अच् affix (III. I. 134) to the root, with adding the prefix प्रति ॥ Thus ग्राममद्य प्रवेक्ष्यामि भव मे त्व प्रतिष्कशः 'I shall inspect the town to-day, be thou my emissary'. The word प्रतिष्कशः means "a messenger, a herald, an emissary". Why do we say "to the *root* कश"? Observe प्रतिगतः कशां=प्रतिकशोऽश्वः 'a horse guided by the whip'. Here though कशा is derived from कश, yet the augment does not take place, because the augment comes to the *root* कश्, and not to a derivative word.

प्रस्कण्वहरिश्चन्द्रावृषी ॥ १५३ ॥ पदानि ॥ प्रस्कण्व हरिश्चन्द्रौ, ऋषी ॥

वृत्तिः ॥ प्रस्कण्वो हरिश्चन्द्र इति सुट् निपात्यते ऋषी चेदभिधेयौ भवतः ॥

153. The words प्रस्कण्व and हरिश्चन्द्र are formed by सुट्, meaning the two Rishis of that name.

Thus प्रस्कण्व ऋषिः, हरिश्चन्द्र ऋषिः ॥ The word हरिश्चन्द्र could be formed by VI. I. 151 in the Mantra, here it refers to other than Mantras. When not referring to Rishis, we have प्रकण्वो देशः, (कण्वं पापं तत्प्रगतं यस्मात्) हरिश्चन्द्रो मानवकः (हरिः चन्द्रो यस्य मुग्धस्य) ॥

मस्करमस्करिणौ वेणुपरिव्राजकयोः ॥ १५४ ॥ पदानि ॥ मस्कर मस्करिणौ, वेणु परिव्राजकयोः ॥

वृत्तिः ॥ मस्कर मस्करिन् इत्येतौ यथासंख्यं वेणौ परिव्राजके च निपात्येते ॥

154. The word **मस्कर** means 'a bamboo', and **मस्करिन्** means 'a mendicant monk'.

When not having these meanings, the form is मकरः ॥ This is an underived nominal stem, having no derivation, to which सुट् is added when 'a bamboo' is meant; and the affix इनि in addition, when a mendicant is to be expressed and thus we have मस्कर and मस्करिन् ॥ Why do we say "when meaning a bamboo or a mendicant". Observe मकरोग्राहः "an alligator", मकरो समुद्र "an ocean". Some say the word मस्कर is a derivative word, being derived from कृ 'to do' with the negative particle मा and the affix अच्, the long आ being shortened. Thus मा क्रियते येन प्रतिषिध्यते=मस्करः 'a bamboo or stick by which the prohibition is made'. So also by adding इनि in the sense of ताच्छील्य to the root कृ preceded by the upapada मा; we get मस्करिन् ॥ Thus मा करणशीलो=मस्करी "a monk, who has renounced all works". A mendicant always says "मा कुरुत: कर्माणि शान्तिर्वः श्रेयसी"—"Do no works ye men, for peace is your highest end".

कास्तीराजस्तुन्दे नगरे ॥ १५५ ॥ पदानि ॥ कास्तीर, अजस्तुन्दे, नगरे ॥

वृत्तिः ॥ कास्तीर अजस्तुन्द इत्येतौ शब्दौ निपात्येते नगरे ऽभिधेये ॥

155. The words **कास्तीर** and **अजस्तुन्द** are names of cities.

When not meaning cities, we have कातीरम् (ईषत् तीरमस्य); and अजतुन्दम् (अजस्येव तुन्दमस्य) ॥

कारस्करो वृक्षः ॥ १५६ ॥ पदानि ॥ कारस्करः, वृक्षः ॥

वृत्तिः ॥ कारस्कर इति सुट् निपात्यते वृक्षश्चेद्भवति ॥

156. The word **कारस्कर** means 'a tree'.

This word is formed from कार+कृ+ट (III. 2. 21)=कारस्करः ॥ When not meaning a tree, the form is कारकरः ॥ Some do not make this a separate sûtra, but include it in the next aphorism.

पारस्करप्रभृतीनि च संज्ञायाम् ॥ १५७ ॥ पदानि ॥ पारस्कर प्रभृतीनि, च, संज्ञायाम् ॥

वृत्ति ॥ पारस्करप्रभृतीनि च शब्दरूपाणि निपात्यन्ते संज्ञायां विषये ॥

157.. The words **पारस्कर** &c are Names.

These words are irregularly formed by adding सुट् ॥ Thus पारस्करः 'a country called Pâraskara'. कारस्करः 'N. of a tree', रथस्या 'N. of a river', किष्कुः 'N. of a measure', किष्किन्धा 'N. of a cave', तस्कर 'a thief', formed by inserting सुट् in the compound of तत्+कर, and eliding त् ॥ बृहस्पति 'N. of a Diety', formed similarly by inserting सुट् between बृहत्+पति and eliding the त् ॥ Why do we say when meaning a thief and a diety? Observe तस्करः, बृहस्पतिः ॥ The words चोर and देवता are used in the Ganapâtha merely for the sake of diversity, the word संज्ञा would have connoted that प्रस्तुम्पति गौः ॥ When the root तुप तुम्प 'to injure' is preceded by the preposition प्र, there is added सुट् to प्र, when the agent of the verb is a cow. Why do we say 'when the agent is cow'? Observe प्रतुम्पति वनस्पतिः ॥ In प्रस्तुम्पति the सुट् is added to a finite verb, which is thus conjugated :—प्रस्तुम्पति गौः, प्रस्तुम्पती गावौ, प्रस्तुम्पन्ति गावः ॥ This is an âkritigaṇa. Thus प्रायश्चित्तम्, प्रायश्चित्तिः ॥

1 पारस्करो देशः, 2 कारस्करो वृक्षः, 3 रथस्या नदी, 4 किष्कुः प्रमाणम्, 5 किष्किन्धा गुहा, 6 तद्बृहतोः करपत्योश्चोरदेवतयोः सुट् तलोपश्च (तस्करः चोरः, बृहस्पतिः = देवता), 7 प्रात् तुम्पतौ गवि कर्तरि (प्रस्तुम्पति गौः) ॥ आकृतिगणः ॥

अनुदात्तं पदमेकवर्जम् ॥ १५८ ॥ पदानि ॥ अनुदात्तम्, पदम्, एक-वर्ज्जम् ॥

वृत्तिः ॥ परिभाषेयं स्वरविधिविषया। यत्रान्यः स्वर उदात्तः स्वरितो वा विधीयते तत्रानुदात्तं पदमेकं वर्जयित्वा भवतीत्येतदुपस्थितं द्रष्टव्यम् ॥

Kârikâ आगमस्य विकारस्य प्रकृतेः प्रत्ययस्य च।
पृथक्स्वरनिवृत्त्यर्थमेकवर्जं पदस्वरः ॥

वार्त्तिकम् ॥ विभक्तिस्वरान्नञ्स्वरो बलीयानिति वक्तव्यम् ॥

वा० ॥ विभक्तिनिमित्तस्वराच्चनञ्स्वरो बलीयानिति वक्तव्यम् ॥

158. A word is, with the exception of one syllable, unaccented.

That is, only one syllable in a word is accented, all the rest are anudâtta or unaccented. This is a Paribhâshâ or maxim of interpretation with regard to the laws of accent. Wherever an accent—be it acute (udâtta) or a circumflex (svarita)—is ordained with regard to a word, there this maxim must be applied, to make all the other syllables of that word unaccented. The word अनुदात्त means 'having an anudâtta vowel'. What is the *one* to be excepted? That one about which any particular accent has been taught in the rules here-in-after given. Thus VI. 1. 162 teaches that a root has acute accent on the final. Therefore, with the exception of the last syllable, all the other syllables are unaccented. Thus in गोपायँति the acute accent is on य, all the rest are unaccented. The root accent is superseded by आ accent, thus लुनाँति has acute accent on ना ॥ The आ accent is superseded by तस् accent, as लुनीतँः, has accent on तः ॥ The तस् accent is superseded by आम् accent, as लुनीतस्तराँम् ॥

आगमस्य विकारस्य प्रकृतेः प्रत्ययस्य च, पृथक् स्वरनिवृत्त्यर्थमेकवर्जं पदस्वरः ॥ The words 'with the exception of one syllable' show that the separate accent of an augment, or a preparative element, or a stem or an affix should cease, when a particular accent is taught for a word'. Thus as to (1) augment:—VII. 1. 98 teaches "आम् acutely accented is the augment of चतुर् and अनडुह् when a sarvanâmsthâna affix follows". Thus चत्वाँरः, अनड्वाँहः, here the augment-accent supersedes the accent of the stem, for चतुर was acutely accented on the first syllable, so also अनडुह्, these being formed by the affixes उरन् and असुन् respectively. Thus चत्+उरन्=चतुर (चतेरुरन् Un V. 58, accent VI. 1. 197); अनडुह् is thus derived: अनो वहति=अनस्+वह्+क्विप्, the स् is replaced by ड्, and there is vocalisation of व् of वह् VI. 1. 15=अनडुह् II This word is formed by a Krit affix with a kârâka upapada, therefore, the second term will retain its original accent, namely the final acute of a root. (VI. 1. 162 and VI. 2. 139) अनस् itself is derived by adding the affix (Un IV. 189) असुन् which makes the word acutely accented on the first syllable. (2). Similarly as to विकार (Vikaraṇa):—VII. 1. 75 teaches "instead of अस्थि, दधि, सक्थि, and अक्षि, there shall be अनङ् acutely accented when टा follows or any of the subsequent terminations beginning with a vowel". This अन will supersede the acute accent of the first अ of the stem: as अस्थ्नि ॥ The word अस्थि is derived from अस् by adding the affix क्थिन् (Un III. 154) which makes the word accutely accented on the first (VI. 1. 197). This is an example of विकार ॥ (3) Similarly in गोपायति the accent of the stem taught in VI. 1. 162 'a root has an accent on its final', supersedes the accent of the vikaraṇa आय (III. 1. 28, 3), i. e. the acute accent on आ in आय gives way to the root-accent which makes य acute. (4) So also the accent of the affix supersedes that of the stem: as कर्त्तव्यम्, and हर्तव्यम्, which are formed by the affix तव्यत् (III. 1. 96) here VI. 1. 185 debars the accent of the root (VI. 1. 162).

The determination of the proper accent of a word depends upon considering the various rules that have gone to form it, and the sequence of those rules, e. g. a latter rule (पर) superseding a prior rule, a nitya rule superseding an anitya rule, an antaranga superseding a bahiranga, an apavâda rule superseding an utsarga rule. But another test is, what is the remaining rule that applies after giving scope to all. A rule, that in spite of another rule, finds scope or activity, bars that former rule. Thus गोपायति II It is derived from गुप् root, which as a root has accent on the syllable गु (VI. 1. 162). When the affix आय is added to it by III. 1. 28, the word becomes गोपाय and it takes the accent of the affix (III. 1. 3), i. e. the accent now falls on पा; but now comes rule III. 1. 32 which says that a word taking the affix आय is a root. Thus गोपाय gets the designation of root (धातु), and thus takes the accent of a dhâtu (VI. 1. 162), and the accent falls on य II

The rule is that except one special accent taught in a sûtra the other syllables take anudâtta. Therefore, where there is a conflict of rules, the accent is guided by the follwing maxim: "परनित्यान्तरङ्गापवादैः स्वरैर्व्यवस्था सतिशिष्टेनच" II namely (1) the sequence, a succeeding rule setting aside a prior rule (2) a Nitya rule is stronger then Anitya, (3) Antaranga stronger than Bahiranga, (4) the Apavâda is stronger then Utsarga. When all these are exhausted, as we have illustrated above, then we apply the rule of सतिशिष्ट ॥ What is this rule? To quote the words of Kâsikâ: यो हि यस्मिन् सति शिष्यते स तस्य बाधको भवति "that which does remain and must last in spite of the presence of another, debars such other". Thus in गोपायति; here the प्रत्ययस्वरः "the accent of the affix" (III. 1. 3) by which the acute is on the first syllable of the *affix* is an apavâda to the धातुस्वरः (VI. 1, 192) by which the final of a dhâtu is acute, and it debars the dhâtu-accent; but this affix-accent is in its turn debarred in the case of derivative verbs formed with affixes, by the rule of सतिशिष्ट, because even ofter the addition of the affix, these words *retain* the designation of dhâtu. Similarly in कार्ष्णोत्तरासङ्गपुत्रः, "The son of him whose upper garment (uttarâsanga) is of black color—the Son of Baladeva" the Bahuvrihi-accent (VI.2.1) being an apavâda to Samâsa-accent (VI. 1. 223), debars the samâsa-accent; but this Bahuvrihi-accent is in its turn debarred by the rule of सतिशिष्ट when a further compound is formed and the final word is a compound only and not a Bahuvrîhi. Though the accent of the Vikarana is a सतिशिष्ट, yet it does not debar the Sârvadhâtuka accent (VI. 1. 186). Thus in लुनीतः, the accent of the vikarana श्ना does not debar the accent of तस् ॥

Vârt:—The नञ्-accent is stronger than the case-affix accent. Thus in अतिस्रः, here the accent of जस् vibhakti after तिसृ (VI. 1. 166) though सतिशिष्ट is debarred by नञ् accent taught in VI. 2. 2, for Negative compounds are Tatpurusha.

Vârt:—The accent of नञ् is stronger than the accent of that which is caused or occasioned by a vibhakti. Thus अचत्वारः ॥ Here the augment आम् in चत्वार is occasioned because of the case-affix, for it is added only then when a Sarvanâma case-affix follows (VII. 1. 98). This आँ is udâtta (VI. 1. 98). But this udâtta is superseded by the accent of the Negative particle.

Why do we say 'in the body of a *pada*'? In a *sentence*, every word will retain its accent. As हे देवदत्त! गामभ्याज शुक्लाम् "O Devadatta, drive away the white cow". The word पद is in fact used in this sûtra in its secondary sense, namely that which will get the designation of पद when completed; had it meant the full ready made pada, this word would not have been repeated in पदाधिकार sûtra (VIII. 1. 16, 17). Had a full 'pada' been meant, the incongruity would arise in the following. The word कुवल is acutely accented on the first as belonging to ग्रामादि class (Phit II. 15), adding the feminine affix ङीष् to it by its belonging to गौरादि class, we get कुवली, which will retain its acute on the first because it is not technically a पद ॥ But it is not so, the word कुवली has anudâtta accent on the first syllable (Phit II. 15), and hence we can apply the अञ् affix to it by IV. 2. 44, thus कुवल्या विकारः = कौवलम् ॥ Similarly the word गर्भिणी formed from गर्भ (belonging to Grâmâdi class Phit II. 15), with, the affix इनि (V. 2. 115) and the feminine ङीप् ॥ If here the affix इनि being udâtta causes all the rest syllables anudâtta, just at the very moment of its application, without seeing whether the word was a pada or not, then the word गर्भिणी being anudâttâdi would have taken अञ्, and therefore its exception is proper in the भिक्षादि class

(IV. 2. 38). But if the anudatta-hood of the remaining syllables were to follow *after* a word had got the designation of पद, then the word गर्भिणी would remain acutely accented on the first, and its enumeration in IV. 2. 38 would be useless.

कर्षात्वतो घञो ऽन्त उदात्तः ॥ १५९ ॥ पदानि ॥ कर्ष, अत्वतः, घञः, अन्तः, उदात्तः ॥

वृत्तिः ॥ कर्षतेर्धातोराकारवतश्च घञन्तस्यान्त उदात्तो भवति ॥

159. A stem formed with the Kṛita-affix घञ् has the acute accent on the end-syllable, if it is formed from the root कृष् (कर्षति) or has a long आ in it.

Thus कर्षः, पाकः, त्यागः, रागः, दायः, धायः ॥ This is an exception to VI. 1. 197 by which affixes having an indicatory ञ् have acute accent on the first syllable. The word कर्ष is used in the aphorism instead of कृष्, to indicate that कृष of Bhvâdi gaṇa is affected by this rule, and not कृष्—कृषति of Tudâdigaṇa. The word कर्षः derived from Tudâdi कृष् has acute accent on the first syllable.

उञ्छादीनां च ॥ १६० ॥ पदानि ॥ उञ्छादीनाम्, च ॥

वृत्तिः ॥ उञ्छ इत्येवमादीनामन्त उदात्तो भवति ॥

160. The words उञ्छ &c. have acute accent on the last syllable.

Thus 1. उञ्छः, 2. म्लेच्छः, 3. जञ्जः, 4. जल्पः ॥ These are formed by घञ्, and would have taken acute-accent on the first. 5. जपः, 6. बधः are formed by अप् affix (III. 3. 61) which being grave (III. 1. 4), these words would have taken the accent of the dhâtu (VI. 1. 162), i. e. acute on the first syllable. Some read व्यधः also here. 7. युगः is derived from युज by घञ् affix, the non-causing of guṇa is irregular, and the word means 'a cycle of time', 'a part of a carriage'. In other senses, the form is योगः ॥ 8. गरः = (दूष्ये); is formed by अप्, and has this accent when it means 'poison', in other senses, the acute is on the first syllable. 9. वेगः, वेदः, वेष्टः (चेष्टः), and बन्धः, करणे ॥ These words are formed by घञ् by III. 3. 121. When denoting instrument (करण) they take the above accent, when denoting भाव the accent falls on the first syllable. 10. स्तुयुद्रुवश्छन्दसि, e. g. परिष्टुत्, परिद्रुत्, संयुत् ॥ 11. वर्त्तनिः स्तोत्रे, the stotra means Sâma Veda, the word वर्त्तनिः occurring in the Sâma Veda has acute on the last: in other places, it has the accent on the middle. 12. श्वभ्रे दरः, the दरः has end-acute when meaning 'a cave', otherwise when formed by अप् affix it has acute on the first. 13. साम्बतापौ भावगर्हायाम्, thus साम्बः, तापः, in other senses, the acute is on the first. 14. उत्तमशश्वत्तमौ सर्वत्र, e. g. उत्तमः, शश्वत्तमः ॥ Some read the limitation of भावगर्हा into this also. 15. भक्षमन्थभोगमन्थाः (भोगदेहा) ॥ These are formed by घञ्, भक्ष though a ण्यन्त root is here घञन्तं ॥

1 उञ्छ, 2 म्लेच्छ, 3 जञ्ज, 4 जल्प, 5 जप, 6 वध (व्यध), 7 युग, 8 गरो दूष्ये, 9 वेद-वेगवेष्टबन्धाः, (चेष्ट वेष्ट) करणे, 10 स्तुयुद्रुवश्छन्दसि (परिष्टुत्, संयुत्, परिद्रुत्), 11 वर्तनिः स्तोत्रे 12 श्वभ्रे दरः, 13 साम्बतापौ भावगर्हायाम्, 14 उत्तमशश्वत्तमौ (उत्तमशश्वत्तमशब्दौ) सर्वत्र, 15 भक्षमन्थ-, भोगमन्थाः (भक्षमन्थभोगदेहाः) ॥

अनुदात्तस्य च यत्रोदात्तलोपः ॥ १६१ ॥ पदानि ॥ अनुदात्तस्य, च, यत्र, उदात्त-लोपः ॥

वृत्तिः ॥ उदात्त इति वर्तते । यस्मिन्ननुदात्ते परत उदात्तो लुप्यते तस्यानुदात्तस्यादिरुदात्तो भवति ॥

161. An unaccented vowel gets also the acute accent, when on account of it the preceding acute is elided.

The word udâtta is understood here. Thus कुमारँ + ई = कुमारी ॥ The word कुमार has acute on the last, when the unaccented (anudâtta) ङीप् is added to it, the अँ is elided (VI. 1. 148), the anudâtta ई becomes udâtta. So also पथिन् + शस् = पथः (VII. 1. 88), पथिन् + ए = पथे, पथिन् + आ = पथा ॥ The पथिन् has acute on the last. So also कुमुद + ड्मतुप् = कुमुद्वान् (IV. 2. 87), नड्वत्, वेतस्वत् ॥ The words कुमुद &c, are end-acute, and the affix मत् (वत्) is anudâtta (III. 1. 4).

Why 'an *anudâtta* vowel gets &c'. Observe प्रासङ्गः + यत् = प्रासङ्ग्यः ॥ (प्रासङ्गं वहति IV. 4. 76). Here though प्रसङ्ग is end-acute (VI. 2. 144 formed by घञ् with gati) it is followed by यं which is svarita (VI. 1. 185), this svarita causes the lopa of अँ udâtta: but it does not itself become udâtta. No, this is not a proper counter-example. For by the general rule of accent VI. 1. 158, when one syllable is ordained to be udâtta or svarita, all the other syllables of that word become anudatta. Therefore when य is taught to be svarita, all the other syllables (like ङ्ग) will become anudâtta. So there is no *lopa* of udâtta when यं comes. The word अनुदात्त is used to indicate that the *initial* anudâtta becomes udâtta. Had anudâtta not been used, the sûtra would have been यत्रोदात्तलोपश्च, which would mean यस्मिन् प्रत्यये परतः उदात्तो लुप्यते तस्यान्त उदात्तो भवति, for the anuvritti of अन्त would then be read from the last. There would then be anomaly in the case of मा हि धुक्षाताम्, and माहि धुक्षाथाम् ॥ From the root दुह we have formed धुक्षाताम् and धुक्षाथाम् in the Aorist Atmanepada, dual. दुह् + क्सँ + आताम् = दुह् + स् (VII. 3. 72) + आताम् ॥ Here आताम् causes the elision of the udâtta अ of स ॥ Therefore the *final* of आताम् would be udâtta, which is not desired. The augment अ is not added because of मा, had it been added, the अँ would have been udâtta (VI. 4. 71). Had हि not been given, then also the whole of धुक्षाताम् would have become anudatta in माधुक्षाताम् because of तिङ्ङतिङः (VIII. 1. 28). See VIII. 1. 34 (हि च). Why have we used the word यत्र in the sûtra? If it was not employed, then the subsequent anudâtta may be such which would not have *caused* the elision of the previous udâtta; such udâtta being elided by some other operator, and still such anudâtta would have become udâtta. Thus in भार्गवः, भार्गवौ, भृगवः ॥ Here भृगवः is plural of भार्गवः ॥ The word भार्गव is end-acute and this acute (अण्) was elided in the plural, before the affix जस् was added.

The elision here is not *caused* by जस्, but is a subject of जस् (not निमित्त but विषय). Therefore जस् does not become udâtta, which would have been the case, had यत्र not been used. प्राक् सुबुत्पत्तेः गोत्रप्रत्ययस्य लुक् ॥ The gotra affix was elided prior to the adding of the case-ending. Why do we say "when an *udâtta* is elided"? Observe बिद+अञ् (IV. 1. 104)=बैद ॥ The feminine of this will be बैद+ङीन् (IV. 1. 73=बैदी ॥ Here ई causes the elision of auûdâtta अ of द, and hence remains unchanged. So also और्वी ॥

धातोः ॥ १६२ ॥ पदानि ॥ धातोः, (अन्तः, उदात्तः) ॥

वृत्तिः ॥ अन्त इत्येव । धातोरन्त उदात्तो भवति ॥

162. A root has the acute on the end-syllable.

The word अन्त is understood here. Thus पचति, पठति, ऊर्णोति, गोपायति, याति ॥

चितः ॥ १६३ ॥ पदानि ॥ चितः, (अन्तः उदात्तः) ॥

वृत्तिः ॥ चितो ऽन्त उदात्तो भवति ॥

163. A stem (formed by an affix or augment or substitute) having an indicatory च् gets acute on the end syllable.

Thus भङ्गुरम्, भासुरम्, मेदुरम्. These are formed by घुरच् III. 2. 161. So also कुण्डिनाः by II. 4. 70 where the substitute कुण्डिनच् is employed. To कुण्ड is added इन in the sense of मतुप्, then is added the feminine affix ङीप, thus कुण्डिनी has middle-acute. The descendants of Kuṇḍinî will be कौण्डिन्यः (by यञ् of Gargâdi). The plural of Kauṇḍinya will be formed by eliding यञ् and substituting कुण्डिनच् for the remaining portion. In the cases of affixes having an indicatory च्, the acute accent falls on the final, taking the stem and the affix in an aggregate. Thus बहुपटुः ॥ The affix बहुच् is one of those few affixes which are really prefixes. (V. 3. 68), The accent will not, therefore, fall on हु, but on the last syllable of the whole word compounded of the prefix + the base. So also with the affix अकच्. It is added in the *middle* of the word, but the accent will fall on the *end*; as उच्चकैः (V. 3. 71).

तद्धितस्य ॥ १६४ ॥ पदानि ॥ तद्धितस्य, (अन्तः, उदात्तः) ॥

वृत्तिः ॥ चित इत्येव । चितस्तद्धितस्यान्त उदात्तो भवति ॥

164. A stem formed with a Taddhita-affix having an indicatory च्, has acute on the end syllable.

Thus कौञ्जायनाः formed by the affix च्फञ् (IV. 1. 98). कुञ्ज+च् फञ्+ ञ्य=कौञ्जायन्यः dual कौञ्जायन्यौ, pl. कौञ्जायनाः (ञ्य being elided by II. 4. 62, and thus giving scope to च्फञ् accent). In this affix there are two indicatory letters च and ञ ; the च has only one function, namely, regulating the accent according to this rule, while ञ has two functions, one to regulate accent by VI. 1. 197, and another to cause Vṛiddhi by VII. 2. 117. Now arises the question, should the word get the accent of च or of ञ ॥ The present rule declares that it should get the accent of च and not of प्र, for the latter finds still a function left to it, while if प्र was to regulate the accent, च would have no scope.

कितः ॥ १६५ ॥ पदानि ॥ कितः ॥

वृत्तिः ॥ तद्धितस्येत्येव । तद्धितस्य कितोन्त उदात्तो भवति ॥

165. A stem formed by a Taddhita affix having an indicatory क, has acute accent on the end syllable.

Thus नाड्ायनः formed by फक् (IV. 1. 99), so also चारायणः ॥ Similarly आक्षिकः, शालाकिकः formed by ठक् (IV. 4. 1).

तिसृभ्यो जसः ॥ १६६ ॥ पदानि ॥ तिसृभ्यः, जसः, (अन्तः, उदात्तः) ॥

वृत्तिः ॥ तिसृभ्य उत्तरस्य जसोन्त उदात्तो भवति ॥

166. The Nominative plural (जस्) of तिसृ has acute accent on the last syllable.

Thus तिस्रस्तिष्ठन्ति ॥ This debars the Svarita accent ordained by VIII. 2. 4. The word तिसृ (feminine of त्रि VII. 2. 99) meaning 'three' is always plural. There are no singular or dual cases of this numeral; of the seven plural cases, the accusative plural will have acute on the final by VI. 1. 174; the remaining cases (Instrumental, Dative, Ablative, Genitive and Locative) have affixes beginning with a consonant, and by VI. 1. 179 they will be udâtta. Thus the only case not covered by any special rule is जस् (nom. pl); which would have been Ŝvarita, but for this rule. If जस् be the only case not provided for, then merely saying तिसृभ्यः would have sufficed to make the rule applicable to जस् only, why has then it been employed in the sûtra? This is done, in order that in compounds, where तिसृ may come as a subordinate member, and where singular and dual endings will also be added, this rule will not apply. Had जस् been not used in tois sûtra, then in the case of simple तिसृ there would be no harm, but when it is seconed member in a compound there would be anomaly. Thus अतितिसृौ would have become end-acnte. But that is not desired. It is svarita on the final by VIII. 2. 4.

चतुरः शसि ॥ १६७ ॥ पदानि ॥ चतुरः, शसि (अन्तउदात्तः) ॥

वृत्तिः ॥ चतुरः शसि परतो ऽन्त उदात्तो भवति ॥

167. The word चतुर्, followed by the accusative plural, has acute accent on the last syllable.

Thus चतुरः पश्य the accent is on तु ॥ The feminine of चतुर् is चतसृ (VII. 2. 99), which has acute accent on the first (VII. 2. 99 Vârt), and its accusative plural will not have accent on the last syllable, This is so, because चतुर् has acute on the first, as formed by उरन् affix. Its substitute चतसृ will also be so, by the rule of स्थानिवत् ॥ The special enunciation of आद्युदात्त with regard to चतसृ in the Vârtika चतसर्याद्युदात्तनिपातनं कर्तव्यं (VII. 2. 99) indicates that the present rule does not apply to चतसृ ॥ Another reason for this is as follows: चतसृ + शस् = चतस्र + शस् ॥ Now comes the present Sûtra ; here, however, the र् substitute of ऋ being sthânivat, will prevent the udâtta formation of the अ of स्र ; nor will ऋ be considered as final and take the acute, as there exists no vowel ऋ but a consonant र् which cannot take an accent. As चतस्रः पश्य ॥ Professor Bohtlingk places the accent thus चतुरः, Pro. Mäx Muller चतुरः ॥ I have followed Prof. Mäx Muller in interpreting this sûtra; for Bohtlingk's interpretation would make the ending शस् accented, and not the final of चतुर् ॥

सावेकाचस्तृतीयादिर्विभक्तिः ॥ १६८ ॥ पदानि ॥ सौ, एकाचः, तृतीयादिः, विभक्तिः ॥

वृत्तिः ॥ साविति सप्तमीबहुवचनस्य सुशब्दस्य ग्रहणम् । तत्र सौ य एकाच् तस्मात्परा तृतीयादिर्विभक्तिरुदात्ता भवति ॥

168. The case-affixes of the Instrumental and of the cases that follow it have the acute accent, if the stem in the Locative Plural is monosyllabic.

The word सौ (locative of सु) refers to the सु of the Locative plural. Thus वाचा, वाग्भ्याम्, वाग्भिः, वाग्भ्यः त्वचा, त्वग्भ्याम्, त्वग्भिः ॥ Why do we say, 'in the Locative plural'? Observe राज्ञा, राज्ञे ॥ Why do we say 'monosyllabic'? Observe हरिणा, गिरिणा, राजसु ॥ Why do we say 'the Instrumentals and the rest'? Observe वाचौ, वाचः ॥ Why do we say "the case-endings (विभक्तिः)?" Observe वाक्तरा, वाक्तमा ॥ The plural of the Locative being taken in the sûtra, the rule does not apply to त्वया and त्वयि, as in the *plural* of the Locative they have more than one syllable, though in *singular* locative their stem has one syllable.

अन्तोदात्तादुत्तरपदादन्यतरस्यामनित्यसमासे ॥ १६९ ॥ पदानि ॥ अन्तोदात्तात्, उत्तरपदात्, अन्यतरस्याम्, अनित्यसमासे ॥

वृत्तिः ॥ एकाच इति वर्तते, तृतीयादिर्विभक्तिरिति च । नित्यशब्दः स्वर्यते । तेन नित्याधिकारविहितः समासः पर्युदस्यते । नित्यसमासादन्यत्रानित्यसमासे यदुत्तरपदमन्तोदात्तमेकाच् तस्मात्परा तृतीयादिर्विभक्तिरन्यतरस्यामुदात्ता भवति ॥

169. The same case endings may optionally have the acute accent, if the monosyllabic word stands at the end of a compound, and has acute accent on the final, when the compound can be easily unloosened.

The phrases "एकाचः" and तृतीयादिर्विभक्तिः are understood here also. The nitya or *invariable* compounds are excluded by this rule. Thus परमवाचा or परमवाचा, परमवाचे or वाचे ; परमवाचः or °वाचः ॥ So also परमत्वचा or °त्वचे &c. According to VI. 1. 223, the compounds have acute accent on the final : that rule applies in the alternative when the case-affixes are not acute and gives us the alternative forms. Why do we say 'is acutely accented on the final'? Observe भँवाचा, सुँवाचा, सुत्वचा ॥ These are Tatpurusha compounds and by VI. 2. 2. the first term of the compound retains its original accent. Why have we used the word 'standing at the end of a compound' when the word नित्यसमासे indicated that the compound was meant? Had we not used the word उत्तरपदात्, the aphorism would have stood as, अन्तोदात्तादन्यतरस्यामनित्यसमासे 'In a loose compound having acute on the final, the above affixes are acute, if the compound consists of a monosyllable'. The word एकाचः will thus qualify the compound and not the second member of the compound, which is intended. And thus the rule will apply to श्वोर्क्र (शुन ऊर्क्) Ins. श्वोर्जा, श्वोर्जे: &c, and not to compounds having more than one syllable. Why do we say 'in loose compounds'? Observe अग्निचिता, सोमसुता ॥ These words form invariable (nitya) compounds by II. 2. 19, and by VI. 2. 139, the second member retains its original accent, which makes चि udâtta.

अञ्चेश्छन्दस्यसर्वनामस्थानम् ॥ १७० ॥ पदानि ॥ अञ्चेः, छन्दसि, असर्वनामस्थानम् ॥

वृत्तिः ॥ अञ्चेः परा ऽसर्वनामस्थानविभक्तिरुदात्ता भवति छन्दसि विषये ॥

170. In the Chhandas, the case-endings other than the sarvanâmasthâna, get the acute accent when coming after अञ्चि ॥

In the Vedas, a stem ending in the word अञ्च्, has the acute not only on the affixes previously mentioned, but on the accusative plural affix also. Thus इन्द्रा दधीचो अस्थभिः (Rig I. 84. 13). Here the word दधीच् had accent on धी by VI. 1. 222, but by the present sûtra, the accent falls on the case-affix अस् ॥ Though the anuvritti of "Instrumentals and the rest" was understood here, the word asarvanâmasthâna has been used here to include the ending शस् also. As प्रतीचो बाहून् प्रतिभङ्ध्येषाम् ॥

ऊडिदम्पदाद्यप्पुम्रैद्युभ्यः ॥ १७१ ॥ पदानि ॥ ऊठ्, इदम्, पदादि, अप्, पुम्, रै, द्युभ्यः ॥

वृत्तिः ॥ ऊठ् इदम् पदादि अप् पुम् रै दिव् इत्येतेभ्यो ऽसर्वनामस्थानविभक्तिरुदात्ता भवति ॥

171. The same (asarvanâmasthâna) case-endings have the acute accent, when the stem ends in वाह्, also after इदम्, after पद् &c (upto निश् VI. 1. 63), after अप्, पुंस्, रै and दिव् ॥

The ऊठ् is the substitute of the वा of वाह् (VI. 4. 132) and not the ऊठ् taught in VI. 4. 19 &c). Thus प्रष्ठौहः, प्रष्ठौहा, but not in अक्षद्युवा (Ins. sing of अक्षद्यूः derived by ऊठ् substitution of व् in अक्षदिव् VI. 4. 19 &c). इदम्—आभ्याम्, एभिः The anuvritti of "अन्तोदात्तात्" is unsderstood here, therefore, when the word

इदम् is not end-acute, this rule will not apply. When, therefore, there is anvâdeśa under II. 4. 32, the final being anudâtta, this rule does not apply, as अथो आभ्यां निपुणमधीत ॥ The पदादि words are पद, दत् &c upto निश् in VI. 1. 63. Thus निपदश्चतुरो जहि, या दन्तोधावति, अपः पश्यः, आङ्गिः, अद्भ्यः, पुंसः, पुम्भ्याम्, पुम्भ्यः, पुंसो पुंसः, रायः पश्य, राभ्याम्, राभिः, दिवः, दिवौ, दिवे ॥ As regards the other cases of दिव् the accent is governed by VI. 1. 183. The word असन् and those which follow it, in VI. 1. 63, are not governed by this rule because they consist of more than one vowel, and the anuvritti of एकाच: is understood here from VI. 1. 168. When these become monosyllable by the elision of अ (penultimate), then the vibhakti will be udâtta by VI. 1. 161 even after these. The case endings after these words are of course, anudâtta, except when these words become monosyllabic:—As ग्रीवायां बद्धो अपि कक्ष आसनि, मत्स्यं न दीन उदनि क्षियन्तं ॥

अष्टनो दीर्घात् ॥ १७२ ॥ पदानि ॥ अष्टनः, दीर्घात् ॥

वृत्तिः ॥ अष्टनो दीर्घान्तादसर्वनामस्थानविभक्तिरुदात्ता भवति ॥

172. The asarvanâmasthâna case-endings after अष्टन् 'eight', have acute accent, when it gets the form अष्टा ॥

The word अष्टन् has two forms in the acc. pl. and the other cases that follow it, namely अष्टा and अष्ट ॥ The affixes of acc. pl. &c are udâtta after the long form अष्टा and not after अष्ट ॥ Thus अष्टाभिः opposed to अष्टभिः, अष्टाभ्यः con. अष्टभ्यः, अष्टासु con. अष्टसु ॥ The word अष्टन् has acute on the last syllable, as it belongs to the class of घृतादि words (Phit I. 21); and by VI. 1. 180 the accent would have been on the penultimate syllable. This rule debars it. The use of दीर्घात् indicates that the word अष्टन् has two forms, and the substitution of long अ taught in VII. 2. 84, thus becomes *optional*, because of this indication. Otherwise the employment of the word दीर्घात् would be useless, for by VII. 2. 84 which is couched in general terms, अष्टन् would *always* end in a long vowel. There is another use of the word दीर्घात्, namely, it makes the word अष्टान् with long आ (VII. 2. 84) to get also the designation of षट् ॥ For if अष्टान् was not to be called a षट्, like अष्टन्, then there would be scope to the present sûtra in the case of अष्टान् while it would be debarred in the case of अष्टन् without long आ, by the subsequent rule VI. 1. 180 which applies to षट् word, and hence the employment of the word दीर्घात् would become useless.

शतुरनुमो नद्यजादी ॥ १७३ ॥ पदानि ॥ शतुः, अनुमः, नदी, अजादी ॥

वृत्तिः ॥ अन्तोदात्तादिति वर्त्तते । अनुम् यः शतृप्रत्ययस्तदन्तादन्तोदात्तात्परा नदी अजादिर्विभक्तिरसर्वनामस्थानमुदात्ता भवति ॥

वार्त्तिकम् ॥ बृहन्महतोरुपसंख्यानम् ॥

173. After an oxytone Participle in अत् the feminine suffix ई,(nadi) and the case endings beginning with vowels

(with the exception of strong cases) have acute accent, when the participial affix has not the augment न् (i. e. is not अन्त).

The word अन्तोदात्तात् 'after an oxytoned word' is understood here. Thus तुदती, तुदती, लुनती, पुनती, तुदतो, लुनतो, पुनतो, सुनतो from तुदत्, तुदत्, लुनत् and पुनत् ॥

Why do we say "not having the augment नुम्?" Observe तुदन्ता, तुदन्ती ॥ Here also by VI. 1. 186, after the root तुद् which has an indicatory श, in the Dhâtupâṭha, being written तुद, the sârvadhâtuka affix शतृ (अत्) is anudâtta. This anudâtta अत्, coalescing with the udâtta अ of तुद (VI. 1. 162), becomes udâtta (VIII. 2. 5); and Rule VIII. 2. 1 not being held applicable here, the Participle gets the accent, and not the feminine affix. Why do we say "a नदी (feminine in ई) word and before vowel-endings?' Observe तुदद्भ्याम्, तुदद्भ्याम् &c. If the participle is not an oxytone, the rule does not apply. As रुदती, ईषती ॥ Here the accent is on the first syllable by VI. 1. 189.

Vârt:—The words बृहती and महती should also be included: as बृहती महती, बृहतो, महतो ॥

उदात्तयणो हल्पूर्वात् ॥ १७४ ॥ पदानि ॥ उदात्त, यणः, हल्, पूर्वात् ॥

वृत्तिः ॥ उदात्तस्थाने यो यण् हल्पूर्वस्तस्मात्परा नदी अजादिर्या ऽसर्वनामस्थानविभक्तिरुदात्ता भवति ॥

वार्त्तिकम् ॥ नकारग्रहणं च कर्त्तव्यम् ॥

174. The same endings have the acute accent, when for the acutely accented final vowel of the stem, a semi-vowel is substituted, and which is preceded by a consonant.

Thus कर्तृ+ई=कर्त्री ; कत्रा, हर्त्रा, हर्त्री, प्रलवित्री, प्रलवित्रा ॥ प्रसवित्री, प्रसवित्रा ॥ All these are तृच् ending words and have consequently acute accent on the final (VI. 1. 163). Why '*actuely* accented final vowel is replaced &c'? Observe कर्त्री, कर्त्रा, हर्त्री, हर्त्रा, formed by तृन् having acute on the first syllable. Why do we say 'preceded by a consonant'? Observe बहुतितउ—बहुतितवा ब्राह्मण्या (VIII. 2. 4) बहूनि तितऊनि अस्या इति बहुतितिः ॥ This compound with बहु gets udâtta on the final by VI. 2. 175. In making the Instrumental singular of बहुतितउ, the उ is replaced by व्, but as this व् is preceded by a vowel, the affix gets the svarita accent.

Vârt:—The rule applies when the stem ends in न् though not in a semi-vowel, as वाक्पत्नी, चित्पत्नी ॥

नोङ्धात्वोः ॥ १७५ ॥ पदानि ॥ न, ऊङ्, धात्वोः ॥

वृत्तिः ॥ ऊङो धातोश्च य उदात्तयण् हल्पूर्वस्तस्मात्परा ऽजाद्यसर्वनामस्थानविभक्तिर्नोदात्ता भवति ॥

175. But not so, when the vowel is of the feminine affix ऊ (IV. 1. 66), or the final of a root.

After the semi-vowel substitutes of the udâtta ऊ (IV. 1. 66) or of the udâtta final vowels of the root, when preceded by a consonant, the weak case-endings beginning with a vowel do not take the acute accent. Thus ब्रह्मबन्ध्वा, ब्रह्मबन्ध्वे, धीरबन्ध्वा, धीर बन्ध्वे from धीरबन्धू, which has acute accent on ऊ, because ऊङ् is udâtta (III. 1. 3), and the ekadeśa of it, when it combines with the preceding vowel is also udâtta (VIII. 2. 5). The व substituted for ऊ before the ending आ, is a semi-vowel substitute of an udâtta (उदात्तयण्) the affix after it would have become udâtta by the last sûtra, but not being so, the general rule VIII, 2. 4 applies and makes it svarita. Let us take an example of a semi-vowel substitute of the vowel of a root (धातु-यण्):—सकुल्ल्वा, सकुल्ल्वे; खलप्वे from सकुल्लू, खलपू formed by क्विप् affix, the second member of the compound retaining its original accent, namely, the oxytone, the semi-vowel being substituted by VI. 4. 83 before the vowel case-endings.

ह्रस्वनुड्भ्यां मतुप् ॥ १७६ ॥ पदानि ॥ ह्रस्व, नुडभ्याम्, मतुप् ॥

वृत्तिः ॥ अन्तोदात्तादित्येव । ह्रस्वान्तादन्तोदात्तान्नुटश्चपरोमतुब् उदात्तो भवति ॥

वार्त्तिकम् ॥ रेशब्दाच मतुप उदात्तत्वं वक्तव्यम् ॥ वा० ॥ त्रेश्च प्रतिषेधो वक्तव्यः ॥

176. The otherwise unaccented मत् (वत्) takes the acute accent, when an oxytoned stem ends in a light vowel, or the affix has before it the augment नु (VIII. 2. 16).

The word अन्तोदात्तात् is understood here also. Thus अग्निमान्, वायुमान्, कर्तृमान्, हर्तृमान् ॥ So also when मतुप् takes नुट्, as अक्षण्वता, शीर्षण्वता ॥ Here by VII. 1. 76, the word अक्षि takes अनङ् and becomes अक्षन्, then is added नुट् by VIII. 2. 16, and we have अक्षन् न् मतुप् ॥ The preceding न् is elided. When the stem is not oxytone (antodâtta) this rule does not apply: as वसुमान् ॥ The word वसु has acute on the first syllable, as it is formed from वस् with the affix उ (Uṇ I. 10) which is नित् (Uṇ I. 9) so the मतुप् retains its anudâtta here. So also in the case of मरुत्वान्, the affix does not become acute, though the word मरुत् has acute on the final as the intervening त् makes the उ of रु *heavy* when the affix is added: the general maxim स्वरविधौ व्यंजनमविद्यमानवत् does not apply here, because the very fact that नु is only taken as an exception, shows this.

Vârt:—The affix मतुप् becomes acute after the heavy vowel of रे: as रेवान् = रयिरस्यास्ति ॥ There is vocalisation of यु of रयि, as र इ इ then substitution of one, as र इ, then guṇa, रे ॥

Vârt:—The prohibition should be stated after त्रि; as त्रिवतीर्याज्यानुवाक्या भवन्ति ॥

नामन्यतरस्याम् ॥ १७७ ॥ पदानि ॥ नाम्, अन्यतरस्याम् ॥

वृत्तिः ॥ ह्रस्वग्रहणमनुवर्त्तते मतुब्ग्रहणं च । तेन मतुपा ह्रस्वो विशेष्यते । मतुपि यो ह्रस्वस्तदन्तादन्तोदात्तादन्यतरस्यां नाम् उदात्तो भवति ॥

177. After an oxytoned stem which ends in a light vowel, the genitive ending नाम् has optionally the acute accent.

Thus भग्नीनाम् or भग्नीनाम्, वायूनाम् or वायूनाम्, कर्तृणाम् or कर्तृणाम् (see VII. 1. 54). It might be objected, that नाम् is not preceded by a short vowel, as is shown in the above examples, then how can the anuvritti of ह्रस्व 'short or light vowel' be read into this sûtra? The reply is that the anuvritti of मतुप् should also be read into this sûtra, the meaning being "a stem which has a light vowel when followed by मतुप्, will cause the नाम् acute, though the light vowel may become heavy before this ending, in its present form". Otherwise, this rule will apply to forms like तिसृणाम्, चतसृणाम् having light vowels before नाम् and not to the forms above given. Why do we read नाम् with the नुट् augment (VII. 1. 54) and not आम्? The rule will not apply to धेन्वाम् शकट्याम् which get the acute on the final by VI. 1. 174. Why do we say 'after a stem ending in a light vowel'? Observe कुमारीणाम् (the word कुमारी is end-acute by Uṇ III. 138 and so is कुमारी by VI. 1. 161). Why do we say after an oxytoned word? Observe वैपूणाम्, वैसूनाम् the words वपु and वसु have acute on the first syllable.

ङ्याश्छन्दसि बहुलम् ॥ १७८ ॥ पदानि ॥ ङ्याः, छन्दसि, बहुलम् ॥

वृत्तिः ॥ ङ्यन्ताच्छन्दसि विषये नामुदात्तो भवति बहुलम् ॥

178. In the Chhandas, the ending नाम् has diversely the acute accent after the feminine affix ई ॥

Thus देवसेनानाम् अभिभञ्जतीनाम्, बह्वीनाम् पिता ॥ Sometimes it does not take place, as नदीनाम् पारे; जयन्तीनाम् मरुतः ॥

षट्त्रिचतुर्भ्यो हलादिः ॥ १७९ ॥ पदानि ॥ षट्, त्रि, चतुर्भ्यः, हलादिः ॥

वृत्तिः ॥ अन्तोदात्तादित्येतन्निवृत्तम् । षट्संज्ञकेभ्यस्त्रि चतुर् इत्येताभ्यां च परा हलादिर्विभक्तिरुदात्ता भवति ॥

179. The case-endings beginning with a consonant, have the acute accent after the Numerals called षट् (I. 1. 24), as well as after त्रि and चतुर् ॥

The anuvritti of अन्तोदात्तात् ceases, for the present rule applies even to words like पंचन् and नवन् which are acute on the initial by Phit II. 5. Thus षण्णाम्, षड्भिः, षड्भ्यः, पंचानाम्, सप्तानाम्, त्रिभिः त्रिभ्यः, त्रयाणाम्, चतुर्णाम् (See VII. 1. 55). Why do we say 'before case-affixes beginning with consonants'? Observe चतस्रः पश्य (VI. 1. 167 and VII. 2. 99).

झल्युपोत्तमम् ॥ १८० ॥ पदानि ॥ झलि, उपोत्तमम् ॥

वृत्तिः ॥ षट्त्रिचतुर्भ्यो या झलादिर्विभक्तिस्तदन्ते पदे उपोत्तममुदात्तं भवति । त्रिप्रभृतीनामन्त्यमुत्तमं तत्समीपे च यत्तदुपोत्तमम् ॥

180. The above numerals, when taking a case-affix beginning with a भ् or स्, get the acute accent on the penultimate syllable, when the said numerals assume a form consisting of three or more syllables.

The numerals षट्, त्रि and चतुर् when ending in a case-affix beginning with a झल् consonant, form a full word (पद), in such a word the penultimate syllable gets the acute accent. The very word penultimate shows that the पद must be of three syllables at least. Thus पंचभिः, सप्तभिः, तिसृभिः, चतुर्भिः ॥ Why do we say 'beginning with भ् and स्'? Observe, पञ्चानाम्' सप्तानाम् ॥ Why do we say 'the penultimate syllable'? Observe षड्भिः, षड्भ्यः ॥

विभाषा भाषायाम् ॥ १८१ ॥ पदानि ॥ विभाषा, भाषायाम् ॥

वृत्तिः ॥ षट्त्रिचतुर्भ्यो या झलादिर्विभक्तिस्तदन्ते पदे उपोत्तममुदात्तं भवति विभाषा भाषायां विषये ॥

181. In the Secular language this is optional.

The झलादि case-affixes coming after the above numerals षट्, त्रि and चतुर् may make the words so formed take the acute on the penultimate optionally, in the spoken ordinary language. Thus पंचभिः or पंचभिः ॥ In the alternative VI. 1. 179 applies. So also सप्तभिः or सप्तभिः, तिसृभिः or तिसृभिः ॥

न गोश्वन्त्साववर्णराडङ्क्रुङ्कृद्भ्यः ॥ १८२ ॥ पदानि ॥ न, गो, श्वन्, सौ अवर्ण, राट्, अङ्, क्रुङ्, कृद्भ्यः ॥

वृत्तिः ॥ गो श्वन् साववर्ण सौ प्रथमैकवचने यदवर्णान्तं राट् अङ् क्रुङ् कृद् इत्येतेभ्यो यदुक्तं तत्र भवति ॥

182. The foregoing rules from VI. 1. 168 downwards have no applicability after गो, and श्वन् and words ending in them; nor after a stem which before the case ending of the Nominative singular has अ or आ, nor after राज्, or after a stem ending in अञ्च्, nor as well as after क्रुञ्च् and कृत् ॥

Thus गवा, गवे, गोभ्याम् ॥ Here by VI. 1. 168, the case-endings would have got otherwise the accent, which is however prohibited. So also सुगुना, सुगवे and सुगुभ्याम् ॥ Here VI. 1. 169 is prohibited. So also शुना, शुने, श्वभ्याम्, परमशुना, परमशुने and परमश्वभ्याम् ॥ The word साववर्णः (सौ अवर्णः) means 'what has अ or आ before सु (1st. sing.)" Thus येभ्यः, तेभ्यः, केभ्यः ॥ राज्ः—राजा, राज्ञे, परमराजा ॥ (The word राज is formed by क्विप् affix): अङ्=अञ्च्+क्विन्; the prohibition applies to that form of this word wherein the nasal is not elided (VI. 4. 30). Thus प्राञ्चा, प्राङ्भ्याम् ॥ Where the nasal is elided, there the case-ending must take the accent; as प्राचा, प्राचे प्राग्भ्याम् ॥ क्रुङ् is also a क्विन् formed word. Thus क्रुञ्चा, क्रुञ्चे, परमक्रुञ्चा ॥ कृत् is derived from कृ 'to do' or from कृत् 'to cut' by क्विप्; as कृता कृते and परमकृता ॥ Why has the word श्वन् been especially mentioned in this sûtra, when the rule would have applied to it even without such enumeration, because in the Nominative Singular this word assumes the form श्वा and consequently it is साववर्णः? The inclusion of श्वन् indicates that the elision of न should not be considered asiddha for the purposes of this rule. Therefore, the present rule will not apply to words like नृ and पितृ which in Nom. Sing. end in आ, as ना and पिता after the elision of न् of अनङ् (VII. 3. 94). Thus the Locative Singular of नृ will be नरि by VI. 1. 168, this prohilition not applying, and the affix मतुप् will get udâtta after पिता by VI. 1. 176 as पितृमान् ॥ But rule VI. 1. 176 will be debarred by the present in the case of वृक्षवान् because वृक्ष is a सावर्ण ॥

दिवो झल् ॥ १८३ ॥ पदानि ॥ दिवः, झल् ॥

वृत्तिः ॥ दिवः परा झलादिर्विभक्तिर्नोदात्ता भवति ॥

183. After दिव् a case-ending beginning with भ or स is unaccented.

Thus द्युभ्याम्, द्युभिः ॥ This debars VI. 1. 168, 171. Why do we say 'beginning with a झल् consonant'? Observe दिवौ, दिवे ॥

नृ चान्यतरस्याम् ॥ १८४ ॥ पदानि ॥ नृ, च, अन्यतरस्याम् ॥

वृत्तिः ॥ नृ इत्येतस्मात्परा झलादिर्विभक्तिरन्यतरस्यां नोदात्ता भवति ॥

184. After नृ, a case ending beginning with भ or स is optionally unaccented.

Thus नृभिः or नृभिः, नृभ्यः, नृभ्यः, नृभ्याम्, नृभ्याम्, नृषु, नृषु ॥ But not so नरौ, नरे ॥

तित्स्वरितम् ॥ १८५ ॥ पदानि ॥ तित्, स्वरितम्, ॥

वृत्तिः ॥ तित्स्वरितं भवति ॥

185. An affix having an indicatory त्, is svarita i. e. has circumflex accent.

Thus चिकीर्ष्यम्, जिहीर्ष्यम्, formed by यत् (III. 1. 97). कार्यम्, हार्यम् with ण्यत् (III. 1. 124). This is an exception to III. 1. 3 which makes all affixes âdyudâtta. For exception to this rule see VI. 1. 213 &c.

तास्यनुदात्तेन्ङिददुपदेशाल्लसार्वधातुकमनुदात्तमह्न्विङोः ॥ १८६ ॥ पदानि ॥ तासि, अनुदात्तेत्, ङिद्, अदुपदेशात्, ल, सार्वधातुकम्, अनुदात्तम्, अ-ह्नु, इङो, ॥

वृत्तिः ॥ तासेरनुदात्तेतोङितो ऽकारान्तोपदेशाच्च शब्दात्परं लसार्वधातुकमनुदात्तं च भवति ह्नुङ् इङ् इत्येताभ्यां परं वर्जयित्वा ॥

186. The Personal-endings and their substitutes (III. 2. 124-126) are, when they are sârvadhâtuka (III. 4. 113 &c), unaccented, after the characteristic of the Periphrastic future (तासि), after a root which in the Dhâtupâṭha has an unaccented vowel or a ङ् (with the exception of ह्नुङ् and इङ्) as indicatory letter, as well as after what has a final अ in the Grammatical system of Instruction (upadeśa).

Thus तासि :—कर्त्ता, कर्त्तारौ, कर्त्तारः, this debars the affix accent (III. 1. 3). Anudáttet :—as, आस्—आस्ते, वस्—वस्ते ॥ ङित् :—षूङ्=सूते, शीङ्—शेते ॥ अत् उपदेशः :—as तुदतः, तुदतः, पचतः, पठतः ॥ A root taking शप् (अ) is considered as taught (upadeśa) as if ending with an अ, as the indicatory letters श and च् are disregarded on the maxim अनुबन्धस्यानैकान्तिकत्वं (= अनवयवत्वं) ॥ Thus पचमानः, यजमानः ॥ The augment मुक is added by आने मुक् VII. 2. 82 which may be explained in two ways; *first*, the augment मुक् is added to the final अ of the base (aṅga) when आन (आनच् &c) follows; or *secondly*, the the augment मुक is added to the base (aṅga) which ends in अ, when आन follows. In the first case मुक् becomes part and parcel of अ and will be taken and included by the enunciation of अ, and therefore अदुपदेश will mean and include an अ having such मुक्, on the maxim यदागमास्तद्गुणीभूतास्तद्ग्रहणेन गृह्यन्ते "That to which an augment is added denotes, because the augment forms part of it, not merely itself, but it denotes also whatever results from its combination with that augment". Therefore मुक् will not prevent the verb becoming अदुपदेश ॥ But if secondly मक be taken as part of the *base* which ends in अ, then the लसार्वधातुक does not follow an अदुपदेश, because म intervenes. But we get rid of this difficulty by considering मुक् augment as Bahiranga and therefore asiddha, when the Antaranga operation of accent is to be performed. The augment मुक (म्) in the last two examples consequently does not prevent the application of the rule. Though the affix शानच् has an indicatory च, yet चित् accent (VI. 1. 163) is debarred by this rule, as it is *subsequent*.

Why do we say after तासि &c. Observe चिनुतः चिन्वन्ति ॥ The vikaraṇa श्नु is ङित् (I. 2. 4) with regard to operations affecting the prior term, and not those which affect the subsequent. Therefore though श्नु is considered as ङित् for the purposes of preventing the guṇa of the prior term चि, it will not be considered so for the purposes of subsequent accent. Or the word ङित् in this sûtra may be taken as equal to ङिदुपदेश and not the आतिदेशिक ङित् like इनु ॥ Why do we use the word upadeśa? So that the rule may apply to पचावः, पचामः, but not to हतः, हथः the dual of हन् which ends in न् in upadesa. though before तस् and थस it has assuned the form ह ॥ Therefore हतः हथः ॥ Why do we use the word ल (Personal endings)? Observe कतीह पवमाना formed by शानन् added to पू (III.2.128),which not being a substitute of लट्, is not a personal ending like शानच् ॥ Why do we use the word Sârvadhâtuka? Observe शिश्ये, शिश्याते, शिश्यिरे ॥ Why do we say with the exception of ह्नुङ् and इङ्? Observe ह्नुते, यद् अधीते ॥

आदिः सिचो ऽन्यतरस्याम् ॥ १८७ ॥ पदानि ॥ आदिः, सिचः, अन्यतरस्याम्,

वृत्तिः ॥ उदात्त इति वर्त्तते । सिजन्तस्यान्यतरस्यामादिरुदात्तो भवति ॥

वार्त्तिकम् ॥ सिच आद्युदात्तत्वे ऽनिटः पितः पक्षे उदात्तत्वं वक्तव्यम् ॥

187. In सिच् Aorist, the first syllable may optionally have the acute accent.

The word उदात्त is understood here. Thus मा हि कार्ष्टाम्, मा हि कार्ष्टाम्; मा हि लाविष्टाम or मा हि लविष्टाम् ॥ In the last example the accent is on पि; and the reason why मां and हि are used in these illustrations, has already been explained in VI. 1. 161. The indicatory च् of सिंच् shows that by VI. 1. 163 the acute will be on the otherwise unaccented augment इट्, when it takes this augment. The सिच् being a वलादि affix will take the augment इट् (VII. 2. 35), and it is a general rule that augments are unaccented; so in the above the षि would have been unaccented, and the accent would have been on the final, but for the indicatory च् of सिच्, which otherwise would find no scope. Thus वि gets acute.

Vârt:—An affix having an indicatory प् (पित्) when coming after an Aorist formed by सिंच् without the augment इट् (अनिट् सिंच्) is in one alternative udâtta (in the other, it is non-acute). This vârtika restricts the scope of the sûtra with regard to पित् affixes. Thus we get the following two forms, which otherwise would have one form only by dhâtu-accent, namely, acute on the first, for पित् is anudâtta. Thus माहि कार्षम् or मा हि कार्षम् ॥ But when it takes the इट् augment, there are two forms (1st.) मा हि लाविषम् as a तिङन्त, (2nd.) मा हि लाविषम् accent on वि (VI. 1. 163). but never मा हि लाविषम् ॥ When however the augment अ is added, the accent falls on this augment (VI. 4. 71).

स्वपादिर्हिंसामच्यनिटि ॥ १८८ ॥ पदानि ॥ स्वपादि, हिंसाम्, अचि, अनिटि ॥

वृत्तिः ॥ लसार्वधातुकग्रहणं यदनुवर्तते तदच्यनिटीति सम्बन्धादिह सप्तम्यन्तं भवति स्वपादीनां हिंसेश्चाजादावनिटि लसार्वधातुके परतो ऽन्यतरस्यामादिरुदात्तो भवति ॥

188. The acute accent is optionally on the first syllable when a Personal-ending, being a Sârvadhâtuka tense affix beginning with a vowel, provided that the vowel is not the augment इट्, follows after स्वप् &c, or after हिंस् ॥

The phrase लसार्वधातुके in the locative case is understood here. Thus स्वपन्ति or स्वपन्ति, श्वसन्ति or श्वसन्ति, हिंसन्ति or हिंसन्ति ॥ The accent on the middle falls by the accent of the affix III. 1. 3. Why do we say 'before an affix beginning with a *vowel*'? Observe स्वप्यात्, हिंस्यात् ॥ Why do we say 'not taking the augment इट्?' Observe स्वपितः and श्वसितः ॥ This rule applies to those vowel-beginning affixes which are ङित्; it does not apply to स्वपानि, हिनसानि ॥

अभ्यस्तानामादिः ॥ १८९ ॥ पदानि ॥ अभ्यस्तानाम्, आदिः ॥

वृत्तिः ॥ अभ्यस्तानामजादावनिटि लसार्वधातुके परत आदिरुदात्तो भवति ॥

189. The acute accent falls on the first syllable of the reduplicate verbs when followed by an affix beginning with a vowel (the vowel being not इट्) and being a sârvadhâtuka personal ending.

Thus ददति, ददतु, दधति, दधतु, जक्षति, जक्षतुः, जाग्रति, जाग्रतुः ॥ Before consonant affixes: दद्यात् ॥ Before सेट् affixes :—जक्षितः ॥ Though the word भादि was understood here from the last aphorism, the repetition is for the sake of making this an *invariable* rule and not an *optional* rule as those in the foregoing.

अनुदात्ते च ॥ १९० ॥ पदानि ॥ अनुदात्ते, च, ॥

वृत्तिः ॥ अविद्यमानोदात्ते च लसार्वधातुके परतो ऽभ्यस्तानामादिरुदात्तो भवति ॥

190. Also when the unaccented endings of the three persons in the singular follow, the first syllable of the reduplicate has the acute.

The endings तिप् सिप् and मिप् are anudâtta (III. 1. 4). This sûtra applies to those personal endings which do not begin with a vowel. Thus ददाति, जहाति, दधाति, जिहीते, मिमीते ॥ The word अनुदात्त is to be construed here as a Bahuvrihi i. e. an affix in which there is no udâtta vowel, so that the rule may apply when a portion of the affix is elided or a semivowel is substituted : as मा हि स्म दधात्, and दधात्यत्र ॥

सर्वस्य सुपि ॥ १९१ ॥ पदानि ॥ सर्वस्य, सुपि ॥

वृत्तिः ॥ सर्वशब्दस्य सुपि परत आदिरुदात्तो भवति ॥

वार्त्तिकम् ॥ सर्वस्वरो ऽनकच्कस्येति वक्तव्यम् ॥

191. The acute is on the first syllable of सर्व when the case-endings follow.

Thus सर्वः, सर्वाः सर्वे ॥ Why do we say when the *case-endings* follow ? Observe सर्वतरः, सर्वतमः the acute is on र्व ॥ The word सर्व has acute on the final, as it is so taught in the Uṇâdi list by निपातन् ॥ It thus being anudâttâdi takes the affix अञ् and forms सार्वः (सर्वस्य विकारः) This rule applies even when the case affix is elided in spite of the prohibition of न लुमताङ्गस्य (I. 1. 63) : as सर्वस्तोमः ॥

Vârt :—The rule does not apply when the affix अकच् is put in : as सर्वकेः ॥ Here the accent is on the final by चित् accent (VI. 1. 163).

भीह्रीभृहुमदजनधनदरिद्राजागरां प्रत्ययात्पूर्वं पिति ॥ १९२ ॥ पदानि ॥ भी, ह्री, भृ, हु, मद, जन, धन, दरिद्रा, जागराम्, प्रत्ययात्, पूर्वम्, पिति ॥

वृत्तिः ॥ भी ह्री भृ हु मद जन धन दरिद्रा जागृ इत्येतेषामभ्यस्तानां लसार्वधातुके पिति प्रत्ययात्पूर्वमुदात्तं भवति ॥

192. In भी, ह्री, भृ, हु, मद्, जन्, धन्, दरिद्रा, and जागृ, in their reduplicates, the acute accent is, before the sârvadhâtuka unaccented endings of the three persons in singular, (पित्), on the syllable which precedes the affix.

This debars the accent on the beginning. Thus बिभेति, जिह्रेति, बिभर्ति, जुहोति, ममत्तु नः परिज्मा ॥ Here the root मद् has diversely taken in the Chhandas the vikaraṇa श्लु, though it belongs to Divâḍi class. जजनत्, इन्द्रम् ॥ The verb is here लेट् or the Vedic Subjunctive, so also is the next example. दधनत् from धन धान्ये,

the इ of ति being elided by III. 4. 97, and the augment अट् being added by III. 4. 94. दर्धनत्, दरिद्रति, जागर्ति ॥ In the case of other verbs we have देदाति ॥ Before affixes which have not the indicatory प् (i. e. all endings other than the three singular endings), the accent will be on the first syllable: as देरिद्रति ॥

लिति ॥ १९३ ॥ पदानि ॥ लिति ॥

वृत्तिः ॥ लिति प्रत्ययात्पूर्वमुदात्तं भवति ।

193. The acute accent falls on the syllable immediately preceding the affix that has an indicatory ल् ॥

Thus चिकीर्षकः, जिहीर्षकः with the affix ण्वुल् (III. 1. 133), भौरिकिविधम् and ऐषुकारिभक्तम् with the affixes विधल् and भक्तल् (IV. 2. 54) accent on the कि and रि ॥

आदिर्णमुल्यन्यतरस्याम् ॥ १९४ ॥ पदानि ॥ आदिः, णमुलि, अन्यतरस्याम् ॥

वृत्तिः । णमुलि परतो ऽन्यतरस्यामादिरुदात्तो भवति ।

194. The first syllable may be optionally acute when the absolutive affix णमुल् follows.

Thus लोलूयम् or लोलूयम् ॥ In the reduplicate form लोलू, the second part लू is unaccented by VIII. 1. 3. The present sûtra makes लो accented. When लो is not accented, लू will get the accent by लित् accent. This rule is confined to polysyllabic Absolutives, namely to reduplicated Absolutives (VIII. 1. 4).

अचः कर्तृयकि ॥ १९५ ॥ पदानि ॥ अचः, कर्तृ-यकि ॥

वृत्तिः । उपदेशइति वर्त्तते । अजन्ता ये उपदेशे धातवस्तेषां कर्तृयकि अन्यतरस्यामादिरुदात्तो भवति ।

195. The roots which are exhibited in Dhâtupâṭha with a final vowel, may optionally have the acute on the first syllable, before the affixes of the Passive (यक्), when the sense of the verb is Reflexive.

The word उपदेश is understood here. Thus लूयते or लूयते केदारः स्वयमेव ॥ स्तीर्यते or स्तीर्यते केदारः स्वयमेव ॥ When the accent does not fall on the first syllable, it falls on य (VI. 1. 186). This rule applies to जन्, खन्, and सन् when they get the form जायते, सायते and खायते; the long आ (VI. 4. 43) substitute is considered as if these verbs were taught in the Dhâtupâṭha with long आ ॥ Thus जायते or जायते स्वयमेव सायते or सायते स्वयमेव; खायते or खायते स्वयमेव ॥ Why do we say 'when ending in a *vowel*'? Observe भिद्यते स्वयमेव ॥ Why do we say "when the sense is Reflexive (कर्तृ)"? Observe लूयते केदारो देवदत्तेन ॥

थलि च सेटीडन्तो वा ॥ १९६ ॥ पदानि ॥ थलि, च, सेटि, इडन्तः, वा ॥

वृत्तिः ॥ सेटि थलि इट वा उदात्तो भवति अन्तो वा आदिर्वा ऽन्यतरस्याम् ।

196. Before the ending थ of the Perfect, second person singular, when this ending takes the augment इ; the acute accent falls either on the first syllable, or on this इ, or on the personal ending.

Thus लुलविथ, लुलविथ, लुलविथ, and लुलविथ. As थल् has an indicatory ल्, the syllable preceding the affix may have also the accent (VI. 1. 193). Thus we get the four forms given above. In short, with इथ termination, the accent may fall on any syllable. When the थ is not सेट्, the accent falls on the root and we have one form only by लिट् accent (VI. 1. 193):—ययाथ ॥

ञ्नित्यादिर्नित्यम् ॥ १९७ ॥ पदानि ॥ ञ्निति, आदिः, नित्यम् ॥

वृत्तिः ॥ ञिति निति च नित्यमादिरुदात्तो भवति ।

197. Whatever is derived with an affix having an indicatory ञ् or न्, has the acute accent invariably on the first syllable.

Thus गार्ग्य with यञ् (IV. 1. 105), वासुदेवकः, अर्जुनकः with वुन् (IV. 3. 98). This is an exception to III. 1. 3. When the affixes are, however, elided, the word loses this accent, i. e. the affix does not leave its mark behind, as it generally does by I. 1. 62. Therefore गर्गाः, बिदाः, चञ्चाः having lost यञ्, अञ् and कन्, have lost their accent also.

आमन्त्रितस्य च ॥ १९८ ॥ पदानि ॥ आमन्त्रितस्य, च ॥

वृत्तिः ॥ आमन्त्रितस्यादिरुदात्तो भवति ।

198. The first syllable of a Vocative gets the acute accent.

Thus देवदत्त !, देवदत्तौ !, देवदत्ताः ॥ This debars the final accent ordained by VI. 2. 148. Though the affix may be elided by a लुमान् word (लुक्, लुप् or श्लु), yet the effect of the affix remains behind in spite of I. 1. 63. As सर्पिरागच्छ ! सप्ता गच्छत ! ॥

पथिमथोः सर्वनामस्थाने ॥ १९९ ॥ पदानि ॥ पथि, मथोः, सर्वनामस्थाने ॥

वृत्तिः ॥ पथिमथिशब्दावौणादिकाविनिप्रत्ययान्तौ प्रत्ययस्वरेणान्तोदात्तौ तयोः सर्वनामस्थाने परत आदिरुदात्तो भवति ।

199. The acute accent is on the first syllable of पथिन् and मथिन् when followed by a strong case-ending.

The words पथिन् and मथिन् are derived by the Uṇâdi affix इनि, (IV. 12. and 13) and are oxytone by III. 1. 3. They become âdyudâtta before strong cases. Thus पन्थाः, पन्थानौ, पन्थानः, मन्थाः, मन्थानौ, मन्थानः ॥ Before other cases we have:—पथः पश्य, मथः पश्य ॥ The accent is on the final by VI. 1. 162, there being elision of the udâtta इन् ॥ The rule I. 1. 62, about the remaining effect of the affix, does not apply here. As पथिप्रियः, has acute on the final of the first word, by retaining its original accent.

अन्तश्च तवै युगपत् ॥ २०० ॥ पदानि ॥ अन्तः, च, तवै, युगपत्, ॥

वृत्तिः ॥ तवैप्रत्ययान्तस्यान्तश्चशब्दादिश्च युगपदुदात्तो भवतः ।

200. The Infinitive in तवै has the acute on the first syllable and on the last syllable at one and the same time.

Thus कर्तवै, हर्तवै ॥ This is an exception to III. 1. 3 by which त of तवै ought to have got the accent, and it also countermands rule VI. 1. 158 by which there can be only a single acute in a single word.

क्षयो निवासे ॥ २०१ ॥ पदानि ॥ क्षयः, निवासे ॥

वृत्तिः ॥ क्षयशब्दो निवासे ऽभिधेये आद्युदात्तो भवति ।

201. The word क्षय has the acute on the first syllable in the sense of 'house, dwelling'.

Thus क्षये जागृहि प्रपश्यन् ॥ The word is formed by घ affix (III. 1. 118) and would have had accent on the affix (III. 1. 3). When not meaning a house we have: क्षयो वर्त्तते दस्यूनाम् ॥ The word is formed by अच् (III. 2. 31).

जयः करणम् ॥ २०२ ॥ पदानि ॥ जयः, करणम् ॥

वृत्तिः ॥ जयशब्दः करणवाची आद्युदात्तो भवति ॥

202. The acute accent falls on the first syllable of जय, in the sense of 'whereby one attains victory'.

Thus जयोऽश्वः, but otherwise जयो वर्तते ब्राह्मणानाम् ॥ The former जय is by घ affix, (III. 1. 118) the second by अच् (III. 2. 31) ॥

वृषादीनां च ॥ २०३ ॥ पदानि ॥ वृषादीनाम्, च, ॥

वृत्तिः ॥ वृष इत्येवमादीनामादिरुदात्तो भवति ॥

203. The words वृष &c have the acute on the first syllable.

Thus 1. वृषः, 2. जनः, 3. ज्वरः, 4. ग्रहः, 5. हयः, 6. गयः ॥ These are formed by अच् (III. 1. 134). The word गय is from गै-गायते, irregularly it is treated as गे ॥ 7. नयः, 8. तायः, 9. तयः, 10. चयः, 11. अमः, 12. वेदः, 13. सूदः, 14. वदः (formed by अच् numbers 8 to 11 are not in Kâśika). सूद is formed by क (III. 1. 135) 15. अंशः, 16. गुहा (formed by अङ् III. 3. 104). 17. शमरणौ संज्ञायां संमतौ भावकर्मणोः :— शमः and रणः, 18. मन्त्रः (formed by अच् III. 1. 134), 19. शान्तिः formed by क्तिच्, 20. कामः, 21. यामः, both formed by घञ्, 22. आरा, 23. धारा, 24. कारा, (all three formed by अङ् III. 3. 104), 25. वहः = गौश्चरादिषु formed by घञ् 26. कल्पः, 27. पादः formed by घञ्, which may either take the accent indicated by the affix or by VI. 1. 159, 28. पदः, 29. दवः ॥ It is आकृतिगणः ॥ All words which are acutely accented on the first, should be considerd as belouging to this class, if their accent cannot be accounted for by any other rule.

1 वृषः, 2 जनः, 3 ज्वर 4 ग्रहः 5 हयः, 6 गयः, 7 नयः, 8 ताय*, 9 तयः, 10 चयः*, 11 भ्रम*:, 12 वेदः, 13 सूदः°, 14 अंशः, 15 गुहा, 16 शमरणौ संज्ञायां संमतौ भावकर्मणोः, 17 मन्त्रः, 18 शान्तिः, 19 कामः, 20 यामः, 21 आरा, 22 धारा, 23 कारा, 24 वहः, 25 कल्पः, 26 पादः 27 पद्यः, 28 द्रवः, 29 आकृतिगण ॥

संज्ञायामुपमानम् ॥ २०४ ॥ पदानि ॥ संज्ञायाम्, उपमानम् ॥

वृत्तिः ॥ उपमानशब्दः संज्ञायामाद्युदात्तो भवति ॥

204. The acute accent falls on the first syllable of that word with which something is likened, provided that it is a name.

Thus चञ्चा, वध्रिका, खरकुटी, दासी ॥ All these are उपमान words used as names of the उपमेय (the thing compared). The affix कन् (V. 3, 96) is elided here by V. 3. 98. It might be asked when कन् is elided, its mark, namely causing the first syllable to be acute (VI. 1. 197), will remain behind by virtue of I. 1. 62, where is then the necessity of this sûtra. The formation of this sûtra indicates that the प्रत्ययलक्षण rule is not of universal application in the rules relating to accent.

When the word is not a Name, we have अग्निर्माणवकः ॥ When it is not an upamâna we have देवदत्तः (VI. 2. 148).

निष्ठा च द्व्यजनात् ॥ २०५ ॥ पदानि ॥ निष्ठा, च, द्व्यच्, अनात् ॥

वृत्तिः ॥ निष्ठान्तं च द्व्यच् संज्ञायां विषये आद्युदात्तं भवति चेदादिराकारो न भवति ॥

205. A disyllabic Participle in त (Nishṭhâ), when a Name has the acute on the first syllable, but not if the first syllable has an आ ॥

Thus दत्तः, बुद्धः, दत्तः ॥ This debars the affix accent (III. 1. 3). In non-participles we have देवः, भीमः ॥ In polysyllabic Participles we have चिन्तितः, रक्षितः ॥ In Participles having long आ in the first syllable, we have, घातः, आप्तः ॥ When the Participle is not a Name we have, कृतम्, हृतम् ॥

शुष्कधृष्टौ ॥ २०६ ॥ पदानि ॥ शुष्क, धृष्टौ ॥

वृत्तिः ॥ आदिरुदात्त इति वर्त्तते । शुष्क धृष्ट इत्येतावाद्युदात्तौ भवतः ॥

206. Also शुष्क and धृष्ट have acute on the first syllable.

These are non-Names. Thus शुष्कः and धृष्टः ॥

आशितः कर्ता ॥ २०७ ॥ पदानि ॥ आशितः, कर्त्ता ॥

वृत्तिः ॥ आशितशब्दः कर्तृवाची आद्युदात्तो भवति ॥

207. The word आशित meaning 'having eaten' has acute on the first syllable.

Thus आशितो देवदत्तः 'Devadatta, having eaten'. Here it is used as an active participle. The क्त is added to अश् preceded by आ, to form both Active and Passive Participles: which by VI. 2. 144 would have taken acute on the final. This debars that. In the Passive Participle we have आशितम् देवदत्तेन 'eaten by Devadatta'. आशितमन्नम् 'the eaten food'. The former is भावे क्त, the second is कर्मणि क्त ॥

रिक्ते विभाषा ॥ २०८ ॥ पदानि ॥ रिक्ते, विभाषा ॥

वृत्तिः ॥ रिक्तशब्दे विभाषा आदिरुदात्तो भवति ॥

208. The word रिक्त may have optionally the acute on the first syllable.

Thus रिक्तः or रिक्तः ॥ This debars VI. 1. 204 and 205.

जुष्टार्पिते च छन्दसि ॥ २०९ ॥ पदानि ॥ जुष्टा, अर्पिते, च, छन्दसि ॥

वृत्तिः ॥ जुष्ट अर्पित इत्येते शब्दरूपे छन्दसि विषये विभाषा आद्युदात्ते भवतः ॥

209. In the Chhandas, the words जुष्ट and अर्पित have optionally the acute on the first syllable.

Thus जुष्टः or जुष्टः ; अर्पितः or अर्पितः ॥ In the secular literature the accent is always on the last syllable (III. 1. 3).

नित्यं मन्त्रे ॥ २१० ॥ पदानि ॥ नित्यम्, मन्त्रे ॥

वृत्तिः ॥ जुष्ट अर्पित इत्येते शब्दरूपे मन्त्रविषये नित्यमाद्युदात्ते भवतः ॥

210. In the Mantras, these words जुष्ट and अर्पित have always the acute on the first syllable.

Thus जुष्ट देवानामर्पितं पितॄणाम् ॥ Some say that this rule applies only to जुष्ट and not to अर्पित ; in which option is allowed even in the Mantra : so that it has acute on the last in the Mantra even : e. g. तस्मिन्साकं त्रिशता न शंकवोऽर्पिताः ॥

युष्मदस्मदोर्ङसि ॥ २११ ॥ पदानि ॥ युष्मद्-अस्मदोः-, ङसि ॥

वृत्तिः ॥ युष्मदस्मदी मदिक्प्रत्ययान्ते ऽन्तोदात्ते तयोर्ङसि परत आदिरुदात्तो भवति ॥

211. The acute accent is on the first syllable of युष्मद् and अस्मद् in the Genitive Singular.

This applies when the forms are मम and तव, and not मे and ते ॥ Thus मम स्वम्, तव स्वम् ॥ The word युष्मद् and अस्मद् are derived from युष and अस by adding the affix मदिक् (Un I. 139) युष्मद्+ङस्=युष्मद्+अश् (VII. 1. 27)=तव अद्+अश् (VI. 2. 96)=तवँ+अँश् (VII. 2. 90)=तव (VI. 1. 97). Here by VIII. 2. 5, व would have been udâtta, the present sûtra makes त udâtta. So also with मम ॥

ङयि च ॥ २१२ ॥ पदानि ॥ ङयि, च ॥

वृत्तिः ॥ युष्मदस्मदोरिति वर्तते, आदिरुदात्त इति च । इत्येतस्मिंश्च परतो युष्मदस्मदोरादिरुदात्तो भवति ॥

212. The acute accent is on the first syllable of युष्मद् and अस्मद् in the Dative Singular.

Thus तुभ्यम् and मह्यम्, the forms ते and मे are not governed by this rule. The making of two separate sûtras is for the sake of preventing the application of यथासंख्य rule (I. 3. 10). Had the sûtra been युष्मदस्मदोर्ङिङसोः, then yushmad in the Dative, and asmad in the Genitive alone would have taken this accent.

यतोऽनावः ॥ २१३ ॥ पदानि ॥ यतः, अनावः ॥

वृत्तिः । निष्ठा च द्व्यजनाद्दित्यतो द्व्यज्ग्रहणमनुवर्त्तते । यत्प्रत्ययान्तस्य द्व्यच आदिरुदात्तो भवति न चेन्नौशब्दात्परो भवति ।

213. Whatever is formed by the affix यत्, has, if it is a disyllabic word, the acute on the first syllable, with the exception of नाव्यः from नौ ॥

The word द्व्यच् is understood here from VI. 1. 205. Thus चेयम्, जेयम् (III. 1. 97); कण्ठ्यम्, ओष्ठ्यम् (V. 1. 6). This rule debars the Svarita accent required by तित् (VI. 1. 185) ॥ But नौ—नाव्यम् ॥ The rule does not apply to words of more than two syllables, thus:—चिकीर्ष्यम्, ललाट्यम् ॥

ईडवन्दवृशंसदुहां ण्यतः ॥२१४॥ पदानि ॥ ईड, वन्द, वृ, शंस्, दुहाम्, ण्यतः ॥

वृत्तिः ॥ ईड वन्द वृ शंस दुह इत्येतेषां यो ण्यत् तदन्तस्यादिरुदात्तो भवति ।

214. The acute accent is on the first syllable of ईड्, वन्द्, वृ, शंस् and दुह्, when they are followed by the affix ण्यत् ॥

Thus ईड्यम्, वन्द्यम्, वार्यम्, शंस्यम्, दोह्या धेनुः ॥ The two letters ण् and त् being indicatory, the 'ṇyat' is not included in 'yat' of the last sûtra. The accent would be regulated by त् ॥ The accent of त् however is debarred by this rule. The वृ in the sûtra is वृङ् संभक्तौ of Kriyadi class; the वृञ् of स्वादि class takes kyap affix. See III. 1. 109.

विभाषा वेण्विन्धानयोः ॥ २१५ ॥ पदानि ॥ विभाषा, वेणु, इन्धानयोः ॥

वृत्तिः ॥ वेणु इन्धान इत्येतयोर्विभाषा आदिरुदात्तो भवति ।

215. The acute accent is optionally on the first syllable of वेणु and इन्धान ॥

Thus वेणुः or वेणुः; इन्धानः or इन्धानः or इन्धानः ॥ The word वेणु is derived by the Uṇâdi affix णु (III. 38), which being a नित् would *always* have acute on the first. This allows an option. The word इन्धान, if it is formed by चानश् it will have the accent on the final. If it is considered to be formed by शानच्, the affix being a sârvadhâtuka is anudâtta, and as it replaces udâtta final of the root, it becomes udâtta (VI. 1. 161), and thus इन्धान gets acute on the middle. It would never have acute on the first syllable, the present rule ordains that also. When वेणु is used as an upamâna वेणुरिव वेणुः, then it is *invariably* acutely accented on the first (VI. 1. 204).

त्यागरागहासकुहश्वठक्रथानाम् ॥ २१६ ॥ पदानि ॥ त्याग, राग, हास, कुह, श्वठ, क्रथानाम् ॥

वृत्तिः । त्याग राग हास कुह श्वठ क्रथ इत्येतेषां विभाषा आदिरुदात्तो भवति ।

216. The acute accent is optionally on the first syllables of त्याग, राग, हास, कुह, श्वठ, and क्रथ ॥

Thus त्यागः or त्यागः, रागः, रागः, हासः, हासः ॥ These are formed by घञ् affix and by VI. 1. 159 would take acute on the final, this ordains acute on the first syllable also. कुहः or कुहः, श्वठः or श्वठः, क्रथः or क्रथः formed by अच् (III. 1. 13).

उपोत्तमं रिति ॥ २१७ ॥ पदानि ॥ उपोत्तमम्, रिति ॥

वृत्तिः ॥ रिदन्तस्योपोत्तममुदात्तं भवति । त्रिप्रभृतीनामन्त्यमुत्तमं तस्य समीपे यत्तदुपोत्तमम् ।

217. What is formed by an affix having an indicatory र, has acute on the penultimate syllable, the full word consisting of more than two syllables.

A penultimate syllable can be only in a word consisting of three syllables or more. Thus करणीयम् and हरणीयम् formed by अनीयर् (III. 1. 96); पटुजातीयः, मृदुजातीयः by जातीयर् (V. 3. 19). This debars III. 1. 3.

चङ्यन्यतरस्याम् ॥ २१८ ॥ पदानि ॥ चङि, अन्यतरस्याम् ॥

वृत्तिः ॥ चङन्ते ऽन्यतरस्यामुपोत्तममुदात्तं भवति ।

218. The acute accent may be optionally on the penultimate syllable of the reduplicated Aorist in चङ्, the word consisting of more than two syllables.

Thus मा हि चीकरताम् or चीकरताम् ॥ The augment अट् is elided by the addition of मा, VI. 4. 74; हि prevents the verb from becoming anudatta VIII. 1. 34 then comes the चित् accent of चङ् ॥ The augmented form with अट् has acute always on the first syllable VI. 4. 71. When the word is of less than three syllables, the rule does not apply, as, माहि दधत् ॥

मतोः पूर्वमात्संज्ञायां स्त्रियाम् ॥ २१९ ॥ पदानि ॥ मतोः, पूर्वम्, आत्, संज्ञायाम्, स्त्रियाम् ॥

वृत्तिः ॥ मतोः पूर्वं आकार उदात्तो भवति तच्चेन्मत्वन्तं स्त्रीलिङ्गं संज्ञा भवति ।

219. The आ before the affix मत् has the acute accent, when the word is a name in the Feminine Gender.

Thus उदुम्बरावती, पुष्करावती, शरावती (IV. 2. 85). The lengthening takes place by VI. 3. 120. वीरणावती ॥ Why do we say 'the आ'? Observe इक्षुमती, द्रुमवती ॥ The words इक्षु Un. III. 157 and द्रुम (V. 2. 108) are end-acute, so accent is on मतुप् by VI. 1, 176. Why do we say when a name? Observe खट्वावती ॥ खट्वा is formed by क्वन् and has acute on the first (Un. I. 151). Why do we say in the Feminine Gender? Observe धरावान् ॥ Why do we say when followed by मतु? Observe गवाहिनी ॥

अन्तो ऽवत्याः ॥ २२० ॥ पदानि ॥ अन्तः, अवत्याः ॥

वृत्तिः ॥ संज्ञायामित्येव । अवतीशब्दान्तस्य संज्ञायामन्त उदात्तो भवति।

220. The Names ending in अवती have the acute accent on the last syllable.

Thus अजिरवती, खदिरवती, हंसवती, कारण्डवती ॥ These words being formed by ङीप् would have been unaccented on the final (III. 1. 4). Why do we use अवती and not वती? Then the rule would apply to राजवती also, for this word is really राजन्वती ending in अन्वती, the subsequent elision of न् is held to be non-valid for the purposes of the application of this rule (VIII. 2. 2). But the change of म into व (मत् = वत्) is considered asiddha for the purposes of this rule.

ईवत्याः ॥ २२१ ॥ पदानि ॥ ईवत्याः, (उदात्तः) ॥

वृत्तिः ॥ ईवतीशब्दान्तस्यान्त उदात्तो भवति स्त्रियां संज्ञायां विषये।

221. The Names ending in ईवती have the acute on the last syllable.

Thus अहीवती, कृषीवती, मुनीवती ॥

चौ ॥ २२२ ॥ पदानि ॥ चौ ॥

वृत्तिः ॥ चाविस्यञ्चतिर्लुप्तनकारो गृह्यते। तस्मिन्परतः पूर्वस्यान्त उदात्तो भवति।

वार्तिकम् ॥ चावतद्धितइति वक्तव्यम् ॥

222. In compound words ending in अञ्च्, the final vowel of the preceding word has the acute accent in the weak cases in which only च् of अञ्च् remains.

Thus दधीचः पश्य; दधीचा, दधीचे: मधूचः पश्य, मधूचा, मधूचे ॥ This is an exception to VI. 1. 161, 170 and VI. 2. 52.

Vârt:—This rule does not apply before a Taddhita affix. As दाधीचः. माधूचः ॥ Here the accent is regulated by the affix (III. 1. 3).

समासस्य ॥ २२३ ॥ पदानि ॥ समासस्य, (उदात्तः) ॥

वृत्तिः ॥ समासस्यान्त उदात्तो भवति।

223. A compound word has the acute on the last syllable.

Thus राजपुरुषः ब्राह्मणकम्बलः, कन्याखनः, पटहशब्दः, नदीघोषः, राजदृषत्, ब्राह्मणसमित् ॥ The consonants being held to be non-existent for the purposes of accent, the udâtta will fall on the vowel though it may not be final, the final being a consonant. The exceptions to this rule will be mentioned in the next chapter.

ओ३म् ।

षष्ठाध्यायस्य द्वितीयः पादः ।

BOOK SIXTH.

CHAPTER SECOND.

बहुव्रीहौ प्रकृत्या पूर्वपदम् ॥ १ ॥ पदानि ॥ बहुव्रीहौ, प्रकृत्या, पूर्वपदम् ॥

वृत्तिः ॥ पूर्वपदग्रहणमत्र पूर्वपदस्थे स्वरे उदात्ते स्वरिते वा वर्त्तते । बहुव्रीहौ समासे पूर्वपदस्य यः स्वरः स प्रकृत्या भवति, स्वभावेनावतिष्ठते, न विकारमनुदात्तत्वमापद्यते ॥

I. In a Bahuvrîhi, the first member preserves its own original accent.

The word पूर्वपद means here the accent—whether udâtta or swarita—which is in the first member: प्रकृत्या means, retains its own nature, does not become modified into an anudâtta accent. By the rule VI. 1. 223, the final of a compound gets the accent, so that all the preceding members lose their accent and become anudâtta, as in one word all syllables are unaccented except one. VI. 1. 158. Thus the first member of a Bahuvrîhi would have lost its accent and become anudâtta; with the present sûtra commences the exceptions to the rule that the final of a compound is always udâtta. Thus कार्ष्णोत्तरासङ्गाः ॥ The word कार्ष्ण is derived by the Taddhita affix अण् (IV. 3. 154) from कृष्ण 'a kind of antelope;' and has the ञित् accent (VI. 1. 197) i. e. on the first syllable: which the word preserves in the compound also. So also यूपवलजः; the word यूप is derived from यु by the Uṇâdi affix प (Uṇ III. 27), before which the vowel becomes lengthened (Uṇ III. 25) and the affix is treated as नित् (Un III. 26), and hence the word is acutely accented on the first syllable (VI. 1. 197). So also ब्रह्मचारिपरिस्कन्दः; the word ब्रह्मचारिन् has a Kṛit-formed word as its second part, and gets the acute on the final (VI. 2. 139). So also स्नातकपुत्रः, the word स्नातक is derived by कन् (V. 4. 29) affix and has नित् accent (VI. 1. 197) i. e. udâtta on the first syllable. So also अध्यापकपुत्रः, the word अध्यापक is accented on the middle as it is formed by वुञ् लित् affix (III. 1. 133, VI. 1. 193). श्रोत्रियपुत्रः, the श्रोत्रिय being enounced with an indicatory न् in Sûtra V. 2. 84 is acutely accented on the first. मनुष्यनाथः, the word मनुष्य being formed by यत् (IV. 1. 161) a तित् affix is svarita (VI. 1. 185),

The words udâtta and svarita are understood in this aphorism. Therefore if *all* the syllables of the pûrvapada are anudâtta, the present rule has no scope there, and such a compound will get udâtta on the final by the universal rule enunciated in VI. 1. 223. Thus समभागः, here सम being *all* anudâtta, the accent falls on ग ॥

तत्पुरुषे तुल्यार्थतृतीयासप्तम्युपमानाव्ययद्वितीयाकृत्याः ॥ २ ॥ पदानि ॥ तत्पुरुषे, तुल्यार्थ, तृतीया, सप्तमी, उपमान, अव्यय, द्वितीया, कृत्याः ॥

वृत्तिः ॥ तत्पुरुषे समासे तुल्यार्थं तृतीयान्तं सप्तम्यन्तमुपमानवाचि अव्ययं द्वितीयान्तं कृत्यान्तं च यत्पूर्वपदं तत्प्रकृतिस्वरं भवति ॥

वार्त्तिकम् ॥ अव्यये नञ्कुनिपातानामिति वक्तव्यम् ॥

2. In a Tatpurusha, the first member preserves its original accent, when it is a word (1) meaning "a resemblance", or (2) an Instrumental or (3) a Locative or (4) a word with which the second member is compared, (5) or an Indeclinable, or (6) an Accusative, or (7) a Future Passive Participle.

Thus (1) तुल्यश्वेतः, तुल्यलोहित, तुल्यमहान्, सदृक्श्वेतः, सदृग्लोहितः, सदृङ्महान् ॥ These are Karmadhâraya compounds formed under II. 1. 68: and तुल्य being formed by यत् is acutely accented on the first (VI. 1. 216). The word सदृश् is formed by क्विन् (III. 2. 60 Vârt), and has acute on the final (VI. 1. 197 and VI. 2. 139). So also सदृशश्वेतः सदृशलोहितः, सदृशमहान् ॥ The word सदृश is formed by कञ् added to दृश्, and by VI. I. 197 the accent falls on दृ (VI. 2. 139). (2) When the first member is in the Instrumental case, as:—शङ्कुलया खण्डः = शंकुलाखण्डः, so also किरिकाणः (II. 1. 30) शंकुला is derived from शंकु+ला ॥ To the root ला is added the affix क with the force of घञ्, and thus the noun ला is udâtta: or the whole word शंकुला is a word formed by क affix and hence VI. 1. 165 applies and is final-acute. किरिः is formed by the Uṇâdi affix इ to कॄ (Uṇ IV. 143), and it being treated as a कित् (Uṇ. IV. 142) has udâtta on the final.

(3) When the first member is a word in the Locative case, as:—अक्षेषु शौण्डः = अक्षशौण्डः, so also पानशौण्डः ॥ The word अक्ष is formed by the affix स added to अश् (Uṇ III. 65), and is final acute (III. 1. 3). The word पान is formed by ल्युट् affix added to पा, and is acute on the first (VI. 1. 193) owing to the लित् accent. (4) When the first member is a word with which the second member is compared, as:—शस्त्रीश्यामा, कुमुदश्येनी, हंसगद्गदा, न्यग्रोधपरिमण्डला, दूर्वाकाण्डश्यामा, शरकाण्डगौरी ॥ These compounds are formed by II. 1. 55. शस्त्री is formed by ङीष् and is final-acute; कुमुद is formed by क affix (कौ मोदते = कुमुद) see III. 2. 5. Vârt: and is acutely accented on the first, or by Phit sûtra II. 3 it has acute on the first. हंस is formed by the Uṇâdi affix स added to हन्

(Uṇ III. 62), and is finally accented (III. 1. 3). न्यग्रोहति = न्यग्रोधः formed by अच् (III. 1. 134), and ह is irregularly changed into ध as Pânini himself uses this form (VII. 3. 5): and it is accented in the middle. The words दूर्वाकाण्ड, शरकाण्ड are Genitive Tatpurusha, and their second member has accent on the first syllable (VI. 2. 135). (5) When the first member is an Indeclinable, as, अब्राह्मणः, अवृषलः, कुब्राह्मणः, कुवृषलः ॥ निष्कौशाम्बिः, निर्वाराणसिः, अतिखट्वः, अतिमालः ॥ All these Indeclinable compounds have udâtta on the first. they are formed by II. 2. 5 &c.

Vârt:—In cases of Indeclinable compounds. the rule applies only to those which are formed by the negative Particle अ, by कु, and by Particles (nipâta). Though नञ् is one of the Nipâtas, its separate mention indicates that नञ्-accent debars even the subsequent कृत्-accent as अकरणिः ॥ Therefore, it does not apply here स्नात्वाकालकः which has acute on the final and belongs to Mayuravyṅsakâdi class.

(6) When the first member as in the accusative case, as:—मुहूर्तसुखम्, मुहूर्तरमणीयम्, सर्वरात्रकल्याणी, सर्वरात्रशोभना ॥ They are formed by II. 1. 29. मुहूर्त belongs to पृषोदरादि class and is acutely accented on the last. सर्वरात्र is formed by the samâsanta affix अच and is finally accented.

(7) When the first member is a Kritya-formed word, as, भोज्यलवणम्, भोज्योष्णम्, पानीयशीतम्, हरणीयचूर्णम् (II. 1. 68). भोज्य is formed by ण्यत् and has svarita on the final: पानीय and हरणाय are formed by अनीयर् and are accented on the penultimate (VI. 1. 185 and 217) i. e. on ई ॥

वर्णोवर्णेष्वनेते ॥ ३ ॥ पदानि ॥ वर्णः, वर्णेषु, अनेते ॥

वृत्तिः ॥ प्रकृत्या पूर्वपदं, तत्पुरुषइति च वर्तते। वर्णे वर्णवाचि पूर्वपदं वर्णवाचिष्वेवोत्तरपदेषु एतशब्दवर्जितेषु परतस्तत्पुरुषे समासे प्रकृतिस्वरं भवति ॥

3. The first member of a Tatpurusha preserves its original accent, when a word denoting color is compounded with another color denoting word, but not when it is the word एत ॥

Thus कृष्णसारङ्गी, लोहितसारङ्गी, कृष्णकल्माषः, लोहितकल्माषः ॥ कृष्ण is formed by नक affix (Uṇ. III. 4) and has acute on the final (III. 1. 3). लोहित is formed by the affix तन् added to रुह् (Uṇ. III. 94) and has accent on the first (VI. 1. 197).

Why do we say 'color-denoting word'? Observe परमकृष्णः (VI. 1. 223). Why do we say 'with another color denoting word'? Observe कृष्णतिलाः (VI. 1. 223). Why do we say 'but not when it is एत'? Observe कृष्णैतः, लोहितैतः ॥ The compounding takes place by II. 1. 69.

गाधलवणयोः प्रमाणे ॥ ४ ॥ पदानि ॥ गाध, लवणयोः, प्रमाणे ॥

वृत्तिः ॥ प्रमाणवाचिनि तत्पुरुषे समासे गाध लवण इत्येतयोरुत्तरपदयोः पूर्वपदं प्रकृतिस्वरं भवति ॥

4. The first member of a Tatpurusha preserves its original accent, when the second term is गाध or लवण, and the compound expresses a 'measure or mass'.

Thus शाम्बगाधमुदकम्, अरित्रगाधमुदकम् 'water as low or fordable as a Śamba or an Aritra i. e. of the depth of an oar or a pestle'. गोलवणम्, अश्वलवणम् 'so much salt as may be given to a cow or a horse'. These are Genitive Tatpurusha compounds. शाम्ब is formed by adding वन् to शम् (Uṇ. IV. 94), and has acute on the first (VI. 1. 197). अरित्र is formed by the affix इत्र added to ऋ (III. 2. 184), and has acute on the middle (III. 1. 3): गो is formed by डो (Uṇ II. 68) and has acute on the final ओ; अश्व is formed by क्वन् affix added to अश् (Uṇ. I. 151), and has acute on the first (VI. 1. 197). The word प्रमाण here denotes 'quantity', 'measure', 'mass', 'limit', and not merely the length. The power of denoting measure by these words is here indicated by and is dependent upon accent.

When not denoting प्रमाण we have परमगाधम् and परमलवणम् ॥

दायाद्यं दायादे ॥ ५ ॥ पदानि ॥ दायाद्यम्, दायादे ॥

वृत्तिः ॥ तत्पुरुषे समासे दायादशब्दउत्तरपदे दायाद्यवाचि पूर्वपदं प्रकृतिस्वरं भवति ॥

5. In a Tatpurusha compound, having the word दायाद as its second member, the first member denoting inheritance preserves its original accent.

Thus विद्यादायादः, धनदायादः ॥ The word विद्या is formed by the affix क्यप् (III. 3. 99) which is udâtta (III. 3. 96). The word धन is derived by adding क्यु to धाञ् (Uṇ. II. 81). Though the Uṇâdi Sûtra II. 81 ordains क्यु after the root धा preceded by नि, yet by बहुल (III. 3. 1) rule it comes after धा also when it is not preceded by नि and धन has acute on the first (III. 1. 3).

In the forms विद्यादायादः &c, what Genitive case has been taken? If it is the Genitive case which the word दायाद requires by Rule II. 3. 39, then by the Vârtika प्रतिपदविधाना च षष्ठी न समस्यते (II. 2. 10 Vart), there can be no compounding. The Genitive case there is the ordinary Genitive case of II. 3. 50. i. e. a शैषिक Genitive case, and not a प्रतिपद Genitive. If it is a शेषलक्षण Genitive case, then why the other Geintive case is taught in II. 3. 39 with regard to दायाद &c. That sûtra only indicates the existence of the Locative case in the *alternative*, and does not pervent the Genitive. In fact, had merely Locative been ordianed in that sûtra, this particular case would have prevented the Genitive on the maxim that a particular rule debars the general. But the employment of both terms Genitive and Locative in that sûtra indicates the *alternative* nature of the rule and shows that the Genitive case so taught is not a प्रतिपद Genitive, but a general Genitive. In short the Genitive taught in II.

3. 39, is not an apûrva-vidhi, the words naturally would have taken Genitive; the taking of the Locative is the only new thing taught there.

Why do we say 'when meaning inheritance'? Observe परमदायादः (VI. 1. 223) taking the final acute of a compound.

प्रतिबन्धि चिरकृच्छ्रयोः ॥ ६ ॥ पदानि ॥ प्रतिबन्धि, चिर, कृच्छ्रयोः ॥

वृत्तिः ॥ तत्पुरुषे समासे चिरकृच्छ्रयोरुत्तरपदयोः प्रतिबन्धिवाचि पूर्वपदं प्रकृतिस्वरं भवति ॥

6. In a Tatpurusha compound, having the words चिर or कृच्छ्र as its second member, the first member, when it denotes that which experiences an obstacle, preserves its original accent.

Thus गमनचिरम्, गमनकृच्छ्रम्, व्याहरणचिरम् or व्याहरणकृच्छ्रम् ॥ The words गमन and व्याहरण are formed by ल्युट् affix, and have लित् accent (VI. 1. 193). This compound belongs either to the class of Mayûra-vyaṅsakâdi (II. 1. 72), or of an attribute and the thing qualified. When *going* to a place is *delayed* owing to some defective arrangement or cause, or becomes *difficult*, there is produced an *obstacle* or hinderance, and is called गमनचिरं or गमनकृच्छ्रं ॥ Why do we say 'which experiences a hinderance'? Observe मूत्रकृच्छ्रम् ॥

पदे ऽपदेशे ॥ ७ ॥ पदानि ॥ पदे, अपदेशे ॥

वृत्तिः ॥ अपदेशो व्याजस्तद्वाचिनि तत्पुरुषे समासे पदशब्दउत्तरपदे पूर्वपदं प्रकृतिस्वरं भवति ॥

7. In a Tatpurusha compound the first member preserves its original accent, when the second member is the word पद denoting 'a pretext'.

The word अपदेश means 'a pretext', 'a contrivance'. Thus मूत्रपदेन प्रस्थितः, उच्चारपदेन प्रस्थितः ॥ Gone on pretext of voiding urine or excreta.

The word मूत्र is derived by adding the affix ष्ट्रन् to the root मुच्, the ऊ being substituted for उच् of मुच्, (Uṇ. IV. 163), and has acute on the first (VI. 1. 197) or it may be a word formed by घञ् to the root मूत्रयति ॥ The word उच्चार is also formed by घञ् and by VI. 2. 144 has acute on the final. The compounding takes place by II. 1. 72 or it is an attributive compound.

Why do we say "when meaning a pretext?" Observe विष्णोः पदम्=विष्णुपदम् ॥

निवाते वातत्राणे ॥ ८ ॥ पदानि ॥ निवाते, वात-त्राणे ॥

वृत्तिः ॥ निवातशब्दउत्तरपदे वातत्राणवाचिनि तत्पुरुषे समासे पूर्वं पदं प्रकृतिस्वरं भवति ॥

8. In a Tatpurusha compound, the first member preserves its original accent, when the second member is the word निवात in the sense of 'a protection from wind'.

Thus कुट्याः निवात = कुटीनिवातम् 'a hut as the only shelter from the wind'. So also शमीनिवातम्, कुड्यनिवातम् or कुड्यनिवातम् ॥ The word निवात is an Avyayîbhâva compound = वातस्य अभावः (II. 1. 6): or a Bahuvrîhi = निरुद्धो वातोऽस्मिन् ॥ The words कुटीनिवातम् &c, are examples of compounds of two words in apposition. कुटी and शमी are formed by ङीष् (IV. 1. 41) and have acute on the last (III. 1. 3). Some say that कुड्य is derived from कु by adding यत् with the augment डुक् and treating it as कित्, is has the acute on the first; others hold that it is derived by the affix ड्यक् to कु and the affix has the accent.

Why do we say when meaning 'a shelter from wind'? Observe राज-निवाते वसति, सुखं मातृनिवाते = 'he lives under the shelter of the king'; 'pleasant is the shelter or the protection of the mother'. Here निवात = पार्श्वः or vicinity.

शारदे ऽनार्तवे ॥ ९ ॥ पदानि ॥ शारदे, अनार्त्तवे ॥

वृत्तिः ॥ ऋतौ भवमार्तवम्। अनार्तववाचिनि शारदशब्दउत्तरपदे तत्पुरुषे समासे पूर्वपदं प्रकृतिस्वरं भवति ॥

9. In a Tatpurusha compound the first member preserves its original accent, when the second member is the word शारद, having any other sense than that of 'autumnal'.

The word आर्तव means appertaining to season (ऋतु) i. e. when the word शारद does not refer to the season of शरत् or autumn. Thus रज्जुशारदमुदकम् 'fresh drawn water'. So also दर्षत् शारदाः सक्तवः 'the saktu flour fresh from the mill'. The word शारद means here 'fresh' 'new': and it forms an invariable compound. The word रज्जु is formed by उ affix added to सृज् (Uṇ. I. 15), the स being elided. The affix उ is treated as नित् (Uṇ. I. 9) and the accent falls on the first syllable (VI. 1. 197). The word दर्षत् is formed by the augment ष and shortening of the vowel of the root दृ 'to tear' (दृणाति), and the affix अदिक् (Uṇ. I. 131) and has accent on the final (III. 1. 3).

Why do we say 'when not meaning autumnal'? Observe परमशारदम्, उत्तमशारदम् 'the best autumnal grass &c'. (VI. 1. 223).

अध्वर्युकषाययोर्जातौ ॥ १० ॥ पदानि ॥ अध्वर्यु, कषाययोः, जातौ ॥

वृत्तिः ॥ अध्वर्युकषाय इत्येतयोर्जातिवाचिनि तत्पुरुषे समासे पूर्वपदं प्रकृतिस्वरं भवति ॥

10. In a Tatpurusha compound denoting a genus, the first member preserves its original accent, when the second member is the word अध्वर्यु or कषाय ॥

Thus प्राच्याध्वर्युः, कठाध्वर्युः, कालापाध्वर्युः ॥ These are Appositional compounds denoting 'genus or kind', with a fixed meaning. प्राच्य is formed by यत्, and has accent on the first (VI, 1. 213). कठ is derived by अच् affix (III. 1. 34), and to it is added the Taddhita affix णिनि (IV. 3. 104), in the sense of कठेन प्रोक्तं (IV. 3. 101), and the affix is then elided by IV. 3. 107. The word कालाप comes from कलापिन् + अण् (IV. 3. 108) in the sense of कलापिना प्रोक्तं (IV. 3.

101), and it would have preserved its form without change before this affix (VI. 4. 164) but for a vârtika which declares that the इन् of कलापिन् will be elided (See VI. 1. 144 vart). Thus कालॅाप gets accent on the final (III. 1. 3). So also सर्पिर्मण्डकषायम्, उमापुष्पकषायम्, शैवारिककषायम् ॥ These are Genitive compounds. The words सर्पिमण्ड and उमापुष्प are Genitive compounds and have accent on the final (VI. 1. 223). The word शैवारिक is formed by ठक् affix added to शार and has acute on the final (VI. 1. 165). Why do we say when meaning a 'genus'? Observe, परमाध्वर्युः, परमकषायः (VI. 1. 223).

सदृशप्रतिरूपयोः सादृश्ये ॥ ११ ॥ पदानि ॥ सदृश, प्रतिरूपयोः, सादृश्ये ॥

वृत्तिः ॥ सदृश प्रतिरूप इत्येतयोरुत्तरपदयोः सादृश्यवाचिनि तत्पुरुषे समासे पूर्वपदं प्रकृतिस्वरं भवति ॥

11. In a Tatpurusha compound expressing resemblance with some one or something, the first member preserves its original accent, when the second member is सदृश or प्रतिरूप ॥

Thus पितृसदृशः, मातृसदृशः ॥ The words पितृ and मातृ are formed by Uṇâdi affix तृच् (Un. II. 95) and are finally accented. By II. 1. 31, सदृश forms Instrumental Tatpurusha. That case, however, is governed by VI. 2. 2, which provides for Instrumental compounds. The examples here given are of Genitive Tatpurusha: and it applies to cases where the case-ending is not elided. As दास्याः सदृशो, वृषल्याः सदृशः ॥ Here दासी and वृषली are finally acute, and the case-affix gets the accent when semivowel is substituted (VI. 1. 174). So also पितृप्रतिरूपः, मातृप्रतिरूपः ॥ Why do we say 'when meaning resemblance'? Observe परमसदृशः, उत्तमसदृशः (VI, 1. 223): here the sense of the compound is that of 'honor' and not 'resemblance'.

द्विगौ प्रमाणे ॥ १२ ॥ पदानि ॥ द्विगौ, प्रमाणे ॥

वृत्तिः ॥ द्विगावुत्तरपदे प्रमाणवाचिनि तत्पुरुषे समासे पूर्वपदं प्रकृतिस्वरं भवति ॥

12. In a Tatpurusha compound denoting 'measure or quantity', the first member preserves its original accent, when the second member is a Dvigu.

Thus प्राच्यसप्तसमः and गान्धारिसप्तसमः ॥ The word सप्तसमः = सप्तसमाः प्रमाणमस्य, the affix मात्रच् denoting 'measure' (V. 2. 37) is elided (See V. 2. 37 Vart) प्राच्यश्चासौ सप्तसमश्च = प्राच्यसप्तसमः "an Eastern seven-years old". So also गान्धारिसप्तसमः or °षट्समः ॥ प्राच्य has acute on the first; while गान्धारि is either accented on the first or on the middle; as it belongs to the Kardamâdi class (Phit III. 10). Why do we say 'before a Dvigu'? Observe व्रीहिप्रस्थः ॥ Why do we say 'when denoting measure?' Observe परमसप्तसमः ॥

गन्तव्यपण्यं वाणिजे ॥ १३ ॥ पदानि ॥ गन्तव्य, पण्यम्, वाणिजे ॥

वृत्तिः ॥ वाणिजशब्दउत्तरपदे तत्पुरुषे समासे गन्तव्यवाचि पण्यवाचि च पूर्वपदं प्रकृतिस्वरं भवति ॥

13. Before the word वाणिज 'a trader', the first member of a Tatpurusha preserves its accent, when it is a word specifying the place whither one has to go, or the ware in which one deals.

Thus मद्रवाणिजः, काश्मीरवाणिजः, गान्धारिवाणिजः = मद्रादिषु गत्वा व्यवहरन्ति 'the Madra-merchants i. e. who trade by going to Madra &c' All these are Locative compounds. मद्र is derived by रक affix (Uṇ II, 13) and is acutely accented on the last (VI. 1. 165). काश्मार belongs to Kṛshodarâdi class (VI. 3. 109), and has acute either on the first or the second syllable. The word गान्धारि belongs to the Kardamâdi class, and is consequently acute on the first or the second (Phit III. 10) In the sense of पण्य we have: गोवाणिजः 'a dealer in cows', अश्ववाणिजः &c. गो is finally accented (Un II. 67): and अश्व has acute on the first (Un I. 151) the affix being क्वन् ॥

Why do we say 'the place whither one goes, or the goods in which one deals?' Observe परमवाणिजः, उत्तमवणिजः ॥

मात्रोपज्ञोपक्रमच्छाये नपुंसके ॥ १४ ॥ पदानि ॥ मात्रा, उपज्ञा, उपक्रम, छाये, नपुंसके ॥

वृत्तिः ॥ मात्रा उपज्ञा उपक्रम छाया एतेषूत्तरपदेषु नपुंसकवाचिनि तत्पुरुषे समासे पूर्वपदं प्रकृतिस्वरं भवति ॥

14. The first member of a Tatpurusha preserves its accent before the words मात्रा, उपज्ञा, उपक्रम and छाया when these words appear as neuter.

Thus भिक्षामात्रं न ददाति याचितः, समुद्रमात्रं न सरोऽस्ति किंचन ॥ The word मात्रा is here synonymous with तुल्य, the phrase being = भिक्षायास्तुल्यप्रमाणं, and is a Genitive compound. The word भिक्षा is derived from भिक्ष, by the feminine affix अ (III. 3. 103), and has acute on the final (III. 1. 3). The word समुद्र has also acute on the final as it is a word denoting 'a sea', (Phiṭ sûtra I. 2). So also with उपज्ञा, as पाणिनोपज्ञमकालकं व्याकरणम् ; व्याड्युपज्ञं दुष्करणम् आपिशल्युपज्ञ गुरुलाघव (see II. 4. 21). All these are Genitive compounds. The word पाणिन is derived by अण् affix from पणिन् (पणिनोऽपत्यम् = पाणिनः), and has acute on the final, (III. 1. 3). The word व्याडि being formed by इञ् affix has acute on the first (VI 1. 197), so also आपिशलि ॥ So also with उपक्रम, as आढ्योपक्रमं प्रासादः, दर्शनीयोपक्रमम्, सुकुमारोपक्रमम्, नन्दोपक्रमाणि मानानि ॥ All these are Genitive compounds. The word आढ्य (तत्रैनं ध्यायन्ति) is derived from आ+ध्यै+क affix added with the force of घञ्, the ध being changed to ढ the word belonging to पृषोदरादि class (VI. 3. 109), and it has acute on the final by VI. 2. 144. The word दर्शनीय is formed by अनीयर् and has acute on the penultimate नी owing to the indicatory र् (VI. 1. 217). The word सुकुमार has acute on the final by VI. 2. 172. The word नन्द is formed by अच् (III. 1. 134). The Tatpurusha compounds ending in उपज्ञा and उपक्रम are neuter by II. 4. 21. So also with छाया, as इषुच्छायम्,

धैनुश्छायम् ॥ The word इषु is derived from इष् by उ affix (Un I. 13), and it being treated as नित् (Un I. 9) the acute falls on इ the first syllable (VI. 1. 197). The word धनुस् has also acute on the first by Phiṭ sûtra II. 3. The compound is a Genitive Tatpurusha—इषूणां छाया ; and it is Neuter by II. 4. 22. When the compound is not a Neuter we have कुड्यछाया (II. 4. 25).

सुखप्रिययोर्हिते ॥ १५ ॥ पदानि ॥ सुख, प्रिययोः, हिते ॥

वृत्तिः ॥ सुख प्रिय इत्येतयोरुत्तरपदयोर्हितवाचिनि तत्पुरुषे समासे पूर्वपदं प्रकृतिस्वरं भवति ॥

15. The first member of a Tatpurusha preserves its accent, when the second term is सुख or प्रिय, and the sense is 'to feel delight, or is good'.

Thus गैमनसुखम् 'the pleasure of going'. So also वैचनसुखम्, व्याहैरणसुखम्, गैमनप्रियम्, वैचनप्रियम्, व्याहैरणप्रियम् ॥ These are appositional compounds. All the above words are formed by ल्युट् affix and have acute on the syllable preceding the affix (VI. 1. 193). The words sukha and priya have the sense of हित or 'well *good* 'beneficial', i. e. when the thing denoted by the first term is the cause of pleasure or delght. When this is not the sense we have परमसुखैम्, परमप्रियैम् ॥

प्रीतौ च ॥ १६ ॥ पदानि ॥ प्रीतौ, च ॥

वृत्तिः ॥ प्रीतौ गम्यमानायां सुख प्रिय इत्येतयोरुत्तरपदयोस्तत्पुरुषे समासे पूर्वपदं प्रकृतिस्वरं भवति ॥

16. The first member of a Tatpurusha preserves its accent, the second term being सुख or प्रिय, in the sense of "agreeable to one, or desired".

Thus ब्राह्मणैसुखं पायसं "the sweetmilk desired by or agreeable to the Brâhmanas", छात्रैप्रियोऽनध्यायः ॥ कन्याप्रियो मृदङ्गः ॥ &c. The words ब्राह्मण and छात्र have acute on the final being formed by the affixes अण् and ण (V. 4. 62) respectively (III. 1. 3) and कन्या has svarita on the final. When not meaning agreeable to or desired, we have राजसुखैम्, राजप्रियैम् ॥

स्वं स्वामिनि ॥ १७ ॥ पदानि ॥ स्वम्, स्वामिति ॥

वृत्तिः ॥ स्वामिशब्दउत्तरपदे तत्पुरुषे समासे स्ववाचि पूर्वपदं प्रकृतिस्वरं भवति ॥

17. In a Tatpurusha compound, having the word स्वामिन् as its second member, the first term, when it denotes the thing possessed, retains its original accent.

Thus गैस्वामी, अैश्वस्वामी, धैनस्वामी ॥ The accents of गो, अश्व and धन have already been mentioned before in VI. 2. 14.. When the first member is not a word denoting possession, we have परमस्वामी ॥

पत्यावैश्वर्ये ॥ १८ ॥ पदानि ॥ पत्यौ, ऐश्वर्ये ॥

वृत्तिः ॥ पतिशब्दउत्तरपदे ऐश्वर्यवाचिनि तत्पुरुषे पूर्वपदं प्रकृतिस्वर भवति ॥

18. In a Tatpurusha ending in पति when it means 'master' or lord', the first member preserves its original accent.

Thus गृहपति:, सेनापतिः, नरपतिः, धान्यपतिः ॥ The word गृह is formed by क (III. 1. 144) and has acute on the final (III. 1. 3). The word सेना is a Bahuvrihi (सह इनेन वर्त्तते = सेना), and by VI. 2. 1 the first member retains its accent. The word नर is derived from नृ 'to lead' by the affix अप् (III. 3. 57) and has acute on the first (III. 1. 4), the word धान्य has svarita on the final (See Phit II. 23 ?) Why do we say when meaning 'lord'? Observe ब्राह्मणो वृषलीपतिः "a Brahmana, husband of a Sûdrâ".

न भू वाक्चिद्दिधिषु ॥ १९ ॥ पदानि ॥ न, भू, वाक्, चित्, दिधिषु ॥

वृत्तिः ॥ पतिशब्दउत्तरपदे ऐश्वर्यवाचिनि तत्पुरुषे समासे भू वाक् चित् दिधिषू इत्येतानि पूर्वपदानि प्रकृतिस्वराणि न भवन्ति ॥

19. The words भू, वाक्, चित् and दिधिषू, however, do not preserve their original accent in a Tatpurusha when coming before the word पति denoting 'lord'.

This debars the accent taught by the last aphorism. Thus भूपतिः, वाक्पतिः, चित्पतिः, दिधिषूपतिः ॥ All these are Genitive compounds and are finally accented by VI. 1. 223.

वा भुवनम् ॥ २० ॥ पदानि ॥ वा, भुवनम् ॥

वृत्तिः ॥ पतिशब्दउत्तरपदे ऐश्वर्यवाचिनि तत्पुरुषे समासे भुवनशब्दः पूर्वपदं वा प्रकृतिस्वरं भवति ॥

20. The word भुवन may optionally keep its accent in a Tatpurusha, before पति denoting 'lord'.

Thus भुवनपतिः or भुवनपतिः ॥ The word भुवन is formed by क्युन् (Uṇ. II. 80), and has acute on the first (VI. 1. 197). Though Sûtra II. 80 (Unadi) ordains क्युन् after भू in the Vedas only, yet on the theory of बहुल (III. 1. 3), it comes in the secular literature also, as भुवनपतिरादित्यः ॥

आशङ्काबाधनेदीयस्सु संभावने ॥ २१ ॥ पदानि ॥ आशङ्क, आ बाध, नेदीयस्सु, संभावने ॥

वृत्तिः ॥ प्रकृत्या पूर्वपदं तत्पुरुषइति वर्त्तते । आशङ्क आबाध नेदीयस् इत्येतेषूत्तरपदेषु संभावनवाचिनि तत्पुरुषे समासे पूर्वपदं प्रकृतिस्वरं भवति ॥

21. Before आशङ्क, आबाध and नेदीयस्, the first member in a Tatpurusha compound preserves its original accent, when it treats about a supposition.

The word संभावनम् = अस्तित्वाध्यवसायः "the hesitation about the existence of a thing'. Thus गमनाशङ्कं वर्त्तते 'one fears the journey'; so also वचनाशङ्कं, व्याहरणाशङ्कं, &c. Similarly गमनाबाधम् वर्तते = गमनं बाध्यते इति संभाव्यते "it has stepped in as an obstacle to journey". So also वैघनाबाधम्, व्याहैरणाबाधम् ॥ Similarly गैमननेदीयो वर्तते, वैघननेदीयः व्याहैरणनेदीयः = गमनमिति निकटतरमिति संभाव्यते "the journey stands directly before".

Why do we say when a supposition is meant? Observe परमनेदीयः ॥ All the above words are formed by ल्युट् affix and have लित् accent. (VI. 1. 193).

पूर्वे भूतपूर्वे ॥ २२ ॥ पदानि ॥ पूर्वे, भूतपूर्वे ॥

वृत्तिः ॥ पूर्वशब्दउत्तरपदे भूतपूर्ववाचिनि तत्पुरुषे समासे पूर्वपदं प्रकृतिस्वरं भवति ॥

22. The first member of a Tatpurusha compound preserves its original accent when the word पूर्व is the second member, and the sense is "this had been lately——".

Thus आढ्यो भुतपूर्वः = आढ्यपूर्वः "formely had been rich". The compound must be analysed in the above way. The compounding takes place by II. 1. 57 or it belongs to Mayura-vyaṅsakâdi class. So also दर्शनीयपूर्वः, सुकुमारपूर्वः ॥

Why do we say when meaning 'had been lately'. Observe परमपूर्वः, उत्तमपूर्वः, which should be analysed as परमश्चासौ पूर्वश्चेति ॥ If it is analysed as परमो भूतपूर्वः then it becomes an example under the rule and not a counter-example. In order therefore, to make this rule applicable we must know the sense of the compound.

सविधसनीडसमर्यादसवेशसदेशेषु सामीप्ये ॥ २३ ॥ पदानि ॥ सविध, सनीड, समर्याद, सवेश, सदेशेषु, सामीप्ये ॥

वृत्तिः ॥ सविध सनीड समर्याद सवेश इत्येतेषूत्तरपदेषु सामीप्यवाचिनि तत्पुरुषे समासे पूर्वपदं प्रकृतिस्वरं भवति ॥

23. The first member of a Tatpurusha compound preserves its original accent, when the second member is सविध, सनीड, समर्याद, सवेश, and सदेश in the sense of "what can be found in the vicinity thereof".

Thus मद्रसविधम्, गान्धारिसविधम्, काश्मीरसविधम् ॥ So also मद्रसनीडम्, मद्रसमर्यादम्, मद्रसवेशम् and मद्रसदेशम् So also with गान्धारि and काश्मीर ॥ The accents of these words have been taught before in Sûtra VI. 2. 12, 13. The words सविध &c, are derived from सह विधया &c, but they all mean 'in the vicinity': मद्रसविधं = मद्राणां सामिप्यम् ॥ Why do we say when meaning in the vicinity thereof? Observe सह मर्यादया वर्तते = समर्यादं क्षेत्रम् 'a field having boundary'. देवदत्तस्य समर्यादं = देवदत्तसमर्यादम् "the bounded field of D'. Why do we say सविध &c? Observe देवदत्तसमर्या ॥

विस्पष्टादीनि गुणवचनेषु ॥ २४ ॥ पदानि ॥ विस्पष्ट, आदीनि-गुणवचनेषु ॥

वृत्तिः ॥ विस्पष्टादीनि पूर्वपदानि गुणवचनेषूत्तरपदेषु प्रकृतिस्वराणि भवन्ति ॥

24. The words विस्पष्ट &c preserve their accent when followed by an Adjective word in a compound,

Thus वि॑स्पष्ट कटुकम्, वि॑चित्रकटुकम् व्य॑क्तकटुकम्, वि॑स्पष्टलवणम्, विचित्रलवणम्, व्यक्त-लवणम् ॥ The compounding takes place by II. 1. 4, and it should be analysed thus विस्पष्टं कटुकम् &c.

The words विस्पष्ट &c, are indeed here adjectives, and in conjunction with कटु &c, they denote an object possessing those qualities ; and therefore not being in apposition, the compound is not a Karmadhâraya.

The word विस्पष्ट has acute on the first by VI. 2. 49. The word विचित्र is also acute on the first as it gets the accent of the Indeclinable. Some read the word as वि॑चित्तः, which being a Bahuvṛîhi has also first acute. The word व्य॑क्त has svarita on the first by VIII. 2. 4. The remaining words of this class are संपन्नँ, पटु or कटु, पण्डितँ, कुशलँ, चपलँ and निपुणँ. Of these, the word संपन्नँ has acute on the final by VI. 2. 144; पटु is formed by उ (Uṇ I. 18), which being considered as नित् (Uṇ I. 9), it has acute on the first. पण्डित is formed by क्त to the root पडि, and is finally acute (VI. 2. 144). कुशल has accent on the final being formed by a kṛit affix (कुशान् लाति = कुशलः, ला आदाने, or Uṇ I. 106), चपल being formed by a चित् affix (Uṇ I. 111), has acute on the final (VI. 1. 163), for चित् is understood in the Uṇadi sûtra Uṇ. I. 111 from sûtra Uṇ. I. 106. The word निपुण has acute on the final by VI. 2. 144, being formed by क affix added to पुण &c.

Why do we say 'of विस्पष्ट &c' Observe परमलवणँम् उत्तमलवणँम्, both having acute on the final. Why do we say "when followed by a word expressing a quality"? Observe विस्पष्टब्राह्मणः ॥

श्रज्यावमकन्पापवत्सु भावे कर्मधारये ॥ २५ ॥ पदानि ॥ श्र, ज्य, अवम, कन्, पापवत्सु, भावे, कर्मधारये ॥

वृत्तिः ॥ श्र ज्य अवम कन् इत्येतेषु पापशब्दवति चोत्तरपदे कर्मधारये समासे भाववाचि पूर्वपदं प्रकृतिस्वरं भवति ॥

25. In a Karmadhâraya compound, the first member consisting of a Verbal noun (भाव), preserves its original accent before adjective forms built from श्र (V. 3. 60), ज्य (V. 3. 61) अवम and कन् (V. 3. 64), and before a form built from the word पाप ॥

Thus ग॑मनश्रेष्ठम्, or ग॑मनश्रेयः, व॑चनज्येष्ठम् or वचनज्यायः; ग॑मनावमम्, व॑चनावमम्, ग॑मनकनिष्ठम् or गमनकनीयः ॥ So also ग॑मनपापिष्ठम्, ग॑मनपापीयः ॥ All the first members are ल्युट् formed words and have लित् accent i. e. on the first syllable. (VI. 1. 193). The words श्र, ज्य and कन् are substitutes which certain adjectives take in the comparative and superlative degree, and the employment of these forms in the sûtra indicates that the comparative and superlative words having these elements should be taken as second members, and so also of पाप, the comparative and superlative are taken, for this is the meaning here of the word पापवत् ॥

Why do we say "भ्र &c" ? Observe गमनशोभनम् ॥ Why do we say 'a verbal Noun'? Observe गमनश्रेयः, where the word गमन is = गम्यते ऽनेन 'a carraige'. Why do we say 'a Karmadhâraya compound'? Observe गमनं श्रेयः = गमनश्रेयः ॥

कुमारश्च ॥ २६ ॥ पदानि ॥ कुमारः, च ॥

वृत्तिः ॥ कुमारशब्दः पूर्वपदं कर्मधारये समासे प्रकृतिस्वरं भवति ॥

26. The word कुमार preserves its original accent when standing as a first member in a Karmadhâraya compound.

Thus कुमारकुलटा, कुमारश्रमणा, कुमारतापसी ॥ The word कुमार has acute on the final as it is derived from the root कुमार क्रीडायाम् with the affix अच् of पचादि ॥ By II. 1. 70, it is ordained that कुमार is compounded with श्रमण &c. Some commentators hold that the word कुमार must be followed by श्रमण &c. (II. 1. 70) to make this rule applicable. They refer to the maxim लक्षणप्रतिपदोक्तयोः प्रतिपदोक्तस्यैव ग्रहणम् "whenever a term is employed which might denote both something original and also something else resulting from a rule of grammar, or when a term is employed in a rule which might denote both something formed by another rule in which the same individual term has been employed, and also something else formed by a general rule, such a term should be taken to denote, in the former case, only that which is original, and in the latter case, only that which is formed by that rule in which the same individual term has been employed." Other Grammarians, however do not make any such limitation, but apply the rule to all Karmadhâraya compounds of कुमार ॥

आदिः प्रत्येनसि ॥ २७ ॥ पदानि ॥ आदिः, प्रत्येनसि ॥

वृत्तिः ॥ कर्मधारयइति वर्त्तते । प्रतिगत एनसा प्रतिगतमेनो वा यस्य सः प्रत्येनाः । तस्मिन्नुत्तरपदे कर्मधारस्यादिरुदात्तो भवति ॥

27. In a Karmadhârya compound of Kumâra followed by प्रत्येनस्, the acute falls on the first syllable of Kumâra.

The word प्रत्येनस् = प्रतिगत एनसा or प्रतिगतमेनो यस्य ॥ Thus कुमारप्रत्येनाः ॥ The word udâtta is required to be read into the sûtra to complete the sense: for the construction of the sûtra requires it, and the anuvritti of the 'first member preserves its accent' would be inappropriate because the word आदि is employed here.

पूगेष्वन्यतरस्याम् ॥ २८ ॥ पदानि ॥ पूगेषु, अन्यतरस्याम् ॥

वृत्तिः ॥ पूगा गणास्तद्वाचिन्युत्तरपदे कर्मधारये समासे कुमारस्यान्यतरस्यामादिरुदात्तो भवति ॥

28. The first syllable of Kumâra is acute optionally, when the second member is a word denoting 'the name of a horde'.

The word घृग means 'a multitude, a collection &c'. See V. 3. 112 also. Thus कुँमारघातकाः or कुमारँघातका (VI. 2. 26), or कुमारघातकाँः ॥ So also कुँमारलोहध्वजाः or कुमारँलोहध्वजाः or कुमारलोहध्वजाँः ॥ So also with कुँमारँवलाहकाः, कुँमारँ-जीमूतकाः ॥ Here घातक &c, are horde-names; and the affix ञ्य is added to them by V. 3. 112: which is elided in the Plural by II. 4. 62. In the above examples when the word 'Kumâra' is not accented on the first syllable, it gets accent on the last by VI. 2. 26, when the प्रतिपदोक्त maxim is not applied: when that maxim is applied, the final of the compound takes the accent by the general rule VI. 1. 223.

इगन्तकालकपालभगालशरावेषु द्विगौ ॥ २९ ॥ पदानि ॥ इगन्त, काल, कपाल, भगाल, शरावेषु, द्विगौ ॥

वृत्तिः ॥ इगन्तउत्तरपदे कालवाचिनि कपाल भगाल शराव इत्येतेषु च द्विगौ समासे पूर्वपदं प्रकृतिस्वरं भवति ॥

29. In a Dvigu compound, the first member preserves its original accent, before a stem ending in a simple vowel, with the exception of अ (इक्), before a word denoting time, as well as before कपाल, भगाल and शराव ॥

Thus पँञ्चारत्निः, दँशारत्निः ॥ The above are examples of Taddhitârtha Dvigu (II. 1. 52), equal to पंचारत्नयः प्रमाणमस्य, the प्रमाण denoting-affix मात्रच् is always elided in Dvigu (V. 2. 3 Vârt). So also पँञ्चमास्यः, दँशमास्यः = पञ्च मासान् भृतो भूतो भावी वा. This is also a Taddhitârtha Dvigu (II. 1. 52), formed by the affix यप् (V. 1. 80—82). So also पँञ्चवर्षः दँशवर्षः the affix ठञ् being elided (V. 1. 88). So also पँञ्चकपालः, दँशकपालः, पँञ्चभगालः, दँशभगालः, पँञ्चशरावः, दँशशरावः ॥ These are also Taddhitartha Dvigu formed by IV. 2. 16 the affix अण् being elided by IV. 1. 88.

Why do we say "before an इगन्त stem &c"? Observe पंचभिरश्वैः क्रीतः = पञ्चाश्वैः, दशाश्वैः ॥ Why do we say "in a Dvigu Compound?" Observe परमारत्निः, परमशरावँम् ॥

When these Dvigu compounds, by case-modifications do not end in इक् vowel, but the vowel is replaced by a semi vowel or Guṇa, the rule will still apply. Thus पुँञ्चारत्न्यः or पँञ्चारत्नयः ॥ This is done on the strength of the maxim असिद्धं बहिरङ्गमन्तरङ्गे. "That which is bahiranga is regarded as not having taken effect or as not existing, when that which is antaranga is to take effect:" because the substitution of semivowel or guṇa is a bahiranga operation in relation to accent. Or the substitutes may be considered as sthânivat to the short-vowel which they replace.

बह्वन्यतरस्याम् ॥ ३० ॥ पदानि ॥ बहु, अन्यतरस्याम् ॥

वृत्तिः ॥ बहुशब्दः पूर्वपदमिगन्तादिषूत्तरपदेषु द्विगौ समासे ऽन्यतरस्यां प्रकृतिस्वरं भवति ॥

30. In a Dvigu compound, the word बहु may optionally preserve its accent when followed by an ik-ending stem, or by a time-word, or by kapâla, bhagâla and śarâva.

This allows option where the last rule required the accent necessarily. Thus बहुरत्निः or बहुरत्निः, बहुमास्यः or बहुमास्यः, बहुकपालः or बहुकपालः, बहुभगालः or बहुभगालः, बहुशरावः or बहुशरावः ॥ The word बहु has acute on the final being formed by the affix कु (Uṇ I. 29). When the उ is changed to व्, as in the first example, the anudatta अ is changed into svarita by VIII. 2. 4 : when the first member preserves its acccent. In the other alternative, the accent falls on the last syllable.

दिष्टिवितस्त्योश्च ॥ ३१ ॥ पदानि ॥ दिष्टि, वितस्त्योः, च ॥

वृत्तिः ॥ दिष्टि वितस्ति इत्येतयोरुत्तरपदयोर्द्विगौ समासे पूर्वपदमन्यतरस्यां प्रकृतिस्वरं भवति ॥

31. In a Dvigu compound, the first member may optionally preserve its accent, when followed by the words दिष्टि and वितस्ति as second members.

Thus पञ्चदिष्टिः or पञ्चदिष्टिः, पञ्चवितस्तिः or पञ्चवितस्तिः ॥ The affix मात्रच् is elided after the प्रमाण denoting words dishṭi and vitasti (V. 2. 37).

सप्तमी सिद्धशुष्कपक्वबन्धेष्वकालात् ॥ ३२ ॥ पदानि ॥ सप्तमी, सिद्ध, शुष्क, पक्व, बन्धेषु, अकालात् ॥

वृत्तिः ॥ सप्तम्यन्तं पूर्वपदं सिद्ध शुष्क पक्व बन्ध इत्येतेषूत्तरपदेषुप्रकृतिस्वरं भवति सा चेत्सप्तमी कालान्न भवति ॥

32. A locative-ending word when it does not denote time, preserves its original accent, when followed by सिद्ध, शुष्क, पक्व and बन्ध in a compound.

Thus सांकाश्यसिद्धः or सांकाश्यसिद्धः, काम्पिल्यसिद्धः or काम्पिल्यसिद्धः ॥ The words sâṁkâśya and kâmpilya have acute on the final, and by Phiṭ Sûtra (III. 16) in the alternative the accent falls on the middle also. So also निधनशुष्कः, ऊकशुष्कः ॥ The word निधन is derived by क्यु affix added to नि-धाञ् and has acute on the middle; the word ऊक is formed from अव् root by the affix कक्, and has acute on the final. So also भ्राष्ट्रपक्वः, कुम्भीपक्वः, कलशीपक्वः ॥ The words Kumbhî and Kalaśî are formed by ङीष् affix and have acute on the final; the word भ्राष्ट्र is formed by ष्ट्रन् affix, and has acute on the beginning. So also चक्रबन्धः चारकबन्धः ॥ The word chakra has acute on the final, and châraka being formed by ण्वुल् has acute on the first.

Why do we say 'when not denoting time'? Observe पूर्वाह्णसिद्धः, अपराह्णसिद्धः ॥ The compounding takes place by II. 1. 41. The accent of the Locative Tatpurusha taught in VI. 2. 1 was debarrd by Kṛit-accent taught VI. 2. 144. The present sûtra debars this last rule regarding Kṛit accent, and re-ordains the Locative Tatpurusha accent when the Kṛit-words are सिद्ध &c.

परिप्रत्युपापा वर्ज्यमानाहोरात्रावयवेषु ॥ ३३ ॥ पदानि ॥ परि,प्राति, उप, अपाः, वर्ज्यमान, अहोरात्रावयवेषु ॥

वृत्तिः ॥ परि प्रति उप अप इत्येते पूर्वपदभूता वर्ज्यमानवाचिनि अहोरात्रावयव वाचिनि रात्र्यवयववाचिनि चोत्तरपदे प्रकृतिस्वरा भवन्ति ।

33. The particles परि, प्रति, उप and अप preserve their accent before that word, which specifies an exclusion, or a portion of day and night, (in an Avyayîbhâva compound also).

Thus परित्रिगर्त्तं वृष्टो देवः "It rained all round (but not in) Trigarta". (See II. 1. 11 and 12). So also परिसौवीरम् परिसार्वसनि, परिपूर्वरात्रम ॥ So also प्रतिपूर्वाह्णम, प्रत्यपराह्णम, प्रत्यपररात्रम, उपपूर्वाह्णम, उपापराह्णम, उपपूर्वरात्रम, उपापररात्रम् ॥ अपत्रिगर्तं वृष्टो देवः, अपसौवीरम्, अपसार्वसेनी (II. 1. 11 and 12).

By Phiṭ Sûtras IV. 12, and 13 all Particles (Nipâta) have acute on the first syllable. So also upasargas with the exception of अभि ॥ Therefore परि &c, have acute on the first. In a Tatpurusha and Bahuvrîhi compounds, these words 'pari', 'prati' &c, as first members would have retained their accent by the rules already gone before; the present sûtra, therefore, extends the principle of the preservation of the accent to Avyayibhâva compounds also. The prepositions अप and परि alone denote the limit exclusive or वर्जन, and it is therefore with these two prepositions only that the second member can denote the thing excluded, and not with प्रति and उप ॥ With these prepositions अप and परि, the second term if denoting a member of day or night, are also taken even as *excluded*, therefore no separate illustrations of those are given.

Why do we say 'before a word which is excluded, or is a part of a day and night'? Observe प्रत्यग्नि शलभाः पतन्ति ॥ In प्रतिवनम् "all round the forest, but not in it', the accent falls on the last by VI. 2. 178, which debars this general rule, as well as all special rules which might affect वन in a compound.

राजन्यबहुवचनद्वन्द्वेऽन्धकवृष्णिषु ॥ ३४ ॥ पदानि ॥ राजन्य, बहु वचन, द्वन्द्वे, अन्धक, वृष्णिषु, (पूर्वपदप्रकृतस्वरम्)

वृत्तिः ॥ राजन्यवाचिनां बहुवचनान्तानां यो द्वन्द्वो ऽन्धकवृष्णिषु वर्त्तते तत्र पूर्वपदं प्रकृतिस्वरं भवति ।

34. The first member of a Dvandva compound, formed of names denoting the Kshatriya (warrior) clans in

the plural number, retains its original accent when the warrior belongs to the clan of Andhaka or Vṛishṇi.

Thus श्वाफल्कचैत्रकाः, चैत्रकरोधकाः, शिनिवासुदेवाः ॥ The words Śvâphalka and Chaitraka are formed by अण् affix (IV. 1. 114) and have acute on the last (III. 1. 3). The word शिनि has acute on the first syllable, and does not change in denoting Patronymic. Why do we say 'in denoting a Warrior clan'? Observe द्वैप्यहैमायनाः ॥ Here द्वैप्य is derived from द्वीप by the affix यञ् (IV. 3. 10) = द्वीपे भवाः; हैमायनः = हैमेरपत्यं युवा ॥ These names belong to Andhaka and Vṛishṇi clans, but are not the warrior-names. The word राजन्य here means those Kshatriyas who belong to the family of annointed kings and warriors (अभिषिक्तवंश्याः); these (Dvaipya and Haimâyana) do not belong to any such family. Why do we say 'in the Plural number'? Observe संकर्षणवासुदेवौ ॥ Why do we say 'in a Dvandva compound'? Observe वृष्णीनां कुमाराः = वृष्णिकुमाराः ॥ Why do we say 'of Andhaka and Vṛishni clans'? Observe कुरुपञ्चालाः ॥

संख्या ॥ ३५ ॥ पदानि ॥ संख्या ॥

वृत्तिः ॥ द्वन्द्वसमासे संख्यावाचि पूर्वपदं प्रकृतिस्वरं भवति ।

35. The Numeral word, standing as the first member of a Dvandva compound, preserves its accent.

Thus एकादश, द्वादश, त्रयोदश or त्रयोदश ॥ The word एक is derived from इण् by कन् affix (Uṇ III. 43) and has acute on the first (VI. 1. 197). The त्रयस् is the substitute of त्रि (VI. 3. 48) and has acute on the final.

आचार्योपसर्जनश्चान्तेवासी ॥ ३६ ॥ पदानि । आचार्य्योपसर्जनः, च, अन्तेवासी, (प्रकृतिस्वरम्)

वृत्तिः ॥ आचार्योपसर्जनान्तेवासिनां यो द्वन्द्वस्तत्रपूर्वपदं प्रकृतिस्वरं भवति ।

36. When words denoting scholars are named after their teachers and are compounded into a Dvandva, the first member retains its accent.

The word अन्तेवासी means 'a pupil' 'a boarding not a day scholar'. When the scholar is named by an epithet derived from the name of his teacher, that name is आचार्योपसर्जनः or teacher-derived name. Thus आपिशलपाणिनीयाः, पाणिनीय-रौढीयाः, रौढीयकाशकृत्स्नाः ॥ The son of Apiśala is आपिशलि the name of a Teacher or founder of a school—an âchârya: formed by इञ् affix (IV. 1. 95). The science taught by him is called आपिशलम्, formed by adding अण् affix to आपिशलाः (IV. 3. 101 and IV. 2. 11). The scholars who study the Apiśalam are also called आपिशलाः the affix denoting 'to study' is elided by (IV. 2. 59 and 64). Or the pupils of Apiśali will be also called Apiśalâḥ. Thus in both ways Apiśalâḥ is a scholar name derived from the name of a teacher. The word आचार्योपसर्जन qualifies the whole Dvandva compound and not the first member only. That is, the whole compound in all its parts should denote scholars, whose names are derived from those of their teachers. Therefore not here पाणिनीय-देवदत्तौ where though the first is a teacher-derived name, the second is not. Why do we say "names derived from the teacher's"? Observe छान्दसवैयाकरणाः ॥ Why do we say "a Scholar"? Observe आपिशलपाणिनीये शास्त्रे ॥

कार्तकौजपादयश्च ॥ ३७ ॥ पदानि ॥ कार्त्तकौजप, आद्यः, च ॥

वृत्तिः ॥ कार्तकौजपादयो ये द्वन्द्वास्तेषु पूर्वपदं प्रकृतिस्वरं भवति ।

37. Also in the Dvandvas कार्तकौजप &c, the first members retain their accent.

Those words of this list which end in a dual or plural affix have been so exhibited for the sake of distinctness. The following is a list of these words. 1. कार्त-कौजपौ (formed by अण् IV. 1. 114 in the sense of Patronymic, from कृत and कुजप these being Rishi names) ॥ 2. सावर्णिमाण्डूकेयौ (sâvarni is formed by इञ् Patron. affix and माण्डूकेय by ढक् IV. 1. 119). 3. आवन्त्यश्मकाः The word Avanti is end-acute, to which is added thePatron affix ñyaṅ by IV. 1. 171, which being a Tadrâj is elided in the plural; अवन्तीनां निवासो जनपद = अवन्ति the quadruple significant अण् being elided.

4. पैलश्यापर्णेयाः (Paila is derived from Pilâ the son of Pîlâ is Paila, the yuvan descendent of Paila will be formed by adding फिञ् IV. 1. 156, which is, however, elided by II. 4. 59.) The word Śyâparna belongs to Bidâdi class IV. 1. 104, the female descendant will be Śyâparnî, the yuvan descendant of her will be Śyâparneya. It is not necessary that the compound should be plural always We have पैलश्यापर्णेयौ also.

5. कपिश्यापर्णेयाः (Kapi has acute on the final. The son of Kapi will be formed by यञ् IV. 1. 107, which is however elided by II. 4. 64. This compound must, therefore, be always in the plural.

6. शैतिकाक्षपांचालेयाः (Śitikâksha is the name of a Rishi, his son will be Śaitikâksha by अण्, IV. 1. 114, the yuvan descendant of the latter will be formed by इञ् which is elided by II. 4. 58. Pâñchâla's female descendant is Pâñchâlî, her yuvan descendant is Pâñchâleya. The plural number here is not compulsory. We have शैतकाक्षपाञ्चालेयौ also.)

7. कटुकवार्धलेयाः or कटुकवार्चलेयाः (The son of Kaṭuka will be formed by इञ् IV. 1. 59, which is elided in the Plural by II. 4. 66. The son of Varchalâ is Vârchaleya).

8. शाकलशुनकाः (The son of Śakala is Śâkalya, his pupils are Śâkalâḥ by अण् IV. 2. 111. The son of Śunak will be Śaunaka by अञ् IV. 1. 104, which will be elided in the Plural by II. 4. 64). Some read it as शकलसणकाः, where the इञ affix after Saṇaka is elided by II. 4. 66. So also शुनकधात्रेयः ॥

9. शणकबाभ्रवाः (the son of Babhru is Bâbhrava). 10. आर्चाभिमौद्गलाः (Archâvinaḥ are those who study the work produced by Ṛichâva, the affix

णिनि being added by IV. 3. 104. Mudgala belongs to Kaṅvâdi class IV. 2. 111 ; Maudgalâḥ are pupils of the son of Mudgala). 11. कुन्तिसुराष्ट्राः. This a Dvandva of Kunti and Surâshṭra in the plural or of the country-names derived from them like Avanti. Kunti and Chinti have acute on the final. 12. चिन्तिसुराष्ट्राः as the last. 13. तण्डवतण्डाः (Both belong to Pachâdi class formed by अच् III. 1. 134, from तडि ताडने Bhvâdi 300, वतण्ड is formed from the same root with the prefix अव, the अ being elided, and both have acute on the final: and are enumerated in the Gargâdi list IV. 1. 105. In the plural the patronymic affix यञ् is elided by II. 4. 64. 14. गर्गवत्साः Here also यञ् affix is elided II. 4. 64. 15. अविमत्तकामविधाः or °विद्धाः ॥ Avimatta has acute on the first being formed by the नञ् particle. Both the words lose इञ् patronymic by II. 4. 66.

16. बाभ्रवशालङ्कायनाः The son of Babhru is Bâbhrava, and the son of Śalaṅku or Śalaṅka of नडादि IV. 1. 99 is Śâlaṅkâyana.

17. बाभ्रवदानच्युताः Dânchyuta takes इञ् in the patronymic which is elided by II. 4. 66.

18. कठकालापाः, Kaṭhâḥ are those who read the work of Kaṭha, the affix णिनि (IV. 3. 104) being elided by IV. 3. 107. Those who study the work of Kalâpin are Kâlâpâḥ, the अण् being added by IV. 3. 108, which required the इन् of kalâpin to be retained by VI. 4. 164 but by a Vârtika under VI. 4. 144 the इन् portion is elided before अण् II

19. कठकौथुमाः Those who study the work of Kuthumin are कौथुमाः formed by अण् IV. 1. 83 the इन् being elided before अण् by VI. 4. 144 Vârt already referred to above.

20. कौथुमलौकाक्षाः Those who study the work of Lokâksha are Laukâkshâḥ. Or the son of Lokâksha is Laukâkshi, the pupils of latter are Laukâkshâḥ.

21. स्त्रीकुमारम् ॥ Strî has accent on the final.

22. मौदपैप्पलादाः, the son of Muda is Maudi, the pupils of latter are Maudâḥ. So also Paippalâdâḥ.

23. मौदपैप्पलादाः The double reading of this word indicates that Rule VI. 1. 223 also applies.

24. वत्सजरत् or वत्सजरन्तः = वत्स + जरत् ॥ Vatsa has acute on the final.

25. So also सौश्रुतपार्थवाः, The pupils of Suśruta and Pṛithu are so called they take अण् IV. 1. 83. 26. जरामृत्यू, 27. याज्यानुवाक्ये Yâjya is formed by ण्यत्, added to यज्, the ज् is not changed to a Guttural by VII. 3. 66. It has svarita on the final by तित् accent (VI. 1. 185). Anuvâkya is derived from anu + vach + ण्यत्.॥

महान् व्रीह्यपराह्णगृष्टीष्वासजाबालभारभारतहैलिहिलरौरवप्रवृद्धेषु ॥ ३८ ॥ पदानि ॥ महान्, व्रीहि, अपराह्ण, गृष्टि, इष्वास, जाबाल, भार, भारत, हैलिहिल, रौरव, प्रवृद्धेषु, (प्रकृतिस्वरम्) ॥

वृत्तिः ॥ प्रकृत्या पूर्वपदमिति वर्त्तते, द्वन्द्वइति निवृत्तम् । महानित्येतत्पूर्वपदं व्रीहि अपराह्ण, गृष्टि इष्वास जाबाल भार भारत हैलिहिल रौरव प्रवृद्ध इत्येतेषूत्तरपदेषु प्रकृतिस्वरं भवति ।

38. The word महत् (महा) retains its accent before the following : व्रीहि, अपराह्ण, गृष्टि, इष्वास, जाबाल, भार, भारत, हैलिहिल, रौरव' and प्रवृद्ध ॥

Thus महाव्रीहिः, महापराह्णः, महागृष्टिः, महेष्वासः, महाजाबालः, महाभारः, महाभारतः, महाहैलिहलः, महारौरवः, महाप्रवृद्धः ॥ The महत् has acute on the final. (Uṇ II. 84) On the पतिपदोक्त maxim already mentioned under VI. 2. 26, this accent will apply to that compound of महत् which it forms under rule II. 1. 61, for that is the particular rule of Karmadhâraya compounding relating to mahat (pratipadokta). This rule therefore, will not apply to Genitive Tatpurusha. Thus महतो व्रीहिः = महद्व्रीहिः which has accent on the final by VI. 1. 223.

Q. The word प्रवृद्ध is a Participle formed by क्त affix, and by rule VI. 2. 46, in a Karmadhâraya compound, the first member will retain its original accent. What is then the necessity of reading this word in this sûtra? Ans. That sûtra VI. 2 46 applies, cn the maxim of pradipadokta, to the special participles and nouns mentioned in II. 1. 59 and not to every participle and noun.

क्षुल्लकश्च वैश्वदेवे ॥ ३९ ॥ पदानि ॥ क्षुल्लकः, च, वैश्वदेवे ॥

वृत्तिः ॥ क्षुल्लक इत्येतत्पूर्वपदं महांश्च वैश्वदेवउत्तरपदे प्रकृतिस्वरं भवति ।

39. The words mahat and kshullaka retain their accent before the word Vaiśvadeva.

Thus महावैश्वदेवम्, and क्षुल्लकवैश्वदेवम् ॥ The word kshullaka is derived thus क्षुधं लाति = क्षुल्लः to which the Diminutive क (V. 3. 73 &c) is added : and the word has udâtta on the final.

उष्ट्रः सादिवाम्योः ॥ ४० ॥ पदानि ॥ उष्ट्रः, सादि, वाम्योः ॥

वृत्तिः ॥ उष्ट्रशब्दः पूर्वपदं सादिवाम्योरुत्तरपदयोःप्रकृतिस्वरं भवति ॥

40. The word 'ushṭra' retains its accent before 'sâdi' and 'vâmi'.

Thus उष्ट्रसादि and उष्ट्रवामि ॥ The word उष्ट्र is derived from उष् by ष्ट्रन् affix (Uṇ IV. 162) and has acute on the first (VI. 1. 197). This is either a Karmadhâraya or a Genitive compound. In some texts the above examples are given with a visarga in the masculine, and not Neuter.

गौः सादसादिसारथिषु ॥ ४१ ॥ पदानि ॥ गौः, साद, सादि, सारथिषु, प्रकृति स्वरम् ॥

वृत्तिः ॥ गोशब्दः पूर्वपदं साद सादि सारथि इत्येतेषूत्तरपदेषु प्रकृतिस्वरं भवति ॥

41. The word 'गो' retains its accent before 'sâda', 'sâdi', and 'sârathi'.

Thus गो:साद: or गां सादयति = गोॅसाद:, गो: सादि: = गो सॅादि:, and गोॅसारथि: ॥ साद is formed from सद् with the affix घञ् and forms a Genitive compound (गो: साद:). Or from the causative verb सादयति, we get गोसाद: by adding अण् (III. 9. 1) गोसादी is formed by णिनि from the same causative root. The Kṛit-accent is debarred in the case of साद and सादिन्, the Samâsa-accent VI. 1. 223 in the case of सारथि ॥

कुरुगार्हपतरिक्तगुर्वसूतजरत्यश्लीलदृढरूपा पारेवडवा तैतिलकद्रूः पण्यकम्बलो दासीभाराणां च ॥ ४२ ॥ पदानि ॥ कुरुगार्हपत, रिक्तगुरु, असूतजरती, अश्लीलदृढरूपा, पारेवडवा, तैतिलकद्रूः, पण्यकम्बलः, दासीभाराणाम्, च, प्रकृतिस्वरम् ॥

वृत्तिः ॥ कुरुगार्हपत रिक्तगुरु असूतजरती अश्लीलदृढरूपा पारेवडवा तैतिलकद्रू पण्यकम्बल इत्येते समासास्तेषां दासीभारादीनां च पूर्वपदप्रकृतिस्वरं भवति ॥

वार्त्तिकम् ॥ कुरुवृज्योर्गार्हपतइति वक्तव्यम् ॥ वा० ॥ संज्ञायामिति वक्तव्यम् ॥

42. The first member retains its accent in the following :—'Kuru-gârhapata', 'Rikta-guru', 'Asûta-jaratî', 'Aślîla-dṛiḍha-rûpâ', 'Pâre-vaḍabâ', 'Taitila-kadrûḥ', 'Paṇya-kambalaḥ' and 'Dâsî-bhâra &c'.

The first seven words are compounds, the first two of these are exhibited without any case-ending, the renaining five are in nom. Singular. Thus कुॅरुगार्हपतम् (कुरूणां गार्हपत, Kuru is formed by कु affix added to कृ Uṇ I. 24,) and has acute on the final.

Vârt:—So also वॅृजिगार्हपतम्, the word Vṛiji has acute accent on the first.

So also रिक्तो गुरुः = रिॅक्तगुरुः or रिक्तॅगुरुः for rikta has acute either on the first or on the second (VI. 1. 208). So also असूता जरती = अॅसूतजरती, अश्लीलादृढरूपा = अॅश्लील दृढरूपा ॥ Asûtâ and aslîlâ being formed by नञ् particle have acute on the first: (VI. 2. 2). That which has श्री is called श्लील, the affix लच् being added by its belonging to Sidhmâdi class, and र changed to ल by its belonging to kapilakâdi class. So also पारेॅवडवा, this is = पारेवडवेव ॥ This is a samâsa with the force of इव, and there is elision of the case ending. The word पार belongs to Ghṛitâdi class, and has acute on the final. तैतिलानां कद्रूः = तैतिलॅकद्रूः, the son or pupil of Titilin is Taitila formed by अण् affix. पण्यकम्बलः, panya ends in यत् and has acute on the first (VI. 1. 213).

Vârt:—पॅण्यकम्बलः has acute on the first only when it is a name. Otherwise in पणितव्ये कम्बले compound, the accent will be on the final by the general rule VI. 1. 223. The word पण्य being frrmed by यत् affix (III. 1. 101) is acutely accented on the first (VI. 1. 213). The word पण्यकम्बलः is as Name when it means the market-blanket i. e. a blanket of a well known determinate size and fixed price, which is generally kept for sale by the blanket-sellers. But when the compound means a saleable blanket, it takes the samasa accent (VI. 1. 223). If it be objected what is the use this Vartika, for the word पण्य being formed by a kritya affix, will retain its accent in the Tatpurusha, by VI. 2. 2, we reply that the कृत्य used in VI. 2. 2 relates to pratipadokta kritya compounds such as ordained by कृत्यतुल्याख्या अजात्या II. 1. 68, while here the compound is by विशेषणं विशेष्येण II. 1. 51 and is a general compound. So also दास्याभारः = दासीभारः II The words belonging to Dâsi bhârâdi class are all those Tatpurusha compound words, not governed by any of the rules of accent, in which it is desired that the first member should retain its accent. Some of them are देवहूतिः, देवसूतिः, देववीतिः, वसुनीतिः ॥ Vasu has acute on the first being formed by a नित् affix Un I. 9 10). ओषधिः = ओषोधीयतेऽस्याम्, formed by कि affix (III. 3. 93), ओष being formed by घञ् has acute on the first (VI. 1. 197). चन्द्रमाः is formed by असि affix added to the root माङ् माने preceded by the upapada चन्द्र as, चन्द्र + मा + अस् = चन्द्रमस्, the affix being treated as ङित् (Uṇ IV. 228), and चन्द्र is formed by रक affix (Uṇ II. 13) and has acute on the final.

चतुर्थी तदर्थे ॥ ४३ ॥ पदानि ॥ चतुर्थी, तदर्थे, प्रकृतिस्वरम् ॥

वृत्तिः ॥ चतुर्थ्यन्तं पूर्वपदं तदर्थउत्तरपदे तदभिधेयार्थे यत्तद्वाचिन्युत्तरपदे प्रकृतिस्वरं भवति । तदिति चतुर्थ्यन्तस्यार्थः परामृश्यते ।

43. A word in the Dative case as the first member retains its accent, when the second member expresses that which is suited to become the former.

Thus यूपदारु, कुण्डलहिरण्यम् II The word यूप has accent on the first syllable, as it is formed by प (Uṇ III. 27) treated as a नित् (Uṇ III. 26). The word कुण्डल is formed by कल affix which is treated as चित् (Uṇ. I. 108) and has acute on the final. So also रथदारु, वल्लीहिरण्यम् ॥ Ratha is first-acute formed by kthan affix (Uṇ II. 2). Vallî has acute on the final formed by ङीष् affix. (IV. 1. 41) Why do we say 'it being suited to the first'? Observe कुबेरबलिः II This accent applies when the second member denoting the material is modified into the first by workmanship. The composition takes place by II. 1. 36.

अर्थे ॥ ४४ ॥ पदानि ॥ अर्थे, प्रकृतिस्वरम् ॥

वृत्तिः ॥ चतुर्थीति वर्तते । अर्थशब्दउत्तरपदे चतुर्थ्यन्तं पूर्वपदं प्रकृतिस्वरं भवति ।

44. Before the word 'artha', the first member in the Dative retains its accent.

Thus मात्रे इदं = मात्रर्थम्, देवतार्थम्, अतिथ्यर्थम् ॥ The words मातृ and पितृ are finally acute as taught so in Uṇâdi sûtra (Uṇ II. 95): देवता being formed by a लित् affix (V. 4. 27) has acute on the middle ; अतिथि is formed by इथिन् affix and has acute on the first.

The difference between तदर्थ and अर्थ is that the former, like दारु 'wood', हिरण्य 'gold', has not inherent in it the sense of adaptibility, while अर्थ means 'adapted'. Some say that the making of two sûtras, one with तदर्थ and the other with अर्थ indicates, that the former rule is applicable only to that compound where the material itself is changed into the substance of the first. Therefore the rule does not apply to अश्वघासः, श्वश्रूसुरम् &c, though 'grass be suited for the horse' &c.

क्तेच ॥ ४५ ॥ पदानि ॥ क्ते, च, प्रकृतिस्वरम् ॥

वृत्तिः ॥ क्तान्ते चोत्तरपदे चतुर्थ्यन्तं पूर्वपदं प्रकृतिस्वरं भवति ।

45. The first member in the Dative case retains its accent before a Past Participle in क्त ॥

Thus गोहितम्, मनुष्यहितम्, अश्वहितम्, गोरक्षितम्, अश्वरक्षितम्, तापसरक्षितम् वनम् ॥ The compounding takes place by II. 1. 36. The compound गोरक्षितं means गोभ्योरक्षितं and is a sampradana Dative.

कर्मधारयेऽनिष्ठा ॥ ४६ ॥ पदानि ॥ कर्मधारये, अनिष्ठा, प्रकृतिस्वरम् ॥

वृत्तिः ॥ कर्मधारये समासे क्तान्तउत्तरपदे ऽनिष्ठान्तं पूर्वपदं प्रकृतिस्वरं भवति ॥

46. Before a Past Participle in 'kta', the first member, when it itself is not a Past Participle, retains its original accent in a Karmadhâraya compound.

This rule is confined to the Past Participles and the Nouns specifically mentioned in II. 1. 59; on the maxim of pratipadokta &c. Thus श्रेणिकृताः, पूगकृताः, ऊककृताः, निधनकृताः ॥ The word श्रेणि has acute on the first as it is formed by the affix णि which is considered नित् (Uṇ IV. 51). The word पूग is end-acute as it is formed by the affix गक् (Uṇ I. 124). The word ऊक is also end-acute (VI. 2. 32). The word निधन has acute on the middle. Why do we say in a Karmadhâraya compound? Observe श्रेण्या कृतं = श्रेणिकृतम् ॥ Why do we say 'when it is a non-nishṭhâ word?' Observe कृताकृतम् ॥ Here the compounding is by II. 1. 60.

अहीने द्वितीया ॥ ४७ ॥ पदानि ॥ अहीने, द्वितीया ॥

वृत्तिः ॥ अहीनवाचिनि समासे क्तान्तउत्तरपदे द्वितीयान्तं पूर्वपदं प्रकृतिस्वरं भवति ॥

वार्त्तिकम् ॥ द्वितीयानुपसर्गइति वक्तव्यम् ॥

47. Before a Past Participle in 'kta', a word ending in the Accusative case retains its accent, when it does not mean a separation.

Thus कष्टश्रितः, त्रिशकलपतितः, ग्रामगतः ॥ Kashṭa has acute on the end, triśakala is a Bahuvrihi compound (triṇi śakalâni asya), and consequently acute on the first: grâma has acute on the first as it is formed by the नित् affix

मन् added to ग्रस्, the final being replaced by आ (Uṇ I. 143) ॥ Why do we say 'when not meaning separation'? Observe कान्तारातीतः, योजनातीतः, because one has taken himself beyond kântâra and yojana.

Vârt:—This rule does not apply when the Past Participle has an upasarga attached; as सुखप्राप्तः, दुःखप्राप्तः सुखापन्नः, दुःखापन्नः (VI. 4. 144). This is an exception to rule VI. 2. 144.

तृतीया कर्मणि ॥ ४८ ॥ पदानि ॥ तृतीया, कर्मणि, (पूर्वपदप्रकृतिस्वरम्) ॥

वृत्तिः ॥ कर्मवाचिनि क्तान्तउत्तरपदे तृतीयान्तं पूर्वपदं प्रकृतिस्वरं भवति ॥

48. A word ending in an Instrumental case retains its accent before the Past Participle in 'kta', when it has a Passive meaning.

Thus अहिहतः or अहि हतः रुद्रहतः, वज्रहतः, महाराजहतः, नखनिर्भिन्ना, दात्रलूना ॥ The word 'ahi' is derived from हन् with the proposition आ which is shortened, and the affix इण् (Uṇ IV. 138), and has acute on the final, according to others the acute is on the first: Rudra is formed by रक् affix (Uṇ II. 22) added to the causative रोदि; Mahârâja is formed by the Samâsanta affix टच्; nakha is formed by ख affix added to नह् (Uṇ V. 23) or it may be a Bahuvrihi नास्य खमस्ति = नखः, formed by अच् (V. 4. 121), and has acute on the final: Dâtra is formed by ष्ट्रन् (III. 2. 182). Why do we say when having a Passive signification? Observe रथेन यातः = रथयातः, the 'kta' is added to a verb of motion with an Active significance.

गतिरनन्तरः ॥ ४९ ॥ पदानि ॥ गति, अनन्तरः (प्रकृतिस्वरम्) ॥

वृत्तिः ॥ क्ते कर्मणीति वर्त्तते । कर्मवाचिनि क्तान्तउत्तरपदे गतिरनन्तरः पूर्वपदं प्रकृतिस्वरं भवति ॥

49. A word called Gati (I. 4. 60) when standing immediately before a Participle in 'kta' having a Passive significance, retains its accent.

Thus प्रकृतः, प्रहृतः ॥ Here one of the following rules would have applied otherwise, namely, either (1) the Samasa end-acute IV. 1. 223 (2) or the Indeclinable first member to retain its accent VI. 2. 2, (3) or the end acute by VI. 2. 139 and 144. The present sûtra debars all these. Why do we say 'immediately?' Observe अभ्युद्धतः, समुद्धृतः, समुदाहृतः ॥ Where the distant Gati words अभि and सम् do not preserve their accent, but the immediately preceding Gati, as उत् does retain its accent, though it is not the first member of the compound word. Compare also VIII. 2. 70. But in दूरात् + आगतः (âgata being governed by this rule) we have दूरादागतः, (II. 1. 39 and VI. 3. 2) where VI. 2. 144 has its scope, though it had not its scope in अभि + उद्धृतः = अभ्युद्धृतः ॥ In the former case this maxim applies कृद्ग्रहणे गतिकारकपूर्वस्यापि ग्रहणं ॥ "A Kṛit affix denotes whenever it is employed, a word-form which begins with that to which that

Kṛit affix has been added, and which ends with the Kṛit affix, but moreover should a Gati or a noun such as denotes a case-relation have been prefixed to that word-form, then the Kṛit affix must denote the same word-form together with the Gati or the noun which may have been prefixed to it". In the second example, this maxim is not applied, because scope should be given to the word अनन्तर in this aphorism. When the Participle has not a Passive significance, the rule does not apply because the word कर्मणि is understood here also; as, प्रकृतः कटं देवदत्तः ॥ This sûtra debars VI. 2. 144.

तादौ च निति कृत्यतौ ॥ ५० ॥ पदानि ॥ तादौ, च, निति, कृति, अ-तौ ॥

वृत्तिः ॥ तकारादौ च तुशब्दवर्जिते निति कृति परतो गतिरनन्तरः प्रकृतिस्वरो भवति ॥

50. An immediately preceding Gati retains its original accent before (a word formed by) a Kṛit-affix beginning with त्, which has an indicatory न्, but not before तु ॥

Thus प्रकर्ता (with तृन्) प्रकर्तुम् (with तुमुन्), प्रकृतिः (with क्तिन्) ॥ This sûtra debars the Kṛit-affix accent (VI. 2. 139). Why do we say "before an affix beginning with त्"? Observe प्रजल्पाकः formed with the affix षाकन् (III. 2. 155), and the Gati प्र, the accent being governed by VI. 2. 139. Why do we say 'which is नित्'? Observe प्रकर्ता formed by तृच् affix. When a Kṛit-affix takes the augment इट्, it does not lose its character of beginning with त् on the Vartika कृदुपदेशो वा ताद्यर्थमिडर्थम् ॥ Thus प्रलपिता, प्रलपितुम् ॥ Why do we say "but not before तु"? Observe आगन्तुः with the Uṇâdi affix तुन् ॥

तवै चान्तश्च युगपत् ॥ ५१ ॥ पदानि ॥ तवै च, अन्तः, च, युगपत्, (उदात्तः प्रकृतिस्वरम्) ॥

वृत्तिः ॥ तवैप्रत्ययस्यान्त उदात्तो भवति गतिश्चानन्तरः प्रकृतिस्वर इति एतदुभयं युगपद्भवति ॥

51. An immediately preceding Gati retains its original accent before an Infinitive in तवै (III. 4. 14) but whereby simultaneously the final has the acute as well.

Thus अन्वेतवै, परिस्तरितवै, परिपातवै, अभिचरितवै ॥ All upasargas have acute on the first except 'abhi': which therefore has acute on the final. (Phit Su IV. 13) which declares उपसर्गा आद्युदात्ता अभिवर्जम् ॥ This debars कृत् accent (VI. 2. 139) and is an exception to the rule that in a single word, a single syllable only has acute.

अनिगन्तोऽञ्चतौ वप्रत्यये ॥ ५२ ॥ पदानि ॥ अनिगन्तः, अञ्चतौ, वप्रत्यये, (प्रकृतिस्वरः)

वृत्तिः ॥ अनिगन्तो गतिः प्रकृतिस्वरो भवत्यञ्चतौ वप्रत्यये परतः ॥

52. An immediately preceding Gati not ending in इ or उ, retains its original accent before अञ्च् when an affix having a व् follows.

Thus प्राङ्, प्राञ्चौ, प्राञ्चः or प्राङ्, प्राञ्चौ, प्राञ्चः ॥ The accent is acute and optionally svarita by VIII. 2. 6. So also पराङ्, पराञ्चौ, पराञ्चः, पराचः, पराचा ॥ But with प्रति which ends in इ, we have प्रत्यङ्, प्रत्यञ्चौ, प्रत्यञ्चः here by VI. 2. 139 the second member retains its original accent. Why do we say 'before an affix व्'? Observe उदञ्चनः ॥ When the nasal of 'añch' is elided, then rule VI. 1. 222 presents itself; but that rule is superseded when a Gati not ending in इ or उ precedes, because the present rule is subsequent. Thus पराचः and पराचा ॥ In some texts, the reading is अञ्चतावप्रत्यये ॥ The affix व् is like क्विप् &c, (VI. 1. 67).

न्यधी च ॥ ५३ ॥ पदानि ॥ नि, अधी, च, (प्रकृतिस्वरौ) ॥

वृत्तिः ॥ नि अधि इत्येतौ चाञ्चतौ वप्रत्यये परतः प्रकृतिस्वरौ भवतः ॥

53. The Gatis नि and अधि, however, retain their original accent before 'añch' followed by a व् affix.

Thus न्यङ्, न्यञ्चौ, न्यञ्चः ॥ The अ becomes svarita by VIII. 2. 4. So also अध्यङ्, अध्यञ्चौ, अध्यञ्चः, अधीचः, अधीचः, नीचः, नीचा ॥

ईषदन्यतरस्याम् ॥ ५४ ॥ पदानि ॥ ईषत्, अन्यतरस्या, (प्रकृतिस्वरम्) ॥

वृत्तिः ॥ ईषदित्येतत्पूर्वपदमन्यतरस्यां प्रकृतिस्वरं भवति ॥

54. The word ईषत् when first member of a compound may optionally preserve its original accent.

Thus ईषत्कडारः or ईषत्कडारः, ईषत्पिङ्गलः or ईषत्पिङ्गलः ॥ ईषत् has acute on the final. But in ईषद्भेदः &c, the Kṛit-accent will necessarily take place (VI. 2. 139); no option being allowed; because the compounds to which the present rule applies are, on the maxim of pratipadokta, those formed by ईषत् with non-Kṛit words under II. 2. 7.

हिरण्यपरिमाणं धने ॥ ५५ ॥ पदानि ॥ हिरण्य-परिमाणम्, धने, (प्रकृतिस्वरम्)॥

वृत्तिः ॥ हिरण्यपरिमाणवाचि पूर्वपदं धनशब्दउत्तरपदे ऽन्यतरस्यां प्रकृतिस्वरं भवति ॥

55. The first member, denoting the quantity of gold, retains optionally its original accent, before the word धन ॥

Thus द्विसुवर्णधनम् or द्विसुवर्णधनम् ॥ This is a Karmadhâraya compound द्वौसुवर्णौ परिमाणमस्य = द्विसुवर्णं, तदेव धनम् ॥ It may also be treated as a Bahuvrihi compound, then the accent will be of that compound, as द्विसुवर्णधनः or द्विसुवर्णधनः ॥ Why do we say 'gold'? Observe प्रस्थधनम् ॥ Why do we say 'quantity'? Observe काञ्चनधनम् ॥ Why do we say 'धन'? Observe निष्कमाला ॥

प्रथमो ऽचिरोपसंपत्तौ ॥५६॥ पदानि ॥ प्रथमः,अचिरः,उपसम्पत्तौ (प्रकृतिस्वरम्)॥

वृत्तिः ॥ प्रथमशब्दः पूर्वपदमचिरोपसंपत्तौ गम्यमानायामन्यतरस्यां प्रकृतिस्वरं भवति । अचिरोपसंपत्तिरचिरोपश्लेषोऽभिनवत्वम् ॥

56. The word प्रथम when standing first in a compound, retains optionally its original accent when meaning 'a novice'.

The word अचिरोपसंपत्ति = अचिरोपश्लेष or अभिनवत्वम् ॥ Thus प्रथमवैयाकरणः or प्रथमवैयाकरणः = सम्प्रतिव्याकरणमध्येतुं प्रवृत्तः 'one who has recently commenced to study Grammar'. The word प्रथम is derived from प्रथ by अमच् (Uṇ V. 68) and by चित् accent the acute falls on the last. Why do we say when meaning 'a Novice?' Observe प्रथमवैयाकरणः (वैयाकरणानामाद्यो मुख्यो वा यः सः) 'the first Grammarian or a Grammarian of the first rank'. It will *always* have acute on the final.

कतरकतमौ कर्मधारये ॥ ५७ ॥ पदानि ॥ कतर-कतमौ, कर्मधारये, प्रकृतिस्वरम्॥

वृत्तिः ॥ कतरशब्दः कतमशब्दश्च पूर्वपदं कर्मधारये समासे ऽन्यतरस्यां प्रकृतिस्वरं भवति ॥

57. The words कतर and कतम standing as the first member of a compound retain optionally their original accent in a Karmadhâraya.

Thus कतरकठः or कतरकठः, कतमकठः or कतमकठः ॥ The word Karmadhâraya is used for the sake of the next sûtra, this sûtra could have done without it, as 'katara' and 'katama' by the maxim of pratipadokta, form only Karmadhâraya compound by II. 1. 63.

आर्यो ब्राह्मणकुमारयोः ॥५८॥ पदानि ॥ आर्यः, ब्राह्मण-कुमारयोः, प्रकृतिस्वरम् ॥

वृत्तिः ॥ आर्यशब्दः पूर्वपदं ब्राह्मणकुमारशब्दयोरुत्तरपदयोः कर्मधारये समासे ऽन्यतरस्यां प्रकृतिस्वरं भवति ॥

58. The word आर्य optionally retains its original accent in a Karmadhâraya, before the words ब्राह्मण and कुमार ॥

Thus आर्यब्राह्मणः or आर्यब्राह्मणः, आर्यकुमारः or आर्यकुमारः ॥ The word आर्य is formed by ण्यत् affix and has svarita on the final. Why do we say 'Arya'? Observe परमब्राह्मणः, परमकुमारः ॥ Why do we say before 'Brâhmaṇa' and 'Kumâra'? Observe आर्यक्षत्रियः ॥ Why 'Karmadhâraya?' Observe आर्यस्य ब्राह्मणः = आर्यब्राह्मणः ॥ According to the Accentuated Text the accent is आर्य (Pro. Bohtlingk).

राजा च ॥ ५९ ॥ पदानि ॥ राजा, च ॥

वृत्तिः ॥ राजा च पूर्वपदं ब्राह्मणकुमारयोरुत्तरपदयोः कर्मधारये समासे ऽन्यतरस्यां प्रकृतिस्वरं भवति ॥

59. The word राजन् retains optionally its accent before the words 'Brâhmaṇa' and 'Kumâra', in a Karmadhâraya.

Thus राजब्राह्मणः or राजब्राह्मणः, राजकुमारः or राजकुमारः ॥ The word राजन् is formed by the affix कनिन् added to राज् (Uṇ I. 156). But राज्ञो ब्राह्मण = राजब्राह्मणः where the compound is not Karmadhâraya. The making of this a separate aphorism is for the purpose of preventing the yathâsankhya rule and also for the sake of the subsequent sûtra into which the anuvritti of राजन् runs and not of आर्य ॥

षष्ठी प्रत्येनसि ॥ ६० ॥ पदानि ॥ षष्ठी, प्रत्येनसि, (अन्यतरस्याम् राजा प्रकृतिस्वरम्) ॥

वृत्तिः ॥ राजेति वर्त्तते, ऽन्यतरस्यामिति च । षष्ठ्यन्तो राजशब्दः पूर्वपद प्रत्येनस्युत्तरे ऽन्यतरस्यां प्रकृतिस्वरं भवति ॥

60. The word 'râjan' ending in the Genitive case optionally retains its accent before the word प्रत्येनस् ॥

The words राजन् and अन्यतरस्याम् are understood here also. Thus राज्ञः प्रत्येनाः or राज्ञः प्रत्येनाः ॥ The sign of the Genitive is not elided by VI.3. 21. When आक्रोश is not meant we have, राजप्रत्येनाः or राजप्रत्येनाः ॥ Why do we say 'ending in the Genitive'? Observe राजा चासौ प्रत्येनाश्च = राजप्रत्येनाः no option.

क्ते नित्यार्थे ॥ ६१ ॥ पदानि ॥ क्ते, नित्यार्थे (पूर्वपदम् अन्यतरस्याम् प्रकृतिस्वरम्) ॥

वृत्तिः ॥ क्तान्तउत्तरपदे नित्यार्थे समासे पूर्वपदमन्यतरस्यां प्रकृतिस्वरं भवति ॥

61. A word having the sense of 'always', retains optionally its accent before a Past Participle in क्त ॥

Thus नित्यप्रहसितः or नित्यप्रहसितः, सततप्रहसितः or सततप्रहसितः ॥ These are Accusative compounds formed under Rule II. 1. 28. नित्य is formed by त्यप् affix added to the upasarga नि (IV. 2. 104 Vârt); and has acute on the first, the upasarga retaining its accent, the affix being anudâtta (III. 1. 4). The word सतत being formed by क्त affix with the force of भावः, has acute on final by VI. 2. 144. If it be considered to have been formed by कर्मणि क्त, then the accent will be on the beginning by VI. 2. 49. Why do we say when the first term means 'always'? Observe मुहूर्त्तप्रहसितः ॥ In the case of नित्यप्रहसितः &c the samâsa accent VI. 1. 223 was first set aside by the Accusative Tatpurusha accent VI. 2, 2. this in its turn was set aside by क्त accent VI. 2. 144, which is again debarred by the present.

ग्रामः शिल्पिनि ॥ ६२ ॥ पदानि ॥ ग्रामः, शिल्पिनि, (अन्यतरस्याम् प्रकृतिस्वरम्) ॥

वृत्तिः ॥ ग्रामशब्दः पूर्वपदं शिल्पिवाचिन्युत्तरपदे ऽन्यतरस्यां प्रकृतिस्वरं भवति ॥

62. The word ग्राम when first member of a compound, optionally retains its accent before a word denoting "a professional man or artisan".

Thus ग्रामनापितः or ग्रामनापितः, ग्रामकुलालः or ग्रामकुलालः ॥ The word ग्राम has acute on the first. Why do we say "ग्राम"? Observe परमनापितः ॥ Why do we say 'a śilpî a professional workman'? Observe ग्रामरथ्या; where there is no option.

राजा च प्रशंसायाम् ॥ ६३ ॥ पदानि ॥ राजा, च, प्रशंसायाम्, (अन्यतरस्याम् प्रकृति स्वरम्) ॥

वृत्तिः ॥ राजशब्दः पूर्वपदं शिल्पिवाचिन्युत्तरपदे प्रशंसायां गम्यमानायां मन्यतरस्यां प्रकृतिस्वरं भवति ॥

63. The word राजन् followed by a profession-denoting noun, optionally retains its accent, when praise is to be expressed.

Thus राजनापितः or राजनापितः, राजकुलालः or राजकुलालः "A royal barber i. e. a skillful barber or one fit to serve the king even" &c. It may be either a Karmadhâraya or a Genitive compound. Why do we say 'राजन्'? Observe परमनापितः ॥ Why do we say 'when denoting praise'? Observe राजनापितः 'king's barber'. Why do we say 'a professional man'? Observe राजहस्ती 'a royal elephant'.

आदिरुदात्तः ॥ ६४ ॥ पदानि ॥ आदिः, उदात्तः, ॥

वृत्तिः ॥ आदिरुदात्त इत्येतदधिकृतमित उत्तरं यद्वक्ष्यामस्तत्र पूर्वपदस्यादिरुदात्तो भवतीत्येवं तद्वेदितव्यम् ॥

64. In the following up to VI. 2. 91 inclusive the phrase "the first syllable in—(the word standing in the Nominative) has the acute", is to be always supplied.

This is an adhikâra aphorism. The first syllable of the पूर्वपद will get the acute in the following aphorisms. In short, the phrase 'âdir udâtta' should be supplied to complete the sense of the subsequent sûtras. The very next sûtra illustrates it. That sûtra literally means "a word in the Locative case or a word denoting the name of the receiver of a tax or tribute, standing before a word denoting that which is lawful, but not before हरण". To complete the sense we must supply the words "has acute on the first syllable". Thus स्तूपेशाणः, मुकुटे कार्षापणम्, याज्ञिकाश्वः, वैयाकरणहस्ती ॥ The word आदि 'the first syllable' is understood upto VI. 2. 91, the word उदात्त has longer stretch: it governs upto VI. 2. 137.

सप्तमीहारिणौ धर्म्येऽहरणे ॥ ६५ ॥ पदानि ॥ सप्तमी, हारिणौ, धर्म्ये, अहरणे, (आद्युदात्तम्) ॥

वृत्तिः ॥ सप्तम्यन्तं हारिवाचि च पूर्वपदं धर्म्यवाचिनि हरणशब्दादन्यास्मिन्नुत्तरपदे आद्युदात्तं भवति ॥

65. The first member of a compound, if in the Locative case or denoting the name of the Receiver of a tax, has acute on the first syllable, when the second member is a word denoting 'what is lawful', but not when it is हरण ॥

The word हारिण् means 'appropriates the dues or taxes': and धर्म्यम् means 'the due or tax which has been determined by the custom or usage, of the country, town, sect or family. that which one is lawfully entitled to get'. The word धर्म्य is formed by यत् under IV. 4. 91 and 92 and has the sense of both. Of Locative words we have the following examples: —स्तूपे-शाणः मुकुटे-कार्षापणम्, हले-द्विपदिका, हले-त्रिपदिका, दृषदि-माषकः ॥ These compounds are formed under II. 1. 44, and the sign of the Locative is not elided by VI. 3. 9 and 10. With the name of a due-receiver हारी we have the following:—याज्ञिकाश्वः 'the horse which is the customary due of the sacrificer'. So also वैयाकरणहस्ती, मातुलाश्वः, पितृव्यगवः ॥ In some places the established usage is to give a शाण coin in every sacred Tope &c, or to give a horse to a sacrificer &c. Why do we say 'what is lawful'? Observe स्तम्बेरमैः, कर्मकर वर्द्धितकैः वर्द्धितकों नाम मूले स्थूलोग्रे सूक्ष्म ओदन पिण्डः, स कर्मकराय दीयते, अन्यथा कर्म न कुर्यादिति, न त्वयं धर्मः ॥ Why do we say "but not before हरण"? Observe वाडबहरणम् 'that which is given to a mare'. हरण is that customary food which is given to a mare after she has been covored, in order to strengthen her. The word हरण is a Kṛit-formed word, its exclusion here indicates that other Kṛit-formed words however are governed by this rule when preceded by a हारी denoting word; and thus this sûtra supersedes the Kṛit accent enjoined by VI. 2. 139, so far. Thus वाडबहायः has acute on the first by this rule, the subsequent VI. 2. 139 not applying.

युक्ते च ॥ ६६ ॥ पदानि ॥ युक्ते, च, (आद्युदात्तम्) ॥

वृत्तिः ॥ युक्तवाचिनि च समासे पूर्वपदमाद्युदात्तं भवति ।

66. The first member of a compound has acute on the first syllable, when the second member denotes that by whom the things denoted by the first are regulated or kept in order.

The word युक्त means 'he who is prompt in the discharge of his appointed duty' i. e. the person appointed to look after. Thus गोबल्लवः 'a cowherd looking after cow': अश्वबल्लवः, गोमणिन्द्रः, अश्वमणिन्द्रः, गोसंख्यः, अश्वसंख्यः ॥ All these word बल्लवः, माणिन्द्रः, सख्यः &c mean पालकः 'the protector &c.

विभाषा ऽध्यक्षे ॥ ६७ ॥ पदानि ॥ विभाषा, अध्यक्षे, (आद्युदात्तम्) ॥

वृत्तिः ॥ अध्यक्षशब्दउत्तरपदे विभाषा पूर्वपदमाद्युदात्तं भवति ॥

67. The acute is optionally on the first syllable when the word अध्यक्ष follows.

Thus गवाध्यक्षः or गवाध्यक्षः: 'a superintendent of cows': अश्वाध्यक्षः or अश्वाध्यक्षः ॥

पापं च शिल्पिनि ॥ ६८ ॥ पदानि ॥ पापम्, च, शिल्पिनि, (विभाषा)(आद्युदात्तः) ॥

वृत्तिः ॥ पापशब्दः शिल्पिवाचिन्युत्तरपदे विभाषा ऽऽद्युदात्तो भवति ॥

68. The word पाप has optionally acute on the first syllable when followed by a word denoting a professional man.

Thus पा॑पनापितः or पापनापि॒तः, पा॑पकुलालः or पापकुला॒लः ॥ This rule applies to the pratipadokta samâsa of पाप in the sense of censure as taught in II. 1. 54, when it is an appositional compound; and not when it forms a Genitive compound. Thus पापस्यनापितः = पापनापि॒तः ॥

गोत्रान्तेवासिमाणवब्राह्मणेषु क्षेपे ॥ ६९ ॥ पदानि ॥ गोत्र, अन्तेवासि, माणव, ब्राह्मणेषु, क्षेपे, (पूर्वपदम् आद्युदात्तम्) ॥

वृत्तिः ॥ गोत्रवाचिन्यन्तेवासिवाचिनि चोत्तरपदे माणवब्राह्मणयोश्च क्षेपवाचिनि समासे पूर्वपदमाद्युदात्तम् भवति ॥

69. The first syllable of the first member of a compound has the acute accent before a Patronymic name or a scholar-name, as well as before माणव and ब्राह्मण, when a reproach is meant.

Thus जं॑घावात्स्यः = यो जंघाशनं ददान्यहमिति वात्स्यः, संपद्यते सः; यत्र श्राद्धादौ वात्स्यानामिद पादप्रक्षालनं क्रियते, तत्रावात्स्यः सन् वात्स्योऽहमिति ब्रूते तल्लाभाय सः ॥ भार्या॑सौश्रुतः 'a descendant of Suśruta under the petticoat government of his wife'. The compounding takes place by the analogy of शाकपार्थिवः ॥ दै॑शाब्राह्मकृतयः (Brahmakrita belongs to Subhrâdi class). The above are examples of Gotra words. Now with scholar names. कु॑मारीदाक्षाः 'the pupils of Daksha for the sake of marriage i. e. who study the work of Daksha or make themselves the pupils of Daksha for the sake of girls'. क॑म्बलचारायणीयाः, घृ॑तरौढीयाः, and ओ॑दनपाणिनीयाः &c. भि॑क्षामाणवः = भिक्षांलप्स्येऽहमिति माणवो भवति ॥ दा॑सीब्राह्मणः, वृ॑षली ब्राह्मणः, भ॑यब्राह्मणः = यो भयेन ब्राह्मणः संपद्यते ॥ Compounding by II. 1. 4 where no other rule applies. Why do we say 'when followed by a Gotra word?' Observe दासीश्रोत्रि॒यः ॥ Why do we say 'when reproach is meant?' Observe महाब्राह्मणः ॥

अङ्गानि मैरेये ॥ ७० ॥ पदानि ॥ अङ्गानि, मैरेये, (आद्युदात्तानि) ॥

वृत्तिः ॥ मैरेयशब्दउत्तरपदे तदङ्गवाचीनि पूर्वपदान्याद्युदात्तानि भवन्ति ॥

70. The first syllable of the word preceding मैरेय, gets the acute, when it denotes the ingredient of the same.

Thus गु॑डमैरेयः 'the wine maireya prepared from treacle or molasses'. म॑धुमैरेयः 'the maireya prepared from honey'. Why do we say when denoting 'an ingredient?' Observe परममैरे॒यः ॥ Why do we say "before मैरेय?" Observe पुष्पास॒वः ॥ Every sort of spirituous liquor except सुरा is called मैरेय ॥

भक्ताख्यास्तदर्थेषु ॥ ७१ ॥ पदानि ॥ भक्ताख्याः, तदर्थेषु, (आद्युदात्ताः) ॥

वृत्तिः ॥ भक्तमन्नं तदाख्यास्तद्वाचिनः शब्दास्तदर्थेषूत्तरपदेषु आद्युदात्ता भवन्ति ॥

71. A word denoting food gets the acute on the first syllable, when standing before a word which denotes a repository suited to contain that.

Thus भिँक्षाकंसः, भैँक्तकंसः, श्रौँणाकंसः, भाँजीकंसः ॥ The words like भिक्षा, भक्त &c, are names of food. Why do we say 'when denoting the name of food'? Observe समाशशाल्यैँः (the word समाश = समशनं is the name of an 'action' and not of a 'substance'). Why do we say 'tadartheshu suited to contain that'? Observe भिक्षाँप्रियः. which is a Bahuvrihi, and the first member gets acute on the final.

गोबिडालसिंहसैन्धवेषूपमाने ॥ ७२ ॥ पदानि ॥ गो, बिडाल, सिंह, सैन्धवेषु, उपमाने, (आदूयुदात्तम्) ॥

वृत्तिः ॥ गवादिषूपमानवाचिषूत्तरपदेषु पूर्वपदमाद्युदात्तं भवति ॥

72. A word denoting the object of comparison gets the acute on the first syllable when standing before गो, बिडाल, सिंह, and सैन्धव ॥

Thus धाँन्यगवः = धान्यं गौरिव ॥ The compounding takes place by II. 1. 56, the words गो &c, being considered to belong to Vyâghrâdi class, which is an Akṛitigana. The meaning of the compound must be given according to usage and appropriateness. Thus धान्यगवः means गवाकृत्याऽवस्थितं धान्यं ॥ So also हिँरण्यगवः, भिँक्षाबिडालः, ब्राँह्मणबिडालः, तृँणसिंहः, काँष्ठसिंहः, सँक्तुसैन्धवः, पाँनसैन्धवः ॥ Why do we say "when denoting the object of comparision"? Observe परमसिंहः ॥

अके जीविकार्थे ॥ ७३ ॥ पदानि ॥ अके, जीविकार्थे, (आदूयुदात्तम्) ॥

वृत्तिः ॥ अकप्रत्ययान्त उत्तरपदे जीविकार्थवाचिनि समासे पूर्वपदमाद्युदात्तं भवति ॥

73. The first member of a compound has the acute on the first syllable when the second member is a word ending in the affix अक, and the compound expresses a calling by which one gets his living.

Thus दँन्तलेखकः, नँखलेखकः, अँवस्करशोधकः, रँमणीयकारकः = दन्तलेखनादिभिर्येषां जीविका ॥ The compounding takes place by II. 2. 17. Why do we say when meaning 'means of living'? Observe इक्षुभक्षिकां मे धारयसि ॥ All affixes which ultimately become अक by taking substitutes, are called अक affixes. Thus ण्वुल्, वुन् &c are अक affixes (VII. 1. 1). Why do we say "ending in the affix अक"? Observe रमणीयकर्त्ता ॥ Here the compounding takes place by II. 2. 17, and the affix तृच् is added in the sense of sport and not of livelihood.

प्राचां क्रीडायाम् ॥ ७४ ॥ पदानि ॥ प्राचाम्, क्रीडायाम्, (आदूयुदात्तम्)

वृत्तिः ॥ प्राग्देशवर्त्तिनां या क्रीडा तद्वाचिनि समासे ऽकप्रत्ययान्तउत्तरपदे पूर्वपदमाद्युदात्तं भवति ॥

74. A compound the second member of which is a word ending in अक affix, and which denotes the sport of the Eastern people, gets the the acute accent on the first syllable.

Thus उद्दालकपुष्पभञ्जिका, वीरणपुष्पप्रचायिका, शालभञ्जिका, तालभञ्जिका ॥ These are formed by ण्वुल् affix (III. 3. 109), and the compounding takes place by II. 2. 17. Why do we say 'of the Eastern Folk'? Observe जीवपुत्रप्रचायिका, which is a sport of the Western People. Why do we say 'when denoting a sport'? Observe तवपुष्पप्रचायिका 'thy turn for &c,' which is formed by ण्वुच् (III. 3. 111) and denotes 'rotation or turn'.

अणि नियुक्ते ॥ ७५ ॥ पदानि ॥ अणि, नियुक्ते, (आद्युदात्तम्) ॥

वृत्तिः ॥ अणन्तउत्तरपदे नियुक्तवाचिनि समासे पूर्वपदमाद्युदात्तं भवति ॥

75. A compound, the second member of which is a word ending in the Kṛit-affix अण्, and which denotes a functionary, gets the acute on the first syllable.

Thus छत्रधारः, तूणीधारः, कमण्डलुग्राहः, भृङ्गारधारः ॥ Why do we say when meaning 'a functionary'? Observe काण्डलावः, शरलावः ॥

शिल्पिनि चाकृञः ॥ ७६ ॥ शिल्पिनि, च, अकृञः, (पूर्वपदम् आद्युदात्तम्) ॥

वृत्तिः ॥ शिल्पिवाचिनि समासे ऽणन्तउत्तरपदे पूर्वपदमाद्युदात्तं भवति स चेदण् कृञो न भवति ॥

76. And when such a compound ending in अण् affix denotes the name of a professional man, but not when the second term is कार (derived from कृञ्), the acute is on the first syllable of the first word.

Here also the second term ends in अण् affix. Thus तन्तुवायः, तुन्नवायः, वालवायः ॥ Why do we say when denoting 'a work-man or professional person'? Observe काण्डलावः, शरलावः ॥ Why do we say 'but not when the affix अण् comes after कृ'? Observe कुम्भकारः, अयस्कारः ॥

संज्ञायां च ॥ ७७ ॥ पदानि ॥ संज्ञायाम्, च, (पूर्वपदम् आद्युदात्तम्) ॥

वृत्तिः ॥ संज्ञायां विषये ऽणन्तउत्तरपदे ऽकृञः पूर्वपदमाद्युदात्तं भवति ॥

77. Also when such an upapada compound ending in अण् affix denotes a Name, the acute falls on the first syllable : but not when the second term is कार ॥

Thus तन्तुवायः 'a kind of insect, spider'. वालवायः 'the hill Vâlavâya'. But not so अण् with कृ ; as रथकारः 'the name of a Brâhmaṇa caste'.

गोतन्तियवं पाले ॥ ७८ ॥ पदानि ॥ गो, तन्ति, यवम्, पाले, (आद्युदात्तानि) ॥

वृत्तिः ॥ गो तन्ति यव इत्येतानि पूर्वपदानि पालशब्दउत्तरपदे आद्युदात्तानि भवन्ति ॥

78. The words गो, तन्ति and यव get the acute on the first syllable when followed by पाल ॥

Thus गोपालः, तन्तिपालः, यवपालः ॥ The word तन्ति is the rope with which calves are tied. (तनु विस्तारे + क्तिच्). This applies to words not denoting a functionary, which would be governed by VI. 2. 75. Why do we say गो &c ? Observe वत्सपालः ॥ Why do we say 'followed by पाल'? Observe गोरक्षः ॥

णिनि ॥ ७९ ॥ पदानि ॥ णिनि, (पूर्वपदम् आद्युदात्तम्) ॥

वृत्तिः ॥ णिनन्तउत्तरपदे पूर्वपदमाद्युदात्तं भवति ॥

79. A compound ending in the Kṛit-affix णिनि (इन्) has the acute on the first syllable of the first member.

Thus पुष्पहारिन्, फलहारिन्, पर्णहारिन् ॥

उपमानं शब्दार्थप्रकृतावेव ॥ ८० ॥ पदानि ॥ उपमानम्, शब्दार्थे, प्रकृतौ, एव, (आद्युदात्तत्) ॥

वृत्तिः ॥ उपमानवाचि पूर्वपदं शब्दार्थ प्रकृतावेव णिनन्तउत्तरपदआद्युदात्तं भवति ॥

80. When the first member of a compound expresses that with which resemblance is denoted, then it has acute on the first syllable, before a word formed by णिनि affix, only then, when such latter word is a radical without any preposition, and means 'giving out a definite sound like so and so'.

The word उपमान means the object with which something is likened: शब्दार्थ means 'expressing a sound'; प्रकृति means 'root, without any preposition'. Thus उष्ट्रक्रोशिन्, ध्वाङ्क्षराविन्, खरनादिन् ॥ The word उपमान shows the scope of this sûtra as distinguished from the last. So that, when the first term is an उपमान word, the preceding sûtra will not apply, though the second member may be a णिनि formed word. When the second term is not a word denoting sound, the rule will not apply. As वृकवञ्चिन्, वृकप्रेक्षिन् which retain kṛit accent (VI. 2. 139) Why do we say 'a radical word without any preposition'? Observe गर्दभोच्चारिन्, कोकिलभिव्याहारिन् ॥ Here the second terms radically (i. e. chârin and hârin) do not denote sounds, but it is with the help of the Prepositions उत् and अभि, वि and आ that they mean sound. The force of एव is that the उपमान words are restricted. Such words get acute on the first syllable *only then*, when the second member is a radical sound name. According to Patanjali, the first syllable gets acute, whether it denotes उपमान or not, when the second word is a radical denoting sound. (शब्दार्थ प्रकृतौ ह्युपमानं चानुपमानं चाद्युदात्तमिष्यते) ॥ As पुष्कलजल्पिन्, for had एव not been used, the sûtra would have run thus: उपमानं शब्दार्थप्रकृतौ and would mean:—"If the second member is a sound denoting radical word, then the upamâna first member and no other will get the acute". But this is not what is intended : because when the second member is a sound-denoting radical, the first member will get the acute, whether it is upamâna word or not. The word एव therefore restricts upamâna; i. e. a first member denoting उपमानं will get the accent then only, when the second term is a sound-denoting radical. If the second term is not a sound denoting radical, the first term denoting upamâna will not get the accent. The compounding takes place by III. 2. 79.

युक्तारोह्यादयश्च ॥ ८१ ॥ पदानि ॥ युक्तारोह्यादयः, च (आद्युदात्ताः) ॥

वृत्तिः ॥ युक्तारोह्यादयः समासा आद्युदात्ता भवन्ति ॥

81. The compounds युक्तारोहिन् &c, have acute on the first syllable.

Thus 1 युक्तारोही, 2 आगतरोही, 3 आगतयोधी, 4 आगतवञ्ची, 5 आगतनर्दी, 6 आगतनन्दी, 7 आगतप्रहारी ॥ These are formed by णिनि affix, and are illustrations of Rule VI. 2. 79. Some say, these delare a restrictive rule with regard to the first and second member of these terms. Thus रोहिन् &c must be preceded by युक्त, &c and युक्त &c followed by रोहिन् &c to make this rule VI. 2. 79 applicable. Thus वृक्षारोहिन् though ending in णिनि does not take acute on the first, so युक्ताध्यायिन् ॥ 8 आगतमत्स्या or °त्स्य, 9 क्षीरहोता, 10 भगिनीभर्त्ता ॥ The last two are Genitive compounds under Rule II. 2. 9. 11 ग्रामगोधुक्, 12 अश्वत्रिरात्रः, 13 गर्गत्रिरात्रः, 14 व्युष्टत्रिरात्रः, 15 शनपादः (गणपादः), 16 समपादः ॥ All these are Genitive compounds. 17 एकशितिपात्=एकःशितिःपादोऽस्य ॥ This is a Bahuvrîhi of three terms. The word एकशितिः is a Taddhitârtha Samâsa (II. 1. 51), and being a Tatpurusha, required acute on the final, as the Tatpurusha accent is stronger. This declares acute on the first. Moreover by VI. 2. 29, this word एकशितिः would have acute on the first, as it is a Dvigu ending in a simple vowel. But the very fact that this word is enumerated here, shows that other Dvigu compounds in शिति are not governed by VI. 2. 29, therefore द्विशितिपाद् has acute on ति ॥ The enumeration of the एकशितिपात् further proves by implication that the (एकशितिपात् स्वरवचनं ज्ञापक निमित्तस्वरबलीयस्त्वस्य) accent for the application of which a case is present is stronger. (See Mahâbhashya II. 1. 1.) The class of compounds known as पात्रेसमित &c, (II. 1. 48) also belong to this class.

1 युक्तारोही, 2 आगतरोही, 3 आगतयोधी, 4 आगतवञ्ची, 5 आगतनन्दी (आगतनर्दी), 6 आगतप्रहारी, 7 आगतमत्स्यः (आगतमत्स्या), 8 क्षीरहोता, 9 भगिनीभर्त्ता, 10 ग्रामगोधुक्, 11 अश्वत्रिरात्रः 12 गर्गत्रिरात्रः, 13 व्युष्टित्रिरात्रः, 14 गणपादः (शणपादः), 15 एकशितिपात्, 16 पात्रेसंमितादयश्च (पात्रेसमितादयश्च), 17 समपादः ॥

दीर्घकाशतुषभ्राष्ट्रवटं जे ॥ ८२ ॥ पदानि ॥ दीर्घ, काश, तुष, भ्राष्ट्र, वटम्, जे, (आद्युदात्तानि) ॥

वृत्तिः ॥ दीर्घान्तं पूर्वपदं काश तुष भ्राष्ट्र वट-इत्येतानि च जउत्तरपदे आद्युदात्तानि भवन्ति ॥

82. When the first member is a word ending in a long vowel, or is काश, तुष, भ्राष्ट्र or वट, and is followed by ज, the acute falls on the first syllable.

Thus कुटीजः, शमीजः, काशजः, तुषजः, भ्राष्ट्रजः वटजः These are formed by the affix ड added to जन् (III. 2. 97).

अन्त्यात्पूर्वं बह्वचः ॥ ८३ ॥ पदानि ॥ अन्त्यात्, पूर्वम्, बह्वचः (उदात्तम् जे) ॥

वृत्तिः ॥ जउत्तरपदे बह्वचः पूर्वपदस्यान्त्यात्पूर्वमुदात्तं भवति ॥

83. In a word consisting of more than two syllables, followed by ज, the acute falls on the syllable before the last.

Thus उपसरजः, मन्दुरजः, आमलकीजः, and वडबाजः (though the last two words have upapadas ending in long vowel, the accent is governed by this sûtra and not the last). Why do we say "a Polysyllabic first member"? Observe दग्धजानि तृणानि ॥

ग्रामेऽनिवसन्तः ॥ ८४ ॥ पदानि ॥ ग्रामे, अनिवसन्तः ॥

वृत्तिः ॥ ग्रामशब्दउत्तरपदे पूर्वपदमाद्युदात्तं भवति न चेन्निवसद्वाचिभवति ॥

84. Before ग्राम, the first syllable of the first member has acute, when thereby inhabitants are not meant.

Thus मल्लग्रामः, वणिग्ग्रामः ॥ Here ग्राम is equal to समूह 'an assemby'. देवग्रामः = देवस्वामिकः ॥ Why do we say 'when not meaning inhabitants'. Observe दाक्षिग्रामः 'a village inhabited by the descendants of Daksha', माहिकग्रामः 'a village inhabited by Mâhikas'.

घोषादिषु च ॥ ८५ ॥ पदानि ॥ घोषादिषु, च, (पूर्वपदम् आद्युदात्तम्) ॥

वृत्तिः ॥ घोषादिषु चोत्तरपदेषु पूर्वपदमाद्युदात्तं भवति ॥

85. The first member has acute on the first syllable when followed by घोष &c.

Thus दाक्षिघोषः, दाक्षिकटः, दाक्षिपल्वलः, दाक्षिबदरी, दाक्षिवल्लभः, दाक्षिह्रदः, दाक्षिपिङ्गलः, दाक्षिपिशङ्गः, दाक्षिमाला, दाक्षिरक्षा, दाक्षिशाला, or (°रक्षः or °शालः), दाक्षिशिल्पी, दाक्ष्यश्वत्थः, दाक्षिशाल्मली, कुन्दतृणम्, आश्रममुनिः, दाक्षिपुंसा, दाक्षिकूटः ॥

Of the above, those which denote places of habitation, there the first members though denoting inhabitants get the acute accent. Some do not read the anuvritti of अनिवसन्तः in this aphorism, others however read it.

1 घोष, 2 कट (घट), 3 वल्लभ (पल्वल), 4 ह्रद, 5 बदरी (बदर), 6 पिङ्गल, 7 पिशङ्ग, 8 माला, 9 रक्षा (रक्षः), 10 शाला (शालः), 11 कूट, 12 शाल्मली, 13 अश्वत्थ, 14 तृण, 15 शिल्पी, 16 मुनि, 17 प्रेक्षा (प्रेक्षाकू ; पुंसा) ॥.

छात्र्यादयः शालायाम् ॥८६॥ पदानि ॥ छात्र्यादयः, शालायाम्, (आद्युदात्ताः) ॥

वृत्तिः ॥ शालायामुत्तरपदे छात्र्यादय आद्युदात्ता भवन्ति ॥

86. The words छात्रि &c, get acute on the first syllable when followed by the word शाला ॥

Thus छात्रिशाला, ऐलिशाला' भाण्डिशाला ॥

Where the Tatpurusha compound ending in शाला becomes Neuter, by the option allowed in II. 4. 25; there also in the case of these words, the acute falls on the first syllable of the first term; thus superseding VI. 2. 123 which specifically applies to Neuter Tatpurushas. Thus छात्रिशालम्, ऐलिशालम् ॥

1 छात्रि, 2 पेलि (ऐलि), 3 भाण्डि, 4 व्याडि, 5 आखण्डि, 6 आटि, 7 गामि (गौमि) ॥

प्रस्थे ऽवृद्धमकर्क्यादीनाम् ॥ ८७ ॥ पदानि ॥ प्रस्थे, अवृद्धम्, अकर्क्यादीनाम्, (पूर्वपदम् आद्युदात्तम्) ॥

वृत्तिः ॥ प्रस्थशब्दउत्तरपदे कर्क्यादिवर्जितमवृद्धं पूर्वपदमाद्युदात्तं भवति ॥

87. The first member, which has not a Vṛiddhi in the first syllable, or which is not कर्की &c, gets the acute on the first syallblə before प्रस्थ ॥

Thus इन्द्रप्रस्थः, कुण्डप्रस्थः, ह्रदप्रस्थः, सुवर्णप्रस्थः ॥ But not in दाक्षिप्रस्थः, माहिकप्रस्थः which have Vṛiddhi in the first syllable; nor also in कर्कीप्रस्थः मघीप्रस्थः &c.

1 कर्की, 2 मघी (मघी), 3 मकरी, 4 कर्कन्धु (कर्कन्धू), 5 शमी, 6 करीर, 7 कन्दुक (कटुक), 8 कवल (कुवल; कूरल), 9 बदरी (बदर) ॥

मालादीनां च ॥ ८८ ॥ पदानि ॥ मालादीनाम्, च, (आदिः उदात्तः) ॥

वृत्तिः ॥ प्रस्थइति वर्त्तते । प्रस्थउत्तरपदे मालादीनामादिरुदात्तो भवति ॥

88. The first syllable of माला &c, gets the acute when प्रस्थ follows.

Thus मालाप्रस्थः, शालाप्रस्थः ॥ This sûtra applies even though the first syllables are Vṛiddhi vowel. In the words एक and शोणा the letters ए and ओ are treated as Vṛiddhi (I. 1. 75).

1 माला, 2 शाला, 3 शोणा (शोण), 4 द्राक्षा, 5 आक्षा, 6 क्षामा, 7 काञ्ची, 8 एक, 9 काम, 10 क्षौमा ॥

अमहन्नवं नगरे ऽनुदीचाम् ॥ ८९ ॥ पदानि ॥ अ, महत्, नवम्, नगरे, अनुदीचाम् ॥

वृत्तिः ॥ नगरशब्दउत्तरपदे महन्नवशब्दवर्जितं पूर्वपदमाद्युदात्तं भवति तच्चेदुदीचां न भवति ॥

89. The first member has acute on the first syllable before the word नगर, but not when it is the word महत् or नव, nor when it refers to a city in the lands of the Northern People.

Thus सुह्मनगरम्, पुण्ड्रनगरम्, विराटनगरम् ॥ But not in महानगरम् and नवनगरम्, Why do we say "but not of Northern People"? Observe नान्दीनगरम् कान्तीनगरम् ॥

अर्मे चावर्णं द्व्यच्त्र्यच् ॥ ९० ॥ पदानि ॥ अर्मे, च, अवर्णम्, द्व्यच्, त्र्यच्, (पूर्वपदम् आद्युदात्तम्) ॥

वृत्तिः ॥ अर्मशब्दउत्तरपदे द्व्यच् त्र्यच् पूर्वपदमवर्णान्तमाद्युदात्तं भवति ॥

90. A word of two or three syllables ending in अ or आ (with the exception of महा and नव), standing before the word अर्म has acute on the first syllable.

Thus दत्तार्मम्, गुप्तार्मम्, कुक्कुटार्मम्, वायसार्मम् ॥ Why do we say 'ending in अ (long or short)'? Observe बृहदर्मम् ॥ Why do we say 'consisting of two or three syllables'? Observe कपिञ्जलार्मम् ॥ The words महा and नव are to be read here also. The rule therefore does not apply to महार्मम् and नवार्मम् ॥

न भूताधिकसंजीवमद्राश्मकज्जलम् ॥ ९१ ॥ पदानि ॥ न, भूत, अधिक, संजीव, मद्र, अश्म, कज्जलम्, (आद्युदात्तानि) ॥

वृत्तिः ॥ भूत अधिक संजीव मद्र अश्मन् कज्जल इत्येतानि पूर्वपदानि अर्मशब्दउत्तरपदे नाद्युदात्तानि भवन्ति ॥

वार्त्तिकम् ॥ आद्युदात्तप्रकरणे दिवोदासादीनां छन्दस्युपसंख्यानम् ॥

91. The following words do not get acute on the first syllable, when standing before 'arma', viz: भूत, अधिक, संजीव, मद्र, अश्मन् and कज्जल ॥

Thus भूतार्मम्, अधिकार्मम्, संजीवार्मम्, मद्रार्मम्, अश्मार्मम्, मद्राश्मार्मम् (because the sûtra shows the compounding of those words in madrâsmam) कज्जलार्मम् ॥ All these compounds have acute on the final by VI. 1. 223.

Vârt:—In the Vedas the words दिवोदास &c, have acute on the first syllable. Thus दिवोदासाय गायत, वध्र्यश्वाय दाशुषे ॥

अन्तः ॥ ९२ ॥ पदानि ॥ अन्तः ॥

वृत्तिः ॥ अन्त इत्यधिकृतमित उत्तरं यद्वक्ष्यामस्तत्र पूर्वपदस्यान्त उदात्तो भवतीत्येवं वेदितव्यम् ॥

92. In the following sûtras upto VI. 2. 110 inclusive, is to be supplied the phrase "the last syllable in a word standing in the Nominative case has the acute".

This is an adhikâra aphorism. In the succeeding sûtras, the last syllable of the first member of a compound gets the acute accent. Thus in the next sûtra the word सर्व gets acute on the final. This adhikâra extends upto VI. 2. 110 inclusive.

सर्वं गुणकार्त्स्न्ये ॥ ९३ ॥ पदानि ॥ सर्वम्, गुण, कार्त्स्न्ये ॥

वृत्तिः ॥ सर्वशब्दः पूर्वपदं गुणकार्त्स्न्ये वर्त्तमानमन्तोदात्तं भवति ॥

93. The acute is on the final of the word सर्व standing as first member before an attributive word, in the sense of 'whole, through and through'.

Thus सर्वश्वेतः॰ सर्वकृष्णः, सर्वमहान् ॥ Why do we say सर्व ? Observe परमश्वेतः, here the attribute of श्वेत pervades through and through the object referred: but the accent is not on the final of परम ॥ Why do we say 'attributive word'? Observe सर्वसौवर्णः, 'golden', सर्वराजतः 'silvery', which do not denote any attribute in their original state but modification. In fact it is not गुणकार्त्स्न्यं here at all, but a विकारकार्त्स्न्यं ॥ Why do we use the word 'Kârtsnya or complete pervasion". Observe सर्वेषां श्वेततरः = सर्वश्वेतः here the compounding takes place by the elision of the affix तरप् denoting comparison, and as it shows only comparitive, not absolute, whiteness, the rule does not apply. Moreover, in this example, the "kârtsnya" is not that of "guṇa" but of "guṇî", not of the 'attribute', but of the 'substance'. *Objection*:—How do you form such a compound सर्वेषां श्वेततरः = सर्वश्वेतः, for it is prohibited by II. 2. 11.? *Ans.* We do it on the strength of the following Vârtika गुणात्तरेण समासो वक्तव्यः, तरलोपश्च ॥

संज्ञायां गिरिनिकाययोः ॥ ९४ ॥ पदानि ॥ संज्ञायाम्, गिरि, निकाययोः ॥

वृत्तिः ॥ संज्ञायां विषये गिरि निकाय इत्येतयोरुत्तरपदयोः पूर्वपदमन्तोदात्तं भवति ॥

94. The last syllable of the first member before गिरि and निकाय has the acute, when the compound is a Name.

Thus अञ्जनागिरिः, भञ्जनागिरिः, The finals of añjana and bhañjana are lengthened by VI. 3. 117. शापिण्डिनिकायः, मौण्डिनिकायः, चिखिल्लिनिकायः ॥ Why do we say 'when it is a Name'? Observe परमगिरिः, ब्राह्मणनिकायः ॥

कुमार्यां वयसि ॥ ९५ ॥ पदानि ॥ कुमार्य्याम्, वयसि, (पूर्वपदम् अन्तोदात्तम्)॥

वृत्तिः ॥ कुमार्यामुत्तरपदे वयसि गम्यमाने पूर्वपदमन्तोदात्तं भवति ॥

95. The last syllable of the first member gets the acute when the word कुमारी follows, the compound denoting age.

Thus वृद्धकुमारी 'an old maid'. The compounding is by II. 1. 57. जरत्कुमारी ॥ This compound is formed by II. 1. 49 with जरती ॥ The words become masculine by VI. 3. 42 in both examples. Q. The word कुमारी was formed by ङीप् by IV. 1. 20 in denoting the prime of youth, how can this word be now applied to denote old age by being coupled with वृद्धा or जरती; it is a contradiction in terms. *Ans*; The word कुमारी has two senses; one denoting "a young maiden" and second "unmarried virgin". It is in the latter sense, that the attribute वृद्धा or जरती is applied. Why do we say "when the compound denotes age"? Observe परमकुमारी ॥

उदकेऽकेवले ॥ ९६ ॥ पदानि ॥ उदके, अ, केवले, (पूर्वपदम् अन्तोदात्तम्) ॥

वृत्तिः ॥ अकेवलं मिश्रं तद्वाचिनि समासे उदकशब्दउत्तरपदे पूर्वपदमन्तोदात्तं भवति ॥

96. Before the word उदक, when the compound denotes a mixture, the last syllable of the first member has the acute.

Thus गुडोदकम् or गुडोदकम्, तिलोदकम् or तिलोदकम् ॥ When we have already made the ड and ल acute by this rule, then the svarita accent may result optionally, by the combination of the acute अ of guḍa and tila and the subsequent grave उ of उदक, by Rule VIII. 2. 6. The word अकेवल means mixture. When mixture is not meant, this rule does not apply. As शीतोदकम्, उष्णोदकम् ॥

द्विगौ क्रतौ ॥ ९७ ॥ पदानि ॥ द्विगौ, क्रतौ, (पूर्वपदम् अन्तोदात्तम्) ॥

वृत्तिः ॥ द्विगावुत्तरपदे क्रतुवाचिनि समासे पूर्वपदमन्तोदात्तं भवति ॥

97. Before a Dvigu, when the compound denotes a sacrifice, the last syllable of the first member has the acute.

Thus गर्गत्रिरात्रः, चारकत्रिरात्रः, कुसुरुबिन्दसप्तरात्रः = गर्गाणां त्रिरात्रः &c. Why do we say 'before a Dvigu compound'? Observe अतिरात्रः (रात्रिमतिक्रान्त इति प्रादिसमासः) which being formed by the Samasânta affix अच् (V. 4. 87) has acute on the final (VI. 1, 163). Why do we say 'when denoting a sacrifice'? Observe बिल्वसप्तरात्रः = बिल्वशतस्य बिल्वहोमस्य वा सप्तरात्रः ॥

सभायां नपुंसके ॥ ९८ ॥ पदानि ॥ सभायाम्, नपुंसके, (पूर्वपदम् अन्तोदात्तम्)॥

वृत्तिः ॥ सभाशब्दउत्तरपदे नपुंसकलिङ्गेसमासे पूर्वपदमन्तोदात्तं भवति ॥

98. Before the word सभा when it is exhibited as Neuter, the first member of the compound gets acute on the last syllable.

Thus गोपालसभम्, पशुपालसभम्, स्त्रीसभम्, दासीसभम्, गावडालसभम् ॥ Why do we say 'before सभा'? Observe ब्राह्मणसभम् ॥ Why do we say 'when in the Neuter'? Observe राजसभा, ब्राह्मणसभा ॥ The word सभा becomes Neuter under Rules II. 4. 23-24: therefore when the word सभा does not become Neuter under those rules, then by the maxim of Pratipadokta &c: the accent does not fall on the final of the preceding term as, रमणीयसभं, here the word सभा is neuter not by the force of any particular rules, but because the thing designated (अभिधेय) is neuter.

पुरे प्राचाम् ॥ ९९ ॥ पदानि ॥ पुरे, प्राचाम्, (पूर्वपदमन्तोदात्तम्) ॥

वृत्तिः ॥ पुरशब्दउत्तरपदे प्राचां देशे पूर्वपदमन्तोदात्तं भवति ॥

99. Before the word पुर, when the compound denotes a city of the Eastern People, the final of the first member has the acute.

Thus ललाटपुरम्, काञ्चीपुरम्, शिवदत्तपुरम्, कार्ष्णपुरम्, नान्दीपुरम् ॥ Why do we say 'of the Eastern people'? Observe शिवपुरम् ॥

अरिष्टगौडपूर्वे च ॥१००॥ पदानि ॥ अरिष्ट, गौड, पूर्वे, च, (पूर्वपदम् अन्तोदात्तम्)

वृत्तिः ॥ अरिष्ट गौड इत्येवं पूर्वे समासे पुरशब्दउत्तरपदे पूर्वपदमन्तोदात्तं भवति ॥

100. When the words अरिष्ट and गौड stand first, the first member has the acute on the final before the word पुर ॥

Thus अरिष्टपुरम्, गौडपुरम् ॥ By the force of the word पूर्व in the aphorism, we can apply the rule to अरिष्टाश्रितपुरम्, गौडभृत्यपुरम् ॥

न हास्तिनफलकमार्देयाः ॥ १०१ ॥ पदानि ॥ न, हास्तिन, फलक, मार्देयाः, (अन्तोदात्तानि) ॥

वृत्तिः ॥ हास्तिन फलक मार्देय इत्येतानि पूर्वपदानि पुरशब्द उत्तरपदे नान्तोदात्तानि भवन्ति ॥

101. But when the words हास्तिन, फलक and मार्देय precede पुर, the acute does not fall on their final.

This is an exception to VI. 2, 99. Thus हास्तिनपुरम्, फलकपुरम्, मार्देयपुरम् ॥ The son of मृदु is मार्देय formed by ढक्, the word belonging to Śubhrâdi class. The उ is elided by VI. 4. 147.

कुसूलकूपकुम्भशालं बिले ॥ १०२ ॥ पदानि ॥ कुसूल, कूप, कुम्भ, शालम्, बिले॥

वृत्तिः ॥ कुसूल कूप कुम्भ शाला इत्येतानि पूर्वपदानि बिलशब्दउत्तरपदे ऽन्तोदात्तानि भवन्ति ॥

102. The words कुसूल, कूप, कुम्भ and शाला have the acute on the last syllable before the word बिल ॥

Thus कुसूलबिलम्, कूपबिलम्, कुम्भबिलम्, शालाबिलम् ॥ But not so here सर्पबिलम् ॥ Why do we say 'before बिल'? Observe कुसूलस्वामी ॥

दिक्शब्दा ग्रामजनपदाख्यानचानराटेषु ॥ १०३ ॥ पदानि ॥ दिक्शब्दाः, ग्रामजनपदाख्यान, चानराटेषु ॥

वृत्तिः ॥ दिक्शब्दाः पूर्वपदानि अन्तोदात्तानि भवन्ति ग्रामजनपदाख्यानचानराटेषूत्तरपदेषु चानराटशब्दे च ॥

103. Words expressing direction (in space or time) have acute on the last syllable, when followed by a word denoting a village, or a country or a narrative, and before the word चानराट ॥

Thus पूर्वेषुकामशमी, अपरेषुकामशमी or पूर्वे and अपरे (VIII. 2. 6). The compounding takes place by II. 1. 50. पूर्वकृष्णमृत्तिका, अपरकृष्णमृत्तिका ॥ Country name—पूर्वपञ्चालाः, अपरपञ्चालाः ॥ These are Karmadhâraya compounds (II. 1. 58). Story name:—पूर्वाधिरामम् or पूर्वा, पूर्वयायातम्' पूर्वाधिरामकम्, अपरयायातम् ॥ So also पूर्वचानराटम्, अपरचानराटम् ॥ The employment of the term शब्द in the aphorism shows that time-denoting दिक् words as in पूर्वयायातं should also be included. The word आधिरामम् is derived from अधिराममधिकृत्य कृतो ग्रन्थः (IV. 3. 87).

आचार्योपसर्जनश्चान्तेवासिनि ॥ १०४ ॥ पदानि ॥ आचार्योपसर्जनः, च, अन्तेवासिनि, (अन्तोदात्ताः) ॥

वृत्तिः ॥ आचार्योपसर्जनान्तेवासिवाचिन्युत्तरपदे दिक्शब्दा अन्तोदात्ता भवन्ति ॥

104. The direction denoting words have acute on the final, before the names of scholars, when such names are derived from those of their teachers.

Thus पूर्वपाणिनीयाः, अपरपाणिनीयाः, पूर्वकाशकृत्स्नाः, अपरकाशकृत्स्नाः ॥ Compare VI. 2. 36 Why do we say 'when derived from the names of their Teachers'? Observe पूर्वशिष्याः ॥ Why do we say 'Scholar-names'? Observe पूर्वपाणिनीयं शास्त्रम् ॥ (पाणिनीयं शास्त्रं पूर्वं चिरन्तनम्) ॥

उत्तरपदवृद्धौ सर्वं च ॥ १०५ ॥ पदानि ॥ उत्तर-पद-वृद्धौ, सर्वम् च ॥

वृत्तिः ॥ उत्तरपदस्येत्यधिकृत्य या विहिता वृद्धिस्तद्वत्युत्तरपदे सर्वशब्दोदिक्शब्दाश्चान्तोदात्ता भवन्ति ॥

105. Words denoting direction and the word सर्व have acute on the final, before a word which takes Vṛiddhi in the first syllable of the second term by VII. 3. 12 and 13.

By the sûtra उत्तरपदस्य VII. 3. 10. 12, the Vṛiddhi of the Uttarapada is ordained when the Taddhita affixes having ञ्, ण् or क् follow, the Purvapada being सु, सर्व and अर्ध ॥ The word उत्तरपदवृद्धि: therefore, means that word which takes Vṛiddhi, under the rule relating to uttarapada, i. e. under rule VII. 3. 12 and 13. Thus पूर्वपाञ्चालकः, अपरपांचालकः, सर्वपाञ्चालकः ॥ These are formed by वुञ् affix (IV. 2. 125). Why do we say "which takes Vṛiddhi in the second term?" Had the word उत्तरपद not been used, then the sûtra would have run thus वृद्धौ सर्वं च, and would have applied to cases like सर्वमासः, सर्वकारकः where मासः and कारकः are Vṛiddha words not by virtue of VII. 3. 12.

बहुव्रीहौ विश्वं संज्ञायाम् ॥ १०६ ॥ पदानि ॥ बहुव्रीहौ, विश्वम्, संज्ञायाम् ॥

वृत्तिः ॥ बहुव्रीहौ समासे विश्वशब्दः पूर्वपदं संज्ञायां विषये ऽन्तोदात्तं भवति ॥

106. The word विश्व has acute on the final, being first member in a Bahuvrîhi, when it is a Name.

Thus विश्वदेवः, विश्वयशाः, विश्वमहान् ॥ This is an exception to VI. 2. 1 by which the first member in a Bahuvrihi would have retained its original accent. Why do we say in a Bahuvrîhi compound? Observe विश्वे च देवाः = विश्वदेवाः ॥ Why do we say 'when a name'? Observe विश्वेदेवा अस्य = विश्वदेवः ॥ But विश्वामित्रः and विश्वाजिनः have acute on the final, as they are governed by the subsequent rule VI, 2. 165 which supersedes this. The word Bahuvrîhi governs the succeeding sûtras upto VI. 2. 120 inclusive. The word विश्व is originally acute on the first, as it is formed by the affix क्वन् added to विश् ॥ This rule has unrestricted scope in विश्वदेवः, विश्वयशाः. and rule VI. 2. 165 has unrestricted scope in कुलमित्रः, कुलाजिनः ॥ But in विश्वामित्रः and विश्वाजिनः there is a conflict, as both these rules would apply, therefore by the maxim of vipratishedha, VI. 2. 165 supersedes this.

उदराश्वेषुषु ॥ १०७ ॥ पदानि ॥ उदर, अश्व, इषु षु ।

वृत्तिः ॥ उदर अश्व इषु इत्येतेषूत्तरपदेषु बहुव्रीहौ समासे संज्ञायां विषये पूर्वपदमन्तोदात्तं भवति ॥

107. The first member in a Bahuvrîhi, before the words उदर, अश्व and इषु, gets acute on the final syllable, when the compound denotes a Name.

Thus वृकोदरः, दामोदरः, हर्यश्वः, यौवनाश्वः, सुवर्णपुङ्खेषुः and महेषुः ॥ This sûtra is also an exception to VI. 2 1 by which the first term would have retained its original accent. The word वृक has acute on the first by Phit II. 7. The word दाम is formed by मनिन् affix (Uṇ IV. 145) and is first acute; हरि is also first acute as formed by इन् (Uṇ IV. 118). The word यौवन if considered as an underived primitive, has acute on the first by Phit II. 19. If it be considered as derived from युवन् with the affix अण् then it is already end-acute and would retain its accent even by VI. 2. 1. The first Bahuvrîhi word सुवर्ण has acute on the final by VI. 2. 172, the second Bahuvrîhi compound सुवर्णपुङ्खाः has acute on र्ण by VI. 2. 1, the third Bahuvrihi with इषु gets accent on ङ्ख ॥ The word महत् is end-acute by V. 2. 38. Its mention here appears redundant.

क्षेपे ॥ १०८ ॥ पदानि ॥ क्षेपे ॥

वृत्तिः ॥ क्षेपे गम्यमाने उदरादिषूत्तरपदेषु बहुव्रीहौ समासे संज्ञायां विषये पूर्वपदमन्तोदात्तं भवति ॥

108. A word before उदर, अश्व and इषु in a Bahuvrîhi gets acute on the final, when reproach is meant.

Thus कुण्डोदरः, घटोदरः, कटुकाश्वः, स्यन्दिताश्वः, अनिघातेषुः, चलाचलेषुः ॥ The word कुण्ड has acute on the first as it is a Neuter name (Phiṭ II. 3), and it would have retained this accent in the Bahuvrihi by VI. 2. 1. but for this sûtra. The word घट is formed by अच् (III. 1. 134) and has acute on the final, and so it would have retained this accent by VI. 2. 1. even with out this sûtra. The word कटुक being formed by कन् (V. 3. 75) has acute on the first. स्यन्दित is formed by the Nishṭâ affix क्त ॥ The word अनिघात being an avyayîbhâva, the first member would have retained its original accent. In this and the last sûtra, all the acutes may optionally be changed into svarita by VIII. 2. 6. But अनुदरः and सूदरः have acute on the final by VI. 2. 172, which being a subsequent sûtra supersedes this present, so far as अन् and सु are concerned.

नदी बन्धुनि ॥ १०९ ॥ पदानि ॥ नदी, बन्धुनि ॥

वृत्तिः ॥ बहुव्रीहौ समासे बन्धुन्युत्तरपदे नद्यन्तं पूर्वपदमन्तोदात्तं भवति ॥

109. In a Bahuvrîhi compound having the word बन्धु as its second member, the first member ending in the Feminine affix ई (नदी word) has the acute on its final syllable.

Thus गार्गीबन्धुः, वात्सीबन्धुः ॥ The words गार्गी and वात्सी are formed by adding ङीप् (IV. 1. 16) to गार्ग्य and वात्स्य ending in यञ् (IV. 1. 105), and therefore, they are first acute. By VI. 2. 1 this accent would have been retained, but for the present sûtra. Why do we say "a Nadi (Feminine in ई) word"? Observe ब्रह्मबन्धुः, the word ब्रह्म has acute on the first syllable as it is formed by मनिन् (Uṇ IV. 146) and it retains that accent (VI. 2. 1). Why do we say "before बन्धु"? Observe गार्गीप्रियः ॥

निष्ठोपसर्गपूर्वमन्यतरस्याम् ॥ ११० ॥ पदानि ॥ निष्ठा, उपसर्ग-पूर्वम्, अन्यतरस्याम् ॥

वृत्तिः ॥ बहुव्रीहौ समासे निष्ठान्तमुपसर्गपूर्वं पूर्वपदमन्यतरस्यामन्तोदात्तं भवति ॥

110. In a Bahuvrîhi compound, a Participle in क्त preceded by a preposition, standing as the first member of the compound, has optionally acute on the last syllable.

Thus प्रधौतमुखः or प्रधौतमुखः (VI. 2. 169), or प्रधौतमुखः (VI. 2. 49 and 1) प्रक्षालितपादः or प्रक्षालितपादः ॥ When the word मुख means (mouth) then by VI. 2. 167 which is an optional rule, the accent falls on the last syllable खः ॥ When the other alternative is taken or when it does not mean (mouth) then by VI. 2. 49 the acute falls on प्र, which accent is retained (VI. 2. 1). Why do we say "a Nishṭhâ"? Observe प्रसारकमुखः which is acute in the middle by the kṛit accent being retained ofter प्र (VI. 2. 139). Why do we say 'preceded by a preposition'? Observe शुष्कमुखः which has acute on the first by VI. 1. 206.

उत्तरपदादिः ॥ १११ ॥ पदानि ॥ उत्तर, पदादिः, (उदात्तः) ॥

वृत्तिः ॥ उत्तरपदादिरित्येतदधिकृतम् । यदित ऊर्ध्वमनुक्रमिष्याम उत्तरपदस्यादिरुदात्तो भवतीत्येवं तद्वेदितव्यम्॥

111. In the following sûtras, upto VI. 2. 136 inclusive, should always be supplied the phrase "the first syllable of the second member has the acute".

This is an adhikâra aphorism and the word उत्तरपद exerts its influence upto the end of the chapter, while the word आदि has scope upto VI. 2. 187 exclusive.

कर्णो वर्णलक्षणात् ॥ ११२ ॥ पदानि ॥ कर्णः, वर्ण, लक्षणात्, (आद्युदात्तम्) ॥

वृत्तिः ॥ बहुव्रीहौ समासे वर्णवाचिनो लक्षणवाचिनश्च कर्णशब्दउत्तरपदमाद्युदात्तं भवति ॥

112. In a Bahuvrîhi compound, the word कर्ण standing as second member, has acute on the first syllable, when it is preceded by a word denoting color or mark.

Thus with color we have शुक्लकर्णः, कृष्णकर्णः, and with mark-name, we have दात्राकर्णः शङ्कुकर्णः, the lengthening of दात्र and शंकु takes place by VI. 3. 115.

The marks of 'scythe', 'arrow' &c, are made on the ears of cattle to mark and distinguish them. It is such a 'mark' which is meant here, therefore, the rule does not apply to स्थूलकर्णः ॥ Why do we say कर्ण ? Observe श्वेतपादः, कूटशृङ्गः here श्वेत being formed by अच् (II. 1. 134) is end-acute, and कूट being formed by क्र (III. 1. 135) is also end-acute and these accents are retained in the compound. Why do we say "when preceded by a word denoting color or mark"? Observe शोभनपादः where शोभन being formed by युच् (III. 2. 149) is end-acute and this accent is retained (VI. 2. 1).

संज्ञौपम्ययोश्च ॥ ११३ ॥ पदानि ॥ संज्ञा, औपम्ययोः, च ॥

वृत्तिः ॥ संज्ञायामौपम्ये च यो बहुव्रीहिर्वर्त्तते तत्र कर्णशब्द उत्तरपदमाद्युदात्तं भवति संज्ञायाम् ॥

113. In a Bahuvrîhi the second member कर्ण has acute on the first syllable, when the compound denotes a Name or a Resemblance.

Thus कुञ्चिकर्णः, मणिकर्णः, are Names. गोकर्णः, खरकर्णः denote resemblance i. e. "persons having ears like a cow or an ass".

कण्ठपृष्ठग्रीवाजङ्घं च ॥ ११४ ॥ पदानि ॥ कण्ठ, पृष्ठ, ग्रीवा, जंघम्, च, (आद्युदात्तानि) ॥

वृत्तिः ॥ कण्ठ पृष्ठ ग्रीवा जङ्घा इत्येतानि उत्तरपदानि बहुव्रीहौ समासे संज्ञौपम्ययोराद्युदात्तानि भवन्ति ॥

114. In a Bahuvrîhi expressing a Name or comparision, the second members कण्ठ, पृष्ठ, ग्रीवा and जङ्घा have acute on the first syllable.

Thus Name: शितिकण्ठः, नीलकण्ठः ॥ Comparision खरकण्ठः, उष्ट्रकण्ठः ॥ Name काण्डपृष्ठः, नाकपृष्ठः ॥ Resemblance गोपृष्ठः अजपृष्ठः ॥ Name सुग्रीवः, नीलग्रीवः, दशग्रीवः ॥ Resemblauce गोग्रीवः, अश्वग्रीवः ॥ Name नाडीजङ्घः, तालजङ्घः ॥ Resemblance गोजङ्घः, अश्वजङ्घः, एणीजङ्घः ॥

The sûtra कण्ठपृष्ठग्रीवाजंघ is in Neuter gender, and जंघा is shortened as it is a Samâhâra Dvandva. In the case of सुग्रीव, the accent would have fallen on the final व by VI. 2. 172, this ordains acute on ग्री ॥

शृङ्गमवस्थायां च ॥ ११५ ॥ पदानि ॥ शृङ्गम्, अवस्थयाम्, च (आद्युदात्तम्) ॥

वृत्तिः ॥ शृङ्गशब्द उत्तरपदमवस्थायां संज्ञौपम्ययोश्च बहुव्रीहौ आद्युदात्तं भवति ॥

115. In a Bahuvrîhi denoting age, (as well as a Name or a Resemblance), the second member शृङ्ग gets acute on the first syllable.

Thus उद्गतशृङ्गः, द्व्यंगुलशृङ्गः, त्र्यंगुलशृङ्गः ॥ Here the word शृङ्ग denotes the particular age of the cattle at which the horns come out, or become one or two inches long. Name :—ऋष्यशृङ्गः comparison : गोशृङ्गः, मेषशृङ्गः ॥ Why do we say when denoting 'age &c'. Observe स्थूलशृङ्गः ॥

नञो जरमरमित्रमृताः ॥ ११६ ॥ पदानि ॥ नञः, जर, मर, मित्र, मृताः, (आद्युदात्ताः) ॥

वृत्तिः ॥ नञ उत्तरे जरमरमित्रमृता बहुव्रीहौ समासे आद्युदात्ता भवन्ति ॥

116. After a Negative Particle, in a Bahuvrîhi, the acute falls on the first syllable of जर, मर, मित्र and मृत ॥

Thus अजॅरः, अमॅरः, अमित्रः and अमृतः ॥ Why do we say after a Negative Particle? Observe ब्राह्मणमित्रः ॥ Why do we say "जर &c". Observe अशत्रुः when the final gets the acute by VI. 2. 172.

सोर्मनसी अलोमोषसी ॥ ११७॥ पदानि ॥ सोः, मन्-असी, अ लोम, उषसी ॥

वृत्तिः ॥ सोरुत्तरमनन्तमसन्तं च बहुव्रीहौ समासे आद्युदात्तं भवति लोमोषसीवर्जयित्वा ॥

117. After the adjective सु in a Bahuvrîhi, a stem ending in मन् and अस्, with the exception of लोमन् and उषस् has acute on the first syllable.

Thus सुकॅर्मन्, सुधॅर्मन्, सुप्रॅथिमन्, सुपॅयस्, सुयॅशस्, सुस्रॅोतस् so also सुस्रॅत् and सुध्वॅत् from the root स्रंस् and ध्वंस् with the affix क्विप् ॥ The final स् is changed to द् by VIII. 2. 72. But this substitution is considered asiddha for the purposes of accent, and these words are taken as if still ending in अस् ॥ Why do we say 'after सु?' Observe कृतकर्मन्, कृतयशस् ॥ Why do we say 'ending in मन् and अस्?' Observe सुराजन् and सुतक्षन् formed by the affix कनिन् (Uṇ I. 156), and the accent is on रा and त, but with सु, the accent is thrown on the final by VI. 2. 172. Why do we say with the exception of लोमन and उषत्? Observe सुलोमॅन् and सूषॅस् (VI. 2. 172). The following maxim applies here: अनिनस्मन् ग्रहणान्यर्थवता चानर्थकेन च तदन्तविधिं प्रयोजयन्ति "whenever अन्, or इन् or अस् or मन्, when they are employed in Grammar, denote by I. 1. 72, something that ends with अन् or इन् or अस् or मन्, there (अन्, इन्, अस् and मन्) represent these combinations of letters, both in so far as they possess and also in so far as they are void of, a meaning". Therefore the मन् and अस् void of meaning are also included here. Thus धर्मन् is formed by मन् (Uṇ I. 140), but कर्मन् is formed by मनिन् (Uṇ. IV. 145), and प्रथिमन् is formed by इमनिच् affix (V. 1. 122) in which मन् is only a part. Similarly यशस् is formed by असुन् (Uṇ IV. 191), and so also स्रोतस् (Uṇ IV. 202); but in सुध्वॅस् (सुध्वस् from ध्वंस् with the affix क्विप III. 2. 76) the rule applies also, though अस् is here part of the root. But when the samâsânta affix कप् is added (V. 4. 154), then the accent falls on the syllable immediately preceding कप्, for there the subsequent Rule VI. 2. 173 supersedes the present rule: thus सुकर्मॅकः, सुस्रोतॅस्कः ॥

क्रत्वादयश्च ॥ ११८॥ पदानि ॥ क्रत्वादयः, च, ॥

वृत्तिः ॥ क्रत्वादयः सोरुत्तरे बहुव्रीहौ समासे आद्युदात्ता भवन्ति ।

118. After सु in a Bahuvrîhi, the acute falls on the first syllable of क्रतु &c.

Thus सुक्रतुः, सुप्रतीकः, सुप्रपूर्तिः, सुहव्यः, सुभगः, सुप्रतिक्रः ॥

आद्युदात्तं द्व्यच्छन्दसि ॥ ११९ ॥ पदानि ॥ आद्युदात्तम्, द्व्यच्, छन्दसि ॥

वृत्तिः ॥ आद्युदात्तं द्व्यच् उत्तरपदं बहुव्रीहौ समासे सोरुत्तरं तदाद्युदात्तमेव भवति छन्दसि विषये ॥

119. In a Bahuvrîhi compound in the Chhandas, a word of two syllables with acute on the first syllable, when preceded by सु, gets acute on the first syllable.

In other words, such a word retains its accent. Thus:—स्वश्वासिन्धुः सुरथा सुवासा (Rig Veda X. 76. 8). Here स्वश्वः and सुरथः have acute on अ and र, which they had originally also, for अश्व and रथ are formed by क्वन् (Uṇ I. 151) and क्थन् (Uṇ II. 2) respectively and have the नित् accent (VI. 1. 197). Why do we say 'having acute on the first syllable'? Observe या सुबाहुः स्वङ्गुरिः (Rig II. 32. 7). Here बाहु has acute on the final (Uṇ I. 27 formed by उ affix and has the accent of the affix III. 1. 3). Why do we say 'having two syllables'? Observe सुगुरसत्, सुहिरण्यः ॥ This sûtra is an exception to VI. 2. 172.

वीरवीर्यौ च ॥ १२० ॥ पदानि ॥ वीर, वीर्य्यौ, च, ॥

वृत्तिः ॥ वीर वीर्य इत्येतौ च शब्दौ सोरुत्तरौ बहुव्रीहौ समासे छन्दसि विषये आद्युदात्तौ भवतः ।

120. In a Bahuvrîhi compound in the Chhandas, after सु, the words वीर and वीर्य have acute on the first syllable.

Thus सुवीरेण ते, सुवीरस्ते जनिता (Rig IV. 17. 4) सुवीर्यस्य स्वश्व्यस्य (Rig VIII. 13. 36) where सुवीर्य has acute on वी ॥ So also सुवीर्यस्य पतयः स्याम ॥ The word वीर्य is formed by यत् affix and by VI. 1. 213, it would have acute on the first. But its enumeration in this sûtra shows that Rule VI. 1. 213 does not apply to वीर्य ॥ The word वीर्य has svarita on the final in the Chhandas, by Phit IV. 9. In the secular literature it is âdyudâtta.

कूलतीरतूलमूलशालाक्षसममव्ययीभावे ॥ १२१ ॥ पदानि ॥ कूल, तीर, तूल, मूल, शाला, अक्ष, समम, अव्ययीभावे ॥

वृत्तिः ॥ कूल तीर तूल मूल शाला अक्ष सम इत्येतानि उत्तरपदानि अव्ययीभावसमासे आद्युदात्तानि भवन्ति ॥

121. In an Avyayîbhâva compound, the following second terms have acute on their first syllable : कूल, तीर, तूल, मूल, शाला, अक्ष and सम ॥

Thus परिकूलम्, उपकूलम्, परितीरम्, उपतीरम्, परितूलम्, उपतूलम्, परिमूलम्, उपमूलम्, परिशालम्, उपशालम्, उपाक्षम्, पर्यक्षम्, सुषमम्, विषमम्, निषमम् and दुःषमम् ॥ These last four are to be found in Tishṭhadgu class of compounds (II. 1. 17). Why do we say 'कूल &c'? Observe उपकुम्भम् ॥ Why do we say "in an Avyayîbhâva compound?" Observe परमकूलम्, उत्तमकूलम् ॥ After the prepositions परि, प्रति, उप and अप, the words कूल &c would have become accentless by VI. 2. 33, the present sûtra supersedes VI. 2. 33, and we have accent on कूल &c and not on the Prepositions.

कंसमन्थशूर्पपाय्यकाण्डं द्विगौ ॥ १२२ ॥ पदानि ॥ कंस, मन्थ, शूर्प, पाय्य, काण्डम, द्विगौ ॥

वृत्तिः ॥ कंस मन्थ शूर्प पाय्य काण्ड इत्येतान्युत्तरपदानि द्विगौ समासआद्युदात्तानि भवन्ति ॥

122. In a Dvigu Compound the following second members get acute on their first syllable :—कंस, मन्थ, शूर्प, पाय्य and काण्ड ॥

Thus द्विकंसः, (द्वाभ्यां कंसाभ्यां क्रीतः the affix टिठन् V. 1. 25 is elided by V. 1. 28) त्रिकंसः, द्विमन्थः, (the affix ठक् V. 1. 19 is elided by V. 1. 28) त्रिमन्थः, द्विशूर्पः, (the affix अञ् V. 1. 26 is elided) त्रिशूर्पः, द्विपाय्यः, त्रिपाय्यः, द्विकाण्डः, त्रिकाण्डः ॥ Why do we say in a Dvigu? Observe परमकंसः, उत्तमकंसः ॥

तत्पुरुषे शालायां नपुंसके ॥ १२३ ॥ पदानि ॥ तत्पुरुषे, शालायाम, नपुंसके ॥

वृत्तिः ॥ शालाशब्दान्ते तत्पुरुषे समासे नपुंसकलिङ्गे उत्तरपदमाद्युदात्तं भवति ॥

123. The word शाला at the end of a Tatpurusha compound when exhibited in the Neuter has acute on the first syllable.

Thus ब्राह्मणशालम्, क्षत्रियशालम् ॥ The compound becomes Neuter by II. 4. 25. Why do we say "in a Tatpurusha"? Observe दृढशालं ब्राह्मणकुलम् which is a Bahuvrîhi compound and therefore first member retains its accent VI. 2. 1, and as the first member is a Nishṭhâ word, it has acute on the final. Why do we say "the word शाला?" Observe ब्राह्मणसेनम् ॥ Why do we say 'in the Neuter'? Observe ब्राह्मणशाला ॥ Compare VI. 2. 86.

कन्था च ॥ १२४ ॥ पदानि ॥ कन्था, च, ॥

वृत्तिः ॥ तत्पुरुषे समासे नपुंसकलिङ्गे कथाशब्द उत्तरपदमाद्युदात्तं भवति ॥

124. In a Neuter Tatpurusha ending in कन्था, the acute falls on the first syllable of the second member.

Thus सौशमिकन्थम्, आह्वरकन्थम्, चप्यकन्थम् ॥ The word सौशमिः denotes the descendant of सुशमः (शोभनः शमो यस्य) आह्वर is formed by the preposition आ with the verb ह्वृ and the affix क (III. 1. 136) The compound is Neuter by II. 4. 20. These are Genitive compounds. When the word is not Neuter we have दाक्षिकन्था ॥

आदिश्चिहणादीनाम् ॥ १२५ ॥ पदानि ॥ आदिः, चिहणादीनाम् ॥

वृत्तिः ॥ कन्थान्ते तत्पुरुषे समासे नपुंसकलिङ्गे चिहणादीनामादिरुदात्तो भवति ॥

125. In a Neuter Tatpurusha ending in कन्था, the first syllable of चिहण &c have the acute.

As चिँहणकन्थम्, मैँडरकन्थम्, मैँड्डरकन्थम् ॥ The repetition of the word आद्ये in this sûtra, though its anuvritti was present, indicates that the first syllable of the *first member* gets the acute. The word चिहण is derived from the root चिनोति with क्विप् which gives चित् and हन is formed by adding अच् (III. 1. 134) to हन् ॥ चित + हन = चिहण the elision of त् is irregular.

चेलखेटकटुककाण्डं गर्हायाम् ॥ १२६ ॥ पदानि ॥ चेल, खेट, कटुक, काण्डम्, गर्हायाम्, ॥

वृत्तिः ॥ चेल खेट कटुक काण्ड इत्येतान्युत्तरपदानि तत्पुरुषे समासे गर्हायां गम्यमानायामाद्युदात्तानि भवन्ति ॥

126. The words चेल, खेट, कटुक and काण्ड at the end of a Tatpurushá have acute on the first syllable, when a reproach is meant.

Thus पुत्रचेँलम्, भार्याचेँलम, उपानत्खेँटम्, नगरखेँटम्, (खेट इति तृणनाम, तद्वद् दुर्बला उपानत्) दधिकँटुकम् (कटुकमस्वादु) उदश्वित्कँटुकम्, भूतकाँण्डम् (काण्डमिति शरनाम, तद्यथा सत्वपीडाकर मेवं भूतमपि) प्रजाकाँण्डम् ॥ The reproach is denoted of the sons &c by comparing them to चेल &c. The analysis will be पुत्रश्चेलमिव i. e. चेलवत् तुच्छम् and the compounding takes place under II. 1. 56: the Vyaghrâdi class being an akṛtigaṇa. When reproach is not meant, we have परमचेलम् ॥

चीरमुपमानम् ॥ १२७ ॥ पदानि ॥ चीरम्, उपमानम् ॥

वृत्तिः ॥ चीरमुत्तरपदमुपमानवाचि तत्पुरुषे समासे आद्युदात्तं भवति ॥

127. The word चीर, at the end of a Tatpurusha, has acute on the first syllable, when something is compared with it.

Thus वस्त्रम् चीरमिव = वस्त्रचीँरम्, पटचीँरम्, कम्बलचीँरम् ॥ Why do we say 'when comparison is meant?' Observe परमचीरम् ॥

पललसूपशाकं मिश्रे ॥ १२८ ॥ पदानि ॥ पलल, सूप, शाकम्, मिश्रे ॥

वृत्तिः ॥ पलल सूप शाक इत्येतान्युत्तरपदानि मिश्रवाचीनि तत्पुरुषे समासे आद्युदात्तानि भवन्ति ॥

128. In a Tatpurusha ending in पलल, सूप and शाक the acute falls on the first syllable of these, when the compound denotes a food mixed or seasoned with something.

Thus गुडपँललम्, घृतपँललम्, घृतसूपः, मूलकसूँपः, घृतशाँकम्, मुद्गशाँकम् = गुडेन मिश्रं पललं &c. The compounding takes place by II. 1. 35. Why do we say "when meaning mixed or seasoned?' Observe परमपललम् ॥

कूलसूदस्थलकर्षाः संज्ञायाम् ॥ १२९ ॥ पदानि ॥ कूल, सूद, स्थल, कर्षाः, संज्ञायाम् ॥

वृत्तिः ॥ कूल सूद स्थल कर्ष इत्येतान्युत्तरपदानि तत्पुरुषे समासे संज्ञायां विषये आद्युदात्तानि भवन्ति ॥

129. The words कूल, सूद, स्थल and कर्ष have acute on their first syllable, when at the end of a Tatpurusha denoting a Name.

Thus दाक्षिकूलम्, आहकिकूलम्, देवसूदम्, भाजीसूदम्, दाण्डायनस्थली, माहकिस्थली, दाक्षिकर्षः ॥ All these are names of villages. The feminine of स्थल is taken here, formed by ङीष् (IV. 1. 42). When not a name we have परमकूलम् ॥

अकर्मधारये राज्यम् ॥ १३० ॥ पदानि ॥ अ, कर्मधारये, राज्यम् (आद्युदात्तम्) ॥

वृत्तिः ॥ कर्मधारयवर्जिते तत्पुरुषे समासे राज्यमित्येतदुत्तरपदमाद्युदात्तं भवति ॥

130. The word राज्यम् has acute on the first syllable, when at the end of a Tatpurusha compound, which is not a Karmadhâraya.

Thus ब्राह्मणराज्यम्, क्षत्रियराज्यम् ॥ In a Karmadhâraya we have परमराज्यम् ॥ The accent taught in VI. 2. 126 to 130 is superseded by the accent of the Indeclinable taught in VI. 2. 2, though that rule stands first and this subsequent. As कुचेलम्, कुराज्यम् ॥

वर्ग्यादयश्च ॥ १३१ ॥ पदानि ॥ वर्ग्यादयः, च, (आद्युदात्तानि)

वृत्तिः ॥ वर्ग्य इत्येवमादीन्युत्तरपदानि अकर्मधारये तत्पुरुषे समासे आद्युदात्तानि भवन्ति ॥

131. At the end of a non-Karmadhâraya Tatpurusha compound, the words वर्ग्य &c have acute on the first syllable.

Thus वासुदेववर्ग्यः, वासुदेवपक्ष्यः, अर्जुनवर्ग्यः, अर्जुनपक्ष्यः ॥ In a Karmadhâraya we have परमवर्ग्यः ॥ The words वर्ग्य &c are no where exhibited as such; the primitive words वर्ग, पूग, गण &c sub-divisionof दिगादि (IV. 3. 54) are here referred to, as ending with यत् affix.

पुत्रः पुम्भ्यः ॥ १३२ ॥ पदानि ॥ पुत्रः, पुम्भ्यः (आद्युदात्तः) ॥

वृत्तिः ॥ पुत्रशब्दः पुंशब्देभ्य उत्तरस्तत्पुरुषे समासे आद्युदात्तो भवति ॥

132. The word पुत्र coming after a Masculine noun in a Tatpurusha has acute on the first syllable.

Thus कौनटिपुत्रः, दामकपुत्रः, माहिषपुत्रः ॥ Why do we say 'a पुत्र'? Observe कौनटिमातुलः ॥ Why do we say 'after a masculine word'? Observe गार्गीपुत्रः, वात्सीपुत्रः ॥

नाचार्यराजर्त्विक्संयुक्तज्ञात्याख्येभ्यः ॥ १३३ ॥ पदानि ॥ न, आचार्य्य, राज, ऋत्विक्, संयुक्त, ज्ञात्याख्येभ्यः, (आद्युदात्तः) ॥

वृत्तिः ॥ आचार्य उपाध्यायः । राजा ईश्वरः । ऋत्विजो याजकाः । संयुक्ताः स्त्रीसंबन्धिनः श्यालादयः । ज्ञातयो मातृपितृसंबन्धिनो बान्धवाः । आचार्याद्याख्येभ्यः परः पुत्रशब्दो नाद्युदात्तो भवति ।

133. The word पुत्र has not acute on the first syllable, when preceded by a word which falls under the category of teachers, kings, priests, wife's relations, and agnates and cognates.

The word आचार्य means 'teacher', राजा 'prince, king', ऋत्विज् 'a sacrificing priest', संयुक्ताः 'relations through the wife's side' as श्याला 'brother-in-law' &c: ज्ञाति means 'all kinsmen related through father and mother or blood-relations'. The word आख्या shows that the rule applies to the synonyms of 'teacher' &c, as well as to particular 'teacher' &c. Thus आचार्यपुत्रः, उपाध्यायपुत्रः, शाकटायनकपुत्रः, राजपुत्रः, ईश्वरपुत्रः, नन्दपुत्रः, ऋत्विकपुत्रः, याजकपुत्रः, होतुःपुत्रः, (VI. 3. 23) संयुक्तपुत्रः, संबन्धिपुत्रः, श्यालकपुत्रः, ज्ञातिपुत्रः, भ्रातुष्पुत्रः (VI. 3. 23). Here the special accent of पुत्र taught in the last sûtra being prohibited, the accent falls on the last syllable by the general rule VI. 1. 2 23.

चूर्णादीन्यप्राणिषष्ठ्याः ॥ १३४ ॥ पदानि ॥ चूर्णादीनि, अ, प्राणि, षष्ठ्याः, (आद्युदात्तानि) ॥

वृत्तिः ॥ उत्तरपदादिरिति वर्त्तते तत्पुरुषइति च । चूर्णादीन्युत्तरपदानि अप्राणिवाचिनः षष्ठ्यन्तात्पराणि तत्पुरुषे समासे आद्युदात्तानि भवन्ति ॥

134. The words चूर्ण &c, in a Tatpurusha compound have acute on the first syllable, when the preceding word ends in a Genitive and does not denote a living being.

Thus मुद्गचूर्णम्, मसूरचूर्णम, but मत्स्यचूर्णम् where the first term is a living being, and परमचूर्णम् where it is not Genitive. Another reading of the sûtra is चूर्णादीन्यप्राण्युपग्रहात्, the word उपग्रह being rhe ancient name of षष्ठी given by old Grammarians.

1 चूर्ण, 2 करिव, 3 करिप, 4 शाकिन, 5 शाकट, 6 द्राक्षा, 7 तूस्त, 8 कुन्दुम (कुन्दम), 9 दलप, 10 चमसी, 11 चक्कन (चकन चक्वन), 12 चौल ॥

The word चूर्ण is derived from the root चुरी दाहे (Div 50) with the affix क्त ; करिव and करिप are formed with the upapada करि and the verbs वा 'to go' and पा 'to protect' respectively, and the affix क (करिणंवाति = करिव) (III. 2. 3); शाक with the affix इनण् added diversely (Uṇ II. 56); शक with अटच (Uṇ IV. 81) gives शकट ; this with अण् (तद्वहति) gives शाकट ; द्राक् क्षराति = द्राक्षा (Prishodarâdi); तुस (शब्दे) with क्त gives तूस्त the penultimate being lengthened; the word कुन्दु is formed by the affix क्विप added to the root दु with the upapada कु (कुंदुनोति कुत्सितं वा दुनोति) the angment मुम् being added to कु ॥ कुन्दुं मिमीते = कुन्दुमः ॥ दल with the âffix कपन् gives दलपः, चम with असच् forms चमस, then is added ङीष् ; चक्कन is formed by अच् (III. 1. 134) added to कन् and reduplication., चोलस्यापत्यं = चौलः ॥

षट् च काण्डादीनि ॥ १३५ ॥ पदानि ॥ षट्, च, काण्डादीनि, (आद्युदात्तानि) ॥

वृत्तिः ॥ षट् पूर्वोक्तानि काण्डादीन्युत्तरपदानि अप्राणिषष्ठ्या आद्युदात्तानि भवन्ति ॥

135. The six words काण्ड, चीर, पलल, सूप, शाक and कूल of Sûtras VI. 2. 126–129, preceded by a non-living genitive word, have acute on the first syllable.

As दर्भकाण्डम्, शरकाण्डम्; दर्भचीरम्, कुशचीरम् ॥ In the last two examples चीर is not used as a comparision, that case being governed by VI. 2. 127, तिलपललम्, मूलकशाकम्, मुद्गसूपः ॥ Here पलल, सूप and शाक do not denote mixing, which is governed by VI. 2. 128. नदीकूलम्, समुद्रकूलम्, here the compound does not denote a Name, which would be the case under VI. 2, 129. Why these 'six' only? Observe राजसूदः ॥

कुण्डं वनम् ॥ १३६ ॥ पदानि ॥ कुण्डम्, वनम् (आद्युदात्तम्) ॥

वृत्तिः ॥ कुण्डशब्दोऽत्र कुण्डसादृश्येन वने वर्त्तते । कुण्डमित्येतदुत्तरपदं वनवाचि तत्पुरुषे समासे आद्युदात्तं भवति ॥

136. The word कुण्ड at the end of a Tatpurusha compound denoting 'a wood or forest', has acute on the first syllable.

The word कुण्ड here denotes 'a wood' by metaphor. Thus दर्भकुण्डम्, शरकुण्डम् ॥ Why do we say when denoting 'a wood'? Observe मृत्कुण्डम् ॥ The word कुण्ड means (1) a basin (2) a caste called kuṇḍa. Some say it means 'forest' also primarily and metaphorically. The force here is that of समुदाय, i. e. शरवणसमुदायः = शरकुण्डम् ॥

प्रकृत्या भगालम् ॥ १३७ ॥ पदानि ॥ प्रकृत्या, भगालम्, (प्रकृतिस्वरम्) ॥

वृत्तिः ॥ भगालवाच्युत्तरपदे तत्पुरुषे समासे प्रकृतिस्वरं भवति ॥

137. The word भगाल at the end of a Tatpurusha, preserves its original accent.

The synonyms of भगाल are also included. As कुम्भीभगालम्, कुम्भीकपालम्, कुम्भीनदालम् ॥ The words भगाल &c, have acute on the middle. Phit II. 9. The word प्रकृत्य governs the subsequent sûtras upto VI. 2. 143.

शितेर्नित्याबह्वज् बहुव्रीहावभसत् ॥ १३८ ॥ पदानि ॥ शितेः, नित्य, अबह्वच्, बहुव्रीहौ, अभसत्, (प्रकृतिस्वरम्) ॥

वृत्तिः ॥ शितेरुत्तरपदं नित्यं यदबह्वज्भसच्छब्दवर्जितं बहुव्रीहौ समासे तत्प्रकृतिस्वरं भवति ॥

138. After शिति, a word retains in a Bahuvrîhi its original accent, when it is always of not more than two syllables, with the exception of भसद् ॥

Thus शितिपादः, शित्यंसः, शित्योष्ठः ॥ The word पाद belongs to वृषादि class (VI. 1. 203) and has acute on the first, and अंसः and ओष्ठ: being formed by सन् (Uṇ V. 21) and थन् (Uṇ II. 4) affixes, have acute on the first (VI. 1. 197). Why do we say 'after शिति'? Observe दर्शनीयपादः which being formed by the affix अनीयर् has acute on the penultimate syllable नी by VI. 1. 217 ॥ Why do we say 'always'? Observe शितिककुत्, for though ककुत् is here of two syllables, it is an abbreviated form of ककुद, the final अ being elided in denoting condition of life (V. 4. 146), in compounds other than those denoting 'age', we have शितिककुदः, hence this word is not such which is *always* of two syllables. The word शिति has acute on the first syllable, by Phiṭ II. 10, and retains this accent in the Bahuvrihi (VI. 2. 1). Why do we say 'abahvach or not many-syllable'? Observe शितिपिल्लाटः ॥. Why do we say in a Bahuvrihi? Observe शितेः पादः = शितिपादः ॥ Why do we say 'with the exception of भसत्'? Observe शितिभसत् ॥ This sûtra is an exception to VI. 2. 1.

गतिकारकोपपदात्कृत् ॥ १३९ ॥ पदानि ॥ गति, कारक, उपपदात्, कृत, (प्रकृतिस्वरम्) ॥

वृत्तिः ॥ तत्पुरुषइति वर्त्तते न बहुव्रीहाविति । गतेः कारकादुपपदाच्च कृदन्तमुत्तरपदं तत्पुरुषे समासे प्रकृतिस्वरं भवति ॥

139. In a Tatpurusha, a word ending in a Kṛit-affix preserves its original accent, when preceded by an Indeclinable called Gati (I. 4. 60), or a noun standing in intimate relation to a verb (Kâraka), or any word which gives occasion for compounding (Upapada see III. 1. 92).

The above is according to Professor Bohtlingk. Thus प्रकारकः, प्रकरणम्, प्रहारकः, प्रहरणम् ॥ The compounding is here by II. 2. 18. With kâraka-word we have :—इध्मप्रव्रश्चनः. पलाशशातनः, श्मश्रुकल्पनः (III. 3. 117). With upapada words, we have :—ईषत्करः, दुष्करः, सुकरः ॥ All these are formed by लित् affixes and the accent is governed by VI. 1. 193. i. e. the word व्रश्चन is formed by ल्युट् (इध्मं प्रवृश्च्यते येन) ; so also with शातन (पलाशानि शात्यन्ते येन स दण्डः) ; so also with कल्पन (श्मश्रु कल्पते येन स क्षुरादिः) Why do we say "after a Gati, Kâraka, or an Upapada word?" Observe देवदत्तस्यकारकः = देवदत्तकारकः ॥ Here the Genitive in देवदत्त does not express a kâraka relation. The genitive is here a शेष लक्षणा षष्ठी denoting a possessor and not a कर्मलक्षणा one: for had it been latter, there would have been no compounding at all, by II. 2. 16. see also II. 3. 65. The word कृत् is employed in the sûtra for the sake of distinctness ; for a gati, karaka or upapada could not be followed by any other word than a kṛit-formed word, if there is to be a samasa. For two sorts of affixes come after a root (dhatu) namely तिङ् and कृत् ॥ A samâsa can take place with kṛit-formed words, but not with tiṅanta words. So that without employing कृत् in the sûtra, we could have inferred that कृत् was meant. Therefore, it is said the 'Kṛit' is employed in the sûtra for the sake of distinctness. According to this view we explain the accent in प्रपचतितराम्, प्रपचतितमाम्, by saying that first compounding takes place with प्र and the words पचतितर and पचतितम ending in तरप् and तमप् and then आम्, is added and the accent of the whole word is regulated by आम् by the rule of सतिशिष्ट (see V. 3. 56. and V. 4. 11). According to others, the कृत् is taken in this sûtra, in order to prevent the gati accent applying to verbal compounds in words like प्रपचति देश्यः,or प्रपचति देशीयं (V. 3. 67), or प्रपचतिरूपम् (V. 3. 66). The accent of these will be governed by the rule of the Indeclinable first term retaining its accent.

उभे वनस्पत्यादिषु युगपत् ॥ १४० ॥ पदानि ॥ उभे, वनस्पत्यादिषु, युगपत्, (प्रकृतिस्वरम्) ॥

वृत्तिः ॥ प्रकृत्येति वर्त्तते । वनस्पत्यादिषु समासेषु उभे पूर्वोत्तरपदे युगपत् प्रकृतिस्वरे भवतः ॥

140. In वनस्पति &c, both members of the compound preserve their original accent simultaneously.

Thus वनस्पतिः, both वन and पति have acute on the first syllable, and सुट् augment comes by VI. 1. 157. (2) बृहस्पतिः or बृहस्पतिः = बृहतां पतिः (VI. 1. 157) The word बृहत् is acutely accented on the final, some say it has acute on the first. (3) शचीपतिः (Sachî being formed by ङीष्), some make Sachî acute on the first शचीपतिः, by including it in Sarangrava class (IV. 1. 73). (4) तनूनपात् (tanû being formed by ऊ Un I. 80 has acute on the final, according to others it has acute on the first and napât = na pâti or na palayati with क्विप् and has acute on the first). (5) नराशंसः नरा अस्मिन्नासीनाः शंसन्ति or नरा एव शंसन्ति (nara is formed by अप् and has acute on the first, Saṅsa is formed by घञ्, the lengthening takes place by VI. 3. 137). (6) शुनःशेपः = शुन इव शेपोऽस्य is a Bahuvrihi: the Genitive is not elided by (VI. 3. 21. Vârt.), and both have acute on the first. (7) शण्डामर्कौ both 'Sanda' and 'Marka' being formed by घञ् have acute on the first: the lengthening takes place by VI. 3. 137. (8) तृष्णावरूत्री ॥ Tṛishṇa has acute on the first, वरूत्री has acute on the final. The lengthening here also is by VI. 3. 137. (9) बम्बाविश्ववयसौ ॥ Bamba is finally acute, and viśva by VI. 2. 106 has acute on the final, as viśvavayas is a Bahuvrihi. The lengthening takes place as before by VI. 3. 137. (10) मर्मृत्युः ॥ मर् is formed by विच् affix and मृत्यु has acute on the final. The words governed by this sûtra are those which would not be included in the next two sûtras.

देवताद्वन्द्वे च ॥ १४१ ॥ पदानि ॥ देवता, द्वन्द्वे, च ॥

वृत्तिः ॥ देवतावाचिनां यो द्वन्द्वस्तत्र युगपदुभे पूर्वोत्तरपदे प्रकृतिस्वरे भवतः ॥

141. In a Dvandva compound ofnames of Divinities, the both members retain their original accent.

Thus इन्द्रासोमौ, इन्द्रावरुणौ, इन्द्राबृहस्पती ॥ The word इन्द्र has acute on the first (by nipatana), सोम is formed by मन् (Uṇ I. 140), and has acute on the first (VI. 1. 197), वरुण is formed by उनन् (Uṇ III. 53) and by VI. 1. 197 has acute on the first. बृहस्पति has two acutes by VI. 2. 140, and Indra-Brihaspati has three acutes. Why do we say "names of divinities"? Observe प्लक्षन्यग्रोधौ ॥ Why do we say 'a Dvandva'? Observe अग्निष्टोमः ॥

नोत्तरपदे ऽनुदात्तादावपृथिवीरुद्रपूषमन्थिषु ॥ १४२ ॥ पदानि ॥ न, उत्तरपदे, अनुदात्तादौ, अ पृथिवी, रुद्र, पूष, मन्थिषु ॥

वृत्तिः ॥ उत्तरपदे ऽनुदात्तादौ पृथिवीरुद्रपूषमन्थिवर्जिते देवताद्वन्द्वे नोभे युगपत्प्रकृतिस्वरे भवतः ॥

142. In a Dvandva compound of the names of divinities, both members of the compound simultaneously do not retain their accent, when the first syllable of the second word is anudâtta, with the exception of पृथिवी, रुद्र, पूषन्, and मन्थिन् ॥

Thus इन्द्राग्नी, इन्द्रवायू, the words Agni and Vâyu have acute on the final. The word uttarapada is repeated in the sûtra, in order that it should be qualified by the word 'anudâttâdau', which latter would otherwise have qualified Dvandva. The word "anudattadau" shows the scope of the prohibition and the injunction. Why do we say with the exception of 'prthivi' &c? Observe द्यावापृथिव्यौ or द्यौ dvyâvâ has acute on the first, 'prithivi' being formed by 'ṅish', has acute on the final. सोमारुद्रौ, Rudra is formed by 'rak' affix (Uṇ II. 22.), and has acute on the final. इन्द्रापूषणौ, Pûshan has acute on the end. (Uṇ I. 159) शुक्रामन्थिनौ, the words Śukra and manthin have acute on the final.

अन्तः ॥ १४३ ॥ पदानि ॥ अन्तः, ॥

वृत्तिः ॥ अन्त इत्यधिकारो यदित ऊर्ध्वमनुक्रमिष्यामस्तत्र समासस्योत्तरपदस्यान्त उदात्तो भवतीत्येवं तद्वेदितव्यम् ॥

143. In the following sûtrâs up to the end of the chapter, should always be supplied the phrase "the last syllable of the second member has the acute".

The application is given in the next sûtra.

थाथघञ्क्ताजबित्रकाणाम् ॥ १४४ ॥ पदानि ॥ थ, अथ, घञ्, क्त, अच्, अप्, इत्र, काणाम्, (अन्त उदात्तः,) ॥

वृत्तिः ॥ थ अथ घञ् क्त अच् अप् इत्र क इत्येवमन्तानामुत्तरपदानां गतिकारकोपपदात्परेषामन्त उदात्तो भवति ॥

144. The last syllable of the second member has the acute, in the verbal nouns ending in थ, अथ, घञ्, क्त, अच्, अप्, इत्र and क, when preceded by a Gati, a Kâraka or an Upapada (VI. 2. 139).

Thus सुनीथः, अवभृथः formed by क्थन् affix (Uṇ II. 2 and 3), and but for this sûtra, by VI. 2. 139 these words would have retained their original accent which was acute on the first. अथः—आवसथः, उपवसथः formed by अथन् affix (Uṇ III. 116). घञ्—प्रभेदः, काष्ठभेदः, रज्जुभेदः ॥ क्तः—दूरादागतः, Here क्त has the force of कर्म, and the gati आ would retain its accent (VI. 2. 49) therefore, आगत is first acute: this accent would have been retained when compounded with the kâraka word dûra, but for this sûtra. विशुष्कः आतपशुष्कः ॥ अच् (III. 3. 56) :—प्रक्षयः, प्रजयः, the words क्षय 'dwelling', and जय 'victory' are acute otherwise on the first (VI. 1. 201, 202). अप्—प्रलवः, प्रसवः ॥ इत्र—प्रलवित्रम्, प्रसवित्रम् ॥ क—खरोवृषः गोवृषः = गां वर्षति, खरो वर्षति (III. 2. 5 Vârt) : प्रवृषः, प्रहृषः, (क being added by III. 1. 135). The word वृष has acute on the first as it belongs to वृषादि class (VI. 1. 203). When the preceding words are not Gati, Kâraka or Upapada, this rule does not apply : as सुस्तुतं भवता, अतिस्तुतं भवता, where सु and अति being Karmapravachaniya, the words get the accent of the Indeclinable.

सूपमानात् क्तः ॥ १४५ ॥ पदानि ॥ सु, उपमानात्, क्तः, ॥

वृत्तिः ॥ सु इत्येतस्मादुपमानाच्च परं क्तान्तमुत्तरपदमन्तोदात्तं भवति ॥

145. The Participle in क्त has acute on the final, when it is preceded by सु or by a word with which the second member is compared.

Thus सुकृतम्, सुभुक्तम्, सुपीतम् ॥ With Upamâna words we have—वृकावलुप्तम्, शशप्लुतम्, सिंहविनर्दितम् ॥ This debars VI. 2. 49 and 48. When सु is not a Gati, the rule does not apply, as सुस्तुतम् भवता ॥

संज्ञायामनाचितादीनाम् ॥ १४६ ॥ पदानि ॥ संज्ञायाम्, अनाचितादीनाम् ॥

वृत्तिः ॥ संज्ञायां विषये गतिकारकोपपदात् क्तान्तमुत्तरपदमन्तोदात्तं भवति आचितादीन्वर्जयित्वा ॥

146. The Participle in 'kta' has acute on the last syllable, when preceded by a Gati, or a Karaka or an Upapada, if the compound denotes a Name, but not in आचित &c.

Thus संभूतो रामायणः, उपहूतः शाकल्यः, परिजग्धः कौण्डिन्यः ॥ This debars VI. 2. 49, धनुषखाता नदी, कुद्दालखातम् नगरम्, हस्तिमृदिता भूमिः ॥ Here VI. 2. 48 is debarred. Why do we say "when it is not आचित &c" Observe आचितम् &c.

1 आचित, 2 पर्याचित, 3 आस्थापित, 4 परिगृहीत, 5 निरुक्त, 6 प्रतिपन्न, 7 अपश्लिष्ट*, 8 प्रश्लिष्ट, 9 उपहित (उपहत) 10 उपस्थित, 11 संहितागवि (संहिताशब्दो यदा गोरन्यस्य संज्ञा तदान्तोदात्तो न भवति । यदा तु गोः संज्ञा तदान्तोदात्त एव ॥)

The word संहिता in the above list does not take acute on the final, when it is the name of anything else than a 'cow'; but when it denotes 'a cow' it has acute on the final.

प्रवृद्धादीनां च ॥ १४७ ॥ पदानि ॥ प्रवृद्धादीनाम्, च, (अन्तोदात्तम्) ॥

वृत्तिः ॥ प्रवृद्धादीनां च क्तान्तमुत्तरपदमन्तोदात्तं भवति ॥

147. The words प्रवृद्ध &c. ending in 'kta' have acute on the final.

Thus प्रवृद्धं यानम्, प्रवृद्धो वृषलः, प्रयुक्ताः सक्तवः, आकर्षेऽवहितः, अवहितो भोगेषु, खट्वारूढः, कविशस्तः ॥ It is an Akritigaṇa. The words have acute on the final, even when not followed by यान &c, though in the Ganapâṭha they are read along with these words. Some hold it is only in connection with यान &c that these words have acute on the final. This being an Akritigaṇa we have पुनरुत्स्यूतं वासो देयं, पुनर्निष्कृतो रथः &c.

1 प्रवृद्धं यानम्, 2 प्रवृद्धो वृषलः, 3 प्रयुक्तास्सक्तवः or प्रयुक्ताः सक्तव 4 आकर्षे ऽवहितः, 5 अवहितो भोगेषु, 6 खट्वारूढः 7 कविशस्तः, आकृतिगण.

कारकाद्दत्तश्रुतयोरेवाशिषि ॥ १४८ ॥ पदानि ॥ कारकात्, दत्त, श्रुतयोः, एव, आशिषि ॥

वृत्तिः ॥ संज्ञायामिति वर्त्तते, क्त इति च। संज्ञायां विषये आशिषि गम्यमानायां कारकादुत्तरयोर्दत्तश्रुतयोरेव क्तान्तयोरन्त उदात्तो भवति ॥

148. The final of Part Participles दत्त and श्रुत alone has acute, in a compound denoting a Name and a benediction, the preceding word being a word standing in close relation to an action (kâraka).

Thus देवा एनं देयासुः = देवदत्तः, विष्णुरेनं श्रूयाद् = विष्णुश्रुतः ॥

Why do we say "of दत्त and श्रुत"? Observe देवपालितः (VI. 2. 48), which, though a Name, is not governed by VI. 2. 146, and does not take acute on the final, for the present rule makes a restriction with regard to that rule even. So that where a Participle in क्त is preceded by a kâraka, and the compound donotes a benediction and a Name, the accent is not on the final, as required by VI. 2. 146, but such a word is governed by VI. 2. 48, unless the Participle be Datta and Śruta, when the present rule applies. The word कारक indicates that the ru'e will not apply when a gati or upapada precedes. Why do we use 'एव (*alone*)'? So that the restriction should apply to 'kâraka', and not to 'Datta' and 'Śruta'. For the words 'Datta' and 'Sruta' will have acute on the final even after a nonkâraka word. As सम्भूतः, विश्रुतः ॥ Why do we say 'when denoting henediction'? The rule will not apply where benediction is not meant. As देवैः खाता = देवखाता ॥ This rule applies to Datta and Sruta after a kâraka-word, only when benediction is meant. It therefore does not apply to देवदत्त 'the name of Arjuna's conch', as आहतानदति देवदत्तः, which is governed by VI. 2. 48.

इत्थंभूतेन कृतमिति च ॥ १४९ ॥ पदानि ॥ इत्थंभूतेन, कृतम्, इति, च, (अन्तोदात्तम्) ॥

वृत्तिः ॥ इमं प्रकारमापन्न इत्थंभूतः । इत्थंभूतेन कृतमित्येतस्मिन्नर्थे यः समासो वर्त्तते तत्र क्तान्तमुत्तरपदमन्तोदात्तं भवति ॥

149. The Participle in क्त has acute on the final, when the compound denotes 'done by one in such a condition'.

The word इत्थंभूत means 'being in such a condition'. Thus सुप्रप्रलपितम्, उन्मत्तप्रलपितम्, प्रमत्तगीतम्, विपन्नश्रुतम् as Adjectives and Abstract verbal nouns. This is an exception to VI. 2. 48. When the words प्रलपित &c are used to denote Noun of Action (भाव, then by VI. 2. 144 they get of course acute on the final.

अनो भावकर्मवचनः ॥ १५० ॥ पदानि ॥ अनः, भाव, कर्मवचनः, (अन्तोदात्तम्) ॥

वृत्ति. ॥ अन प्रत्ययान्तमुत्तरपदं भाववचनं कर्मवचनं च कारकात्परमन्तोदात्तं भवति ॥

150. After a kâraka as mentioned in VI. 2. 148, the second member ending in the affix अन, and denoting an action in the Abstract or the object (i. e. having the senses of a Passive Adjective), has acute on the final.

Thus ओदनभोजनं सुखम, पयपानं सुखम्, चन्दनप्रियङ्गुकालेपनं सुखम् ॥ All these are examples of भाव or Abstract Verbal Nouns. राजभोजनाः शालयः, राजाच्छादनानि वासांसि, are examples of कर्मवचन or Passive Adjectives. These are formed by ल्युट् under III. 3. 116. For the Sûtra III. 3. 116 may be explained by saying that (1) ल्युट् is applied when the Upapada is in the objective case and bhâva is meant, (2) as well as when object is to be expressed. When the first explanation is taken, the above are examples of Bhâva; when the second explanation is taken, they are examples of Karma. Why do we say "ending in अन्"? Observe, हस्तहार्यमुर्शभित ॥ Why do we say "when expressing an action in the abstract (bhâva), or an Object (karma)"? Observe दन्तधावनम्, here ल्युट् is added after an Instrumental kâraka (III. 3. 117). Why do we say "after a kâraka"? Observe निदर्शनम्, अवलेखनम् ॥ In all the counter-examples, the second members retain there original accent.

मन्क्तिन्व्याख्यानशयनासनस्थानयाजकादिक्रीताः ॥ १५१ ॥ पदानि ॥ मन्, क्तिन्, व्याख्यान, शयन, आसन, स्थान, याजकादि, क्रीताः ॥

वृत्तिः ॥ मन्नन्तं क्तिन्नन्तं व्याख्यान शयन आसन स्थान इत्येतानि याजकादयः क्रीतशब्दश्चोत्तरपदमन्तोदात्तं भवति ॥

151. The words ending in मन् or क्तिन् affixes, and the words व्याख्यान, शयन, आसन, स्थान and क्रीत as well as याजक &c, have acute on the final, when at the end of a compound, preceded by a kâraka word.

Thus मन्—रथवर्त्मन्, शकटवर्त्मन् ॥ क्तिन्—पाणिनिकृतिः, आपिशलिकृतिः ॥ व्याख्यान—ऋगयनव्याख्यानम्, छन्दोव्याख्यानम् ॥ शयन—राजशयनम्, ब्राह्मणशयनम् ॥ आसन—राजासनम्, ब्राह्मणासनम् ॥ स्थान—गोस्थानम्, अश्वस्थानम् ॥ याजकादि words are those which form Genitive compounds under II. 2. 9, and those compounds only are to be taken here; as ब्राह्मणयाजकः, क्षत्रिययाजकः, ब्राह्मणपूजकः, क्षत्रियपूजकः ॥ क्रीत—गोक्रीतः, अश्वक्रीतः ॥ This is an exception to VI. 2. 139. and in the case of क्रीत, rule VI. 2. 48 is superseded. The words व्याख्यान &c do not denote here भाव or कर्म, had they done so, rule

VI. 2. 149 would have covered them. When the first member is not a kâraka, we have प्रक्रान्तिः and प्रहृतिः ॥

1 याजक. 2 पूजक, 3 परिचारक, 4 परिषेचक परिवेषक 5 स्नापक स्नानक 6 अध्यापक, 7 उत्सादक (उत्सादक) 8 उद्वर्तक, 9 होतृ, 10 भर्तृ, 11 रथगणक, 12 पत्तिगणक, 13 पोतृ, 14 हातृ, 15 वर्तक,

सप्तम्याः पुण्यम् ॥ १५२ ॥ पदानि ॥ सप्तम्याः, पुण्यम् ॥

वृत्तिः ॥ सप्तम्यन्तात्परं पुण्यमित्येतदुत्तरपदमन्तोदात्तं भवति ॥

152. The word पुण्य has acute on the final when preceded by a noun in the Locative case.

Thus अध्ययने पुण्यम् = अध्ययनपुण्यम्, वेदपुण्यम् ॥ The compounding takes place by II. 1. 40 by the process of splitting the sûtra (yoga-vibhâga), taking सप्तमी there as a full sûtra, and शौण्डैः another. Here by VI. 2. 2, the first member would have preserved its accent, the present sûtra supersedes that and ordains acute on the final. The word पुण्य is derived by the Uṇâdi affix यत् (Uṇ V. 15) and would have retained its natural accent (VI. 1. 213) and thus get acute on the first syllable by kṛit-accent. (VI. 2. 139). Why do we say 'a locative case'? Observe वेदेन पुण्यं = वेदपुण्यम् ॥

ऊनार्थकलहं तृतीयायाः ॥ १५३ ॥ पदानि ॥ ऊनार्थ, कलहम, तृतीयायाः ॥

वृत्तिः ॥ ऊनार्थान्युत्तरपदानि कलहशब्दश्च तृतीयान्तात्पराण्यन्तोदात्तानि भवन्ति ॥

153. The acute falls on the final of words having the sense of ऊन, and of कलह, when they are second members in a compound, preceded by a term in the instrumental case.

Thus माषोनम्, कार्षापणोनम्, माषविकलम्, कार्षापणविकलम्, असिकलहः, वाक्कलहः ॥ The compounding takes place by II. 1. 31. This is an exception to VI, 2. 2 by which the first member being in the third case, would have retained its original accent. Some say that the word अर्थ in the sûtra means the word-form अर्थ, so that the aphorism would mean—"after an Instrumental case, the words ऊन, अर्थ, and कलह get acute on the final". The examples will be in addition to the above,:—धान्येनार्थाः = धान्यार्थः ॥ If this be so, then the word-form ऊन alone will be taken and not its synonyms like विकल &c. To this we reply, that ऊन will denote its synonyms also, by the fact of its being followed by the word अर्थ ॥ By sûtra II. 1. 31, ऊनार्थ and कलह always take the Instrumental case, so we could have omitted the word तृतीयायाः, from this sûtra, for by the maxim of pratipadokta &c, ऊनार्थकलहं would have referred to the compound ordained by II. 1. 31. The mention of तृतीया here is only for the sake of clearness.

मिश्रं चानुपसर्गमसंधौ ॥ १५४ ॥ पदानि ॥ मिश्रम्, च, अनुपसर्गम्, असंधौ ॥

वृत्तिः ॥ तृतीयेति वर्तते । मिश्र इत्येतदुत्तरपदमनुपसर्गं तृतीयान्तात्परमन्तोदात्तं भवत्यसंधौ गम्यमाने ॥

154. The word मिश्र has acute on the final after an Instrumental case, when it is not joined with any Preposition and does not mean a 'compact or alliance'.

Thus गुडमिश्रः, तिलमिश्रः, सर्पिर्मिश्राः ॥ Why do we say मिश्र? Observe गुडधानाः ॥ Why do we say 'not having a Preposition'? Observe गुडसंमिश्राः ॥ The employment in this sûtra of the phrase 'anupasargam' implies, that wherever else, the word miśra is used, it includes miśra with a preposition also. Therefore in II. 1. 31 where the word मिश्र is used, we can form the Instrumental compounds with मिश्र preceded by a preposition also. Why do we say 'not denoting a compact'? Observe ब्राह्मणमिश्रो राजा = ब्राह्मणैः सह संहित ऐकार्थ्यमापन्नः ॥ The word सन्धि here means a contract formed by reciprocal promises, if you do this thing for me, I will do this for you. Others say, it means close proximity, without losing identity, and thus differs from मिश्र in which two things blend together into one. Therefore though the King and the Brâhmaṇa may be in close proximity as regards space, they both retain their several individualities: hence the counter-example ब्राह्मणमिश्रोराजा ॥ While in the examples गुडमिश्राः &c there is no possibility of separating the two.

नञो गुणप्रतिषेधे संपाद्यर्हहितालमर्थास्तद्धिताः ॥ १५५ ॥ पदानि ॥ नञः, गुण, प्रतिषेधे, संपादि, अर्ह, हित, अलम, अर्थाः, तद्धिताः, ॥

वृत्तिः ॥ संपादि अर्ह हित अलम् इत्येवमर्था ये तद्धितास्तदन्तान्युत्तरपदानि नञो गुणप्रतिषेधे वर्त्तमानात्पराण्यन्तोदात्तानि भवन्ति ॥

155. The words formed with the Taddhita affixes denoting 'fitted for that' (V. 1. 99), 'deserving that' (V. 1. 63), 'good for that' (V. 1. 5), 'capable to effect that' (V. 1. 101), have acute on the final, when preceded by the Negative Particle नञ्, when it makes a negation with regard to the above mentioned attributes.

Thus संपादि 'suited for that' (V. 1. 99):—अकार्णवेष्टकिकं मुखम् = न कार्णवेष्टकिकं (कर्णवेष्टकाभ्यां सम्पादि) ॥ The affix is ठञ् ॥ अर्ह 'deserving that' (V. 1. 63):—अच्छैदिकः = न छैदिकः (छेदमर्हति). The affix is ठक् (V. 1. 64 and V. 1. 19). हित 'good for that' (V. 1. 5):—अवत्सीयः = न वत्सीयः ॥ The affix is छ V. I. 1. अलमर्थः 'capable to effect that' (V. 1. 101):—असंतापिकः = न संतापिकः ॥ The affix is ठञ् (V. 1. 18) Why do we say 'after नञ्'? Observe गार्हपत्यमर्हति = गार्हपत्यिकः, विगार्हपत्यिकः, where the negative वि is used and therefore the avyaya वि retains its accent by VI. 2. 2. Why do we say 'negation of that attribute'? Observe गार्हपत्यिकादन्यः = अगार्हपत्यिकः ॥ The word गुण here means the attribute denoted by the Taddhita affix, and not any attribute in general. Thus अकार्णवेष्टकिकं मुखं =

कर्णवेष्टकाभ्याम् न संपादि मुखम् ॥ Why do we say 'in the sense of sampâdi &c'? Observe पाणिनीयमधीयते = पाणिनीयः; न पाणिनीयः, = अपाणिनीयः ॥ Why do we say "Taddhita affixes"? Observe कन्यां वोढुमर्हति = कन्यावोढा, न वोढा – अवोढा ॥ Here तृच् a kṛit affix is added in the sense of 'deserving' (III. 3. 169).

ययतोश्चातदर्थे ॥ १५६ ॥ पदानि ॥ य, यतो, च, अतदर्थे ॥

वृत्तिः ॥ य यत् इत्येतौ यौ तद्धितावतदर्थे वर्तेते तदन्तस्योत्तरपदस्य नञो गुणप्रतिषेधविषयादन्त उदात्तो भवति ॥

156. The words formed with the Taddhita affixes य and यत् when not denoting 'useful for that', have acute on the last syllable, after the particle नञ् negativing the attribute.

Thus पाशानां समूहः = पाश्याः, न पाश्याः = अपाश्याः, So also अतृण्याः (IV. 2. 49); दन्तेषु भवं = दन्त्यम्, न दन्त्यं = अदन्त्यम्, अकर्ण्यम् (V. 1. 6). Why do we say 'atadartha:— not useful for that'. Observe पादार्थमुदकम् = पाद्यम्, न पाद्यम् = अपाद्यम् (V. 4. 25). This rule does not apply when the affixes are not Taddhita, as अदेयम् formed with the kṛit affix यत् ॥ There must be negation of the attribute, otherwise दन्त्यादन्यत् = अदन्त्यम् ॥ The affix य and यत्, one without any anubandha and, the other with the anubandha त् being specifically mentioned, excludes all other affixes having य as their effective element, such as ड्य &c. (IV. 2. 9), thus न वामदेव्यं = अवामदेव्यम् ॥ See IV. 2. 9.

अच्कावशक्तौ ॥ १५७ ॥ पदानि ॥ अच, कौ, अ शक्तौ ॥

वृत्तिः ॥ अच् क इत्येवमन्तमशक्तौ गम्यमानायामुत्तरपदं नञः परमन्तोदात्तं भवति ॥

157. A word formed with the kṛit affix अच् and क, preceded by the particle नञ्. has acute on the final, when the meaning is 'not capable.'

Thus अपचः = य पक्तुं न शक्नोति, so also अजयः, अपठः, अविक्षिपः, अविलिखः (III. 1. 134 &c). Why do we say when meaning 'not capable'? Observe अपचो दीक्षितः, अपचः परिव्राजकः ॥ A दीक्षित and a परिव्राजक do not cook their food, not because they are physically incapable of cooking, but because by the vows of their particular order they are prohibited from cooking.

आक्रोशे च ॥ १५८ ॥ पदानि ॥ आक्रोशे, च ॥

वृत्तिः ॥ आक्रोशे च गम्यमाने नञ उत्तरमच्कान्तमन्तोदात्तं भवति ॥

158. A word formed by the kṛit-affixes अच् or क, preceded by the Negative particle, has acute on the final when one abuses somebody by that word.

Thus अपचोऽयं जाल्मः 'this rogue does not cook, though he can do so'. Here avarice is indicated, the fellow wants more pay before he will cook: and not his incapacity. So also अपठोऽयं जाल्मः, so also अविक्षिपः, अविलिखः ॥

संज्ञायाम् ॥ १५९ ॥ पदानि ॥ संज्ञायाम्, (अन्तो दात्तम्) ॥

वृत्तिः ॥ आक्रोशे गम्यमाने नञः परमुत्तरपदं संज्ञायां वर्त्तमानमन्तोदात्तं भवति ॥

159. When abuse is meant, a word preceded by नञ्, has acute on the final, in denoting a Name.

Thus अदेवदत्तः 'No Devadatta, not deserving of this name' अयज्ञदत्तः, अविष्णुमित्रः ॥

कृत्योकेष्णुच्चार्वादयश्च ॥ १६० ॥ पदानि ॥ कृत्य, उक, इष्णुच्, चार्वादयः, च ॥

वृत्तिः ॥ कृत्य उक इष्णुच् इत्येवमन्ताश्चार्वादयश्च नञ उत्तरेऽन्तोदात्ता भवन्ति ॥

160. After the Negative particle, the words formed by the kritya affixes (III. 1. 95), by उक, and इष्णुच्, and the words चारु &c. have acute on the final.

Thus kritya:—अकर्तव्यम्, अकरणीयम्, उकः—अनागामुकम्, अनपलाषुकम् ॥ इष्णुच्-अनलंकरिष्णुः, अनिराकरिष्णुः ॥ The affix इष्णुच् includes खिष्णुच् also: अनाढ्यंभविष्णुः, असुभगंभविष्णुः ॥ चारु &c:—अचारुः, असाधुः, अयौधिकः, अवदान्यः, अनङ्गमेजयः (double negation). अनकस्मात् (double negation), The words वर्तमान, वर्धमान त्वरमाण, ध्रियमाण, रोचमान, क्रीयमाण, and शोभमान preceded by अ (नञ्) when denoting names have acute on the final. अविकारः, असदृशः and अविकारसदृशः (विकार and सदृश taken jointly & separately). अगृहपति, अगृहपतिकः ॥ अराजा and अनहः in the Vedas only. In the Vernacular they have the accent of नञ्, i. e. udâtta on the first.

1 चारु, 2 साधु, 3 यौधाकि (यौधिक) 4 अनङ्गमेजय, 5 वदान्य 6 अकस्मात्, 7 वर्तमानवर्धमानत्वरमाणध्रियमाणक्रीयमाणरोचमानशोभमानाः (क्रियमाण क्रीयमाण) संज्ञायाम्, 8 विकारसदृशे व्यस्ते समस्ते (अविकार, असदृश अविकारसदृश), 9 गृहपति, 10 गृहपतिक, 11 राजाह्नोश्छन्दसि.

विभाषा तृन्नन्नतीक्ष्णशुचिषु ॥ १६१ ॥ पदानि ॥ विभाषा, तृन्, अन्न, तीक्ष्ण, शुचिषु, (अन्तोदात्तः) ॥

वृत्तिः ॥ तृन्नन्त अन्न तीक्ष्ण शुचि इत्येतेषु नञ उत्तरेषु विभाषाऽन्त उदात्तो भवति ॥

161. After the Negative particle, the final of the following is optionally acute :—a word formed with the affix तृन्, and the words अन्न, तीक्ष्ण, and शुचि ॥

Thus तृन्—अकर्ता or अकर्ता ; अन्न &c—अनन्नम् or अनन्नम्, अतीक्ष्णम्, or अतीक्ष्णम्, अशुचिः or अशुचिः ॥ The alternative accent is that of the Indeclinable. (VI. 2. 2)

बहुव्रीहाविदमेतत्तद्भ्यः प्रथमपूरयोः क्रियागणने ॥ १६२ ॥ पदानि ॥ बहुव्रीहौ, इदम्, एतत्, तद्भ्यः, प्रथम, पूरयोः, क्रिया-गणने, (अन्तउदात्तः) ॥

वृत्तिः ॥ बहुव्रीहौ समासे इदम् एतद् तदित्येतेभ्य उत्तरस्य प्रथमशब्दस्य पूरणप्रत्ययान्तस्य च क्रियागणने वर्तमानस्यान्त उदात्तो भवति ॥

162. In a Bahuvrihi, after the words इदम्, एतद् and तद्, the last syllable of प्रथम and of a proper Ordinal Numeral, has the acute, when the number of times of an action is meant.

Thus इदं प्रथमं गमनं भोजनं वा = स इदमप्रथमः 'this is the first time of going or eating'. इदं द्वितीयः, इदं तृतीयः, एतत्प्रथमः, एतद्द्वितीयः, एतत्तृतीयः तत्प्रथमः, तद्द्वितीयः तत् तृतीयः ॥ Why do we say 'in a Bahuvrihi?' Observe अनेन प्रथमः=इदंप्रथमः ॥ Here the first member being in the third case retains its accent by VI. 2. 2. Why do we say "after idam &c". Observe यत्प्रथमः=यःप्रथम एषाम्, here the first term retains its accent by VI. 2. 1. Why do we say 'of prathama and the Ordinals'? Observe तानि बहून्यस्य=तद्बहुः ॥ Why do we say 'in counting an action'? Observe अयं प्रथम एषां=त इद प्रथमाः ॥ Here *substances* are counted and not *action*. Why do we say 'in counting'? Observe अयं प्रथम एषां=इदं प्रथमाः i. e. इदं प्रधानाः ॥ and the word प्रथम means here 'foremost', and is not a numeral. When the कप् affix is added, the acute falls on the last syllable preceding कप् ॥ As इदं प्रथमकाः ॥ The Bahuvrîhi governs the subsequent sûtras upto VI. 2. 178.

संख्यायाः स्तनः ॥ १६३ ॥ पदानि ॥ संख्यायाः, स्तनः ॥

वृत्तिः ॥ संख्यायाः परः स्तनशब्दो बहुव्रीहौ समासेऽन्तोदात्तो भवति ॥

163. In a Bahuvrîhi, after a Numeral, the word स्तन has acute on the final.

Thus द्विस्तनाः, त्रिस्तनाः, चतुःस्तनाः ॥ Why do we say after a Numeral? Observe दर्शनीयस्तना ॥ Why do we say 'स्तन'? Observe द्विशिराः ॥

विभाषा छन्दसि ॥ १६४ ॥ पदानि ॥ विभाषा, छन्दसि, (अन्तोदात्तः) ॥

वृत्तिः ॥ छन्दसि विषये बहुव्रीहौ समासे संख्यायाः परः स्तनशब्दो विभाषाऽन्तोदात्तो भवति ॥

164. Optionally so, in the Vedas, the stana after a Numeral has acute on the final.

Thus द्विस्तनाँ or द्विस्तना, चतुःस्तनाँ or चतुःस्तना ॥

संज्ञायां मित्राजिनयोः ॥ १६५ ॥ पदानि ॥ संज्ञायाम्, मित्र, अजिनयोः (अन्तउदात्तः) ॥

वृत्तिः ॥ संज्ञायां विषये बहुव्रीहौ समासे मित्र अजिन इत्येतयोरुत्तरपदयोरन्त उदात्तो भवति ॥

वार्त्तिकम् ॥ ऋषिप्रतिषेधो मित्रे ॥

165. In a Bahuvrîhi, ending in मित्र and अजिन, the acute falls on the last syllable, when the compound denotes a Name.

As देवमित्रः, ब्रह्ममित्रः, वृकाजिनः, कूलाजिनः कृष्णाजिनः ॥ Why do we say 'a Name'? Observe प्रियमित्रः, महाजिनः ॥

Vart:—Prohibition must be stated in the case of मित्र when the name is that of a Rishi. As विश्वामित्रः which is governed by VI. 2. 106 ॥

व्यवायिनो ऽन्तरम् ॥ १६६ ॥ पदानि ॥ व्यवायिनः, अन्तरम्, (अन्तोदात्तम्)॥

वृत्तिः ॥ व्यवायी व्यवधाता । तद्वाचिनः परमन्तरं बहुव्रीहौ समासेऽन्तोदात्तं भवति ॥

166. In a Bahuvrîhi ending in अन्तर, the acute falls on the final, after a word which denotes 'that which lies between'.

Thus वस्त्रान्तरम् 'through an intervened cloth or drapery', पटान्तरम्, कम्बलान्तरम्=वस्त्रमन्तरं व्यवधायकं यस्य &c. Why do we say 'when meaning lying between'? Observe आत्मान्तरम्=आत्मा स्वभावोऽन्तरोऽन्योयस्य ॥

मुखं स्वाङ्गम् ॥ १६७ ॥ पदानि ॥ मुखम्, स्वाङ्गम्, (अन्तोदात्तम्) ॥

वृत्तिः ॥ मुखमुत्तरपदं स्वाङ्गवाचि बहुव्रीहौ समासे ऽन्तोदात्तं भवति ॥

167. In a Bahuvrîhi the acute is on the final, when the second member is मुख meaning mouth i. e. the actual bodily part of an animal and not used metaphorically.

Thus गौरमुखः, भद्रमुखः ॥ Why do we say 'an actual part of a body'? Observe दीर्घमुखा शाला ॥ Here मुख means "entrance or door". The word स्वाङ्ग means "a non liquid substance actually to be found in living beings &c". as explained in III. 4. 54.

नाव्ययदिक्शब्दगोमहत्स्थूलमुष्टिपृथुवत्सेभ्यः ॥ १६८ ॥ पदानि ॥ न, अव्यय, दिक्शब्द, गो, महत्, स्थूल, मुष्टि, पृथु, वत्सेभ्यः ॥

वृत्तिः ॥ अव्यय दिक्शब्द गो महत् स्थूल मुष्टि पृथु वत्स इत्येतेभ्यः परं मुखं स्वाङ्गवाचि बहुव्रीहौ समासे नान्तोदात्तं भवति ॥

168. In a Bahuvrîhi, the acute does not fall on such मुख denoting a real mouth, when it comes after an Indeclinable, and a name of a direction, or after गो, महत्, स्थूल, मुष्टि, पृथु and वत्स ॥

Thus: अव्ययः—उच्चैर्मुखः, नीचैर्मुखः ॥ The words उच्चैः and नीचैः are finally acute and retain their accent. दिक्—प्राङ्मुखः, प्रत्यङ्मुखः ॥ The word प्राङ् has acute on the first by VI. 2, 52, and प्रत्यङ् is finally acute by VI. 3. 139. गो &c :—गोमुखः, महामुखः, स्थूलमुखः, मुष्टिमुखः पृथुमुखः and वत्समुखः ॥ In these the first members of the Bahuvrîhi preserve their respective accents under Rule VI. 2. 1 and in the case of compounds preceded by गो, मुष्टि and वत्स, the optional rule taught in the next sûtra is also superseded by anticipation, though the words may denote comparison.

निष्ठोपमानादन्यतरस्याम् ॥ १६९ ॥ पदानि ॥ निष्ठा, उपमानात्, अन्यतरस्याम् ॥

वृत्तिः ॥ निष्ठान्तादुपमानवाचिनश्च मुखं स्वाङ्गमुत्तरपदमन्यतरस्यां बहुव्रीहौ समासेऽन्तोदात्तं भवति ॥

169. In a Bahuvrîhi, the word मुख denoting 'an actual mouth', has optionally the acute on the final, when preceded by a participle in त, or by that wherewith something is compared.

Thus प्रक्षालितमुखः or प्रक्षालितमुखः or प्रक्षालितमुखः ॥ When the final is not acute, then Rule VI. 2. 110 applies which makes the first member have acute on the final optionally, and when that also does not apply, then by VI. 2. 1. the first member preserves its original accent, which is that of the gati (VI. 2. 49). Thus there are three forms. So also with a word denoting comparison:— सिंहमुखः or सिंहमुखः, व्याघ्रमुखः or व्याघ्रमुखः ॥

जातिकालसुखादिभ्यो ऽनाच्छादनात् क्तो ऽकृतमितप्रतिपन्नाः ॥ १७० ॥ पदानि ॥ जातिकाल, सुखादिभ्यः, अनाच्छादनात्, क्तः, अकृतमितप्रतिपन्नाः ॥

वृत्तिः ॥ जातिवाचिन आच्छादनवर्जितात् कालवाचिनः सुखादिभ्यश्च परं क्तान्तं कृतमितप्रतिपन्नान्वर्जयित्वा बहुव्रीहौ समासेऽन्तोदात्तं भवति ॥

170. After a word denoting a species (with the exception of a word for 'garment or covering'), and after a time-denoting word as well as after सुख &c. the Participle in क्त has acute on the final, in a Bahuvrîhi, but not so when the participles are कृत, मित and प्रतिपन्न ॥

Thus सारङ्गजग्धः, पलाण्डुभक्षितः, सुरापीतः ॥ कालः—मासजातः, संवत्सरजातः, द्व्यहजातः, त्र्यहजातः ॥ सुख &c:—सुखजातः दुःखजातः, तृप्रजातः ॥ Why do we say "after a Species, a time or सुख &c. word"? Observe पुत्रजातः (II. 2. 37), the participle being placed after the word Putra. Why do we say 'when not meaning a garment'? Observe वसनच्छन्नः, वसनच्छन्नः from the root वस् with the affixes ष्ट्रन् and ल्युट् respectively. Why do we say "when not कृत &c."? Observe कुण्डकृतः, कुण्डमितः कुण्डप्रतिपन्नः; कुण्ड is first acute by Phit II. 3 being neuter. These three participles do not stand first in a compound (contrary to II. 2. 36), as this sûtra implies. In the counter-examples, above given, the first members retain their original accent (VI. 2. 1). The words सुख &c are given under III. 1. 18.

1 सुख, 2 दुःख, 3 तृप्र (तृप्र तीव्र) 4 कृच्छ्र, 5 अस्र, 6 आस्र*, 7 अलीक 8 प्रतीप, 9 करुण, 10 कृपण, 11 सोढ. 12 गहन.

वा जाते ॥ १७१ ॥ पदानि ॥ वा, जाते, (अन्तोदात्तः) ॥

वृत्तिः ॥ जातशब्दउत्तरपदे वा ऽन्त उदात्तो भवति बहुव्रीहौ समासे जातिकालसुखादिभ्यः ॥

171. After a species (with the exception of garment) or a time denoting word, or after सुख &c. in a Bahuvrîhi, the word जात has optionally acute on the final.

Thus दन्तजातः or दन्तजातः, स्तनजातः or स्तनजातः, मासजातः or मासजातः, संवत्सरजातः or संवत्सरजातः; सुखजातः or सुखजातः, दुःखजातः or दुःखजातः &c. The words दन्त and स्तन are first-acute by Phit II. 6; मास is first-acute by Phit II. 15, संवत्सर is finally-acute by Phit I. 7. बहिष्ठवत्सरति शत्यान्ताम् "words ending in बहिष्ठ, वत्स, ति, शत् and थ are finally acute", as बहिष्ठः, संवत्सरः, सप्ततिः, त्रिंशत्, गूर्थम् ॥ The words सुख and दुःख are end-acute by Phit I. 6.

नञ्सुभ्याम् ॥ १७२ ॥ पदानि ॥ नञ्, सुभ्याम्, (अन्तोदात्तम्) ॥

वृत्तिः ॥ नञ्सुभ्यां परमुत्तरपदं बहुव्रीहौ समासेन्तोदात्तं भवति ॥

172. A Bahuvrîhi formed by the Negative particle नञ् or by सु has acute on the last syllable of the compound.

Thus अयवो देशः अव्रीहिः अमाषः, सुयवः, सुव्रीहिः, सुमाषः ॥ The acute here rests on the last syllable of the completed compound ; so that the rule applies to the compounds which have fully developed themselves by taking the samâsânta affixes. Thus अनृचः (formed by the samâsânta affix अ V. 4. 74). Though the word समास and उत्तरपद are both present here by context, yet the operation is performed on samâsa. This is to be inferred, because of the next sûtra. For had the present sûtra meant that the final of the second member (उत्तरपद) preceded by नञ् and सु gets the acute, then there would have been no necessity of the next sûtra, for the present would have covered the case of सुकुमारीक &c because कप् is not a part of the *second term* (uttarapada) कुमारी but of the *compound* (Samasa) सुकुमारी; and therefore, if we translated the present sûtra, by saying that the end of second term gets acute, the accent would have fallen on ई in सुकुमारीकः even by this sûtra. But this is not intended, because of the accent of the samasanta words अनृचः and बहृचः ॥ There is necessity of the next sûtra, because a samâsa includes not only the simple samâsa, but one ending with a samâsânta affix. Therefore, had not the next sûtra been made, the accent would have fallen on क and not on ई, for the affix कप् is considered part of the samasa and not of the uttarapada समासान्तः समासस्यैवावयवा नोत्तरपदस्य ॥

कपि पूर्वम् ॥ १७३ ॥ पदानि ॥ कपि, पूर्वम् ॥

वृत्तिः ॥ नञ्सुभ्यां कपि परतः पूर्वमन्तोदात्तं भवति ॥

173. A Bahuvrîhi formed by नञ् or सु and ending in the affix कप्, (V. 4. 153) has acute on the syllable preceding the affix.

By the last sûtra the accent would have fallen on कप्, this makes it fall on the vowel preceding it. Thus अकुमारीको देशः अवृषलीकः, अब्रह्मबन्धूकः, सुकुमारीकः, सुवृषलीकः, सुब्रह्मबन्धूकः ॥

ह्रस्वान्ते ऽन्त्यात्पूर्वम् ॥ १७४ ॥ पदानि ॥ ह्रस्वान्ते, अन्त्यात्, पूर्वम्,(उदात्तम्)॥

वृत्तिः ॥ ह्रस्वो ऽन्तो यस्य तदिदं ह्रस्वान्तमुत्तरपदं समासो वा, तत्रान्त्यात्पूर्वमुदात्तं भवति कपि परतो नञ्सुभ्यां परं बहुव्रीहौ समासे ॥

174. When the compound ends in a light vowel, the acute falls on the syllable before such last, in a Bahuvrîhi preceded by नञ् and सु to which कप् is added.

Thus अयवको देशः, अव्रीहिकः, अमाषकः, सुयवकः, सुव्रीहिकः, सुमाषकः ॥ The repetition of पूर्व in this sûtra, though its anuvritti was present from the last, shows, that in the last aphorism, the syllable preceding कप् takes the acute, while here the syllable preceding the short-vowel-ending final syllable has the acute and not the syllable preceding कप्॥ This is possible with a word which is, at least, of two syllables (not counting, of course, सु and क or कप्). Therefore, in अज्ञकः and सुज्ञकः, the acute is on the syllable preceding कप् by VI. 2. 173, because it has here no 'antyât-purvam.

बहोर्नञ्वदुत्तरपदभूम्नि ॥ १७५ ॥ पदानि ॥ बहोः, नञ्वदुत्तरपदभूम्नि ॥

वृत्तिः ॥ उत्तरपदार्थबहुत्वे यो बहुशब्दो वर्त्तते तस्मान्नञइव स्वरो भवति । नञ्सुभ्यामित्युक्तम् । बहोरपि तथा भवति ॥

175. A Bahuvrîhi with बहु, has the same accent as नञ्, when it denotes muchness of the object expressed by the second member.

In other words a Bahuvrîhi with the word बहु in the first member, is governed by all those rules which apply to a Bahuvrihi with a Negative Particle such as Rules VI. 2. 172 &c. when this gives the sense of multiety of the objects denoted by the second member. Thus बहुयवो देशः, बहुव्रीहिः, बहुतिलः the same as VI. 2. 172. बहुयवकः, बहुव्रीहिकः, बहुमाषकः by VI. 2. 174. बहुजरः, बहुमरः' बहुमित्रः, बहुमृतः by VI. 2. 116: these examples of VI. 2. 116 are not given by Dr. Bohtlingk.

Why do we say 'uttara-pada-bhumni—when multeity of the objects denoted by the second member is meant'? Observe बहुषु मनोऽस्य = बहुमना भयम् (VI. 2. 1).

न गुणादयोऽवयवाः ॥ १७६ ॥ पदानि ॥ न, गुणादयः, अवयवाः (अन्तोदात्ताः)

वृत्तिः ॥ गुणादयोऽवयववाचिनोबहोरुत्तरे बहुव्रीहौ नान्तोदात्ता भवन्ति ॥

176. In a Bahuvrîhi, after बहु, the acute does not fall on the final of गुण &c. when they appear in the compound as ingredient of something else.

Thus बहुगुणाः रज्जुः, बह्वक्षरं पदम्, बहुच्छन्दोमानम्, बह्वध्यायः (VI. 2. I). गुणादि is an Akrtigana. Why do we say " when it denotes an avayava or ingredient " ? As बहुगुणोब्राह्मणः = अध्ययनश्रुतसदाचारादयोऽत्रगुणाः ॥

1 गुण, 2 अक्षर, 3 अध्याय, 4 सूक्त, 5 छन्दोमान. आकृतिगण.

उपसर्गात् स्वाङ्गं ध्रुवमपर्शु ॥ १७७ ॥ पदानि ॥ उपसर्गात्, स्वाङ्गम्, ध्रुवम्, अपर्शु, (अन्तोदात्तम्) ॥

वृत्तिः ॥ उपसर्गात् स्वाङ्गं ध्रुवं पर्शुवर्जितमन्तोदात्तं भवति बहुव्रीहौ समासे ॥

177. A word denoting a part of the body, which is constant (and indispensable), with the exception of पर्शु, has, after a Preposition in a Bahuvrîhi compound, the acute on the last syllable.

Thus प्रपृष्ठैः, प्रोदरैः, प्रललाटैः; सततं यस्य प्रगतं पृष्ठं भवति स प्रपृष्ठः ॥ Why do we say 'after a Preposition'? Observe दर्शनीयललाटः ॥ Why do we say 'part of the body'? Observe प्रशाखो वृक्षः ॥ Why do we say 'dhruva—constant and indispensable'? Observe उद्बाहुः क्रोशति ॥ Here the hand is raised up only at the time of cursing and not *always*, so the state of उद्बाहु is temporary and not permanent. Why do we say with the exception of पर्शु? Observe ईत्पर्शुः, विपर्शुः (VI. 2. 1).

वनं समासे ॥ १७८ ॥ पदानि ॥ वनम्, समासे, (अन्तोदात्तम्) ॥

वृत्तिः ॥ समासमात्रे वनमित्येतदुत्तरपदमुपसर्गात्परमन्तोदात्तं भवति ॥

178. After a preposition, वन has acute on the final in compounds of every kind.

Thus प्रवणे यष्टव्यम्, निर्वणे प्रणिधीयते, the न changed to ण by VIII. 4. 5. The word 'samâsa' is used in the sûtra to indicate that all sorts of compounds are meant, otherwise only Bahuvrihi would have been meant.

अन्तः ॥ १७९ ॥ पदानि ॥ अन्तः ॥

वृत्तिः ॥ अन्तश्शब्दादुत्तरं वनमन्तोदात्तं भवति ॥

179. After अन्तर् the acute falls on the final of वन ॥

Thus अन्तर्वणो देशः ॥ This sûtra is made in order to make वन oxytoned, when a preposition (upasarga) does not precede.

अन्तश्च ॥ १८० ॥ पदानि ॥ अन्तः, च ॥

वृत्तिः ॥ अन्तश्शब्दश्चोत्तरपदमुपसर्गादन्तोदात्तं भवति ॥

180. The word अन्तर् has acute on the final when preceded by a Preposition.

Thus प्रान्तः, पर्यन्तः ॥ This is a Bahuvrîhi or a प्रादि compound.

न निविभ्याम् ॥ १८१ ॥ पदानि ॥ न, नि, विभ्याम्, (अन्तोदात्तः) ॥

वृत्तिः ॥ नि वि इत्येताभ्यामुत्तरोन्तश्शब्दो नान्तोदात्तो भवति ॥

181. The word antar has not acute on the final, after the prepositions नि and वि ॥

Thus न्यन्तः, व्यन्तः, here the first member retains its acute, and semivowel is then substituted for the vowel इ, then the subsequent grave is changed to svarita by VIII. 2. 4.

परेरभितोभावि मण्डलम् ॥ १८२ ॥ पदानि ॥ परेः, अभितः-भावि, मण्डलम् ॥

वृत्तिः ॥ परेरुत्तरमभितोभाविवचनं मण्डलं चान्तोदात्तं भवति ॥

182. After परि, a word, which expresses something, which has both this side and that side, as well as the word मण्डल, has acute on the final.

Thus परिकूलम्, परितीरम्, परिमण्डलम् ॥ This is a Bahuvrihi or प्रादि compound or an Avyayîbhâva. If it is an Avyayibhâva, then rule VI. 2, 33 is superseded, and the first member does not retain its original accent. अभितः = उभयतः 'on both sides, अभितोभावोऽस्यास्ति = अभितोभाविन् 'that which has both sides: namely those things which have naturally two sides such as 'banks', 'shores' &c.

प्रादस्वाङ्गं संज्ञायाम् ॥ १८३ ॥ पदानि ॥ प्रात्, अस्वाङ्गम्, संज्ञायाम्, ॥

वृत्तिः ॥ प्रादुत्तरपदमस्वाङ्गवाचि संज्ञायां विषये ऽन्तोदात्तं भवति ॥

183. After प्र, a word, which does not denote a part of body, has acute on the final, when the compound is a name.

Thus प्रकोष्ठम्, प्रगृहम्, प्रद्वारम् ॥ Why do we say 'not denoting a body part'? Observe प्रहस्तम्, प्रपदम् ॥ Why do we say 'when a Name'? Observe प्रपीठम् ॥

निरुदकादीनि च ॥ १८४ ॥ पदानि ॥ निरुदकादीनि, च, (अन्तोदात्तम्) ॥

वृत्तिः ॥ निरुदकादीनि च शब्दरूपाण्यन्तोदात्तानि भवन्ति ॥

184. The words निरुदक &c, have acute on the final.

Thus निरुदकम्, निरुलपम्, निरुपलम् &c.

1 निरुदक, 2 निरुपल निरुलप 3 निर्मक्षिक, 4 निर्मशक, 5 निष्कालक, 6 निष्कालिक, 7 निष्पेष, 8 दुस्तरीप, 9 निस्तरीप, 10 निस्तरीक, 11 निराजिन, 12 उदजिन, 13 उपाजिन, 14 परेर्हस्तपादकेशकर्षाः आकृतिगण.

These may he considered either as प्रादि समास or Bahuvrîhi. If they be considered as avyayî bhâva compounds then they are end acute already by VI. I. 223. The word निष्कालकः = निष्कान्तः कालकात्, is a Prâdi-samâsa with the word काल ending in the affix कन् ॥ The word दुस्तरीपः is thus formed: to the root तॄ is added the affix ई and we have तरी (Uṇ III. 158) तरीम् पाति = तरीपः; कुत्सित स्तरीपः = दुस्तरीपः ॥ The word निस्तरीकः is formed by adding the affix कप् to the Bahuvrihi निस्तरी ॥ The words हस्त, पाद, केश anb कर्ष have acute on the final after परि, as, परिहस्तः, परिपादः, परिकेशः, and परिकर्षः ॥

अभेर्मुखम् ॥ १८५ ॥ पदानि ॥ अभेः, मुखम्, (अन्तोदात्तम्) ॥

वृत्तिः ॥ अभेरुत्तरं मुखमन्तोदात्तं भवति ॥

185. The word मुख has acute on the final when preceded by अभि ॥

As, अभिमुखम् ॥ It is a Bahuvrihi or a प्रादि samâsa. If it is an Avyayîbhâva, then it would have acute on the final by VI. 1. 223 also. By VI. 2. 177, even मुख would have oxytone after an upasarga, the present sûtra makes the additional declaration that मुख is oxytone even when the compound is not a Bahuvrihi, when it does not denote an indispensable part of body, or a part of body even, as was the case in VI. 2. 177. Thus अभिमुखा शाला ॥

अपाच्च ॥ १८६ ॥ पदानि ॥ अपात्, च, (अन्तोदात्तम्) ॥

वृत्तिः ॥ अपाच्चोत्तरं मुखमन्तोदात्तं भवति ।

186. The word मुख has acute on the final, after the preposition अप् ॥

Thus अपमुखम्, अपमुखैः ॥ The compound is in one case Avyayibhâva also, when rule VI. 2. 33 will be superseded. The separation of this from the last sûtra, is for the sake of the subsequent aphorism, in which the anuvritti of अप only goes.

स्फिगपूतवीणाञ्जोऽध्वकुक्षिसीरनाम नाम च १८७ ॥ पदानि ॥ स्फिग, पूत, वीण, अञ्जः, उध्वम् कुक्षि, सीर नाम, नाम, च,

वृत्तिः ॥ स्फिग पूत वीणा अञ्जस् अध्वम कुक्षि इत्येतान्युत्तरपदानि सीरनामानि नामशब्दश्चापादुत्तराण्यन्तोदात्तानि भवन्ति ।

187. The words स्फिग, पूत, वीणा, अञ्जस्, अध्वम, कुक्षि, नामन् and a word denoting 'a plough', have acute on the final when preceded by अप ॥

Thus अपस्फिगम्, अपपूतम्, अपवीणम्, अपाञ्जः, अपाध्वा (This ordains acute on the final where the compound apâdhwa does not take the samâsanta affix अच् by V. 4. 85, when it takes that affix, the acute will also fall on the final because अच् is a चित् affix.) This further shows that the samâsanta affixes are not compulsory. (अनित्यश्च समासान्तः), अपकुक्षिः, अपसीरः अपहलः, अपलाङ्गलम्, अपनाम ॥ These are प्रादि compounds or Bahuvrihi or Avyayibhavas. Some of these viz. स्फिग, पूत and कुक्षिः will be end-acute by VI. 2. 177, also when they denote parts of body and a permanent condition and the compound is a Bahuvrihi. Here the compound must not be a Bahuvrihi, nor should these words denote parts of body and permanent condition of these parts.

अधेरुपरिस्थम ॥ १८८ ॥ पदानि ॥ अधेः, उपरिस्थम, (अन्तोदात्तम) ॥

वृत्तिः ॥ अधेरुत्तरमुपरिस्थवाचि अन्तोदात्तं भवति ।

188. After अधि, that word, which denotes that thing which overlaps or stands upon, has acute on the final.

Thus अधिदन्तः = दन्तस्योपरि योऽन्योदन्तो जायते 'a tooth that grows over another tooth'. अधिकर्णः, अधिकेशः ॥ These are प्रादि samâsa or an appositional compound in which the second member has been dropped. Why do we say when meaning 'standing upon'? Observe अधिकरणम् Here the acute is on क, the krit-formed second member retaining its accent (VI. 2. 139).

अनोरप्रधानकनीयसी ॥ १८९ ॥ पदानि ॥ अनोः, अप्रधान, कनीयसी, (अन्तोदात्तम)

वृत्तिः ॥ अनोरुत्तरमप्रधानवाचि कनीयश्चान्तोदात्तं भवति ।

189. After अनु, a word which is not the Principal, as well as कनीयस् has acute on the final.

The word अप्रधान means a word which stands in a dependant relation in a compound. Thus अनुगतो ज्येष्ठम् = अनुज्येष्ठः, अनुमध्यमः ॥ These are प्रादि samâsa in which the first member is the principal or Pradhâna. अनुगतः कनीयान्=अनुकनीयान्, here the second member is the Principal: the word कनीयस् is taken as प्रधान ॥ Had it been non-pradhâna, it would be covered by the first portion of the sûtra, and there would have been no necessity of its separate enumeration. Why do we say "अप्रधान"? Observe अनुगतो ज्येष्ठः=अनुज्येष्ठः, where ज्येष्ठ is the Principal.

पुरुषश्चान्वादिष्टः ॥ १९० ॥ पदानि ॥ पुरुषः, च, अन्वादिष्टः ॥

वृत्तिः ॥ पुरुषशब्दो ऽन्वादिष्टवाची चानोरुत्तरोऽन्तोदात्तो भवति ।

190. After अनु, the acute falls on the final of पुरुष, when it means a man of whom mention was already made.

The word अन्वादिष्ट means 'of a secondary importance, inferior', or 'mentioned again after having already been mentioned'. Thus अन्वादिष्टः पुरुषः=अनुपुरुषः; but अनुगतः पुरुषः=अनुपुरुषः ॥

अतेरकृत्पदे ॥ १९१ ॥ पदानि ॥ अतेः, अकृत्पदे ॥

वृत्तिः ॥ अतेः परमकृदन्तं पदशब्दश्चान्तोदात्तो भवति ।

वार्त्तिकम् ॥ अतेर्धातुलोपइति वक्तव्यम् ॥

191. After अति, a word not formed by a kṛit-affix, and the word पद, have acute on the last syllable.

Thus अत्यङ्कुशो नागः, अतिकशोऽश्वः, अतिपदा शक्वरी ॥ Why do we say 'non-krit-word and पद'? Observe अतिकारकः ॥

Vârt:—The rule is restricted to those compounds in which a root has been elided. That is, when in analysing the compound a verb like क्रम् is to be employed to complete the sense. Therefore it does not apply to शोभनो गार्ग्यः=अतिगार्ग्यः ॥ But it would apply to अतिकारकः, which when analysed becomes equal to अतिक्रान्तः कारकम् ॥

नेरनिधाने ॥ १९२ ॥ पदानि ॥ नेः, अनिधाने, (अन्तोदात्तम्) ॥

वृत्तिः ॥ नेः परमुत्तरपदमन्तोदात्तं भवति ।

192. After नि, the second member has the acute on the last syllable, when the sense is of 'not laying down'.

The word निधानं=अप्रकाशता 'not making manifest'. Thus निमूलम्, न्यक्षम्, नितृणम् ॥ These are either Bahuvrihi or prâdisamâsa. In the case of their being Avyayîbhâva, they would have acute on the final by VI. 1. 223. Why do we say when meaning 'not laying down'? Observe निवाक्=निहितवाक् as निवाग्वृषलः ; निदण्डः=निहितदण्डः ॥ The force of नि is that of निधान here.

प्रतेरंश्वादयस्तत्पुरुषे ॥१९३॥ पदानि ॥ प्रतेः, अंश्वादयः, तत्पुरुषे, (अन्तोदात्ताः)

वृत्तिः ॥ प्रतेरंश्वादयस्तत्पुरुषे समासेऽन्तोदात्ता भवन्ति ।

193. In a Tatpurusha compound, the words अंशु &c have acute on the final when preceded by प्रति ॥

Thus प्रत्यंशुः, प्रतिजनैः, प्रतियज्ञौ ॥ In the case of राजन् this rule applies when the Samâsânta affix टच् is not added, when that affix is added, the acute will also be on the final by virtue of टच् which is a चित् affix.

1 अंशु, 2 जन, 3 राजन्, 4 उष्ट्र, 5 खेटक (रोटक), 6 अजिर, 7 आर्द्रा, 8 श्रवण, 9 कृत्तिका, 10 अर्ध, 11 पुर (आर्धपुर आर्धपुरः) ॥

The word अंशु is formed by the affix कु under the general class मृगय्वः (Uṇ I. 37), राजन् is formed by the affix कनिन् (Uṇ I. 156), उष्ट्र by adding ष्ट्रन् to उष् 'to burn'. (Uṇ IV. 162), खिट् + ण्वुल् = खेटक ; अजिर is formed by किरच् (Uṇ I. 53) आ + द्रा + अङ् (III. 3. 106), with the augment रुक् added to आ = आर्द्रा ॥ श्रु + ल्युट् = श्रवण, कृत + तिकन् = कृत्तिका (Uṇ III. 147) ऋधु + अच् (III. 1. 134) = अर्द्ध ; पुर् + क = पुर ॥

Why do we say 'in the Tatpurusha'? Observe प्रतिगता अंशवोऽस्य = प्रत्यंशुरयमुष्ट्रः ॥

उपाद् द्व्यजजिनमगौरादयः ॥ १९४ ॥ पदानि ॥ उपाद्, द्व्यच् अजिनम्, अगौरादयः, (अन्तोदात्तम्) ॥

वृत्तिः ॥ उपादुत्तरं द्व्यजजिनं चान्तोदात्तं भवति तत्पुरुषे समासे गौरादीन्वर्जयित्वा ॥

194. In a Tatpurusha, the words of two syllables and अजिन have acute on the final when preceded by उप, but not when they are गौर and the rest.

Thus उपगतो देवः = उपदेवः, उपेन्द्रः, उपसोमः, उपहोडः, उपाजिनम् ॥ But not so in उपगौरः, उपनैषः &c.

1 गौर, 2 नैष (नैप) 3 तैल, 4 लेट, 5 लोट, 6 जिह्वा, 7 कृष्ण (कृष्णा) 8 कन्या, 9 गुध (गुड) 10 कल्प, 11 पाद

Why "in a Tatpurusha"? Observe उपगतः सोमोऽस्य = उपसोमः ॥

सोरवक्षेपणे ॥ १९५ ॥ पदानि ॥ सोः, अवक्षेपणे ॥

वृत्तिः ॥ सुशब्दात्परमुत्तरपदं तत्पुरुषे समासेऽन्तोदात्तं भवति अवक्षेपणे गम्यमाने ॥

195. After सु, the second member has acute on the final in a Tatpurusha compound, when reproach is meant, in spite of the addition of सु which denotes praise.

Thus इह खल्विदानीं, सुस्थण्डिले सुस्फिताभ्यां सुप्रत्यवसितैः ॥ The word सु here verily denotes praise, but it is the sense of the whole sentence that indicates reproach or censure. Why do we say "after सु"? Observe कुब्राह्मणः ॥ Why 'when reproach is meant'? Observe शोभनेषु तृणेषु = सुतृणेषु ॥

विभाषोत्पुच्छे ॥ १९६ ॥ पदानि ॥ विभाषा, उत्पुच्छे, (अन्तउदात्तः) ॥

वृत्तिः ॥ उत्पुच्छशब्दे तत्पुरुषे विभाषाऽन्त उदात्तो भवति ॥

196. In a Tatpurusha, the word उत्पुच्छ may optionally have acute on the final.

Thus उत्क्रान्तः पुच्छात् = उत्पुच्छः or उत्पुच्छः (VI. 2. 2) ॥ When this word is derived by the affix अच् from पुच्छमुदस्यति = उत्पुच्छयति, then it would always have taken acute on the final by VI. 2. 144, the present sûtra ordains option there also. The rule does not apply to a non-Tatpurusha : as, उद्स्तं पुच्छमस्य = उत्पुच्छः ॥

द्वित्रिभ्यां पाद्दन्मूर्द्धसु बहुव्रीहौ ॥ १९७ ॥ पदानि ॥ द्वि, त्रिभ्याम्, पात्, दत्, मूर्द्ध सु, बहुव्रीहौ, ॥

वृत्तिः ॥ द्वि त्रि इत्येताभ्यामुत्तरेषु पाद् दत् मूर्द्धन् इत्येतेषूत्तरपदेषु यो बहुव्रीहिस्तत्र विभाषा ऽन्त उदात्तो भवति ॥

197. In a Bahuvrîhi, the words पाद्, दत् and मूर्धन् have optionally acute on the final after द्वि and त्रि ॥

Thus द्वौ पादावस्य = द्विपात् or द्विपात्, त्रिपाद् or त्रिपाद्, द्विदन् or द्विदन्, त्रिदन् or त्रिदन्, द्विमूर्द्धा or द्विमूर्धा ॥ The word पाद् is पाद with its अ elided, (V. 4. 140) दत् is the substitute of दन्त (V. 4. 141) and मूर्धन् retains its न् not allowing samâsanta affix. This also indicates that the samâsanta rule is not universal. When the samâsanta affix is added, then also the acute is on the final, for the कार्यी is here the Bahuvrihi compound, and this is only a part of it. Thus द्विमूर्द्धः, त्रिमूर्द्धः ॥ Why after द्वि and त्रि? Observe कल्याणमूर्धा here the first member is middle acute by Phiṭ II. 19 and this accent is retained VI. 2. 1. Why 'पाद् &c'? Observe द्विहस्तम्, त्रिहस्तम् ॥ Why 'Bahuvrihi'? Observe द्वयोर्मूर्द्धा = द्विमूर्द्धा ॥

सक्थं चाक्रान्तात् ॥ १९८ ॥ पदानि ॥ सक्थम्, च, अ क्रान्तात्, (अन्तोदात्तः) (विभाषा) ॥

वृत्तिः ॥ सक्थमिति कृतसमासान्तः सक्थिशब्दोऽत्र गृह्यते सोऽक्रान्तात्परो विभाषान्तोदात्तो भवति ॥

198. The word सक्थ has acute on the final optionally, when preceded by any word other than what ends in क्र ॥

The word सक्थ is the samâsânta form of सक्थि (V. 4. 113,). Thus गौरसक्थः or गौरसक्थः, श्लक्ष्णसक्थः or श्लक्ष्णसक्थः The word गौर being formed by प्रज्ञादि अण् and श्लक्ष्ण by क्स्न (Uṇ III. 19) are both end-acute. Why 'not after a word ending in क्र'? Observe चक्रसक्थः which is *always* oxytone as it is formed by षच् (V. 4. 113) a चित् affix.

परादिश्छन्दसि बहुलम् ॥ १९९ ॥ पदानि ॥ परादिः, छन्दसि, बहुलम् ॥

वृत्तिः ॥ छन्दसि विषये परादिरुदात्तो भवति बहुलम् ॥

Karika—परादिश्च परान्तश्च पूर्वान्तश्चापि दृश्यते ।
पूर्वादयश्च दृश्यन्ते व्यत्ययो बहुलं ततः ॥

वार्त्तिकम् ॥ अन्तोदात्तप्रकरणे त्रिचक्रादीनांछन्दस्युपसंख्यानम् ॥

वा० ॥ पूर्वपदान्तोदात्तप्रकरणे मरुद्वृद्धादीनां छन्दस्युपसंख्यानम् ॥

वा० ॥ पूर्वपदाद्युदात्तप्रकरणे दिवोदासादीनां छन्दस्युपसंख्यानम् ॥

199. The first syllable of the second member is diversely acute, in the Veda.

The word पर "the second member" refers to सक्थ, as well as to any other word in general. Thus अञ्जिसक्थमालभेत, but लोमशसक्थः so also ऋजुबाहुः, वाक्पतिः, चित्पति ॥ In the non-Vedic literative these last two compounds will be final acute by VI. 1. 223, rule VI. 2. 18 not applying because of the prohibition contained in VI. 2. 19.

The rule is rather too restricted. It ought to be: "In the Veda, the *first* syllable and the *final* syllable of the *second* member, as well as the *final* syllable and the *first* syllable of the *preceding* member are seen to have the acute accent, in supersession of all the foregoing rules".

As to where the final of the second terms takes the acute, we have this *Vârtika*—In the Veda, त्रिचक्र &c have acute on the final of the second term. As त्रिचक्रेण, त्रिबन्धुरेण, त्रिवृतारथेन, ॥ नियेनं मुष्टिहत्यया ॥

As to where the final of the preceding takes the acute, we have this *Vârtika*:—The words मरुद्वृद्ध &c in the Vedas have acute on the final of the first term. As मरुद्वृद्धः and त्रिश्वायुः ॥

As to where the first syllable of the preceding takes the acute, we have this *Vârtika*:—In the Veda, the words दिवोदास &c have acute on the first syllable of the first member. As दिवोदासाय सामगाय ते ॥

ओम् ३ ।

षष्ठाध्यायस्य तृतीयः पादः ।

BOOK SIXTH.

CHAPTER THIRD

अलुगुत्तरपदे ॥ १ ॥ पदानि ॥ अलुक्, उत्तरपदे ॥

वृत्तिः ॥ अलुगिति च उत्तरपदे इति च एतदधिकृतं वेदितव्यम् । यदित ऊर्ध्वमनुक्रमिष्यामो ऽलुगुत्तरपदइत्येव तद्वेदितव्यम् ॥

1. In the following upto VI. 3. 24 inclusive is always to be supplied the phrase "the elision does not take place before the second member of the compound".

The words अलुक् 'there is no elision', and उत्तरपदे "before the second member" are to be supplied in the subsequent sûtras. Both these words govern the sûtras upto VI. 3. 24, jointly; while उत्तरपदे extends further upto that point whence commences the jurisdiction of अङ्ग (VI.4. 1). Thus sûtra VI. 3. 2 says "the affixes of the Ablative after 'stôka' &c". The present sûtra should be read there to complete the sense, e. g. "the affixes of the Ablative after stoka &c are not elided before the second member of the compound". Thus स्तोकात् मुक्तः = स्तोकान्मुक्तः, अल्पान्मुक्तः ॥ Why do we say "before the second member"? Observe निष्क्रान्तः स्तोकात् = निःस्तोकः ॥ The maxim of pratipadokta does not apply here.

पञ्चम्याः स्तोकादिभ्यः ॥ २ ॥ पदानि ॥ पञ्चम्याः, स्तोकादिभ्यः, (अलुक्) ॥

वृत्तिः ॥ स्तोकान्तिकदूरार्थकृच्छ्राणि स्तोकादीनि तेभ्यः परस्याः पञ्चम्या उत्तरपदे ऽलुग्भवति ॥

2. The Ablative-ending after स्तोक &c is not elided before the second member of a compound.

Thus स्तोकान्मुक्तः, अल्पान्मुक्तः, अन्तिकादागतः. अभ्याशादागतः, दूरादागतः, विप्रकृष्टादागतः, कृच्छ्रान्मुक्तः ॥ By I. 2. 46, a case-inflected word when forming part of a compound is called prâtipadika, and by II. 4. 71 the endings of a Prâtipadika are elided. Therefore, in forming the compound of स्तोकात् मुक्तः, the ablative ending required to be dropped. The present sûtra prevents that. The words स्तोक &c in the dual and plural are never compounded, and consequently this rule does not apply to them. Thus स्तोकाभ्यां मुक्तः, स्तोकेभ्यः मुक्तः are separate words and not compounds, for not being treated as compounds, these are not one Pada (एकपद) or one word, and do not have *one* accent, for in *one* word, there is only *one* acute. Thus while स्तोकान्मुक्तः being *one* compound word will have *one* acute (VI. 1. 158, VI. 2. 144), the word स्तोकाभ्यां मुक्तः being treated as *two* words, wlll have separate acute accents. The above compounding takes place by II. 1. 39.

Vârt:—The word ब्राह्मणाच्छंसिन् should be enumerated in this connection. Here also the Ablative is not elided. Thus ब्राह्मणाद्गृह्य शंसति = ब्राह्मणाच्छंसिन् "a kind of Ritvik priest".

ओजः सहोम्भस्तमसस्तृतीयायाः ॥ ३ ॥ पदानि ॥ ओजस्, सहस्, अम्भस् तमसः, तृतीयायाः (अलुक्) ॥

वृत्तिः ॥ ओजस् सहस् अम्भस् तमस् इत्येतेभ्य उत्तरस्यास्तृतीयाया अलुग्भवति उत्तरपदे ॥

वार्त्तिकम् ॥ अञ्जस उपसंख्यानम् ॥ वा० ॥ पुंसानुजो जनुषान्ध इति वक्तव्यम् ॥

3. The Instrumental endings after ओजस्, सहस्, अम्भस् and तमस् are not elided before the second member of a compound.

Thus ओजसाकृतम्, सहसाकृतम्, अम्भसाकृतम्, तमसाकृतम् ॥

Vârt—अञ्जस् also should be enumerated. Thus अञ्जसाकृतम् ॥

Vârt:—The compounds पुंसानुजः and जनुषान्धः should also be mentioned. Thus पुंसा हेतुनानुजः = पुंसानुजः ॥ जनुषा हेतुनाऽन्धः = जनुषान्धः ॥ The word जनु is another name of जन्मन् 'birth'.

मनसः संज्ञायाम् ॥ ४ ॥ पदानि ॥ मनसः, संज्ञायाम्, (अलुक्) ॥

वृत्तिः ॥ मनस उत्तरस्यास्तृतीयायाः संज्ञायामलुग्भवति ॥

4. After मनस् when the compound is a Name, the Instrumental endings are not elided before the second member.

Thus मनसादत्ता, मनसागुप्ता, मनसासंगता ॥ Why do we say 'when a Name'? Observe मनोदत्ता, मनोगुप्ता ॥

आज्ञायिनि च ॥ ५ ॥ पदानि ॥ आज्ञायिनि, च, (अलुक्) ॥

वृत्तिः ॥ आज्ञायिन्युत्तरपदे मनस उत्तरस्यास्तृतीयाया अलुग्भवति ॥

5. Also before आज्ञायिन्, the Instrumental endings of मनस् are not elided.

Thus मनसाज्ञायिन् = मनसाऽऽज्ञातु शीलमस्य ॥

आत्मनश्च पूरणे ॥ ६ ॥ पदानि ॥ आत्मनः, च, पूरणे, (अलुक्) ॥

वृत्तिः ॥ आत्मन उत्तरस्यास्तृतीयायाः पूरणप्रत्ययान्तउत्तरपदे ऽलुग्भवति ॥

6. The Instrumental endings after आत्मन् are not elided when an Ordinal Numeral follows.

Thus आत्मनापंचमः, आत्मनाषष्ठः ॥ The Instrumental case here takes place under the Vârtika तृतीयाविधाने प्रकृत्यादीनामुपसंख्यानं (II. 3. 18 Vârt). And compounding takes place by II. 1. 30, by separating तृतीया of that aphorism and making it a separate sûtra or in this way :—आत्मना कृतः पंचमः = आत्मनापंचमः ॥ How do you explain the form आत्मचतुर्थ in जनार्दनस्त्वात्मचतुर्थ एव? It is a Bahuvrîhi compound = आत्मा चतुर्थोऽस्य ॥ The word पूरणे is a later addition of the Vârtikakâra.

वैयाकरणाख्यायां चतुर्थ्याः ॥ ७ ॥ पदानि ॥ वैयाकरणाख्यायाम्, चतुर्थ्याः, (अलुक्) ॥

वृत्तिः ॥ वैयकारणस्याख्या वैयाकरणाख्या । आख्या संज्ञा । यया संज्ञया वैयाकरणा एव व्यवहरन्ति तस्यामात्मन उत्तरस्याश्चतुर्थ्या अलुग्भवति ॥

7. The Dative case ending is not elided after आत्मन् when the compound is the name of a technical term of grammar.

Thus आत्मनेपदम्, आत्मनेभाषा ॥ The compounding takes place by the yoga-bibhâga of sûtra II. 1. 36, and the force of the Dative is here that of tadartha.

परस्य च ॥ ८ ॥ पदानि ॥ परस्य, च, (अलुक्) ॥

वृत्तिः ॥ परस्य च या चतुर्थी तस्यां वैयाकरणाख्यायामलुग्भवति ॥

8. The Dative ending is not elided after पर, when the compound is the name of a technical term of grammar.

Thus परस्मैपदम्, परस्मैभाषा ॥

हलदन्तात्सप्तम्याः संज्ञायाम् ॥ ९ ॥ पदानि ॥ हल्, अदन्तात्, सप्तम्याः, संज्ञायाम्, (अलुक्) ॥

वृत्तिः ॥ हलन्तादन्ताच्चोत्तरस्याः सप्तम्याः संज्ञायामलुग्भवति ॥

वार्त्तिकम् ॥ हृद्द्युभ्यां ङेः ॥

9. The Locative ending is not elided after a stem ending in a consonant or a short अ, when the compound is a Name.

Thus युधिष्ठिरः, त्वचिसारः, गविष्ठिरः ॥ Though गो does not end in a consonant, yet it retains its Locative ending by virtue of VIII. 3. 95 (गवियुधिभ्यां स्थिरः) which shows by implication that गवि is governed by this rule. So also अ ending words: as अरण्येतिलकाः, अरण्येभाषकाः, वनेकिंशुकाः, वनेहरिद्रकाः, वनेबल्बजकाः, पूर्वाह्णेस्फोटकाः, कूपेपिशाचकाः ॥ Why do we say "after a word ending in a consonant or अ"? Observe नद्यां कुक्कुटिका = नदीकुक्कुटिका, भूम्यां पाशाः = भूमिपाशाः ॥ Why do we say 'when a Name'? Observe अक्षशौण्डः ॥

Vârt:—The Locative ending is not elided after हृद् and दिव्; as : हृदिस्पृक्, दिविस्पृक् ॥

कारनाम्नि च प्राचां हलादौ ॥ १० ॥ पदानि ॥ कारनाम्नि, च, प्राचाम्, हलादौ, (अलुक्) ॥

वृत्तिः ॥ प्राचां देशे यत्कारनाम तत्र हलादावुत्तरपदे हलदन्तादुत्तरस्याः सप्तम्या अलुग्भवति ॥

10. The Locative-case affix is not elided after a stem ending in a consonant or a short अ, in the name of a tax of the Eastern people, when the second member begins with a consonant.

Thus सूपेशाणः, दृषदिमाषकः, हलेद्विपदिका, हलेत्रिपदिका ॥ All these are names of taxes, and would have retained the Locative ending even by the last rule. The present rule makes a niyama or restriction, which is threefold, namely (1) when it is the name of a tax, and no other word, (2) when it belongs to the Eastern people and no other people, (3) and when the second member begins with a consonant.

Why do we say when it is the name of a tax. ? Observe अभ्यर्हितेपशुः = अभ्यर्हितपशुः ॥ It is the name of 'a duty or dues', but not of a 'tax'. Why do we say "of the Eastern people"? Observe यूथेपशुः = यूथपशुः ॥ Why do we say 'before a second member beginning with a consonant'? Observe अविकटे उरणः = अविकटोरणः ॥ So also नद्यां दोहनी = नदीदोहनी ॥ For accent of these words see VI. 2. 65.

मध्याद्गुरौ ॥ ११ ॥ पदानि ॥ मध्यात्, गुरौ, अलुक् ॥

वृत्तिः ॥ मध्यादुत्तरस्याः सप्तम्या गुरावुत्तरपदेऽलुग्भवति ॥

वार्त्तिकम् ॥ अन्ताच्चेति वक्तव्यम् ॥

11. The Locative case-affix is not elided after मध्य when गुरु follows.

As, मध्येगुरुः ॥

Vârt:—So also after अन्त ; as अन्तेगुरुः ॥

अमूर्द्धमस्तकात् स्वाङ्गादकामे ॥ १२ ॥ पदानि ॥ अ मूर्द्ध, मस्तकात्, स्वाङ्गात्, अकामे, (अलुक्) ॥

वृत्तिः ॥ मूर्द्धमस्तकवर्जितात्स्वाङ्गादुत्तरस्याः सप्तम्या अकामउत्तरपदेऽलुग्भवति ॥

12. The Locative case-affix is not elided after a word denoting a part of the body (with the exception of मूर्धन् and मस्तक), before every word other than काम ॥

Thus कण्ठे कालोऽस्य = कण्ठेकालः, उरसिलोमा, उदरेमणिः ॥ But मूर्धशिखः, मस्तकशिखः, मुखे कामोऽस्य = मुखकामः ॥ When the first member does not denote the name of a part of the body, the rule does not apply: as अक्षशौण्डः, nor does it apply when the first member does not end in a consonant or अ, as अंगुलित्राणः, जङ्घाबलिः ॥

बन्धे च विभाषा ॥ १३ ॥ पदानि ॥ बन्धे, च, विभाषा, (अलुक्) ॥

वृत्तिः ॥ बन्ध इति घञन्तो गृह्यते । तस्मिन्नुत्तरपदे हलदन्तादुत्तरस्याः सप्तम्या विभाषा ऽलुग्भवति ॥

13. The Locative case-affix is optionally not elided after a word ending in a consonant or अ before बन्ध ॥

Thus हस्तेबन्धः or हस्तबन्धः, चक्रेबन्धः or चक्रबन्धः ॥ This declares an option, with regard to the last rule, in a Bahuvrihi when the first member is a स्वाङ्ग word, and also it is an option to VI. 3. 19, when the compound is a Tatpurusha, whether the first be स्वांग or not. The word बन्धः is घञ् formed word. When the first member ends in a vowel (other than अ), the rule does not apply. As गुप्तिबन्धः ॥

तत्पुरुषे कृति बहुलम् ॥ १४ ॥ पदानि ॥ तत् पुरुषे, कृति, बहुलम्, (अलुक्) ॥

वृत्तिः ॥ तत्पुरुषे समासे कृदन्तउत्तरपदे सप्तम्या बहुलमलुग्भवति ॥

14. In a Tatpurusha compound, when the second member is a word formed with a kṛit affix, the Locative ending is optionally preserved.

As स्तम्बेरमः, कर्णेजपः, but also कुरुचरः, मद्रचरः ॥

प्रावृड्शरत्कालदिवां जे ॥१५॥ पदानि ॥ प्रावृड्, शरत्, काल, दिवाम्, जे, (अलुक्)॥

वृत्तिः ॥ प्रावृड् शरत् काल दिव् इत्येतेषां ज उत्तरपदे सप्तम्या अलुग्भवति ॥

15. The Locative ending is retained after प्रावृट्, शरत्, काल and दिव् when ज follows.

Thus प्रावृषिजः, शरदिजः, कालेजः, दिविजः ॥ This sûtra is but an extension or amplification of the previous sûtra.

विभाषा वर्षक्षरशरवरात् ॥ १६ ॥ पदानि ॥ विभाषा, वर्ष, क्षर, शर, वरात्, (अलुक्) ॥

वृत्तिः ॥ वर्ष क्षर शर वर इत्येतेभ्य उत्तरस्याः सप्तम्या ज उत्तरपदे विभाषा ऽलुग्भवति ॥

16. The Locative ending is optionally retained after वर्ष, क्षर, शर, and वर when ज follows.

Thus वर्षेजः or वर्षजः, क्षरेजः or क्षरजः, शरेजः or शरजः, वरेजः or वरजः ॥

घकालतनेषु कालनाम्नः ॥ १७ ॥ पदानि ॥ घ, काल, तनेषु, काल नाम्नः, (अलुक्)

वृत्तिः ॥ घसंज्ञके प्रत्यये कालशब्दे तनप्रत्यये च परतः कालनाम्न उत्तरस्याः सप्तम्या विभाषा ऽलुग्भवति ॥

17. The Locative ending is optionally retained after a word denoting time ending in a consonant or अ when तरप् or तमप्, or the word काल or the affix तन follows.

The affixes तर and तम are called घ (I. 1. 22). Thus घः—पूर्वाह्णेतरे or पूर्वाह्णतरे, पूर्वाह्णेतमे or पूर्वाह्णतमे ॥ काल :—पूर्वाह्णेकाले or पूर्वाह्णकाले ॥ तन :—पूर्वाह्णेतने or पूर्वाह्णतने ॥ Why do we say 'after a time—name'? Observe शुक्लतरे, शुक्लतमे ॥ The condition that the preceding word should end in a consonant or अ applies here also. Thus no option is allowed in रात्रितरायाम् ॥

As a general maxim, an affix denotes whenever it is employed in Grammar a word-form which begins with that to which that affix has been added, and ends with the affix itself (प्रत्ययग्रहणे यस्मात् स विहित स्तदादे स्तदन्तस्य ग्रहणम्) ॥ Thus the word थ, अथ &c in VI. 2. 144 means a word ending in थ affix &c. But in this chapter, so far as the jurisdiction of उत्तरपदं goes, an affix does not denote a word-form ending in that affix, on the following maxim: उत्तरपदाधिकारे प्रत्ययग्रहणे न तदन्त ग्रहणम्; on the contrary the affix denotes its own-form. Thus तर, तम and तन here do not denote a word ending in these affixes. This rule we infer from the fact that in sûtra VI. 3. 50, the author declares "हृद् is the substitute of हृदय when the word लेख, and the affixes यत्, अण्, and लास follow". Had the affix अण् here meant the word-form ending in अण्, then there would have been no necessity of using the word लेख in the sûtra, as लेख is formed with the अण् affix. The word काल in the aphorism means the word-form काल ॥ See Sûtra IV. 3. 23 for the affix तन ॥

शयवासवासिष्वकालात् ॥१८॥ पदानि ॥ शय, वास, वासिषु, अकालात्, (अलुक्)

वृत्तिः ॥ शय वास वासिन् इत्येतेषूत्तरपदेष्वकालवाचिन उत्तरस्याः सप्तम्या विभाषा ऽलुग्भवति ॥

18. The Locative ending is optionally retained before the words शय, वास and वासिन् when the preceding word does not denote time, and ends in a consonant or short अ ॥

Thus खेशयः, or खशयः, ग्रामेवासः or ग्रामवासः, ग्रामेवासिन् or ग्रामवासिन् ॥ After a time-name we have पूर्वाह्णशयः ॥ After a vowel ending word (other than अ) we have भूमिशयः ॥

Vârt:—The Locative case-affix is retained after अप् when योनि, or the affix यत् or मतुप् follows. Thus अप्सुयोनिः, अप्सव्यः, अप्सुमन्तौ ॥ The affix यत् is added by treating अप् as belonging to the दिगादि class (अप्सु भवः, IV. 3. 54).

नेन्सिद्धबध्नातिषु च ॥ १९ ॥ पदानि ॥ न, इन्, सिद्ध, बध्नातिषु, च, (अलुक्) ॥

वृत्तिः ॥ इन्नन्ते सिद्धशब्दे बध्नातौ च परतः सप्तम्या अलुग्न भवति ॥

19. The Locative ending is not preserved before a stem ending in इन्, before the word सिद्ध, and before a word derived from बन्ध् ॥

Thus स्थण्डिलशायिन्, सांकाश्यसिद्धः, काम्पिल्यसिद्धः, चक्रबन्धकः, चरकबन्धकः ॥ The compounding takes place by yoga-vibhâga of sûtra II. 1. 40. Some use the word चक्रबन्धः as an illustration under this rule: बन्ध then is derived by अच् of III. 1. 134. The बन्ध ending in घञ् is governed by VI. 3. 13. This sûtra is an exception to VI. 3. 14.

स्थे च भाषायाम् ॥ २० ॥ पदानि ॥ स्थे, च, भाषायाम्, (न) (अलुक्) ॥

वृत्तिः ॥ स्थे चोत्तरपदे भाषायां सप्तम्या अलुग्न भवति ॥

20. The Locative ending is not preserved before स्थ in the spoken language.

Thus विषमस्थः, कूटस्थः, पर्वतस्थः ॥ But आखरेष्ठः in the Veda, as in कृष्णोस्याखरेष्ठः ॥ स is changed to ष by VIII. 3. 106.

षष्ठ्या आक्रोशे ॥ २१ ॥ पदानि ॥ षष्ठ्याः. आक्रोशे, (अलुक्) ॥

वृत्तिः ॥ आक्रोशे गम्यमाने उत्तरपदे षष्ठ्या अलुग्भवति ॥

वार्त्तिकम् ॥ षष्ठीप्रकरणे वाग् दिक्पश्यद्भ्यो युक्तिदण्डहरेषु यथासंख्यमलुग्वक्तव्यः ॥

वा० ॥ आमुष्यायणामुष्यपुत्रिकामुष्यकुलिकेति चालुग्वक्तव्यः ॥

वा० ॥ देवानां प्रिय इत्यत्र च षष्ठ्या अलुग् वक्तव्यः ॥

वा० ॥ शेपपुच्छलाङ्गूलेषु शुनः संज्ञायां षष्ठ्या अलुग्वक्तव्यः ॥

वा० ॥ दिवश्च दासे षष्ठ्या अलुग्वक्तव्यः ॥

21. The Genitive case affix is retained when the compound expresses an 'affront or insult'.

Thus चौरस्यकुलम्, वृषलस्यकुलम् ॥ Why do we say when insult is meant?. Observe ब्राह्मणकुलम् ॥

Vârt:—The Genitive is not elided after वाक् when followed by युक्ति, after दिश् before दण्ड, and after पश्यत् before हर ॥ As, वाचोयुक्तिः, दिशोदण्डः, पश्यतोहरः ॥

Vârt:—The Genitive affix is not elided in the following words आमुष्यायणः, आमुष्यपुत्रिका and आमुष्यकुलिका ॥ अमुष्य is the Genitive Singular of the Pronoun अदस्, and is enumerated in the नडादि class (IV. 1. 99) and takes फक् in forming the Patronymic, अमुष्यापत्यम्=आमुष्यायणः, अमुष्यपुत्रस्य भावः=आमुष्यपुत्रिका formed by वुञ् (V. 1. 133) ॥ So also आमुष्यकुलिका ॥

Vârt:—The Genitive affix is not elided in the compound देवानांप्रियः ॥ The author of Siddhânta Kaumudi says "when the sense is that of a fool, the affix is not elided in devânâm-priya" There is no authority for this, either in the Mahâbhâshya or the Kâśikâ. This was the title of the famous Buddhist monarch Aśoka, who would not have adopted it, had it meant 'a fool'. The phrase इति च मूर्खे has been added by Bhattoji Dikshit through Brahmanical spite.

Vârt:—The Genitive affix is not elided after श्वन् when शेप, पुच्छ and लांगुल follow it:—शुनःशेपः, शुनःपुच्छः, शुनोलांगुलः ॥

Vârt:—The Genitive affix is not elided after दिव् when दास follows: as दिवोदासः ॥

पुत्रेऽन्यतरस्याम् ॥ २२ ॥ पदानि ॥ पुत्रे, अन्यतरस्याम्, (अलुक्) ॥

वृत्तिः ॥ पुत्रशब्दउत्तरपदे आक्रोशे गम्यमाने ऽन्यतरस्यां षष्ठ्या अलुग्भवति ।

22. The genitive affix is optionally retained when insult is meant, when पुत्र follows.

Thus दास्याःपुत्रः or दासीपुत्रः, वृषल्याःपुत्रः, or वृषलीपुत्रः ॥ But when insult is not meant we have ब्राह्मणीपुत्रः ॥

ऋतो विद्यायोनिसम्बन्धेभ्यः ॥२३॥ पदानि ॥ ऋतः, विद्या, योनि, सम्बन्धेभ्यः, (अलुक्) ॥

anomalous use there being no Dvandva compounding here. द्यावा चिदस्मै पृथिवी नमेते ॥

उषासोषसः ॥ ३१ ॥ पदानि ॥ उषासा, उषसः, (देवताद्वन्द्वे) ॥
वृत्तिः ॥ उषस उषासा इत्ययमादेशो भवति देवताद्वन्द्वे उत्तरपदे ॥

31. For उषस् is substituted उषासा in a devatâ-dvandva.

Thus :—उषासासूर्यम्, उषासानक्ता ॥

मातरपितरावुदीचाम् ॥ ३२ ॥ पदानि ॥ मातर, पितरौ, उदीचाम्, ॥
वृत्तिः ॥ मातरपितराविस्युदीचामाचार्याणां मतेनारङादेशो मातृशब्दस्य निपात्यते ॥

32. According to the Northern Grammarians, मातरपितरौ is a valid form.

This is formed by अरङ् substitution of the ऋ of मातृ ॥ The other form is मातापितरौ ॥

पितरामातरा च च्छन्दसि ॥ ३३ ॥ पदानि ॥ पितरा, मातरा, च, छन्दसि, ॥
वृत्तिः ॥ पितरामातरा इति छन्दसि निपात्यते ॥

33. In the Vedas the form पितरामातरा is valid.

In the ordinary language मातापितरौ is the proper form. The Vedic form is derived by adding अङ् to the first member, and आ is added to the second by VII. 1. 39 : and then Guṇa by VII. 3. 110. Thus आ मा गन्तां पितरा-मातरा च ॥

स्त्रियाः पुंवद्भाषितपुंस्कादनूङ्, समानाधिकरणे स्त्रियामपूरणीप्रियादिषु ॥ ३४ ॥ पदानि ॥ स्त्रियाः, पुम्वत्, भाषितपुंस्कात्, अनूङ्, समानाधिकरणे स्त्रियाम्, अपूरणी, प्रियादिषु, ॥
वृत्तिः ॥ भाषितपुंस्कादनूङः स्त्रीशब्दस्य पुंशब्दस्येव रूपं भवति समानाधिकरणउत्तरपदे स्त्रीलिङ्गे पूरणीप्रिया-दिवर्जिते ॥

34. In the room of a feminine word there is substituted an equivalent and uniform masculine form, when it is a word which has an actual corresponding masculine, and does not end in the feminine affix ऊङ्, and is followed by another feminine word in the relation of apposition with it; but not when such subsequent word is an ordinal numeral, nor प्रिय &c.

The words of this sûtra require a detailed analysis ; स्त्रियाः 'for a feminine word', पुंवत् "like the mascul ine", i. e. a substitute like the masculine takes the room of a feminine word. भाषितपुंस्कात् = भाषितपुमान्येन, by which a masculine is spoken of i. e. a word which has an equivalent masculine, the correspondence must be in the *form* (आकृति) and the *connotation* (आयाम) of the two words; that is when both the words are coextensive in their denotation, applying to the same objects, but of different genders. A word which has not the affix ऊङ् is called अनूङ् ॥ That feminine word which does not end in ऊङ् and has a corresponding masculine word, having the same form and connotation, (of course, with the exception of affixes) is called a भाषितपुंस्कादनूङ् स्त्रीशब्दः ॥ The word भाषितपुंस्कादनूङ् is a Bahuvrihi, the fifth affix is not elided anomalously. Of such a भाषितपुंस्कादनूङ् feminine word, there is the substitution of a masculine form. Provided that, the second member is a (समानाधिकरण) i. e. a word in apposition with the first, and (स्त्रियाम्) of the feminine gender: with the exception of an Ordinal numeral (पूरण) and of प्रिय &c.

Thus दर्शनीयभार्यः (=दर्शनीयाभार्या यस्य). Here दर्शनीया is a feminine word having a corresponding masculine word of the same form and force, namely, दर्शनीयः, moreover this feminine does not end in the affix ऊङ्, but in the affix आ; it is followed by another feminine word भार्या which is in the same case with it, and which is not a Numeral nor included in the प्रियादि class; hence this word दर्शनीया is changed to the corresponding masculine word दर्शनीय ॥ So also श्लक्ष्णचूडः, दीर्घजङ्घः ॥ Why do we say स्त्रियाः 'for a feminine word'? Observe ग्रामणि ब्राह्मणकुलं दृष्टिरस्य = ग्रामणिदृष्टिः ॥ Why do we say which has an appropriate masculine (भाषितपुंस्कः)? Observe खट्वाभार्यः ॥ There is no corresponding masculine of खट्वा ॥ Why do we say "of the same connotation and form समानायामाकृतौ"? Observe द्रोणीभार्यः, the masculine word द्रोण has not the same significance as द्रोणी ॥ The words गर्भिभार्यः, प्रसूतभार्यः, and प्रजातभार्यः are anomalous. Why do we say not ending in ऊङ्? Observe ब्रह्मबन्धूभार्यः ॥ Why do we say 'both words being in the same case and referring to another person'? Observe कल्याण्यामाता = कल्याणीमाता "the mother of Kalyâṇi". Why do we say स्त्रियाम् 'followed by a feminine word'? Observe कल्याणी प्रधानमेषां = कल्याणीप्रधानाः (इमे) ॥ Here the second member प्रधान is a Neuter word. Why do we say 'not being an ordinal Numeral'? Observe कल्याणी पञ्चमी यासां ताः = कल्याणी पञ्चमारात्रयः, so also कल्याणीदशमाः ॥ The Ordinal Numbers must be the Principal Ordinal and not the secondary Derivative Ordinals. Therefore the rule applies here कल्याणपञ्चमीकः पक्षः ॥ The samâsânta affix अप् (V. 4. 116) also applies to an Ordinal which is a Principal and not what is used as a secondary word: and therefore the above compound does not take अप् ॥ Why do we say not before प्रिय &c. Observe कल्याणीप्रियः ॥

1 प्रिया, 2 मनोज्ञा, 3 कल्याणी, 4 सुभगा, 5 दुर्भगा, 6 भक्ति, 7 सचिवा, 8 स्वा (स्वसा), 9 कान्ता, 10 क्षान्ता, 11 समा, 12 चपला, 13 दुहिता, 14 वामना (वामा) 15 तनया, 16 अम्बा ॥ The compound दृढभक्तिः is anomalous.

तसिलादिष्वाकृत्वसुचः ॥ ३५ ॥ पदानि ॥ तसिलादिषु, आकृत्वसुचः ॥

वृत्तिः ॥ पञ्चम्यास्तसिलित्यतः प्रभृति संख्यायाः क्रियाभ्यावृत्तिगणने कृत्वसुजिति प्रागेतस्माद् ये प्रत्ययास्तेषु भाषितपुंस्कादनूङ्स्त्रियाः पुंवद्भवति ॥

वार्त्तिकम् ॥ शसि बह्वल्पार्थस्य पुंवद्भावो वक्तव्यः ॥ वा० ॥ त्वतलोर्गुणवचनस्य पुंवद्भावो वक्तव्यः ॥ वा० ॥ भस्याढे तद्धिते पुंवद्भावो वक्तव्यः ॥ वा० ॥ ठक्छसोश्च पुंवद्भावो वक्तव्यः ॥

35. A feminine word not ending in the affix ऊङ्, and having an equivalent and uniform masculine, is changed to such masculine form, before the affixes beginning with तसिल् &c (V. 3. 7) and ending with कृत्वसुच् (V. 4. 17)

Thus तस्याः शालायाः = ततः, तस्यां = तत्र, यस्यां = यत्र, यस्या = यतः ॥ The following are the affixes before which the feminine is changed to masculine: त्र and तस्, तरप् and तमप्, चरट्, जातीयर्, कल्पप्, देश्य, देशीयर् रूपप्, पाशप्, थम, थाल्, श and र्हिल तिल् तातिल् ॥ All other affixes do not affect the gender. Thus तरप् तमप् &c दर्शनीयतरा, दर्शनीयतमा, पटुचरी, पटुजातीया, दर्शनीयकल्पा, दर्शनीयदेशीया, दर्शनीयरूपा, दर्शनीयपाशा ॥ कया प्रकृत्या = कथम्, यया प्रकृत्या = यथा, तस्यां वेलाया = तदा, तर्हि &c.

Vârt:—The feminine of बहु and अल्प is changed to masculine before the Taddhita affix शस्:—as बह्वीभ्यो देहि = बहुशो देहि; अल्पाभ्यो देहि = अल्पशो देहि ॥

Vârt:—A feminine Adjective is changed into masculine before the affixes त्व and तल् ॥ As पट्व्या भावः = पटुत्वम् or पटुता ॥ Why do we say 'an adjective'? Observe कठ्या भावः = कण्ठीत्वं or कठीता ॥

Vârt: The feminine word is changed to masculine before all Taddhita affixes, except ढ, when the word gets the designation of भ ॥ Thus हस्तिनीनां समूहः = हास्तिकम् ॥ Had the word not become masculine, then हस्तिनी having lost its ई (VI. 4. 148), the word न् of हस्तिन् would not be elided be fore the Taddhta affix, because the lopa-elision being sthânivat, would have prevented the application of the rule VI. 4. 144, ordaining the elision of the final syllable. So the form would have been something like हास्तिनिकम् instead of हास्तिकम् ॥ Why do we say 'with the exception of ढ'? Observe श्यैनेयः, रौहिणेयः the masculine being श्येत and रोहित ॥ The word आग्नेयः (= अग्नायी देवता अस्य स्थालीपाकस्य) is an exception to this rule.

Vârt:—The masculine-change takes place before the affixes ठक् and छस् ॥ As भवत्या छात्रा = भावत्काः, भवदीयाः ॥

क्यङ्मानिनोश्च ॥ ३६ ॥ पदानि ॥ क्यङ्, मानिनोः, च, ॥

वृत्तिः ॥ क्यङि परतो मानिनि च स्त्रिया भाषितपुंस्कादनूङ् पुंवद्भवति ॥

36. A feminine word not ending in ऊङ् and having an equivalent and uniform masculine, is changed into masculine before the Denominative क्यङ्, and the affix मानिन् ॥

Thus from एनी—एतायते, श्येनी—श्येतायते ॥ मानिन् :—दर्शनीयमानी अयमस्याः "He esteems her as handsome". दर्शनीयमानिनीयमस्याः (इयम् अस्याः "She esteems her as handsome'. The word मानिन् is employed for the sake of non-feminine and non-appositional words. Thus non-feminine words:—दर्शनीयां मन्यते देवदत्तो यज्ञदत्तां =

दर्शनीयमानी अयमस्याः ॥ For non-appositional words :—as, दर्शनीयां मन्यते देवदत्तां यज्ञदत्ता = दर्शनीयमानिनी इयमस्याः ॥

न कोपधायाः ॥ ३७ ॥ पदानि ॥ न, क, उपधायाः, ॥

वृत्तिः ॥ कोपधायाः स्त्रियाः पुंवद्भावो न भवति ॥

वार्त्तिकम् ॥ कोपधप्रतिषेधे वु तद्धितग्रहणं कर्त्तव्यम् ॥

37. A Feminine word having a penultimate क्, does not assume the Masculine form.

Thus पाचिकाभार्यः, कारिकाभार्यः, वृजिकाभार्यः, मद्रिकाभार्यः, मद्रिकाकल्पा, मद्रिकायते ॥ वृजिकायते, मद्रिकामानिनी, वृजिकामानिनी, वैलेपिकं (वैलेपिकाया धर्म्यं). This rule is an exception to all the previous rules VI. 3. 34—36 : and not only to VI. 3. 34.

Vârt :—The rule applies to the क of the affix वु and the Taddhita क and not to every क ॥ Therefore the masculine transformation takes place here पाकभार्यः, भेकभार्यः ॥ The word पाका means "young"; and भेकी means 'action'.

संज्ञापूरण्योश्च ॥ ३८ ॥ पदानि ॥ संज्ञा, पूरण्योः, च, ॥

वृत्तिः ॥ संज्ञायाः पूरण्याश्च स्त्रियाः पुंवद्भावो न भवति ॥

38. The feminine is not changed to masculine, when it is a Name or an Ordinal Numeral.

Thus दत्ताभार्यः । गुप्ताभार्यः । दत्तापाशा । गुप्तापाशा । दत्तायते । गुप्तायते । दत्तामानिनी । गुप्तामानिनी । पूरण्याः । पञ्चमीभार्यः । दशमीभार्यः । पञ्चमीपाशा । दशमीपाशा । पञ्चमीयते । दशमीयते । पञ्चमीमानिनी । दशमीमानिनी ॥

वृद्धिनिमित्तस्य च तद्धितस्यारक्तविकारे ॥ ३९ ॥ पदानि ॥ वृद्धिनिमित्तस्य, च, तद्धितस्य, अरक्तविकारे, ॥

वृत्तिः ॥ वृद्धिनिमित्तस्तद्धितः स यदि रक्तेर्थे विकारे च न विहितः, तदन्तस्य स्त्रीशब्दस्य न पुंवद्भवति ॥

39. The feminine is not changed into Masculine, when it is formed by such a Taddhita affix, which causes the Vṛiddhi of the first syllable, with the exception however of the Taddhitas meaning 'colored therewith', and 'made there of'.

Thus स्रौघ्नीभार्यः, माथुरीभार्यः, स्रौघ्नीपाशा, माथुरीपाशा, स्रौघ्नीयते, माथुरीयते, स्रौघ्नीमानिनी and माथुरीमानिनी ॥

Why do we say 'which causes Vriddhi'? Observe मध्यमभार्यः (मध्ये भवा = मध्यमा formed by the affix म IV. 3. 8 which does not canse Vṛiddhi). Why do we say 'of a Taddhita'? Observe काण्डलावभार्यः (काण्डं लुनाति = काण्डलावी with अण् (कर्मण्यण्) and ङीप्). Why do we say when not meaning 'colored there with' or 'made thereof'? Observe. कषायेण रक्ता = काषायी, काषायी बृहतिका यस्य = काषायबृहतिकः, लोहस्य विकारो लौही लौही ईषा यस्य रथस्य = लौहेषः (IV. 3. 134). The word वृद्धिनिमित्तस्य should be explained as a Bahuvrihi, and not a Tatpurusha, i. e. a taddhita affix, in which there is an element like ञ or ण् or क् &c which causes

Vriddhi. Therefore this exception does not apply to तावद्भार्यः यावद्भार्यः (तावती भार्या यस्य &c). Here the affix वतुप् V. 2. 39 added to तद् does not cause Vriddhi by its own force, but by VI. 3. 91.

स्वाङ्गाच्चेतो ऽमानिनि ॥ ४० ॥ पदानि ॥ स्वाङ्गात्, च, इतः, अमानिनि, ॥

वृत्तिः ॥ स्वाङ्गादुत्तरो य ईकारस्तदन्तायाः स्त्रिया न पुंवद्भवति अमानिनि परतः ॥

40. A feminine in ई ending in the name of a part of body, does not become masculine, except when the word मानिन् follows.

Thus दीर्घकेशीभार्यः, शुक्लकेशीभार्यः, दीर्घकेशीपाशा, श्लक्ष्णकेशीपाशा, दीर्घकेशीयते, श्लक्ष्णकेशीयते, but पटुभार्यः (पटु not denoting any bodily member), अकेशभार्यः (अकेशा भार्या, not ending in long ई), and दीर्घकेशमानिनी ॥ The exception अमानिनि has been added from the Vârtika and is no part of the original sûtra.

जातेश्च ॥ ४१ ॥ पदानि ॥ जातेः, च, (न) (अमानिनि) ॥

वृत्तिः ॥ जातेश्च स्त्रिया न पुंवद्भवति अमानिनि परतः ॥

41. A feminine noun expressing a class or kind does not become masculine.

Thus कठीभार्यः, बह्वृचीभार्यः कठीपाशा, बह्वृचीपाशा, कठीयते, बह्वृचीयते ॥ But not so when मानिन् follows, as कठमानिनी, बह्वृचमानिनी ॥

The exception does not apply to हस्तिनीनां समूहः = हास्तिकम् ॥

पुंवत्कर्मधारयजातीयदेशीयेषु ॥ ४२ ॥ पदानि ॥ पुम्वत्, कर्मधारय, जातीय, देशीयेषु, ॥

वृत्तिः ॥ कर्मधारये समासे जातीय देशीय इत्येतयोश्च प्रत्यययोर्भाषितपुंस्कादनूङ् स्त्रियाः पुंवद्भवति ॥

वार्त्तिकम् ॥ कुक्कुट्यादीनामण्डादिषु पुंवद्भावो वक्तव्यः ॥

42. The feminine (unless it ends in ऊ), having an equivalent and uniform masculine, becomes masculine in a Karmadhâraya, and before जातीय and देशीय ॥

This sûtra is enunciated as a prohibition to the preceding sûtras. Thus it applies even to words having a penultimate क (VI. 3. 37). Thus पाचकवृन्दारिका, पाचकजातीया, पाचकदेशीया ॥ It applies even to Names and the feminines which are ordinals in opposition to VI. 3. 38. Thus दत्तवृन्दारिका, दत्तजातीया, दत्तदेशीया, पंचमवृन्दारिका, पंचमजातीया, पंचमदेशीया ॥ It applies even in opposition to VI. 3. 39 : स्रौघ्नवृन्दारिका, स्रौघ्नजातीया, स्रौघ्नदेशीया ॥ So also in opposition to VI. 3. 40, as श्लक्ष्णमुखवृन्दारिका, श्लक्ष्णमुखजातीया and श्लक्ष्णमुखदेशीया ॥ So also in opposition to VI. 3. 41, as कठवृन्दारिका, कठजातीया, कठदेशीया ॥

The feminine must have a corresponding masculine (भाषितपुंस्क), So the rule does not apply खट्वावृन्दारिका, as खट्वा has no corresponding masculine. The feminine should not end in ऊ ; as ब्रह्मबन्धूवृन्दारिका ॥

Vârt :—The words कुक्कुटी &c become masculine before अण्ड &c : as, कुक्कुट्या अण्डं = कुक्कुटाण्डम् ॥ मृग्याः पदं = मृगपदम्, मृग्याः क्षीरं = मृगक्षीरम्, काक्याः शावः = काक-

शावः ॥ This rule need not be made, as the first member in these compounds may be considered as class denoting words of common gender.

Vârt :—When a word formed by an affix having an indicatory ख, or the affixes तर and तम &c (VI. 3. 43) follow, the final long vowel of the first term becomes short instead of its becoming masculine. As कालीमात्मानं मन्यते काल्येवाहम्=कालिमन्या (compare VI. 3. 66) हरिणिमन्या, पट्वितरा, पट्वितमा, पट्विरूपा, पट्विकल्पा, पट्विका, मृद्विका ॥ We have said that the rule does not apply to the feminines in ऊ ॥ The words इडविद्, दरद्, पृथ and उशिज are names of countries denoting Kshatriya clans. The tadrâja affix (VI. 1. 168 and 170), is elided in forming the feminine of these (IV. 1. 177). Thus we have the compouud of इडविद् वृन्दारिका ॥ When the first words become masculine, we have ऐडाविड, दारद, &c. Thus ऐडविडवृन्दारिका, औशिजवृन्दारिका ॥

घरूपकल्पचेलडब्रुवगोत्रमतहतेषु ङ्योऽनेकाचो ह्रस्वः ॥ ४३ ॥ पदानि ॥ घ, रूप, कल्प, चेलड, ब्रुव, गोत्र, मत, हतेषु, ङ्यः, अनेकाचः, ह्रस्वः, ॥

वृत्तिः ॥ घ रूप कल्प चेलट् ब्रुव गोत्र मत हत इत्येतेषु परतो भाषितपुंस्कात्परो यो ङीप्रत्ययस्तदन्तस्यानेकाचो ह्रस्वो भवति ॥

43. Before the affixes तर, तम, रूप, कल्प, before चेल (with the feminine in ई), ब्रुव, गोत्र, मत and हत, a word ending in the feminine affix ङी becomes short, when the feminine consists of two or more syllables, and has an equivalent and uniform masculine.

Thus घ—ब्राह्मणितरा, ब्राह्मणितमा ब्राह्मणिरूपा, ब्राह्मणिकल्पा, ब्राह्मणिचेली, ब्राह्मणिब्रुवा ब्राह्मणिगोत्रा, ब्राह्मणिमता and ब्राह्मणिहता ॥ घ, रूप and कल्प are affixes, चेलट् &c are words as second members; ब्रुवः is formed by अच् (III. 1. 134) added to ब्रू, guṇa and वच substitution being prevented anomalously. Why do we say ending in ई (ङी)? Observe दत्तातरा, गुप्ततरा ॥ Why do we say consisting of more than one syllable? Because words of one syllable *optionally* become shortened by the next rule. Why do we say having a corresponding masculine? Observe आमलकीतरा कुवलीतरा, where आमलकी and कुवली have no equivalent masculine forms.

नद्याः शेषस्यान्यतरस्याम् ॥ ४४ ॥ पदानि ॥ नद्याः, शेषस्य, अन्यतरस्याम्, ॥

वृत्तिः ॥ नद्याः शेषस्य घादिषु परतो ह्रस्वो भवति अन्यतरस्याम् । कश्च शेषः । अङी च या नदी ङ्यन्तं च यदेकाच् ॥

वार्त्तिकम् ॥ कृन्नद्याः प्रतिषेधो वक्तव्यः ॥

44. In all the remaining feminine words called Nadî (I. 4. 3 and 4), the substitution of short vowel under the preceding circumstances is optional.

What are the शेष or the remnants? Those feminines which are not formed by long ई (ङी), and are called Nadi; and those feminines which end-in long ई but consist of one syllable. Thus ब्रह्मबन्धूतरा or ब्रह्मबन्धुतरा वीरबन्धूतरा or वीरबन्धुतरा, स्त्रितरा or स्त्रीतरा, स्त्रितमा or स्त्रीतमा ॥

Vârt: – Nadî words formed by कृत् affixes are excepted: as लक्ष्मीतरा, तन्त्रीतरा formed by the Uṇâdi affix ई (Uṇ III. 158, 160)

उगितश्च ॥ ४५ ॥ पदानि ॥ उगितः, च, (ह्रस्वः) (अन्यतरस्यां) ॥

वृत्तिः ॥ उगितश्च परस्या नद्या घादिषु अन्यतरस्यां ह्रस्वो भवति ॥

45. The feminine ई (ङी) added to a word formed by a Taddhita-affix having an indicatory उ or ऋ, is optionally shortened before the घ &c (VI. 3. 43).

Thus श्रेयसितरा or श्रेयसीतरा, or श्रेयस्तरा, विदुषितरा or विदुषीतरा or विद्वत्तरा ॥ The first is formed by the Taddhita affix ईयसुन्, and the second by क्वसु ॥ In one alternative, there is masculisation also when we get the forms श्रेयस्तरा &c. Or this latter form may be considered to have been evolved from श्रेयस्, to which is added the affixes denoting comparison, and then the feminine affix, in denoting a feminine.

आन्महतः समानाधिकरणजातीययोः ॥ ४६ ॥ पदानि ॥ आत्, महतः, समानाधिकरण, जातीययोः, ॥

वृत्तिः ॥ समानाधिकरणउत्तरपदे जातीये च प्रत्यये परतो महत आकारादेशो भवति ॥

वार्त्तिकम् ॥ महदात्वे घासकरविशिष्टेषूपसंख्यानं पुंवद्वचनं चासमानाधिकरणार्थम् ॥

वा० ॥ अष्टनः कपाले हविष्युपसंख्यानम् ॥ वा० ॥ गवि च युक्ते ऽष्टन उपसंख्यानं कर्त्तव्यम् ॥

46. For the final of महत्, is substituted आत् (आ) before a word which is in apposition with it and before जातीय ॥

As महादेवः, महाब्राह्मणः, महाबाहुः, महाबलः, महाजातीयः ॥ But महतः पुत्रः = महत्पुत्रः "the son of the great man": the two words are not in apposition. The compounding with महत् takes place under II. 1. 61. This rule applies to compounds under that rule, as well as to Bahuvrihis, when also the two words are in apposition, as in महाबाहुः ॥ In fact this is the object of using the word samânâdhikarana in this sûtra. Had it not been used, then by the maxim of pratipadokta, the rule would have applied only to the Tatpurasha compounds of mahat taught under II. 1. 61 but not to Bahuvrihis. In महद्भूतश्चन्द्रमा = अमहान् महान् संपन्नः, the long आ is not substituted, as the sense of महत् is here secondary.

Vart:—आ is substituted for the final of महत् before घास, कर and विशिष्ट, the feminine महती being changed to masculine, though the words may not be in apposition. As महत्या घासः = महाघासः, महत्याः करः = महाकरः, महत्याविशिष्टः = महाविशिष्टः ॥

Vârt:—आ is substituted for the final of अष्टन् before कपाल, when a sacrificial offering is meant. As अष्टाकपालं चरुं निर्वपेत ॥ Why do we say when meaning a sacrificial offering? Observe अष्टकपालं ब्राह्मणस्य ॥

Vârt:—आ is substituted for the final of अष्टन् before गो, when the meaning is that of 'yoked'. As, अष्टागवेन शकटेन ॥ But अष्टगवं ब्राह्मणस्य, where 'yoking' is not meant. The त् in आत् is for the sake of distinctness.

द्व्यष्टनः संख्यायामबहुव्रीह्यशीत्योः ॥ ४७ ॥ पदानि ॥ द्व्यष्टनः, संख्यायाम्, अबहुव्रीहि, अशीत्योः, ॥

वृत्तिः ॥ द्वि अष्टन् इत्येतयोराकारादेशो भवति संख्यायामुत्तरपदे अबहुव्रीह्यशीत्योः ॥

वार्त्तिकम् ॥ प्राक् शतादिति वक्तव्यम् ॥

47. आ is substituted for the final of द्वि and अष्टन् when another Numeral follows, but not in a Bahuvrîhi or before अशीति ॥

Thus द्वादश, द्वाविंशतिः, द्वात्रिंशत्, अष्टादश, अष्टाविंशतिः, अष्टात्रिंशत् ॥ Why do we say द्वि and अष्टन्? Observe पञ्चदश ॥ Why do we say 'when followed by a Numeral'? Observe द्वैमातुरः, आष्टमातुरः ॥ Why do we say 'not when the compound is a Bahuvrîhi, or the word अशीति follows'? Observe द्वित्राः, त्रिदशाः, द्व्यशीतिः ॥

Vârt:—This rule applies upto one hundred. Therefore not here, द्विशतम्, द्विसहस्रम्, अष्टशतम्, अष्टसहस्रम् ॥

त्रेस्त्रयः ॥ ४८ ॥ पदानि ॥ त्रेः, त्रयस्, ॥

वृत्तिः ॥ त्रि इत्येतस्य त्रयमित्ययमादेशो भवति संख्यायामबहुव्रीह्यशीत्योः ॥

48. For त्रि is substituted त्रयस् when another Numeral follows, but not in a Bahuvrîhi or before अशीतिः ॥

As, त्रयोदश, त्रयोविंशतिः, त्रयस्त्रिंशत् ॥ But not in त्रैमातुरः (the second word not being a Numeral), nor in त्रिदशाः which is a Bahuvrihi, (II. 2. 25) त्र्यशीति ॥ This substitution takes place upto hundred : not here, त्रिशतम्, त्रिसहस्रम् ॥

विभाषा चत्वारिंशत्प्रभृतौ सर्वेषाम् ॥ ४९ ॥ पदानि ॥ विभाषा, चत्वारिंशत्, प्रभृतौ, सर्वेषाम्, ॥

वृत्तिः ॥ चत्वारिंशत्प्रभृतौ संख्यायामुत्तरपदे ऽबहुव्रीह्यशीत्योः सर्वेषां द्व्यष्टन् त्रि इत्येतेषां यदुक्तं तद्विभाषा भवति ॥

49. The above substitution in the case of all (द्वि, त्रि and अष्टन्), is optional, when the word चत्वारिंशत् and the numerals which follow it are the second member.

Thus द्विचत्वारिंशत् or द्वाचत्वारिंशत्, त्रिपञ्चाशत् or त्रयःपञ्चाशत्, अष्टपञ्चाशत् or अष्टापञ्चाशत् ॥ This also before hundred : as, द्विशतम् and अष्टशतम्, त्रिशतम् ॥

हृदयस्य हृल्लेखयदण्लासेषु ॥ ५० ॥ पदानि ॥ हृदयस्य, हृत्, लेख, यत्, अण्, लासे षु, ॥

वृत्तिः ॥ हृदयस्य हृदित्ययमादेशो भवति लेख यत् अण् लास इत्येतेषु परतः ॥

50. हृद् is substituted for हृदय, before लेख, and the affixes यत् and अण् and before लास ॥

Thus हृदयं लिखाति = हृल्लेखः, हृदयस्य प्रियं = हृद्यम्, हृदयस्येदम् = हार्दम्, हृदयस्य लासो = हृल्लासः ॥ The word लेख is derived by अण् affix from लिख् ॥ Before the word लेख formed by घञ् affix, this substitution does not take place, as हृदयलेखः ॥ The inclusion of लेख in this sûtra proves the existence of this maxim "उत्तरपदाधिकारे प्रत्ययग्रहणे न तदन्तग्रहणम्" ॥ See VI. 3. 17.

वा शोकष्यञ्रोगेषु ॥ ५१ ॥ पदानि ॥ वा, शोक, ष्यञ्, रोगेषु ॥

वृत्तिः ॥ शोक ष्यञ् रोग इत्येतेषु परतो हृदयस्य वा हृदित्ययमादेशो भवति ॥

51. हृद् is optionally the substitute for हृदय, when the words शोक, and रोग or the affix ष्यङ् follows.

Thus हृच्छोकः or हृदयशोकः, सौहार्द्यम् or सौहृदय्यम् ॥ Here ष्यङ् is added as हृदय belongs to Brâhmaṇâdi class V. 1. 124. When हृद् is substituted there is Vṛiddhi of both the members सु and हृ by VII. 3. 19. So also हृद्रोगः or हृदयरोगः ॥ All these forms could have been got from हृत् which is a *full* word *sui generis*, having the same meaning as हृदयः ॥ The substitution taught in this sûtra is rather unnecessary.

पादस्य पदाज्यातिगोपहतेषु ॥ ५२ ॥ पदानि ॥ पादस्य, पत्, आजि, आति, ग, उपहतेषु, ॥

वृत्तिः ॥ पादस्य पद इत्ययमादेशो भवति आजि आति ग उपहत इत्येतेषूत्तरपदेषु ॥

52. पद् is substituted for पाद, before आजि, आति, ग and उपहत ॥

Thus पदाजिः = पादाभ्यामजति ; पदातिः = पादाभ्यामतति ॥ आजिः and आतिः are formed by इण् from अज् and अत् (Uṇ IV. 131), and irregularly अज् is not changed to वी though required by II. 4. 56 ; before this affix. So also पदगः = पादाभ्यां गच्छति ; पदोपहतः = पादेनोपहतः ॥ पाद belongs to Vṛishâdi class (VI. 1. 203) and has therefore acute on the first syllable, the पद् substitute however has acute on the final, only in the उपदेश (VI. 1. 171), therefore in पदोपहतः, पद् retains its accent (VI. 2. 48), and it becomes acute on the final. While पदाजिः, पदातिः and पदगः have acute on the final (VI. 1. 223 and kṛit-accent).

पद्यत्यतदर्थे ॥ ५३ ॥ पदानि ॥ पद, यति, अतदर्थे, ॥

वृत्तिः ॥ यत्प्रत्यये परतः पादस्य पदित्ययमादेशो भवत्यतदर्थे ॥

वार्त्तिकम् ॥ पद्भावे इके चरतावुपसंख्यानम् ॥

53. पद् is substituted for पाद before the affix यत् used in any sense other then that of "suited there to.;

Thus पादौविध्यन्ति = पद्याः शर्कराः, पद्याः कण्टकाः ॥ When यत् has the force of "suited there to" we have पाद्यम् = पादार्थमुदकं ॥ (see IV. 4. 83 and V. 4. 25).

Vart:—Before the affix इक्, in the sense of 'he walks there by', पद् is substituted for पाद; as पादाभ्यां चरति = पदिकः (IV. 4. 10) by ष्ठन् affix. The word पाद in this sûtra means 'the actual foot', a part of animal organism. Therefore पद् is not substituted before the यत् of V. I. 34, as द्विपाद्यम्, त्रिपाद्यम् because पाद here denotes ,a measure'.

हिमकाषिहतिषु च ॥ ५४ ॥ पदानि ॥ हिम, काषि, हतिषु, च, (पद्) ॥

वृत्तिः ॥ हिम काषिन् हति इत्येतेषु पादशब्दस्य पदित्ययमादेशो भवति ॥

54. पद् is substituted for पाद before हिम, काषिन् and हति ॥

Thus पद्धिमम्, (= पादस्य शीतं) पत्काषिन् (= पादचारिणः) as in अथ पत्काषिणा यान्ति, and पद्धतिः (पद्भ्यां हन्यते) ॥

ऋचः शे ॥ ५५ ॥ पदानि ॥ ऋचः, शे ॥

वृत्तिः ॥ ऋक्संबन्धिमः पादशब्दस्य शे परतः पदित्ययमादेशो भवति ॥

55. पद् is the substitute for पाद before the affix शस्, when the meaning is that of a Hymn (Rik).

Thus पच्छो गायत्रीं शंसति = पादं पादं शंसति, the affix शस् being added by V. 4. 43. Why do we say 'when meaning a Hymn'? Observe पादशः कार्षापणं ददाति ॥

वा घोषमिश्रशब्देषु ॥ ५६ ॥ पदानि ॥ वा, घोष, मिश्र, शब्देषु, (पद्) ॥

वृत्तिः ॥ घोष मिश्र शब्द इत्येतेषु चोत्तरपदेषु पादस्य वा पदित्ययमादेशो भवति ॥

वार्त्तिकम् ॥ निष्के चेति वक्तव्यम् ॥

56. This substitution of पद् for पाद is optional before घोष, मिश्र and शब्द ॥

Thus पद्घोषः or पादघोषः, पन्मिश्रः or पादमिश्रः, पच्छब्दः or पादशब्दः ॥

Vârt:—So also before निष्कः as पन्निष्कः or पादनिष्कः ॥

उदकस्योदः संज्ञायाम् ॥ ५७ ॥ पदानि ॥ उदकस्य, उदः, संज्ञायाम् (उत्तरपदे) ॥

वृत्तिः ॥ उदकशब्दस्य संज्ञायां विषये उद इत्ययमादेशो भवति उत्तरपदे परतः ॥

वार्त्तिकम् ॥ संज्ञायामुत्तरपदस्य उदकशब्दस्य उदादेशो भवतीति वक्तव्यम् ॥

57. उद is substituted for उदक, when the compound is a Name.

Thus उदमेघः 'a person called Udamegha', उदवाहः "a person named Uda vâhah." The well-known Patronymics from these are औदमेघिः and औदवाहिः ॥ Why do we say 'when it is a Name'? Observe उदकगिरिः ॥

Vârt—उद is the substitute for उदक when it stands as the second member of a compound and denotes a Name: as, लोहितोदः, नीलोदः, क्षीरोदः ॥

पेषंवासवाहनधिषु च ॥ ५८ ॥ पदानि ॥ पेषम्, वास, वाहन, धिषु, च, ॥

वृत्तिः ॥ पेषं वास वाहन धि इत्येतेषु चोत्तरपदेषु उदकस्य उद इत्ययमादेशो भवति ॥

58. उद is substituted for उदक before पेषं, वास, वाहन, and धि ॥

Thus उदपेषं पिनष्टि formed by णमुल् by III. 4. 38; उदवासः = उदकस्यवासः, so also उदवाहनः ॥ उदकं धीयतेऽस्मिन् = उदधिः 'a water jar'.

एकहलादौ पूरयितव्ये ऽन्यतरस्याम् ॥५९॥ पदानि ॥ एक, हलादौ, पूरयितव्ये, अन्यतरस्याम्, ॥

वृत्तिः ॥ हल् आदिर्यस्योत्तरपदस्य तदेकहलादिस्तस्मिन्नेकहलादौ पूरयितव्यवाचिन्यन्यतरस्यामुदकस्य उद इत्ययमादेशो भवति ॥

59. उद is optionally substituted for उदक, before a word biginning with a single consonant, and which expresses that which is filled with water.

Thus उदकुम्भः, or उदककुम्भः, उदपात्रम् or उदकपात्रम् ॥ The word एकहलादि means 'a word beginning with a single simple consonant'. The rule does not apply to उदकस्थालम् as the second member begins with a conjunct consonant: nor to उदकपर्वतः, as the पर्वतः is not a vessel which is to be filled.

मन्थौदनसक्तुबिन्दुवज्रभारहारवीवधगाहेषु च ॥ ६० ॥ पदानि ॥ मन्थ, ओदन, सक्तु, बिन्दु, वज्र, भार, हार, वीवध, गाहेषु, च, ॥

वृत्तिः ॥ मन्थ ओदन सक्तु विन्दु वज्र भार हार वीवध गाह इत्येतेषूत्तरपदेषूदकस्य उद इत्ययमादेशो भवति अन्यतरस्याम् ॥

60. उद is optionally substituted for उदक, before मन्थ, ओदन, सक्तु, विन्दु, वज्र, भार, हार, वीवध, and गाह ॥

Thus उदकेन मन्थः = उदमन्थ or उदकमन्थः । उदकेनौदन, उदौदनः or उदकौदनः । सक्तु । उदकेन सक्तुः, उदसक्तु or उदकसक्तुः । बिन्दु । उदकस्य बिन्दुः, उदबिन्दुः or उदकबिन्दुः । वज्र । उदकस्य वज्रः, उदवज्रः or उदकवज्रः । भार । उदकं बिभर्तीति उदभारः or उदकभारः । हार । उदकं हरतीति, उदहारः or उदकहारः । वीवध । उदकस्य वीवध, उदवीवधः or उदकवीवधः । गाह । उदकं गाहत इति, उदगाहः or उदकगाहः ॥

इको ह्रस्वोऽङ्यो गालवस्य ॥ ६१ ॥ पदानि ॥ इकः, ह्रस्वः, अङ्यः, गालवस्य, अन्यतरस्याम् ॥

वृत्तिः ॥ इगन्तस्याङ्यन्तस्योत्तरपदे ह्रस्वो भवति गालवस्याचार्यस्य मतेनान्यतरस्याम् ॥

वार्त्तिकम् ॥ भ्रूकुंसादीनामकारो भवतीति वक्तव्यम् ॥

61. According to the opinion of Gâlava, a short vowel is substituted, in a compound, before the second member, for the long इक् vowels (ई, ऊ, ॠ), unless it is the long vowel of the Feminine affix ई (ङी).

In other words, for ई, when it is not the Feminine affix ई (ङी) and for ऊ, a short इ and उ are substituted in a compound before the second member. Thus ग्रामणिपुत्रः or ग्रामणीपुत्रः, ब्रह्मबन्धुपुत्रः or ब्रह्मबन्धूपुत्रः ॥ Why do we say इक् vowels? Observe खट्वापादः, मालापादः ॥ Why do we say 'not the long ई of the Feminine affix ङी'? Observe गार्गीपुत्रः, वात्सीपुत्रः ॥ The name of Gâlava is mentioned pujârtha for the anuvritti of 'optionally' was present in this sûtra. It is a limited option pujârtha, (vyavasthita vibhâsha), and does not apply to कारीषगन्धीपति &c which are governed by VI. 3. 139.

Vârt:—It does not apply to Avyayibhâva compounds, nor to those words which take इयङ् or उवङ् augment in their declension, as श्रीकुलम्, भ्रूकुलम्, काण्डीभूतम्, कुडचीभूतं, वृषलीभूतम् ॥

Vart :—It does however apply to भ्रुकुंस &c, as भ्रुकुंसः, भ्रुकुटिः ॥ Others say भ्र is substituted for भ्र &c as भ्रकुंसः and भ्रकुटिः

एक तद्धिते च ॥ ६२ ॥ पदानि ॥ एक तद्धिते, च, (ह्रस्वः) (उत्तरपदे) ॥

वृत्तिः ॥ एकशब्दस्य तद्धिते उत्तरपदे ह्रस्वो भवति ॥

62. The short is substituted for the long of एका, before a Taddhita affix, and when a second member follows.

As एकस्या आगतं = एकरूप्यम्, एकमयम्, एकस्या भावः = एकत्वम्, एकता ॥ So also एकस्याः क्षीरं = एकक्षीरम्, एकदुग्धम् ॥ The shortening takes place of the Feminine word एका, having the affix आ ॥ When एक is an adjective (गुणवचन) then the above forms could be evolved by the help of the rules of masculation, such as VI. 3. 35, i. e. when एक means the numeral one. But when it means 'aione', then those rules will not apply. The word एक is exhibited in the sûtra without any case-affix as a Chhandas irregularity. The examples given are of एका in the feminine which alone can be shortened, and not of एक whose final is already short. Nor can the rule of shortening be applied to ए of एक, for the rule applies to the *final* letter, aud not to a vowel situeated in the body of a word.

ङ्यापोः संज्ञाछन्दसोर्बहुलम् ॥६३॥ पदानि ॥ ङ्यापोः, संज्ञा, छन्दसोः, बहुलम्, ॥

वृत्तिः ॥ ङ्यन्तस्याबन्तस्य च संज्ञाछन्दसोर्बहुलं ह्रस्वो भवति ॥

63. The short is diversely substituted for the feminine affixes ई and आ (ङी and आप्) in a Name and in the Vedas.

As रेवतिपुत्रः, रोहिणिपुत्रः, भरणिपुत्रः ॥ Sometimes not, as नान्दीकरः, नान्दीघोषः, नान्दीविशालः ॥ So also in the Vedas, as कुमारिदारा, प्रदर्विदा; sometimes the shortening does not take place, as फाल्गुनीपौर्णमासी, जगतीछन्दः ॥ आप् ending words in Name: शिलवहम्, शिलप्रस्थम्; sometimes there is no shortening, as, लोमकागृहम्, लोमकाखण्डम् ॥ So also in the Vedas:—अजक्षीरेण जुहोति, ऊर्णम्रदा पृथिवीं विश्वधायसम् ॥ Sometimes there is no shortening, as, ऊर्णासूत्रेण कवयो वयन्ति ॥

त्वे च ॥ ६४ ॥ पदानि ॥ त्वे, च, (ह्रस्वः) ॥

वृत्तिः ॥ त्वप्रत्यये परतो ङ्यापोर्बहुलं ह्रस्वो भवति ॥

64. The feminine affixes ई and आ diversely become short, before the affix त्व ॥

Thus अजाया भावः = अजत्वं or अजात्वं, रोहिणित्वं or रोहिणीत्वम् ॥ These are Vedic illustrations, no Names can be formed in त्व ॥

इष्टकेषीकामालानां चिततूलभारिषु ॥ ६५ ॥ पदानि ॥ इष्ट का, इषी का, मालानाम्, चित, तूल, भारिषु, ॥

वृत्तिः ॥ इष्टकेषीकामालानां चित तूल भारिन् इत्येतेषूत्तरपदेषु यथासंख्य ह्रस्वो भवति ॥

65. For the long vowel, a short is substituted, in इष्टका before चित, in इषीका before तूल, and in माला before भारिन् ॥

Thus इष्टकचितम्, इषीकतूलम् and मालभारिणी कन्या ॥ The rule of tadanta applies to इष्टका &c, so that the compounds ending in इष्टका &c are also governed by this rule : as पक्वेष्टकचितम्, मुञ्जेषीकतूलम्, उत्पलमालभारिणी कन्या ॥

खित्यनव्ययस्य ॥ ६६ ॥ पदानि ॥ खिति, अनव्ययस्य, (ह्रस्वः) ॥

वृत्तिः ॥ खिदन्तउत्तरपदे ऽनव्ययस्य ह्रस्वो भवति ॥

66. A short is always substituted for the final of the first member, when the second member is a word formed by an affix having an indicatory ख, but not when the first member is an Indeclinable.

Thus कालिमन्या, हरिणिमन्या ॥ The augment मुम् does not prevent the shortening, had it done so, the rule would have been unnecessary. But दोषामन्यमहः, दिवामन्यारात्रिः, where दोषा and दिवा are Indeclinables there is no shortening. The above words are formed by खश् (III. 2. 83). The phrase anavyayasya indicates by implication that the word खित् here means खिदन्तः, contrary to the maxim enunciated in VI. 3. 17 उत्तरपदाधिकारे प्रत्ययग्रहणे तदन्तविधिर्नेष्यते ॥ For an Avyaya can never take a खित् affix which are ordained only after dhâtus.

अरुर्द्विषदजन्तस्य मुम् ॥ ६७ ॥ पदानि ॥ अरुस्, द्विषत्, अजन्तस्य, मुम्, ॥

वृत्तिः ॥ अरुस् द्विषत् इत्येतयोरजन्तानां च खिदन्तउत्तरपदे मुमागमो भवति अनव्ययस्य ॥

67. मुम् is the augment added immediately after the final vowel, of अरुस्, द्विषत्, and of a stem ending in a vowel, unless it is an Indeclinable, when a word formed by a खित् affix follows.

Thus अरुन्तुदः, द्विषन्तपः, कालिमन्या &c. See III. 2. 35, 39, 83. The स् of अरुस and the त् of द्विषत् are dropped by VIII. 2. 23.

Why do we say 'of अरुस् &c'? Observe विद्वन्मन्या ॥ Why do we say 'not an Indeclinable'? Observe दोषामन्यमहः, दिवामन्यारात्रिः ॥ Why do we use the word अन्त in अजन्त, when merely saying अचः would have sufficed by the rule of tadanta-vidhi? This indicates that the shortening taught in the preceding sûtra does not debar the मुम् augment, nor does मुम debar the shortening. So that मुम् is added after the shortening has taken place.

इच एकाचोऽम्प्रत्ययवच्च ॥ ६८ ॥ पदानि ॥ इचः, एकाचः, अम्, प्रत्ययवत्, च, ॥

वृत्तिः ॥ इजन्तस्य एकाच खिदन्तउत्तरपदे ऽमागमो भवति अम्प्रत्ययवच्चास्मिन्द्वितीयैकवचनवच्च स भवति ॥

68. A monosyllabic word, ending in any vowel other than अ, when followed by a word formed by a खित् affix, receives the augment अम, which is added in the same way as the affix अम् of the Accusative singular.

The word अम् is to be repeated here thus, इच एकाचोऽम्, अमप्रत्ययवच्च ॥ Thus गांमन्यः, स्त्रींमन्यः, or स्त्रियंमन्यः, श्रियंमन्यः, भ्रुवंमन्यः ॥ By force of the atideśa अमप्रत्ययवत्, the changes produced by the Accusative ending are caused by this augment also : viz : the substitution of long आ, the substitution of a vowel homogenous with the first, the guṇa, the substitutes इयङ् and उवङ् As आ—गांमन्यः (VI. 1. 93); पूर्वसवर्ण as स्त्रींमन्यः (VI. 1. 107); guṇa, as,—नरंमन्यः (VII. 3. 110) and इयङ् and उवङ्, as श्रियंमन्यः, भ्रुवंमन्यः (VI. 4. 81 &c). Why do we say ending in a vowel other than अ (इच्)? Observe स्वंमन्यः ॥ Why do we say 'a monosyllable'? Observe लेखाभ्रुं मन्याः ॥

The affix अम is elided after a Neuter noun (VII. 1. 23), therefore, will this अम् also be elided when श्री is treated as Neuter? As श्रियमात्मानं मन्यते ब्राह्मणकुलं = श्रियंमन्यम् or श्रिमन्यम्? The second is the valid form according to Patanjali.

वाचंयमपुरंदरौ च ॥ ६९ ॥ पदानि ॥ वाचंयम, पुरन्दरौ, च, ॥

वृत्तिः ॥ वाचंयम पुरंदर इत्येतौ निपात्येते ॥

69. **वाचंयम** and **पुरन्दर** are irregularly formed.

Thus वाचंयमः आस्ते (III. 2. 40 खच् affix). पुरं दारयति = पुरन्दरः (III. 2. 42). The shortening of याम and दार takes place by VI. 4. 94.

कारे सत्यागदस्य ॥ ७० ॥ पदानि ॥ कारे, सत्य, अगदस्य, ॥

वृत्तिः ॥ कारशब्दउत्तरपदे सत्य अगद इत्येतयोर्मुमागमो भवति ॥

वार्त्तिकम् ॥ अस्तुसत्यागदस्य कारइति वक्तव्यम् ॥ वा० ॥ भक्षस्य छन्दसि कारे मुम वक्तव्यः ॥

वा० ॥ धेनोर्भव्यायां मुम्वक्तव्यः ॥ वा० ॥ लोकस्य पृणे मुम्वक्तव्यः ॥

वा० ॥ इत्ये ऽनभ्याशस्य मुम्वक्तव्यः ॥ वा० ॥ भ्राष्ट्राग्न्योरिन्धे मुम्वक्तव्य ॥

वा० ॥ गिलि ऽगिलस्य मुम्वक्तव्यः ॥ वा० ॥ गिलगिले चेति वक्तव्यम् ॥

वा० ॥ उष्णभद्रयोः करणे मुम्वक्तव्यः ॥ सुतोग्रराजभोजमेर्वित्ये तेभ्य उत्तरस्य दुहितृशब्दस्य पुत्त्रडादेशो वा वक्तव्यः ॥

70. **मुम्** is the augment of **सत्य** and **अगद** when the word **कार** follows.

As सत्यंकारः = सत्यंकरोति or सत्यस्यकारः ॥ So also अगदंकारः ॥

Vârt:—So also of अस्तु, as अस्तुंकारः ॥

Vârt:—So also in Vedas, of भक्ष before कारः—e. g. भक्षंकार, in secular language भक्षकारः ॥

Vârt:—Of धेनु before भव्या, e. g. धेनुंभव्या ॥

Vârt:—Of लोक before पृण, e. g. लोकंपृणा ॥

Vârt:—Of अनभ्याश before इत्य as अनभ्याशमित्यः ॥

Vârt:—Of भ्राष्ट्र and अग्नि, before इन्धः, as भ्राष्ट्रमिन्धः, अग्निमिन्धः ॥

Vârt:—A word before गिल takes मुम् augment, unless it is also गिल e. g. तिमिङ्गिलः, but गिलगिलः ॥

Vârt:—So also before गिलगिल, e. g. तिमिङ्गिलगिलः ॥

Vârt:—Of उष्ण and भद्र before करण, e. g. उष्णं करणं, भद्रंकरणं ॥

Vârt:—पुत्रङ् is optionally the substitute of दुहितृ when the words सूत, उग्र, राज, भोज, and मेरु precede it e. g. सूतपुत्री or सूतदुहिता, उग्रपुत्री or उग्रदुहिता, राजपुत्री or राजदुहिता, भोजपुत्री or भोजदुहिता, मेरुपुत्री or मेरुदुहिता ॥ Some read पुत्र in the Śârangaravâdi class (IV. 1. 73), and then this word has its feminine पुत्री ॥ This is seen in other places also, e. g. शैलपुत्री ॥

श्येनतिलस्य पाते ञे ॥ ७१ ॥ पदानि ॥ श्येन, तिलस्य, पाते, ञे, ॥

वृत्तिः ॥ श्येन तिलइत्येतयोः पातशब्दउत्तरपदे ञप्रत्यये ममागमो भवति ॥

71. मुम् is the augment of the words श्येन and तिल, before पात, when the affix ञ is added.

Thus श्येनपातोऽस्यां क्रीडायां = श्यैनंपाता, तैलंपाता ॥ See IV. 2. 58. Why do we say before ञ ? Observe श्येनपातः ॥

रात्रेः कृति विभाषा ॥ ७२ ॥ पदानि ॥ रात्रेः, कृति, विभाषा, (मुम्) ॥

वृत्तिः ॥ रात्रेः कृदन्तउत्तरपदे विभाषा मुमागमो भवति ॥

72. The word रात्रि optionally takes मुम् before a word formed by kṛt-affix.

As रात्रिचरः or रात्रिंचरः, रात्रिमटः or रात्र्यटः ॥ This is an aprâpta-vibhâshâ. The augment is compulsory before a krit-affix having an indicatory ख, As, रात्रिंमन्यः ॥

नलोपो नञः ॥ ७३ ॥ पदानि ॥ न, लोपः, नञः, (उत्तरपदे) ॥

वृत्तिः ॥ नञो नकारस्य लोपो भवत्युत्तरपदे ॥

वार्त्तिकम् ॥ नञो नलोपो ऽवक्षेपे तिङ्युपसंख्यानम् ॥

The न of the Negative particle नञ्, is elided when it is the first member of a compound.

Thus अब्राह्मणः, अवृषलः, असुरापः, असोमपः ॥

Vârt:—The न of नञ् is elided before a verb also, when reproach is meant: as, अपचसि त्वं जाल्मः, अकरोषि त्वं जाल्मः ॥

तस्मान्नुडचि ॥ ७४ ॥ पदानि ॥ तस्मात्, नुट्, अचि, (उत्तरपदे) ॥

वृत्तिः ॥ तस्माल्लुप्तनकारान्नञः नुडागमो भवति अजादावुत्तरपदे ॥

74. After the above न-elided नञ् (i. e. after अ) is added the augment नुट्, to a word beginning with a vowel.

Thus अनजः, अनश्वः, अनुष्ट्रः ॥ Why do we use तस्मात् "after such a नञ्"? Otherwise नुट् would have been the augment of नञ्, and not of the subsequent word for: the sûtra would have read thus नुडाचि ॥ Adding नुट् to नञ् or rather to अ, we have अन् (granting that नुट् is not to be added *before* अ but *after* it, against I. 1. 46). Now अन्+अजः will be अन्नजः and not अनजः for VIII. 3. 32 will cause the doubling of the final न of अन् ॥ Hence to prevent this contingency, नुट् is ordained with regard to the second member and not with regard to अ or नञ् ॥

नभ्राण्नपान्नवेदानासत्यानमुचिनकुलनखनपुंसकनक्षत्रनक्रनाकेषु प्रकृत्या ॥ ७५ ॥ पदानि ॥ नभ्राट्, नपात्, नवेदा, नासत्या, नमुचि, नकुल, नख, नपुंसक, नक्षत्र, नक्र, नाकेषु, प्रकृत्या, ॥

वृत्तिः ॥ नभ्राट् नपात् नवेदाः नासत्या नमुचि नकुल नख नपुंसक नक्षत्र नख नक्र नाक इत्येतेषु नञ् प्रकृत्या भवति ॥

75. The Negative particle remains unchanged in **नभ्राज्, नपात्, नवेदस्, नासत्या** (dual), **नमुचि, नकुल, नख, नपुंसक, नक्षत्र, नक्र** and **नाक** ॥

Upto नासत्या the words are exhibited in the Nominative case in the sûtra, the rest are exhibited in the Locative ! नभ्राजते=नभ्राट्, formed by क्विप् and नञ् composition. न पाति=नपात् formed by शतृ affix. न वेत्ति=नवेदा, formed by असुन् ॥ सत्सु साधवः=सत्याः, न सत्याः=असत्याः, न असत्याः=नासत्याः ॥ न मुञ्चति=न मुचि, formed by कि affix (Uṇadi), नास्य कुलमस्ति=नकुलः ॥ नास्य खमस्ति=नखम् ॥ न स्त्री न पुमान्=नपुंसकम् ॥ न क्षरते क्षीयते वा=नक्षत्रम् ॥ न क्रामति=नक्र by ड affix. न अस्मिन् अकम्=नाकम् ॥

एकादिश्चैकस्य चादुक् ॥ ७६ ॥ पदानि ॥ एकादिः, च, एकस्य, च, अदुक्, ॥

वृत्तिः ॥ एकादिश्च नञ्प्रकृत्या भवति एकशब्दस्यादुगागमो भवति ॥

76. The Negative particle remains unchanged in a word which begins with **एक**, and of this **एक**, there is the augment **अदुक्** (**अद्**).

Thus एकेन न विंशतिः=एकान्नविंशतिः, एकान्नविंशत् ॥ These are Instrumental compounds. The augment आदुक् is added to the final of the first member, so that we have optionally two forms एकात् न विंशतिः and एकान् न विंशति by VIII. 4. 45.

नगो ऽप्राणिष्वन्यतरस्याम् ॥ ७७ ॥ पदानि ॥ नगः, अप्राणिषु, अन्यतरस्याम्, ॥

वृत्तिः ॥ नञ्प्रकृत्या भवति ॥

77. The Negative particle is optionally retained unchanged in **नग**, when it does not mean a living animate being.

Thus नगाः or अगाः 'trees', or 'mountains', literally 'what do not move'. The affix ड is added to गम् ॥ Why do we say when not referring to animate beings. Observe अग: वृषलः शीतेन ॥ No alternative form is allowed here.

सहस्य सः संज्ञायाम् ॥ ७८ ॥ पदानि ॥ सहस्य, सः, संज्ञायाम् ॥

वृत्तिः ॥ सहशब्दस्य स इत्ययमादेशो भवति संज्ञायां विषये ॥

78. स is substituted for सह, in a Name.

Thus साश्वत्थम्, सपलाशम्, साशिंशपम् ॥ Why when it is a Name? Observe सहयुध्वा, सहकृत्वा ॥ The word सँह has acute on the first syllable, because all Particles have acute on the first syllable. The substitute स coming in the room of the acute स and the grave ह, will have an accent mid-way between सँ acute and ह grave, namely, it would have the svarita accent. But, as a matter of fact, it has the acute accent. As सँपुत्रः, सँभार्यः ॥ These are Bahuvrihi. In Avyayîbhâva, the samâsa-accent will prevail (VI. 1. 223), as सेष्टिँ, सपशुबन्धँम् ॥

ग्रन्थान्ताधिके च ॥ ७९ ॥ पदानि ॥ ग्रन्थान्त, अधिके, च, ॥

वृत्तिः ॥ ग्रन्थान्ते ऽधिके च वर्त्तमानस्य सहशब्दस्य स इत्ययमादेशो भवति ॥

79. स is the substitute for सह, when it has the sense of 'upto the end' (in connection with a literary work), or 'more'.

Thus सकलं = कलान्तं ज्योतिषमधीते ॥ So also समुहूर्तम् = (मुहूर्तान्तम्) ॥ स संग्रह (= संग्रहान्तम्) व्याकरणमधीते ॥ These are all Avyayîbhâva compounds by ° अन्तवचने (II. 1. 6). Therefore, when a word, denoting time, is the second member, सह would not be changed to स, because of the prohibition in VI. 3. 81. The present sûtra removes that prohibition by anticipation, with regard to time-denoting words even, when the meaning is that 'of the end of a book'. When the sense is that of 'more', we have सद्रोणाखारी, समाषः कार्षापणः सकाकिणीको माषः ॥

द्वितीये चानुपाख्ये ॥ ८० ॥ पदानि ॥ द्वितीये, च, अनुपाख्ये, (सहस्यसः) ॥

वृत्तिः ॥ द्वितीये ऽनुपाख्ये सहस्य स इत्ययमादेशो भवति ॥

80. स is the substitute for सह, when it is in connection with a word which refers to a second object, which latter however is not directly perceived.

Of the two things which are generally found co-existing, the non-principal is called the 'second' or द्वितीय ॥ That which is perceived, observed or is known is called उपाख्य, that which is not perceived &c is अनुपाख्य, i. e. what is to be inferred. That is, when the second object is to be inferred from the presence of the first, स is added to such second word. Thus साग्निः (कपोतः) 'a pigeon which points out that conflagration has taken place some where'. सपिशाचा वात्या "a storm-wind which announces the Piśâchas". सराक्षसीका शाला ॥ Here the fire, the Piśâcha or the Râkshasas are not directly perceived, but their existence is inferred from the presence of the pigeon &c.

अव्ययीभावे चाकाले ॥ ८१ ॥ पदानि ॥ अव्ययीभावे, च, अकाले, (सहस्यसः) ॥

वृत्तिः ॥ अव्ययीभावे च समासे ऽकालवाचिन्युत्तरपदे सहस्य स इत्ययमादेशो भवति ॥

81. स is the substitute of सह, in an Avyayîbhâva when the second member is not a word denoting time.

Thus सचक्रंधेहि, मधुरं प्राज्ञः, but सहपूर्वाह्णम् the second member being a time denoting word (II. 1. 5).

वोपसर्जनस्य ॥ ८२ ॥ पदानि ॥ वा, उपसर्जनस्य ॥

वृत्तिः ॥ सर्वोपसर्जनो बहुव्रीहिर्गृह्यते । तदवयवस्य सहशब्दस्य वा स इत्ययमादेशो भवति ॥

82. स is optionally the substitute of सह, when the compound is a Bahuvrîhi.

That compound in which all members are secondary—उपसर्जन—is a सर्वोपसर्जन, and the Bahuvrihi is such a compound, because in it all the members are secondary, the Principal being understood. Thus सपुत्रः or सहपुत्रः, सच्छात्रः or सहच्छात्रः ॥ Why do we say of a Bahuvrihi ? Observe सहयुध्वा, सहकृत्वा ॥ The substitution does not however take place in a Bahuvrîhi like सहकृत्वप्रियः or सहयुध्वप्रियः ॥

प्रकृत्याशिष्यगोवत्सहलेषु ॥ ८३ ॥ पदानि ॥ प्रकृत्या, आशिषि, अ, गोवत्सहलेषु, ॥

वृत्तिः ॥ प्रकृत्या सहशब्दो भवति आशिषि विषये ऽगोवत्सहलेषु ॥

83. The word सह retains its original form when the sentence denotes benediction, except when it is गो, वत्स or हल ॥

Thus स्वस्ति देवदत्ताय सहपुत्राय, सहच्छात्राय, सहामात्याय ॥ But optionally here, as स्वस्ति भवते सहगवे or सगवे, सहवत्साय or सवत्साय, सहहलाय, or सहलाय ॥ The phrase अगोवत्सहलेषु is no part of the original sûtra, but has been added by the Kâśikâ from a Vârtika.

समानस्य छन्दस्यमूर्द्धप्रभृत्युदर्केषु ॥ ८४ ॥ पदानि ॥ समानस्य, छन्दसि, अ, मूर्द्ध, प्रभृति, उदर्केषु, ॥

वृत्तिः ॥ समानस्य स इत्ययमादेशो भवति छन्दसि विषये मूर्द्धन् प्रभृति उदर्क इत्येतान्युत्तरपदानि वर्ज्जयित्वा ॥

84. स is the substitute of समान in the Chhandas, but not before मूर्धन्, प्रभृति and उदर्क ॥

Thus अनुभ्राता सगर्भ्यः, अनुसखा सयूथ्यः, योनः सनुत्यः (See IV. 4. 114). समानो गर्भः = सगर्भः, तत्र भवः = सगर्भ्यः formed by यत् affix IV. 4. 114. But समानमूर्द्धा, समानप्रभृतयः, समानोदर्काः ॥ This substitution takes place in secular literature also, as सपक्षः, साधर्म्यम्, सजातीयः &c.

ज्योतिर्जनपदरात्रिनाभिनामगोत्ररूपस्थानवर्णवयोवचनबन्धुषु ॥ ८५ ॥ पदानि ॥ ज्योतिः, जनपद, रात्रि, नाभि, नाम, गोत्ररूप, स्थान, वर्ण, वयोवचन, बन्धुषु, (समानस्यसः)

वृत्तिः ॥ ज्योतिस् जनपद रात्रि नाभि नामन् गोत्र रूप स्थान वर्ण वयस् वचन बन्धु इत्येतेषूत्तरपदेषु समानस्य स इत्ययमादेशो भवति ॥

85. This substitution of स for समान् takes place before ज्योतिस्, जनपद, रात्रि, नाभि, नामन्, गोत्र, रूप, स्थान वर्ण, वयस्, वचन and बन्धु in the common language also.

Thus सज्योतिः, सजनपदः, सरात्रिः, सनाभिः, सनामा, सगोत्रः, सरूपः, सस्थानः, सवर्णः, सवयाः, सवचनः, सबन्धुः ॥

चरणे ब्रह्मचारिणि ॥ ८६ ॥ पदानि ॥ चरणे, ब्रह्मचारिणि, (समानस्यसः)(उत्तरपदे)

वृत्तिः ॥ चरणे गम्यमाने ब्रह्मचारिण्युत्तरपदे समानस्य स इत्ययमादेशो भवति ॥

86. स is substituted for समान before ब्रह्मचारिन् when it denotes persons engaged in fulfilling a common vow of studying the Vedas.

Thus समानो ब्रह्मचारी = सब्रह्मचारी ॥ ब्रह्म means the Vedas. The vow of studying the Veda, is also called ब्रह्म ॥ He who is engaged in the performance of that vow is called ब्रह्मचारिन् ॥ समान refers to the vow, the vow of studying being common to both : i. e. समाने ब्रह्मणि व्रतचारी = सब्रह्मचारी ॥ According to Bhattoji Dikshit चरणे in the sûtra means a शाखा or a department of Vedic study. He who has a common (samâna) branch (charaṇa) is a sabrahmchârî.

तीर्थे ये ॥ ८७ ॥ पदानि ॥ तीर्थे, ये, (समानस्यसः) ॥

वृत्तिः ॥ तीर्थशब्दउत्तरपदे यत्प्रत्ययपरे परतः समानस्य स इत्ययमादेशो भवति ॥

87. स is substituted for समान, before तीर्थ when the affix यत् is added to it.

Thus सतीर्थ्यः = समाने तीर्थे वासी (IV. 4. 107). 'a fellow-student ?

विभाषोदरे ॥ ८८ ॥ पदानि ॥ विभाषा, उदरे, (समानस्यसः) (उत्तरपदे) ॥

वृत्तिः ॥ उदरशब्दउत्तरपदे यत्प्रत्ययान्ते समानस्य विभाषा स इत्ययमादेशो भवति ॥

88. The substitution of स for समान is optional before उदर when the affix यत् is added to it.

Thus सोदर्यः or समानोदर्यः (IV. 4. 108).

दृग्दृशवतुषु ॥ ८९ ॥ पदानि ॥ दृक्, दृश, वतुषु, (समानस्यसः) ॥

वृत्तिः ॥ दृक् दृश वतु इत्येतेषु परतः समानस्य स इत्ययमादेशो भवति ॥

वार्त्तिकम् ॥ दृक्षे चेति वक्तव्यम् ॥ वा० ॥ दृशेः क्सप्रत्ययोपि तत्रैव वक्तव्यः ॥

89. स is substituted for समान, before दृक्, दृश and the affix वत् ॥

Thus सदृक्, सदृशः ॥ The affixes कञ् and क्विन् are added to दृश् under III. 2. 60. *Vârt* :—which give as the forms दृक् and दृश ॥ *Vârt* :—So also before दृक्ष : as सदृक्षः ॥ दृक्ष is formed by क्स affix under III. 2. 60. Vârtika. The affix वतु is taken for the sake of the subsequent sûtra.

इदंकिमोरीश्की ॥ ९० ॥ पदानि ॥ इदम्, किमोः, ईश्, की, (दृग्दृशवतुषु) ॥

वृत्तिः ॥ इदं किम् इत्येतयोरीश् की इत्येतौ यथासंख्यमादेशौ भवतो दृग्दृशवतुषु ॥

वार्त्तिकम् ॥ दृक्षे चेति वक्तव्यम् ॥

90. ई is substituted for इदम् and की for किम् before the words दृक्, दृश and the affix वत् ॥

Thus ईदृक्, ईदृशः and इयान्, कीदृक्, कीदृशः and कियान् ॥ ईवत् and कीवत् are changed to ई+इयत् and की+इयत् by V. 2. 40 and the long ई is elided by VI. 4. 148: and we get इयत् and कियत् ॥

Vârt:—So also before दृक्ष, as ईदृक्षः and कीदृक्षः ॥

आ सर्वनाम्नः ॥ ९१ ॥ पदानि ॥ आ, सर्वनाम्नः, (दृग्दृशवतुषु) ॥
वृत्तिः ॥ सर्वनाम्न आकारादेशो भवति दृग्दृशवतुषु ॥
वार्त्तिकम् ॥ दृक्षे चेति वक्तव्यम् ॥

91. आ is substituted for the final of the Pronouns (I. 1: 27) before these words दृक्, दृश and the affix वत् ॥

Thus तादृक्, तादृशः. तावान्, यादृक्, यादृशः, यावान् ॥

Vârt:—So also before दृक्ष, as तादृक्षः and यादृक्षः ॥

विष्वग्देवयोश्च टेरद्र्यञ्चतौ (ता) वप्रत्यये ॥ ९२ ॥ पदानि ॥ विष्वक्, देवयोः, च, टेः, अद्रि, अञ्चतौ, वप्रत्यये ॥
वृत्तिः ॥ विष्वक् देव इत्येतयोः सर्वनाम्नश्च टेरद्रीत्ययमादेशो भवति अञ्चतौ वप्रत्ययान्त उत्तरपदे ॥
वार्त्तिकम् ॥ छन्दसि स्त्रियां बहुलमिति वक्तव्यम् ॥

92. In the room of the last vowel with the consonant that follows it, of a Pronoun, and of the words विष्वक and देव, is substituted अद्रि, when अञ्च with the affix व follows.

Thus विष्वगञ्चति = विष्वद्र्यङ्, This form is thus evolved. अञ्च + क्विन् = अञ्च् + O = अञ्च् + नुम् (VII. 1. 70) Then there is elision of the final conjunct consonaut ञ्च्, then the final dental is changed to guttural because of the क्विन् affix (VIII. 2. 62), e. i. न् is changed to ङ् and we have अङ् which with विष्वद्रि gives the above form. देवद्र्यङ्, तद्र्यङ्, यद्र्यङ् ॥ आद्रि and सध्रि (VI. 3. 95) have acute on the final irregularly (nipâtan) in order to prevent the krit-accent. and when इ is changed into य the following vowel becomes svarita (VIII. 2. 4). Why do we say of विष्वग् and देव? Observe अश्वाची = अश्वमञ्चति, the feminine ङीप् being added by IV. 1. 6 *Vârt.* The अ of अच् is elided by VI. 4. 138. and the final of अश्व is lengthened by VI. 3. 138. Why 'when अञ्च follows'? Observe विष्वग्युक् ॥ Why do we say 'when the affix व् follows'? Observe विष्वगञ्चनं ॥ The व is totally elided by VI. 1. 67. Another reading of the sûtra is अप्रत्यये (अञ्चतावप्रत्यये). It would give the same result, the meaning then being when no affix follows. The word वप्रत्यये or अप्रत्यये indicates by implication that in other places where simply a verb is mentioned, it means a word-form beginning with that verb which ends with some affix. For had अप्रत्यये not been used, then the rule would have applied not only when añch followed, but when añchana ending in ल्युट् also followed. The maxim धातुग्रहणे तदादि विधिरिष्यते is illustrated in अयस्कृतं and

अयस्कारः; for VIII. 3. 46 teaches that visarga is changed into स् when कृ follows. There the कृ denotes not only the root कृ but a word derived from कृ, therefore which begins with कृ, such as कारः and कृतः ॥ Therefore the rule applies to forms like अयस्कृत् which is followed merely by the verb कृ; as well as to forms like अयस्कृतः ॥

Vârt:—In the Vedas, diversely before the feminine nouns: thus in "विश्वाची च. घृताची च" there is no substitution in विश्वाची, but in कद्रीची there is this substitution. कद्रीची is derived from किम्+अञ्च्=कद्रि+अञ्च् ॥ Then is added ङीप् and then like अश्वाची ॥

समः समि ॥ ९३ ॥ पदानि ॥ समः, समि, ॥

वृत्तिः ॥ समित्येतस्य समि इत्ययमादेशो भवति अञ्चतौ व (अ) प्रत्ययान्त उत्तरपदे ॥

93. समि is substituted for सम्, before this अञ्च when no affix (or व affix) follows.

Thus सम्यक्, सम्यञ्चौ, सम्यञ्चः ॥

तिरसस्तिर्यलोपे ॥ ९४ ॥ पदानि ॥ तिरसः, तिरि, अलोपे, ॥

वृत्तिः ॥ तिरस् इत्येतस्य तिरि इत्ययमादेशो भवत्यञ्चतौ व (अ) प्रत्ययान्तउत्तरपदे ऽलोपे । यदा ऽस्य लोपो न भवति ॥

94. तिरि is substituted for तिरस् before this अञ्च् when no affix (or व affix) follows, provided that the अ of अञ्च् is not elided.

Thus तिर्यङ्, तिर्यञ्चौ, तिर्यञ्चः ॥ Why do we say 'when there is no elision'? Observe तिरश्चा, तिरश्चे ॥ Here अ is elided by VI. 4. 138. The word अलोपे in the sûtra is ambiguous. It may mean elither (1) " where अ is elided" or (2) "Where there is no elision" The latter meaning should be taken however.

सहस्य सध्रिः ९५ ॥ पदानि ॥ सहस्य, सध्रिः, ॥

वृत्तिः ॥ सहेत्यस्य सध्रिरित्ययमादेशो भवत्यञ्चतौ व (अ) प्रत्ययान्तउत्तरपदे ।

95. सध्रि is the substitute of सह, before अञ्च् followed by no affix (or व affix).

Thus सध्र्यङ्, सध्र्यञ्चौ, सध्र्यञ्चः; and सध्रीचः, सध्रीचा ॥ See VI. 3. 138 for long vowel.

सध मादस्थयोश्छन्दसि ॥ ९६ ॥ पदानि ॥ सध, माद, स्थयोः, छन्दसि, ॥

वृत्तिः ॥ छन्दसि विषये माद स्थ इत्येतयोरुत्तरपदयोः सहस्य सध इत्ययमादेशो भवति ॥

96. सध is substituted for सह in the Veda, when माद and स्थ follow.

Thus सधमादो द्युम्न्य एकास्ताः, सधस्थाः ॥ Another example is आत्वा वहन्तो हरयो युजाना, अर्वागिन्द्र सधमादो वहन्तु (Rig III. 3. 7) सहमादन्ति देवा अस्मिन् ॥

द्व्यन्तरुपसर्गेभ्यो ऽप ईत् ॥ ९७ ॥ पदानि ॥ द्वि, अन्तर्, उपसर्गेभ्यः, अपः, ईत्, ॥

वृत्तिः ॥ द्वि अन्तरित्येताभ्यामुपसर्गाच्चोत्तरस्याबित्येतस्य ईकारादेशो भवति ॥

वार्त्तिकम् ॥ समापईत्वे प्रतिषेधो वक्तव्यः ॥ वा० ॥ ईत्वमनवर्णादिति वक्तव्यम् ॥

97. After द्वि, अन्तर् and Prepositions, long ई is the substitute of अप् ॥

By I. 1. 54, ई replaces the *first-letter* of अप् viz अ only. Thus द्वीपः, अन्तरीपः, नीपम्, वीपम्, समीपम् ॥ The samâsanta अ is added by V. 4. 74.

Vârt :—Prohibition should be stated with regard to समाप ॥ समापं नाम देवयजनम् ॥ Others say after a Preposition in अ, the long ई substitution does not take place. Thus प्रापम्, परापम् ॥ The word upasarga strictly speaking denotes adverbs, and cannot be applied to nouns like अप्; here however, this word is used in a loose sense in the sûtra. It means प्र &c.

ऊदनोर्देशे ॥ ९८ ॥ पदानि ॥ उत्, अनोः, देशे, ॥

वृत्तिः ॥ अनोरुत्तरस्याप ऊकारादेशो भवति देशाभिधाने ॥

98. After अनु, ऊ is substituted for (the अ of) अप्, when the sense is that of a locality.

Thus अनूपो देशः, but अन्वीपम् when locality is not meant. The long ऊ is taught for the sake of showing how the word is to be analysed; as अनु ऊपः = अनूपः ॥ The form अनूपः could have been evolved with a short उ also, as अनु + उपः = अनूपः ॥ But this analysis is not intended.

अषष्ठ्यतृतीयास्थस्यान्यस्य दुगाशीराशास्थास्थितोत्सुकोतिकारकरागच्छेषु ॥९९॥ पदानि ॥ अषष्ठी, अतृतीयास्थस्य, अन्यस्य, दुक्, आशीः, आशा, आस्था, आस्थित, उत्सुक, ऊति, कारक, राग, च्छेषु, ॥

वृत्तिः ॥ अषष्ठीस्थस्य अतृतीयास्थस्य चान्यशब्दस्य दुगागमो भवति आशिस् आशा आस्था आस्थित उत्सुक ऊति कारक राग छ इत्येतेषु परतः ॥

Kârikâ—दुगागमोऽविशेषेण वक्तव्यः कारकच्छयोः ।
षष्ठीतृतीययोर्नेष्ट आशीरादिषु सप्तसु ॥

99. अन्य, when not used in the Genitive or the Instrumental, gets the augment दुक् (द्), before आशिस्, आशा, आस्था, आस्थित, उत्सुक, ऊति, कारक and राग, as well as before the affix छ (ईय).

Thus अन्या आशीः = अन्यदाशीः अन्या आशा = अन्यदाशा, अन्या आस्था = अन्यदास्था, अन्य आस्थितः = अन्यदास्थितः, अन्य उत्सुकः = अन्यदुत्सुकः, अन्या ऊतिः = अन्यदूतिः, अन्यः कारकः अन्यत्कारकः, अन्यो रागः = अन्यद्रागः ॥ So also with छ as अन्यस्मिन् भवः = अन्यदीयः ॥ It takes छ because it belongs to गहादि class (IV. 2. 138.)

The word अन्य belongs to गहादि class (IV. 2. 138). Why do we say when not in Genitive or the Instrumental ?. Observe अन्यस्य आशीः = अन्याशीः, अन्येन आस्थितः = अन्यास्थितः &c. With regard to the word कारक and the affix छ, the दुक् augment is universal, though अन्य may be even in the Genitive case &c : as अन्यस्य कारकः = अन्यत् कारकम्, अन्यस्येदम् = अन्यदीयम् ॥ The unusual occurrence of two negatives in the sûtra (अषष्ठी and अतृतीया), implies this.

अर्थे विभाषा ॥ १०० ॥ पदानि ॥ अर्थे, विभाषा, (उत्तरपदे) ॥
वृत्तिः ॥ अर्थशब्द उत्तरपदे अन्यस्य विभाषा दुगागमो भवति ॥

100. दुक् is optionally the augment of अन्य when अर्थ follows.

As अन्यदर्थः or अन्यार्थः ॥

कोः कत्तत्पुरुषेऽचि ॥ १०१ ॥ पदानि ॥ कोः, कत् तत्पुरुषे, अचि, ॥
वृत्तिः ॥ कु इत्येतस्य कदित्ययमादेशो भवति तत्पुरुषे समासे ऽजादावुत्तरपदे ॥
वार्त्तिकम् ॥ कत्त्रावि चापुपसंख्यानम् ॥

101. कत् is substituted for कु in a Tatpurusha, when a word beginning with a vowel follows as the second member.

As कदजः, कदश्वः, कदुष्ट्रः, कदन्नम् ॥ Why do we say in a Tatpurusha? Observe कुष्ट्रो राजा ॥ Why do we say "when the second member begins with a vowel"? Observe कुब्राह्मणः, कुपुरुषः ॥

Vârt:—कत् is substituted before त्रय, as कत्त्रयः = कुत्सितास्त्रयः ॥

रथवदयोश्च ॥ १०२ ॥ पदानि ॥ रथ, वदयोः, च, ॥
वृत्तिः ॥ रथ वद इत्येतयोश्चोत्तरपदयोः कोः कदित्ययमादेशो भवति ॥

102. कद् is substituted for कु before रथ and वद also.

Thus कद्रथः, कद्वदः ॥

तृणे च जातौ ॥ १०३ ॥ पदानि ॥ तृणे, च, जातौ, ॥
वृत्तिः ॥ तृणशब्द उत्तरपदे जातावभिधेयायां कोः कदादेशो भवति ॥

103. कत् is substituted for कु, when तृण follows denoting a species.

As कत्तृणा नाम जातिः ॥ But कुत्सितानि तृणानि = कुतृणानि ॥

का पथ्यक्षयोः ॥ १०४ ॥ पदानि ॥ का, पथि, अक्षयोः, ॥
वृत्तिः ॥ पथिन् अक्ष इत्येतयोरुत्तरपदयोः कोः का इत्ययमादेशो भवति ॥

104. का is the substitute of कु, before पथिन् and अक्ष ॥

Thus कापथः and काक्षः ॥

ईषदर्थे ॥ १०५ ॥ पदानि ॥ ईषत्-अर्थे ॥
वृत्तिः ॥ ईषदर्थे वर्त्तमानस्य कोः का इत्ययमादेशो भवति ॥

105. का is the substitution for कु, when the meaning is 'a small'.

As कामधुरम्, कालवणम्, काम्लम ॥ Though the second member may begin with a vowel, yet this substitution takes place, in spite of VI. 3. 101 : as कोष्णम् ॥

विभाषा पुरुषे ॥ १०६ ॥ पदानि ॥ विभाषा, पुरुषे, ॥
वृत्तिः ॥ पुरुषशब्द उत्तरपदे विभाषा कोः का इत्ययमादेशो भवति ॥

106. का is optionally substituted for कु, when the word पुरुष follows.

Thus कापुरुषः or कुपुरुषः ॥ This is an aprâpta-vibhâshâ. In the sense of 'a little ईषद्', the substitution is compulsory; as ईषत् पुरुषः = का पुरुषः ॥

कवञ्चोष्णे ॥ १०७ ॥ पदानि ॥ कवम्, च, उष्णे, ॥

वृत्तिः ॥ उष्णशब्द उत्तरपदे कोः कवङित्ययमादेशो भवति का च विभाषा ॥

107. का and कवङ् are optionally the substitutes of कु when उष्ण follows.

As कवोष्णम्, कोष्णम् or कदुष्णम् ॥

पथि चच्छन्दसि ॥ १०८ ॥ पदानि ॥ पथि, च, छन्दसि, ॥

वृत्तिः ॥ पथिशब्द उत्तरपदे छन्दसि विषये कोः कव का इत्येतावादेशौ भवतो विभाषा ॥

108. This substitution of का, and कव for कु takes place in the Veda, before पथ ॥

Thus कवपथः, कापथः and कुपथः ॥

पृषोदरादीनि यथोपदिष्टम् ॥ १०९ ॥ पदानि ॥ पृषोदरादीनि, यथोपदिष्टम्, ॥

वृत्तिः ॥ पृषोदरादीनि शब्दरूपाणि येषु लोपागमवर्णविकाराः शास्त्रेण न विहिता दृश्यन्ते च तानि यथोपदिष्टानि साधूनि भवन्ति ॥

वार्त्तिकम् ॥ दिक्शब्देभ्य उत्तरस्य तीरस्य तार भावो वा भवति ॥

वा० ॥ वाचो वादे डत्वं च लभावश्चोत्तरपदस्येञि प्रत्यये ॥

वा० ॥ षषउत्वं दतृदशधासूत्तरपदादेष्टुत्वं च ॥

वा० ॥ दुरोदाशनाशदभध्येषूत्वं वक्तव्यमुत्तरपदादेश्च ष्टुत्वम् ॥

वा० ॥ स्वरो रोहतौ छन्दस्युत्वं वक्तव्यम् ॥ वा० ॥ पीवोपवसनादीनां च लोपो वक्तव्यः ॥

Kârikâ—वर्णागमो वर्णविपर्ययश्च द्वौ चापरौ वर्णविकारनाशौ ।
धातोस्तदर्थातिशयेन योगस्तदुच्यते पञ्चविधं निरुक्तम् ॥

109. The elision, augment and mutation of letters to be seen in पृषादर &c, though not found taught in treatises of Grammar, are valid, to that extent and in the mode, as taught by the usage of the sages.

The word यथोपदिष्टम् = शिष्टैरुच्चारितानि ॥ Thus पृषदुदरो यस्य = पृषोदरम्, पृषद् उद्वानं यस्य = पृषोद्वानम् ॥ Here there is elision of द् ॥ So also वारिवाहकः = बलाहकः, here वारि is replaced by ब, and ल replaces व of वाहक; जीवनस्य मूतः = जीमूतः, here वन has been elided; शवानां शयनं = श्मशानम्; here श्म replaces शव; and शान for शयन ॥ ऊर्ध्वं खमस्य = उलूखलम्; here उल replaces ऊध, and खल replaces खम ॥ पिशिताशः = पिशाचः ॥ ब्रुवन्तोस्यां सीदन्ति = बृसी ॥ Here सद् takes the affix ड्ट् in the locative, and ब्रुव is replaced by ब ॥ मह्यां रौति = मयूरः ॥ Here मही is replaced by मयू, and the final of रु is elided before the affix अच ॥ And so on with अश्वत्थ, कपित्थ &c.

Vârt:—तीर becomes optionally तार after a word denoting direction, as दक्षिणतीरम् or दक्षिणतारम्, उत्तरतीरम्, or उत्तरतारम् ॥

Vârt:—Before the Patronymic इञ् affix, वाग्वाद becomes वाड्वाल as, वाग्वादस्यापत्यं = वाड्वालिः ॥

Vârt:—The final of षष् is changed to उ before दत्, दश, and धा (meaning 'location'): and the first letter of the second member is changed to ड or ढ॥ Thus षड् दन्ता अस्य = षाडन्; so षोडश ; षड्धा or षोढा कुरु॥ The addition of ड is optional here. The putting of धासु in the plural number indicates that धा has here the meaning of "in many parts or ways" (नानाधिकरण). In fact it has the force of an affix here. The rule therefore does not apply to these:—षट् दधाति or धयति = षड्धा॥

Vârt.—The final of दुर् is changed to उ, before दाश, नाश, दभ and ध्यै and the first letters of these are changed to their corresponding cerebrals. Thus दुःखेन दाश्यते, नाश्यते, दभ्यते यः = दूडाशः, दूणाशः, दूडभः, In the last (दम्भ) there is elision of the nasal also. दुष्टं ध्यायति = दूढ्यः॥ Here is added the affix क to the root ध्या (ध्यै) preceded by the upapada दुः, by III. I. 136.

Vârt:—उ is substituted for the final of स्वर् when the verb दह follows in the Vedas: as एहिस्वं जायेस्वो रोहावं (रोहाव is Imperative Ist. Pers. Dual).

Vârt:—The final of पीवस्, पयस् &c. is elided in the Vedas. as पीवोप वसनानां, पयोपवसनानाम्॥

संख्याविसायपूर्वस्याह्नस्याहनन्यतरस्यां ङौ॥ ११०॥ पदानि॥ संख्या, वि, साय, पूर्वस्य, अह्नस्य, अहन्, अन्यतरस्याम्, ङौ॥

वृत्तिः॥ संख्या वि साय इत्येवंपूर्वस्याह्नशब्दस्य स्थाने अहनित्ययमादेशो भवत्यन्यतरस्यां ङौ परतः॥

110. अहन् may optionally be substituted for अह्न, in the Locative singular, when a Numeral, or वि or साय precedes it.

Thus द्वयोरह्नोर्भवः = द्व्यह्नः, त्र्यह्नः॥ The Locative singular of these are द्व्यह्नि or द्व्यहनि, त्र्यह्नि or त्र्यहनि॥ So also द्व्यह्ने, त्र्यह्ने॥ With वि—व्यह्नि, व्यहनि or व्यह्ने; साय—सायाह्नि, सायाहनि, सायाह्ने॥ These are एकदेशिसमासः, and this very sûtra is an indicator that अहन् may be compounded with other words than a Numeral, or वि or साय॥ Thus we have मध्याह्ने = मध्यमह्नः (II. 2. 1). But पूर्वाह्णे and अपराह्णे only.

ढ्रलोपे पूर्वस्य दीर्घोऽणः॥ १११॥ पदानि॥ ढ्रलोपे, पूर्वस्य, दीर्घः, अणः॥

वृत्तिः॥ ढकाररेफयोर्लोपो यस्मिन् स ढ्रलोपः, तत्र पूर्वस्याणो दीर्घो भवति॥

111. When ढ् or र् is elided, for the preceding अ, इ and उ a corresponding Long vowel is substituted.

Thus लीढम्, मीढम्, उपगूढम्॥ रलोपे-निर्-रक्तम् = नीरक्तम्, अग्निर् रथः = अग्नीरथः, इन्दू रथः, पुना रक्तम् वासः, प्राता राजक्रयः॥ For the elision of ढ see VIII. 3. 13, and for the elision of र् see VIII. 3. 14. But आवृढम्, the ऋ is not lengthened because it is not included in the pratyahâra अण् which is formed with the ण् of अ इ उ ण्॥

सहिवहोरोदवर्णस्य॥ ११२॥ पदानि॥ सहि, वहोः, ओत्, अवर्णस्य,॥

वृत्तिः॥ सहि वहि इत्येतयोरवर्णस्योकार आदेशो भवति ढ्रलोपे॥

112. When ढ् or र् are elided, there is the substitution of ओ for the अ or आ of the verbs सह् and वह्॥

Thus सोढा, सोढुम्, सोढव्यम्, वोढा, वोढुम् and वोढव्यम् ॥ Why do we say of अ or आ? Observe ऊढः, ऊढवान् ॥ Why do we say अवर्ण which includes long आ also? The rule will apply even when the short अ of सह and वह is changed to आ by Vṛiddhi: as उद्वोढाम्, उद्वोढम् ॥ Had merely अ been read into the sûtra, instead of अवर्ण then coming after the त् of ओत्, it would have denoted only short अ (तादपि परः = तपरः I. 1. 75).

साढ्यै साढ्वा साढेति निगमे ॥ ११३ ॥ पदानि ॥ साढ्यै, साढ्वा, साढा, इति, निगमे ॥

वृत्तिः ॥ साढ्यै साढ्वा साढा इति निगमे निपात्यन्ते ॥

113. साढ्यै, साढ्वा and साढा are irregularly formed in the Vedas.

Thus साढ्यै समन्तात्, साढ्वा शत्रून् ॥ The latter is formed by क्त्वा affix, the ओ substitution not taking place. In the other alternative क्त्वा is changed to ध्वै ॥ साढा is formed by तृच् affix. In the secular literature सोढा and सोढ्वा are the proper forms.

संहितायाम् ॥ ११४ ॥ पदानि ॥ संहितायाम्, ॥

वृत्तिः ॥ संहितायामित्ययमधिकारः । यदित ऊर्ध्वमनुक्रमिष्यामः संहितायामित्येवं तद्वेदितव्यम् ॥

114. In the following sûtras upto the end of the pâda, are to be supplied the following words :—"In an uninterrupted flow of speech".

Thus sûtra VI. 3. 135 declares "अ at the end of a two-syllabic inflected verb becomes long in the Hymns". Thus विद्माहित्वा सत्पतिं शूर गोनाम् The word संहितायाम् should be read into that sûtra to complete the sense. So that when the above words stand separately, we have विद्म, हि, त्वा, सत्पतिं, शूर, गोनाम् ॥

कर्णे लक्षणस्याविष्टाष्टपञ्चमणिभिन्नच्छिन्नच्छिद्रस्रुवस्वस्तिकस्य ॥ ११५ ॥ पदानि ॥ कर्णे, लक्षणस्य, अ विष्ट, अष्ट, पञ्च, मणि, भिन्न, छिन्न, छिद्र, स्रुव, स्वस्तिकस्य (दीर्घः) ॥

वृत्तिः ॥ कर्णशब्दे उत्तरपदे लक्षणवाचिनो दीर्घो भवति विष्ट अष्टन् पञ्चन् मणि भिन्न छिन्न छिद्र स्रुव स्वस्तिक इत्येतान्वर्जयित्वा ॥

115. Before कर्ण, there is the substitution of a long vowel for the final of the preceding word, when it denotes a proprietorship mark on the ears of cattle, but not when the words are विष्ट, अष्टन्, पञ्चन्, मणि, भिन्न, छिन्न, छिद्र, स्रुव and स्वस्तिक ॥

Thus दात्राकर्णः, द्विगुणाकर्णः, त्रिगुणाकर्णः, द्व्यङ्गुलाकर्णः, अङ्गुलाकर्णः ॥ The word लक्षण here means any peculiar mark showing the proprietorship, put or made on the ears of animals. Why do we say when it denotes such a mark?

Observe सामककर्णः ॥ Why do we say 'with the exception of विष्ट &c'? Observe विष्टकर्णः ॥ भट्टकर्णः, पञ्चकर्णः, भिन्नकर्णः, छिन्नकर्णः, छिद्रकर्णः, स्रुवकर्णः, स्वस्तिककर्णः and मणिकर्णः॥

नहिवृतिवृषिव्यधिरुचिसहितनिषु क्वौ ॥११६॥ पदानि ॥ नहि, वृति, वृषि, व्यधि, रुचि, सहि, तनिषु, क्वौ ॥

वृत्तिः ॥ नहि वृति वृषि व्यधि रुचि सहि तनि इत्येतेषु क्विप्प्रत्ययान्तेषूत्तरपदेषु पूर्वपदस्य दीर्घो भवति संहितायां विषये ॥

116. A long vowel is substituted for the final vowel of the preceding word, before the verbs नह्, वृत्, वृष्, व्यध्, रुच्, सह् and तन्, when these roots take the affix क्वि ॥

Thus उपानह् (उपानत् Nom. S.), so also, परीणत्, नीवृत्, उपावृत्, (with vṛt) प्रावृट्, उपावृट्, (with vṛsh) मर्माविध्, हृदयाविध्, श्वाविध्, (with vyadh) नीरुक्, अभीरुक्, (with ruch) ऋतीषट्, (with sah) तरीतत् (with tan). The nasal is elided after गम् before क्वि (VI. 4. 40), by an extension of that rule, it is elided after तन् also. Why do we say when क्वि follows? Observe परिणहनम् ॥

वनगिर्योः संज्ञायां कोटरकिंशुलकादीनाम् ॥ ११७ ॥ पदानि ॥ वन, गिर्योः, संज्ञायाम्, कोटर, किंशुलकादीनाम्, ॥

वृत्तिः ॥ वन गिरि इत्येतयोरुत्तरपदयोर्यथासंख्यं कोटरादीनां किंशुलकादीनां च दीर्घो भवति संज्ञायां विषये॥

117. For the final vowel of कोटर &c. a long vowel is substituted before वन, and so also of किंशुलक &c. before गिरि, when the compound is a Name.

Thus कोटरावणम्, मिश्रकावणम्, सिध्रकावणम्, सारिकावणम् ॥

So also किंशुलकागिरिः, अञ्जनागिरिः, &c.

The न is changed to ण in वन by VIII. 4. 4. But असिपत्रवनम् and कृष्णगिरि as these words do not belong to the above classes.

1 कोटर, 2 मिश्रक, 3 सिध्रक, 4 पुरग (पुरक), 5 सारिक (सारिका) ॥

1 किंशुलक (किंशुलक), 2 साल्व (साल्वक), 3 नड*, 4 अञ्जन, 5 भञ्जन, 6 लोहित, 7 कुक्कुट ॥

वले ॥ ११८ ॥ पदानि ॥ वले, (पूर्वस्य दीर्घः) ॥

वृत्तिः ॥ वले परतः पूर्वस्य दीर्घो भवति ॥

वार्त्तिकम् ॥ अनुत्साहभ्रातृपितॄणामिति ॥

118. The final of the preceding word is lengthened before the affix वल ॥

Thus आसुतीवलः, कृषीवलः, दन्तावलः ॥ These are formed by the affix वलच् (V. 2. 112).

Vârt:—Not so, of उत्साह, भ्रातृ and पितृ : as उत्साहवलः, भ्रातृवलः and पितृवलः ॥

मतौ बह्वचो ऽनजिरादीनाम् ॥ ११९ ॥ पदानि ॥ मतौ, बह्वचः, अनजिरादीनाम्, (संज्ञायाम्) ॥

वृत्तिः ॥ मतौ परतो बह्वचो ऽजिरादिवर्जितस्य दीर्घो भवति संज्ञायां विषये ॥

119. The final vowel of a word consisting of more than two syllables is lengthened before the affix मत्, when it is a name, but not of the words अजिर &c.

Thus उदुम्बरावती, मशकावती, वीरणावती, पुष्करावती, अमरावती ॥ These are formed by the affix मतुप् (IV. 2. 85) The मत् is changed to वत्, by VIII. 2. 11. Why do we say 'of a word consisting of more than two syllables? Observe व्रीहिमती ॥ Why 'with the exception of अजिर &c'. Observe अजिरवती, खदिरवती, पुलिनवती, हंसकारण्डवती, चक्रवाकवती ॥ When the word is not a name, there is no lengthening, as वलयवती ॥

1 अजिर, 2 खदिर, 3 पुलिन. 4 हंस, 5 कारण्डव (हंसकारण्डव) 6 चक्रवाक.

शरादीनां च ॥ १२० ॥ पदानि ॥ शरादीनाम्, च, (दीर्घः) ॥

वृत्तिः ॥ शरादीनां च मतौ दीर्घो भवति संज्ञायां विषये ॥

120. The final vowel of शर &c. is lengthened before मत् when it is a Name.

As शरावती, वंशावती ॥ The म of मत् is changed to व because it is a Name (VIII. 2. 11). But not so after व्रीहि &c as these belong to यवादि class (VIII. 2. 9).

1 शर, 2 वंश, 3 धूम, 4 अहि, 5 कपि 6 मणि, 7 मुनि, 8 शुचि, 9 हनु.

इको वहे ऽपीलोः ॥ १२१ ॥ पदानि ॥ इकः, वहे, अपीलोः ॥

वृत्तिः ॥ इगन्तस्य पूर्वपदस्य पीलुवर्जितस्य वहउत्तरपदे दीर्घो भवति ॥

वार्त्तिकम् ॥ अपील्वादीनामिति वक्तव्यम् ॥

121. The final इ and the उ of a word, with the exception of पीलु, are lengthened before वह ॥

Thus ऋषीवहम्, कपीवहम्, मुनीवहम् ॥ Why do we say 'ending in इक् vowels'? Observe पिण्डवहम् ॥ Why not of पीलु? Observe पीलुवहम् ॥

Vârt:—It should be stated "with the exception of पीलु and the rest." As दारुवहम् ॥

उपसर्गस्य घञ्यमनुष्ये बहुलम् ॥ १२२ ॥ पदानि ॥ उपसर्गस्य, घञि, अमनुष्ये, बहुलम्, ॥

वृत्तिः ॥ उपसर्गस्य घञन्तउत्तरपदे ऽमनुष्येऽभिधेये बहुलं दीर्घो भवति ॥

122. The final vowel of a Preposition is diversely lengthened, before a word formed by the kṛit-affix घञ्, but not when the compound denotes a human being.

Thus नीक्लेदः, वीमार्गः, अपामार्गः ॥ It does not take place, as प्रसेवः, प्रसारः ॥ It is lengthened before सार and कार, when building is meant, as प्रासारः and प्राकारः, otherwise प्रसारः and प्रकारः ॥ Optionally in वेश &c. as प्रतिवेशः or प्रतीवेशः, प्रतिरोधः or प्रतीरोधः ॥ When human beings are meant, there is no lengthening, as निषादो मनुष्यः ॥

इकः काशे ॥ १२३ ॥ पदानि ॥ इकः, काशे, (दीर्घः) ॥
वृत्तिः ॥ इगन्तस्योपसर्गस्य काशशब्दउत्तरपदे दीर्घो भवति ॥

123. A Preposition ending in इ, or उ lengthens its final before काश ॥

As नीकाशः, वीकाशः, अनूकाशः ॥ काश is formed by अच् (III. 1. 134). Why do we say 'ending in इ or उ'? Observe प्रकाशः where the Preposition does not end in इक् ॥

दस्ति ॥ १२४ ॥ पदानि ॥ दः, ति, (दीर्घः इकः उपसर्गस्य) ॥
वृत्तिः ॥ दा इत्येतस्य यस्तकारादिरादेशस्तस्मिन्परत इगन्तस्योपसर्गस्य दीर्घो भवति ॥

124. A Preposition ending in इ or उ lengthens its final vowel, before the verb दा, when the latter is changed to त ॥

Thus नीत्तम्, वीत्तम्, परीत्तम् ॥ See VII. 4. 47 for the change of दा to त ॥ But प्रत्तम्, अवत्तम्, where the prepositions do not end in इ or उ ॥ Why do we say 'दा is changed to त'? Observe वितीर्णम् नितीर्णम् ॥ Why do we say ति 'a substitute of दा, beginning with a त'? Observe सुदत्तम्, here दद् is the substitute of दा (VII. 4. 46).

अष्टनः संज्ञायाम् ॥ १२५ ॥ पदानि ॥ अष्टनः, संज्ञायाम्, (दीर्घः) ॥
वृत्तिः ॥ अष्टनित्येतस्योत्तरपदे संज्ञायां दीर्घो भवति ॥

125. A long vowel is substituted for the final of अष्टन् before the second member, when the compound is a name.

Thus अष्टावक्रः, अष्टाबन्धुरः अष्टापदम् ॥ But अष्टपुत्रः, अष्टभार्यः where the compounds are not names.

छन्दसि च ॥ १२६ ॥ पदानि ॥ छन्दसि, च, (दीर्घः) ॥
वृत्तिः ॥ छन्दसि विषये ऽष्टन उत्तरपदे दीर्घो भवति ॥
वार्त्तिकम् ॥ गवि च युक्ते भाषायामष्टनो दीर्घो भवतीति वक्तव्यम् ॥

126. In the Veda also, the long vowel is substituted for the final of अष्टन् before a second member.

Thus आग्नेयमष्टाकपालं निर्वपेत्, अष्टाहिरण्या दक्षिणा, अष्टापदी देवता सुमती ॥ The form अष्टापदी is the feminine in ङीप् (IV. 1. 8) of अष्टपात् (V. 4. 138 the अ of पाद being elided in a Bahuvrihi), पद् being substituted for पात् by VI. 4, 130.

Vârt:—The final of अष्टन् is lengthened before गो even in the vernacular, when yoking is meant. Thus अष्टागवं शकटम् ॥

चितेः कपि ॥ १२७ ॥ पदानि ॥ चितेः, कपि, (दीर्घः) ॥
वृत्तिः ॥ चितिशब्दस्य कपि परतो दीर्घो भवति ॥

127. The final vowel of चिति is lengthened before the affix कप् ॥

Thus एकचितीकः, द्विचितीकः, त्रिचितीक ॥

विश्वस्य वसुराटोः ॥ १२८ ॥ पदानि ॥ विश्वस्य, वसु, राटोः, (दीर्घः) ॥

वृत्तिः ॥ विश्वशब्दस्य वसु राडित्येतयोरुत्तरपदयोर्दीर्घ आदेशो भवति ॥

128. The final vowel of विश्व is lengthened before वसु and राट् (the form assumed by राज्).

Thus विश्वावसुः, विश्वाराट् ॥ The rule applies to the राट् form of राज in the Nominative singular, and not when it retains its own form: as विश्वराजौ, विश्वराजः ॥

नरे संज्ञायाम् ॥ १२९ ॥ पदानि ॥ नरे, संज्ञायाम, (दीर्घः) ॥

वृत्तिः ॥ नरशब्दउत्तरपदे संज्ञायां विषये विश्वस्य दीर्घो भवति ॥

129. The final of विश्व is lengthened before नर, when the compound is a Name.

Thus विश्वानरः, वैश्वानरिः (the son of Vishvânara). But विश्वनरः = विश्वे नरा यस्य when it is not a name.

मित्रे चर्षौ ॥ १३० ॥ पदानि ॥ मित्रे, च, ऋषौ, (दीर्घः) ॥

वृत्तिः ॥ मित्रे चोत्तरपदे ऋषावभिधेये विश्वस्य दीर्घो भवति ॥

130. The final of विश्व is lengthened before मित्र when it is the name of a Rishi.

As विश्वामित्रः 'the sage Viśvâmitra'. But विश्वमित्रः 'a boy called Viśvamitra'.

मन्त्रे सोमाश्वेन्द्रियविश्वदेव्यस्य मतौ ॥ १३१ ॥ पदानि ॥ मन्त्रे, सोम, अश्व, इन्द्रिय, विश्वदेव्यस्य, मतौ, (दीर्घः) ॥

वृत्तिः ॥ मन्त्रविषये सोम अश्व इन्द्रिय विश्वदेव्य इत्येतेषां मतुप्प्रत्यये परतो दीर्घो भवति ॥

131. In a Mantra, the final vowels of सोम, अश्व, इन्द्रिय and विश्वदेव्य are lengthened when the affix मतुप् follows.

Thus सोमावती, अश्वावती, इन्द्रियावती, विश्वदेव्यावती ॥

ओषधेश्च विभक्तावप्रथमायाम् ॥ १३२ ॥ पदानि ॥ ओषधेः, च, विभक्तौ, अप्रथमायाम, (मन्त्रे) ॥

वृत्तिः ॥ ओषधिशब्दस्य विभक्तावप्रथमायां परतो दीर्घो भवति ॥

132. In a Mantra, the final of ओषधि is lengthened before the case-endings, but not in the Nominative.

Thus ओषधीभिरपीपतत्, नमः पृथिव्यै नमः ओषधीभ्यः ॥ Why do we say 'before case-endings'? Observe ओषधिपते ॥ Why do we say 'but not in the Nominative'? Observe स्थिरेयमस्त्वौषधिः ॥

ऋचि तुनुघमक्षुतङ्कुत्रोरुष्याणाम् ॥ १३३ ॥ पदानि ॥ ऋचि, तु, नु, घ, मक्षु, तङ्, कुत्र, उरुष्याणाम, (दीर्घः) ॥

वृत्तिः ॥ ऋचि विषये तु नु घ मक्षु तङ् कु त्र उरुष्य इत्येषां दीर्घो भवति ॥

133. In the Rig-Veda the finals of the particles तु, तु, घ, मक्षु, the tense-affix तङ्, कु, the ending त्र and the word उरुष्य are lengthened.

Thus तु :—आ तू न इन्द्र वृत्रहन् (Rig IV. 32. 1) नु—नू करणे ॥ घ : —उत वाघा स्यालात् ॥ मक्षु:—मक्षू गोमन्तमीमहे ॥ तङ् :—भरता जातवेदसम् (Rig X. 176. 2). तङ् is the त substitute of था, when it is treated as ङित्, therefore it does not apply here, शृणोत ग्रावाणः (I. 2. 4). कु—कूमनस ; त्र—अत्रा गौः ; उरुष्या णोम्रेः ॥

इकः सुञि ॥ १३४ ॥ पदानि ॥ इकः, सुञि, (दीर्घः) ॥

वृत्तिः ॥ सुञ् निपातो गृह्यते । इगन्तस्य सुञि परतो मन्त्रविषये दीर्घो भवति ॥

134. In a Mantra, the finals of the preceding member ending in इ or उ are lengthened before the particle सु ॥

Thus अभी षु णः सखीनाम् (Rig. IV. 31. 3) ऊर्ध्व ऊ षुण ऊतये (Rig I. 36. 13). The स is changed to ष by VIII. 3. 107: and न changed to ण by VIII. 4. 27.

द्व्यचोतस्तिङः ॥ १३५ ॥ पदानि ॥ द्व्यचः, अतः, तिङः, (ऋचि दीर्घः) ॥

वृत्तिः ॥ द्व्यचस्तिङन्तस्यात ऋग्विषये दीर्घो भवति ॥

135. A tense affix ending in अ is lengthened in the Rig-veda, when the Verb consists of two syllables.

Thus विद्मा हि त्वा सत्पतिं शूर गोनाम् &c. See Rig III. 42. 6, विद्मा हि तस्य पितरम् &c. But not here देवा भवत वाजिनः, as the verb consists of more than two syllables: not also here आ देवान् वक्षि यक्षि च as the verbs do not end in अ ॥

निपातस्य च ॥ १३६ ॥ पदानि ॥ निपातस्य, च, (ऋचि) (दीर्घः) ॥

वृत्तिः ॥ निपातस्य च ऋग्विषये दीर्घ आदेशो भवति ॥

136. In the Rig Veda the final of a particle is lengthened.

Thus एवा ते, अच्छाते, अच्छा जरितारः (R. 1. 2. 2).

अन्येषामपि दृश्यते ॥ १३७ ॥ पदानि ॥ अन्येषाम्, अपि, दृश्यते, (दीर्घः) ॥

वृत्तिः ॥ अन्येषामपि दीर्घो दृश्यते स शिष्टप्रयोगादनुगन्तव्यः ॥ यस्य दीर्घत्वं न विहितं दृश्यते च प्रयोगे तद्नेन कर्त्तव्यम् ॥

वार्त्तिकम् ॥ शुनो दन्तदंष्ट्राकर्णकुन्दवराहपुच्छपदेषु ॥

137. The elongation of the final is to be found in other words also.

Here we must follow the usage of the Sishthas. Where the lengthening is not ordained by any of the rules of Grammar, but occurs in the writing of standard authors, there we should accept such lengthening as valid. Thus केशाकेशि, कचाकचि, अलाषाट्, नारकः, पूरुषः ॥

Vârt:—The final of श्वन् is lengthened before the following दन्त, दंष्ट्रा, कर्ण कुन्द, वराह, पुच्छ, and पद:—as श्वादन्तः श्वादंष्ट्रः, श्वाकर्णः, श्वाकुन्दः, श्वावराहः, श्वापुच्छः, श्वापदः ॥

चौ ॥ १३८ ॥ पदानि ॥ चौ, (पूर्वस्यदीर्घः) ॥

वृत्तिः ॥ चौ परतः पूर्वपदस्य दीर्घो भवति ॥ चावित्यञ्चतिर्लुप्तनकाराकारो गृह्यते ॥

138. The final vowel of the preceding member is lengthened before अञ्च, when it assumes the form च, having lost its nasal and the vowel.

Thus दधीचः पश्य, दधीचा, दधीचे, मधूचः पश्य, मधूचा, मधूचे ॥ The nasal of अञ्च is elided by VI. 4. 24, and the अ by VI. 4. 138. In दधि+अच् the इ is not changed to its semivowel, though that is an antaranga rule, because the present sûtra ordains specifically long ई, and so also दधी+अच् and मधू+अच् ॥ See also VI. 3. 92.

संप्रसारणस्य ॥ १३९ ॥ पदानि ॥ संप्रसारणस्य, (उत्तरपदे दीर्घः) ॥

वृत्तिः ॥ संप्रसारणान्तस्य पूर्वपदस्योत्तरपदे दीर्घो भवति ॥

139. The vowel substituted for a semivowel is lengthened, when it stands as the first member of a compound.

As कारीषगन्धीपुत्रः, कारीषगन्धीपतिः, कौमुदगन्धीपतिः ॥ See. VI. 1. 13. करीषस्येव गन्धोऽस्य=करीषगन्धिः (इ being added as samâsânta by V. 4. 136 and 137). The optional shortening ordained by VI. 3. 61. does not apply here, for that option is a definite and restricted option; moreover, on the maxim of परत्व, 'a subsequent rule superseding a precedent,' rule VI. 3. 61 is superseded by VI. 3. 139; and the rule VI. 3. 61 can not be revived by the maxim पुनः प्रसङ्ग विज्ञानं "occasional ly the formation of a particular form is accounted for by the fact that a preceding rule is allowed to apply again, after it had previously been superseded, by a subsequent rule." For here the following maxim will prevent the revival सकृद्गतौ विप्रतिषेधेयद्बाधितं तद्बाधितमेव "when two rules, while they apply simultaneously, mutually prohibit each other, that rule of the two which is once superseded by the other, is superseded altogether, and cannot, therefore, apply again, after the latter rule has taken effect."

ओ३म् ।

षष्ठाध्यायस्य चतुर्थः पादः ।

BOOK SIXTH.

CHAPTER FOURTH

अङ्गस्य ॥ १ ॥ पदानि ॥ अङ्गस्य, ॥

वृत्तिः ॥ अधिकारोयमाऽऽसप्तमाध्यायपरिसमाप्तेः । यदित ऊर्द्धमनुक्रमिष्यामोऽङ्गस्येत्येवं तद्वेदितव्यम् ॥

1. Whatever will be taught here after upto the end of the Seventh Adhyâya, is consequent upon the stem (aṅga).

This is an adhikâra sûtra. Thus in VI. 4. 2 is taught the lengthening of the vowel of a samprasâraṇa : as हूतः, जीतः, संवीतः ॥ That means that the vowel preceded by a consonant belonging to the stem is lengthened. Therefore in निर्+वेञ्+क्त=निरुतम्, the vocalised vowel उ is not lengthened, as निर् is upasarga and not stem. So दुरुतम् ॥ Similarly VI. 4. 3, teaches the lengthening of the final before नाम्, as अग्नीनाम्, वायूनाम् ॥ But क्रिमिणाम् पश्य, पामनां पश्य, as मि and न are not the end-portions of a stem. The stem is क्रिमिणा and पामना 'a female having क्रिमि or पामन्', formed by न affix (V. 2. 100). The forms क्रिमिणाम् and पामनाम् are Accusative Singular. Similarly VII. 1. 9 teaches that after अ, भिस् is changed into ऐस् ॥ As वृक्षैः, प्लक्षैः ॥ There also, the अ must be the अ final in an aṅga or stem : hence not here ब्राह्मणभिस्सा, ओदनभिस्सटा, the भिस् does not follow an aṅga. भिस्सा means boiled rice and भिस्सटा means दग्धिः ॥

The maxim of अर्थवद्ग्रहणे नानर्थकस्य does not apply here ; for had it been so, there would have been no necessity of making this sûtra. For example, in the sûtra नामि (VI. 4. 3), the affix नाम् having a meaning would have been meant, and not any other नाम् ॥

The word अङ्गस्य must be read in the following sûtras, otherwise there would arise incongruity : *first*; sûtras teaching the lengthening of the vowel when सन् or Samprasaraṇa follows, thus : VI. 4. 16 ordains the lengthening of vowel before सन्, as विवीषति ; but not here दधि सनोति for इ of दधि is not that of aṅga. So also in Samprasârana, but not in निरुत &c as shown above.

2ndly—For the purposes of एत्वं in sûtra VI. 4. 68. The optional change of आ into ए must refer to anga,, as ग्लेयात् or ग्लायात्, but not here निर्यायात् or निर्वायात्, for here र् is not part of the aṅga, and so र्य cannot be considered a conjunct part of anga.

3rdly—For the change of तु to तात् in VII. 1. 35. There also तु must be portion of the aṅga, and not the particle तु, therefore, जीवतु or जीवतात्, but hot here जीव तु त्वम् ॥

4thly—For the substitution of इयङ् aud उवङ् in VI. 4. 77. Therefore not here इयर्थम् and वर्थम् ॥

5thly—For the sake of नुट् augment in VII. 1. 54. But not here कुमारी आमिति आह ॥

6thly—For the sake of shortening of vowels. Thus VII. 4. 13 ordains the shortening of अण् vowels before क ॥ It refers to the aṅga-vowel, as कुमारिका ॥ But not here, कुमारी कस्मै स्पृहयति or कुमार्याः कं सुखं = कुमारीकं ॥

And lastly for तत्व or त substitution. Thus VII. 4. 48 ordains the change of प into त् in the case of अप् before भ ॥ It refers to aṅga, as अद्भिः ॥ But not here अब्भारः, for अप् here is not aṅga.

To sum up in Sanskrit: सन् सम्प्रसारण दीर्घत्वेत्वतातार्ङ्यङुवङ्नुट ह्रस्वत्व तत्वे च अङ्गस्येत्यधिकारे प्रयोजनं ॥

The word अङ्गस्य is in the Genitive case. But the force of Genitive is here not only that taught in I. 1. 49 (स्थाने योगः), but of mere relation-ship. Or अङ्गस्य may be considered as a mere prâtipadika, without any case-affix. In the subsequent aphorisms, it should be read with proper case-affixes as the exigencies of each sûtra may require. Thus in अतो भिस ऐस् (VII. 1. 9) अङ्ग should be read in the ablative case: अकारान्ताद् अङ्गाद् भिसः ऐस् ॥ The Genitive case has force of स्थानषष्ठी in sûtras like हन्तेर्जः, where the *whole* of हन् is replaced (VI. 4. 36). It has the force of अवयवषष्ठी in sûtras like ऊदुपधाया गोहः (VI. 4. 89). It has the force of निमित्तनिमित्ति सम्बन्धः in युवोरनाकौ (VII. 1. 1). Or the Genitive case in अङ्गस्य may be changed into any other case, as already shown.

हलः ॥ २ ॥ पदानि ॥ हलः, (अङ्गस्य सम्प्रसारणम् दीर्घः) ॥

वृत्तिः ॥ अङ्गावयवाद्धलो यदुत्तरं संप्रसारणं तदन्तस्याङ्गस्य दीर्घो भवति ॥

2. The long vowel is substituted for a vocalised half-vowel अ, इ and उ at the end of a stem, when it is preceded by a consonant which is a portion of the stem.

Both the words दीर्घ and अणः from VI. 3. 111, and सम्प्रसारण from VI. 3. 139 are understood here. Thus हूतः from ह्वा, जीनः from ज्या, संवीतः from व्या ॥ Why do we say 'preceded by a consonant'? Observe उतः and उतवान् from वेञ्॥ Why do we say that the preceding consonant should be a portion of the stem?

Observe निरुतम्, here र is not an integral part of the stem, but a portion of the upasarga निर् and therefore उ is not lengthened. Why do we say 'at the end of a stem'? Observe विद्धः, विचितः from व्यध् and व्यच्; here the vowel इ is in the *middle* of the stem. Why do we say 'अ, इ and उ substitutes of semivowels'? Observe तृतीयः ॥ Here त्रि has been vocalised into तृ, ऋ being substituted for र् before the affix तीय (V. 2. 55). The ऋ will not be lengthened. Or the absence of lengthening in तृतीय is an irregularity countenanced by Pâṇini himself in sûtras like II. 1. 30 &c. The word अङ्ग should be repeated in this sûtra, first to qualify the word हल, and then to qualify the letters अ, इ and उ ॥

नामि ॥ ३ ॥ पदानि ॥ नामि, (अङ्गस्य दीर्घः) ॥

वृत्तिः ॥ नामीत्येतत्षष्ठीबहुवचनम् आगतनुट्कं गृह्यते ॥ तस्मिन्परतोऽङ्गस्य दीर्घो भवति ॥

Kârikâ—नामि दीर्घ आमि चेत्स्यात्कृते दीर्घे न नुट् भवेत् ।

वचनाद्यत्र तन्नास्ति, नोपधायाश्च चर्मणाम् ॥

3. The long vowel is substituted for the final of the stem before the Genitive Plural affix नाम् (having the augment नुट्).

Thus अग्नीनाम्, वायूनाम्, कर्तॄणाम्, हर्तॄणाम् ॥ The anuvritti of अण् (VI. 3. 111) ceases. The augment नुट् (VII. 1. 54) in नाम् is for the sake of the subsequent sûtra; like VI.4.7. and the lengthening takes place after the addition of नुट् to the genitive affix आम् ॥ For if the lengthening took place before the addition of नुट्, there would be no occasion for नुट् which comes only after short stems.

न तिसृचतसृ ॥ ४ ॥ पदानि ॥ न, तिसृ, चतसृ, (नामि दीर्घः) ॥

वृत्तिः ॥ तिसृ चतसृ इत्येतयोर्नामि दीर्घो न भवति ॥

4. The finals of तिसृ and चतसृ are not lengthened before नाम् ॥

As तिसृणाम्, चतसृणाम् ॥ The very fact of this prohibition proves by implication that the final ऋ of these words is not changed to र before a genitive plural, VII. 2. 100 notwithstanding. In fact नुट् is added before scope is given to that rule, and thus the preceding rule VII. 1. 54 prevents the application of the subsequent rule VII. 2. 100.

छन्दस्युभयथा ॥ ५ ॥ पदानि ॥ छन्दसि, उभय था ॥

वृत्तिः ॥ छन्दसि विषये तिसृचतस्रोर्नामि परत उभयथा दृश्यते, दीर्घश्चादीर्घश्च ॥

5. In the Veda, the finals of तिसृ and चतसृ are found in both ways, before the Genitive plural नाम् ॥

In some places they are seen as lengthened, in others not. As तिसृणाम् मध्यंदिने or तिसृणाम् मध्यंदिने ॥ So also चतसृणाम् and चतसृणाम् ॥

नृ च ॥ ६ ॥ पदानि ॥ नृ, च, ॥

वृत्तिः ॥ नृ इत्येतस्य नामि पर्युभयथा भवति ॥

6. So also नृ before the Genitive Plural नाम is lengthened optionally.

As त्वं नृणां नृपते, and त्वं नृणां नृपते ॥ According to some this option is confined to the Vedas, according to others, it extends to secular literature also.

नोपधायाः ॥ ७ ॥ पदानि ॥ न, उपधायाः, (नामि दीर्घः) ॥

वृत्तिः ॥ नान्तस्याङ्गस्योपधाया नामि परतो दीर्घो भवति ॥

7. In a stem ending in न्, the preceding vowel is lengthened before the affix नाम ॥

Thus पञ्चन् + नाम (VII. 1. 55) = पञ्चान् + नाम् (VI. 4. 7) = पञ्चानाम् (VIII. 2. 7); सप्तानाम्, नवानाम्, दशानाम् ॥ Why do we say 'ending in न्'? Observe चतुर्णाम् ॥ But not in चर्म्मणाम् where the affix is not नाम् but आम् without नुट् ॥

सर्वनामस्थाने चासंबुद्धौ ॥ ८ ॥ पदानि ॥ सर्वनामस्थाने, च, असम्बुद्धौ (नोपधायाः दीर्घः) ॥

वृत्तिः ॥ सर्वनामस्थाने च परतो ऽसंबुद्धौ नोपधाया दीर्घो भवति ॥

8. In a stem ending in न्, the preceding vowel is lengthened in strong cases, with the exception of the Vocative singular.

As राजा, राजानौ, राजानः, राजानम्, राजानौ ॥ So also सामानि तिष्ठन्ति ॥ राजा was राजान्स्, the स् was elided by VI. 1. 68, and न् by VIII. 2. 7. Why do we say 'in strong cases'? Observe राजनि (Loc-Sing); सामनि (Loc. Sing). Why do we say 'but not in the Vocative Singular'? Observe हे राजन्! हे तक्षन्!

वा षपूर्वस्य निगमे ॥ ९ ॥ पदानि ॥ वा, ष, पूर्वस्य, निगमे ॥

वृत्तिः ॥ षपूर्वस्याचो नोपधाया निगमविषये सर्वनामस्थाने परतो ऽसंबुद्धौ वा दीर्घो भवति ॥

9. The lengthening of the penultimate vowel of a stem ending in न्, before the affixes of the strong-case, is optional in the Veda, when ष precedes such a vowel.

Thus स तक्षाणं or तक्षणं, तिष्ठन्तमब्रवीत् । ऋभुक्षाणं or ऋभुक्षणमिन्द्रम् ॥

Why do we say 'in the Veda'? In the secular literature we have तक्षा, तक्षाणौ तक्षाणः always.

सान्तमहतः संयोगस्य ॥ १० ॥ पदानि ॥ सान्त, महतः, संयोगस्य, (दीर्घः) ॥

वृत्तिः ॥ सकारान्तस्य संयोगस्य यो नकारः महतश्च तस्यौपधाया दीर्घो भवति सर्वनामस्थाने परतो ऽसंबुद्धौ ॥

10. In the strong cases with the exception of Vocative singular, the penultimate vowel is lengthened, in the case of a stem ending in स्, with a Nasal consonant preceding it, and of महत् ॥

That is, a stemending in the conjunct consonant न्स्, elongates its penultimate vowel before the affixes of the first five cases. Thus श्रेयान्, श्रेयांसौ, श्रेयांसः, श्रेयांसि, पयांसि, यशांसि ॥ महत्—महान्, महान्तौ, महान्तः ॥ But हे श्रेयन्, हे महन् in Vocative Singular. The Nasal is inserted by VII. 1. 70.

अप्तृन्तृच्स्वसृनप्तृनेष्टृत्वष्टृक्षत्तृहोतृपोतृप्रशास्तॄणाम् ॥११॥ पदानि ॥ अप्, तृन्, तृच्, स्वसृ, नप्तृ, नेष्टृ, त्वष्टृ, क्षत्तृ, होतृ, पोतृ, प्रशास्तॄणाम् ॥

वृत्तिः ॥ अप् इत्येतस्य तृजन्तस्य स्वसृ नप्तृ नेष्टृ त्वष्टृ क्षत्तृ होतृ पोतृ प्रशास्तृ इत्येतेषां चाङ्गानामुपधाया दीर्घो भवति सर्वनामस्थाने परतो ऽसंबुद्धौ ॥

11. In the strong cases, with the exception of the Vocative Singular, the penultimate vowel is lengthened in अप्, in stems formed by तृन् and तृच् affixes, and in स्वसृ, नप्तृ, नेष्टृ, त्वष्टृ, क्षत्तृ, होतृ, पोतृ and प्रशास्तृ ॥

Thus आपः तिष्ठन्ति ॥ Some would have it even in compounds; as बह्वाम्पि तडाग्यानि ॥ The Samâsânta rule is not applied here, because it is *anitya*. If it be considered *nitya*, then also there is lengthening, but without the addition of the nasal. तत्र समासान्तो विधिरनित्य इति समासान्तो न क्रियते। नित्यमपि च नुममकृत्वा दीर्घत्वमिष्यते। तृन्। कर्त्तारौ कटान्। वदितारौ जनापवादान्। कर्त्तारः। तृच्। कर्त्तारौ कटस्य। कर्त्तारः। हर्त्तारौ भारस्य, हर्त्तारः। स्वसृ। स्वसा। स्वसारौ। स्वसारः। नप्तृ। नप्ता। नप्तारौ। नप्तारः। नेष्टृ। नेष्टारौ। नेष्टारः। त्वष्टृ। त्वष्टारौ। त्वष्टारः। क्षत्तृ। क्षत्तारौ। क्षत्तारः। होतृ। होतारौ। होतारः। पोतृ। पोतारौ। पोतारः। प्रशास्तृ। प्रशास्तारौ। प्रशास्तारः। नप्त्रादीनां ग्रहणमव्युत्पत्तिपक्षे विध्यर्थम्। व्युत्पत्तिपक्षे नियमार्थम्। एवंभूतानामन्येषां संज्ञाशब्दानां दीर्घो मा भूदिति। पितरौ। पितरः। मातरौ। मातरः। असंबुद्धाविति किम्। हेकर्त्तः। हेस्वसः ॥

If the words नप्तृ &c. be considered as रूढि, not derived from any root, then their enumeration is here for the sake of Vidhi (injunction); if they be considered as derivative words formed by Uṇadi affixes, then their enumeration is for the sake of niyama (restriction), so that other words formed similarly are not to be governed by this rule. As पितरौ, पितरः, मातरौ, मातरः ॥ Why do we say 'not in the Vocative Singular'? Observe हे कर्त्तः, हे स्वसः ॥ In the above examples अर् is substituted for ऋ by VII. 3. 110.

इन्हन्पूषार्यम्णां शौ ॥ १२ ॥ पदानि ॥ इन्, हन्, पूष अर्यम्णां, शौ, (दीर्घः) ॥

वृत्तिः ॥ इन् हन् पूषन् अर्यमन् इत्येवमन्तानामङ्गानां शौ परत उपधाया दीर्घो भवति ॥

12. The penultimate vowel is lengthened before the affix शि (Nominative and Accusative Pl.), when the stem ends in इन्, or हन्, or पूषन् or अर्यमन् ॥

According to the maxim (See VI. 4. 14 also) that "अन्, इन्, अस्, मन् ग्रहणान्यर्थवता चानर्थकेन च तदन्त विधिं प्रयोजयन्ति", the employment of इन् in this sûtra includes and means "words *ending* in the syllable इन्" ॥ As regards the rest (हन् &c.), the affix शि (Neuter Pl.) is never added to them alone, but when they are parts of a compound. Thus इन् is a noun formed by the addition of the affix क्विप् to the root हन्; and the affix Kvip is added to it only then, when it is preceded by another word like "Brahma" &c. See III. 2. 87. Similarly the words पूषन् and अर्यमन् are masculine and cannot take the Neuter Plural affix शि in their original state. They must be parts of a neuter compound, to admit this affix. Hence we have used words "when the stem *ends* in इन् &c."

Thus बहुदण्डीनि and बहुच्छत्रीणि । बहुवृत्रहाणि । बहुभ्रूणहाणि । बहुपूषाणि । बह्वर्यमाणि ॥ सिद्धे सत्यारम्भो नियमार्थः । इन्हन्पूषार्यम्णामुपधायाः शावेव दीर्घो भवति नान्यत्र । दण्डिनौ । छत्रिणौ । वृत्रहणौ । पूषणौ । अर्यमणौ ॥

Though this result could have been obtained by VI. 4. 8, the special mention of these words shows that except in Accusative and Nom. Pl. the lengthening does not take place in other strong cases. As दण्डिनौ, छत्रिणौ, वृत्रहणौ, पूषणौ, अर्यमणौ ॥

Kârikâ :—Regarding the rule of lengthening taught about इन् &c here, let the wise reader, after making a restrictive rule with regard to सुट् (sarvanâmas thâna) affixes in general, make again another rule regarding the affix शि in particular, (i. e., make a yoga-bibhâga). By so doing, the form भ्रूणहनि (Loc. sin.) of the Achârya, will not be found fault with.

2. (But if yoga-vibhaga be not made) then I rule that the anuvritti of सुट् being dropped, let the rule be made with regard to शि affix in general (without regarding it as a Sarvanâmasthâna affix). And as the rule of lengthening applies to penultimates, there would arise no fault, if the vowel of हन् is lengthened before the demonstrative affix य (in words like वृत्रहायते = वृत्रहा इव आचरति, This refers to VII, 4. 25).

3. Or if the anuvṛitti of सुट् (Sarvanamasthana) be taken into this Sûtra, because of the context, then the mention of शि in this Sûtra, (would be redundant, because the word Sarvanâmasthâna includes it, so far as the strong cases are concerned) but it would find scope and utility in preventing the lengthening in those cases to which the context of Sarvanâmasthâna does not apply. That is, the Sarvanâmasthâna will be restricted with regard to इन् &c to the affix शि and not to सुट् affixes generally.

Note :—शि is the affix of the Nom. aud Acc. Pl. in Neuter (VII. 1. 20.) It it a Sarvanamasthana by I. 1. 42. But the word Sarvanamasthana may be read into this sutra from the preceding VI. 4. 8. What is then the necessity of employing शि in this? The above karika answers this.

In the case of हन् ending words, the subsequent rule VI. 4. 15, which required the lengthening of the penultimate vowel before an affix having an indicatory क् or ङ्, is however debarred by the present restrictive rule. Thus the Locative Singular (ङि) is वृत्रहनि, and भ्रूणहनि ॥ How do you make this? By splitting up the present sutra into two parts, the first part being इन् हन् पूषार्यम्णाम्, and the second being शौ ॥ It would then mean :—

(1) The penultimate vowel is lengthened, in strong cases only and no where else, when the stem ends in इन् or हन् or in पूषन् or अर्यमन् ॥ (2) So also it is lengthened before the strong case शि and no where else. These two restrictive rules therefore, would debar all other rules of penultimate lengthening which would otherwise have been applicable. But a rule which does not relate to *penultimate* vowel, is not debarred by this restriction, but does take effect. Thus वृत्रहायते, भ्रूणहायते denominative verbs in क्यङ् ॥

Or even though the Sarvanâmasthâna may be read into the sûtra by anuvṛitti, yet this may be considered a Restrictive Rule in general, and not only with regard to शि considered a Sarvanâmasthâna or a Neuter affix शि is the Sarvanâmasthâna affix of the Neuter: which has no other Sarvanâmasthâna, therefore, it is a general Niyama and not only a Sarvanâmasthâna or a Neuter niyama. Therefore in this niyama the word "नपुंसकस्य"—"of the Neuter"—is not to be taken.

For if it be taken, then the Sûtra would mean, the neuter stems in इन् &c are lengthened in शि only and no where else. The result would be that in examples like भ्रूणहनि ब्राह्मणकुले (loc. sin), there would be no lengthening at all (i.e. we shall never have the form भ्रूणहानि in loc. sin. by force of VI. 4. 15); moreover, by so doing, there wou'd arise this anomaly also, that words other than Neuter would also not be lengthened.

The force of the definition of Sarvanâmasthâna applies to Neuter also in certain cases, therefore, any rule (niyama) made with regard to Sarvanâmasthâna would apply to Neuter also.

सौ च ॥ १३ ॥ पदानि ॥ सौ, च, (उपधायाः दीर्घः) ॥

वृत्तिः ॥ सावसंबुद्धौ परत इन्हन्पूषार्यम्णामुपधाया दीर्घो भवति ॥

13. The penultimate vowels of a stem ending in इन्, हन्, पूषन् or अर्यमन् are lengthened before the affix सु of the Nominative Singular but not in Vocative Singular.

Thus दण्डी, वृत्रहा, पूषा, अर्यमा ॥ The न् is elided by VIII. 2. 7, and the case-affix by VI. 1. 68. In the Vocative singular we have हे दण्डिन्, हे पूषन्, हे वृत्रहन् हे अर्यमन् ॥

अत्वसन्तस्य चाधातोः ॥ १४ ॥ पदानि ॥ अतु, असन्तस्य, च, अधातोः ॥

वृत्तिः ॥ अतु अस इत्येवमन्तस्य अधातोरुपधायाः सावसंबुद्धौ परतो दीर्घो भवति ॥

14. In the Nominative Singular (with the exception of the Vocative Singular) the penultimate vowel is lengthened in a stem ending in अतु, and अस् when the consonant (अस्) does not belong to a root.

Thus भवान् (with डवतुप् Uṇ I. 63 from भा to shine), कृतवान् (with क्तवतु); गोमान् and यवमान् (with मतुप्) ॥ The नुम् (न्) is added to the above by VII. 1. 70, after the elongation has taken place, for if added *before* elongation, the vowel no longer being *penultimate*, will not be lengthened at all. अस्:—as सुपयाः, सुयशाः, सुश्रोताः ॥ Why do we say 'not belonging to a dhâtu'? Observe पिण्डग्रः where स् belongs to the root ग्रस् (पिण्डं ग्रसते), so also चर्मवः (चर्म वस्ते) ॥ The अस् having no significance as an affix &c is also included here, on the strength of the maxim "whenever अन् or इन् or अस् or मन्, when they are taught in Grammar denote by I. 1. 72, something that ends with these, there they represent these combination of letters both in so far as they possess, and also in so far as they are void of a meaning". (अनिनस्मन् ग्रहणानि अर्थवता चानर्थकेन च तदन्तविधिं प्रयोजयन्ति) ॥ The word अन्त in the sûtra indicates whatever *ends* in अतु whether when first enunciated (उपदेश), such as डवतु, क्तवतु &c, or which assumes the form अतु in grammatical inflection, such as मतुप् which in upadeśa ends in अतुप्, but becomes अतु in प्रयोग or application. In Vocative singular we have हे गोमन्, हे सुपयः this rule not applying there.

अनुनासिकस्य क्विझलोः क्ङिति ॥ १५ ॥ पदानि ॥ अनुनासिकस्य, क्वि, झलोः, क्ङिति, (दीर्घः) ॥

वृत्तिः ॥ अनुनासिकान्तस्याङ्गस्य उपधाया दीर्घो भवति क्विप्रत्यये परतो झलादौ च क्ङिति ॥

15. The penultimate vowel of a stem, ending in a nasal, is lengthened before the affix क्वि, and before an affix having an indicatory क् or ङ्, which begins with a consonant other than a semivowel or a nasal.

Thus प्रशान् and प्रतान् from the roots शम् and तम् by VIII. 2. 64. So also before an affix beginning with a झल् consonant (any consonant but a nasal and a semivowel). As शान्तः (with क्त), शान्तवान् (with क्तवतु), शान्त्वा (with क्त्वा), and शान्तिः (with क्तिन्). These are all formed with कित् affixes. As to ङित् affixes we have शंशान्तः and तन्तान्तः formed by तस् 3rd Person Dual added to the Intensive roots शम् and तम् ॥ तस् is ङित् by I. 2. 4. Why do we say 'ending in a Nasal'? Observe ओदनपक्, पक्वः, पक्ववान् ॥ Why do we say 'before क्वि and jhalâdi affix'? Observe गम्यते, रम्यते ॥ Why do we say a ङित् or a कित् affix? Observe गन्ता and रन्ता ॥

अज्झनगमां सनि ॥ १६ ॥ पदानि ॥ अच्, हन्, गमाम्. सनि, (वा दीर्घः) ॥

वृत्तिः ॥ अजन्तानामङ्गानां हनिगम्योश्च सनि झलादौ परे वा दीर्घो भवति ॥

वार्त्तिकम् ॥ गमेरिङादेशस्येति वक्तव्यम् ॥

16, The lengthening of the vowel takes place in the case of a stem ending in a vowel, as well as of हन् and गम्, when the Desiderative affix सन् being jhalâdi (i. e. not taking the augment इट्) follows.

Thus of roots ending in vowel we have:—चिचीषति, तुष्टूषति, चिकीर्षति, जिहीर्षति (VII. 1. 100); of हन् and गम्, जिघांसति, and अधिजिगांसते ॥

Vârt:—The rule applies to that गम which is the substitute of इङ् (II. 4. 48) 'to study'. Therefore, not here, संजिगंसते वत्सौ मात्रा (cf. VII. 2. 58); In the Veda we read स्वर्गं लोकं समजिगांसत्, where though गम् means 'to go' and is not, therefore, the substitute of इङ्, the lengthening takes place by the rule VI. 3, 137. Or the word अच् should not be added in the sûtra at all: which should be read as हनगमां सनि meaning "There is lengthening of the stem when the Desiderative सन् follows". This would apply of course, to vowel-ending stems, because the sentence would mean that, for there cannot be lengthening of a consonant. This will apply to गम् also, in this way:—"A stem ending in a vowel is lengthened in the Desiderative, and so also of गम which is a substitute of the vowel-stem इ" ॥ In this way, we may see, that there is no necessity of the Vârtika.

तनोतेर्विभाषा ॥ १७ ॥ पदानि ॥ तनोतेः, विभाषा ॥

वृत्तिः ॥ तनोतेरङ्गस्य सनि झलादौ विभाषा दीर्घो भवति ॥

17. The lengthening of the stem of तन् is optional, before the Desiderative सन्, when it does not take the augment इट् ॥

Thus तितांसति or तितंसति ॥ But in िततनिषति no alternative is allowed, as इट् is added to सन् by VII. 2. 49 Vârt: optionally.

क्रमश्च क्त्वि ॥ १८ ॥ पदानि ॥ क्रमः, च, क्त्वि, (झलि) ॥

वृत्तिः ॥ क्रम उपधाया विभाषा दीर्घो भवति क्त्वाप्रत्यये झलादौ परतः ॥

18. The penultimate of क्रम् is optionally lengthened, before the affix क्त्वा, when it is without the augment इट् ॥

Thus क्रन्त्वा or क्रान्त्वा; but क्रमित्वा only, with इट् augment. But when क्त्वा is replaced by ल्यप्, the rule does not apply: as प्रक्रम्य, उपक्रम्य ॥ This is on the maxim अन्तरङ्गानपि विधीन् बहिरङ्गोल्यप् बाधते 'a bahiranga substitution of ल्यप् supersedes even antaranga rule".

च्छ्वोः शूडनुनासिके च ॥ १९ ॥ पदानि ॥ च्छ्वोः, शूठ्, अनुनासिके, च, (क्किझलोः) ॥

वृत्तिः ॥ छ इत्येतस्य सतुक्कस्य वकारस्य च स्थाने यथासंख्यं श ऊठ् इत्येतावादेशौ भवतः, अनुनासिकादौ प्रत्यये परतः क्वौ झलादौ च क्ङिति ॥

19. For च्छ (including the augment तुक्) is substituted श्, and for व is substituted ऊठ्, before an affix beginning with a Nasal, as well as before क्वि and jhalâdi ङित् and कित् affixes (VI. 4. 15).

Thus प्रश्नः, विश्नः from प्रच्छ and विच्छ, with the affix नङ् (III. 3. 90) the च्छ being replaced by श ॥ Similarly from the root सिव् we have स्योनः thus: सिव्+न (Un III. 9).=सि+ऊ+न=स्यू+न=स्योनः (VII. 3. 84). Here the ऊ is added to the stem prior to the scope being given to the guṇa rule of VII. 3. 86, otherwise the form would be सिव्+न=सेव्+न=से+ऊ+न ॥ Having thus added ऊ,

before scope could be given to the guṇa rule VII. 3. 86, we make sandhi of सि+ऊ=स्यू, because semivowel substitution is antaranga operation and of wider scope than guṇa, and the maxim of वार्णादाङ्गं बलीयो भवति has no scope here. "An operation which is taught in the Aṅgâdhikâra, and affects the anga or stem, possesses greater force than an operation which concerns a combination of letters (i. e. is taught in a sandhi rule)".

With ऊठ् we have शब्दप्राश् formed with क्विप् (Uṇ II. 57) added to प्रच्छ, there is no vocalisation of the semivowel र, and there is lengthening of अं, and च्छ changed to श. So also गोविश् ॥

Of the change of व into ऊ we have the following :—अक्षद्यूः, हिरण्यद्यूः (दिव्+क्विप्=दि+ऊ=द्यूः) ॥ Here the ऊ substitution is Bahiranga, and दि+ऊ=द्यू, the change of इ into य is antaranga, therefore on the maxim of असिद्धं बहिरङ्गमन्तरङ्गे (a bahiranga is non-existent for the purposes of an antaranga), there should be no change of इ into य, for ऊ is non-existent. That maxim is however set aside by नाजानन्तर्ये बहिष्ट्व प्रक्लृप्तिः "A bahiranga operation is not regarded as bahiranga, and consequently asiddha, when an antaranga operation is to take effect, which depends on the immediate sequence of a vowel and something else".

So also before a jhalâdi affix; as प्रच्छ+क्त=पृष्टः, पृष्टवान् (क्तवतु), पृष्ट्वा (क्त्वा); here च्छ is changed to श, there is vocalisation by VI. 1. 16, and श changed to ष by VIII. 2. 36.

So also व is changed to ऊ as, द्यूतः, द्यूतवान्, द्यूत्वा ॥

When the affixes are not ङित् or कित्, the rule does not apply: as द्युभ्याम्, द्युभिः ॥ Some do not read the anuvritti of कित् and ङित् into this sûtra, and explain द्युभ्याम् and द्युभिः by VI. 1. 131 : उ short being substituted for व of दिव् ॥

In "छशां ष" (VIII. 2. 36) the letter छ should not be taken, because by the force of the present sûtra, श is ordained to come every where in the place of छ ॥

The indicatory ठ् in ऊठ् is for the sake of distinguishing this ऊ in sûtras like एत्येधत्यूठ्सु (VI. 1. 89). In the sutra वाह ऊठ् (VI. 4. 132) there is also indicatory ठ् ॥

ज्वरत्वरश्रिव्यविमवामुपधायाश्च ॥ २० ॥ पदानि ॥ ज्वर, त्वर, श्रिवि, अवि, मवाम्, उपधायाः, च, (क्विझलोः वस्य) ॥

वृत्तिः ॥ ज्वर त्वर श्रिवि अव मव इत्येतेषामङ्गानां वकारस्य उपधायाश्च स्थाने ऊडित्ययमादेशो भवति क्वौ परतो ऽनुनासिके झलादौ च क्ङिति ॥

20. In ज्वर, त्वर् श्रिव्, अव, and मव्, before the above-mentioned affixes (क्वि, a Nasal or a jhalâdi 'कित्' or ङित्) there is the single substitution of ऊठ् for the व् and the vowel preceding the final consonant.

Thus ज्रूः, ज्रुरौ, ज्रुरः, ज्रूर्त्तिः ॥ त्वरः—तूः, तुरौ, तुरः, तूर्णिः ॥ श्रिविः—श्रूः, श्रुवौ, श्रुवः, श्रूतः श्रूतवान, श्रूतिः ॥ अवः—ऊः, उवौ, उवः, ऊतिः ॥ मवः—मूः, मुवौ, मुवः, मूतः, मूतवान्, मूतिः ॥ ज्वरत्वरो-रुपधा वकारात् परा, श्रिव्य वमवां पूर्वा ॥

In ज्वर् and त्वर् the ऊ replaces व् as well as the अ which *follows* व्; and in श्रिव्, अव् and मव् it replaces the व् and the vowel इ and अ which *precede* व् ॥ Another reading is स्रिव् ॥

राल्लोपः ॥ २१ ॥ पदानि ॥ रात्, लोपः, (क्विझलोः) ॥

वृत्तिः ॥ रेफादुत्तरयोश्छ्वोर्लोपो भवति क्वौ परतो झलादौ क्ङिति च परतः ॥

21. After र् there is the elision of छ् and व् before 'क्वि' and jhalâdi 'कित्' and 'ङित्' affixes.

Thus from मुर्छा—मूर्, मुरौ, मुरः, मूर्तः मूर्तवान्, मूर्तिः, the त of Nishṭhâ is not changed into न by VIII. 2. 57. So also from हुर्छा we have हूर्, हुरौ, हुरः, हूर्णः, हूर्णवान्, हूर्त्तिः ॥ So also the व is elided, as from तुर्वी:—तूर्, तुरौ, तुरः, तूर्णः, तूर्णवान्, तूर्त्तिः ॥ धुर्वी:—धूः, धुरौ, धुरः, धूर्णः, धूर्णवान्, धूर्त्ति ॥

असिद्धवदत्राऽऽभात् ॥ २२ ॥ पदानि ॥ असिद्धवत्, अत्र, आभात् ॥

वृत्तिः ॥ असिद्धवदित्ययमधिकारो यदित ऊर्द्ध्वमनुक्रमिष्याम आ अध्यायपरिसमाप्तेस्तद् असिद्धवद्वेदितव्यम् ॥

वार्त्तिकम् ॥ कुग्युटावुवङ्यणोः सिद्धौ भवत इति वक्तव्यम् ॥

22. The change, which a stem will undergo by the application of any of the rules from this sûtra upto VI. 4. 129, is to be considered as not to have taken effect, when we have to apply any other rule of this very section VI. 4. 23 to 129.

This is an adhikâra rule. The above translation is given according to Prof. Bohtlingk. According to Kâsika the असिद्धवत् extends up to the end of the chapter. Dr. Ballantyne translates it thus :—"The rules, reckoning from this one to the end of the chapter, are called Abhîya, because the chapter ends with a series of rules dependant on the aphorism 'bhasya' VI. 4. 129. When that (i. e. one of the âbhîya rules) is to be brought into operation, having the same place for coming into operation as another âbhiya, which has already taken effect, that one which has taken effect, shall be regarded as not having taken effect".

The word आभात् means 'up to भ' i. e. upto VI. 4. 129. in which last sûtra the word भ occurs : i. e. in applying the rules taught upto VI. 4. 129. The word अत्र shows that the two rules must have the same आश्रय or place of operation, where their places of operation are different, they are not asiddha to each other. The word असिद्ध shows that an utsarga or general rule must take effect, as if existing in spite of a special rule, and that an 'âdesa' or substitution taught by another rule should not be considered to have taken effect in applying the special rule. Thus in forming एधि and शाधि (Imperative 2nd person)

ए is first substituted for अस् 'to be' by VI, 4. 119: and शा for शास् by VI. 4. 35 and then is धि added by VI. 4. 101. The latter rule says that धि is added in the Imperative, only after those roots which end in a consonant of झल् class. Now अस् and शास् end in a *jhal* consonant, and can take धि, but their substitute ए and शा end in a vowel and not a consonant and should not take धि ॥ The present rule helps us here, and for the application of धि (VI. 4. 101) the substitution of ए for अस् or शा for शास् should be considered as asiddha or not to have taken effect. Similarly in आगहि (Vedic Imperative, शप् being elided by II. 4. 73) and जहि from गम् and हन्, the nasal being elided in the case of गम्, VI. 4. 36 and ज being substituted for हन् (VI. 2. 36) we have the stems आग and ज, which ending in अ would require the elision of हि by VI. 4. 105. But since the change of ज &c is not regarded as having been accomplished, the elision of हि does not take place.

Why do we say आभात् 'up to VI. 4. 129'? In applying any other rule the changes ordained by âbhiya rules would not be considered as asiddha. Thus अभाजि and रागः from भञ्ज् and रञ्ज ॥ Here the nasals of rañj and bhañj have been elided by VI. 4. 27-28 and 33 before the affixes घञ् and चिण् respectively, and we have the stems रज्, and भज् to which rule VII. 2. 116 applies and we have Vṛiddhi of अ preceding the final consonant. Had the elision of the nasal been considered as non-effective for the purposes of VII. 2. 116, then अ could not have taken Vṛiddhi, as it would not then be उपधा or penultimate.

Why do we use the word अत्र in the aphorism? The rules are asiddha to each other with regard to a common place of operation and not otherwise. Thus पा+वस् (क्वसु)+अस् (शस् Acc. Pl). = पपा + उस् + अस् (VI. 4. 131 vocalisation of व). If this उ substitute be considered as asiddha for the purposes of sûtra VI. 4. 64, then we cannot elide the आ of पा, because आ is not then followed by a vowel (उ being non-existent). उ however is not considered as asiddha, and आ being thus elided, we have पपुषः in पपुषः पश्य ॥ Similarly चि+वस्+अस्=चिचि+उस् +अस् ॥ Here also उ is not considered asiddha, and we apply rule VI. 4. 82, and substitute य for इ as चिच्युषः पश्य ॥ Similarly लू+वस्+अस् लुलू+उस्+अस्=लुलुवुषः ॥ Here also उ is not considered asiddha, and we change the ऊ of लू into उव् by VI. 4. 77. In all the above three cases, the elision of आ, or change of इ to य, or of ऊ to उव्, takes place in reference to वस्, while the samprasâraṇa of व takes place with reference to the Accusative plural case-ending अस् which makes the stem Bha. So they have not the same आश्रय ॥ Nor does the maxim of असिद्धं बहिरङ्गमन्तरङ्गे apply here, because the special maxim of Abhîya governs the sûtras of this section, so there cannot be the relation of Antaranga and Bahiranga among these sûtras, simultaneously with their being asiddha to each other.

Vârt:—The substitute वुक् (VI. 4. 88), and युट् (VI. 4. 63) should however be considered as not asiddha, and rule VI. 4. 77 teaching उवङ् and VI. 4. 82, teaching य् substitution should not be applied simultaneously with them. Thus भू—बभूव, बभूवतुः बभूवः with वुक्, and उपदिदीये, उपदिदीयाते, उपदिदीयिरे with युट् of VI. 4. 63. In the case of भू, when वुक् is added, there is not the addition of उवङ्, and in the case of दीङ्, when युट् is added, there is not यणादेश ॥

The आ in आभात् has the force of limit inclusive, so that, the asiddha rule applies to the sûtras governed by भ ॥

श्नान्नलोपः ॥ २३ ॥ पदानि ॥ श्नात्, न लोपः, ॥

वृत्तिः ॥ श्नादिति श्नमयमुत्सृष्टमकारो गृह्यते तत उत्तरस्य नकारस्य लोपो भवति ॥

23. After श्न, which is added to the roots of the seventh class as a characteristic (i. e. the vikaraṇa श्नम्), there is the elision of the following न ॥

Thus अनक्ति and भनक्ति from अञ्ज 'to anoint', and भञ्ज 'to break'. Thus अञ्ज् + श्नम् + तिप् = अनञ्ज् + ति (I. 1. 47) = अनज् + ति (VI. 4. 23) = अनक्ति ॥ So also हिनस्ति from हिंसि (हिन्स्) 'to injure'. Why do we say 'after श्न' and not merely 'after न', without the indicatory श? Observe यज्ञानाम्, यत्नानाम्, where the न of नाम् is not elided after the न of यज्ञ and यत्न, the lengthening of अ by VII. 3. 102 being sthânivat would not have prevented the elision. In the case of विश्नानाम् and प्रश्नानाम् (formed by विश्न + नाम् and प्रश्न + नाम्) also; the न of नाम् is not elided after श्न of विश्न ॥ For the श्न of the sûtra is the *technical* श्न the vikaraṇa, and not any combination of the letters श and न ॥ The pratipadokta maxim applies here. लक्षणप्रतिपदोक्तयोः प्रतिपदोक्तस्यैव ग्रहणम् ॥

अनिदितां हल उपधायाः क्ङिति ॥ २४ ॥ पदानि ॥ अनिदिताम्, हलः, उपधायाः, क्ङिति ॥

वृत्तिः ॥ अनिदितामङ्गानां हलन्तानामुपधाया नकारस्य लोपो भवति क्ङिति प्रत्यये परतः ॥
वार्त्तिकम् ॥ अनिदितां नलोप लङ्गिकम्प्योरुपतापशरीरविकारयोरुपसंख्यानं कर्त्तव्यम् ॥
वा० ॥ रञ्जेर्णौ मृगरमणउपसंख्यानं कर्त्तव्यन् ॥ वा० ॥ घिनुणि च रञ्जेरुपसंख्यानं कर्त्तव्यम ॥
वा० ॥ रजकरजनरजः सूपसंख्यानं कर्त्तव्यम् ॥

24. In a root-stem ending in a consonant preceded by न्,—this न not being added to the root owing to its having an indicatory इ (VII. 1. 58)—the न् is elided when an affix having an indicatory क् or ङ् follows.

Thus from स्रन्स् and ध्वन्स् are formed स्रस्तः and ध्वस्तः with क्त, स्रस्यते, ध्वस्यते with यक्, सनीस्रस्यते, दनीध्वस्यते with यङ् the नी being added by VII. 4. 84. But नन्द्यते and नानन्द्यते, the न् is not elided, the root being written in the Dhâtupâṭha as टुणदि समृद्धौ, and न being added by VII. 1. 58. Why do we say ending in a consonant? Observe नीयते, नेनीयते from नी which has a penultimate nasal, but ends in a vowel. Why do we say 'penultimate'? Observe नह्यते, नानह्यते ॥ Why do we say having an indicatory क or ङ? Observe स्रंसनं, ध्वंसनं with ल्युट् ॥

Vârt:—The roots लङ्ग (लगि) and कम्प् (कपि) are exceptions, where meaning 'to feel pain or difficulty' and 'a disease of the body'. These, though exhibited in the Dhâtupaṭha with an indicatory इ, are treated as exceptions to the rule of अनिदित्: thus विलगितः and विकपितः, when not having the above meanings, we have विलङ्गितं and विकम्पितं ॥

Vârt:—The causative of the root रञ्ज, loses its nasal when meaning 'to hunt deer': as, रजयति मृगान् 'he hunts the deer', but रञ्जयति वस्त्राणि 'he colors the clothes'.

Vârt:—रञ्ज loses its nasal before the affix घिनुण्, as रागी ॥

Vârt:—The words रजकः, रजनम्, and रजः are formed from रञ्ज by the elision of the nasal.

दंशसञ्जस्वञ्जां शपि ॥ २५ ॥ पदानि ॥ दंश, सञ्ज, स्वञ्जाम्, शपि ॥

वृत्तिः ॥ दंश सञ्ज ष्वञ्ज इत्येतेषामङ्गानां शपि परत उपधाया नकारस्य लोपो भवति ॥

25. The nasal of दंश्, संज् and स्वञ्ज् is elided before the vikaraṇa शप् of the roots of the 1st class.

Thus दशति, सजति and परिष्वजते for the change of the स् of स्वञ्ज् to ष see VIII. 3. 65

रञ्जेश्च ॥ २६ ॥ पदानि ॥ रञ्जेः, च, ॥

वृत्तिः ॥ रञ्जेश्च शपि परत उपधाया नकारस्य लोपो भवति ॥

26. The nasal of रञ्ज is also elided before शप् ॥

As रजति, रजतः, रजन्ति ॥ The separation of this from the preceding is for the sake of the subsequent sûtras in which the anuvṛiti of rañj only runs and not of dañs &c.

घञि च भावकरणयोः ॥ २७ ॥ पदानि ॥ घञि, च, भावकरणयोः ॥

वृत्तिः ॥ भावकरणवाचिनि घञि परतो रञ्जेरुपधाया नकारस्य लोपो भवति ॥

27. The penultimate nasal of रञ्ज् is elided before घञ्, when the word formed with it expresses a state or an instrument.

Thus रागः 'passion, color, or the coloring stuff'. Thus आश्चर्यो रागः, विचित्र रागः denote भाव, while रज्यतेऽनेनेति रागः denotes instrument. The घञ् is added by III. 3. 121; and च् changed to क् by VII. 3. 52. But रङ्गः = रजन्ति तस्मिन् 'a theatre;

स्यदो जवे ॥ २८ ॥ स्यदः, जवे, ॥

वृत्तिः ॥ जवे ऽभिधेये स्यद इति घञि निपात्यते । स्यन्देर्नलोपो वृद्ध्यभावश्च ॥

28. The word स्यद is formed by घञ् in the sense of 'speed'.

This word is derived from स्यन्द, the nasal is elided, and the Vriddhi prohibited irregularly. Though the ârdhadhâtuka affix घञ् causes here the elision of a portion of the root, viz of न् of स्यन्द्, yet rule I. 1. 4 does not apply here. That rule prohibits Guṇa and Vṛiddhi, only in case of इक् vowels, here the Vṛiddhi is prevented with regard to अ ॥ The prevention of this Vṛiddhi is irregular and not governed by I. 1. 4. Thus गोस्यदः' अश्वस्यदः meaning "cow-speed," "horse-speed." but तैलस्यन्दः, and घृतस्यन्दः meaning "dripping of oil or ghee".

अवोदैधौद्मप्रश्रथहिमश्रथाः ॥२९॥ पदानि ॥ अवोद,एध,ओद्म,प्रश्रथ,हिमश्रथाः

वृत्तिः ॥ अवोद एध ओद्मप्रश्रथ हिमश्रथ इत्येते निपात्यन्ते ।

29. अवोद, एध, ओद्म, प्रश्रथ, and हिमश्रथ are irregularly formed by the elision of न ॥

Thus उन्द्—अव + उन्द् + घञ् = अवोदः ; इन्ध् + घञ् = एधः, the guṇa is irregular, for I. 1. 4 applied here, and prevented guṇa. उन्द् + मन् = ओद्म (Uṇadi मन्). प्र + श्रन्थ + घञ् = प्रश्रथः (The want of Vṛiddhi is the irregularity). So also हिमश्रथः ॥

नाञ्चेः पूजायाम् ॥ ३० ॥ पदानि ॥ न, अञ्चेः, पूजायाम्, ॥

वृत्तिः ॥ अञ्चेः पूजायामर्थे नकारस्य लोपो न भवति ॥

30. The nasal of अञ्च is not elided when the meaning is to honor.

Thus अञ्चिता अस्य गुरवः, अञ्चितमिव शिरो वहति ॥ The इट् augment is added by VII. 2. 53. When the sense is not that of 'honoring', we have उदक्तमुदकं कूपात् "the water was *drawn* from the well." Here the इट् is prohibited by VII. 2. 15.

क्त्वि स्कन्दिस्यन्दोः ॥ ३१ ॥ पदानि ॥ क्त्वि, स्कन्दि, स्यन्दोः, (न लोपः) ॥

वृत्तिः ॥ क्त्वाप्रत्यये परतः स्कन्द स्यन्द इत्येतयोर्नकारलोपो न भवति ॥

31. स्कन्द् and स्यन्द retain their nasal before the affix क्त्व ॥

Thus स्कन्त्वा, and स्यन्दित्वा or स्यन्त्वा, the इट् being added when स्यन्द is considered as having an indicatory ऊ in the dhatupâtha. When इट् is added, क्त्वा is no longer कित् by virtue of the rule I. 2. 18, and elision would not take place, for no rule of elision would apply in that case.

जान्तनशां विभाषा ॥ ३२ ॥ पदानि ॥ जान्त, नशाम्, विभाषा (न लोपः) ॥

वृत्तिः ॥ जान्तानामङ्गानां नशेश्च क्त्वाप्रत्यये परतो विभाषा नकारलोपो न भवति ॥

32. The nasal may be optionally elided before क्त्वा in a root ending in ज् and in नश् ॥

Thus रङ्क्त्वा or रक्त्वा, भङ्क्त्वा or भक्त्वा, नष्ट्वा or नंष्ट्वा See ॥ VII. 1. 60 for the augment न् in नश् ॥ When इट् comes, we have नशित्वा ॥

भञ्जेश्च चिणि ॥ ३३ ॥ पदानि ॥ भञ्जेः, च, चिणि, (विभाषा न लोपः) ॥

वृत्तिः ॥ भञ्जेश्च चिणि परतो विभाषा नकारलोपो भवति ॥

33. The nasal may be optionally elided in भञ्ज before the third person Passive of the Aorist in चिण् (इ)

Thus अभाजि or अभञ्जि ॥ This is an aprâpta vibhâshâ, and teaches for the first time the elision of न in a certain contingency.

शास इदङ्हलोः ॥ ३४ ॥ पदानि ॥ शासः, इत्, अङ्, हलोः, (क्ङिति) ॥

वृत्तिः ॥ शास उपधाया इकारादेशो भवति अङि परतो हलादौ च क्ङिति ॥

वार्त्तिकम् ॥ क्वौ च शास इत्वं भवतीति वक्तव्यम् ॥ वा० ॥ क्विप् प्रत्यये तस्यापि भवतीति वक्तव्यम् ॥

34. Before the Aorist in अङ् and before an affix beginning with a consonant having an indicatory क् or ङ्, there is the substitution of इ for the vowel of शास् ॥

Thus अन्वाशिषत्, अन्वशिषताम् and अन्वशिषन्; so also शिष्टः (with क्त), शिष्टवान् (with क्तवतु), तौ शिष्टः वयं शिष्मः (with the tense-affixes तः and मः which are ङित् by I. 2. 4). The स is changed to ष by VIII. 3. 60. Why do we say 'before the affixes of अ Aorist and consonant affixes'? Observe शासति, शशासतु, शशासुः ॥

Vart:—There is the substitution of इ for the vowel of शास् before the affix क्वि ॥ As आर्यशीः = आर्यान् शास्ति ॥ So also मित्रशीः ॥ The form is thus evolved, शास् + क्वि = शिस् + ० = शिर + ० = शीः (the short इ being lengthened by VIII. 2. 76.

The root शास् is that root which takes अङ् aorist; namely the second Adâdi शास् (शासु अनुशिष्टौ), and not the Bhvâdi and the first Adâdi शास (आङ् शासु इच्छायाम्) ॥ Therefore not here आशास्ते, आशास्यमानः ॥

Vârt:—But before क्विप्, this शास् also is changed, as आशीः, आशिषौ, आशिषः॥ Or this is an irregular form indicated by the author in the word क्षियाशीः used in VIII. 2. 104.

शा हौ ॥ ३५ ॥ पदानि ॥ शा, हौ, ॥

वृत्तिः ॥ शासो हौ परतः शा इत्ययमादेशो भवति ॥

35. Before the Imperative affix हि, शा is substituted for शास् ॥

Thus अनुशाधि, प्रशाधि ॥ The हि is changed to धि by VI. 4. 101. See VI 4. 22. The anuvritti of उपधायाः is not here; so शा is substituted in the room of the full word शास् and not only for the penultimate vowel of शास् ॥ The anuvritti of कित् and ङित् also is not here. Therefore, when this हि is treated as पित् (III. 4. 88), then too the substitution takes place, though a पित् Sârvadhâtuka is not ङित् (I. 2. 4). Thus शाधि is also found in the Vedas as having acute on the first syllable, which can only be when धि is पित् and conseqaently anudâtta (III. 1. 4)

हन्तेर्जः ॥ ३६ ॥ पदानि ॥ हन्तेः, जः, (हौ) ॥

वृत्तिः ॥ हन्तेर्धातोर्ज इत्ययमादेशो भवति हौ परतः ॥

36. ज is substituted for हन् before हि ॥

Thus जहि शत्रून् ॥

अनुदात्तोपदेशवनतितनोत्यादीनामनुनासिकलोपो झलि क्ङिति ॥ ३७ ॥ पदानि ॥ अनुदात्तोपदेश, वनति, तनोत्यादीनाम्, अनुनासिक लोपः, झलि, क्ङिति ॥

वृत्तिः ॥ अनुदात्तोपदेशानामङ्गानां वनतेस्तनोत्यादीनां चानुनासिकलोपो भवति झलादौ क्ङिति प्रत्यये परतः ॥

37. The final nasal of those roots which in the Dhâtupâṭha have an unaccented root-vowel, as well as of वन and तन &c, is elided before an affix beginning with a consonant (except a semi-vowel or nasal), when these have an indicatory क् or ङ् ॥

Thus यमु gives us यत्वा (with क्त्वा), यतः (with क्त), यतवान् (with क्तवतु), यतिः (with क्तिन्), Similarly रमु gives us रत्वा, रतः, रतवान्, रतिः ॥ यम्, रम्, नम्, गम्, हन् and मन् which end in a nasal are to be considered as unaccented roots, though taught as accented in the Dhâtupâtha. So also of वन्: i. e. वतिः with क्तिन्; with क्तिच् the nasal is not elided as वन्ति; (VI. 4. 39): and before other jhalâdi affixes व, retains न् as all those affixes take the augment इट् ॥ The तनादि roots belong to the eighth class. Thus ततः, ततवान्. The Tanâdi roots are ten in number, तन् सन्, क्षण्, क्षिण्, ऋण्, तृण, घृण्, वन्, मन् and कृञ् ॥ Of these सन् takes long आ also (VI. 4. 45). क्षण्—क्षतः, क्षतवान्, ऋण्—ऋतः, ऋतवान्; तृण्—तृतः, तृतवान्; घृण्—घृतः घृतवान्; वन्—वतः, वतवान्; मन्—मतः, मतवान् ॥

Why do we say before a ङित् affix? Observe अतत, अतथाः (I. 2. 11 these affixes are ङित्) So also not in शान्तः, शान्तवान्, तान्तः, तान्तवान्, दान्तः, दान्तवान्, not being anudâtta in the Dhâtupâṭha. If the root does not end in a nasal, the rule does not apply, as in पक्वः, पक्ववान् ॥ If the affix does not begin with a *jhal* consonant, the rule does not apply: as गम्यते, रम्यते ॥ If the affix is not कित् or ङित् the rule does not apply: as, यन्ता, यन्तव्यम् ॥ Why do we say "anudâtta by *upadesa*"? So that the rule may apply to गम् root, as गतिः, but not to शम्, as शान्तः शान्तवान् ॥ For गतिः is formed by क्तिन् affix and is accented with udâtta on the first, but it is a secondary udâtta and not of upadeśa or dhâtupâṭha, and does not prevent the elision of म् of गम् ॥ Similarly शम् is udâtta-upadesa though in शान्त it has become अनुदात्तः ॥ The former though taught in the Dhâtupâṭha as udâtta, has been specifically mentioned above as anudâtta, and शम् is taught as udatta in the Dhâtupâṭha, and no where *else* taught as anudâtta.

वा ल्यपि ॥ ३८ ॥ पदानि ॥ वा, ल्यपि, ॥

वृत्तिः ॥ ल्यपि परतोऽनुदात्तोपदेशवनतितनोत्यादीनामनुनासिकलोपो वा भवति ॥

38. The nasal of the above roots (i. e. anudâtta ending in a nasal, and वन and तनादि) is optionally elided before the Absolutive affix ल्यप् ॥

This is a vyavasthita-vibhâshâ. The option applies to roots ending in म्. In the case of roots ending in other nasals, the elision is compulsory. Thus प्रयत्य or प्रयम्य, प्ररत्य or प्ररम्य, प्रणत्य or प्रणम्य, आगत्य आगम्य, but no option in आहत्य, प्रमत्य, प्रवत्य, प्रक्षत्य ॥

नं क्तिचि दीर्घश्च ॥ ३९ ॥ पदानि ॥ न, क्तिचि, दीर्घः, च ॥

वृत्तिः ॥ क्तिचि परतो ऽनुदात्तोपदेशादीनामनुनासिकलोपो दीर्घश्च न भवति ।

39. Before the affix क्तिच्, the above roots neither drop their nasal nor lengthen their root-vowel.

The above roots i. e. anudâttopadeśa, ending in a nasal, and वन and तनादि, do not lose their nasal before क्तिच्. Thus यन्तिः, तन्तिः, वन्तिः ॥ The lengthening would have taken place by VI. 4. 15, when the nasal was not elided: that also is prohibited.

गमः क्वौ ॥ ४० ॥ पदानि ॥ गमः, क्वौ, (अनुनासिकलोपः) ॥

वृत्तिः ॥ अनुनासिकलोप इति वर्तते । गमः क्वौ परतो ऽनुनासिकलोपो भवति ।

वार्त्तिक म् ॥ गमादीनामिति वक्तव्यम् ॥ वा० ॥ ऊङ् च गमादीनामितिवक्तव्यम् ॥

40. The nasal of गम् is always elided before क्वि ॥

Thus अङ्गगत्, कलिङ्गगत्, अध्वगतो हरयः ॥ The त् is added by VI. 1. 71.

Vârt:—It should be stated of गम् and the rest. The elision takes place here also संयत्, परीतत् ॥

Vârt:—The nasal of गम् &c. is elided before ऊङ्: as, अग्रेगूः, अग्रेभूः ॥

विड्वनोरनुनासिकस्यात् ॥ ४१ ॥ पदानि ॥ विट्-वनोः, अनुनासिकस्य आत् ॥

वृत्तिः ॥ विटि वनो च प्रत्यये परतो ऽनुनासिकान्तस्याङ्गस्याकार आदेशो भवति ॥

41. A stem ending in a nasal, and followed by the affix विट् or वन्, always substitutes long आ for its nasal.

Thus अब्जाः, गोजाः, ऋतजाः, अद्रिजाः, गोषाः (e. g. गोषा इन्द्रोनृषा असि Rig V.), कूपखाः, शतखाः, सहस्रखाः, दधिक्राः, अग्रेगा उन्नेतृणाम् ॥ The affix विट् (which is totally elided) is added under III. 2. 67. The स of सन् is changed to ष by VIII. 3. 108. in गोषा ॥ With the affix वन् we have the following:—विजावा, अग्रेजावा (III. 2. 75). The repetition of the word अनुनासिक in this sûtra shows that the limitation of anudâttopadeśa &c. which applied to the अनुनासिक of sûtra VI. 4. 37 does not apply here.

जनसनखनां सञ्झलोः ॥ ४२ ॥ पदानि ॥ जन-सन-खनाम् सन्-झलोः, (आत्) ॥

वृत्तिः ॥ जन सन खन इत्येतेषामङ्गानां सनि झलादौ क्ङिति झलादौ प्रत्यय परत आकार आदेशो भवति ।

42. The long आ is substituted for the final of जन्, सन् and खन् before the consonant beginning Desiderative affix सन्, and before any other affix beginning with a jhal consonant, which has an indicatory क् or ङ् ॥

Thus जातः, जातवान्, जातिः, सातः, सातवान्, सातिः, सिषासति; खातः, खातवान्, खातिः॥ In जन् and खन् the Desiderative does not begin with a consonant, but takes the augment इट्, the न् is not therefore elided, as जिजनिषति, चिखनिषति॥ In the case of the root सन्, the Desiderative takes इ, so we have two forms सिषासति and सिसनिषति (VII. 2. 49). The Desiderative has, therefore, been mentioned in the aphorism, only for the sake of the root सन्॥

If the phrase सन्झलोः be taken to mean 'the Desiderative beginning with a consonant', then we should read the anuvṛitti of झलि क्ङिति from the preceding sûtras, to complete the sense of this; and if the phrase means "when the Desiderative of a jhalâdi affix follows", then we should qualify the word Desiderative by the word jhal from the preceding sûtras. Or we may divide the sûtra into two (1) Before a कित् or ङित् jhalâdi affix long आ is the substitute of the न् of 'jan', 'san' and 'khan'. (2) And so is the case, when the Desiderative affix follows, not having the augment इ, for then also the न् of 'jan', 'san' and 'khan' is replaced by long आ॥

The न् of the root सन् would have required elision by VI. 4. 37, because this verb belongs to Tanâdi class, still the आ substitution taught in this sûtra takes place, by preference, on the maxim of विप्रतिषेधे परं कार्यम् (I. 4. 2). In fact, though in this section of asiddha (VI. 4. 22) one rule is considered as asiddha for the purposes of the operations of another rule, yet one rule *supersedes* another by the maxim of vipratisedha. That that maxim applies in this section also, is to be inferred from the employment of the term हल् in VI. 4. 66, which supersedes the lopa of आ taught in VI. 4. 64, and substitutes instead the long ई॥

ये विभाषा ॥ ४३ ॥ पदानि ॥ ये, विभाषा, (जनसनखनाम् आत्) ॥

वृत्तिः ॥ यकारादौ क्ङिति प्रत्यये परतो जनसनखनामाकार आदेशो भवति विभाषा ।

43. There is optionally the substitution of long आ for the finals of जन्, सन् and खन् before an affix beginning with य and marked with an indicatory क् or ङ्॥

Thus जायते or जन्यते (with यक्) जाजायते or जञ्जन्यते (with यङ्)। So also सायते or सन्यते, सासायते, or संसन्यते, खायते, or खन्यते, चाखायते or चङ्खन्यते॥ Before the vikaraṇa श्यन् of the Fourth class, which is ङित् according to I. 2. 4; the जा is *always* substituted for जन् by VII. 3. 79. No option is allowed there.

तनोतेर्यकि ॥ ४४ ॥ पदानि ॥ तेनोतेः, यकि, (विभाषा आत्) ॥

वृत्तिः ॥ तेनोतेर्यकि परतो विभाषा आकार आदेशो भवति ।

44. The long आ may be optionally substituted for the final of तन् before the Passive characteristic यक्॥

Thus तायते or तन्यते; but no option is allowed in तन्तन्यते with यङ्॥

सनः क्तिचि लोपश्चास्यान्यतरस्याम् ॥ ४५ ॥ पदानि ॥ सनः, क्तिचि, लोपः, च, अस्य, अन्यतरस्याम्, ॥

वृत्तिः ॥ सनोतेरङ्गस्य क्तिचि प्रत्यये परत आकार आदेशो भवति लोपश्चास्यान्यतरस्याम् ।

45. The long आ is optionally substituted for the final of सन् before the affix क्तिच्; and there is also elision optionally of the Nasal.

Thus we have three forms सातिः, सन्तिः and सतिः ॥ The word अन्यतरस्याम् 'optionally' has been employed in the sûtra for the sake of clearness only; for the विभाषा of VI. 4. 43 could have been read into it by annvṛitti. Lest any one should doubt, that the annvṛitti of विभाषा had ceased with the last aphorism, this word अन्यतरस्याम् is employed here.

आर्द्धधातुके ॥ ४६ ॥ पदानि ॥ आर्द्धधातु के ।

वृत्तिः ॥ आर्द्धधातुकइत्यधिकारो न ल्यपीति प्रागेतस्माद्यदित ऊर्ध्वमनुक्रमिष्याम आर्द्धधातुकइत्येवं तद्वेदितव्यम् ।

46. From this upto VI. 4. 68 inclusive, is always to be supplied "before an affix called ârdhadhâtuka (III. 4. 114 &c)."

This is an adhikâra sûtra and extends upto VI. 4. 69 (exclusive). In all the sûtras upto VI. 4. 68 should be supplied the phrase "before an affix called ârdhadhâtuka". Thus VI. 4. 48 teaches "the अ standing at the end of a verbal stem is elided". To complete the sense we should add: "before an ardhadhâtuka affix". Thus the final अ of the verbal stem चिकीर्ष is elided before the ârdhâtuka affix तृ, as चिकीर्षितृ, जिहीर्षितृ, but the final अ is not elided before a sârvadhatuka affix, as the अ of भव in भवति, भवतः ॥ The *luk*-elision of शप् after roots of भवादि class, implies that there is never *lopa* of शप् ॥

The following purposes are served by this sûtra, i. e. an ârdhâtuka affix causes the following special changes (1) अतोलोपः— The elision of अ of a stem, as shown above, in चिकीर्षिता, चिकीर्षितुम्, (2) यलोपश्च, The elision of य by VI. 4. 49, 50: as बेभिदिता, बेभिदितुम्, बेभिदितव्यम् from बेभिद्य the Intensive stem. Before Sârvadhâtuka, we have बेभिद्यते, चेच्छिद्यते ॥ (3) णिलोपश्च प्रयोजनम्, The elision of णि by VI. 4. 51, as कारणा हारणा पाच्यते (पाचि + यक् + ते = पाच् + य + ते), याज्यते ॥ In Śârvadhâtuka, पाचयति, याजयति, कारयति, हारयति ॥ (4) आल्लोपः, the elision of आ, VI. 4. 64— as पपतुः, पपुः, ववतुः वबुः, In Sârvadhâtuka, यान्ति, वान्ति (5) ईत्वम्— The substitntion of long ई for आ in some roots, VI. 4. 65 as धीयते, दीयते; in Sârvadhâtuka अदाताम्, अधाताम् (6) एत्वम्—The substitution of ए for आ, VI. 4. 68; as स्नेयात्, ग्लेयात्; in Sârvadhâtuka, स्नायात्, ग्लायात् ॥ This is confined to the Precative (âsirlin). (7) चिण्वद्भावश्च सीयुटि, the treatment of the Precative like Aorist Passive in चिण्, by VI. 4. 62. as कारिषीष्ट, हारिषीष्ट ॥ In Sârvadhâtuka, क्रियेत, ह्रियेत ॥

Kâsikâ:—अतो लोपो यलोपश्च णिलोपश्च प्रयोजनम् ।
आल्लोप ईत्वमेत्वं च चिण्वद्भावश्च सीयुटि ॥

भ्रस्जो रोपधयोरमन्यतरस्याम् ॥ ४७ ॥ पदानि । भ्रस्जः, र-उपधयोः, रम्, अन्यतरस्याम् ॥

वृत्तिः ॥ भ्रस्जो रेफस्योपधायाश्च रमन्यतरस्यां भवति ।

47. In the room of the ऋ and the penultimate letter स् of the root भ्रस्ज, there is optionally the substitute रम्, when an ârdhadhâtuka affix follows.

The ऋ and स् cease to exist and र takes their place. The substitute having an indicatory म् comes after the final vowel (I. 1. 49). Thus भ्रस्ज+तृ= भर्ज+तृ= भर्ष्टा the ज being changed to ष by VIII. 2. 36, and त to ट by VIII. 4. 41. The other form will be भ्रष्टा; so also भ्रष्टुम् and भर्ष्टुम्, भ्रष्टव्यम् and भर्ष्टव्यम्, भ्रज्जनम् or भर्ज्जनम् ॥ But भृष्टः and भृष्टवान् by VI. 1. 16, in spite of this rule. The word उपदेश (VI. 4. 37). is understood here also. The rule therefore applies to the simple root bhrasj as originally taught in the Dhatupâṭha, and not to any Derivative root from it. As the Intensive (यङ्) is बरीभृज्यते ॥

अतो लोपः ॥ ४८ ॥ पदानि ॥ अतः, लोपः, (आर्द्धधातुके) ॥

वृत्तिः ॥ अकारान्तस्यार्द्धधातुके लोपो भवति ।

वार्त्तिकम् ॥ वृद्धिदीर्घाभ्यामतो लोपः पूर्वविप्रतिषेधेन ॥

48. The अ standing at the end of a stem is elided before an ârdhadhâtuka affix.

Thus चिकीर्षिता, चिकीर्षितुम्, and चिकीर्षितव्यम्, from the Desiderative stem चिकीर्ष ॥ So also धिनुतः and कृणुतः from the roots धिन्व् and कृण्व् thus, धिन्व्+उ (III. 1. 80)=धिन्+अ+उ (III, 1. 80)=धिन्+उ (अ being elided before the ârdhâtuka उ)=धिनु, the 3rd Personal dual of it is धिनुतः ॥ The addition of अ by III. 1. 80 and its subsequent elision by the present sûtra, may appear a redundancy, but the elided अ being sthânivat, prevents guṇa of धि ॥ So also कृणुतः ॥ See sûtra III. 1. 80. Why do we say "the अ is elided'? Observe चेता, स्तोता here इ and उ have not been elided. Why do we say "अतः with a त"? The long आ will not be elided: as याता, वाता ॥ Why do we say 'before an Ardhadhâtuka'? Before a Sârvadhâtuka there will be no elision of अ nor before a Taddhita: as वृक्षत्वम् and वृक्षता ॥

Vârt:—The elision of such अ takes place even to the supersession of the subsequent rules relating to Vṛiddhi and lengthening. As चिकीर्षकः, जिहीर्षकः, चिकीर्ष्यते and जिहीर्ष्यते ॥

यस्य हलः ॥ ४९ ॥ पदानि ॥ यस्य, हलः ॥

वृत्तिः ॥ हल उत्तरस्य यशब्दस्यार्द्धधातुके लोपो भवति ।

49. When a consonant precedes the final य in a verbal stem, this य is elided also before an ârdhadhâtuka affix.

Thus बेभिदिता, बेभिदितुम्, बेभिदितव्यम् from the Intensive stem बेभिद्य ॥ In the sûtra यस्य is given, which is the Genitive singular of य namely of the letters य् अ ॥ By the rule of अलोऽन्त्यस्य (I. 1. 52), the अ of य ought to be elided and not य्; but that rule is evidently inapplicable here, since the elision of अ would have taken place by the preceding rule: the present rule therefore teaches the elision of य (ya). Or the word हलः may be considered as in the ablative case, and then by I. 1. 54, the first letter would be elided namely य ॥ Why have we taken [the two letters (संघात) conjointly viz.] य and not य्? Observe ईर्ष्यिता, मव्यिता, शुच्यिता from the simple *roots* ईर्ष्य, मव्य्, and शुच्य् ॥ Here य् not being followed by अ, is not elided (see Bhvadi 541—546). Why do we say 'when preceded by a consonant?' Observe लोलूयिता, पोपूयिता ॥

क्यस्य विभाषा ॥ ५० ॥ पदानि ॥ क्यस्य, विभाषा, (आर्द्धधातुके) ॥

वृत्तिः ॥ क्यस्य हल उत्तरस्य विभाषा लोपो भवति आर्द्धधातुके ।

50. The elision of य of the Denominative stem (क्य) is optional, when preceded by a consonant and followed by an ârdhadhâtuka affix.

The क्य denotes the affixes क्यच् and क्यङ् ॥ Thus समिध्यिता or समिधिता, दृषद्यिता or दृषदिता meaning समिधमात्मन इच्छति or समिध इवाचरति &c.

णेरनिटि ॥ ५१ ॥ पदानि ॥ णेः, अनिटि, (आर्द्धधातुके) ॥

वृत्तिः ॥ अनिडादावार्द्धधातुके णेर्लोपो भवति ।

51. The इ of the verbal stem formed with the affix णि, is elided before an ârdhadhâtuka affix which does not take the augment इट् ॥

This debars इयङ्, the semi-vowel य, the guṇa, Vṛiddhi and the long substitutions. Thus अततक्षत्, अररक्षत्, आटिटत्, आशिशत्, कारणा, हारणा, कारकः, हारकः, कार्यते, हार्यते and ज्ञीप्सति (see VII. 4. 1 for the shortening of the stem of the Aorists in these). Why do we say 'not having the augment इट्?' Observe कारयिता and हारयिता ॥

निष्ठायां सेटि ॥ ५२ ॥ पदानि ॥ निष्ठायाम्, सेटि ॥

वृत्तिः ॥ निष्ठायां सेटि परतो णेर्लोपो भवति ।

52. The affix णि is elided before the affixes क्त and क्तवतु when these take the augment इट् ॥

Thus कारितम्, हारितम्, गणितम्, लक्षितम् ॥ Why do we say "before an ardhadhâtuka affix having the augment इट्"? Observe संज्ञपितः पशुः ॥ This is the part participle of the causative, the इ being the sign of the causative. By VII. 2. 15 read with VII. 2. 49, ज्ञप् is a root which takes no इट् augment in the Nishṭhâ. It may be objected that VII. 2. 15 preventing इट् augment applies to verbs of one syllable (VII. 2. 10), and the causative ज्ञपि being of two syllables will always have इट् in the Nishṭhâ, and so it is useless to use the word सेटि in the sûtra. The word सेटि in the sûtra fixes the *time* when the elision of णि should take place. Namely, *first* there should be added the augment इट् and *then*, there should take place the elision of णि ॥ Otherwise we shall have this difficulty कारि + त, here let us elide the णि *first*: and we get कार् + त, now we cannot add इट् to त, for कार् being a verb of one syllable will not take इट् by VII. 2. 10. Therefore, the reverse process must be adopted. We must elide इट् *first*. For ज्ञपितः see also VII. 2. 27.

जनिता मन्त्रे ॥ ५३ ॥ पदानि ॥ जनिता, मन्त्रे ॥

वृत्तिः ॥ जनितेति मन्त्रविषये इडादौ णिलोपो निपात्यते ।

53. In a Mantra, the word जनिता is formed irregularly by the elision of णि before the affix तृ with the augment इट् ॥

Thus यो नः पिता जनिता ॥ Otherwise जनयिता in secular literature. It is an exception to VI. 4. 51.

शमिता यज्ञे ॥ ५४ ॥ पदानि ॥ शमिता, यज्ञे ॥

वृत्तिः ॥ यज्ञकर्म्मणि शमितेति इडादौ णिलोपो निपात्यते ।

54. शमिता is formed irregularly by the elision of णि before an इट् augmented affix, when meaning a sacrificial act.

Thus शृतं हविः शमितः ॥ It is formed by शमु and is in the Vocative case. Why do we say 'when referring to a sacrificial act'? See शृतं हविः शमयितः ॥ See Śatpatha Br. III. 8. 3, 4 and 5.

अयामन्ताल्वाय्येत्न्विष्णुषु ॥ ५५ ॥ पदानि ॥ अय, आम्-अन्त-आलु-आय्य-इत्नु-इष्णुषु, ॥

वृत्तिः ॥ आम् अन्त आलु आय्य इत्नु इष्णु इत्येतेषु परतो णेरयादेशो भवति ।

55. अय् is substituted for the इ of णि, before the affixes आम्, अन्त, आलु, आय्य, इत्नु, and इष्णु ॥

Thus कारयां चकार, हारयां चकार, गण्डयन्तः, मण्डयन्तः (formed by the Uṇâdi affix झच्, झ = अन्त, added to the roots गंड and मंड) आलु । स्पृहयालुः । आय्य, स्पृहयाय्यः, गृहयाय्यः ॥ इत्नुः—स्तनयित्नुः ॥ इष्णुः—पोषयिष्णुः ॥ Thus sûtra could have been well dispensed with; for the इ of णि would take guṇa ए which will be changed to अय by the rules of Sandhi, be fore these affixes. This substitution of अय् for इ is for the sake of the subsequent sûtra however, because there इ could not be changed to अय by any sandhi-rules.

ल्यपि लघुपूर्वात् ॥ ५६ ॥ पदानि ॥ ल्यपि, लघु पूर्वात (णेः अय ॥

वृत्तिः ॥ ल्यपि परतो लघुपूर्वादुत्तरस्य णेरयादेशो भवति ।

56. अय् is substituted for the इ of णि, before the Absolutive affix ल्यप्, when the vowel preceding the इ is light.

Thus प्रशमय्य गतः, संदमय्य गतः, प्रबेभिदय्य, प्रगणय्य ॥ But प्रपात्य गतः the vowel preceding the इ being long. Here VI. 4. 51 applies. The shortening, the elision of य and the elision of अ should not be considered as asiddha, as their place of operation is not the same. Thus शम् + णिच् = शामि ; this आ is shortened by VI. 4. 92, and we have शमि ॥ This shortening is not to be considered as asiddha, for if asiddha, there being no laghu pûrva, the present rule would not apply. Similarly बेभिद्य is the Intensive root, its य is elided by VI. 4. 49, this elision is not considered as asiddha, if it were asiddha, the इ of भि would not be laghu. Similarly the elision of अ in गण which is a root which ends in अ, (see Dhâtupâṭha Churadi 309), is not considered as asiddha for similar reasons.

विभाषा, ऽऽपः ॥ ५७ ॥ पदानि ॥ विभाषा, आपः, ॥

वृत्तिः ॥ आप उत्तरस्य णेर्ल्यपि परतो विभाषा ऽयादेशो भवति ॥

57. अय् is optionally substituted for the इ of णि before the affix ल्यप्, after the verb आप् ॥

Thus प्रापय्य or प्राप्य गतः ॥ This however does not apply to the आप् substitute for इङ्, as अध्याप्य गतः (VI. 1. 48, VII. 3. 36). The maxim of Pratipadokta applies here.

युप्लुवोर्दीर्घश्छन्दसि ॥ ५८ ॥ पदानि ॥ यु-प्लुवोः, दीर्घः, छन्दसि, (ल्यपि) ॥

वृत्तिः ॥ यु प्लु इत्येतयोर्ल्यपि परतश्छन्दसि विषये दीर्घो भवति ॥

58. In यु and प्लु, long is substituted for उ, before ल्यप् in the Veda.

Thus दान्त्यनुपूर्वं वियूय ; यत्रा यो दक्षिणा परिप्लूय ॥ Why do we say 'in the Chhandas'? Observe संयुत्य, आप्लुत्य in the secular literature.

क्षियः ॥ ५९ ॥ पदानि ॥ क्षियः, (दीर्घः ल्यपि) ॥

वृत्तिः ॥ क्षियश्च दीर्घो भवति ल्यपि परतः ॥

59. A long is substituted for the इ of क्षि before ल्यप् ॥

As प्रक्षीय, उपक्षीय ॥

निष्ठायामण्यदर्थे ॥ ६० ॥ पदानि ॥ निष्ठायाम्. अ-ण्यदर्थे, (दीर्घः) ॥

वृत्तिः ॥ ण्यतः कृत्यस्यार्थो भावकर्म्मणी ताभ्यामन्यत्र या निष्ठा तस्यां क्षियो दीर्घो भवति ।

60. A long is substituted for the इ of क्षि before the Participle in क्त, when it has not the sense of the future Passive Participle in ण्यत् ॥

The force of ण्यत् is to denote condition (Impersonal action) and object (passive). When the Past Participle has not the force of ण्यत्, the vowel of क्षि is lengthened. Thus आक्षीणः, प्रक्षीणः, परिक्षीणः all used in the active sense. The क्त is added to the Intransitive क्षि to denote the agent (III. 4. 72). Thus प्रक्षीणमिदं देवदत्तस्य 'this is the spot where Devadatta perished'. Here क्त is used with a Locative force (III. 4. 76). Why do we say 'not having the force of

ण्यत् ?' Observe अक्षितमसिमक्षेत्राः ॥ Here च is added with the force of condition, and akshitam means 'imperishable'. The vowel not being lengthened the त is not changed to न (VIII. 2. 46).

वा ऽऽक्रोशदैन्ययोः ॥ ६१ ॥ पदानि ॥ वा, आक्रोश-दैन्ययोः (क्षियः दीर्घः विभाषा)

वृत्ति ॥ आक्रोश गम्यमाने दैन्ये च क्षियो निष्ठायामण्यदर्थे वा दीर्घो भवति ॥

61. The long is optionally substituted, for the इ of क्षि, before the Past Participle क्त, not having the sense of the Future Passive Participle ण्यत्, when the word means 'imprecation' or 'a miserable plight'.

Thus क्षितायुरेधि or क्षीणायुरेधि, क्षितकः or क्षीणकः, क्षितोयं तपस्वी, क्षीणोऽयं तपस्वी ॥ When not having the sense of cursing or miserable condition, we have one form only, as क्षीणमन्त्रः ॥

स्यसिच्सीयुट्तासिषु भावकर्म्मणोरुपदेश ऽज्झनग्रहदृशां वा चिण्वदिट् च ॥६२॥ पदानि ॥ स्य-सिच्-सीयुट्-तासि, भाव-कर्मणोः, उपदेशे, अच्-हन्-ग्रह-दृशाम्, वा, चिण्वत्, इट्, च, ॥

वृत्तिः ॥ स्य सिच् सीयुट् तासि इत्येतेषु भावकर्म्मविषयेषु परत उपदेशे ऽजन्तानामङ्गानां हन् ग्रह दृश इत्येतेषां च चिण्वत्कार्यं भवति वा । यदा चिण्वत् तदा इडागमो भवति ।

62. Before the affixes स्य (First Future and Conditional), सिच् (S-Aorist), सीयुट् (Benedictive) and तासि (the Priphrastic Future), when there are used in the Impersonal (भाव) and Passive (कर्म) Voices, (1) the verbal stems ending in a vowel in the Grammatical system of instruction (उपदेश), as well as the verbs (2) हन् (3) ग्रह् and (4) दृश् are treated optionally in the same way as in the third person of the Passive Aorist in चिण्, and when so treated, they have the augment इट् ॥

The augment इट् is, of course, added to the affixes स्य, सिच्, सीयुट् and तासि and not to the stem. What are the special objects served by this atideśa aphorism? They are given in the following verse :—

Kârikâ चिण्वद् वृद्धिर्युक् च हन्तेश्च घत्वं
दीर्घश्चोक्तो यो मितां वा चिणीति ।
इट् चासिद्धस्तेन मे लुप्यते णि-
र्नित्यश्चायं वलनिमित्तोऽविघाती ॥

First :—The Vṛiddhi takes place as in चिण् (VII. 2. 116, VII. 3. 34), secondly, there is the addition of युक् augment (VII. 3. 33), thirdly घ is substituted for the ह of हन् (VII. 3. 54), fourthly, the roots having indicatory म

(Bhuâdi 809 to 873) optionally lengthen their vowel (VI. 4. 93), and lastly the addition of the augment इट् being considered as asiddha or not to have taken effect by VI. 4. 22, the rule VI. 4. 51 applies and the causative affix णि is elided : and this इट् is added irrespective of the conditions and limitations of VII. 2. 35 &c.

(1) Roots ending in a vowel in the Dhâtûpâṭha with the affix स्य as, चि:—चायिष्यते or चेष्यते, अचायिष्यत or अचेष्यत ॥ So also with शा, as, शायिष्यते or शास्यते, अशायिष्यत or अशास्यत ॥

In शमि there are three forms, the two शामिष्यते or शमिष्यते, अशामिष्यत and अशमिष्यत being given by the elision of the causative ending by VI. 4. 51, in spite of the इट् augment which is considered as asiddha : and शम् being a root of मित् class, the अ is lengthened optionally by VI. 4. 93. The forms शमयिष्यते and अशमयिष्यत are given when not treated as चिण्, the causative is retained, the penultimate being shortened by VI. 4. 92. With the affix सिच्—अचायिषाताम् or अचेषाताम्, अशायिषाताम्, or अशिषाताम् and अशामिषाताम् or अशमिषाताम् ॥ With the affix सीयुट्—चायिषीष्ट or चेषीष्ट, शायिषीष्ट or शासीष्ट and शामिषीष्ट or शमिषीष्ट ॥ With the affix तासि :—चायिता or चेता, शायिता or शाता, शामिता or शमिता ॥ The चिण् aorist model of these roots is अचायि, अशायि (VII. 3. 33), and अशामि (VII. 3. 34) or अशमि (VI. 4. 93).

(2) हन् :—Fut. घानिष्यते or हनिष्यते; Con. अघानिष्यत or अहनिष्यत, Aor. अघानिषाताम् or अवाधिषाताम् and अहसाताम् (II. 4. 44); Ben घानिषीष्ट or वधिषीष्ट ; Per. Fut. घानिता or हन्ता ॥ The चिण् model is अघानि ॥

(3) ग्रह:—Fut. ग्राहिष्यते or ग्रहीष्यते Con. अग्राहिष्यत or अग्रहीष्यत; Aor. अग्राहिषाताम् or अग्रहीषाताम् (अग्रहिषाताम्) ? ; Ben. ग्राहिषीष्ट or (ग्रहिषीष्ट) ? ग्रहीषीष्ट, Per. Fut. ग्राहिता or ग्रहिता ॥ The lengthening of ही takes place by VII. 2. 37. The चिण् model is अग्राहि ॥

(4) दृश:— Fut. दर्शिष्यते or द्रक्ष्यते, Con. अदर्शिष्यत or अद्रक्ष्यत ; Aor. अदर्शिषाताम् or अदृक्षाताम् ; Ben दर्शिषीष्ट or दृक्षीष्ट; Per. Fut. दर्शिता or द्रष्टा (दर्ष्टा)? ॥ The चिण् model is अदर्शि ॥

Why do we say before स्य &c ? Observe चेतव्यम्, शातव्यम् ॥ Why in the Impersonal and Passive ? Observe चेष्यते and शास्यते ॥ Why in Upadeśa ? The rule applies to कारिष्यते also, though कार् (after guṇa change) ends in a consonant, but in its original ennuciation it ends with a vowel. The atideśa rule being enunciated with regard to stems (aṅga), prevents the substitutions of हन् and इङ् and इण् ॥ Thus हानिष्यते, घानिष्यते, एष्यते or आयिष्यते, अध्येष्यते or अध्यायिष्यते ॥ The substitutes वध or गा (II. 4. 42, 43, 45, 50) do not come according to the Kâśikâ, when these roots are treated as चिण् ॥

दीङो युडचि क्ङिति ॥ ६३ ॥ पदानि ॥ दीङः, युट्, अचि, क्ङिति ॥

वृत्तिः ॥ दीङो युडागमो भवति अजादौ क्ङिति प्रत्यये परतः ॥

63. युट् is the augment after दीङ्, of an ârdhadhâtuka affix beginning with a vowel and having an indicatory क् or ङ् ॥

Thus उपदिदीये, उपदिदीयाते and उपदिदीयिरे ॥ The Personal ending is कित् by I. 2. 5. दीङः being in the Ablative case, the augment is applied to the affix. This augment, however, is not to be considered as asiddha (VI. 4. 22) for the purposes of semi-vowel substitution under VI. 4. 82. If that substitution were allowed, the augment would become useless. Why before an affix having क् or ङ्? Observe उपदानम् ॥

आतो लोप इटि च ॥ ६४ ॥ पदानि ॥ आतः, लोपः, इटि, च, ॥

वृत्तिः ॥ इडादावार्द्धधातुके क्ङिति चाकारान्तस्याङ्गस्य लोपो भवति ॥

64. The final आ of a root is elided before an ârdhadhâtuka affix with the augment इट् as well as when it begins with a vowel and has an indicatory क् or ङ् ॥

Thus पपिथ and तस्थिथ ॥ Here the affix has the इट् augment. पपतुः, पपुः, तस्थतुः, तस्थुः ॥ Here the affixes are कित् by I. 2. 5 गोदः, कम्बलदः with the affix क (III. 2. 3). So also प्रदा (fem), प्रधा (fem) by अङ् III. 3. 106. Before Sârvadhâtuka affixes, we have यान्ति, वान्ति, व्यत्यरे and व्यत्यले ॥ The two latter are the Imperfect 1st Pers. Sing. Atm. of रा and ला with the affix इ (इट्). When it does not begin with a vowel, we have ग्लायते, दासीय ॥

ईद्यति ॥ ६५ ॥ पदानि ॥ ईत्, यति, ॥

वृत्तिः ॥ ईकार आदेशो भवति आकारान्तस्याङ्गस्य यति परतः ॥

65. The final आ of a stem is changed into ई before the Kṛit-affix यत् ॥

Thus देयम्, धेयम्, हेयम्, and स्तेयम् ॥ The Guṇa takes place according to VII. 3. 84.

घुमास्थागापाजहातिसां हलि ॥ ६६ ॥ पदानि ॥ घु, मा, स्था, गा, पा, जहाति साम्, हलि ॥

वृत्तिः ॥ घुसंज्ञकानामङ्गानां मा स्था गा पा जहाति सा इत्येतेषां हलादौ क्ङिति प्रत्यये परत ईकारादेशो भवति ॥

66. For the final of the roots of the form of दा and धा (घु), as well as for that of the roots मा, स्था, गा, पा, हा (जहाति) and सा (सो), there is substituted ई before an ârdhadhâtuka affix beginning with a consonant, which has an indicatory क् or ङ् ॥

Thus दीयते, धीयते with यक्, देदीयते, देधीयते with यङ् ॥ So also मीयते मेमीयते स्थीयते, तेष्ठीयते, गीयते, जेगीयते, अध्यगीष्ट, अध्यगीषाताम्, अध्यगीषत, पीयते, पेपीयते, हीयते, जेहीयते, अवसीयते, अवसेसीयते ॥

The पा 'to protect' of Adadi (47) is not meant here. be come the vikarana शप् is elided in roots of that class. Its form will be पायते. It is Bhvâdi पा 'to drink' that is taken here. So also हा-जिहीते is not to be taken here. Its form is हायते ॥

Why do we say 'before a consonant'? Observe ददतुः, ददुः ॥ Here had हल् not been used in the sûtra, the आ of दा would be replaced by ई by the present sûtra, even before a vowel-affix अतुः o उस्; for the lopa of आ taught in VI. 4. 64 is prevented by this *subsequent* sûtra teaching ई substitution. In fact, the employment of the word हल् in the aphorism is a jñâpaka that the rule of vipratishedha (I.4.2) applies in this section of asiddha (VI. 4. 22), and the lopa of आ is *superseded* by the present rule substituting ई instead. So also दाता and धाता before non-कित् and non ङित् affixes.

एर्लिङि ॥ ६७ ॥ पदानि ॥ एः, लिङि, ॥

वृत्तिः ॥ घुमास्थागापाजहातिसामङ्गानां लिङि परत एकारादेशो भवति ॥

67. ए is substituted for the आ of the above roots in the Benedictive mood Active.

Thus देयात्, मेयात्, धेयात्, स्थेयात्, गेयात्, पेयात् and अवसेयात् ॥ Before non-कित् and non-ङित् we have दासीष्ट and धासीष्ट ॥ By the word लिङ् is here meant the आशीर्लिङ् or the Precative mood; the Personal endings of which mood are ârdhadhâtuka by III. 4. 116. More-over by III. 4. 104 the Parasmaipada affixes only of the Benedictive are कित्, so the present rule does not apply to the Atmanepada affixes of the Precative.

वाऽन्यस्य संयोगादेः ॥ ६८ ॥ पदानि ॥ वा, अन्यस्य-संयोग, आदेः, (लिङि) (आतः) ॥

वृत्तिः ॥ घ्वादिभ्योऽन्यस्य संयोगादेराकारान्तस्य वा एकारादेशो भवति लिङि परतः ॥

68. For the final आ of any other root than those mentioned in VI. 4. 66, ए may optionally be substituted, in the Benedictive active, when the root begins with a conjunct consonant.

The स्था was the only root of VI. 4. 66, which could have been affected by this rule. It has been, however, specially exempted by the word अन्यस्य ॥ Thus ग्लेयात् or ग्लायात्, म्लेयात् or म्लायात्, but only स्थेयात् (VI. 4. 66), and यायात् (not commencing with a double consonant). The phrase किङति is understood here and therefore the rule applies to Parasmaepada affixes (III. 4. 104). Thus ग्लासीष्ट in Atmanepada. The root considered as an aṅga, should consist of a double consonant, therefore in निर्यायात् (from निर्+या), यै is not to be considered as a root having a double consonant, for र is no part of the aṅga, but of the preposition.

न ल्यपि ॥ ६९ ॥ पदानि ॥ न, ल्यपि, घुमास्थागापाजहातिसाम् ॥

वृत्तिः ॥ ल्यपि प्रत्यये परतो घुमास्थागापाजहातिसां यदुक्तं तन्न ॥

69. The ई substitution for आ under rule VI. 4. 66, does not apply when the absolutive affix ल्यप् follows घु मा, स्था, गा, पा, हा and सा ॥

Thus प्रदाय, प्रधाय, प्रमाय, प्रस्थाय, प्रगाय, प्रपाय, प्रहाय and अवसाय ॥ The affix ल्यप् as the substitute of क्त्वा, is a कित् affix by I. 1. 56.

मयतेरिदन्यतरस्याम् ॥ ७० ॥ पदानि ॥ मयतेः, इत्, अन्यतरस्याम्, (ल्यपि) ॥

वृत्तिः ॥ मयतेरिकारादेशो वा भवति ॥

70. इ may optionally be substituted for the आ of मा, (मयति) before ल्यप् ॥

Thus अपमित्य or अपमाय ॥

लुङ्लङ्लृङ्क्ष्वडुदात्तः ॥ ७१ ॥ पदानि ॥ लुङ्, लङ्, लृङ् क्षु, अट्, उदात्तः (अङ्गस्य) ॥

वृत्तिः ॥ लुङ् लङ् लृङ् इत्येतेषु परतोऽङ्गस्याडागमो भवति, उदात्तश्च स भवति ॥

71. अट् acutely accented is the augment of the verbal stem in the Aorist, Imperfect and the Conditional.

Thus अकार्षीत्, अहार्षीत्, अकरोत्, अहरत् and अकरिष्यत्, अहरिष्यत् ॥

आडजादीनाम् ॥७२॥ पदानि ॥ आट्, अच्-आदीनाम्, (उदात्तः) ॥

वृत्तिः ॥ आडागमो भवत्यजादीनां लुङ्लङ्लृङ्क्षु परत उदात्तश्च स भवति ॥

72. आट् acutely accented is the augment of a verbal stem beginning with a vowel, in the Aorist, Imperfect and the Conditional.

Thus ऐक्षिष्ट, ऐक्षत, ऐक्षिष्यत; औञ्जीत्, औब्जत्, औब्जिष्यत् ॥ ऐहिष्ट, ऐहत and ऐहिष्य औम्भीत्, औम्भत्, and औम्भिष्यत् ॥ The Vriddhi takes place by VI. 1. 90.

The Passive Imperfect (लङ्) of यज्, वप् and वह are ऐज्यत, औप्यत and औह्यत formed by आट् and not अट् ॥ First, the affixes of the Imperfect are added and then the Passive characteristic यक् is added to these roots, which causes the vocalisation of the semi-vowels, and we have इज्यत, उप्यत, and उह्यत stems (VI. I. 15). The stems having now assumed a form in which they begin with a vowel, take आट् ॥ The addition of tense-affixes being an antaranga operation precedes the addition of augment. After the affixes have been added, the vikaraṇa यक्, being nitya, is added and precedes in order the augment, the latter being so far anitya; after यक् addition the roots assume a form in which we can add आट् ॥ Why आट् is considered anitya depends on the following maxim :—शब्दान्तरस्य प्राप्नुवन् विधिरनित्यो भवति "when the word-form in reference to which a rule teaches something; after the taking effect of another rule that applies simultaneously would be different from what it was before that other rule had taken effect, then the former rule is not nitya."

छन्दस्यपि दृश्यते ॥ ७३ ॥ पदानि ॥ छन्दसि, अपि, दृश्यते, आट् ॥

वृत्तिः ॥ छन्दसि विषये आडागमो दृश्यते । यत्र हि विहितस्ततोऽन्यत्रापि दृश्यते ।

73. The आट् augment is found in the Veda also.

It is found there before the roots beginning with a vowel as well as before consonant roots. Thus आवः, आनक्, and आयुनक् ॥ आवः is the Aorist of वृञ्, the affix being elided by II. 4. 80. आनक् from नश् (II. 4. 80), and आयुनक् is the Imperfect of युञ् ॥

न माङ्योगे ॥ ७४ ॥ पदानि ॥ न, माङ्, योगे (लुङ् लङ् लृङ्क्षु) ॥

वृत्तिः ॥ माङ्योगे लुङ्लङ्लृङ्क्षु यदुक्तं तन्न भवति ॥

74. In connection with the prohibitive particle मा, the augment अट् or आट् is not added in the Aorist, Imperfect and the Conditional.

Thus मा भवान् कार्षीत्, मा भवान् हार्षीत्, मा स्म करोत्, मा स्म हरत्, मा भवानीहिष्टमा, भवानीक्षिष्ट, मा स्म भवानीहत, मा स्म भवानीक्षत ॥

बहुलं छन्दस्यमाङ्योगे ऽपि ॥ ७५ ॥ पदानि ॥ बहुलम्, छन्दसि, अ माङ योगे, अपि ॥

वृत्तिः ॥ छन्दसि विषये माङ्योगे ऽपि बहुलमडाटौ भवतः अमाङ्योगेपि न भवतः ॥

75. There is diversity in the Veda: the augment अट् or आट् is added even with मा, and sometimes not added even when there is no मा ॥

Thus in जनिष्ठा उग्रः (Rig X. 73. 1), काममूनयीत् (Rig I. 53. 3) and काममर्दयीत्; the augment is not added though there is no मा ॥ In मा वः क्षेत्रे परबीजान्यवाप्सुः, मा भिरित्थाः, मा आवः, the augment is not elided, though the particle मा is added.

इरयो रे ॥ ७६ ॥ पदानि ॥ इरयोः, रे, (बहुलंछन्दसि) ॥

वृत्तिः ॥ इरे इत्येतस्य छन्दसि विषये बहुलं रे इत्ययमादेशो भवति ॥

76. रे is diversely substituted for इरे in the Veda.

Thus कं स्विद्गर्भं प्रथमं दध्रे आपः (Rig X. 82. 5) या स्व परिदध्रे ॥ In दध्रे, the आ of धा is elided before the affix इरे by VI. 4. 64, the रे substitution being considered as asiddha (VI. 4. 22) for the purposes of the elision of आ ॥ Sometimes the substitution does not take place, as परमाया धियोग्निम्र्माणि चक्रिरे ॥ Here इट् augment is first added to रे after the सेट् roots and the affix thus becomes इरे, then रे is substituted again for this इरे by this sûtra, thus the affix is brought back to its original condition. To show this repetition—रे—इरे—रे the sûtra has exhibited the word इरयोः in the dual number.

अचि श्नुधातुभ्रुवां य्वोरियङुवङौ ॥ ७७ ॥ पदानि ॥ अचि, श्नु, धातु, भ्रुवाम्, य्वोः, इयङ्, उवङौ, ॥

वृत्तिः ॥ श्नुप्रत्ययान्तस्याङ्गस्य धातोरिवर्णोवर्णान्तस्य भ्रु इत्येतस्य इयङुवङ् इत्येतावादेशौ भवतोऽचि परतः ॥
वार्त्तिकम् ॥ इयङुवङ्प्रकरणे तन्वादीनां छन्दसि बहुलमुपसंख्यानं कर्त्तव्यम् ॥

77. Before an affix beginning with a vowel, there are substituted for the उ of नु, the characteristic of the roots of the fifth class, for the final इ, ई, उ and ऊ of a root, as well as for the ऊ of भ्रू, the इय् (for इ or ई) and उव् (for उ or ऊ).

Thus आप्नुवन्ति, राध्नुवन्ति, शक्नुवन्ति, from roots of the 5th class. चिक्षियतुः, लुलुवतुः, लुलुवुः, नियौ, नियः, लुवौ, लुवः and भ्रुवौ and भ्रुवः ॥

Why do we say before an affix beginning with a vowel'? Observe आप्नुयात्, शक्नुयात्, राध्नुयात् ॥ Why "of श्नु &c."? Observe लक्ष्म्यै, लक्ष्म्याः, वध्वै, वध्वाः ॥ Why "of इ and उ"? Observe चक्रतुः, चक्रुः where the vowel is ऋ ॥

Vârt:—The Guṇa (VII. 3. 84) and Vṛiddhi (VII. 2. 115) however take place to the supersession of इयङ् and उवङ्: as from चि—चयनम् and चायकः, लू—लवनम् and लावकः, with ल्युट् and ण्वुल् ॥

Vârt:—In the Chhandas there is deversely the substitution of इयङ् and उवङ् in the case of तनू &c. Thus तन्वं पुषेम or तनुवं पुषेम ॥ विषुवं पुषेम, स्वर्गो लोकः, सुवर्गो लोकः, त्र्यम्बकं यजामहे, त्रियम्बकं यजामहे ॥

अभ्यासस्यासवर्णे ॥७८॥ पदानि ॥ अभ्यासस्य, अ, सवर्णे ॥
वृत्तिः ॥ अभ्यासस्येवर्णोवर्णान्तस्यासवर्णेऽचि परत इयङ् उवङ् इत्येतावादेशौ भवतः ॥

78. इयङ् and उवङ् are substituted for the इ and उ of a reduplicate, before a non-homogenous vowel.

Thus इयेष, उवोष, इयर्त्ति, (VII. 4. 77) but ईषतुः and ईषुः, ऊषतुः and ऊषुः before homogenous vowels and इयाय and उवाय before a non-vowel.

स्त्रियाः ॥ ७९ ॥ पदानि ॥ स्त्रियाः, (अचि इयङ्) ॥
वृत्तिः ॥ स्त्रीइत्येतस्याजादौ प्रत्यये परतः इयङादेशो भवति ॥

79. इयङ् is substituted for the ई of स्त्री before an affix beginning with a vowel.

As स्त्री, स्त्रियौ, स्त्रियः; but स्त्रीणाम् the न् being added by a subsequent rule, supersedes this rule. The making this a separate sûtra is for the sake of the subsequent aphorisms.

वाऽम्शसोः ॥ ८० ॥ पदानि ॥ वा, अम्, शसोः (इयङ् स्त्रियाः) ॥
वृत्तिः ॥ अमि शसि परतः स्त्रिया वा इयङादेशो भवति ॥

80. The substitution of इयङ् for the ई of strî is optional before the accusative endings अम् and शस् (अस्) ॥

Thus स्त्रीं पश्य or स्त्रियं पश्य, स्त्रीः पश्य or स्त्रियः पश्य ॥

इणो यण् ॥ ८१ ॥ पदानि ॥ इणः, यण्, (अङ्गस्य अचि) ॥
वृत्तिः ॥ इणोङ्गस्य यणादेशो भवति अचि परतः ॥

81. For the इ of the root इण् (एति) is substituted a semivowel (य), before an affix beginning with a vowel.

Thus यन्ति, यन्तु, आयन् ॥ This supersedes इयङ् substitution, and is itself superseded by VII. 2. 115, and VII. 3. 84 which ordain Vṛiddhi and Guṇa: on the maxim मध्ये ऽपवादाः पूर्वान् विधीन् बाधन्ते, नोत्तरान् ॥ "Apavâdas that are surrounded by the rules which teach operations that have to be superseded by the apavâda operations, supersede only those rules that precede, not those that follow them." So we have अयनम् and आयकः ॥

एरनेकाचो ऽसंयोगपूर्वस्य ॥ ८२ ॥ पदानि ॥ एः, अनेकाचः, अ संयोगपूर्वस्य, (धातोः अचिं प्रत्यये) ॥

वृत्तिः ॥ धातोरवयवः संयोगः पूर्वो यस्मादिवर्णान्न भवति असावसंयोगपूर्वस्तदन्तस्याङ्गस्यानेकाचोऽचि परतो यणादेशो भवति ॥

82. A semivowel is substituted before an affix beginning with a vowel, for the final इ or ई of a root, not preceded by a conjunct consonant forming part of the root, when the stem is not a monosyllable.

The word धातोः is understood here, and the word संयोग is qualified by that: i. e. the इ or ई which is not preceded by conjunct consonant forming part of the root is called an asamyoga pûrva इ ॥ Thus निन्यतुः, निन्युः, उन्न्यौ, उन्न्यः, ग्रामण्यौ, ग्रामण्यः ॥ All the above examples are of the soot नी preceded by the gati prepositions नि and उत्, or a Kâraka-upapada ग्राम ॥ The rule will not apply however if the preceding word is neither a gati nor a Kâraka, but an adjective, as परमनी, its dual and plural will be परमनियौ and परमनियः by इयङ् ॥ Why do we say 'of इ or ई'? Observe लुलुवतुः and लुलुवः from लुलू which ending in ऊ takes उवङ् substitution. This is also shown in the next sûtra. Why do we say the stem should be of more than one syllable? Observe नी; its dual and plural are नियौ and नियः by इयङ् ॥ Why do we say the इ or ई should not be preceded by a conjunct consonant? Observe यवक्री d. यवक्रियौ pl. यवक्रियः by इयङ् ॥ Why do we say "forming part of the root"? So that the rule may apply to उन्नी also. Here though ई is preceded by a conjunct न्न्, yet the latter is not part of the root, one न् being part of the upasarga उत् ॥ Thus we have उन्न्यौ and उन्न्यः ॥ The phrase असंयोगपुर्व should in fact be taken as qualifying the letter ई, and not as qualifying the word अङ्ग ॥

ओः सुपि ॥८३॥ पदानि ॥ ओः, सुपि, (यण्, धातोः, असंयोगपूर्वस्य, अनेकाचः अङ्गस्य) ॥

वृत्तिः ॥ धात्ववयवः संयोगः पूर्वो यस्मादुवर्णान्न भवति तदन्तस्याङ्गस्या नेकाचो ऽजादौ सुपि परतो यणादेशो भवति ॥

83. When a case-affix, beginning with a vowel follows, then the semivowel व् is substituted for the final

ऊ of a stem containing more than one syllable, if the stem ends with a verbal root ending in ऊ not preceded by a conjunct consonant forming part of the root.

As no roots at the end of a stem end in short उ, the latter is not mentioned in the translation. Thus खलपू 'a sweeper':—d. खलप्वौ, pl. खलप्वः; so also शतस्वौ and शतस्वः, and सकृल्लू: dual सकृल्ल्वौ and सकृल्ल्वः ॥ But लुलुवतुः and लुलुवः before tense-affixes, (non—सुप्); लू—लुवौ, लुवः (because consisting of one syllable only), and कटप्रू—कटप्रुवौ, कटप्रुवः (because ऊ is preceded by a conjunct consonant forming part of the root). The rule does not apply if the first member is not a Gati or a Kâraka word: as परमलू:—परमलुवौ and परमलुवः ॥[1]

वर्षाभ्वश्च ॥ ८४ ॥ पदानि ॥ वर्षा भ्वः, च, अचि सुपि यण् ॥

वृत्तिः ॥ वर्षाभू इत्येतस्याजादौ सुपि परतो यणादेशो भवति ॥

वार्त्तिकम् ॥ पुनर्भ्वश्चेतिवक्तव्यम् ॥

84. व् is substituted for the ऊ of वर्षाभू also, when a case-affix beginning with a vowel follows.

As वर्षाभ्वौ, वर्षाभ्वः ॥ वर्षाभू 'what is born in the rains, a kind of herb.' This is an exception to the subsequent rule.

Vârt:—The semi-vowel substitution takes place when दृन्, कार and पुनर् precede भू; as दृन्भ्वौ, दृन्भ्वः, पुनर्भ्वौ, पुनर्भ्वः, कारभ्वौ (काराभ्वौ), कारभ्वः (काराभ्वः) ॥

न भूसुधियोः ॥ ८५ ॥ पदानि ॥ न, भू, सुधियोः, यण्, ॥

वृत्तिः ॥ भू सुधी इत्येतयोर्यणादेशो न भवति ॥

85. The semi-vowel substitution does not take place in the case of stems ending in भू or the word सुधी, before affixes beginning with a vowel.

Thus प्रतिभु—प्रतिभुवौ, प्रतिभुवः; सुधी—सुधियौ, सुधियः ॥ VI. 4. 77.

छन्दस्युभयथा ॥ ८६ ॥ पदानि ॥ छन्दसि, उभयथा, भूसुधियोः ॥

वृत्तिः ॥ छन्दसि विषये भू सुधी इत्येतयोरुभयथा दृश्यते यण् ॥

86. In the Chhandas, in the case of a stem in भू and सुधी, are found sometimes the इयङ्, उवङ् and sometimes the semivowel substitution.

As विभ्वम्,विभुवम्,सुध्यः and सुधियः; वनेषु चित्रं विभ्वं विशे, विशे विभुवम्, सुध्यो हव्यमग्ने, सुधियो हव्यमग्ने ॥

हुश्नुवोः सार्वधातुके ॥ ८७ ॥ पदानि ॥ हुश्नु वोः, सार्वधातु के, अङ्गस्य, अनेकाचः, असंयोगं, पूर्वस्य, अचि ॥

वृत्तिः ॥ हु इत्येतस्याङ्गस्य श्नुप्रत्ययान्तस्यानेकाचो ऽसंयोगपूर्वस्याजादौ सार्वधातुके परतो यणादेशो भवति.॥

87. The semi-vowel व् is substituted for the उ of हु, and for that of नु (the characteristic of the fifth class roots),

before a sârvadhâtuka affix (III. 4. 113) beginning with a vowel, when the stem consists of more than one syllable and the उ is not preceded by a conjunct consonant.

Thus हु—जुह्वति, जुह्वतु ; अजुह्वन्, so also with सु—as सुन्वन्ति, सुन्वन्तु, असुन्वन् ॥ Why do we say "of हु and श्नु formed stems"? Observe योयुवति, रोरुवति, from Intensive bases, by the elision of the यङ् affix. The यङ् is elided in the secular literature also, by the implication (jnâpaka) of this aphorism, for no counter-example can be formed of a root consisting of more than one syllable and ending in उ, not preceded by a conjunct consonant and followed by a Sârvadhâtuka affix, unless the Intensive roots with the elision of यङ् be taken. Nor can we get examples from the Chhandas, for the preceding rule applies only to ârdhadhâtuka affixes. Why do we say before a Sârvadhâtuka? Observe जुहुवतुः, जुहुवुः (VI. 4. 77). So also not in आप्नुवन्ति and राध्नुवन्ति as the उ is preceded by a conjunct consonant.

भुवो वुग्लुङ्लिटोः ॥ ८८ ॥ पदानि ॥ भुवः, वुक्, लुङ्, लिटोः, अचि, ॥
वृत्तिः ॥ भुवो वुगागमो भवति लुङि लिटि चाजादौ परतः ॥

88. भू gets the augment व् (वुक्) before the tense-affixes of the Aorist and the Perfect, when beginning with a vowel.

Thus अभूवन्, अभूवम् ; बभूव:, बभूवतुः, बभूवुः ॥

ऊदुपधाया गोहः ॥८९॥ पदानि ॥ ऊत, उपधायाः, गोहः, अङ्गस्य, अचि, प्रत्यये ॥
वृत्तिः ॥ गोहो ऽङ्गस्य उपधाया ऊकारादेशो भवति अजादौ प्रत्यये परतः ॥

89. For the penultimate ओ of the guṇated stem गोह् (from गुह्), there is substituted ऊ before an affix beginning with a vowel.

Thus नि गूहति, निगूहकः, साधुनिगूहिन्, निगूहम्, निगूहन्ति, गूहे वर्तते ॥ Why do we say 'penultimate'? So that the substitution should not apply any where else. The form गोह् is taken in the sûtra to prohibit the application of the rule to cases where गुह् does not assume the form गोह् ॥ Therefore not here, निजुगुहतुः, निजुगुहुः ॥ This change will not take place before the affixes beginning with a consonant; as निगोढा, निगोढुम् ॥ Some say, the word is exhibited as गोह in order to prohibit the अय् substitution of णि before ल्यप् ॥ As निगोहि + ल्यप् = निगूह्य (VI. 4. 56 not applied), the ऊ substitution being considered as asiddha (VI. 4. 22) would have brought in अय्, गूह् being considered as a word having a light vowel for its penultimate. According to Kâśikâ the ऊ substitution, however, is not asiddha, as their places of operation are different.

दोषो णौ ॥ ९० ॥ पदानि ॥ दोषः, णौ, उदुपधायाः ॥
वृत्तिः ॥ दोष उपधाया ऊकार आदेशो भवति णौ परतः ॥

90. The ओ of दोष् is replaced by ऊ before the causative णि ॥

Thus दूषयति, दूषयतः, दूषयन्ति ॥ Similar reasons as in गोह, may be given for the root दुष being exhibited as दोष in the sûtra. When not followed by णि, we have दोषो वर्त्तते ॥

वा चित्तविरागे ॥ ९१ ॥ पदानि ॥ वा, चित्त-विरागे, उदुपधायाः णौ, ॥

वृत्तिः ॥ चित्तविकारार्थे दोष उपधाया वा ऊकारादेशो भवति णौ परतः ॥

91. The ऊ substitution for the ओ of दोष् is optional, when the sense is that of the disturbing of the mind.

As चित्तं or प्रज्ञां दूषयति or दोषयति ॥ Otherwise साधनं दूषयति when mental agitation is not meant.

मितां ह्रस्वः ॥ ९२ ॥ पदानि ॥ मिताम्, ह्रस्वः, णौ, उपधायाः, ॥

वृत्तिः ॥ मितो धातवो घटादयो मित इत्येवमादयो ये प्रतिपादितास्तेषामुपधाया ह्रस्वो भवति णौ परतः ॥

92. The roots having an indicatory म्, retain their penultimate short vowel before the causative णि ॥

The मित् roots are घटादि a subdivision of Bhwâdi (800 to 873), and all other roots that end in अम् as शम् and तम् of Divâdi class. Thus घटयति, व्यथयति, जनयति, रजयति, शमयति, तपयति ॥ Some read the anuvṛitti of the word 'optionally' from the last sûra into this. This will then be a limited option only (vyavasthita-vibhâshâ). The forms उत्कामयति and संक्रामयति are thus explained.

93. Optionally a long may be substituted for the penultimate of the causative of मित् roots, before the third person of the Passive Aorist in चिण् (इ), and before the Absolutive affix णमुल् (अम्) ॥

चिण्णमुलोर्दीर्घो ऽन्यतरस्याम् ॥ ९३ ॥ पदानि ॥ चिण्, णमुलोः, दीर्घः, अन्यतरस्याम्, णौ, मितः उपधायाः ॥

वृत्तिः ॥ चिण्परे णमुल्परे च णौ परतो मितामङ्गानामुपधाया दीर्घो भवति अन्यतरस्याम् ॥

Thus अशमि or अशामि, अतमि or अतामि with चिण्; and शमंशमम्, and शामंशामं; तमंतमम् or तामंतामम् with णमुल् ॥ Why have we used the word दीर्घ in the sûtra? The rule does not teach merely the *optional shortening*. So that in the alternative of short, we have अशमि and in the other alternative we have अशामि, so that there is long. For had दीर्घ not been used, it would have taught optional short only, i. e. it would be a ह्रस्वविकल्पविधि only, and there will be this difficulty :—when the causative of causative is taken, as in शमयन्तं प्रयुङ्क्ते, there would not be lengthening in the alternative. Because the lopa substitute of णि would be sthânivat : therefore, the णि which would be followed by

चिण् or णमुल्, would not have in it the मित् aṅga, because the first णि intervenes between the मित् anga and the चिण् and णमुल् affix, and that णि which is preceded by a मित् anga is not followed by चिण् and णमुल्, because the second णि (though elided) intervenes. Therefore, there would not be *optional* short here, but *compulsory* short, by the preceding sûtra and no lengthening. The rule, therefore, teaches the optional substitution of the *long* (दीर्घ). For there arises no such anomaly in this view. For taking this rule to be a दीर्घविधि, the lopa-substitution of णि would *not* be sthânivat, by the express prohibition contained in I. 1. 58, and so we can get forms of double causatives. But if we take it a ह्रस्वविकल्पविधि, then the lopa-adeśa of णि being sthânivat, would prevent getting the alternative long form. Therefore the word दीर्घ is used in the sûtra to make this rule a दीर्घविधि, and prevent sthânivat-bhâva. Thus take the causative of शम्, which will be शामि by the last sûtra. Take its Intensive with यङ्, शामि + यङ् which causes doubling by VI. 1. 9 = शमि शामि + यङ् = शशामि + यङ् (VII. 4. 60) = शं शामि + यङ् (नुक् or nasal being added to the abhyâsa by VII. 4. 85) = शंशामि + यङ् = शंशम् + य (VI. 4. 51) = शंशम्य. Add णिच् to this ie. make the causative of the Intensive. शंशम् + य + इ ॥ Then the अ of य is elided by VI. 4. 48 = शंशम् + य् + इ. Then य् is elided by VI. 4. 49 = शंशम + इ = शंशामि ॥ This शंशामि is the causative root of the Intensive of the causative शम् ॥ Now add चिण् or णमुल् to this root; and we get two forms short and long अशंशमि or अशंशामि with चिण् and शंशमम् or शंशामम् with णमुल् ॥ The long forms could not have been obtained had this not been a दीर्घविधि, for then the lopa-adeśâ of णिच् being sthânivat would have prevented the application of दीर्घ ॥ The roots शम् and तम् (both Divâdi) ending in म् do not ever lengthen the root vowel before चिण् and णमुल् by VII. 3. 34. The present sûtra, therefore, does not apply to the simple roots. The derivative causative roots of these, namely, शमि — शमयति, तमि — तमयति, optionally lengthen the penultimate before these affixes. Thus शमि + चिण् = शम् + चिण् (the इ of णि being elided by VI. 4. 51) = शामि or शमि (with the augment अ = अशामि or अशमि) ॥ This rule applies when the Causative of the Causative root takes these affixes. In fact the mention of the word दीर्घ implies as much, otherwise the sûtra could have been made without this word, for the word 'optionally' would have brought in both 'short' and 'long'. Thus in शमयन्तं प्रयुङ्क्ते 'he causes another to make quiet,' we add णि (the Causative sign.), to the Causative root शमि, as शमि + णि = शम् + इ (VI. 4. 51) = शामि, the lopâdeśa here is not sthânivat for the purposes of *lengthening* (दीर्घविधि) the अ of शम् (I. 1. 58) ॥ From this शामि with चिण् we get अशामि, and with णमुल् we get शामम् ॥ But we cannot get the short forms, by taking the other alternative, as the lopâdeśa will then be sthânivat. Hence the necessity of the word दीर्घ in the sûtra. Thus the चिण् and णमुल् forms of the Causative of the Causative (i. e. the double Causative) of शम् are अशमि or अशामि ; शमंशमम् or शामंशामम् and from the form शंशमयति, we have अशंशमि or अशंशामि, शंशमंशंशमम् or शंशामंशं-

शामय ॥ These latter are from the Causative stems of the Intensive root. The sign यङ् of the Intensive has been elided (VI. 4. 49) as shown above.

खचि ह्रस्वः ॥ ९४ ॥ पदानि ॥ खचि, ह्रस्वः, (उपधायाः अङ्गस्य) ॥

वृत्तिः ॥ खच्परे णौ परतो ह्रस्वो भवत्यङ्गस्योपधायाः ॥

94. The penultimate of the Causative stem is shortened before the affix खच् ॥

Thus द्विषन्तपः, परंतपः, पुरंदरः ॥ See III. 2. 29 and 41.

ह्लादो निष्ठायाम् ॥ ९५ ॥ पदानि ॥ ह्लादः, निष्ठायाम्, (ह्रस्वः उपधायाः अङ्गस्य) ॥

वृत्तिः ॥ ह्लादो ऽङ्गस्योपधाया ह्रस्वो भवति निष्ठायां परतः ॥

95. The penultimate of the Causative of ह्लद् (ह्लादि) is shortened before the Participle affixes क्त and क्तवतु ॥

Thus प्रह्लन्नः, प्रह्लन्नवान्, but प्रह्लादयति before non-nishṭhâ. The rule applies also when क्तिन् follows as प्रह्लत्तिः ॥ This is done by splitting up the aphorism into two (1) ह्लादः (2) निष्ठायाम् ॥

छादेर्घे ऽद्व्युपसर्गस्य ॥ ९६ ॥ पदानि ॥ छादेः, घे, अ द्व्युपसर्गस्य, (उपधायाः ह्रस्वः) ॥

वृत्तिः ॥ छादेरङ्गस्याद्व्युपसर्गस्य घप्रत्यये परत उपधाया ह्रस्वो भवति ॥

वार्त्तिकम् ॥ अद्विप्रभृत्युपसर्गस्येति वक्तव्यम् ॥

96. The penultimate of the Churâdi छद् is shortened before the affix घ (III. 3. 118), when not preceded by two prepositions (or more).

As उरश्छदः, प्रच्छदः, दन्तच्छदः ॥ But समुपच्छादः with two prepositions. The same when preceded by more than two prepositions, as समुपातिच्छादः ॥ The elision of णि of छादि &c., by VI. 4. 51, should not be considered as asiddha (VI. 4. 22) or sthânivat (I. 1. 57), otherwise there would be no *penultimate* to be shortened.

Vârt:—The prohibition with regard to द्वि should be extended to numbers more than two.

इस्मन्त्रन्क्विषु च ॥ ९७ ॥ पदानि ॥ इस्, मन्, त्रन्, क्विषु, च, छादेः (उपधायाः ह्रस्वः) ॥

वृत्ति॥इस् मन् त्रन् क्वि इत्येतेषु परतश्छादेरुपधाया ह्रस्वो भवति ।

97. The penultimate of छादि is shortened before the affixes इस्; मन्, त्रन् and क्वि ॥

Thus छदिस्, छद्मन् (neuter), छत्रम्, धामच्छत् and उपच्छत् ॥ The first three are Uṇâdi affixes.

गमहनजनखनघसां लोपः क्ङित्यनङि ॥ ९८ ॥ पदानि ॥ गम, हन, जन, खन, घसाम्, लोपः, क्ङिति अनङि, ॥

वृत्तिः ॥ गम हन जन खन घस इत्येतेषामङ्गानामुपधाया लोपो भवत्यजादौ प्रत्यये क्ङित्यनङि परतः ॥

98. The root-vowel of गम्, हन्, जन्, खन्, and घस् is elided before an affix beginning with a vowel, when it has an indicatory क् or ङ्; but not before the Aorist affix अङ् ॥

Thus जग्मतुः, जग्मुः जघ्नतुः, जघ्नुः, जज्ञे, जज्ञाते, जज्ञिरे, चख्नतुः, चख्नुः, जक्षतुः, जक्षुः, अक्षन्नमीमदन्त पितरः, ॥ क्ङितीति किम्, गमनम्, हननम्, ॥ अनङीति किम्, अगमत्, अघसत्, ॥ अचीत्येव, गम्यते, हन्यते ॥

Why 'having indicatory क् or ङ्'? See गमनम्, हननम् ॥ Why 'not अङ्'? See अगमत्, अघसत् ॥ Why 'beginning with a vowel,'? See गम्यते and हन्यते ॥

तनिपत्योश्छन्दसि ॥ ९९ ॥ पदानि ॥ तनि, पत्योः, छन्दसि, (क्ङिति उपधायाः लोपः) ॥

वृत्तिः ॥ तनि पति इत्येतयोश्छन्दसि विषये उपधाया लोपो भवति अजादौ क्ङिति प्रत्यये परतः ॥

99. In the Chhandas, the root-vowel of तन् and पत् is elided before an affix beginning with a vowel, when it has an indicatory क् or ङ् ॥

As वितत्निरे कवयः, शकुना इव पप्तिम ॥ In secular language वितेनिरे, पेतिम ॥

घसिभसोर्हलि च ॥१००॥ पदानि ॥ घसि, भसोः, हलि, च, (अचि क्ङिति)॥

वृत्तिः ॥ घसि भस इत्येतयोश्छन्दसि उपधाया लोपो भवति हलादावजादौ च क्ङिति प्रत्यये परतः ।

100. The root-vowel of घस् and भस् is elided in the Chhandas, before any affix, whether beginning with a vowel or a consonant, which has an indicatory क् or ङ् ॥

Thus सग्धिश्च मे सपीतिश्च मे, बब्धां ते हरी धानाः ॥ सग्धिः is thus derived: क्तिन् is added to the root अद्; then by II. 4. 39, घस् is substituted for अद्; thus घस्+ति = घस+ति (अ being elided by the present sûtra) = घ्+ति (स् being elided by VIII. 2. 26), then त is changed to ध, and घ to ग and we have ग्धिः ॥ Then समाना ग्धिः = सग्धिः (समान changed to स VI. 3. 84). The word बब्धाम् is the Imperative of भस्, thus भस्+श्लु+ताम् = भ भस्+ताम् = ब भ्स्+ताम् (VI. 4. 100) = बभ्+ताम् (VIII. 2. 26) = ब ब्+धाम् = बब्धाम् ॥ This rule of elision being a nitya and a subsequent rule ought to have operated first, but, as a Vedic anomaly, the reduplication takes place first. See VII. 2. 67

Why do we read "before an affix beginning *also* with a consonant"? Because the elision takes place before a vowel affix also, as बप्सति = भस्+श्लु+झि = ब भ्स्+अति (VII. 1. 4) = बप्सति (VIII. 4. 55).

Why having an indicatory क् or ङ्? Observe भस्मन् बभस्ति ॥ The च has been added into the aphorism by the Vârtikakâra.

हुझल्भ्यो हेर्धिः ॥ १०१ ॥ पदानि ॥ हु-झल्भ्योः, हेः, धिः, ॥

वृत्तिः ॥ हु इत्येतस्मात् झलन्तेभ्यश्चोत्तरस्य हलादेर्हेः स्थाने धिरादेशो भवति ।

101. After हु and after a consonant (with the exception of semi-vowels and nasals), धि is substituted for the

Imperative affix हि, when the latter does not take the augment इट् ॥

Thus हु—जुहुधि; झल् consonants; भिद्—भिन्द्धि, छिद्—छिन्द्धि ॥ But क्रीणीहि, प्रीणीहि (VI. 4. 113) not ending in consonants. Why 'हि only'? Observe जुहुताम् ॥ Why do we read the anuvritti of हलि into this sûtra? When हि does not begin with a consonant, but with a vowel, i. e. when it takes the augment इट्, the rule does not apply. As रुदिहि, स्वपिहि ॥ In the case of जुहुतात्, भिन्तात्, when हि is replaced by तात् (VII. 1. 35) this substitution does not take place because तात् is a later rule in the order of Ashṭâdhyâyî, and because सकृद्गतौ विप्रतिषेधे यद्बाधितं तद्बाधितमेव "When two rules, while they apply simultaneously mutually prohibit each other, that rule of the two which is once superseded by the other, is superseded altogether". When अकच् is added by V. 3. 71, धि substitution takes place, as भिन्द्धकि, छिन्द्धकि ॥ The maxim पुनः प्रसङ्ग विज्ञानात् सिद्धम् applies here:—"Occasionally the formation of a particular form is accounted for by the fact that a preceding rule is allowed to apply again, after it had been previously superseded by a subsequent rule."

श्रुशृणुपॄकृवृभ्यश्छन्दसि ॥ १०२ ॥ पदानि ॥ श्रु-शृणु-पॄ-कृ-वृ-भ्यः, छन्दसि, हेर्धिः ॥

वृत्तिः ॥ श्रु शृणु पॄ कृ वृ इत्येतेभ्य उत्तरस्य हेर्धिरादेशो भवति छन्दसि विषये ।

102. धि is substituted for हि in the Vedas, after श्रु, शृणु, पॄ, कृ and वृ ॥

As श्रुधी हवमिन्द्र, शृणुधी, गिरः, पूर्धि, उरुणस्कृधि and अपावृधि, ॥

In शृणुधी, the हि is not elided after the उ of शृ, as it was required by VI. 4. 106, since the present aphorism specifically mentions it. The lengthening takes place by VI. 3. 137. The forms other than शृणुधि are irregular; शप् being added *diversely* by III. 1. 85, and then elided diversely by बहुलं छन्दसि II. 4. 73

अङितश्च ॥ १०३ ॥ पदानि ॥ अङ्-इतः, च, हेर्धिः ॥

वृत्तिः ॥ अङितश्च हेर्धिरादेशो भवति ॥

103. धि is substituted for हि, when the tense-affix is not ङित् ॥

Under III. 4. 88 हि is also पित् in the Vedas: and when it is पित्, it is not ङित् by I. 2. 4. Thus रारन्धि, यन्धि and युयोधि in the following सोमरारन्धि अस्मभ्यं तद्धर्यश्व प्रयन्धि, युयोध्यस्मज्जुहुराणमेनः

Why do we say 'when it is not ङित्'? Observe प्रीणीहि ॥ रारन्धि is irregularly Parasmaipada of रम; the शप being replaced by श्लु, and the reduplicate lengthened as a Vedic form. The म is not elided, by VI. 4. 37 as the affix is not ङित् ॥ प्रयन्धि is from यम, the शप् is elided: and युयोधि from यु (यौति), the शप being replaced by श्लु ॥

च्विणो लुक् ॥ १०४ ॥ पदानि ॥ चिणः, लुक्, प्रत्ययस्य ॥

वृत्ति ॥ चिण उत्तरस्य प्रत्ययस्य लुग्भवति ॥

104. The personal-endings are elided after चिण्, the third person, singular Passive of the Aorist.

As अहारि, अलावि, अकारि, अपाचि ॥ So also अकारितराम्, अहारितमाम्, here the elision of the personal affix त (III. 1. 60) of the Aorist being considered as *asiddha*, the affixes तरप् and तमप् are not elided: though if the sûtra were to be literally interpreted, *every affix* after चिण्, ought to be elided. Or the word क्ङिति is understood here; so that कित् and ङित् affixes of चिण् are elided and not every affix.

अतो हेः ॥ १०५ ॥ पदानि ॥ अतः, हेः, अङ्गस्य ॥

वृत्तिः ॥ अकारान्तादङ्गादुत्तरस्य हेर्लुग्भवति ॥

105. The Imperative affix हि is elided after a stem ending in short अ ॥

Thus पच, पठ, गच्छ, धाव ॥ But युहि, रुहि after stems ending in उ. Why do we say "*short* अ"? Observe लुनीहि, पुनीहि (लुना + हि, the ई substitution by VI. 4. 113, should be considered *asiddha*), here हि is not elided after the long आ ॥

उतश्च प्रत्ययादसंयोगपूर्वात् ॥ १०६ ॥ पदानि ॥ उतः, च, प्रत्ययात्, असंयोग पूर्वात् ॥

वृत्तिः ॥ उकारो यो ऽसंयोगपूर्वस्तदन्तात्प्रत्ययादुत्तरस्य हेर्लुग्भवति ।

वार्तिकम् ॥ उतश्च प्रत्ययादित्यत्र छन्दसि वेति वक्तव्यं ॥

106 The Imperative हि is elided after the उ of an affix, in the vikaraṇa with which the Present-stem (special conjugation) is made, provided that the उ is not preceded by a conjunct consonant.

The affix उ with which the Present-stem is made is उ and श्नु ॥ Thus चिनु, सुनु, कुरु ॥ Why after 'उ'? Observe लुनीहि, पुनीहि ॥ Why do we say "उ being part of the vikaraṇa or affix"? Observe रुहि, युहि, here उ is part of the *root* itself, and not of the vikaraṇa. Why de we say 'not preceded by a conjunct consonant,? Observe प्राप्नुहि, राध्नुहि, तक्ष्णुहि ॥

Vârt:—The elision of हि after the उ of the vikaraṇa उ and श्नु is optional in the Vedas; as आतनुहि यातुधानान्, धिनुहि यज्ञपतिम्, तेन मा भागिनं कृणुहि ॥

लोपश्चास्यान्यतरस्यां म्वोः ॥ १०७ ॥ पदानि ॥ लोपः, च, अस्य, अन्यतरस्याम्, म्वोः, ॥

वृत्तिः ॥ योऽयमुकारो ऽसंयोगपूर्वस्तदन्तस्य प्रत्ययस्यान्यतरस्यां लोपो भवति ॥

107. The उ of the vikaraṇa उ and श्नु, where not preceded by a conjunct consonant, may be elided optionally before a personal ending beginning with म or व् ॥

Thus सुन्वः or सुनुवः, सुन्मः, सुनुमः, तन्वः, तनुवः, तन्मः, तनुमः ॥ The उ must belong to the affix, and should not be part of the root. Therefore not in युवः, युमः ॥

Why do we say 'not preceded by a conjunct consonant'? Observe शक्नुवः, शक्नुमः only. Though the elision word लुक् was understood in this sûtra, the mention of लोप indicates that the *final* is only to be elided, and not the whole affix नु ॥ It is a general maxim that the words लुक्, श्लु and लुप् cause the elision of the *whole* affix, while 'lopa' will cause elision of the final letter only of the affix. If the whole affix be elided, we could not get सुन्वः &c., Moreover, in कुर्वः and कुर्मः formed by guṇa of कृ, there would have been no guṇa, had the word लुक् been used, for I. 1. 63, would have prevented guṇa; but by using the word लोप we have such guṇa also by I. 1. 62.

नित्यं करोतेः ॥ १०८ ॥ पदानि ॥ नित्यम्, करोतेः, ॥

वृत्ति ॥ करोतेरुत्तरस्य उकारप्रत्ययस्य वकारमकारादौ प्रत्यये परतो नित्यं लोपो भवति ॥

108. The elision of उ is invariable before व् and म् in the case of कृ (करोति).

Thus कुर्वः and कुर्मः ॥ Thus कृ+उ+वः=कुर्+उ+वः (VI. 4. 110)=कुर्+०+वः (VI. 4. 108). Now the lopa being not sthânivat, when a vowel is to be lengthened (I. 1. 58), उ of कु should be lengthened by VIII. 2. 77. This contingency is prevented by VIII. 2. 79.

ये च ॥ १०९ ॥ पदानि ॥ ये, च, लोपः नित्यंकरोतेः ॥

वृत्तिः ॥ यकारादौ च प्रत्यये परतः करोतेरुत्तरस्योकारप्रत्ययस्य नित्यं लोपो भवति ॥

109. The affix उ of the stem कुरु is always elided before a personal ending beginning with a य ॥

Thus कुर्यात्, कुर्याताम् and कुर्युः ॥ The augment यासुट् is treated here as an affix, and it makes the personal ending to which it is added, as an affix beginning with य ॥

अत उत्सार्वधातुके ॥ ११० ॥ पदानि ॥ अतः, उत्, सार्वधातु के, क्ङिति ॥

वृत्तिः ॥ उकारप्रत्ययान्तस्य करोतेरकारस्य स्थाने उकार आदेशो भवति सार्वधातुके क्ङिति परतः ।

110. Before a Sârvadhâtuka affix with an indicatory क् or ङ्, short उ is substituted for the अ of कृ (कर्+उ) when gunated.

Thus कृ+उ+तस्=कर्+उ+तस्(VII. 3. 84)=कुर्+उ+तस्=कुरुतः (VI. 4. 110) The तस् is ङित् by I. 2. 4. So also कुर्वन्ति, कुरु ॥ Why do we say 'before a Sârvadhatukâ'? So that the rule may apply to what was once a Sârvadhâtuka, though no longer existent. Thus कुरु where the personal ending हि is elided, but it leaves its effect behind. The त् in उत् shows that this उ is not to be gunated by VII. 3. 86. When the affix is not कित् or ङित् we have करोति, करोषि and करोमि (I. 2. 4).

श्नसोरल्लोपः ॥ १११ ॥ पदानि ॥ श्न-असोः, अत्-लोपः, सार्वधातुके क्ङिति ॥

वृत्तिः । अस्यास्तेश्चाकारस्य लोपो भवति सार्वधातुके क्ङिति परतः ।

111. Before a Sârvadhâtuka कित् or ङित् affix, the अ of श्न and अस् is elided.

श्न is the characteristic of the roots of the Rudhâdi class, while अस् is the root itself. Thus रुन्धः; रुन्धन्ति, भिन्तः, भिन्दन्ति; So also of अस्:—स्तः, सन्ति ॥ But भिनत्ति and अस्ति before non—कित् and non—ङित् affixes. श्न + अस् ought to be श्नास्, instead of that we have श्नस् in the sûtra. The पररूप single substitution is an irregularity.

श्नाभ्यस्तयोरातः ॥ ११२ ॥ पदानि ॥ श्ना-अभ्यस्तयोः, आतः, लोपः सार्वधातुके क्ङिति ॥

वृत्तिः ॥ श्ना इत्येतस्याभ्यस्तानां चाङ्गानामाकारस्य लोपो भवति सार्वधातुके क्ङिति परतः ।

112. Before a Sârvadhâtuka कित् or ङित् affix beginning with a vowel, the long आ of श्ना (the vikaraṇa of the 9th class) and of the reduplicate stems is elided.

Thus लुनते, लुनताम्, अलुनत; मिमते, मिमताम्, अमिमत, संजिहते, संजिहताम् and समजिहत ॥ Why do we say 'of श्ना and the reduplicates'? Observe यान्ति, वान्ति ॥ Why 'of long आ'? Observe बिभ्रति ॥ Why 'before कित् and ङित्'? Observe अलुनात्, अजहात् ॥

ई हल्यघोः ॥ ११३ ॥ पदानि ॥ ई, हलि, अ-घोः (श्नाभ्यस्तयोरातः सार्वधातुके क्ङिति) ॥

वृत्तिः ॥ श्नान्तानामङ्गानामभ्यस्तानां च घुवर्जितानामात ईकारादेशो भवति हलादौ सार्वधातुके क्ङिति परतः ॥

113. Before a Sârvadhâtuka कित् or ङित् affix beginning with a consonant, the आ of श्ना and of the reduplicate stems is replaced by ई, except when the root is दा or धा (घु) ॥

Thus लुनीतः, पुनीतः, लुनीथः, पुनीथः, लुनीते and पुनीते ॥ Of reduplicates we have मिमीते, मिमीषे, मिमीध्वे, संजिहीते, संजिहीषे, संजिहीध्वे ॥ Why do we say 'beginning with a consonant'? Observe लुनन्ति, मिमते ॥ Why with the exception of घु? Observe दत्तः, धत्तः ॥ So also लुनाति and जहाति before non-कित् and non-ङित् affixes.

इद्दरिद्रस्य ॥ ११४ ॥ पदानि ॥ इत्, दरिद्रस्य, (हलि सार्वधातुके क्ङिति) ॥

वृत्तिः ॥ दरिद्रातेर्हलादौ सार्वधातुके क्ङिति परत इकारादेशो भवति ।

वार्त्तिकम् ॥ दरिद्रातेरार्धधातुके लोपो वक्तव्यः ॥ वा० ॥ सिद्धश्च प्रत्ययविधौ भवतीति वक्तव्यम् ॥

Kârikâ ॥ न दरिद्रायके लोपो दरिद्राणे च नेष्यते ।
दिदरिद्रासतीत्येके दिदरिद्रिषतीति वा ॥

वा० ॥ अद्यतन्यां वेति वक्तव्यम् ॥

114. इ is substituted for the आ of दरिद्रा before a Sârvadhâtuka कित् or ङित् affix beginning with a consonant.

Thus दरिद्रितः, दरिद्रिथः, दरिद्रिवः, दरिद्रिमः ॥ But दरिद्रति before a vowel affix (VI. 4. 112) and दरिद्राति before a non-ङित् affix.

Vârt :—The final of दरिद्रा is elided before an Ârdhadhâtuka affix. *Vârt* :—And this elision should be considered as siddha, in applying rules relating to affixes. Thus दरिद्रा by loosing आ becomes दरिद्र्, and we should apply those affixes which would come after a form like 'daridr', and not what would have come after a form like 'daridrâ'. Thus ण comes after roots ending in long आ (III. 1. 141): but this affix would not be applied here, but the general affix अच् (III. 1. 134). Thus दरिद्राति = दरिद्रः ॥

Kârikâ :—The elision does not take place in the forms दरिद्रायक and दरिद्राण, and the Desiderative may be either दिदरिद्रासति or दिदरिद्रिषति ॥ Siddhânta Kaumudi gives the following rule: "आ of दरिद्रा should be considered as elided when applying an ârdhadhâtuka affix, but optionally so before लुङ् (Aorist), and not at all before सन् (Desiderative), ण्वुल् and ल्युट्" ॥

Vârt :—Optionally so in the Aorist (adyatana-past) as, अदरिद्रीत् or अदरिद्रासीत् ॥ The latter form is evolved by VII. 2. 73 and elision of सिच् ॥ The form दरिद्रस्य in the sûtra is Vedic, the root being shortened from दरिद्रा to दरिद्र ॥

भियो ऽन्यतरस्याम् ॥ ११५ ॥ पदानि ॥ भियः, अन्यतरस्याम्, (इतहलि क्ङिति सार्वधातु के) ॥

वृत्तिः ॥ भी इत्येतस्याङ्गस्यान्यतरस्यामिकारादेशो भवति हलादौ क्ङिति सार्वधातुके परतः ॥

115. इ is optionally substituted for the ई of भी before a Sârvadhâtuka affix beginning with a consonant and having an indicatory क् or ङ् ॥

Thus बिभितः or बिभीतः, बिभिथः or बिभीथः, बिभिवः or बिभीवः; बिभिमः or बिभीमः॥ But बिभ्यति before a vowel-beginning affix and बिभेति before a non-ङित् affix and भीयते before an ârdhadhâtuka affix.

जहातेश्च ॥ ११६ ॥ पदानि ॥ जहातेः, च, (इ हलि अन्यतरस्याम् क्ङितिसार्वधातुके) ॥

वृत्तिः ॥ जहातेश्च इकारादेशो भवति अन्यतरस्यां हलादौ क्ङिति सार्वधातुके परतः ॥

116. इ is optionally substituted for the आ of हा (जहाति) before a Sârvadhâtuka कित् or ङित् affix beginning with a consonant.

Thus जहितः or जहीतः (VI. 4. 113) जहिथः or जहीथः (VI. 4. 113). But जहति before a vowel affix, and जहाति before a non-ङित् affix, and हीयते and जिहीयते before an ârdhadhâtuka. The separation of this sûtra from the last, is for the sake of subsequent aphorisms.

आ च हौ ॥ ११७ ॥ पदानि ॥ आ, च, हौ, (इ अन्यतरस्याम्) ॥

वृत्तिः ॥ जहातेराकारश्चान्तादेशो भवति इकारश्चान्यतरस्यां हौ परतः ।

117. आ as well as इ may optionally be substituted for the final of the stem of हा before the Imperative ending हि ॥

Thus जहाहि, जहिहि or जहीहि (VI. 4. 113).

लोपो यि ॥ ११८ ॥ पदानि ॥ लोपः, यि, (जहातेः सार्वधातुके क्ङिति) ॥

वृत्तिः ॥ लोपो भवति जहातेर्यकारादौ क्ङिति सार्वधातुके परतः ।

118. The final of the stem of हा is elided before an affix beginning with य being a Sârvadhâtuka कित् or ङित् affix.

Thus जह्यात्, जह्याताम् and जह्युः ॥

घ्वसोरेद्धावभ्यासलोपश्च ॥ ११९ ॥ पदानि ॥ घु-असोः, एत्, हौ, अभ्यास-लोपः, च, ॥

वृत्तिः ॥ घुसंज्ञकानामङ्गानामस्तेश्च एकारादेशो भवति हौ परतो ऽभ्यासलोपश्च ॥

119. For the final vowel of the roots दा and धा (घु), and for the स् of अस्, is substituted ए before the Imperative ending हि; and thereby the reduplicated syllable of दा and धा is elided.

Thus देहि, and धेहि, of घु, and एधि of अस्, the स being elided by this sûtra, and अ being elided by VI. 4. 111. This लोप of the present sûtra should be considered as having an indicatory श् so that the *whole* of the reduplicated and not only the final letter of the abhyâsa (I. 1. 55) is elided.

अत एकहल्मध्ये ऽनादेशादेर्लिटि ॥ १२० ॥ पदानि ॥ अतः, एक-हल्, मध्ये, अनादेशादेः, लिटि ॥

वृत्तिः ॥ क्ङितीतिवर्तते ॥ लिटि परत आदेश आदिर्यस्याङ्गस्य नास्ति, तस्य एकहल्मध्ये, असहाययोर्हलोर्मध्ये यो ऽकारस्तस्य एकारादेशो भवति, अभ्यासलोपश्च लिटि क्ङिति परतः ॥

वार्त्तिकम् ॥ दम्भेरेत्वं वक्तव्यम् ॥ वा० ॥ नशिमन्योरलिट्येत्वं वक्तव्यम् ॥

वा० ॥ छन्दस्यमिपचोरप्यलिटि एत्वं वक्तव्यम् ॥ वा० ॥ यजिवप्योश्च ॥

120. ए is substituted for the short अ standing between two simple consonants of a verbal stem, before the personal endings of the Perfect which have an indicatory क् (I. 2. 5), provided that, at the beginning of the root, in the reduplication, no other consonant has been substituted; and when this ए is substituted, the reduplicate is elided.

Thus रेणतुः, रेणुः, येमतुः, येमुः, पेचतुः, पेचुः, देभतुः, देभुः ॥ Why 'for अ'? Observe सिस्वितुः, सिस्विदुः the इ is not replaced. Why do we say '*short* अ'? Observe रराशे, रराशाते, रराशिरे ॥ Why do we say 'standing between two *simple* consonants'? Observe ररक्षतुः, ररक्षुः ॥ Some say this example is not appropriate, for by I. 2. 5, the Perfect affixes are not कित् here, as they come after a conjunct consonant. The following is then more appropriate:—तत्सरतुः and तत्सरुः ॥ Why do we say 'which has no substituted consonant in the reduplicate'? Observe चकणतुः, चकणुः, जगणतुः, जगणुः, बभणतुः, बभणुः ॥

The substitution referred to here must be caused by the affixes of the Perfect, therefore, the rule will apply to नेमतुः, नेमुः, सेहे and सेहाते, सेहिरे though णम् and षह् are the roots, and ण् and ष् are changed to न and स ॥ The substitution of जश् consonant or a चर् consonant in the reduplicate, should not be here considered asiddha (VIII. 4. 54, read with VIII. 2. 1). That substitution will be considered a substitution for the purposes of this sûtra and will make the stem आदेशादिः, as is indicated by the special exception made in favor of फल् and भज् (VI. 4. 122). If the form of the letter is not changed in the reduplicate, by substitution, then such substitution will not make the stem आदेशादिः ॥ Thus by VIII. 4. 54, a चर् letter (च, ट, त, क, प, श, ष, स) is substituted for a consonant (other than a nasal and a semi-vowel) in the reduplicate.

Thus in पच् the reduplicate is पपच्, the first प is also a *substitute*, for the चर् substitute of प will be प ॥ Such substitutes, however, are not meant here. This we learn from the implication (jñâpaka) of sûtra VI. 4. 126 where exception is made in case of शस् and दद् ॥ Therefore, where the substitute is a *different* letter, then the reduplicate becomes âdeśâdî: otherwise not.

When the affixes are not कित् or ङित् the rule does not apply: as अहं पपच, अहं पपठ ॥

Vârt:—ए is substituted for the अ of दम्भ under similar circumstances:—thus देभतुः, देभुः ॥ The elision of the nasal by VI. 4. 24, would be considered asiddha by VI. 4. 22, hence this vârtika.

Vârt:—ए is substituted for the अ of नश and मन before affixes other than those of लिट् ॥ As अनेशम्, मेनका ॥ अनेशम् is the Aorist in अङ् of नश् which belongs to Pushâdi roots (III. 1. 55). मेनका is formed by वुन् (III. 1. 150). Padamanjari gives अनेशन् (3 rd Pl.), and quotes अनेशन्नस्येषवः ॥

Vârt:—In the Vedas, ए is substituted for the अ of अम् and पच् before affixes other than those of the Perfect, as व्येमानम्, (वि + अम् + चानश्, the augment मुक् being dropped); पेचिरन् instead of पचेरन्, the Imperfect of पच् ॥ The shortening is also a Vedic irregularity.

Vârt:—So also of यज् and वप, as आयेजे and आवेपे the Imperfect Vedic forms. The augment आट् being added by VI. 4. 73.

थलि च सेटि ॥१२१॥ पदानि ॥ थलि, च, सेटि, (अत एक हल् मध्ये अनादेशादेः)

वृत्तिः ॥ थलि च सेटि परतो ऽनादेशादेरङ्गस्य एकहल्मध्यगतस्यातः स्थाने एकार आदेशो भवति अभ्यासलोपश्च ॥

121. ए is substituted for अ, of a verbal stem standing between two simple consonants, the stem not having any different letter substituted in the reduplicate, when the ending थल् of the Perfect having the augment इट् follows, and thereby, the reduplicate is elided.

Thus पेचिथ, शेकिथ ॥ But पपक्थ before aniṭ थ; दिदेविथ, the vowel being इ and not अ; ततक्षिथ, ररक्षिथ, the अ not standing between two *simple* consonants; and चकणिथ, बभणिथ, the reduplicate having the substitutes च and ब different from क and भ ॥ This sûtra applies even when the affix is not कित्; and थल् is read in the sûtra only for the sake of clearness, no non-kit Perfect ending can take इट् except थल् ॥

तॄफलभजत्रपश्च ॥ १२२ ॥ पदानि ॥ तॄ, फल, भज, त्रपः, च, (अत एक हलमध्ये अनादेशादेर्लिटिथलिचसेटि) ॥

वृत्तिः ॥ तॄ फल भज त्रप इत्येतेषामङ्गानामत एकारादेशो भवति, अभ्यासलोपश्च, लिटि क्ङिति परतस्थलि च सेटि ॥

वार्त्तिकम् ॥ श्रन्थेश्चेति वक्तव्यम् ॥

122. ए is substituted for the अ of तॄ, फल, भज and त्रप, and the reduplicate is elided, when the affixes of the Perfect having an indicatory क् (or ङ्) follow, as well as when थल् with the इट् augment follows.

Thus तेरतुः, तेरुः, तेरिथ, फेलतुः, फेलुः, फेलिथ, भेजतु, भेजुः, भेजिथ, त्रेपे, त्रेपाते, त्रेपिरे ॥ In the case of तॄ the rule applies to the अ obtained by Guṇa, contrary to VI. 4. 126, in फल् and भज् the rule, that no different substitute should be in the reduplicate, is not adhered to, and in त्रप the अ does not stand between two *simple* consonants.

Vârt: It should be stated that the rule opplies to श्रन्थ also:-as, श्रेथतुः, श्रेथुः ॥

राधो हिंसायाम् ॥ १२३ ॥ पदानि ॥ राधो हिंसायाम् ॥

वृत्तिः ॥ राधो हिंसायामर्थेऽवर्णस्य एकार आदेशो भवति, अभ्यासलोपश्च लिटि क्ङिति परतस्थलि च सेटि ॥

123. ए is substituted for the आ of राध when meaning 'to hurt some one', and the reduplicate is elided, before the affixes of the Perfect having an indicatory क् (or ङ्), as well as before थल् with the इट् augment.

Thus अपरेधतुः, अपरेधुः, अपरेधिथ, but रराधतुः, रराधुः, रराधिथ in any other sense than that of 'hurting'. In this sûtra the *long* आ of राध is to be replaced by ए, the anuvṛitti of short अ (अतः VI. 4. 120) is therefore not appropriate here. We should either read the annuvṛitti of आ from VI. 4. 112, or we should read the word एकहलमध्ये in this way "in राध् *whatever* stands between two simple consonants is replaced by ए".

वा जॄभ्रमुत्रसाम् ॥ १२४ ॥ पदानि ॥ वा, जॄ, भ्रमु, त्रसाम्, ॥

वृत्तिः ॥ जॄ भ्रमु त्रस इत्येतेषामङ्गानामतः स्थाने वा एकार आदेशो भवति अभ्यासलोपश्च लिटि क्ङिति परतस्थलि च सेटि ॥

124. ए is optionally substituted for the अ of the stems जर् (जॄ), भ्रम, and त्रस, and the reduplicate is thereby elided, before the affixes of the Perfect having an indicatory क् (or ङ्), as well as before the थल् with the augment इट्॥

Thus जेरतुः, जेरुः, जेरिथ, or जजरतुः, जजरुः, जजरिथ, भ्रेमतुः, भ्रेमुः, भ्रेमिथ, or बभ्र मतुः, बभ्रमुः, बभ्रमिथ, त्रेसतुः, त्रेसुः, त्रेसिथ, or तत्रसतुः, तत्रसुः, तत्रसिथ ॥

फणां च सप्तानाम् ॥ १२५ ॥ पदानि ॥ फणाम्, च, सप्तानाम्, ॥

वृत्तिः ॥ फणादीनां सप्तानां धातूनामवर्णस्य स्थाने वा एकार आदेशो भवति, अभ्यासलोपश्च लिटि क्ङिति परत, स्थलि च सेटि ॥

125. ए is optionally substituted for the अ and आ of the seven roots फण्, राज्, भ्राज्, भ्राश्, भ्लाश्, स्यम and स्वन् ; and the reduplicate is elided thereby, before the affixes of the Perfect having an indicatory क् (or ङ्) as well as before the थ with the इट् augment.

Thus फेणतुः, फेणुः, फेणिथ or पफणतुः, पफणुः, पफणिथ; रेजतुः, रेजुः, रेजिथ, or रराजतुः, रराजुः, रराजिथ; भ्रेजे, भ्रेजाते, भ्रेजिरे, or बभ्राजे, बभ्राजाते, बभ्राजिरे; भ्रेशे, भ्रेशाते, भ्रेशिरे, or बभ्राशे, बभ्राशाते, बभ्राशिरे; भ्लेशे, भ्लेशाते, भ्लेशिरे, or बभ्लाशे, बभ्लाशाते, बभ्लाशिरे; स्येमतुः, स्येमुः, स्येमिथ, or सस्यमतुः, सस्यमुः, सस्यमिथ; स्वेनतुः, स्वेनुः, स्वेनिथ, or सस्वनतुः, सस्वनुः, सस्वनिथ, Why of 'seven"? Observe, दध्वनतुः, दध्वनुः, दध्वनिथ ॥ The Phaṇâdi is a subdivision of Bhuâdi (873-879)

न शसददवादिगुणानाम् ॥ १२६ ॥ पदानि ॥ न, शस, दद, वादि, गुणानाम्, (अत एक हल्मध्येऽनादेशादेर्लिटि) ॥

वृत्तिः ॥ शस दद इत्येतयोर्वकारादीनां च धातूनां गुण इत्येवमभिनिर्वृत्तस्य च योऽकारस्तस्य स्थाने एकारादेशो न भवति, अभ्यासलोपश्च ॥

126. ए is not substituted for the अ of शस्, दद्, or of roots beginning with a व, or of such verbal stems in which the अ results through the substitution of Guṇa, though the affixes of the Perfect being कित् or ङित् follow, or the seṭ थल्, nor is the reduplicate elided.

Thus विशशसतुः, विशशसुः, विशशसिथे, ददरे, ददशाते, ददशिरे, Of roots beginning with वः-ववमतुः, ववमुः, ववमिथ, ॥ Of roots where अ is the result of Guṇa, विशशरतुः, विशशरुः, विशशरिथ, लुलविथ, पुपविथ ॥ गुणशब्दाभिनिर्वृत्तस्यार्थोऽस्यौकारस्य चायमकार इति एत्वं प्रतिषिध्यते ॥

The अ of Guṇa may result either from the guṇa of ऋ as ॠ changed to कर् or of उ changed to ओ again changed to अव् as लु—लव ॥

अर्वणस्त्रसावनञः ॥ १२७ ॥ पदानि ॥ अर्वणः, तृ, असौ, अनञः, ॥

वृत्तिः ॥ अर्वन्नित्येतस्याङ्गस्यत् इत्ययमादेशो भवति, सुश्चेत्ततः परो न भवति, स च नञ उत्तरो न भवति ॥

127. तृ (which is changed to न्त in the strong cases, and forms the feminine in ई unaccented) is substituted for the final of the stem अर्वन्, except in the Nominative singular or when the word is joined with the Negative particle.

The real substitute is तृ, the ऋ is for the sake of making this affix an उगित्, so that in sarvanâmasthâna cases we have नुम् augment VII. I. 70. Thus अर्वन्तौ, अर्वन्तः, अर्वन्तम्, अर्वन्तौ, अर्वतः, अर्वता, अर्वद्भ्याम्, अर्वद्भिः, अर्वती, आर्वतम् ॥ असाविति किम्, अर्वा ॥ अनञ इति किम्, अनर्वाणौ, अनर्वाणः, अनर्वाणं वृषभं मन्द्रजिह्वम् ॥

But अर्वा in the Nominative Sing: and अनर्वाणौ, अनर्वाणः, अनर्वाणं वृषभं मन्द्रजिह्वम् with the Negative Particle नञ् ॥

मघवा बहुलम् ॥ १५८ ॥ पदानि ॥ मघवा, बहुलम्, (तृ) ॥

वृत्तिः ॥ मघवन्नित्येतस्याङ्गस्य बहुलं तृ इत्ययमादेशो भवति ॥

128. तृ is diversely substituted for the final of मघवन् ॥

As मघवान्, मघवन्तौ, मघवन्तः, मघवन्तम्, मघवन्तौ, मघवतः, मघवता, मघवती, माघवतम्, ॥ न च भवति, मघवा, मघवानौ, मघवानः, मघवानम्, मघवानौ, मघोनः, मघोना, मघवभ्याम्, मघवभिः मघोनी, माघवनम् ॥

भस्य ॥ १५९ ॥ पदानि ॥ भस्य ॥

वृत्तिः ॥ भस्येत्ययमधिकार, आ अध्यायपरिसमाप्तेः, यदित ऊर्ध्वमनुक्रमिष्यामो भस्येत्येवं तद्वेदितव्यम् ॥

129. Whatever will be taught in the following upto the end of the Adhyâya, should be understood to apply to the nominal stems called Bha (I. 4. 18, 19).

Thus sûtra VI. 4. 130 says 'पद् is the substitute of पाद्' ॥ It means पद् is substituted for पाद् when the latter gets the designation of भ ॥ Thus द्विपदः पश्य, द्विपदा कृतम् but द्विपादौ, द्विपादः where the affixes are those of Sarvanâmasthâna.

पादः पत् ॥ १३० ॥ पादः, पत् ॥

वृत्तिः ॥ पादिति पादशब्दो लुप्ताकारो गृह्यते । तदन्तस्याङ्गस्य भस्य पदित्ययमादेशो भवति । स च पाच्छब्दस्यैव भवति ॥

130. For पाद् is substituted पद् when the former is Bha.

The substitute replaces the whole form पाद् and not only the final, on the maxim निर्दिश्यमानस्यादेशा भवन्ति "substitutes take the place of that which is actually enunciated in a rule." ॥ Thus द्विपदः पश्य, द्विपदा, द्विपदे, द्विपदिकां ददाति (V. 4. 1), त्रिपदिकां ददाति, वैयाघ्रपद्यः ॥

वसोः संप्रसारणम् ॥ १३१ ॥ पदानि ॥ वसोः, सम्प्रसारणम् ॥

वृत्तिः ॥ वस्वन्तस्य भस्य संप्रसारणं भवति ॥

131. The semi-vowel of the affix वस् (वंसु) is vocalised to उ in a Bha stem.

Thus विदुषः पश्य, विदुषा, विदुषे, पेचुषः पश्य, पेचुषा, पेचुषे, ययुषः पश्य ॥ For the purposes ofthe elision of आ (VI. 4. 64), vocalisation under the present sûtra should not be considered as asiddha (VI. 4. 22). Thus पा + क्वसु (III. 2. 107) = पपा + वस् = पपा + उस् + शस् (VI. 4. 131, VI. 1. 108). Now if उ were to be considered as asiddha, then the affix does not begin with a vowel, and we can not apply VI. 4. 64, which requires the elision of आ, but the samprasâraṇa is not considered assiddha, and we have पप् + उस् + अस् = पपुषः पश्य ॥ In the nominative, where the stem is not भ, we have पपा + वस् + स् = पपी + वस् + स (VI. 4. 66) = पपीवान् (VII. 1. 70, VI. 4. 10, VI. 1. 68 and VIII. 2. 23). The affix क्वसु is included in वसु for the purposes of samprasâraṇa.

वाह ऊठ् ॥ १३२ ॥ पदानि ॥ वाहः, ऊठ् ॥

वृत्तिः ॥ वाह इत्येवमन्तस्य भस्य ऊठ् इत्येतत्संप्रसारणं भवति ॥

132. The व् in वाह् is vocalised to ऊ (ऊठ्), when the compound stem is Bha.

The word वाह् is a ण्वि formed stem by III. 2. 64. It can never stand alone, but, must be preceded by an upapada: hence we have used the word "compound." Thus प्रष्ठौहः, प्रष्ठौहा, प्रष्ठौहे, दित्यौहः, दित्यौहा, दित्यौहे ॥ By VI. 1. 108, ऊ + आ (of वा) = ऊ ;and then प्रष्ठ + ऊह् = प्रष्ठौह् ; the Vṛiddhi being substituted by VI. 1. 89. This form could have been evolved by simple samprasâraṇa thus: प्रष्ठ + वह् + शस् = प्रष्ठ + उह् + अस् (VI. 1. 108) = प्रष्ठ + ओह् + अस् (the affix ण्वि III. 2. 64, will produce guṇa) = प्रष्ठौहः (VI. 1. 88). In fact ण्वि is never added to वह् (III. 2. 64) unless the preceding member ends in अ and that अ + ओ of वा will always produce औ ॥ The making of this special samprasâraṇa in ऊठ्, indicates the existence of following maxim: असिद्धं बहिरङ्गमन्तरङ्गे ; and the samprasâraṇa being a bahiranga operation, is considered as asiddha for the purposes of guṇa which is an antaranga operation : therefore, we can never get the form ओह ॥

श्वयुवमघोनामतद्धिते ॥ १३३ ॥ पदानि ॥ श्व, युव, मघोनाम्, अतद्धिते ॥

वृत्तिः ॥ श्वन् युवन् मघवन् इत्येतेषामङ्गानामतद्धिते प्रत्यये परतः संप्रसारणं भवति ॥

133. The व of श्वन्, युवन् and मघवन् becomes vocalised, but not before a Taddhita affix.

Thus शुनः, शुना, शुने, यूनः, यूना, यूने, मघोनः, मघोना, मघोने ॥ But शौवनं मांसम् यौवनं वर्तते, माघवनः स्थालीपाकः with Taddhita affixes. शौवन is formed by अञ् affix (IV. 3. 154) and औ being added by VII. 3. 4 as श्वन belongs dvârâdi class.

This vocalisation takes place of the nouns ending in न्, but not when they become feminine or do not end in न्, as युवतीः पश्य, मघवतः, मघवते, मघवता ॥ The word अनः of the next sûtra, in a way, qualifies this sûtra also.

अल्लोपोऽनः ॥ १३४ ॥ पदानि ॥ अल्, लोपः, अनः ॥

वृत्तिः ॥ अनित्येवमन्तस्य भस्य अकारलोपो भवति ॥

वार्त्तिकम् ॥ अनो नकारान्तस्याय लोप इष्यते ॥

134. Of a Bha stem ending in अन्, the अ is elided.

As राज्ञः पश्य, राज्ञा, राज्ञे, तक्ष्णः पश्य, तक्ष्णा and तक्ष्णे ॥ *Vârt*:—The elision takes place of a stem which actually ends in न्, therefore, it does not take place here, राजकीयम् ॥

षपूर्वहन्धृतराज्ञामणि ॥ १३५ ॥ पदानि ॥ ष पूर्व, हन्, धृतराज्ञाम्, अणि ॥

वृत्तिः ॥ षकारपूर्वो यो ऽन् हनो धृतराज्ञश्च तस्याकारलोपो भवति ॥

135. Of a Bha stem ending in अन् with a preceding ष, as well as of हन् and धृतराजन्, the अ is elided before the affix अण् ॥

Thus औक्ष्णः, ताक्ष्णः, भ्रौणघ्नः, धार्तराज्ञः ॥ But सामनः, वैमन ॥ Why do we say before the affix अण्? Observe ताक्षण्यः ॥ Why do we say 'preceded by a ष'? Observe सामनः and वैमनः from सामन् and विमन् formed with the affix अण्; here neither the अ of मन् nor the final syllable अन् is elided, since VI. 4. 167 keeps these words in their primitive state so far.

विभाषा ङिश्योः ॥ १३६ ॥ पदानि ॥ विभाषा, ङि, श्योः (अल्लोपोऽनः) ॥

वृत्तिः ॥ ङौ परतः शीशब्दे च अनो विभाषा अकारलोपो भवति ॥

136. In a stem ending in अन्, the अ is optionally elided before the Locative ending इ and before the ending शी (ई) of the Nominative and Accusative Dual Neuter.

As राज्ञि or राजनि, साम्नि or सामनि, साम्नी or सामनी (VII. 1. 19).

न संयोगाद्वमन्तात् ॥ १३७ ॥ पदानि ॥ न, संयोगात्, व्, म्, अन्तात्, (अल्लोपोऽनः) ॥

वृत्तिः ॥ वकारमकारान्तात्संयोगादुत्तरस्यानो ऽकारस्य लोपो न भवति ॥

137. The अ in अन् is not elided when the Bha stem ends in वन् or मन् with a consonant preceding व् or म् ॥

Thus पर्वणा, पर्वण, अथर्वणा, अथर्वणे, चर्मणा and चर्मणे ॥ Why do we say 'preceded by a consonant'? Observe प्रतिदीव्ना, प्रातर्दीव्ने, साम्ना, साम्ने ॥ Why do we say 'stems in वन् and मन्'? Observe तक्ष्णा, and तक्ष्णे ॥

अचः ॥ १३८ ॥ पदानि ॥ अचः, (भस्य अल्लोपः) ॥

वृत्तिः ॥ अच इत्ययमञ्चतिर्लुप्तनकारो गृह्यते । तदन्तस्य भस्य अकारस्य लोपो भवति ॥

138. The अ of अच् (अञ्च्) is elided at the end of a Bha stem.

Thus दधीचः पश्य, दधीचा, दधीचे, मधूचः पश्य, मधूचा, मधूचे ॥ The lengthening of the first member takes place by VI. 3. 138: and न् of अञ्च is elided by VI. 4. 24.

उद ईत् ॥ १३९ ॥ पदानि ॥ उदः, ईत्, (अचः) ॥

वृत्तिः ॥ उद उत्तरस्याच ईकारादेशो भवति ॥

139. Long ई is substituted for the अ of अच् (अञ्च्), after the word उत् when the stem is Bha.

As उदीचः, उदीचा, उदीचे ॥

आतो धातोः ॥ १४० ॥ पदानि ॥ आतः, धातोः, (भस्य लोपः) ॥

वृत्तिः ॥ आकारान्तस्य धातोर्भस्य लोपो भवति ॥

140. The final आ of a Bha stem, when it ends in a root, is elided.

Thus कीलालपः पश्य, कीलालपा, कीलालपे, शुभंयः पश्य, शुभंया, and शुभंये from कीलालपा and शुभंया ॥ Why do we say 'the आ *of a root*'? Observe खट्वाः पश्य, मालाः पश्य ॥ This sûtra should be divided into two (1) आतः (2) धातोः; so that the long आ in general may be elided. For Pâṇini himself has declined क्त्वा and श्ना by the elision of आ, see VII. 1. 37, (क्त्वो ल्यप्) and III. 1. 83, (श्नः शानच्) ॥

मन्त्रेष्वाङ्यादेरात्मनः ॥ १४१ ॥ पदानि ॥ मन्त्रेषु, आङि, आदेः, आत्मनः ॥

वृत्तिः ॥ मन्त्रेषु आङि परत आत्मन आदेर्लोपो भवति ॥

वार्तिकम् ॥ आङोऽन्यत्रापि छन्दसि लोपो दृश्यते ॥

141. In the Mantras, the beginning of आत्मन् is elided, when the affix of the Instrumental Singular follows.

आङ् is the name of the Instrumental singular affix, given by ancient Grammarians. Thus त्मना देवेभ्यः, त्मना सोमेषु ॥ Why in the Mantras? Observe आत्मनो कृतम् ॥ Why in the Instrumental Singular? यत्रात्मन स्तन्वो वरिष्ठा ॥

Vârt:—The elision of आ of 'âtman' is found in other cases also, but not so frequently as in the Instrumental, as त्मन्यासमञ्जत मह्यम् ॥

ति विंशतेर्डिति ॥ १४२ ॥ पदानि ॥ ति, विंशतेः, डिति, (भस्य, लोपः) ॥

वृत्तिः ॥ भस्य विंशतेस्तिशब्दस्य डिति प्रत्यये परतो लोपो भवति ॥

142. Of the Bha stem विंशति, before an affix having an indicatory ड, the ति is elided.

Thus विंशकः = विंशत्या क्रीतः (with ड्वुन् V. 1. 24), विंशं शतम्, (विंशतेः पूरणो विंशः, with डट affix V. 2. 48), एकविंशः ॥ Why do we say 'having an indicatory ड'? Observe विंशत्या ॥

टेः ॥ १४३ ॥ पदानि ॥ टेः, (डिति, लोपः) ॥

वृत्तिः ॥ टिसंज्ञकस्य डिति प्रत्ययेपरतो लोपो भवति ॥

143. Before an affix having an indicatory ड्, the last vowel, with the consonant, if any, that follows it, is elided.

Thus कुमुद्वत्, नड्वत् and वेतस्वत् with ड्मतुप् (IV. 2. 87). So also त्रिंशता क्रीतः = त्रिंशकः with ड्वुन् of V. 1. 24. The rule applies even to non-bha bases, for effect must be given to the indicatory ड ॥ Thus उपसरजः, मन्दुरजः (III. 2. 97 with the krit affix ड) ॥

नस्तद्धिते ॥ १४४ ॥ पदानि ॥ नः, तद्धिते, (भस्य, टेः, लोपः) ॥

वृत्तिः ॥ नकारान्तस्य भस्य टेर्लोपो भवति तद्धिते परतः ॥

वार्तिकम् ॥ नान्तस्य टिलोपे सब्रह्मचारिपीठसर्पिकलापिकुथुमितैतिलिजाजलिलाङ्गलिशिलालिशिखण्डिसूकरसद्मसुपर्वणामुपसंख्यानं कर्तव्यम् ॥ वार्तिकम् ॥ अश्मनो विकार उपसंख्यानम् ॥

वा० ॥ चर्मणः कोश उपसंख्यानम् ॥ वा० ॥ शुनः सङ्कोच उपसंख्यानम् ॥

वा० ॥ अव्ययानां च सायंप्रातिकाद्यर्थमुपसंख्यानम् ॥

144. Of the stem bha, the final न् with the vowel that precedes it, is elided, before a Taddhita affix.

Thus आग्निशर्मिः, औडुलोमिः, सारलोमिः from अग्निशर्मन्, उडुलोमन्, and सरलोमन् with the Taddhita affix इञ् (IV. 1. 96). Why do we say 'ending in न्'? Observe सात्वतः ॥ Why 'before a Taddhita affix'? Observe शर्मणा, शर्मणे ॥

Vârt:—The final न् with the vowel that precedes it, is dropped before a Taddhita in the following: 1. सब्रह्मचारिन्—साब्रह्मचाराः (IV. 3. 120), 2. पीठसर्पिन्—पैठसर्पाः (IV. 3. 120), 3. कलापिन्—कालापाः (IV. 3. 108 and IV. 2. 59), 4. कुथुमिन्—कौथुमाः (IV. 3. 101), 5. तैतिलिन्—तैतिलाः (IV. 3. 116), 6. जाजलिन्—जाजलाः (IV. 2. 59), 7. लाङ्गलिन्—लाङ्गलाः, 8. शिलालिन्—शैलालाः, 9. शिखण्डिन्—शैखण्डाः, 10. सुकरसद्मन्—सौकर सद्माः, 11. सुपर्वन्—सौपर्वाः ॥ In the above those which end in इन्, elide the इन् in spite of VI, 4. 164, and those in अन् contradict VI. 4. 167.

Vârt:—अश्मन् loses its अन् before a Taddhita affix meaning 'prepared there with': as, आश्मः, otherwise आश्मनः ॥

Vârt:—Of चर्मन्, the अन् is elided when meaning 'a sheath or purse': as, चार्मः कोशः (IV. 3. 134), otherwise चार्मणः ॥

Vârt:—The अन् of श्वन् is elided when the sense is 'to contract', as शौवः संकोचः (IV. 3. 120), otherwise शौवनः ॥

Vârt:—The Indeclinables like सायंप्रातिकः &c are formed by the टि elision: as सायंप्रातिकः, पौनः पुनिकः, बाह्यः, कौतस्कुतः (formed by ठञ् IV. 3. 11). But not before the affixes ख्यु and ख्युल्, as आरातीयः, शाश्वतिकः ॥ Pâṇini himself has shown the exception, in the case of शाश्वतिक, by using it in II. 4. 9. So also शाश्वतम् ॥

अह्नष्टखोरेव ॥ १४५ ॥ पदानि ॥ अह्नः, ट, खोः, एव ॥

वृत्ति ॥ अहन्नित्येतस्य टखोरेव परतष्टिलोपो भवति ।

वार्तिक ॥ अह्नः समूहे खो वक्तव्यः ॥

145. The अन् of अहन् is elided only before the affixes ट and ख ॥

Thus द्वे अहनी समाहृते = द्व्यहः, त्र्यहः (V. 4. 91 with टच्). द्वे अहनी अधीष्टो भृतो भूतो भावी वा = द्व्यहीनः, त्र्यहीनः (with ख V. 1. 87).

Vârt:—ख is added to अहन् in the sense of तस्य समूहः, when referring to a sacrifice. अह्नां समूहः क्रतुः = अहीनः (IV. 2. 42).

Though the अन् of अहन् would have been elided by the last aphorism also, before the affixes ट and ख, the present sûtra makes a restrictive rule: अहन् does not lose its final अन् before any other Taddhita affix, thus अह्ना निर्वृत्तम् = आह्निकम् (with ठञ् V. 1. 79). The word एव 'only' is for the sake of perspicuity. अहन् alone does not lose its final अन् before ट and ख, other stems also do the same. This we infer, from the exception made in the case of âtman and adhvan, before ख, in VI. 4. 169.

ओर्गुणः ॥ १४६ ॥ पदानि ॥ ओः, गुणः ॥

वृत्तिः ॥ उवर्णान्तस्य भस्य गुणो भवति तद्धिते परतः ॥

146. For उ or ऊ of a bha stem, there is substituted Guṇa, before a Taddhita affix.

Thus बाभ्रव्यः from बभ्रु, माण्डव्यः from मण्डु, शाङ्कव्यं दारु (from शंकु), पिचव्यः कार्पासः, (from पिचु) कमण्डलव्या मृत्तिका (from कमण्डलू), परशव्यमयः, औपगवः, कापटवः &c. Instead of making the sûtra simpler by saying ओरोत् 'let ओ be substituted for उ or ऊ', the employment of the technical phrase गुणः in the aphorism indicates the existence of the following maxim संज्ञा पूर्वको विधिरनित्यः "A rule is not universally valid, when that which is taught in it, is denoted by a technical term". The present sûtra is, therefore, anitya, and we have forms like स्वायंभुवः from स्वयंभू without guṇa. See VII. 4. 30 also.

ढे लोपोऽकद्र्वाः ॥ १४७ ॥ पदानि ॥ ढे, लोपः, अ, कद्र्वाः ॥

वृत्तिः ॥ ढे परत उवर्णान्तस्य भस्याकद्र्वा लोपो भवति ॥

147. The ऊ or उ of a bha stem is elided before the affix एय (ढ), but not of the stem 'Kaṭrû'.

Thus कामण्डलेयः, शैतिवाहेयः, जाम्बेयः, माद्रवाहेयः, but काद्रवेयो मन्त्रमपश्यत् ॥

यस्येति च ॥ १४८ ॥ पदानि ॥ यस्य, ईति, च, (भस्य, तद्धिते, लोपः) ॥

वृत्तिः ॥ इवर्णान्तस्यावर्णान्तस्य च भस्य ईकारे परे तद्धिते च लोपो भवति ॥

वार्त्तिकम् ॥ यस्येत्यौङः श्यां प्रतिषेधो वक्तव्यः ॥

वार्त्तिकम् ॥ इयङ् उवङ्भ्यां लोपो भवति विप्रतिषेधेन ॥

148. The final इ and अ (both long and short), of a bha stem, are elided before a Taddhita affix and before the feminine affix ई ॥

Thus दाक्षी, प्लाक्षी, सखी from दाक्षि, प्लाक्षि and सखि with the feminine affix ई

(IV. 1. 65) The above forms could also have been evolved by the simple rules of sandhi, as शाक्षि + ई = शाक्षी ॥ It might be asked, where was then the necessity of eliding इ ? There would arise difficulty in the forms like अति सखि ॥ From the word सखी formed by ङीष् under IV. 1. 62, we form the compound सखीमतिक्रान्तः = अतिसखि, the final becoming short by I. 2. 48 (the samâsânta affix टच् is not added here as required by V. 4. 91, that rule applying to the masculine form सखि and not to the feminine सखी). Now if in forming सखि + ई = सखी, had we not elided the letter इ of खि, then the long ई being the single substitute for both इ + ई, would be considered as like the final इ of सखि by VI. 1. 85. That being so, the word अतिसखि would be considered a non – घि word by I. 4. 7, for सखि has been specifically excluded form घि class. Not being a घि, we cannot have the form अतिसखेः in the Ablative and Genitive singular. Hence the necessity of eliding इ before the feminine ई, so that the ekâdeśa rule VI. 1. 85, should not apply.

The short इ is elided before Taddhita affixes :—दुलि – दौलेयः, बलि – बालेयः, अग्नि – आग्नेयः ॥ अ is elided before ई as :—कुमार – कुमारी, गौर – गौरी, शार्ङ्गरव – शार्ङ्गरवी ॥ अ and आ are elided before the Taddhita :—दक्ष – दाक्षिः, प्लक्ष – प्लाक्षिः, चूड – चौडिः, बलाका – बालाकिः, सुमित्रा – सौमित्रिः ॥

Vârt :—Prohibition must be stated in the case of ई (शी), when it is the substitute of औ (VII. 1. 18), being the case-affix of the nom. and acc. dual in the neuter, and of certain feminine in long आ ॥ Before this ई, the preceding vowel, इ and अ are not elided. The stem before this ई is also bha by I. 4. 18 in the case of Neuter nouns. Thus काण्ड + ई = काण्डे ; कुड्ये ॥ सौर्य + ई = सौर्ये (the य would have beeen elided by VI. 4. 149). It is owing to this Vârtika, that we have inserted the word 'feminine' in the translation of the sûtra. This may also be done by reading the anuvṛitti of श्यां (VI. 4. 136); and च (VI. 4. 137) into this sûtra.

Vârt :—इयङ् and उवङ् are superseded, when they would apply simultaneously with this lopa. Thus इयङ् and उवङ् have unimpeded scope in श्री or भ्रू + औ or अस् (जस्), as श्रियौ, श्रियः, भ्रुवौ, भ्रुवः ॥ Lopa has unimpeded scope in कमण्डलु – कामण्डलेयः (with ढञ् IV. 1. 135), and माद्रबाहेयः ॥ But in वत्सप्री + ढञ् (IV. 1. 135), both the rules VI. 4. 77 and VI. 4. 148, present themselves. The former is superseded, and we have वात्सप्रेयः (वत्सं प्रीणाति = वत्सप्रीः, तस्यापत्यं) ; so also लेखाभ्रूः – लैखाभ्रेयः with the ढक् affix, this word belonging to Śubhrâdi class (IV. 1. 123).

सूर्यतिष्यागस्त्यमत्स्यानां य उपधायाः ॥ १४९ ॥ पदानि ॥ सूर्य, तिष्य, अगस्त्य, मत्स्यानाम्, यः, उपधायाः, (ईति, तद्धिते, लोपः) ॥

वृत्तिः ॥ सूर्य तिष्य अगस्त्य मत्स्य इत्येतेषां यकारस्य उपधाया भस्य लोपो भवति ईति परतस्तद्धिते च ॥

वार्त्तिकम् ॥ मत्स्यस्य ङ्यामिति वक्तव्यम् ॥ वा० ॥ सूर्यागस्त्ययोश्छे च ङ्यां च ॥

वा० ॥ तिष्यपुष्ययोर्नक्षत्राणि ॥
वा० ॥ अन्तिकशब्दस्य तसिप्रत्यये परतः ककारादिशब्दस्य लोपो वक्तव्य, आद्युदात्तं च ॥
वा० ॥ तमे तादेश्च ॥ वा० ॥ कादिलोपे बहुलमिति वक्तव्यम् ॥ वा० ॥ ये च ॥

149. Of the bha stems सूर्य, तिष्य, अगस्त्य and मत्स्य, (and their derivatives when they are Bha) the penultimate य् is also elided before the long ई and a Taddhita affix.

Thus सूर्येणैकादिक्=सौरी (सूर्य+अण् under IV, 3, 112=सौर्य, then ई of ङीप्= सौरी), as सौरी बलाका ॥

So also तिष्य—तैषमहः, तैषी रात्रिः ॥ So also अगस्त्यस्यापत्यं स्त्री=आगस्ती (IV. 1. 114), आगस्तीयः ; So also मत्स्य—मत्सी with ङीष् as it belongs to Gaurâdi class (IV. 1. 40). If the words सूर्य &c, were to be qualified by the word भ, then the sûtra would mean सूर्यादीनां भसंज्ञानां "of सूर्य &c, when they get the designation of भ"; and the result of this interpretation would be, that the rule would apply to cases like सूर्यस्य स्त्री=सूरी, आगस्त्यस्य स्त्री=आगस्ती, &c, only, where the forms सूर्य &c, are Bha, and not to their derivatives, as सौर्य &c: and there would not have been the forms like सौरी बलाका ; because, here the word सूर्य is not Bha before the affix ई, but the word सौर्य is Bha. Hence we have introduced the words "and their derivatives" in the translation, so as to cover the cases like सौरी बलाका ॥

In the last example, we again have an illustration, of the rule VI. 4. 22, which says that for purposes of asiddha the आश्रय must be the same. Thus सौर्य+ई=सौर्य्+अ lopa+ई=सौरी ॥ But सौर्य itself was formed by the elision of अ of सूर्य before the affix अण्, thus, सूर्य+अण्=सौर्य्+०+अण् (last sûtra) =सौर्य ॥ But if this lopa be considered as asiddha by VI. 4. 22, then we have the following equation सौर्य्+०+अ (of अण्)+ई=सौर्य्+०+० (अ of अण् being elided by VI. 4. 148)+ई ॥ Here य् cannot be elided, as it is not upadhâ or penultimate: because the first lopa is considered asiddha. But it is not to be so considered, as their scopes (आश्रय) are different. Hence we have the elision of य् by this sûtra. It should not be objected that the य् here is not penultimate, but ultimate: as सौर्य+ई=सौर्य्+०+ई (अ elided by the last sûtra), and thus य् is ultimate. Here, however, rule VI. 4. 22, applies. This elision of अ will be considered asiddha for the purposes of the elision of य्, their scope being the same. So being considered asibdha, य् still retains its designation of upadhâ and is elided by the present sûtra. It should be remembered here, that we could not take help of the rule of sthanîvat-bhâva, because for purposes of यलोप, that rule is set aside. See I. 1. 58.

Why do we say the penultimate य्? Observe मत्स्यचरी ॥ This word is thus formed. The affix चरट् is added to मत्सी by V. 3. 53, in the sense of मत्सी भूतपूर्वा ॥ Then the मत्सी becomes masculine मत्स्य by VI. 4. 35, and we have मत्स्यचर ॥ This word takes ङीप् by IV. 1. 15, because it is formed by an affix having an indicatory ट् ॥ Thus मत्स्यचर+ई, and the word is भ, but the य is not elided, because it is not penultimate. The य has been read for the sake of the subsequent sûtras : उपधायाः alone would have been enough for the purposes of this aphorism. The rule contained in this sûtra is rather too general ; it is limited by the following vârtikas, which enumerate the conditions under which the elision takes place.

Vart :—The य of मत्स्य is elided before the feminine ई only : therefore not here मत्स्यस्येदं मांसं=मात्स्यम् ॥

Vârt :—Of सूर्य and अगस्त्य before the affixes छ, and ई (of the feminine) : as सौरीयः, सौरी, आगस्तीयः, आगस्ती ॥ But not here सौर्यं चरुं निर्वपेत्, आगस्त्य formed with the Patronymic अण् (IV. I. 114)

Vârt :—Of तिष्य and पुष्य when referring to asterisms, as, तिष्येण नक्षत्रेण युक्तः कालः=तैषः, पौषः (IV. 2. 3).

Vârt :—Of अन्तिक before the affix तसि, the क is elided, and the word has acute on the first syllable : as, अन्तितः in अन्तितो न दूरात् (V. 4. 45).

Vârt:—Before the affix तम, it loses the syllable तिक as well as क, as अन्तमः or अन्तितमः, in अग्ने त्वं नो अन्तिमः अन्तितमे अवरोहति ॥

Vârt :—The elision of क of अन्तिक takes place diversely, before the second member also, as अन्तिके सीदति=अन्तिषत् (स changed to ष by VIII. 3. 106)

Vârt :—The elision takes place also before the affix य, as अन्तियः, this is found in the Atharva-Veda, (अन्तिके भवः, with the affix यत् IV. 4. 110).

हलस्तद्धितस्य ॥ १५० ॥ पदानि ॥ हलः, तद्धितस्य, (य उपधायाः लोपः ईति)॥

वृत्तिः ॥ हल उत्तरस्य तद्धितयकारस्य उपधाया ईति परतो लोपो भवति ॥

150. The य् of a Taddhita when preceded by a consonant, and penultimate in a stem, is elided before the feminine ई ॥

The anuvritti of "taddhita" ceases, because of its mention in the next sûtra. Hence this sûtra applies to feminine ई only. As गार्गी, वात्सी from गार्ग्य and वात्स्य ॥ Why do we say 'when preceded by a consonant'? Observe कारिकेयी ॥ Why do we say 'of a Taddhita'. Observe वैश्यस्य भार्या=वैश्यी ॥

आपत्यस्य च तद्धितेऽनाति ॥ १५१ ॥ पदानि ॥ आपत्यस्य, च, तद्धिते, अनाति (लोपः) ॥

वृत्तिः ॥ अपत्ययकारस्य हल उत्तरस्य तद्धिते अनाकारादौ लोपो भवति ॥

151. The य, belonging to a Patronymic affix, preceded by a consonant, is elided before a Taddhita, when it does not begin with an आ ॥

Thus गर्गाणां समूहः = गार्गकम् from गार्ग्य, वात्सकम् from वात्स्य (IV. 2. 37-40). Why do we say 'a Patronymic य'? Observe सांकाश्यकः, काम्पिल्यकः (IV. 2. 80).

The repetition of the word Taddhita indicates that the elision takes place some-times of the non-patronymic य also, as सौमी इष्टिः ॥

Why do we say 'not beginning with a long आ'? Observe गार्ग्यायणः, वात्स्यायनः ॥ The य should be preceded by a consonant, otherwise we have कारिकेयस्यापत्यं = कारिकेयिः ॥ Why do we say 'when followed by a Taddhita affix'? Observe गार्ग्ययोः, वात्स्ययोः (before the Genitive and Locative dual affixes).

क्यच्व्योश्च ॥ १५२ ॥ पदानि ॥ क्य, च्व्योः, च, (हलः, लोपः) ॥

वृत्तिः ॥ क्य च्वि इत्येतयोश्च परत आपत्ययकारस्य हल उत्तरस्य लोपो भवति ॥

152. The य् belonging to a Patronymic affix, preceded by a consonant, is elided before the Denominative affix क्य, and the adverbial affix च्वि ॥

Thus वात्सीयति or वात्सीयते गार्गीयति, or गार्गीयते ॥ So also गार्गीभूतः, वात्सीभूतः ॥ But सांकाश्यायते (where य is not Patronymic) and so also सांकाश्यीभूतः; and not also in कारिकेयीयति, कारिकेयीभूतः, the य not being preceded by a consonant.

बिल्वकादिभ्यश्छस्य लुक् ॥ १५३ ॥ पदानि ॥ बिल्वक-आदिभ्यः, छस्य, लुक् (भस्य तद्धिते) ॥

वृत्तिः ॥ नडादिषु बिल्वादयः पठ्यन्ते ॥ नडादीनां कुक् च इति कृतकुगागमा बिल्वकादयो भवन्ति तेभ्य उत्तरस्य छस्य भस्य तद्धिते परतो लुग् भवति ॥

153. The affix छ of the bha stems बिल्वक &c is elided before a Taddhita affix.

The बिल्व &c are a subdivision of Naḍâdi class (IV. 2. 91), and the augment क is added to them by IV. 2. 91. After these words, with the augment क, the affix छ is elided. Thus बिल्वा यस्यां सन्ति = बिल्वकीयाः ; तस्यां भवाः (IV. 3. 53) = बैल्वकाः ॥ Similarly वेणुकीयाः—वैणुकाः, वेत्रकीयाः, वैत्रकाः, वेतसकीयाः, वैतसकाः, तृणकीयाः, तार्णकाः इक्षुकीयाः, ऐक्षुकाः, काष्ठकीयाः, काष्ठकाः, कपोतकीयाः, कापोतकाः ॥ There is shortening of the final of कुंचा by the Vârtika कुञ्चा ह्रस्वत्वं च ॥ कुञ्चकीयाः, कौञ्चकाः ॥ छग्रहणं किम, छमात्रस्य लुग्यथा स्यात् कुको निवृत्तिर्मा भूदिति, ॥ अन्यथा हि संनियोगशिष्टानामन्यतरापाये उभयोरप्यभाव इति कुगपि निवर्त्तेत ॥ लुग्ग्रहणं सर्वलोपो यथा स्याद् यकारमात्रस्य मा भूत् ॥

The affix छ is specifically mentioned in order to show that the *affix only* should be elided and not the augment क ॥ Otherwise क् would also have been elided on the strength of the maxim :—संनियोगशिष्टानामन्यतरापाये (or अभावे) उभयोरप्यभावः (or अपायः), "When of the two things which are taught together, one disappears, then the other disappears likewise". The लुक् indicates the elision of the *whole* affix ईय, and not merely of य ॥

तुरिष्ठेमेयस्सु ॥ १५४ ॥ पदानि ॥ तुः, इष्ठ, इम, ईयस्सु, (लोपः) ॥

वृत्तिः ॥ इष्ठन् इमनिच् ईयसुन् इत्येतेषु परतः तृशब्दस्य लोपो भवति ॥

154. The affix तृ is elided before the affixes इष्ठन्, इमनिच् and ईयसुन् ॥

Thus करिष्ठः, विजयिष्ठः, दोहिष्ठः, दोहीयसी धेनुः ॥ The whole affix तृ is elided, otherwise only the last vowel (टि) with the following consonant would have been elided by the following rules. The anuvṛitti of लुक् of the last aphorism should not be read into this, for had the elision taken place by लुक्, then the mark of the affix would also have disappeared likewise (I. 1. 63), and there would have remained no guṇa in विजयिष्ठ and करिष्ठ ॥ See V. 1. 122, and V. 3. 59; for these affixes. The affix इमन् has been read into this aphorism for the sake of the subsequent sûtra, there being no example of तृ followed by इमन्; तृ is followed by इष्ठ and ईयस् by V. 3. 59.

टेः ॥ १५५ ॥ पदानि ॥ टेः, (भस्य लोपः इष्ठेमेयस्सु) ॥

वृत्तिः ॥ भस्य टेर्लोपो भवति इष्ठेमेयस्सु परतः ।

वार्तिकम् ॥ णाविष्ठवत्प्रातिपदिकस्य कार्यं भवतीति वक्तव्यम् ॥

वा० ॥ णाविष्ठवत्प्रातिपदिकस्य पुंवद्भावरभावटिलोपयणादिपरविन्मतोर्लुक्कनर्थमिति ॥

155. The last vowel, with consonant, if any, that follows it, is elided when the affixes इष्ठ, इमन् and ईयस् follow.

Thus पटिष्ठः, पटिमा, and पटीयान् from पटु, and लघिष्ठः, लघिमा and लघीयान् from लघु ॥

Vârt:—The Prâtipadika followed by the causative णि, undergoes all the changes, as it would have undergone, had the affix इष्ठ followed it. Those changes are (1) पुंवद्भावः the feminine noun becomes masculine: as, एनीमाचष्टे = एतयति, श्येतयति ॥ इष्ठ belongs to तसिलादि affixes and causes masculation by VI. 3. 35, (2) रभावः—the change of ऋ to र, as पृथुमाचष्टे = प्रथयति, म्रदयति, see VI. 4. 161. (3) टिलोपः—as, पटुमाचष्टे = पटयति, लघयति by this sûtra, (4) यणादिपरम् i. e. the application of Rule VI. 4. 156; as, स्थूलमाचष्टे = स्थवयति ॥ According to the school of Bhâradvâja, three more purposes are served: (5) विन् मतोर्लुक्—as स्रग्विणमाचष्टे = स्रजयति, वसुमन्तमाचष्टे = वसयति, see V. 3. 65. (6) कन्विधिः—the substitution of कन् for युवन् and अल्प (V. 3. 64)—as युवानमाचष्टे or अल्पमाचष्टे = कनयति ॥ (7) प्रादि substitution, as required by VI. 4. 157: as, प्रियमाचष्टे = प्रापयति ॥

स्थूलदूरयुवह्रस्वक्षिप्रक्षुद्राणां यणादिपरं पूर्वस्य च गुणः ॥ १५६ ॥ पदानि ॥ स्थूल, दूर, युव, ह्रस्व, क्षिप्र, क्षुद्राणाम, यण्, आदिपरम, पूर्वस्य, च गुणः, ॥

वृत्तिः ॥ स्थूल दूर युव ह्रस्व क्षिप्र क्षुद्र इत्येतेषां यणादिपरं लुप्यते इष्ठेमेयस्सु परतः, पूर्वस्य च गुणो भवति ॥

156. Before the affixes इष्ठ, इमन् and ईयस्, is elided the last semi-vowel with that which follows it, and for the first vowel, a Guṇa is substituted, in स्थूल, दूर, युवन्, ह्रस्व, क्षिप्र and क्षुद्र ॥

That is ल, र, वन्, व, र, and. र are elided. Thus स्थविष्ठः, स्थवीयान्; दविष्ठः दवीयान्; यविष्ठ, यवीयान्; ह्रसिष्ठः, ह्रसीयान्, ह्रसिमा; क्षेपिष्ठः, क्षेपीयान्, क्षेपिमा ॥ The words ह्रस्व, क्षिप्र, and क्षुद्र are read in Pṛithvâdi class and take 'iman' affix (V. 1. 122). क्षोदिष्ठः, क्षोदीयान्, क्षोदिमा ॥ Why do we say परं in यणादिपरं i. e. 'the *last* semi-vowel'? The *first* semi-vowel of युवन् and ह्रस्व i. e. य of यु and र of ह्र should not be elided. The word पूर्व is employed for the sake of distinctness.

प्रियस्थिरस्फिरोरुबहुलगुरुवृद्धतृप्रदीर्घवृन्दारकाणां प्रस्थस्फवर्बंहिगर्वर्षित्रब्द्राघिवृन्दाः ॥ १५७ ॥ पदानि ॥ प्रिय, स्थिर, स्फिर, उरु, बहुल, गुरु, वृद्ध, तृप्र, दीर्घ, वृन्दारकाणाम्, प्र, स्थ, स्फ, वर्, बंहि, गर्, वर्षि, त्रप्, द्राघि, वृन्दाः, (इष्ठेमेयस्सु) ॥

वृत्तिः ॥ प्रिय स्थिर स्फिर उरु बहुल गुरु वृद्ध तृप्र दीर्घ वृन्दारक इत्येतेषां प्र स्थ स्फ वर् बंहि गर् वर्षि त्रप् द्राघि वृन्द इत्येते यथासंख्यमादेशा भवन्ति इष्ठेमेयस्सुपरतः ॥

157. Before the affixes इष्ठ, इमन् and ईयस् the following substitutions take place :—प्र for प्रिय; स्थ for स्थिर, स्फ for स्फिर, वर् for उरु, बंह् for बहुल, गर् for गुरु, वर्ष् for वृद्ध, त्रप् for तृप्, द्राघ for दीर्घ, and वृन्द् for वृन्दारक ॥

Thus प्रेष्ठः, प्रेमा, प्रेयान्; स्थिर, स्थेष्ठः, स्थेयान्, स्थेमा; स्फिर, स्फेष्ठः, स्फेयान्; उरु, वरिष्ठः, वरिमा, वरीयान्; बहुल, बंहिष्ठः, बंहीयान्, बंहिमा; गुरु, गरिष्ठः, गरीयान्, गरिमा; वृद्ध, वर्षिष्ठः, वर्षीयान्; तृप, त्रपिष्ठः, त्रपीयान्; दीर्घ, द्राघिष्ठः, द्राघीयान्, द्राघिमा; वृन्दारक, वृन्दिष्ठः, वृन्दीयान्; प्रियोरुगुरुबहुलदीर्घाः पृथ्वादिषु पठ्यन्ते, तेनान्येषामिमानिज् न भवतीति नोदाह्रियते ॥

Of the above, priya, uru, guru and bahula are read in Prithvâdi class and take इमन् (V. 1. 122), others do not.

बहोर्लोपो भू च बहोः ॥ १५८ ॥ पदानि ॥ बहोः, लोपः, भू, च, बहोः ॥

वृत्तिः ॥ बहोरुत्तरेषामिष्ठेमेयसां लोपो भवति तस्य च बहोः स्थाने भू इत्ययमादेशो भवति ॥

158. The इ and ई of these affixes (इमन् and ईयस्) are elided after बहु, and for बहु is substituted भू ॥

Thus भूयान्, भूमा ॥ In the case of इष्ठ, the following rule 159 will apply. Under I. 1. 54 and 67, बहोः being in the Ablative, the first letter of the succeeding term is elided, viz. इ or ई; in this case. ॥ बहु belongs to Prithvâdi class and takes इमन् affix. (V. 1. 122) The repetition of बहोः is for the sake of pointing out the sthânî, for which the word भू is to be substituted : otherwise भू would have replaced these affixes.

इष्ठस्य यिट् च ॥ १५९ ॥ पदानि ॥ इष्ठस्य, यिट्, च, (बहोः भू च बहोः) ॥

वृत्तिः ॥ बहोरुत्तरस्य इष्ठस्य यिडागमो भवति बहोश्च भूरादेशो भवति ॥

159. After बहु, the augment यिट् is added to इष्ठ, and भू replaces बहु ॥

As भूयिष्ठ. ॥ This augment यिट् debars the lopa substitution, of the last sûtra, in the case of इष्ठ ॥ The इ in यिट् is for the sake of pronunciation, the augment being य् ॥ Or इष्ठ may be taken to have lost its इ by the foregoing sûtra, and to the ष्ठ, the augment थि may be added.

ज्यादादीयसः ॥ १६० ॥ पदानि ॥ ज्यात्, आत्, ईयसः ॥

वृत्तिः ॥ ज्यादुत्तरस्य ईयस आकार आदेशो भवति ॥

160. आ is substituted for the first letter of ईयस्, after ज्य ॥

As ज्यायान् ॥ ज्य is substituted for प्रशस्य by V. 3. 61. 'Lopa' being shut out by the intervening थिट् VI. 4. 159, the आत् is read in this sûtra. If the anuvṛitti of 'lopa' were present here, then the अ of ज्य would be lengthened before यस् by VII. 4. 25, and we would get the form ज्यायान् ॥ The peculiar construction of this sûtra indicates the existence of the following maxim:—अङ्गवृत्ते पुनर्वृत्तावविधिः 'when an operation which is taught in the angâdhikâra (VI. 4, end—VII. 4, end) has taken place, and another operation of the angâdhikâra is subsequently applicable, this latter operation is not allowed to take place." In VII. 4. 25, however, क्ङित् is understood, and lengthening could not have taken place by that rule.

र ऋतो हलादेर्लघोः ॥१६१॥ पदानि ॥ र, ऋतः, हल, आदेः, लघोः, (इष्ठेमेयस्सु) ॥

वृत्तिः ॥ रशब्द आदेशो भवति ऋकारस्य हलादेर्लघोरिष्ठेमेयस्सु परतः ॥

Kârikâ पृथुं मृदुं भृशं चैव कृशं च दृढमेव च ।
परिपूर्वं वृढं चैव षडेतान् रविधौ स्मरेत् ॥

161. Before the affixes इष्ठ, इमन् and ईयस्, र is substituted for the ऋ in a stem, when this ऋ is preceded by a consonant, and is not prosodially long (on account of being followed by a double consonant).

Thus प्रथिष्ठः, प्रथीयान् and प्रथिमा from पृथु (V. 1. 122), म्रदिष्ठः, म्रदीयान् and म्रदिमा ॥ Why do we say 'the ऋ'? Observe पटिष्ठः &c. Why do we say 'preceded by a consonant'? Observe ऋजिष्ठः, ऋजीयान् ॥ Why do we say 'when prosodially short'? Observe कृष्णिष्ठः, कृष्णीयान्, कृष्णिमा ॥ The following are the six words to which this rule applies and to none else:—पृथु, मृदु, भृश, कृश, दृढ, परिवृढ ॥ It therefore, does not apply to words like कृत, मातृ, भ्रातृ, &c, as कृतमाचष्टे = कृतयति, मातरमाचष्टे = मातयति, भ्रातरमाचष्टे = भ्रातयति ॥

विभाषर्जोश्छन्दसि ॥१६२॥ पदानि ॥ विभाषा, ऋजोः, छन्दसि, (इष्ठेमेयस्सु) ॥

वृत्तिः ॥ ऋजु इत्येतस्य ऋतः स्थाने विभाषा रेफ आदेशो भवति इष्ठेमेयस्सु परतश्छन्दसि विषये ॥

162. Before the affixes इष्ठ, इमन् and ईयस्, the ऋ of ऋजु may optionally be changed to र, in the Chhandas.

As रजिष्ठः and ऋजिष्ठः, in रजिष्ठमेति पन्थानम्, स्वमृजिष्ठः ॥

प्रकृत्यैकाच् ॥ १६३ ॥ पदानि ॥ प्रकृत्या, एक-अच्, (इष्ठेमेयस्सु) ॥

वृत्तिः ॥ एकाज् यद्भसञ्ज्ञकं तदिष्ठेमेयस्सु परतः प्रकृत्या भवति ॥
वार्त्तिकम् ॥ प्रकृत्या ऽके राजन्यमनुष्ययुवानः ॥

163. A monosyllabic bha stem retains its original form, without undergoing any change, before the affixes इष्ठ, इमन्, and ईयस् ॥

Thus स्रजिष्ठः, स्रजीयान्, स्रजयति from स्रग्विन्, the विन् being elided by V. 3. 65, the stem thus becoming monosyllabic. स्रजयति is the causative, formed on the model of इष्ठ by the Vârtika under VI. 4. 155. So also स्रुचिष्ठः, स्रुचीयान् and स्रुचयति from स्रुग्वत्, the मतुप् being elided as before. Why do we say 'a monosyllabic stem'? Observe वसिष्ठः from वसुमत् ॥ This rule is an exception to VI. 4. 155.

Vârt:—राजन्य, मनुष्य and युवन् retain their original form unchanged, before the affix अक ॥ As, राजन्यानां समूहः = राजन्यकम्, मानुष्यकम् ॥ This debars the elision of य required by VI. 4. 151. So यूनो भावः = यौवनिकः with वुञ् affix (V. 1. 133), in supersession of VI. 4. 144.

इनण्यनपत्ये ॥ १६४ ॥ पदानि ॥ इन्, अणि, अ नपत्ये, (प्रकृत्या) ॥
वृत्तिः ॥ इन्नन्तमनपत्यार्थेणि परतः प्रकृत्या भवति ॥

164. The final इन् of a bha stem remains unaltered before the non-Patronymic अण् affix.

Thus सांकुटिनम्, सांराविणम्, सांमार्जिनम् (III. 3. 44 and V. 4. 15). These are formed by the Krit-affix इनुण् (III. 3. 44), and then अण् is added in स्वार्थ by V. 4. 15. So also स्राग्विणम् from स्रग्विन् ॥ Why 'when अण् follows'? Observe दण्डिनां समूहः = दाण्डम् ॥ It is formed by अञ् (IV. 2. 44). Why do we say 'non-Patronymic'? Observe मेधाविनोऽपत्यं = मैधावः ॥

गाथिविदथिकेशिगणिपणिनश्च ॥ १६५ ॥ पदानि ॥ गाथि, विदथि, केशि, गणि, पणिनः, च, (अणिप्रकृत्या) ॥
वृत्तिः ॥ गाथिन् विदथिन् केशिन् गणिन् पणिन् इत्येते चाणि प्रकृत्या भवन्ति ॥

165. गाथिन्, विदथिन्, केशिन्, गणिन् and पणिन् remain unchanged before the Patronymic अण् also.

Thus गाथिनोऽपत्यं = गाथिनः, वैदथिनः, कैशिनः, गाणिनः, and पाणिनः ॥ This sûtra applies to Patronymics.

संयोगादिश्च ॥ १६६ ॥ पदानि ॥ संयोग- आदिः, च, (इन् अणि प्रकृत्या) ॥
वृत्तिः ॥ संयोगादिश्च इनणि प्रकृत्या भवति ॥

166. The syllable इन् of a stem ending in इन् remains unchanged before अण्, when a conjunct consonant precedes it.

Thus शाङ्खिनोऽपत्यं = शाङ्खिनः, याज्रिणः, वार्ज्जिणः ॥

अन्, ॥ १६७ ॥ पदानि ॥ अन्, (अणि प्रकृत्या) ॥

वृत्तिः ॥ अन्नन्तमणि प्रकृत्या भवति अपत्ये चानपत्ये च ॥

167. The syllable अन् of a stem ending in अन् remains unchanged, before अण् affix, whether Patronymic or otherwise.

As सामानः, वैमनः, सौत्वनः, जैत्वनः, from सामन्, वेमन्, सुत्वन् and जित्वन् ॥

ये चाभावकर्मणोः ॥ १६८ ॥ पदानि ॥ ये, च, अभाव, कर्मणोः, (तद्धिते अन् प्रकृत्या) ॥

वृत्तिः ॥ यकारादौ च तद्धिते ऽभावकर्मणोरर्थयोरन् प्रकृत्या भवति ॥

168. The syllable अन् of a stem ending in अन्, remains unchanged before a Taddhita beginning with य, when it does not denote existence in abstract or the avocation of some one.

Thus सामसु साधुः = सामन्यः, ब्राह्मण्यः ॥ But राज्ञो भावः कर्म वा = राज्यम् ॥ राजन् belongs to Purohitâdi class and takes यक् (V. 1. 128).

आत्माध्वानौ खे ॥ १६९ ॥ पदानि ॥ आत्म, अध्वानौ, खे, ॥

वृत्तिः ॥ आत्मन् अध्वन् इत्येतौ खे परतः प्रकृत्या भवतः ॥

169. The finals of the stems आत्मन् and अध्वन् remain unchanged before the affix ख ॥

Thus आत्मने हितं = आत्मनीनः (V. 1. 9), अध्वानमलङ्गामी (V. 2. 16) = अध्वनीनः ॥ But प्रत्यात्मम् and प्राध्वम् ॥ The first is formed by the samâsanta affix टच् added to the avyayîbhâva (V. 4. 108), and the latter by अच् (V. 4. 85).

न मपूर्वो ऽपत्ये ऽवर्म्मणः ॥१७०॥ पदानि ॥ न, म, पूर्वः, अपत्ये, अवर्मणः, (अणि) ॥

वृत्तिः ॥ मपूर्वो ऽन् अवर्म्मणोऽणि परतो ऽपत्येऽर्थे न प्रकृत्या भवति ॥

वार्त्तिकम् ॥ मपूर्वप्रतिषेधे वा हितनाम्न इति वक्तव्यम ॥

170. In a stem in अन् with a preceding म, with the exception of वर्मन्, the ending अन् does not remain unchanged before the patronymic affix अण् ॥

Thus सुषाम्णोऽपत्यं = सौषामः, चान्द्रसामः from चन्द्रसामन् ॥ Why do we say 'preceded by म'? Observe सौत्वनः, preceded by व ॥ Why do we use 'Patronymic'? Observe चमर्णा परिवृतो रथः = चामर्णः, the अन् not being changed by VI. 4. 167. Why do we say 'with the exception of वर्मन'? Observe चक्रवर्मणोऽपत्यं = चाक्रवर्मणः ॥

Vârt :—Optionally so in हितनामन्, as हितनाम्नोऽपत्यं = हैतनामः or हैतनामनः ॥

ब्राह्मो जातौ ॥ १७१ ॥ पदानि ॥ ब्राह्मः, अजातौ, ॥

वृत्तिः ॥ ब्राह्म इत्येतदपत्याधिकारेऽपि सामर्थ्यादपत्यादन्यत्राणि टिलोपार्थं निपात्यते ततोऽजातौ अपत्यइत्येव अपत्ये जातावणि ब्रह्मणष्टिलोपो न भवति ॥

171. ब्राह्म is irregularly formed from ब्रह्मन्, when not meaning 'a kind or jâti.'

This sûtra should be divided into two (1) ब्राह्मः, the final अन् of ब्रह्मन् is elided, when the अण् affix with the force of the Patronymic, as well as with any other force, comes after it. Thus ब्राह्मो गर्भः, ब्राह्मं हविः, ब्राह्ममस्त्रम् ; ब्राह्मो नारदः ॥ (2) अजातौ, but not so, when the Patronymic denotes a jâti ; for then the अन् of ब्रह्मन् is not elided before the अण् affix : as ब्रह्मणोऽपत्यं = ब्राह्मणः 'a Brahmana'. When jâti is expressed, but अण् has not the force of the Patronymic, the अन् of ब्रह्मन् is elided, As ब्राह्मी औषधिः ॥

कार्म्मस्ताच्छील्ये ॥ १७२ ॥ पदानि ॥ कार्मः, ताच्छील्ये, ॥

वृत्तिः ॥ कार्म्म इति ताच्छील्ये टिलोपो निपात्यते ॥

172. कार्म is irregularly formed from कर्मन्, by the elision of the final अन्, when the sense is 'accustomed to such an occupation or prompt therein'.

This is formed by ण affix (IV. 4. 62). If this is the case, then by VI. 4. 144, the form कार्म is regularly evolved. The fact is, that ण् and अण् affixes, in the sense of tâchchhilika are considered as one, and therefore VI. 4. 167, would have prevented the elision of the final अन् syllable. In fact this proves the existence of the following maxim :—ताच्छीलिके णेऽण् कृतानि भवन्ति ॥ "The same operations which are occasioned by the addition of the affix अण्, take place, whenever the affix ण is added in the sense of one accustomed to that." Thus though ङीप् is added, to अण्-formed words, it is also added to ण-formed words, in the feminine : as चौरी ; तापसी &c. The ण taught in V. 2. 101, and III. 1. 140, is excepted. Why do we say, having the sense of accustomed to that? Observe कर्मणः इदम् = कार्मणम् ॥

औक्षमनपत्ये ॥ १७३ ॥ पदानि ॥ औक्षम्, अ नपत्ये ॥

वृत्तिः ॥ औक्षमित्यनपत्येणि टिलोपो निपात्यते ॥

173. From उक्षन् is formed औक्ष, when not meaning a descendant.

As औक्षं पदम् but औक्ष्णः = उक्ष्णोऽपत्यम्, the अ is elided in the latter example by VI. 4. 135.

दाण्डिनायनहास्तिनायनाथर्वणिकजैह्माशिनेयवासिनायनिभ्रौणहत्यधैवत्यसारवैक्ष्वाकमैत्रेयहिरण्मयानि ॥ १७४ ॥ पदानि ॥ दाण्डिनायन, हास्तिनायन, आथर्वणिक, जैह्माशिनेय, वासिनायनि, भ्रौणहत्य, धैवत्य, सारव, ऐक्ष्वाक, मैत्रेय, हिरण्मयानि, ॥

वृत्तिः ॥ दाण्डिनायन हास्तिनायन आथर्वणिक जैह्माशिनेय वासिनायनि भ्रौणहत्य धैवत्य सारव ऐक्ष्वाक मैत्रेय हिरण्मय इत्येतानि निपात्यन्ते ॥

174. The following are irregularly formed ; 1.

Dâṇḍinâyana, 2. Hâstinâyana, 3. Âtharvaṇika, 4. Jaihmâśineya, 5. Vâsinâyani, 6. Bhrauṇahatya, 7. Dhaivatya. 8. Sârava, 9. Aikshvâka, 10. Maitreya and 11. Hiraṇmaya.

These words are thus derived (1 and 2) शाण्डिनायन and हास्तिनायन from शण्डिन् and हस्तिन् belonging to नडादि class. The affix is फक् (IV. 2. 91). If they do not belong to that class, the affix is added irregularly: शण्डिनोऽपत्यं = शाण्डिनायनः &c. The final इन् is not elided. (3) अथर्वन् belongs to Vasantâdi class (IV. 2. 63). The science or work of Atharvan Rishi is also called Atharvan. He who studies that work is called Atharvaṇika: the final is not elided before the ठक् affix. (4 and 5) The descendants of जिह्माशिन् and वासिन् are Jaihmâśineya and Vâsinâyani, the former with the affix ढक् of the Subhrâdi class (IV. 1. 123), and the latter with the affix फिञ् of IV. 1. 157. The finals of the stems are not dropped. (6 and 7) These are derived from भ्रूणहन् and धीवन् with the affix ष्यञ्, and न् being replaced by त = भ्रूणघ्नो भावः, धीव्नो भावः ॥ हन् takes त before affixes having an indicatory ण् or ञ् by VII. 3. 32: it might be said त would be added to भ्रूणहन् before ष्यञ् by that rule. That rule is, however, confined to affixes which come after roots only, and not to Taddhita affixes. That rule does not apply to cases like भ्रौणघ्नी, वार्त्रघ्नः ॥ The त in Bhrauṇhatya is therefore, an irregularity. (8) सारव is from सरयू with the affix अण्, the final अयू being elided, सरय्वां भवः = सारवमुदकं ॥ (9) The son of इक्ष्वाकु, with अञ् affix (IV. 1. 168), the final उ is elided, or इक्ष्वाकुषु जनपदेषु भवः = ऐक्ष्वाकः with अण् affix (IV. 2. 132). Accent on the first or the final. The irregularity consists in the elision of final उ ॥ As one word is ऐ॑क्ष्वाकः and the other ऐक्ष्वाक॑ः, the sûtra ought to have read this word twice, strictly speaking. The single reading may be justified on the ground, that the sûtra gives ऐक्ष्वाक without any accent (eka-śruti), and consequently includes both (एकश्रुतिः स्वर सर्वनाम) ॥

(10) मैत्रेय is from मित्रयु of Grishtyâdi class IV. 1. 136, and takes ढञ् as मित्रयु + एय, here VI. 4. 146, requires Guṇa, but VI. 4. 146, prevents it, and requires lopa of उ, but VII. 3. 2, required the substitution of इय for यु ॥ The irregularity consists in eliding यु altogether as मैत्रेय, the अ of मित्र cannot be elided by VI. 4. 148, befor एय, as the lopa of यु is considered asiddha VI. 4. 22; however the result is the same, for अ + ए = ए by VI. 1. 97; the single substitute being the form of the subsequent. The plural of मैत्रेय will be मित्रयवः (the plural of मित्रयु); as it belongs of Yaskâdi class and loses the affix in the plural (II. 4. 63). Another form of this word is मैत्रेयिक formed under VII. 3. 2. It might be objected that had मित्रयु been read in Bidâdi class (IV. 1. 104), it would have taken the affix अञ्, and the form मैत्रेय would have been evolved regularly: as मित्रयु + अञ् = मित्र + इय (VII. 3. 2) + अ = मैत्रेयः ॥ This would have prevented also the necessity of including this word in the Yaskâdi class (II. 4.

63), for then by II. 4. 63, अञ् formed words would lose the affix in the plural and we would have got the form मिश्रवः in the plural. So far it would have been all right, but if मैश्रेय were to be formed with अञ् affix, as proposed, then the संघ derivative of this word would have required to be formed with अण् affix under IV. 3. 127, and not with वुञ् under IV. 3. 126; but we require वुञ्, as मैश्रेयकः संघः ॥ (11) हिरण्मय from हिरण्य with मयट् with the elision of य, हिरण्यस्य विकारः = हिरण्मयः ॥

ऋत्व्यवास्त्व्यवास्त्वमाध्वीहिरण्ययानिच्छन्दसि ॥ १७५ ॥ पदानि ॥ ऋत्व्य, वास्त्व्य, वास्त्व, माध्वी, हिरण्ययानि, छन्दसि, ॥

वृत्तिः ॥ ऋत्व्य वास्त्व्य वास्त्व माध्वी हिरण्यय इत्येतानि निपात्यन्ते छन्दसि विषये ॥

175. In the Veda the following are irregularly formed: Ṛitvya, Vastvya Vâstva, Mâdhvî, and Hiraṇyaya.

The word ऋत्व्य is derived from ऋतु, and वास्त्व्य from वास्तु with the affix यत्, उ being changed to व ॥ ऋतौ भवम् = ऋत्व्यम्, वास्तौ भवम् = वास्त्व्यम् ॥ वास्त्व is from वस्तु, as वस्तुनि भवः = वास्त्वः with the affix अण् ॥ माध्वी from मधु with the affix अण् in the feminine, as माध्वीर्नः सन्त्वोषधीः ॥ हिरण्यय is from हिरण्य with the affix मयट्, the म being elided.

Printed by Freeman & Co., Ld., at the Târâ Printing Works, Benares.

[illegible] natural
[illegible] have
[illegible] then
[illegible]
[illegible]
[illegible]
[illegible] from
[illegible]

[illegible]
[illegible]
[illegible]

[illegible] apparently
[illegible]
[illegible]
[illegible]
[illegible]

BOOK VII.

THE

ASHTÁDHYÁYI OF PÁṆINI.

TRANSLATED INTO ENGLISH

BY

SRISA CHANDRA VASU, B. A.,

Provincial Civil Service, N. W. P.

Benares:

PUBLISHED BY SINDHU CHARAN BOSE,

at the Panini Office,

1897.

TO

Hon'ble Sir John Edge, Kt. Q. C.,

ATE CHIEF JUSTICE OF THE NORTH-WESTERN PROVINCES

THIS WORK

IS,

WITH HIS LORDSHIP'S PERMISSION,

AND IN RESPECTFUL APPRECIATION OF HIS LORDSHIP'S SERVICES TO THE CAUSE OF ADMINISTRATION OF JUSTICE AND OF EDUCATION

IN

THESE PROVINCES,

Dedicated

BY HIS LORDSHIP'S HUMBLE SERVANT

THE TRANSLATOR.

ओ३म् ।

अथ सप्तमाध्यायस्य प्रथमः पादः ।

BOOK SEVENTH.

CHAPTER FIRST.

युवोरनाकौ ॥ १ ॥ पदानि ॥ यु-वोः, अन-अकौ ।

वृत्तिः ॥ यु वु इत्येतयोरुत्सृष्टविशेषणयोरनूनासिकयणोः प्रत्यययोर्ग्रहणं तयोः स्थाने यथासङ्ख्य मन अक इत्येतावादेशौ भवतः ।

Kârikâ युवोश्चेद् द्विस्वनिर्देशो द्वित्वे यण्तु प्रसज्यते । अथ चेदेकवद्भावः कथ पुंवद्भवेदयम् ॥
द्वित्ये नैगमिको लोप एकत्वे नुमनित्यता । आशिष्यत्वाद्धि लिङ्गस्य पुंस्त्वं वेहि समाश्रितम ।

1. For यु and वु (nasalised) in an affix, are substituted respectively अन and अक ॥

यु and वु are taken here as stripped of all other indicatory letters, and the semi-vowels are also to be understood to have been nasalised. The अन replaces यु, and अक replaces वु ॥ Thus ल्यु (III. 1. 134)=अन, as नन्द+ल्यु=नन्दनः रमणः ॥ So also ट्यु and ट्युल् (IV. 3. 23), as सायंतनः, चिरंतनः ॥ वु we find in ण्वुल् (III. 1. 133), as कृ+ण्वुल्=कारकः, हारकः ॥ So also वुञ् (IV. 3. 98) as वासुदेवकः, अर्जुनकः ॥

Why do we say nasalised यु and वु? Observe ऊर्णाया युस् (V. 2. 123) Here the यु is not replaced by अन, and we have ऊर्णायुः ॥ So also in भुजिमृङ्भ्यां युक्त्युकौ ॥ Here the यु of युक् and त्युक् (Uṇ III. 21) are not replaced by अन; as भुज्युः and मृत्युः ॥ In the affixes above mentioned, the semi-vowel is not considered to have the nasal. There are no visible marks of nasality on any affixes, but the maxim is प्रतिज्ञानुनासिक्याः पाणिनीयाः ॥

The word युवोः is the Genitive Singular of युवु considered as a single word, i. e. a Samâhâra Dvandva compound in the singular, and such compounds are always neuter (II. 4. 17), The Genitive Singular of युवु is therefore युवुनः the augment being added by VII. 1. 73. The anomalous form युवोः shows the existence of the maxim that a rule ordaining an augment is not universally valid (अनित्यमागमशासनम्) ॥ Or the युवु may be considered as masculine Dvandva, and then it proves the maxim that the gender need not be taught, the usage of the people settles the gender of a word (लिङ्गमशिष्यं, लोकाश्रयत्वाल्लिङ्गस्य) ॥ If, however, युवू be considered an itaretara-yoga Dvandva compound, then its Genitive dual will be युव्वोः, one व् is elided as a Chhandas irregularity, or the ऊ is elided, and we have the युव्+ओः=युवोः an anomalous dual.

Kârikâ :—If युवू is taken as a *dual*, then there ought to be a semi-vowel (i.e. युव्नोः); if it is considered as Aggregate Singular, then it ought to be neuter, how is then युवोः masculine? (To this we answer), if it be taken as dual युवू, then there is elision of the यणादेश (i.e. व्); if it be taken as singular युवु, then the augment नुम् which comes in the Genitive Singular of Neuters, does not come here, proving that the rule of नुम् augment is Anitya (not of universal application). Or the word युवु is taken as masculine, because the Gender depends upon usage.

आयनेयीनीयियः फढखच्छघां प्रत्ययादीनाम् ॥ २ ॥ पदानि ॥ आयन्-एय्-ईन् ईय्-इयः, फ-ढ-ख-छ-घाम्, प्रत्यय-आदीनाम् ॥

वृत्तिः ॥ आयन् एय् ईन् ईय् ईय् इत्येते आदेशा भवन्ति यथासंख्यं फ ढ ख छ घ इत्येतेषां प्रत्ययादीनाम् ।

2. **आयन्, for फ्, एय् for ढ्, ईन् for ख् ईय् for छ्, and इय् for घ्, are substituted, when these consonants stand in the beginning of an affix.**

Thus फक् (IV. 1. 99)=आयन, as नड+फक्=नाडायनः, चारायणः ॥ ढक् (IV. 1. 120)=एय as सौपर्णेयः, वैनतेयः ॥ ख (IV. 1. 139) ईन, as आढ्यकुलीनः; श्रोत्रियकुलीनः ॥ छ (IV. 2. 114)=ईय, as गार्गीयः, वात्सीयः ॥ घ (IV. 1. 138)=इय, as क्षत्रियः ॥

Why do we say 'of an *affix*'? Observe फक्कति, ढौकते, खनति, छिनत्ति and घूर्णते, where these consonants are in the beginning of a *root*. Why do we say 'in the beginning'? Observe उरुदघ्नम् जानुदघ्नम्, where घ is in the *middle* of the affix; and remains consequently unchanged.

These आयन &c, substitutions should be understood to have taken place at the very time the affixes फक् &c, are taught, and these substitutions being made, the rule of accent, which makes an affix acute on the first syllable, applies. Thus ख is not acute, but ई of ईन् substituted for it. Similarly in IV. 4. 117, the affix taught is घच् with an indicatory च्, showing that the final of the affix इयँ will be acute (VI. 1. 163), and not of घ, for घ would have been acute by the general rule affix.

In शमे ढः (Uṇ I. 99), शमेः ख (Uṇ I: 102), the affixes ढ and ख remain unchanged, and we have शण्ढः, and शंखः ॥ This is explained on the maxim of उणादयो बहुलम् (III. 3. 1). In the sûtra ऋतेरीयङ् (III. 1. 29), the affix ईयङ् has been taught and not छङ्, this shows that the rule of substitution herein taught does not apply to the affixes to be added to the verbal roots. Thus एजेः खश् (III. 2. 28), पदरुजविशस्पृशो घञ् (III. 3. 16). Here the ख and घ are not be replaced by ईन and इय ॥ In fact, they cannot be regarded as affixes, but only as इत् or servile letters. By I. 3. 8, the gutturals are इत् except in Taddhita: therefore, the substitutions take place in Taddhita affixes, where the ख and घ are not इत् ॥

The final न् in आयन् and इन् should not, however, be considered as servile (इत्) though they be final consonants. This we infer from the sûtra

प्राचामवृद्धात् फिन् बहुलम् ॥ Here the न् of फिन् is indicatory, showing the position of the accent. But फ is replaced by आयन्, so if the न् of आयन् were also to be indicatory (इत्) there would have been no necessity of adding न् in फिन् ॥ Hence the fact of this न् in फिन् shows that the न् in आयन् and इन् are not इत् ॥

झोऽन्तः ॥ ३ ॥ पदानि ॥ झः, अन्तः, ॥

वृत्तिः ॥ प्रत्ययावयवस्य झस्य अन्त इत्ययमादेशो भवति ॥

3 अन्त् is substituted for the झ of an affix.

The word प्रत्यय is understood here, but not so the word आदिः ॥ Thus झि becomes अन्ति aud झ becomes अन्त (III. 4. 78). As कुर्वन्ति, सुन्वन्ति and चिन्वन्ति, so also शयान्ते, the लेट् of शीङ् ॥ Thus शी + लेट् = शी + शप् + आट् + झ (III. 4. 54) = शी + शप् + आ + झे (III. 4. 79) = शी + शप् + आ + झै (III. 4 96) = शी + शप् + आ + अन्तै (VII. 1. 3) = शी + आ + अन्तै = शयान्तै (after guna): as अद्य श्वो विजगिष्यमाणाः पतिभिः सह शयान्तै ॥ So also in the Uṇadi affix झच् (Uṇ III. 126): as जॄ + झच् = जरन्तैः, वेशन्तः ॥ This substitution does not take place when झ is not part of an affix: as उज्झिता, उज्झितुम्, उज्झितव्यम् ॥ Here also the accent falls on the substitute, according as it is चित् or otherwise. Thus the substitute अ॑न्त of झ is first-acute by the rule III. 1. 3; but the substitute अन्तँ of झच् is final acute because of the indicatory च (VI. 1. 763) ॥

अदभ्यस्तात् ॥ ४ ॥ पदानि ॥ अत्, अभ्यस्तात्, ॥

वृत्तिः ॥ अभ्यस्तादङ्गादुत्तरस्य झकारस्य अदित्ययमादेशो भवति ॥

4. अत् is substitute for झ after a reduplicated verbal stem.

As दँदति, ददतु, दधति, दधतु; जक्षति, जक्षतु; जाग्रति, जाग्रतु ॥ This अत् is replaced by जुस्, as अददुः, अदधुः ॥ Here also the accent will be on the firstsyllable of the substitute. Thus अँति, अँत, अँते, अँतु, अँताम् in the subsequent sûtras. The accent of the reduplicates, however, is governed by VI. 1. 189, (अभ्यस्तानामादिः) ॥

आत्मनेपदेष्वनतः ॥ ५ ॥ पदानि ॥ आत्मनेपदेषु, अ नतः, (अत्) ॥

वृत्तिः ॥ आत्मनेपदेषु यो झकारस्तस्यानकारान्तादङ्गादुत्तरस्यादित्ययमादेशो भवति ॥

5. अत् is always substituted for the झ in the Atmanepada, when it is not preceded by a verbal stem ending in अ ॥

Thus चिन्वते, चिन्वताम, अचिन्वत; लुनते, लुनताम्, अलुनत ॥ Why in the Atmanepada? Observe चिन्वन्ति, लुनन्ति ॥ Why "when not preceded by an अ"? Observe च्यवन्ते, प्लवन्ते, in which, though the roots are च्यु and प्लु, they assume the form च्यव and प्लव when the Vikaraṇa शप् is added; the vikaraṇa is added *first*, because it is nitya; and then the substitution of अन्त or अत for झ, as the case may be. The word अनतः qualifies झ, the झ should be *immediately* preceded by a stem ending in a non-अ; if some other letter intervenes, the rule will not apply. Thus from शी—शयान्तै, here between शी and झ, intervenes the augment आट्, therefore झ is not preceded by a stem ending in non अ, but by आट् ॥

शीङो रुट् ॥ ६ ॥ पदानि ॥ शीङः, रुट् ॥
वृत्तिः ॥ शीङोऽङ्गादुत्तरस्य झादेशस्यातो रुडागमो भवति ॥

6. The अत् substitute of झ्, gets the augment रुट्, after the root शी ॥

Thus शेरते, शेरताम्, अशेरत ॥ The augment र् is added at the beginning of the affix, making अत्=रत् ॥ Had this र् been an augment of झ, then like the आट् augment in शयान्तै, it would have intervened between the शी and झ, and झ not immediately following a non-अ stem, अत् would not have been substituted for झ at all. Therefore रुट् is made the augment of the *substitute* अत, and not of झ ॥ The root शी is read in the sûtra with its anubandha ङ् in order to indicate, that there is no रुट् augment when there is elision of the Intensive affix यङ्, nor any Guṇa. As व्यति शेश्यते ॥

It is a general rule that an operation applying to a root which is exhibited with an anubandha, will not apply to the same root in its Intensive-yañ-luk form. The following verse shows when operations applying to simple roots will not apply to their Intensive forms :—

श्तिपा शपानुबन्धेन निर्दिष्टं यद्गणेन च ।
यत्रैकाज् ग्रहणं चैव पंचैतानि न यङ्लुकि ॥

"These five sorts of operations will not apply to Intensive-yañ-luk forms : 1. When the simple root is exhibited in the sûtra with श्तिप् as भू in VII. 4. 73 is shown as भवति ॥ In Intensive, the perfect will be बोभवाम्चकार and not बभवाम्चकार ॥ 2. Where the root is exhibited with शप्, as the root भृ in VII. 2. 49 is shown as भर ॥ There is इट् after the Desiderative of simple root but not in Intensive. 3. When a simple root is exhibited with an anubhandha, as शीङ् here. 4. Where a gaṇa is mentioned in a rule, as श्यन् is taught after Divâdi-roots (III. 1. 69). It will apply to simple roots of Divâdi gaṅa, and not to their Intensive. 5. Lastly, where the word एकाच् is used in a sûtra. As VII. 2. 10. That rule will apply to एकाच् simple roots and not to their Intensives.

वेत्तेर्विभाषा ॥ ७ ॥ पदानि ॥ वेत्तेः, विभाषा ॥
वृत्तिः ॥ वेत्तेरङ्गादुत्तरस्य झादेशस्यातो विभाषा रुडागमो भवति ॥

7. The अत् substitute of झ optionally gets the augment रुट् after the verbal stem विद् (वेत्ति) ॥

As संविद्रते or संविद्रते ; संविदताम् or संविद्रताम् ; समविदत or समविद्रत ॥ The विद् is the Adâdi root here, and does not apply to विन्ते, विन्दाति, विन्दते, which belongs to the Rudhâdi class (विद विचारणे) ॥

There is no augment in यङ्लुक् here also, as व्यतिवेविदते ॥

बहुलं छन्दसि ॥ ८ ॥ पदानि ॥ बहुलम्, छन्दसि, (रुट्) ॥
वृत्तिः ॥ छन्दसि विषये बहुलं रुडागमो भवति ॥

8. The augment रुट् is diversely applied in the Veda.

Thus देवा अदुह्र ; गन्धर्वा अप्सरसो अदुह्र ॥ Here अदुह्र is the Imperfect (लङ्) plural of दुह् ॥ Thus दुह्+झ=दुह्+रत्=अदुह्र, the त् being elided by VII. 1. 41. Sometimes, the augment does not take place, as अदुहत ॥ Owing to the word बहुल, 'diversely', the augment र is added to other affixes also, than झ ॥ As अदृश्रम् in अदृश्रमस्य केतवः ॥ This is the aorist in अङ् of the root दृश by III. 1. 57, the guṇa ordained by VII. 4. 16, does not '*diversely*' take place.

अतो भिस ऐस् ॥ ९ ॥ पदानि ॥ अतः, भिसः, ऐस् ॥

वृत्तिः ॥ अकारान्तादङ्गादुत्तरस्य भिस ऐसित्ययमादेशो भवति ॥

Kârîkâ ॥ एत्वं भिसि परत्वाच्चेदत ऐस्क्व भविष्यति । कृतेऽप्येत्वे भौतपूर्व्यादैस्तु नित्यस्तथा सति ॥

9. After a nominal stem ending in अ, ऐस् is substituted for the case-ending भिस् ॥

As वृक्षैः, प्लक्षैः, अतिजरसैः ॥ Why do we say ending in अ? Observe अग्निभिः, वायुभिः ॥ Why '*short* अ'? Observe खट्वाभिः, मालाभिः ॥ The adhikâra of "अतः" ('after a short अ'), extends up to VII. 1. 17.

The form अतिजरसैः illustrates some important principles of grammar. अति+जरा=(जरामतिक्रान्तः) अतिजर (अ being shortened by I. 2. 48). The word अतिजर ends in अ, and there fore forms its Ins. pl. by ऐस् ॥ Thus अतिजर+ऐस् ॥ Now we apply VII. 2. 101, which says for जरा is substituted जरस् before vowel-beginning case-endings. It should not be objected, that the substitution is ordained for जरा and not जर; for the maxim एकदेशविकृतमनन्यवद् भवति (a tail-less dog is still a dog) applies here. Having made this substitution, we get अतिजरसैः॥ Nor should you object that it was the अ of जर which had given occasion to the existence of ऐस्, and that अ should not be destroyed, on the maxim संनिपातलक्षणो विधिरनिमित्तं तद् विघातस्य, for this maxim is not uni versal, as Pâṇini himself shows in employing the form कष्टाय (III. 1. 14), in which ए of the Dative is changed into य by VII. 1. 13, and then this very य causes the destruction of अ and makes it आ (See VII. 1. 13 also).

Kârikâ :—If there be substitution of ए for the final अ before the affix भिस् by the subsequent sûtra VII. 3. 103, where will then the present sûtra, causing the substitution of ऐस् for भिस् after stems ending in अ, find its scope, (because there will be no stem left ending in अ)? If even after changing अ into ए, you change the भिस् into ऐस्, because the ए was once अ (भौतपूर्व्यात्); then the rule of changing भिस् into ऐस् becomes a nitya rule, because it takes effect even after the application of rule VII. 3. 103, and being nitya it debars that rule. Thus वृक्ष+भिस् ॥ Here the subsequent rule VII. 3. 103, requires the अ to be changed into ए ॥ Thus वृक्षे+भिः Now the present rule cannot apply because there is no अदन्त stem. However, if considering that वृक्षे once was अदन्त, we change भिः to ऐस् then the rule becomes a *nitya* rule. In fact, it is a nitya rule and debars the application of VII. 3. 103, within its jurisdiction, VII. 3. 103, finds its scope in वृक्ष + सु = वृक्षेषु ॥

बहुलं छन्दसि ॥ १० ॥ पदानि ॥ बहुलम्, छन्दसि, (ऐस्) ॥

वृत्तिः ॥ छन्दसि विषये बहुलमैसादेशो भवति ॥

10. In the Veda the substitution takes place diversely.

That is ऐस् is substituted for भिस् even after stems which do not end in short अ; as नद्यैः; and some times the substitution does not take place even after stems ending in short अ, as, देवेभिः सर्वेभिः प्रोक्तम् ॥ देवो देवेभिरागमत् (Rig Veda I. 1. 4).

नेदमदसोरकोः ॥ ११ ॥ पदानि ॥ न, इदम्, अदसोः, अ, कोः, (भिस ऐस्) ॥

वृत्तिः ॥ इदम् अदस् इत्येतयोरककारयोर्भिस ऐस भवति ॥

11. This substitution of ऐस् does not take place after इदम् and अदस्, except when they end in क ॥

As एभिः, अमीभिः, but इमकैः, अमुकैः ॥ By VII. 2. 102, अ is substiuted for the final of इदम्, as इद + अ = इद (VI. 1. 97). By VII. 2. 113, the इद् is elided before भिस, and the only portion left is अ, which becomes ए according to VII. 3. 103. For the final of अदस् is simlarly by VII. 2. 102, अ substituted, and अद + अ = अद (VI. 1. 97), and according to our present sûtra, the form in Ins.pl. would be अदेभिः, but द् is changed to म् by VIII. 2. 80, and ए to ई by VIII. 2. 81.

The exception made with regard to these forms ending in क, shows the existence of the following maxim : तदूमध्यपतितस्तद्ग्रहणेन गृह्यते "Any term that may be employed in Grammar denotes not merely what is actually denoted by it, but it denotes also whatever word-form may result when something is inserted in that which is actually denoted by it."

The sûtra has not been made as इदमदसोः कात्, for had it been so constructed the rule would have applied to the क ending इदम् and अदस् and to no other क ending pronoun, and we could not get the forms सर्वकैः, विश्वकैः ॥ Moreover such a construction would have made ऐस् applicable to इदम् and अदस् also in their simple states : i. e. we could not have got the forms एभिः or अमीभिः ॥ Therefore the negative construction न अकोः is used in sutra in order to prevent the rule of contrariety.

टाङसिङसामिनात्स्याः ॥ १२ ॥ पदानि ॥ टा, ङसि, ङसाम्, इन, आत्, स्याः, ॥

वृत्तिः ॥ अकारान्तादङ्गादुत्तरेषां टाङसिङसाम् इन आत् स्य इत्येते आदेशा भवन्ति यथासंख्यम् ॥

12. After a stem ending in अ, are substituted इन for the Instrumental ending; आ आत् for the Ablative ending अस्, and स्य for the Genitive ending अस् ॥

Thus वृक्षेण and प्लक्षेण; वृक्षात् and प्लक्षात्; and वृक्षस्य and प्लक्षस्य ॥ After stems not ending in अ we have the original ending, as पद्या, सख्या ॥ Some would have the forms अतिजरसिन and अतिजरसात् from अतिजर ॥ This is on the analogy of अतिजरसैः [See Sûtra 9 *ante*]. Thus अति + जरा = अतिजर (I. 2. 48). Then by VII. 2. 101, जरस् is substituted for जर before the vowel-affixes. These forms are not supported however by Patanjali. According to him the forms will be either अतिजरेण, अतिजरात्, or अतिजरसा and अतिजरसः but never अतिजरसिन and अतिजरसात् ॥

ङेर्यः ॥ १३ ॥ पदानि ॥ ङेः, यः, (अतः अङ्गस्य) ॥

वृत्तिः ॥ ङेरिति चतुर्थ्येकवचनस्य ग्रहणम् अकारान्तादङ्गादुत्तरस्य ङे इत्येतस्य य इत्ययमादेशो भवति ॥

13. After a stem ending in अ, there is substituted य for the Dative ending ए ॥

Thus वृक्षाय, प्लक्षाय, the अ is lengthended by VII. 3. 102, in spite of the maxim संनिपातलक्षणो विधि रनिमित्तम् तद्विघातस्य ॥ "That which is taught in a rule the application of which is occasioned by the combination of two things, does not become the cause of the destruction of that combination". Thus य is substituted here, because the preceding word ends in a short अ, thus this short अ occasioned the existence of य, therefore this य cannot occasion the destruction of अ ॥ But that however it does, for it is on account of this य, that the preceding अ is replaced by आ ॥

The ङेः is the anomalous genitive case of the Dative ending ङे; this affix is exhibited without any vibhakti in VII. 1. 28. The ङेः should not be taken as the Genitive singular of ङि the affix of the Locative singular.

सर्वनाम्नः स्मै ॥ १४ ॥ पदानि ॥ सर्वनाम्नः, स्मै, (अतः ङे) ॥

वृत्तिः ॥ अकारान्तात्सर्वनाम्न उत्तरस्य ङेः स्मै इत्ययमादेशो भवति ॥

14. After a Pronominal stem ending in अ, स्मै is substituted for the ए of the Dative.

As सर्वस्मै' विश्वस्मै, यस्मै, कस्मै, तस्मै ॥ But भवते where the Pronoun does not end in अ ॥ When अश् is substituted for इदम् (II. 4. 32) in anvâdeśa sentences, then we have the form अस्मै ॥ But in अत्र इदम् + ङे = अत्र अ + ए = अत्रा + ए, here the preceding word ends in आ and we could not have ए replaced by स्मै ॥ Therefore we infer that स्मै being an antaranga operation should be substituted first, and the sandhi afterward and we get अत्रास्मै ॥ (See VII. 2. 102 for the change of यद्, तद् &c into य, त &c). The change of ए into स्मै is antaranga as it depends upon one word, while the एकादेश long आ is bahiranga because it is an operation depending upon two words.

ङसिङ्योः स्मात्स्मिनौ ॥ १५ ॥ पदानि ॥ ङसि, ङ्योः, स्मात्, स्मिनौ, (अतः सर्वनाम्नः) ॥

वृत्तिः ॥ ङसि ङि इत्येतयोरकारान्तात्सर्वनाम्न उत्तरयोः स्मात् स्मिन् इत्येतावादेशौ भवतः ॥

15. After a Pronominal stem ending in अ, स्मात्

is substituted for the Ablative ending अस् and स्मिन् for the Locative ending इ ॥

Thus सर्वस्मात्, विश्वस्मात्, यस्मात्, तस्मात् and कस्मात् ॥ सर्वस्मिन्, विश्वस्मिन् यस्मिन्, तस्मिन् and अन्यस्मिन् ॥ But भवतः and भवति from भवत् ending in a non-अ, and वृक्षात् and वृक्षे in non-pronouns. See VII. 2. 102 for यद् तद् &c.

पूर्वादिभ्यो नवभ्यो वा ॥ १६ ॥ पदानि ॥ पूर्व-आदिभ्यः, नवभ्यः, वा, (सर्वनाम्नः ङसिङ्योः स्मात् स्मिनौ) ॥

वृत्तिः ॥ पूर्वादिभ्यो नवभ्यः सर्वनाम्न उत्तरयोर्ङसिङ्योः स्मात् स्मिन् इत्येतावादेशौ वा भवतः ॥

16. स्मात् and स्मिन् are optionally substituted for the Ablative and Locative endings, after पूर्व and the eight that follow it (I. 1. 34).

Thus पूर्वस्मात् or पूर्वात्, पूर्वस्मिन् or पूर्वे, परस्मात् or परात्, परस्मिन् or परे, अवरस्मात्, or अवरात्, अवरस्मिन् or अवरे, दक्षिणस्मात् or दक्षिणात्, दक्षिणस्मिन् or दक्षिणे, उत्तरस्मात्, or उत्तरात्, उत्तरस्मिन्, or उत्तरे, अपरस्मात्, or अपरात्, अपरस्मिन्, or अपरे, अधरस्मात्, or अधरात्, अधरस्मिन्, or अधरे, स्वस्मात्, or स्वात्, स्वस्मिन् or स्वे, अन्तरस्मात् or अन्तरात्, अन्तरस्मिन् or अन्तरे ॥ नवभ्य इति किम्, त्यस्मात्, त्यस्मिन् ॥

Why do we say 'nine only'? Observe त्यस्मात् and त्यस्मिन्, no option is allowed here.

जसः शी ॥ १७ ॥ पदानि ॥ जसः, शी, ॥

वृत्तिः ॥ आकारान्तात्सर्वनाम्न उत्तरस्य जसः शीत्ययमादेशो भवति ॥

17. After a Pronominal stem ending in अ, ई is substituted for the nominative plural अस् ॥

Thus सर्वे (सर्व+ई), विश्वे, ये, के, ते ॥ Though सर्व+इ would have also given सर्वे, the long ई is taken for the sake of subsequent sûtras, in forming त्रपुणी, जतुनी ॥

औङ आपः ॥ १८ ॥ पदानि ॥ औङः, आपः, ॥

वृत्तिः ॥ आबन्तादङ्गादुत्तरस्यौङः शीत्ययमादेशो भवति ॥

Kârikâ—औकारोयं शीविधौ ङिद्गृहीतो ङिच्चास्माकं नास्ति कोयं प्रकारः ।
सामान्यार्थस्तस्य चासंजनेस्मिन्ङित्कार्यं ते स्यां प्रसक्तं स दोषः ॥
ङित्त्वे विद्याद्वर्णनिर्देशमात्रं वर्णे यत्स्यात्तच्च विद्यात्तदादौ ।
वर्णश्चायं तेन ङित्त्वेप्यदोषो निर्देशोयं पूर्वसूत्रेण वा स्यात् ॥

18. After a stem ending in the feminine affix आ, ई is substituted for the dual endings औ of the Nominative and Accusative.

Thus खट्वे तिष्ठतः, खट्वे पश्य, बहुराजे (IV. 1. 13), कारीषगन्ध्ये ॥ The ङ् in औङ् is for the purposes of included औट् also. There is, in fact, no such affix as औङ् taught by Panini any where. The following Karika raises this question and certain doubts in the first verse and then answers them in the second.

Kârikâ :—In this rule about शी, the letter औ has been enunciated with an indicatory ङ् ; but we have no औ with a ङ्, taught any where. What sort of sûtra construction is this? If you say, the use of ङ् is to form a common term for the two affixes औ and औट्, then by so doing, ङित् operations must be performed with regard to this शी of yours, and this is an error. [शी replacing ङित् औङ् will be considered as ङित्, and being ङित्, it will take the augment याट् by VII. 3, 113: and the form will be खट्वायै and not खट्वे] ॥

Ans :—The ङ् should be considered here as merely indicating the letter औ, and as not an इत्, so that whatever will apply to the letter औ will apply to any form beginning with it, by the maxim यस्मिन् विधि तदादावल् ग्रहणे ॥ Or औङ् may be considered as merely the letter औ and not any particular *affix*, and ङ् is added only for the sake of facility of pronounciation, like ट् in ऋटोरच्। औ being merely a letter, will include all affixes having the letter औ as their significant part: and thus the औङ् not being a ङित् affix the rule VII. 3. 113, will not apply: and so there is no anomaly. Or the form औङ् may be considered as the affix of the dual, for Nominative and Accusative in the terminology of Ancient Grammarians, and will not produce ङित् effects, because the anubandhas of the Ancients do not produce their effects in this Grammar of Pâṇini: i.e. the rules regarding anubandhas made by Pâṇini refer to the anubandhas made by him and not by older authors.

नपुंसकाच्च ॥ १९ ॥ पदानि ॥ नपुंसकात्, च (औङः शी) ॥
वृत्तिः ॥ नपुंसकादङ्गादुत्तरस्य औङः शी इत्ययमादेशो भवति ॥
वार्त्तिकम् ॥ श्यां प्रतिषेधो वक्तव्यः ॥

19. After a neutral stem, ई is substituted for the nom. and acc. dual औ ॥

Thus कुण्डे: तिष्ठतः, कुण्डे पश्य ॥ कुण्ड+ई=कुण्डे, the अ of कुण्ड required to be elided by VI. 4. 148. This is, however, not done by the following

Vârt:—Prohibition should be stated in the case of the affix शी ॥ Therefore the अ is not elided.

Similarly दधिनी, मधुनी, त्रपुणी, जतुनी ॥ The augment न् is added by VII. 1. 73.

जश्शसोः शिः ॥ २० ॥ पदानि ॥ जस्, शसोः, शिः, ॥
वृत्तिः ॥ नपुंसकादङ्गादुत्तरयोर्जश्शसोः शि इत्ययमादेशो भवति ॥

20. After a neutral stem, इ is substituted for the endings of the Nominative and Accusative Plural (जस् and शस्) ॥

Thus कुण्डानि तिष्ठन्ति, कुण्डानि पश्य, दधीनि' मधूनि, त्रपूणि, जतूनि ॥ The augment न् is by VII. 1. 72. The word शस् in the sûtra being read along with जस्

denotes the Accusative Plural ending शस् and not the Taddhita affix शस् (V. 4. 43); as कुण्डशो ददाति, वनशः प्रविशति ॥

अष्टाभ्य औश् ॥ २१ ॥ पदानि ॥ अष्टाभ्यः, औश्, ॥

वृत्तिः ॥ अष्टाभ्य इति कृताकारोऽष्टशब्दो गृह्यते तस्मादुत्तरयोर्जश्शसोरौशित्ययमादेशो भवति ॥

21. After the stem अष्टा (the form assumed by अष्टन् VII. 2. 84), औश् is substituted for the endings of the Nominative and Accusative Plural.

As अष्टौ तिष्ठन्ति, अष्टौ पश्य ॥ Why have we taken the form अष्टा and not अष्ट? Observe अष्ट तिष्ठन्ति, अष्ट पश्य ॥ This peculiar construction of the present sûtra (अष्टाभ्यः instead of अष्टनः) indicates, that the आ substitution for the न् of अष्टन् is optional. This sûtra is, moreover, an exception by anticipation, to the following sûtra, by which the plural Nom. and Acc. endings are elided after the numerals called षष् ॥ The elision of case-endings taught by II. 4. 71, is not, however, barred by this rule; the elision taught therein will take place, whether this rule applies or not. Thus अष्टपुत्रः, अष्टभार्यः ॥

The present rule applies even when अष्ट is at the end of a compound, as परमाष्टौ, उत्तमाष्टौ ॥ But in प्रियाष्टानः, औ does not come, as अष्टन् has not assumed the form अष्टा here i. e. it has not lost its न् ॥

षड्भ्यो लुक् ॥ २२ ॥ षड्भ्यः, लुक्, ॥

वृत्तिः ॥ षट्संज्ञकेभ्य उत्तरयोर्जश्शसोर्लुग्भवति ॥

22. The Nom. and Acc. Plural endings are elided after the Numerals called षष् (I. 1. 24).

As षट् तिष्ठन्ति, षट् पश्य, पञ्च, सप्त, नव, दश ॥ The rule applies even to compounds ending with 'shash' words: as परमषट्, उत्तमषट्, but the 'shash' should be the principal; if it is only a secondary member of the compound, the rule will not apply: as प्रियषषः, प्रियपञ्चानः ॥ For the elision of न् see VIII. 2. 7.

स्वमोर्नपुंसकात् ॥ २३ ॥ पदानि ॥ सु, अमोः, नपुंसकात्, ॥

वृत्तिः ॥ सु अम् इत्येतयोर्नपुंसकादुत्तरयोर्लुग्भवति ॥

23. The nom. and acc. singular case-endings सु and अम् are elided after a Neutral stem.

As दधि तिष्ठति, दधि पश्य, मधु तिष्ठति, मधु पश्य ॥ So also त्रपु and जतु ॥ In तद् ब्राह्मणकुलम् the word तद् has lost its nom. sing. ending by this rule, which has thus superseded the subsequent rule VII. 2. 102, by anticipation, by which अ replaces the final द् of तद् ॥ Or this *luk* rule of the present sûtra is a Nitya rule compared with VII. 2. 102. How can this be a nitya rule when it is set aside by the next rule अतोऽम् ॥ We still call this rule nitya, on the maxim

यस्य च लक्षणान्तरेण निमित्तं विहन्यते न तदनित्यम् "(an operation) the cause of which would, (after the taking effect of another operation that applies simultaneously), be removed by another (third rule), is not, (on that account regarded as) not nitya". For here the cause which is luk-elision, is removed by the following aphorism अतोऽम् which ordains an अम् instead of *luk*, and not by VII. 2. 102. For the application of rule VII. 2. 102, the necessary condition is that a case-affix should follow तद् &c. But when the case-affix itself is luk-elided, the substitution taught in that sûtra cannot take place.

अतोऽम् ॥ २४ ॥ पदानि ॥ अतः, अम्, ॥

वृत्तिः ॥ अकारान्तान्नपुंसकादुत्तरयोः स्वमोरमित्ययमादेशो भवति ॥

24. After a Neutral stem in अ, अम् is substituted for सु and अम् the endings of the nom. and acc. sing.

As कुण्डं तिष्ठति, कुण्डं पश्य ॥ So also वनम्, पीठम् ॥ Why do we not say "म् is substituted'? कुण्ड + म = कुण्डाम्, thus there would be lengthening if only म् was taught (VII. 3. 101), while कुण्ड + अम् = कुण्डम् (the single substitution of the form of the antecedent by VI. 1. 107).

अद्ड् डतरादिभ्यः पञ्चभ्यः ॥ २५ ॥ पदानि ॥ अद्ड्, डतरादिभ्यः, पञ्चभ्यः ॥

वृत्तिः ॥ डतरादिभ्यः परयोः स्वमोरद्ड् इत्ययमादेशो भवति ॥

Kârikâ अपृक्तश्चेदमो दोषो निवृत्ते डतरादिषु । अद्डित्वाड्डतरादीनां न लोपो नापि दीर्घता ॥

25. अद्ड् is substituted for the Nom. and Acc. singular endings सु and अम् after the five Pronouns डतर &c. (i. e. the stems formed with the affixes 1. डतर, and 2. डतम्, and the stems 3. इतर, 4. अन्य and 5. अन्यतर).

These are the five pronouns, which in the list of Sarvanâmans are read together (See I. 1. 27) :—डतर, डतम, इतर, अन्य and अन्यतर ॥ Thus कतर + अद्ड् = कतरत् (the अ of katara elided by ड्) : as कतरत् तिष्ठन्ति, कतरत् पश्य ॥ So also कतमत्, इतरत्, अन्यतरत् and अन्यत् ॥ Why after these five only? Observe नेमं तिष्ठन्ति, नेमं पश्य ॥ Why do we make the affix have an indicatory ड्? In order to prevent the lengthening of the vowel in the nominative singular: as कतर + अत् = कतरात् by VI. 1. 102. In the case of the accusative, अत् being the substitute of अम् will be sthânivat, and give us कतरत् by VI. 1. 107 even without ड् ॥ Why not make the affix merely त् and not अत्ड्; it would give कतरत् &c without the application of any rule of Sandhi? The simple त् would not give us the Vocative हे कतरत्, The final would have been elided in the Vocative, as being an apṛikta. See however VI. 1. 69.

Kârikâ :—If in the sûtra VI. 1. 69, there is the anuvṛitti of the word 'apṛkta', then there is fault with regard to अम् (i. e. the vocative of members in अम् will not be elided, हे कुण्डम् will be the form required and not हे कुण्ड) ; if however, the anuvṛitti of apṛkta ceases, there will be anomaly with regard to pronouns कतरत् &c (i. e. we shall not have the form हे कतरत् but हे कतर) Therefore, by reading the affix अत् with an indicatory ड् i. e reading it as अद्ड्, we get out of this dilemma, and so there is not the elision of अत् in कतरत् &c in the vocative ; nor is there lengthening of the vowel (कतरात्, which would have been the form had there been no ड्).

नेतराच्छन्दसि ॥ २६ ॥ पदानि ॥ न, इतरात्, छन्दसि, ॥

वृत्तिः ॥ इतरशब्दादुत्तरयोः स्वमोश्छन्दसि विषये अद्डादेशो न भवति ॥

26. In the Veda, अत् (or अद्) is not the substitute of सु and अम् Nom. and Acc. Sg. endings, after इतर ॥

As इतरमितरमण्डमजायत ; वार्त्रघ्नमितरम् ॥ Why in the Vedas? See इतरत् काष्ठम्, इतरत् कुड्यम् ॥ Had this sûtra been placed immediately after अतोऽम् (VII. 1. 24), we could have made it simpler by saying इतराच्छन्दसि ; the present position of the sûtra indicates that we should divide it into two, to include other cases. In the case of एकतर, the अद्ड् substitution does not take place, either in the Veda or in the Common Language. As एकतरं तिष्ठति, एकतरं पश्य ॥

युष्मदस्मद्भ्यां ङसो ऽश् ॥ २७ ॥ पदानि ॥ युष्मदस्मद्भ्याम्, ङसः, अश् ॥

वृत्तिः ॥ युष्मदस्मदित्येताभ्यामुत्तरस्य ङसो ऽशित्ययमादेशो भवति ॥

27. अश् (I. 1. 55), is substituted for the Genitive ending अस्, after युष्मद् and अस्मद् ॥

Thus तव and मम ॥ The indicatory श् of अश् shows that by I. 1. 55, the *whole* of the affix अस् is to be replaced : otherwise it would have replaced only the first letter of the affix ; and the affix not being a substitute-affix, rule VII. 2. 89, would not be applicable to it. The तव is substituted for युष्मद्, and मम for अस्मद् by VII. 2. 96 ; and तव + अ (अश्), and मम + अ = तव and मम by VI. 1. 97.

ङे प्रथमयोरम् ॥ २८ ॥ पदानि ॥ ङे, प्रथमयोः, अम्, ॥

वृत्तिः ॥ ङे इत्यविभक्तिको निर्देशः ङे इत्येतस्य प्रथमयोश्च विभक्त्योः प्रथमाद्वितीययोर्युष्मदस्मद्भ्यामुत्तरयो-रमित्ययमादेशो भवति ॥

28. अम् is substituted for the Dative ending ए and for the endings of the nom. and acc. in all numbers, after the stems युष्मद् and अस्मद् ॥

The ङे the ending of the Dative is exibited anomalously in the sûtra without any case ending (compare VII. 1. 13, ङेः) प्रथमयोः means 'of the first and second cases.' Thus युष्मद् + ङे = तुभ्यद् + ङे (VII. 2. 95) = तुभ्य + ङे (VII. 1. 102) = तुभ्य + अम् (VII. 1. 28) = तुभ्यम् (VI. 1. 107 or 97) ; similarly मह्यम् ॥ So also युष्मद् + सु = त्वद् + सु (VII. 2. 94) = त्व + सु (VII. 2. 94) = त्व + सु (VII. 2. 102) = त्व + अम्

(VII. 1. 28)=त्वम् (VI. 1. 97 or 107). Similarly अहम् ॥ So also युवाम् and आवाम् by VII. 2. 92 and VI. 2. 88; यूयम् and वयम् by VII. 2. 93 and VI. 1. 97 or 107, त्वाम् and माम् by VII. 2. 97 and VII. 2. 87; and युवाम् and आवाम् as before.

शसो न ॥ २६ ॥ पदानि ॥ शसः, न, ॥

वृत्तिः ॥ युष्मदस्मद्भ्यामुत्तरस्य शसो नकारादेशो भवति ॥

29. **न्** is substituted for the **स्** of **अस्** the affix of the Accusative Plural after **युष्मद्** and **अस्मद्** ॥

As युष्मान् and अस्मान् (द् elided by VII. 2. 90, and lengthening by VII. 2. 87). युष्मान् ब्राह्मणान्। अस्मान् ब्राह्मणान्। युष्मान् ब्राह्मणीः। अस्मान् ब्राह्मणीः। युष्मान् कुलानि। अस्मान्कुलानि ॥

भ्यसो भ्यम् ॥ ३० ॥ पदानि ॥ भ्यसः, भ्यम् ॥

वृत्तिः ॥ युष्मदस्मद्भ्यामुत्तरस्य भ्यसो भ्यमित्ययमादेशो भवति ॥

30. **अभ्यम्** is substituted for the Dative **भ्यस्** after 'yushmad' and 'asmad.'

As युष्मभ्यम् and अस्मभ्यम् ॥ As the sûtra is constructed (भ्यसो भ्यम्) it is not easy to say whether the substitute is भ्यम् or अभ्यम् ॥ If it is भ्यम्, then we have two cases, (1) eliding the final द् of yushmad and asmad, by VII. 2. 90, and adding भ्यम् (2) eliding अद् of yushmad and asmad by VII. 2. 90, and adding भ्यम् ॥ It will be shown hereafter that VII. 2. 90, is capable of two explanations, one by which yushmad and asmad lose their द् only, and by another अद् ॥ Similarly with अभ्यम् we have also two cases: Thus we have four cases. as (1) yushma+bhyam, (2) yushm+bhyam, (3) yushma+abhyam, (4) yushm+abhyam. In the case of the first (yushma+bhyam) we can get the proper form, though it may be objected that yushma+bhyam should be equal to युष्मेभ्यम् by VII. 3. 103: this ए substitution will not take place, however, by force of the maxim अङ्गवृत्त पुनर्वृत्तावविधि र्निष्ठितस्य "when an operation which is taught in the angâdhikâra has taken place, and another operation of the angâdhikâra is subsequently applicable, this latter operation is not allowed to take place."

The second case is an impossibility, namely, yushm+bhyam can give us no form. The third case yushma+abhyam will give us the proper form युष्मभ्यम् (अ+अ=अ by VI. 1. 97). Moreover the accent also will be on the middle युष्मभ्यम् by VI. 1. 161, the udâtta अ of yushma being elided by the anudâtta अ of अभ्यम्, the acute will be on the anudâtta अ ॥ It should not be objected that in VI. I. 161, the word अन्त of VI. 1. 159 is understood, and the accent will be on the final. We have shown in that sûtra, that the udâtta will fall on the आदि (*beginning*) of the anudâtta term which causes the elision The fourth alternative yushm+abhyam is free from all objections.

पञ्चम्या अत् ॥ ३१ ॥ पदानि ॥ पञ्चम्या, अत् ॥

वृत्तिः ॥ पञ्चम्या भ्यसो युष्मदस्मद्भ्यामुत्तरस्य अदित्ययमादेशो भवति ॥

31. अत् is substituted for the Ablative भ्यस्, after युष्मद् and अस्मद् ॥

As युष्मत्, अस्मत् ॥ The द् is elided by VII. 2. 95, before the case ending भ्यस्, and युष्म + अत् = युष्मत् by VI. 1. 97.

एकवचनस्य च ॥ ३२ ॥ पदानि ॥ एकवचनस्य, च ॥

वृत्तिः ॥ पञ्चम्या एकवचनस्य युष्मदस्मद्भ्यामुत्तरस्यादित्ययमादेशो भवति ॥

32. This substitution of अत् is made in the singular number also of the ablative, after yushmad and asmad.

As त्वद् and मद् ॥ For the substitution of त्व and म see VII. 2. 97.; and त्व and म + अत् = त्वत् and मत् by VI. 1. 97.

साम आकम् ॥ ३३ ॥ पदानि ॥ सामः आकम् ॥

वृत्तिः ॥ साम इति षष्ठीबहुवचनमागतसुट्कं गृह्यते, तस्य युष्मदस्मद्भ्यामुत्तरस्याकमित्ययमादेशो भवति ॥

33. आकम् is substituted for the Genitive plural affix साम् (VII. 1. 52), after yushmad, and asmad.

साम् is the affix आम् of the Genitive plural with the augment स ॥ Thus युष्माकम् and अस्माकम् ॥ Why is it read साम् and not आम्. when there is no स् at the time when the substitution is ordained? It is read as साम् in order to indicate that आकम् will not get the augment स्, for otherwise 'yushma' and 'asma' having lost their 'd' by VII. 2. 90, end in अ, and so by VII. 1. 52, would cause the genitive affix to get the augment स; the present sûtra removes that also. The substitute is exhibited with a long आ, in order to make अ + आ = आ in युष्म + आकम्, had it been short अ, then there would have been no lengthening but अ + अ = अ by VI. 1. 97. If you say 'the very fact that अकम् was taught and not कम्, would prevent para-rûpa and cause lengthening'; we reply, that the अ of अकम् would find its scope in preventing ए substitution. For without अ, we should have युष्म + कम् = युष्मेकम् (VII. 3. 103).

आत औ णलः ॥ ३४ ॥ पदानि ॥ आतः, औ, णलः ॥

वृत्तिः ॥ आकारान्ताद्धातुरुत्तरस्य णल औकारादेशो भवति ॥

34. औ is substituted for णल्, the affix of the first and third person singular of the perfect, after roots ending in long आ ॥

Thus पपौ, तस्थौ, जग्लौ, मम्लौ, from पा, स्था, ग्लै (ग्ला) and म्लै (म्ला) ॥ The form पपौ is thus evolved, पा + णल् = पा + अ ॥ Here three operations simultaneously present themselves for application, namely; 1. Reduplication, 2. Lengthening; by the single substitution of one long vowel आ, for आ + अ; and 3. The substitution of औ for आ by the present sûtra. In what order should these operations be then performed? First the affix अ should be replaced by औ. then the single substitution of औ for आ + औ; and then treating it as sthânivat, and then reduplication. For if the single substitution of आ for आ + अ had taken place first, then there would be no scope for औ substitution, therefore the औ substitution, should take place first. Thus we have पा + औ = पौ; this vṛiddhi-ekâdeśa, is treated as sthânivat by I. 1. 59, and it causes reduplication. The vṛiddhi-ekâdeśa should first take place (i. e. आ + औ = औ) and then the reduplication, because the former rule is subsequent to the latter.

तुह्योस्तातङ्ङाशिष्यन्यतरस्याम् ॥ ३५ ॥ पदानि ॥ तु, ह्योः, तातङ्, आशिषि, अन्यतरस्याम् ॥

वृत्तिः ॥ तु हि इत्येतयोराशिषि विषये तातङादेशो भवत्यन्यतरस्याम् ॥

35. तातङ् is optionally substituted for the affixes तु and हि of the Imperative, when benediction is meant.

As जीवताद् भवान्, जीवतात् त्वम्, जीवतु भवान्, जीव त्वम् ॥ The ङ् prevents Guṇa and Vṛiddhi, (I. 1. 4), and the substitute replaces the whole affix (I. 1. 53 notwithstanding). The substitute is not sthânivat पित्, though it replaces a पित् affix, because it has its own indicatory letter ङ्, and ङित् does not become पित्; and consequently in ब्रूतात् ई is not added to the affix, by VII. 3. 93, ई being added only to पित् affixes after ब्रू ॥ When not denoting benediction, we have not this substitution: as ग्रामं गच्छतु भवान् or गच्छ ग्रामम् ॥

The affix तातङ् being a substitu e of हि, is like हि, and, therefore, rules propounded with regard to हि, will apply to तातङ् also. Thus VI. 4. 105 says that after stems ending in short अ, the हि is elided: therefore, after such words तातङ् should also be elided. Therefore we cannot get the form जीवतात् त्वम् for जीवत्वम् ॥ This objection, however, is futile; for, in the sûtra अतो हेः (VI. 4. 105), there is the anuvritti of हि from sûtra VI. 4. 101 (हु झल्भ्यो हेर्धिः) ॥ So that अतो हेः should be construed as meaning "there is the elision of हि when it is of the form हि, and not when it assumes the form तातङ्" ॥

The object of ङ् in तातङ् is, as we have said above, for the sake of preventing Guṇa and Vṛiddhi. It should not be said that the object of ङ् in तातङ् is for the sake of अन्त्यविधिः by the application of sûtra ङिच्च (I. 1. 53), just as the substitutes अनङ् &c (VII. 1. 93 and 94) apply to the finals. For by so doing, तातङ् would replace only the उ of तु and the इ of हि, which is not desired. And the case of तातङ् is to be distinguished from अनङ्, for in अनङ् the ङ् has no other object but to prevent sarvâdeśa; but in तातङ् we see that ङ् has another object, namely, the prevention of Guṇa and Vṛiddhi; and ङ् having thus found scope, the तातङ् substitute will be governed by the general rule अनेकाल् शित् सर्वस्य (I. 1. 55).

The Kârikâ given below raises these points.

Kárika:—तातङि ङित्त्वं संक्रमकृत्स्यादन्त्यविधिश्चेत्तन्न तथा न ।
हेरधिकारे हेरधिकारो लोपविधौ तु ज्ञापकमाह ॥
तातङो ङित्त्वसामर्थ्यान्नायमन्त्यविधिः स्मृतः ।
न तद्वदनङादीनां तेन ते ऽन्त्यविकारजाः ॥

Kârikâ:—In तातङ् the ङ् is for the sake of preventing Guṇa and Vṛiddhi (संक्रम = गुणवृद्धिप्रतिषेधः) ॥ If it be said, it is for the sake of अन्त्यविधि by I. 1. 53; we say it is not so. (If you say that after roots ending in short अ, तात् should be elided, by VI. 4. 105 read with I. 1. 56, we reply): when the anuvṛtti or adhikâra of हि was already existent in the sûtra VI. 4. 105 from sûtra VI. 4. 101, the express employment of हि in VI. 4. 105, indicates that the lopa rule does not apply to तातङ् ॥ (The lopa-rule not applying to तातङ्, it follows that it replaces the *whole* of हि and not only its final). The ङ् in तातङ् finds its scope in preventing Guṇa and Vriddhi, therefore, it is not for the sake of antya-vidhi (I. 1. 53). The ङित्त्व in अनङ् &c has no other scope, therefore, these substitutes replace the final only.

विदेः शतुर्वसुः ॥ ३६ ॥ पदानि ॥ विदेः, शतुः, वसुः ॥

वृत्तिः ॥ विद ज्ञाने इत्येतस्माद्धातोरुत्तरस्य शतुर्वसुरादेशो भवति ॥

36. वसु is substituted for the Present Participle affix शतृ after the root विद् 'to know'.

Thus विद्वस् (n. s. विद्वान्), विद्वांसौ, विद्वांसः ॥ The words formed with affixes having an indicatory उ or ऋ (उगित्) add a न् in their strong cases (VII. 1. 70), and form their feminine with unaccented ई ॥ शतृ is an affix having an indicatory ऋ, therefore its substitute would also be considered as having an indicatory ऋ, the उ of वसु therefore is not absolutely necessary for the purposes of उगित् operations. वसु is so written, in order that in the sûtra वसोः संप्रसारणं (VI. 4. 131.), both क्वसु and वसु should be included. Nor can we object that in the above mentioned sûtra, वसु with one indicatory letter being taken, cannot include an affix like क्वसु having two indicatory letters,—on the maxim एकानुबन्धकग्रहणे न द्व्यनुबन्धकस्य—for if that were so, there was no necessity of उ in वसु ॥ Some read the anuvṛtti of the word optionally into this: and we have विदन्, विदन्तौ, विदन्तः formed with शतृ (see V. 4. 38).

समासे ऽनञ्पूर्वे क्त्वो ल्यप् ॥ ३७ ॥ पदानि ॥ समासे, अनञ्, पूर्वे, क्त्वः ल्यप् ॥

वृत्तिः ॥ समासे ऽनञ्पूर्वे क्त्वा इत्येतस्य ल्यबित्ययमादेशो भवति ॥

37. In a compound, the first member of which is an Indeclinable but not नञ्; ल्यप् is substituted for क्त्वा ॥

Thus प्रकृत्य, प्रहृत्य ॥ The tvâ is added by III. 4. 21, the compounding is by II. 2. 18, and तुक् by VI. 1. 71. पार्श्वतःकृत्य, The tvâ is added by III. 4. 61. and compounding is by II. 2. 22. नानाकृत्य; द्विधाकृत्य The tvâ is added by III. 4. 62. Why do we say 'in a compound'? Observe कृत्वा हृत्वा. Here the counter example is हत्वा, which is preceded by an Indeclinable कृत्वा, but as it is not compounded, there is no substitution. Why do we say 'not preceded by नञ्'? Observe अकृत्वा, अहृत्वा, परमकृत्वा, उत्तमकृत्वा ॥ The word अनञ् means 'other than नञ्', and means words of the same class as नञ्, i. e. Indeclinables : and does not mean words which are not Indeclinables. The compounds like स्नात्वाकालक contained in the class of मयूरव्यंसक &c (II. 1. 72.), do not take ल्यप anomalously. Or the word समासे is in the Locative with the force of specification : and means those compounds which are specifically formed with क्त्वा and not any compound in general.

Now by the rule I. 1. 72, ktvâ would denote a form ending with ktvâ; and would include the case of a compound ending in ktvâ. But this general rule is modified by the maxim प्रत्यय ग्रहणे यस्मात् स विहित स्तदादेस्तदन्तस्य ग्रहणम् "an affix denotes, whenever it is employed in grammar, a word-form which begins with that to which that affix has been added and ends with the affix itself." But the affix ktvâ is never ordained after a compound. Therefore, the case of compounds ending in ktvâ, would not be covered by the mere employment of ktvâ. Then comes the maxim कृद् ग्रहणे गति कारक पूर्वस्यापि ग्रहणं 'a kṛit affix denotes whenever it is employed in grammar, a word-form which begins with that to which that kṛit affix has been added and which ends with the kṛit affix, but moreover should a gati, or a noun such as denotes a case-relation have been prefixed to that word-form, then the kṛit affix must denote the same word-form together with the gati or the noun which may have been prefixed to it." By this a compound also may end in ktvâ. This maxim will cover cases like प्रकृत्य, पार्श्वतः कृत्य but not उच्चैः कृत्य &c because उच्चैः is neither a gati nor a kâraka. Hence the employment of the word समासे in the sûtrâ, and also of the word अनञ्पूर्वे, for नञ् is neither a Gati nor a Kâraka.

In the case of प्रधाय and प्रस्थाय this maxim applies :—अन्तरङ्गानपि विधीन् बहिरङ्गो ल्यप् बाधते "a Bahiranga substitution of ल्यप् supersedes even antaranga rule". What are these antaranga rules superseded by the substitute ल्यप्? (1) हित्वं—the substitution of हि for धा (VII. 4. 42). Thus हित्वा but प्रधाय and not प्रहित्वा ॥ (2) दत्वं—the substitution of दद् for दो (VII. 4. 46)—as दत्त्वा, but प्रदाय and not प्रदत्त्वा ॥ (3) आत्वं as required by VI. 4. 42 : as खात्वा, प्रखाय and प्रखन्य ॥ (4) इत्वं—as स्थित्वा but प्रस्थाय ॥ (5) ईत्वं by VI. 4. 66, as पीत्वा but प्रपाय ॥ (6) दीर्घत्वं by VI. 4. 15, as शान्त्वा but प्रशम्य ॥ (7) शुट् by VI. 4. 19, as पृष्ट्वा but आपृच्छय ॥ (8) ऊठ्—as द्यूत्वा ॥ (9) इट् (VII. 2. 56)—देवित्वा but प्रदीव्य ॥

क्त्वापि छन्दसि ॥ ३८ ॥ पदानि ॥ क्त्वा, अपि, छन्दसि ॥

वृत्तिः ॥ समासे ऽनञ्पूर्वे क्त्वा इत्येतस्य क्त्वा इत्ययमादेशो भवति अपिशब्दाल्ल्यबपि भवति छन्दसि विषये ॥

38. In the Veda the क्त्वा also, as well as ल्यप, is substituted for क्त्वा, after an Indeclinable compound, other than one preceded by the Negative नञ् ॥

Thus कृष्णं वासो यजमानं परिधापयित्वा, प्रत्यञ्चमर्कं प्रत्यर्पयित्वा ॥ So also we have ल्यप्, as उद्धृत्य जुहोति ॥ The sûtra could have been made shorter by saying merely वा छन्दसि; not doing so indicates that conditions and limitations are set aside in the Vedas in applying this affix. Therefore ल्यप् is applied even when there is no compound, as, अर्च्य तान् देवान् गतः ॥ The word छन्दसि governs the following sûtras upto VII. 1. 50, inclusive.

सुपां सुलुक्पूर्वसवर्णाच्छेयाडाड्यायाजालः ॥ ३९ ॥ पदानि ॥ सुपाम्, सु, लुक्, पूर्वसवर्ण, आ, आत्, शे, या, डा, ड्या, याच्, आलः ॥

वृत्तिः ॥ छान्दसि विषये सुपां स्थाने सु लुक् पूर्वसवर्ण आ आत् शे या डाड्या याच् आल इत्येते आदेशा भवन्ति ॥

वार्त्तिकम् ॥ सुपां सुपो भवन्ति इति वक्तव्यम् ॥ वार्त्तिकम् ॥ तिङां तिङो भवन्तीति वक्तव्यम् ॥

वार्त्तिकम् ॥ इयाडियाजीकाराणामुपसंख्यानम् ॥ वार्त्तिकम् ॥ आङ्याजयारामुपसंख्यानम् ॥

39. The following irregular endings are substituted for the various case endings in the Veda: (1) स् of the Nom. Sg. for अस् of the Plural, (2) the *luk*-elision of the case-endings, (3) the single substitution of the homogeneous long vowel for the end vowel of the stem, (4) आ, (5) आत्, (6) ए (शे) for the ending of the Nom. Plural, (7) या, (8) आ (डा), with the elision of the last vowel and the consonant, if any, that follows it in the stem, (9) या (ड्या) with the similar shortening of the stem (10) याँ (याच्) and आ (accent of ल) ॥

Thus (1) अनृक्षरा ऋजवः सन्तु पन्थाः (for पन्थानः) Rig Veda X. 85. 23.

Vârt:—It should be stated that case-endings replace case-endings promiscuously, as, धुरि दक्षिणायाः (for दक्षिणायाम् Rig I. 164. 9).

Vârt:—One personal ending replaces another personal ending in the Vedas चषालं ये अश्वयूपाय तक्षति (for तक्षन्ति) Rig I. 162. 6.

(2) लुक्-elision:—As आर्द्रे चर्मन्, लोहिते चर्मन् for चर्मणि; हविर्धाने यत् सुन्वन्ति, तत् सामिधेनीरन्वाह (यद् for यस्मिन् and तद् for तस्मिन्) ॥

(3) Lengthening:—धीती, मती, सुष्टुती for धीत्या, मत्या and सुष्टुत्या ॥

(4) आ—उभा यन्तारौ (for उभौ) ॥

(5) आत्—न ताद् ब्राह्मणाद् निन्दामि for तान् ब्राह्मणान् ॥

(6) शे—न युष्मे (for यूयम्) वाजबन्धवः, Rig VIII. 68. 19. अस्मे (for वयं) इन्द्राबृहस्पती; Rig IV. 49. 4, the यूय and वय substitution has not taken place as a Vedic usage.

(7) या—उरुया, धृष्णुया for उरुणा and धृष्णुना ॥

(8) डा—नाभा (for नाभौ) पृथिव्याः Rig I. 143. 4.

(9) ड्या—अनुष्ट्या च्यावयतात् for अनुष्टुभा Ait Br. II. 6. 15.

(10) याच्—साधुयाँ for साधु, there was required the elision of सु ॥

(11) आल्—वसन्ता यजेत for वसन्ते ॥

Vârt:—The following substitutes should also be enumerated, (*a*) इया, (*b*) डियाच् with elision of the final vowel and the consonant, if any, that follows it, and (*c*) long ई ॥ As (*a*) उर्विया परिधानम्, for उरुणा, so also दार्विया for दारुणा ॥ (*b*) सुक्षेत्रिया for सुक्षेत्रिणा, and सुगात्रिया for सुगात्रिणा ॥ (*c*) दृति न शुष्कं सरसी शयानम् for सरसि ॥

Vârt:—So also (*a*) आङ्, (*b*) अयाच् and (*c*) अयार्: as प्रबाहवा for प्रबाहुना, (*b*) स्वप्नया सच सेवनम् for स्वप्नेन, (*c*) सिन्धुमिव नावया for नावा ॥

The word आच्छे in the sûtra is compounded of three words आ + आत् + शे, the word आत् = आ + आत् ॥

अमो मश् ॥ ४० ॥ पदानि ॥ अमः, मश् ॥

वृत्तिः ॥ अम् इति मिबादेशो गृह्यते । तस्य छन्दसि विषये मशादेशो भवति ॥

40. For the Personal ending अम् of the First Person Singular (in the Aorist) म (I. 1. 55) is substituted in the Veda.

The अम् here is the substitution of मिप्, and not the accusative singular affix. As वधीं वृत्रम् (for अवधिषम्) Rig I. 165. 8: क्रमीम वृक्षस्य शाखाम् ॥ The अट् augment is diversely elided (VI. 4. 75). The indicatory श् of मश् shows that the *whole* of the affix अम् is to be replaced. The substitution of म् for म् is to prevent the change of म् into anusvâra as in VIII. 3. 25.

लोपस्त आत्मनेपदेषु ॥ ४१ ॥ पदानि ॥ लोपः, त, आत्मनेपदेषु ॥

वृत्तिः ॥ आत्मनेपदेषु यस्तकारस्तस्य छन्दसि विषये लोपो भवति ॥

41. In the Veda the त of the Atmanepada Personal ending is elided.

As देवा अदुह and गन्धर्वा अप्सरसो अदुह्र for अदुहत (see VII. 1. 8); दुहाम् (for दुग्धाम्) अश्विभ्यां पयो अघ्न्येयम् ॥ Rig I. 164. 27. दक्षिणतः शये for शेते ॥ Owing to the anuvritti of अपि from VII. 1. 38, this substitution sometimes does not take place; as: आत्मानमनृतं कुरुते ॥ Why in the Atmanepada? Observe वत्सं दुहन्ति कलशं चतुर्बिलम् ॥

ध्वमो ध्वात् ॥ ४२ ॥ पदानि ॥ ध्वमः, ध्वात् ॥

वृत्तिः ॥ छन्दसि विषये ध्वमो ध्वादित्ययमादेशो भवति ॥

42. In the Veda, ध्वात् is substituted for the Personal ending ध्वम् ॥

As अन्तरेवोष्माणं वारयध्वात् for वारयध्वम् ॥ Ait Br. II. 6. 14.

यजध्वैनमिति च ॥ ४३ ॥ पदानि ॥ यजध्वैनम्, इति, च ॥

वृत्तिः ॥ यजध्वमित्येतस्य एनमित्येतस्मिन्परतो मकारलोपो निपात्यते वकारस्य च यकारश्छन्दसि विषये ॥

43. यजध्वैनम् is irregularly formed in the Veda for यजध्वमेनम् ॥

The word यजध्वम् followed by एनम् loses its final म् in the Veda. As यजध्वैनं प्रियमेधाः (Rig VIII. 2. 37). The Kasika adds "that व् is also irregularly changed into य": the form would then be यजध्यैनम् ॥ This is, however, a mistake as pointed out by Bhattoji Dikshit.

तस्य तात् ॥ ४४ ॥ पदानि ॥ तस्य, तात् ॥

वृत्तिः ॥ तशब्दस्य लोण्मध्यमपुरुषबहुवचनस्य स्थाने तादित्ययमादेशो भवति ॥

44. For the ending त of the 2nd Pers. Pl. Imperative is substituted तात् in the Veda.

As गात्रं गात्रमस्या नूनं कृणुतात् (for कृणुत), and ऊवध्ये गोहं पार्थिवं खनतात् (for खनत) Ait Br. II. 6. 15, 16. अस्मारक्ष संसृजतात् (=संसृजत), सूर्यं चक्षुर्गमयतात् (=गमयत).

तप्तनप्तनथनाश्च ॥ ४६ ॥ पदानि ॥ तप्, तनप्, तन, थनाः, च ॥

वृत्तिः ॥ तस्येति वर्त्तते । छन्दसि विषये तस्य स्थाने तप् तनप् तन थन इत्येते आदेशा भवन्ति ॥

45. Also त and तन (before both, on account of the indicatory प् the preceding vowel of the verbal stem is strengthened, or if weak not shortened), तन and थन are substituted for the त of the 2nd Pers. Pl. Imperative in the Veda.

This शृणोत ग्रावाणः (for शृणुत), सुनोत (=सुनुत), संवरत्रा दधातन (for धत्त), जुजुष्टन (for जुषत) the ślu vikaraṇa being added as a Vedic irregularity; यदिष्टन for यदिच्छत ॥ The indicatory प् makes तप् and तनप् non-ङित् affixes (I. 2. 4).

इदन्तो मसि ॥ ४७ ॥ पदानि ॥ इदन्तः, मसि ॥

वृत्तिः ॥ छन्दसि विषये मसित्ययं शब्द इकारान्तो भवति । मसः सकारान्तस्य इकारागमो भवति स च तस्यान्तो भवति ॥

46. The Personal ending मस् becomes in the Veda मसि ending with an इ ॥

Thus पुनस्त्वां दीपयामसि (for दीपयामः) शलभं भञ्जयामसि (for भञ्जयामः), त्वयि रात्रि वासयामसि for वासयामः ॥

क्त्वोयक् ॥ ४८ ॥ पदानि ॥ क्त्वः, यक् ॥

वृत्तिः ॥ क्त्वा इत्येतस्य यगागमो भवति छन्दसि विषये ॥

47. In the Veda, the Absolutive affix क्त्वा gets at the end, the augment य ॥

Thus दत्वाय सविता धियः (for दत्वा). This sûtra is not read immediately after VII. 1. 38, as in that sûtra, the anuvṛitti of samâsa is understood, while there is no such anuvṛitti here.

इष्ट्वीनमिति च ॥ ४९ ॥ पदानि ॥ इष्ट्वीनम्, इति, च ॥

वृत्तिः ॥ इष्ट्वीनमित्यय शब्दो निपात्यते छन्दसि विषये । यजेः क्त्वाप्रत्ययान्तस्य ईनमादेशोऽन्त्यस्य निपात्यते ॥ वार्त्तिकम् ॥ पीत्वीनमित्यपीष्यते ॥

48. In the Veda, the Absolutive इष्ट्वीनम् is irregularly formed for इष्ट्वा ॥

To the root यज् is added क्त्वा, and the final आ is replaced by ईनम् ॥ As इष्ट्वीनम् देवान् for इष्ट्वा देवान् ॥ The च in the sûtra indicates that there are other forms like this, as पीत्वीनम् for पीत्वा ॥

स्नात्व्यादयश्च ॥ ४६ ॥ पदानि ॥ स्नात्वी-आदयः, च ॥

वृत्तिः ॥ स्नात्वी इत्येवमादयः शब्दा निपात्यन्ते छन्दसि विषये ॥

49. **स्नात्वी** &c. are irregularly formed in the Veda.

Thus स्नात्वी मलादिव, for स्नात्वा ; पीत्वी सोमस्य वावृधे for पीत्वा ॥ The word आदि 'et cetera' means "of the form of", namely words having form like स्नात्वी, as पीत्वी &c.

आज्जसेरसुक् ॥ ५० ॥ पदानि ॥ आत्, जसेः, असुक् ॥

वृत्तिः ॥ अवर्णान्तादङ्गादुत्तरस्य जसेरसुगागमो भवति छन्दसि विषये ॥

50. After a stem ending in अ or आ, the affix अस् of the Nom. Pl. gets, in the Veda, the augment अस् (असुक्) at the end.

Thus ब्राह्मणासः पितरः सोम्यासः for ब्राह्मणाः and सोम्याः ॥ Rig VI. 75. 10. ये पूर्वासो य उपरासः (Rig X. 15. 2) for पूर्वे and उपरे ॥ So also पुत्रासः (R. I. 3. 4) Why is not, after the adding of the augment असुक्, the जस् changed to शी in the last example, as required by VII. 1. 17, and on the maxim पुनः प्रसङ्गः विज्ञानात्? No, the maxim that applies here is सकृद् गतौ विप्रतिषेधे यद्बाधितं, तद्बाधितमेव ॥

अश्वक्षीरवृषलवणानामात्मप्रीतौ क्यचि ॥ ५१ ॥ अश्व, क्षीर, वृष, लवणानाम्, आत्मा प्रीतौ, क्यचि ॥

वृत्तिः ॥ छन्दसीत्यत्र: प्रभृति निवृत्तम् । अश्व क्षीर वृष लवण इत्येतेषामङ्गानामात्मप्रीतिविषये क्यचि परतोऽसुगागमो भवति ॥

वार्त्तिकम् ॥ अश्ववृषयोर्मैथुनेच्छायामिति वक्तव्यम् ॥ वा० ॥ क्षीरलवणयोर्लालसायामिति वक्तव्यम् ॥

वा० ॥ सर्वप्रातिपदिकेभ्यो लालसायामसुग्वक्तव्यः ॥ वा० ॥ सुग्वक्तव्यः ॥

51. The same augment असुक् is added after the words अश्व, क्षीर, वृष and लवण before the Denominative affix क्यच्, when the delight of the subject in these things is to be expressed.

The anuvṛitti of छन्दसि does not extend to this sûtra or any further. Thus अश्वस्यति वडवा, क्षीरस्यति माणवकः, वृषस्यति गौः, लवणस्यत्युष्ट्रः ॥ अश्व + अस् + य + ति = अश्वस्यति (VI. 1. 97). Why 'when the delight of the subject is meant'? Observe अश्वीयति, क्षीरीयति, वृषीयति and लवणीयति ॥

Vârt:—After अश्व and वृष, the force of the augment is that of desiring sexual connection. *Vârt*:—After क्षीर and लवण it has the force of ardently wishing for, i. e. an intense thirsting after the thing. The augment is not added, though the sense may be that of delight, if it has not the above meanings. Others say *Vârt*:—असुक् should be added after every nominal stem when the sense is that of intense yearning after that thing: as दध्यस्यति, मध्वस्यति &c. Others say *Vârt*:—That the augment सुक् should be added, as दधिस्यति, मधुस्यति &c.

आमि सर्वनाम्नः सुट् ॥ ५२ ॥ पदानि ॥ आमि, सर्वनाम्नः, सुट् ॥

वृत्तिः ॥ आमिति वर्त्तते अवर्णात्सर्वनाम्न उत्तरस्यामः सुडागमो भवति ॥

52. After a Pronominal stem ending in अ or आ, the affix आम् of the Genitive Plural gets the augment स् at the beginning.

The word आत् of the last sûtra is understood here. Thus सर्वेषाम्, विश्वेषाम्, येषाम्, तेषाम्, सर्वासाम्, यासाम्, तासाम् ॥ But भवताम् of भवत् ॥ The आम् of the sûtra is the Genitive Plural ending आम्, and not the आम् of the Locative Singular ordained by VII. 3. 116; for that आम् takes the augments याट्, आट् or स्याट् (VII. 3. 112-114), while the present आम् takes सुट् or नुट् ॥ Nor the आम् of the Perfect Tense (III. I. 35 &c), because that refers to verb and Sarvanâma nor the आम् of V. 4. 11, for the same reason. The word आमि is exhibited in the sûtra in the locative case, for the sake of the subsequent sûtra VII. I. 53. For the purposes of the present sûtra, it should be construed, as if it was in the Genitive case (आमः सर्वनाम्नः सुट्), because सर्वनाम्नः being in the Ablative case, the augment सुट् will be added at the beginning of the affix following it, on the maxim तस्मादित्युत्तरस्य ॥

त्रेस्त्रयः ॥ ५३ ॥ पदानि ॥ त्रेः, त्रयः ॥

वृत्तिः ॥ त्रिइत्येतस्य आमि परे त्रय इत्ययमादेशो भवति ॥

53. त्रय is substituted for त्रि before the Genitive Pl. affix.

As त्रयाणाम् ॥ त्रीणाम् however appears in the Veda: as श्रीणामपि समुद्राणाम् ॥

ह्रस्वनद्यापो नुट् ॥ ५४ ॥ पदानि ॥ ह्रस्व, नदी, आपः, नुट् ॥

वृत्तिः ॥ ह्रस्वान्तान्नद्यन्तादाबन्ताश्चोत्तरस्यामो नुडागमो भवति ॥

54. The augment न् is added before the Genitive Pl. ending आम्, after stems ending in a short vowel, after stems called Nadî (I. 4. 3 &c), and after the stems ending in the Feminine affix आ ॥

As वृक्षाणाम्, प्लक्षानाम्, अग्नीणाम्, वायूनाम्, कर्तृणाम् ॥ नद्यन्तात्ः—कुमारीणाम्, किशोरीणाम्, गौरीणाम्, शार्ङ्गरवीणाम्, लक्ष्मीणाम्, ब्रह्मबन्धूनाम्, वीरबन्धूनाम् ॥ आबन्तात्ः—खट्वानाम्, मालानाम्, बहुराजानाम्, कारीषगन्ध्यानाम् ॥

The lengthening of the short final vowel takes place by VI. 4. 3.

षट्चतुर्भ्यश्च ॥ ५५ ॥ पदानि ॥ षट्, चतुर्भ्यः, च ॥

वृत्तिः ॥ षट्संज्ञकेभ्यश्चतुर्भ्यश्च शब्दाचोत्तरस्यामो नुडागमो भवति ॥

55. The augment न् is added before the Genitive pl. ending आम् after the Numerals called 'shash', and after चतुर् ॥

As षण्णाम्, पञ्चानाम्, (VI. 4. 7), सप्तानाम्, नवानाम्, दशानाम्, चतुर्णाम् ॥ A numeral ending in र् is not 'shash', hence the specific mention of चतुर ॥

This rule applies to compounds ending with these numerals, when these latter are the principal member, as परमषण्णाम्, परमपञ्चानाम्, परमचतुर्णाम्, but प्रियषषाम्, प्रियपञ्चाम्, प्रियचतुराम् where the Numerals are secondary (upasarjana).

श्रीग्रामण्योश्छन्दसि ॥ ५६ ॥ पदानि ॥ श्री, ग्रामण्योः, छन्दसि ॥

वृत्तिः ॥ श्री ग्रामणी इत्येतयोश्छन्दसि विषये आमो नुडागमो भवति ॥

56. In the Veda after the words श्री and ग्रामणी, the Gen. Pl. आम gets the augment न् ॥

As श्रीणामुदारो धरुणो रयीणाम्, अन्यत्र सूतग्रामणीनाम् ॥ This sûtra could be well dispensed with: by I. 4. 5. श्री is optionally a Nadi in the Genitive plural. We make the option of that sûtra a vyavasthita-vibhâshâ, by saying श्री is *always* Nadi in the Veda, and *optionally* every where else. As regards सूतग्रामणीनाम्, we have सूतश्च ग्रामणीश्च = सूतग्रामणि, the Genitive Pl. of which by VII. I. 54 will be सूतग्रामणीनाम् ॥

The necessity of this sûtra will, however, arise if the compound be सूताश्च ते ग्रामण्यश्च सूतग्रामण्यः ॥

गोः पादान्ते ॥ ५७ ॥ पदानि ॥ गोः, पादान्ते ॥

वृत्तिः ॥ गो इत्येतस्मादृक्पादान्ते वर्त्तमानादुत्तरस्यामो नुडागमो भवति ॥

57. After गो, when standing at the end of a Rik verse, the augment न comes before the Gen. Pl. आम् ॥

As विद्माहि त्वा सत्पतिं शूरगोनाम्; but गवां गोत्रमुदसृजो यदङ्गिरः in the beginning of a Pâda. "All rules have exceptions in the Vedas" is an established maxim, so at the end of a Pâda, sometimes this rule does not apply, as हन्तारं शत्रूणां कृधि विराजं गोपतिं गवाम् ॥

इदितो नुम् धातोः ॥ ५८ ॥ पदानि ॥ इदितः, नुम्, धातोः ॥

वृत्तिः ॥ इदितो धातोर्नुमागमो भवति ॥

58. न् is added after the vowel of the root, in a root which has an indicatory इ in the Dhâtupâṭha.

Thus from कुडि—कुण्डितृ, कुण्डितुम्, कुण्डितव्यम्; from हुडि—हुण्डितृ, हुण्डितुम्, हुण्डितव्यम् &c. But पचति, पठति where इ is not इत् ॥ The न् is added to the root from its very inception, and they must be considered to have got a न, for the purposes of the application of the grammatical rules. Thus III. 3. 103 says that अ is added in the feminine to a root which ends in a consonant and has a prosodially long vowel. The root कुडि must be considered to be such a root and कुण्डा, हुण्डा are thus formed. Similarly though the roots in the Dhâṭupâtha are धिवि and कृवि, in applying affixes we must consider them as धिन्व् and कृन्व्, as the author himself has indicated in III. 1. 80. In short, in adding affixes, these roots should be considered as having a न् ॥ Moreover the *root* (*dhâtu*) should have इ, and not the *stem* (anga). The affixes तासि (Future) and सिच् (Aorist) when added to roots, will not make those roots

इदित्; for the इ in तासि and सिच् is merely for the sake of pronunciation, and is not to be considered as इत् in the strict sense of the word: in fact it should be considered as non-nasalised. If you say that "the इ in सिच् should be considered as इत्, for because of its being इत्, the न् of मन् is not elided by VI. 4. 24 in अमंस्ता", we reply, "not so, the न् is not elided, because sûtra हनः सिच् I. 2. 14 makes सिच् a कित् after हन् only, the result of which is that हन् only loses its न् by VI. 4. 37, and no other root". In मन्ता = मन् + तासि + डा = मन् + त् + आ (the आस् is elided VI. 4. 143). For the purposes of the elision of न्, the elided आस् would be considered as asiddha (VI. 4. 22), for both VI. 4. 143, and VI. 4. 37, requiring the elision of न् are âbhîya sûtras. In भेत्ता, छेत्ता from भिदिर् and छिदिर् the whole combination इर् is इत्, and not इ and र् separately, and hence नुम् is not added. But even if these roots be considered as इदित्, the syllable इर् having an इ, yet they will not get the नुम् augment, because the word अन्त of पाद्यन्ते (VII. 1. 57) is understood here in this sûtra also, so that the roots must have a *final* इ as इत् for the application of this rule.

शे मुचादीनाम् ॥ ५९ ॥ पदानि ॥ शे, मुचादीनाम् ॥

वृत्तिः ॥ शे प्रत्यये परतो मुचादीनां नुमागमो भवति ॥

वार्त्तिकम् ॥ शेतृम्फादीनामुपसंख्यानंकर्त्तव्यम् ॥

59. In मुच् &c, before the characteristic श of the Tudâdi class, the न् is placed after the vowel of the root.

Thus मुच्ल—मुञ्चति, लुम्पति, विन्दति, लिम्पति, सिञ्चति, कृन्तति, खिन्दति, पिंशति ॥ Why "before श"? Observe मोक्ता, मोक्तुम्, मोक्तव्यम् ॥ Why "of मुच् &c"? Observe तुदति, नुदति ॥

Vârt:—The तृम्फ &c should be also enumerated. These are the following roots of Tudâdi class: 24. तृप (तृफ), 25. तृम्फ तृप्तौ, 26. तुप तुम्प, 27. तुफ तुम्फ, हिंसायाम्, 28. दृफ (दृप), 29. दृम्फ उत्क्लेशे, 30. ऋफ (रिफ), ऋम्फ (रिम्फ), हिंसायाम्, 31. गुफ, गुम्फ ग्रन्थे, 32. उभ उम्भ पूरणे, 33. शुभ, शुम्भ शोभार्थे ॥ Of these, those which have a nasal, lose it by VI. 4. 24, and then get the नुम् augment by the present rule, which being specifically ordained, cannot be again dropped. Thus तृम्फति, तुम्फति, तुम्पति, दृम्फति &c. Those which have no nasal, are conjugated as तृफति, तुफति, दृफति गुफति, उभति and शुभति ॥

मस्जिनशोर्झलि ॥ ६० ॥ पदानि ॥ मस्जि, नशोः, झलि ॥

वृत्तिः ॥ मस्जि नशि इत्येतयोरङ्गयोर्झलादौ प्रत्यये नुमागमो भवति ॥

60. The augment नुम् is added after the vowel of the root in मस्ज् and नश, before an affix, beginning with any consonant, other than a semi-vowel or a nasal.

As मङ्क्ता, मस्ज् + तृच् (no इट् by VII. 2. 10), add न् = मस् न् ज् + तृ, elide स् by VIII. 2. 29, change ज् to क्, and न् to anusvâra, which then becomes ङ् ॥ मङ्क्तुम्, मङ्क्तव्यम्, नंष्टा, नंष्टुम् and नंष्टव्यम् ॥ But मज्जनम् and नशिता, and मग्न (VI. 4. 32). In मग्नः and मग्नवान्, the नुम् is supposed to be placed the last consonant in मस्ज्, in order that it ma, get elded.

रधिजभोरचि ॥ ६१ ॥ रधि, जभोः, अचि ॥

वृत्तिः ॥ रधि जभि इत्येतयोरजादौ प्रत्यये नुमागमो भवति ॥

61. The augment नुम् is added after the root-vowel in रध् and जभ्, before affixes beginning with a consonant.

Thus रन्धयति, रन्धकः, साधुरन्धी, रन्धो वर्त्तते ॥ जम्भयति, जम्भकः, साधुजम्भी, जम्भंजम्भम्, जम्भो वर्त्तते ॥ Though the वृद्धि rule is subsequent, it is superseded by the augment. Why do we say 'before an affix beginning with a vowel'? Observe रद्धा, जभ्यम् ॥

नेट्यलिटि रधेः ॥ ६२ ॥ पदानि ॥ न, इटि, अ लिटि, रधेः ॥

वृत्तिः ॥ इडादावलिटि प्रत्यये परे रधेर्नुमागमो न भवति ॥

62, The augment नुम् is not added to रध्, before an affix beginning with the augment इट्, except in the Perfect.

As रधिता, रधितुम्, रधितव्यम्, but रन्धनम्, रन्धकः before Aniṭ affixes, and ररन्धिव, ररन्धिम in the Perfect. When नुम् is added रन्ध् becomes a root ending in a conjunct consonant, and therefore the लिट् affixes after it are not कित् (असंयोगात् लिट् कित् I. 2. 5), and therefore the न् is not elided by VI. 4. 24. But when the affix क्वसु of the Perfect is added, we have रेधिवस् Nom. Sg. रेधिवान् ॥ Here the affix being expressly taught with an indicatory क the न् is elided. The reduplicate is elided, the अ changed into ए, then इट् is added, then नुम्, and then the नुम् is elided by the expressly taught कित् ॥

Why was not the sûtra made as इटि लिटि रधेः when by so doing, the augment नुम् would have been added only in the Perfect when it had इट् and no where else? This form of sûtra would have also meant that नुम् would be added in that Perfect which took इट् and in no other Perfect, while cases other than Perfect might take it. That being so, there would be no नुम् in ररन्ध, while रधिता would require नुम् ॥ See, however, the Mahabhâshya for the *contra*.

रभेरशब्लिटोः ॥ ६३ ॥ पदानि ॥ रभेः, अ शप्, लिटोः ॥

वृत्तिः ॥ रभेरङ्गस्य शब्लिड्वर्जिते ऽजादौ प्रत्यये परतो नुमागमो भवति ॥

63. The augment नुम् is added after the vowel of the root रभ् before an affix beginning with a vowel, but not before the vikaraṇa शप् or the affixes of the Perfect.

Thus आरम्भयति, आरम्भकः, साध्वारम्भी, आरम्भमारम्भम्, आरम्भो वर्त्तते ॥ But आरभते in शप्, and आरेभे in लिट्, and आरब्धा before an affix beginning with a con sonant.

लभेश्च ॥ ६४ ॥ पदानि ॥ लभेः, च ॥

वृत्तिः ॥ लभेश्चाजादौ प्रत्यये शब्लिड्वर्जिते नुमागमो भवति ॥

64. So also of लभ्, before an affix beginning with a vowel, with the exception of शप् and लिट्, there is the augment नुम् ॥

As लम्भयति, लम्भकः, साधुलम्भी, लम्भंलम्भम्, लम्भो वर्तते ॥ But लभते with शप्, and लेभे in the Perfect, and लब्धा before an affix beginning with a consonant. The separation of this from the last, is for the sake of the subsequent aphorisms.

आङो यि ॥ ६५ ॥ पदानि ॥ आङः, यि ॥

वृत्तिः ॥ आङ उत्तरस्य लभेर्यकारादिप्रत्ययविषये नुमागमो भवति ॥

65. The augment नुम is added to लभ् preceded by आ, before an affix beginning with य ॥

As आलम्भ्यो गौः ॥ The नुम् is added before the addition of the affix, and by so doing लभ् becomes लम्भ् and thus loses its character of having a penultimate अ, and therefore by III. 1. 124, we shall have ण्यत् affix, and not यत् affix by III. 1. 98. Had the नुम् been added *after* the addition of the affix, then यत् would be added by III. 1. 98. Though in both cases the form will be आलम्भ्या, the difference will be in the accent: यत् would throw the acute on the first syllable (यतोऽनावः) while the word has svarita on the final; thus instead of आलँम्भ्या (by VI. 1. 213 and VI. 2. 139), which यत् gives, we have आलम्भ्यां (तित् svar).

Why do we say 'when preceded by आ'? Observe लभ्य ॥ How do you explain अग्निष्टोम आलभ्यः? All rules are optionally applied in the Vedas. Or आलभ्य may be explained by saying that the नुम् having been added, is again dropped.

उपात्प्रशंसायाम् ॥ ६६ ॥ पदानि ॥ उपात्, प्रशंसायाम् ॥

वृत्तिः ॥ उपादुत्तरस्य लभेः प्रशंसायां गम्यमानायां यकारादिप्रत्ययविषये नुमागमो भवति ॥

66. The augment नुम is added to लभ् preceded by उप, before य, when the reference is to something praiseworthy.

As उपलम्भ्या भवता विद्या, उपलम्भ्यानि धनानि ॥ These words are formed by ण्यत् and have svarita on the final. Why do we say 'when referring to something praise worthy'? Observe उपलभ्यमस्माद् वृषलात् किंचित्, this is formed with the यत् affix (III. 1. 98).

उपसर्गात्खल्घञोः ॥ ६७ ॥ पदानि ॥ उप सर्गात्, खल्, घञोः ॥

वृत्तिः ॥ उपसर्गादुत्तरस्य लभेः खल्घञोः परतो नुमागमो भवति ॥

67. The augment नुम is added to लभ् preceded by a Preposition, before the affixes खल् (III. 3. 126) and घञ् ॥

Thus ईषत्प्रलम्भः, सुप्रलम्भः, दुष्प्रलम्भः, प्रलम्भः, विप्रलम्भः ॥ This is a Niyama rule, and restricts the scope of VII. 1. 64. Before the vowel affixes खल् and घञ्, the root लभ् gets the augment नुम् only then when it is preceded by a Preposition, and not otherwise, as ईषल्लभः, लाभो वर्तते ॥

न सुदुर्भ्यां केवलाभ्याम् ॥ ६८ ॥ पदानि ॥ न, सु, दुर्भ्याम, केवलाभ्याम् ॥

वृत्तिः ॥ सु दुरित्येताभ्यां केवलाभ्यामन्योपसर्गरहिताभ्यामुपसृष्टस्य लभेःखल्घञोः परतो नुमागमो न भवति ॥

68. The augment नुम् is not added to लभ् before खल् and घञ् when सु or दुः alone (without another Preposition along with them) precede the root.

Thus सुलभम्, दुर्लभम्, सुलाभो, दुर्लाभः ॥ But सुप्रलम्भः, दुष्प्रलम्भः ॥ The word केवल is used in the sûtra because सुदुर्भ्यां is in the Instrumental case and not in the Ablative. Had it been in the Ablative, there would have been no necessity of using the word केवलं, for the rule would not have applied, when a preposition intervened between these and the root. In अतिसुलभम्, the word अति is not an Upasarga but a Karmapravachaniya; when अति is used as an Upasarga, we have अतिसुलम्भः ॥ If the words सुदुर्भ्याम् be construed as Ablative, then also the use of केवल is for a purpose similar to that as above.

विभाषा चिण्णमुलोः ॥ ६९ ॥ पदानि ॥ वि भाषा, चिण्, णमुलोः ॥

वृत्तिः ॥ चिण् णमुल् इत्येतयोर्विभाषा लभेर्नुम्भवति ॥

69. The नुम् is optionally added to लभ् not preceded by a Preposition, before the चिण् Aorist and the Absolutive णमुल् ॥

Thus अलाभि or अलम्भि, लाभंलाभम् or लम्भंलम्भम् ॥ This is a Vyavasthita-vibhâshâ, the option is allowed where there is no Preposition along with the root; and no option is allowed but नुम् must be added, when a Preposition precedes: as प्रालम्भि, प्रलम्भम् ॥

उगिदचां सर्वनामस्थानेऽधातोः ॥ ७० ॥ पदानि ॥ उगित्, अ चाम्, सर्वनामस्थाने, अ धातोः ॥

वृत्तिः ॥ उगितामङ्गानां धातुवर्जितानामञ्चतेश्च सर्वनामस्थाने परतो नुमागमो भवति ॥

70. Whatever has an indicatory उ, ऋ and ऌ, (with the exception of a root), and the stem अच्, (अञ्चति) get the augment नुम् in the strong cases.

Thus भवतु has an indicatory उ, formed by the Uṇâdi affix डवतुप्, and it is declined as भवान्, भवन्तौ, भवन्तः ॥ Similarly ईयसुन्—श्रेयान्, श्रेयांसौ, श्रेयांसः ; शतृ—पचन्, पचन्तौ, पचन्तः ॥ अञ्च—प्राङ्, प्राञ्चौ, प्राञ्चः ॥

Why do we say 'having an indicatory उक् vowel or the stem अच्'? Observe दृषत्, दृषदौ, दृषदः ॥

Why do we say in strong cases? Observe भवतः पश्य, श्रेयसः पश्य ॥ अञ्चु root is mentioned for the sake of niyama, i.e. of the roots, only अञ्चु gets नुम् and no other root. Therefore उखास्रत्, पर्णध्वत् formed from the roots स्रंसु and ध्वंसु having indicatory उ ॥ (See III. 2. 76, IV. 1. 6, VIII. 2. 72). For the lengthening in भवान् &c, see VI. 4. 10, 14: the च् is elided in प्राङ् by VIII. 2. 23, and न् becomes ङ् by VIII. 2. 62: and त् in स्रत् by VIII. 2. 72.

Why do we say 'with the exception of a root' when by the mere fact of including *one* root अच् all other roots would have been excluded from the scope of this sûtra? The specific mention of अधातोः shows that the prohibition applies to *original* roots, and not to those roots which are *derived* from nouns. Thus गोमन्तमिच्छति = गोमत्यति formed by क्यच् ॥ Here गोमत्य is a derivative root, in its primitive state it was a noun. The prohibition of अधातोः will not apply to this root and नुम् will be added. Thus गोमत्य + क्विप् = गोमत्य् + ० (the अ is dropped by VI. 4. 48) = गोमत् + ० (the य् is elided by VI. 4. 50). Now is added नुम् and we have गोमान् ॥

युजेरसमासे ॥ ७१ ॥ पदानि ॥ युजेः, अ समासे ॥

वृत्तिः ॥ युजेरसमासे सर्वनामस्थाने परतो नुमागमो भवति ॥

71. The nominal stem युज् gets before the strong cases the augment न्, when it does nôt stand in a compound.

Thus युङ् (VIII. 2. 23, 62) युञ्जौ, युञ्जः; but अश्वयुक्, अश्वयुजौ, अश्वयुजः in a compound. The root युज समाधौ (Divâdi 68) is not to be taken here; therefore not here युजमापन्ना ऋषयः ॥ But युजिर् योगे (Rudhâdi 7) is to be taken.

नपुंसकस्य झलचः ॥ ७२ ॥ पदानि ॥ नपुंकस्य, झल्, अचः ॥

वृत्तिः ॥ नपुंसकस्य झलन्तस्याजन्तस्य च सर्वनामस्थाने परतो नुमागमो भवति ॥

वार्त्तिकम् ॥ बहूर्जि प्रतिषेधो वक्तव्यः ॥ वा० ॥ अन्त्यात्पूर्वं नुममेकइच्छन्ति ॥

72. The augment नुम् is added in the strong cases to a Neuter stem ending in a consonant (other than a nasal or a semivowel), or ending in a vowel.

Thus उदश्विन्ति, शकृन्ति (VI. 4. 10) यशांसि, पयांसि; कुण्डानि, वनानि (VI. 4. 8), त्रपूणि, जतूनि ॥ Why 'of a Neuter'? Observe अग्निचिद् ब्राह्मणः ॥ Why do we say 'not ending in a semivowel or a nasal'? Observe बहुपुरि, बहुधुरि, विमलदिवि, चत्वारि, अहानि (VII. 1. 98). A neuter having an indicatory उक् vowel gets नुम् by this sûtra and not by VII. 1. 70, as that is superseded by this, this being the subsequent. As श्रेयांसि, भूयांसि कुर्वन्ति कृषन्ति ब्राह्मणकुलानि ॥

Vârt:—Prohibition should be stated with regard to बहूर्जि; as बहूर्जि ब्राह्मणकुलानि ॥ Some would have न् added between र् and ज् of this word, as बहूर्ञ्जि ब्राह्मणकुलानि ॥ See I. 4. 13.

इकोऽचि विभक्तौ ॥ ७३ ॥ पदानि ॥ इकः, अचि, विभक्तौ ॥

वृत्तिः ॥ इगन्तस्य नपुंसकस्याङ्गस्याजादौ विभक्तौ नुमागमो भवति ॥

Kârikâ—इकोचि व्यञ्जने मा भूदस्तु लोपः स्वरः कथम्।
स्वरो वै श्रूयमाणो पि लुप्ते किं न भविष्यति ॥
रायास्त्वं तिसृभावश्च व्यवधानान्नुमा अपि।
नुड् वाच्य उत्तरार्थं तु इह किं त्रिपो इति ॥

73. The augment नुम् is added to a Neuter-stem ending in a simple vowel, except अ, before a case-affix beginning with a vowel.

Thus त्रपुणी, जतुनी, तुम्बुरुणी, त्रपुणे, जतुने, तुम्बुरुणे ॥ Why "with the exception of अ"? Observe कुण्डे, पीठे ॥ The phrase "before an affix beginning with a vowel" is employed here for the sake of the subsequent sûtras like VII. 1. 75. Here we could have dispensed with it: for before affixes beginning with a consonant, नुम् would be elided by VIII. 2. 7. The only object that it serves here is that we can form हे त्रपो! or हे त्रपु! in the Vocative singular. For had we त्रपुन्+स in the vocative, the form would have been हे त्रपुन् like हे राजन्, for न् would not be elided here, see VIII. 2. 8.

If it be objected that by the sûtra न लुमताङ्गस्य (I. 1 63) when the affix स् is elided in the Vocative, it will leave no trace behind, and there being no affix at all, नुम् will not be added in the Vocative. We reply: that this very employment of the word अच् in this sûtra indicates (jñâpaka) that the rule prohibiting the effect of an affix (I. 1. 63) does not apply here. Therefore, though the affix is elided, it produces its effect in spite of I. 1. 63, and we have the guṇa of the vowel in the Vocative, as हे त्रपो by VII. 3. 108.

Why have we used the word विभक्तौ 'when a case-affix follows'? Observe तुम्बुरवं चूर्णम्, where the *taddhita* affix अण् is added to तुम्बुरु by IV. 3. 139.

Kârikâ:—The employment of the words इकः अचि in the sûtra shows that नुम् will not come when the affix begins with a consonant, as त्रपुभ्यां, त्रपुभिः ॥ An objector says, the employment of अचि in the sûtra is useless for नुम् may be added even before an affix beginning with a consonant, for having added it, it will be elided by न लोपःप्रातिपदिकान्तस्य (VIII. 2. 7). We reply, yes it can be so done, but how will you then manage the accent? For in पैञ्चत्रपुभ्यां, पैञ्चत्रपुभिः, the accent is regulated by the rule VI. 2. 29 which says that in a Dvigu compound, the first member preserves its original accent if the second member ends in an इक् vowel. But if there was a नुम्, then the second member would not end in इक् but in न्: and the elision of this न् by VII. 2. 7. is asiddha for the purposes of accent. To this the objector answers, that even where न् is not elided the accent is governed by VI. 2. 29, namely the accent of पैञ्चत्रपुणे or पञ्चत्रपुण: is by VI. 2. 29, why should it not be so when न् is elided. So the objection about accent has no strength.

Well if नुम् be added even before consonant-affix, then there will arise this anomaly: अतिरि + भ्यां = अतिरिन् + भ्यां (by adding नुम्). Here rule VII. 2. 85 cannot apply: because न् intervenes between रि and भ्यां, therefore इ of रि is not changed to आ, and therefore we cannot get the proper from अतिराभ्यां ॥ Moreover in प्रियत्रि + भ्यां, the त्रि cannot be changed to तिसृ if there be नुम्, and so we cannot get the form प्रियतिसृभ्यां ब्राह्मणकुलानि ॥

To this it is answered, the change of इ into आ in the case of रि, and the substitution of तिसृ for त्रि will take place even when the नुम् intervenes, on the maxim विभक्तिविधानदशायां यदानन्तर्यं तत् तत्राश्रीयते न स्वादिशविधानदशायाम् ॥ And this is done in this way: अतिरि + भ्यां, and प्रियात्रि + भ्यां, here नुम् is superseded by the subsequent rule requiring आ and तिसृ respectively.

If this be so, then the employment of अच् in the sûtra is for the sake of the supersession of नुम् by नुट् (VII. 1. 54). Thus नुट् has unrestricted scope in अग्नीनां, वायूनां, and नुम् has unrestricted scope in त्रपुणे and जतुने ॥ But in त्रपूणाम् and जतूनाम्, both नुट् and नुम् present themselves. Here however नुम् is superseded by नुट् by purva-vipratishedha and so there is lengthening of the vowel by VI. 4. 3. This supersession is indicated by the employment of अच्, for नुट् and नुम् being both *anitya* and of equal force, had there been no अच्, नुम् would have come and not नुट् ॥

But this is also not valid, for नुट् would have to be added, even if there had been no अच् in the sûtra.

The employment of अच् is for the sake of the subsequent sûtra VII. 1. 75. The only object that अच् serves in this sûtra, is in forming the vocative हे त्रपो as shown above.

तृतीयादिषु भाषितपुंस्कं पुंवद्गालवस्य ॥ ७४ ॥ पदानि ॥ तृतीयदिषु, भाषित पुंस्कम्, पुम्वत्, गालवस्य ॥

वृत्तिः ॥ तृतीयादिषु विभक्तिष्वजादिषु भाषितपुंस्कंनपुं सकलिङ्गमिगन्तं गालवस्याचार्यस्य मतेन पुंवद्भवति । यथा पुंसि ह्रस्वनुमौ न भवतस्तद्वत्रापि न भवत इत्यर्थः ।

74. A neuter stem ending in a vowel, except अ, of which there exists an equivalent, uniform masculine, is treated like the masculine, in the opinion of Gâlava, before the vowel beginning affixes of the Instrumental and the cases that follow it.

As in the Masculine there is no shortening, nor the addition of नुम्, so here also. As ग्रामणी is the equivalent, uniform masculine of the neuter form ग्रामणि, we have either Ins. ग्रामणिना or ग्रामण्या ब्राह्मणकुलेन, the Ins. Sg. of ग्रामणि n. Similarly Dat. ग्रामणिने or ग्रामण्ये ब्राह्मणकुलाय; Abl. ग्रामणिनो or ग्रामण्यो ब्राह्मणकुलात्, Gen. Sg.. ग्रामणिनो or ग्रामण्यो ब्राह्मणकुलस्य, Gen. Du. ग्रामणिनोर्ब्राह्मणकुलयोः or ग्रामण्योः; Gen. Pl. ग्रामणीनां or ग्रामण्यां ब्राह्मणकुलानां ॥ Loc. ग्रामणिनि or ग्रामण्यां ब्राह्मणकुले ॥ Similarly: Ins. शुचिना (same form in mas. and neu.), Dat. शुचये or शुचिने; Abl. and Gen. शुचेः or शुचिनः Gen. Du. शुच्योः or शुचिनोः Loc. शुचौ or शुचिनि॥

Why do we say after the 3rd case and the rest? Observe ग्रामणिनी ब्राह्मणकुले, and शुचिनी Nom. dual. Why do we say having an appropriate masculine of the same form and meaning? Observe त्रपुणं, जतुने ॥ Why have we only one form पीलुने फलाय, when पीलुर्वृक्षः and पीलुफलं show that पालु has a masculine form also. The word पीलु is masculine when it applies to 'trees', and पालु is neuter when it refers to 'fruits'; so this word पीलु cannot be said to be भाषितपुंस्कः, the masculine पीलु not having the same meaning as the neuter पीलु ॥ See VI. 3. 34.

Why do we say "ending in a vowel except अ"? Observe कीलालपा ब्राह्मणः and कीलालपं ब्राह्मणकुलं; the Ins. &c of कीलालपा will not be the Ins. &c of कीलालपं ॥ The latter will have only one form कीलालपेन ब्राह्मणकुलेन ॥ &c.

Before case affixes beginning with a consonant we have one form only, as ग्रामणिभ्यां ब्राह्मणकुलाभ्याम् ॥

अस्थिदधिसक्थ्यक्ष्णामनङुदात्तः ॥ ७५ ॥ पदानि ॥ अस्थि, दधि, सक्थि, अक्ष्णाम, अनङ्, उदात्तः ॥

वृत्तिः ॥ अस्थि दधि सक्थि अक्षि इत्येतेषां नपुंसकानां तृतीयादिष्वजादिषु विभक्तिषु परतो ऽनङित्ययमादेशो भवति, स चोदात्तो भवति ॥

75. The acutely accented अन् (अनङ्) is substituted for the finals of asthi, dadhi, sakthi and akshi, before the affixes of the Instrumental and the cases that follow it, which begin with a vowel.

Thus अस्थ्ना, अस्थ्ने, दध्ना, दध्ने, सक्थ्ना, सक्थ्ने, अक्ष्णा, अक्ष्णे ॥ The words अस्थि &c have acute on the first syllable, the substitute अनङ would have been also anudâtta, but for this sûtra. The stem getting the designation भ, we elide the अ (VI. 4. 134), the udâtta अ being thus elided, the case-ending, which was anudâtta before, now becomes udâtta (VI. 1. 161). The stems ending with 'asthi &c' and though not neuter, are governed by this rule. As प्रियास्थ्ना ब्राह्मणेन, प्रियदध्ना ॥ Why 'before the affixes of the Instrumental and the rest?' Observe अस्थिनी, दधिनी ॥ Before affixes beginning with a consonant, we have अस्थिभ्याम्, दधिभ्याम् ॥

छन्दस्यपि दृश्यते ॥ ७६ ॥ पदानि ॥ छन्दसि, अपि, दृश्यते ॥

वृत्तिः ॥ अस्थिदधिसक्थ्यक्ष्णामनङ् छन्दस्यपि दृश्यते । यत्र विहितस्ततोऽन्यत्रापि दृश्यते ॥

76. In the Veda also, the stems 'asthi', 'dadhi', 'sakthi' and 'akshi', are found to take the substitute अनङ्, before endings other than those mentioned above.

Thus the substitute is ordained before endings beginning with a vowel. In the Veda it comes before affixes beginning with a consonant. As इन्द्रो दधीचो अस्थभिः, भद्रं पश्येमाक्षभिः ॥ The substitute is ordained to come after the Instrumental &c. In the Vedic literature it is found in the Acc. &c. As अस्थानि in अस्थान्युत्कृत्य जुहोति ॥ The substitute comes before case-endings (vibhakti), in the Vedic literature it comes before affixes which are not case-endings, as अक्षण्वता लाङ्गलेन, अस्थन्वन्तं यदनस्था बिभर्त्ति ॥ See VI. 1. 176.

ई च द्विवचने ॥ ७७ ॥ पदानि ॥ ई, च, द्विवचने ॥

वृत्तिः ॥ द्विवचने परतश्छन्दसि विषये ऽस्थ्यादीनामीकारादेशो भवति, स चोदात्तः ॥

77. The acutely accented ई is substituted for the final of asthi, dadhi, sakthi and akshi, in the Veda, when the case-affixes of the dual follow.

As अक्षी ते इन्द्रपिङ्गले कपेरिव ॥ अक्षीभ्यान् ते नासिकाभ्याम् ॥ In अक्षी the augment नुम् is not added to the stem before the vowel-beginning ending, because VII. 1. 73, which ordained नुम्, is superseded by the present sûtra, and being once superseded, it is superseded for good. (सकृद् गतौ विप्रतिषेधे यद्बाधितं तद्बाधितमेव) ॥

नाभ्यस्ताच्छतुः ॥ ७८ ॥ पदानिं ॥ न, अभ्यस्तात्, शतुः ॥

वृत्तिः ॥ अभ्यस्तादङ्गादुत्तरस्य शतुर्नुम्न भवति ॥

78. The Participial-affix शतृ (अत्-अन्त्), does not take the augment नुम् after a reduplicate stem.

Thus ददत्, ददतौ, ददतः, जक्षत्, जक्षतौ, जक्षतः, जाग्रत्, जाग्रतौ, जाग्रतः ॥ This is an exception to VII. 1. 70, and applies of course to sarvanâmasthâna or strong cases. The नुम् is to be read into this sûtra from VII. 1. 70; for the negation of this sûtra cannot apply to ई taught in the preceding sûtra, for ई is never ordained after śatṛi : therefore, though several other operations intervene, yet नुम् is to be read here.

वा नपुंसकस्य ॥ ७९ ॥ पदानि ॥ वा, नपुंसकस्य ॥

वृत्तिः ॥ अभ्यस्तादङ्गादुत्तरो यः शतृप्रत्ययस्तदन्तस्य नपुंसकस्य वा नुमागमो भवति ॥

79. The Participial-affix शतृ optionally takes the augment नुम् after a reduplicate stem, in Neuter nouns.

Thus ददति or ददन्ति, कुलानि; दधति or दधन्ति कुलानि, जक्षति or जक्षन्ति कुलानि, जाग्रति or जाग्रन्ति कुलानि॥ This of course applies to sarvanâmasthâna or strong cases.

आच्छीनद्योर्नुम् ॥ ८० ॥ पदानि ॥ आत्, शी, नद्योः, नुम् ॥

वृत्तिः ॥ अवर्णान्तादङ्गादुत्तरस्य शतुर्वा नुमागमो भवति शीनद्योः परतः ॥

80. When the affix शतृ comes after a verbal stem ending in अ or आ, it may optionally take the augment नुम्, before the neutral case-ending शी and before the feminine affix ई ॥

Thus तुदती कुले or तुदन्ती कुले, तुदन्ती ब्राह्मणी, तुदती ब्राह्मणी, याती कुले, यान्ती कुले याती ब्राह्मणी, यान्ती ब्राह्मणी, करिष्यती कुले, करिष्यन्ती कुले, करिष्यती ब्राह्मणी, करिष्यन्ती ब्राह्मणी ॥ अत्रान्तरङ्गत्वादेकादेशे कृते व्यपवर्गाभावादवर्णान्तादङ्गादुत्तरस्य शतुरिति न युज्यते वक्तुम्, उभयत आश्रये नान्तादिवदित्यन्तादिवद्भावोऽपि नास्ति भूतपूर्वगत्याश्रयणो वा ऽदतो प्रतीत्येवमादिष्वतिप्रसङ्ग इति, अत्र समाधि

के चिदाहुः, शतुरवयवे शतृशब्दो वर्त्तते, अवर्णान्ताद्ङ्गादुत्तरो यः शत्रवयव इति ॥ अपरे पुनराहुः, आदित्येतेन शीनद्यावेव विशेष्यते, अवर्णान्ताद्ङ्गादुत्तरे ये शीनद्या तयोः परतः शत्रन्तस्य नुम्भवतीति, तत्र येन नाव्यवधानं तेन व्यवहितेपि वचनप्रमाण्याच्छिति तकारेणैव व्यवधानमाश्रयिष्यते ॥ आदिरिति किम्, कुर्वती, सुन्वती ॥ शीनद्योरिति किम्, तुदताम्, तुदताम् ॥

The form तुदती is thus evolved. तुद्+श+शतृ+ङीप् ॥ The vikaraṇa श is added by III. I. 77, & ङीप् by IV. I. 6. This is equal to तुद्+अ+अत्+ई= तुदती the अ+अ becoming अ by the rule of पररूप ekâdeśa (VI. I. 97). This ekâdeśa operation being antaranga, now there is no शतृ affix coming after a stem ending in अ, and therefore this sûtra will not apply. If you say the ekâdeśa will be considered as the final of तुद् by VI. I. 85, we reply, that the antâchvadbhâva of that sûtra will not apply when simultaneous operations are to be performed, for अ cannot be said at one and the same time as the final of तुद् and the beginning of अत् (शतृ). If you say the maxim सांप्रतिकाभावे भूतपूर्वं गतिः (when a word cannot denote something which actually is what is expressed by the word; it must be understood to denote something which formerly was what is expressed by it), will apply here, and that तुद् will be considered to end in अ because it formerly did end in the affix अ of श; we reply that then the present rule should apply to forms like अदती घ्नती &c. For here also we have अद्+शप् लोप+शतृ+ङीप्; and अद् should be considered to end in अ, because it had the affix शप् after it, though it was afterwards elided. The maxim quoted, therefore, proves too much.

To solve these objections, some say, that the word शतृ in this sûtra means 'a portion of the affix शतृ, such as त्' and the sûtra means 'after a stem ending in अ, to the portion त् of the affix शतृ there is added नुम्.' Others say, the word आत् in the sûtra qualifies शी and नदी and not शतृ; and the sutra means "नुम् is added to a stem ending in शतृ, when शी or नदी affixes follow after a stem ending in अ." Therefore in तुदती the affix ई is considered to come after the अ of तुद, the intervening त् not debarring it.

Why do we say "after अ"? Observe कुर्वती and सुन्वती, no optional नुम् is added here. Why do we say "शी and नदी following"? Observe तुदताम् and तुदताम्

शप्श्यनोर्नित्यम् ॥ ८१ ॥ पदानि ॥ शप्, श्यनोः, नित्यम् ॥

वृत्तिः ॥ शप् श्यन् इत्येतयोः शतुः शीनद्योः परतो नित्यं नुमागमो भवति ॥

81. When the affix शतृ comes after a verbal stem ending in the vikaraṇas शप् and श्यन्, it invariably takes the augment नुम् before the neutral case-ending शी (ई), and the feminine ending ई (Nadî).

Thus पचन्ती कुले, पचन्ती ब्राह्मणी, दीव्यन्ती कुले, दीव्यन्ती ब्राह्मणी, सीव्यन्ती कुले, सीव्यन्ती ब्राह्मणी ॥ The word नित्य stops the anuvṛitti of वा (VII. I. 79).

सावनडुहः ॥ ८२ ॥ पदानि ॥ सौ, अनडुहः ॥

वृत्तिः ॥ सौ परतो ऽनडुहोऽङ्गस्य नुमागमो भवति ॥

82. अनडुह् gets the augment नुम् before the ending सु of the Nom. Sg. (and Vocative).

By VII. 1. 98 अनडुह् gets the augment आ after उ in the strong cases, and अ in Vocative Singular (VII. 1. 99). It thus becomes अनड्वाह् and अनड्वह् ॥ By the present sûtra न् is added after this आ and अ ॥ The case-ending is elided by VI. 1. 68, and the final ह् by VIII. 2. 23. Thus we have अनड्वान् Nominative Singular; and अनड्वन् in the Vocative Singular. The augments आम् and अम् (VII. 1. 98, 99), do not supersede नुम्, nor are they superseded by नुम् ॥

In this sûtra, some read the annvṛitti of आत् from VII. 1. 80; and by so doing they add नुम् to that form of अनडुह् where there is an आ or अ, namely, after the word has taken the augment आम् in the nominative singular by VII. 1. 98, and अम् in the Vocative by VII. 1. 99. Therefore, the नुम् does not debar आम् or अम्, nor is it debarred by आम् or अम् ॥ Others hold that though one is a general rule and the other is a particular rule, yet in this instance, आम् (or अम्) and नुम् are applied simultaneously, one not debarring the other, there is no relationship of बाध्य and बाधक among them, just as in चिचीषति the rule of lengthening (VI. 4. 16) and reduplication are applied simultaneously, one not debarring the other. In बह्वनड्वांहि ब्राह्मणकुलानि, we add first आम् because it is subsequent, and them we add नुम् by VII. 1. 72 on the maxim of पुनः प्रसङ्गविज्ञान &c ॥

इक्स्ववस्स्वतवसां छन्दसि ॥ ८३ ॥ पदानि ॥ इक्, स्ववस्, स्वतवसाम्, छन्दसि ॥

वृत्तिः ॥ इक् स्ववस् स्वतवसित्येतेषां सौ परतो नुमागमो भवति छन्दसिविषये ॥

83. इश्, स्ववस् and स्वतवस् take the augment नुम् before the affix सु (Nominative and Vocative Singular) in the Veda.

Thus ईदृङ्, तादृङ्, यादृङ्, सदृङ्, स्ववान्, स्वतवान् ॥ The श् of ईदृश् (formed by III. 2. 60), is elided by VIII. 2. 23; and ङ् substituted for न् by VIII. 2. 62. The lengthening in स्ववान् and स्वतवान् is through VI. 4. 14.

दिव औत् ॥ ८४ ॥ पदानि ॥ दिवः, औत् ॥

वृत्तिः ॥ दिवित्येतस्य सौ परतो औदित्ययमादेशो भवति ॥

84. औ is substituted for the final of दिव् before सु (Nom. Sg. and Voc. Sg).

As द्यौः ॥ There is a nominal-stem दिव् which is taken here. It has no indicatory letters annexed to it. The root दिव् is not to be taken here, as it has the indicatory letter उ and is exhibited in the Dhâtupâṭha as दिवु ॥ The nominal-stem derived from दिवु, does not take औ, but ऊ, the Nom. Sg. of which is द्युः as अक्षद्युः (See VI. 4. 19, and VI. 1. 131).

पथिमथ्यृभुक्षामात् ॥ ८५ ॥ पदानि ॥ पथि, मथि, ऋभुक्षाम्, आत् ॥

वृत्तिः ॥ पथिन् मथिन् ऋभुक्षिन् इत्येतेषामङ्गानां सौ परत आकार आदेशो भवति ॥

85. आत् (आ) is substituted for the final of 'pathin' 'mathin' and 'ṛbhukshin', before the ending सु (of the Nom. Sg).

As पन्थाः, मन्थाः, ऋभुक्षाः ॥ Though the sthânin here is a nasal (i.e. न्), yet the substitute आ is not to be nasalised, but to be pronounced purely. For न्थ see VII. 1. 87. The nasal आँ is not to be taken on the maxim भाव्यमानेन सवर्णानां ग्रहणं न भवति ॥ "A letter which is taught in a rule does not denote the letters homogeneous with it.'

इतोत्सर्वनामस्थाने ॥ ८६ ॥ पदानि ॥ इतः, अत्, सर्वनामस्थाने ॥

वृत्तिः ॥ पथ्यादीनामिकारस्य स्थाने आकारादेशो भवति ॥

86. अ is substituted for the इ of 'pathin, mathin and ṛbhukshin,' in the strong cases.

Thus पन्थाः, पन्थानौ, पन्थानः, पन्थानम्, पन्थानौ, मन्थाः, मन्थानौ, मन्थानः, मन्थानम्, मन्थानौ, ऋभुक्षाः, ऋभुक्षाणौ, ऋभुक्षाणः, ऋभुक्षाणम्, ऋभुक्षाणौ ॥ आदिति वर्त्तमाने पुनरद्वचनं पपूर्वार्थम्, ऋभुक्षणमित्यत्र वा षपूर्वस्य निगमइति दीर्घविकल्पः ॥

Though the anuvṛitti of आत् was here, the separate mention of अत् is for the sake of VI. 4. 9: by which in the case of ऋभुक्षिन् we have two forms, ऋभुक्षाणम् and ऋभुक्षणम् ॥

थोन्थः ॥ ८७ ॥ पदानि ॥ थः, न्थः ॥

वृत्तिः ॥ पथिमथोस्थकारस्य स्थाने न्थ इत्ययमादेशो भवति सर्वनामस्थाने परतः ॥

87. न्थ् is substituted for the थ् of pathin and mathin in the strong cases.

As पन्थाः, पन्थानौ, पन्थानः, मन्थाः, मन्थानौ मन्थानः ॥

भस्य टेर्लोपः ॥ ८८ ॥ पदानि ॥ भस्य, टेः, लोपः ॥

वृत्तिः ॥ पथ्यादीनां भसंज्ञकानां टेर्लोपो भवति ॥

88. The last vowel, with the consonant that follows it, is dropped in pathin, mathin and ṛbhukshin, before a weak case-ending beginning with a vowel (before which the stem is called Bha I. 4. 18).

As पथः, पथा, पथे, मथः, मथा, मथे, ऋभुक्षः, ऋभुक्षा, ऋभुक्षे ॥ The anuvṛitti of sarvanâmasthâna, of course, is inappropriate here: though its anuvṛitti is current as will be seen in the next sûtra.

पुंसोऽसुङ् ॥ ८९ ॥ पदानि ॥ पुंसः, असुङ् ॥

वृत्तिः ॥ पुंस इत्येतस्य सर्वनामस्थाने परतोऽसुङित्ययमादेशो भवति ॥

89. असुङ् (अस्) is substituted for the final of पुंस् in the strong cases.

The word पुंस् is derived from पा (to protect)+डुम्सुन् (Uṇ IV. 178), the स् being changed to anusvâra. So when स् of पुंस् is replaced by अस् we get the form पुमस्, the उ of असुङ् indicates that न् should be added in the strong cases after अ (VII. 1. 70), so we have पुमान्, पुमांसौ, पुमांसः ॥

This substitution must take place in its incipient stage before the affixes are added, (उपदेशिवद्भावः): otherwise the accent will be wrong. The compounds have acute on the final, (VI. 1. 223), therefore, परमपुंस् has acute on पु. and in the Nominative Singular परमपुमान् the acute will remain on पु, but it is intended that it should be on मा, thus परमपुमाॅन् ॥ The simple word पुमान् of course, has accent on पु ॥

गोतो णित् ॥ ९० ॥ पदानि ॥ गोतो, णित् ॥

वृत्तिः ॥ गोशब्दात्परं सर्वनामस्थानं णिद्भवति ॥

90. The endings of the strong cases are णित् after गो ॥

That is, these affixes produce all the णित् operations: such as Vṛiddhi &c. As गौः, गावौ, गावः ॥ Why have we added a त् after गो? The rule applies to the form गो, and not when it assumes the form गु, as in चित्रगुः, शबलगुः ॥

How do you explain the forms हे चित्रगो, हे शबलगवः? This is done on the maxim अङ्गवृत्ते पुनर्वृत्तावविधि र्निष्ठितस्य, (when an operation which is taught in the Aṅgâdhikâra VI. 4.—VII. 4. has taken place, and another operation of the Aṅgâdhikâra is subsequently applicable, this latter operation is not allowed to take place). For when Guṇa once takes place before the Vocative and the Nominative Plural affix by VII. 3. 108-109, the णित्व operation of this rule will not again take place. Or गोतः in the sûtra may be construed as Sambandha-lakshaṇâ Sasṭhî (a Genitive denoting a general relation): and the meaning will be "that sarvanâmasthâna affix, denoting singular, dual, plural, which refers to the meaning of गो or 'cow.' While in चित्रगु, the sarvanâmasthâna affix does not refer to 'cow' but to another *object*, namely to a '*person*' who possesses brindled cows. त् in गोत् in this view is for specification only.

Some read the sûtra as ओतः णित्, so that the rule will apply to द्यो also: as, द्यौः, द्यावौ, द्यावः ॥ If the reading be taken गोतः, then we extend this rule to द्यो also, by taking गो as merely illustrative of all words ending in ओ; and this is done by the letter त् in गोतः, for the तपर rule applies to *letters*, and not to *words*, so that गोतः means and includes गो and words ending in ओ ॥

णलुत्तमो वा ॥ ९१ ॥ पदानि ॥ णल्, उत्तमः, वा ॥

वृत्तिः ॥ उत्तमो णल्वा णित् भवति णित्कार्यं तत्र वा भवतीत्यर्थः ॥

91. The ending of the First Pers. Sg. in the Perfect optionally acts as णित् ॥

The Vṛiddhi is optional, as अहं चकार or चकर, अहं पपाच or पपच ॥

सख्युरसम्बुद्धौ ॥ ९२ ॥ पदानि ॥ सख्युः, अ सम्बुद्धौ ॥

वृत्तिः ॥ असंबुद्धौ यः सखिशब्दः तस्मात्परं सर्वनामस्थानं णिद्भवति ॥

92. After सखि, the endings of the strong cases, with the exception of the Vocative singular, are णित् ॥

That is, they cause Vṛiddhi. As सखायौ, सखायः, but हे सखे ॥

अनङ् सौ ॥ ९३ ॥ पदानि ॥ अनङ्, सौ ॥

वृत्तिः ॥ सखिशब्दस्य सौ परतोऽनङित्ययमादेशो भवति स चेत्सुशब्दः संबुद्धिर्न भवति ॥

93. अनङ् (अन्) is substituted for the इ of सखि before सु of the Nominative Singular, (but not in the Vocative Singular).

As सखा, but हे सखे ॥

ऋदुशनस्पुरुदंशोनेहसां च॥९४॥ पदानि॥ऋत्, उशनस्, पुरुदंशः अनेहसाम् च ॥

वृत्तिः ॥ ऋकारान्तानामङ्गानामुशनस् पुरुदंशस् इत्येतेषां चासंबुद्धौ सौ परतोऽनङादेशो भवति ॥

वार्तिकम् ॥ उशनसः सम्बुद्धावपि पक्षेऽनङ् इष्यते । न ङिसम्बुद्ध्योरिति नलोपप्रतिषेधोऽपि पक्षइष्यते ॥

Kárika:—संबोधने तूशनसस्त्रिरूपं सान्तं तथा नान्तमथाप्यदन्तम् ॥
माध्यंदिनिर्वष्टि गुणं त्विगन्ते नपुंसके व्याघ्रपदां वरिष्ठः ॥

94. Anaṅ (अन्) is substituted for the final of the stems ending in ऋ, as well as for the final of uśanas, purudanśas, and anehas, in the Nominative Singular (but not in the Vocative Singular).

As कर्ता, हर्ता, माता, पिता, भ्राता, उशना, पुरुदंशा, अनेहा ॥ In the Voc. Sg. we have हे कर्तः, हे मातः, पितः पुरुदंशः, अनेहः and उशनः ॥

Vârt:—अनङ् is substituted for the final of उशनस् in the Voc. Sg. also, as हे उशनन्, the final न् not being elided (See VIII. 2. 8). Otherwise we have हे उशन! Thus it has three forms in the Vocative Singular: as हे उशनस्, हे उशनन्, and हे उशन! ॥

Kârikâ:—In the vocative, the word उशनस् has three forms, (1) ending in स् when अनङ् is not added, (2) ending in न्, when न् is not elided, (3) ending in अ when न् is elided. This is the opinion of the Achârya Mâdhyandini. So also according to the Achârya Vaiyâghrapadya, (the best of the Vyâghrapadas), there is Guṇa in the Neuter of the stems ending in इक् vowels; as हे त्रपो ॥

The त् in ऋत् is for the sake of distinctness.

तृज्वत्क्रोष्टुः ॥ ९५ ॥ पदानि ॥ तृज्वत्, क्रोष्टुः ॥

वृत्तिः ॥ क्रोष्टुशब्दस्तुन्प्रत्ययान्तः संज्ञाशब्दः सर्वनामस्थानेऽसंबुद्धौ परतः तृज्वद्भवति ॥

95. The word क्रोष्टु 'a jackal' is treated in the strong cases (with the exception of Vocative Singular) as if it ended in तृच् (तृ) ॥

The word क्रोष्टु is declined like क्रोष्टृ in the strong cases. As क्रोष्टा, क्रोष्टारौ, क्रोष्टारः, क्रोष्टारम्, क्रोष्टारौ ॥ But क्रोष्टून् in weak cases, and हे क्रोष्टो in the Vocative Singular. The accent in the strong cases is also that of the तृच् affix, i.e. acute on the final. The word क्रोष्टु is formed by the affix तुन् (Uṇ सितनिगमि &c, I. 69).

स्त्रियां च ॥ ९६ ॥ पदानि ॥ स्त्रियां, च ॥

वृत्तिः ॥ असर्वनामस्थानार्थमारम्भः । स्त्रियां च क्रोष्टुशब्दस्य तृज्वद्भवति ॥

96. The word क्रोष्टु is treated as if it ended in तृच्, in the feminine, before all case-endings.

This sûtra is commenced for the sake of cases other than strong ones. In strong cases, whether of masculine or feminine, the former sûtra applies; but in the feminine, in other cases also there is tṛich-treatment. Thus क्रोष्ट्री, क्रोष्ट्रीभ्याम्, क्रोष्ट्रीभिः ॥ Some read the word क्रोष्टु in the Gaurâdi class (IV. 1. 41), and they treat it is a तृच् ending word before the feminine affix ङीष्, as क्रोष्ट्री ॥ According to them, in forming the Taddhitârtha compounds like पञ्चभिः क्रोष्ट्रीभिः क्रीतैः = पञ्चक्रोष्टृभी रथैः, we could not get the form पञ्चक्रोष्टृभिः, because when the affix ठक् is elided by V. 1. 28, the feminine is also elided by I. 2. 49, and the ङीष् being thus luk-elided, there would be no तृज्वद्भाव, because the affix leaves no trace behind I. 1. 63. To get out of the difficulty, we can only say, that the form is so, in spite of the apparent inconsistency.

Those who do not read क्रोष्टु in the Gaurâdi class, they explain this sûtra by saying that the word स्त्रियां indicates the sense, namely, क्रोष्टु is treated like a तृच् word, when it denotes a female, wherever it may occur.

And because क्रोष्टु is treated as if it was क्रोष्टृ, the feminine will be formed by the affix ङीप् by IV. 1. 5, and the form क्रोष्ट्री will be end-acute by VI. 1. 174. So that whether क्रोष्ट्री be formed by ङीष् under Gaurâdi class, or by ङीप् under IV. 1. 5, the accent remains the same: while under this second view, we have not to face any such difficulty as in the first.

विभाषा तृतीयादिष्वचि ॥ ९७ ॥ पदानि ॥ विभाषा, तृतीयादिषु, अचि ॥

वृत्तिः ॥ तृतीयादिषु विभक्तिष्वजादिषु क्रोष्टुर्विभाषा तृज्वद्भवति ॥

वार्त्तिकम् ॥ तृज्वद्भावात् पूर्वविप्रतिषेधेन नुमटुटौ भवतः ॥

97. क्रोष्टु may optionally be treated as Kroshṭṛ, before the endings beginning with a vowel, in the Instrumental and the cases that follow it.

As क्रोष्ट्रा or क्रोष्टुना, क्रोष्ट्रे or क्रोष्टवे, क्रोष्टुः or क्रोष्टोः, क्रोष्टरि or क्रोष्टौ, क्रोष्ट्रोः or क्रोष्ट्वोः ॥ But क्रोष्टून् in the Accusative Plural, and क्रोष्टुभ्यां before consonant-beginning affixes.

Vârt:—नुम् and नुट् augments come in supersession of the Trich-vadbhâva ordained by the preceding sûtras. Thus the Dative of the Neuter noun प्रियक्रोष्टु will be प्रियक्रोष्टुने ऽरण्याय, हितक्रोष्टुने वृषलकुलाय, and not °क्रोष्ट्रे ॥ Similarly with नुट्, as क्रोष्टूनाम् ॥

चतुरनडुहोरामुदात्तः ॥ ९८ ॥ पदानि ॥ चतुर्, अनडुहोः, आम्, उदात्तः ॥

वृत्तिः ॥ चतुर् अनडुह् इत्येतयोः सर्वनामस्थाने परत आमागमो भवति, स चोदात्तः ॥

वार्त्तिकम् ॥ अनडुहः स्त्रियां वेति वक्तव्यम् ॥

98. चतुर् and अनडुह् get the acutely accented augment आ (आम्) after the उ in the strong cases.

Thus चत्वारः, अनड्वान्, अनड्वाहौ, अनड्वाहः, अनड्वाहम् ॥ The rule applies to compounds ending with चत्वार् and अनडुह्, as प्रियचत्वार्, प्रियचत्वारौ, प्रियचत्वारः, प्रियानड्वान्, प्रियानड्वाहौ, प्रियानड्वाहः ॥

Vârt:—In the case of अनडुह् there is option in the feminine, as अनडुही, or अनड्वाही ॥ This would be so, because it occurs in Gaurâdi class IV. 1. 41.

अम्संबुद्धौ ॥ ९९ ॥ पदानि ॥ अम्, सम्बुद्धौ ॥

वृत्तिः ॥ संबुद्धौ परतश्चतुरनडुहोरमागमो भवति ॥

99. चतुर् and अनडुह् get the augment अ after the उ in the Vocative Singular.

This debars the previous rule, as हे प्रियचत्वः (a Bahuvrîhi), हे प्रियनड्वन् ॥

ॠत इद्धातोः ॥ १०० ॥ पदानि ॥ ॠतः, इत्, धातोः ॥

वृत्तिः ॥ ॠकारान्तस्य धातोरङ्गस्य इकारादेशो भवति ॥

100. For the final long ॠ of a root, there is substituted इर् (I. 1. 51).

As किरति, गिरति from कॄ and गॄ of the Tudâdi class. आस्तीर्णम् विस्तीर्णम् from स्तॄ, the lengthening by VIII. 2. 77. Why do we say of a root? Observe पितॄणाम्, मातॄणाम् ॥

This substitution will apply to Derivative roots also, as चिकीर्षति from कॄ 'to scatter'.

उपधायाश्च ॥ १०१ ॥ पदानि ॥ उपधायाः, च ॥

वृत्तिः ॥ उपधायाश्च ॠकारस्य इकारादेशो भवति ॥

101. इर् is also substituted for the penultimate long ॠ of a root.

As कीर्तयति, कीर्तयतः, कीर्तयन्ति ; from कॄत् ॥ Lengthening by VIII. 2. 77.

उदोष्ठ्यपूर्वस्य ॥ १०२ ॥ पदानि ॥ उत्, ओष्ठ्य, पूर्वस्य ॥

वृत्तिः ॥ ओष्ठ्यः पूर्वो यस्मात् ॠकारात्तस्मादोष्ठ्यपूर्वस्तदन्तस्य धातोरङ्गस्य उकारादेशो भवति ॥

वार्त्तिकम् ॥ इत्त्वोत्त्वाभ्यां गुणवृद्धी भवतो विप्रतिषेधेन ॥

102. उर् is substituted for the final long ॠ of a root, when it is preceded by a labial consonant belonging to the root.

As पूर्त and पुपूर्षति from पॄ, so also मुमूर्षति ॥ The lengthening is by VIII. 2. 77. The rule applies when the dento-labial व precedes: as वुवूर्षति ऋत्विजम् from वॄ; so also प्रावुवूर्षति कम्बलम् ॥ The labial consonant must be the consonant of the root. Therefore when ॠ 'to go' is preceded by सम्, the rule will not apply, for म् is not part of the root: as समीर्णम् by VII. 1. 100.

Vârt:—The Guṇa and Vṛiddhi do take place in supersession of इर् and उर् substitution. Thus आस्तरणम् and आस्तारकः (from स्तॄ with ल्युट् and ण्वुल्), निपरणम्, निपारकः from पॄ, निगरणम्, निगारकः from गॄ ॥

बहुलं छन्दसि ॥ १०३ ॥ पदानि ॥ बहुलम्, छन्दसि ॥

वृत्तिः ॥ छन्दसि विषये ॠकारान्तस्य धातोरङ्गस्य बहुलमुकारादेशो भवति ॥

103. In the Veda, the उर् substitution for ॠ of a root-stem is diverse.

That is, it takes place even when the preceding letter is not labial, and does not take place even when the letter is labial. Thus मित्रा वरुणौ ततुरिः, दूरे ह्यध्वा जगुरिः, पप्रितमम् (no change), and पपुरिः, from तॄ. गॄ and पॄ ॥ All these words ततुरि, जगुरि and पप्रि are formed by the affix किन् (III. 1. 171).

ओ३म् ।

अथ सप्तमाध्यायस्य द्वितीयः पादः ।

BOOK SEVENTH.

CHAPTER SECOND.

सिचि वृद्धिः परस्मैपदेषु ॥ १ ॥ पदानि ॥ सिचि, वृद्धिः, परस्मैपदेषु ॥

वृत्तिः ॥ परस्मैपदे परे सिचि परत इगन्तस्याङ्गस्य वृद्धिर्भवति ॥

1. Before the Aorist-characteristic स् (सिच्), Vṛiddhi is substituted in the Parasmaipada, for the final of a stem ending in इ, उ, ऋ (long or short, I. 1. 3).

The word इकः is to be read into this sûtra by virtue of I. 1. 3. As अचैषीत्, अनैषीत्, अलावीत्, अपावीत्, अकार्षीत्, अहार्षीत् (VII. 3. 96 and VIII. 2. 28) The antaranga guṇa substitution is superseded by the express mention of Vṛiddhi. If the antaranga guṇa is superseded by this vṛiddhi, why is not the antaranga उवङ् also superseded in न्युवीत्, न्युधुवीत्? The Vṛiddhi does not take place, as these roots belong to कुटादि class, after which this affix is ङित् (I. 2. 1). The Vṛiddhi being thus superseded, we have उवङ् substitution. Why do we say in the Parasmaipada? Observe अच्योष्ट, अप्लोष्ट ॥

अतो ल्रान्तस्य ॥ २ ॥ पदानि ॥ अतः, ल्रान्तस्य ॥

वृत्तिः ॥ रेफलकारौ यावतः समीपौ तदन्तस्याङ्गस्य अत एव स्थाने वृद्धिर्भवति ॥

2. Vṛiddhi is substituted for the short अ, when it is immediately followed by the final र् or ल् of a root, before the Parasmaipada s-Aorist.

As क्षर्—अक्षारीत्, त्सर्—अत्सारीत्, ज्वल्—अज्वालीत्, ह्मल्—अह्मालीत् ॥ This debars the option of VII. 2. 7. Why 'short अ'? Observe न्यखारीत् न्यमीलीत् ॥ Why do we say "ending in र or ल"? Observe मा भवानश्चीत्, मा भवानटीत् ॥ The word अन्त means here 'proximity', as in the sentence उदकान्तं गतः = उदकसमीपं गतः ॥ The अ must be in the proximity of the र and ल ॥ Therefore the rule does not apply to अवभ्रीत्, अभ्वलीत्, for though र and ल are here *final* of the stem, yet are not in the proximity of अ ॥

वदव्रजहलन्तस्याचः ॥ ३ ॥ पदानि ॥ वद, व्रज, हलन्तस्य, अचः ॥

वृत्तिः ॥ वदव्रजोर्हलन्तानां चाङ्गानामचः स्थाने वृद्धिर्भवति सिचि परस्मैपदे परतः ॥

6

3. In the Parasmaipada s-Aorist there is Vṛiddhi of the अ of वद्, व्रज्, and of any vowel, without distinction, of the stems ending in a consonant.

As अवादीत्, अव्राजीत् ॥ This debars the option in the case of these two roots, which would have otherwise obtained by VII. 2. 7. So also of stems ending in consonants: as अपाक्षीत्, अभैत्सीत्, अच्छैत्सीत्, अरौत्सीत् ॥ By the splitting up of the sûtra (yoga-vibhaga) these forms could be evolved without using the word हलन्त in the sûtra. Thus (1) वदिव्रज्योः "In the room of the अ of वद and व्रज् there is Vṛiddhi". (2) अचः "In the room of the vowel of the stem there is Vṛiddhi". The word "stem" is understood throughout these chapters. If the vowel be at the *end* of the stem, there would be Vṛiddhi by VII. 2. 1, and if in the *middle* of the stem, then the verb *ends* with a *consonant*, and still there will be Vṛiddhi by our rule. The use of the word हलन्त in the sûtra indicates that the rule applies when more than one consonant even is at the end: as अराङ्क्षीत्, अभाङ्क्षीत् ॥

Had the word हलन्तस्य not been used in the sûtra, then the following maxim would have applied "येन नाव्यवधानं तेन व्यवहितेऽपि वचनप्रामाण्यात्" ॥ The rule would have applied where only *one* consonant intervened between the vowel and the affix, but not when more than one consonant intervened. But it is intended that the rule should apply to such cases also.

The form उदवोढाम् is thus evolved. To the root वह् we add सिच् in the second Person singular. Thus वह्+स्ताम् ॥ Now there appears the Vṛiddhi rule on the one side; and the rule requiring the change of ह to ढ (VIII. 2. 31) the rule requiring the elision of स् (VIII. 2. 26), the rule requiring the change of त into ध (VIII. 2. 40), then the rule requiring the change of ध into ढ, and then the elision of one ढ (VIII. 3. 13) on the other. What rule is to be applied first—the Vṛiddhi or the other rules? The Vṛiddhi rule is to be applied first, because the other rules are considered as asiddha (VIII. 2. 1): and after that we apply the other rules: and afterwards on account of the elsion of ढ, we change the Vṛiddhi आ into ओ (VI. 3. 112). The equation will be something like this:—वह्+स्ताम=वाह्+स्ताम् (VII. 2. 3)=वाढ्+स्ताम् (VIII. 2. 31)=वाढ्+ताम् (VIII. 2. 26)=वाढ्+धाम् (VIII. 2. 80)=वाढ्+ढाम् (VIII. 4. 41)=वा+ढाम् (VIII. 3. 13)=वोढाम् (VI. 3. 112). This with the upasarga उत् and the augment अ becomes उदवोढाम् ॥ Similar is the evolution of उदवोढम् with स्तम ॥ Once the अ has been Vṛiddhied into आ, there is no Vṛiddhi of ओ ॥ Had we not first Vṛiddhied the वह् into वाह्, but applied the vṛiddhi rule last, then there would have been vṛiddhi of ओ, as वौढाम् which is wrong. In fact where there has not taken place vṛiddhi first, there ओ is vṛiddhied, as=सोढामित्रस्यापत्यं =सौढामित्रिः ॥

नेटि ॥ ४ ॥ पदानि ॥ न, इटि ॥

वृत्तिः ॥ इडादौ सिचि हलन्तस्याङ्गस्य वृद्धिर्न भवति ।

4. The vowel of a stem, ending in a consonant, does not get Vṛiddhi, when the सिच् takes the augment इट् ॥

As अदेवीत्, असेवीत्, अकोषीत्, अमोषीत्, but अलावीत् where the root ends in a vowel. Will not लू by taking Guṇa (which is an antaraṅga operation) and the substitution of अव्, become a root ending in a consonant? No, though Guṇa is antaraṅga, it is superseded by the express Vṛiddhi.

ह्मयन्तक्षणश्वसजागृणिश्व्येदिताम् ॥ ५ ॥ पदानि ॥ ह्, म्, य्, अन्त, क्षण, श्वस्, जागृ, णि, श्वि, एदिताम् ॥

वृत्तिः ॥ हकारान्तानां मकारान्तानां यकारान्तानामङ्गानां क्षण श्वस जागृ णि श्वि इत्येतेषामेदितां च इडादौ सिचि परस्मैपदे परतो वृद्धिर्न भवति ।

5. The Vṛiddhi of the vowel of the following stems, does not take place before the इट् augment s-Aorist in the Parasmaipada; namely—the stems ending in ह्, म् or य्, the roots क्षण्, श्वस्, जागृ, a stem formed with णि, the root श्वि, and the roots having an indicatory ए in the Dhâtupâṭha.

Thus ग्रह, 'to catch' अग्रहीत्, स्यम, 'to sound' अस्यमीत्, व्यय, 'to expend' अव्ययीत्, टुवम्, 'to vomit' अवमीत्, क्षण 'to hurt' अक्षणीत्, श्वस् 'to breathe' अश्वसीत्, जागृ 'to be awake' अजागरीत्, णि, ऊन (churâdi) 'to lose' ऊनयीत्, ईल् 'to send' ईलयीत्, श्वि, अश्वयीत् ॥ एदिताम्, रगे 'to cover' अरगीत्. कखे, अकखीत् ॥

ह्मयन्तक्षणश्वसामेदितां च अतो हलादेर्लघोरिति विकल्पे प्राप्ते प्रतिषेधः ॥ जागृणिश्वीनां तु सिचि वृद्धिः प्राप्ता, सा च नेटीति न प्रतिषिध्यते, न चान्तरङ्गत्वादत्र पूर्वं गुणो भवति सिचि वृद्धेरनवकाशत्वात् ॥ यदि पूर्वं गुणः स्यादिहणिश्विग्रहणमनर्थकं स्यात् ॥ गुणायादेशयोः कृतयोर्यकारान्तत्वादेव प्रतिषेधस्य सिद्धत्वात् ॥ तस्मादिदमेव णिश्विग्रहणं ज्ञापकं न सिच्यन्तरङ्गमस्तीति ॥ अथ जागृग्रहणं किमर्थम् ॥ जाग्रो विचिण्णल्ङित्सु इति जागर्तेर्गुणो वृद्धेरपवादो विधीयते ॥ स यथा अचो ञ्णितीति वृद्धिं बाधते, तथा सिचि वृद्धिमपि बाधिष्यते ॥ नैतदस्ति ॥ कृते गुण ऽतो ल्रान्तस्येति या वृद्धिः प्राप्नोति सा प्रतिषिध्यते, ॥ अथ गुणविधानसामर्थ्यादुत्तरकालभाविन्यपि वृद्धिर्बाध्यते, ॥ यथा जागरयतीत्यत्रात उपधाया इत्यपि वृद्धिर्न भवति, तथा चिण्णलोः प्रतिषेधोऽर्थवान्भवति इति शक्यमिह जागृग्रहणमकर्त्तुम् ॥ नत्तु क्रियते विस्पष्टार्थम् ॥

In the case of roots ऊन and ईल in the above examples, the चङ् is prohibited by III. 1. 51. This is an exception to VII. 2. 7: so far as stems in ह्, य् and म् are concerned. There is no option allowed here. In the case of जागृ, णि-roots, and श्वि, the Vṛiddhi would have taken place by VII. 1. 1; and VII. 1. 4, could not have debarred Vṛiddhi, hence the special mention of these roots.

Nor can it be said, in the case of these roots, that "they will take first guṇa, on account of its being an Antaranga operation", because, then the rule of Vṛiddhi ordained by VII. 1. 1 will find no scope. Moreover, if the guṇa took place first and then Vṛiddhi, the mention of णि-roots and श्वि in the sûtra would be redundant. For in ऊनयीत् and अश्वयीत्, having guṇated the roots ऊनि and श्वि to ऊने and श्वे, and then substituting अय् (which is also antaranga) for ए before ईत्, we have ऊनय् + ईत्, and श्वय् + ईत् ॥ Now these are roots which end in य् and would be covered by the first portion of the present sûtra, viz, "h-m-y-anta", so the especial mention of णि-roots and श्वि would be superflûous, if guṇa was to take place first. The very mention of णि-roots and श्वि in this sûtra, is a jnâpaka (indicator) of the following maxim न सिचि अन्तरङ्गमस्ति ॥

Why have we used the root जागृ in the sûtra, when the special sûtra VII. 3. 85 will cause guṇa by superseding Vṛiddhi in the case of जागृ? This supersession will take place on the analogy of अचोऽञ्णिति (VII. 2. 115); for as this vṛiddhi rule VII. 2. 115 is superseded by VII. 3. 85, so will the present Vṛiddhi rule VII. 2. 1. *Ans.* No, this is not so. No doubt VII. 3. 85 does supersede the vṛiddhi rule VII. 2. 1 and we have guṇa, as जागर् + ईत् ॥ Then comes in VII. 2. 2, which would cause vṛiddhi, because now it is a root ending in र; this second vṛiddhi is prohibited by the present sûtra. You can say, that by the very fact that the guṇa rule VII. 3. 85 takes effect, will prevent every future Vṛiddhi, as in जागरयति there is no penultimate vṛiddhi by VII. 2. 116 [जागृ + णि = जागर् + णि (VII. 3. 85) = जागरि the rule VII. 2. 116 does not apply after guna] You can, of course, say so, and there is no answer to this but by saying that the mention of जागृ is only for the sake of distinctness.

In case the reading of जागृ in the sûtra be held necessary, then the operations which it undergoes, are shown below:

जागृ + इस् + ईत् ॥ Now appears (1) the rule VI. 1. 77. requiring the change of ऋ into र ॥ (2) This यणादेश is however, debarred by the rule VII. 3. 84 which causes guṇa of the finals of verbal stems before all sârvadhâtuka and ârdhadhâtuka affixes, because this guṇa rule is an apavâda to यणादेश ॥ (3) But this guṇa in its turn is debarred by the rule VII. 2. 1 requiring the vṛiddhi. (4) But this vṛiddhi is, however, superseded by VII. 3. 85, which causes the guṇa of the final of जागृ ॥ Now having gunated it, we get this form:—

जागर् + इस् + ईत् ॥ Now appears VII. 2. 3 which requires vṛiddhi, because it is a root ending in a consonant. (2) But that vṛiddhi is superseded by VII. 2. 4 because the affix सिच् has taken the इट् augment. (3) Then appears the rule VII. 2. 7 requiring optional vṛiddhi, (4) But that optional vṛiddhi is superseded by the compulsory vṛiddhi requirred by VII. 2. 2, because it is a root ending in र ॥ (5) And this last vṛiddhi is prohibited by the present sûtra VII. 2. 5 These nine stages through which the form अजागरीत् is evolved, is abbreviated in the following mnemonic verse:—गुणो वृद्धि र्गुणो वृद्धिः प्रतिषेधो विकल्पनम् ॥ पुन र्वृद्धि र्निषेधोऽतो यण्पूर्वाः प्राप्तयो नव ॥

ऊर्णोतेर्विभाषा ॥ ६ ॥ पदानि ॥ ऊर्णोतेः, विभाषा ॥

वृत्तिः ॥ ऊर्णोतेरिडादौ सिचि परस्मैपदपरे परतो विभाषा वृद्धिर्न भवति ।

6. Before an इट्-beginning s-Aorist of the Parasmaipada, there is optional Vṛiddhi of the vowel of ऊर्णु ॥

As और्णावीत् or प्रौर्णवीत् ॥ This option applies when the सिच् is not treated as ङित् ॥ But after ऊर्णु, सिच् is optionally ङित्, (I. 2. 6): when it is ङित्, there being neither guṇa nor vṛiddhi; we have उवङ् substitution, as प्रौर्णुवीत् (VI. 4. 77).

अतो हलादेर्लघोः ॥ ७ ॥ पदानि ॥ अतः, हल् आदेः, लघोः ॥

वृत्तिः ॥ हलादेरङ्गस्य लघोरकारस्य इडादौ सिचि परस्मैपदपरे परतो विभाषा वृद्धिर्न भवति ।

7. Before an इट्-beginning s-Aorist of the Parasmaipada, the short अ of the root gets optionally Vṛiddhi, when the stem begins with a consonant, and the अ is prosodially short by being followed by a simple consonant.

Thus अकणीत् or अकाणीत्, अरणीत् or अराणीत् ॥ Why do we say 'of अ'? Observe असेवीत्, असेवीत् ॥ Besides this patent objection, there is another, not so manifest. If we had not taken अतः, the sûtra would have ordained Vṛiddhi of every *vowel* (अचः VII. 2. 3), the Vṛiddhi so ordained would be an अच् pertaining Vṛiddhi, and not an इक्-pertaining Vṛiddhi. Therefore ङित् affixes will not debar such Vṛiddhi, for the क्ङिति च (I. 1. 5), debars only इग्लक्षणा Vṛiddhi. Therefore कुटादि roots after which सिच् is ङित् (I. 2. 1), will get Vṛiddhi, which is not desired. Therefore we have only one form of न्यकुटीत्, न्यपुटीत् ॥

Why do we say 'beginning with a consonant'? Observe मा भवानशीत्, मा भवानदीत् from अश् and अद् ॥ Why do we say 'prosodially short'? Observe अतक्षीत्, अरक्षीत् ॥

But why does not vṛiddhi take place in अचकासीत् from the root चकास् (Ad. 65)? The vṛiddhi does not take place on the maxim येन ना व्यवधानं तेन व्यवहितेऽपि वचन प्रामाण्यात्; for the rule applies to short अ only when a consonant intervenes between it and the affix, and not when both consonants and vowels intervene. In चकास् not only the consonants क् and स् intervene but also the vowel आ ॥ Hence there is no vṛiddhi. Moreover, the व्यवधान can be by one letter and not by more than one letter. Therefore, applying this maxim, the word लघोः might have been omitted from the sûtra without any detriment. In that case, the form अतक्षीत् from the root तक्ष (Bhu 685) will be explained by saying that rule VII. 2. 7 does not apply to it, because *two* consonants intervene between अ and the affix. In this view of the case, the employment of the word लघोः in the sûtra is for the sake of distinctness only.

The word इट् is understood in this sûtra, so that the rule applies to सेट् aorist. The rule therefore, does not apply to Aniṭ aorist, as अपाक्षित् ॥

The form आपिपाठिषीत् the aorist of the Desiderative root, is explained by saying that the long आ of vṛiddhi is elided by VI. 4. 64.

नेड्वशि कृति ॥ ८ ॥ पदानि ॥ न, इट्, वशि, कृति ॥

वृत्तिः ॥ वशादौ कृति प्रत्यये परत इडागमो न भवति ।

8. The augment इट् is not added to a kṛit-affix beginning with a sonant consonant (वश् pratyâhâra).

The वश् pratayâhâra is rather vague. The rule really applies to Kṛit-affixes beginning with व, र (ल) म and न, and no कृत् affix begins with any other letter of वश् class. Thus ईशिता, ईशितुम् non-vaś letters get the augment, but not ईश्वरः, (III. 2. 175) so also दीपिता, दीपितुम् but not दीप्रम् (III. 2. 167 र) भसिता, भसितुम् but not भस्म, (III. 2. 75. मनिन्) यतिता, यतितुम् but not यत्नः (III. 3. 90 नङ्) The Vârtika नेड् वरमनादौ कृति gives the rule in a more definite form. Of course, in the Uṇâdi Kṛit-affixes, there is diversity. There we get the affix ड, for example, which of course does not take the augment, as दम् + ड = दण्डः (Uṇ I. 113). Why do we say कृत् affixes? Observe रुदिव, रुदिम ॥

Here by VII. 2. 76 the Sârvadhâtuka affixes beginning with a वल् consonant take इट् augment after the roots रुद् &c ; but this इट् will also be prohibited by the present sûtra, if the word कृति be not read in the sûtra. So that rule VII. 2. 76 would find scope before those वलादि affixes only which do not begin with a वश् letter; as रुदितः ॥ In some texts of Kâsika the counter-example is रुरुदिम in the Perfect. This is wrong, according to Padamnjari (क्रादिनियमादेव इटः सिद्धत्वात्) because इट् always comes in the Perfect except after the root कृ &c. (VII. 2. 13): so the counter-example from the Perfect Tense is not valid. This sûtra is an exception to VII. 2. 35. The Kṛit-affixes beginning with वश् letters as given by Pâṇini are the following: वन् (वनिप्, क्वनिप्, ङ्वनिप्), वर (वरच and क्वरप्), वस् (क्वसु), रु (क्रु), लुक् (क्लुकन्), मन् (मनिन्), मर (क्मरच्) न (नङ्, नन्), नज् (नजिङ्), नु (क्नु) ॥ This list will show the truth of the above vârtika.

तितुत्रतथसिसुसरकसेषु च ॥ ९ ॥ पदानि ॥ ति, तु, त्र, त, थ, सि, सु, सर, क, सेषु, ॥

वृत्तिः ॥ ति तु त्र त थ सि सु सर क स इत्येतेषु कृत्सु इडागमो न भवति ।

वार्त्तिकम् ॥ तितुत्रेषु अग्रहादीनाम् इति वक्तव्यम् ॥

9. The इट् augment is not taken by the following Kṛit-affixes :—ति, तु, त्र, त, थ, सि, सु, सर, क and स ॥

Thus (1) क्तिच्—तन्तिः but तनिता, तनितुम्, क्तिन्—दीप्तिः but दीपिता, दीपितुम् ॥ (2) तुन् (Uṇ I. 70)—सक्तुः but साचिता, साचितुम् ॥ (3) ष्ट्रन् (III. 2. 182)—पत्रं but पतिता, पतितुम्, so also Uṇâdi ष्ट्रन् (Uṇ IV. 158), as तन्त्रम् from तन् ॥ (4) तन् (Uṇ III. 86)—हस्तः but हसिता, हसितुम् ; so also लीतः, पीतः, धूर्त्तः from लू, पू, धूर्वि forming सेट् लविता, पविता, धूर्विता ॥ The त affix mentioned in the sûtra refers to this Uṇâdi त (Uṇ III. 86), and not to the त (क्त) of Nishṭhâ, for the Nishṭhâ त takes the augment, as हसितम् ॥ (5) क्थन् (Uṇ II. 2)—कुष्ठम् but कोषिता, कोषितुम्, काष्ठम् but काशिता, काशितुम् ॥ (6) क्सि (Uṇ III. 155), as कुक्षिः but कोषिता, कोषितुम् ॥ (7) क्सु (Uṇ III. 157)—इक्षुः but एषिता, एषितुम् ; (8) सरन् (Uṇ III. 70)—अक्षरम्,

but अशिता, अशितुम् ॥ (9) कन् (Uṇ III. 43)—शल्कः but शलिता, शलितुम् ॥ (10) स (Uṇ III. 62)—वत्सः but वदिता, वदितुम् ॥

Vârt:—The affix ति, तु and त्र take इट् augment after ग्रह् and words of similar formations:—as विगृहीतिः, उपस्निहितिः, निकुचिति निपाठितिः ॥.

Before non-kṛit ति &c, we have इट्, as रोदिति, स्वपिति ॥

एकाच उपदेशे ऽनुदात्तात् ॥ १० ॥ पदानि ॥ एकाचः, उपदेशे, अनुदात्तात्, ॥

वृत्तिः ॥ उपदेशे य एकाच् धातुरनुदात्तश्च तस्मादिडागमो न भवति ।

10. The augment इट् is not added to that affix which is joined to a root, which in the Grammatical system of Instruction (i. e. in the Dhâtupâṭha) is of one syllable, and is without accent (anudâtta).

A list of such roots has been collected by the *Anit—Kârikâ*. They are given below.

Kârikâ:—अनिट्स्वरान्तो भवतीति दृश्यतामिमांस्तु सेटः प्रवदन्ति तद्विदः ।
अदन्तमृदन्तमृतां च वृङ्वृञौ श्विडीङ्विर्णेष्वथ शीङ्श्रिञावपि ॥
गणस्थमूदन्तमुतां च रुस्नुवौ क्षुवन्तयोर्णोतिमथो युणुक्ष्णवः ।
इति स्वरान्ता निपुणैः समुच्चितास्ततो हलन्तानपि सन्निबोधत ॥

As a general rule all monosyllabic roots ending in a *vowel* except अ, long ऊ and long ॠ are anudâtta, and do not take इट् augment: as दातृ, नेतृ, चेतृ, स्तोतृ, कर्तृ, हर्तृ ॥ The following are the exceptions:—

(1) All roots ending in short अ are Udâtta and take इट्; as अवधिष्ट ॥

(2) All roots ending in long ॠ are सेट्, as तॄ—तरिता or तरीता ॥

(3) All roots ending in short ऋ are अनिट् except वृङ् (IX. 38 the references are to the class and number in the Dhâtupâṭha) and वृञ् (V. 8, X. 271): as निर्वरिता or निर्वरीता, प्रवरिता or प्रवरीता ॥

(4) All roots in short इ are Aniṭ, except श्वि (I. 1059), 'to grow' and श्रिञ् 'to attend' (I. 945), as श्वयिता, श्रयिता ॥

(5) All roots in long ई are Aniṭ, except शीङ् 'to rest' (II. 22), and डीङ् 'to fly' (I. 1017. IV. 27), as शयिता, उड्डयिता ॥

(6) All roots in long ऊ are सेट्, as लविता, पविता from लू and पू ॥

(7) All monosyllabic roots in short उ are Aniṭ, except, रुङ् 'to sound' (II. 24, I. 1008), स्नु 'to flow' (II. 29), क्षु 'to sound' (II. 27), यु 'to mix' (II. 23) नु 'to praise' (II. 26), क्ष्णु 'to sharpen', (II. 28): and ऊर्णुञ् 'to cover' (II. 30, though consisting of more than one syllable, is treated like नु for the purposes of यङ्) ॥ Thus रविता, प्रस्नविता, क्षविता, यविता, नविता, क्ष्णविता and प्रोर्णविता ॥

Of the roots ending in consonants, all are सेट् except the following:—

Kârikâ:—इति स्वरान्ता निपुणैः समुच्चितास्ततो हलन्तानपि सन्निबोधत ।
शकिस्तु कान्तेष्वनिडेक इष्यते घसिश्च सान्तेषु वसिः प्रसारणी ॥
रभिस्तु भान्तेष्वथ मैथुने यभिस्ततस्तृतीयो लभिरेव नेतरे ॥

यमिर्यमन्तेष्वनिडेक इष्यते रमिश्च यश्च श्यनि पठ्यते मनिः ।
नमिश्चतुर्थो हनिरेव पञ्चमो गमिश्च षष्ठः प्रतिषेधवाचिनाम् ॥
शिहिर्दुहिर्मेहतिरोहती वहिर्नहिस्तु षष्ठो दहतिस्तथा लिहिः ।
इमे ऽनिटोऽष्टाविह मुक्तसंशया गणेषु हान्ताः प्रविभज्य कीर्त्तिताः ॥
दिशिं दृशिं दंशिमथो मृशिं स्पृशिं रिशिं रुशिं क्रोशतिमष्टमं विशिम् ।
लिशं च शान्ताननिटः पुराणगाः पठन्ति पाठेषु दशैव नेतरान् ॥
रुधिः सराधिर्युधिबन्धिसाधयः क्रुधिक्षुधी शुध्यतिबुध्यती व्यधिः ।
इमे तु धान्ता दश येऽनिटो मतास्ततः परं सिध्यतिरेव नेतरे ॥
शिषिं पिषिं शुष्यतिपुष्यती त्विषिं विषिं श्लिषिं तुष्यतिदुष्यती द्विषिम् ।
इमान्दशैवोपदिशन्त्यनिड्विधौ गणेषु षान्तान्कृषिकर्षती तथा ॥
तपिं तिपिं चापिमथो वपिं स्वपिं लिपिं लुपिं तृप्यति दृप्यती सृपिम् ।
स्वरेण नीचेन शपिं छुपिं क्षिपिं प्रतीहि पान्तान्पठितांस्त्रयोदश ॥
अदिं हदिं स्कन्दिभिदिच्छिदिक्षुदीन् शदिं सदिं स्विद्यतिपद्यती खिदिम् ।
तुदिं नुदिं विद्यतिविन्त इत्यपि प्रतीहि दान्तान्दश पञ्च चानिटः ॥
पचिं वचिं विचिरिचिरञ्जिपृच्छतीन् निजिं सिचिं मुचिभजिभञ्जिभृज्जतीन् ।
त्यजिं यजिं युजिरुजिसञ्जिमज्जतीन् भुजिं स्वजिसृजिमृजी विद्ध्यनिट्स्वरान् ॥

(1.) क—शक् 'to be able' (IV. 78, V. 15). शक्ता, शक्ष्यति

(2.) स्—घस् 'to eat' (I. 747, and also substitute of अद्), as, घस्ता ; वस् 'to dwell' (I. 1054), as वस्ता ॥ The वस् which takes Samprasâraṇa by VI. 1. 15, is meant here, and not वस् 'to cover' (II. 13), which does not vocalise, as वसिता वस्त्राणाम्, but उषितः from वस 'to dwell' (VII. 2. 52).

(3.) भ्—Three roots: रभ् 'to desire' (I. 1023), as, आरब्धा, यभ् coire (I. 1029), यब्धा, लभ् 'to take' (I. 1024), लब्धा ॥

(4.) म्—Four roots, यम् 'to cease' (I. 1033), यन्ता ; रम् 'to play' (I. 906) रन्ता, नम् 'to bow' (I. 867, 1030) नन्ता, गम्लृ 'to go' (I. 1031) गन्ता ॥

5. न्—Two roots मन् 'to think' (IV. 67), मन्ता, हन् 'to kill' (II. 2), हन्ता ॥ The Divâdi मन् should be taken, otherwise मनिता from मन्—मनुते (VIII. 9).

(6.) ह्—Eight roots:—दिह् 'to smear' (II. 5), देग्धा ; दुह् 'to milk' (II. 4), दोग्धा ; मिह् 'to sprinkle' (I. 1041) मीढा, रुह् 'to grow' (I. 912) रोढा ; वह् 'to carry' (I. 1053) वोढा, नह् 'to bind' (IV. 57) नद्धा; दह् 'to burn' (I. 1041) दग्धा, लिह् 'to lick' (II. 6) लेढा ॥ In other collections सह् (I. 905, IV. 20), मुह् (IV. 89), रिह (VI. 23), लुह् (?), are also enumerated; of these सह् takes इट् optionally before affixes beginning with त, so also मुह् because it belongs to the class of रधादि (VII. 2. 45) the other two are not found (?) in root-collections, hence the Kârika uses the words मुक्तसंशयः ॥

(7.) श्—Ten roots:—दिश् 'to show' (VI. 3), दृश् 'to see' (I. 1037), दंश 'to bite' (I. 1038), मृश् 'to rub' (VI. 131), स्पृश् 'to touch' (VI. 128), रिश् (VI. 126), रुश् (VI. 126) both meaning 'to hurt', विश् 'to enter' (VI. 130), लिश् 'to be small' (IV. 70, VI. 127). As देष्टा, द्रष्टा, दंष्टा, आम्रष्टा or आमर्ष्टा, स्पर्ष्टा or स्प्रष्टा, The roots with a penultimate ऋ short, which are anudâtta in the dhâtupâṭha, with th exception of मृज् and दृश्, take optionally the augment अम् (VI. 1. 59), ॥ रेष्टा, रोष्टा, क्रोष्टा, प्रवेष्टा, लेष्टा ॥

(8.) ध्–Ten roots:—रुध् with अनु, 'to love'. रुध् 'to obstruct' (IV. 65) रोद्धा. राध् 'to accomplish' (IV. 71, V. 16) राद्धा; युध् 'to fight' (IV. 64) योद्धा; बन्ध् 'to bind' (I. 1022), बन्द्धा; साध् 'to accomplish' (V. 17) साद्धा; क्रुध् 'to be angry' (IV. 80) क्रोद्धा, क्षुध् 'to be hungry' (IV. 81) क्षोद्धा; शुध् 'to be pure' (IV. 82) शोद्धा, बुध् 'to be aware' (IV. 63) बोद्धा; व्यध् 'to pierce' (IV. 72) व्यद्धा; सिध् 'to be accomplished' (IV. 83) सेद्धा ॥ The roots बुध् and सिध् are exhibited in the above Kârikâ with श्यन् vikarana (बुध्यति, सिध्यति); therefore बुध् and सिध् take इट् in other ganas than the Fourth; as बोधिता and सेधिता ॥ There being want of prohibition with regard to निष्ठा, we have बुधितं and सिधितं ॥

(9.) ष्-roots. Ten. शिष् 'to distinguish' (VII, 14) शेष्टा; पिष् 'to pound' (VII. 15) पेष्टा, शुष् 'to become dry' (IV. 74) शोष्टा; पुष् 'to be nourished' (IV. 73), पोष्टा, त्विष् 'to shine' (I. 1050) त्वेष्टा, विष् 'to pervade, to sprinkle' (I. 729, III. 13, IX. 54) वेष्टा, श्लिष् 'to embrace' (I. 734. IV. 77) श्लेष्टा; तुष् 'to be satisfied' (IV. 75) तोष्टा, दुष् 'to be sinful' (IV. 76) दोष्टा. दोक्ष्यति, द्विष् 'to hate' (II. 3) द्वेष्टा, द्वेक्ष्यति, कृष् 'to draw' (I. 1059, VI. 6 both Bhuâdi and Tudâdi are taken, as the kârikâ uses the two forms), आक्रष्टा and आकर्ष्टा ॥

(10.) प्–Thirteen roots: तप् 'to burn' (I. 1034, IV. 51) तप्ता, तप्स्यति, तिप् 'to distil' (I. 385) तेप्ता, आप् 'to obtain' (V 14, X. 295) आप्ता; वप् 'to sow' (I. 1052) वप्ता; स्वप् 'to sleep' (II. 59) स्वप्ता; लिप् 'to anoint' (VI. 139) लेप्ता; लुप् (VI. 137) 'to break', लोप्ता ॥ The roots तृप् and दृप् optionally take इट्, as they belong to रधादि class (VII. 2. 45, Divâdi 84–91). The special mention of these two roots in the kârikâ, is for the sake of indicating that these roots take अम् augment; as त्रप्ता or तर्प्ता, or तर्पिता; द्रप्ता, or दर्प्ता or दर्पिता ॥ The तृप् and दृप् belonging to Tudâdi class, are Udâtta and सेट् ॥ सृप् (I. 1032) 'to creep' स्रप्ता, सर्प्ता; शप् 'to curse' (I. 1049) शप्ता; छुप् 'to touch' (VI. 125) छोप्ता; क्षिप् 'to throw' (IV. 14) क्षेप्ता ॥

(11.) द्–Fifteen roots. अद् 'to eat' [II. 1] अत्ता; हद् 'to void excrement' (I. 1026) हत्ता; स्कन्द् 'to leap' (I. 1028) स्कन्ता; भिद् 'to break' (VII. 2) भेत्ता, छिद् 'to cut' (VII. 3) छेत्ता; क्षुद् 'to pound' (VII. 6) क्षोत्ता, क्षोत्स्यति, शद् 'to perish' (I. 908, VI. 134) शत्ता, सद् 'to sink' (I. 907, VI. 133) सत्ता, स्विद् 'to sweat' (IV. 79) स्वेत्ता ॥ The root is exhibited as स्विद्यति in the above kârikâ, showing that the Fourth class root is to be taken, and not the Bhuâdi (I. 780), which is udâtta and takes इट् ॥ पद् 'to go' (IV. 60), पत्ता; खिद् 'to be troubled' (IV. 61, VI. 142, VII. 12) खेत्ता, तुद् 'to strike' (VI. 1) तोत्ता; नुद् 'to impel' (VI. 2) नोत्ता; विद् (IV. 62) वेत्ता ॥ The root विद् is exhibited in the kârikâ, as विद्यति and विन्त, therefore, the rule applies to विद्यति and रुधादि विद् ॥ The Adâdi (वत्ति) and Tudâdi (विन्दति) विद् is सेट्, as वेदिता विद्यानाम्, वेदिताधनस्य ॥

(12.) च्–six roots:—पच् 'to cook' (I. 187) पक्ता, पक्ष्यति; वच् 'to speak' (II. 54) वक्ता, विच् 'to separate' (VII. 5) विवेक्ता; रिच् 'to make empty' (VII. 4) रेक्ता; सिच् 'to sprinkle' (VI. 140) सेक्ता; मुच् (VI. 136) 'to loose' मोक्ता ॥

(13.) छ्–One root प्रछ् 'to ask' (VI. 120) प्रष्टा, प्रक्ष्यति ॥

(14.) ज्–Fifteen roots :—रञ्ज् 'to colour' (I. 865. 1048) रङ्क्त्वा; निज् 'to cleanse' (III. 11) निर्णेक्ता, नेक्ष्यति ; भज् 'to honor' (I. 1047) भक्ता; भञ्ज् 'to break' (VII. 16) भङ्क्त्वा; भ्रस्ज् 'to fry' (I. 181) भ्रष्टा or भर्ष्टा; त्यज् 'to quit' (I. 1035) त्यक्ता; यज् 'to sacrifice' (I. 1051) यष्टा, युज् 'to join' (IV. 68, VII. 7) योक्ता; रुज् 'to break' (VI. 123) रोक्ता; सञ्ज् 'to adhere' (I. 1036) सङ्क्त्वा, मस्ज् to be immersed' (VI. 122) मङ्क्त्वा; भुज् 'to bend' (VI. 124) 'to enjoy' (VII. 17). भोक्ता, स्वज् 'to embrace' (I. 1025) परि-ष्वक्ता; सृज 'to emit' 'to create' (IV. 69, VI. 121) स्रष्टा; मृज् 'to cleanse' (I. 269, II. 57), मार्ष्टा, मर्जिता ॥ The root मृज् is exhibited in the Dhâtupâṭha with a long indicatory ऊ, e-s, मृजू शुद्धौ (II. 57). It, therefore, optionally would take इट् ॥ Nor does this root take अम् augment. The inclusion of this root in the above list is, therefore, questionable. Others read विज instead of मृज ॥ The निजादि root विज is Aniṭ (III. 12) i. e. विज् 'to separate' the विज् of Rudhâdi takes इट् ॥

Why do we say "a monosyllabic root"? Observe अवधीत् ॥ The root is taught as वध with a final अ (II. 4. 42) in order to prevent vṛiddhi. Why do we say "in upadeśa or Dhâtupâṭha" ?

The rule will not apply to roots which have become anudâtta during evolution i. e. when taking affixes. Therefore, we have परिष्यति and लविष्यति with इट्, but not here, कर्ता कटान्, कर्तुम् ॥

श्र्युकः किति ॥ ११ ॥ पदानि ॥ श्री, उकः, किति ॥

वृत्तिः ॥ श्रि इत्येतस्योगन्तानां च किति प्रत्यये परत इडागमो न भवति ।

Kârikâ :—वाच्य ऊर्णोर्नुवद्भावो यङ्प्रसिद्धिः प्रयोजनम् । आमश्च प्रतिषेधार्थमेकाचश्चेड्उपग्रहात् ॥

11. The augment इट् is not added to an affix having an indicatory क्, when it comes after the root श्रि, or after a monosyllabic root ending in उ, ऊ, ऋ or ॠ in the Dhâtupâṭha.

As श्रित्वा, श्रितः, श्रितवान् ॥ So also with roots ending in उक् vowels : as युत्वा, युतः, युतवान् ; लूत्वा, लूनः, लूनवान् ; वृत्वा, वृतः, वृतवान् ; तीर्त्वा, तीर्णः, तीर्णवान् ॥

Why 'श्रि and उक् ending roots only'? Observe विदितः ॥ Why having an indicatory क् ? Observe श्रयितृ, श्रयितुम्, श्रयितव्यम् ॥ Some read two क's in the sûtra and would apply it to the indicatory ग् also, as भूष्णु (III. 2. 139).

This rule applies to those roots, which have not been enumerated above. In the case of यु the Nishṭhâ will not take इट् even by VII. 2. 49 read with VII. 2. 15.

When two क are read in the sûtra, one standing for ग्; there arises a little difficulty of combination. Thus ग् coming after the visarga of उकः would require that the visarga be changed to उ by VI. 1. 114. If ग be changed to क् (VIII. 4. 55) then also, the visarga required to be changed into upadhmanîya by VIII. 3. 37. If the change of ग् into क् (VIII. 4. 55) be considered asiddha

(VIII. 2. 1.), then also the visarga must be changed to उ (VI. 1. 114), and the sûtra should be श्र्युकोकिति ॥ This, however, is not done as an anomaly allowable in sûtra construction. According to Kâsikâ, this difficulty would not at all arise, if in the sûtra ग्लाजिस्थश्चक्स्नुः (III. 2. 139), the स्था + आ be taken as compounded into स्था; so that that rule would apply to that स्था which ends in आ, and not to that स्था whose final is changed to ई; so that the form स्थास्नुः is evolved without anomaly : and the affix will be कित् (क्स्नु) and not गित् (ग्स्नु). The affix being कित्, the above sandhi difficulty will not arise at all.

The word उपदेश is understood here also, so that the rule will apply to roots which end in उक् vowel, in their original states and not to the transformed base before the affix. Thus तॄ is a उक्-ending root, which is transformed to तीर् before the Nishṭha त ॥ The rule will apply to it, as तीर्णः ॥ If you object saying, that तॄ ends in long ॠ and its Desiderative optionally takes इट् by VII. 2. 41, and therefore, its Nishṭhâ will always take no इट् by VII. 2. 15. we reply, that the option taught in VII. 2. 41 applies to roots ending in long ॠ; but when the root vowel is changed to ई, it is no longer a ॠ-ending root. If you say, the rule of sthânivad bhâva will apply : we say, that that rule is not applicable to अल् विधि, and this is an अल्विधि ॥ Therefore, the word उपदेश should be read into this sûtra. If this be so, the rule ought to apply to जागृ, and we could not get the forms जागरितः and जागरितवान् ॥ To explain this we should also read the anuvṛitti of एकाच् into this sûtra. The root ऊर्णु, however is an exception and is governed by this rule, in spite of its consisting of more than one vowel. Thus प्रोर्णुतः and प्रोर्णुतवान् ॥

Kârikâ :—ऊर्णु is treated as if it was नु, when the affix यङ् is to be applied, आम् is to be prohibited, or इट् is to be debarred.

सनि ग्रहगुहोश्च ॥ १२ ॥ पदानि ॥ सनि, ग्रह, गुहोः, च ॥

वृत्तिः ॥ ग्रह गुह इत्येतयोरुगन्तानां च सनि प्रत्यये परत इडागमो न भवति ।

12. The Desiderative affix सन् does not get the augment इट्, not only after roots ending in उ, ऊ, ऋ and ॠ, but also after ग्रह and गुह ॥

As जिघृक्षति, जुघुक्षति, रुरूषति, लुलूषति ॥ The anuvṛitti of श्रि is not drawn into this sûtra, as option is allowed regarding it by VII. 2. 49. ग्रह would always get इट्, गुह् (I. 944) being ऊदित् (in the Dhâtupâṭha), would have optionally taken इट् (VII. 2. 44)

The forms जिघृक्षति and जुघुक्षति are thus evolved :—ग्रह् + सन् (the affix is कित् by I. 2. 8) = गृह् + सन् (VI. 1. 16) = गृढ् + सन् (VIII. 2. 31) = गृक् + सन् (VIII. 2. 41) = जिघृक्षति (VIII. 2. 37). So also with गुहू संवरणे, the सन् is कित् here by I. 2. 10.

कृसृभृवृस्तुद्रुस्रुश्रुवो लिटि ॥१३॥ पदानि ॥ कृ. सृ, भृ, वृ, स्तु, द्रु, स्रु, श्रुवः, लिटि ॥

वृत्तिः ॥ कृ सृ भृ वृ स्तु द्रु स्रु श्रु इत्येतेषां लिटि प्रत्यये इडागमो न भवति ।
वार्त्तिकम् ॥ कृञोऽसुट इति वक्तव्यम् ॥

13. The Personal endings of the Perfect do not get the augment इट्, after कृ, सृ, भृ, वृ, स्तु, द्रु, स्रु, श्रु ॥

Thus कृ—चकृव, चकृम ; सृ, ससृव, ससृम ; भृ, बभृव, बभृम ; वृञ्, ववृव, ववृम ; वृङ्, ववृवहे, ववृमहे ; स्तु, तुष्टुव, तुष्टुम ; द्रु, दुद्रुव, दुद्रुम ; स्रु; सुस्रुव, सुस्रुम ; श्रु; शुश्रुव, शुश्रुम ॥ सिद्धे सत्यारम्भो नियमार्थः, क्रादय एव लिट्यनिटस्ततोऽन्ये सेट इति ॥

These roots with the exception of वृ are Aniṭ by rule VII. 2. 10 ; their special mention here is for the sake of niyama, namely, these roots alone are Aniṭ in the Perfect, other roots are all Seṭ in the Perfect. Thus बिभिदिव, बिभिदिम, लुलुविव, लुलुविम ॥ All anudâtta roots of the Dhâtupâṭha are to be understood, by this rule, to get इट् ॥ The affix थ of the Perfect gets इट् after वृञ्, as the irregular form ववर्थ in VII. 2. 64, indicates that in the Veda, थ does not get इट् after वृञ्, but in the secular literature it does. By VII. 2. 63, the थ would have got इट् after स्तु, द्रु, स्रु and श्रु ; that इट् is also prohibited by the present sûtra. As तुष्टोथ, दुद्रोथ, सुस्रोथ, शुश्रोथ ॥

Vârt :—इट् is added when कृ takes the सुट् augment : as संचस्करिव, संचस्करिम ॥ The rule VII. 2. 63, applies here also, as संचस्करिथ ॥

श्वीदितो निष्ठायाम् ॥ १४ ॥ पदानि ॥ श्वि, ईदितः, निष्ठायाम्, ॥

वृत्तिः ॥ श्वयतेरीदितश्च निष्ठायामिडागमो न भवति ॥

14. The Participial affixes त and तवत् (kta and ktavatu), do not get the इट् augment after श्वि, and after the root which has an indicatory ई ॥

As शूनः, शूनवान ; ओलजी (VI. 10),—लग्न, लग्नवान् ; ओविजी (VI. 9), उद्विग्नः, उद्विग्नवान् ॥ The त is changed to न because of the indicatory ओ (VIII. 2. 45). So also दीपी (IV. 42), दीप्तः, दीप्तवान् ॥ In the Dhâtupâṭha, डीङ् (IV. 27), is classed among ओदित् roots, and it indicates that the Nishṭhâ is aniṭ after it : and ओ is for न-change (VIII. 2. 45) as, उड्डीनः, उड्डीनवान् ॥ The word निष्ठायाम् governs the following sûtras upto VII. 2. 35.

यस्य विभाषा ॥ १५ ॥ पदानि ॥ यस्य, विभाषा ॥

वृत्तिः ॥ यस्य धातोर्विभाषा क्वचिदिडुक्तस्तस्य निष्ठायां परत इडागमो न भवति ॥

15. The Participial-affixes do not take इट्, after those roots, to which another suffix can optionally be added, with or without this augment इ ॥

That is, a root which is *optionally* Seṭ before other affixes, is *invariably* aniṭ before Nishṭhâ. Thus by VII. 2. 44, वल् consonant beginning affixes are optionally सेट् after the roots धू &c. The Nishthâ after धू &c, will be invariably aniṭ. Thus विधूतः, विधूतवान् ; गूढः, गूढवान् ॥ By VII. 2. 56, the roots having an indicatory उ, *optionally* are followed by Seṭ क्त्वा ॥ The Nishṭhâ after उदित् roots will *invariably* be aniṭ : as वृद्धः, वृद्धवान् ॥

By the vârtika तनि पति शरिद्राणामुपसङ्ख्यानम् the roots तन्, पत and दरिद्रा take optional इट् in the Desiderative (VII. 2. 49). Though पत् is a root which thus *optionally* takes इट् in the Desiderative, yet its Nishṭhâ is always सेट्, for Pâṇini himself has employed the word पतित in Sûtra II. 1. 24, 38. According to Padamanjari this rule of यस्य विभाषा is anitya and not of universal application. Because had this rule been of universal application then the root कृत which is *optionally* aniṭ by VII. 2. 57, would be *universally* aniṭ by the present sûtra: and there would be no necessity of reading it with a long ई in the Dhâtupâṭha, as कृती छेदने (VI. 141) to make its nishthâ aniṭ under VII. 2. 14.

आदितश्च ॥ १६ ॥ पदानि ॥ आदितः, च, ॥

वृत्तिः ॥ आदितश्च धातोर्निष्ठायामिडागमो न भवति ॥

16. The Participial-affixes do not get इट् augment after a root which has an indicatory आ ॥

As ञिमिदा — मिन्नः, मिन्नवान् ; ञिक्ष्विदा — क्ष्विण्णः, क्ष्विण्णवान् ; ञिष्विदा — स्विन्नः, स्विन्नवान् ॥ The च implies that other roots not enumerated are to be also included, as आश्वस्तः, वान्तः ॥

This and the sûtra following it could have been made into one, as आदितश्च विभाषा भावादिकर्मणोः ॥ The separate making of two sûtras indicates that the rule of यस्य विभाषा (VII. 2. 15), applies with the restrictions and limitations of the rule ordaining 'option', i. e., the prohibition of इट् augment, with regard to the participial-affixes is limited by the same conditions, which apply to the optional employment of इट् before other affixes in the विभाषा rules (यदुपाधेर्विभाषा, तदुपाधेः प्रतिषेधः) ॥ Thus VII. 2. 68 ordains इट् optionally to the affix वसु after the roots गम्, हन्, विद् and विश् ॥ The root विद् there is the Tudâdi root meaning 'to acquire'. The rule यस्य विभाषा will apply to this विद् with this meaning: and not to विद् meaning 'to know', the Past Participles of which are विदितः, विदितवान् ॥

विभाषा भावादिकर्म्मणोः ॥ १७ ॥ पदानि ॥ विभाषा, भाव, आदिकर्म्मणोः ॥

वृत्तिः ॥ भावे आदिकर्म्मणि च आदितो धातोर्विभाषा निष्ठायामिडागमो न भवति ॥

17. The participial affixes after roots having an indicatory आ, may optionally take the augment इट्, when the affixes have an Impersonal sense, or denote the beginning of an action.

Thus मिन्नमनेन or मेदितमनेन, प्रमिन्नः, प्रमेदितः ॥ The Saunâgas optionally make the Nishṭhâ seṭ after the root शक्, when the affix has a Passive significance even, as शकितो घटः कर्त्तुम् or शक्तो घटः कर्त्तुम् ॥ Not so, when the affix has Impersonal force, as शक्तमनेन् ॥ The root असु 'to throw' (अस्यति), is followed by सेट् Nishṭhâ, when the sense is Impersonal: as असितमनेन ; but not when the beginning of action is meant, as अस्तः काण्डः ॥

क्षुब्धस्वान्तध्वान्तलग्नम्लिष्टविरिब्धफाण्टबाढानि मन्थमनस्तमःसक्ताविस्पष्टस्वरा-

नायासभृशेषु ॥ १८ ॥ पदानि ॥ क्षुब्ध, स्वान्त, ध्वान्त लग्न, म्लिष्ट, विरिब्ध, फाण्ट, बाढानि, मन्थ, मनः, तमः, सक्त, अविस्पष्ट, स्वर, अनायास, भृशेषु ॥

वृत्तिः ॥ क्षुब्ध स्वान्त ध्वान्त लग्न म्लिष्ट विरिब्ध फाण्ट बाढ इत्येते निपात्यन्ते यथासंख्यं मन्थ मनस्तमः सक्ताविस्पष्ट स्वरानायासभृश इत्येतेष्वर्थेषु ॥

18. The following words are made without इट् augment in the senses given against them :—

1. क्षुब्धः 'a churning stick', 2. स्वान्तः 'the mind', 3. ध्वान्तः darkness', 4. लग्नः 'attached', 5. म्लिष्टः 'indistinct or unintelligible', 6. विरिब्धः 'a note or tone', 7. फाण्टः 'made without an effort or by an easy process', and 8. बाढः 'excessive'.

When the words have not the above sense, we have 1. क्षुभितं 'disturbed or agitated'. The phrase क्षुब्धो गिरिः or नदी is a metaphorical use of the word. 2. स्वनितः as स्वनितो मृदङ्गः, स्वनितं मनसा ॥ 3. ध्वनितो मृदङ्गः or ध्वनितं मनसा ॥ 4. लगितं, 5. म्लेच्छितं, (= अपभाषितं) 6. विरेभितं from रेभृ 'to sound', or विरिभितं from रिभि ॥ 7. फाणितं ॥ फाण्ट is a decoction, prepared without much trouble, by simply slightly heating the substance with some water, without powdering or pasting it. (यदशृतमपिष्टं च कषायमुदकसंपर्कमात्राद् विभक्तरसमीषदुष्णं) a medicine for any disease may be administered in five forms :—रसः or essence, कल्कः paste or powder, शृतः decoction or extract, शीतः cold extract prepared by throwing pounded drugs into cold water, and keeping that all night to soak. This watery extract, to be drunk in the morning, is so called. फाण्ट is a similar hot preparation, but for immediate use, when the drugs are put in boiling water and the decoction after purification is ready for use as a drink. 8. बाहितं from बाहृ 'to strive'.

धृषिशसी वैयात्ये ॥ १९ ॥ पदानि ॥ धृषि, शसी, वैयात्ये, ॥

वृत्तिः ॥ वियातस्य भावो वैयात्यम् प्रागल्भ्यमविनीतता ॥ तत्र धृष् शस् इत्येतयोर्निष्ठायामिडागमो न भवति ॥

19. The Participial affix does not get इट् augment, after the roots धृष् and शस्, when meaning 'bold, impudent and arrogant'.

As धृष्टः, विशस्तः ॥ The root धृष् is exhibited in the Dhâtupâṭha as ञिधृषा 'to be impudent' (V. 22), and as it has an indicatory आ, its past-participle would be अनिट् by VII. 2. 16. शस् is शसु in the Dhâtupâṭha (I. 763), and as it has an indicatory उ by VII. 2. 56. read with VII. 2. 15, its Nishṭhâ is also Aniṭ. The special mention of these roots here, is for the sake of making a niyama rule: namely, अनिट् only then when meaning 'impudent', and सेट् in other senses: as धर्षितः, विशसितः "धृष् never forms past participle with the force of भाव (Impersonal action) or आदिकर्म (beginning of action), and therefore VII. 2. 17 cannot apply to it"—This is Kâśikâ. According to Bhattoji Dikshit who quotes Haradatta and Mâdhava, धृष् forms participles in those senses, when option is allowed, as, धृष्टं or धर्षितं, प्रधृष्टः or प्रधर्षितः not meaning 'impudent'.

दृढः स्थूलबलयोः ॥ २० ॥ पदानि ॥ दृढः, स्थूल, बलयोः, ॥

वृत्तिः ॥ दृढ इति निपात्यते स्थूले बलवति चार्थे ॥

20. The irregularly formed Past Participle दृढ means 'stout' and 'strong'.

It is derived from दृंह् with क्त affix. In other senses, the forms are दृंहितम् or दृहितम् ॥ There are two roots one दृह् (I. 769) without nasal, and the other दृंह् (I. 770) with the nasal. दृढ can be derived from any one of these by eliding ह्, and the nasal, and changing त to ढ, and not adding the augment इट् ॥

The difference between स्थूल and बल is that a man may be stout or स्थूल without being strong (बलवान्) and *vice versa.* The word बल in the sûtra is equal to बलवत्; in fact, the word बल is formed by अच् affix. The irregularity in the formation of दृढ consists in the absence of इट् and the elision of ह् (and of न्, if the root दृंह be taken) : and the change of त into ढ ॥ This irregular elision of ह is for the sake of preventing the application of the rule पूर्वत्रासिद्धम् (VIII. 2. 1). The form could have been obtained in the regular way by the elision of ढ, thus : दृह्+त=दृढ्+त (VIII. 2. 31)=दृढ्+ध=दृढ्+ढ=दृ+ढ (VIII. 3. 13)=दृढ ॥ But then when ढ is elided, the rule पूर्वत्रासिद्धम् will apply, and the forms द्रढिमा, द्रढीयान्, द्रढयति could not be obtained. For ऋ is changed to र by VI. 4. 161 only when it is *laghu* or light, but ढ-lopa being considered asiddha, the ऋ would be heavy as standing before a conjunct consonant. So also the form परिदृढय्याऽगतः could not be obtained : for the णि would not be changed to अय् before ल्यप when the ऋ is not light or laghu (VI. 4. 56). So also, परिदृढस्यापत्यं=पारिदृढी (the daughter of Paridṛḍha) could not be formed. For ऋ being considered guru or heavy, the affix ष्यङ् would have come in the feminine (IV. 1. 78).

प्रभौ परिवृढः ॥ २१ ॥ पदानि ॥ प्रभौ, परिवृढः ॥

वृत्तिः ॥ परिवृढ इति निपात्यते प्रभुश्चेद्भवति ॥

21. The irregularly formed परिवृढ means 'Lord'.

This is formed, like दृढ, from वृह् or वृंह् ॥ When not having the sense of 'Lord', we have परिवृहितम् and परिवृंहितम् ॥

The ह is elided first as an anomaly. By so doing we can get the forms like परिव्रढयति, परिव्रढय्यगतः; पारिवृढीकन्या ॥ The form परिव्रढय्य is formed by ल्यप् instead of ktvâ ॥ Though the full noun is परिवृढ and णिच् is added to such a noun, yet for the purposes of ktvâ it is considered as a compound verb, having परि as upasarga. In fact, णिच् is added to वृढ, and the root becomes व्रढि, and then ktvâ is added to this root, and then there is compounding of परि with this word ending in ktvâ, and then by the regular process the ktvâ is replaced by ल्यप् ॥ The general rule is that Derivative roots formed from nouns, like परिवृढ, उत्मनस्, सुमनस् &c which have an upasarga as one of their formative elements, are treated as if they were compound verbs having those upasargas. The result of this is, that though the full noun is सुमनस्, yet in the derivative verb, सु will be treated as an upasarga, as in ordinary compound verbs. Thus the augment अ in the Imperfect is added after सु and not before it, as स्वमनायत, उद्मनायत ॥ The rule is उपसर्गसमानाकारं पूर्वपदं धातुसंज्ञाप्रयोजके प्रत्यये चिकीर्षिते पृथक् क्रियते ॥ The Participial form of these words is therefore with ल्यप् and not क्त्वा, as सुमनाय्य and उन्मनाय्य ॥ The only exception to this rule is the noun संग्राम, in which the upasarga सम् is not considered as a separate member in the Derivative verb. This being the general rule, in परिव्रश्चयति the portion परि is treated as an upasarga, and व्रश्चयति as the verb, and its accent is governed by तिङ्ङतिङः (VIII. 1. 28) i. e. it becomes altogether unaccented and परि retains its accent. So also परिव्रश्च्य, where is परि is compounded with the Participial form व्रश्चित्वा, and then क्त्वा is changed to ल्यप् by VII. 1. 37.

कृच्छ्रगहनयोः कषः ॥ २२ ॥ पदानि ॥ कृच्छ्र, गहनयोः, कषः, ॥

वृत्तिः ॥ कृच्छ्र गहन इत्येतयोरर्थयोः कषेर्धातोर्निष्ठायामिडागमो न भवति ॥

22. The Participial affix does not take the augment इट् after the root कष्, when the participle means 'difficult' and 'impenetrable'.

As कष्टो ऽग्निः, कष्टं व्याकरणं, ततोऽपि कष्टतराणि सामानि ॥ "Difficult is Fire-sacrifice i. e. it is difficult to completely master the ritual connected with the worship of fire; and difficult enough is Grammar, but the Sâmâns are worst of all". कष्टानि वनानि 'impervious forests.' कष्टाः पर्वताः ॥ When not havig these senses, we have कषितं सुवर्णम् ॥

घुषिरविशब्दने ॥ २३ ॥ पदानि ॥ घुषिः, अविशब्दने ॥

वृत्तिः ॥ घुषेर्धातोरविशब्दनेऽर्थे निष्ठायामिडागमो न भवति ॥

23. The Participial affix does not take the augment इट्, after the root घुष् in any sense other than that of 'proclaimed'.

As घुष्टा रज्जुः, घुष्टो पादौ but अवघुषितं वाक्यमाह ॥ विशब्दन = प्रतिज्ञानम् 'assertion, affirmation, agreement'. घुषिर् अविशब्दने is Bhvâdi (I. 683), and घुषिर् विशब्दने is Churâdi (X. 187), both of these are referred to in the sûtra. The prohibition of विशब्दन in the sûtra, indicates by jñâpaka thât the णिच् added to the root in the Churâdi class in the sense of विशब्दन is anitya. So the following construction becomes valid:-as महीपालवचः श्रुत्वा जुघुषुः पुष्पमाणवाः "expressed their opinions in words".

In short the णिच् is optionally added to the घुषिर् of the Churâdi class.

Some say the Churâdi णिच् is anitya generally and not only after घुषिर् (अनित्य ण्यन्ताश्चुरादयः) ॥ This is inferred from the mention of the root चिति स्मृत्याम् (X. 2) in this class. The indicatory इ in चिति shows that the augment

नुम् will be added to the root, which will thus become चिन्त and this न will be retained throughout and never dropped. (VII. 1. 48). Now had the णिच् been nitya, then the root ought to have been taught as चिन्त स्मृत्याम्, because no rule would have caused the elision of the न of चिन्त when णिच् was added. The enunciation of the root as चिति, therefore, indicates that the churâdi णिच् is anitya, and thus we get the forms like चिन्तितः, चिन्त्यात्, चिन्त्यते, चिन्तति, चिन्तेत् &c.

अर्दैः सन्निविभ्यः ॥ २४ ॥ पदानि ॥ अर्दैः, सम, नि, विभ्यः ॥

वृत्तिः ॥ सं नि वि इत्येतेभ्य उत्तरस्यार्देर्निष्ठायामिडागमो न भवति ॥

24. The Participial affix does not take the इट्, after the root अर्द when it is preceded by सं, नि or वि ॥

As समर्णः, 'plagued' न्यर्णः, व्यर्णः ॥ Why 'of अर्द'? Observe समेधितः ॥ Why 'सम, नि or वि'? Observe आर्दितः ॥

अभेश्चाविदूर्ये ॥ २५ ॥ पदानि ॥ अभेः, च, आविदूर्य्ये ॥

वृत्तिः ॥ अभिशब्दादुत्तरस्यार्देराविदूर्येर्थे निष्ठायामिडागमो न भवति ॥

25. The Participial affix does not take the इट्, after अर्द preceded by अभि, when the meaning is that of 'near'.

As अभ्यर्णा सेना, अभ्यर्णा शरत् ॥ Why 'when meaning near'? See अभ्यर्दितो वृषलः शीतेन meaning पीड़ितः॥ विदूरं means 'remote,' that which is not remote is अविदूरं 'non-remote,' the state of being non-remote is आविदूर्य्यम् 'non-remote-ness.' The affix ष्यञ् is added irregularly, in spite of the prohibition contained in V. 1. 121.

णेरध्ययने वृत्तम् ॥ २६ ॥ पदानि ॥ णेः, अध्ययने, वृत्तम् , ॥

वृत्तिः ॥ ण्यन्तस्य वृत्तेर्निष्ठायामध्ययनार्थे वृत्तमितीडभावो णिलुक् च निपात्यते ॥

26. The word वृत्त is formed from the causative of वृत्, in the sense of 'studied through or read.'

There is absence of इट् and luk-elision of the causative sign. As वृत्तो गुणो देवदत्तेन 'Devadatta has read or gone through Guṇa.' (गुणः पाठः पदक्रमसंहिता रूपोऽध्ययनविशेषः) II वृत्तं पारायणं देवदत्तेन ॥ When the sense is not that of 'read', we have वर्त्तितम् ॥ The root वृत् is intransitive, and becomes Transitive when employed in the Causative. The participle is formed from this Transitive causative verb, otherwise it could not have governed an object as shown above. " The affix क्त is added with a Passive force to वृत्, as we find the author himself using this form in निर्वृत्तम् in sûtras IV. 2. 68, and V. 1. 79; on the analogy of निर्वृत्त the word वृत्तः could also have been formed without this sûtra."

वा दान्तशान्तपूर्णदस्तस्पष्टच्छन्नज्ञप्ताः ॥२७॥ पदानि ॥ वा, दान्त, शान्त, पूर्ण, दस्त, स्पष्ट, छन्न, ज्ञप्ताः, ॥

वृत्तिः ॥ णेरित्यनुवर्त्तते। दम् शम् पूरी दस् स्पश् छद् ज्ञप् इत्येतेषां ण्यन्तानां धातूनां वा अनिट्त्वं निपात्यते ॥

27. The following irregularly formed Participles, from the causative roots, may optionally take **इट्**, namely, **दान्त, शान्त, पूर्ण, दस्त, स्पष्ट, छन्न, ज्ञप्त ॥**

These words are formed either from the causative base or from the primary roots दम् &c. The other forms are दमितः, शमितः, पूरितः, दासितः, स्पाशितः, छादितः and ज्ञपितः ॥ The words दान्त &c. are formed by the luk-elision of णि (Causative), and not taking the इट् Augment. By VII. 2. 49 ज्ञप् optionally is सेट् and, therefore, by VII. 2. 15, its Participle would have been *always* अनिट्, hence, this sûtra makes an option.

रुष्यमत्वरसंघुषास्वनाम् ॥ २८॥ पदानि ॥ रुषि, अम, त्वर, संघुष, आस्वनाम् ॥

वृत्तिः ॥ वेति वर्त्तते । रुषि अम त्वर संघुष आस्वन इत्येतेषां निष्ठायां वा इडागमो न भवति ॥

28. The Participial affix may optionally get **इट्** augment, after **रुष्, अम्; त्वर्, संघुष्,** and **आस्वन् ॥**

As रुष्टः or रुषितः ॥ By VII. 2. 48, the affixes after रुष् are *optionally* सेट्, and therefore by VII. 2. 15, the Nishṭhâ after this verb would have been *always* aniṭ; hence this optional rule. अभ्यान्तः or अभ्यमितः; तूर्णः or त्वरितः ॥ The त्वर् is exhibited in the Dhâtupâṭha as ञित्वरा (I. 812) i. e. with an indicatory long आ, and hence by VII. 2. 16. would have been aniṭ always, this rule makes it optionally aniṭ. So also, संघुष्टौ पादौ, or संघुषितौ पादौ संघुष्टं or संघुषितं वाक्यमाह, संघुष्टौ or संघुषितौ दम्भौ ॥ घुष preceded by सम् will be optionally aniṭ, even when having any sense other than that of 'proclaimed', as this *subsequent* sûtra supersedes VII. 2. 23 so far. So also आस्वान्तः or आस्वनितो देवदत्तः, आस्वान्तम् or आस्वनितं मनः ॥ स्वन् when preceded by आ, though denoting 'mind,' is *optionally* aniṭ, in spite of VII. 2. 18, that rule being superseded so far by this *subsequent* rule.

हृषेर्लोमसु ॥ २९ ॥ पदानि ॥ हृषेः, लोमसु, ॥

वृत्तिः ॥ लोमसु वर्त्तमानस्य हृषेर्निष्ठायां वा इडागमो न भवति ॥

वार्त्तिकम् ॥ विस्मितप्रतिघातयोश्चेति वक्तव्यम् ॥

29. The Participial affix optionally takes **इट्**, after **हृष्** when the word **लोमन्** or its synonym is in construction with it.

As हृष्टानि लोमानि or हृषितानि लोमानि; हृष्टाः केशाः or हृषिताः केशाः; हृष्टं or हृषितं लोमभिः or केशैः ॥ हृषु 'to lie' (I. 741) is exhibited with an indicatory उ in the Dhâtupâṭha, and would have been consequently *always* aniṭ, in the Nishṭhâ (VII. 2. 15) because it was optionally aniṭ before ktvâ (VII. 2. 56) hence this rule. हृष् 'to be delighted' (IV. 119) is also included here, this verb is सेट् ॥ The option appertains to both these verbs. The word लोम means the hair of the body as well as of the head: as in the sentence लोमनखं स्पृष्ट्वा शौचं कर्तव्यम् ॥ The sense of हृष in connection with लोम will be that of bristling up, horipillation. Why do we say "in connection with लोम?" Observe हृष्टो (bhuadi) देवदत्तः 'the deceived Deva Datta' and हृषितो (Divâdi) देवदत्तः 'the delighted Devadatta.

Vârt:—The option is allowed also in the senses of 'astonished' and 'beaten back', as हृष्टो or हृषितो देवदत्तः 'the astonished D'. हृष्टाः or हृषिता दन्ताः 'the bent or destroyed teeth'.

अपचितश्च ॥ ३० ॥ पदानि ॥ अपचितः, च, ॥

वृत्तिः ॥ अपचित इति वा निपात्यते । अपपूर्वस्य चायतेर्निष्ठायामनिट्त्वं चिभावश्च निपात्यते ।

वार्त्तिकम् ॥ क्तिनि नित्यमिति वक्तव्यम् ॥

30. And अपचित has also a second form with the augment इ ॥

The word अपचित is formed with the preposition अप added to the root चाय् (I. 929) 'to honor, to fear, to see' and चाय् changed irregularly to चि before क्त ॥ The other form is अपचायितः, as अपचितो or अपचायितो ऽनेनगुरुः 'the teacher is feared by him'. This example is given when the sense is that of 'fear'; when the word means 'honor', then the participle must govern the genitive case, as required by III. 2. 188.

Vârt:—Before क्तिन् affix, चाय् is always changed to चि, as अपचितिः 'Loss, destruction, showing reverence'. The affix क्तिन् is added to चाय्, by considering it as belonging to the class of आप् &c. See III. 3. 94 *Vârt.* Otherwise it would take the affix अ by III. 3. 103.

ह्रु ह्वरेश्छन्दसि ॥ ३१ ॥ पदानि ॥ ह्रु ह्वरेः, छन्दसि ॥

वृत्तिः ॥ ह्वरतेर्धातोर्निष्ठायां छन्दसि ह्रु इत्ययमादेशो भवति ।

31. ह्रु is substituted for ह्वर् (I. 978) in the Veda, before the Participial-affix.

As ह्रुतस्य चाह्रुतस्य च, अह्रुतमसि हविर्धानम् (Vaj San. I. 9). But ह्वृतम् in secular literature.

अपरिह्वृताश्च ॥ ३२ ॥ पदानि ॥ अपरिह्वृताः, च ॥

वृत्तिः ॥ अपरिह्वृता इति निपात्यते छन्दसि विषये । ह्रु इत्येतस्यादेशस्याभावो निपात्यते ।

32. The word 'aparihvṛitâ' is irregularly formed in the Veda.

The ह्रु substitution required by the last sûtra, does not take place here. As अपरिह्वृताः सनुयाम वाजम् (Rig I. 100. 19).

सोमे ह्वरितः ॥ ३३ ॥ पदानि ॥ सोमे, ह्वरितः ॥

वृत्तिः ॥ ह्वरित इति ह्वरतेर्निष्ठायामिडागमो गुणश्च निपात्यते छन्दसि विषये, सोमश्चेद्भवति ।

33. ह्वरित is irregularly formed from ह्वृ in the Veda, by guṇa substitution and इट् augment, when it refers to Soma.

As मा नः सोमो ह्वरितो, विह्वरितस्त्वम् ॥

ग्रसितस्कभितस्तभितोत्तभितचत्तविकस्ता विशस्तृशंस्तृशास्तृतरुतृतरूतृवरुतृवरूतृवरूत्रीरुज्ज्वलिति क्षरिति क्षमिति वमित्यमितीति च ॥ ३४ ॥ पदानि ॥ ग्रसित, स्कभित, स्तभित, उत्तभित, चत्त, विकस्त, विशस्तृ, शंस्तृ, शास्तृ, तरुतृ, तरूतृ, वरुतृ, वरूतृ, वरूत्रीः, उज्ज्वलिति, क्षरिति, क्षमिति, वमिति, अमिति, इति, च ॥

वृत्तिः ॥ ग्रसित स्कभित स्तभित उत्तभित चत्त विकस्त विशस्तृ शंस्तृ शा स्तृ तरुतृ तरूतृ वरुतृ वरूतृ वरूत्रीः उज्ज्वलिति क्षरिति क्षमिति वमित्यमिति इत्येतानि छन्दसि निपात्यन्ते ।

34. In the Veda, the following irregular forms are found, some with, and some without the augment इट—1 grasita, 2 skabhita, 3 stabhita, 4 uttabhita, 5 chatta, 6 vikasta, 7 viśastṛi, 8 śanstṛi, 9 śâstṛi, 10 tarutṛi, 11 tarûtṛi, 12 varutṛi, 13 varûtṛi, 14 varûtrîḥ, 15 ujjvaliti, 16 kshariti, 17 kshamiti; 18 vamiti and 19 amiti.

Of the above nineteen words, 1, 2, 3, and 4 are from roots ग्रसु, 'to swallow' (I. 661) स्कम्भु 'to stop' (I. 414) and स्तम्भु (I. 413) all having an indicatory उ, and therefore by VII. 2. 56 read with VII. 2. 15, their Nishṭhâ would not have taken इट् ॥ Thus ग्रसितं (ver. ग्रस्त) वा एतत् सोमस्य ॥ विष्कभिते अजरे (=विष्कब्धः); येन स्वस्तभितम् (=स्तब्धम्), सत्येनोत्तभिता भूमिः (=उत्तब्धः) ॥ The irregularity is only with the preposition उत्, with other prepositions, the form स्तभित is not employed. Similarly (5) चत्ता (=चतिता) वर्षेण विद्युत् from चते याच्ने॥ (6)उत्तानाया हृदयं यद् विकस्तम् (=विकासितम्) The forms, 7 8, and 9 are from the roots शसु हिंसायाम् and शंसु स्तुतौ, and शासु अनुशिष्टौ with the affix तृच् and no augment; as एकस्त्वष्टुरश्वस्याविशस्ता (=विशसिता), उत शंस्ता सुविप्रः (=शंसिता), प्रशास्ता (=प्रशासितम्)॥ The forms 10, 11, 12, 13 and 14 are from the roots तॄ and वृ (वृङ् and वृञ्), with the affix तृच्, and the augment उट् and ऊट् ॥ As तरुतारं or तरूतारं रथानाम् (=तरितारम् or तरीतारम्), वरुतारम् or वरूतारम् रथानाम् (=वरितारम् or वरीतारम्); वरूत्रीष्ट्वा देवीर्विश्वदेव्यावती ॥ वरूत्रीः is exhibited in this form of Nom. pl. of the feminine वरूत्री merely for the sake of showing one form in which it is found: another form is अहोरात्राणि वैवरूत्रयः ॥ Here the plural is formed irregularly, by taking the word as वरूत्रि ॥ The feminine form could have been easily obtained from वरूतृ, by adding ङीप्, the special mention is explanatory. The rest 15, 16, 17, 18 and 19 are from उत्-ज्वल, क्षर्, क्षम्, वम्, and अम्, formed with the vikaraṇa शप् and the affix of the 3rd Per Sing तिप्, इ being substituted for अ of शप, or शप् is elided and the augment इट् is added॥ As अग्निरुज्ज्वलिति (=उज्ज्वलति), स्तोमं क्षमिति (=क्षमति), स्तोकं क्षरिति (=क्षरति), यः सोमं वमिति (=वमति), अभ्यमिति वरुणः (=अभ्यमति) ॥ Sometimes we have अभ्यमीत, as रथमभ्यमीति ॥

आर्द्धधातुकस्येड्वलादेः ॥ ३५ ॥ पदानि ॥ आर्द्धधातुकस्य, इट्, वलादेः ॥

वृत्तिः ॥ छन्दसीति निवृत्तम् । आर्द्धधातुकस्य वलादेरिडागमो भवति ।

35. An ârdhadhâtuka affix (III. 4. 114 &c) beginning with a consonant (except य), gets the augment इट् (in these rules).

Thus लविता, लवितुम्, लवितव्यम्, पविता, पवितुम्, पवितव्यम् ॥ Why 'ârdhadhâtuka'? Observe आस्ते, वस्ते ॥ The niyama rule of VII. 2. 76 ordaining इट् augment to sârvadhâtuka affixes of Rudâdi verbs, would prevent इट् augment before sârvadhâtuka affixes when coming after other roots. The employment of ârdhadhâtuka here can be dispensed with. Why before affixes beginning with a वल्-consonant? Observe लव्यम्, पव्यम्, लवनीयम, पवनीयम् ॥ Though the anuvritti of इट् was understood here, its repetition is for the sake of preventing the prohibition of the foregoing sûtras like VII. 2. 8.

स्नुक्रमोरनात्मनेपदनिमित्ते ॥ ३६ ॥ पदानि ॥ स्नु, क्रमोः, अनात्मनेपदनिमित्ते ॥

वृत्तिः ॥ नियमार्थमिदम् । स्नुक्रमोरार्द्धधातुकस्य वलादेरिडागमो भवति, न चेत्स्नुक्रमौ आत्मनेपदस्य निमित्तं भवतः ।

वार्त्तिकम् ॥ क्रमस्तु कर्त्तर्यात्मनेपदविषयादसत्यात्मनेपदे कृति प्रतिषेधो वक्तव्यः ॥

36. The augment इट् is added to ârdhadhâtuka valâdi affixes after स्नु and क्रम, only then when they do not occasion the taking of the Personal endings of the Atmanepada.

The roots स्नु and क्रम् are udâtta, and will get इट् augment naturally, the sûtra makes a restriction or niyama. The restriction is that when the roots themselves occasion atmanepada affixes, then they do not take इट्, otherwise they will.

When do rootsgive occasion to Atmanepada affixes? The roots occasion atmanepada affixes when employed in the Impersonal, Passive, and Intensive senses. Sutras I. 3. 38-43, teach us when क्रम takes Âtmanepada affixes. Thus प्रस्नाविता, प्रस्नावितुम्, प्रस्नवितव्यम्, प्रक्रमिता, प्रक्रमितुम, प्रक्रमितव्यम् ॥ Why do we say 'when not the occasion of getting the Atmanepada affixes'? Observe, प्रस्नोषीष्ट, प्रक्रंसीष्ट, प्रस्नोष्यते, प्रक्रंस्यते, प्रस्नुषिष्यते, प्रचिक्रंसिष्यते ॥ In all these examples स्नु and क्रम् have become the causes of taking the Atmanepada affixes. The Desiderative is also Atmanepadi because of I. 3. 62.

Why have we used the word निमित्त in the sûtra? Would it not have been simpler to say स्नुक्रमोरनात्मनपदे? This form of sûtra would have indicated that whenever an âtmanepada affix followed, then there would be no इट् augment. Now the rule is that all words exhibited in the Locative case in this Grammar, have the force of परसप्तमी, i. e. when that word *follows*. Therefore आत्मनेपदे would mean when an âtmanependa affix followed. If then this "âtmanepada" be taken as qualifying स्नु and क्रम्, then it must follow *immediately* after those roots, as in प्रस्नोषीष्ट and प्रक्रंसीष्ट; but we would not get the forms प्रस्नोष्यते and प्रक्रस्यत, becanse स्य intervenes between the atmanepada and the affix. On the other hand if "atmanepada" be taken to qualify the word "ârdhadhâtuka affix" understood, viz, if the sûtra ment स्नुक्रमिभ्यां परस्यार्धधातुकस्यात्मनेपदेऽनन्तर then the forms प्रस्नोष्यते and प्रक्रंस्यते would be valid, but we should not get the forms प्रस्नोषीट and प्रक्रंसीष्ट, because the augment सीयुट् is a portion of the âtmanepada affix, and there is no ârdhdhâtuka affix here. If the sûtra be taken to have both the above senses, then we could not get the form प्रचिक्रंसिष्यते in the Desiderative, because here the âtmanepada does not follow immediately after the sârvadhâtuka affix that follows क्रम् ॥ Therefore, the word निमित्त should be taken. For by so doing, there takes place prohibition with regard to सीयुट &c, and also with regard to that after which comes the âtmanepada, as the स्य in प्राचक्रंसिष्यते, and also with regard to that which precedes the latter, as the सन् affix in the above. In प्रस्नाविचीयते (प्रस्नवितेवाचरति), the root स्नु has not occasioned the âtmanepada affix, but the affix क्यङ्, hence the prohibition of this sûtra does not apply.

Vârt:—Prohibition of इट् augment should be stated with regard to क्रम् when an Kṛit-affix, with active force, follows not in the âtmanepada, though in the Active voice such क्रम् was subject of Atmanepada. When क्रम् takes no upasargas, we have according to one view two forms क्रन्ता and क्रमिता (I. 3. 43) because the âtmanepada here is optional. According to the other view there will be only one form, as कामता ॥ But with प्र and उप् we have प्रक्रन्ता and उपक्रन्ता ॥ Why do we say 'the Kṛit-affix should have an active force'? Observe प्रक्रमितव्यम्, उपक्रमितव्यम् ॥ Why do we say "when it was subject of Atmanepada"? Observe निष्क्रमिता ॥ Here there is इट् augment; for by I. 3. 42, क्रम् is subject of atmanepada, when the upasargas प्र and उप precede, but not otherwise.

With regard to स्नु, it will take no इट् in the Desiderative, and before a कित् affix, by virtue of VII. 2. 11 and 12. Therefore, we have the forms प्रसुस्नुषति, प्रस्नुतः, प्रस्नुतवान् ॥

ग्रहो ऽलिटि दीर्घः ॥ ३७ ॥ पदानि ॥ ग्रहः, अ लिटि, दीर्घः ॥

वृत्तिः ॥ ग्रह उत्तरस्य इटः अलिटि दीर्घो भवति ।

37. The augment इट added to valâdi ârdhadhâtuka affixes, becomes lengthened, except in the Personal endings of the Perfect, after the root ग्रह ॥

As ग्रहीता, ग्रहीतुम्, ग्रहीतव्यम् ॥ Why not in the Perfect? Observe जगृहिव जगृहिम ॥ The lengthening takes place of the इट् taught in VII. 2. 35, and does not refer to the चिण्वद् इट् of VI. 4. 62: as ग्राहिता, ग्राहिष्यते ॥

वॄतो वा ॥ ३८ ॥ पदानि ॥ वॄतः वा ॥

वृत्तिः ॥ वॄ इति वृङ्वृञोः सामान्येन ग्रहणं तस्मादुत्तरस्य ॠकारान्तेभ्यश्चेटो वा दीर्घो भवति ।

38. The इट् is optionally lengthened after वृङ्, वृञ् and after roots ending in long ॠ, except in the Perfect.

As वरिता । वरीता । प्रावरिता । प्रावरीता ॥ ॠकारान्तेभ्यः । तरिता । तरीता । आस्तरिता । आस्तरीता ॥ वृत इति किम् । करिष्यति हरिष्यति । अभिलिलविथ । ववरिथ । तेरिथ ॥ Why do we say 'after वृ and long ॠ ending roots'? Observe करिष्यति and हरिष्यति ॥ Why do we say except in the Perfect? Observe ववरिथ and तेरिथ ॥

न लिङि ॥ ३९ ॥ पदानि ॥ न, लिङि ॥

वृत्तिः ॥ वृत उत्तरस्य इटो लिङि दीर्घो न भवति ।

39. The इट् is not lengthened after the same roots वृ, and ॠ ending roots, in the endings of the Benedictive.

As विवरिषीष्ट, प्रावरिषीष्ट, आस्तरिषीष्ट, विस्तरिषीष्ट ॥

सिचि च परस्मैपदेषु ॥ ४० ॥ पदानि ॥ सिचि, च, परस्मैपदेषु ॥

वृत्तिः ॥ परस्मैपदपरे सिचि वृत उत्तरस्य इटो दीर्घो न भवति ।

40. The इट् is not lengthened after वृ and ॠ ending roots, in the s-Aorist of the Parasmaipada.

As प्रावारिष्टाम्, प्रावारिषुः, अतारिष्टाम्, from तॄ प्लवनतरणयोः ॥ आस्तारिष्टाम्, आस्तारिषुः, from स्तॄञ् आच्छादने; but प्रावरिष्ट, प्रावरीष्ट in the Atmanepada.

इट् सनि वा ॥ ४१ ॥ पदानि ॥ इट्, सनि, वा ॥

वृत्तिः ॥ वृतः सनो वा इडागमो भवति ।

41. The Desiderative स् may optionaly take इट् (which is optionally lengthened also) after the said वृ and ॠ ending roots.

As वुवूर्षति । विवरिषते । विवरीषते । प्रावुवूर्षति । प्राविवरिषति । प्राविवरीषति । ॠकारान्तेभ्यः। तितीर्षति । तितरिषति । तितरीषति । आतिस्तीर्षति । This Parasmaipada form is not valid, according to Padamanjari. आतिस्तरिषति । आतिस्तरीषति । सनि ग्रहगुहश्चेति इट्प्रतिषेधे प्राप्ते पक्षे इडागमो विधीयते । इटश्च वृतो वेति पक्षेदीर्घः । चिकीर्षति जिहीर्षति इत्यत्रोपदेशोधिकाराल्लाक्षणिकत्वाच्च इडागमो न भवति ॥

The इट् was prohibited by VII. 2. 12, in case of the Desideratives, hence this sûtra: when इट् is added, it may be lengthened by VII. 2. 38. The augment इट् however is not added in चिकीर्षति and जिहीर्षति, as they are formed from कृ 'to do' and हृ 'to lose', which do not take इट् at all. Because here, though the short ऋ is lengthened before सन् by VI. 4. 16, yet such lengthening will not make the roots long ॠ ending roots. Because the anuvṛitti of the word upadeśa is understood here from VII. 2. 10, so that the rule applies to those roots only which in 'upadeśa' or Dhâtupâṭha end in long ॠ and not those whose ऋ is lengthened by some Grammatical rule. Moreover, the long ॠ in कृ and हृ is temporary only, as it is replaced by long ई ॥ (See VI. 4. 16, for lengthening). The Desiderative of कॄ—चिकरिषति, however, does not lengthen its vowel (VII. 2. 75).

लिङ्सिचोरात्मनेपदेषु ॥ ४२ ॥ पदानि ॥ लिङ्, सिचोः, आत्मनेपदेषु ॥

वृत्तिः ॥ लिङि सिचि च आत्मनेपदे परे वा इडागमो भवति ।

42. The इट् is optionally added to the endings of the Atmanepada Benedictive and s-Aorist, after the ॠ and ऋ ending roots.

As वृषीष्ट or वरिषीष्ट, प्रावृषीष्ट (I. 2. 12 no guṇa) प्रावरिषीष्ट, आस्तरिषीष्ट, आस्तीर्षीष्ट ॥ सिचिखल्वपि, अवृत, अवरिष्ट, अवरीष्ट, प्रावृत, प्रावरिष्ट, प्रावरीष्ट, आस्तीर्ष्ट, आस्तरिष्ट, आस्तरीष्ट॥ आत्मनेपदेष्विति किम्, ? प्रावारिष्टाम्, प्रावारिषुः ॥ लिङः प्रत्युदाहरणं न दर्शितमसम्भवादिटो ऽवलादित्वादिति ॥

Why in the Atmanepada? Observe प्रावारिष्टाम्, प्रावारिषुः ॥ No counter-examples of Benedictive Parasmaipadi are given, as the affixes not being वलादि, the इट् can never be added to them.

ऋतश्च संयोगादेः ॥ ४३ ॥ पदानि ॥ ऋतः, च, संयोगादेः ॥

वृत्तिः ॥ ऋदन्ताद्धातोः संयोगादेरुत्तरयोर्लिङ्सिचोरात्मनेपदेषु वा इडागमो भवति ।

43. The इट् is optionally added to the endings of the Atmanepada Benedictive and S-Aorist, after a root, which ends in short ऋ, which is preceded by a conjunct consonant.

As ध्वृषीष्ट or ध्वरिषीष्ट ; स्मृषीष्ट, or स्मरिषीष्ट ; अध्वृषाताम्, or अध्वरिषाताम् ; अस्मृषाताम्, or अस्मरिषाताम् ॥ ऋत इति किम् । च्योषीष्ट, प्लोषीष्ट; अच्योष्ट, अप्लोष्ट ॥ संयोगादेरिति किम् । कृषीष्ट, हृषीष्ट; अकृत, अहृत ॥ आत्मनेपदेष्वित्येव । अध्वार्षीत्, अस्मार्षीत् ॥ संस्कृषीष्ट समस्कृतेत्यत्रोपदेशाधिकारादभक्तत्वाच्च सुट् इडागमो न भवति ॥

Why ending in short ऋ? Observe च्योषीष्ट, अच्योष्ट, प्लोषीष्ट and अप्लोष्ट ॥ Why 'beginning with a conjunct consonant'? Observe कृषीष्ट, हृषीष्ट, अकृत and अहृत ॥ Why 'in the Atmanepada'? Observe अध्वार्षीत्, अस्मार्षीत् ॥ In संस्कृषीष्ट and समस्कृत there is not इट्, first because स्कृ (the form assumed by कृ with सुट् augment) is not so enunciated in the Dhâtupaṭha; the word upadeśa VII. 2. 10, is understood here; so that the rule applies to those roots only which in the Dhâtupaṭha are ऋ ending and preceded by conjunct consonant; and secondly' सुट् augment is considered as not attached to the root (VI. 1. 135), and therefore स्कृ is not considered a root beginning with a conjunct consonant.

स्वरतिसूतिसूयतिधूञूदितो वा ॥ ४४ ॥ पदानि ॥ स्वरति, सूति, सूयति, धूञ, ऊदितः, वा ॥

वृत्तिः ॥ स्वरति सूति सूयति धूञ् इत्येतेभ्य ऊदिद्भ्यश्चोत्तरस्य वलादेरार्द्धधातुकस्य वा इडागमो भवति ।

44. A Valâdi-ârdhadhâtuka affix optionally takes इट्, after svṛi, after the two roots सू (sûti and sûyati), after धूञ्, and after a root which has an indicatory long ऊ ॥

As स्वरिता or स्वर्त्ता ॥ प्रसोता, प्रसविता ॥ सूयति, सोता, सविता ॥ धूञ्, धोता, धविता ॥ ऊदिद्भ्यः खल्वपि । गाहू, विगाढा, विगाहिता ; गुपू, गोप्ता, गोपिता ॥ वेति वर्त्तमाने पुनर्वाग्रहणं लिङ्सिचोर्निवृत्त्यर्थम । सूतिसूयत्योर्विकरणनिर्देशः षू प्रेरणइत्यस्य निवृत्त्यर्थः । धूञिति सानुबन्धकस्य निर्देशो धू

विधूननइत्यस्य निवृत्त्यर्थः । सविता धवितेत्येव नित्यमेतयोर्भवति । स्वरतेरेतस्माद्विकल्पाद्दूद्गनोः स्यइत्येतद्भ-वति विप्रतिषधेन । स्वारिष्यति । किति तु प्रत्यये श्रुधकः कितीति नित्यः प्रतिषेधो भवति पूर्वप्रतिषेधेन ॥ स्वृत्वा, सूत्वा, धूत्वा ॥

Though the anuvṛitti of वा was current, the second employment of वा is to stop the anuvṛitti of the Benedictive and the S-Aorist. The roots सू of Adâdi (21) and Divâdi (24) are to be taken, as the special forms सूति and सूयति indicate, and not the सू of the Tudâdi (115) class. The धू is exhibited with the anubandha ञ्, in order to exclude धू विधूनने of Tudâdi (105). In the case of these latter the इट् augment is invariable, as सविता and धविता ॥ The root स्वृ takes invariably इट् in the Future, by virtue of the subsequent superseding rule VII. 2. 70, as स्वारिष्यति ॥ And before कित् affixes, the prior rule VII. 2. 11, invariably debars इट्, as स्वृत्वा, सूत्वा, धूत्वा ॥

रधादिभ्यश्च ॥ ४५ ॥ पदानि ॥ रध-आदिभ्यः, च ॥

वृत्तिः ॥ रध हिंसासंसिद्धावित्येवमादिभ्यो ऽष्टाभ्य उत्तरस्य वलादेरार्द्धधातुकस्य वा इडागमो भवति ॥

45. A valâdi-ârdhadhâtuka affix optionally takes इट् after रध् and the seven roots that follow it (Divâdi. 84 to 91).

As रधिता or रद्धा ; नंष्टा, (VII. 1. 60 नुम्) नशिता ; त्रप्ता, (VI. 1. 59 अम्) तर्प्ता, तर्पिता : द्रप्ता, दर्प्ता, दर्पिता ; द्रोग्धा, द्रोढा, (VIII. 2. 33) द्रोहिता ; मोग्धा, मोढा, मोहिता ; स्नोढा, स्नोहिता, स्नोग्धा, स्नेग्धा, स्नेढा, स्नेहिता ॥

Some hold that the रधादि roots *optionally* take इट् in the Perfect Tense also, because the present sûtra being subsequent to VII. 2. 13, debars that sûtra so far. Others hold that the रधादि roots will *always* take इट् in the Perfect, because the former rule VII. 2. 13 is stronger than the present, in as much as that is a prohibitory rule. So they form ररन्धिव and ररन्धिम ॥

निरः कुषः ॥ ४६ ॥ पदानि ॥ निरः, कुषः ॥

वृत्तिः ॥ निर इत्येवंपूर्वात् कुश उत्तरस्य वलादेरार्द्धधातुकस्य वा इडागमो भवति ।

46. A valâdi-ârdhadhâtuka affix gets optionally the augment इट्, after कुष् when it is preceded by निर् ॥

As निष्क्रोष्टा or निष्क्रोषिता, निष्क्रोष्टुम् or निष्क्रोषितुम्, निष्क्रोष्टव्यम् or निष्क्रोषितव्यम् ॥ But only कोषिता, कोषितुं, कोषितव्यम् without निर् ॥ The exhibition of निर् instead of निस् indicates the existence of a separate and distinct preposition निर्, besides निस् ॥ It is the र् of this निर् which is changed to ल् by VIII. 2. 19, in निलयनम् ; for the र् of निस् being asiddha could not be changed to ल् ॥

इण्निष्ठायाम् ॥ ४७ ॥ पदानि ॥ इट्, निष्ठायाम् ॥

वृत्तिः ॥ निरः कुषो निष्ठायामिडागमो भवति ।

47. The augment इट् is added to the Participial affixes त and तवत्, after कुष् preceded by निर् ॥

As निष्कुषितवान्, निष्कुषितः ॥ The special mention of इट् in the sûtra is for the sake of making its addition invariable, otherwise it would have been optional, or debarred by VII. 2. 15. In the subsequent sûtra, the addition becomes again optional.

तीषसहलुभरुषरिषः ॥ ४८ ॥ पदानि ॥ ति, इष, सह, लुभ, रुष, रिषः ॥

वृत्तिः ॥ तकारादावार्द्धधातुके इषु सह लुभ रुष रिष् इत्येतेभ्यो वा इडागमो भवति ।

48. An ârdhadhâtuka affix beginning with a त may optionally take the इट्, after the roots इष्, सह्, लुभ्, रुष् and रिष् ॥

As एष्टा or एषिता ॥ The इष् 'to wish' (VI. 59) is taken here, and not the इष् (IV. 19. IX. 53) of the Divâdi and Kryâdi class. Of the Divâdi इष् 'to send, to go' we have invariably प्रेषिता, प्रेषितुं, प्रेषितव्यं ; and the इष् 'to repeat' of the Kryâdi is governed also by this rule and has the same forms. Therefore some read the anuvṛitti of उदित् into this sûtra. सह। सोढा । सहिता । लुभ। लोभिता । लोब्धा । रुष। रोष्टा । रोषिता। रिष् । रेष्टा । रेषिता ॥ Why do we say 'beginning with a त'? Observe एषिष्यति ॥

सनीवन्तर्द्धभ्रस्जदम्भुश्रिस्वृयूर्णुभरज्ञपिसनाम् ॥ ४६ ॥ पदानि ॥ सनि, इवन्त, ऋध, भ्रस्ज, दम्भ, श्रि, स्वृ, यु, ऊर्णु, भर, ज्ञपि, सनाम् ॥

वृत्तिः ॥ इवान्तानाम धातूनाम् । ऋधु भ्रस्ज दम्भु श्रि स्वृ यु ऊर्णु भर ज्ञपि सन् इत्येतेषां च सनि वा इडागमो भवति।

49. The desiderative स् may optionally take इट्, after a root ending in इव्, and after ऋधु, भ्रस्ज, दम्भु, श्रि, स्वृ, यु, ऊर्णु, भृ, ज्ञप्, and सन् ॥

Thus दिदेविषति or दुद्यूषति, सिसेविषति, सुस्यूषति ॥ ऋध्, अर्दिधिषति, ईर्त्सति ॥ भ्रस्ज, बिभ्रज्जिषति, (VI. 4. 47) बिभ्रक्षति, (VIII. 2. 36 and 41) बिभर्ज्जिषति, बिभर्क्षति ॥ दम्भु. दिदम्भिषति, धिप्सति, (VII. 4. 56) धीप्सति, श्रि, उच्छिश्रयिषति, उच्छिश्रीषति ॥ स्वृ, सिस्वरिषति, सुस्वूर्षति ॥ यु, यियविषति, (VII. 4. 80) युयूषति, ऊर्णु, प्रोर्णुनविषति, प्रोर्णुनुविषति, प्रोर्णुनूषति, ॥ The root भृञ् of the Bhuâdi class is to be taken, as the form भर with शप् in the sûtra indicates. बिभरिषति, बुभूर्षति,॥ ज्ञपि, जिज्ञपयिषति, ज्ञीप्सति ॥ सन्, सिसनिषति, सिषासति ॥ केचिदत्रभरज्ञपिसनितनिपतिदरिद्राणामिति पठन्ति, ॥ तितनिषति, तितंसति, तितांसति, पिपतिषति, पित्सति, दिदरिद्रिषति, दिदरिद्रासति ॥ सनीति किम, देविता, भ्रष्टा ॥

Some add तन्, पत् and दरिद्रा also, as तितनिषति or तितंसति or तितांसति, (VI. 4. 17) पिपतिषति or पित्सति (VII. 4. 54, VIII. 2. 29. VII. 4. 58) दिदरिद्रिषति or दिदरिद्रासति ॥ Why do we say 'Desiderative'? Observe देविता, भ्रष्टा ॥ The form अर्दिधिषति is thus evolved. The Desiderative root is अर्धिस, the ऋ being guṇated by VII. 3. 86 before सन् ॥ Now we reduplicate it, and the second syllable धिस् will be reduplicated by VI. 1. 2. and the रेफ is not duplicated by VI. 1. 3: so we get धिस् to reduplicate, and ध is changed to द ॥ The form ईर्त्सति is thus evolved. By VII. 4. 55, the ऋ is changed to long ई, which is followed by र् by I. 1. 57. Thus we have ईर्ध्स् as root, and ध्स is reduplicated, and the reduplicate is elided (VII. 4. 58). The forms धिप्सति and धीप्सति are similarly formed.

क्लिशः क्त्वानिष्ठयोः ॥ ५० ॥ पदानि ॥ क्लिशः, क्त्वा, निष्ठयोः ॥ ५० ॥
वृत्तिः । क्लिशः क्त्वानिष्ठयोर्वा इडागमो भवति ।

50. The affixes ktvâ, क्त and क्तवतु, may optionally take इट् after क्लिश् ॥

As क्लिष्ट्वा or क्लिशित्वा, क्लिष्टः or क्लिशितः, क्लिष्टवान् or क्लिशितवान् ॥ क्लिशू (IX. 50) having an indicatory ऊ would have optionally taken इट् before ktvâ by VII. 2. 44, but then the Nishṭhâ affixes by VII. 2. 15 would never have taken the augment. क्लिश् (Divâdi 52) उपतापे, being anudâtta would *always* have taken इट् before ktvâ and Nishṭhâ. Hence this rule ordains option with regard to ktvâ.

पूङश्च ॥ ५१ ॥ पदानि ॥ पूङः, च ॥
वृत्तिः ॥ पूङश्च क्त्वानिष्ठयोर्वा इडागमो भवति ।

51. The affixes ktvâ, क्त and क्तवतु optionally get इट् after पू ॥

As पूत्वा or पवित्वा, सोमोतिपूतः, सोमोतिपवितः पूतवान् or पवितवान् ॥ This allows option where by VII. 2. 11 there would have been prohibition. See I. 2. 22.

वसतिक्षुधोरिट् ॥ ५२ ॥ पदानि ॥ वसति, क्षुधोः, इट् ॥
वृत्तिः ॥ वसतेः क्षुधेश्च क्त्वानिष्ठयोरिडागमो भवति ।

52. The affix ktvâ, kta and ktavatu always receive the augment इट् after वस् (वसति) and क्षुध् ॥

As उषित्वा, उषितः and उषितवान्, क्षुधित्वा, क्षुधितः, क्षुधितवान् ॥ The वस् of the Adâdi class will get इट् as it is enumerated in the list of सेट् roots. The repetition of इट् shows that the rule is invariable, the 'optionally' of the preceding sûtra does not affect it.

अञ्चेः पूजायाम् ॥ ५३ ॥ पदानि ॥ अञ्चेः, पूजायाम् ॥
वृत्तिः ॥ अञ्चेः पूजायामर्थे क्त्वानिष्ठयोरिडागमो भवति ।

53. The affixes ktvâ, kta and ktavatu take the augment इट् after the root अञ्च्, when meaning 'to honor or do something to show honor'.

As अञ्चित्वा जानु जुहोति, अञ्चिता अस्य गुरवः (III. 2. 188, VI. 4. 30, II. 3. 67) By VII. 2. 56 अञ्चु would optionally have caused इट् to come before ktvâ, and hence by VII. 2. 15 never before the Nishṭhâ. This sûtra ordains invariable addition of this augment. Why do we say when meaning 'to honor'? Observe उदक्तमुदकं कूपात्, 'the water is raised from the well'.

लुभो विमोहने ॥ ५४ ॥ पदानि ॥ लुभः, विमोहने ॥
वृत्तिः ॥ लुभो विमोहनेर्थे वर्तमानात् क्त्वानिष्ठयोरिडागमो भवति ।

54. The affixes ktvâ, kta and ktavatu take इट् after the root लुभ् (Tud. 22) when meaning 'entangled or confused'.

As लुभित्वा and लोभित्वा, विलुभिताः केशाः, विलुभितः सीमन्तः, विलुभितानि पदानि ॥ विमोहनं = आकुलीकरणं ॥ By VII. 2. 48 लुभ would have optionally caused इट् to come before ktvâ, and then by VII. 2. 15 the Nishṭhâ would never have been सेट् ॥ Hence this sûtra. Why do we say when meaning 'to entangle'? See लुब्धः वृषलः = शीतेन पीडितः, ॥ लुभ् 'to be greedy' (Div. 128) is not governed by this rule, but by VII. 2. 48. As लुब्ध्वा or लोभित्वा and लुभित्वा (I. 2. 26) ॥

जॄव्रश्चोः क्त्वि ॥ ५५ ॥ पदानि ॥ जॄ, व्रश्चोः, क्त्वि ॥

वृत्तिः ॥ जॄ व्रश्चि इत्येतयोः क्त्वाप्रत्यये इडागमो भवति ।

55. The affix ktvâ takes the augment इट्, after जॄ and व्रश्च् ॥

As जरित्वा or जरीत्वा, (VII. 2. 38) and व्रश्चित्वा ॥ जॄ was prohibited by VII. 2. 11. and व्रश्च would have been optionally सेट्, as it has an indicatory long ऊ, by VII. 2. 44. Hence this rule. The special mention of ktvâ, stops the anuvṛitti of kta and ktavatu.

उदितो वा ॥ ५६ ॥ पदानि ॥ उदितः, वा ॥

वृत्तिः ॥ उदितो धातोः क्त्वाप्रत्यये परतो वा इडागमो भवति ।

56. The इट् is optionally the augment of ktvâ, after a root which has an indicatory short उ ॥

As शमु—शमित्वा or शान्त्वा; तमु—तमित्वा or तान्त्वा; दमु—दमित्वा or दान्त्वा ॥

से ऽसिचि कृतचृतच्छृदतृदनृतः ॥ ५७ ॥ पदानि ॥ से, असिचि, कृत, चृत, छृद, तृद, नृतः ॥

वृत्तिः ॥ सकारादावसिच्यार्द्धधातुके कृत चृत छृद तृद नृत इत्येतेभ्यो धातुभ्यो वा इडागमो भवति ।

57. An ârdhadhâtuka affix beginning with a स् (except सिच् the characteristic of the s-Aorist) may optionally take the augment इट्, after the verbs कृत्, (Tud 141, Rudh. 11) चृत, (Tud. 35) छृद् (Rudh. 8) तृद् (Tud. 9) and नृत् (Div. 9).

As कर्त्स्यति, अकर्त्स्यत्, चिकृत्सति कर्तिष्यति, अकर्तिष्यत् चिकर्तिषति । चृत, चर्त्स्यति अचर्त्स्यत्, चिचृत्सति, चर्तिष्यति, अचर्तिष्यत्, चिचर्तिषति । छृद्, छर्त्स्यति । अच्छर्त्स्यत्, चिच्छृत्सति । छर्दिष्यति, अच्छर्दिष्यत् । चिच्छर्दिषति । तृद्, तर्त्स्यति, अतर्त्स्यत्, तितृत्सति, तर्दिष्यति । अतर्दिष्यत् । तितर्दिषति । नृत्, नर्त्स्यति, अनर्त्स्यत्, निनृत्सति, नर्तिष्यति । अनर्तिष्यत् । निनर्तिषति ।

Why do we say 'beginning with a स्'? Observe कर्तिता ॥ Why असिचि? Observe अकर्तीत् ॥

गमेरिट् परस्मैपदेषु ॥ ५८ ॥ पदानि ॥ गमेः, इट्, परस्मैपदेषु ॥

वृत्तिः ॥ गमेर्धातोः सकारादेरार्द्धधातुकस्य परस्मैपदेष्विडागमो भवति ।

इष्टिः ॥ आत्मनेपदेन समानपदस्थस्य गमेरयमिडागमोनेष्यते ॥

58. An ârdhadhatuka affix beginning with a स् gets the इट् augment, after गम् in the Parasmaipada.

As गमिष्यति, अगमिष्यत्, जिगमिषति ॥ Why of गम्? Observe चेष्यति ॥ The repetition of इट् shows that the rule is invariable. Why 'in the Parasmaipada'? Observe संगंसीष्ट; संगसीष्ट, संगंस्यते, संजिगंसते, संजिगंसिष्यते, अधिजिगांसते, अधिजिगांसिष्यते ॥

The lengthening takes place by VI 4 16 when गम् is the substitute of the root इङ् (II. 4. 48) Why before स्? Observe गन्तास्मि, गन्तास्वः, गन्तास्मः ॥

Ishti: This इट् augment is not desired of the root गम standing in the same pada with an atmanepada affix. But it occurs every where else. As जिगमिषिता इव आचरति = जिगमिषित्रीयते, here there is इट् augment, because âtmanepada affix is not in the same pada with गम्, but is bahiranga. Compare VII. 2. 36 *vart.* It occurs before kṛit affixes, and even where is luk-elsion of Parasmaipada affix, and where therefore the affix generally would have left no trace behind by I. 1. 63. As संजिगमिषिता and अधिजिगमिषिता व्याकरणस्य ॥ So also जिगमिषस्व, here there is luk-elision of the Imperative affix ह्रि ॥ The opinion of the author of Padaśeshakâra is that the employment of the term Parsmaipada in the sûtra is illustrative. He explains it by saying:—परस्मैपदेषु यो गमिरुपलक्षित स्तस्मात् सकारादेरार्धधातुकस्य इट् भवति ॥ According to him we have the forms सजिगसिता and अधिजिगंसिता व्याकरणस्य ॥

न वृद्भ्यश्चतुर्भ्यः ॥ ५६ ॥ पदानि ॥ न, वृद्भ्यः, चतुर्भ्यः, ॥

वृत्तिः ॥ वृतादिभ्यश्चतुर्भ्य उत्तरस्य सकारादेरार्द्धधातुकस्य परस्मैपदेषु इडागमो न भवति ।

59. The Parasmaipada ârdhadhâtuka affixes beginning with स् do not get the augment इट् after वृत् and the three roots that follow it.

Thus वृत्—वर्त्स्यति, अवर्त्स्यत्, विवृत्सति । वृध् वर्त्स्यति । अवर्त्स्यत् । विवृत्सति । शृधु । शर्त्स्यति । अशर्त्स्यत् शिशृत्सति । स्यन्दू । स्यन्त्सति । अस्यन्त्स्यत् ।

The वृतादि roots are four वृत्, वृध्, शृध् and स्यन्द (Bhu. 795-798). In the examples, the Parasmaipada forms are shown, because these roots are optionally Parasmaipadi by I. 3. 92 before स्य and सन् ॥

Obj :—The word चतुर्भ्यः may conveniently have been omitted from the sûtra. A reference to the Dhâtupâṭha will show that the वृतादि roots form a subdivision of द्युतादि roots, and stand at the end of Dyutâdi class. So that the sûtra न वृद्भ्यः would have been enough, and there would have been no uncertainty or vagueness about it, for the word वृतादि would mean 'the roots वृत् &c. with which the Dyutâdi class ends'. Thus we shall get the *five* roots 795 वृतु वर्तने 796 वृधु वृद्धौ, 797 शृधु शब्दकुत्सायाम्; 798 स्यन्दू प्रस्रवणे and कृपू सामर्थ्ये ॥ As regards the last root कृपू, we shall find from the next sûtra, that the present sûtra applies to this root also. Or we can change the order of the roots, putting कृपू first, and वृतु &c after it, so that वृतादि will mean *four* roots only. Whether vṛitâdi be taken to mean the *five* or the *four* roots, the word चतुर्भ्यः is redundant.

Ans :—The word चतुर्भ्यः is used in order that the prohibition contained in this sûtra may debar the 'option' which the root स्यन्दू would have taken, because of its indicatory long ऊ (VII. 2. 44). For this 'option' is an antaranga operation, because it applies to *all* ârdhadhâtuka affixes ; while the 'prohibition' of the present sûtra is a bahiranga, because it applies to those affixes only which begin with च ॥ So that the 'prohibition' of this sûtra would not have debarred the 'option' of VII. 2. 44 : and in the Parasmaipada स्यन्दू would have had two forms; which, however, is not the case because of the word चतुर्भ्यः by which the 'prohibiton' is extended to स्यन्दू also. Thus in the Parasmaipada, we have only one form, as, स्यन्त्स्यति; but in the Atmanepada we have *two* forms स्यन्दिष्यते or स्यन्त्स्यते ॥

The word 'Parsmaipada' is understood in this sûtra, so that the prohibition does not apply to âtmanepada affixes: as वर्त्तिषीष्ट, वर्तिष्यते, अवर्तिष्यत्, विवर्तिष्यते, स्यन्दिषीष्ट or स्यन्त्सीष्ट ॥ Moreover, with regard to Atmanepada also, the इट् is added to these roots when they stand in the same 'pada' with the affixes. But when the Atmanepada affixes are added not to the *roots* 'vṛit &c', but to the *roots* which are derived from the *nominal* bases formed from 'vṛit &c', then the '*root*' is not in the same pada with the affix, and the prohibition of this sûtra will apply. As विवृत्सित्रीयते ॥ Moreover, the rule applies, as we have said, to the affixes standing in the same 'pada' with the 'roots'; therefore it will apply to Desiderative roots, as विवृत्सति, though शप् here intervenes between the ârdhadhatuka affix सन् and the Parasmaipada तिप्; so also, an ekâdeśa though sthânivat and therefore an intervention, will not be considered so for the purposes of this rule, as विवृत्सिष्यति; so also in विवृत्सयति ॥ The prohibition, moreover, applies to कृत् affixes, and where there is luk-elision of Parasmaipada affixes. As विवृत्सिता; and विवृत्स स्वम् where the Imperative हि is luk-elided, and being so elided, the force of Parasmaipada does not here remain by न लुमताङ्गस्य (I. 1. 63); hence the above *Ishti.*

तासि च क्लृपः ॥ ६० ॥ पदानि ॥ तासि, च, क्लृपः ॥

वृत्तिः ॥ कृप उत्तरस्य तासेः सकारादेश्चार्द्धधातुकस्य परस्मैपदेषु इडागमो न भवति ।

60. The Parasmaipada ârdhadhâtuka affixes beginning with स्, and the affix तास् (the sign of the Periphrastic Future) do not get the augment इट्, after the root क्लृप् ॥

Thus कल्प्ता, कल्प्स्यति, अकल्प्स्यत्, चिक्लप्स्यति ॥ But कल्पितासे, कल्पिषीष्ट, कल्पिष्यते, अकल्पिष्यत, चिकल्पिषते in the Âtmanepada.

In the case of क्लृप् also, the इट् is added to the ârdhadhâtuka affixes in the Atmanepada, when the root stands in the same pada with the affixes and there is prohibition everywhere else. So also there is prohibition before kṛit-affixes, and the luk-elision of Parasmaipada. As चिक्लप्सिता, चिक्लप्स त्वं ॥

According to Padamanjari, these two sûtras could have been shortened thus:—(1) न वृद्भ्यः पञ्चभ्यः, (2) तासि च; and "क्लृपः" could well have been omitted. The तास् comes only after क्लृप and not after other roots of Vṛitâdi class, in Parasmaipada [L 3. 92 and 93]. Therefore, there is no fear that the prohibition तासि च will apply to the other roots of vṛitâdi, but only to 'klip', because the word परस्मैपदेषु is understood here; and as no roots of vṛitadi class take Parasmaipada in the Periphrastic Future except 'klip', there is no fear of any ambiguity.

अचस्तास्वत्थल्यनिटो नित्यम् ॥ ६१ ॥ पदानि ॥ अचः, तास्वत्, थलि, अनिटः, नित्यम्, ॥

वृत्तिः ॥ तासौ ये नित्यानिटो धातवोऽजन्तास्तेभ्यस्तासाविव थलीडागमो न भवति ।

61. After a root, which ends in a vowel, and after which the Per. Fut. affix tâsi is always devoid of the augment इट्; (after such a root) थल् the personal ending of the Perfect, like तास्, does not also get the augment इट् ॥

Those vowel-ending roots in Dhâtupâṭha which are *invariably* aniṭ before the affix तास् (Peri. Future), are also aniṭ before the Perfect ending थल् ॥ As याता (Peri-Fut.), ययाथ (Per), चेता, चिचेथ, नेता, निनेथ; होता जुहोथ ॥ Why 'ending in a vowel'? Observe भत्ता, बिभेदिथ ॥ Why 'like तास्? Observe लूत्वा but लुलविथ, Why 'थल्'? Observe याता but ययिव, ययिम ॥ The word नित्य qualifies अनिट्, if therefore तास् be *optionally* aniṭ, then the थल् will be सेट् *always*. As तास्—विधोता or विधविता; the थल् is विदुधविथ ॥

Here इट् is optional before तास् by VII. 2. 44. Similarly चक्रमिथ, for क्रम् is aniṭ in âtmanepada, and सेट् in Parasmaipada. In fact, whereever there is want of इट्, whether by complete prohibition or optional prohibition, all that is regulated by VII. 2. 13: this is the view adopted by the Kâśikâ. But another view is that the prohibition of this sûtra applies to the इट् of VII. 2. 13 only, but does not debar the option of VII. 2. 44; so they have two forms विदुधोथ and विदुधविथ ॥ This view is applied by them to VII. 2. 46, as सस्वर्थ or सस्वरिथ (VII. 2. 44).

Why have we used the word वत् in तास्वत्? The force of वत् is that the root should have a form in तास् and then be aniṭ; and if a root has no Periphrastic Future form, and thus its तास् is aniṭ,, such a root is not governed by this sûtra. As जघसिथ and उवयिथ ॥ Here the roots घस् and वय् the substitutes of अद् and वेञ् respectively have no Periphrastic Future form, and hence this rule does not apply to them.

उपदेशेऽत्वतः ॥ ६२ ॥ पदानि ॥ उपदेशे, अत्वतः ॥

वृत्तिः ॥ उपदेशे यो धातुरकारवान् तासौ नित्यानिट् तस्मात्तासाविव थलीडागमो न भवति ।

62. After a root which possesses a short अ as its root-vowel in the original enunciation (the Dhâtupâṭha), and after which the Peri-Fut. तास् is always devoid of the augment इट्, थल् the Personal ending of the Perfect, like तास्, does not get the augment इट् ॥

As Fut. पक्ता, Per. पपक्थ, यष्टा, इयष्ठ, शक्ता, शशक्थ ॥ Why do we say 'in the Original Enunciation'? Observe Fut. कर्ष्टा Per. चकर्षिथ in which the अ of 'karsh' is the result of guṇa substitution. Why do we say 'having an अ'? Observe Fut भेत्ता Per बिभेदिथ, here the root-vowel is इ ॥ Why do we say "*short* अ"? Observe Fut. राद्धा Per. रराधिथ from राध् the root-vowel being long आ ॥ The word तास्वत् is understood here also. Therefore we have जिघृक्षति, जिग्रहिथ ॥ Here the root ग्रह is aniṭ before सन् (VII. 2. 12) and not before तास् so it will not be aniṭ before थ ॥ The words नित्यं अनिटः are also understood here. Therefore the rule does not apply to आनञ्जिथ (VII. 4. 71, 72). For the root अञ्जू (VII. 21) takes *optionally* इट् before तास् (VII. 2. 44) as अञ्जिता and अङ्क्ता ॥

ऋतो भारद्वाजस्य ॥ ६३ ॥ पदानि ॥ ऋतः, भारद्वाजस्य ॥

वृत्तिः ॥ ऋकारान्ताद्धातोर्भारद्वाजस्याचार्यस्य मतेन तासाविव नित्यानिटस्थलि इडागमो न भवति ।

63. In the opinion of Bhâradvâja, it is only after a root which ends in short ऋ, and after which the Peri-Fut. तास् is always devoid of the augment इट्, that थल् also, like तास्, does not take the augment इट् ॥

As स्मर्त्ता, सस्मर्थ, ध्वर्त्ता, दध्वर्थ ॥ The ऋ roots are covered by VII. 2. 61; the specification of these roots makes a restriction, so that *all* other roots, are not auiṭ, though the Peri-Fut in तास् be aniṭ. So that according to Bhâradwâja, we have forms like ययिथ, वविथ, पेचिथ, शेकिथ ॥ Thus this sûtra makes the preceding two sûtras optional, except so far as short ऋ-ending roots are concerned.

As a general rule, all roots ending in long ॠ are सेट्; therefore, the sutra mentions *short* ऋ, in order to debar its application to long ॠ ending words. Had it not been so, this rule would have been a *vidhi* rule and not a *niyama*: because rule VII. 2. 61 does not apply to long ॠ ending roots, and so if the present sûtra were to include long ॠ also, it could not be called a *niyama* (restriction) of VII. 2. 61.

बभूथाततन्थजगृम्भववर्थेति निगमे ॥ ६४ ॥ पदानि ॥ बभुथ, आततन्थ, जगृम्भ ववर्थ, इति, निगमे ॥

वृत्तिः ॥ बभूथ आततन्थ जगृम्भ ववर्थ इत्येतानि निपात्यन्ते निगमविषये ।

64. In the Veda are found the irregular forms बभूथ, आततन्थ, जगृम्भ and ववर्थ ॥

As त्वं हि होता प्रथमो बभूथ (=बभूविथ); येनान्तरिक्षमुर्वाततन्थ (=आतेनिथ), जगृम्भा ते दक्षिणमिन्द्र हस्तम् (=जगृहिम), ववर्थ त्वं हि ज्योतिषा (=ववरिथ). See VII. 2. 13. This is also a niyama rule with regard to वृ for by VII.2.13 the root वृ was already aniṭ, and its Perfect would have been ववर्थ by that rule. The special mention of this form shows that in secular literature this root is always सेट् before थ of the Perfect.

विभाषा सृजिदृशोः ॥ ६५ ॥ विभाषा, सृजि-दृशोः ॥
वृत्तिः ॥ सृजि दृशि इत्येतयोस्थलि विभाषा इडागमो न भवति ।

65. थल् the Personal ending of the Perfect, optionally gets the augment इट् after सृज् and दृश् ॥

As सस्रष्ठ or ससर्जिथ, दद्रष्ठ or ददर्शिथ ॥ See VI. 1. 58 for अम् augment.

इडत्त्यर्तिव्ययतीनाम् ॥ ६६ ॥ पदानि ॥ इट्, अत्ति-आर्ति-व्ययतीनाम् ॥
वृत्तिः ॥ अत्ति अर्ति व्ययति इत्येतेषां थलीडागमो भवति ।

66. The affix थल् gets always the augment इट् after अद्, ऋ and व्यय् ॥

As आदिथ, आरिथ, and संविव्ययिथ ॥ The root व्येञ् is not changed to व्या (VI. 1. 46) in the Perfect. By VII. 2. 63, the roots अद् and व्ये would have *optionally* been सेट्, and ऋ never; therefore, the present sûtra makes the इट् augment compulsory. The इट् is repeated in the aphorism for the sake of clearness, the rule could have stood without it, for the anuvṛitti of 'optionally' could not have run into it from the last sûtra: for if it was an optional sûtra, the enumeration of अद् and व्ये was useless, as they were already provided for by VII. 2. 63. Therefore, this sûtra makes an invariable rule.

वस्वेकाजाद्घसाम् ॥ ६७ ॥ पदानि ॥ वसु, एकाच्-आत्-घसाम् ॥
वृत्तिः ॥ कृतद्विर्वचनानामेकाचां धातूनाम् आकारान्तानां घसेश्च वसाविडागमो भवति ।

67. The Participial affix वसु (वस्) gets the augment इट् only then when the reduplicated root before it consists of one syllable, or when it comes after a root ending in long आ, and after घस् ॥

Thus आदिवान्, आशिवान्, पेचिवान्, शेकिवान् ॥ In the first two of these, the reduplicate stems आद् and आश् become of one syllable by the coalescence of अ अद् and अअश् ॥ In पेच् and शेक् the reduplicate is elided and the vowel अ changed to ए, and thus the reduplicate has become of one syllable. Of roots ending in आ we have, ययिवान्, तस्थिवान्, of घस्—जक्षिवान् ॥ This वस् would have taken the augment by the general rule of इट् increment, the present sûtra makes a niyama, so that the roots which are not monosyllabic in their reduplicate form are aniṭ: as बिभिद्वान्, चिच्छिद्वान्, बिभूवान्, शिश्रिवान् ॥ The niyama is made with regard to the roots which would have taken इट् generally, as not being governed by the prohibition in VII.2.13. The roots ending in long आ may consist of more than one syllable in their reduplicate form, as याया + वस्, hence their separate enumeration: as a matter of fact, however, these reduplicates also become monosyllabic ultimately by losing their आ ॥ The root दरिद्रा is not governed by this rule, for its Perfect will be formed periphrastically by III. 1. 35 Vârt, because it consists of more than one syllable: as दरिद्रांचकार ॥ And when आम् is not added, there also दरिद्रा loses its final आ before ârdhadhâtuka affixes by the vârtika under VI. 4. 114. So the आ being elided before the adding of any affix, this becomes a root which no longer ends in आ, and so the cause of adding इट् under this sûtra no longer exists, and so no इट् is added. Thus we have दद्रिद्वान्, for before ârdhadhâtuka affixes दरिद्रा loses its आ (VI. 4. 114 Vârt), and this elision being considered as *siddha*, (VI. 4. 114 Vârt), no occasion remains for the augment इट् ॥ The घस् becomes जक्ष् in its reduplicate form (a stem of one syllable), but had it not been separately mentioned, then by VI. 4. 100, the penultimate अ of घस् would have been elided first, before reduplication, because VI. 4. 100, is subsequent in order to the rule ordaining reduplication (VI. 1. 14 &c). The अ being elided, we should have घ्स् only, which not having any vowel, could not be reduplicated. By its separate enumeration here, the augment इट् being ordained by a subsequent rule (VII. 2. 67), prevents even the rule of elision (VI. 4. 100). Having, therefore, *first* added इट्, we *then* elide the penultimate अ by VI. 4. 98, this elided अ, however, becomes sthânivat for the purposes of reduplication only by I. 1. 59. Thus घस् + इवस् = घ्स् + इवस् (VI. 4. 98) = जक्ष् + इवस् = जक्षिवान् ॥

विभाषा गमहनविदविशाम् ॥ ६८ ॥ पदानि ॥ विभाषा, गम-हन-विद्-विशाम्॥

वृत्तिः ॥ गम हन विद विश इत्येतेषां धातूनां वसौ विभाषा इडागमो भवति ।

वार्त्तिकम् ॥ दृशेश्चेति वक्तव्यम् ॥

68. The affix वस् (वंस्) optionally takes इट् after गम्, हन्, विद् and विश् ॥

As गम् — जग्मिवान् or जगन्वान् (म् changed to न् by VIII. 2. 64); हन् — जघ्निवान् or जघन्वान्, (VII. 2. 54 and 55) विद् — विविदिवान् or विविद्वान्, विश् — विविशिवान् or विविश्वान् ॥ The root विद् 'to acquire' belongs to the Tudâdi class, as it is read here with the Tudâdi विश् ॥ The root विद् 'to know' (II. 55. IV. 62), forms *invariably* विविद्वान् because it is âtmanepadi and cannot take इट् augment before वस् affix.

Vârt:—The root दृश् should also be enumerated. As ददृशिवान् and ददृश्वान् ॥

सनिं ससनिवांसम् ॥ ६९ ॥ पदानि ॥ सनिम्-ससनिवांसम् ॥

वृत्तिः ॥ सनोतेः सनतेर्वा धातोः सनिंससनिवांसमिति निपात्यते ।

69. The form ससनिवांसम् with सनिं is irregularly formed.

This is derived from सनोति or सनति root. As अग्निज्योतिषं सनिं ससनिवांसम् ॥ The augment इट् is added, there is no change of अ of सन् to ए, nor the elision of the reduplicate before वस् ॥ The other form is सेनिवांसम् when not preceded by सनिम् ॥ This form ससनिवांसम् is Vedic, in secular literature we have सेनिवांसम् ॥

ऋद्धनोः स्ये ॥ ७० ॥ पदानि ॥ ऋत-हनोः, स्ये ॥

वृत्तिः ॥ ऋकारान्तानां धातूनां हन्तेश्च स्ये इडागमो भवति ।

70. स्य the sign of the Future and Conditional gets the augment इट्, after a root ending in short ऋ and after हन् ॥

As करिष्यति, हनिष्यति, हरिष्यति ॥ The root स्वृ takes always इट् before स्य, though it does so optionally before other affixes (see VII. 2. 44): as स्वरिष्यति ॥ Similarly अकरिष्यत्, अहरिष्यत्, अहनिष्यत् &c ॥

अञ्जेः सिचि ॥ ७१ ॥ अञ्जेः, सिचि ॥

वृत्तिः ॥ अञ्जेः सिचि इडागमो भवति ।

71. The स् of the s-Aorist always takes the इट् after अञ्ज् (Rudh. 21).

As आञ्जीत्, आञ्जिष्टाम्, आञ्जिषुः ॥ But अङ्क्ता or अञ्जिता in tenses other than Aorist. The root having an indicatory long ऊ optionally takes इट् (VII. 2. 44.)

स्तुसुधूञ्भ्यः परस्मैपदेषु ॥ ७२ ॥ पदानि ॥ स्तु, सु, धूञ्भ्यः, परस्मैपदेषु ॥

वृत्तिः ॥ स्तु सु धूञ् इत्येतेभ्यः सिचि परस्मैपदे परत इडागमो भवति ॥

72. The सिच् of the s-Aorist gets the इट् in the Parasmaipada after the roots स्तु, सु and धूञ् ॥

As अस्तावीत्, असावीत्, अधावीत् ॥ But अस्तोष्ट, असोष्ट, अधोष्ट or अधविष्ट in Atmanepada. Exception to VII. 2. 10 and 44.

यमरमनमातां सक्च ॥ ७३ ॥ पदानि ॥ यम, रम, नम, आताम्, सक्, च ॥

वृत्तिः ॥ यम रम नम इत्येतेषामङ्गानामाकारान्तानां च सगागमो भवति परस्मैपदे सिचि इडागमश्च ॥

73. The सिच् of the Aorist in the Parasmaipada takes the augment इट् after यम, रम, नम and roots ending in long आ, and स् (सक्) is added at the end of these stems.

Thus अयंसीत्, अयंसिष्टाम्, अयंसिषुः ॥ व्यरंसीत्। व्यरंसिष्टाम्। व्यरंसिषुः ॥ The root रम is Parasmaipadi when preceded by वि or आ (I. 3. 83). अनंसीत्। अनंसिष्टाम् अनंसिषुः ॥ आकारान्तानाम्। अयासीत्। अयासिष्टाम्; अयासिषुः। यमादीनां हलन्तलक्षणा वृद्धिः प्राप्ता सा नेटीति प्रतिषिध्यते। परस्मैपदेष्वित्येव। आयंस्त। अरंस्त। अनंस्त ॥

The Vṛiddhi in the case of यम् &c. ordained by VII. 2. 3, does not take place by VII. 2. 4. In the Atmanepada we have आयंस्त ॥ The root यम् is âtmanepadi, as it is preceded by आ (I. 3. 75) अरंस्त, अनंस्त (III. 1. 85). Exception to VII. 2. 10, 44.

स्मिपूङ्रञ्ज्वशां सनि ॥ ७४ ॥ पदानि ॥ स्मि, पूङ्, ऋ अञ्जू, अशू सनि ॥

वृत्तिः ॥ स्मिङ् पूङ् ऋ अञ्जू अशू इत्येतेषां धातूनां सनीडागमो भवति ॥

74. The Desiderative सन् gets the augment इट् after the roots स्मिङ्, पूङ्, ऋ, अञ्जू and अशू ॥

Thus सिस्मयिषते, पिपविषते (VII.4.80) अरिरिषति, अञ्जिजिषति (VI. 1. 2 and 3) and अशिशिषते ॥ The root पूङ् is not governed by this rule, as पुपूषति ॥ The अशू (V. 18) of Suâdi class is taken here, and not अश् (IX. 51) of Kryâdi class, for the latter *always* has इट्, while the former having an indicatory long ऊ has *optionally* इट् ॥

किरश्च पञ्चभ्यः ॥ ७५ ॥ पदानि ॥ किरः, च, पञ्चभ्यः ॥

वृत्तिः ॥ किरादिभ्यः पञ्चभ्यः सनि इडागमो भवति ॥

75. The desiderative सन् takes इट् after कृ and the four roots that follow it (Tud. 116-120)

Thus चिकरिषति, जिगरिषति, दिदरिषते, दिधरिषते, पिप्रच्छिषति (I. 2. 8; VI. 1. 16). But सिसृक्षति not included in the five. The roots कॄ and गॄ would have optionally got इट् in the desiderative by VII. 2. 41, which would have been optionally lengthened by VII. 2. 38. But the इट् here being specifically ordained, does not get lengthened by VII. 2. 38.

रुदादिभ्यः सार्वधातुके ॥ ७६ ॥ पदानि ॥ रुदादिभ्यः, सार्वधातुके ॥

वृत्तिः ॥ रुदादिभ्य उत्तरस्य वलादेः सार्वधातुकस्य इडागमो भवति ॥

76. A sârvadhâtuka affix beginning with a consonant other than a य, gets the augment इट् after the root रुद् and the four that follow it (Ad. 58-62)

Thus रोदिति, स्वपिति, श्वसिति, प्राणिति, जक्षिति ॥ But जागर्ति which is beyond the five, and स्वप्ता before ârdhadhâtuka affixes, and रुदन्ति before a vowel beginning affix.

ईशः से ॥ ७७ ॥ पदानि ॥ ईशः, से ॥

वृत्तिः ॥ ईश उत्तरस्य से इत्येतस्य सार्वधातुकस्य इडागमो भवति ॥

77. The sârvadhâtuka affix से (the ending of the second Person Present and Imperative Atmanepada) gets the augment इट् after ईश् (Ad. 10)

As ईशिषे and ईशिष्व ॥ से becomes स्व by III. 4. 91 and 80. The से is exhibited in the sûtra without any case-ending.

ईडजनोर्ध्वे च ॥ ७८ ॥ पदानि ॥ ईड्, जनोः, ध्वे, च ॥

वृत्तिः ॥ ईड जन इत्येताभ्यामुत्तरस्य ध्वे इत्येतस्य से इत्येतस्य च सार्वधातुकस्य इडागमो भवति ॥

78. The sârvadhâtuka affix से and ध्वे, (the endings of the Present and Imperative Atmanepadi) get the augment इट् after the roots ईड् (Ad. 9) and जन् ॥

Thus ईडिध्वे, ईडिध्वम्, ईडिषे, ईडिष्व, जनिध्वे, जनिध्वम्, जनिषे, जनिष्व ॥ The root जनी (IV. 41) is taken here. The Vikaraṇa श्यन् has been elided in this case, as a Vedic irregularity, and so also there is not elision of the penultimate.

In the secular literature the form is जायसि ॥ Here the य would prohibit इट् always. The जन् of the third class (III. 24) is also to be included, thus we have व्यतिजज्ञिषे, व्यतिजज्ञिष्व, व्यतिजज्ञिध्वे, व्यतिजज्ञिध्वम् in karma vyatihâra. Otherwise this root is Parasmaipadi. ध्व takes इट after ईश् also, as ईशिध्वम् ॥

For this purpose, some read the sûtra as ईडजनोः स्ध्वे च; and स stands here for से having its Locative dropped, and therefore the force of च in the sûtra, according to this reading, is to draw in the anuvritti of ईश from the previous sûtra. Those who do not follow this reading, draw the whole of the last sûtra by force of च ll From these it may be asked, what is then the necessity of *two* sûtras? Could not one sûtra, like this, ईशीडिजनां सध्वयोः, have sufficed, as being shorter and more general? To this there is no better valid answer than this विचित्रा हि सूत्रस्य कृतिः पाणिनेः ॥

The form ध्वे being taken in the sûtra, the rule will not apply to the ध्वम् of लङ् (Imperfect): which will not take इट् ॥ But इट् will apply to the ध्वम् of the Imperative on the maxim एकदेशविकृतस्यानन्यत्वात् ॥

लिङः सलोपो ऽनन्त्यस्य ॥ ७९ ॥ पदानि ॥ लिङः, स, लोपः, अनन्त्यस्य ॥

वृत्तिः ॥ सार्वधातुकइति वर्तते, सार्वधातुके यो लिङ् तस्य अनन्त्यस्य सकारस्य लोपो भवति ॥

79. In the sârvadhâtuka Liṅ (i. e. Potential), the स् which is not final (i.e. the स् of the augments यास् and सीय्), is elided.

What is the स which is not final? The स of the augments यासुट्, सुट् and सीयुट् ॥ Thus कुर्यात्, कुर्याताम्, कुर्युः, कुर्वीत, कुर्वीयाताम्, कुर्वीरन् ॥ Why 'not the final'? Observe कुर्युः, कुर्याः ॥ Why in the Sârvadhâtuka? Observe क्रियास्ताम्, क्रियासुः, कृषीष्ट, कृषीयास्ताम्, कृषीरन् in the Benedictive.

अतो येयः ॥ ८० ॥ पदानि ॥ अतः, या, इयः ॥

वृत्तिः ॥ अकारान्तादङ्गादुत्तरस्य या इत्येतस्य सार्वधातुकस्य इय् इत्ययमादेशो भवति ॥

80. After a Present stem ending in short अ, इय् is substituted for the sârvadhâtuka या (i.e. for the या of the augment यास् of the Potential).

Thus पचेत्, पचेताम् and पचेयुः ॥ The य् of इय् is elided before affixes beginning with a consonant by VI. 1. 66. In the case of पचेयुः, the pararûpa of VI. 1. 96 is prevented. Why 'ending in a short अ'? Observe चिनुयात्, सुनुयात् ॥ Why '*short*'? Observe यायात् ॥ Why sârvadhâtuka? Observe चिकीर्ष्यात् ॥

The objector may say, the form चिकीर्ष्यात् will be so by the elision of अ under VI. 4. 48, and so there is no necessity of reading the anuvṛtti of sârvadhâtuka in this sûtra; for when अ is elided by अतोलोपः VI. 4. 48, in the case of ârdhadhâtuka या the present rule cannot apply, as there is no base left which ends in अ ॥ To this we reply, this is not a good reason: for then in the case of पचेत् and यजेत् also, the rule अतो दीर्घो यञि (VII. 3. 101) would apply, and the अ of पच would require to be lengthened. But that is not so. The fact is that the present sûtra debars rule VII. 3. 101. Therfore, as this इय् substitute debars the lengthening of VII. 3. 101, so it would debar the *lopa* of VI. 4. 48. Therefore, if the anuvṛitti of sârvadhâtuka be not read into this sûtra, the इय् substitute would apply to ârdhadhâtuka also, and the lopa-elision VI. 4. 48 would not help, as that would be superseded by this special rule. Therefore the aunvṛitti of "sârvadhâtuka" should be read into this sûtra.

The above is stated on general grounds. But if the maxim मध्येऽपवादाः पूर्वान् विधीन् बाधन्ते नोत्तरान् (Apavâdas that are surrounded by the rules which teach operations that have to be superseded by the apavâda operations, supersede only those rules that precede, not those that follow them) be applied here, then the present sûtra would supersede only the preceding sûtra VI. 4. 48 and not the following sûtra VII. 3. 101 which would not be superseded by the present sûtra. In this view also, the lopa being superseded at all events, the anuvṛitti of 'Sârvadhâtuka' must be read into this sûtra.

In the दीर्घ rule VII. 3. 101, the word 'sârvadhâtuka' is understood from VII. 3. 95. But according to some, the word तिङि of VII. 3. 88 is also understood there, so that they would lengthen the अ, before a sârvadhâtuka personal termination (तिङ्) only, and not before every sârvadhâtuka affix in general. According to this view, the present sûtra will debar only the dirgha rule (VII. 3. 101) and not the lopa rule (VI. 4. 48), on the maxim येन ना प्राप्ते &c.

The word येयः in the sûtra is formed by या+इयः; and या is exhibited without any case-termination. Others say, the word is यः the sixth case of या formed on the analogy of विश्वपः by the elision of आ (VI. 4. 140). Then यः+इयः=य+इयः (VIII. 3. 19) after this elision, there ordinarily would take place no sandhi; as this elision is considered asiddha (VIII. 2. 1) for the purposes of VI. 1. 87. Contrary to this general rule, however, the sandhi takes place here and we have येयः by VI. 1. 87. The अ in इयः is for the sake of pronunciation only. The real substitute is इय् ॥

Some read the sûtra as अतो यासियः ॥ So that the sthâni is यास् and not या, and यासियः is a genitive compound.

आतो ङितः ॥ ८१ ॥ पदानि ॥ आतः, ङितः ॥

वृत्तिः ॥ आकारस्य ङित्वयवस्य अकारान्तादङ्गादुत्तरस्य सार्वधातुकस्य इय् इत्ययमादेशो भवति ॥

81. For the आ being a portion of a sarvadhâtuka Personal ending which is ङित् (i.e. आते, आथे, आताम् and आथाम्), coming after a Verbal stem ending in short अ, there is substituted इय् ॥

Thus पचेते, पचेथे, पचेताम्, पचेथाम्, यजेते, यजेथे, यजेथाम्, शास्येथे, शास्येते ॥ The य् of इय् drops by VI. 1. 66. Why do we say "the long आ"? Observe पचन्ति, यजन्ति, पचन्ते, यजन्ते ॥ Why do we say 'a ङित् affix'? Observe पचावहै, पचामहै (I. 2. 4). Why do we say 'ending in short अ'? Observe भिन्दाते, छुन्दाते ॥ Why 'short'? Observe मिमाते, मिमाथे ॥

All sârvadhâtuka affixes which have not an indicatory प् are ङित् by I. 2. 4. Now सार्वधातुकमपित् (I. 2. 4) is a sûtra in which the word ङित् is understood from I. 2. 1. But the grammatical construction of the word ङित् in the two sûtras I. 2. 1 and I. 2. 4 is not the same. In the first sûtra, it means ङिति इव = ङित्वत्, i. e. the roots गा कुट् &c are treated in the same way as they would have been treated, had a ङित् affix *followed.* But in the second sûtra I. 2. 4, the word ङिद्वत् is equal to ङित इव "like of ङित्" ॥ The sûtra I. 2. 1. is so explained in order to evolve the form उच्चुकुटिषति ॥ For when the सन् is added to कुट्, the root कुट् is treated as if the सन् was a ङित् affix, and so there is no guṇa. But if सन् itself had become ङित् then the Desiderative root चुकुटिष्, being a ङित् root would require âtmanepada affixes by अनुदात्तङित आत्मनेपदम् (I. 3. 12). In the case, however, of sârvadhâtuka-apit-affixes, the affixes themselves become like ङित्, and are treated as ङित् affixes, not only with regard to the stem *preceding* them, but with regard to their own selves also, as we see in the present sûtra.

आने मुक् ॥ ८२ ॥ पदानि ॥ आने, मुक् ॥

वृत्तिः ॥ आने परतोऽङ्गस्यातो मुगागमो भवति ॥

82. Before the Participial ending आन, a verbal stem ending in short अ, gets the augment मुक् ॥

Thus पचमानः, यजमानः ॥

This मुक् is part and parcel of अ only, and not of the anga. For if मुक् be considered as part of the aṅga, then it will be an intervention, and make the aṅga end in a consonant and so there will be anomaly in accent. For by VI. 1. 186, the ल sârvadhâtuka affix is anudâtta after a stem ending in अ; so if मुक् be considered part of the anga, the stem no longer ends in अ but म्; but if it be considered as a portion of अ only, then the aṅga still remains अदुपदेश (VI. 1. 186). So the accent of पचमानः and यजमानः is governed by VI. 1. 186.

An objector may say, "if this be so, then the stem पचम् is still considered as ending in अ, and therefore in पचम् + आन, we should apply the previous sûtra VII. 2. 81, and change अ into इय्" ॥ To this we reply, 'no, it cannot be so; for the त् in अत् (VII. 2. 80) shows that the अ consisting of *one mâtrâ* is to be taken, but when मुक् is added, this अ becmes *one mâtrâ and half*, so the rule VII. 2. 81 will not apply; because it applies only to अ of *one mâtrâ*" The objector:—"If this is so, then the anudâtta of VI. 1. 186 will not also hold good, for there also the अत् means the अ of one mâtrâ." This is no valid objection. For there the word उपदेश is taken, so that a stem which at the time of upadeśa or first enunciation, ends in a short अ of one mâtrâ, is governed by that rule; though after the enunciation, the short अ may be lengthened in its mâtrâ. It is for this reason that the rule VI. 1.186 applies to पचावः and पचामः; though the short अ is subsequently lengthened before व and म by VII. 3. 101.

Or the sûtra may have been made, as आनस्य मुट्, and the augment म् would then be added to आन and not to the verbal stem. All the above difficulties would be removed by this view. But then the final अ of पच &c would require to be lengthened before मान by VII. 3. 101. This objection, however, is not insuperable, for one view of VII. 3. 101 is that the word तिङि is understood there, so that the lengthening would take place only before a तिङ् affix beginning with a यञ् vowel : and not before any other affix.

ईदासः ॥ ८३ ॥ पदानि ॥ ईत्, आसः ॥

वृत्तिः ॥ आस उत्तरस्यानस्य ईकारादेशो भवति ॥

83. ई is substituted for the आ of आन, after आस् ॥

Thus आसीनो यजते ॥ (See I. 1. 54 by which the *first* letter of the *second* term after आसः which is exhibited in the Ablative is taken here). The आने which is in the 7th case in the last aphorism, should be taken in the 6th case in this.

अष्टन आ विभक्तौ ॥ ८४ ॥ पदानि ॥ अष्टनः, आ, विभक्तौ ॥

वृत्तिः ॥ अष्टनो विभक्तौ परत आकारादेशो भवति ॥

84. आ is substituted for the final of अष्टन् before a case-ending.

Thus अष्टाभिः, अष्टाभ्यः, अष्टानाम, अष्टासु ॥ Why 'before a *case-ending*'? Observe अष्टत्वम्, अष्टता ॥ The rule of this sûtra is an optional one, and we have in the alternative अष्टभिः, अष्टभ्यः ॥ The आ in the sûtra indicates the *individual* letter आ, and not आ belonging to the general class आ ॥ For the generic आ would include the nasalised आं also, and as the letter replaced (अन्) is a nasal, the substitute would have been also nasal आँ, but it is not so. See VI. 1. 172 and VII. 1. 22. This rule applies also when the word stands at the end of a compound, as प्रियाष्टानः or प्रियाष्टौः (VII. 1. 22). The word विभक्ति governs the subsequent sûtras upto VII. 2. 114.

रायो हलि ॥ ८५ ॥ पदानि ॥ रायः, हलि ॥

वृत्तिः ॥ रै इत्येतस्य हलादौ विभक्तौ परत आकारादेशो भवति ॥

85. Before a case-ending beginning with a consonant, आ is substituted for the final of रै ॥

As राभ्याम्, राभिः, ॥ But रायौ, रायः before affixes beginning with a vowel. Why 'a case ending'? Observe रैत्वम्, रैता ॥

युष्मदस्मदोरनादेशे ॥ ८६ ॥ पदानि ॥ युष्मद, अस्मदोः, अनादेशे ॥

वृत्तिः ॥ युष्मदस्मदित्येतयोरनादेश विभक्तौ परत आकारादेशो भवति ॥

86. आ is substituted for the final of युष्मद् and अस्मद् before a case-ending, beginning with a consonant, when it is not a substitute.

The substitute case-endings are given in VII. 1. 27 &c. Thus युष्माभिः अस्माभिः, युष्मासु, अस्मासु ॥ Why do we say 'when it is not a substitute'? Observe युष्मत् and अस्मत् (VII. 1 31). The anuvṛitti of हलि need not be read into this sûtra from the preceding, for if that were so, the mention of अनादेशे would become redundant, because as a matter of fact no *substitute* case-ending begins with a consonant. However, reading this sûtra with VII. 2. 89, we find that the scope of the present sûtra is before consonant beginning affixes.

द्वितीयायां च ॥ ८७ ॥ पदानि ॥ द्वितीयायाम्, च ॥

वृत्तिः ॥ द्वितीयायां च परतो युष्मदस्मदोराकारादेशो भवति ॥

87. आ is substituted for the final of युष्मद् and अस्मद् before the endings of the Accusative.

As त्वाम्, माम्, युवाम्, आवाम्, युष्मान् and अस्मान् ॥ This rule applies to endings which are even substitutes, otherwise the last rule would have been sufficient. See VII. 2. 28, 29, and VII. 2. 92 and 97.

प्रथमायाश्च द्विवचने भाषायाम् ॥ ८८ ॥ पदानि ॥ प्रथमायाः, च, द्विवचने, भाषायाम् ॥

वृत्तिः ॥ प्रथमायाश्च द्विवचने परतो भाषायां विषये युष्मदस्मदोराकारादेशो भवति ॥

88. आ is substituted for the final of युष्मद् and अस्मद् before the ending of the Nom. Du. in the Secular literature.

As युवाम्, आवाम् ॥ Why of the nomnative? Observe युवयोः, आवयोः ॥ Why in the Dual? Observe त्वं, अहं, यूयं, वयं ॥ Why in the secular literature? Observe युवं वस्त्राणि पीवसा वसाथे in the Veda, so also आवम् ॥

योऽचि ॥ ८९ ॥ पदानि ॥ यः, अचि ॥

वृत्तिः ॥ अजादौ विभक्तावनादेशे युष्मदस्मदोर्यकारादेशो भवति ॥

89. य is substituted for the final of युष्मद् and अस्मद् before a case-ending, which is not a substitute, and which begins with a vowel.

Thus त्वया, मया, त्वयि, मयि, युवयोः, आवयोः ॥ Why do we say 'beginning with a vowel'? Observe युवाभ्याम्, आवाभ्याम् ॥ If in the sûtra VII. 2. 86, we read the anuvṛitti of हलि, we need not use अचि in the present sûtra. For then this sûtra will be a general (utsarga) aphorism, ordaining य before *all* non-substitute case-endings; and the sûtra VII. 2. 86, will be considered an exception (apavâda) to this, with regard to those case-endings which begin with a consonant, where आ will be ordained. In this view of the case, the use of अचि here si explanatory. Why 'when the ending is not a substitute'? Observe त्वद् गच्छति, मद् गच्छति ॥

शेषे लोपः ॥ ९० ॥ पदानि ॥ शेषे, लोपः ॥

वृत्तिः ॥ शेषे विभक्तौ युष्मदस्मदोर्लोपो भवति ॥

90. In the remaining cases where (आ or य is not substituted) there is elision of the final of yushmad and asmad.

This elision finds scope in the Singular and Plural of the Ablative, Dative, Genitive, and the Nominative. Thus त्वम्. अहम्, यूयम्, वयम्, तुभ्यम्, मह्यम्, युष्मभ्यम्, अस्मभ्यम्, त्वत्, मत्, युष्मत्, अस्मत्, तव, मम, युष्माकम्, अस्माकम् ॥ The following śloka gives the cases which are included in the word शेष :—

पञ्चम्याश्च चतुर्थ्याश्च षष्ठीप्रथमयोरपि ।
यान्यद्विवचनान्यत्र तेषु लोपो विधीयते ॥

The word शेष is employed in the sûtra for the sake of clearness. For there will be elision *universally* before *all* case-affixes. This is the *general* rule. To this there is the exception that before non-substitute case-affixes there will be य (VII. 2. 89). To this latter, there is an exception that before non-substitute case-endings beginning with a consonant, आ comes. Thus without any confusion, the आ, the य, and the lopa find their respective scopes.

When there is elision, why is not टाप् added in the Feminine; in त्वं ब्राह्मणी ; अहं ब्राह्मणी ? The टाप् is not added on the maxim सन्निपात लक्षणो विधिरनिमित्तं तद्विघातस्य 'a rule which is occasioned by a certain combination, does not become the cause of the destruction of that combination.' Because the ending in अ of युष्मद् and अस्मद् was occasioned by vibhakti combination, if this latter occasion टाप्, then it will destroy its own fruit.

Or the words युष्मद् and अस्मद् may be taken to have no gender, and equally applicable to both masculine and feminine.

In order to avoid all this difficulty about टाप् some would elide the अद् (or टि portion) of युष्मद् and अस्मद् under this sûtra. They argue that by the next sûtra VII. 2. 91, the portions 'yushm' and 'asm', namely the portions upto म of युष्मद् and अस्मद् are replaced by substitutes. The portion that *remains* (शेष) is अद्, and it is this अद् which is to be elided.

Why is this 'lopa' taught again, when by VII. 2. 102, all त्यदादि pronouns have अ substituted for their finals before case-endngs ; and so would yushmad and asmad, lose their finals and become yushma and asma by that rule? That rule does not apply to yushmad and asmad, because by an ishṭi that rule is restricted to tyadâdi pronouns upto द्वि, thus excluding युष्मद्, अस्मद्, भवतु and किम् ॥

मपर्यन्तस्य ॥ ९१ ॥ पदानि ॥ म पर्य्यन्तस्य ॥

वृत्तिः ॥ मपर्यन्तस्येत्ययमधिकारो, यदित ऊर्ध्वमनुक्रमिष्यामो मपर्यन्तस्येत्येवं तद्वेदितव्यम् ॥

91. The substitutions taught hereafter upto VII.2. 98 take effect with regard to the portions of युष्मद् and अस्मद् upto म, i. e. the substitutes replace युष्म and अस्म ॥

Thus VII. 2. 92 teaches that युव and आव are substituted for yushmad and asmad in the dual. The substitutes replace युष्म् and अस्म्. Thus युवाम्, आवाम् ॥ Why 'upto म'? Observe युवकाम्, आवकाम् ॥ The क (V. 3. 71), is not replaced. Similarly VII. 2. 97 teaches that त्व and म replace 'yushmad' and 'asmad' in the singular; by this sûtra 'yushm' and 'asm' are only replaced. Thus त्वया, मया, the अद् portion remains for which य is substituted by VII. 2. 89. Had the whole been replaced, then the अ of त्व and म would have been replaced by य (VII. 2. 89), and given us undesired forms like त्व्या and म्या ॥ Why is the word पर्यन्त employed in the sûtra and not the word अन्त, as मान्तस्य? In the first place the word अन्त is ambiguous, it may mean ending with म् but excluding म्, or ending with म् and including म् ॥ In the second place, the word पर्यन्त is used to indicate the limit, or portion taken out of the whole. The word मान्त would have meant, that form of yusmad and asmad which ends with म् ॥ Now these words have a form which ends in म्, as युष्मानाचष्टे or अस्मानाचष्टे = युष्मते or अस्मते formed by णिच् (the टि portion अद् is elided by VII. 4. 155, *vârtika*). Now a noun formed from this derivative root युष्मि and अस्मि by क्विप् affix will be युष्म् and अस्म् ॥ These are the two forms of yusmad and asmad which are complete words ending in म ॥ The present sûtra does not apply to these words.

In declining these nouns युष्म् and अस्म्, we shall apply the rules VII. 2. 89 and 86, thus :—

	Sing.	Dual.	Plural.		Sing.	Dual.	Plural.
Nom.	त्वं	युषां	युयं	Acc.	युषां	युषां	युषान्
Ins.	युष्या	युष्याभ्यां	युषाभिः	Dat.	तुभ्यं	युषाभ्यां	युषभ्यं
Abl.	युषत्	युषाभ्यां	युषत्	Gen.	तव	युष्योः	युषाकं
Loc.	युष्यि	युष्योः	युषासु ‖ (Padamanjari).				

युवावौ द्विवचने ॥ ६२ ॥ पदानि ॥ युव, आवौ, द्विवचने ॥

वृत्तिः ॥ द्विवचनइत्यर्थग्रहणम् । द्विवचने ये युष्मदस्मदी द्व्यर्थाभिधानविषये तयोर्मपर्यन्तस्य स्थाने युव आव इत्येतावादेशौ भवतः ॥

92. In the Dual, युव is substituted for युष्म् and आव for अस्म् ॥

Thus युवाम्, आवाम्, युवाभ्याम्, आवाभ्याम्, युवयोः, आवयोः ॥ This substitution takes place even in compounds, where the sense of duality is prominent, if some other substitute like VII. 2. 94 &c. does not intervene. As अतिक्रान्तं युवाम् = अतियुवाम्, so also अत्यावाम्; अतियुवान्, अत्यावान् (= अतिक्रान्तान् युवाम् &c.) अतियुवया and अत्यावया (= अतिक्रान्तेन युवाम्) Similarly अतियुवाभिः, (अतिक्रान्तैर्युवां) अत्यावाभिः, अतियुवभ्यम्, (अतिकान्तेभ्योयुवां) अत्यावभ्यम्, अतियुवत्, (अतिकान्ताद् युवां) अत्यावत्, अतियुवाकम्, (अतिकान्तानां युवां) अत्यावाकम, अतियुवयि, (अतिकान्ते युवां) अत्यावयि, अतियुवासु, अतिक्रान्तेषु युवां अत्यावासु ॥ But where त्व &c are to be substituted, there those will be substituted, as अतित्वम् (= अतिक्रान्तो युवाम्), अत्यहम्, अतियूयम्, अतिवयम्, अतितुभ्यम्, अतिमह्यम्, अतितव, अतिमम ॥ This substitution does not take place when 'yushmad' and 'asmad' denote *one* or *many* (more than two), though the compound may denote a duality: as अतिक्रान्तौ त्वाम् = अतित्वाम्, अतिमाम्, अतियुष्मान्, अत्यस्मान् ॥

If in a compound, the words yushmad and asmad are employed in a dual signification, though the compound as a whole may have a singular or plural number, for the number of a compound does not depend upon the number of the words composing it, yet even in such a compound the युव and आव substitution should be made for the dual-significant yushmad and asmad: unless such substitution is debarred by some other substitutes like त्व and अह (VII. 2. 94 &c). Thus अतिक्रान्तं युवां = अतियुवाम्, similarly अति-आवाम ॥ The whole declension is given lelow :—

	Sing.	Pl.	Sing.	Pl.
Nom.	अतित्वम्	अतियूयम्	अत्यहम्	अतिवयम्
Acc.	अतियुवाम्	अतियुवाम्	अत्यावाम्	अत्यावान्
Ins.	अतियुवया	अतियुवभिः,	अत्यावया	अत्यावाभिः
Date.	अतितुभ्यं	अतियुवभ्यं	अतिमह्यम	अत्यावभ्यं
Abl.	अतियुवत्	अतियुवत्	अत्यावत्	अत्यावत्
Gen.	अतितव	अतियुवाकम	अतिमम	अत्यावाकम्
Loc.	अतियुवयि	अतियुवासु	अत्यावयि	अत्यावासु

But when the words yushmad and asmad denote singular or plural ,nbt the compound denotes a dual, then the yuva and âva substitutions do not take place. As अतिक्रान्तौ त्वाम् = अतित्वाम्, so also अतिक्रान्तौ युष्मान् = अतियुष्मान् so also अत्यस्मान् ॥ So on in other cases.

यूयवयौ जसि ॥ ९३ ॥ पदानि ॥ यूय, वयौ, जसि ॥

वृत्तिः ॥ युष्मदस्मदोर्मपर्यन्तस्य जसि परतो यूव वय इत्येतावादेशौ भवतः ॥

93. In the Nom. Pl. यूय is substituted for युष्म, and वय for अस्म ॥

As यूयम्, वयम्, परमयूयम्, परमवयम्, अतियूयम्, अतिवयम् ॥ The Tadanta-vidhi applies here. That rule applies in this angâdhikâra on the maxim अङ्गाधिकारे तस्य च तदुत्तरपदस्य च ॥ See also VII. 3. 10. In यूयम् and वयम्, the final द् is elided by VII. 2. 90, and we have यूय and वय + अ + अम् (VII. 1. 28) = यूयम् and वयम् (VI. 1. 97 and 107).

त्वाहौ सौ ॥ ९४ ॥ पदानि ॥ त्व, अहौ, सौ ॥

वृत्तिः ॥ युष्मदस्मदोर्मपर्यन्तस्य सौ परे त्व अह इत्येतावादेशौ भवतः ॥

94. In the Nominative Singular त्व is substituted for युष्म and अह for अस्म ॥

Thus त्वम् and अहम्, परमत्वम्, परमाहम्, अतित्वम् and अत्यहम् ॥ See VII. 1. 28, VI. 1. 97 and 107.

तुभ्यमह्यौ ङयि ॥ ९५ ॥ पदानि ॥ तुभ्य, मह्यौ, ङयि ॥

वृत्तिः ॥ युष्मदस्मदोर्मपर्यन्तस्य तुभ्य मह्य इत्येतावादेशौ भवतो ङयि परतः ॥

95. In the Dative Singular तुभ्य is substituted for युष्म and मह्य for अस्म ॥

As तुभ्यम, मह्यम्, परमतुभ्यम्, परममह्यम्, अतितुभ्यम्, अतिमह्यम् ॥

तवममौ ङसि ॥ ९६ ॥ पदानि ॥ तव, ममौ, ङसि ॥

वृत्तिः ॥ युष्मदस्मदोर्मपर्यन्तस्य तव मम इत्येतावादेशौ भवतो ङसि परतः ॥

96. In the Genitive Singular तव is substituted for युष्म् and मम for अस्म् ॥

As तव, मम, परमतव, परमसम, अतितव, अतिमम ॥ The द् is elided by VII. 2. 90, and तव and मम+अ+अ (VII. 1. 27)=तव and मम by VI. 1. 97.

त्वमावेकवचने ॥ ९७ ॥ पदानि ॥ त्वमौ, एक वचने ॥

वृत्तिः ॥ एकवचनइत्यर्थनिर्देशः । एकवचने ये युष्मदस्मदी एकार्थाभिधानविषये तयोर्मपर्यन्तस्य स्थाने त्व म इत्येतावादेशौ भवतः ॥

97. In the remaining cases of the Singular, त्व is substituted for युष्म् and म for अस्म् ॥

As त्वाम्, माम्, त्वया, मया, त्वत्, मत्, त्वयि, मयि ॥ The compounds also take this substitution according to the sense: as अतिक्रान्तस्त्वाम्=अतित्वम्, अत्यहम्, अतिक्रान्तौ मम=अतिमाम्, अतित्वाम्, अतिक्रान्तान् त्वाम्=अतित्वान्, अतिमान्, अतिक्रान्ताभ्यां त्वां=अतित्वाभ्याम्, अतिमाभ्याम्, अतिक्रान्तैस्त्वाम्=अतित्वाभिः, अतिमाभिः ॥

When in a compound, the words yushmad and asmad denote one, though the compound may denote two or many, thereeven the त्व and म substitutions must take place. And as regards different substitutes, like त्व and आह before सु &c, those prior taught substitutes debar this latter by the rule of पूर्वविप्रतिषेधः ॥ Some examples have already been given above, others are अतियूयम्, अतितुभ्यम्, अतितव ॥ So also with asmad. Similarly अतित्वां पश्य, अतित्वान्, अतित्वाभ्याम्, अतित्वाभिः, अतित्वभ्यम, अतित्वत्, अतित्वयोः, अतित्वाकम्, अतित्वयि, अतित्वयोः, अतित्वासु ॥

प्रत्ययोत्तरपदयोश्च ॥ ९८ ॥ पदानि ॥ प्रत्यय, उत्तरपदयोः, च ॥

वृत्तिः ॥ एकवचनइत्यनुवर्त्तते । प्रत्यये उत्तरपदे च परत एकत्वे वर्त्तमानयोर्युष्मदस्मदोर्मपर्यन्तस्य त्व म इत्येतावादेशौ भवतः ॥

98. त्व is substituted for युष्म् and म for अस्म्, when they signify a single individual, even when an affix follows, or a word is in composition.

As त्वदीयः, मदीयः, with the affix छ (IV. 2. 114, I. 1. 74) त्वत्तरः (=अतिशयेन त्वं), मत्तरः, त्वयति (=त्वामिच्छति), मयति; त्वयते (=त्वमिवाचरते), मयते ॥ Similarly when a second member of the compound follows. As तव पुत्रः=त्वत्पुत्रः, मत्पुत्रः ॥ त्वं नाथोऽस्य=त्वन्नाथः, मन्नाथः ॥ When more than one individual is signified, the substitution does not take place, as युष्मदीयं (=युष्माकमिदं), अस्मदीयं, युष्मत्पुत्रः (=युष्माकं पुत्रः), अस्मत्पुत्रः ॥

The sûtra VII. 2. 97 referred to the vibhaktis or case-endings, as that word from VII. 2. 84 governs these sûtras, the present sûtra refers to other affixes, and to compounds. It might be objected, that even before other affixes and compounds these words had in them vibhaktis, though those vibhaktis were elided when these affixes were added or when the words became part of a compound;

and that having in them suppressed vibhaktis, the substitutions would take place in spite of this sûtra. This objection is not valid, for there the vibhaktis have been elided. But is not elision a Bahiranga and the substitute an antaranga process; and should not, therefore, the substitute come first and then the vibhakti elided? The substitution specially taught in this sûtra is, therefore, a jñâpaka and proves the existence of the following maxim :—अन्तरङ्गानपि विधीन् बहिरङ्गोलुग्बाधते 'a bahiranga substitution of लुक् supersedes even antaranga rules'. Thus गोमान् प्रियोऽस्य = गोमत्प्रियः, here the antaranga नुम् augment is superseded by the bahiranga लुक् ॥ This sûtra further indicates, that all other substitutes of 'yushmad' and 'asmad' which take place in the singular, such as तव, मम, तुभ्य, मह्य, त्व, अह, do not take effect, before general affixes or in compounds, but that त्व and म are the only substitutes there even. As तुभ्यं हितं = त्वद्धितं, मद्धितं ॥ तव पुत्रः = त्वत्पुत्रः, मत्पुत्रः ॥

त्रिचतुरोस्त्रियां तिसृचतसृ ॥ ९९ ॥ पदानि ॥ त्रि, चतुरोः, स्त्रियाम्, तिसृ चतसृ ॥

वृत्तिः ॥ त्रि चतुर् इत्येतयोः स्त्रियां वर्तमानयोस्तिसृ चतसृ इत्येतावादेशौ भवतो विभक्तौ परतः ।

वार्त्तिकम् ॥ तिसृभावे सञ्ज्ञायां कन्युपसंख्यानं कर्तव्यम् ॥ वा० ॥ चतसर्याद्युदात्त निपातनं कर्तव्यम् ॥

99. **तिसृ** is substituted for **त्रि**. and **चतसृ** for **चतुर्** in the feminine, when a case-ending follows.

Thus तिस्रः, चतस्रः, तिसृभिः, चतसृभिः ॥ Why 'in the Feminine'? Observe त्रयः, चत्वारः, त्रीणि, चत्वारि ॥ The word स्त्रियाम् qualifies त्रि and चतुर् and not the word अङ्ग 'stem' which is of course understood here. Therefore, the substitution will take place even where the anga refers to a Masculine, or a Neuter; when त्रि and चतुर् refer to a Feminine; as प्रियास्तिस्रो ब्राह्मण्योऽस्य ब्राह्मणस्य = प्रियतिसा ब्राह्मणः (VII. 1.94) प्रियतिस्रौ, प्रियतिस्रः ॥ The guṇa of VII. 3. 110 is debarred in anticipation by VII. 2. 100 ordaining र ॥ प्रियतिसृ ब्राह्मणकुलं, प्रियतिसृणी, प्रियतिसृणि ॥ Similarly प्रियचतसा. °चतस्रौ, °चतस्रः, प्रियचतसृ, °चतसृणी, °चतसृणि ॥ The samâsânta affix कप् (V. 4. 153) is however not added in the above, because तिसृ &c are bahiranga substitutions. Conversely, the aṅga may be feminine, but if त्रि and चतुर् refer to Masculine or Neuter nouns, the substitution will not take place: as प्रियास्त्रयोऽस्याः or प्रियाणि त्रीणि वा अस्या ब्राह्मण्याः = प्रियत्रिः 'a Brahmani to whom three are beloved.' dual. प्रियत्री:, प्रियत्रयः ॥ Similarly प्रियचत्वाः, प्रियचत्वारौ, प्रियचत्वारः ॥

Vârt:—The substitution of तिसृ for त्रि takes place before the affix कन्; as तिसृका नाम ग्रामः ॥

Vârt:—चतसृ has acute on the first, as चतस्रः पश्य ॥ Rule VI. 1. 167 does not apply. But चतसृणाम् according to VI. 1. 179: the हलादि debars the निपातन accent.

अचि र ऋतः ॥ १०० ॥ पदानि ॥ अचि, र, ऋतः ॥

वृत्तिः ॥ तिसृ चतसृ इत्येतयोर्ऋतः स्थाने रेफादेशो भवति अजादौ विभक्तौ परतः ।

100. **र्** is substituted for the **ऋ** of **तिसृ** and **चतसृ** before case-affixes beginning with a vowel.

Thus तिस्रः, (in तिस्रस्तिष्ठन्ति, तिस्रः पश्य) चतस्रस्तिष्ठन्ति, चतस्रः पश्य ॥ प्रियतिस्र आनय, प्रियचतस्र आनय; प्रियतिस्रः स्वम्, प्रियचतस्रः स्वम् ॥ प्रियतिस्रि निधेहि, प्रियचतस्रि निधेहि ॥ This supersedes VI. 1. 102 (ordaining the single long substitution of the form of the first), VI. 1. 111 (substitution of उर् for ऋ), and VII. 3. 110 (the substitution of guṇa). The last rule VII. 3. 110, though subsequent in order, is however superseded by this rule. Why 'before the affixes beginning with a vowel?' Observe तिसृभिः, चतसृभिः ॥ The ऋतः of the sûtra refers to the ऋ of तिसृ and चतसृ and not to a ऋ ending stem in general: and had it not been used in the sûtra, the latter would have stood thus अचिरः "र् is substituted for the final of the words above-mentioned before an affix beginning with a vowel." So र् would have been substituted for the final of त्रि and चतुर् also.

जराया जरसन्यतरस्याम् ॥ १०१ ॥ पदानि ॥ जरायाः, जरस्, अन्यतरस्याम्, ॥

वृत्तिः ॥ जरा इत्येतस्य जरसित्ययमादेशो भवति अन्यतरस्यामजादौ विभक्तौ परतः ।

101. जरस् may be substituted for जरा, optionally before a case-affix beginning with a vowel.

As जरया or जरसा, in जरसा or जरयादन्ताः शीर्यन्ते ॥ जरायै or जरसे (जरसे or जरायै त्वा परिदद्युः) ॥ But only जराभ्याम्, जराभिः before an affix biginning with a consonant. The जरस् substitution takes place in the Neuter plural, when the augment नुम् is added: as अतिजरांसि ब्राह्मणकुलानि ॥ In अतिजरसं ब्राह्मणकुलं पश्य the affix is not elided. The form is thus evolved: अतिजर+अम् ॥ Here three rules present themselves simultaneously; first, luk-elision of the affix अम् by VII. 1, 23, (2) then the अम् substitution by VII. 1. 24, (3) and thirdly, जरस् for जर by this rule. Of these लुक्-elision is superseded by अम् of VII. 1. 24 which is an exception to VII. 1. 23; and in its turn अम् is replaced by the जरस् of this sûtra. जरस् being substituted for जर, we have अतिजरस्, now luk cannot again appear and cause elision, as it has already lost the opportunity: and we are left with अम् alone, and have अतिजरसं ॥ In the Nom. Sg. and Ins. Pl we have अतिजरं and अतिजरैः according to the opinion of Gonardîya. The reason being सन्निपातलक्षणो विधिरनिमित्तं तद्विघातस्य 'that which is taught in a rule the application of which is occasioned by the combination of two things, does not become the cause of the destruction of that combination'. Because अम् was added to अतिजर because it ended in अ (VII. 1. 24), and similarly भिः was replaced by ऐस् (VII. 1. 9). Now अ has *caused* the production of अम् and ऐस्, therefore, these latter affixes, though beginning with a vowel will not cause जरस् to be substituted for जर by this rule, for then the produced will cause the destruction of the producer. Others hold that the above maxim is anitya, and we have Nom. Sg. अतिजरसं, and Ins. Pl. अतिजरसैः ॥

The form अतिजरांसि is thus evolved अतिजर+इ ॥ Here if the नुम् augment be added first, it will be a portion of the aṅga, and will not be an intervention to anything which is to be added or operated upon the aṅga. But this augment will be an intervention with regard to जरा which is but a portion of the word अतिजर ॥ So that an operation applicable to जरा will not take effect, because of this नुम intervention. And though tadantaviddhi applies in these chapters (पदाङ्गाधिकारे तस्य च तदन्तस्य च), yet the maxim is that the substitutes only replace those which are specifically exlibited in a rule (निर्दिश्यमानस्य आदेशा भवन्ति), therefore जरस् would not replace जरा which forms only a portion of a full word अतिजर ॥ Even if the substitution does take place, the नुम् would be found after the स् of जरस् ॥ Therefore, the जरस् substitution should be made first, because this is a subsequent rule; and having done so, the नुम् should be added afterwards under VII. 1. 72.

The form अतिजरसं is thus evolved. We have अतिजर + अम् ॥ Here on the maxim एकदेशविकृतस्य अनन्यत्वात्, we substitute जरस् for जर also, (for जर and जरा are considered as one). Then appears VII 1. 23 ordaining the luk of अम and VII. 1. 24, teaching अम् ॥ The latter rule is preferred for the reasons given above.

त्यदादीनामः ॥ १०२ ॥ पदानि ॥ त्यदादीनाम्, अः ॥

वृत्तिः ॥ त्यदित्येवमादीनामकारादेशो भवति विभक्तौ परतः ।

102. For the final of त्यद् and the rest, there is substituted अ, when an affix, called vibhakti, follows.

Thus त्यद्—स्यः, त्यौ, त्ये ॥ तद्—सः, तौ, ते; यद्—यः, यौ, ये; एतद्—एषः, एतौ, एते; इदम्—अयम्, इमौ, इमे; अदस्—असौ, अमू, अमी; द्वि, द्वौ, द्वाभ्याम् ॥ The tyadâdi words extend upto द्वि, in the list of the pronouns, for the purposes of this अ substitution. Therefore, the substitution does not take place here in भवत् which forms भवान् ॥ When the word त्यद् &c are employed as names, or as a secondary member in a compound, the substitution does not take place, as त्यद्, त्यदौ, त्यदः, अतित्यद्, अतित्यदौ, अतित्यदः See also I. 1. 27 commentary. But when they form the principal member of a compound, the substitution takes place, as परमसः, परमतौ, परमते ॥ For case affix (vibhakti) see V. 3. 1. also. Those affixes are also called vibhakti and cause these substitutions.

किमः कः ॥ १०३ ॥ पदानि ॥ किमः, कः, ॥

वृत्तिः ॥ किम् इत्येतस्य क इत्ययमादेशो भवति विभक्तौ परतः ।

103. क is substituted for किम् before a vibhakti affix.

As कः, कौ, के ॥ The substitution takes place even when the augment अकच् is added. Therefore, the substitute is here क and not अ which latter would have been sufficient for किम् ॥ For म् of किम् being replaced by अ (VII. 2. 102), the इ would be left, which would be replaced by अ, had the sûtra been किमोऽत् and the forms would have been the same (क् + अ + अ = क VI. 1. 97). See V. 3. 1, 13 &c.

कु तिहोः ॥ १०४ ॥ पदानि ॥ कु, तिहोः, ॥

वृत्तिः ॥ तकारादौ हकारादौ च विभक्तौ परतः किमित्येतस्य कु इत्ययमादेशो भवति ।

104. कु is substituted for किम् before a vibhakti affix beginning with a त or a ह ॥

Thus कुतः, कुत्र, कुह (V. 3. 13, 7). The इ in ति means beginning with a त ॥

काति ॥ १०५ ॥ पदानि ॥ क, आति ॥

वृत्तिः ॥ अतीत्येतस्यां विभक्तौ परतः किमित्येतस्य कु इत्ययमादेशो भवति ।

105. क is substituted for किम् before the vibhakti अत् (V, 3. 13).

As कु गमिष्यसि, कु भोक्ष्यते ॥ The substitute कु of the last rule, before the affix अ would have become कु, but that it would have caused guṇa, hence this separate substitute. Had the sûtra been किमोऽङ्कुत् it would not have included the अकच् augmented किम् ॥

तदोः सः सावनन्त्ययोः ॥ १०६ पदानि ॥ तदोः, सः, सौ, अनन्त्ययोः ॥

वृत्तिः ॥ त्यदादीनां तकारदकारयोरनन्त्ययोः सकारादेशो भवति सौ परतः ।

106. For the non-final त् and द् of त्यद् &c. there is substituted स् in the Nominative Singular.

As त्यद् + सु = त्य + अ + सु (VII. 2. 102) = स्य + अ + सु (VII. 2. 106) = स्यः (VI. 1. 97). Similarly सः from तद्, एषः from एतद् as एतद् + सु = एत + अ + स् (VII. 2. 102) = एस + अ + स् (VII. 2. 106) = एषः (VI. 1. 97). So असौ from अदस् by the following sûtra. Why do we say 'non-final'? Observe हे से, सा ॥ Had not this word been used, the case-affix would not be elided in the vocative, as then there would have been no short vowel, as required by VI. 1. 69.

अदस औ सुलोपश्च ॥ १०७ ॥ पदानि ॥ अदसः, औ, सुलोपश्च ॥

वृत्तिः ॥ अदसः सौ परतः सकारस्य औकारादेशो भवति सोश्च लोपो भवति ।

वार्त्तिकम् ॥ औत्वप्रतिषेधः साकच्काद्वा वक्तव्यः सादुत्वं च ॥

वा० ॥ उत्तरपदभूतानां त्यदादीनामकृतसन्धीनामादेशा वक्तव्याः ॥

Kârikâ अदसः सोर्भवेदौत्वं किं सुलोपो विधीयते ।
ह्रस्वाल्लुप्येत संबुद्धिर्न हलः प्रकृतं हि तत् ॥
आप एत्वं भवेत्तस्मिन्न झलीत्यनुवर्तनात् ।
प्रत्ययस्थाच्च कादित्वं शीभावश्च प्रसज्यते ॥

107. For the स् of अदस् there is substituted औ, whereby the Nom. affix सु is elided.

As अदस् + सु = अद + औ + सु (VII. 2. 107) = अस + औ (VII. 2. 106) = असौ ॥

Vârt:—When the augment अकच् is added, the औ substitution is optional, and in that alternative उ is added after स्, as असुकः or असकौ ॥

Vârt:—When त्यद् &c. form second members of a compound, the above mentioned substitutions take place before the application of sandhi: as परमाहम्, परमायम्, परमानेन ॥

The form असुकः is thus evolved :—अदकस् + सु, now औ substitution of the present sûtra is prohibited; therefore, the अ substitution of VII. 2. 102 takes place, and the द् is changed to स् by VII. 2. 106, and the अ of अकच् after म् is changed to उ ॥

The following observations may be made with regard to the forms परमाहम् &c A substitute would be a bahiraṅga with regard to a case-affix that should be added to a compound. Therefore, being an antaraṅga rule, the ekadeśa should be made first, and this ekadeśa being considered as the beginning of the subsequent word, we should get erroneous forms like परमहम्. परमयं instead of परमाहम् and परमायम् &c. Hence the necessity of the above vârtika.

Kârikâ:—Let the sûtra be अदस औ without the words सुलोपश्च ॥ The word सौ is understood here from the preceding aphorism. The word अदसः is in the ablative case, the word सौ which is in the 7th case, should be changed here into the 6th case सोः ॥ The sûtra would then mean अदस उत्तरस्य सोरौकारो भवति— औ is substituted for the सु after अदस् ॥ Then the final अस् of अदस् is changed to अ by VII. 2. 102, and द् is changed to स् by VII. 2. 106, and we have असौ ॥ So where is the necessity of using the words सुलोपश्च in the sûtra.

Obj : If औ be substituted for सु, then in the vocative this औ should be elided by VI. 1. 69, as it comes after a short vowel अ of VII. 2. 102. Ans. औ will not be elided by VI. 1. 69, for that rule refers to the elision of a consonantal affix only, the word हलः being understood in that sûtra, from the preceding sûtra VI. 1. 68.

Obj : If this be so, then in the Feminine Vocative we have असा+औ, and by the rule VII. 3. 106, the आ should be changed to ए before this औ ॥ Ans. No, this will not be so, for the ए substitution takes place only before a हल् beginning affix, for the word हलि is understood in the sûtra VII. 3. 106 from the sûtra VII. 3. 103.

Obj : If this be so, then in the feminnine with अकच्, we have, असका+ औ, and here rule VII. 3. 44 shows itself and requires the अ of स to be changed to इ (असिका) before the क of an affix. Ans. That rule VII. 3. 44 applies where the feminine affix आ is audible and remains unchanged, but here it is changed to औ (Vṛddhi आ + औ = औ) in असकौ ॥

Obj : But then in असा+औ, the औ would require to be changed to शी by VII. 1. 18. Ans. This objection is partial only, for औङ् in VII. I. 18 is explained by some, to be the common name given by ancient grammarians to the औ of Dual; and not to this औ ; moreover, in the masculine no objection can apply. Hence the words सुलोपश्च may well be omitted.

इदमो मः ॥ १०८ ॥ पदानि ॥ इदमः, मः ॥

वृत्तिः । इदमः सौ परतो मकारोन्तादेशो भवति ।

108. म is substituted for the final म of इदम् in the Nominative Singular.

As इयम्, अयम् ॥ The substitution of म् for म् is to prevent the अ substitution of VII. 2. 102. The case-ending is elided by VI. 1. 68, and य substituted by VII. 2. 110.

दश्च ॥ १०९ ॥ पदानि ॥ दः,च, ॥

वृत्तिः । इदमो दकारस्य स्थाने मकारादेशो भवति विभक्तौ परतः ।

109. And म is substituted for the द् of इदम् before a case-affix.

As इमौ, इमे, इमम्, इमौ, इमान् ॥ Thus इदम्+अम्=इदअ+अम् (VII. 2. 102)= इमअ+अम् (VII. 2. 109)=इमम् (VI. 1. 97, 107).

यः सौ ॥ ११० ॥ पदानि ॥ यः,सौ, ॥

वृत्तिः । इदमो दकारस्य यकारादेशो भवति सौ परतः ।

110. य् is substituted for the द् of इदम् in the Nom. Sg. in the feminine.

As इयम् ॥ This is confined to the Feminine, as the following sûtra relates to the masculine; and in the Neuter, the सु is लुक् elided by स्वमोर्नपुंसकात् and so leaves no trace behind.

इदोऽय् पुंसि ॥ १११ ॥ पदानि ॥ इदः,अय्,पुंसि ॥

वृत्तिः । इदम इद्रूपस्य पुंसि सौ परतो ऽय् इत्ययमादेशो भवति ।

111. अय् is substituted for the इद् of इदम् in the Nom. Sg. masculine.

As अयम् ॥ In the Feminine इयम् ॥ As अयं ब्राह्मणः, and इयं ब्राह्मणी ॥

अनाप्यकः ॥ ११२ ॥ पदानि ॥ अन, आपि, अकः, ॥

वृत्तिः । इदमो ऽककारस्य इद्रूपस्य स्थाने अन इत्ययमादेशो भवति आपि विभक्तौ परतः ।

112. अन is substituted for the इद् of इदम् in the Instrumental singular and the cases that follow, provided that the augment akach is not added.

As अनेन, अनयोः ॥ Why do we say "not when क is added by V. 3. 71"? Observe इमकेन, इमकयोः ॥ The word आप् (आपि) in the sûtra is a pratyâhâra, formed with the आ of टा (Ins. Sg), and प् of सुप् (Loc. Pl).

हलि लोपः ॥ ११३ ॥ पदानि ॥ हलि, लोपः, ॥

वृत्तिः । हलादौ विभक्तौ परत इदमो ऽककारस्य इद्रूपस्य लोपो भवति ।

113. The इद् of इदम् is elided before a case-affix beginning with a consonant.

As आभ्याम्, एभिः, (VII. 1. 11) एभ्यः एषाम्, एषु ॥ For म् is substituted अ by VII. 2. 102, and for अ+अ=अ by VI. 1. 97. The rule I. 1. 52 by which a substitute replaces only the final *letter*, does not apply here, on the maxim नानर्थके ऽलोऽन्त्यविधिः ॥ For no purpose is served by eliding merely the final इ

of इदम् ॥ Hence इद् is elided. Or it may be said that the sûtra does not teach the elision of इद्, but of अन् which was substituted for इद् by the preceding sûtra.

मृजेर्वृद्धिः ॥११४॥ पदानि ॥ मृजेः, वृद्धिः ॥

वृत्तिः ॥ विभक्ताविति निवृत्तम् मृजेरङ्गस्य इको वृद्धिर्भवति ॥

114. The Vṛiddhi (आर्) is substituted for the root vowel (ऋ) of the stem मृज् before an affix.

As मार्ष्टा, मार्ष्टुम्, मार्ष्टव्यम् ॥ The मृज् here is a root, and the affixes before which this Vṛiddhi takes place are those which come after *roots*, and not which come after Prâtipadikas. Therefore, not before the affixes भ्यां &c, as कंसपरिमृड्भ्याम्, मृड्भिः ॥ The anuvṛitti of the word vibhakti has ceased. This sûtra debars guṇa of VII. 3. 84.

अचो ञ्णिति ॥ ११५ ॥ पदानि ॥ अचः, ञ्, णिति ॥

वृत्तिः ॥ अजन्ताङ्गस्य ञिति णिति च वृद्धिर्भवति ॥

115. Before the affixes having an indicatory ञ् or ण्, Vṛiddhi is substituted for the end-vowel of a stem.

Thus एकस्तण्डुलनिषावः, (III. 3. 20) द्वौ शूर्पनिष्पावौ, कारः and हारः (with घञ्); गौः, गावौ, गावः, सखायौ, सखायः where the case-endings are णित् by VII. 1. 90, 92. जैत्रम्, यौत्रम् with the Uṇâdi ष्ट्रण् from जि and यु ॥ च्यौत्नः with त्नण् and means 'strength'. It is an obsolete Vedic word.

अत उपधायाः ॥ ११६ ॥ पदानि ॥ अतः, उपधायाः ॥

वृत्तिः ॥ अङ्गोपधाया अकारस्य स्थाने ञिति णिति च प्रत्यये वृद्धिर्भवति ॥

116. In a stem ending in a consonant with an अ immediately preceding it, the Vṛiddhi is substituted for such अ, when an affix having an indicatory ञ् or ण् follows.

As पाकः, त्यागः, यागः with घञ्, पाचि with the causative णि, पाचकः with ण्वुल् ॥ Why do we say 'अ'? Observe भेदयति, भेदकः with guṇa only from भिद् where इ is penultimate and not अ ॥ Why do we say 'penultimate'? Observe चकासयति, तक्षकः ॥

तद्धितेष्वचामादेः ॥ ११७ ॥ पदानि ॥ तद्धितेषु, अचाम्, आदेः ॥

वृत्तिः ॥ तद्धिते ञिति णिति च प्रत्यये परतोऽङ्गस्याचामादेरचः स्थाने वृद्धिर्भवति ॥

117. The Vṛiddhi is substituted for the first vowel of the stem, when a Taddhita-affix having an indicatory ञ् or ण् follows.

As गार्ग्यः from गर्ग + यञ्, so also वात्स्यः ॥ दाक्षिः (दक्ष + इञ्), प्लाक्षिः, औपगवः (with अण् from उपगु), कापटवः &c. This debars the Vṛiddhi of VII. 2. 115 and 116. as स्वाङ्गः from स्वङ्, and जागतः from जगत् ॥

किति च ॥ ११८ ॥ पदानि ॥ किति, च, ॥

वृत्तिः ॥ किति च तद्धिते परतोऽङ्गस्याचामादेरचः स्थाने वृद्धिर्भवति ॥

118. The Vṛiddhi is substituted for the first vowel of the stem, when a Taddhita affix with an indicatory क् follows.

As नाडायन with फक्, so also चारायणः (IV. 1. 99), and आक्षिकः and शालाकिकः with ठक् (IV. 4. 1).

ओ३म् ।

अथ सप्तमाध्यायस्य तृतीयः पादः ।

BOOK SEVENTH.

CHAPTER THIRD.

देविकाशिंशपादित्यवाड्दीर्घसत्रश्रेयसामात् ॥ १ ॥ पदानि ॥ देविका, शिंशपा, दित्यवाट्, दीर्घसत्र, श्रेयसाम्, आत् ॥

वृत्तिः ॥ देविका शिंशपा दित्यवाट् दीर्घसत्र श्रेयस् इत्येतेषामङ्गानामचामादेरचः स्थाने वृद्धिप्रसङ्गे आकारो भवति ञिति णिति किति तद्धिते परतः ॥

वार्त्तिकम् ॥ वहीनरस्येद्वचनम् ॥

1. When a Taddhita-affix having an indicatory ञ्, ण् or क् follows, आ is substituted instead of Vṛiddhi for the first vowels of the following: devikâ, *s*im*s*apâ, dityavâṭ, dîrghasatra, and *s*reyas.

Thus दाविकम् (=देविकायां भवम्) in दाविकमुदकम्; दाविकाकूलाः शालयः (=देविकाकूले भवाः), पूर्वदाविकः from पूर्वदेविका 'the name of a village of the Eastern people'. Here the vṛiddhi of the second member ordained by VII. 3. 14, becomes आ ॥ Similarly शांशपश्चमसः (=शिंशपायाविकारः) ॥ The word belongs to the Palâsâdi class (IV. 3. 141), and takes अण् or अञ्, the difference being in accent. So also शांशपास्थलाः (=शिंशपास्थले भवाः), and पूर्वशांशप from पूर्वशिंशपः 'the name of a village' See VII. 3. 14. Similarly दात्यौहम् from दित्यवाह्, (दित्यौह इदं) and दार्घसत्रम् (दीर्घसत्रे भवं) and श्रायसम् (श्रेयसि भवं) ॥

Vârt:—The Vṛiddhi of वहीनर under similar circumstances is with an ऐ as if व was वि, as वहीनरस्यापत्यं=वैहीनरिः ॥ Some say the original word itself is विहीनर (विहीनोनरः), and so its taddhita derivative is regular.

केकयमित्रयुप्रलयानां यादेरियः ॥ २ ॥ पदानि ॥ केकय, मित्रयु, प्रलयानाम्, य-आदेः, इयः, ॥

वृत्तिः ॥ केकय मित्रयु प्रलय इत्येतेषां यकारादेरिय इत्ययमादेशो भवति तद्धिते ञिति णिति किति च परतः ॥

2. When a Taddhita affix with an indicatory ञ्, ण् or क् follows, इय् is substituted for the य and यु of केकय, मित्रयु and प्रलय ॥

As कैकेयः (=केकयस्यापत्यं), with the affix अञ् (IV. 1. 168): similarly मैत्रेयिका formed with वुञ् (V. 1. 134) in the sentence मैत्रेयिकया श्लाघते ॥ The word Gotra in that sûtra V. 1. 134 means a Rishi name, for in ordinary parlance the name of a Rishi is called Gotra. Similarly प्रालेयम् (=प्रलयादागत). As प्रालेयमुदकं ॥

न य्वाभ्यां पदान्ताभ्यां पूर्वौ तु ताभ्यामैच् ॥ ३ ॥ पदानि ॥ न, य्वाभ्याम्, पदान्ताभ्याम्, पूर्वौ, तु, ताभ्याम्, ऐच् ॥

वृत्तिः ॥ यकारवकाराभ्यामुत्तरस्य अचामादेरचः स्थाने वृद्धिर्न भवति; ताभ्यां तु यकारवकाराभ्यां पूर्वमैचावागमौ भवतो ञिति णिति किति च तद्धिते परतः ॥

वार्त्तिकम् ॥ अव्ययानां भमात्रे टिलोपः ॥

3. Before a Taddhita affix having an indicatory ञ्, ण् or क्, the Vṛiddhi is not substituted for the first vowel in a compound, when it follows a word ending in य् or व्, but ऐ and औ are respectively placed before the semi-vowels.

That is ऐ is placed before य्, and औ before व् ॥ As वैयसनम् from व्यसन; (व्यसने भवं) वैयाकरणः from व्याकरण (व्याकरणमधीते) सौवश्वः from स्वश्वः (स्वश्वस्यापत्यं) ॥ Why after य् or व् only? Observe वार्थिः son of वर्थः ॥ Why do we say 'य् or व् *final* of a pada or *word*'? Observe याष्टीकः from यष्टिः, (यष्टिः प्रहरणमस्य) IV. 4. 59 वातः from व्रति (व्रतेश्छात्राः or व्रत इमे छात्राः) ॥ The rule does not apply to दाध्याश्वि and माध्वश्वि, for no rule ordains the Vṛiddhi of ध्य or ध्व, and so no occasion for the prohibition of this rule arises. These are Patronyms formed by इञ् (IV. 1. 95) from दध्यश्व and मध्वश्व (दधि प्रियोऽश्वोयस्य &c). The present rule applies to that Vṛiddhi also which takes place in the second member of the compound by VII. 3. 10 &c. As पूर्वैवैयालिन्दः from पूर्वैव्यालिन्द (पूर्वव्यालिन्दे भवः) ॥ But this prohibition does not apply where the य् or व् are not the parts of the second member, as द्व्याशीतिक (=द्वे अशीतीं भृतो, भृतो भावी वा) ॥

द्वारादीनां च ॥ ४ ॥ पदानि ॥ द्वार, आदीनाम्, च, ॥

वृत्तिः ॥ द्वार इत्येवमादीनां य्वाभ्याम् उत्तरपदस्याचामादेरचः स्थाने वृद्धिर्न भवति पूर्वौ तु ताभ्यामैजागमौ भवतः ॥

4. Before a Taddhita-affix with an indicatory ञ्, ण् or क the Vṛiddhi is not substituted for the first vowel after य् or व्, but ऐ and औ are respectively placed before these semi-vowels in द्वार &c.

As द्वारे नियुक्तः=दौवारिकः, दौवारपालम् from द्वारपाल ॥ The Tadâdi rule applies here. सैावरः from स्वर,(स्वरमधिकृत्य कृतो मन्थः)॥ So also सौवरोऽध्यायः, सैावर्यः सप्तम्यः॥ वैयल्कशः from व्यल्कश, (व्यल्कशे भवः) सौवस्तिकः from स्वास्ति, (स्वस्तीति आह) सौवः from स्वर् (स्वर्भवः)॥

Vârt:—The last vowel, with the consonant, if any, which follows it, is elided in the Indeclinables: as सौवर्गमिकः (=स्वर्गमनमाह) ॥

Some read the word स्वाध्याय also in this list, but it is unnecessary, as it would be governed by the last rule, because it is a compound of सु + अध्याय (शोभनोऽध्याय), or it may be a compound of स्व + अध्याय, then also it is unnecessary, as स्व is separately mentioned, in this list, and therefore when स्व begins a word it would get this peculiar substitution then also. Similarly स्फैयकृतः from स्फ्यकृत; सौवादुमृदुम् from स्वादुमृदु, शौवनम् from श्वन् the prakṛiti-bhâva is by (VI. 4. 167) while शौवम् from श्वन् where there is no prakṛitibhâva (by अण् IV. 3. 154): शौवादंष्ट्रः (श्वादंष्ट्रयां भवः). Similarly सौवम् from स्व (=स्वस्येदं); सौवग्रामिकः from स्वग्राम with the affix ठञ् (अध्यात्मादित्वाद् ठञ्). This sûtra is made because the य् and व् here are not finals of a पद or word, as they were in the preceding sûtra. The following is a list of Dvârâdi words.

1 द्वार, 2 स्वर, 3 स्वाध्याय, 4 व्यल्कश, 5 स्वस्ति, 6 स्वर् (स्वर), 7 स्फ्यकृत, 8 स्वादुमृदु, 9 श्वस्*, 10 श्वन्, 11 स्व ॥

न्यग्रोधस्य च केवलस्य ॥ ५ ॥ पदानि ॥ न्यग्रोधस्य, च, केवलस्य, ॥

वृत्तिः ॥ न्यग्रोधशब्दस्य केवलस्य यकारादुत्तरस्याचामादेरचः स्थाने वृद्धिर्न भवति तस्माच्च पूर्वमैकार आगमो भवति ॥

5. ऐ is placed before the य् of न्यग्रोध, instead of Vṛiddhi, when the word stands alone, and is not a member of a compound, and is followed by a Taddhita affix with the indicatory ञ्, ण् or क् ॥

As नैयग्रोधश्चमसः (=न्यग्रोधस्य विकारः). Why do we say 'when it is alone'? Observe न्यग्रोधमूले भवाः शालयः = न्यग्रोधमूलाः ॥ If न्यग्रोध is a derivative word (from न्यग्रोहयति = नीचैर्गतौ परोहैर्वधते), then it would have been governed by VII. 3. 3, this separate, sûtra is then for the sake of making a restrictive rule (niyama) with regard to this word. If it is a primary word, then this sûtra makes a Vidhi rule. The word केवल is a jñâpaka that the rule of Tadâdi applies in this section. See VII. 3. 8, also.

न कर्मव्यतिहारे ॥ ६ ॥ पदानि ॥ न, कर्मव्यतिहारे ॥

वृत्तिः ॥ कर्मव्यतिहारे यदुक्तं तन्न भवति ॥

6. The prohibition and the augment, ordained by VII. 3. 3, do not apply to a word which expresses the reciprocity of an action.

As व्यावक्रोशी, व्यावलेखी, व्यावर्त्ती, व्यावहासी ॥ See III. 3. 43 and V. 4. 14.

स्वागतादीनां च ॥ ७ ॥ पदानि ॥ स्वागत, आदीनाम्, च, ॥

वृत्तिः ॥ स्वागत इत्येवमादीनां यदुक्तं तन्न भवति ॥

7. The prohibition and augment taught in VII. 3. 3 does not apply also to स्वागत &c.

As स्वागतिकः, (=स्वागतमिति आह) स्वाध्वरिकः, (=स्वधरेण चरति) स्वाङ्गिः, व्याङ्गिः, व्याडिः (sons of Svanga, Vyanga and Vyaḍa). व्यावहारिकः and स्वापतेयः (=स्वपतौ साधुः) ॥ The word व्यवहार does not mean reciprocity of action, for then it would have been governed by the last sûtra. स्वपत being a compound with स्व, would have been governed by VII. 3. 4 as it is included in the Dvârâdi list, hence its specific mention here. The following is the list of svâgatâdi words.

1 स्वागत, 2 स्वध्वर, 3 स्वङ्ग, 4 व्यङ्ग, 5 व्यड, 6 व्यवहार, 7 स्वपति ॥

श्वादेरिञि ॥ ८ ॥ पदानि ॥ श्व, आदेः, इञि ॥

वृत्तिः ॥ श्वादेरङ्गस्य इञि परतो यदुक्तं तन्न भवति ॥

वार्त्तिकम् ॥ इकारादिग्रहणं कर्तव्यं पूर्वगणिकाद्यर्थम् ॥

8. A compound beginning with श्वन्, and followed by the Taddhita affix इञ्, is not governed by the prohibition, nor takes the augment, taught in VII. 3. 4.

Thus the descendant of श्वभस्त्र is श्वाभस्त्रिः, so also श्वादंष्ट्रिः ॥ The word श्वन् is included in the list of Dvâṛâdi words VII. 3, 4., the present sûtra implies that the rule VII. 3. 4 applies not only to those words, but to compounds beginning with those words.

Vârt:—This rule applies when any Taddhita affix beginning with इ follows; as श्वगणेन चरति=श्वागणिकः, श्वायूथिकः (IV. 4. 11).

The prohibition applies, when other Taddhita affixes follow such a word ending with इञ् (an affix beginning with इ): as from श्वाभस्त्रि we have श्वाभस्त्रम् (श्वाभस्त्रेरिदं) ॥

पदान्तस्यान्यतरस्याम् ॥ ९ ॥ पदानि ॥ पदान्तस्य, अन्यतरस्याम् ॥

वृत्तिः ॥ श्वादेरङ्गस्य पदशब्दान्तस्यान्यतरस्यां यदुक्तं तन्न भवति ॥

9. The rule VII. 3. 4. is optionally applied to श्वन् followed by पद ॥

As श्वापदस्येदं=श्वापदम् or शौवापदम् ॥

उत्तरपदस्य ॥ १० ॥ पदानि ॥ उत्तर पदस्य ॥

वृत्तिः ॥ उत्तरपदस्येत्ययमधिकारः, हनस्तोऽचिण्णलोरिति प्रागेतस्मात् । यदित ऊर्ध्वमनुक्रमिष्याम उत्तरपदस्येत्येवं तद्वेदितव्यम् ॥

10. Upto VII. 3. 31 inclusive, the substitution of Vṛiddhi will take place, for the first vowel of the second member in a compound.

This is an adhikâra sûtra, and exerts governing influence upto VII. 3. 32 exclusive. The phrase "of the second member of the compound" should be supplied in all those sûtras, to complete the sense. Thus in VII. 3. 11, the word उत्तरपदस्य should be supplied. As पूर्ववार्षिकं, अपरवार्षिकम्, पूर्वहैमनम्, अपरहैमनम् ॥

In those sûtras, where the word denoting the first member is not exhibited in the Ablative case, as in VII. 3. 18, 19, 20, 21, the present sûtra is absolutely necessary for causing the vṛiddhi of the second member. But in those sûtras, where the first member is exhibited in the ablative case, as in VII. 3. 11 (अवयवात्), there this sûtra is only explanatory (and not absolutely necessary), and serves also the purpose of placing such vṛiddhis under the category of 'uttarapada-vṛiddhi'. This peculiar vṛiddhi is liable to certain rules of accent, as in VI. 2. 105. Hence the importance of the present aphorism in those sûtras also, where the word is exhibited in the fifth case.

अवयवादृतोः ॥ ११ ॥ पदानि ॥ अवयवात्, ऋतोः ॥

वृत्तिः ॥ अवयववाचिन उत्तरस्य ऋतुवाचिन उत्तरपदस्याचामादेरचो वृद्धिर्भवति तद्धिते ञिति णिति किति च परतः ॥

11. Before a Taddhita affix having an indicatory ञ्, ण् or क्, Vṛiddhi is substituted for the first vowel of a word denoting season, when it is preceded by a word denoting a part.

As पूर्ववार्षिकम्, पूर्वहैमनम्, अपरवार्षिकम्, अपरहैमनम् ॥ The composition with पूर्व and अपर &c takes place by II. 2. 1. and then by IV. 3. 18 there is ठक् after वर्ष, and अण् after हेमन्त with the elision of त by IV. 3. 22. The Tadanta-viddhi, as a general rule, does not apply to compounds, so that a rule made applicable to a particular word, will not apply to a compound which ends with that word: but tadanta-viddhi applies to a word denoting season when it takes an affix causing Vṛiddhi, and is preceded by a word denoting a portion. We draw this rule from the present sûtra, for हैमनं being formed from हेमन्त by a vṛiddhi-causing affix (IV. 3. 22), the affix अण will be applied to हेमन्त even when it is the second member of a compound, the first member of which denotes a part. (ऋतोर्वृद्धि मद्विधावयवात् I. 1. 72 Vârt. Mahâbhâshya).

Why do we say 'denoting a portion'? Observe पूर्वासु वर्षासु भवं पौर्ववर्षिकम् with ठञ् (IV. 3. 11). The tadanta-vidhi applies only when the first member denotes a portion.

सुसर्वार्द्धाज्जनपदस्य ॥ १२ ॥ पदानि ॥ सु, सर्व, अर्द्धात्, जनपदस्य ॥

वृत्तिः ॥ सु सर्व अर्द्ध इत्येतेभ्य उत्तरस्य जनपदवाचिन उत्तरपदस्याचामादेरचो वृद्धिर्भवति तद्धिते ञिति णिति किति च परतः ॥

12. After सु, सर्व and अर्ध, the first vowel of the name of a country gets the Vṛiddhi, when a Taddhita affix with an indicatory ञ्, ण् or क् follows.

As सुपाञ्चालकः, सर्वपाञ्चालकः and अर्धपाञ्चालकः, formed with वुञ् (IV.2.125). This sûtra also gives rise to the following rule सुसर्वार्धदिक् शब्देभ्यो जनपदस्य "The tadantavidhi applies to words denoting country, when the first member is सु, सर्व, अर्ध or a direction-denoting word". As shown in the above examples, and for direction denoting words see the following sûtra. (I. 1. 72 Vârt. Mahâbhâshya).

दिशोऽमद्राणाम् ॥ १३ ॥ पदानि ॥ दिशः, अ मद्राणाम् ॥

वृत्तिः ॥ दिग्वाचिन उत्तरस्य जनपदवाचिनो मद्रवर्जितस्याचामादेरचोवृद्धिर्भवति तद्धिते ञिति णिति किति च परतः ॥

13. After a word denoting direction, the first vowel of the name of a country, with the exception of मद्र, gets Vṛiddhi before a Taddhita-affix having an indicatory ञ्, ण्, or क् ॥

As पूर्वपाञ्चालकः, अपरपाञ्चालकः, दाक्षिणपाञ्चालकः, उत्तरपाञ्चालकः (IV. 2. 125, 107, 108. VI. 2. 105 accent). The Tadanta-vidhi applies here, as shown in the preceding sûtra. Why do we say 'denoting direction'? Observe पूर्वः पञ्चालानां = पूर्वपञ्चालं, तत्र भवः, = पौर्वपञ्चालकः, आपरपञ्चालकः ॥ With मद्र we have पौर्वमद्रः, आपरमद्रः with अञ् (IV. 2. 108). The separation of this sûtra from the last is for the sake of the subsequent sûtra.

प्राचां ग्रामनगराणाम् ॥ १४ ॥ पदानि ॥ प्राचाम्, ग्राम, नगराणाम् ॥

वृत्तिः ॥ प्राचां देशे ग्रामनगराणां दिश उत्तरेषामचामादेरचो वृद्धिर्भवति तद्धिते ञिति णिति किति च परतः ॥

14. After a word denoting direction, the first vowel of the name of a village or city in the land of the eastern people, gets the Vṛiddhi before a Taddhita affix having an indicatory ञ्, ण् or क् ॥

Thus पूर्वैषुकामशमः, अपरैषुकामशमः, पूर्वकार्ष्णमृत्तिकः, अपरकार्ष्णमृत्तिकः (IV. 2. 107). These are village names. पूर्वपाटलिपुत्रकः, अपरपाटलिपुत्रकः पूर्वकान्यकुब्जः, अपरकान्यकुब्जः ॥

The word प्राचां in this sûtra, as well as in VII. 3. 24, does not here mean 'the eastern grammarians', but 'the eastern countries', because of the context. पूर्वैषुकामशमः is thus formed. पूर्वा च असौ इषुकामशमी = पूर्वेषुकामशमी ॥ The compounding takes place by II. 1. 50. Then the affix अ is added to it, in the sense of ततो भवः by IV. 2. 107. In पूर्वपाटलिपुत्रकः the affix वुञ् is added by IV. 2. 123. Though Pâṭaliputra is the name of *one* city, Purva-pâṭaliputra means the Eastern portion of the city Pâṭaliputra.

That place is called 'grâma', where people reside; and a 'nagara' is also a 'grâma' in this sense. Therefore, the rules which good men observe with regard to 'grâma', are obsered by them in 'nagara' also. Thus the rule is अभक्ष्यो ग्रामकुक्कुटः, therefore, the नागर cock is also not eaten. So also ग्रामे नाध्येयम् is applied to nagara also. In this grammar also, we see that 'grâma' includes 'nagara' also, as in IV. 2. 109, 117, VI. 2. 103. Therefore, where is the necessity of employing the word नगर separately in this aphorism?' The two words are separately used, in order to indicate the separate nature and relation of the two kinds of words. The *full* word पूर्वेषुकामशमी is the name of a 'grâma', and not the portion इषुकामशमी ॥ But in पूर्वपाटलिपुत्र, the word पाटलिपुत्र itself is the name of the 'nagara'. In the present sûtra, there is the adhikâra of अङ्गस्य and of उत्तरपदस्य ॥ We apply these separately to these two classes of words: namely ग्रामवाचिनाम् अङ्गानाम and नगरवाचिनाम् उत्तरपदानाम् ॥ This we could not have done without employing these words in the sûtra.' Therefore, in the case of 'grâma' word, the vṛiddhi takes place in that *portion* of it which follows a direction denoting word (ग्रामवाचिनामङ्गानामवयवस्य दिक्शब्दादुत्तरस्य वृद्धिर्भवति). While a *nagara* word itself gets vṛiddhi when it is preceded by a direction denoting word (दिशः उत्तरेषां नगराणाम्) ॥ In पूर्वैषुकामशमः, the vṛiddhi of इषुकामशमी takes place first, and then the combination by sandhi. See on this point VII. 3. 22.

संख्यायाः संवत्सरसंख्यस्य च ॥ १५ ॥ पदानि ॥ संख्यायाः, संवत्सर, संख्यस्य, च ॥

वृत्तिः ॥ सख्याया उत्तरपदस्य संवत्सरशब्दस्य संख्यायाश्चाचामादेरचः स्थाने वृद्धिर्भवति तद्धिते ञिति णिति किति च परतः ॥

15. After a Numeral, the first vowel of संवत्सर and of a Numeral, gets the Vṛiddhi, before a Taddhita having an indicatory ञ्, ण्, or क ॥

Thus द्विसांवत्सरिकः = द्वौ संवत्सरावधीष्टो भृतो भूतो or भावी (V. 1. 80), त्रिसांवत्सरिकः, द्विषाष्टिकः = द्वे षष्टी अधीष्टो भृतो भूतो भावी वा ॥ द्विसाप्ततिकः ॥ The words द्वि, षष्टी &c when applied to वर्ष (VII. 3. 16) and Numerals give rise to the affixes taught under kâlâdhikâra (V. 1. 78-97). The special mention of संवत्सर here, (though this is a परिमाण word and would have been included in the sûtra VII. 3. 17) implies that the word परिमाण in that sûtra does not mean the measure of *time*, but a measure of any other thing than time. Therefore, with other time-words than samvatsara, the Vṛiddhi takes place in the regular way: as द्वैसमिकः, त्रैसमिकः ॥ Similarly in sûtra IV. 1. 22, the word परिमाण does not mean the measure of time or numerals, as त्रिवर्षा. द्विवर्षा माणविका ॥ In short, the word परिमाण in these sûtras (and elsewhere III. 2. 23, II. 3. 46 &c.) means "mass or bulk", and not a measure in general.

वर्षस्याभविष्यति ॥ १६ ॥ पदानि ॥ वर्षस्य, अ-भविष्यति, ॥

वृत्तिः ॥ संख्याया उत्तरस्य वर्षशब्दस्याचामादेरचो वृद्धिर्भवति तद्धिते ञिति णिति किति च परतः, स चेत्तद्धितो भविष्यत्यर्थे न भवति ।

16. After a numeral, the first vowel of वर्ष gets the Vṛiddhi, before a Taddhita affix having an indicatory ञ्, ण् or क्, when the affix does not refer to a Future time.

As द्विवर्षे अधीष्टो भृतो भूतो वा = द्विवार्षिकः, त्रिवार्षिकः ॥ But when denoting future time, we have द्वैवर्षिकः, त्रैवर्षिकः "calculated to last two or three years" as in the sentence यस्य त्रैवर्षिकं धान्यं निहितं भृत्यवृत्तये अधिकं वापि विद्येत स सोमं पातुमर्हति ॥ (= त्रीणि वर्षाणि भावी). The word अभविष्यत् does not qualify the words अधीष्ट and भृत (V. 1. 80), the sense of futurity is there denoted by the sentence and not by the taddhita-affix: as द्वे वर्षे अधीष्टो भृतो वा कर्म करिष्यति = द्विवार्षिको मनुष्यः ॥

परिमाणान्तस्यासंज्ञाशाणयोः ॥१७॥ पदानि ॥ परिमाणान्तस्य, असंज्ञा, शाणयोः॥

वृत्तिः ॥ परिमाणान्तस्याङ्गस्य संख्यायाः परं यदुत्तरपदं तस्याचामादेरचो वृद्धिर्भवति तद्धिते ञिति णिति किति च परतः, संज्ञायां विषये शाणे चोत्तरपदे न भवति ॥

17. After a numeral, the first vowel of a word denoting mass in its widest sense (with the exception of शाण) gets the Vṛiddhi before a Taddhita affix having an indicatory ञ्, ण् or क्, when the word so formed does not mean a Name.

As द्वौ कुडवौ प्रयोजनमस्य = द्विकौडविकः (V. 1. 109) द्वाभ्यां सुवर्णाभ्यां क्रीतं = द्विसौवर्णिकम् (V. 1. 37), त्रिसौवर्णिकम् ॥ The taddhita affix is optionally elided, see vârtika to V. 1. 29. When the affix is elided there can be no Vṛiddhi, as द्विसुवर्णम् ॥ Similarly द्विनैष्किकम्, त्रिनैष्किकम् (V. 1. 30). Why 'when it is not a name'? Observe पाञ्चलोहितिकम्, पाञ्चकपालिकम् (= पञ्चलोहित्यः or कपलानि परिमाणमस्य V. 1. 30) The whole word is a Name here. Why with the exception of शाण? Observe द्विशाणम्. त्रैशाणम् formed with अण् (V. 1. 35 and 36). Some read the sûtra as असंज्ञाशाणकुलिजानाम् so that कुलिज is also excepted, as द्वैकुलिजिकः (V. 1. 55 द्वे कुलिजे प्रयोजनमस्य) ॥

जे प्रोष्ठपदानाम् ॥ १८ ॥ पदानि ॥ जे, प्रोष्ठपदानाम् ॥

वृत्तिः ॥ जइति जातार्थो निर्दिश्यते । तत्र यस्तद्धितो विहितस्तस्मिन् ञिति णिति किति च परतः प्रोष्ठपदानामुत्तरस्याचामादेरचो वृद्धिर्भवति ॥

18. In प्रोष्ठपद and its synonyms, the first vowel of the second member gets the Vṛiddhi, before a Taddhita affix meaning 'born in that time', and having an indicatory ञ्, ण् or क् ॥

The word ज means 'born', the affixes denoting 'born under that asterism' are meant here. प्रोष्ठपद is the name of an asterism, the time appertaining there to is also called प्रोष्ठपद (the affix अण् of IV. 3. 3, is elided by IV. 2. 4). प्रोष्ठपदासु जातः = प्रोष्ठपादो माणवकः (with अण् IV. 3. 16). Why do we say 'born in that time'? Observe यदा प्रौष्ठपदोमेघः (= प्रोष्ठपदासु भवः) धरणीमभिवर्षति ॥ The plural number प्रोष्ठपदानां indicates that the synonyms of प्रोष्ठपद such as भद्रपाद are also to be included.

हृद्भगसिन्ध्वन्ते पूर्वपदस्य च ॥१९॥ पदानि ॥ हृद्, भग, सिन्धु, अन्त, पूर्वपदस्य च॥

वृत्तिः ॥ हृद् भग सिन्धु इत्येवमन्तेऽङ्गे पूर्वपदस्योत्तरपदस्याचामादेरचो वृद्धिर्भवति तद्धिते ञिति णिति किति च परतः ॥

19. The Vṛiddhi is substituted for the first vowels of both (the first and second) members in a compound ending with हृद्, भग, and सिन्धु, before a Taddhita affix having an indicatory ञ्, ण् or क् ॥

As सुहृदयस्येदं = सौहार्दम्, सौभाग्यम्, दौर्भाग्यम् सौभागिनेयः (= सुभगाया अपत्यं), दौर्भागिनेयः (IV. 1. 126). The words सुभगा and दुर्भगा occur in the Kalyâṇâdi class (IV. 1. 126), and the affix ढक् and इन् augment are added. सुभग also occurs in Udgâtṛi class (V. 1. 129). That word, however, does not get the Vṛiddhi in the second member, As महते सौभगाय ॥ This is a Vedic anomaly. Similarly from सक्तुसिन्धवः (= सक्तुप्रधानाः सिन्धवः) we have साक्तुसैन्धवः (= सक्तुसिन्धुषु भवः) so also पानसिन्धवः ॥ The word सिन्धु occurs in Kachchhâdi class, and सैन्धवः is formed by अण् ॥ The Tadanta-rule applies to words formed there-under.

The words सुहृद् and दुर्हृद् are anomalously formed by V. 4. 150. But the reading adopted by Kâśikâ is सुहृदयस्येदम् ; so the word hṛidaya is changed to hṛid by VI. 3. 50 or VI. 3. 51. The word sindhu means 'a country', 'a river' or 'an ocean'.

अनुशतिकादीनां च ॥ २० ॥ पदानि ॥ अनुशतिकादिनाम्, च ॥

वृत्तिः ॥ अनुशतिक इत्येवमादीनां चाङ्गानां पूर्वपदस्य चोत्तरपदस्याचामादेरचः स्थाने वृद्धिर्भवति तद्धिते ञिति णिति किति वा परतः ॥

वार्त्तिकम् ॥ कल्याण्यादीनामिनङ्ङितिनङ् ॥

20. Before a Taddhita affix having an indicatory ञ्, ण् or क्, the Vṛiddhi is substituted for the first vowel of both members of the compounds अनुशतिक &c.

Thus (1) आनुशातिकम् (= अनुशतिकस्येदम्) V.1.21 and IV.3.120; (2) आनुहौडिकः (= अनुहोडेन चरति IV.4.8). (3) आनुसांवरणम् (= अनुसंवरणे दीयते V. 1. 96). (4) आनुसांवत्सरिकः (IV. 3. 60 formed by ठञ् from अनुसम्वत्सरेण दीयते) (5) आंगारवैणवः (son of अङ्गारवेणु). (6) आसिहात्यम् (= असिहत्ये भवं). Some read this word as अस्यहत्य; this will also take अण् as belonging to विमुक्तादि class. As आस्यहात्यः (= अस्यहत्यशब्दोऽस्मिन्नध्यायेऽस्ति) Others read this as अस्यहेतिः, as आस्यहैतिकः (= अस्यहेतिः प्रयोजनमस्य). The word अस्य in these is treated like a Prâtipadika, its case-affix is not elided. (7) वाध्यौगः (= वध्योगस्य अपत्यं). It belongs to Bidâdi class. (8) पुष्करसदोऽपत्यं = पौष्करसादिः ॥ This belongs to Bâhvâdi class. (9) आनुहारत from अनुहरत् II The same as above. (10) कुरुकतः belongs to Gargâdi class. Its partonymic is कौरुकात्यः (11) कौरुपाञ्चालः (कुरुपञ्चालेषु भवः) ॥ The affix वुञ् is not added here, because जनपदसमुदायो जनपदग्रहणेन गृह्यते ॥

(12) औदुकशौद्धिः (son of उदकशुद्धिः) ॥ (13, 14) ऐहलौकिकः, पारलौकिकः, from इहलोकः and परलोकः by adding ठञ् in the sense of तत्र भवः (लोकोत्तरपदस्य च) ॥ (15) सार्वलौकिकः from सर्वलोकः by ठञ् under V. 1, 44. (16) सार्वपौरुषम् from सर्वपुरुषः in the

sense of तस्येदम् ॥ (17) सार्वभौम: (=सर्वभूमेर्निमित्तं संयोगो or उत्पातो वा V 1. 41) ॥ (18) प्रयोग:—प्रायोगिक: (तत्र भवः, प्रयोगाधिदेवाधिभूतत्यध्यात्मादय:) (19) परस्त्री—पारस्त्रैणेय: formed by ढ्नक् (IV. 1. 126).

(20) So also of राजपुरुष before the affix ष्यञ्, as राजपौरुष्यम् ॥ Why do we say before ष्यञ् only? Observe राजपुरुषस्यापत्यं=राजपुरुषायणि:; formed by फिञ् (IV. 1. 157).

(21) शतकुम्भे भवः=शातकौम्भ:, (21 a) सौखशायनिक: from सुखशयन (21 b) पारदारिक: from परदार ॥ (22) सौत्रनाडि=सूत्रनडस्यापत्यं ॥

This is an Akṛitigaṇa class; therefore, we have forms like these, आभिगामिक: (अभिगममर्हति), आधिदैविकम् (अधिदेवभवः), आधिभौतिकं; चातुर्वैद्यम् (चतस्र एव विद्या) ॥ The affix ष्यञ् is added in svârtha.

1 अनुशतिक, 2 अनुहोड, 3 अनुसंवरण (अनुसंचरण), 4 अनुसंवत्सर. 5 अङ्गारवेणु, 6 असिहत्य (अस्यहत्य), 7 अस्यहेति, 8 वध्योग, 9 पुष्करसद्, 10 अनुहरत्, 11 कुरुकत्, 12 कुरुपञ्चाल, 13 उदकशुद्ध, 14 इहलोक, 15 परलोक, 16 सर्वलोक, 17 सर्वपुरुष, 18 सर्वभूमि, 19 प्रयोग, 20 परस्त्री, 21 राजपुरुषात् ष्यञि; 22 सूत्रनड ॥ आकृतिगण, 23 अभिगम, 24 अधिभूत, 25 अधिदेव 26 चतुर्विद्या, 27 सुखशयन 28 शतकुम्भ 29 परदार ॥

देवताद्वन्द्वे च ॥ २१ ॥ पदानि ॥ देवता-द्वन्द्वे, च ॥

वृत्ति: ॥ देवताद्वन्द्वे च पूर्वपदस्योत्तरपदस्य चाचामादेरचः स्थाने वृद्धिर्भवति तद्धिते ञिति णिति किति वा परतः ॥

21. Before a Taddhita affix having an indicatory ञ्, ण् or क्, the Vṛiddhi is substituted for the first vowels of both members a Dvanda compound of the names of Devas.

As अग्निमारुती in अग्निमारुतीमनड्वाहीमालभेत् ॥ आग्निमारुतं कर्म ॥ The rule applies to Dvandas relating to hymns (सूक्त) and sacrificial offerings (हवि). Therefore, not here, स्कान्दविशाखा देवतेऽस्य=स्कान्दविशाख: (IV. 2. 24). So also ब्राह्मप्रजापत्यम् by ण्य from ब्रह्मप्रजापती ॥ See VI. 3. 26.

The short इ in the आग्नि in आग्निमारुत, आग्निवारुणम is by VI. 3. 28. A compound relates to a sûkta, which worships a deva through hymns; and that by which a 'havis' is determined, is a compound relating to sacrificial offering.

नेन्द्रस्य परस्य ॥ २२ ॥ पदानि ॥ न, इन्द्रस्य, परस्य ॥

वृत्ति: ॥ इन्द्रशब्दस्य परस्य यदुक्तं तन्न भवति ॥

22. But the Vṛiddhi of the first vowel of Indra, when it stands as the second member of a Dvanda compound, does not take place before a Taddhita affix having an indicatory ञ्, ण् or क् ॥

As सौमेन्द्र:, आग्नेन्द्र: ॥ Why "when it stands as the subsequent member"? Observe ऐन्द्राग्न मेकादशकपालं चरुं निर्वपेत् ॥ There are two vowels in the word इन्द्र, and when a Taddhita affix is added, then one of these i. e. the अ or the last vowel is elided by VI. 4. 148, and the other (i. e. the इ, coalesces with the last vowel of the first term, as सोम + इन्द्र + अण् = सोम + इन्द्र + अ = सोमे + न्द्र + अ ॥ Now, *no* vowel is left of इन्द्र when it gets the form न्द्र, so what is the necessity of the present prohibitory rule? This prohibition indicates the existence of the following maxim: बहिरङ्गमपि पूर्वोत्तरपदयोः पूर्वं कार्यं भवति, पश्चादेकादेशः or in other words पूर्वोत्तरनिमित्तकार्यात् पूर्वमन्तरङ्गोऽप्येकादेशो न ॥ "The substitution of one vowel for the final of the first and the initial of the second member of a-compound does, even when it is antaranga, not take place previously to an operation which concerns the first or the second member of the compound". It is on this maxim that the forms पूर्वैषुकामशम (VII. 3. 14) &c are constructed, otherwise उ being the first vowel of the second member (इ of इषु having merged in पूर्व), would have been vriddhied.

दीर्घाच्च वरुणस्य ॥ २३ ॥ पदानि ॥ दीर्घात्, च वरुणस्य ॥

वृत्तिः ॥ दीर्घादुत्तरस्य वरुणस्य यदुक्तं तन्न भवति ॥

23. Before a Taddhita affix having an indicatory ञ्, ण् or क्, in a Dvandva compound of god-names, the vriddhi is not substituted for the first vowel of वरुण, when a long vowel precedes it.

As ऐन्द्रावरुणम्, मैत्रावरुणम् from इन्द्रावरुणौ &c. (VI. 3. 26). But आग्निवारुणीं in आग्निवारुणीमनड्वाहीं मालभेत् when a short vowel precedes it. This word is derived from the compound word अग्नीवरुणौ the इ of अग्नि being lengthened by VI. 3. 27. But in forming a Taddhita-derivative from this word, the long ई is shortened by VI. 3. 28, and therefore, it cannot be said that a long vowel precedes वरुण ॥

प्राचां नगरान्ते ॥ २४ ॥ पदानि ॥ प्राचाम्, नगरान्ते ॥

वृत्तिः ॥ प्राचां देशे नगरान्तेऽङ्गे पूर्वपदस्योत्तरपदस्याचामादेरचो वृद्धिर्भवति तद्धिते ञिति णिति किति च परतः ॥

24. Before a Taddhita affix having an indicatory ञ्, ण् or क्, the Vriddhi is substituted for the first vowels of both members of the compound, which is the name of a city of the Eastern People, and which ends in the word नगर ॥

As सौह्मनागरः (= सुह्मनगरे भवः), पौण्ड्रनागरः ॥ Why do we say 'of the Eastern people'? Observe माद्रनगरः, from मद्रनगर: the city of the Northern people.

जङ्गलधेनुवलजान्तस्य विभाषितमुत्तरम् ॥ २५ ॥ पदानि ॥ जङ्गल, धेनु, वलज, अन्तस्य, विभाषितम्, उत्तरम् ॥

वृत्तिः ॥ जङ्गल धेनु वलज इत्येवमन्तस्याङ्गस्य पूर्वपदस्याचामादेरचो वृद्धिर्भवति विभाषितमुत्तर मुत्तरपदस्य विभाषितं तद्धिते ञिति णिति किति वा परतः ।

25. Before a Tahhita affix having an indicatory ञ्, ण्, or क्, the Vriddhi is substituted for the first vowel of

the compound ending in जङ्गल, धेनु and बलज, and optionally for the first vowel of these second members also.

As कौरुजङ्गलम् or कौरुजाङ्गलम्, वैश्वधेनवम् or वैश्वधैनवम्, सौवर्णबलजः or सौवर्णबालजः॥

अर्द्धात्परिमाणस्य पूर्वस्य तु वा ॥२६॥ पदानि ॥ अर्द्धात्, परिमाणस्य, पूर्वस्य, तु, वा ॥

वृत्तिः ॥ अर्द्धशब्दात्परस्य परिमाणवाचिन उत्तरस्याचामादेरचः स्थाने वृद्धिर्भवति पूर्वस्य तु वा भवति तद्धिते ञिति णिति किति वा परतः।

26. Before a Taddhita affix having an indicatory ञ्, ण्, or क्, the Vṛiddhi is substituted for the first vowel of the second member, denoting a mass in its widest sense, when the word अर्ध precedes it, but optionally for the first vowel of अर्ध ॥

As अर्धद्रौणिकम् or आर्धद्रौणिकम्, अर्धकौडविकम् or आर्धकौडविकम् with ठञ् (V. I. 18). Why do we say when denoting a mass? Observe आर्धक्रोशिकम् only (=अर्धक्रोशः प्रयोजनमस्य)॥

नातः परस्य ॥ २७ ॥ पदानि ॥ न, अतः, परस्य ॥

वृत्तिः ॥ अर्द्धात्परस्य परिमाणाकारस्य वृद्धिर्न भवति, पूर्वस्य तु वा भवति, तद्धिते ञिति णिति किति वा परतः ॥

27. When the first vowel of the second member, preceded by अर्ध and denoting mass is short अ, the Vṛiddhi is not substituted for this अ, before a Taddhita affix having an indicatory ञ्, ण् or क्; and optionally so for the first vowel of the first member (i. e. अर्ध) ॥

Thus अर्धप्रस्थिकः or आर्धप्रस्थिकः (V. I. 18) ॥ अर्धकंसिकः or आर्धकंसिकः ॥ Why do we say 'when it is a short अ'? Observe आर्धकौडविकः ॥ Why 'short अ'? Observe अर्धं खार्याम् भवः = अर्धखारी ॥ Here Vṛiddhi is substituted for the आ of खारी, and though the form remains the same, the power of this word is changed. For अर्धखारी being formed by a Taddhita affix causing Vṛiddhi, in forming a Bahuvṛihi compound, this word will retain its feminine form and will not be changed into masculine under VI. 3. 39. as अर्धखारीभार्यः (=अर्धखारीभार्यायस्य)(वृद्धिनिमित्तस्य च तद्धितस्य &c.) Whereever Vṛiddhi is prohibited with regard to a Taddhita affix, that affix cannot be called वृद्धिनिमित्त, and a word formed with such an affix will become masculine in a Bahuvṛihi compound referring to a male person, वैयाकरणी भार्या अस्य = वैयाकरणभार्यः ॥ The word वैयाकरण is formed by *prohibition* of Vṛiddhi. See VII. 3. 3.

प्रवाहणस्य ढे ॥ २८ ॥ पदानि ॥ प्रवाहणस्य, ढे ॥

वृत्तिः ॥ प्रवाहणस्य ढे परत उत्तरपदस्याचामादेरचो वृद्धिर्भवति पूर्वपदस्य वा भवति ॥

28. Before the affix ढ (एय), the Vṛiddhi is substituted for the first vowel of the second member of प्रवाहण, but optionally so for the first vowel of the first member (i. e. प्र) ॥

Thus प्रवाहणस्यापत्यं = प्रावाहणेयः or प्रवाहणेयः ॥ The affix ढक् IV. 1. 123, is added, similarly प्रवाहणेयी भार्याऽस्य = प्रवाहणेयीभार्यः (VI. 3. 39, masculation probibited). Or we may translate the sûtra as "Before the affix ढ, the vowel of प्र in प्रवाहण optionally gets Vṛiddhi", and omit the rest. The masculation will still be prohibited by VI. 3. 41, (आत) ॥

. तत्प्रत्ययस्य च ॥ २६ ॥ पदानि ॥ तत्प्रत्ययस्य, च ॥

वृत्तिः ॥ प्रवाहणस्येति वर्तते, तदिति ढप्रत्ययस्य प्रत्यवमर्षः, ढक् प्रत्ययान्तस्य प्रवाहणशब्दस्य तद्धितेषु परत उत्तरपदस्याचामादेरचो वृद्धिर्भवति पूर्वस्य तु वा ॥

29. Even so in a new derivative from this stem ending in ढ, formed with a Taddhita affix having an indicatory ञ्, ण् or क्, there is vṛiddhi substitution for the first vowel of the second member, and optionally for the first vowel of the first member, in प्रवाहणेय and प्रावाहणेय ॥

As प्रवाहणेयस्यापत्यं = प्रावाहणेयिः or प्रवाहणेयिः, प्रा or प्र-वाहणेयकम् ॥

नञः शुचीश्वरक्षेत्रज्ञकुशलनिपुणानाम् ॥ ३० ॥ पदानि ॥ नञः, शुचि, ईश्वर, क्षेत्रज्ञ, कुशल, निपुणानाम् ॥

वृत्तिः ॥ नञ उत्तरेषां शुचि ईश्वर क्षेत्रज्ञ कुशल निपुण इत्येतेषामचामादेरचो वृद्धिर्भवति, पूर्वपदस्य वा भवति तद्धिते ञिति णिति किति वा परतः ॥

30. Before a Taddhita affix having an indicatory ञ्, ण् or क्, the Vṛiddhi is always substituted for the first vowel of शुचि, ईश्वर, क्षेत्रज्ञ, कुशल and निपुण when preceded by the Negative particle, but this substitution is optional for the vowel of the Negative particle.

As अशौचम् or आशौचम्, अनैश्वर्यम् or आनैश्वर्यम्, अक्षेत्रज्ञ्यम् or आक्षेत्रज्ञ्यम्, अकौशलम् or आकौशलम्, अनैपुणम् or आनैपुणम् ॥ Some say the optional vṛiddhi of the negative particle is an aprâpta-vibhâsha, no other rule would have caused its vṛiddhi had this rule not existed. They argue that by V. 1. 121, all affixes denoting भाव are prohibited after a Tatpurusha compound with the negative particle; therefore, the words शुचि &c, should be first developed by the addition of भाव-affixes, and then they should be compounded with the negative particle, which may be optionally vṛiddhied by this rule, which would apply to it, though it is not an aṅga, because the rule teaches vṛiddhi. Others controvert this opinion, and hold that other affixes causing vṛiddhi than भाव-affixes, also come after negative-Tatpurusha compounds, such as affixes denoting descendant &c: and भाव-affixes are added to Bahuvṛihi negative compounds also, therefore, the force of the anuvṛitti of अङ्ग, which is understood up to the end of the Seventh Adhyâya (VI. 1. 1), and *a fortiori* in this sûtra also, should not be set aside as the above interpretation would do. Moreover the full Taddhita compounds अक्षेत्रज्ञ and अनीश्वर are read in the list of Brâhmaṇâdi words (V. 1. 124), and as such they take the भाव affix ष्यञ् which would have *always* caused the vṛiddhi of अ, but for this sûtra which makes it optional. Therefore it is a prâpta-vibhâshâ.

यथातथयथापुरयोः पर्यायेण ॥३१॥ पदानि ॥ यथातथ, यथापुरयोः, पर्य्यायेण ॥

वृत्तिः ॥ यथातथ यथापुर इत्येतयोर्नञ उत्तरयोः पर्यायेणाचामादेरचो वृद्धिर्भवति तद्धिते ञिति णिति किति वा परतः ॥

31. Before a Taddhita affix having an indicatory ञ्, ण् or क्, the words अयथातथ and अयथापुर may have vṛiddhi of the first vowel of their first member, or that of the second member, in alternation.

That is, when the Negative particle gets the vṛiddhi, the words remain unchanged; and when these words are vṛiddhied, the negative particle remains unaltered. As आयथातथ्यम् or अयाथातथ्यम्, आयथापुर्यम् or अयाथापुर्यम् ॥ The words अयथातथ and अयथापुर should be considered to belong, as negative compounds, to Brâhmaṇâdi class (V. 1. 124): and take ष्यञ् ॥ In the sûtra the compounds यथातथ and यथापुर are exhibited and are Avyayîbhâvas (II. 1. 7), and being neuters, the आ of तथा and पुरा are shortened. According to Patanjali this sûtra is superfluous When the negative particle takes Vṛiddhi, the compound should be analysed as, न यथातथा = अयथातथा, अयथातथा भावः = आयथातथ्यम् ॥ When the second member gets the vṛiddhi, the compound should be analysed as, यथातथा भावः = याथातथ्यं, न याथातथ्यम् = अयाथातथ्यम् ॥

हनस्तोऽचिण्णलोः ॥ ३२ ॥ पदानि ॥ हनः, तः, अ, चिण् णलोः ॥

वृत्तिः ॥ तद्धितेष्विति निवृत्तम् । तत्संबद्धं कितीत्यपि । ञ्णितीति वर्त्तते । हनस्तकारादेशो भवति ञ्णिति प्रत्यये परतः चिण्णलौ वर्जयित्वा ॥

32. त् is substituted for the न् of the root हन् before an affix with an indicatory ञ् or ण्, which causes also the vṛiddhi of the penultimate अ, but the augment is not added before the Aorist-sign चिण्, nor before the Personal ending णल् of the Perfect.

The anuvṛitti of 'Taddhita' ceases, and with it that of कित् also which causes Vṛiddhi in Taddhita only. The ञित् and णित् do govern still. Thus घातः (with घञ्), घातयति (with णिच्), घातकः (with ण्वुल्), साधुघातिन् with इनि; घातंघातम् with णमुल् ॥ But अघानि and जघान with चिण् and णल् ॥ This sûtra has reference to roots, and refers to those affixes only which come after roots (धातु-प्रत्यय), therefore not here वार्त्रघ्नः from वृत्रहन् ॥

आतो युक्चिण्कृतोः ॥ ३३ ॥ पदानि ॥ आतः, युक्, चिण्, कृतोः ॥

वृत्तिः ॥ आकारान्तस्याङ्गस्य चिणि कृति ञ्णिति युगागमो भवति ।

33. A root-stem ending in आ receives the augment युक् (य्), before the Aorist sign चिण्, and before a krit-affix with an indicatory ञ् or ण्, which causes also the Vriddhi of the root-vowel.

As अदायि, अधायि with चिण्, दायः and दायकः, धायः, धायकः with ण and ण्वुल् ॥ Why 'चिण् and krit only'? Observe ददौ, दधौ in the Perfect, and चैडिः, बालाकिः with इञ् a Taddhita affix (IV. 1. 96). So also ज्ञा देवता अस्य = ज्ञः ॥

नोदात्तोपदेशस्य मान्तस्यानाचमेः ॥ ३४ ॥ पदानि ॥ न, उदात्तोपदेशस्य, मान्तस्य, अनाचमे ॥

वृत्तिः ॥ उदात्तोपदेशस्य मान्तस्याङ्गस्याचमिवर्जितस्य चिणि कृति च ञ्णिति यदुक्तं तन्न भवति ॥

वा० ॥ अनाचमिकमिवमीनामिति वक्तव्यम् ॥

34. The Vriddhi is not substituted before the Aorist चिण् or a krit-affix with indicatory ञ् or ण् for the vowel of that root which ends in म and is acutely accented in its original enunciation (Dhâtupâṭha), but not so in चम् after आ ॥

The vriddhi of the penultimate अ takes place before णित् and ञित् affixes (VII. 2. 116), that vriddhi does not take place in the case of udâtta roots ending in म ॥ Thus अशमि, अतमि, and अदमि in चिण् ॥ Compare VI. 4. 92, 93. Similarly with कृत् affixes, as शमकः, तमकः, दमकः, शमः, तमः दमः ॥ Why do we say 'acutely accented'? Observe, यामकः, रामकः ॥ How do you explain उद्यम and उपरम? These are irregular forms exhibited by Pânini himself in the Dhâtupâṭha भडउद्यमे (Bhu. 380), यम उपरमे (Bhu. 1033) Why do we use "in the original enunciation or upadeśa"? So that the rule may apply to शमी दमी, तमी, but not to याममः, रामकः ॥ Here to the root शम्, तम् and दम् is added the affix घिनुण् (III. 2. 141). The words शमिन् &c. get the affix-accent, namely acute इ; and thus the root-vowel becomes anudâtta. Though the root *now* becomes anudâtta, yet because in its upadeśa it was udâtta, the present sûtra will apply and prevent vriddhi. The roots यम्, रम् are anudâtta in upadeśa, but in यामकः, रामकः they become udâtta by लित् accent. This accent is a secondary accent and not the 'original' accent; and hence the present rule does not apply and there is vriddhi. Why do we say ending in म्? Observe चारकः पाठकः ॥ Why with the exception of आचम्? Observe आचामकः ॥

Vârt:—Prohibition must be stated in the case of the roots आ-चम्, कम् and वम्, as वामः, कामः and आचामः ॥ In the case of कम्, the affix घञ् is added in that alternative, when the root does not take the affix णिङ् (III. 1. 31). It thus gets vṛiddhi.

The word भ्रमः is formed from the Churâdi भ्रम्, which with the affix णिच् gets Vṛiddhi, because णिच् is not a kṛit-affix, and is not therefore governed by this rule. If you say "let there be vṛiddhi of णिच्, but this vṛiddhi will be shortened by VI. 4. 92 because it is a मित् root", we reply "this root is not मित्" ॥ The मित् roots are those enumerated in Bhuâdi class, subdivision घटादिः (800). No doubt, there it is said that the roots ending in अम् are मित् (in अमन्ताश्च). But a root is regarded मित् only with regard to the Causative णिच् affix, and not with regard to that णिच् of the Churâdi class where the sense of the causative is not involved in it. Therefore this root is not मित् (VI. 4. 93).

The phrases सूर्यविश्रामा भूमिः and others like it are incorrect. Why do we say 'चिण् and kṛit only'? Observe शशाम, ददाम, चचाम ॥

जनिवध्योश्च ॥ ३५ ॥ पदानि ॥ जनि, वध्योः, च ॥

वृत्तिः ॥ जनि वधि इत्येतयोश्चिणि कृति च ञ्णिति यदुक्तं तन्न भवति ।

35. The Vṛiddhi is not substituted for the vowels of जन् and वध् before the Aorist-sign चिण् and the kṛit-affixes with an indicatory ञ् and ण् ॥

As अजनि and अवधि with चिण्, and जनकः and वधकः (with ण्वुल्), प्रजनः, वधः ॥ This rule refers to the separate and the distinct root वध and not to the substitute of हन् ॥ This we see in the line भक्षकश्चेन्न विद्येत वधकोऽपि न विद्यते ॥ The form from हन् will be घातकः ॥ Moreover the substitute वध ends with अ i. e. it is of two syllables 'badha', and as such it also does not admit Vṛiddhi. (See II. 4 42). The prohibition refers to चिण् and kṛit-affixes, therefore not here, as जजान गर्भं महिमानमिन्द्रम् ॥

अर्त्तिह्रीव्लीरीक्नूयीक्ष्माय्यातां पुङ्णौ ॥ ३६ ॥ अर्त्ति, ह्री, व्ली, री, क्नूयी, क्ष्मायी, आताम्, पुक्, णौ ॥

वृत्तिः ॥ सर्वं निवृत्तमङ्गस्येति वर्त्तते । अर्त्ति ह्री व्ली री क्नूयी क्ष्मायी इत्येतेषामङ्गानामाकारान्तानां च पुगागमो भवति णौ परतः ।

36. The augment पुक् (प्) is added to the roots ऋ, ह्री, व्ली, री, क्नूय्, क्ष्माय्, and to a root ending in long आ, when the affix णि (the Causative) follows.

As अर्पयति, ह्रेपयति, व्लेपयति, रेपयति, क्नोपयति, क्ष्मापयति ॥ The anuvṛitti of every word other than अङ्ग (VI. 4. 1.) ceases. The य of क्नूय and क्ष्माय् drops by VI. 1. 66. The guṇa takes place by VII. 3. 86. Of the roots ending in long आ, we have दापयति, धापयति ॥ The root ऋ (Bhu. 983) गतिप्रापणयोः, and ऋ (Juhotyâdi 16) गतौ are both meant here. Similarly री includes रीङ् स्रवणे (Di-Aâdi 30). and री गतिरेषणयोः (Kryâdi 30). The augment is added at the end of the preceding stem of root, and not to the affix. Being added to the root it becomes part of the root-stem, and in forming the reduplicate Aorist of such stems, the vowel before पू is shortened by VII. 4. 1. If पू were not the part of the stem, that vowel would not be shortened. Thus from ज्ञापयति; we have Aorist अजीज्ञपत् ॥

शाच्छासाह्वाव्यावेपां युक् ॥ ३७ ॥ पदानि ॥ शा, छा, सा, ह्वा, व्या, वे पाम्, युक् ॥

वृत्तिः ॥ शा छा सा ह्वा व्या वे पा इत्येतेषामङ्गानां युगागमो भवति णौ परतः ॥

वार्तिकम् ॥ लुगागमस्तु तस्य वक्तव्यः ॥ वा० ॥ धुञ्प्रीञोर्नुग्वक्तव्यः ॥

37. The augment युक् (य्) is added to the verbal stems शा, छा, सा, ह्वा, वे and पा before the affix णि (Causative).

As निशाययति, अवच्छाययति, अवसाययति, ह्वाययति, संव्याययति, वाययति, and पाययति॥ The word पा includes the root पा 'to drink'. (Bhu 972) पै 'to dry' (Bhu 968). but not पा 'to protect' (Ad. 47): because the latter looses the शप् vikaraṇa.

Vârt:—The root पा 'to protect' takes the augment लुक् before णि, as पालयति ॥

Vârt:—The roots धुञ् and प्रीञ् take the augment नुक् before णि, as धूनयति, प्रीणयति ॥

All these augments are added to the roots, in order that VII. 4. 1. should cause the shortening of the vowel preceding these. Thus the Aorist of the above are: अशीशयत्, अपीपलत्, अदूधुनत्, अपिप्रिणत् ॥

The roots शा, छा, सा, ह्वा, व्या and पा are exhibited as ending in long आ their Dhâtupâṭha forms are शो, शा, छो, सै, सो, ह्वे, व्ये and पै ॥ This indicates that these roots would have taken पुक् by the last sûtra, the word आत् 'ending in long आ' means the roots which actually end in long आ, as well as those which get long आ by VI. 1. 45. This also indicates, that in this subdivision or section, the maxim of lakshaṇa protipadokta &c does not apply. Therefore when the roots इ with अधि, and जि assume the form अधि-आ and जा before the affix णि by VI. 1. 48, the augment पुक् is added to them, thus अध्यापयति, जापयति ॥

वो विधूनने जुक् ॥ ३८ ॥ पदानि ॥ वः, विधूनने, जुक् ॥

वृत्तिः ॥ वा इत्येतस्य विधूननेऽर्थे वर्तमानस्य जुगागमो भवति णौ परतः ।

38. वा gets the augment जुक् (ज्) before the affix णि when the Causative has the sense of 'shaking'.

As पक्षेणोपवाजयति ॥ But आ वापयति केशान् when the sense is not that of shaking. This form could have been obtained from the root वज 'to move', (Bhu 271) with the affix णि in the ordinary way without any augment. The special augment ज् to वा indicates that this root will not take पुक्, which it would have otherwise done by the last sûtra. The root वा belongs to Bhu. 969 [ओवै शोषणे) ॥

लीलोर्नुग्लुकावन्यतरस्यां स्नेहविपातने ॥ ३९ ॥ पदानि ॥ ली, लोः, नुक्, लुकौ, अन्यतरस्याम्, स्नेह विपातने ॥
वृत्तिः ॥ ली ला इत्येतयोरङ्गयोरन्यतरस्यां नुक् लुक् इत्येतावागमौ भवतो णौ परतः स्नेहविपातनेऽर्थे ॥

39. The roots ली and ला get optionally नुक् and लुक् augment respectively, before the affix णि, when the causative means 'the melting of a fatty substance'.

As वि लीनयति, वि लालयति, वि लाययति, or वि लापयति घृतम् ॥ The augment नुक् is added to ली when the root ends in long ई, and that also optionally. When the augment is not added, the regular causative लाययति is formed. But when ली gets the form ला by VI. 1. 51, it does not take the augment नुक् ॥ The root ली includes both ली and लीङ् of Kryâdi and Divâdi The root ला includes ला 'to give' (adâdi 49), and ला the form assumed by ली under VI. 1. 51. When लुक् is not added to ला, पुक् is added by VII. 3. 36. Why do we say when meaning 'to melt fat'? Observe only लोहं विलापयति, जटाभिरालापयते (I. 3. 70).

भियो हेतुभये षुक् ॥ ४० ॥ पदानि ॥ भियः, हेतुभये, षुक् ॥
वृत्तिः ॥ भी इत्येतस्य हेतुभयेऽर्थे षुगागमो भवति णौ परतः ॥

40. The augment षुक् is added to the root भी before the affix णि, when fear is caused immediately owing to the agent of the Causative.

As मुण्डो भीषयते, जटिलो भीषयते ॥ See I. 3.68. Herealso भी with long ई being employed in the sûtra, indicates that षुक् is added then only, when the root has the form भी, but when it assumes the form भा by VI. 1. 56, the proper augment पुक् will come: as मुण्डो भापयते ॥ Why do we say 'when the agent of the causative is himself the direct cause of fear'? Observe कुञ्चिकयैनं भाययति, for here कुञ्चिका causes fear and not the agent of the verb. The ई is vriddhied and भाय् substituted.

स्फायो वः ॥ ४१ ॥ पदानि ॥ स्फायः, वः ॥
वृत्तिः ॥ स्फाय् इत्येतस्याङ्गस्य वकारादेशो भवति णौ परतः ॥

41. For the final of the stem स्फाय् is substituted व् in the causative.

As स्फावयति ॥

शदेरगतौ तः ॥ ४२ ॥ पदानि ॥ शदेः, अ गतौ तः ॥
वृत्तिः ॥ शदे रङ्गस्यागतावर्थे वर्तमानस्य तकारादेशो भवति णौ परतः ॥

42. For the final of the शद् is substituted त, in the Causative, when it does not mean 'to drive'.

As पुष्पाणि शातयति, फलानि शातयति, but गाः शादयति गोपालकः ॥

रुहः पोऽन्यतरस्याम् ॥ ४३ ॥ पदानि ॥ रुहः, पः, अन्यतरस्याम् ॥

वृत्तिः ॥ रुहेरकारस्यान्यतरस्यां पकारादेशो भवति णौ परतः ॥

43. प् may optionally be substituted for the final of रुह् in the Causative.

As व्रीहीन् रोपयति or रोहयति ॥ According to Padamanjari this sûtra could be dispensed with. The form रोपयति could be obtained from the root रुप् of Divâdi class: which though meaning मोहन may be taken to mean 'grow' also; अनेकार्थत्वाद् धातूनाम् ॥

प्रत्ययस्थात्कात्पूर्वस्यात इदाप्यसुपः ॥ ४४ ॥ पदानि ॥ प्रत्ययस्यात्, कात्, पूर्वस्य, अतः, इत्, आपि, असुपः ॥

वृत्तिः ॥ प्रत्यये तिष्ठतीति प्रत्ययस्थः तस्मात् प्रत्ययस्थात्ककारात् पूर्वस्याकारस्य इकारादेशो भवति आपि परतः, स चेदाप्सुपः परो न भवति ।

वार्त्तिकम् ॥ मामकनरकयोरुपसंख्यानं कर्तव्यमप्रत्ययस्थत्वात् ॥

वार्त्तिकम् ॥ प्रत्ययनिषेधे त्यकन्त्यपोश्चोपसंख्यानम् ॥

44. इ is substituted for the अ which stands before the क् belonging to an affix, when the Feminine-ending आ follows, provided that, it does not come after a case-affix (i.e. when such a word in अक does not stand at the end of a Bahuvrihi).

That which stands in an affix is called प्रत्ययस्थ, i. e. क् must be the part of the affix. The अक् is changed into इक् in the feminine in आ ॥ As जटिलिका, मुण्डिका, गुणिका, दत्तिका, कारिका, हारिका ॥ So also एतिका from एतद् + अकच् + आप् एतकद् + आप् ॥ The द is then replaced by अ (VII. 2. 102). The क् must belong to the affix, therefore, not in शका from शक्नोति ॥ The स्थ in प्रत्ययस्थ is for the sake of distinctness, there is no affix which is only क ॥ The rule applies to क, therefore, not to नन्दना, रमणा ॥ The इ is substituted for the अ which precedes (पूर्वस्य) क, and not the अ which follows क्, as पटुका, मृदुका ॥ The क् must be preceded by short अ, therefore, not here गोका, नौका, nor in राका, धाका ॥ The substitution takes place when आ follows, therefore, not in कारकी ॥ The word आपि qualifies क् ॥ The क् should be followed by आ ॥ Obj. But in कारिका from कारक + आ, क् is not directly followed by आ, but by अ? Ans. When अ + आ = आ there is ekâdeśa, the क is followed by आ, there being no third letter intervening then. Obj. But an ekâdeśa is sthânivat to what it replaces when a pûrva-vidhi is to be applied, therefore there still exists the intervention. Ans. The express text of this sûtra will remove the intervention. Obj. Then इ should be substituted in रथकट्या and गर्गकाम्या ॥ These words are formed by the affixes कट्यच् and काम्यच्, as रथानां समूहः, (IV. 2. 51) and गर्गमिच्छति आत्मनः (III. 1. 9) = रथकट्य and गर्गकाम्य ॥ Here also before the क् of the affix, the अ should be replaced by इ, when the feminine affix आ is added: for there is no intervention between क् and आ (the intermediate letters being non-existent, as you say). Ans. We say that intervention is no intervention, when it consists of only *one* letter, which even does not *actually* exist, but only through the fiction of sthânivat. Therefore, the feminine of the above words will not take इ, as क् is not *followed immediately* (in the sense above expressed) by आप्, as रथकात्या and गार्ग्यकाम्या, because in these *actually* many letters are *heard* as intervening between the क् and आप् ॥

Why do we say असुपः 'provided that the feminine affix आप् does not come after a case-affix'? Observe बहवः परिव्राजका अस्यां मथुरायां = बहुपरिव्राजका मथुरा॥ Here आप comes after the noun बहुपरिव्राजक which ends in a case-affix, and hence the अ of ज is not changed to इ ॥ The case-affix is elided by II. 4. 71, and it still exerts its influence by I. 1. 62. The word असुपः is a प्रसज्यप्रतिषेधः (a simple prohibition of the particular matter specified without mentioning what is different from it): and not a पर्युदासः or exception. Had it been a Paryudâsa, (सुपोऽन्यः = असुपः) then आप् coming after a full word not having a case-affix, would have caused the इ substitution in the last example. Nor should असुपः be explained as that in which there exists no case-affix. Had it been so, then in बहूनि चर्माण्यस्यां = बहुचर्मिका no इ ought to be added.

Vârt:—मामक and नरक should be enumerated, for the क् of these is not part of the affix: as मामिका, नरिका ॥ Here ममक is substituted for मम before the affix अण् (IV. 3. 3), to which is then added टाप् ॥ The word ममक takes long ई in the feminine only when it is a Name or in the Vedas (IV. 1. 30): therefore though मामक ends in अण्, it does not take ङीप् (IV. 1. 15) but टाप् (IV. 1. 4), नरान् कायति = नरक formed with the affix क (अ III. 2. 3).

Vârt:—The rule applies to the words ending in त्यक् (IV. 2. 98) and त्यप्, (IV. 2. 104) in spite of the prohibition in VII. 3. 46. As दाक्षिणात्यिका, इहत्यिका ॥

The word in the sûtra is कात् the fifth case of क ending in अ ॥ If then this be the condition, that the affix must end in ka क and not in k क्, then the rule will not apply to एतिका ॥ Because here the augment is अकच् (अक्) with क; the final अ in अकच् is for euphony only, and not a portion of the affix, as we find in भिन्धकि, छिन्धकि, रुन्धकि ॥ The word कात् therefore, is construed to mean ending in the *consonant* क् ॥

न यासयोः ॥ ४५ ॥ पदानि ॥ न, या, सयोः ॥

वृत्तिः ॥ या सा इत्येतयोरिकारादेशो न भवति ॥

वार्त्तिकम् ॥ यत्तदोः प्रतिषेधे त्यकन उपसंख्यानम् ॥ वा० ॥ पावकादीनां छन्दस्युपसंख्यानम् ॥

वा० ॥ आशिषि चोपसंख्यानम् ॥ वा० ॥ उत्तरपदलोपे चोपसंख्यानम् ॥

वा० ॥ क्षिपकादीनां चोपसंख्यानम् ॥ वा० ॥ तारका ज्योतिष्युपसंख्यानम् ॥

वा० ॥ वर्णका तान्तव उपसंख्यानम ॥ वा० ॥ वर्तका शकुनौ प्राचामुपसंख्यानम् ॥

वा० ॥ अष्टका पितृदैवत्ये ॥ वा० ॥ वा सूतकापुत्रकावृन्दारकाणामुपसंख्यानम ॥

45. The इ is not substituted for the अ of य and स, with the augment क, when the feminine आ follows.

As यका. सका ॥ The या and सा simply stand for यद् and तद्, and the prohibition is not confined to the nominative case only, as the forms या and सा may lead one to think. न यत् तदोः would have been a better sûtra. The prohibition applies in every case, as यकामधीते. तकां पचामहे ॥ Or यकांयकामधीमहे (i. e. ऋचां गाथां च), and तकां तकाम्पचामहे (i. e. ओषधीं शाकिनीं वा)

Vârt:—The affix त्यकन् (V. 3. 34) should be enumerated also along with यत् and तद् ॥ As उपत्यका, अधित्यका ॥

Vârt:—The feminine of पावक &c in the Veda does not take इ for अ ॥ As हिरण्यवर्णः शुचयः पावकाः, यासु अ लोमकाः, अलकाः &c. But पाविकाः, अलोमिकाः in secular literature.

Vârt:—So also in the affix वुन् used in benediction: as जीवताद् जीवका, नन्दताद् नन्दका, भवताद् भवका ॥ See III. 1. 150.

Vârt:—So also when the second member is elided in a compound: as देवका, यज्ञका, the second member दत्त is elided, the fuller forms being देवदत्तिका, यज्ञदत्तिका (अनजादौ च विभाषा लोपो वक्तव्यः) See V. 3. 83 Vârt.

Vârt:—क्षिपक &c should be enumerated in this prohibition: as क्षिपका, ध्रुवका, धुवका, चटका ॥

Vârt:—तारका is formed when it means 'stars', but तारिका 'a maid-servant' from तारयति ॥

Vârt:—वर्णका is formed when it means 'a mantle or mask', but वर्णिका 'an expounder': as वर्णिका भागुरी लोकायते 'Bhâguri is a commentary of Lokâyata'

Vârt:—वर्तका 'a bird' according to the Eastern grammarians, but वर्तिका according to the Northern authorities. Why do we say 'when meaning a bird'? Observe वर्त्तिका भागुरी लोकायतस्य ॥

Vârt:—अष्टका when meaning a पितृदैवत्य ceremony, but अष्टिका खारी ॥ The ceremony related to Pitridevata is called Pitridaivatya, the affix is यत् ॥ The former is derived from the root अश् with the affix तकन् (अश्नान्ति ब्राह्मणा ओदनमस्यां), the other is derived from the numeral अष्ट by the affix कन् (V. 1. 22).

Vârt:—Optionally सूतका, पुत्रका and वृन्दारका, the other forms are सूतिका, पुत्रिका, and वृन्दारिका ॥

उदीचामातः स्थाने यकपूर्वायाः ॥ ४६ ॥ पदानि ॥ उदीचाम्, आतः, स्थाने, यक, पूर्वायाः, ॥

वृत्तिः ॥ उदीचामाचार्याणां मतेन यकारपूर्वायाः ककारपूर्वायाश्चातः स्थाने योऽकारस्तस्यातः स्थाने इकारादेशो भवति ॥

वार्त्तिकम् ॥ यकपूर्वत्वे धात्वन्तप्रतिषेधः ॥

46. According to the opinion of Northern grammarians, इ is not substituted for that अ which is obtained by

shortening the long आ of the feminine (under rule VII. 4. 13 before the affix क), which is preceded by a य् or a क् ॥

The mention of 'northern grammarians' makes this an optional rule. As इभ्यका or इभ्यिका, क्षत्रियका or क्षत्रियिका, चटकका or चटकिका, मूषिकका, मूषिकिका ॥ Why do we say preceded by य or क? Observe अश्वक-अश्विका only (from अश्वा)॥ The word यकपूर्वायाः is exhibited in the feminine, in order to indicate that the rule applies when the *feminine* affix आ is shortened to अ ॥ Therefore not here शुभंयिका from शुभंया (शुभं याति). So also भद्रयिका from भद्रया, where आ is part of the root या (see III. 2. 74).

Vârt:—Prohibition must be stated of the य and क being finals of a root. When the य or क preceding this अ, is the final of the root, the prohibition contained in the sûtra, does not apply: as सुनयिका, सुशयिका, सुपाकिका, and अशोकिका॥

Why do we say 'of long आ'? Observe सांकाश्ये भवा = सांकाशियका ॥ The word संकाश्य is formed from संकाश by the affix ण्य (संकाशे निर्वृत्तं) ॥ Then is added the affix वुञ् (IV. 2. 121). Here there is no shortening of a long आ, and hence no option is allowed. But in इभ्यका or इभ्यिका the long आ has been shortened. Because this word is thus derived: इभमर्हति = इभ्या (दण्डादिभ्यो यः V. 1. 66). To this क is added, and the long आ is shortened.

Why is the word स्थाने used in the sûtra, when by the general rule षष्ठी स्थाने योगः this word would be understood here? The special mention is for the sake of pointing out that the अ which takes the place of आ is intended here: i. e. the इ replaces this short अ; but had the word स्थाने not been used in the sûtra the इ would have replaced the long आ ॥

भस्त्रैषाजाज्ञाद्वास्वा नञ्पूर्वाणामपि ॥ ४७.॥ पदानि ॥ भस्त्रा, एषा, अजा, ज्ञा, द्वा, स्वा, नञ्, पूर्वाणाम्, अपि ॥

वृत्तिः ॥ उदीचामातः स्थाने इति वर्तते ॥ भातः स्थाने योकारस्तस्य इत्वं न भवति उदीचामाचार्याणां मतेन ॥

47. According to the opinion of Northern grammarians, इ is not substituted for that अ which is obtained by shortening the आ (before क by VII. 4. 13), of भस्त्रा, एषा, अजा, ज्ञा, द्वा (VII. 2. 102), and स्वा; even not then when the negative particle precedes them.

As भस्त्रका or भस्त्रिका, अभस्त्रका or अभस्त्रिका, एषका or एषिका, अजका or अजिका, ज्ञका or ज्ञिका, अज्ञका or अज्ञिका, द्वके or द्विके, स्वका or स्विका, अस्वका or अस्विका ॥ Of एषा and द्वि there are no examples with the negative particle. For if the compounding with नञ् takes place after the addition of the अकच्, or on the contrary, if first अकच् be added and then the नञ् compounding takes place; in both alternatives, the case-affixes must be added in order to substitute अ for the final by VII. 2. 102: and it is only when this अ is substituted that the feminine टाप् can come. So that the case-affix is the principal ingredient, and टाप् comes after सुप्, and therefore by the prohibition of असुपः in VII. 3. 44, there can arise no occasion for the substitution of इ ॥ Therefore अनेषका and अज्ञका are the invariable forms of these words with the negative particle. स्व meaning agnates and property, takes the negative particle. भस्त्रा is a word which has no corresponding masculine form, and as such, by the following rule VII. 3. 48 it would not have taken इ; its special mention here indicates that it should be the secondary member of the compound here: as अविद्यमाना भस्त्रा यस्या = अभस्त्रा, the Diminutive of which is अभस्त्रका or अभस्त्रिका ॥ Here first the भस्त्रा is shortened as it is a secondary member (upasarjana), then when the Bahuvrihi is made, the feminine affix टाप् is added to this भाषितपुंस्क word, then this आ is shortened before क by VII. 4. 13. This short अ (VII. 4. 13) does not come in the room of the आ which is ordained to come after a word having no corresponding masculine.

The force of अपि shows that the rule applies, when words other than नञ् also precede, and even when no words precede. As निर्भस्त्रिका or निर्भस्त्रका, बहुभस्त्रिका or बहुभस्त्रका ॥

Note:—The form द्वके is from the word द्विक, dual number, the final इ is changed to अ (त्यदाद्यत्व), then the feminine आ (टाप्) is added (द्वका), and then ङी is substituted for औ ॥

अभाषितपुंस्काच्च ॥ ४८ ॥ पदानि ॥ अ, भाषितपुंस्कात्, च, ॥

वृत्तिः ॥ अभाषितपुंस्काद्विहितस्यातः स्थाने योकारस्तस्योदीचामाचार्याणांमतेन इकारादेशो न भवति ॥

48. According to the opinion of Northern Grammarians, इ is not substituted for an अ obtained from the shortening of the Feminine आ (VII. 4. 13), when to the feminine in long आ there is no equivalent masculine, even when the Negative particle precedes.

As खट्वका or खट्विका, अखट्विका or अखट्वका, परमखट्वका or परमखट्विका ॥ When before the affix कप्, the stem is shortened in a Bahuvrihi, this rule will apply (VII. 4. 15). There also, the अ must be substituted for the आ of a feminine word which has no corresponding masculine. But this rule does not apply when the negative compound is the synthesis of अविद्यमाना खट्वा अस्याः = अखट्वा, अल्पा अखट्वा = अखट्विका ॥ Similarly अतिक्रान्ता खट्वाम् = अतिखट्वा, अल्पा अतिखट्वा = अतिखट्विका ॥

Note:—The word खट्वा is always feminine and has no corresponding masculine.

आदाचार्याणाम् ॥ ४९ ॥ आत्, आचार्य्याणाम् ॥

वृत्तिः ॥ अभाषितपुंस्कादातः स्थाने योऽकारस्तस्याचार्याणामाकारादेशो भवति ॥

49. According to the opinion of other Teachers, आ is substituted for the अ which arose from the shortening of the feminine आ of a word which has no corresponding masculine form.

As खट्वाका, अखट्वाका or परमखट्वाका॥

Note:—The "Teachers" referred to here are either those other than the Northern Grammarians, or it may refer to the Teacher of Pânini, the plural being for the sake of respect. Thus there are three forms अखट्वका, अखट्विका, and अखट्वाका ॥

ठस्येकः ॥ ५० ॥ पदानि ॥ ठस्य, इकः ॥

वृत्तिः ॥ अङ्गस्य निमित्तं यष्ठः, कश्चाङ्गस्य निमित्तं, प्रत्यय, स्तस्य प्रत्ययठस्य इक इत्ययमादेशो भवति ॥

50. For ठ in the beginning of a Taddhita affix there is substituted इक ॥

As आक्षिकः, शालाकिकः (ठक् IV. 4. 1), लावणिकः (ठञ् IV. 4. 52). In the affixes ठक्, ठञ् &c, if the affix is the consonant ठ्, and अ is only for euphony, then here also the अ is for pronunciation only: but if on the contrary, the aggregate ठ (ठ्+अ) is the affix, then the same is the case here. This rule does not apply in Unâdi affixes always, as कणेश् ठः = कण्ठः (Uṇ I. 103), for there is diversity (बहुल) in the Uṇâdi.

माथितिकः (= मथितं पण्यमस्य IV. 4. 51) is thus formed मथित + ठक् = मथित् + इक (VI. 4. 148 the अ is dropped). Now arises the doubt, should इक be replaced by क as taught in the next aphorism VII. 3. 51, as it comes after a त् ॥ This substitution, however, does not take place, because it was इक् which caused the elision of अ, and now त् which became final by such elision cannot cause the destruction of इक its producer (सन्निपातलक्षणो विधिरनिमित्तं तद्विघातस्य). Or the elided अ (VI. 4. 148) may be considered as sthânivat, and would thus prevent क substitution.

There are two views about this ठ ॥ Some say that the consonant ठ् only is the sthâni, and the अ is only for the sake of pronunciation. The others hold that ठ, the consonant and the vowel are sthâni in the aggregate. In the first view, the rule would apply to the consonant ठ् at the end of roots like पठ् in पठिता, पठितुं; in the other view the rule would apply to the affix अठच् in कर्मठः॥ Hence, the commentary uses the word, that ठ must be the cause of अङ्ग ॥

इसुसुक्तान्तात्कः ॥ ५१ ॥ पदानि ॥ इस्, उस्, उक्, त, अन्तात्, कः, ॥

वृत्तिः ॥ इस् उस् इत्येवमन्तानामुगन्तानां तान्तानां चाङ्गानामुत्तरस्य ठस्य क इत्ययमादेशो भवति ॥

वार्त्तिकम् ॥ दोष उपसंख्यानम् ॥

51. क is substituted for ठ after a stem ending in इस्, उस्, उ or ऊ, ऋ and त् ॥

As सार्पिष्कः, धानुष्कः, याजुष्कः, नैषादकर्षुकः, शाम्बरजम्बुकः; मातृकम्, पैतृकम्; औदश्वि-

तूक . शाक्रतूक . याक्रतूक ॥ The इस् and उस् are the affixes of that name, therefore not here, आशिषिकः (= आशिषा चरति), औषिका (= उषा चरति) ॥

Vârt:—So also after दोस्, as दौष्क. (दोर्भ्यांचरति) ॥

The word सार्पिष्कः is formed by ठक् of तस्य पण्यं, (IV. 4. 51) and स is changed to ष by इणः षः (VIII. 3. 39). भातुष्कः is by ठक् of प्रहरण ॥ याजुष्का is by ठक् of दीव्यति ॥ नैषादकर्षुकः &c by ठञ् of भवाद्यर्थे औदेर्षे ठञ् ॥ मातृकः by ठञ् of तत आगतः, ऋतठञ् ॥ औशश्वत्कः by ठक् (IV. 2. 19) शाकुलकः by ठञ् of संसृष्ट (IV. 4. 12).

चजोः कु घिण्ण्यतोः ॥ ५२ ॥ पदानि ॥ चजोः, कु, घित्, ण्यतोः, ॥

वृत्तिः ॥ चकारजकारयोः कवर्गादेशो भवति घिति ण्यति च प्रत्यये परतः ॥

52. For the final च् or ज् of a root, there is substituted a corresponding guttural, before an affix having an indicatory घ्, and before ण्यत् ॥

As पाक, त्यागः, रागः with घञ्, and पाक्यम्, वाक्यम् and रेक्यम् with ण्यत् ॥ Compare VII. 3. 59.

न्यङ्क्वादीनां च ॥ ५३ ॥ पदानि ॥ न्यङ्कु, आदीनाम्, च, ॥

वृत्ति ॥ न्यङ्कु इत्येवमादीनां कवर्गादेशो भवति ॥

53. The guttural is substituted in न्यङ्कु and the rest.

Thus न्यङ्कुः from नि + अञ्च् + उ; So also मद्गुः ॥

(1) By the sûtra नावञ्चेः (Uṇ I. 17), the affix उ is added to the root अञ्च् preceded by नि ॥ (2) मद्गु is formed by adding उ to the root मस्ज (Uṇ I. 7) (3) भृगुः, is formed by the affix उ added to the root भ्रस्ज, the स् is elided, and र is vocalised (Uṇ I. 28). (4 and 5) दूरेपाकः, फलेपाक formed by the अच् affix of पचादि class, (= दूरे पच्यते स्वयमेव, फले पच्यते स्वयमेव) ॥ The vṛiddhi is by nipâtana. The seventh case-affix is not elided in these compound words by VI. 3. 14. (6) क्षणेपाकः ॥ This word is read by some. Others read these as दूरेपाका, फलेपाका with टाप् ॥ A third reading is दूरेपाकु फलेपाकुः, by the affix उ added irregularly. (7 and 8) तक्र and वक्र ॥ These are formed from the roots तञ्च and वञ्च with the affix रक् Uṇ II. 13). (9) व्यतिषङ्गः formed from व्यतिषजति with पचादि अच् ॥ (10) अनुषङ्गः ॥ (11) अवसर्गः ॥ (12) उपसर्गः ॥ (13) मेघः ॥ (14) श्वपाकः ॥ (15) मांसपाकः ॥ (16) कपोतपाकः ॥ (17) उलूकपाकः ॥ (18) पिण्डपाकः formed by the affix अण् with an accusative word in construction as upapada. (19) अघः when it denotes a name meaning 'price'. This is formed from the root अर्ह with the affix घञ् ॥ When it is not a name, the form is अर्ह ॥ (20 and 21) अवदाघः and निदाघः, when they are names meaning "Summer or Hot season". These are formed from the root दह् preceded by अव and नि ॥ But when they are not names, the forms are अवदाहः, निदाहः ॥ (22) न्यग्रोधः formed from the root रुह् preceded by न्यक् and by adding the पचादि अच् ॥ The ह् is changed to ध ॥ (23) वीरुत् ॥ Formed from रुह् with वि and the affix क्विप्, and ह changed to ध ॥ न्यग्राहयति and विरोहयति ॥

1 न्यङ्कु, 2 मद्गु, 3 भृगु, 4 दूरेपाक, 5 फलेपाक, 6 क्षणेपाक, 7 दूरेपाका, 8 फलेपाका' 9 दूरेपाकु, 10 फलेपाकु, 11 तक्र, 12 वक्र, 13 व्यतिषङ्ग, 14 अनुषङ्ग, 15 अवसर्ग, 16 उपसर्ग, 17 श्वपाक, 18 मांसपाक, 19 मूलपाक, 20 कपोतपाक, 21 उलूकपाक, 22 संज्ञायां मेघनिदाघावदाघार्घाः मेघ 23 न्यग्रोध, 24 वीरुध् ॥

हो हन्तेर्ञ्णिन्नेषु ॥ ५४ ॥ पदानि ॥ हः, हन्तेः, ञ्णित्, नेषु, ॥

वृत्तिः ॥ हन्तेर्हकारस्य कवर्गादेशो भवति ञिति णिति प्रत्यये परतो नकारे च ॥

54. A guttural is substituted for the ह in हन् before an affix having an indicatory ञ्. or ण् and before न् ॥

As घातयति with णिच्, घातिकः with ण्वुल्, साधुघातिन् with इनि, घातघातम् with णमुल्, घातः with घञ्, घ्नन्ति, घ्नन्तु, and अघ्नन् before न् ॥ Why do we specify ह? Otherwise the substitute would replace the final letter. Why of हन्? Observe प्रहारः, प्रहारकः ॥ ण् and ञ् qualify the affixes, and न् means the न् of हन् which becomes joined with ह् when the intermediate अ is dropped. This न् comes in immediate contact with ह, because it is *heard* in pronouncing, and in writing. If the elided अ be considered as sthânivat, then ह can never be followed by न्, for there will exist the intervention of this latent अ, but by virtue of the special text of this sûtra, such an elided अ should not be considered as an intervention. And if ञ्, ण् and न् be all considered as qualifying the ह of हन्, still on the maxim येन नाव्यवधानं तेन व्यवहितेऽपि वचनप्रामाण्यात् therefore ण or ञ are considered to come after ह् though a portion of the root intervenes. But not so here, हननमिच्छति हननीयति, add ण्वुल to this Denominative root, and we have हननायकः ॥

अभ्यासाच्च ॥ ५५ ॥ पदानि ॥ अभ्यासात्, च, ॥

वृत्तिः ॥ अभ्यासादुत्तरस्य हन्तिहकारस्य कवर्गादेशो भवति ॥

55. A Guttural is substituted for the ह in हन् after a reduplication also.

As जिघांसति, जङ्घन्यते, अहं जघान ॥ The rule applies when such an affix follows which causes the reduplication of the stem (aṅga) हन्, therefore not here हननीयितुमिच्छति = जिहननीयिषति ॥

हेरचङि ॥ ५६ ॥ पदानि ॥ हेः, अ, चङि, ॥

वृत्तिः ॥ हिनोतेर्हकारस्याभ्यासादुत्तरस्य कवर्गादेशो भवति अचङि ॥

56. A guttural is substituted for the ह of हि (हिनोति) after a reduplication, but not in the Reduplicated Aorist.

As जिघीषति, प्र जेघीयते, प्रजिघाय; but प्राजीहयद् दूतम् in the simple Aorist. Obj. The word अचङि could be dispensed with from the sûtra, in as much as चङ् can never come after the simple root हि, but after the causative of हि, and the causative stem of हि is a different verb than, हि. Ans. The fact of this word अचङि being employed in the sûtra indicates the existence of the following maxim: प्रकृतिग्रहणे ण्यधिकस्यापि ग्रहणम् "A radical denotes whenever it is employed in Grammar, not only that radical itself, but it denotes also whatever stem may result from the addition to it of the causative affix णि" ॥ Therefore we have प्रजिघाययिषति ॥

The word प्राजीह्रयत् is the Aorist of the causative of ह्रि, with चङ्, the elision of णि, the shortening of the penultimate the reduplication, guttural change by कुहोश्चुः and lengthening by दीर्घोलघोः ॥

सन्लिटोर्जेः ॥ ५७ ॥ पदानि ॥ सन्, लिटोः, जेः, ॥

वृत्तिः ॥ सनि लिटि च प्रत्यये जेरङ्गस्य योऽभ्यासस्तस्मादुत्तरस्य कवर्गादेशो भवति ॥

57. A guttural is substituted for the ज् in जि after a reduplication before the Desiderative affix सन्, and in the Perfect.

As जिगीषति, जिगाय ॥ Why in the Desiderative and Perfect only? Observe जेजीयते ॥ Though the root ज्या also assumes the form जि by vocalisation (VI. 1. 16, 17) yet that जि is not to be taken here. That will form जिज्यतुः, जिज्युः ॥

विभाषा चेः ॥ ५८ ॥ पदानि ॥ विभाषा, चेः, ॥

वृत्तिः ॥ चिनोतेरङ्गस्य सन्लिटोरभ्यासादुत्तरस्य विभाषा कवर्गादेशो भवति ॥

58. A guttural is optionally substituted for the च of चि after a reduplication in the Desiderative and Perfect.

As चिचीषति or चिकीषति, चिचाय or चिकाय ॥ But चेचीयते in other cases.

न क्वादेः ॥ ५९ ॥ पदानि ॥ न, कु, आदेः, ॥

वृत्तिः ॥ कवर्गादेर्धातोश्चजोः कवर्गादेशो न भवति ॥

59. A guttural is not substituted for the final च् ज् of a root which begins with a guttural, before an affix having an indicatory घ and before ण्यत् ॥

As कूजः, खर्जः and गर्जः with घञ्; कूज्यः, खर्ज्यः and गर्ज्यः with ण्यत् ॥ This is an exception to VII. 3. 52.

अजिव्रज्योश्च ॥ ६० ॥ पदानि ॥ अजि, व्रज्योः, च ॥

वृत्तिः ॥ अजि व्रजि इत्येतयोश्च कवर्गादेशो न भवति ॥

60. A guttural is not substituted for the final or ज् of अज् and व्रज् before an affix having an indicatory घ and before ण्यत् ॥

This is an exception to VII. 3. 52. Thus समाजः, उदाजः, परिव्राजः and परिव्राज्यम् ॥ There is no example of अज् with the affix ण्यत्, because by II. 4. 56, वी replaces अज् before all ârdhadhâtuka affixes except घञ् and अप् ॥ The च of the sûtra implies that the rule applies to other roots also not mentioned, as वाजः, वाज्यम् from वज् ॥

भुजन्युब्जौ पाण्युपतापयोः ॥ ६१ ॥ पदानि ॥ भुज, न्युब्जौ, पाणि, उपतापयोः, ॥

वृत्तिः ॥ भुज न्युब्ज इत्येतौ शब्दौ निपात्येते यथासंख्यम् पाणावुपतापे च ॥

61. भुज 'an arm', and न्युब्ज 'a kind of bodily disease', are irregularly formed, without any change of their ज before घञ् ॥

The word भुजः = भुज्यतेऽनेन, with घञ् (III. 3. 121). The irregularity consists in the absence of Guṇa, as well as of gutturalisation. न्युब्जिमताः शरतेऽस्मिन् = न्युब्जः from the root उब्ज आर्जवे (Tudâdi 20). The irregularity consists in the non-changing of ज ॥ When not meaning 'an arm' and 'a disease', we have भोगः, समुद्गः ॥

प्रयाजानुयाजौ यज्ञाङ्गे ॥ ६२ ॥ पदानि ॥ प्रयाज, अनुयाजौ, यज्ञ, अङ्गे, ॥

वृत्तिः ॥ कुत्वप्रतिषेधोऽनुवर्तते ॥ प्रयाज अनुयाज इत्येतौ निपात्येते यज्ञाङ्गेऽभिधेये ॥ प्रपूर्वस्य यजेर्घञि कुत्वाभावो निपात्यते ॥

62. प्रयाज and अनुयाज are irregularly formed with घञ्, when meaning a portion of a sacrificial offering.

These words are derived from यज् with घञ् without the guttural substitution; as पञ्च प्रयाजाः; त्रयोनुयाजाः, त्वमग्ने प्रयाजाना पश्चात् त्वं पुरस्तात् ॥ But प्रयागः and अनुयागः when not referring to portions of a sacrifice. The प्रयाज and अनुयाज are illustrative only. The guttural change does not take place with other prepositions &c. also, as उपयाजः, उपांशुयाजः, संयाजः, ऋतुयाजः, as in the sentences एकादशोपयाजाः, उपांशु याजमन्तरा यजति, अष्टौ पत्नी संयाजा भवन्ति, ऋतुयाजै श्चरन्ति ॥

वञ्चेर्गतौ ॥ ६३ ॥ पदानि ॥ वञ्चेः, गतौ, ॥

वृत्तिः ॥ वञ्चेरङ्गस्य गतौ वर्तमानस्य कवर्गादेशो न भवति ॥

63. A guttural is not substituted for the palatal of वञ्च् in the sense of 'going'.

As वञ्च्यं वञ्चन्ति वणिजः, but वाङ्क्यं काष्ठं = कुटिलं ॥ Why is गतौ used, when we know from the Dhatupâṭha (Bhuadi 204) that वंचु means 'to go'? The specification shows that the roots possess many meanings other than those assigned to them in the Dhâtupâṭha.

ओक उचः के ॥ ६४ ॥ पदानि ॥ ओकः, उचः, के, ॥

वृत्तिः ॥ उचेर्धातोः के प्रत्यये ओक इति निपात्यते ॥

64, ओक is irregularly formed from the root उच् with the affix क (अ) ॥

The change of च् into क्, and the Guṇa are the irregularities. As न्योकः 'a bird, a tree'. The affix क is added under III. 1. 135. The क is added with the force of घञ् the Kâraka relation being that of Location &c. The घञ् affix would have given the form regularly, but then the word would have been acutely accented on the first syllable, but it is desired that the acute should be on the last. The words दिवौकसः, जनौकसः &c are also irregular, formed with the Uṇadi affix असुन् the क being substituted for च् as an Uṇadi diversity (bahulam).

ण्यआवश्यके ॥ ६५ ॥ पदानि ॥ ण्यः, आवश्यके, ॥

वृत्तिः ॥ आवश्यकेऽर्थे यो ण्यप्रत्ययस्तस्मिन् परतः चजोः कुत्वं न भवति ॥

65. A guttural is not substituted for the palatal, before the affix ण्य, when it means 'to do as absolute necessity'.

As अवश्य पाच्यम्, अवश्य वाच्यम्, अवश्यरेच्यम्, but पाक्यं, वाक्यं and रेक्यं when the sense is not that of necessity.

यजयाचरुचप्रवचर्चश्च ॥ ६६ ॥ पदानि ॥ यज, याच, रुच, प्रवच, ऋचः, च, ॥

वृत्तिः ॥ यज याच रुच प्रवच ऋच इत्येतेषां ण्ये परतः कवर्गादेशो न भवति ॥

वार्त्तिकम् ॥ ण्यति प्रतिषेधे त्यजेरुपसंख्यानम् ॥

66. A guttural is not substituted for the final palatals of यज्, याच, रुच्, प्र-वच्, and ऋच् before the affix ण्यत् ॥

As याज्यम्, याच्यम्, रोच्यम्, प्रवाच्यम्, and अर्च्यम् ॥ Though ऋच् has a penultimate ऋ and therefore by III. 1. 110 would have taken क्यप्, it takes ण्यत् by force of this sûtra. प्रवच् shows that the present sûtra applies to it, though it means 'a word or speech', and the prohibition of VII. 3. 67 does not apply. प्रवाच्य is the name of a particular book. Others say that the prohibition applies to वच् only when it is preceded by प्र, and does not mean word or speech (VII. 3. 67) and not when it is preceded by any other preposition. As अविवाक्य-महरिति पठन्ति ॥ This even in a very restricted sense, namely on the tenth day of the Daśarâtra ceremony. In other places we have अविव च्यं ॥

Vârt :—त्यज् should he enumerated in this connection i. e. before ण्यत्, the ज remains unaltered, as त्याज्यम् ॥

वचोऽशब्दसंज्ञायाम् ॥ ६७ ॥ पदानि ॥ वचः, अ, शब्द, संज्ञायाम् ॥

वृत्तिः ॥ ण्यइति वर्तते वचोऽशब्दसंज्ञायां ण्यति परतः कवर्गो न भवति ॥

67. The guttural is not substituted for the final of वच् before ण्यत्, when it does not mean 'a word or speech'.

As वाच्यमाह, अवाच्यमाह, but अवद्युषितं वाक्यमाह ॥

प्रयोज्यनियोज्यौ शक्यार्थे ॥ ६८ ॥ पदानि ॥ प्रयोज्य, नियोज्यौ, शक्य, अर्थे, ॥

वृत्तिः ॥ प्रपूर्वस्य निपूर्वस्य च युजेः प्रयोज्य नियोज्य इत्येतौ शब्दौ शक्यार्थे निपात्येते ॥

68. प्रयोज्य and नियोज्य preserve their palatal in the sense of 'capable to do this'.

As प्रयोज्यः = प्रयोक्तुंशक्यः ; नियोज्यः = नियोक्तुंशक्यः, but प्रयोग्य and नियोग्य in other senses.

भोज्यं भक्ष्ये ॥ ६९ ॥ पदानि ॥ भोज्यम्, भक्ष्ये, ॥

वृत्तिः ॥ भोज्यं निपात्यते भक्ष्येऽभिधेये ॥ भुजेर्ण्यति कुत्वाभावो निपात्यते शक्यार्थे ॥

69. भोज्य preserves its palatal in the sense of 'eatable'.

The word is derived from भुज with ण्यत् in the sense of 'able'. As भोज्य ओदनः 'eatable rice', भोज्या यवागूः 'eatable barley-gruel'. भक्ष्य here means anything which is fit for being eaten. When not having this sense, we have भोग्यः कम्बलः ॥

घोर्लोपो लेटि वा ॥ ७० ॥ पदानि ॥ घोः, लोपः, लेटि, वा, ॥

वृत्तिः ॥ घुसंज्ञकानां लेटि परतो वा लोपो भवति ॥

70. The final of दा and धा (घु roots) may optionally be elided in the Subjunctive (लेट्) ॥

As दधद्रत्नानि दाशुषे Rig I. 35. 8. सोमो ददद् गन्धर्वाय Rig X. 85. 41. But also यदग्निरग्नये ददात् ॥ The form ददात्, however, may also be deduced even when the final of दा is elided, for then by the आट् augment (III. 4. 94) we get this form. The word वा is therefore employed in the sûtra only for the sake of distinctness, for the sûtra without वा would have also given the above forms, as we have shown. Or the वा is used to remove the doubt which one may entertain to this effect "ददात् is the form which may be deduced by the general rule, since लोप is taught, this form will be excluded altogether and will never appear".

The form दधत् is thus evolved. We add तिप् to the root धा; then the इ of ति is elided (III. 4. 97). दाशुषे = यजमानाय रत्नानिदद्यात् ॥ Others say, the दधत् is the form of the root with the शतृ affix. ददत् is from the root दाञ् ॥

Some say that वा is jnâpaka and indicates the existence of the following maxim :—अनित्यमागमशासनम् "the rule about augments is *anitya*". So that the augment आट् being *anitya*, we could not have got the form ददात् ॥ Hence the employment of the word वा ॥

ओतः श्यनि ॥ ७१ ॥ पदानि ॥ ओतः, श्यनि, ॥

वृत्तिः ॥ ओकारान्तस्याङ्गस्य श्यनि परतो लोपो भवति ॥

71. A stem ending in ओ loses its final before the Present characteristic श्यन् of the Divâdi class.

As निश्यति from शो, अवच्छ्यति from छो, अवद्यति from दो, and अवस्यति from सो ॥ The त् in ओत् is for the sake of euphony or ease of pronunciation.

According to Padamanjari, the sûtra should have been ओतः शिति, and thereby there would be the saving of half a mâtrâ, and also there would be no necessity of repeating the word शिति in VII. 3. 75.

क्सस्याचि ॥ ७२ ॥ पदानि ॥ क्सस्य, अचि, ॥

वृत्तिः ॥ क्सस्याजादौ प्रत्यये लोपो भवति ॥

72. The अ of the Aorist characteristic क्स is elided before an affix beginning with a vowel.

As अधुक्षाताम, अधुक्षाथाम्, अधुक्षि from the root दुह् ॥ Had the अ not been elided before आताम् and आथाम्, then इय् must have been substituted for it according to VII. 2. 81. Why do we say before an affix beginning with a vowel? Observe अधुक्षत्, अधुक्षताम् ॥ Why do we say क्स and not only स? So that the elision should not take place here, as उत्सौ, उत्साः, वत्सौ, बत्साः, तृणसौ, तृणसः ॥

लुग्वा दुहदिहलिहगुहामात्मनेपदे दन्त्ये ॥ ७३ ॥ पदानि ॥ लुक्, वा, दुह, दिह, लिह, गुहाम्, आत्मनेपदे, दन्त्ये, ॥

वृत्तिः ॥ दुह दिह लिह गुह इत्येतेषामात्मनेपदे दन्त्यादौ परतः क्सस्य वा लुग्भवति ॥

73. The whole of the affix क्स is elided optionally before the personal endings of the Atmanepada beginning with a dental, after दुह्, दिह् लिह् and गुह् ॥

As अदुग्ध or अधुक्षत, अदुग्धाः or अधुक्षथाः, अदुग्ध्वम् or अधुक्षध्वम्, अदुह्वहि or अधुक्षावहि, अदिग्ध or अधिक्षत, अलीढ or अलिक्षत, न्यगुढ or न्यघुक्षत ॥

Why दुह् &c. only? Observe व्यत्यरुक्षत ॥ Why in the Atmanepada? Observe अधुक्षत only. Why before an affix beginning with a dental? Observe अधुक्षामहि only. Though the anuvṛitti of लोप was understood in this sûtrá; the employment of the term लुक् indicates that the *whole* of the affix is to be elided. For लोप would have elided only the final अ of स ॥ But even with the elision of अ alone we would have got all the above forms, except those in वहि ॥ For अ being elided, we have स् between ह् (a consonant of झल् class) and a dental (which is also a letter of झल् class). This स् situate between two झल् will be elided by VIII. 2. 26. Nor can it be objected that the elided अ is sthânivat, for by पूर्वत्रासिद्धं VIII. 2. 1, such an elision cannot be sthânivat. Though व् is a dento-labial, yet it is included in the word dental. Had it not been meant to be so included, तो (letters of त class) would have been taken in the sûtra. See III. 1. 45, for this Aorist-affix.

शमामष्टानां दीर्घः श्यनि ॥ ७४ ॥ पदानि ॥ शमाम्, अष्टानाम्, दीर्घः, श्यनि, ॥

वृत्तिः ॥ शमादीनामष्टानां दीर्घो भवति श्यनि परतः ॥

74. Before the Present character श्यन्, a long is substituted for the root-vowel in शम् and the seven roots that follow it.

As शाम्यति, ताम्यति, दाम्यति, श्राम्यति, भ्राम्यति, क्षाम्यति क्लाम्यति and माद्यति ॥ Why of these eight only? Observe अस्यति ॥ Why before श्यन्? Observe भ्रमति; the श्यन् being optional after this root by III. 1. 70.

ष्ठिवुक्लम्याचमां शिति ॥ ७५ ॥ पदानि ॥ ष्ठिवु, क्लमु, आचमाम्, शिति, ॥

वृत्तिः ॥ दीर्घ इति वर्तते ॥ ष्ठिवु क्लम आचम इत्येतेषां दीर्घो भवति शिति परतः ॥

75. Before any other Present character (शित्), the root vowel of ष्ठिव्, क्लम्, and आ-चम् is lengthened.

As ष्ठीवति, क्लामति, and आ चामति ॥ क्लम् lengthens its vowel before श्यन् by the last rule, the present rule produces this change before the affix शप् also, which it gets by III. 1. 70. चम् lengthens its vowel only when it is preceded by आ; therefore not here: चमति, विचमति or उच्चमति ॥ The sûtra is exhibited as ष्ठिवुक्लमु चमां शिति in the original text of Pâṇini; the present form, owes its existence to the insertion of आ from the vârtika दीर्घत्वमाङि चमः ॥

क्रमः परस्मैपदेषु ॥ ७६ ॥ पदानि ॥ क्रमः, परस्मैपदेषु, ॥

वृत्तिः ॥ दीर्घ इति वर्तते ॥ क्रमः परस्मैपदपरे शिति परतो दीर्घो भवति ॥

76. The long is substituted in क्रम्, before a शित् affix, in the Parasmaipada.

As क्रामति, क्रामतः, क्रामन्ति ॥ Why in the Parasmaipada? Observe आक्रमते आदित्यः ॥ How do you explain the lengthening in उत्क्राम and संक्राम (Imperative 2nd Per. Sg.)? For when हि is elided by लुक्, (VI. 4. 105) then by I. 1. 63, the affix being dropped by a लु-elision, it would produce no effect and so there ought to have been no lengthening? This is no valid objection. The prohibition of I. 1. 63, applies to the अङ्ग *stem* after which the affix is elided. Here क्रम् is not a stem or aṅga with regard to हि, but it is a *stem* with regard to शप्, as क्रम + शप् + हि ॥ Therefore, though हि is elided, the lengthening will take place by I. 1. 62, (प्रत्यय लक्षणम्) ॥

इषुगमियमां छः ॥ ७७ ॥ पदानि ॥ इषु, गमि, यमाम्, छः, ॥

वृत्तिः ॥ शितीति वर्तते ॥ इषु गमि यम इत्येतेषां शिति प्रत्यये परतश्छकारादेशो भवति ॥

77. छ is substituted for the final of इष्, गम् and यम् before a Present-character (शित्) ॥

As इच्छति, गच्छति, यच्छति ॥ The इषु with the indicatory उ is taken here, (Tud. 59), and not इष् of Divâdi (19) class or of Kryâdi class (53). There we have इष्यति and इष्णाति respectively. Those who do not read the sûtra as इषु &c, but as इषगमि &c, read the anuvṛitti of the word आचि from VII. 3. 72 into this sûtra; so that the शित् is qualified by the word अच्, i. e. a शित् affix which is merely a vowel, and has no consonant in it; (and not a शित् affix which *begins* with a vowel). Therefore though शानच् is a शित् affix beginning with a vowel, yet as it contains a consonant, the छ substitution does not take place, as इषाणः (III. 1. 83) The reading of the text according to Patanjali and Kâtyayana is इषगमियमां छः, and hence the necessity of the above explanation. The reading इषु, though convenient, is not ârsha.

पाघ्राध्मास्थाम्नादाण्दृश्यर्त्तिसर्त्तिशदसदां पिबजिघ्रधमतिष्ठमनयच्छपश्यर्च्छधौशीयसीदाः ॥ ७८ ॥ पदानि ॥ पा, घ्रा, ध्मा, स्था, म्ना, दाण्, दृशि, अर्त्ति, सर्त्ति, शद, सदाम्, पिब, जिघ्र, धम, तिष्ठ, मन, यच्छ, पश्य, ऋच्छ, धौ, शीय, सीदाः ॥

वृत्तिः ॥ पा घ्रा ध्मा स्था म्ना दाण् दृशि अर्ति सर्ति शद सद इत्येतेषां पिब जिघ्र धम तिष्ठ मन यच्छ पश्य ऋच्छ धौ शीय सीद इत्येते आदेशा भवन्ति शिति परतः ॥

78. Before a Present-character (शित्), the following substitutions take place :—पिब् for पा, जिघ्र for घ्रा, धम for ध्मा, तिष्ठ् for स्था, मन् for म्ना, यच्छ् for दा (दाण्), पश्य् for दृश्, ऋच्छ् for ऋ, धौ for सृ, शीय् for शद् and सीद् for सद् ॥

As पिबति, जिघ्रति, धमति, तिष्ठति, मनति, यच्छति, पश्यति, ऋच्छति, धावति, शीयते and सीदति ॥ पिब् + शप् + तिप् required Guṇa of the इ of पि by VII. 3. 86, it however does not take place on the maxim अङ्गवृत्ते पुनर्वृत्तावविधिः "when an operation which is taught in the angâdhikâra, has taken place, and another operation of the angâdhikâra is subsequently applicable, this latter operation is not allowed to take place". Or the substitute पिब is one which ends with अ, and is acutely accented on the first. It must be acutely accented on the first; otherwise by VI. 1. 162, the acute will be on the last पिबॆ ॥ Then when there is ekâdeśa with शप्, the acute will be on the middle in पिबति, which is not desired. धौ is substituted for सृ when the sense is 'to run, move quickly'; in any other sense, we have प्रसरति, अनुसरति ॥

ज्ञाजनोर्जा ॥ ७९ ॥ पदानि ॥ ज्ञा, जनोः, जा, ॥

वृत्तिः ॥ ज्ञा जन इत्येतयोर्जादेशो भवति शिति परतः ॥

79. Before a शित् affix, जा is substituted for ज्ञा and जन् ॥

As जानाति and जायते ॥ The जन् here belongs to Divâdi class, meaning 'to be produced', and not जन् of the Juhotyâdi class. Why जा (long) and not ज, for this ज would assume the form जा by VII. 3. 101? This long आ of जा indicates the existence of the maxim given above in VII. 3. 78; and had ज been the substitute, VII. 3. 101, could not have lengthened it.

प्वादीनां ह्रस्वः ॥ ८० ॥ पदानि ॥ पू, आदीनाम्, ह्रस्वः, ॥

वृत्तिः ॥ पू इत्येवमादीनां ह्रस्वो भवति शिति परतः ॥

80. A short is substituted for पू &c, before a शित् affix.

The Pvâdi roots form a subdivision of the Kryâdi class, beginning with पूञ् पवने (2) and ending with प्ली गतौ (32). The ल्वादि roots (VIII. 2. 44) are a portion of प्वादि (nos 13 to 32). Others hold that upto the end of the Kryâdi class are Pvâdi. Thus पुनाति, लुनाति, स्तृणाति ॥ Those who hold that Pvâdi roots are upto the end of the Class, explain the non-shortening of जानाति (for ज्ञा would also then become Pvâdi), by saying that the express text of VII. 3. 79, substituting long आ prevents the shortening. They say had ज्ञा been also shortened, then merely ज substitute would have been enough and not जा ; and this ज would have been lengthened in the case of जन् by VII. 3. 101, to form जायते ॥

मीनातेर्निगमे ॥ ८१ ॥ पदानि ॥ मीनातेः, निगमे, ॥
वृत्तिः ॥ मीनातेरङ्गस्य शिति प्रत्यये परतो ह्रस्वो भवति निगमविषय ॥

81. In the Veda मी is shortened before a शित् affix.

As प्रमिनन्ति व्रतानि Rig. X. 10. 5. The न becomes ण (प्रमिणन्ति according to Kâśika) by VIII. 4. 15. Why in the Veda? Observe प्र मीणाति ॥

मिदेर्गुणः ॥ ८२ ॥ पदानि ॥ मिदेः, गुणः, ॥
वृत्तिः ॥ मिदेरङ्गस्येको गुणो भवति शिति प्रत्यये परतः ॥

82. For इ in मिद्, there is substituted a guṇa before a शित् affix.

As मेद्यति, मेद्यतः, मेद्यन्ति ॥ Why मिद् only? Observe स्विद्यन्ति, क्लिद्यन्ति ॥ The root ञिमिदा belongs both to the Bhvâdi and the Divâdi classes. The Bhvâdi मिद् will get guṇa before शप् by virtue of VII. 3. 86, but the Divâdi मिद् would not have got guṇa before श्यन्, as this affix is ङित् (I. 2. 4): hence the necessity of this sûtra. Before non शित् affixes there is no guṇa, as मिद्यते, मेमिद्यते ॥

जुसि च ॥ ८३ ॥ पदानि ॥ जुसि, च, ॥
वृत्तिः ॥ जुसि च प्रत्यये परत इगन्तस्याङ्गस्य गुणो भवति ॥

83. Before the personal-ending जुस् (उस्) of the Imperfect, guṇa is substituted for the final इ, ई, उ, ऊ, ऋ, and ॠ, ऌ of the stem.

As अजुहवुः, अबिभयुः, अबिभरुः, अजागरुः ॥ This Personal ending is ङित् according to I. 2. 4, and would not have caused guṇa (I. 1. 5), but for this sûtra. The ending जुस (III. 4. 108) comes in the लिङ् also. There, however, it does not cause guṇa. As चिनुयुः, सुनुयुः ॥ Here there are two ङित् affixes, the augment यासुट्, and the sârvadhâtuka जुस् ; and the यासुट् prevents guṇa. The इक् is read into the sûtra from I. 1. 3.

सार्वधातुकार्द्धधातुकयोः ॥ ८४ ॥ पदानि ॥ सार्वधातुक, आर्द्धधातुकयोः, ॥
वृत्तिः ॥ सार्वधातुके आर्द्धधातुके च प्रत्यये परत इगन्तस्याङ्गस्य गुणो भवति ॥

84. The Guṇa is substituted for the final इक् vowel of a stem before the affixes called sârvadhâtuka and ârdhadhâtuka (III. 4. 113 &c).

As तरति, नयति, भवति ; कर्तृ, चेतृ, स्तोतृ, ॥ Why sârvadhâtuka and ârdhadhâtuka affixes only ? Observe अग्नित्वम्, अग्निकाम्यति ॥ For had the sûtra been सङि then the rule would have applied to affixes like सन् काम्यच &c which go to form Denominative verbs. सङ् includes all affixes beginning with सन and ending with महिङ् ॥ If the sûtra had been प्रत्यये, then the rule would have applied to the affixes like त्वम् &c. To exclude these cases, the two words sârvadhâtuka and ârdhadhâtuka are used. For exceptions See I. 1. 4, 5, 6.

जाग्रोऽविचिण्णल्ङित्सु ॥ ८५ ॥ पदानि ॥ जाग्रः, अ, विच्, चिण्, णल्, ङित्सु ॥

वृत्तिः ॥ जागृ इत्येतस्याङ्गस्य गुणो भवति अविचिण्णल्ङित्सु परतः ॥

85. The Guṇa is substituted for the ऋ of the stem जागृ, except before the affix वि, before the Aorist-character चिण्, before the Personal ending, णल् of the Perfect, and before an affix with an indicatory ङ् ॥

As जागरयति, with णिच्, जागरकः (with ण्वुल्) साधुजागरी, जागरं जागरम् (with णमुल्) जागरो वर्तते (with घञ्), जागरितः (with क्त), जागरितवान् (with क्तवतु) ॥ This is an exception to the Vṛiddhi rule of VII. 2. 115, and to the prohibition in I. 1. 5. When this guṇa is substituted, there does not take effect that rule, which causes Vṛiddhi of the penultimate short अ of जागर; (अत उपधायाः VII. 2. 116). Had that been the case, then the guṇa substitution would become simply useless, and the prohibition with regard to चिण् and णल् superfluous. Why do we say not before वि, चिण् and णल् and ङित्? Observe जागृविः (with the affix विन् Uṇâdi) अजागारि with चिण् which causes Vṛiddhi, and अजागार with णल्, and जागृतः and जागृथः with a ङित् (I. 2. 4) affix. Some hold that the इ in वि is for the sake of pronunciation only, and the prohibition applies to all affixes beginning with a व्, such as क्वसु, as जजागृवान्, here there is no guṇa. In अजागरुः with जुस् the guṇa takes place by virtue of VII. 3. 83 : for though it is a ङित् affix also, the prohibition ङित्सु of this sûtra does not affect it. Similarly अहं जजागर with णल् the optional guṇa VII. 1. 91 is also not prohibited by the णल् of this sûtra. In fact the phrase अविचिण् णल् ङित्सु is a Paryudâsa prohibition : for had it been a prasayya-pratishedha, then the guṇa before जुस् and the 1st Pers. णल् would also have been prohibited. In short this sûtra positively ordains guṇa of जागृ before every affix, other than वि, चिण्, णल् and ङित्, and if by any other rule these latter would cause guṇa, that guṇa is not *prohibited.* That is the result of Paryudâsa negation.

But if the sûtra be construed as a Prasayyapratishedha, then we shall apply the maxim अनन्तरस्य-विधिर्वा भवति प्रतिषेधो वा ॥ The prohibition is therefore stated with regard to जाग in connection with the affixes वि, चिण्, णल् and ङित् ॥ But the Guṇa ordained by VII. 3 84, 83 is not prohibited.

पुगन्तलघूपधस्य च ॥ ८६ ॥ पदानि ॥ पुक् अन्त, लघु उपधस्य, च, ॥

वृत्तिः ॥ पुगन्तस्याङ्गस्य लघूपधस्य च सार्वधातुकार्द्धधातुकयोर्गुणो भवति ॥

Kârikâ:—संयोगे गुरुसंज्ञायां गुणो भेत्तुर्न सिध्यति ।
विध्यपेक्षं लघोश्चासौ कथं कुण्डिर्न दुष्यति ॥
धातोर्हिनुम कथं रञ्जे, स्यदिश्रथ्योर्निपातनात् ।
अनल्लोपशिदीर्घत्वे विध्यपेक्षे न सिध्यतः ॥
अभ्यस्तस्य यदाहाचि लङर्थं तत्कृतं भवेत् ।
क्नुसनो यत्कृतं कित्त्वं ज्ञापकं स्याल्लघोर्गुणे ॥

86. Guṇa is substituted before a sârvadhâtuka and an ârdhadhâtuka affix, for the इक् vowels of the Causative stems which take the augment पु (VII. 3. 36), and for the short penultimate vowel of a root which ends in a single consonant.

As ब्लेपयति, ह्रेपयति, क्नोपयति, भेदनम्, छेदनम्, भेत्ता, छेत्ता ॥ Of course the vowel should be laghu or light, before the addition of the affix; the heaviness caused by the addition of the affix, will not prevent guṇa. Thus भिद् + तृ, though द् + तृ = त्तृ causes the इ to become heavy, that will not prevent guṇa: for विध्यपेक्षं लघु ग्रहणम् ॥ Obj: If this be so, why the forms कुण्डितृ, हुण्डितृ are not incorrect, for in them also the vowel is laghu (the roots are कुड् and हुड्), and the augment नुम् is added afterwards by a Vidhi rule? Ans. The augment नुम् is added to the *root*, and becomes upadeśivat. (See VII. 1. 58). Obj. If so, how do you cause Vṛiddhi in रञ्ज्, as in रागः with घञ्; as रञ्ज् + घञ् = रज् + घञ् (the ञ् being dropped by VI. 4. 27), for it is *after* the elision of ञ्, that the अ of रज् becomes penultimate and can admit of Vṛiddhi by VII. 2. 116? Ans. The exceptional forms स्यदः from स्यन्द् + घञ्, and श्रथः from श्रन्थ + घञ्, taught in VI. 4. 28, 29 teach by implication that roots of this form take Vṛiddhi as a *general* rule. Obj. If the विध्यपेक्ष maxim is not of universal application: though by VI. 4. 134, the अ of अन् &e. is elided in bha stems, like राजन् thus राज्ञा; yet the अ shoud not be elided if you be consistent, in अनङ् augment added by VII. 1. 75 to दधि, अस्थि &c. In fact, you could not get the forms दध्ना सक्थ्ना &c. Moreover though there can be the lengthening of the penultimate in सामन्—सामानि (before शि affix Nom. Pl). yet not in the case of कुण्डानि from कुण्ड for here न् is added by another rule VII. 1. 72. If you say, the maxim is not of universal application, then there can be no guṇa of इ in भिद् to form भेत्तृ ॥ Ans. The guṇa takes place in forms like भेत्तृ &c, because the prohibition of the following rule VII. 3. 87, with regard to the affixes beginning with a *vowel*, proves by implication that before affixes beginning with a consonant, as तृ, the guṇa also takes place. Obj. The prohibiton in the case of vowel beginning affixes is for the sake of लङ्, to form अनेनेक् ॥ This is derived from णिजिर् (Juhotyadi 11), in the Imperfect, as अ + निज् + शप्श्लु, + तिप् then reduplication (VI. 1. 10), then guṇa of the reduplicate, (VII. 4. 75), then तिप् which had become त् in the Imperfect, is elided by VI. 1. 68. Thus अनिज्+श्लु+त्=अ+निनिज्+त् (VI. 1. 10)=अ नेनिज्+त् (VII. 4. 75)=अ नेनिज् (VI. 1. 98)=अनेनक्. The elided त् produces its effect, the guṇa by VII. 3. 86. This is why अचि is taken in sûtra VII. 3. 87, namely अजादि affixes do not cause guṇa, the हलादि affixes like त् cause guṇa. You cannot therefore say that अचि in VII. 3. 87 is a jñâpaka. Ans. The sûtra त्रसिगृधिधृषिक्षिपेः क्नुः (III. 2. 140) teaches the addition of नु to त्रस &c, as गृध्नुः; if this नु had not tended to cause the guṇa of the penultimate vowels of these roots, what was the necessity of making this affix a कित्? Similarly I. 2. 10 teaches that सन् (Desiderative) is कित् after roots ending in consonants. These rules show that words like भेत्ता &c get guṇa, and the final consonant of the root plus the initial consonant of the affix, does not make the root vowel heavy. Obj: The कित् of सन् is for the sake of the elision of the nasal, in घिप्सति, धीप्सति (VI. 4. 24). Ans. Let it be so. still the कित् of क्नु is enough for us.

The "upadhâ short" must be the vowels of the इक् pratyâhâra. Therefore in भिनत्ति, the penultimate is short अ (of श्नम्) and it does not take guṇa. In fact, the word penultimate qualifies the word इक् understood. Others explain it by saying that पुगन्त is to be analysed by पुकिमन्त "in the vicinity of प्" ॥ The word अन्त means समीप, and means the इक् vowel in the *proximity* of पुक् ॥ The word लघूपधा should be analysed as लघ्वी उपधा and is a Karmadhâraya compound, and means "a short or light penultimate". The word पुगन्तलघूपध is a Samâhara Dvandva.

नाभ्यस्तस्याचि पिति सार्वधातुके ॥ ८७ ॥ पदानि ॥ न, अभ्यस्तस्य, अचि, पिति, सार्वधातु के ॥

वृत्तिः ॥ अभ्यस्तसंज्ञकस्याङ्गस्य लघूपधस्याजादौ पिति सार्वधातुके गुणो न भवति ॥

वार्त्तिकम् ॥ बहुलं छन्दसीति वक्तव्यम् ॥

87. The guṇa is not substituted for the penultimate light इक् vowel in the reduplicated form of a root, before a Sârvadhâtuka affix beginning with a vowel and having an indicatory प् ॥

As नेनिजानि, अनेनिजम्; परि वेविषाणि, पर्यवेविषम् ॥ Why of a reduplicated root? Observe वेदानि ॥ Why beginning with a vowel? Observe नेनेक्ति ॥ The word पित् is read here for the sake of the subsequent sûtras like VII. 3. 92. For here in cases other than पित्, guṇa will be prevented by ङित् because of सार्वधातुकमपित् ॥ Why a sârvadhâtuka affix? Observe निनेज in the Perfect, the affixes of which are ârdhadhâtuka (III. 4. 115). Why do we say a penultimate light vowel? Observe जुहवानि, अजुहवम् ॥

Vârt:—There is diversity in the Vedas. As जुजोषत् the लेट् of जुष् ॥

The forms पस्पशात, चाकशीति, वावसीतीः are irregular. स्पश्+लेट्=स्पश्+आट्+त=स्पश्+शप्श्लु+आते=पस्पशाते ॥

The above forms are thus evolved. 1. नेनिजानि is लोट् (Imperative 1st Per Sing). the मि is changed to नि, the augment आट् is added which is पित् (आडुत्तमस्य पिच्च III. 4. 92), श्लु is substituted for शप्, then there is reduplication, then guṇa by VII. 4. 75. 2. अनेनिजम् is लङ्, the मिप् is changed to अम् ॥ 3. वेविषाणि is 1st Pers. Sing. Imperative of विष् ॥ 4. नेनेक्ति is 3rd Person singular of the Present. 5. निनेज is the Perfect with णल् which is ârdhâdhtuka III. 4. 115. 6. जुजोषत् is the लेट् of जुषी प्रीतिसेवनयोः (Tudâdi 8), in the Parasmaipada, the इ of तिप is elided (III. 4. 97), then is added the augment अट् (III. 4. 94) then शप् is irregularly replaced by श्लु, then reduplication.

In the words पस्पशाते &c. the reduplicate has been shortened, as a Vedic form, in the Intensive यङ् लुक् ॥ चाकशीति is from काशृ दीप्तौ there is (यङ् लुक्, लट्, तिप्, and ईट् augment by यङो वा (VII. 3. 94). वावशीती: is from वाशृ दीप्तौ, in the Intensive (यङ्लुक), लट्, शतृ, ङीप् and शस् i. e. it is the Accusative plural of the Feminine Present Participle from the Intensive root of वाशृ ॥ The reading in the Kâsikâ is वावशीति ॥ In these two काशृ and वाशृ the roots have been shortened. Or the above forms may be derived regularly, without shortening, from the roots कशृ and वशृ ॥

भूसुवोस्तिङि ॥ ८८ ॥ पदानि ॥ भू, सुवोः, तिङि ॥

वृत्तिः ॥ भू सू इत्येतयोस्तिङि सार्वधातुके गुणो न भवति ॥

88. भू and सू get no guṇa before an immediately following Personal ending which is Sârvadhâtuka.

As अभूत्, अभूः, अभुवम्; सुवै, सुवावहै, सुवामहै ॥ The सू refers to the Adâdi root (21) in which the Present character is dropped, and does not refer to Divâdi (24) or Tudâdi (115) roots, because there the Present character श्यन् and श *intervene* between the Personal endings (तिङ्) and the root: and moreover the affixes श्यन् and श are ङित् (I. 2. 4) and would not cause guṇa. Why do we say before तिङ्? Observe भवति where the guṇa takes place before शप् ॥ Why before a sârvadhâtuka affix? Observe भ्यति भविषीष्ट, where the Benedictive is not a Sârvadhâtuka (III. 4. 116), and the augment is of course considered as a portion of the personal ending. Why the guṇa is not prohibited in बोभवीति when the Intensive यङ् is dropped, and the Personal ending is added directly to the root. Because the form बोभूतु in VII. 4. 65 indicates by implication that guṇa takes place in यङ्लुक् except in बोभूतु ॥

But of सू we have सोषुवीति where guṇa has been prohibited in the Intensive, because there is no jñâpaka with regard to it.

The forms सुवै &c are the 1st Per. Imperative of सू ॥

उतो वृद्धिर्लुकि हलि ॥ ८९ ॥ पदानि ॥ उतः, वृद्धिः, लुकि, हलि ॥

वृत्तिः ॥ सार्वधातुके पितीति वर्तते ॥ उकारान्तस्याङ्गस्य वृद्धिर्भवति लुकि सति हलादौ पिति सार्वधातुके ॥

89. A root ending in short उ, which has no Present

characteristic (i. e. the vikaraṇa is dropped by luk elision), gets vṛiddhi, before a पित् Sârvadhâtuka affix beginning with a consonant, but not if the stem is reduplicated.

Thus यौति, यौषि, यौमि ; नौति, नौषि, नौमि, स्तौति, स्तौषि, स्तौमि ॥ Why ending in उ ? Observe एति, एषि, एमि ॥ Why do we say whose vikaraṇa is elided by लुक् ? Observe सुनोति, सुनोषि, सुनोमि ॥ Why beginning with a हल् ? Observe यवानि, रवाणि, the First Person of the Imperative is पित् by III. 4. 92. Why before a पित् affix ? Observe युतः, रुतः ॥ The augment यासुट् being ङित् (III. 4. 103), prevents पित् action in अपि स्तुयात् राजानम् ॥ The phrase नाभ्यस्तस्य should be read into the sûtra from VII. 3. 87: therefore Vṛiddhi does not take place here योयोति नोनोति ॥ Here there is luk-elision of यङ् ॥

ऊर्णोतेर्विभाषा ॥ ९० ॥ पदानि ॥ ऊर्णोतेः, विभाषा ॥

वृत्तिः ॥ ऊर्णोतेर्विभाषा वृद्धिर्भवति हलादौ पिति सार्वधातुके ॥

90. Before a पित् Sârvadhâtuka affix beginning with a consonant, the final उ of ऊर्णु gets optionally vṛiddhi.

As प्रोर्णोति or प्रोर्णौति, प्रोर्णोषि or प्रोर्णौषि, प्रोर्णोमि or प्रोर्णौमि ; but प्रोर्णवानि before an affix beginning with a vowel.

गुणोऽपृक्ते ॥ ९१ ॥ पदानि ॥ गुणः, अपृक्ते ॥

वृत्तिः ॥ ऊर्णोतेर्धातोरपृक्ते हलि पिति सार्वधातुके गुणो भवति ॥

91. Before a पित् Sârvadhâtuka affix which is a single consonant, Guṇa is substituted for the final of ऊर्णु ॥

As प्रोर्णोत्, प्रौर्णोः ॥ Though the anuvṛitti of हलि was understood in this sûtra from the last aphorism, the employment of the term अपृक्त implies the existence of the following maxim :—यस्मिन् विधि स्तदादावल् ग्रहणे "when a term which denotes a letter is exhibited in a rule, in the form of a Locative case, and qualifies something else which likewise stands in the Locative case, that which is qualified by it must be regarded as beginning with the letter which is denoted by the term in question, and not as ending with it".

तृणह इम् ॥ ९२ ॥ पदानि ॥ तृणहः, इम् ॥

वृत्तिः ॥ तृणह इत्येतस्याङ्गस्य इमागमो भवति हलि पिति सार्वधातुके ॥

92. Before a पित् Sârvadhâtuka affix beginning with a consonant, इ is added after अ of the verbal stem तृणह् ॥

As तृणेढि, तृणेक्षि, तृणेह्मि, अतृणेट् ॥ In the last example though the affix vanishes altogether, yet it produces its effect. Why beginning with a consonant? Observe तृणहानि ॥ Why a पित् affix ? Observe तृण्ढः with तस् ॥ The stem तृणह is formed from the root तृह् (Rudhâdi) with the vikaraṇa श्नम्, and is so exhibited in the sûtra in order to indicate that the augment इम् is added *after* the vikarana श्नम् has been added, and that the root तृह of Tudâdi class is not to be taken.

The above forms are thus derived :—

तृह् + श्नम् + तिप् = तृणह् + इम् + ति = तृणइह + ति = तृणेह् + ति (VI. 1. 87) = तृणेढ् + ति (VIII. 2. 31) = तृणेढ् + धि (VIII. 2. 40) = तृणेढ् + ढि (VIII. 4. 41) = तृणेढि with the elision of one ढ (VIII. 3. 13). The form तृणेक्षि is similarly formed by VIII. 2. 41, the ढ् being changed to क before सि of सिप् ॥ अतृणेट् is the लङ् 2nd and 3rd Per. Sing.

ब्रुव ईट् ॥ ९३ ॥ पदानि ॥ ब्रुवः, ईट् ॥

वृत्तिः ॥ ब्रु इत्येतस्मादुत्तरस्य हलादेः पितः सार्वधातुकस्य ईडागमो भवति ॥

93. Before a पित् Sârvadhâtuka affix beginning with a consonant, the augment ईट् is placed after ब्रू ॥

As ब्रवीति, ब्रवीषि, ब्रवीमि, अब्रवीत् ॥ But ब्रवाणि before such an affix beginning with a vowel, and ब्रूतः before an affix which is not पित् ॥

यङो वा ॥ ९४ ॥ पदानि ॥ यङः, वा, ॥

वृत्तिः ॥ यङ उत्तरस्य हलादेः पितः सार्वधातुकस्य ईडागमो भवति वा ॥

94. The पित् Sârvadhâtuka affixes, beginning with a consonant, optionally get the augment ईट् in the Intensive.

As लालपीति in शाकुनिको लालपीति, so also दुन्दुभिर्वावदीति, त्रिधाबद्धो वृषभो रोरवीति महादेवोमर्त्यां आविवेश ॥ (Rig. IV. 58. 3). Also not, as वर्वर्त्ति चक्रम् and वर्वर्मि ॥ These are all examples of the Intensive with the elision of यङ् ॥ When the stem retains यङ्, there can be no पित् Sârvadhâtuka affix beginning with a consonant after it, because then शप् will intervene between the affix and the stem. Hence no examples of the same can be given.

तुरुस्तुशम्यमः सार्वधातुके ॥ ९५ ॥ पदानि ॥ तु, रु, स्तु, शमि, अमः, सार्वधातु के ॥

वृत्तिः ॥ तु इति सौत्रोयं धातुः, रु शब्दे ष्टुञ् स्तुतौ शम उपशमे अम गत्यादिषु इत्येतेभ्यः परस्य सार्वधातुकस्य हलादेर्वा ईडागमो भवति ।

95. A sârvadhâtuka affix, beginning with a consonant, optionally gets ईट् augment, after the roots तु, रु, स्तु, शम् and अम् ॥

The root तु (Adâdi 25) means 'to increase', रु (Adâdi 24) 'to make a sound', स्तु (Adâdi 34) 'to praise', शम् 'to be satisfied', and अम् 'to go'. According to Kâśikâ तु is a Sautra dhâtu. Thus उत्तौति or उत्तवीति, उपरौति or उपरवीति, उपस्तौति or उपस्तवीति, शाम्यध्वम् or शमीध्वम्, अभ्यमति or अभ्यमीति ॥ शम् and अम् can then be followed by a consonant beginning sârvadhatuka affix, when they lose their Present character (vikaraṇa) as a Vedic anomaly (bahulam chhandasi).

The Apiśalâs read the sûtra as तुरुस्तुशम्यमः सार्वधातुकासुच्छन्दसि ॥ This will then become a विधि rule for the Vedic forms. The word सार्वधातुका is here exhibited in the feminine.

The repetition of 'sârvadhâtuka', though its anuvṛitti was present is for the sake of stopping the anuvṛitti of पित्, and this rule applies to अपित् affixes also, as सुवीत, शमीध्वम् ॥

अस्तिसिचोऽपृक्ते ॥ ९६ ॥ पदानि ॥ अस्ति, सिचः, अ, पृक्ते ॥

वृत्तिः ॥ अस्तेरङ्गात् सिजन्ताच्च परस्यापृक्तस्य सार्वधातुकस्य ईडागमो भवति ॥

वार्त्तिकम् ॥ आहिभुवोरीटि प्रतिषेधः ॥

96. A single consonantal sârvadhâtuka affix gets the augment ईट्, after अस् (अस्ति) and after the Aorist character सिच् ॥

As आसीत्, आसीः ; अकार्षीत्, असावीत् ॥ Why do we say a single-consonant affix? Observe अस्ति, अकार्षम् ॥

Vârt:—Prohibition of the sthânivad-bhâva must be stated when आह् is substituted for ब्रू (III. 4. 84), and भू for अस् (II. 4. 52), before the augment ईट् ॥ Therefore not here आत्थ and अभूत् ॥ The word आत्थ is thus formed. आह्+सिप्=आह्+थल् (III. 4. 84)=आथ्+थ (VIII. 2. 35)=आत्+थ (VIII. 4. 55) =आत्थ ॥

बहुलं छन्दसि ॥ ९७ ॥ पदानि ॥ बहुलम्, छन्दसि ॥

वृत्तिः ॥ अस्तिसिचोरपृक्तस्य सार्वधातुकस्य ईडागमो भवति बहुलं छन्दसि विषये ॥

97. In the Veda, a single consonantal Sârvadhâtuka affix gets diversely the augment ईट्, after अस् and सिच् ॥

As आप एवेदं सलिलं सर्वमाः ॥ Here आः is used instead of आसीत् ; but also अहेवासीन्न रात्रिः (See Maitr. S. I. 5. 12). So also with s-Aorist, as गोभिरक्षाः (Rig IX. 107. 9), प्रत्यञ्चमत्साः (Rig X. 28. 4). And अभैषीर्मा पुत्रक, the अट् is not elided though मा is added (VI. 4. 75). अक्षाः and अत्साः are examples of सिच् without इट्. Compare VIII. 2. 73.

The word आः is the लङ् of अस्, there is added तिप्, then तप् is elided, then स् is changed to रु, and it is turned to visarjaniya. The words अक्षाः and अत्साः are derived from the roots क्षर् (संचलने) and त्सर् (छद्मगतौ), in the Aorist, the तिप् is elided (VI. 1. 68), the सिच् is elided by VIII. 2. 24 and the र् of the roots is changed to visarga. The augment इट् is not added as a Vedic irregularity.

रुदश्च पञ्चभ्यः ॥ ९८ ॥ पदानि ॥ रुदः, च, पञ्चभ्यः ॥

वृत्ति ॥ रुदादिभ्यः परस्य सार्वधातुकस्य हलादेरपृक्तस्य ईडागमो भवति ॥

98. After रुद् and the four roots that follow it, comes the augment ईट् to a sârvadhâtuka affix consisting of a single consonant.

As अरोदीत्, अरोदीः, अस्वपीत् and अस्वपीः, अश्वसीत्, अश्वसीः, प्राणीत्, प्राणीः, अजक्षीत्, अजक्षीः ॥ Why of these five only? Observe अजागर्, अयात् ॥ Why an apṛikta affix? Observe रोदिति ॥ The word रुदः is singular, though it ought to have been plural.

अड्गार्ग्यगालवयोः ॥ ९९ ॥ पदानि ॥ अद्, गार्ग्य, गालवयाः ॥

वृत्तिः ॥ रुदादिभ्यः पञ्चभ्यः परस्य अपृक्तस्य सार्वधातुकस्याडागमो भवति गार्ग्यगालवयोर्मतेन ॥

99. According to the opinon of Gârgya, and Gâlâva, the augment अद् comes before a Sârvadhâtuka affix consisting of a single consonant, after the above five roots रुद &c.

As अरोदत्, अरोदः, अस्वपत्, अस्वपः, अश्वसत् अश्वसः, प्राणत् प्राणः, अजक्षत्, अजक्षः ॥ The names of Gârgya and Gâlava are mentioned for honoris causa.

The mention of these names is not for the sake of "option" (विकल्पार्थम्). Because the very injunction about अद्, would make the ईद् of the preceding sûtra optional. The mention of more than one Achârya in the sûtra is also for this very reason.

अदः सर्वेषाम् ॥ १०० ॥ पदानि ॥ अदः, सर्वेषाम् ॥

वृत्तिः ॥ अद भक्षणे अस्मादुत्तरस्यापृक्तस्य सार्वधातुकस्याडागमो भवति सर्वेषामाचार्याणां मतेन ॥

100. After अद् 'to eat', comes the augment अद् before a Sârvadhâtuka affix consisting of a single consonant, according to the opinion of all grammarians.

As आदत् and आदः ॥ Before a non-aprikta we have अत्ति, अत्सि ॥ The word सर्वेषाम् makes it a necessary rule and not optional, like the last.

अतो दीर्घो यञि ॥ १०१ ॥ पदानि ॥ अतः, दीर्घः, यञि ॥

वृत्तिः ॥ अकारान्तस्याङ्गस्य दीर्घो भवति यञादौ सार्वधातुके परतः ॥

101. The long आ is substituted for the final अ of a Tense-stem, before a Sârvadhâtuka affix beginning with व् or म (lit. a consonant of यञ् pratyâhâra).

As पचामि, पचावः, पचामः, पक्ष्यामि, पक्ष्यावः, पक्ष्यामः ॥ Why 'for the अ only'? Observe चिनुवः, चिनुमः ॥ Why before a यञ् consonant (semivowels, nasals and झ and भ) only? Observe पचतः, पचथः ॥ Why a 'Sârvadhâtuka'? Observe भक्ता, केशवः ॥ Some read the anuvṛitti of तिङ् into this sûtra, from VII. 3. 88 so that the lengthening takes place only before Personal-endings. According to them before क्वसु there is no lengthening, as भववान् ॥

The word भववान् is thus formed. To भू is added क्वसु, then comes शप्, treating kvasu as a sârvadhâtuka under III. 4. 117; the reduplication of the root ending in शप् is prevented, because the word dhâtu is used in VI. 1. 8 which ordains reduplication of a *root* only, and not of a root plus a vikaraṇa like the form भव (भू-।-शप्) ॥ Those who do not read the anuvṛitti of तिङ् in this sûtra, but only of the word सार्वधातुके, they explain the form भववान् as a Vedic anomaly.

सुपि च ॥ १०२ ॥ पदानि ॥ सुपि, च ॥

वृत्ति ॥ अतो दीर्घो यञीत्यनुवर्तते । सुपि च यञादौ परतो ऽकारान्तस्याङ्गस्य दीर्घो भवति ॥

102. Before a case-ending beginning with य or भ (lit a consonant of यञ् Pratyâhâra), the final अ of a Nominal-stem is also lengthened.

The whole of the phrase अतो दीर्घो यञि is understood here. Thus वृक्षाय, प्लक्षाय, वृक्षाभ्याम, प्लक्षाभ्याम् ॥ But अग्निभ्याम् where the stem ends in इ, and वृक्षस्य प्लक्षस्य where the affix does not begin with a यञ consonant.

बहुवचने झल्येत् ॥ १०३ ॥ पदानि ॥ बहुवचने, झलि, एत् ॥

वृत्तिः ॥ बहुवचने झलादौ सुपि परतो ऽकारान्तस्याङ्गस्य एकारादेशो भवति ॥

103. Before a case-ending beginning with भ् or स् (lit. a झल consonant), in the Plural, ए is substituted for the final अ of a Nominal stem.

As वृक्षेभ्यः, प्लक्षेभ्यः, वृक्षेषु, प्लक्षेषु ॥ Why in the Plural? Observe वृक्षाभ्याम् प्लक्षाभ्याम् ॥ Why before a case-affix beginning with a झल् consonant? Observe वृक्षाणाम् (the lengthening here is by VI. 4. 3). Why a case-affix? Observe यजध्वम्, पचध्वम् ॥

ओसि च ॥ २०४ ॥ पदानि ॥ ओसि, च ॥

वृत्तिः ॥ ओसि परतोकारान्तस्याङ्गस्य एकारादेशो भवति ॥

104. Before the case-ending ओस्, ए is substituted for the final अ of a Nominal-stem.

As वृक्षयोः (Gen. dual) स्वं, प्लक्षयोः स्वम्, वृक्षयोः (Loc. dual) as वृक्षयोर्निधेहि, प्लक्षयोर्निधेहि ॥

आङि चापः ॥ १०५ ॥ पदानि ॥ आङि, च, आपः ॥

वृत्तिः ॥ आङिति पूर्वाचार्यनिर्देशेन तृतीयैकवचनं गृह्यते । तस्मिन्नाङि परतश्चकारादोसि च आबन्तस्याङ्गस्यैकारादेशो भवति ।

105. Before the case-endings ओस् and before आ of the Instrumental, ए is substituted for the final आ of the Feminine-affix.

आङ is the name given to the affix टा, the Ins. Sg. by the ancient grammarians. As खट्वया, मालया, खट्वयोः, मालयोः, बहुराजया, कारीषगन्ध्यया, बहुराजयोः, कारीषगन्ध्ययोः ॥ Why the आ of the Feminine affix only? Observe कीलालपा ब्राह्मणेन कीलालपोः ब्राह्मणकुलयोः ॥ Where ever ङी or आप् is employed in Grammar, they mean the long forms ई and आ, and not when they are shortened, therefore, not here, अतिखट्वेन ब्राह्मणकुलेन ॥

The word कीलालपा is derived from कीलालं पिबति with the affix विच् (III. 2. 74). In the Ins. Sing. the final आ is elided by VI. 4. 140. Had therefore, आ only been used in the sûtra, instead of आप्, there would have been ए substitution in the case of कीलालपा also; for the लोप् rule VI. 4. 140 would find its scope in कीलालपः पश्य &c, and would be debarred here by the present sûtra.

The maxim ङ्याप् ग्रहणेऽदीर्घग्रहणम् is necessary, because otherwise on the maxim of sthânivadbhâva, the short substitutes of ङी and आप् would also be included. In fact, in the sûtra prohibiting sthânivad bhâva, we find this vârtika ङ्याप् ग्रहणेऽदीर्घः "A short (not long) substitute of ङी and आप् is not sthânivat".

संबुद्धौ च ॥ १०६ ॥ पदानि ॥ सम्बुद्धौ, च ॥

वृत्तिः ॥ आप इति वर्त्तते । संबुद्धौ च परत आबन्तस्याङ्गस्य एत्वं भवति ॥

106. ए is substituted for the final आ of a Feminine stem, in the Vocative Singular.

As हे खट्वे, हे बहुराजे, हे कारीषगन्ध्ये ॥

अम्बार्थनद्योर्ह्रस्वः ॥ १०७ ॥ पदानि ॥ अम्बार्थ, नद्योः, ह्रस्वः ॥

वृत्तिः ॥ संबुद्धाविति वर्त्तते । अम्बार्थानामङ्गानां नद्यन्तानां ह्रस्वो भवति, संबुद्धौ परतः ॥

वार्त्तिकम् ॥ डलकवतीनां प्रतिषेधो वक्तव्यः ॥ वा० ॥ छन्दसि वेति वक्तव्यम् ॥

वार्त्तिकम् ॥ तलो ह्रस्वो वा ङिसंबुद्ध्योरिति वक्तव्यम् ॥

वार्त्तिकम् ॥ छन्दस्येव ह्रस्व त्वमिष्यते ॥ मातॄणां मातच् पुत्रार्थमर्हते ॥

107. A short vowel is substituted in the Voc. Sg. for the आ of the feminine, in the sense of 'mother, mother-dear', as well as for the long vowel of the Feminines called Nadî (I. 4. 3 &c).

As हे अम्ब ! हे अक्क ! हे अल्ल ! हे कुमारि ! हे शार्ङ्गरवि ! हे ब्रह्मबन्धु ! हे वीरबन्धु !

Vârt:—Prohibition must be stated when the endearing terms denoting mother have an uncombined ड, ल or क, as हे अम्बाडे ! हे अम्बाले ! हे अम्बिके ! But हे अक्क and हे अल्ल where the ल and क are conjunct.

Vârt:—Optionally so in the Veda: as हे अम्बाड ! or हे अम्बाडे ! हे अम्बाल ! or हे अम्बाले, हे अम्बिक ! हे अम्बिके ॥

Vârt:—A feminine stem formed with the affix तल् optionally becomes short before the Loc. Sg. and Voc. Sg. As देवते भक्तिः or देवतायां भक्तिः, हे देवत ! or हे देवते ॥ This shortening takes place in the Veda only.

Vârt:—In a Bahuvrîhi compound ending with मातृ, there is substituted मातच् for मातृ in the Voc. Sg. when the word means a son worthy of such a mother. As हे गार्गीमात ! = मात्रा व्यपदेशमर्हति श्लाघनीयत्वाद् यः पुत्रः ॥ This debars the कप् affix of V. 4. 153. The च् of मातच् makes the final acute.

ह्रस्वस्य गुणः ॥ १०८ ॥ पदानि ॥ ह्रस्वस्य, गुणः, ॥

वृत्तिः ॥ संबुद्धाविति वर्त्तते । ह्रस्वान्तस्याङ्गस्य गुणो भवति संबुद्धौ परतः ।

108. For short इ and उ final in a nominal-stem, a guṇa is substituted in the Vocative Singular.

As हे अग्ने, हे वायो, हे पटो ॥ But there is no guṇa in हे कुमारि, हे ब्रह्मबन्धु, because ई and ऊ were shortened specifically, and to substitute guṇa for them would make their shortening a useless operation. Moreover, had guṇa been intended in the case of these nadî words, the sûtra would have been अम्बार्थानांह्रस्वः, २ नदीह्रस्वयो॰ : ॥

जसि गुण च ॥ १०९ ॥ पदानि ॥ जसि, च ॥

वृत्तिः ॥ जसि परतो ह्रस्वान्तस्याङ्गस्य गुणो भवति ॥

वार्त्तिकम् ॥ जसादिषु छन्दसि वावचनं प्राक् णौ चङ्युपधाया ह्रस्व इत्येतस्मात् ॥

109. Before the affix अस् of the Nom. Pl., Guṇa is substituted for the final short vowel of a nominal stem.

As अग्नयः, वायवः, पटवः, धेनवः, बुद्धयः ॥

Vârt:—All these rules upto the end of this chapter are of optional application in the Veda. As अम्बे or अम्ब, पूर्वा दर्वि or पूर्णा दर्वी, अधा शतक्रत्वः or शतक्रतवः, पश्वे नृभ्यः or पशवे नृभ्यः, किकिदीव्या or किकिदीविना ॥

The forms दर्वि and दर्वी could have been regularly obtained by the optional use of ङीष् (कृदिकारादक्तिनः) ॥ शतक्रत्वः is formed by adding अस् to शतक्रतु without guṇa of उ, and उ being changed to व् ॥ The rule of lengthening the prior vowel (VI. 1. 102) which would have otherwise come, in the absence of guṇa does not take place, as a Vedic option (VI. 1. 106). किकिदीव्या is the Instrumental singular, the ना of VII. 3. 120 does not come. The word किकिदीवि is formed by Uṇâdi nipâtan (कृविधृष्वि &c Uṇ IV. 56).

ऋतो ङिसर्वनामस्थानयोः ॥ ११० ॥ पदानि ॥ ऋतः, ङि, सर्वनामस्थानयोः ॥

वृत्तिः ॥ गुण इति वर्तते ऋकारान्तस्याङ्गस्य ङौ परतः सर्वनामस्थाने च गुणो भवति ॥

110. Guṇa is substituted for the final ऋ of a stem, in the Locative singular and in the Strong cases.

As मातरि, पितरि. भ्रातरि, कर्तरि; मातरौ, पितरौ, भ्रातरौ, कर्तारौ, कर्तारः ॥ For the long in कर्तारौ and कर्तारः see VI. 4. 11. The त् in ऋत् is for the sake of facility of utterance.

Because before ङि and strong cases, it is impossible, for a stem to end in a long vowel ॠ nor a dhâtu noun can so come, since in that case, long ॠ would be changed to इर् by VII. 1. 100, and in forms like कर्तॄणि there is नुम् ॥

घेर्ङिति ॥ १११ ॥ पदानि ॥ घेः, ङिति, ॥

वृत्तिः ॥ घ्यन्तस्याङ्गस्य ङिति प्रत्यये परतो गुणो भवति ॥

111. For the इ and उ of the stems called घि (I.4.3.) Guṇa is substituted in Dative, Ablative and Genitive Singular.

As अग्नये, वायवे, अग्नेः, वायोः, (VI. 1. 110). Why of घि stems ? Observe सख्ये, पत्ये ॥ Why in the Singulars of the Dat. Abl. and Loc. only? Observe अग्निभ्याम् ॥ The word case ending (सुपि) is understood here also, as the counter-examples are पट्वी, कुरुतः ॥

The word पट्वी is formed by adding ङीष् to पटु (IV. 1. 44). ङीष् is not a case-affix, though it is ङित् and is added to पटु which is घि ॥ कुरुतः is no proper example: for though तस् which is added to कुरु, is ङित्, it is only so by atideśa (सार्वधातुकमपित्), and moreover कुरु is not घि ॥

आण्नद्याः ॥ ११२ ॥ पदानि ॥ आट्, नद्याः, ॥

वृत्तिः ॥ नद्यन्तात्परेषां ङितां प्रत्ययानामाडागमो भवति ॥

112. The augment आट् is added to the case-endings of the Dat. Abl. and Gen. Sg. after the stem called Nadî (I. 4. 3. &c.).

As कुमार्यै, किशोर्यै, ब्रह्मबन्ध्वै, धीरबन्ध्वै, कुमार्याः, किशोर्याः, ब्रह्मबन्ध्वाः, धीरबन्ध्वाः ॥

याडापः ॥ ११३ ॥ पदानि ॥ याट्, आपः, ॥

वृत्तिः ॥ आबन्तात्परेषां ङितां प्रत्ययानां याडागमो भवति ॥

113. The augment याट् is added to the Dat. Abl. and Gen. Sg. after a Feminine stem ending in आ ॥

As खट्वायै, बहुराजायै, कारीषगन्ध्यायै, खट्वायाः, बहुराजायाः, कारीषगन्ध्यायाः ॥ But in the compound अतिखट्व, (from खट्वामतिक्रान्तः), this rule does not apply, on the maxim ङ्याप् ग्रहणेऽदीर्घः as the आ has been shortened here. Even when the word अतिखट्व assumes the form अतिखट्वा in the Dative by VII. 3. 102, the affix does not take the augment याट्, because this long आ is a lâkshaṇika आ only, while the आ of the sûtra is a pratipadokta (लक्षणप्रतिपदोक्तयोः प्रतिपदस्यैव) ॥

सर्वनाम्नः स्याड्ढ्रस्वश्च ॥ ११४ ॥ पदानि ॥ सर्वनाम्नः, स्याट्, ह्रस्वः च, ॥

वृत्तिः ॥ सर्वनाम्न आबन्तात्परेषां ङितां प्रत्ययानां स्याडागमो ह्रस्वश्च भवति ॥

114. After a Pronominal stem ending in long आ of the Feminine, the Dat. Abl. and Gen. Sg. receive the augment स्याट् and the आ of the stem is shortened.

As सर्वस्यै, विश्वस्यै, यस्यै, तस्यै, कस्यै, भवत्यै, भवत्याः, सर्वस्याः, विश्वस्याः, यस्याः, तस्याः, कस्याः, अन्यस्यै अन्यस्याः ॥

But अमुष्यै where the stem does not end in long आ of the Feminine.

विभाषा द्वितीयातृतीयाभ्याम् ॥ ११५ ॥ पदानि ॥ विभाषा, द्वितीया, तृतीयाभ्याम्, ॥

वृत्तिः ॥ द्वितीया तृतीया इत्येताभ्यां परेषां ङितां प्रत्ययानां विभाषा स्याडागमो भवति ॥

115. After द्वितीया and तृतीया the Dat. Abl. and Gen. Sg. may optionally get the augment स्याट् before which the आ is shortened.

As द्वितीयस्यै or द्वितीयायै; तृतीयस्यै or तृतीयायै, द्वितीयस्याः or द्वितीयायाः, तृतीयस्याः or तृतीयायाः ॥

ङेराम्नद्याम्नीभ्यः ॥ ११६ ॥ पदानि ॥ ङेः, आम्, नदी, आप्, नीभ्यः, ॥

वृत्तिः ॥ नद्यन्तादाबन्तान्नीत्येतस्माच्चोत्तरस्य ङेरामित्ययमादेशो भवति ॥

116. For the ending इ of the Loc. Sg. there is substituted आम्, after a stem called Nadî (I. 4. 3. &c), after the Feminines in आ, and after नी ॥

As कुमार्याम्, किशोर्याम्, गौर्याम्, ब्रह्मबन्ध्वाम्, धीरबन्ध्वाम्, खट्वायाम्, बहुराज्ञायाम्, कारीषगन्ध्यायाम्, नी--ग्रामण्याम्, सेनान्याम् ॥

The word ग्रामणी is formed by क्विप् affix added under III. 2. 61, the न is changed to ण by अग्र ग्रामाभ्याम्; and the यण् substitute in the Locative is by VI. 4. 82.

इदुद्भ्याम् ॥ ११७ ॥ पदानि ॥ इत्, उद्भ्याम्, ॥

वृत्तिः ॥ इकारोकाराभ्यां नदीसंज्ञकाभ्यामुत्तरस्य ङेराम् आदेशो भवति ॥

117. After the Feminine nadî words ending in इ and उ short, आम् is substituted for the इ of the Loc. Sg.

As कृत्याम्, धेन्वाम् ॥ See I. 4. 6.

The word नदी is understood here also. Obj. If this be so, it is not a really separate sûtra, because it is included in the last, and these forms could be obtained by the last sûtra : so that we ought to make only one sûtra of 117 and 118, as इदुद्भ्यामौत् ॥ Ans. We could not have done so, for then in the case of कृति and धेनु, the औ would have come and not आ, in this way. The आम् would have found scope in nadî words like कुमार्याम्, the औ would have undisputed scope in पत्यौ and सख्यौ; but in the case of कृति when getting the designation नदी the औ would have come, being subsequently taught, and the form would have been कृत्यौ instead of कृत्याम् ॥

औत् ॥ ११८ ॥ पदानि ॥ औत् ॥

वृत्तिः ॥ इदुद्भ्यामुत्तरस्य ङेरौकारादेशो भवति ॥

118. After a stem ending in इ or उ short, and which is not a Nadî or a Ghi, औ is substituted for the इ of the Loc. Sg.

As सख्यौ, पत्यौ ॥

In the case of नदी words आम् is taught by the previous sûtras; in the case of घि words औ preceded by अ substitution of घि letters will be taught in the next sûtra, so by the rule of exclusion, the present sûtra applies to words other than nadî and ghi.

अच्च घेः ॥ ११९ ॥ पदानि ॥ अत्, च, घेः, ॥

वृत्तिः ॥ औदिति वर्तते घिसंज्ञकादुत्तरस्य ङेरौकारादेशो भवति तस्य च घेरकारादेशो भवति ॥

119. After a Ghi (I. 4. 7) stem ending in short इ or उ, औ is substituted for the इ of the Loc. Sg. and अ is substituted for the final of such Ghi stem.

As अग्नौ, वायौ, कृतौ, धेनौ, पटौ ॥ The short अ is substituted, in order to prevent the टाप् affix in the Feminine. Those who read 118 and 119 combined as औत्त्च घेः translate it thus: "After every other stem ending in इ and उ (i. e. which is not a Nadî), औ is substituted for the Locative Singular इ, whereby for the final of Ghi stems, अ is substituted". They do so on the analogy of the sûtra कर्तुः क्यङ् सलोपश्च (III 1. 11).

आङो नाऽस्त्रियाम् ॥ १२० ॥ पदानि ॥ आङः, ना, अ स्त्रियाम् ॥

वृत्तिः ॥ घेरुत्तरस्याङो नाभावो भवति अस्त्रियाम् ॥

120. ना is substituted for the ending आ of the Instrumental singular, after the Ghi stems, when they are not Feminine.

As अग्निना, वायुना, पटुना ॥ Why do we not say आङो ना पुंसि 'ना is substituted for आ in the Masculine'? Ans. In order to form the neuter Instrumentals also, as त्रपुणा, जतुना ॥ Obj. These can be formed by the augment नुम् under rule VII. 1. 73, and not by the ना of this sûtra. Ans. But अमुना will not be so formed as अमुना ब्राह्मणकुले ॥ Because मु substituted for दस् of अदस् VIII. 2. 80 is considered as asiddha or non-existent (VIII.2.1) for the purposes of the application of VII. 1. 73, and as अमु cannot take नुम्, it will take ना by this rule. Why do we say " not in the Feminine?" Observe कृत्या, धेन्वा ॥

ओ३म् ।

अथ सप्तमाध्यायस्य चतुर्थः पादः ।

BOOK SEVENTH.

CHAPTER FOURTH.

णौ चङ्युपधाया ह्रस्वः ॥ १ ॥ पदानि ॥ णौ, चङि, उपधायाः, ह्रस्वः, ॥

वृत्तिः ॥ अङ्गस्येति वर्तते चङ्परे णौ यदङ्गं तस्योपधाया ह्रस्वो भवति ॥

वार्त्तिकम् ॥ उपधाह्रस्वत्वे णौणिच्युपसंख्यानम् ॥

1. A short is substituted for the vowel, standing in a penultimate position, in the Causative stem, when the affix चङ् (sign of the Reduplicate Aorist of the Causatives) follows.

As अचीकरत्, अजीहरत्, अलीलवत्, अपीपठत् ॥ Here the rules of reduplication and shortening of the penultimate both present themselves simultaneously. The rule about shortening, being subsequent in order, is applied first, and then the reduplication takes place. Thus कारि + अत् = कार् + अत् (णि being elided VI. 4. 51) = कर् + अत् (shortening VII. 4. 1) = चकर् + अत् (VI. 1. 11) = चिकर् + अत् (VII. 4. 93, 79) = चीकरत् (VII. 4. 94). The necessity of maintaining this order will appear from the following considerations. The Causative stem of अट् is आटि; the Aorist of which is आटि + चङ् + त् = आट् + अत् (VI. 4. 51). Now if reduplication took place first we shall have आटिट् + अत् (I. 1. 59 the elided इ will be present for the purposes of reduplication) and as the penultimate is short already, the form will be आटिटत्, which with the augment अ will be अ + आटिटत् = आटिटत् ॥ This is a correct form, so far as it goes; but when the augment is elided in connection with the negative मा, the form will be मा भवान् आटिटत्, the correct form however is मा भवान् अटिटत् with a short अ, which can be formed if we shorten first and then reduplicate, as आट् + अत् = अट् + अत् = अटिट् + अत् = अटिटत्, which with the augment अ, will be आटिटत् ॥ In fact, though the reduplication of the second syllable (VI. 1. 2) is a *nitya* rule, because it applies even where a penultimate is shortened and where not, yet the rule about shortening takes effect first, because the author has himself indicated this, by making the root

ओण have an indicatory ऋ in the Dhâtupâṭha (See VII. 4. 2 about ऋदित् verbs). For had the reduplication taken place first in the case of ओणृ (Bhu. 482), as ओणिण्, there would be no long vowel to be shortened, and there would be no necessity of the probibition (VII. 4. 2).

Obj: Why do we say 'in the Causative'? The चङ् Aorist is formed of Causatives only (See III. I. 48), the only exceptions being the simple roots श्रि, द्रु, स्रु, कमु and श्वि, none of which have any vowel in the penultimate and कम and गुप् have already short upadhâ. The sûtra चङ्युपधाया ह्रस्वः would have been enough. Ans. Had the sûtra been, as proposed, then it would have meant, 'that which is penultimate when चङ् follows, should be shortened'. Therefore in the Aorist of the Causative of लू, we have लू+णि+चङ्+त्=लू+इ+अत् here the penultimate *with regard* to चङ् is ऊ, which would be shortened, debarring Vṛiddhi and आव् substitute, and there would have come the उवङ् substitute instead. But that is not the case. We have अलीलवत्, and not अलुलुवत् ॥ Similarly, in the Aorist of the Causative of दा, we shall have दा+इ+अत्, and आ being shortened we have द+इ+अत, so that we cannot add the augment पुक् (VII. 3. 36), and form अदीदपत् ॥ And the forms like अपीपचत् (पच्+इ+अत्) would not at all admit of shortening.

Why do we say when चङ् follows? Observe कारयति, हारयति where there is no shortening in the Present Tense. Why do we say of the penultimate? Observe अचकाङ्क्षत् from काङ्क्ष्, and अववाञ्छत् from वाञ्छ, where the penultimate being a consonant, there can be no shortening. Had the word penultimate been not used, the vowels of these would be shortened. And the word 'upadhâ' is also absolutely necessary for the sake of the subsequent sûtras like VII. 4. 4, and it prevents shortening in the above case, which would have otherwise tâken place, on the maxim येन नाव्यवधानं तेन व्यवहितेऽपि वचन प्रामाण्यात् which qualifies I. 1. 67.

Vârt:—The rule of shortening of the penultimate applies to the चङ् Aorist of the Causative of the Causative i. e. to the double Causative even. Thus अवीवदत् (=वादितवन्तं प्रयोजितवान्) वीणां परिवादकेन ॥ Otherwise वादि+इ+अत्=वाद्+इ+अत्=वाद्+०+अत् ॥ Here the elided इ being sthanivat, will prevent shortening, or because the stem has lost a simple-vowel (अग्लोपिन्), it will not be shortened. The present vârtika makes it so however.

नाग्लोपिशास्वृदिताम् ॥ २ ॥ पदानि ॥ न, अक्, लोपि, शासु, ऋदिताम् ॥

वृत्तिः ॥ अग्लोपिनामङ्गानां शासेर्ऋदितां च णौ चङ्युपधाया ह्रस्वो न भवति ॥

2. The shortening of the penultimate of the stem, before the causative affix, in the reduplicated-Aorist, does not take place, when it is a (Denominative) stem, which has lost

a simple (end vowel of the Nominal-stem), before the Causative sign and also not, when it is the verb शास्, or a root which has an indicatory ऋ ॥

The word अग्लोपिन् means literally a stem, in which a simple vowel (अक् pratyâhâra) or a portion containing an अक् vowel has been dropped. As the final vowels of Denominative stems are so elided before the Causative sign णि, the sûtra has been translated accordingly. Thus अममालत् = मालामाख्यत्; अममातरत् = मातरमाख्यत्, अत्यरराजत् = राजानमतिक्रान्तवान्, अन्वलुलामत् = लोमान्यनुमृष्टवान् ॥ Where a simple अक् vowel *alone* is elided, as in the case of माला, there the elided आ being sthânivat, would prevent the shortening, the आ of मा not being then considered penultimate. So that अग्लोपिन् could be spared from the sûtra, since the sthânivad-bhâva would prevent shortening. But where an अक् vowel plus a consonant is dropped, as in राजन् and लोमन्, there the sthânivad-bhâva does not apply (I. 1. 57), hence the necessity of employing the term अग्लोपिन् in the sûtra. Similarly अशशासत् with शास् ; and अबबाधत् from बाधृ, अययाचत् from याचृ, and अडुढौकत from ढौकृ ॥ See III. 1. 21 and 25.

भ्राजभासभाषदीपजीवमीलपीडामन्यतरस्याम् ॥ ३ ॥ पदानि ॥ भ्राज, भास, भाष, दीप, जीव, मील, पीडाम्, अन्यतरस्याम् ॥

वृत्तिः ॥ भ्राज भास भाष दीप जीव मील पीड इत्येतेषामङ्गानां णौ चङ्युपधाया ह्रस्वो भवत्यन्यतरस्याम् ॥
वार्त्तिकम् ॥ काण्यादीनां वेति वक्तव्यम् ॥

3. The shortening of the penultimate of the Causative stem, in the reduplicated Aorist, is optional in the following:—bhrâj, bhâs, bhâsh, dîp, jîv, mîl and pîḍ.

As अबिभ्रजत् or अबभ्राजत्, अबीभसत् or अबभासत्, अबीभषत् or अबभाषत्, अदीदिपत् or अदिदीपत्, अजीजिवत् or अजिजीवत्, अमीमिलत् or अमिमीलत्, अपीपिडत् or अपिपीडत् ॥ The Dhâtupâṭha reads भ्राजृ (Bhu. 194) and भासृ (Bh. 655). The indicatory ऋ is unnecessary and not countenanced by Pâṇini, as shown in this sûtra. Had they been ऋदित्, they would have been governed by the last aphorism.

Vârt:—The words काणि, वाणि, राणि, हेठि, लोपि should be enumerated: as अचकाणत् or अचीकणत्, अरराणत् or अरीरणत्, अशश्राणत् or अशिश्रणत्, अबभाणत् or अबीभणत्, अजीहिठत्, अजिहेठत्, अलुलोपत् or अलूलुपत् ॥

लोपः पिबतेरीच्चाभ्यासस्य ॥ ४ ॥ पदानि ॥ लोपः, पिबतेः, ईत्, च, अभ्यासस्य ॥

वृत्तिः ॥ पिबतेरङ्गस्य णौ चङ्युपधाया लोपो भवति अभ्यासस्येकारादेशो भवति ॥

4. The penultimate vowel, in the Causative stem of पा 'to drink' is elided in the Aorist, and for the vowel of the Reduplicate there is substituted long ई ॥

As पा + णि + अत् = पाइ + इ + अत् (VII. 3. 37) = पाय् + अत् (VI. 4. 51) = प्य् + अत् (VII. 4. 8) = पप्य् + अत् (I. 1. 59) = पीप्यत् (VII. 4. 4). Thus अपीप्यत्, अपीप्यतांम्, अपीप्यन् ॥ When the penultimate आ is elided, there remains प् which cannot be reduplicated as having no vowel, but the elided आ is considered as sthânivat and thus पा is reduplicated. Sûtra VII. 4. 80 establishes by implication the principle that the substitutes caused by णि are sthânivat. Thus भू + णि = भावि; in reduplicating, this भा will not be reduplicated, but भू, as बुभावि, भा = भू by sthâinvad-bhâva.

तिष्ठतेरित् ॥ ५ ॥ पदानि ॥ तिष्ठतेः, इत् ॥

वृत्तिः ॥ तिष्ठतेरङ्गस्य णौ चङ्युपधाया इकारादेशो भवति ॥

5. Short इ is substituted for the penultimate vowel of the Causative stem of स्था in the Aorist.

Thus अतिष्ठिपत्, अतिष्ठिपताम्, and अतिष्ठिपन् ॥ The form is thus evolved. स्था + णिच् + अत् = स्थाप् + इ + अत् (VII. 3. 36) = स्थाप् + अत् (VI. 4. 51) = स्थिप् + अत् (VII. 4. 5) = तिष्ठिपत् ॥

जिघ्रतेर्वा ॥ ६ ॥ पदानि ॥ जिघ्रतेः, वा ॥

वृत्तिः ॥ जिघ्रतेरङ्गस्य णौ चङ्युपधाया इकारादेशो वा भवति ॥

6. Short इ is optionally substituted for the penultimate vowel of the Causative stem of घ्रा in the Aorist.

As अजिघ्रिपत् or अजिघ्रपत्, अजिघ्रिपताम् or अजिघ्रपताम्, अजिघ्रिपन् or अजिघ्रपन् ॥ Thus घ्रा + णि + अत् = घ्राप् + इ + अत् (VII. 3. 36) = घ्रिप् + इ + अत् (VII. 4. 6) = घ्रिप् + अत् (VI. 4. 51) = जिघ्रिपत् ॥ When इ is not substituted, आ is shortened by VII. 4. 1.

उर्ऋत् ॥ ७ ॥ पदानि ॥ उः, ऋत् ॥

वृत्तिः ॥ णौ चङ्युपधाया ऋवर्णस्य स्थाने वा ऋकारादेशो भवति ॥

7. Short ऋ is optionally substituted for the penultimate ऋ and ॠ of a Causative stem, in the reduplicated Aorist.

This debars the इर् (VII. 3. 101), अर् (VII. 3. 86), and आर् (VII. 2. 114) substitutes. Thus अचिकीर्तत् (VII. 1. 101) or अचिकृतत् from कृत् (Chur 111): अववर्तत् (VII. 3. 86), or अवीवृतत्; अममार्जत् (VII. 2. 114) or अमीमृजत् ॥ Though the इर्, अर् and आर् substitutes are antaranga operations, they are prohibited by the express text of this sûtra. The short ऋ is substituted even for a long ॠ: the त् of ऋत् shows that, as in अचीकृतत् (VIII. 2. 77). In fact, this ऋ substitute does not take place after the operations of इर्, आर् and अर् substitutions have taken effect, but it is a form which suspends the operation of all those rules.

नित्यं छन्दसि ॥ ८ ॥ पदानि ॥ नित्यम्, छन्दसि ॥

वृत्तिः ॥ छन्दसि विषये णौ चङ्युपधाया ऋवर्णस्य स्थाने ऋकारादेशो भवति नित्यम् ॥

8. Short ऋ is invariably substituted in the Veda, for the penultimate ॠ or ऋ of a Causative stem, in the Reduplicated Aorist.

As अवीवृधत्, अवीवृधताम् and अवीवृधन् ॥

दयतेर्दिगि लिटि ॥ ९ ॥ पदानि ॥ दयतेः, दिगि, लिटि ॥

वृत्तिः ॥ दयतेरङ्गस्य लिटि परतो दिगीत्ययमादेशो भवति ॥

9. दिगि is substituted for दे (दयते), in the Perfect.

As अव दिग्ये, अव दिग्याते, अव दिग्यिरे ॥ The root देङ् 'to protect' (Bhu. 1011) is to be taken, and not दय 'to give' (Bhu. 510), for that root forms its Perfect by आम् (Periphrastic Perfect) as taught in III. 1. 37. The substitute दिगि debars reduplication.

ऋतश्च संयोगादेर्गुणः ॥ १० ॥ पदानि ॥ ऋतः, च, संयोग-आदेः, गुणः ॥

वृत्तिः ॥ ऋकारान्तस्याङ्गस्य संयोगादेर्गुणो भवति लिटि परतः ॥

वार्त्तिकम् ॥ संयोगादेर्गुणविधाने संयोगोपधग्रहणं कृञर्थं कर्तव्यम् ॥

10. A root ending in short ऋ, and preceded by a conjunct consonant, gets Guṇa in the Perfect.

As सस्वरतुः, सस्वरुः from स्वृ, दध्वरतुः, दध्वरुः from ध्वृ, सस्मरतुः, सस्मरुः from स्मृ ॥ Why do we say ending in ऋ? Observe चिक्षियतुः, चिक्षियुः ॥ Why do we say beginning with a conjunct consonant? Observe चक्रतुः, चक्रुः ॥ This sûtra ordains Guṇa where there was prohibition by I. 2. 5 read with I. 1. 5. But this does not debar the Vṛiddhi caused by णल् (VII. 1. 115). In fact, that prior rule supersedes this posterior rule, as सस्वार, दध्वार, सस्मार ॥ The word लिटि is to be supplied in the sûtra, the rule does not apply to Nishṭhâ &c., as स्मृतः, स्मृतवान् ॥

Vârt:—For the sake of कृञ्, the guṇa should be stated even where the double-consonant is in the penultimate position and not in the beginning. As संचस्करतुः, संचस्करुः ॥See VI. 1. 135. On the maxim पूर्वं धातुः साधनेन युज्यते पश्चादुपसर्गेण 'a root is first developed fully and then the preposition is added to it'; we first develop कृ in the Perfect by reduplication, which gives us चकृ+अतुस्, then we add the preposition as संचकृ+अतुः, then we add सुट् though the reduplicate intervenes, by VI. 1. 136 and 137, as संचस्कृ+अतुः, now the root assumes a form in which the penultimate begins with a double consonant, and applying the vârtika we make guṇa, and get संचस्करतुः ॥

It is by this consideration that in संस्कृषीष्ट, उपस्कृषीष्ट, the सुट् augment being Bahiraṅga and consequently considered as non-existent (asiddha), there is no इट् augment added by VII. 2. 43.

ऋच्छत्यृताम् ॥ ११ ॥ पदानि ॥ ऋच्छति, ऋ, ऋताम् ॥

वृत्तिः ॥ ऋच्छतेरङ्गस्य ऋ इत्येतस्य ॠकारान्तानां च लिटि परतो गुणो भवति ॥

11. There is guṇa in the Perfect of ऋच्छ्, ऋ and roots ending in long ॠ.

As आनर्च्छ, आनर्च्छतुः, आनर्च्छुः from ऋच्छ्, आर, आरतुः, आरुः from ऋ, and नि चकरतुः, नि चकरुः, नि जगरतुः, नि जगरुः from कॄ and गॄ ॥ ऋच्छ् not having a light vowel in the penultimate, would not have received guṇa by VII. 3. 86, this sûtra ordains it; roots in long ॠ never received guṇa, but इर् substitution; this ordains guṇa. The Vṛiddhi of VII. 2. 115 supersedes this rule, within its own jurisdiction, a prior superseding the posterior: as निचकार, नि जगार ॥

शॄदॄप्रां ह्रस्वो वा ॥ १२ ॥ पदानि ॥ शॄ, दॄ, प्राम्, ह्रस्वः, वा, ॥

वृत्तिः ॥ शॄ दॄ पॄ इत्येतेषामङ्गानां लिटि परतो वा ह्रस्वो भवति ॥

12. In शॄ, 'to injure' (IX. 18) दॄ 'to tear' (IX. 23) and पॄ to protect' (IX. 19) the vowel may optionally be shortened in the Perfect.

As वि शश्रतुः by shortening or वि शशरतुः, by guṇa, which prevents ए and abhyâsalopa (VI. 4. 126) वि शश्रुः or विशशरुः, विदद्रतुः or विददरतुः, विदद्रुः or विददरुः; निपप्रतुः or नि पपरतुः, नि पप्रुः or नि पपरुः ॥ Why is the word 'short' made optional in the sûtra, and not the word 'guṇa'; for in the absence of guṇa, the long ॠ would have become र before अतुः by यणादेशः, and we would have got the forms विशश्रतुः, विशश्रुः by the regular rules of 'sandhi'? The word 'short' is used in the sûtra, in order to debar the इर् and उर् alternatives. Had the sûtra been "शॄ दॄ प्रां वा" the alternative examples would have been with इर् (VII. 1. 101) as शिशिरतुः विदिरतुः and उर् (VIII. 2. 77) as पिपुरतुः ॥ Some say this sûtra is unnecessary. The above forms like वि शश्रतुः, विशश्रुः, &c. can be regularly obtained from the roots श्रा 'to cook', द्रा 'to abuse', and प्रा 'to fill' and as the roots have many other senses, besides those assigned to them in the Dhâtupâṭha, the roots श्रा, द्रा and प्रा will give the meanings of शॄ, दॄ, and पॄ" ॥ If that were so, the form विशश्रृवान् with the affix क्वसु could not be formed, for we should have either विशशर्वान् from शॄ root or विशश्रिवान् from श्रा root but never विशश्रृवान् ॥ So the rule about shortening is necessary.

केऽणः ॥ १३ ॥ पदानि ॥ के, अणः, ॥

वृत्तिः ॥ के प्रत्यये परतो ऽणो ह्रस्वो भवति ॥

13. Before the affix क, the preceding आ, ई and ऊ are shortened.

As ज्ञका, (VII. 3. 47) कुमारिका, किशोरिका, ब्रह्मबन्धुका ॥ Why आ, ई and ऊ only? Observe गोका, नौका ॥ The words राका, धाका are irregular being formed by Uṇâdi diversity. with the affix क added to रा and धा (Uṇ III. 40) By the following sûtra, the rule does not apply to the affix कप्; it therefore implies that कन् is governed by this rule, though it has the anubandha न् ॥ Kâtyâyana would confine this rule to the Taddhita क, and not the kṛit क of the

Uṇâdi, as राका, धाका; but Uṇâdi words are not derivatives (उणादयोऽव्युत्पन्नानि प्रातिपदिकानि), and hence no necessity of reading Taddhita into the sûtra.

न कपि ॥ १४ ॥ पदानि ॥ न, कपि, ॥

वृत्तिः ॥ कपि प्रत्यये परतो ऽणो ह्रस्वो न भवति ॥

14. But before the samâsanta affix कप coming after Bahuvrihi compounds, the अण vowels are not shortened.

As बहुकुमारीकः, बहुवृषलीकः, बहुवधूकः, बहुलक्ष्मीकः ॥ The shortening ordained by I. 2. 48 even does not operate when कप follows.

For had there been upasarjana shortening (I. 2. 48), the present sûtra would be useless. Therefore, the very existence of this sûtra debars every sort of shortening. Obj. The present sûtra would not be useless, for it will find scope where there is no shortening of the upasarjana by I. 2. 48: namely before non-feminine affixes, as बहुयवागूकः; but there should be shortening in feminine affixes. Ans. The shortening of I. 2. 48 will not take place before कप् affix. Because the affix कप् will first be added to the second member in the sense of the compound, and then the word so ending in कप् will be compounded with the first member. So there is no *prâtipadika* left which ends in a feminine affix, and therefore I. 2. 48, does not apply, because the pratipadika now left is one ending in the affix कप् and not in a feminine affix.

आपोन्यतरस्याम् ॥ १५ ॥ पदानि ॥ आपः, अन्यतरस्याम् ॥

वृत्तिः ॥ आबन्तस्याङ्गस्य कपि ह्रस्वो न भवत्यन्यतरस्याम् ॥

15. Optionally the feminine stem in आ is not shortened before कप् ॥

As बहुखट्वाकः or बहुखट्वकः, बहुमालकः or बहुमालाकः ॥

ऋदृशो ऽङि गुणः ॥ १६ ॥ पदानि ॥ ऋ, दृशः, अङिः, गुणः ॥

वृत्तिः ॥ ऋवर्णान्तानां दृशेश्च अङि परतो गुणो भवति ॥

16. Guṇa is substituted for the vowel of the root, before the affix अङ्, in the roots ending in ऋ or ॠ, as well as in दृश् ॥

As शकलाङ्गुष्ठकोऽकरत्, अहं तेभ्योऽकरं नमः, असरत्, आरत्, अदर्शत्, अदर्शताम्, अदर्शन् ॥ The affix अङ् means the Aorist-character अङ् of which the above examples are given. It also is the kṛit-affix (III. 3. 104). of which we have जॄ—जरा ॥

The word अकरत् is अङ् Aorist formed from कृ by III. 1. 59. The word असरत् is from सृ (III. 1. 56). अदर्शत् by VI. 1. 57.

अस्यतेस्थुक् ॥ १७ ॥ पदानि ॥ अस्यतेः, थुक्, ॥

वृत्ति ॥ अस्यतेरङ्गस्य थुगागमो भवत्यङि परतः ॥

17. The stem अस् (अस्यते) gets the augment थुक् before this Aorist अङ् ॥

As आस्थत्, आस्थताम्, आस्थन् ॥ See III. 1. 52.

श्वयतेरः ॥ १८ ॥ पदानि ॥ श्वयतेः, अः ॥

वृत्तिः ॥ श्वयतेरङ्गस्याकारादेशो भवत्यङि परतः ॥

18. The अ is substituted for the final of श्वि in the अङ् Aorist.

As अश्वत्, अश्वताम्, अश्वन् ॥ For the अ of the stem and the अ of the affix, there is the single substitute of the last by VI. 2. 97. See III. 1. 58.

पतः पुम् ॥ १९ ॥ पदानि ॥ पतः, पुम् ॥

वृत्तिः ॥ पतेरङ्गस्य पुमागमो भवत्यङि परतः ॥

19. The augment पु is added after the vowel of the root पत् in the अङ्-Aorist.

As अपप्तत्, अपप्तताम्, अपप्तन् ॥ The पत् takes the अङ् Aorist as it has an indicatory ऌ in the Dhâtupâṭha (III. 1. 55).

वचउम् ॥ २० ॥ पदानि ॥ वचः, उम् ॥

वृत्तिः ॥ वचेरङ्गस्य अङि परत उमागमो भवति ॥

20. The augment उ is added after the अ of वच् in the अङ्-Aorist.

As अवोचत्, अवोचताम्, अवोचन् ॥ See III. 1. 52.

शीङः सार्वधातुके गुणः ॥ २१ ॥ पदानि ॥ शीङः, सार्वधातुके, गुणः ॥

वृत्तिः ॥ शीङोऽङ्गस्य सार्वधातुके परतो गुणो भवति ॥

21. For the vowel of शी, there is substituted guṇa, when a Sârvadhâtuka affix follows.

As शेते, शयाते, शेरते, but शिश्ये before the ârdhadhâtuka affix (III. 4. 115). Though these sârvadhâtuka affixes were ङित् (I. 2. 4) and would not have caused guṇa (I. 4. 5), they do so by virtue of the present sûtra. The word शीङ् is read in the sûtra with the anubardha ङ्, in order to indicate that the rule does not apply to यङ् लुक् as शेशीतः, शेश्यति ॥

अयङ् यि क्ङिति ॥ २२ ॥ पदानि ॥ अयङ्, यि, क्ङिति, ॥

वृत्तिः ॥ यकारादौ क्ङिति प्रत्यये परतः शीङोऽङ्गस्यायङित्ययमादेशो भवति ॥

22. Before an affix beginning with य् and having an indicatory क् or ङ्, there is substituted अय् for the ई of शी ॥

As शय्यते with यक्, शाशय्यते with यङ्, प्रशय्य and उपशय्य with ल्यप् which being the substitute of क्त्वा is कित् ॥ But शिश्ये where the affix is ए, and शेयम् where the affix is यत् (neither कित् or ङित्) ॥

उपसर्गाद्ध्रस्व ऊहतेः ॥ २३ ॥ पदानि ॥ उपसर्गात्, ह्रस्वः, ऊहतेः ॥

वृत्तिः ॥ उपसर्गादुत्तरस्य ऊहतेरङ्गस्य ह्रस्वो भवति यकारादौ क्ङिति ॥

23. The short is substituted for the ऊ of ऊह् when a Preposition precedes it, and an affix beginning with य with an indicatory क् or ङ् follows.

As समुह्यते, प्रत्युह्यते, समुह्य, अभ्युह्यते, अभ्युह्य ॥ But ऊह्यते without Preposition. Why do we say of ऊह्? Observe समीह्यते ॥ Why do we say 'before य'? Observe समूहितम् ॥ Why do we say having indicatory क् or ङ्? Observe अभ्यूह्यः with यत् ॥ Of course the shortening takes place of ऊ (or अण् vowel, the word अण् being understood here from VII. 4. 13), and not when it assumes the form ओ, as आ ऊह्यते = ओह्यते, समोह्यते ॥

एतेर्लिङि ॥ २४ ॥ पदानि ॥ एतेः, लिङि ॥

वृत्तिः ॥ एतेरङ्गस्योपसर्गादुत्तरस्य लिङि यकारादौ क्ङिति परतो ह्रस्वो भवति ॥

24. The short is substituted for the vowel of the stem इ (एति) before the augment यासु in the Benedictive, when a Preposition precedes it.

As उदियात्, समियात्, अभियात् ॥ This is an exception to the following sûtra by which a long would have been substituted. But ईयात् without a Preposition. The अण् (VII. 4. 13) is understood here also. Therefore ए form of इ will not be shortened, as आ-।-इयात् = एयात्, समेयात् ॥

अकृत्सार्वधातुकयोर्दीर्घः ॥ २५ ॥ पदानि ॥ अकृत, सार्वधातुकयोः, दीर्घः, ॥

वृत्तिः ॥ अकृद्यकारे असार्वधातुकयकारे च क्ङिति परतोऽजन्तस्याङ्गस्य दीर्घो भवति ॥

25. A long is substituted for the final vowel of the stem, before an affix beginning with a य् having an indicatory क् or ङ्, when it is not either a Kṛit or a Sârvadhâtuka affix.

Thus भृशायते, सुखायते, and दुःखायते with the Denominative affix क्यङ् according to III. 1. 12 and 18. चीयते and स्तूयते with the Passive यक्, चेचीयते and तोष्टूयते with the Intensive यङ्, and चीयात् and स्तूयात् in the Benedictive (See III. 4. 116). But प्रकृत्य and प्रहृत्य where the affix ल्यप् is kṛit, and had the vowel been lengthened by this subsequent rule, the antecedent तुक् augment would have been debarred (VI. 1. 71). And चिनुयात् and सुनुयात् where the Personal endings of the Potential are sârvadhâtuka. The phrase क्ङिति is understood in this sûtra, so there is no lengthening before non-kit and non-ṅit affixes, as, उरुया, धृष्णुया, formed by या under VII. 1. 39.

च्वौ च ॥ २६ ॥ पदानि ॥ च्वौ, च ॥

वृत्तिः ॥ च्विप्रत्यये परतोऽजन्तस्याङ्गस्य दीर्घो भवति ॥

26. A long is substituted for the final vowel of the stem, before the Adverbial affix च्वि (V. 4. 50).

As शुची करोति, शुची स्यात्, शुची भवति, पटू करोति, पटू स्यात्, पटू भवति ॥ The च draws in the anuvṛitti of the phrase 'non-krit, and non-sârvadhâtuka' from the last sûtra, which though not of any direct use in this aphorism, is necessary for the sake of subsequent ones. See VII. 4. 32 for words ending in अ ॥

रीङृतः ॥ २७ ॥ पदानि ॥ रीङ्, ऋतः ॥

वृत्तिः ॥ च्वाविति वर्त्तते ॥ अकृत्सार्वधातुकयोरिति च ॥ ऋकारान्तस्याङ्गस्य अकृद्यकारेऽसार्वधातुके यकारे च्वौ च परतो रीङित्ययमादेशो भवति ॥

27. री is substituted for the final short ऋ of a stem, before an affix beginning with य, when it is not a Kṛit nor a Sârvadhâtuka affix, and before the adverbial affix च्वि ॥

The anuvṛitti of क्ङिति is, however, not understood in this sûtra; that of च्वौ and अकृत्सार्वधातुकयोः is present. Thus मात्रीयति and पित्रीयति with क्यच (III. 1. 8), मात्रीयते, पित्रीयते with क्यङ् (III. 1. 11). चेक्रीयते with यङ्, मात्रीभूतः with च्वि ॥ The कित् and ङित् not being understood here, we have पितुरागत = पित्र्यम् (IV. 3. 79), which is thus formed पितृ+यत् = पित्री + य = पित्र्+य (ई being elided by VI. 4. 148). Why do we say short ऋ? Observe चेकीर्यते, from कॄ विक्षेपे, with यङ्, ऋत इद् धातोः and हलि च lengthening. निजेगिल्यते from कॄ and गॄ ॥

रिङ् शयग्लिङ्क्षु ॥ २८ ॥ पदानि ॥ रिङ्, श, यक्, लिङ् क्षु ॥

वृत्तिः ॥ ऋकारान्तस्याङ्गस्य श यक् इत्येतयोर्लिङि च यकारादौ असार्वधातुके परतो रिङित्ययमादेशो भवति ॥

28. For the final short ऋ of a root, there is substituted रि, before the Present-character अ (श), before the Passive-character य, and before the augment यास् in the Benedictive.

The word लिङि in the aphorism is qualified by the phrase यकारादौ असार्वधातुके ॥ A Liṅ affix which begins with a य and is not a Sârvadhâtuka, is necessarily the augment यास् of the Benedictive. Thus श — आ द्रियते and आ ध्रियते (the य comes by VI. 4. 77). यक् — क्रियते, ह्रियते ॥ लिङ् — क्रियात् and ह्रियात् ॥ This short रि debars the long री of the last. The word non-Sârvadhâtuka being understood, the rule does not apply to the Potential, as बिभृयात् ॥ The यि (VII. 4. 22) is understood here also, therefore when the Benedictive affix does not begin with य, the rule does not apply, as कृषीष्ट, हृषीष्ट ॥

गुणोर्त्तिसंयोगाद्योः ॥ २९ ॥ पदानि ॥ गुणः, अर्त्ति, संयोगाद्योः ॥

वृत्तिः ॥ ऋतो यकि लिङि इति वर्तते ॥ शइत्यत्रासंभवान्नानुवर्त्तते ॥ गुणो भवत्यर्त्तेः संयोगादीनामृकारान्तानां यकि परतो, लिङि च यकारादावसार्वधातुके ॥

29. Guṇa is substituted for the final ऋ in the root ऋ (अर्त्ति), and in those roots ending in ऋ, in which

the vowel is preceded by a conjunct consonant, when the Passive character यक् or the Benedictive augment यासु follows.

The words ऋतः, यक्ति and लिङि are understood here. Not so the word च as its anuvṛitti is impossible. Thus अर्यते, अर्यात्, स्मर्यते and स्मर्यात् ॥ This is an exception to I. 1. 5. In सं स्क्रियते and संस्क्रियात् (VI. 1. 135), there is no Guṇa, either because in स्कृ the augment स् is considered as Bahiranga and therefore asiddha, or because it is considered as no part of (or non-attached to) कृ, and therefore स् कृ is not a root beginning with a conjunct consonant. See however VII. 4. 10, where in forming संचस्करतुः, स्कृ is considered as a root beginning with a conjunct consonant. See also Mahâbhâshya on VI. 1. 135. The चि (VII. 4. 22) is understood here also; the Benedictive affix must begin with य, therefore not here स्तृषीष्ट, ध्वृषीष्ट ॥ The word non-sarvadhâtuka is also understood here, the rule does not apply to the Potential, as इयृयात्, there is ślu substitution of śap, reduplication, then there is इ substitution in the reduplicate by VII. 4. 77, then इयङ् by VI. 4. 78.

यङि च ॥ ३० ॥ पदानि ॥ यङि, च ॥

वृत्तिः ॥ यङि च परतो अर्त्तेः संयोगादेश्च ऋतो गुणो भवति ॥

वार्त्तिकम् ॥ न न्द्राः संयोगादय इति द्विर्वचनप्रतिषेधो यकारपरस्य नेष्यते ॥

वा० ॥ हन्तेर्हिंसायां यङि घ्नीभावो वक्तव्यः ॥

30. Guṇa is substituted for the final ऋ of the root ऋ (अर्ति) and in those roots, ending in short ऋ, in which the vowel is preceded by a conjunct consonant, when the Intensive character यङ् follows.

As अरार्यते, सास्वर्यते, दाध्वर्यते, सास्मर्यते ॥ The root ऋ takes यङ् according to a Vârtika under Sûtra III. 1. 22, with Guṇa we have ऋ-।-य=अर्य ॥ By VI. 1. 2, the second member is reduplicated, in spite of the prohibition in VI. 1. 3, for according to Patanjali र् followed by य is not governed by that prohibition. So we have अर्यर्य, and according to VII. 4. 60, the य् is dropped, and we have अरर्य, and by VII. 4. 83, we get अरार्य ॥ This is an exeeption to I. 1. 5.

Vârt:—In the Intensive of हन् 'to kill', घ्नी is substituted for हन् as जेघ्नीयते ॥ The substitute is with a long ई, had it been with a short इ, that might also have been lengthened by VII. 4. 25. Not doing so, however, indicates the existence of the maxim संज्ञापूर्वकविधेरनित्यत्वम् "A rule is not universally valid, when that which is taught in jt is denoted by a technical term". It is through this that स्वायंभुवः is formed from स्वयंभू; because the Guṇa taught by VI. 4. 146, does not take place here before the Taddhita affix अण्, in as much as that rule VI. 4. 146, is taught by employing the technical term गुणः in ओर्गुणः instead of ओरोत्, hence that rule is anitya, and we have उवङ् ॥

Why do we say when meaning 'to kill'? Observe जङ्घन्यते where it means to do.

ई घ्राध्मोः ॥ ३१ ॥ पदानि ॥ ई, घ्रा, ध्मोः, ॥

वृत्तिः ॥ घ्रा ध्मा इत्येतयार्यङि परत ईकारादेशो भवति ॥

31. Long ई is substituted for the vowel of the roots घ्रा and ध्मा in the Intensive.

As जेघ्रीयते, देध्मीयते ॥ The long ई is for the sake of the subsequent sûtra, short इ would have, by VII. 4. 25, given the same forms also.

अस्य च्वौ ॥ ३२ ॥ पदानि ॥ अस्य, च्वौ, ॥

वृत्तिः ॥ ई इति वर्तते अवर्णान्तस्याङ्गस्य च्वौ परत ईकारादेशो भवति ॥

32. Long ई is substituted for the final अ or आ of a Nominal stem, before the Adverbial affix च्वि (V. 4. 50).

As शुक्ली करोति, शुक्ली भवति, शुक्ली स्यात् ॥ खट्वी करोति, खट्वी भवति and खट्वी स्यात् ॥

क्यचि च ॥ ३३ ॥ पदानि ॥ क्यचि, च, ॥

वृत्तिः ॥ अस्येति वर्तते क्यचि परतोवर्णान्तस्याङ्गस्य ईकारादेशो भवति ॥

33. Long ई is substituted for the final अ or आ of a Nominal stem, before the Denominative affix क्यच् ॥

As पुत्रीयति, घटीयति, खट्वीयति, मालीयति ॥ This is an exception to VII. 4. 25. The separating of this aphorism from the preceding, is for the sake of the subsequent aphorism.

अशनायोदन्यधनाया बुभुक्षापिपासागर्द्धेषु ॥ ३४ ॥ पदानि ॥ अशनाय, उदन्य धनायाः, बुभुक्षा, पिपासा, गर्द्धेषु, ॥

वृत्तिः ॥ अशनाय उदन्य धनाय इत्येतानि निपात्यन्ते बुभुक्षा पिपासा गर्द्ध इत्येतेष्वर्थेषु ॥

34. The Denominative roots अशनाय, उदन्य and धनाय are irregularly formed, when they respectively mean 'to be hungry', 'to be thirsty', 'to be greedy'.

Thus अशनायति from अशन+क्यच्, आ instead of ई; the other form being अशनीयति who is not hungry at the time, but wishes to get food for some future occasion, and therefore when not meaning 'to be hungry'; उदन्यति 'he is thirsty', उदन् being substituted for उदक; in any other sense we have उदकीयति, who wants water for purposes of bathing &c. धनायति 'he is greedy'; in any other sense, धनीयति who is poor, and therefore wishes to get riches.

नच्छन्दस्यपुत्रस्य ॥ ३५ ॥ पदानि ॥ न, छन्दसि, अ, पुत्रस्य ॥

वृत्तिः ॥ छन्दसि विषये पुत्रवर्जितस्यावर्णान्तस्याङ्गस्य क्यचि यदुक्तं तन्न भवति ॥

वार्त्तिकम् ॥ अपुत्रादीनामिति वक्तव्यम् ॥

35. In the Veda, the above rules causing lengthening, or the substitution of long ई for the final vowel of the stem, do not apply, except in the case of पुत्र ॥

20

Thus मित्रयुः, संस्वेदयुः, देवाञ् जिगाति सुम्नयुः ॥ But पुत्रीयन्तः, सुदानवः (Rig VII. 96. 4).

Vârt:—It should be rather stated पुत्र and the rest: as जनीयन्तोऽन्वयः ॥ See III. 2. 170, for the affix उ ॥

दुरस्युर्द्रविणस्युर्वृषण्यति रिषण्यति ॥ ३६ ॥ पदानि ॥ दुरस्युः, द्रविणस्युः, वृषण्यति, रिषण्यति, ॥

वृत्तिः ॥ दुरस्युः द्रविणस्युः वृषण्यति रिषण्यति एतानि छन्दसि निपात्यन्ते ॥

36. In the Veda दुरस्यु, द्रविणस्यु, वृषण्यति and रिषण्यति are irregularly formed.

As अवियोना दुरस्युः, (= दुष्टीयति with the affix क्यच् added to दुष्ट), द्रविणस्यु र्विपन्यया (द्रविणीयति, here द्रविणस् is substituted for द्रविण similarly). वृषण्यति = वृषीयति (वृषण् substituted for वृष) ॥ रिषण्यति = रिष्टीयति (रिषण् substituted for रिष्ट) ॥

अश्वाघस्यात् ॥ ३७ ॥ पदानि ॥ अश्व, अघस्य, आत्, ॥

वृत्तिः ॥ अश्व अघ इत्येतयोः क्यचि परतः छन्दसि विषये आकारादेशो भवति ॥

37. In the Veda, long आ is substituted for the final of अश्व and अघ, before the Denominative क्यच् ॥

As अश्वायन्तो मघवन् (Rig VII. 32. 23), मा त्वा वृका अघायवो विदन् ॥ This also indicates that other words do not lengthen their vowel in the Veda before क्यच्, as taught in VII. 4. 35. See Vârtika to III. 1. 8. The word अघायु occurs in Rig I. 120. 7, 27; 3.

देवसुम्नयोर्यजुषि काठके ॥ ३८ ॥ पदानि ॥ देव सुम्नयोः, यजुषि, काठके, ॥

वृत्तिः ॥ देव सुम्न इत्येतयोः क्यचि परत आकारादेशो भवति यजुषि काठके ॥

38. Long आ is substituted for the final of देव and सुम्न before the Denominative क्यच् in Yajush Kâṭhaka.

As देवायन्तो यजमानाः सुम्नायन्तो हवामहे ॥ Why in the Yajus? Observe देवाञ्जिगाय सुम्नयुः ॥ Why do we say in the Kâṭhaka? Observe सुम्नयुरिमासात् ॥

कव्यध्वरपृतनस्यर्चि लोपः ॥ ३९ ॥ पदानि ॥ कवि, अध्वर, पृतनस्यः, ऋचि, लोपः ॥

वृत्तिः ॥ कवि अध्वर पृतना इत्येतेषामङ्गानां क्यचि परतो लोपो भवति ऋचि विषये ॥

39. In the Rig Veda, the final of कवि, अध्वर and पृतना is dropped before the Denominative क्यच् ॥

As कव्यन्तः सुमनसः (not in the Rig Veda), अध्वर्यन्तः (not in this case in the Rig Veda). पृतन्यन्तस्तिष्ठन्ति (not in this connection in the Rig. Veda). The examples given above are of Kâśikâ: according to Pro. Bohtlingk none of them are from the Rig Veda. The following are given by Bhattoji Dikshita in his Siddhanta Kaumudi: स पूर्वया निविदा कव्यतायोः (Rig I. 96. 2). अध्वर्युं वा मधुपाणिम् (Rig X. 41. 3), दमयन्तं पृतन्युम् ॥

द्यतिस्यतिमास्थामित्ति किति ॥ ४० ॥ पदानि ॥ द्यति, स्यति, मा, स्थाम्, इत्, ति, किति ॥

वृत्तिः ॥ द्यति स्यति मा स्था इत्येतेषामङ्गानामिकारादेशो भवति तकारादौ किति प्रत्यये परतः ॥

40. Short इ is substituted for the final of दो, सो, मा and स्था, before an affix beginning with त् and having an indicatory क् ॥

As निर्दितः and निर्दितवान्; अवसितः and अवसितवान्, मितः and मितवान्; स्थितः and स्थितवान्, all with क्त and क्तवतु ॥ Why before त्? Observe अवदाय ॥ Why before a कित् affix? Observe अवदाता with तृच् ॥

शाच्छोरन्यतरस्याम् ॥ ४१ ॥ पदानि ॥ शा, छोः, अन्यतरस्याम् ॥

वृत्तिः ॥ शा छा इत्येतयोरन्यतरस्यामिकारादेशो भवति तकारादौ किति प्रत्यये परतः ॥

वार्त्तिकम् ॥ श्यतेरित्वं व्रते नित्यमिति वक्तव्यम् ॥

Kârikâ:—देवत्रातो गलो ग्राह इतियोगे च सद्विधिः ।
मिथस्ते न विभाष्यन्ते गवाक्षः संशितव्रतः ॥

41. Short इ is optionally substituted for the final of शा (शो) and छा (छो), before an affix beginning with त् and having an indicatory क ॥

As निशितं or निशातम्, निशितवान् or निशातवान्; अवच्छितं, अवच्छितवान् or अवच्छातं, अवच्छातवान् ॥ The शा *always* takes the इ when it means a vow: as संशितो ब्राह्मणः = संशितव्रतः ॥ The rule of this sûtra thus becomes a vyavasthita vibhâshâ. Other examples of such vyavasthita vibhâshâ are to be found in VIII. 2. 56, where त्रात and त्राण past participles are formed with त or ण, but त्रात is *only* employed in names as देवत्रातः &c, and never त्राण, while in denoting action both forms are valid: similarly by VIII. 2. 21, गल and गर are both formed, but गल *alone* is used when 'neck' is meant, and गर *alone* when 'poison' is indicated; optionally both when an action is meant. Similarly by III. 1. 143, ग्राह and ग्रह are formed, but ग्राहः is *only* used when 'a crocodile' is meant, and ग्रहः *alone* is employed when a 'planet' is indicated. Similarly the addition of the Present Participle affix शतृ and शानच् under III. 2. 126, is debarred when इति is added, as हन्ति इति पलायते, वर्षतीति धावति ॥ In all the above examples, the option though taught generically, should be limited to specific cases; as also in the examples गवाक्षः 'a window', and गोऽक्षम् 'cow's eye' (VI. 1. 123) and संशितव्रतः ॥ In short, we should limit a general vibhâshâ to a vyavasthita-vibhâshâ, on the maxim व्यवस्थितविभाषा विज्ञानात् सिद्धम् ॥

दधातेर्हिः ॥ ४२ ॥ पदानि ॥ दधातेः, हिः ॥

वृत्तिः ॥ दधातेरङ्गस्य हीत्ययमादेशो भवति तकारादौ किति प्रत्यये परतः ॥

42. हि is substituted for धा (दधाति) before an affix beginning with त and having an indicatory क ॥

As हितः, हितवत्, हित्वा ॥

जहातेश्च क्त्वि ॥ ४३ ॥ पदानि ॥ जहातेः, च, क्त्वि ॥

वृत्तिः ॥ जहातेरङ्गस्य हीत्ययमादेशो भवति क्त्वाप्रत्यये परतः ॥

43. हि is substituted for हा (जहाति) before क्त्वा ॥

As हित्वा राज्यं वनम गतः, हित्वा गच्छति ॥ The rule does not apply to हा जिहीते ॥ There we have हात्वा गतः ॥

विभाषा छन्दसि ॥ ४४ ॥ पदानि ॥ विभाषा, छन्दसि ॥

वृत्तिः ॥ जहातेरङ्गस्य विभाषा हीत्ययमादेशो भवति छन्दसि विषये क्त्वाप्रत्यये परतः ॥

44. हि is optionally substituted for हा before क्त्वा in the Chhandas.

As हित्वा शरीरं यातव्यं, or हात्वा also. The long ई of VI. 4. 62 does not take place also as a Vedic irregularity.

सुधितवसुधितनेमधितधिष्वधिषीय च ॥ ४५ ॥ पदानि ॥ सुधित, वसुधित, नेमधित, धिष्व, धिषीय, च ॥

वृत्तिः ॥ सुधित वसुधित नेमधित धिष्व धिषीय इत्येतानि छन्दसि विषये निपात्यन्ते ॥

45. These five Vedic forms are irregularly formed, सुधित, वसुधित, नेमधित, धिष्व and धिषीय ॥

Of these five, सुधित, वसुधित and नेमधित are formed from the root धा with the affix क्त, preceded by सु, वसु and नेम ॥ As गर्भं माता सुधितम् (=सुहितम्), वसुधितमग्नौ जुहोति (=वसुहितं), नेमधिता बाधन्ते (=नेमहिता) ॥ धिष्व is Imperative 2nd Per. Sg. of धा, there is no reduplication, as धिष्व सोमम्=धत्स्व ॥ धिषीय is Benedictive Atmanepada 1st Per. Sg. of धा, the regular form being धासीय ॥

दो दद् घोः ॥ ४६ ॥ पदानि ॥ दः, दत्, घोः ॥

वृत्तिः ॥ दा इत्येतस्य घुसंज्ञकस्य ददित्ययमादेशो भवति तकारादौ किति प्रत्यये परतः ॥

46. For दा, when it is a Ghu (I. 1. 20), there is substituted दद् before a कित् affix beginning with त् ॥

As दत्तः, दत्तवान्, दत्तिः ॥ Why of दा? Observe धीतः, धीतवान् from धेट्; and the long ई is by VI. 4. 66. Why when it is a Ghu? Observe दातं बर्हिः from दाप् 'to cut', and अवदातं मुखं from दैप् "to cleanse'. The substitute is दथ् ending in थ, according to an *Ishti*,

Kârikâ:—तान्ते दोषो दीर्घत्वं स्याद्, दान्ते दोषो निष्ठा नत्वम्।
धान्ते दोषो धत्व प्राप्तिस्, थान्तेऽ दोष स्तस्मात् थान्तम् ॥

If the substitute be दत् ending in त्, then it would require the lengthening taught in VI. 3. 124. (N. B. The sûtra दस्ति should be interpreted as 'the vowel of the Preposition is lengthened before a substitute of दा which *ends* in त्', in order to make this objection applicable. That sûtra however is capable of another interpretation). If the substitute be दद् ending in द् then the Nishthâ त would be changed to न by VIII. 2. 42: as in भिद्+त=भिन्नः ॥ If the substitute be दध् ending in ध्, then by VIII. 2. 40; the Nishthâ त would be changed to ध ॥ Hence the substitute is दथ् ॥ If however, the sûtra VI. 3. 124, is interpreted as "the vowel of a preposition is lengthened before a substitute of दा which *begins* with त् ", then the substitute may be तत् also without any harm. Even if the substitute be तद् or तथ्, the apprehended न् and ध् substitutions will not take place, on the maxim सन्निपातलक्षणो विधि रनिमित्तं तद्विघातस्य ॥

The following are exceptions to VII. 4. 47, अवदत्तं, विदत्तं, प्रदत्तं, सुदत्तं, अनुदत्तं and निदत्तं ॥ Or the words अव &c, here are not Upasargas. See I. 4. 57.

Kârikâ:—अवदत्तं विदत्तं च प्रदत्तं चादिकर्म्मणि ।
सुदत्तमनुदत्तं च निदत्तमिति चेष्यते ॥

The word आदिकर्मणि qualifies pradatta only. The word च shows that regular forms अवत्तं, वित्तं, प्रत्तं, &c also are valid.

अच उपसर्गात्तः ॥ ४७ ॥ पदानि ॥ अचः, उपसर्गात्, तः ॥

वृत्तिः ॥ अजन्तादुपसर्गादुत्तरस्य दा इत्येतस्य घुसंज्ञकस्य त इत्ययमादेशो भवति तकारादौ किति ॥

वार्त्तिकम् ॥ घसेरित्वात्त्वस्त इत्येतद्भवति विप्रतिषेधेन ॥

47. त् is substituted for the ghu दा before a कित् affix beginning with त, when a Preposition ending in a vowel precedes it.

The examples under the present sûtra are प्रत्तं, अवत्तं, नीत्तं, परीत्तं ॥ For the lengthening see VI. 3. 124. Why do we say 'ending in a vowel'? Observe निर्दत्तम्, दुर्दत्तम् ॥ Why 'after an Upasarga only''? Observe दधि दत्तम्, मधु दत्तम् ॥ Why 'the दा called Ghu'? Observe अवदात्तं मुखं from दैप् ॥

Obj. The word उपसर्गात् in the sûtra is in the Ablative case, and by I. 1. 67, the substitute त् should replace only the *first* letter of दा, how does it replace the *whole*?

Ans—The word अचः is to be repeated in the sûtra, one अचः being in the Ablative case and qualifying उपसर्गात्, and the other अचः being in the Genitive case, showing the sthânin to be आ, as "after an Upasarga ending in a vowel, त् is substituted *for the vowel* of दा". Or the word अस्य may be read into this sûtra from VII. 4. 32. Or उपसर्गात्त्तः consists of three त्'s, the substitute being त्त, and being a substitute of more than one letter, it replaces the *whole* of दा (I. 1. 55). In the following sûtra अपोभि, the अचः in the Ablative case is understood, and therefore त् replaces only प् ॥

Vârt:—After a Preposition ending in a vowel, त is substituted for दा (दो), when इ would have been substituted otherwise for its final by VII. 4. 40. As अवत्तम्, प्रत्तम् जुहोति and नीत्तं, वीत्तं ॥

अपो भि ॥ ४८ ॥ पदानि ॥ अपः, भिः ॥

वृत्तिः ॥ अप् इत्येतस्याङ्गस्य भकारादौ प्रत्यये परतस्त इत्ययमादेशो भवति ॥

48. त् is substituted for the final of the stem अप् before a case-ending beginning with भ् ॥

As अद्भ्याम, अद्भिः, अद्भ्यः ॥ Why beginning with a भ? Observe अप्सु ॥

In the Veda, त् is substituted before भ, for the final of स्ववस्, from सु + अव् + असुन्; meaning शोभनमवोयेषां; स्वतवस् from the root तु meaning स्वं तवो येषां; मास and उषस्, as स्ववद्भिः, स्वतवद्भिः, माद्भिरिष्टा इन्द्रो वृत्रहा, समुषद्भिरजायथाः ॥ The word मास becomes मास by VI. 1. 63.

सः स्यार्द्धधातुके ॥ ४९ ॥ पदानि ॥ सः, सि, आर्द्धधातुके ॥

वृत्तिः ॥ सकारान्तस्याङ्गस्य सकारादा वार्द्धधातुके परतस्तकारादेशो भवति ॥

49. त् is substituted for the final स् of a root before an Ârdhadhâtuka affix beginning with स् ॥

As वत्स्यति, अवत्स्यत्, विवत्सति, जिघत्सति ॥ Why do we say 'when ending in स'? Observe वक्ष्यति ॥ Why do we say 'beginning with स'? Observe घासः, वासः ॥ Why an ârdhadhâtuka? Observe आस्से, वस्से, from आस् 'to sit' and वस् 'to cover'; both Adâdi roots.

तासस्त्योर्लोपः ॥ ५० ॥ पदानि ॥ तास्अस्त्योः, लोपः ॥

वृत्तिः ॥ तासेरस्तेश्च सकारस्य सकारादौ प्रत्यये लोपो भवति ॥

50. The final स् of तास् (the character of the second Future) and that of अस् 'to be', is elided before an affix beginning with स् ॥

As कर्त्तासि, कर्त्तासे, स्वमसि, व्यति से ॥ See VI. 4. 111. In से the अ and स् both of अस् have been elided, the अ by VI. 4. 111, and स् by the present sûtra, so that the mere suffix से remains, which however here is a finite verb: hence the स, is not changed to ष ॥ See VIII. 3. 111.

रि च ॥ ५१ ॥ पदानि ॥ रि, च ॥

वृत्तिः ॥ रेफादौ च पत्यये परतः तासस्त्योः सकारस्य लोपो भवति ॥

51. The स् of तास् and अस् is dropped before an affix beginning with a र् ॥

As कर्तारौ, कर्त्तारः, अध्येतारौ अध्येतारः ॥ The स् of अस् 'to be' is elided in the Perfect, because it is there that a र् beginning affix can follow it. Thus व्यतिरे (See VI. 4. 111). According to the reading of Padamanjari, there can be no example of अस् ॥ अस्तेरुदाहरणं न प्रदर्शितं, रेफादेरसम्भवात् ॥

ह एति ॥ ५२ ॥ पदानि ॥ हः, एति ॥

वृत्तिः ॥ तासस्त्योः सकारस्य हकारादेशो भवति एति परतः ॥

52. For the स् of तास् and अस् there is substituted ह् before the personal-ending ए ॥

As कर्त्ताहे, and व्यति हे from अस् ॥ See VI. 4. 111. The ह substitution does not take place before the Personal ending एश् (III. 4. 8), as एधामासे ॥ The reason of this is that the ए referred to in this sûtra, is that ए which can come after तास्; and that very ए should also come after अस् ॥ The ए that can come after तास् is the 1st Person singular ए; and not this ए of the Perfect 3rd Person singular. Others say, this even sârvadhâtuka, and therefore not here क्षुभितोऽहं त्वां प्रेक्षामासे ॥

यीवर्णयोर्दीधीवेव्योः ॥ ५३ ॥ पदानि ॥ यि, इवर्णयोः, दीधी, वेव्योः ॥

वृत्तिः ॥ यकारादाविवर्णादौ च परतो दीधीवेव्योर्लोपो भवति ॥

53. The final of दीधी and वेवी falls before an affix beginning with य्, इ or ई ॥

Thus आदीध्य and आवेव्य गतः, आदीध्यते, and आवेव्यते before य् ॥ आदीधितृ, आवेवितृ; आदीधीत and आवेवीत ॥ Why before य, इ or ई? Observe आदीध्यनम् and आवेव्यनम् ॥ The long ई in यी is a sûtra वैचित्र्य, for यिवर्णयोः would have been enough.

सनि मीमाघुरभलभशकपतपदामच इस् ॥ ५४ ॥ पदानि ॥ सनि, मी, मा, घु, रभ, लभ, शक, पत, पदा म, अचः, इस् ॥

वृत्तिः ॥ सनि प्रत्यये सकारादौ परतो मी मा घु रभ लभ शक पत पद इत्येतेषामङ्गानामचः स्थाने इसित्ययमादेशो भवति ॥

वार्त्तिकम् ॥ आशि राधो हिंसायामच इस्वक्तव्यः ॥

54, इस् is substituted for the root-vowel of मी, मा, दा and धा (घु), रभ्, लभ्, शक्, पत् and पद् when the Desiderative सन् beginning with स् (i. e. not taking the augment इ) follows.

The मी includes मीनाति (Kryâdi 4), and मिनोति (मि of Svâdi 4) for मि assumes the form मी by VI. 4. 16 Thus मित्सति, प्रमित्सति ॥ The मा denotes all the roots which assume the form मा, on the maxim गामादा ग्रहणेष्वविशेषः "The terms गा, मा or दा when they are employed in Grammar denote both the original roots गा, मा and दा and also the roots which are changed to गा, मा and दा" ॥ They are मा and माङ् माने, and मेङ् प्रणिदाने ॥ Thus मित्सते, अप मित्सते ॥ घु—दित्सति, धित्सति; रभ्—आरिप्सते, लभ्—आलिप्सते, शक्—शिक्षति, पत्—पित्सति, पद्—प्रपित्सते ॥ In the roots that end in a vowel, the स् of इस् is changed to त् by VII. 4. 49, and in the roots that end in a consonant, this स् is dropped, according to VIII. 2. 29. The reduplication falls by VII. 4. 58.

Why do we say 'when the Desiderative follows'? Observe दास्यति ॥ The word सि is understood here from VII. 4. 49, so the rule will not apply when the Desiderative takes the augment इट्, as प्र पिपतिषति ॥ Here पत् optionally takes इट् under the vârtika तनिपतिदरिद्राणामुपसंख्यानम् ॥

Vârt:—The इस् comes after the root-vowel of राध् in the Desiderative, when the sense is that of to injure. As प्रति रित्सति ॥ Why do we say when the sense is that of 'to injure'? Observe आरि रात्सति ॥

आप्ज्ञप्यृधामीत् ॥ ५५ ॥ पदानि ॥ आप्, ज्ञप्, ऋधाम्, ईत् ॥

वृत्तिः ॥ आप ज्ञपि ऋध इत्येतेषामङ्गानामच ईकारादेशो भवति सनि सकारादौ परतः ॥

55. For the vowel of the roots आप्, ज्ञपि and ऋध् there is substituted long ई before the सन् of the Desiderative, when it begins with स् ॥

Thus आप्—ईप्सति, ज्ञपि—ज्ञीप्सति, ऋध्—ईर्त्सति (I. 1. 51.). The reduplication is dropped by VII. 4. 58. In the Causative stem ज्ञपि there are two vowels, the इ (णि) is dropped by pûrva-vipratishedha (the prior debarring the subsequent) according to VI. 4. 51, and ई substituted for अ according to the present sûtra. The word सन् is to be read into the sûtra, otherwise प्राप्स्यति ॥ The सन् must begin with स् i.e. should not take the इट् augment, as in जिज्ञपयिषति, अर्दिधिषति ॥ The roots ज्ञपि and ऋध् are optionally सेट् in the Desiderative by VII. 2. 49.

दम्भ इच्च ॥ ५६ ॥ पदानि ॥ दम्भः, इत्, च ॥

वृत्तिः ॥ दम्भेरच इकारादेशो भवति चकारादीच्च सनि सकारादौ परतः ॥

56. For the vowel of the root दम्भ् there is substituted इ as well as ई before the सन् of the Desiderative, when it begins with स् ॥

As धीप्सति or धिप्सति ॥ But दिदम्भिषति before the सेट्सन् ॥ The reduplication falls off by VII. 4. 58.

मुचोऽकर्मकस्य गुणो वा ॥ ५७ ॥ पदानि ॥ मुचः, अकर्मकस्य, गुणः वाः ॥

वृत्तिः ॥ मुचोऽकर्म्मकस्य गुणो वा भवति सनि सकारादौ परतः ॥

57. When मुच् has an Intransitive signification, Guṇa is optionally substituted for its vowel before the aniṭ सन् of the Desiderative.

By I. 2. 10, after a root ending in a consonant, the सन् is like कित् and does not cause Guṇa. The present sûtra ordains it optionally. As मोक्षते or मुमुक्षते वत्सः स्वयमेव ॥ In the Transitive there is one form only, as मुमुक्षति वत्सं देवदत्तः ॥ मुच् becomes Intransitive when it has a Reflexive significance, or when it expresses a mere action. The reduplication is elided by VII. 4. 58.

अत्र लोपोऽभ्यासस्य ॥ ५८ ॥ पदानि ॥ अत्र, लोपः, अभ्यासस्य ॥

वृत्तिः ॥ यदेतत्प्रक्रान्तं सनि मीमेत्यादि मुचोऽकर्मकस्य गुणो वेति यावत् अत्राभ्यासलोपो भवति ॥

58. The reduplicate is dropped under the circumstances mentioned in the foregoing sûtras VII. 4. 54 to VII. 4. 57.

The examples are given under the above-mentioned sûtras. The word 'of the reduplicate' अभ्यासस्य is to be supplied in all the subsequent sûtras upto the end of the chapter. Thus Sûtra VII. 4. 59, says 'a short is to be substituted', we must supply the words 'for the reduplicate' to complete the sense: as डुढौकिषते, तुत्रौकिषते ॥ The word अत्र in the sûtra indicates that the reduplication is not to be elided, when an affix is treated *like* सन् but is not actually सन् ॥ Thus चङ्-Aorist is treated like सन् by VII. 4. 93; but the reduplication will not be dropped there: as अमीमपत्, अदीदपत् ॥ Some say the word अत्र here indicates that the *whole* of the reduplicate is dropped, and not only its final letter. Others elide the whole of the reduplicate on the maxim नानर्थकेऽलोऽन्त्यविधिः ॥ "The rule I. 1. 52, by which a substitute should take the place of only the final letter of that which is exhibited in the Genitive case, is not valid, where what is exhibited in the Genitive is meaningless".

ह्रस्वः ॥ ५९ ॥ पदानि ॥ ह्रस्वः ॥

वृत्तिः ॥ ह्रस्वो भवत्यभ्यासस्य ॥

वार्त्तिकम् ॥ अभ्यासस्यानचि ॥

वार्त्तिकम् ॥ चरि चलि पति वदीनां वा द्वित्वमच्याक् चाभ्यासस्य इति वक्तव्यम् ॥

59. A short is substituted for the long vowel of the reduplicate.

As डुढौकिषते, तुत्रौकिषते, डुढौके, तुत्रौके, अडुढौकत्, अतुत्रौकत् ॥

Vârt:—The shortening takes place before affixes other than अच् (III. 1. 134). Before अच्, the roots चर्, चल्, पत् and वद् are reduplicated, and the augment अक् added to the reduplicate. See VI. 1. 12 Vârt. This augment when added to the reduplicate, is not to be shortened by this rule: and because this is not to be shortened, also indicates that the consonants of the reduplicate other than the first are also not dropped: as चराचरः, चलाचलः, पतापतः, वदावदः ॥

हलादिः शेषः ॥ ६० ॥ पदानि ॥ हल् आदिः, शेषः ॥

वृत्तिः ॥ अभ्यासस्य हलादिः शिष्यते अनादिर्लुप्यते ॥

60. Of the consonants of the reduplicate, only the first is retained, the remainders are dropped.

As जग्लौ, मम्लौ; पपाच, पपाठ, आट, आटतुः, आटुः ॥ This rule ordains the retention of the initial consonant, if any, and elision of the non-initials in the reduplicate. If the root begins with a vowel as अट्, there being no initial consonant, in अट् अट्, the ट् will be elided of course. The word हलादिः should not be construed as a Genitive Tatpurusha 'first among the consonants', for then in अक्ष्+लिट्=अक्ष् अक्ष्, the ष् only would be elided, and क् retained.

The word शेषः or शिष्यते here means अवस्थाप्यते 'is retained'. The word हलादिः is not a compound. For had it been a compound, then if it is a Karmadhâraya, the word आदि should stand first; if it be a Genitive compound then the first among compound consonants would be retined and we could not get the form आनक्ष from अक्ष्. The word abhyâsa is to be taken in the sense of jâti or kind, i.e. in the jâti which is collectively called abhyâsa, the consonant that stands first in respect to abhyâsa, is retained, and not the consonant standing in any other portion of it. So that all consonants, where ever they may be situate in the body of an abhyâsa, whether in the begnning or middle or end, are dropped, except one with which the abhyâsa begins. Thus if the abhyâsa begins with a simple consonant, it is retained; if it begins with a conjunct consonant, the first is only retained; and if the consonant or consonants are not in the beginning they are all dropped.

Others say, the word शेषः here means "retention along with the cessation of others". Therefore, tbough literally the word शेषः or retention appears to be the principal word in this sûtra, yet as a matter of fact, it is secondary, because the injunction is not with regard to retention, but with regard to cessation. The rule is not "Retain the first consonant"; but "Drop every consonant but the first, if there be a first consonant". Or the sûtras 59 and 60, may be combined and read thus: ह्रस्वोऽहल् "The abhyâsa becomes short and also without consonant". आदिशेषः "The first consonant is retained". Or the sûtras may be divided thus:—

(1) 'A short vowel is substituted in the abhyâsa'.

(2) 'The consonants of abhyâsa are all elided'.

(3) The first is retained.

The sûtras 59 and 60 must be joined by sandhi "ह्रस्वोऽहलादिशेषः", and then we shall be able to read an elided अ between ह्रस्व and हल्, as if it was a compound of ह्रस्व and अहल् ॥

शर्पूर्वाः खयः ॥ ६१ ॥ पदानि ॥ शर्पूर्वाः, खयः ॥

वृत्तिः ॥ अभ्यासस्य शर्पूर्वाः खयः शिष्यन्ते ॥

वार्त्तिकम् ॥ खर्पूर्वाः खय इति वक्तव्यम् ॥

61. Of a reduplicate, the hard consonants (aspirate and unaspirate) when preceded by a sibilant, are only retained, the other consonants are elided.

As चुश्च्योतिषति, from śchyutir ksharaṇe, तिष्ठासति, पिस्पन्दिषते ॥ Why do we say 'when preceded by a sibilant'? Observe पपाच ॥ Why do we say hard consonants? Observe सस्नौ ॥

Vârt:—It should be said rather, a hard consonant preceded by a hard consonant or a sibilant is only retained: and the खर् consonants are elided: as in उचिच्छिषति, here उछ् becomes उच्छ् by the augment त् (तुक्); in the reduplicate the च् should be elided, and छ् retained out of च्छ; and not च् retained and छ् elided; for the च् represents त्, and if this were retained, it would be त् and not च् that would be heard: for by VIII. 2. 1, the change of त् to च् is asiddha for the purposes of this rule.

कुहोश्चुः ॥ ६२ ॥ पदानि ॥ कुहोः, चुः ॥

वृत्तिः ॥ अभ्यासस्य कवर्गहकारयोश्चवर्गादेशो भवति ॥

62. For the Guttural and ह् of a reduplicate there is substituted a Palatal.

As चकार, चखान, जगाम, जघान, जहार, जिहीर्षति, जहौ ॥

न कवतेर्यङि ॥ ६३ ॥ पदानि ॥ न, कवतेः, यङि ॥

वृत्तिः ॥ कवतेरभ्यासस्य यङि परतश्चुर्न भवति ॥

63. The Palatal is not substituted for the Guttural of the reduplicate of कु (कवते) in the Intensive.

As कोकूयते उष्ट्रः, कोकूयते खरः ॥ The कु here is कुङ् (Bhu. 999), and not कु 'to make sound' (Ad. 33, कौति), nor कुङ् (Tud. 108, कुवति) ॥ Of those two, we have चोकूयते ॥ Why do we say in the Intensive? Observe चुकुवे ॥

कृषेश्छन्दसि ॥ ६४ ॥ पदानि ॥ कृषेः, छन्दसि ॥

वृत्तिः ॥ कृषेश्छन्दसि विषये यङि परतोऽभ्यासस्य चुर्न भवति ॥

64. The Palatal is not substituted for the Guttural of the reduplicate of कृष् in the Veda, when in the Intensive.

As करीकृष्यते यज्ञकुणपः ; otherwise चरीकृष्यते कृषीवलः ॥

दाधर्त्तिदर्द्धर्त्तिदर्द्धर्षिबोभूतुतेतिक्तेलर्ष्यापनीफणत्संसनिष्यदत्करिक्रत्कनिक्रदद्भरिभ्रद्दविध्वतो दविद्युतत्तरित्रतः सरीसृपतंवरीवृजन्मर्मृज्यागनीगन्तीति च ॥ ६५ ॥ पदानि ॥ दाधर्त्ति, दर्द्धर्त्ति, दर्द्धर्षि, बोभूतु, तेतिक्ते, अलर्षि, आपनीफणत्, संसनि ष्यदत्, करिक्रत् कनिक्रदत्, भरिभ्रत्, दविध्वतः, दविद्युतत्, तरित्रतः, सरीसृपतम्, वरीवृजत्, मर्मृज्य, आगनी गन्ति, इति, च ॥

वृत्तिः ॥ दाधर्त्ति दर्धर्ति दर्द्धर्षि बोभूतु तेतिक्ते अलर्षि आपनीफणत् संसनिष्यदत् करिक्रत् कनिक्रदत् भरिभ्रत् दविध्वतः दविद्युतत् तरित्रतः सरीसृपतं वरीवृजत् मर्मृज्य आगनीगन्ति इत्येतानि अष्टादश छन्दसि विषये निपात्यन्ते ॥

65. In the Veda are found the following eighteen irregularly reduplicated forms :—1 dâdharti, 2 dardharti, 3 dardharshi, 4 bobhûtu, 5 tetikte, 6 alarshi, 7 â panîphaṇat, 8 sam sanishyadat. 9 karikrat, 10 kanikradat, 11 bharibhrat, 12 davidhvataḥ, 13 davidyutat, 14 taritrataḥ, 15 sarîsṛpatam, 16 varîvṛjat, 17 marmṛjya and 18 â ganîganti.

The word छन्दसि is drawn in to this sûtra, by force of च ॥ The form दाधर्त्ति, is either from the Causative of the root धृङ् अवस्थाने or from धृञ्, in the श्लु or यङ् लुक्, there is lengthening of the abhyâsa and elision of णि ॥ (2) So also दर्द्धर्त्ति is the form in ślu, with रुक् augment of the abhyâsa. (3) दर्धर्षि if it be a form of यङ् लुक्, there is no irregularity. (4) बोभूतु is from भू in the Intensive (यङ् लुक्), Imperative, irregularly without guṇa. Q. There is no necessity of including this, because there would be no guṇa regularly even under VII. 3.

88? Ans. The inclusion of बोभूतु is a jñâpaka, indicating that in every other case, the guṇa is not prohibited in the Intensive (यङ् लुक्), as बोभोति, बोभवीति (लट् with ईट् VII. 3. 94) (5) तेतिक्ते is from तिज् in the Intensive yaṇ luk, âtmanepada is irregular. Q. The यङ् is ङित् and therefore by pratyaya lakshaṇa rule (I, 1. 62) read with I. 3. 12, the यङ् लुक् will be âtmanepadi, where is the necessity of reading this nipâtan? Ans. The âtmanepada nipâtan is a jñapaka, that in the Intensive yaṇ luk the âtmanepada affixes are not employed. (6) अलर्षि is from the root ऋ (इयर्ति), in Present, 2nd Person, the र् of abhyâsa is not elided, though required by VII. 4. 60, and this र् is changed to ल irregularly. This form is found in the 3rd Person also, as अलर्ति दक्षः ॥ (7) आ पनीफणत् is from फण् with आ augment, and शतृ affix is added to यङ् लुक्, and in the reduplicate नी is added. (8) संसनिष्यदत् is from स्यन्द् with the Preposition सम्, in the Intensive yaṇ luk, with शतृ affix, नि being added in the abhyâsa, the root स is changed to ष ॥ The Preposition सं is not absolutely necessary, with other Prepositions also we have this form, as आ सनिष्यदत् ॥ (9) करिक्रत् is from कृ (करोति), in the Intensive yaṇ luk, with शतृ, in the abhyâsa there is no palatal change (VII. 4.62), and रि is added to the reduplicate. (10) कनिक्रदत् from क्रन्द् in the Aorist with अङ्, reduplication, there is no chutva (VII. 4. 62) of the reduplicate, and the augment नि is added. In the secular literature, the form is अक्रन्दीत् ॥ (11) भरिभ्रत् from भृ (बिभर्ति) in yaṇ luk with शतृ, without इ of VII. 4. 76, without jaśtva, and रि is added to the reduplicate. (12) दविध्वतः from ध्वृ (ध्वरते) in the yaṇ luk, śatṛ, plural number Nominative. The वि is added to the reduplicate, the ऋ is elided, दविध्वतः रश्मयः सूर्यस्य ॥ (13) दविद्युतत् is from dyut, yaṇ luk with śatṛ, there is no vocalisation of the reduplicate, with अ change and वि augment. (14) तरित्रतः from तृ (तरति) with ślu, śatṛ, genitive singular: and रि added to abhyâsa. (15) सरीसृपत् from सृप् with ślu, śatṛ, Accusative with री added to abhyâsa. (16) वरीवृजत् from वृज् with ślu, śatṛ and री augment. (17) मर्मृज्य from मृज् with लिट् (Perfect) णल्, रु added to abhyâsa, and य added to the root, and there is no vṛiddhi, because there is no short penultimate now. In fact VII. 2. 114 is to be qualified by the words लघूपध from VII. 3. 86. (18) आ गनीगन्ति is from गम् with the Preposition आ, in the Perfect, with ślu, there is no chutva (VII. 4. 62), and augment नी is added. सङ्कन्ती वेवा गनीगन्ति कर्णम् ॥

The word इति in the aphorism indicates that other forms, similar to these, are also to be included.

उरत् ॥ ६६ ॥ पदानि ॥ उः, अत् ॥

वृत्तिः ॥ ऋवर्णान्तस्याभ्यासस्याकारादेशो भवति ॥

66. अर् (I. 1. 51) is substituted for the ऋ or ॠ of the reduplicate.

As ववृते, ववृधे, शशृधे, नर्नर्ति, नरिनर्ति नरीनर्ति ॥ The र् is elided by VII. 4. 60. In the Intensives VII. 4. 90 &c, are applied, by which after the substitution of अर्

by the present sûtra, we apply those sûtras and add रिक रुक्, रिक् &c: for the maxim is अभ्यासविकारेषु अपवादो नोत्सर्गान् विधीन् बाधते "so far as the changes of a reduplicative syllable are concerned special (apavâda) rules do not supersede the general (utsarga) rules".

द्युतिस्वाप्योः, संप्रसारणम् ॥ ६७ ॥ पदानि ॥ द्युतिः स्वाप्योः, सम्प्रसारणम् ॥

वृत्तिः ॥ द्युति स्वापि इत्येतयोरभ्यासस्य संप्रसारणं भवति ॥

67. There is vocalisation of the half-vowel of the reduplicate of द्युत् and स्वापि (Causative of स्वप्) ॥

As वि दिद्युतत्, वि दिद्योतिषते, वि दिद्युतिषते, (I. 2. 26) वि देद्युत्यते ॥ स्वापि – सुष्वापयिषति ॥ The Causative of स्वप् is taken here, and the vocalisation takes place then only, when it is immediately followed by an affix which causes reduplication. Therefore not here, स्वापि + ण्वुल् = स्वापकः ; स्वापक + क्यच् = स्वापकीय, स्वापकीय + सन् = सिस्वापकीयिषति ॥

The simple root स्वप् will get vocalised in its reduplicate by VI. 1. 15, 17 in the Perfect. The Desiderative of स्वप् is कित् by I. 2. 8, and therefore the reduplicate of स्वप् will be vocalised before सन् by VI. 1. 15. The reduplicate of स्वप् will be vocalised in the Intensive also by VI. 1. 19.

Quere:—Does the reduplicate of the Desiderative of the Denominative verb द्योतकीयति get vocalised or not.

व्यथो लिटि ॥ ६८ ॥ पदानि ॥ व्यथः, लिटि ॥

वृत्तिः ॥ व्यथेर्लिटि परतोऽभ्यासस्य संप्रसारणं भवति ॥

68. There is vocalisation of the half-vowel of the reduplicate of व्यथ् in the Perfect.

As विव्यथे, विव्यथाते, विव्यथिरे ॥ This ordains the vocalisation of य, which otherwise would have been elided as being a non-initial consonant (VII. 4. 60). The vocalisation of व् is prevented by VI. 1. 37. Why do we say in the Perfect? Observe वाव्यथ्यते ॥

दीर्घ इणः किति ॥ ६९ ॥ पदानि ॥ दीर्घः, इणः, किति ॥

वृत्तिः ॥ इणोऽङ्गस्य योऽभ्यासस्तस्य दीर्घो भवति किति लिटि परतः ॥

69. A long vowel is substituted in the reduplicate of the root इ (एति), before a Personal ending of the Perfect, which has an indicatory क् ॥

As ईयतुः, ईयुः ॥ These are thus formed इ + अतुस् = य् + अतुः (य् substituted for इ by VI. 4. 81). Then there is reduplication, the य becomes sthânivat to इ by I. 1. 59, and we have इ य् + अतुः and then by the present rule ईयतुः ॥ Why do we say before a कित् affix? Observe इयाय, इययिथ ॥

अत आदेः ॥ ७० ॥ पदानि ॥ अतः, आदेः, ॥

वृत्तिः ॥ अभ्यासस्यादेरकारस्य दीर्घो भवति लिटि परतः ॥

70. A long vowel is substituted in the Perfect for the initial अ of a reduplicate.

This debars the single substitute of the form of the subsequent ordained by VI. 1. 97. Thus आट, आटतुः, आटुः ॥ Why do we say 'the *initial*'? Observe पपाच and पपाठ ॥ Thus अट् + अतुः = अट् अट् + अतुः = अ अट् + अतुः = आ अट् + अतुः ॥

तस्मान्नुड् द्विहलः ॥ ७१ ॥ पदानि ॥ तस्मात्, नुट्, द्वि-हलः ॥

वृत्तिः ॥ तस्माद्‌तोऽभ्यासाद्दीर्घीभूतादुत्तरस्य द्विहलोऽङ्गस्य नुडागमो भवति ॥

71. After such a lengthened आ of the reduplicate, there is added the augment नुट् (न्) to the short अ of the root which ends in a double consonant.

As from अञ्च् — आ अञ्च् = आन् अञ्च्, which with the affixes of the Perfect gives us, आनञ्च, आनञ्चतुः, आनञ्चुः ॥ From अञ्ज् — आनञ्ज, आनञ्जतुः, आनञ्जुः ॥ Why do we say 'containing two consonants'? Observe आट, आटतुः, आटुः ॥

With regard to नुट् augment, ऋ is considered like र्, as आनृधतुः, आनृधुः ॥ This proceeds on a vârtika to be found under the Pratyâhâra sûtra ऐ औच् ॥ The vârtika is नुड्विधि—लादेश—विनामासु ऋकारे प्रतिविधातव्यं ॥ The examples of लादेश are क्लृप्तः, क्लृप्तवान्; (See VIII. 2. 18) and of विनाम are कर्तृणाम् and धर्तृणाम् ॥

अश्नोतेश्च ॥ ७२ ॥ पदानि ॥ अश्नोतेः, च ॥

वृत्तिः ॥ अद्विहलर्थ आरम्भः ॥ अश्नोतेश्च दीर्घीभूतादभ्यासादुत्तरस्य नुडागमो भवति ॥

72. After the lengthened आ of the reduplicate of अश् (अश्नोति), comes the augment नुट् (न्) before the short अ of the root in the Perfect.

This applies to a case where the root does not contain a double consonant, Thus व्यानशे, व्यानशाते, व्यानशिरे ॥ The rule applies to अश् (Svâdi 18) and not to अश् (Kryâdi 51); there we have आश, आशतुः, आशुः ॥

भवतेरः ॥ ७३ ॥ पदानि ॥ भवतेः, अः ॥

वृत्तिः ॥ भवतेरभ्यासस्याकारादेशो भवति लिटि परतः ॥

73. अ is substituted for the vowel of the reduplicate of भू in the Perfect.

As बभूव, बभूवतुः, बभूवुः, बभूवे ॥ Why do we say 'in the Perfect'? Observe बुभूषति and बोभूयते ॥

The word भवतेः is shown in the sûtra in the Active Voice, therefore the rule will not apply to Passive and Reflexive forms; as अनुबुभूवे कम्बलो देवदत्तेन ॥ This opinion of Kâśikâ, however, is not endorsed by later Grammarians

ससूवेति निगमे ॥ ७४ ॥ पदानि ॥ ससूव, इति, निगमे ॥

वृत्तिः ॥ ससूव इति निपात्यते सूतेर्लिटि परस्मैपदं वुगागमो ऽभ्यासस्य चात्वं निपात्यते ॥

74. In the Veda ससूव is irregularly formed in the Perfect.

It is derived from सू ॥ Thus ससूव स्थविरं विपश्चितीम् otherwise सुषुवे ॥ Rig. IV. 18 10.

This word ससूव might well have been included in sûtra VII. 4. 65.

निजां त्रयाणां गुणः श्लौ ॥ ७५ ॥ पदानि ॥ निजाम्, त्रयाणाम्, गुणः, श्लौ ॥

वृत्तिः ॥ निजादीनां त्रयाणामभ्यासस्य गुणो भवति श्लौ सति ॥

75. Guṇa is substituted for the vowel of the reduplicate, in the Reduplicated Present form (श्लु) of निज्, विज् and विष् ॥

Thus नेनेक्ति, वेवेक्ति, वेवेष्टि ॥ The word त्रयाणां could have been spared in this sûtra, as these three roots stand at the end of a subdivision, and निजां would have denoted these three without the word trayâṇâm. The word is however used here for the sake of the subsequent sûtra. Why do we say in the reduplicated Present form ? Observe निनेज in the Perfect.

भृञामित् ॥ ७६ ॥ पदानि ॥ भृञाम्, इत् ॥

वृत्तिः ॥ भृञादीनां त्रयाणामभ्यासस्येकारादेशो भवति श्लौ सति ॥

76. In the Reduplicated Present-form of the three roots भृ, मा (माङ्) and हा (ओहाङ्), इ is substituted for the vowel of the reduplicate.

As बिभर्त्ति, मिमीते, (VI. 4. 113) जिहीते ॥ The word 'three' is understood here, therefore not in ओहाक्—जहाति ॥ The rule applies in the Reduplicated Present system (श्लु) only: therefore not in बभार ॥

अर्त्तिपिपर्त्योश्च ॥ ७७ ॥ पदानि ॥ अर्त्ति-पिपर्त्योः, च ॥

वृत्तिः ॥ अर्त्ति पिपर्त्ति इत्येतयोरभ्यासस्येकारादेशो भवति श्लौ ॥

77. इ is substituted for the vowel of the reduplicate of ऋ and पृ in the Reduplicated Present-form.

As इयर्त्ति (VI. 4. 78) धूमम्, पिपर्त्ति सोमम् ॥

बहुलं छन्दसि ॥ ७८ ॥ पदानि ॥ बहुलम्, छन्दसि ॥

वृत्तिः ॥ छन्दसि विषये ऽभ्यासस्य श्लौ बहुलमिकारादेशो भवति ॥

78. इ is diversely substituted in the Veda, for the vowel of the reduplicate, in the Reduplicated Present-form.

As पूर्णां विवष्टि (from वश्), जनिमा विवक्ति (from वच्), वत्सं न माता सिषक्ति (from सच्), and जिघर्त्ति सोमम् ॥ But also ददाति, जजनम्, दधनत् as in ददातीत्येवं ब्रुयात्; जजनमिन्द्रं माता यद्वीरं दधनद् धनिष्ठा ॥ All these three roots belong to Juhotyâdi class.

सन्यतः ॥ ७९ ॥ पदानि ॥ सनि, अतः ॥

वृत्तिः ॥ सनि परतोकारान्ताभ्यासस्येकारादेशो भवति ॥

79. इ is substituted for the final short अ of the reduplicate in the Desiderative.

As पिपक्षति, यियक्षति, (VIII. 2. 36, 41) तिष्ठासति, पिपासति ॥ Why do we say in the Desiderative? Observe पपाच ॥ Why do we say "for the अ"? Observe लुलूषति ॥ Why do we say 'short अ'? Observe पापचिषते the Desiderative of the Intensive पापच्यते ॥

ओः पुयण्ज्यपरे ॥ ८० ॥ पदानि ॥ ओः, पु-यण्-जि-अपरे ॥

वृत्तिः ॥ सनीति वर्त्तते इदिति च ॥ उवर्णान्तस्याभ्यासस्य पवर्गे यणि जकारे चावर्णपरे परत इकारादेशो भवति सनि प्रत्यये परतः ॥

80. इ is substituted for the final उ or ऊ of a reduplicate, before a labial, a semi-vowel and before ज्, when अ or आ follows these consonants, in the Desiderative.

The word पु-यण्-जि is the Locative singular of the samâhâra dvandva compound of those three words—पु, यण् and ज् ॥ The samâsânta affix टच् (V. 4. 106) does not come, as these affixes are anitya. The word अ-परं means that after which is the letter अ ॥

Thus: 1. Labial:—पिपविषते, पिपावयिषति, बिभावयिषति; 2. Semi-vowel:—यियविषति, यियावयिषति, रिरावयिषति, लिलावयिषति; 3. ज—जिजावयिषति from the root जु ॥

The word पिपविषते is from पू which gets इट् augment in सन् (VII. 2. 74), then there is guṇa, and अव् substitutions, but these latter being sthanivât for reduplication (I. 1. 59), पू is doubled: and for ऊ there is substited इ by the present sûtra. पिपावयिषति is the Desiderative of the Causative of पू ॥ बिभावयिषति is the Desiderative of the Causative of भू ॥ यियविषति is the Desiderative of यु 'to mix', which is सेट् by VII. 2. 49. यियावयिषति is the Desiderative of the Causative of this root. The words रिरावयिषति and लिलावयिषति are the Desiderative of the Causatives of रौति and लुनाति ॥

This sûtra indicates the existence of the following maxim:—भाद्विर्वचन निमित्तेऽपि णौ स्थानिवद् भवति, "though not the cause of reduplication, the substitute which takes place when णि follows, becomes like the original". Thus in बिभावयिषति we have भावि + सन् from भू + णि + सन्, here the आव् substitute caused by णि is sthânivat to ऊ, otherwise there would be no उ in the reduplicate to be operated upon by the present sûtra. See VI. 1. 31 also. Why do we say "for the उ or ऊ"? Observe पापच्यते, the Desiderative of which will be पापच्चिषति ॥ Why do we say "followed by a labial, semi-vowel or ज'? Observe भेवं नुनावयिषति, according to Padamanjari it is भव तुता वयिषति from the sautra root तु ॥ तुतावयिषति ॥ Why do we say 'when these consonants are followed by an अ'? Observe बुभूषति ॥

स्रवतिशृणोतिद्रवतिप्रवतिप्लवतिच्यवतीनां वा ॥ ८१ ॥ पदानि ॥ स्रवति-शृणोति-द्रवति-प्रवति-प्लवति-च्यवतीनाम् ॥

वृत्तिः ॥ स्रवति शृणोति द्रवति प्रवति प्लवति च्यवति इत्येतेषामभ्यासस्य ओरवर्णपरे यणि वा इकारादेशो भवति सनि परतः ॥

81. इ is optionally substituted for the final उ of the reduplicate of स्रु, श्रु, द्रु, प्रु, प्लु and च्यु when the semi-vowel is followed by अ or आ in the Desiderative.

Thus सिस्रावयिषति or सुस्रावयिषति; शिश्रावयिषति or शुश्रावयिषति; दिद्रावयिषति or दुद्रावयिषति; पिप्रावयिषति or पुप्रावयिषति; पिप्लावयिषति or पुप्लावयिषति; चिच्यावयिषति or चुच्यावयिषति ॥ All these are Desideratives of the Causatives of the above roots. Here though a letter like स्, श्, द् &c, intervenes between the semi-vowel and the preceding उ of the reduplicate, yet the substitution takes place owing to the express text of this sûtra. In the preceding aphorism, the semi-vowel followed *immediately* after the उ of the reduplicate. The option of the present sûtra is, therefore, an aprâpta-vibhâshâ. The word अपरे is understood here also: therefore not in सुस्रूषति, शुश्रूषति ॥

गुणो यङ्लुकोः ॥ ८२ ॥ पदानि ॥ गुणः, यङ्-लुकोः ॥
वृत्तिः ॥ यङि यङ्लुकि च इगन्तस्याभ्यासस्य गुणो भवति ॥

82. Guṇa is substituted for the इ and उ (with their long) of a reduplicate, when the Intensive character यङ् follows and also when it is elided.

Thus चेचीयते, लोलूयते with यङ्, and जोहवीति with यङ् लुक् ॥ The ईट् is added in the latter by VII. 3. 94. So also चोक्रुशीति from क्रुश् (VII. 3. 94 and 87).

दीर्घोऽकितः ॥ ८३ ॥ पदानि ॥ दीर्घः, अकितः ॥
वृत्तिः ॥ अकितोऽभ्यासस्य दीर्घो भवति यङि यङ्लुकि च परतः ॥

83. A long vowel is substituted for the अ of the reduplicate in the Intensive (with expressed or elided यङ्), when the reduplicate receives no augment having an indicatory क् ॥

The reduplicate receives augments like नीक्, नुक् by the following sûtras. Thus पापच्यते, and पापचीति, यायज्यते and यायजीति ॥ Why do we say "when it gets no augment'? Observe यंयम्यते, यंयमीति, रंरम्यते, रंरमीति ॥

Obj:—When the न् augment is added, the reduplicate will end in a consonant, and as it does not end in a vowel, there will be no occasion for lengthening; hence the employment of the term अकितः is useless.

Ans.—The employment of this term by the Achârya indicates the existence of the following maxim: अभ्यासविकारेष्वपवादा नोत्सर्गान् विधीन् बाधन्ते "so far as changes of a reduplicative syllable are concerned, rules which teach those changes do not supersede one another". What is the necessity of this indication (jñâpaka)? Observe डोढौक्यते, here the rule of lengthening of this sûtra, does not supersede, though it is subsequent, the rule of shortening in VII. 4. 59; so the diphthong औ is shortened to उ, and it is then guṇated by VII. 4. 82. Secondly observe अचीकरत्, here इ is substituted in the reduplicate by VII. 4. 79 plus 93, and then this is lengthened by VII. 4. 94, the latter not superseding the former. Thirdly observe मीमांसते &c, where in मान्+सन् (III. 1. 6), the reduplicate is lengthened, but that does not prevent the इ of VII. 4. 79. Fourthly observe अजीगणत्, where the ई substitute (VII. 4. 97) does not supersede the sûtra VII. 4. 60, by which the ण् of गण् is elided.

नीग्वञ्चुस्रंसुध्वंसुभ्रंसुकसपतपदस्कन्दाम् ॥ ८४ ॥ पदानि ॥ नीक्, वञ्चु - स्रंसु ध्वंसु-भ्रंसु-कस-पत-पद्-स्कन्दाम् ॥

वृत्तिः ॥ वञ्चु स्रंसु ध्वंसु भ्रंसु कस पत पद स्कन्द इत्येतेषामभ्यासस्य नीगागमो भवति यङि यङ्लुकि च ॥

84. The augment नीक् is added to the reduplicate of the Intensive (with the expressed or elided यङ्) in the following :—वञ्च्, स्रंस्, ध्वंस्, भ्रंश्, कस्, पत, पद् and स्कन्द् ॥.

Thus वनीवच्यते and वनीवञ्चीति; सनीस्रस्यते and सनीस्रंसीति; दनीध्वस्यते and दनीध्वंसीति; बनीभ्रस्यते and बनीभ्रंसीति, (बनीभ्रश्यते and बनीभ्रंशीति), चनीकस्यते and चनीकसीति; पनीपत्यते and पनीपतीति, पनीपद्यते and पनीपदीति; चनीस्कद्यते and चनीस्कन्दीति ॥ The nasal is elided in one alternative by VI. 4. 24.

नुगतोनुनासिकान्तस्य ॥ ८५ ॥ पदानि ॥ नुक्, अतः, अनुनासिक-अन्तस्य ॥

वृत्तिः ॥ अनुनासिकान्तस्याङ्गस्य योऽभ्यासस्तस्याकारान्तस्य नुगागमो भवति यङ्यङ्लुकोः परतः ॥

वार्त्तिकम् ॥ पदान्तवच्चेति वक्तव्यम् ॥

85. The augment नुक् (न्) is added after the short अ of a reduplicate in the Intensive (with or without यङ्), when the root ends in a Nasal.

As तन्तन्यते and तन्तनीति; जङ्गम्यते and जङ्गमीति, यंयम्यते and यंयमीति; रंरम्यते and रंरमीति ॥ The augment न् here should be considered as anusvâra, because an âdeśa is indicated by the nature of the sthânin which is replaced; and therefore in यंयम्यते, it remains anusvâra. Had it been न्, it could not have been changed to anusvâra in यंयम्यते, रंरम्यते (See VIII. 3. 24). In तन्तन्यते &c, the anusvâra is changed to न्, ङ् &c, by VIII. 4. 58; the other forms तंतन्यते तंतनीति, जंगम्यते, जंगमीति are derived by the following :—

Vârt:—This anusvâra should be treated as if it was at the end of a Pada or word. That being so, VIII. 4 59 applies, and we have the anusvâra unchanged, as in तंतन्यते &c.

Why do we say "after a short अ"? Observe तेतिम्यते ॥ The त् in अत् indicates that the augment will not be added to a reduplicate which once was long आ but became short by VII. 4. 59 as from भाम 'to be angry', is बाभाम्यते.

(the second lengthening takes place by VII. 4. 83). Why do we say ending in a nasal ? Observe पापच्यते ॥

जपजभदहदशभञ्जपशां च ॥ ८६ ॥ पदानि ॥ जप-जभ-दह-दश-भञ्ज-पशाम्, च ॥

वृत्तिः ॥ जप जभ दह दश भञ्ज पश इत्येतेषामभ्यासस्य नुगागमो भवति यङ्यङ्लुकोः परतः ॥

86. The augment नुक् comes after the reduplicates of जप, जभ, दह, दश, भञ्ज, and पश in the Intensive (with or without यङ्)॥

Thus जंजप्यते and जंजपीति ; जंजभ्यते and जंजभीति, दंदह्यते and दंदहीति ; दंदश्यते and दंदशीति ॥ The root is दंश्, but it is exhibited in the sûtra as दश, showing that even in यङ् लुक्, the root loses its nasal. Similarly बंभज्यते and बंभजीति, and पंपश्यते and पंपशीति ॥ This last is a sautra root.

चरफलोश्च ॥ ८७ ॥ पदानि ॥ चर-फलोः, च ॥

वृत्तिः ॥ चर फल इत्येतयोरभ्यासस्य नुगागमो भवति यङ्यङ्लुकोः परतः ॥

87. The augment नुक् comes after the reduplicate of चर् and फल् in the Intensive (with or without यङ्) ॥

Thus चंचूर्यते and चंचूरीति (the lengthening of उ is by VIII. 2. 77) पंफुल्यते and पंफुलीति ॥ See the following sûtra.

उत्परस्यातः ॥ ८८ ॥ पदानि ॥ उत्, परस्य, अतः ॥

वृत्तिः ॥ चरफलोरभ्यासात्परस्यात उकारादेशो भवति यङ्यङ्लुकोः परतः ॥

88. For the subsequent अ (i. e. for the अ of the root and not of the reduplicate), there is substituted उ in the Intensive (with or without यङ्) of चर् and फल् ॥

The examples have been given above, as चंचूर्यते, चंचूरीति and पंफुल्यते पंफुलीति ॥ Why do we say 'the अ which stands subsequent to the reduplicate'? The substitute does not replace the अ of the reduplicate. Why do we say 'of अ'? The substitute should not replace the final letter, which it otherwise would have done by I. 1. 52. The त् in उत् debars guṇa (VII. 3. 86) in चंचूर्ति and पंफुल्ति, for though उ is lengthened by VIII. 2. 77, in चंचूर्ति, yet that lengthening is considered as non-existent or asiddha (VIII. 2. 1) for the purposes of Guṇa (VII. 3. 86). *Quere.* If the त् in उत् debars guṇa, why should it not debar lengthening also of VIII. 2. 77 ?

ति च ॥ ८९ ॥ पदानि ॥ ति, च ॥

वृत्तिः ॥ तकारादौ प्रत्यये परतश्चरफलोरकारस्य उकारादेशो भवति ॥

89. उ is substituted for the vowel of चर् and फल् before an affix beginning with त ॥

Thus चूर्तिः (= चरणं or भक्षणं), प्रफुल्तिः and प्रफुल्लाः ॥ The anuvṛitti of यङ्लुकोरभ्यासस्य does not apply here, though present. See VIII. 2. 55.

रीगृदुपधस्य च ॥ ९० ॥ पदानि ॥ रीक्, ऋत्-उपधस्य, च ॥
वृत्तिः ॥ ऋदुपधस्याङ्गस्य योऽभ्यासस्तस्य रीगागमो भवति यङ्लुकोः परतः ॥
वार्त्तिकम् ॥ रीगृत्वत इति वक्तव्यम् ॥

90. The reduplicate of a root, which has a ऋ in the penultimate position, gets the augment री in the Intensive (with or without यङ्) ॥

As वरीवृत्यते and वरीवृतीति, वरीवृध्यते and वरीवृधीति, नरीनृत्यते and नरीनृतीति ॥

Vârt:—It should be rather stated 'a root which contains a ऋ': when यङ् follows, whether this ऋ be of upadeśa, or obtained by samprasâraṇa, so that the augment may come in वरीवृश्च्यते and वरीवृश्चीति where the ऋ is of vocalisation, and not penultimate also.

रुग्रिकौ च लुकि ॥ ९१ ॥ पदानि ॥ रुक्-रिकौ, च, लुकि ॥
वृत्तिः ॥ यङ्लुकि ऋदुपधस्याङ्गस्य योऽभ्यासस्तस्य रुग्रिकावागमौ भवतश्चकाराद्रीक्च ॥
वार्त्तिकम् ॥ मर्मृज्यते मर्मृज्यमानास इत्युपसंख्यानम् ॥

91. The augments रीक्, रुक् and रिक् come after the reduplicate of a root which has a ऋ in the penultimate, only when the यङ् of the Intensive is elided.

Thus नर्नर्ति, नरिनर्ति, and नरीनर्ति; वर्वर्ति, वरिवर्ति, वरीवर्ति ॥ The उ in रुक् is for the sake of pronunciation, the augment is र् ॥

Vârt:—मर्मृज्यते and मर्मृज्यमानासः should also be enumerated. These have taken रुक् augment, though the यङ् is not elided here.

ऋतश्च ॥ ९२ ॥ पदानि ॥ ऋतः, च ॥
वृत्तिः ॥ ऋकारान्तस्याङ्गस्य योऽभ्यासस्तस्य रुग्रिकावागमौ भवतो रीक्च यङ्लुकि ॥
Kârikâ:—किरति चर्करीतान्तं पचतीत्यत्र यो नयेत् ।
प्राप्तिज्ञं तमहं मन्ये प्रारब्धस्तेन संग्रहः ॥

92. The reduplicate of a root, which ends in short ऋ, gets, in the Intensive without यङ्, the above augments री, र्, and रि ॥

Thus चर्कर्ति, चरिकर्ति, and चरीकर्ति, जर्हर्ति, जरिहर्ति and जरीहर्ति ॥ Why do we say 'which ends in a *short* ऋ'? The rule does not apply to roots ending in long ॠ as, चाकर्ति, चाकीर्तः, चाकिरति from कॄ ॥ The word ऋतः qualifies the word अङ्ग and not the word अभ्यास, for an abhyâsa is always short, so the त् in ऋत् would become meaningless if the word qualified reduplicate. Therefore कॄ ending in long ॠ does not get री, र् and रि augments in the reduplicate.

Kârikâ:—He who can conjugate, in the Present tense, the yaṇ-luk Intensive of कॄ and of other roots ending in long ॠ, is considered by me to be a person who has attained to the right knowledge of the employment of the augments ऋ, री, रि &c: and he has obtained the right use of words.

The word किरति in the Kârikâ is illustrative of all roots like कॄ (किरति) ending in long ॠ ॥ चर्करीत is the name given to the यङ् लुक् form of the Intensive, by ancient grammarians. चर्करीतान्त means, therefore, a form ending in yan-luk. पचति is illustrative of लट् or Present tense.

सन्वल्लघुनि चङ्परेऽनग्लोपे ॥ ९३ ॥ पदानि ॥ सन्वत्, लघुनि, चङ-परे, अन् अग्लोपे ॥

वृत्तिः ॥ लघुनि धात्वक्षरे परतो योऽभ्यासस्तस्य चङ्परे णौ परतः सनीव कार्यं भवति अनग्लोपे ॥

93. In the reduplicated Aorist of the Causative, the reduplicate adapts itself to that of the Desiderative, when the vowel of the root is light, and the root has not lost its end-vowel before the Causative affix.

The words of this sûtra require a little detailed explanation. The word सन्वत् means "like unto सन् or Desiderative"; i. e. as the Desiderative is treated, so should the चङ् Aorist of the Causative. The words लघुनि and चङ्परे are both in the Locative case, but not in apposition with each other, but refer to different objects. लघुनि means 'when a light vowel follows', namely that reduplicate which is followed by the light root-vowel. The operations to be performed on such a reduplicate, in the चङ् Aorist, after the णि are the same, as on the reduplicate of the Desiderative. अन्-अक्-लोपे "provided that a simple vowel of the Pratyâhâra अक् has not beed elided". We read the word 'causative' into this sûtra, because there can be no other root which will form चङ् Aorist. Causatives form such Aorist. (III. 1. 48), as well as the simple roots श्रि, द्रु and स्रु ॥ The words चङ्परे qualifies the word अङ्ग understood: that *stem* which is followed by चङ्; therefore, it refers to the Causative *stem*, and not to the simple roots śri, dru and sru. The *light* vowel, therefore refers, to the light vowel of the *Causative stem* before चङ् ॥

The word अनग्लोपे is in apposition with चङ्परे ॥ Thus कम + णिङ् (III. 1. 30). = अकामि + इ + अत् (III. 1. 48) = अकामि + अत् (VI. 4. 51) = अकम् + अत् (VII.4.1) = अचकम् + अत् (VI. 1. 11) = अाचकम् + अत् (VII. 4. 79 read with VII. 4. 93) = अची-कमत् (VII. 4. 94).

Thus VII. 4. 79 teaches the substitution of इ for अ in the reduplicate of the Desiderative. The same substitution will take place in the reduplicate of the Aorist: as अचीकरत्, अपीपचत् ॥ Thus by VII. 4. 80, इ is substituted for the उ of the reduplicate in the Desiderative, the same will be the case in the reduplicate of the Aorist, as अपीपवत् and अलीलवत्, and अजीजवत् ॥ Thus by VII. 4. 81, इ is optionally substituted for उ in the Desiderative reduplicate of स्रु &c, the same will hold good in the Aorist-reduplicate, as असिस्रवत् or असुस्रवत्, अशिश्रवत्

or अशुश्रवत्, अविद्रवत् or अदुद्रवत्, अपिप्रवत् or अपुप्रवत्, अपिप्लवत् or अपुप्लवत्, अचिच्यवत् or अचुच्यवत् ॥ Why do we say 'having a light vowel'? Observe अततक्षत्, अररक्षत्, अजजागरत् ॥

Some say, that in अजजागरत्, the syllable ग is *light*, and therefore, the san-vat rule would apply: for a light vowel no where *immediately* follows a reduplicate; therefore, though a long syllable जा intervenes, yet the rule will apply, because of the express text. This reasoning is wrong. The maxim येन नाव्यवधानं तेनव्यवहितेऽपि वचनप्रामाण्यात् cannot be extended to cases like this. It applies only when the intervention consists of one letter and not of more than one. Obj. If so, how do you form अचिक्षणत् for here two letters क् and ष् (क्ष) intervene between the reduplicate and the light vowel. Ans. The author indicates by implication in VII. 4. 95 that these roots like क्षण् do take इ in the reduplicate; for had it not been so, what was the necessity of making an exception in favor of roots like स्मृ, त्वर, स्तॄ, स्पश् in VII. 4. 95. So that a conjunct consonant is not considered an intervention for the purposes of this rule. Therefore, स्मृ &c would have taken इ in the reduplicate by VII. 4. 79, read with the present sûtra, and so the Achârya enjoins अ instead in VII.4.95 with regard to these.

Why do we say 'when चङ् follows'? Observe अहं पपच ॥ Why do we use the word पर "followed by"? The rule would not apply when चङ् *alone* follows without णि, as अचकमत् where कम् has taken चङ् under the vârtika कमेरुपसंख्यानम् ॥

Why do we say 'when an अक vowel has not been dropped'? Observe अचकथत् from the Churâdi root कथ which ends in अ, and this अ is elided by VI. 4. 48. Obj. This lopa being considered sthânivat, will prevent the application of the present rule, as there will be an intervention. Ans. We shall give another example, अवदृषत् from दृषदमाख्यातवान् ॥ Here णिच् is added to दृषद् under the Vârtika तत्करोतितदाचष्टे, and the टि portion is elided by इष्ठवद्भावः, here a vowel and a consonant have been elided, and so the lopa is not sthânivat.

In the double causative Aorist अवीवदत् the present rule applies, though one णि has been elided. अवीवदत् = वादितवन्तं प्रयोजितवान् ॥ In fact, the elision of one णि when followed by another णि is not considered as an ak-lopa; the latter refers to the elision of any other vowel than णि ॥ Therefore we have अवीवदद् वीणां परिवादकेन ॥ In fact, this exception rests on the following vârtika सन्वद्भावदीर्घत्वे णे र्णिच्युपसंख्यानम् ॥

The lopa of the reduplicate which takes place before सन् of the roots मी, मा &c (VII. 4. 54) does not, however, take place in चङ् Aorist. The analogy does not extend so far. In fact, the present sûtra teaches a रूपातिदेश,

namely the *form* which a reduplicate has in Desiderative, will be the *form* in the Aorist. But as मी, मा &c have *no* reduplicate form in the Desiderative, the analogy stops. Therefore, we shall have अमीमपत् ॥ Moreover the word सन्वद् here means the operations that depend *solely* on सन् ॥ Now the total elision of the reduplicate by VII. 4. 54 does not depend upon सन् *alone*, but upon the augment इस् also of VII. 4. 54. But as there can be no इस् in the Aorist, so there will be no elision also. In fact, an atidesà should be confined to general cases and not to particulars.

दीर्घो लघोः ॥ ९४ ॥ पदानि ॥ दीर्घः, लघोः ॥

वृत्तिः ॥ दीर्घो भवति लघोरभ्यासस्य लघुनि णौ चङ्परे ऽनग्लोपे ॥

94. In the reduplicative syllable, a prosodially short vowel is lengthened in the Reduplicated Aorist of the Causative, when the vowel of the root is light, and the root has not lost its end-vowel before the Causative णि ॥

Thus अचीकरत्, the इ (VII. 4. 79) is lengthened. Similarly अजीहरत्, अलीलवत्, अपीपचत् ॥ Why do we say which is prosodially light? Observe आब-भजत् ॥ Why do we say when the vowel of the root is light? Observe अततक्षत्, अररक्षत् ॥ Why do we say in the reduplicated Aorist? Observe अहं पपच ॥ The word पर is understood here also, so the rule will not apply to simple roots as अचकमत् ॥ The words 'anaglope' are to be read here, therefore not so in अचकथत् ॥

अत्स्मृदृत्वरप्रथम्रदस्तृस्पशाम् ॥ ९५ ॥ पदानि ॥ अत, स्मृ-दृ-त्वर-प्रथ-म्रद, स्तृ-स्पशाम् ॥

वृत्तिः ॥ स्मृ दृ त्वर प्रथ म्रद स्तृ स्पश इत्येतेषामभ्यासस्यादित्ययमादेशो भवति चङ्परे णौ परतः ॥

95. Short अ is substituted for the vowel of the reduplicate in the Reduplicated Aorist of the Causative, of the roots smṛi, dṛî, tvar, prath, mrad, stṛî and spaś,

Thus असस्मरत्, अददरत्, अतत्वरत्, अपप्रथत्, अमम्रदत्, अतस्तरत्, अपस्पशत् ॥ This debars the इ which would have come under VII. 4. 93. The '*short* अ indicates that it is not to be lengthened by VII. 4. 94, as अददरत् ॥

विभाषा वेष्टिचेष्ट्योः ॥ ९६ ॥ पदानि ॥ विभाषा, वेष्टि, चेष्ट्योः ॥

वृत्तिः ॥ वेष्टि चेष्टि इत्येतयोरभ्यासस्य विभाषा अदित्ययमादेशो भवति चङ्परे णौ परतः ॥

96. Short अ is optionally substituted for the vowel of the reduplicate in वेष्ट् and चेष्ट् in the Reduplicated Aorist of the Causative.

Thus अववेष्टत् or अविवेष्टत्, अचचेष्टत् and अचिचेष्टत् ॥ In one alternative there is shortening of the reduplicate (VII. 4. 59), and after such shortening, there is अ substituted in the other alternative.

ई च गणः ॥ ९७ ॥ पदानि ॥ ई, च, गणः ॥

वृत्तिः ॥ गणेरभ्यासस्य ईकारादेशो भवति चङ्परे णौ परतः ॥

97. In the Reduplicated Aorist of the Causative, ई is substituted optionally for the vowel of the reduplicate in गण् ॥

As अजीगणत् or अजगणत् ॥ गण is a root which ends in अ, and this अ being elided by VI. 4. 48 before the Causative णि, the rule VII. 4. 93, does not apply to it, because there is an ak-lopa here, so in the other alternative, it has its natural अ ॥

Printed at the Tara Printing Works, Benares City.

BOOK VIII.

THE

ASHTÁDHYÁYI OF PÁNIṆI.

TRANSLATED INTO ENGLISH,

BY

SRISA CHANDRA VASU, B. A.,

Provincial Civil Service, N. W. P.

Benares:

PUBLISHED BY SINDHU CHÁRAN BOSE,

at the Panini Office,

1898.

TO

Hon'ble Sir John Edge, Kt. Q. C.,

LATE CHIEF JUSTICE OF THE NORTH-WESTERN PROVINCES

THIS WORK

IS,

WITH HIS LORDSHIP'S PERMISSION,

AND IN RESPECTFUL APPRECIATION OF HIS LORDSHIP'S SERVICES TO THE CAUSE OF ADMINISTRATION OF JUSTICE AND OF EDUCATION

IN

THESE PROVINCES,

Dedicated

BY HIS LORDSHIP'S HUMBLE SERVANT

THE TRANSLATOR.

ओ३म् ।

अथ अष्टमाध्यायस्य प्रथमः पादः ।

BOOK EIGHTH.

CHAPTER FIRST.

सर्वस्य द्वे ॥ १ ॥ पदानि ॥ सर्वस्य, द्वे ॥

वृत्तिः ॥ सर्वस्येति च द्वे इति चैतदधिकृतं वेदितव्यम्। इत उत्तरं यद्वक्ष्यामः प्राक् पदस्येत्यतः सर्वस्य द्वे भवत इत्येवं तद्वेदितव्यम् ॥

1. From here upto VIII. 1. 15 inclusive, is to be supplied always the phrase "the whole word is repeated".

This is an adhikâra sûtra. Whatever will be taught hereafter upto पदस्य (VIII. 1. 16) exclusive, there the phrase सर्वस्य द्वे should be supplied to complete the sense. Thus VIII. 1. 4. teaches "when the sense is that of 'always', and 'each'." Here the phrase 'the whole word is repeated' should be supplied to complete the sense. i. e. "The whole word is repeated when the sense is that of *always* and *each*". What is to be repeated? That which is most appropriate in sound and sense both. Thus one पचति becomes two, as पचति पचति 'he always cooks'. Similarly ग्रामो ग्रामो रमणीयः 'every village is beautiful'.

The sûtra 'sarvasya dve', should not be confounded as meaning 'the word-form *sarva* is doubled'. For then rules likes VI. 1. 99, and VI. 1. 100 will find no scope. The word sarva has several meanings: (1) the totality of *things* (द्रव्यः) as सर्वस्वंददाति, (2) the totality of *modes* (प्रकारः) सर्वान्नीनोभिक्षुः = सर्वप्रकारमन्नं भक्षयति; (3) the totality of *members* (अवयवः), as सर्वः पटोदग्धः ॥ In the present sûtra, the word *sarva* has this last sense: namely *all* the *members* of a word are doubled, no portion is omitted. The force of the genitive case in sarvasya, is that of sthâna, i. e. in the *room* of the *whole* of the words like पति &c there is doubling. So one meaning of the sûtra is, that in the *room* of the one word, two are *substituted.* In making such *substitution*, we must have regard to the rule of nearness.

Another meaning of the sûtra however is, that it does not teach *substitution* but *repetition* or *employment*, not âdesâ, but prayoga. That is to say, one word is *employed* twice. In this sense, of course, there is no room left for finding out the proper substitute. The very word-form, पचति &c, is employed twice, i. e. is repeated twice or pronounced twice.

The word sarvasya is employed in the sûtra for the sake of distinctness only. Otherwise, one may double only the last *letter* of a word by the rule of अलोऽन्तस्य, though that rule is not, strictly speaking, applicable to such cases.

Obj. The word पदस्य should be employed in the sûtra, in order to prevent the application of the rule to Samâsa (compound), to taddhitas, and to vâkyas (sentences). Thus सप्तपर्णोऽष्टापदम् ॥ Here there is the sense of vîpsâ with regard to seven leaves, and does not mean a tree having seven leaves. There ought to have been doubling; but it would not take place, if we take the word padasya in the aphorism. Similarly द्विपदिकां ददाति, here also the sense is that of vîpsâ, and there ought to have been doubling, before the affixing of the taddhita affix. So also in ग्रामे ग्रामे पानयिम् the *sentence* ग्रामे पानीयम् is not doubled, if we employ padasya. So the word padasya, should be employed in the sûtra. Moreover, it would prevent our employing the word padasya again in VIII. 1. 16.

Ans. We could not employ the word padasya in this sûtra, for then the rule would become very much restricted. Moreover in the above examples, there can be no doubling; for सप्तपर्णः means 'that whose every twig bears seven leaves पर्वाणि पर्वाणि सप्तपर्णानि अस्य,: so that the sense of vîpsâ is not here inherent in the word sapta or parna. In the case of the taddhita example, there would be no doubling, because the *force* of vîpsâ is there denoted by the taddhita *affix* itself, and so doubling is not *necessary*. Moreover, a sentence can never be doubled, because vîpsâ can take place with regard to a *word*, and not a sentence. Therefore the word पदस्य should not be employed in the sûtra.

On the contrary, if we employ the word padasya in the sûtra, it would give rise to the following anomalies. We could not have प्रपचाति प्रपचाति ; for upasarga being considered as a separate pada, only पचति would be doubled, and प्र would not. So also, we have two forms द्रोग्धा and द्रोढा ॥ Here तृच् is added to the root द्रुह्, and ह् is optionally changed to घ by VIII. 2. 77, and in the other alternative there is ढ ॥ As घ and ढ are both asiddha (VIII. 2. 1), the doubling would take place without making this घ or ढ substitution. So that having first doubled the word (something as द्रोह्ता द्रोह्ता) *then* optional घ or ढ change will take place, and we shall get wrong forms, like द्रोग्धा द्रोढा, द्रोढा द्रोग्धा in doubling. While the correct forms are द्रोढा द्रोढा, or द्रोग्धा द्रोग्धा, and not the hybrid doubling as given above. Hence the necessity of the vârtika पूर्वत्रासिद्धीयम-द्विर्वचने (See VIII. 2. 3 last vârtika).

Or the word सर्व may be considered to be formed by अच् affix of अर्श आद्यच्, meaning सर्वं कार्यं यस्मिन्नस्ति तदिदं सर्वं, तस्य द्वे भवतः ॥ That is, all operations having been *first* performed, *then* the word is doubled; so that a word in its inchoate state is not doubled.

तस्य परमाम्रेडितम् ॥ २ ॥ पदानि ॥ तस्य, परम्, आम्रेडितम् ॥

वृत्तिः ॥ तस्य द्विरुक्तस्य यत्परं शब्दरूपं तदाम्रेडितसंज्ञं भवति ॥

2. Of that which is twice uttered, the latter word-form is called âmreḍita (repeated).

Thus in चौर चौर ३, वृषल वृषल ३ दस्यो ३ घातयिष्यामि त्वा, बन्धयिष्यामि त्वा, the second word being âmreḍita is pluta. The word आम्रेडित occurs in Sûtras VI. 1. 99, VIII. 1. 57, VIII. 2. 95, VIII. 10. 3 &c.

The तस्य here denotes avayava-shashṭhi: and the word परः denotes the avayava. In fact, this sûtra indicates by implication, that a Genitive case is employed, when a member (avayava) is denoted. So that the sentences like पूर्वं कायस्य become valid.

In the above examples, the word has become pluta by VIII. 2. 95.

अनुदात्तं च ॥ ३ ॥ पदानि ॥ अनुदात्तम्, च ॥

वृत्तिः ॥ अनुदात्तं च तद्भवति यदाम्रेडितसंज्ञम् ॥

3. That which is called âmreḍita is gravely accented.

Thus भुङ्क्ते भुङ्क्ते ; पशून् पशून् ॥

That is, all the vowels of the âmreḍita become anudâtta or accentless. In the above examples, the root भुज् becomes âtmanepadi by I. 3. 66: the Personal endings are anudâtta by VI. 1. 186; the vikaraṇa श्नम् gets the acute by III. 1. 3; the अ of this नं is elided by VI. 4. 111, and thus भुङ्क्ते becomes finally acute by udâtta-nivṛtti-svara (VI. 1. 161). The âmreḍita bhunkte becomes wholly anudâtta. The word पशु is formed by the affix कु and is finally acute.

नित्यवीप्सयोः ॥ ४ ॥ पदानि ॥ नित्य, वीप्सयोः ॥

वृत्तिः ॥ नित्ये चार्थे वीप्सायां च यद्वर्त्तते तस्य द्वे भवतः ॥

4. The whole word is repeated when the sense is of 'always' and 'each'.

What words express 'always'? The finite verbs, and the Indeclinable words, formed by kṛit affixes. What 'always' is meant here? The word 'nitya' here means 'again and again', and this idea of 'repetition' is the quality of an action. That action which the agent does principally, without cessation, is called "nitya". So that *nitya* refers to an action (See III. 4. 22). Thus पचति पचति 'he cooks continually'. जल्पति जल्पति 'he talks incessantly'. भुक्त्वा भुक्त्वा व्रजति or

भोजं भोजं व्रजति 'each one, when he has eaten goes away.' See III. 4. 22. लुनीहि लुनीहीत्येवायं लुनाति (See III. 4. 2). The affixes ktvâ and ṇamul formed words and the Imperative mood express the idea of 'again and again', only when they are repeated. While the words formed with the affix यङ् (Intensive) express this idea by the inherent force of the affix, without repetition. Thus पुनः पुनः पचति = पापच्यते ॥ And when this intensive action is continually done, then this word also should be repeated; as पापच्यते पापच्यते ॥ In the above, examples have been given of nitya, as illustrated by finite verbs like पचति, Indeclinable kṛit words like भुक्त्वा, and like भोजं ॥ Now for वीप्सा ॥ In what words the वीप्सा is found? It is found in nouns (सुप् formed words). As finite verbs (तिङ्) express nitya, so inflected nouns (सुप्) express vîpsâ or a distributive sense. What is meant by the word vîpsâ? It is the wish of the agent to pervade (vyâptum ichchhâ) an object through and through with a certain quality or action. That is, when many objects are wished to be pervaded by the speaker, with a particular attribute or action simultaneously, it is vîpsâ. Thus ग्रामो ग्रामो रमणीयः : 'every village is beautiful'. So also जनपदो जनपदो रमणीयः पुरुषः पुरुषो निधनमुपैति ॥

When a finite verb is repeated owing to the idea of nityatâ; and we also wish to add to such a verb the affix denoting comparative or superlative degree, such affix must be added after the word has been repeated, as पचति पचतितराम् ॥ But in the case of a noun, which is repeated owing to vîpsâ, the whole superlative or comparative word should be repeated, as आढ्यतरमाढ्यतरमानय॥

परेर्वर्जने ॥ ५ ॥ पदानि ॥ परेः, वर्जने ॥

वृत्तिः ॥ परीत्येतस्य वर्जनेर्थे द्वे भवतः ॥

वार्त्तिकम् ॥ परेर्वर्जनेऽसमासे वेति वक्तव्यम् ॥

5. The word परि is repeated when employed in the sense of 'with the exception or exclusion of'.

As परि परि त्रिगर्तेभ्यो वृष्टो देवः (I. 4. 88 and II. 3. 10) 'It rained round about (but with the exclusion of) Trigarta'. Similarly परि परि सौवीरेभ्यः, परि परि सर्वसेनेभ्यः॥ Why do we say when meaning exclusion? Observe ओदनं परिषिञ्चति ॥

Vârt:—Optionally परि, meaning 'exclusion', is repeated when it occurs not in a compound, as परि परि त्रिगर्तेभ्यः or परि त्रिगर्तेभ्यः ॥ In a compound, there is no repetition as, परित्रिगर्त्तं वृष्टोदेवः, because the word परि has not the meaning of exclusion only here; in fact, the whole compound word denotes here the idea of exclusion, and not the word परि alone

The word परि is here a Karmapravachaniya (I. 4. 88), and governs the fifth case by II. 3. 11. In परिषिञ्चति the word is an upasarga.

प्रसमुपोदः पादपूरणे ॥ ६ ॥ पदानि ॥ प्र, सम्, उप, उदः, पाद पूरणे ॥

वृत्तिः ॥ प्र सम् उप उत् इत्येतेषां पादपूरणे द्वे भवतो द्विर्वचनेन चेत्पादः पूर्यते ॥

6. प्र, सम्, उ· and उत् are repeated, when by so doubling, the foot of a verse is completed.

As प्र प्रायमग्निर्भरतस्य शृण्वे (Rig VII. 8.4), संसमिद्युवसे वृषन् ॥ (Rig X .191. 1), उपोप मे परामृश (Rig I. 126. 7), किं नोदुदु हर्षसे दातवाउ (Rig IV. 21. 9). Why do we say when 'a foot of a verse is completed thereby'? Observe प्रदेवं देव्या धिया ॥ This rule applies only to the Vedic verses, for there alone the Preposition may be used separate from its verb. In the secular literature, this rule has no applicability, as Prepositions are never so used.

उपर्यध्यधसः सामीप्ये ॥ ७ ॥ पदानि ॥ उपरि, अधि, अधसः, सामीप्ये ॥

वृत्तिः ॥ उपरि अधि अधस् इत्येतेषां द्वे भवतः सामीप्ये विवक्षिते ॥

7. उपरि, अधि, and अधस् are repeated, when it expresses uninterrupted nearness.

The word sâmipya means 'proximity' whether in time or space. As उपर्युपरि दुःखम्, or उपर्युपरि ग्रामम्, अध्यधि ग्रामम्, अधोधो नगरम् ॥ Why do we say 'meaning near'? Observe उपरि चन्द्रमाः ॥ Why the word is not repeated here: उपरि शिरसो घटं धारयति ॥ The relation expressed here is not that of nearness, but that of above and below.

उपर्युपरि पश्यन्तः सर्व एव दरिद्रति ।
अधोधो दर्शने कस्य महिमा नोपजायते ॥

Here the doubling is in the sense of vîpsâ.

वाक्यादेरामन्त्रितस्यासूयासंमतिकोपकुत्सनभर्त्सनेषु ॥ ८ ॥ पदानि ॥ वाक्य-आदेः, आमन्त्रितस्य, असूया, सम्मति, कोप, कुत्सन, भर्त्सनेषु ॥

वृत्तिः ॥ एकार्थः पदसमूहो वाक्यम् । वाक्यादेरामन्त्रितस्य द्वे भवतः असूया संमति कोप कुत्सन भर्त्सनइत्येतेषु यदि तद्वाक्यं भवति ॥

8. A Vocative, at the beginning of a sentence, is repeated, when envy, praise, anger, blame, or threat is meant by the speaker.

A collocation of words, expressing one idea, is called a sentence or vâkya. Thus (1) envy :—माणवका ३ माणवक अभिरूपका ३ अभिरूपक रिक्तं ते आभिरूप्यम् ॥ (2) praise — माणवका ३ माणवक अभिरूपका ३ आभिरूपक शोभनः खल्वसि ॥ (3) anger :— माणवका ३ माणवक अविनीतका ३ अविनीतक इदानीं ज्ञास्यसि जाल्म ॥ (4) blame :— शक्तिके ३ शक्तिके यष्टिके ३ यष्टिके रिक्ता ते शक्तिः ॥ (5) Threat—चौर चौरा ३ वृषल वृषला ३ घातयिष्यामि त्वा, बन्धयिष्यामि त्वा ॥ The first word becomes pluta as well as gets svarita accent, by VIII. 2. 103, in the case of the first four; in the case of 'threat', the second word or the âmreḍita becomes pluta by VIII. 2. 95. Why do we say "at the beginning of a sentence"? The Vocative in the middle or the end of a sentence is not to be repeated, as शोभन खल्वसि माणवकः ॥ Why do we say of a Vocative? Observe उदारो देवदत्तः ॥ Why do we say 'when meaning envy &c'. Observe देवदत्त गामभ्याज शुक्लाम् ॥

In some books, the vâkya is defined as 'a collocation of words having one finite verb', (एकतिङ् पदसमूहो वाक्यं) ॥ In the first example, कन् is added.

एकं बहुव्रीहिवत् ॥ ९ ॥ पदानि ॥ एकम्, बहुव्रीहि, वत् ॥

वृत्तिः ॥ एक मित्येतच्छब्दरूपं द्विरुक्तं बहुव्रीहिवद्भवति ॥

9. When एक is repeated, it is treated like a member a of Bahuvrîhi compound.

The making it a Bahuvrihi is for the sake of eliding the case-affix, and treating the word as a masculine, even when it refers to a feminine. Thus ऐकैकमक्षरं पठति (not एकमेकम्), ऐकैकयाहुत्या जुहोति (not एकयैकया). The accent is regulated by VI. 2. 1. the case-affix is elided by II. 4. 71, and masculinising by VI. 3. 34. This double word एकैक should not however be treated like a Bahuvrihi for the purposes of the application of the following three rules, (1) The sûtra I. 1. 29 by which pronouns are not declined as pronouns when members of a Bahuvrihi compound. The word एकैक however is declined like a Pronoun, as एकैकस्मै ॥ For sûtra I. 1. 29 applies to a compound which is *really* a Bahuvrihi, and not to a word-form which is treated *like* a Bahuvrihi. The repetition of the word Bahuvrihi in that sûtra, though its anuvritti was understood from the preceding one; indicates this. (2) The application of the rule of accent. Thus by the following sûtra, a word is repeated when a mental pain or affliction over something is expressed. Thus न न करोति, सुसुजागर्ति ॥ This double-word is treated *like* a Bahuvrîhi, but not for the purposes of accent. For by VI. 2. 172 a Bahuvrihi preceded by न or सु gets acute on the final, but not so नन or सुसु ॥ Here four rules of accent present themselves 1st VI. 1. 223 ordaining acute on the final, 2nd VI. 2. 1 the first member retaining its accent, 3rd VI. 2. 172 already mentioned, 4th VIII. 1. 3 by which the second member becomes anudâtta, The rule VI. 2. 1 however regulates the accent, in supersession of the other three. (3) The third rule which does not apply to this Bahuvrîhi-vat एकैक is the rule of samâsanta affixing. Thus ऋक् ऋक्, पूः पूः (doubled by VIII. 1. 10) do not get the samâsânta affix अ by V. 4. 74.

आबाधेच ॥ १० ॥ पदानि ॥ आ, बाधे, च ॥

वृत्तिः ॥ आबाधनमाबाधः । पीडाप्रयोक्तृ धर्मः । तत्र वर्त्तमानस्य द्वे भवतः बहुव्रीहिवच्चास्य कार्यं भवति ॥

10. A word is repeated, an d is treated like a member of Bahuvrîhi compound, when a mental distress over something is expressed.

Thus गतंगतः 'gone, gone to my affliction', नष्टंनष्टः, पतितंपतितः, in the masculine, and गतगता, नष्टनष्टा, पतितपतिता in the Feminine (not गतागता for the reasons given in the preceding aphorism). The accent is governed by VI. 2. 1.

कर्म्मधारयवदुत्तरेषु ॥ ११ ॥ पदानि ॥ कर्मधारय, वत्, उत्तरेषु ॥

वृत्तिः ॥ इत उत्तरेषु द्विर्वचनेषु कर्म्मधारयवत्कार्यं भवतीत्येतद्वेदितव्यम्। कर्म्मधारयत्वे प्रयोजनं सुब्लोप-पुंवद्भावान्तोदात्तत्वानि ॥

11. In the following rules, the double-word is treated like a Karmadhâraya compound.

The reason for making it a Karmadhâraya is to elide the case-affix (II. 4. 71), to make the first member a masculine term even when the word refers to a feminine (VI. 3. 42), and to regulate the accent by VI. 1. 223. Thus पटुपटुः, मृदुमृदुः where the first member has lost the case-affix. पटुपट्वी, मृदुमृद्वी where the first member is treated as a masculine, even when there is a क in the penultimate as कालककालिका (See VI. 3. 37 and 42); पटुपटुः, पटुपट्वी, the accent falls on the final, for the rule VI. 1. 223 was debarred by VIII. 1. 3, but the present rule re-instates VI. 1 223. The word उत्तरेषु is for the sake of distinctness, the sûtra being an adhikâra one, would have applied to the subsequent aphorisms, without even the word uttareshu.

प्रकारे गुणवचनस्य ॥ १२ ॥ पदानि ॥ प्रकारे, गुण-वचनस्य ॥

वृत्तिः ॥ प्रकारो भेदः सादृश्यं च । तदिह सादृश्यं प्रकारो गृह्यते । प्रकारे वर्त्तमानस्य गुणवचनस्य द्वे भवतः ॥

वार्त्तिकम् ॥ आनुपूर्व्ये द्वे भवत इति वक्तव्यम् ॥ वा० ॥ स्वार्थे अवधार्यमाणेनेकस्मिन्द्वे भवत इति वक्तव्यम् ॥
वा० ॥ चापले द्वेभवत इति वक्तव्यम् ॥ वा० ॥ क्रियासमभिहारे द्वे भवत इति वक्तव्यम् ॥
वा० ॥ आभीक्ष्ण्ये द्वे भवत इति वक्तव्यम् ॥ वा० ॥ डाचि द्वे भवत इति वक्तव्यम् ॥
वा० ॥ पूर्वप्रथमयोरर्थातिशयविवक्षायां द्वेभवत इति वक्तव्यम् ॥
वा० ॥ डतरडतमयोः समसंप्रधारणयोः स्त्री निगदे भावे द्वे भवत इति वक्तव्यम् ॥
वा० ॥ कर्म्मव्यति र ार्वनाम्नो द्वे भवत इति वक्तव्यम् सामासवच्च बहुलम् ॥
वा० ॥ स्त्रीनपुंसकयारुत्तरपदस्य चाम्भावो वक्तव्यः ॥

12. An adjective is repeated, when it is meant to express that the said attribute belongs to a thing only to a limited degree, and the double word is treated like a Karmadhâraya.

The word प्रकार means both 'difference' and 'resemblance'. It means 'resemblance' here: i. e. the person or thing *resembles*, but is not *fully like*, the thing expressing the attribute. Thus पटुपटुः, 'tolerably sharp', मृदुमृदुः "pretty soft", पण्डितपण्डितः &c. The sense is that the attribute is not *fully* possessed by the person. The affix जातीयर् (V. 3. 69) also expressing प्रकार, is not debarred by this sûtra. Thus पटुजातीयः, मृदुजातीयः ॥

Why do we say prakâre "when denoting somewhat like it"? Observe पटुर्देवदत्तः 'the clever Devadatta'. Why do we say 'an attributive or adjective word'? Observe अग्निर्माणवकः, 'a fiery boy', गौ र्वाहीकः 'a cow-like Bâhîka'. Here 'agni' and 'gau' are not naturally adjective words, though employed here like adjectives.

Vârt:—An adjective is repeated when denoting that persons or things possessing that attribute are to be taken in their due order. Thus मूले मूले स्थूलाः, अग्रे अग्रे सूक्ष्माः, ज्येष्ठं ज्येष्ठं प्रवेशय: ॥

Vârt:—A word denoting more than one is repeated without change of sense, when it denotes the limit or extent of the thing. Thus अस्मात् कार्षापणादिह भवद्भ्यां माषं माषं देहि 'give a mâsha, a mâsha out of this kârshâpaṇa to you two': i, e. give only *two* masha one to each. A kârshâpana contains many mâshas, out of them, the extent of gift is *limited* to two only. This therefore is distinguishable from the distributive double (vîpsâ). The words माषं माषं देहि = द्वौ-देहि; the माष does not take the dual case here. Why do we say when it expresses the limit'? Observe अस्मात् कार्षापणादिह भवद्भ्यां माषमेकं देहि, द्वौमाषौ देहि, त्रीन्वा माषान् देहि. Here the word माष itself does not express limit, but the qualifying words एकं, द्वौ, त्रीन् &c. Why do we say 'denoting more than one'? Observe अस्मात् कार्षापणादिह भवद्भ्यां माषमेकं देहि ॥

Vârt:—In expressing perplexity or alarm, a word may be repeated twice. The word चापल in the vârtika means 'a confused state of mind'. As अहिरहिः बुध्यस्व बुध्यस्व "a snake, a snake, beware. beware'. It is not a necessary condition that the word should be repeated twice only, but as many times as one likes, so long as his meaning is not manifest. As: अहिः अहिः अहिः, बुध्यस्व बुध्यस्व बुध्यस्व ॥

Vârt:—When intensity or frequency of an action is denoted, the word is uttered twice: as, स भवान् लुनीहि लुनीहि इत्येवायं लुनाति ॥ See III. 4. 2.

Vârt:—In re-iteration the word is doubled; as, भुक्त्वा भुक्त्वा व्रजति, भोजं भोजं व्रजति ॥ See III. 4. 22. This has also been illustrated under VIII. 1. 4.

Vârt:—The word is repeated when the affix डाच् follows; as, पटपटा करोति, पटपटायते ॥ This doubling takes place when the word denotes an imitation of an inarticulate sound (V. 4. 57). Therefore, not here, द्वितीया करोति, तृतीया करोति, where the affix डाच् denotes 'to plough', (V. 4. 58). Because of this restriction, some read the vârtika as, डाचि बहुलम् ॥

Vârt:—The words पूर्व and प्रथम are repeated when a comparative or superlative sense is to be denoted: as पूर्वं पूर्वं पुष्प्यन्ति, प्रथमं प्रथमं पच्यन्ते ॥ The comparative and superlative affixes are not debarred hereby, as, पूर्वतरं पुष्प्यन्ति, प्रथमतरं पच्यन्ते ॥

Vârt:—The words ending in the affixes डतर and डतम (comparative and superlative), are doubled when they refer to feminine nouns and are employed in determining or pondering upon the relative condition of the superiority of one out of two or many; as उभाविमावाढ्यौ, कतरा कतरा अनयोराढ्यता "Both these are rich: let us ponder how much is their richness." सर्व इमे आढ्याः, कतमा कतमा एषामा-

च्यता ॥ This is found in words other than those ending in तर and तम; as; उभाविमावाढ्यौ, किदृशी किदृशी अनयोराढ्यता ॥ This is also found where the abstract noun denoting condition (as आढ्यता) is not in the feminine: as, उभाविमावाढ्यौ, कतरः कतरोऽनयोर्विभवः "Both these are rich, let us see what is their respective greatness."

Vârt:—In denoting reciprocity of action, the Pronominal is doubled; and diversely it is treated like a compound (II. 2. 27) when it is not treated like a compound, then the first word is always exhibited in the nominative singular. See I. 3. 14, III. 3. 43, and V. 4. 127. Thus. अन्यमन्यमिमे ब्राह्मणा भोजयन्ति "these Brâhmanas feed one another." अन्योऽन्यमिमे ब्राह्मणा भोजयन्ति ॥ अन्योऽन्यस्य ब्राह्मणा भोजयन्ति = इतरेतरान् भोजयन्ति ॥ The word अन्य and पर are never treated as a compound, and इतर is *always* so treated. The following are from Siddhânta Kaumudi:— अन्योऽन्यौ, अन्योऽन्यान् अन्योऽन्येनकृतं, अन्योऽन्यस्मैदत्तं, अन्योऽन्येषां पुष्करैराभृशन्ते. (Mâgh) परस्परं ॥

Vârt:—In the feminine and neuter, the augment आम् is added optionally to the second term under the above circumstances, as, अन्यो ऽन्यामिमे ब्राह्मण्यौ भोजयतः, अन्योऽन्यं भोजयतः, इतरेतरां भोजयतः, इतरेतरं भोजयतः ॥ अन्योऽन्यामिमे ब्राह्मणकुले भोजयतः, इतरेतरामिमे ब्राह्मणकुले भोजयतः, इतरेतरमिमे ब्राह्मणकुले भोजयतः ॥

अकृच्छ्रेप्रियसुखयोरन्यतरस्याम् ॥ १३ ॥ पदानि ॥ अ-कृच्छ्रे, प्रिय, सुखयोः, अन्यतरस्याम् ॥

वृत्तिः ॥ प्रिय सुख इत्येतयोरन्यतरस्यां द्वे भवतः अकृच्छ्रे द्योत्ये ॥

13. The words 'priya' and 'sukha' are repeated optionally, when they mean "easily, without any difficulty".

The word कृच्छ्र means 'difficulty and sorrow', अकृच्छ्र means 'without difficulty or sorrow, i. e pleasantly'. Thus प्रियप्रियेण ददाति, सुखसुखेन ददाति, or प्रियेण ददाति, सुखेन ददाति = अतिप्रियमपि वस्तु नायासेन ददाति ॥ That is, he gives with pleasure, without feeling it as a trouble. Why do we say "when meaning easily"? Observe प्रियः पुत्रः "beloved son". सुखी रथः ॥

यथास्वे यथायथम् ॥ १४ ॥ पदानि ॥ यथा स्वे, यथा यथम् ॥

वृत्तिः ॥ यो य आत्मा यच्चात्मीयं तत्तद्यथास्वं तस्मिन् यथायथमिति निपात्यते । यथाशब्दस्य द्विर्वचनं. नपुंसकलिङ्गता च निपात्यते ॥

14. The word यथायथम् is irregularly formed in the sense of "respectively, fitly, properly".

What is one's own nature, and whatever is natural to one, that is called यथास्व ॥ In this sense is formed यथायथम् there being doubling and neuter gender. It is an Indeclinable. As ज्ञाताः सर्वे पदार्था यथायथम्=यथास्वभावं "all objects have been known according to their respective nature". सर्वेषां तु यथायथं = यथात्मीयं ॥

द्वन्द्वं रहस्यमर्यादावचनव्युत्क्रमणयज्ञपात्रप्रयोगाभिव्यक्तिषु ॥ १५ ॥ पदानि ॥ द्वन्द्वम्, रहस्य, मर्य्यादा वचन, व्युत्क्रमण, यज्ञ पात्र प्रयोग, अभि व्यक्तिषु ॥

2

वृत्तिः ॥ द्वन्द्वमिति द्विशब्दस्य दिर्वचनं पूर्वपदस्याम्भावः अत्वं चोत्तरपदस्य निपात्यते रहस्य मर्यादावचन व्युत्क्रमण यज्ञपात्र प्रयोग अभिव्यक्ति एतेषु अर्थेषु ॥

15. The word "dvandvam" is irregularly formed, in the sense of 'secret', and when it expresses a 'limit', 'a separation', 'employing in a sacrificial vessel', and 'manifestation'.

The word द्वन्द्वं is formed from द्वि by doubling it, changing the first इ into अम्, and the second इ into अ ॥ The word द्वन्द्व itself means रहस्य or secret; while it marks 'limit' मर्यादा &c only secondarily, by context of the sentence. Thus द्वन्द्वं मन्त्रयन्ते 'they are consulting some secret'. Limit or मर्यादावचनः, as, आचतुरं हीमे पशवो द्वन्द्वं मिथुनायन्ते = माता पुत्रेण मिथुनं गच्छति, पौत्रेण, तत्पुत्रेणापि ॥ (See Maitr. S. I. 7. 3 Śâñkh. Br. III. 97). Separation of व्युत्क्रमण—द्वन्द्वं व्युत्क्रान्ता = द्विवर्गसम्बन्धेन पृथगवस्थिताः ॥ Vyutkramana means bheda or separation, placing at a different place. Employment with regard to a sacrificial vessel (यज्ञपात्रप्रयोगः) as — द्वन्द्वं यज्ञपात्राणि प्रयुनक्ति धीरः (See I. 3. 64) ॥ अभिव्यक्ति or manifestation : as— द्वन्द्वं नारदपर्वतौ, द्वन्द्वं संकर्षण वासुदेवौ = द्वावप्यभिव्यक्तौ साहचर्येण ॥

The word द्वन्द्व is found employed in connection with other senses also; as, द्वन्द्वं युद्धं वर्त्तते, द्वन्द्वानि सहते धीरः, चार्थे द्वन्द्वः &c.

पदस्य ॥ १६ ॥ पदानि ॥ पदस्य ॥

वृत्तिः ॥ पदस्येत्ययमधिकारः प्रागपदान्ताधिकारात् । यदित ऊर्ध्वमनुक्रमिस्यामः पदस्येत्येव तद्वेदितव्यम् ॥

16. Upto VIII. 3. 54, inclusive, should be always supplied in every subsequent sûtra, the phrase "of a word", or "to the whole of a word".

This is an adhikâra sûtra, and extends up to VIII. 3. 55. Whatever we shall treat of here-after, should be understood to apply to a full 'pada' or a completed word. Thus VIII. 2. 23, (संयोगान्तस्य लोपः) teaches "there is elision of the final of what ends in a conjunct consonant". The word पदस्य must be supplied here to complete the sense: viz, of a *word* which ends in a conjunct consonant, the final is elided. Thus पचन्, यजन्, from पचन्त् and यजन्त् ॥

Why do we say 'of a Pada'? Observe पचन्तौ, यजन्तौ where the त though sanyogânta is not elided, because the stem is no longer called pada. The force of the Genitive in पदस्य must be construed according to the context, sometimes as sthâna-shashṭhî i. e. "in the room of the *whole* pada"; and sometimes as avayava-shashṭhî i. e. "of a pada-of the *portion* of a pada".

पदात् ॥ १७ ॥ पदानि ॥ पदात् ॥

वृत्तिः ॥ पदादित्ययमधिकार प्राक्कुत्सने च सुप्यगोत्रादावित्येतस्माद्यदित ऊर्द्ध्वमनुक्रमिष्यामः पदादित्येवं तद्वेदितव्यम् ॥

17. Upto VIII. 1. 68, inclusive should always be supplied the phrase "after a pada".

Whatever we shall teach hereafter should be understood to apply to that which comes *after a pada*. Thus the sûtra VIII. 1. 19, teaches "of an Âmantrita". The phrase पदात्, must be supplied to complete the sense. That is, "of a pada, which is in the Vocative case, *and which comes after another pada*, all vowels become anudâtta". Thus पचसि देवदत्त "Cookest thou, O Devadatta". Why do we say, "after a pada"? Observe देवदत्त पचसि ॥ Here Devadatta is not anudâtta (VI. 1. 198).

अनुदात्तं सर्वमपादादौ ॥ १८ ॥ पदानि ॥ अनुदात्तम्, सर्वम्, अ-पाद-आदौ ॥

वृत्तिः ॥ अनुदात्तमिति च सर्वमिति च अपादादाविति च एतत्त्रयमधिकृतं वेदितव्यमापादपरिसमाप्तेः, इत ऊर्ध्वं यद्वक्ष्यामः अनुदात्तं सर्वमपादादावित्येवं तद्वेदितव्यम् ॥

18. Upto VIII. 1. 74, inclusive is to be supplied the phrase "The whole is unaccented, if it does not stand at the beginning of the foot of a verse".

The three words anudâttam "unaccented", sarvam "the whole", and apâdâdau "not in the beginning of a Pâda of a verse", should be understood to exert a governing influence over all the subsequent sûtras of this chapter, upto its end. Whatever we shall treat of hereafter, must be understood to be wholly unaccented, provided that, it does not stand as the first word of a verse or stanza. Thus VIII. 1. 19, says "of a Vocative". The whole of this sûtra should be read there to complete the sense, viz: "all the syllables of a Vocative are unaccented when a word precedes it, and it does not stand as the first word of a hemistich"; as पचसि देवदत्त ॥

Why do we say "when not at the beginning of a hemistich"? Observe यत्ते नियतं रजसं मृत्यो अनवधृष्यम्, here मृत्यो though in the Vocative case, is not anudâtta, as it stands at the beginning of a Pâda.

Similarly VIII. 1. 21, teaches "वः and नः are the substitutes of युष्मद् अस्मद् in the plural". The present sûtra must be read there to complete the sense, viz, when not at the beginning of a verse. Thus ग्रामो वः स्वं, जनपदो नः स्वम् ॥ But at the beginning of a hemistich, we must have the forms युष्माकं and अस्माकं instead of वः and नः ॥ As,

रुद्रो विश्वेश्वरो देवो युष्माकं कुलदेवता ।
स एव नाथो भगवानस्माकं शत्रुमर्दनः ॥

The word पाद in the sûtra refers both to the hemistiches of the sacred Rik hymns, as well as to secular ślokas.

Q. Why do we employ the word सर्वं in the sûtra?

Ans. The word sarvam is used in the sûtra, in order to indicate that a word, which has not acute accent on the first syllable, should also become anudâtta. For the word पदात् (VIII. 1. 17) is in the ablative case, and shows that the operation taught in any sûtra governed by it, will be performed on the *first* syllable, according to the maxim आदेः परस्य ॥ Therefore, by rule VIII. I. 28, the word पँचाति, which is acutely accented on the *first* syllable, (because शप् and तिप् are anudâtta), will only lose its accent in देवदत्तः पचति; but not so the verb करोति which is acutely accented in the middle (by the vikaraṇa accent) in देवदत्तः करोति ॥ But by force of the word सर्वं, करोति also loses its accent.

Q. This cannot be the reason, for the author indicates by his prohibition in Sûtra VIII. I. 29, that a verb loses its accent, *where ever* that accent may be. For there is no verb when conjugated in लुट् which has acute on the *first* syllable.

Ans. The word 'sarvam' is used to prevent the operation of अलोऽन्त्यात्पूर्वः; for where the rule आदेः परस्य will not apply there the other will apply: so that, if "sarvam" was not used, the rule would apply to the finals, and not to cases where there were other than initials to be operated upon. Thus the rule VIII. I. 28 would apply to कुरुतः which is finally acute by VI. I. 186, in देवदत्तयज्ञदत्तौ कुरुतः, but not to देवदत्तः करोति ॥

Q. No; this cannot be the reason of employing the word 'sarvam' in the sûtra, for the author indicates that the rule is not confined to the *finals*, by the prohibition he makes in favor of लृट् in VIII. I. 51; for there is no verb, when conjugated in Lṛit, which has acute on the final. All Lṛit is acute in the middle by VI. I. 186. So the अलोऽन्त्यस्य rule does not apply.

Ans. The word 'sarvam' is used for this reason. Had 'sarvam', not been used, then in those cases where there was no other rule to apply, like VIII. I. 19, there *only* the word would become anudâtta. But in cases where another rule also operated, there this anudâtta rule would not apply, for then there would be two different sentences. For a thing which is already in existence can be made the subject of a rule ordering certain operations to be performed on it; but not so a thing which will come in existence in future time. Thus the words वां and नौ are ordained as substitutes of yushmad and asmad by one sentence VIII. I. 20; while another sentence ordains their anudatta-hood. So here there is separation of sentences (vâkya-bheda): which is not desireable; for a vâkya bheda should be avoided, if possible. But by employing the word 'sarvam', this vakya-bheda is made tolerable.

Another reason for employing this word is that the substitutes वां and नौ should come in the room of the *whole declined* forms of yushmad and asmad, with their case-affixes. Had not this word (sarvam) been used, then वां and नौ would have replaced only ,yushmad' and 'asmad'. Obj. Will not the anuvritti of the word 'padasya', cause the *whole declined word* to be replaced by वां and नौ, not only the crude-forms yushmad and asmad? And there cannot be a full word unless it takes case-affixes; so the whole of yushmad and asmad with their case-affixes will be replaced. Where is the necessity of using the word 'sarvam'? Ans. This objection will apply to those cases where a Pada is a word ending in a case-affix. But the word पद is a technical term also, and applies to crude forms before certain case-affixes. Thus a nominal *stem* (not a *full* word) is also called Pada by I, 4. 17, before non-sarvanamasthana case-affixes. Therefore yushmad and asmad will be *pada* before those affixes. Thus before the affix of Dative Dual, they will be called Pada ; and had सर्वं not been used, then only "yushmad" and "asmad" will be replaced and not their case-affixes. Thus ग्रामो वां दीयते, जनपदो नौ दीयते ॥ Here वां and नौ would require after them the case - affix भ्यां otherwise.

आमन्त्रितस्य च ॥ १६ ॥ पदानि ॥ आमन्त्रितस्य, च ॥

वृत्तिः ॥ आमन्त्रितस्य पदस्य पदात्परस्यापादादौ वर्त्तमानस्य सर्वस्यानुदात्तो भवति ॥

वार्त्तिकम् ॥ समान वाक्ये निघात युष्मद स्मदादेशा वक्तव्याः ॥

19. All the syllables of a Vocative are unaccented when a word precedes it, and it does not stand at the beginning of a hemistich.

Thus पचसि देवदत्त, पचसि यज्ञदत्त ॥ The Vocative is acutely accented on the first by VI. 1. 198, the present makes it all unaccented.

Vârt:—The rules relating to nighâta (by which all syllables of a word become unaccented, such as the present, and VIII. 1. 28 &c) and to the substitutes of yushmad and asmad apply then only, when the preceding word which would cause the nighâta or the substitution, is part of the same sentence with the latter word. Therefore not here;—अयं दण्डो, हरानेन ॥ "This is the staff. Carry by means of it." Here हर does not lose its accent by VIII. I. 28, though preceded by the Noun daṇḍa, because these are parts of two different sentences. ओदनं पच, तव भविष्यति । ओदनं पच, मम भविष्यति ॥ "Cook the food, it will be for thee, Cook the food, it will be for me." That is the rice cooked by thee, will do both for thyself and myself. Here the ते and मे substitutions have not taken place (VIII. I. 22) for yushmad and asmad, for the same reason.

Another example is, भवतीह विष्णुमित्रो, देवदत्तागच्छ "Vishnumitra is here. Come back Devadatta." Here Devadatta, though in the Vocative case, does not lose its accent. Nor can you say that समर्थः पदविधिः will make this vârtika redundant. In all the above examples, the different sentences are connected with each other in sense. Thus in the last example, Devadatta was searching for Vishnumitra, when some one says to him, 'Here is V. come back D." Thus the two sentences are samartha, yet there is no nighâta. But the rule will apply here:—इह देवदत्त । माता ते कथयति । नद्यास्तिष्ठति (VIII. 1. 28) कूले । शालीनां ते ओदनं दास्यामि ॥ In the last examples the Vocatives, the verbs and the substitutes of yushmad and asmad are not in syntactical construction with the words that immediately precede them, and yet the nighâta rule &c does apply: inspite of the general maxim समर्थः पदविधिः (II. 1. 1), for rules relating to completed words apply to such words only which are in construction.

In the last example, the construction is इह स्थिता माता ते देवदत्त, and not इह देवदत्त. Thus इह is in syntactical construction with स्थिता and not देवदत्त, yet it causes nighâta of Devadatta. Similarly in नद्यास्तिष्ठति कूलं, the word नद्याः is not in construction with तिष्ठति, but with कूलं, i.e. नद्याः कूलं तिष्ठति; yet it causes the nighâta of तिष्ठति ॥ Similarly शालीनां is not in construction with ते, but with ओदनं, i. e. शालीनां ओदनं ते दास्यामि ॥ Yet it causes ते substitution of yushmad. Though the preceding words are not *samartha* with regard to the words that follow them, they cause the changes, because the words are in the *same* sentence.

युष्मदस्मदोः षष्ठीचतुर्थीद्वितीयास्थयोर्वान्नावौ ॥ २० ॥ पदानि ॥ युष्मद्, अस्मदोः, षष्ठी, चतुर्थी, द्वितीयास्थयोः, वाम्, नावौ ॥

वृत्तिः ॥ युष्मदस्मद् इत्येतयोः षष्ठीचतुर्थीद्वितीयास्थयोर्यथासंख्यं वान्नावित्येतावादेशौ भवतस्तौ चानुदात्तौ ॥

20. For the Genitive, Dative and Accusative Dual of yushmad and asmad, are substituted वाम् and नौ respectively, when a word precedes, and these substitutes are anudâtta.

All the three sûtras पदस्य, पदात् and अनुदात्तं सर्वमपादादौ are applicable here. Thus ग्रामो वां स्वम् । जनपदो नौ स्वम् । ग्रामो वां दीयते । जनपदो नौ दीयते । ग्रामो वां पश्यति । जनपदो नौ पश्यति ॥

These two वाम् and नौ come in the Dual only, because other substitutes have been taught for the Singular and Plural in the two subsequent sûtras.

Why do we say "for the Genitive, Dative and Accusative"? In other cases there will be no substitution. As, ग्रामो युवाभ्यां कृतम् ॥ The word स्थ in the sûtra indicates that the case affixes must be express and not understood, for the purposes of this substitution. Therefore, not here: इति युष्मत्पुत्रः though here yushmat is preceded by a word in a sentence, and is in the Genitive case yet वः substitution (VIII. 1. 21) does not take place, because the case-affix is elided.

बहुवचनस्य वस्नसौ ॥ २१ ॥ पदानि ॥ बहुवचनस्य, वस्, नसौ ॥

वृत्तिः ॥ बहुवचनान्तयोर्युष्मदस्मदोः षष्ठीचतुर्थीद्वितीयास्थयोर्यथासंख्यं वस् नस् इत्येतावादेशौ भवतः ॥

21. For (the Genitive, Dative, and Accusative) plural of yushmad and asmad are substituted वस् and नस् respectively,(when a word precedes, and these substitutes are anudâtta).

Thus ग्रामो वः स्वम्, जनपदो नः स्वम्; ग्रामो वो दीयते, जनपदो नो दीयते; ग्रामो वः पश्यति जनपदो नः पश्यति ॥

तेमयावेकवचनस्य २२ ॥ पदानि ॥ ते, मयौ, एक, वचनस्य ॥

वृत्तिः ॥ युष्मदस्मदोरेकवचनान्तयोः षष्ठीचतुर्थीस्थयोर्यथासंख्यं ते मे इत्येतावादेशौ भवतः ॥

22. For the Genitive and Dative Singular (of yushmad and asmad are substituted) ते and मे respectively, (when a word precedes and these are anudâtta).

Thus ग्रामस्ते स्वम्, ग्रामो मे स्वम्, ग्रामस्ते दीयते, ग्रामो मे दीयते ॥ For the Accusative singular, other substitutes have been taught in the next sûtra, hence ते and मे come only in Genitive and Dative.

त्वामौ द्वितीयायाः ॥ २३ ॥ पदानि ॥ त्वा, मौ, द्वितीयायाः ॥

वृत्तिः ॥ एकवचनस्येति वर्त्तते । द्वितीयाया यदेकवचनं तदन्तयोर्युष्मदस्मदोर्यथासंख्यंत्वा मा इत्येतावादेशौ भवतः ॥

23. For the Accusative Singular of yushmad and asmad are substituted त्वा and मा respectively, under the same circumstances.

The word एकवचनस्य is understood here. Thus ग्रामस्त्वा पश्यति, ग्रामो मा पश्यति ॥

न चवाहाहैवयुक्ते ॥ २४ ॥ पदानि ॥ न, च, वा, ह, अह, एव, युक्ते ॥

वृत्तिः ॥ च वा ह अह एव एभिर्योगे युष्मदस्मदोर्वान्नावादयो न भवन्ति ॥

24. The above substitutions do not take place when there is in connection with the pronouns any of these:— च, 'and' वा, 'or' ह, 'oh! अह 'wonderful', or एव 'only'.

Thus ग्रामस्तव च स्वम्, ग्रामो मम च स्वम् ॥

युवयोश्च स्वम् । आवयोश्च स्वम् । युष्माकं च स्वम् । अस्माकं च स्वम् । ग्रामस्तुभ्यं च दीयते ग्रामो मह्यं च दीयते । युवाभ्यां च दीयते । आवाभ्यां च दीयते । युष्मभ्यं च दीयते । अस्मभ्यं च दीयते । ग्रामस्त्वां च पश्यति । ग्रामो मां चपश्यति । युवां च पश्यति । आवां च पश्यति । युष्मांश्च पश्यति । अस्मांश्च पश्यति ॥ वा । ग्रामस्तव वा स्वम । ग्रामो मम वा स्वम् । युवयोर्वा स्वम् । आवयोर्वा स्वम । युस्माकं वा स्वम । अस्माकं वा स्वम् । ग्रामस्तुभ्यं वा दीयते । ग्रामो मह्यं वा दीयते । युवाभ्यां वा दीयते । आवाभ्यां वा दीयते । युष्मभ्यं वा दीयते । अस्मभ्यं वा दीतये । ग्रामस्त्वां वा पश्यति । ग्रामो मां वा पश्यति । युवां वा पश्यति । आवां वा पश्यति । युष्मान् वा पश्यति । अस्मान्वा पश्यति । ह । ग्रामस्तव ह स्वम् । ग्रामो मम ह स्वम् । युवयोर्ह स्वम् । आवयोर्ह स्वम । युष्माकं ह स्वम् । अस्माकं ह स्वम् । ग्रामस्तुभ्यं ह दीयते । ग्रामो मह्यं ह दीयते । युवाभ्यां ह दीयते । आवाभ्यां ह दीयते । युष्मभ्यं ह दीयते । अस्मभ्यं ह दीयते । ग्रामस्त्वां ह पश्यति । ग्रामो मां ह पश्यति । युवां ह पश्यति । आवां ह पश्यति । युष्मान्ह पश्यति । अस्मान्ह पश्यति । अह । ग्रामस्तवाह स्वम । ग्रामो ममाह स्वम । युवयोरह स्वम् । आवयोरह स्वम् । युष्माकमह स्वम् । अस्माकमह स्वम् । ग्रामस्तुभ्यमह दीयते । ग्रामोमह्यमह दीयत । युवाभ्यामह दीयते । आवाभ्यामह दीयते । युष्मभ्यमह दीयत । अस्मभ्यमह दीयते । ग्रामस्त्वामह पश्यति । ग्रामो मामह पश्यति । युवामह पश्यति । आवामह पश्यति । युष्मानह पश्यति । अस्मानह पश्यति । एव । ग्रामस्तवैव स्वम । ग्रामो ममैव स्वम् । युवयोरेव स्वम् । आवयोरेव स्वम् । युष्माकमेव स्वम् । अस्माकमेव स्वम् । ग्रामस्तुभ्यमेव दीयते । ग्रामो मह्यमेव दीयते । युवाभ्यामेव दीयते । आवाभ्यामेव दीयते । युष्मभ्यमेव दीयते । अस्मभ्यमेव दीयते । ग्रामस्त्वामेव पश्यति । ग्रामो मामेव पश्यति । युवामेव पश्यति । आवामेव पश्यति । युष्मानेव पश्यति । अस्मानेव पश्यति । युक्तग्रहणं साक्षाद्योगप्रतिपत्त्यर्थम् । युक्तयुक्ते प्रतिषेधो न भवति । ग्रामश्च ते स्वम् । नगरं च मे स्वम् ।

The word युक्त is employed in the sûtra to indicate direct conjunction. There is, therefore, where the conjunction is not direct but intermediate the employment of the shorter forms. As ग्रामश्च ते स्वं, नगरं च मे स्वम ॥

The particles च, वा, & c denote conjunction, 'separation' 'wonder'

&c. Where the sense of 'conjunction.' 'separation' &c are inherent in the pronouns yushmad and asmad, and these particles are employed to manifest that sense, there the present sûtra will apply its prohibition.

पश्यार्थैश्चानालोचने ॥ २५ ॥ पदानि ॥ पश्य, अर्थैः, च, अनालोचने ॥

वृत्तिः ॥ पश्यार्था दर्शनार्थाः। दर्शनं ज्ञानम्। आलोचनं चक्षुर्विज्ञानम्। तैः पश्यार्थैरनालोचने वर्त्तमानैर्युक्ते युष्मदस्मदोर्वान्नावादयो न भवन्ति ॥

25. The above substitutions do not take place also in connection with verbs having the sense of "seeing", when physical seeing is not denoted.

The word पश्यार्थाः is equivalent to दर्शनार्थाः, and दर्शन means 'knowledge', i.e. verbs denoting 'to know', आलोचन means perception obtained through sight i.e. physi cal 'seeing' opposed to metaphorical "seeing"="knowing". The substitutions of वां and नौ &c. for युष्मद् and अस्मद् do not take place when these pronouns are employed in connection with verbs denoting 'seeing' (metaphorically) but not 'looking' (physically).

Thus ग्रामस्तव स्वं समीक्ष्यागतः, ग्रामो मम स्वं समीक्ष्यागतः; ग्रामस्तुभ्यं दीयमानं समीक्ष्यागतः, ग्रामो मह्यं दीयमानं समीक्ष्यागतः, ग्रामस्त्वां समीक्ष्यागतः, ग्रामो मां समीक्ष्यागतः ॥

Why do we say when not meaning 'to look'? Observe ग्रामस्त्वा पश्यति, ग्रामो मा पश्यति ॥

Ishti:—With regard to verbs of "seeing", the rule should apply even where the connection is not direct: as, we have already illustrated above.

सपूर्वायाः प्रथमाया विभाषा ॥ २६ ॥ पदानि ॥ स पूर्वायाः, प्रथमायाः, विभाषा ॥

वृत्तिः ॥ विद्यमानपूर्वात्प्रथमान्तात्पदादुत्तरयोर्युष्मदस्मदोर्विभाषा वान्नावादयो न भवन्ति ॥

वार्त्तिकम् ॥ युष्मदस्मदो र्विभाषा अनन्वादेश इतिवक्तव्य ॥

वा० ॥ सर्व एव वान्नावादयोऽन्वादेश विभाषा वक्तव्यः ॥

26. When the pronoun follows after a Nominative, which itself is preceded by another word, then the above substitutions may take place optionally.

Thus ग्रामे कम्बलस्ते स्वम् or ग्रामे कम्बलस्तवस्वम् ॥ ग्रामे कम्बलोमेस्वम् ॥ ग्रामेकम्बलोममस्वम् ॥ ग्रामेकम्बलस्तेदीयते ॥ ग्रामे कम्बलस्तुभ्यं दीयते ॥ ग्रामे कम्बलो मे दीयते ॥ ग्रामे कम्बलो मह्यं दीयते ॥ ग्रामे छात्रास्त्वा पश्यन्ति ॥ ग्रामे छात्रास्त्वां पश्यन्ति ॥ ग्रामे छात्रा मा पश्यन्ति ॥ ग्रामे छात्रा मां पश्यन्ति ॥

Why do we say "which itself is preceded by another word"? Observe कम्बलस्ते स्वम्, कम्बलो मे स्वम् ॥

Why do we say "after a Nominative"? Observe कम्बलो ग्रामे ते स्वम्, कम्बलो ग्रामे मे स्वम् ॥

Vârt.—The option herein taught is restricted to युष्मद् and अस्मद् when not employed in anvâdeśa. But when there is anvâdeśa, then the substitution is *compulsory* and not optional. This vârtika restricts the scope of the sûtra, and makes it a *vyavasthita vibhâshâ*. Therefore, there is no option here, where there is anvâdeśa:—अथो ग्रामे कम्बलस्ते स्वम्, अथो ग्रामे कम्बलो मे स्वम् ॥

Vârt:—Others say, that the substitutes वां, नौ &c are *all* optional, when not employed in anvâdeśa, whether the nominative is preceded by another noun or not. Thus the rules 20, 21, 22, 23 are optional. As: कम्बलस्ते स्वम्, or कम्बलस्तव स्वम्, कम्बलो मे स्वम् or कम्बलो मम स्वम् ॥ Why do we say "when not in anvâdeśa"? Observe अथो कम्बलस्ते स्वम्, अथो कम्बलोमे स्वम् ॥ *Q.* If this is so, where is the necessity of the present sûtra at all? Ans. The present sûtra is for the sake of anvâdeśâ: i.e. the option taught in the present sûtra will take place only then, when there is anvâdeśa and not otherwise; thus अथो ग्रामे कम्बलस्ते स्वम्, or अथो ग्रामे कम्बलस्तव स्वम्, अथो ग्रामे कम्बलो मे स्वम्, or अथो ग्रामे कम्बलो मम स्वम् ॥ In other words, according to this vârtika, rules 20, 21, 22 and 23 are all *optional* in anvâdeśa, but compulsory where is no anvâdeśâ; but when the pronoun is preceded by a nominative which itself is preceded by another word, then the above rules are not compulsory, even in anvâdeśa: there also the option will apply.

तिङो गोत्रादीनि कुत्सनाभीक्ष्ण्ययोः ॥ २७ ॥ पदानि ॥ तिङः, गोत्रआदीनि, कुत्सन, आभीक्ष्ण्ययोः ॥

वृत्तिः ॥ तिङन्तात्पराणि गोत्रादीनि कुत्सने आभीक्ष्ण्ये चार्थे वर्त्तमानानि अनुदात्तानि भवन्ति ॥

27. The words गोत्र &c, become unaccented after a finite verb, when a contempt or a repetition is intended.

Thus पचति गोत्रम्, जल्पति गोत्रम्, when contempt is meant.

Here पचति गोत्रं means 'he proclaims his Gotra &c, so that he may get food &c'. पचति is from the root पचि व्यक्तिकरणे 'to make evident' (Bhu. 184). Similarly जल्पति गोत्रम् "he repeatedly utters, his descent &c, in order to get married &c". Where contempt is not meant, it has the force of repetition, i. e. he repeatedly utters his Gotra as one is bound to do, in marriage-rites &c. And पचति पचति गोत्रम्, जल्पति जल्पति गोत्रम् when repetition or intensity is denoted. Similarly पचति ब्रुवम्, पचति पचति ब्रुवम् ॥ The word ब्रुवं is a noun derived from the root ब्रू by the affix कन्, the वच् substitution for ब्रू has not taken place, as an anomaly.

1 गोत्र, 2 ब्रुव, 3 प्रवचन, 4 प्रहसन, 5 प्रकथन, 6 प्रत्ययन, 7 प्रपञ्च, 8 प्राय, 9 न्याय, 10 प्रचक्षण, 11 विचक्षण, 12 अवचक्षण, 13 स्वाध्याय, 14 भूयिष्ठ, 15 वा नाम (नाम वा) 16 प्रहसन, 17 प्रयजन,

The word नाम optionally becomes anudâtta: in the alternative, it is first-acute. Thus पचति नाम or पचति नाम ॥

Why do we say 'after a finite verb'? Observe कुत्सितं गोत्रम् ॥

Why do we say "Gotra and the rest"? Observe पचति पापम् ॥ Here पापं is an adverb

Why do we say 'when contempt or repetition is meant'? Observe खनति गोत्रं समेत्य कूपं ॥ "He digs a well having assembled the Gotra".

The words 'contempt and repetition' in the text qualify the whole sentence or sûtra, and not the word गोत्रादि nor the word अनुदात्त understood. For we find that whereever the word गोत्रादि is used in this Chapter, it always implies the sense of 'contempt or repetition'. Thus the word गोत्रादि is used in VIII. 1. 57 and there also the sense is of contempt and repetition.

तिङ्ङतिङः ॥ २८ ॥ पदानि ॥ तिङ्, अतिङः ॥

वृत्तिः ॥ तिङन्तं पदमतिङन्तात्पदात्परमनुदात्तं भवति ॥

28. A finite verb is unaccented, when a word precedes it, which is not a finite verb.

Thus देवदत्तः पचति ॥ Why do we say "a finite verb"? Observe नीलमुत्पलम्, शुक्लं वस्त्रम् ॥

Why do we say 'when the preceding word is not a finite verb'? Observe भवति पचति 'the act of cooking exists' = पाक क्रिया भवति ॥ Here the word भवति is a finite verb, therefore the verb pachati does not lose its accent. So also तरनिरिज् जयति, क्षेति, पुष्यति 'successful he conquers, rules, thrives'. अस्मभ्यं जिषि योत्सिच "for us conquer and fight". The word अतिङः is in one sense redundant, because in one simple sentence, two finite verbs cannot be employed; one sentence consists of one finite verb only. But the very fact of this sûtra indicates that the condition of समानवाक्य does not apply to this sûtra; so that the two words need not be portions of the *same* sentence, for the application of this nighâta: as we have already explained in VIII. 1. 19. Other examples are: अग्निमीळे पुरोहितं (Rv. I. 1. 1). स इद्देवेषु गच्छति (Rv. I. 1. 4), अग्ने सुपायनो भव (Rv. V. 1. 1), यजमानस्य पशून् पाहि ॥

न लुट् ॥ २९ ॥ पदानि ॥ न, लुट् ॥

वृत्तिः ॥ पूर्वेणातिप्रसक्ते प्रतिषेध आरभ्यते । लुडन्तं तिङन्तं नानुदात्तं भवति ॥

29. But the Periphrastic Future is not unaccented, when it is preceded by a word which is not a finite verb.

This restricts the scope of the last sûtra which was rather too wide. Thus श्वः कर्त्ता, श्वः कर्त्तारौ, मासेन कर्त्तारः ॥ The Sârvadhâtuka affixes डा, रौ, रस्, are anudâtta after the affix तासि by VI. 1. 186, the whole affix तास् becomes udâtta (III. 1. 3) and where the टि portion of तास् i. e. the syllable आस्, is elided before the affix डा, there also the आ of डा becomes udâtta, because the udâtta has been elided. See VI. 1. 161.

निपातैर्यद्यदिहन्तकुविन्नेच्चेच्चण्कच्चिद्यत्रयुक्तम् ॥ ३० ॥ पदानि ॥ निपातैः, यद्, यदि, हन्त, कु विन्, नेत्, चेत्, चण्, कच्चित्, यत्र, युक्तम् ॥

वृत्तिः ॥ नेति वर्त्तते । यत् यदि हन्त कुवित् नेत् चेत् चण् कच्चित् यत्र इत्येतैर्निपातैर्युक्तं तिङन्तं नानुदात्तं भवति ॥

30. The finite verb retains its accent in connection with the particles यत्, 'that', 'because'; यदि, 'if', हन्त, 'also'!, 'O!', कुवित्, 'well', नेत्, 'not', चेत्, 'if', च 'if', कच्चित् (interrogative particle, implying 'I hope' or 'I hope not)', and यत्र 'where'.

Thus यत् करोति, यत् पचति, यदि करोति or यदि पचति, हन्त करोति, हन्त पचति, कुवित् करोति, कुवित् पचति, नेज्जिह्मायन्त्यो नरकं पताम (Nir. I. 11), स चेद् भुङ्क्ते, स चेद् अधीते ॥ The particle चण् with the indicatory ण् has the force of चेत् ॥ Thus अयं च मरिष्यति = अयं चेत् मरिष्यति ॥ Other examples are त्वम् च सोम नो वशो जीवातुम् न मरामहे 'if thou, Soma willest us to live, we shall not die' आ च गच्छान् मित्रमेना दधाम "if he will come here, we will make friends with him." इन्द्रश्च मृलयाति नः, नतः पश्चादघं नशत् "If Indra makes us happy &c". This rule does not apply to the च which is a conjunction meaning 'and'. So also: कच्चिद् भुङ्क्ते, कच्चिद् अधीते' यत्र भुङ्क्ते, यत्राधीते॥

Why do we say "with particles"? Observe यत् कूजति शकटम् = गच्छत् कूजति शकटम् ॥ Here यत् is not a particle, but the Present Participle of the root इण् 'to go'. It means गच्छत् 'the car creaks while going'. Rule VIII. 1. 28 applies here.

Q. Now by the rule of Pratipadokta &c. that यत् should only be taken, which is a Particle; moreover it is read in connection with other Particles like यदि &c, so it must be a Particle. How then can the Present Participle यत् be taken at all? Ans.—This sûtra indicates that the प्रतिपदोक्त rule and the साहचर्य rule do not apply here. Thus the word यावत् formed with the affix वतुप् (V. 2. 39) is also included in the word यावत् of this sûtra. As तावदुषो राधो अस्मभ्यं, रास्व यावत् स्तोतृभ्यो अरदो गृणानाः = यावतोऽश्वान प्रतीगृह्णीयात् ॥

Why do we use the word युक्तं "in connection with". Observe यत्र क्व च ते मनो दक्ष दधस उत्तरम् ॥

Other examples are: यं यज्ञं परिभूरसि (Rv. I. 1. 4.) 'what offering thou protectest'. यत्र नः पूर्वे पितरः परेयुः 'whither our fathers of old departed'. अद्या मुरीय यदि यातुधानो अस्मि 'let me die on the spot, if I am a sorcerer', हन्तेयान् पृथिवीम् विभजामहै "come on, let us share up this earth". ब्रह्मा चेद्धस्तम् अग्रहीत् 'if a Brahman has grasped her hand', नेत् त्वा तपाति सूरो अर्चिषा 'that the sun may not burn thee with his beam' उक्थेभिः कुविद् आगमत् 'will he come hither for our praises'(Whitney's Grammar, Para 595).

नह प्रत्यारम्भे ॥ ३१ ॥ पदानि ॥ नह, प्रत्यारम्भे ॥

वृत्तिः ॥ नह इत्येतेन युक्ते प्रत्यारम्भे तिङन्तं नानुदात्तं भवति ॥

31. The finite verb retains its accent in connection with नह when employed in the sense of forbidding.

When something urged by one, is rejected insultingly by another, then the reply made by the first tauntingly, with a negation, is pratyârambha. Thus A says to B: "Eat this please". B rejects the offer repeatedly, in anger or jest. Then A in anger or jest says 'No, you will eat"—as नह भोक्ष्यसे ॥ Here भोक्ष्यसे retains its accent, which is acute on the middle, for स becomes accentless as it follows अदुपदेश (VI. 1. 186), and स्य becomes udâtta by the प्रत्ययस्वर (III. 1. 3).

Another example is नहाध्येष्यसे 'No, you will study'. Why do we say, 'when asseverative'? Observe नह वै तस्मिंश्च लोके दक्षिणमिच्छन्ति "Verily in that world they do not wish for fee". Here it is pure negation. तस्मिन् is first acute by फिट् accent, लोके is final acute because it is formed by अच् of पचादि (III. 1. 134), दक्षिण is first acute, because it is a Pronoun ending in अ (स्वाङ्गशिटामदन्तानाम् Phit II. 6) and इच्छन्ति is anudâtta by VIII. 1. 28.

सत्यं प्रश्ने ॥ ३२ ॥ पदानि ॥ सत्यम्, प्रश्ने ॥

वृत्तिः ॥ सत्यमित्यनेन युक्तं तिङन्तं नानुदात्तं भवति प्रश्ने ॥

32. The finite verb retains its accent in connection with सत्य when used in asking a question.

Thus सत्यं भोक्ष्यसे 'Truly will you eat'? सत्यमध्येष्यसे ॥ Why do we say 'in questioning'? Observe सत्यं वक्ष्यामि नानृतं 'I shall tell the truth, not falsehood'. सत्यमिद्वा उ तं वयमिन्द्रं स्तवाम ॥

अङ्गाप्रातिलोम्ये ॥ ३३ ॥ पदानि ॥ अङ्ग, अप्रातिलोम्ये ॥

वृत्तिः ॥ अङ्ग इत्यनेन युक्तं तिङन्तमप्रातिलोम्ये गम्यमाने नानुदात्तं भवति ॥

33. The finite verb retains its accent in connection with अङ्ग when used in a friendly assertion.

Anything done to injure another is prati-loma, opposite of this is apratiloma, or friendliness. In fact, it is equal to anuloma. Thus अङ्ग पच 'yes, you may cook'. Here aṇga has the force of friendly permission. So also अङ्ग पठ ॥ But when it has the force of pratiloma, we have:—अङ्ग कूज ३ वृषल ॥ इदानीं ज्ञास्यसि जाल्म "Well, chuckle O sinner! soon wilt thou learn, O coward". Here अङ्ग is used in the sense of censure, for chuckling is a thing not liked by the person: and is pratiloma action: for pluta-vowel see VIII. 2. 96.

हि च ॥ ३४ ॥ पदानि ॥ हि, च ॥

वृत्तिः ॥ हिइत्यनेन युक्तं तिङन्तमप्रातिलोम्ये नानुदात्तं भवति ॥

34. The finite verb retains its accent in connection with हि when used in a friendly assertion.

Thus स हि कुरु, सहि पच, सहि पठ ॥ Why do we say 'in friendly assertion'? Observe स हि कूज वृषल । इदानीं ज्ञास्यासि जाल्म ॥

छन्दस्यनेकमपि साकाङ्क्षम् ॥ ३५ ॥ पदानि ॥ छन्दसि, अनेकम्, अपि, साकाङ्क्षम् ॥

वृत्तिः ॥ हि चेत्यनुवर्त्तते छन्दसि विषये हियुक्तं तिङन्तं साकाङ्क्षमनेकमपि नानुदात्तं भवति ॥

35. In the Veda, the finite verb retains its accent (but not always), in connection with हि, when it stands in correlation to another verb, even more than one.

That is sometimes one verb, sometimes more than one verb retain their accent. Thus of more than one verb, we have the following example:—अनृतं हि मत्तो वदति। पाप्मा एनं वि पुनाति 'Because the drunkard tells falsehood, therefore sin will make him impure: i. e. he does incur sin". Here both verbs वदति and विपुनाति retain their accent: and हि has the force of यत् 'because'. According to Kaiyyata the meaning of this sentence is यस्मात् मत्तोऽनृतं वदति, तस्मादनृतवदन दोषेण न युज्यते i. e. a drunkard does not incur the sin of telling a falsehood, because he is not in his senses. See Maitr. Sanhita I. 11. 6. As regards one verb in a correlated sentence retaining its accent and the other losing it,we have:—अग्निर्हि पूर्वमुदजयत् तमिन्द्रोऽनूदजयत् ॥ Here the first retains its accent and the second not. The force of हि is to denote here cause and its effect. So also:—अजा ह्यग्नेरजनिष्ट गर्भात् (or गर्भम्), सा वा अपश्यज् जनितारमग्रे (Taittariya Samhitâ IV. 2. 10, 4). The word अजनिष्ट is first acute, the augment अट् having the accent; while अपश्यत् is all anudâtta.

यावद्यथाभ्याम् ॥ ३६ ॥ पदानि ॥ यावत्, यथाभ्याम् ॥

वृत्तिः ॥ यावद्यथा इत्येताभ्यां युक्तं तिङन्तं नानुदात्तं भवति ॥

36. A finite verb retains its accent in connection with यावत् and यथा ॥

Thus यावद् भुङ्क्ते, यथाभुङ्क्ते; यावदधीते यथाधीते, देवदत्तः पचति यावत्, देवदत्तः पचति यथा ॥ The meaning is that the verb retains its accent, even when यावत् and यथा follow after it. Another example is यथा चित् कण्वमावतम् ॥ The word आवतम् is the Imperative (लोट्) Second Person Dual of the root अव् ॥ यावत् स्तोतृभ्योऽरदोगृणानाः ॥ The verb अरदः is Imperfect (लङ्) Second Person singular of the root रद् 'to scratch'. The accent, is on अ (the augment).

पूजायां नानन्तरम् ॥ ३७ ॥ पदानि ॥ पूजायाम्, न, अनन्तरम् ॥

वृत्तिः ॥ यावद्यथा इत्येताभ्यां युक्तमनन्तरं तिङन्तं पूजायां विषये नानुदात्तं न भवति किं तर्हि अनुदात्तमेव ॥

37. But not so when these particles यावत् and यथा immediately precede the verb and denote 'praise'.

That is, the verb loses its accent, and becomes anudâtta. Thus यावत् पचति शोभनम्, यथा पचति शोभनम्, यावत् करोति चारु ॥

Why do we say when denoting 'praise'? Observe यावद् भुङ्क्ते, यथा भुङ्क्ते ॥
Why do we say 'immediately'? Observe यावद् देवदत्तः पचति शोभनं, यथा देवदत्तः करोति चारु ॥ Here the verbs retain their accent by the last sûtra.

उपसर्गव्यपेतं च ॥ ३८ ॥ पदानि ॥ उपसर्ग, व्यपेतम्, च ॥

वृत्तिः ॥ यावद्यथाभ्यां युक्तं उपसर्गव्यपेतं च पूजायां विषये नानुदात्तं न भवति किं तर्हि अनुदात्तमेव भवति ॥

38. A finite verb loses its accent when it denotes 'praise' and is joined immediately with यावत् and यथा through the intervention of an upasarga or verbal-preposition.

The last sûtra taught that the verb loses its accent when *immediately* preceded by यावत् and यथा ॥ This qualifies the word 'immediately' and teaches that the intervention of a Preposition does not debar immediateness. Thus यथा प्रकरोति चारु, यथा प्रपचति शोभनं, यावत् प्रकरोति चारु, यावत् प्रपचति शोभनम् ॥

The word 'immediately' is understood here also. Thus यावद् देवदत्तः प्रपचति, शोभनं, यथा विष्णु मित्रः प्रकरोति चारु ॥ The upasarga प्र has udâtta accent. Prof. Bohtlingk's Edition reads the sûtra as व्यवेतं ॥

तुपश्यपश्यताहैः पूजायाम् ॥ ३९ ॥ पदानि ॥ तु, पश्य, पश्यत, अहैः, पूजायाम् ॥

वृत्तिः ॥ तु पश्य पश्यत अह इत्येतैर्युक्तं तिङन्तं नानुदात्तं भवति पूजायां विषये ॥

39. A finite verb retains its accent in connection with तु, पश्य, पश्यत, and अह, when meaning 'praise'.

Thus माणवकस्तु भुङ्क्ते शोभनम्; पश्य माणवको भुङ्क्ते शोभनं, पश्यत माणवको भुङ्क्ते शोभनम्, अह माणवको भुङ्क्ते शोभनम् ॥ Why do we say 'when meaning praise'? Observe, पश्य मृगा धावन्ति ॥

The repetition of the word पूजायाम् here, though its anuvritti could have been supplied from VIII. 1. 37, shows that the negation of that sûtra does not extend here: for the पूजायाम् of that sûtra is connected with two negatives, the न of that sûtra, and the न of VIII. 1. 29, but the पूजायाम् of this sûtra is connected with the general न of VIII. 1. 29 only.

Another example is आदह स्वधामनु पुनर्गर्भत्वमेरिरे ॥

अहो च ॥ ४० ॥ पदानि ॥ अहो, च ॥

वृत्तिः ॥ अहो इत्यनेन युक्तं तिङन्तं नानुदात्तं भवति पूजायां विषये ॥

40. A finite verb retains its accent when in connection with अहो meaning 'praise'.

Thus अहो देवदत्तः पचति शोभनं, अहो विष्णुमित्रः करोति चारु ॥ The separation of this अहो from तु &c, of the last sûtra, indicates that the next rule applies to अहो only. Had अहो been joined with तु &c, then Rule VIII. 1. 41, would have applied to तु &c, which is not desired. Hence the making of it a separate sûtra.

शेषे विभाषा ॥ ४१ ॥ पदानि ॥ शेषे, विभाषा ॥

वृत्तिः ॥ अहो इत्यनेन युक्तं तिङन्तं शेषे विभाषा नानुदात्तं भवति ॥

41. A finite verb retains its accent optionally when in connection with अहो in the remaining cases (i. e. where it does not mean praise).

What is the शेष alluded to here? The शेष means here senses other than पूजा or 'praise'. Thus कटमहो करिष्यसि or कटमहो करिष्यसि ॥ This is a speech uttered in anger or envy and not in praise (असूया वचनं) ॥ So also मम गेहमेष्यसि ॥

The word शेष is employed in the sûtra simply for the sake of distinctness; for sûtra 40 applies to cases of pujâ, while this sûtra will give option in cases other than pujâ.

पुरा च परीप्सायाम् ॥ ४२ ॥ पदानि ॥ पुरा, च, परीप्सायाम् ॥

वृत्तिः ॥ पुरा इत्यनेन युक्तं तिङन्तं परीप्सायामर्थे विभाषा नानुदात्तं भवति ॥

42. A finite verb retains its accent optionally in connection with पुरा when it means 'haste' (i. e. when पुरा means 'before').

The word परीप्सा means त्वरा or 'quick'. Thus अधीष्व माणवक पुरा विद्योतते विद्युत्, or पुरा स्तनयति स्तनयित्नु ॥ The word पुरा here expresses the future occurrence which is imminent or very near at hand. It is against the rule of Dharmaśâstras to study while it thunders of lightens.

Why do we say 'when meaning *haste*'? Observe नडेन स्म पुराधीयते ॥ Here the word पुरा expresses a past time; that is, it means "long ago". So also ऊर्णया स्म पुराधीयते ॥ See III. 2. 118 and 122, for the employment of पुरा in the Past Tense, and III. 3. 4, for the Present.

नन्वित्यनुज्ञैषणायाम् ॥ ४३ ॥ पदानि ॥ ननु, इति, अनुज्ञा, एषणायाम् ॥

वृत्तिः ॥ ननु इत्यनेन युक्तं तिङन्तं नानुदात्तं भवति अनुज्ञैषणायां विषये ॥

43. A finite verb retains its accent in connection with ननु, when with this Particle, permission is asked.

The word एषणा means 'asking, praying'. The word अनुज्ञा means 'permission'. The compound अनुज्ञैषणा means 'asking of permission'. Thus ननु करोमि भोः, "may I do it, sir"; ननु गच्छामि भोः 'can I go sir'. The sense is 'give me permission to do or to go'.

Why do we say when 'asking for permission'? Observe अकार्षीः कटं देवदत्त? ननु करोमि भोः 'Devadatta hast thou made the mat? Well, I am making it'. Here ननु has the force of an answering particle, and not used in asking permission and hence the verb loses its accent.

किं क्रियाप्रश्नेनुपसर्गमप्रतिषिद्धम् ॥ ४४ ॥ पदानि ॥ किम्, क्रिया-प्रश्ने, अनु-पसर्गम्-अप्रतिषिद्धम् ॥

वृत्तिः ॥ किमित्येतत्क्रियाप्रश्ने यदा वर्त्तते तदानेन युक्तं तिङन्तमनुपसर्गमप्रतिषिद्धं नानुदात्तं भवति ॥

44. A finite verb retains its accent in connection with किम्, when with this is asked a question relating to an action, and when the verb is not preceded by a Preposition or by a Negation.

Thus किं देवदत्तः पॅचति, आहो स्विद् भुङ्क्ते ॥ किं देवदत्तः शेतें, आहो स्विदधीते ॥ Here some say, that the first verb (पचति or शेते) being directly joined with किं retains its accent, whilst the second verb (भुङ्क्ते or अधीते) not being joined with किं, loses its accent by the general rule VIII. I. 28. Others say, though the word किं is heard in connection with one verb only, yet as both verbs are objects of doubt, therefore, किं is logically connected with both of them, and so both verbs retain their accents. Thus भुङ्क्ते will retain its accent according to this view.

Why do we say when the question relates to a क्रिया or action? The rule will not apply, when the question relates to an object or साधन ॥ Thus किं देवदत्त ओदनं पचति आहोस्विच्छाकं ॥

Why do we say "when a question is asked"? Observe किमधीते देवदत्तः ॥ Here किं is used to express contempt, and not to ask a question.

Why do we say 'not preceded by a Preposition'? Observe किं देवदत्तः प्र पचति आहोस्वित् प्रकरोति ॥

Why do we say "not preceded by a negative particle". Observe, किं देवदत्तो न पठति आहोस्विन् न करोति ॥

लोपे विभाषा ॥ ४५ ॥ पदानि ॥ लोपे, विभाषा ॥

वृत्तिः ॥ किमो लोपे क्रियाप्रश्ने तिङन्तमनुपसर्गमप्रतिषिद्धं विभाषा नानुदात्तं भवति ॥

45. When however किम् is not added in asking such a question, the finite verb may optionally retain its accent.

When किम् is elided in asking a question relating to an action, the finite verb which is not preceded by a Preposition or a Negative Particle, optionally does not become anudâtta. When is there the elision of this किम् because no rule of Pânini has taught it? When the sense is that of an interrogation, but the word किम् is not used. In short, the word 'lopa' here does not mean the Grammatical substitute, but merely non-use. As देवदत्तः पॅचति (or

पचति)आहांरिशत् पैठति(or पठति) Here the sentence is interrogative, even without the employment of किम् ॥ The option of this sûtra is a Prâpta-vibhâsha, as it is connected with the sense of किम् ॥ The counter-examples are the same as in the last aphorism, but without किम् ॥

एहिमन्ये प्रहासे ऌट् ॥ ४६ ॥ पदानि ॥ एहि, मन्ये, प्रहासे, ऌट् ॥

वृत्तिः ॥ एहिमन्ये इत्यनेन युक्तं ऌडन्तं तिङन्तं नानुदात्तं भवति प्रहासे ॥

46. In connection with एहिमन्ये used derisively, the First Future that follows it, retains its accent.

The word प्रहास means great laughter, i.e. derision, mockery, raillery, jeering, gibing, sneering. Thus एहि मन्ये ओदनं भोक्ष्यसे, नहि भोक्ष्यसे, भुक्तः सोऽतिथिभिः ॥ एहि मन्ये रथेन यास्यसि, नहि यास्यसि, यातस् तेन पिता ॥ The word एहि is the Imperative second Person of the root इण् preceded by the preposition आङ् ॥

Why do we say "used derisively'? Observe एहि मन्यसे ओदनं भोक्ष्ये इति; सुष्ठु च मन्यसे, साधु च मन्यसे ॥

By sûtra VIII. I. 51, *infra*, after the Imperative एहि which is a verb of 'motion' (गत्यर्थ), the following First Future (ऌट्) would have retained its accent. The present sûtra makes a niyama or restriction, namely that in connection with the Imperative एहि मन्ये, the ऌट् is accented only then when 'derision' is meant and not otherwise. Thus the ऌट् loses its accent here:— एहि मन्यसे ओदनं भोक्ष्ये ॥ The employment of the First Person in मन्ये in the sûtra is not intended to be taught: for by I. 4. 106, the verb मन् (मन्यते) takes the affix of the First Person instead of the second, when 'derision' is meant and not otherwise. When प्रहास is not intended, the proper personal affix of the Second Person is employed. The employment of the First Person ceases there also by this restrictive rule. Thus एहि मन्यसे ओदनं भोक्ष्ये ॥

The above counter example is given according to Kâśika, according to which एहि मन्ये इति उत्तमोपादानमतन्त्रम् ॥ But according to Mahâbhâshya, the counter-example is एहि मन्ये रथेन यास्यसि ॥ Here यास्यसि loses its accent. The meaning of the above is त्वं रथेन यास्यसि इति अहं मन्ये, एहि ॥ According to Kaiyyata, this would be an example also under the rule, the First Person not being necessary:—एहि मन्यसे रथेन यास्यामि ॥

जात्वपूर्वम् ॥ ४७ ॥ पदानि ॥ जातु, अपूर्वम् ॥

वृत्तिः ॥ जातु इत्येतदविद्यमानपूर्वं तेन युक्तं तिङन्तं नानुदात्तं भवति ॥

47. A finite verb retains its accent after जातु, when this जातु is not preceded by any other word.

Thus जातु भोक्ष्यसे, जातु अध्यर्ष्यसे, जातु करिष्यामि । Here से is anudâtta by VI. 1. 186, as it is an sârvadhâtuka affix coming after an अदुपदेश; the word जातु is first acute, as it is a Nipâta. Why do we say 'when not preceded by any other word'? Observe:—कटं जातु करिष्यति ॥ The word कटं is end-acute as it is a फिट् or noun.

किंवृत्तं च चिदुत्तरम् ॥ ४८ ॥ पदानि ॥ किम्वृत्तम्, च, चिदुत्तरम् ॥

वृत्तिः ॥ किमोवृत्तं किंवृत्तं, किंवृत्तग्रहणेन तद्विभक्त्यन्तं प्रतीयाडुतरडतमौ च प्रत्ययौ, तत्किंवृत्तं चिदुत्तरमविद्यमानपूर्वं यत्तेन युक्तं तिङन्तं नानुदात्तं भवति ॥

48. Also after a form of किम्, when the particle चित् follows it, and when no other word precedes such form of किम्, the finite verb retains its accent.

The word किम्वृत्तं is a Genitive Tatpurusha meaning किमोवृत्तं ॥ The word किम्वृत्तं means any form of किम् with its case-affixes, as well as the forms of किम् when it takes the affixes डतर and डतम ॥ Thus कश्चिद् भुङ्क्ते, कश्चिद् भोजयति, कश्चिद् अधीते, केनचित् करोति, कस्मै चिद् ददाति, कतरश्चित् करोति, कतमश्चिद् भुङ्क्ते ॥

Why do we say 'followed by चित्'? Observe को भुङ्क्ते ॥

The word अपूर्वं of the last sûtra qualifies this also; therefore, the verb loses its accent here:— देवदत्तः किंचित् पठति ॥

आहोउताहो चानन्तरम् ॥ ४९ ॥ पदानि ॥ आहो, उताहो, च, अनन्तरम् ॥

वृत्तिः ॥ निघातप्रतिषेधोनुवर्त्तते ॥ अपूर्वमिति च ॥ आहो उताहो इत्येताभ्यामपूर्वाभ्यां युक्तमनन्तरं तिङन्तं नानुदात्तं भवति ॥

49. Also after an immediately preceding आहो and उताहो, when these follow after no other word, the verb retains its accent.

The prohibition of *nighâta* or want of accentuation is understood here, so also there is the anuvṛitti of अपूर्वं from the last.

Thus आहो or उताहो भुङ्क्ते, उताहो पठति ॥ Why do we say 'immediately preceding'? In the following sûtra will be taught option, when these particles do not immediately precede the verb.

Why do we say "when no word precedes them"? Observe देवदत्त आहो or उताहो भुङ्क्ते ॥

शेषे विभाषा ॥ ५० ॥ पदानि ॥ शेषे, विभाषा ॥

वृत्तिः ॥ आहो उताहो इत्येताभ्यां युक्तं तिङन्तं नानुदात्तं शेषे विभाषा भवति ॥ कश्च शेषः यदन्यदनन्तरात् ॥

50. When the above-mentioned Particles आहो and उताहो do not immediately precede the verb, the verb may optionally retain its accent.

Thus आहो देवदत्तः पॅचाति or पचाति ॥ उताहो देवदत्तः पॅठाति or पठाति ॥

गत्यर्थलोटा लृण्नचेत्कारकं सर्वान्यत् ॥ ५१ ॥ पदानि ॥ गत्यर्थ-लोटा, लृट्, न, चेत्, कारकम्, सर्व-अन्यत् ॥

वृत्तिः ॥ गतिना समानार्था गत्यर्थाः; गत्यर्थानां धातूनां लोट् गत्यर्थलोट्; तेन गत्यर्थलोटा युक्तं लृडन्तं तिङन्तं नानुदात्तं भवति, न चेत्कारकं सर्वान्यद्भवति ॥

यत्रैव कारके कर्त्तरि कर्म्मणि वा लोट् तत्रैव यदि लृडपि भवतीत्यर्थः। कर्तृकर्म्मणी एवात्र तिङन्तवाच्य कारकग्रहणेन गृह्येते न करणादि कारकान्तरम् ॥

51. The First Future retains its accent in connection with the Imperative of a verb denoting 'motion' ('to go, 'to come' to start' &c), but only in that case, when the subject and object of both the verbs are not wholly different one from another.

Those verbs which have similar meaning with the word गति 'motion' are called गत्यर्थाः ॥ The Imperative of the गत्यर्थ verbal roots, is called गत्यर्थ-लोट् ॥ In connection with such an Imperative of verbs of 'motion', the First Futue does not become anudâtta, if the kâraka is not all different. The sense is, with whatever case-relation (kâraka), whether the Subject or Object, the Imperative is employed, with the same kâraka, the First Future must be employed. In connection with the fiinte verb here, the word कारक denotes the Subject and Object only, and not any other kâraka, such as Instrument, &c.

Thus आँगच्छ देवदत्तग्रा॑मं, द्रक्ष्यॅस्येनम् 'Come O Devadatta to the village, thou shalt see it'. Here the subjects of both verbs आगच्छ and द्रक्ष्यसि are the same, and the objects of both verbs are also the same, namely ग्रामं and एनम् ॥ आ is a Preposition and is accented, गच्छ and देवदत्त both lose their accent by VIII. I. 19 and 28, ग्राम is first-acute being formed by the नित् affix मन् ॥ So also आगच्छ देवदत्त ग्रामं, ओदनं भोक्ष्यसे "Come, O Devadatta! to the village, you will eat rice". Here the subjects of both verbs are the same, only the objects are different, and so the rule still applies. आहर देवदत्त शालीन्, यज्ञदत्त एतान् भोक्ष्येतॅ ॥ Here the subjects are different, but the objects are the same, namely शालीन् ॥ Similarly उह्यन्तां देवदत्तेन शालयः, यज्ञदत्तेन भोक्ष्यॅन्ते "Let the rice be carried by Devadatta, and let them be eaten by Yajñadatta."

Why do we say 'verbs of motion'? Observe पच देवदत्त ओदनं, भोक्ष्यसे एनम् ॥

Why do we say 'After the Imperative'? Observe आगच्छेर्देवदत्त ग्रामं, द्रक्ष्यस्येनम् ॥ Here the Potential mood is used.

Why do we say the 'First Future'? Obseve आगच्छ देवदत्त ग्रामं, पश्यसि एनम् ॥ Here the Present Tense is used.

Why do we say 'if the kâraka is not *wholly* different'? Observe

आगच्छ देवदत्त ग्रामं, पिता ते ओदनं मोक्ष्यते ॥ उह्यन्तां देवदत्तेन शालयः, सक्तवस्तेन प्रास्यन्ते ॥ उह्यन्तां is the Imperative of वह 'to carry'.

Why do we use the word सर्व 'wholly'? Observe आगच्छ देवदत्त ग्रामं, त्वं च अहं च द्रक्ष्याव एनम् ॥ Here also there is prohibition of *nighâta* and the First Future retains its accent, for the subject of the Future is not *wholly* different from that of the Imperative. For here the subject of the Imperative is the subject also of the Future, though only partly, in conjunction with another. Moreover, the object here in both is the same. Had सर्व not been used in the sûtra, where the sentence would have remained the same, there the rule would have applied, and not where the sentences became different.

लोट् च ॥ ५२ ॥ पदानि ॥ लोट्, च ॥

वृत्तिः ॥ लोडन्तं तिङन्तं गत्यर्थलोटा युक्तं नानुदात्तं भवति, न चेत्कारकं सर्वान्यद्भवति ॥

52. Also an Imperative, following after an Imperative of verbs of 'motion', retains its accent, when the subject or object of both the verbs, is not wholly different.

Thus आगच्छ देवदत्त ग्रामं पश्य ॥ आव्रज विष्णुमित्र ग्रामं शाधि ॥ आगम्यतां देवदत्तेन ग्रामो दृश्यतां यज्ञदत्तेन ॥

But not here पच देवदत्तौदनं, भुङ्क्ष्वैनम् because the first Imperative is not one of गत्यर्थ verb. Nor here, आगच्छेर्देवदत्त ग्रामं पश्येनम् because the first verb is not Imperative but Potential.

If the subject and object of both Imperatives are wholly different, the rule will not apply. Thus आगच्छ देवदत्त ग्रामं, पश्यतु रामं यज्ञदत्तः ॥

By the force of the anuvritti of सर्व the rule will apply to the following: आगच्छ देवदत्त ग्रामं, त्वं चाहं च पश्याव: ॥

The separation of this sûtra from the last is for the sake of the subsequent sûtra, by which the 'option' is with regard to लोट् and not लृट् ॥

विभाषितं सोपसर्गमनुत्तमम् ॥५३॥ पदानि ॥ विभाषितम्, सोपसर्गम्, अनुत्तमम् ॥

वृत्तिः ॥ सर्वं पूर्वमनुवर्त्तते ॥ प्राप्तविभाषेयं, लोडन्तं सोपसर्गमुत्तमवर्जितं गत्यर्थलोटा युक्तं तिङन्तं विभाषितं नानुदात्तं भवति न चेत्कारकं सर्वान्यद्भवति ॥

53. An Imperative preceded by a Preposition, and not in the First Person, following after an Imperative of verbs of 'motion', may optionally retain its accent, when the Kâraka is not wholly different.

The whole of the preceding sûtra is understood here. This is a Prâpta-vibhâshâ. Thus आगच्छ देवदत्त ग्रामं प्रविश or प्रविश ॥ आगच्छ देवदत्त ग्रामंप्रशाधि or प्रशाधि ॥ When the verb is accented, the upasarga loses its accent by VIII. I. 71.

Why do we say सोपसर्ग 'joined with a Preposition'? When there is no Preposition, there is no *option* allowed, and the last rule will apply. As आगच्छ देवदत्त ग्रामंपश्य ॥

Why do we say अन्—उत्तमं 'not a First Person'? Observe आ गच्छानि देवदत्त, ग्रामं प्रविशानि ॥

हन्त च ॥ ५४ ॥ पदानि ॥ हन्त, च, ॥

वृत्तिः ॥ पूर्वं सर्वमनुवर्त्तते गत्यर्थलोटं वर्जयित्वा हन्त इत्यनेन युक्तं लोडन्तं सोपसर्गमुत्तमवर्जितं विभाषितं नानुदात्तं भवति ॥

54. An Imperative, with a Preposition preceding it, may optionally retain its accent, in connection with हन्त, but not the First Person.

With the exception of गत्यर्थ लोटा &c, the whole of the preceding sûtra is u nderstood here.

Thus हन्त प्रँ विश or प्रविशँ, हन्त प्रँ शाधि or प्रशाधिँ ॥ But no option is allowed here हन्त कुरु, as it is not preceded by a preposition. Here rule VIII. I. 30, makes the accent compulsory after हन्त ॥ So also हन्त प्रभुनँजावहै, हन्त प्रभुनँजामहै, where the 1st Person is used, the verb retains its accent compulsorily by VIII. I. 30.

The word प्रभुनजावहै is Imperative First Person, Dual of the root भुज् in Atmane pada (I. 3. 66). The Personal ending वहै is anudâtta by VI. I. 186, because the verb is anudâtta-it. The vikaraṇa न therefore retains its accent.

आम एकान्तरमामन्त्रितमनन्तिके ॥ ५५ ॥ पदानि ॥ आमः, एक-अन्तरम्, आमन्त्रितम्, अनन्तिके ॥

वृत्तिः ॥ आम उत्तरमेकपदान्तरमामन्त्रितान्तमनान्तिके नानुदात्तं भवति ॥

55. After आम, but separated from it by not more than one word, the Vocative retains its accent, when the person addressed is not near.

Thus आम् पचसि देँवदत्ताँ३ ; आँम् भो देवदत्ता३ ॥ The *nighâta* being hereby prohibited, the vocative gets accent on the first syllable by VI. I. 198. In the second example, though भो itself is a Vocative, it is not considered to be non-existent by VIII. I. 72, but becomes effective by virtue of VIII. I. 73, as it is in apposition with the Vocative that follows.

Why do we say आम्? Observe शाक पचसि देवदत्त ॥ Here it is anudâtta by VIII. I. 19.

Why do we say एकान्तरम् 'separated only by one word'? Observe आम् प्र पचसि देवदत्ता३ ॥

Why do we say 'the Vocative'? See आम् पचति देवदत्त ॥

Why do we say अनन्तिके 'not near'? See आम् पचसि देवदत्त ॥ Here some hold that अनन्तिक is equivalent to दूर 'far off'. Therefore, according to them, the prohibition applies to एकश्रुतिः as well as to निघातः ॥ Had it been merely a prohibition of *nighâta*, then the sûtra would become redundant, as the nighâta is precluded by the rule of eka-śruti (I. 2. 33). Thus arguing, they hold that eka-śruti being asiddha, the pluta-udâtta of VIII. 2. 84, is not prohibited: and so the last vowel is prolated.

Others say that the word अनन्तिक means 'that which is not far off (दूर) nor very near'. It does not mean दूर only. For had it meant दूर, the author could have used the word दूर in the sûtra. Therefore the rule of eka-śruti (I. 2. 33), has no scope here at all, for it applies to दूर vocatives. Not being दूर, the plutodâtta also should not be exhibited in the illustration; for the rule VIII. 2. 84, applies also to दूर Vocatives.

In the example आम भो देवदत्त, the word आम् being a Nipâta is first acute; the word भो is a shortened form of भवत्, (VIII.3.1. Vârt). and it is accentless by VIII. 1. 19, being a Vocative case preceded by another word. देवदत्त would also have become accentless by the same rule, this sûtra prohibits it. The निघात being thus prohibited by this sûtra, two rules make themselves manifest now for application. The one is of एकश्रुतिदूरात्संबुद्धौ (I. 2. 33) causing एकश्रुति or monotony; the other causing प्लुतोदात्तत्वं by दूराद्धूते च (VIII. 2. 84). The opinions referred to above, relate to this doubt.

यद्धितुपरं छन्दसि ॥ ५६ ॥ पदानि ॥ यत्, हि, तु, परम्, छन्दसि ॥

वृत्तिः ॥ आमन्त्रितमित्येतदस्वरितत्वान्नानुवर्त्तते ॥ तिङिति वर्त्ततएव ॥ यत्परं हिपरं तुपरं च तिङन्तं छन्दसि नानुदात्तं भवति ॥

56. A finite verb followed by यत् or हि or तु retains its accent in the Chhandas.

The anuvṛitti of आमन्त्रितं should not be taken in this sûtra, but that of तिङ् ॥ Thus with यत्परं we have:—गवां गोत्रमुदसृजो यदङ्गिरः ॥ The verb उदसृजः is the Imperfect (लङ्) 2nd person singular of सृज् of Tudâdi class. With हि we have, इन्द्रवो वा मुशन्ति हि (Rig Ved. I. 2. 4). The verb उशन्ति is the Present (लट्) Plural of वश् of Adâdi class. The samprasârana takes place because it belongs to गृह्यादि class. With तु we have, आख्यास्यामि तु ते ॥ By the previous sûtra VIII. 1. 30 a verb in connection with यत् would have retained its accent, so also in connection with हि by the sûtra VIII. 1. 34, and in connection with तु by VIII. 1. 39, the present sûtra is, therefore, a niyama rule. The verb retains its accent when these three Particles *only* follow and not any other. If any other Particle follows, the verb need not retain its accent. Thus जाये स्वा रोहावैहि ॥ Here रोहाव is the 1st Person Dual of the Imperative of रुह् (रुह्+शप्+वस्=रोह+

आट् + वस् III. 4. 92 = रोहाव the स् being elided, as लोट् is like लङ् III. 4. 85 and 99). The verb एहि is the 2nd Person Singular of the Imperative of the root इण्, preceded by the Particle आङ् ॥ Here in रोहाव एहि (= रोहाव आइहि), the verb रोहाव is followed by the Particle आ, and does not retain its accent. But for this rule, it would have retained its accent. Because एहि is a गत्यर्थ लोट् (VIII. 1. 51), रोहाव is another लोट् in connection with it, and therefore, by VIII. 1. 52 it would have retained its accent. But now it loses its accent because it is a तिङ् following after a non तिङ् word स्वः ॥ The visarga of स्वः is elided before र् by VIII. 3. 14, then the preceding अ is lengthened and we have स्वा (VI. 3. 111). Another reading is स्वो रोहावेहि ॥ It is a Vedic anomaly, the visarga is changed to उ॥

चनचिदिवगोत्रादितद्धिताम्रेडितेष्वगतेः ॥ ५७ ॥ पदानि ॥ चन, चित्, इव, गोत्र-आदि, तद्धित, आम्रेडितेषु, अगतेः ॥

वृत्तिः ॥ चन चिद् इव गोत्रादि तद्धित आम्रेडित इत्येतेषु परतः अगतेरुत्तरं तिङन्तं नानुदात्तं भवति ॥

57. A finite verb retains its accent, when it is not preceded by a Gati Particle (I. 4. 60 &c), and when it is followed by चन, चिद्, इव, गोत्र &c, a Taddhita affix, or by its own doubled form.

Thus देवदत्तः पचति चन ; देवदत्तः पचति चित्, देवदत्तः पचतीव ॥ The list of Gotrâdi words is given under sûtra VIII. 1. 27. Thus देवदत्त पचति गोत्रम्, देवदत्तः पचति ब्रुवम्, देवदत्त पचति प्रवचनम् &c. The Gotrâdi words, here also, denote censure and contempt.

With a Taddhita affix, देवदत्तः पचति कल्पम्, देवदत्तः पचति रूपम् ॥ The examples should be given with anudâtta Taddhita affixes, like रूपप्, कल्पप् (V. 3. 66 and 67). Any other Taddhita affix added to the verb would cause the verb to lose its accent, the Taddhita accent overpowers the verb accent: as पचतितेराम् (V. 3. 67).

With a doubled verb, as ; देवदत्तः पचति पचति ॥

Why do we say 'when not preceded by a Participle called Gati'? Observe देवदत्तः प्र पचति चन ॥ The word गति in this sûtra as well as in सगतिरपि तिङ् (VIII. 1. 68) should be taken in its restricted sense, namely upasargas treated as Gati, and not the extended definition of Gati as given in I. 4. 61. Therefore the verb retains its accent here: शुक्लीकरोति चन, यत् काष्ठं शुक्लीकरोति, यत् काष्ठं कृष्णीकरोति ॥

According to others, throughout this Book Eighth, the word Gati means, the Upasarga Gati.

चादिषु च ॥ ५८ ॥ पदानि ॥ च, आदिषु, च ॥

वृत्तिः ॥ चादिषु च परतः तिङन्तमगतेः परं नानुदात्तं भवति ॥

58. A finite verb, not preceded by a gati, retains its accent before the Particles च (वा, ह, अह and एव VIII. 1. 24).

The चादि words are those mentioned in sûtra VIII. 1. 24. Thus देवदत्त पँचति च खाँदति च, देवदत्तः पँचति वा खाँदति वा, देवदत्त पँचति ह खाँदति ह, देवदत्तः पँचति अह खाँदत्यह, and देवदत्तः पँचत्येव खाँदत्येव ॥

But when preceded by a gati, we have देवदत्तः प्र पँचति च प्र खादति च ॥ Here the first verb retains its accent by virtue of the next sûtra, but the second verb loses its accent.

चवायोगे प्रथमा ॥ ५६ ॥ पदानि ॥ च, वा, योगे, प्रथमा ॥

वृत्तिः ॥ अगतेरिति पूर्वसूत्रे चानुकृष्टमित्यत्र नानुवर्त्तते। च वा इत्येताभ्यां योगे प्रथमा तिङ्विभक्तिर्नानुदात्ता भवति ॥

59. The first finite verb only retains its accent in connection with च and वा ॥

The anuvṛitti of अगतेः which was drawn in the last sûtra, does not run into this. Thus गर्द्दभांश्च कालँयति, वीणां च वादयति ॥ गर्द्दभान् वा कालँयति, वीणां वा वादयति ॥

The word योग in the sûtra indicates that the mere *connection* with the verb is meant, whether this connection takes place by adding these words च and वा, *before* the verb, or *after* the verb, is immaterial for the purposes of this sûtra, (not so in the last). The word प्रथमा shows that the *first* verb is governed by this rule and not the *second.*

हेति क्षियायाम् ॥ ६० ॥ पदानि ॥ ह, इति, क्षियायाम् ॥

वृत्तिः ॥ ह इत्यनेन युक्ता प्रथमा तिङ्विभक्तिर्नानुदात्ता भवति क्षियायां गम्यमानायाम् ॥

60. In connection with ह, the first verb retains its accent, when an offence against custom is reprimanded.

The word क्षिया means an error or mistake of duty, a breach of etiquette or a fault against good breeding.

Thus स्वयं ह रथेन यॉति३, उपाध्यायं पदाति गमयति 'He himself goes on a car, while he causes his Preceptor to trudge behind on foot'. स्वयं ह ओदनं भुङ्क्ते३, उपाध्यायं सक्तून् पाययति 'Himself eats the rice, and makes the preceptor eat the gruel'. Here in both examples, the nighâta of the first verbs is prohibited. The verbs become svarita-pluta by VIII. 2. 104.

अहेति विनियोगे च ॥ ६१ ॥ पदानि ॥ अह, इति, वि नि योगे, च ॥

वृत्तिः ॥ अह इत्यनेन युक्ता प्रथमा तिङ्विभक्तिर्नानुदात्ता भवति विनियोगे गम्यमाने चशब्दात् क्षियायां च ॥

61. In connection with अह, the first verb retains its accent, when it refers to various commissions, (as well as when a breach of good manners is condemned).

The word विनियोग means sending a person to perform several commissions. The word च in the sûtra draws in the anuvṛitti of क्षिया also.

Thus त्वं अह ग्रामं गच्छ, त्वं अह अरण्यं गच्छ ॥ So also when क्षिया is meant, as स्वयमह रथेन याति ३, उपाध्यायं पदातिं गमयति ॥ स्वयमहौदनं भुङ्क्ते ३, उपाध्यायं सक्तून् पाययति ॥ The prohibition of *nighâta* and prolation are as in the last aphorism.

चाहलोप एवेत्यवधारणम् ॥ ६२ ॥ पदानि ॥ च, अह, लोपे, एव, इति, अवधारणम् ॥

वृत्तिः ॥ चलोपे अहलोपे च प्रथमा तिङ्विभक्तिर्नानुदात्ता भवति एवेत्येतच्चेदवधारणार्थं प्रयुज्यते ॥

62. When च and अह are elided, the first verb still retains its accent, when एव with the force of limitation, takes their place.

When does this लोप take place? Where the sense of च or अह is connoted by the sentence, but these words are not directly employed, there is then the elision of च and अह ॥ There the force of च is that of aggregation (समुच्चय), and of अह is that of 'only' (केवल). The च is elided when the agent is the same, and अह is elided when the agents are several.

Thus where च is elided:—देवदत्त एव ग्रामं गच्छतु, देवदत्त एवारण्यं गच्छतु = ग्रामं चारण्यं च गच्छतु ॥

So where अह is elided: as:—देवदत्त एव ग्रामं गच्छतु, यज्ञदत्त एव अरण्यं गच्छतु = ग्रामं केवलं, अरण्यं केवलं ॥

Why do we say अवधारणं 'when limitation is meant'? See देवदत्तः क्वेव भोक्ष्यते, देवदत्तः क्वेव वाध्येष्यते ॥ The word एव here has the sense of 'never' 'an impossibility'. The first sentence means न क्वचिद् भोक्ष्यते ॥ क्व + एव = क्वेव by पररूप (VI. 1. 94 Vârt).

चादिलोपे विभाषा ॥ ६३ ॥ पदानि ॥ च, आदि, लोपे, विभाषा ॥

वृत्तिः ॥ चादयो नचवाहाहैवयुक्तइति सूत्रनिर्दिष्टा गृह्यन्ते; तेषां लोपे प्रथमा तिङ्विभक्तिर्नानुदात्ता भवति विभाषा ॥

63. When च, (वा, ह, अह and एव) are elided, the first verb optionally retains its accent.

Thus with च लोपः—शुक्ला व्रीहयो भवन्ति or भवन्ति, श्वेता गा आज्याय दुहन्ति ॥ Here भवन्ति optionally may either lose or retain its accent. So also when वा is elided, as:—व्रीहिभि र्यजेत or यजेत, यवै र्यजेत ॥ So also with the remaining.

वैवावेति च च्छन्दसि ॥ ६४ ॥ पदानि ॥ वै वाव, इति, च, छन्दसि ॥

वृत्तिः ॥ वैवाव इत्येताभ्यां युक्ता प्रथमा तिङ्विभक्तिर्विभाषा नानुदात्ता भवति छन्दसि विषये ॥

64. Also in connection with वै and वाव, may optionally, in the Chhandas, the first verb retain its accent.

Thus अहर्वै देवानाम् आसीत् (or आसीत्), रात्रिरसुराणाम् आसीत् ॥ बृहस्पति र्वै देवानां पुरोहित आसीत् (or आसीत्), शण्डामर्कावसुराणां (Taittariya Sanhita VI. 4. 10, 1. but without the particle वै). अयं वाव हस्त आसीत् (or आसीत्), नेतर आसीत् ॥

वै has the force of स्फुट and क्षमा, and वाव that of प्रसिद्धि and स्फुट ॥

एकान्याभ्यां समर्थाभ्याम् ॥ ६५ ॥ पदानि ॥ एक, अन्याभ्याम्, समर्थाभ्याम् ॥

वृत्तिः ॥ एक अन्य इत्येताभ्यां समर्थाभ्यां युक्ता प्रथमा तिङ्विभक्तिर्विभाषा नानुदात्ता भवति छन्दसि विषये ॥

65. Also in connection with एक and अन्य, optionally in the Chhandas, the first verb retains its accent, when these words have the same meaning ('the one —the other').

Thus प्रजामेका जिन्वति (or जिन्वति), ऊर्जमेकारक्षति ॥ तयोरन्यः पिप्पलं स्वाद्वत्ति (or अत्ति), अनश्नन्नन्यो अभिचाकशीति (Rig Veda I. 164. 20, Mundaka Upanishad III. 1).

Why do we say समर्थाभ्यां 'having the same meaning'? See एको देवानुपातिष्ठत् ॥ Here एक is a Numeral and has not the sense of अन्य 'the one another'. The word समर्थ is used, in fact, to restrict the meaning of एक, for it has various meanings: while there is no ambiguity about the word अन्य ॥ एकोऽन्यार्थे प्रधाने च प्रथमे केवले तथा । साधारणे समानेऽल्पे संख्यायां च प्रयुज्यते ॥

यद्वृत्तान्नित्यम् ॥ ६६ ॥ पदानि ॥ यत्, वृत्तात्, नित्यम् ॥

वृत्तिः ॥ प्रथमा छन्दसीति निवृत्तं, निघातप्रतिषेध इत्येव ॥

वार्त्तिकम् ॥ यथाकाम्ये वेति वक्तव्यम् ॥

66. In connection with यद् in all its forms, the verb retains its accent always.

The anuvritti of प्रथमा and छन्दसि ceases. The prohibition of nighâta, which commenced with न लुट् (VIII. 1. 29) is present here also. In what ever sentence the word यद् occurs, that is called यद्वृत्तं ॥ The word वृत्तं denotes here the form of यद् in all its declensions with case affixes. According to Kâsikâ, डतर and डतम are not included, according to Patanjali they should be included. See also the explanation of किंवृत्तं in VIII. 1. 48.

Thus यो भुङ्क्ते, यं भोजयति, येन भुङ्क्ते, यस्मै ददाति, यत् कामास्ते जुहुमः (Rig Veda X. 121. 10) यद्र्यङ् वायुर्वाति (T. S. V. 5. 1. 1.) यद् वायुः पवते ॥ For the form यद्र्यङ् see VI. 3. 92. Though the sûtra is in the Ablative (यद्वृत्तात्) and therefore requires that the verb should *im-mediately* follow it, yet in यद्र्यङ् वायु वाति, the intervention of वायुः does not prevent the operation of this rule, according to the opinion of Pâtanjali.

Vârt:—Optionally when the sense is that of 'wheresoever' or 'whensoever'. The word यथाकाम्यं means यथेच्छं 'as one wishes', without regard of time or space. The *nighâta* is prohibited here also. As यत्र क्व चन यजते तद् देवयजनं एव यजते ॥

पूजनात्पूजितमनुदात्तं काष्ठादिभ्यः ॥ ६७ ॥ पदानि ॥ पूजनात्, पूजितम्, अनुदात्तम्, काष्ठादिभ्यः ॥

वृत्तिः ॥ पूजनेभ्यः काष्ठादिभ्य उत्तरपदं पूजितमनुदात्तं भवति ॥

वार्त्तिकम् ॥ मलोपश्च ॥

67. After a word denoting praise belonging to काष्ठादि class, the word whose praise is denoted, becomes aundâtta.

This refers to compounds, the first members of which are praise-denoting words. The word काष्ठादिभ्यः, is added to the sûtra from a Vârtika.

Thus काष्ठाध्यापकः, काष्ठाभिरूपकः, दारुणाध्यापकः, दारुणाभिरूपकः ॥

अमातापुत्र । अमातापुत्राध्यापकः । अमातापुत्राभिरूपकः । अयुताध्यापकः । अयुताभिरूपकः । अद्भुत । अद्भुताध्यापकः । अनुक्त । अनुक्ताध्यापकः । भृश । भृशाध्यापकः । घोर । घोराध्यापकः । सुखः । सुखाध्यापकः । परम । परमाध्यापकः । सु । स्वध्यापकः । अति । अत्यध्यापकः । द्यौः । द्यौरध्यापकः । द्यौरभिरूपकः । स्वध्यापकः । अपुत्र । अपुत्राध्यापकः । कल्याण । कल्याणाध्यापकः ॥

Vârt:—The final म् should be elided in forming these words. The word दारुणं is an adverb, and therefore in the accusative case, like मांसंगतः ॥ In such a case, there can be no compounding: hence the elision of म् is taught. This is the opinion of Vârtika—kâra Kâtyâyana. According to Kâśikâ, there is compounding under मयूर व्यंसकादि rule, and so म् is elided by the general rule of samâsa. This becoming of अनुदात्त takes place in the compound, and after composition. In fact, it is an exception to the general rule by which a compound is *finally* acute (VI. 1. 223) But there is no elision in दारुणमध्यापकः &c. and there is no loss of accent also of the second word. By the Vârtika 'मलोपश्च', this further fact is also denoted, where the case-affix is not employed and so the म् is not heard, there the second member becomes anudâtta. When there is no compounding, there is no elision of म् as दारुणमधीते, दारुणमध्यापकः ॥

Though the word पूजन would have implied its correlative term पूजित, the specific mention of पूजित in the aphorism indicates, that the word denoting पूजित should follow *immediately* after the word denoting पूजन ॥ In fact, this peculiar construction of the sûtra, is a jñâpaka of the existence of the following rule:—इह प्रकरणे पञ्चमी निर्देशेऽपि नानन्तर्यमाश्रीयते "In this subdivision or context, though a word may be exhibited in the Ablative case, it does not follow that there should be consecutiveness between the Ablative and the word indicated by it". This has been illustrated in the previous rule of यद्वृत्तान् नित्यम्, in explaning forms like यत्रक्व वायुर्वाति &c.

Though the anuvritti of 'anudâtta' was current, the express employment of this term in the sûtra indicates that the *prohibition* (of anudâtta) which also was current, now ceases.

On this subject, the following extract from the Commentary on Siddhânta-Kaumudi, will give the view of later Grammarians:—The words काष्ठ &c, are all synonyms of अद्भुत, meaning *wonderful, prodigious*: and are words denoting *praise.* This is an aphorism appertaining to samâsa subject. In the examples the compounding takes place under the rule of Mayura-vyansakâdi.

Vârt:—The elision of म् should be mentioned. दारुणम्+अध्यापकः, in making the compound of these two words, the elision of the case affix, in this case म्, is natural. The vârtika, therefore, teaches nothing new, but only repeats this general rule in a particular form. This is the opinion of the authors of Kâśikâ. But according to Kayyata, the commentator on the Great Bhâshya, this aphorism is not a samâsa rule : and the words दारुणम् &c, are adverbs not admitting of samâsa ; and so the rule applies to these words when they are not compounded. There is no authority for holding these] to] be compounds under the Mayuravyansakâdi class. Haradatta also says, had this been intended to be a samâsa rule, the word समासे would have been used in the sûtra and this is valid. There is no adhikâra of samâsa here, that could have caused samâsa and in this view, the vârtika मलोपश्च also becomes effective : had it been a samâsa rule, the vârtika would have been redundant.

1 काष्ठ, 2 दारुण, 3 अमातापुत्र, 4 वेश, 5 अनाज्ञात, 6 अनुज्ञात, 7 अपुत्र, 8 अयुत, 9 अद्भुत, 10 अनुक्त, 11 भृश, 12 घोर, 13 सुख, 14 परम, 15 सु, 16 अति, 17 कल्याण

सगतिरपि तिङ् ॥ ६८ ॥ पदानि ॥ स, गतिः, अपि, तिङ् ॥

वृत्तिः ॥ सगतिरगतिरपि पूजनेभ्यः काष्ठादिभ्यः परं पूजितं तिङन्तमनुदात्तं भवति ॥

68. (After such words denoting praise) the finite verb (which is praised) becomes anudâtta, even along with the Gati, if any, that may precede it.

Whether a finite verb is compounded with a gati or stands single, both the compound and the simple verb lose their accent, when it is qualified by the adverbs काष्ठं &c. Thus यत् काष्ठं प्रचति, यत् काष्ठं प्रपचति ॥ By VIII. 1. 28, the finite verb would have lost its accent after the word काष्ठं, but this loss was prohibited by VIII. 1. 30 in connection with यत् ; the present sûtra re-ordains the loss, by setting aside the prohibition of VIII. 1. 30.

The word सगति 'along with its Gati', indicates that the Gati even loses its accent. The word Gati here is restricted to Upasargas. Therefore not here यत् काष्ठं शुक्ली करोति, यत् काष्ठं कृष्णी करोति ॥

The word तिङ् is used in the sûtra to indicate that the words qualified by काष्ठं &c in the preceding sûtra, were non तिङ् words—i. e. were substantives. The rule of मलोपश्च of that sûtra, therefore, does not apply here.

कुत्सने च सुप्यगोत्रादौ ॥ ६९ ॥ पदानि ॥ कुत्सने, च, सुपि, अगोत्रादौ ॥

वृत्तिः ॥ पूजनादिति निवृत्तम् ॥ सगतिरपि तिङिति वर्त्तते ॥ कुत्सने च सुबन्ते गोत्रादिवर्जिते परतः सगतिरपि तिङ् अगतिरप्यनुदात्तो भवति ॥

वार्त्तिकम् ॥ क्रियाकुत्सन इति वक्तव्यम् ॥ वार्त्तिकम् ॥ पूतिश्च चानुबन्धो भवतीति वक्तव्यम् ॥

वा० ॥ विभाषितं चापि बह्वर्थमनुदात्तं भवतीति वक्तव्यम् ॥

Kârikâ. सुपि कुत्सनं क्रियाया मलोप इष्टोऽतिङीति चोक्तार्थे ।
पूतिश्च चानुबन्धो विभाषितं चापि बह्वर्थम् ॥

69. A finite verb, along with its preceding Gati, if any, becomes anudâtta, when a Noun, denoting the fault of the action, follows, with the exception of गोत्र &c.

The anuvṛitti of पदात् (VIII. 1. 17) ceases. But the anuvṛitti of the last sûtra is current. Thus पचति पूति, प्रपचति पूति, पचति मिथ्या, प्रपचति मिथ्या ॥

Why do we say कुत्सने 'denoting the fault of the action'? See पचति शोभनम् ॥

Why do we say सुपि 'a noun'? Observe पचति क्लिश्नाति ॥

Why do we say with the exception of गोत्र &c. See पचति गोत्रम्, पचति ब्रुवम्, पचति प्रवचनम् ॥

Vârt: It should be mentioned that the 'fault' mentioned in the sûtra, must be the fault relating to the mode of doing the action, denoted by the verb. The rule will not apply, if the कुत्सन refers to the agent and not to the action. Thus पचति पूतिर्देवदत्तः, प्रपचति पूतिः ॥

Vârt: It should be stated that पूति has an indicatory च ॥ The effect of this is that the word पूति is finally acute, because of the indicatory च ॥ The word पूति is not a क्तिन् formed word, because it is not feminine, as we find it in sentences like पूतिरयम्; nor is it a word formed by क्तिच् affix, because this is not a संज्ञा word; therefore, it is a word without a derivation. Therefore by प्रातिपदिकस्वर (Phiṭ I. 1) it will be end-acute. The *vârtika*, therefore, indicates that when पूति causes the loss of accent of the verb, then it is end-acute, but in other cases it is acute on the beginning. According to Padamanjari, पूति is derived from पू by adding the Uṇâdi affix तिप् diversely (Uṇ IV. 180), and is first acute.

Vârt: A finite verb in the plural number, loses its accent optionally: when it loses its accent, then पूति is end-acute. Thus पचन्ति पूतिः, or पचन्ति पूतिः, प्रपचन्ति पूतिः or प्रपचन्ति पूतिः ॥

Kârikâ. The following noun denoting fault must refer to the action. The elision of म् is intended only in the case of non-verbs, because it is so said by those of old. The word पूति has an indicatory च, but it is optionally so when the verb is plural. The elision of म् mentioned above refers to the elision of म् in दारुणम्-अध्यापकः = दारुणाध्यापकः ॥ The words उक्तार्थम् mean आचार्यपरंपराकथितप्रयोजनमेतदित्यर्थः ॥

गतिर्गतौ ॥ ७० ॥ पदानि ॥ गतिः, गतौ ॥

वृत्तिः ॥ गतिर्गतौ परतो ऽनुदात्तो भवति ॥

70. A Gati becomes unaccented, when followed by another Gati.

Thus अभ्युद्धरति, समुदानयति, अभिसंपर्यो हरति ॥ Why do we say गतिः "a Gati becomes &c"? Observe देवदत्तः प्रपचति ॥ Here देवदत्त is a Prâtipadika and does not lose its accent. Why do we say 'when followed by a Gati'? Observe आ मन्द्रैरिन्द्र हरिभि र्याहि मयूर रोमभिः ॥ Here आ is a Gati to the verb याहि, the complete verb is आयाहि ॥ But as आ is not followed by a Gati, but by a Prâtipadika मन्द्र, it retains its accent. Had the word गतौ not been used in the sûtra, this आ would have lost its accent, because the rule would have been too wide, without any restriction of what followed it.

तिङि चोदात्तवति ॥ ७१ ॥ पदानि ॥ तिङि, च, उदात्तवति ॥

वृत्तिः ॥ गतिरिति वर्त्तते ॥ तिङन्ते उदात्तवति परतो गतिरनुदात्तो भवति ॥

71. A Gati becomes anudâtta, when followed by an accented finite verb.

The word गतिः is understood here. Thus यत् प्र पचति, यत् प्रकरोति ॥

Why have we used the word तिङि in the sûtra? In order to restrict the scope of the word उदात्तवति; so that a Gati would not become accentless before every udâtta *word*, but only before udâtta *verbs*. Thus आ does not become anudâtta before मन्द्रैः in आ मन्द्रैरिन्द्र हरिभि र्याहि ॥ If it be said that the word गति is a particular name which the Particles get before *verb* only, and therefore गति would always refer to its correlative term *verb*, and not to *noun*, like as the word *father* refers to its correlative term *son* and not *nephew*: and that, therefore, उदात्तवति must refer to the *verb* like याहि and not to a noun like मन्द्रैः; then also we say that the employment of the term तिङि is necessary, in order to indicate that the *verb* must be a *finite* verb, and not a *verbal root.* So that though a verbal root be udâtta, yet if in its conjugated form (तिङन्त) it is not udâtta, the गति will not lose its accent. Thus in यत् प्र करोति, the root कृ is anudâtta, but the तिङन्त form करोति is udâtta, hence the rule will apply here: which would not have been the case had उदात्तवति not been qualified by तिङि ॥ For the maxim is यत्क्रियायुक्ताः प्रादयस् तेषां तं प्रति गत्युपसर्गसंज्ञे भवतः ॥ Therefore in a तिङन्त, the designation of गति is with regard to धातु or verbal root. Obj: If तिङि is used for this purpose, then the rule will not apply to an आम ending forms, like प्र पचतितराम् and प्रपचतितमाम्, for these are not तिङन्त; but as a matter of fact, we find that प्र loses its accent, in these forms also. How is this explained? *Ans.* Here there are two views: some compound the Gati प्र with the completed आमन्त form पचतितराम् ॥ According to them, this प्र would get the accent, on the rule that an Indeclinable first member retains its accent (VI. 2. 2); so that even if the word तिङ् was not used in the sûtra, the form पचतितराम् being the second member of a compound, became anudâtta; and so प्र being followed by an anudâtta never loses its accent. According to them, therefore, the Gati never loses its accent in प्रपचतितराम् &c. Others compound the word ending in तरप् (पचतितर) with the Gati, and having formed प्रपचतितर, then add the affix आम ॥ According to this view, the आम् accent debars all other accents, on the maxim, 'the accent of the *last* prevails' (सतिशिष्ट), and so प्र is anudâtta, not by this rule, but by अनुदात्तसर्वं पदमेकवर्जं ॥ According to them the word is प्रपचतितराम् ॥ According to both of these views, this sûtra is not necessary for the purposes of प्रपचतिराम &c. But there is a third view which makes this sûtra necessary even for this purpose. There is this maxim: गतिकारकोपपदानाम् कृद्भिः सह समासवचनं प्राक् सुबुत्पत्तेः "It should be stated that Gatis, Kârakas and Upapadas are compounded with bases that end with Kṛit-affixes, before a case-termination has been added to the latter". This maxim itself has been explained in two different ways, one saying that the compounding takes place with kṛit-formed words *only* before the addition of case-affixes; but with words formed by Taddhita affixes, the compounding does not take place before a case affix has been added. The other view makes no such difference between kṛit-formed and non-kṛit formed words. This latter view is not necessary for our purposes. According to the first view, the Gati प्र can never be compounded with पचतितराम् as it is not a सुबन्त ॥ So both प्र and पचतितराम् having different accents, the present sûtra became necessary to cause the loss of accent of प्र ॥

Why have we used the word उदात्तवति? See प्रॅ पचति, प्रॅ करोति ॥ Here the verb loses its accent by VIII. 1. 28, hence the Gati retains its accent.

आमन्त्रितं पूर्वमविद्यमानवत् ॥ ७२ ॥ पदानि ॥ आमन्त्रितम्, पूर्वम्, अविद्यमानवत् ॥

वृत्तिः ॥ आमन्त्रितं पूर्वमविद्यमानवद्भवति, तस्मिन्सति यत्कार्यं तन्न भवति ॥

72. A preceding Vocative is considered as non-existent, (for the purposes of the accent of the following word, and the enclitic forms of युष्मद् and अस्मद्).

Such a Vocative is treated as if not at all existing, it is simply ignored. The operation which its presence otherwise would have caused does not take place, and that operation takes place which would have taken place had it not existed. What are the particular purposes served by considering it as non-existent? They are (1) the absence of the accent-less-ness of the subsequent vocative, which the first, taken as a पद, would have caused under VIII. 1. 19. As देँवदत्त ! यँज्ञदत्त ! Here the first Vocative देवदत्त does not cause the second Vocative to lose its accent, but it remains first acute by VI. 1. 198. (2) The accent less-ness of the verb required by VIII. 1. 28 is prevented: as, देँवदत्त पँचासि ॥ (3) The substitution of the shorter forms of युष्मद् and अस्मद्, required by VIII. 1. 20-23 is prevented, as देवदत्त तव (not ते) ग्रामः स्वम्, देवदत्त मम (not मे) ग्रामः स्वम् ॥ (4) The application of VIII. 1. 37 takes place, in spite of the intervention of the Vocative between the Particle and the verb; such intervention is not considered as taking away anything from the immediateness (अनन्तरम्) of the Particle from the verb: as, यावद् देवदत्त पचसि ॥ (5) For the purposes of VIII. 1. 47, though a Vocative may precede जातु, the latter is still considered as अविद्यमानपूर्वं and VIII. 1. 47 applies, as देवदत्त जातु पँचसि ॥ (6) So also in the case of VIII. 1. 49, as आहो देवदत्त पँचासि, उताहो देवदत्त पचसि, no option is allowed here by VIII. 1. 50.

Why do we use the word 'as if' or वत् in the sûtra, instead of saying 'altogether'? In other words, why do we say "it is considered as if non-existent", instead of saying "it is considered altogether non-existent"? The vocative does produce its own particular effect. Thus in आम् भो देवदत्त! the vocative भो is considered as one word (एकान्तर) for the purposes of separating आम् from the vocative देवदत्त under VIII. 1. 55. This is the opinion of Patanjali; but the opinion of the author of Kâsikâ is that भो would have been considered as अविद्यमानवत् but for VIII. 1. 73.

Why do we say 'a Vocative'? Observe देवदत्तः पचति ॥ Why do we say पूर्वं 'with regard to the subsequent word'? The vocative itself will not be considered as non-existent, for the application of rules that would apply to vocative as such. Thus in देवदत्त यज्ञदत्त, the vocative देवदत्त gets its accent by VI. 1. 193 also. In fact, the word पूर्वं connotes its correlative पर 'subsequent'; and the vocative is considered as non-existent, for the purposes of the operations to be performed on such *subsequent* term, whether such operation be caused by the vocative itself, or by any other cause; but it is not to be considered non-existent for the purposes of operations to be performed upon itself. Therefore in देवदत्त पचसि, Devadatta does get the accent of the vocative. In इमं मे गङ्गे यमुने सरस्वति शतुद्रि the first vocative गङ्गे is considered as non-existent with regard to यमुने, and, therefore, यमुने is considered as following immediately after the pada मे and thus यमुने becomes anudâtta, not because of गङ्गे, but because of मे; similarly सरस्वति and शतुद्रि are anudâtta, not because of the preceding Vocative, but because of मे ॥ In other words, the intervention of the vocatives does not stop the action of मे ॥

नामन्त्रिते समानाधिकरणे सामान्यवचनम् ॥ ७३ ॥ पदानि ॥ न, आमन्त्रिते, समानाधिकरणे, सामान्य-वचनम् ॥

वृत्तिः ॥ अविद्यमानवत्त्वस्य प्रतिषेधः ॥ आमन्त्रितान्ते समानाधिकरणेपरतः पूर्वमामन्त्रितान्तं सामान्यवचनं नाविद्यमानवद्भवति ॥

73. A perceding vocative, when it conveys a general idea, is not to be considered as if non-existent, for the purposes of the subsequent Vocative, which stands in apposition with the former.

This sûtra prevents the operation of the last sûtra in the particular case when the two Vocatives are in apposition, and the second qualifies the first. Thus अग्ने गृहपते, माणवकजटिलकाध्यापक ॥ The first vocative being considered as existing, second vocative loses its accent.

Why do we say 'the *vocative* subsequent'? Observe देवदत्त पचसि here the *verb* does not lose its accent. Why do we say 'standing in apposition or समानाधिकरणे? Observe देवदत्त पण्डित यज्ञदत्त, here the word पण्डित qualifies यज्ञदत्त, and is not in apposition with देवदत्त, and hence it retains its accent.

Why do we say समान्यवचनम् 'which is a generic word'? The rule will not apply when the Vocatives are synonyms. Thus अघ्न्ये देवि सरस्वति ईडे काव्ये विहव्ये एतानि ते अघ्न्ये नामानि ॥ All these Vocatives are synonyms of Saraswati, and hence all retain their accent of the Vocative (VI. I. 198). According to Padamanjari the reading given in Taittariya Br. is:-- इडे रन्तेऽदिते सरस्वति प्रिये प्रेयसि महि विश्रुते, एतानि ते अघ्निये नामानि ॥ सामान्यवचनम् means 'a generic term'. When the first is a generic term, and the second is a specific term, (विशेष वचन) qualifying the first, and both are in the singular number, there the present rule will apply.

विभाषितं विशेषवचने बहुवचनम् ॥ ७४ ॥ पदानि ॥ विभाषितम्, विशेषवचने, बहुवचनम् ॥

वृत्तिः ॥ पूर्वेणाविद्यमानवत्त्वे प्रतिषिद्धे विकल्प उच्यते ॥ विशेषवचने समानाधिकरणे आमन्त्रितान्ते परतः पूर्वमामन्त्रितं बहुवचनान्तं विभाषितमविद्यमानवद्भवति ॥

74. When the preceding Vocative is in the Plural number, it is optionally considered as non-existent, if the subsequent Vocative, in apposition with it, is a specific term.

This ordains option, where the last sûtra would have made the consideration of the first vocative as existent compulsory. Thus देवाः शरण्याः or देवा शरण्याः ॥ ब्राह्मणा वैयाकरणाः or ब्राह्मणा वैयाकरणाः ॥

The anuvṛitti of सामान्यवचनम् is understood here; the second vocative, therefore, must be a विशेषवचन, as being the correlative of the former: where is then the necessity of employing the word विशेषवचने in the sûtra? This word is used in the aphorism for the sake of precision only.

Why do we say 'in the plural number'? Observe माणवक जटिलक ॥ No option is allowed here, and the preceding vocative is *always* considered as existent and so rule VIII. I. 73 applies.

The sûtras 73 and 74 as enunciated by Pâṇini are:—73. नामन्त्रिते समानाधिकरणे; 74. सामान्यवचनं विभाषितं विशेषवचने (i. e. 73. The preceding Vocative is not considered as non-existent, if the subsequent word is a Vocative in apposition with it. 74. Optionally so, if the preceding vocative is a general term and the subsequent vocative is a particular term). Patanjali made the amendment by adding सामान्यवचने to 73 also, and the author of Kâśikâ has added बहुवचनम् to 74 from the commentary of Patanjali and has omitted सामान्यवचनम् from it: though he reads its anuvṛitti.

ओ३म् ।

अथ अष्टमाध्यास्य द्वितीयः पादः ।

BOOK EIGHTH.

CHAPTER SECOND.

पूर्वत्रासिद्धम् ॥ १ ॥ पदानि ॥ पूर्वत्र, अ-सिद्धम् ॥

वृत्तिः ॥ पूर्वत्रासिद्धमित्यधिकार आ अध्यायपरिसमाप्तेः । यदित ऊर्ध्वमनुक्रमिष्यामः पूर्वत्रासिद्धमित्येवं तद्वेदितव्यम् । तत्र येयं सपादसप्ताध्याय्यानुक्रान्ता एतस्यामयं पादोनो ऽध्यायो ऽसिद्धो भवति । इत उत्तरं चोत्तरोत्तरो योगः पूर्वमपूर्वत्रासिद्धो भवति । असिद्धवद्भवति । सिद्धकार्यं न करोति इति अर्थः ॥ तदेतदसिद्धवचनं आदेशलक्षणप्रतिषेधार्थं उत्सर्गलक्षणभावार्थं च ॥

1. Whatever will be taught hereafter, upto the end of the work, is to be considered as not taken effect, in relation to the application of a preceding rule.

This is an Adhikâra or governing rule, and extends upto the end of the Book. Whatever we shall teach hereafter is to be understood as non-existent, with regard to the preceding rule. With regard to whatever has been taught in the preceding Seven Books and a quarter, the rules contained in these three last chapters are considered as *asiddha*. And further, in these three chapters, a subsequent rule is, as if it had not taken effect, so far as any preceding rule is concerned. The word असिद्धम्=असिद्धवद्भवति, सिद्धकार्यं न करोति ॥ The rule is "as if non-effective, does not produce the operation of a siddha or effective rule". This rule of non-effectiveness is for the sake of prohibiting the operation of an âdeśa rule, and establishing the operation of an utsarga or general rule. Thus अस्मा उद्धर; द्वा अत्र; द्वा आनय, असा आदित्यः ॥ In all these, the elision of य् and व् by VIII. 3. 19, being considered as not to have taken effect, there is no further sandhi, and आ+उ does not give rise to guṇa, nor आ+अ=आ ॥ In fact, for the purposes of the application of आद्गुणः rule of VI. 1. 87, or the दीर्घ rule of VI. 1. 101, the rule VIII. 3. 19 is considered as not to have taken effect at all.

Similarly अमुष्मै, अमुष्मात्, अमुष्मिन् from अदस् ॥ Thus अदस्+ङे=अद+ङे (VII. 2. 102 अ being substituted for the final स्, which again merges in the preceding अ VI. 1. 97)=अमु+ङे (VIII. 2. 80. उ being substituted for अ, and म् for द् of अद्). Now the substitution of स्मै for ङे takes place only after Pronouns ending in अ; but अमु is a pronoun ending in उ, so this स्मै (VII. 1. 14) should not take place. The present sûtra helps us out of this difficulty, and the change of अ into उ by VIII. 2. 80 is considered *asiddha* for the purposes of the application of VII. 1. 14.

शुष्किका शुष्कजङ्घा च क्षामिमानौजढत्तथा ।
मतोर्वत्वे झलां जश्त्वं, गुडलिण्मान्निदर्शनम् ॥

The forms शुष्किका, शुष्कजङ्घा, क्षामिमान्, औजढत्, and गुडलिण्मान् illustrate this rule excellently.

(1) शुष्किका ॥ To the root शुष् we add the Nishṭhâ त, as शुष्+त=शुष्+क (त changed to क by VIII. 2. 51)=शुष्क ॥ Add the feminine affix टाप् and we have शुष्का ॥ Add to this the affix क (V. 3. 70, 73), as शुष्का+क=शुष्काक, the feminine of which with टाप् will be शुष्कका (the shortening taking place by VII. 4. 13). Now अ is changed to इ by VII. 3. 44 and we have शुष्किका ॥ Now rule VII. 3. 46 makes this इ substitution optional, when a क् precedes the अ, as is the case here: and that rule would require the alternative form शुष्कका ॥ But there is no such alternative form, because the क of शुष्क was the substitute of त by VIII. 2. 51, which is considered as asiddha for the purposes of the application of VII. 3. 46.

(2) शुष्कजङ्घा ॥ Here rule VI. 3. 37 would have required the form to be शुष्काजङ्घा like मद्रिकाकल्पा; there being no puṅ-vad-bhâva when there is a penultimate क ॥ But the क in शुष्का being the result of VIII. 2. 51 is considered as asiddha for the purposes of VI. 3. 37.

(3) क्षामिमान् ॥ This word may be considered to have been formed by adding the affix मतुप् to the Patronymic word क्षामिः or to the noun क्षामिन् [क्षामस्यापत्यं=क्षामिः, or क्षामोऽस्यास्तीति=क्षामिन्] ॥ The word क्षाम is formed by adding the Nishṭhâ त to the root क्षै, as क्षै+त=क्षा+त (VI. 1. 45)=क्षाम (the त being changed to म by VIII. 2. 53). Now this म is considered as non-effectual for the purposes of application of VIII. 2. 9, which requires the change of म of मत् to व, when मत् is added to a word having a penultimate म, as in शमीवान् ॥ Therefore we have क्षामिमान् and not क्षामिवान् ॥

(4) औजढत् ॥ This is the Aorist third person singular of the Derivative root ऊढि, from the Past-Participle of वह् ॥ Thus वह्+त=ऊढ (VI. 1. 15). Add to it णिच् in the sense of तमाख्यत् (III. 1, 26): and then form its लुङ् ॥ The लुङ् is formed by adding चङ् (III. 1. 48), before which the stem is reduplicated (VI. 1. 11). In reduplicating, all the rules that went before in forming ऊढ are considered asiddha; viz. the rule by which ह was changed to ढ (as वह्+त=उह्+त=उढ्+त VIII. 1. 31), the rule by which त was changed to ध (उढ्+त=उढ्+ध VIII. 1.

40), the rule by which ध was changed to ढ (VIII. 4. 41), and the rule by which the first ढ was elided (VIII. 3. 13 as उढ्+ढ=उ+ढ=ऊढ VI. 3. 111). The elision of टि before णि being considered sthânivat, we reduplicate ह्त; as ऊह्तढ+चङ्+त्=ऊहढत् (VII. 4. 60)=ऊझढत् (VII. 4. 62)=ऊजढत् (VIII. 4. 54). There is no इ added by VII. 4. 79, because of the prohibition of अनग्लोपे of VII. 4. 93. With the augment, it becomes औजढत्॥ The form औजिढत् is from ढि ending in the affix क्तिन् ॥

(5) गुडलिण्मान् ॥ This is formed by adding मतुप् to the word गुडलिह्, which is formed by क्विप् (गुडं लेढि) Here also the म of मतुप् is not changed into व by VIII. 2. 10; because the change of ह् to ढ् (VIII. 1. 3), and again of ढ् to ड् are considered asiddha.

The rules of interpretation, however, contained in the previous part will apply to this part also; because such rules connot be considered 'prior' or पूर्व; for they become operative then only when occasion requires to apply them: The maxim which governs such rules is कार्यकालं हि संज्ञा परिभाषम् ॥ The rules, therefore, which are exhibited here in the sixth case such as VIII. 2. 23, or the seventh case, as VIII. 2. 26, or the fifth case, as VIII. 2. 27, should be interpreted in accordance with the sûtras षष्ठी स्थाने योगा, तस्मिन्निति निर्दिष्टे पूर्वस्य, तस्मादिति उत्तरस्य ॥

But with regard to the paribhâshâ विप्रतिषेधे परं कार्यं, the above will not hold good. For, by the very fact, that a subsequent rule in these chapters, is held to be asiddha, with regard to the prior, there cannot arise any conflict of two rules of equal force with regard to them. And it is only where there is such a conflict, that the above rule of interpretation applies. This being so, in विस्फोर्यम्, अवगोर्यम् formed by ण्यत् (III. 1. 124) the guṇa ordained by VII. 3. 86 is not debarred by the दीर्घ rule VIII. 2. 77, because there is no conflict between guṇa rule VII. 3. 86 and the dîrgha-rule VIII. 2. 77, for the latter is simply non-existent with regard to the former.

But though the विप्रपतिषेध rule does not apply in these chapters; yet an apavâda rule here even, does over-ride an utsarga rule, for otherwise, the enunciation of an apavâda rule would be useless. The apavâda rule is therefore, not considered asiddha. Thus the utsarga rule होढः (VIII. 2. 31) is set aside by the apavâda rule दादेर्धातोर्घः (VIII. 2. 32), and thus we have दोग्धा, दोग्धुम (दुह्+तृच्=दोघ्+तृच्) ॥

नलोपः सुप्स्वरसंज्ञातुग्विधिषु कृति ॥ २ ॥ पदानि ॥ न लोपः, सुप्-स्वर-संज्ञा-तुक्-विधिषु, कृति ॥

वृत्तिः ॥ नलोपः पूर्वत्रासिद्धो भवति सुब्विधौ स्वरविधौ संज्ञाविधौ तुग्विधौ च कृति। विधिशब्दोऽयं प्रत्येकमभिसंबध्यमानः स्वरसंज्ञातुकां विधेयत्वात्तैः कर्म्मषष्ठीयुक्तैर्भावसाधनो ऽभिसंबध्यते । सुपा तु संबन्धसामान्यवचनषष्ठ्यन्तेन कर्म्मसाधनः। तेन सुपः स्थाने यो विधिः सुपि च परभूते सर्वोसौ सुब्विधिरिति सर्वत्रासिद्धत्वं भवति ॥

2. The elision of a final न् (VIII. 2. 7) is considered as if not to have taken effect, in applying the following rules; (1) rules regarding case-endings, (2) rules regarding accents, (3) rules regarding any technical term of Grammar, and (4) rules regarding the augment तु before a Kṛit-affix.

The word विधि in the sûtra applies to all the four words preceding it: as सुब्विधि, स्वरविधि &c. The force of the Genitive compound in स्वरविधि, संज्ञाविधि तुग्विधि is that of ordaining the existence of something: e.g. when an accent is to be given to a word, or a particular designation is to be given to it or when तु is to be added to it, (भावसाधन) ॥ The compound सुब्विधि means however, the rule relating to the case-endings themselves, as well as, the rule which would apply to a word, when a case-ending follows (कर्मसाधन) ॥

(1) सुब्विधि :—As राजभिः, तक्षभिः ॥ Here the elision of न् of राजन् and तक्षन् being asiddha, the भिस् is not changed to ऐस् by VII. 1. 9. So also राजभ्याम्, तक्षभ्यां, राजसु, तक्षसु ॥ Here the finals of राज and तक्ष are not lengthened before भ्यां by सुपिच (VII. 3. 102) and nor changed to ए before सु by (VII. 3. 103): as in नराभ्यां and नरेषु of the stem ending in अ ॥

(2) स्वरविधि :—As राजवती and not राजवती ॥ For the elision of न् being asiddha, the rule VI. 1. 220, does not apply, for the word is considered not to end in अवती but न्वती ॥ Similarly in पञ्चार्मम् and दशार्मम्, the elision of न being asiddha, the first member does not become âdy-udâtta by VI. 2. 90. Similarly पञ्चवीजी: the elision of न् being asiddha, the first member does not retain its original accent as required by VI. 2. 29.

The word राजन् is first acute, as it is formed by the affix कनिन् (Uṇ I. 156). राजवती is formed by adding ङीप् to the मतुप् ending word, by IV. 1. 6. पञ्चार्मम् is a compound under rule II. 1. 50 of पञ्चन्-।-अर्म, and when न् is elided, the first member becomes a word ending in अ and would require the accent of VI. 2. 90.

(3) संज्ञाविधि :—As पञ्च ब्राह्मण्यः, दश ब्राह्मण्यः ॥ The elision of न् being asiddha, the words पंच and दश are still called shash though they no longer end in न् (ष्णान्ता षट् I. 1. 24). Being called षष्, they do not take टाप् in the feminine (IV. 1. 10).

According to the Vârtikakâra, there is no necessity of using the word संज्ञा in the sûtra (संज्ञा ग्रहणानर्थक्यं च तन्निमित्तत्वाल्लोपस्य), because the elision of न् is caused by reason of its having such a designation (as षट्). Thus without its having the name of षट् there would be no elision of जस् and शस्, without such elision, there is no pada sañjña of these words, and unless these words get Pada designation, there can be no elision of न् by VIII. 2. 7. The shash designation, however, would not be retained by these words after taking plural affixes, when feminine affixes are to be added to them, but for this sûtra. The पञ्चन् and दशन् ending in न् would require ङीप् in the feminine, which is however prohibited, for when जस् and न् are elided, the words end in अ and require टाप् for their feminine, which is also prohibited, because, by the present sûtra the word still retains its designation of षट् ॥

Q. How can this be the purpose of this sûtra ? There are two views as regard definitions (संज्ञा), the one is that a particular name is given to a thing once for all, *prior* to any operations; and operations are performed afterwards upon it or with it, as occasions arise. This view is embodied in the maxim यथोद्देशं संज्ञापरिभाषम् 'Sanjña, and Paribhâshâs remain where they are taught.' The other view is that the sanjñâ sûtra is to be read with every particular operative sûtra, and the sanjñâ given to the word afresh, with every new operation. In other words, the sanjña sûtra becomes identified with a vidhi sûtra, every time that a vidhi is to be applied. This is embodied in the maxim कार्यकालं संज्ञापरिभाषम् "Sanjñâs and Paribhâsas are attracted by or unite with the rules that enjoin certain operations." In the first view, the षट् sanjñâ will be good throughout, both for the purposes of eliding जस् and शस् and for prohibiting टाप ॥ Hence thus sûtra is not necessary in that view. But in the other view, the sûtra is necessary. For if the view be taken that a sañjñâ is to be applied with regard to each operation, then that षट् sanjñâ which had taken effect for the purposes of eliding जस् and शस्, will no longer hold good for the purposes of preventing the application of the feminine affix. Hence, the word संज्ञा is taken in this sûtra, to prevent the application of the second view.

(4) तुग्विधिः—Thus वृत्रहभ्यां, वृत्रहभिः ॥ On account of the elision of न् being asiddha, the तुक् augment is not added, though required by VI. 1. 71. (ह्रस्वस्य पिति कृति तुक्) ॥

Some hold that तुक् need not be read in the sûtra. They argue in this way:—There is this maxim सन्निपात लक्षणो विधिरनिमित्तं तद्विघातस्य "That which is taught in a rule, the application of which is occasioned by the combination of two things, does not become the cause of the destruction of that combination". Now the elision of न् of वृत्रहन् took place because of the case affix भ्यां, this elision cannot be the cause of adding तुक् ॥ Or the तुक् being a बहिरङ्ग operation would be asiddha with regard to the antaranga elision of न् ॥ This opinion is, however, not sound. The employment of तुक् in this sûtra indicates, that the two maxims above referred to, are not of universal application i.e. they are anitya.

Why do we say before a Kṛt-affix? Observe वृत्रहच्छत्रम, वृत्रहच्छाया ॥ Here तुक् is added by VI. 1. 73.

The elision of न् taught by VIII. 2. 7 &c would be asiddha by the general rule VIII. 2. 1; the specification of the four cases in which it is asiddha shows that it ~~is a~~ restrictive or niyama rule. That is, the elision of न् is considered asiddha only with regard to these four rules, and no other. It is not asiddha in राजीयते (राजन्+क्यच्+ते=राज+य+ते=राजीयते III. 1. 8, VII. 4. 33). There would not have been long ई had the नलोप been asiddha. So also राजायते there is lengthening, (VII. 4. 25) and राजाश्व there is ekâdeśa (VI. 1. 101).

न मु ने ॥ ३ ॥ पदानि ॥ न, मु, ने, ॥

वृत्तिः ॥ मुभावो नाभावे कर्त्तव्ये नासिद्धोभवति किं तर्हि सिद्ध एव ॥

वार्त्तिकम् ॥ एकादेशस्वरोन्तरङ्गः सिद्धो वक्तव्यः ॥ वा० ॥ संयोगान्तस्य लोपो रो रुत्वे सिद्धो वक्तव्यः ॥

वा० ॥ सिज्लोप एकादेशे सिद्धो वक्तव्यः ॥

वा० ॥ निष्टादेशः षत्वस्वरप्रत्ययविधीड्विधिषु सिद्धो वक्तव्यः ॥ वा० ॥ प्लुतविकारस्तुग्विधौ छे सिद्धो वक्तव्यः ॥

वा० ॥ श्चुत्वं धुटि सिद्धं वक्तव्यम् ॥ वा० ॥ अभ्यासजश्त्वचर्त्वे एत्वतुकोः सिद्धे वक्तव्ये ॥

वा० ॥ द्विर्वचने परसवर्णत्व सिद्धं वक्तव्यम् ॥

वा० ॥ पदाधिकारश्चेद्लत्वढत्वघत्वनत्वरुत्वषत्वणत्वानुनासिकछत्वानि सिद्धानि वक्तव्यानि ॥

3. The sûtra VIII. 2. 80, teaching the substitution of मु for the दस् of the Pronoun अदस्, is however not treated as asiddha in relation to the case-ending ना ॥

The existence of मु is not considered uneffected when there is to be added ना ॥ On the contrary, it is considered as siddha or existing. Thus मु being considered as siddha, अमु gets the designation of घि by I. 4. 7, and as such, its Instrumental Singular is by VII. 3. 120, अमुना ॥ Had the मु been considered as non-effected, then the stem would not have been called *ghi*, and there would have been no ना added. But when ना *had been* added, then the मु being asiddha, अमु is considered to be as अद ending in अ, and this अ would require lengthening by सुपि च VII. 3. 102: but it is not done on the maxim सन्निपातलक्षणो विधिरनिमित्तं तद्विघातस्य "that which is taught in a rule the application of which is occasioned by the combination of two things does not become the cause of the destruction of that combination". There being no long आ the उ of अमु remains short. Or this sûtra may be considered to be the condensation of two sûtras (1) मु is siddha when ना is to be added, (2) मु is siddha when any operations, otherwise to be caused when ना is added, are to take place. Or the sense of the sûtra is ने परतो यत् प्राप्नोति तस्मिन् कर्त्तव्ये मुभावो नासिद्धः "the मु is not non-effected in relation to any operation that would otherwise be occasioned when ना followed". From this, it would follow by implication that मु must be considered valid for the purposes of नाभाव itself. So मु being always siddha, ना is added: and there is no lenghening.

Vârt:—That ekâdeśa accent which is antaranga, should be considered as siddha. What is the necessity of this vârtika? In order to regulate the accents of 1. अय्, 2. आय्, 3. आव् substitutions of ए, ऐ and औ; 4. the accent of ekâdeśa substitutes, 5. the accent of the शतृ formed words, 6. for the purposes of rule VI. 1. 158, by which all syllables of a word are anudâtta except one, and 7. for the purposes of VIII. 1. 28, by which *all* syllables become anudâtta.

Thus (1) let us take अय् first. वृक्षे is finally acute by Phiṭ I. 1. The locative of this is वृक्ष+ङि (anudâtta III. 1. 3)=वृक्षे (ए is udâtta VIII. 2. 5). Now combine वृक्षे+इदम=वृक्षय्+इदम=वृक्ष इदम ॥ So also प्लक्ष इदम ॥ The udâtta ekâdeśa ए must be considered as *siddha*, so that the अय् substitute of ए should also become udâtta. (2) आय: As कुमार्यै इदम ॥ Here also आ is udâtta for similar reasons. कुमारी+ङे=कुमारी+आ+ए (VII. 3. 112)=कुमार्य्+आ+ए=कुमार्य्+आँ+ए (VI. 1. 174)=कुमार्य्+ऐ (VI. 2. 90)=कुमार्यै (VIII. 2. 5). The ऐ is udâtta and its आय् substitute will also be udâtta. How do you give this example? This example is then valid, when by VI. 1. 174, first the affix आ is made udâtta, then this आ (आट् VII. 3. 112) augment is added to ङे, and then (आ+ए) there is vṛiddhi ऐ; and then कुमार्य्+ऐ=कुमार्यै ॥ But if the order be reversed and आ+ए be first combined into ऐ, and then this ऐ be made udâtta by VI. 1. 174, then there would be no necessity of this vârtika for the purposes of आय् ॥ The word कुमार is end-acute by Phiṭ accent (Phiṭ I. 1). Add to it ङीप् in the feminine (IV. 1. 20), as कुमार+ई=कुमार्+ई (अ is elided by VI. 4. 148)=कुमार्+ई (VI. 1. 161)=कुमारी ॥

(3) आव्. As वृक्षाविदम् or प्लक्षाविदम्, for the same reasons as above [वृक्ष+औ (anudâtta)=वृक्षौ VIII. 2. 5, वृक्षौ+इदम्].

(4) एकादेश accent. As गाङ्गेऽनूपे ॥ Here गाङ्ग+इ=गाङ्गे ॥ The word गाङ्ग is formed by अण् affix (गंगाया इदम्) and is end-acute. The ekâdeśa ए is udâtta by VIII. 2. 5. This udâtta accent will remain valid: so that when for ए+अ there is pûrva-rûpa-ekâdeśa by VI. 1. 109, this ekâdeśa ए will be udâtta by VIII. 2. 5, or it will be svarita by VIII. 2. 6. The word अनूप is a प्रादि compound, आपोऽनुगतं=अनूपं ॥ Here by VI. 2. 2, the Indeclinable first term would have retained its accent: but the word is end-acute by VI. 2. 189.

(5) शतृ - accent. As तुदती, तुदते ॥ Here in तुद्+श+शतृ, the affix श is udâtta, and शतृ is anudâtta. The ekâdeśa अ will be udâtta by VIII. 2. 5. This ekâdeśa - udâtta should be considered valid for the pur poses of the rule VI. 1. 173 by which the feminine affix and the weak case-ending are udâtta. Thus तुदत्+ई=तुदती, तुदत्+ए=तुदते ॥ The prohibition अनुमः in VI. 1. 173 is a jñâpaka or indicator of the fact, that the ekâdeśa accent should be considered siddha, in the accent of the शतृ, because without this ekâdeśa accent, there is no śatṛi ending word with नुम which is antodâtta.

(6.) एकाननुदात्त: accent. As तुदन्ति, लिखन्ति ॥ Here in तुद्+श+अन्ति (VI. 1. 186) the ekâdeśa अ is udâtta by VIII. 2. 5, and this ekâdeśa accent is considered valid for the purposes of rule VI. 1. 158, by which all the remaining syllables become anudâtta, as तुदन्ति, लिखन्ति ॥

(7) सर्वानुदात्त: accent. As ब्राह्मणास्तुदन्ति, ब्राह्मणा लिखन्ति ॥ Here the ekâdes'a-accent of तुदन्ति and लिखन्ति being valid, rule VIII. 1. 28 applies, and all the syllables become anudâtta.

The word antaranga is used in the vârtika to indicate that the Bahiranga ekâdes'a accent will not be siddha. Thus पचतीति and प्रपचतीति, where the word इति is first acute, as it is an Indeclinable. And सोमसुत् पचतीति ॥ The accent of पचति+इति=पचतीति is governed by VIII. 2. 5. This ekâdeśa accent of long ई has reference to external sandhi, and therefore naturally it is a bahiranga. This bahiranga ekâdeśa accent is not siddha for the purposes of the application of previous sûtras. Thus sûtra VIII. 1. 71. requires that the *gati* should be unaccented before an accented verb: but प्र does not lose its accent, as पचतीति is not considered as an accented verb. In the second example, the ई of सी is not considered as accented, therefore, it does not become anudâtta by VIII. 1. 28.

Vârt:—The rule VIII. 2. 23 causing the elision of the final consonant in a word ending with a conjunct consonant, should be valid for the purposes of changing रु into उ ॥ What is the necessity of this vârtika ? Observe हरिवो मेदिनं त्वा ॥ The word हरिवः is formed by मतुप् affix हरयोऽस्य सन्ति=हरि+मत् ॥ Now by VIII. 2. 15 the म is changed to व, as हरि+वत् or हरिवत्; add सु (Voc.Sg.) as हरिवत्+सु, then add नुम् augment, as हरिवन्त्+सु ॥ Then there is elision of the final consonant=हरिवन् ॥ Now by VIII. 3. 1. the final न् is changed to रु, and we have हरिवरु, the रु would be changed to उ by VI. 1. 114, if the elision of the conjunct consonants be considered as siddha: for then this रु is followed by म, a हश् letter. But if such elision be considered asiddha, then रु is considered not to be followed by हश् letters, but by the consonants which were elided.

Vârt:— When ekâdeśa is to be done, the elision of सिच् is to be considered siddha or valid. As अलावीत् and अपावीत् ॥ Here the सिच् is elided by इट ईटि (VIII. 2. 28.) This elision is considered valid or siddha, and thus we have dîrgha single substitution of ई for इ+ई as अलाव्+इ+सीत्=अलाव्+इ+0+ईत् =अलावीत् ॥

Vârt:— The substitute of the Nishṭhâ affixes should be considered as valid or siddha for the purposes of the rules relating to the (1) changing of स to ष, (2) accent, (3) affix, and (4) इट् augment. As (1) वृक्णः, वृक्णवान् ॥ The root is ओव्रश्चु (VI. 11) the indicatory ओ shows that the nishṭhâ त is changed to न (VIII. 2. 45). This nishṭhâ substitute is considered as valid or siddha, and the final of the root is not changed to ष, as it otherwise would have been by VIII. 2. 36: for न would have been still considered as त or a झल् letter. The equation is as follows:—व्रश्च्+त=वृश्च्+त (VI. 1. 16)=वृश्च्+न (VIII. 2. 45)=वृष्+न (VIII. 2. 29)=वृक्+न (VIII. 2. 30)=वृक्ण: (VIII. 4. 1) The च् is changed to क् by VIII. 2. 30, by considering न as asiddha and therefore equal to त or a झल् letter. Thus it will be seen that this न is सिद्ध for the purposes of rule VIII. 2. 30, but it is सिद्ध only for the purposes of rule VIII. 2. 36.

As regards the other three cases, viz, accent, affix and इट् augment, the one word क्षीब, will illustrate them all. The irregular formation of this word is variously explained. It is formed by "nipâtana" under VIII. 2. 55. It is the Past Participle of the root क्षीब्, thus evolved क्षीब्+इट्+त=क्षीब्+इ+त =क्षीब्+अ (इत् being elided, this is the anomaly)=क्षीब ॥ Here the elision of इत् is considered as valid and siddhà, and therefore, क्षीब is considered as a word of two syllables, for the purposes of accent, under rule निष्ठा च द्व्यजनात् (VI. 1. 205). Had the lopâdeśa of इत् been considered asiddha, the word would have been considered as if of three syllables, and that rule of *accent* would not have applied.

Similarly क्षीबेन तरति=क्षैबिक formed by ठन् (IV. 4. 7) which *affix* is added, because it is considered a word of *two* syllables, the elision of इत् being considered as valid for the purposes of IV. 4. 7.

Similarly क्षीब may be considered to have been formed by eliding the त्; as क्षीब्+त=क्षीब्+अ ॥ In this view of its formation, the augment इट् is not added, because the lopa of त् is considered as valid and siddha for the purposes of इट् augment. In the opinion of Patanjali, the words इट् विधि may well be omitted from the vârtika, for इट् being a *portion* of a प्रत्यय, the word प्रत्ययविधि would include इट्-विधि also.

Vârt:—The prolation modification of a vowel (pluta) should be considered as valid and siddha, for the purposes of the rule relating to तुक् augment before the letter छ ॥ Thus by VIII. 2. 107, the Vocative words अग्ने and पटो assume the forms अग्ना३इ, and पटा३उ ॥ These इ and उ are pluta-vikâras. As अग्ना३ इच्छत्रम्। पटा३ उच्छत्रम् ॥ Here the modification caused by VIII. 2. 107, is considered as valid and siddha; otherwise there would have been no compulsory तुक् augment as required by VI. 1. 73 but optional तुक् under VI. 1. 76.

Vârt:—The श् and palatal change should be considered siddha and valid before धुट् (VIII. 3. 29). The root श्चुतिर् क्षरणे (I. 41) is read as beginning with a स, which is changed to श because of the subsequent च by VIII. 4. 40. This is not considered asiddha. Had it been so, there would come धुट् augment by VIII. 3. 29, in अट् श्च्योतति, रट् श्च्योतति ॥ The words अट् and रट् are अड् and रड् formed from the roots अटति and रटति by क्विप् ॥

Why is the root श्च्युतिर् considered to begin with स् and not with श as we find it written? Because had it been a root beginning with श originally, we could not get the form मधुक् which would have been मधुट् ॥ The form मधुक् is thus evolved. Thus मधु श्च्योतति=मधुश्च्युत् by adding क्विप् ॥ From मधुश्च्युत् we form a Derivative root in णिच् in the sense of मधुश्च्युतमाचष्टे=मधुश्च्ययति ॥ Add again क्विप् to this Derivative root मधुश्चि, the णिच् will be elided, and we have मधुश्च्य्, then श (which represents स्) is elided because it is at the beginning of a compound letter (VIII. 2. 29), and य is elided, because it is at the end of a conjunct letter final in a pada (VIII. 2. 23), and thus there remains मधुच्, and च् is changed to क् (VIII. 2. 30) we have मधुक् ॥ Had the root been शकारादि, then this श could not be elided, and so we should elide only the final च् and श् and the form would be मधुश् which would be changed to ष् and then to ड् and we should get मधुड् which is not desired.

Vârt:—The जश् and चर् substitution of letters in the reduplicate should be considered siddha and valid for the purposes of ए change (VI. 4. 120) and तुक् augment. Thus बभणतुः and बभणुः ॥ Here the जश् change of भ, to ब in the reduplicate should be considered as valid, otherwise this would be अनादेशादि root and the Perfect would be भेणतुः and भेणुः ॥ Similarly from छिद् we have चिच्छित्सति, and from उच्छ, उचिच्छिषति ॥ In the latter, the second syllable छिस् of उछिस् (Desiderative) is reduplicated by VI. 1. 2. Here had the reduplicate substitute च for छ been considered asiddha, there would not have been तुक् augment by छे च (VI. 1. 73)

Vârt:—The change of letter homogeneous with the subsequent is valid and siddha for the purposes of doubling. As सय्य्यन्ता, सव्व्वत्सरः, यल्ल्लोकम्, तल्ल्लोकम् ॥ In सय्यन्ता &c the म् is changed to anusvâra by VIII. 3. 23, and the anusvâra is then changed to a letter homogeneous with the subsequent by VIII. 4. 58. Had the परसवर्ण change been asiddha, there would have been no doubling by VIII. 4. 47.

Vârt:—If there be the adhikâra of the word 'pada' in those sûtras which ordain the following changes, then those changes are considered siddha for doubling, namely, 1. लत्व the change into ल (VIII. 2. 21), 2. डत्व the change into ड (VIII. 2. 31), 3. धत्व the change in to ध (VIII.2.33), 4. नत्व the change into न (VIII. 2. 56), 5. रुत्व the change to रु (VIII. 2. 75), 6. षत्व the change to ष (VIII. 3. 85), 7. णत्व the change to ण (VIII. 4. 11), 8. anunâsika change (VIII. 4. 45), 9. छत्व the change to छ (VIII. 4. 63).

As 1. गलो गलः; गरोगरः ॥ 2. द्रोग्धा द्रोग्धा ॥ 3. द्रोढाद्रोढा ॥ 4. नुन्नो नुन्नः or नुत्तो नुत्तः ॥ 5. अभिनोऽभिनः or अभिनद् अभिनत् This is लङ् second person singular of भिद्, the स् of सिप् is elided by VI. 1. 68, and the final त् changed optionally to रु by VIII. 2.74. The न is the vikarana श्नम् ॥ 6. मातुः ष्वसा मातुः ष्वसा or मातुः स्वसा, मातुः स्वसा, 7. माषवापाणि माषवापाणि or माषवापानि माषवापानि ॥ 8. वाङ् नयनम् वाङ् नयनम् or वाग्नयनम् वाग्नयनं ॥ 9. वाक् च्छयनं वाक्च्छयनं or वाक्शयन वाक्शयनं ॥

The लत्व &c, changes being all optional, had the changes been considered asiddha, we would have got the following double forms also गरोगल, गलोगरः which are not desired.

All these can be explained by dividing the sûtra न मु ने into two. The first being न, and this negative will prohibit all asiddha-ness mentioned in the preceding vârtikas. The second sûtra would be ह्रे, and we would here draw in the anuvṛitti of न from the preceding.

उदात्तस्वरितयोर्यणः स्वरितो ऽनुदात्तस्य ॥ ४ ॥ पदानि ॥ उदात्त-स्वरितयोः, यणः, स्वरितः, अनुदात्तस्य ॥

वृत्तिः ॥ उदात्तयणः स्वरितयणश्च परस्यानुदात्तस्य स्वरित आदेशो भवति ॥

4. A svarita vowel is the substitute of an anudâtta vowel, when the latter follows after such a semi-vowel, which has replaced an udâtta or a svarita vowel.

An unaccented vowel becomes svarita, when it comes after a यण् (semi-vowel), which यण् itself has come in the room of a vowel which was acute or svarita once.

Let us first take the vowel following an udâtta yan. Thus कुमार्यौ, कुमार्यः ॥ The word कुमारी is acutely accented on the final, because the long ई (ङीप्) replaces अ of कुमार (VI. 1. 161). The semi-vowel य् is substituted in the room of this acute ई; the anudâtta औ and अः become svarita after such a य् ॥

Now to take an example of a svarita-yan. The words सकृल्लू and खलपू are finally acute by kṛit-accent (VI. 2. 139). The Locative singular of these words are खलपू+इ=खलप्वि, and सकृल्ल्वि by VI. 4. 83. This व् is a semi-vowel which comes in the room of the acute ऊ, therefore, it is udâtta-yan. After this udâtta-yan, the anudâtta इ of the Locative becomes svarita by the first part of this sûtra. Now when खलप्वि+आशा and सकृल्ल्वि+आशा are combined by sandhi, this svarita इ is changed to य्; it is, therefore, a svarita-yan. The unaccented आ will become svarita, after this svarita-yan. As खलप्व्याशा and सकृल्ल्व्याशा ॥ The word आशा is finally acute and consequently आ is not acute (Phit. I. 18).

Obj :—Here an objector may say: that the svarita accent on इ in खलप्वि is by this very sûtra, this svarita is to be considered as asiddha for the purposes of यण् âdeśa of VI. 4. 83. How can then the य् substituted for this इ be considered as svarita-yan ?

Ans :—This is considered as siddha by âśraya. (आश्रयात् सिद्धत्वम्) ॥

Obj :—If this be so, then उदात्तादनुदात्तस्य स्वरितः (VIII. 4. 66) should also be considered as siddha: and we should have svarita in नध्याशा &c also. For the word नदि is first-acute by Phit II. 3. Therefore दि is svarita by VIII. 4. 66. The य् is svarita yan, the anudâtta आ after this should become svarita according this view, but this is not so.

Ans :—To avoid this difficulty, we have the following.

Vârt :—यण्स्वरो यणादेशे सिद्धो वक्तव्यः ॥ "The यण् accent should be considered as valid, for the purposes of यण् substitution".

Some say, that even in such cases as दध्याशा the above rule applies, and that the unaccented vowel becomes svarita, if it follows a svarita-yaṇ which is preceded by an acute vowel. They quote the following from Taittarîya śâkhâ :—यास्ते विश्वाः समिधः सन्त्यग्ने, where the अ of अग्ने is pronounced as svarita. So also in the Brâhmaṇa portion as: दध्याशयति the आ is read as svarita. But according to Kâtyayana and Patanjali, the unaccented vowel does not become svarita by this sûtra, when it follows a svarita-yaṇ which is preceded by an acute vowel.

To get rid of these anomalies, the Mâhabhâshya proposes several alternatives, two of which will be mentioned here. The first proposal is to divide this composite sûtra into two parts: (1) उदात्तयणः परस्य अनुदात्तस्य स्वरितो भवति "an unaccented vowel becomes svarita when it follows after an udâtta-yaṇ". (2) स्वरितयणश्च परस्य अनुदात्तस्य स्वरितो भवति "an unaccented vowel becomes svarita, when following a svarita yaṇ" and in this second sûtra, we shall read the anuvṛitti of udâtta-yaṇ from the preceding half. So that this half will mean: : उदात्तयण इत्येवं यो निर्वृत्तः स्वरितः, तस्य यणः परस्य अनुदात्तस्य स्वरितो भवति ॥ The svarita must have been obtained by the application of the first half of this sûtra and *this* svarita should be changed to यण्, which would change the anudâtta into svarita. So that the स्वरित यणः means this *particular* svarita obtained by the application of this very sûtra.

The second proposal is not to read svarita into the sûtra at all. The svarita in सकुल्ल्व्याशा would then be explained by udâtta-yanah rule. सकुल्लू + इ + आशा = सकुल्ल्व् + य् + आशा ॥ Here य् is udâtta-yaṇ. This will cause आ to become svarita. The intervening svarita य् is considered as not existent for the purposes of accent स्वरविधौ व्यञ्जनमविद्यमानवत् ॥ Nor is this य् to be considered as sthâni-vad to इ by I. 1. 57, for in applying the rule of accent, such a substitute is not considered as sthânivat by I. 1. 58.

Why do we say "of udâtta and svarita"? Observe बैदी + आशा = बैद्याशा, so also शार्ङ्गरव्याशा ॥ Here the semi-vowel replaces an unaccented ई, and is अनुदात्त यण् ॥ These words are first acute owing to नित् accent (IV. 1. 73).

Why do we say "an *unaccented* vowel becomes svarita"? Observe कुमार्यत्र, किशोर्यत्र ॥ The word अत्र is acutely accented on the first by लित् accent. (VI. 1. 193).

एकादेश उदात्तेनोदात्तः ॥ ५ ॥ पदानि ॥ एकादेशः, उदात्तेन, उदात्तः ॥

वृत्तिः ॥ उदात्तेन सहानुदात्तस्य य एकादेशः स उदात्तो भवति ॥

5. The single substitute of an unaccented with an udâtta vowel is udâtta.

The word "of an anudâtta" is understood here. An unaccented vowel, which combined with the preceding udâtta vowel remains as a single substitute, becomes udâtta. Thus for the udâtta इ of अग्नि॑ and for the case-ending औ which is anudâtta, there is always substituted long ई single by VI. 1. 102. This single substitute will be udâtta according to the present sûtra, as अग्नी॑ ॥ Similarly वायू॑, वृक्षे॑ः प्लक्षे॑ः ॥

Why do we say "with *udâtta* vowel"? Observe पचन्ति, यजन्ति ॥ Here पच्+शप्+अन्ति=पँच्+अ+अन्ति । Here शप् is anudâtta by III. 1. 4, so also अन्ति by VI. 1. 186. The ekâdeśa of these two non-accented अ will be anudâtta. In forming this para-rûpa ekâdeśa by VI. 1. 97, the svarita of the अं of शप् caused by VIII. 4. 66 is considered as invalid or asiddha.

Other examples are क्व॒ वोऽश्वाः (Rig. V. 61. 2) and क्वावरं मरुतः ॥ The word वः is anudâtta by VIII. 1. 21. read with VIII. 1. 18. The word अ॑श्वः is acutely accented on the first, as it is formed by adding क्वन् to अश् (Uṇ. I. 151). The स् of वस् is changed to र् (VIII. 2. 66), which is again changed to उ (VI. 1. 113). Thus वो ऽश्व ॥ Here अ becomes pûrva-rupa by VI. I. 109, which is udâtta. क्व is formed from किम् by अत् affix (V. 3. 12 and VII. 2. 105) and is svarita (VI. 1. 185). The word अ॑वर is acutely accented on the first by the Phiṭ II. 6. The single long substitute is udâtta.

स्वरितो वा ऽनुदात्ते पदादौ ॥ ६ ॥ पदानि ॥ स्वरितः, वा, अनुदात्ते, पदादौ ॥

वृत्तिः ॥ अनुदात्ते पदादौ उदात्तेन सह य एकादेशः स स्वरितो वा भवत्युदात्तो वा ॥

6. The single substitute of an unaccented vowel, standing at the beginning of a word, with an udâtta vowel, may optionally be svarita or udâtta.

Thus सु+उत्थितः=सू॑त्थितः or सूत्थितः ; वि+ईक्षते=वीक्षते or वीक्षते; वसुकः+असि =वसुकोऽसि or वसुको॑ऽसि ॥ Here the word सु is a Karmapravachanîya by I. 4. 94, when it is compounded by प्रादिसमास with the Past Participle, the Avayayîbhâva compound retains the accent of its first member (VI. 2. 2), and so it is acutely accented on the first, and the rest are anudâtta. Thus the udâtta उ of सु is compounded with the anudâtta उ of उत्थितः which stands at the beginning of a Pada, and so the ekâdeśa is optionally svarita. In वीक्षते and वसुकोऽसि also the verbs ईक्षते and असि lose all accent by VIII. 1. 28 and so ई and अ become anudâtta, which when compounded with वि and वसुका become optionally svarita.

The word स्वरितः is employed in the sûtra only for the sake of distinctness, for the sûtra may have well stood as वाऽनुदात्ते पदादौ ॥ In this form of the sûtra, the udâtta of the preceding sûtra would become optional when the second member is a word beginning with anudâtta. Udâtta being optional, in the other alternative, where there will not be udâtta, the svarita will be substituted by reason of the nearness in position.

Why do we say "anudâtta beginning"? Observe रैवस्तोऽश्च ॥ Here श्च begins with udâtta and not anudâtta, and hence no option is allowed.

Why do we say "beginning of a word"? Observe वृक्षैः, वृक्षाः, प्लक्षैः and प्लक्षाः, where anudâtta case-endings are not beginnings of words.

According to Bhattoji Dikshita this is a vyavasthita-vibhâshâ; in this wise. There will *necessarily* be svarita (1) where a long ई is the single substitute of (इ + इ) or of two short इ, (2) where there is pûrva-rupa by the application of एङपदान्तात् अति (VI. 1. 109). There will be udâtta where a long vowel comes in. Thus in वि + इदम् = वीदम् in वीडुं ज्योतिर्हृदये, the long ई is substituted for two short इ's. This substitution of a long ई for two *short* इ's is technically called प्रश्लेष ॥ Where there is Pras'lesha, the long ई is *necessarily* svarita. Similarly when there is अभिनिहतसन्धिः i. e. the peculiar sandhi taught in VI. 1. 109. Thus तेऽवदन्, सोऽयमागात् ॥ So also where there is क्षैप्रः सन्धिः i. e. the substitution of a semi-vowel in the room of an udâtta or svarita vowel, as अभ्यार्षे ॥ The above rules about svarita are thus summarised in the Prâtiśâkhyas: इकारयोश्च प्रश्लेषे क्षैप्राभिनिहतेषु च॥ But where a long ई is substituted as a single substitute for इ + ई (one of the इ's being long), there it must *always* be acute. As अस्य श्लोको दिवीयते (Rig. 1. 190. 4). The words दिवि + ईयते are compounded into दिवीयते ॥ The word दिवि Locative singular is finally acute by VI. 1. 171. ईयते is from the Divâdi root इङ् गतौ, and has lost its accent by VIII. 1. 28.

नलोपः प्रातिपदिकान्तस्य ॥ ७ ॥ पदानि ॥ न, लोपः, प्रातिपदिक, अन्तस्य ॥

वृत्तिः ॥ प्रातिपदिकस्य पदस्य योऽन्त्यो नकारस्तस्य लोपो भवति ॥

वार्त्तिकम् ॥ अह्नो नलोपप्रतिषेधो वक्तव्यः ॥

7. The न् at the end of a Nominal-stem, which is a Pada (I. 4. 17), is elided.

The word पदस्य 'of a Pada' is understood in this sûtra. Thus राजा, राजभ्याम्, राजभिः, राजता, राजतरः, राजतमः ॥ The Nominal stem राजन् gets the designation of Pada, before these affixes, by I. 4 17.

Why do we say 'of a Prâtipadika or Nominal stem'? Observe अहन्नहिम् ॥ Here अहन् is a verb, the 3rd Per. Sg. Imperfect (लङ्) of the root हन् ॥

Why do we say 'at the end'? If the word अन्तस्य had not been used in the sûtra, then the sûtra would have stood thus नलोपः प्रातिपदिकस्य; and as the word पदस्य is understood here, the sûtra would have meant, there is elision of न्, *where ever it may be*, of a Pada called stem. So that the न of नराभ्याम् would also have required elision. In fact, the genitive case here in पदस्य is not sthâna shashṭhî, but viseshaṇa shashṭhî, नलोप अन्तग्रहणं पदाधिकारस्य विशेषणत्वात् ॥

Q. But even if you use the word अन्त in the sûtra, it is compounded with the word प्रातिपदिक, and the sense of the sûtra will be "न् which is at the end of a pratipadika, which (prâtipadika) is a portion of a pada" &c. and not "न् which is at the end of a pada". So that the rule will not apply to अहस्रराभ्यां but will apply to राजानौ &c? Ans. The word प्रातिपदिक is not compounded, with the word अन्त in the sûtra. It is used without any case-affix, on the analogy of Chhandas usage. In fact, it is in the genitive case, the affix being elided by VII. 1. 39.

Vârt: The prohibition must be stated with regard to the elision of the न of अहन् ॥ As अहः, In अहर् the case-affix सु is luk-elided by VII. 1. 23, the pratyaya-lakshana is prohibited by I. 1. 63, and hence the न् of अहन is changed to र् by VIII. 2. 69. अहोभ्याम्, अहोभिः ॥ For the rules VIII. 2. 68 and 69 by which the final of अहन् is changed to र्, are asiddha with regard to this present rule requiring elision of न्, hence this vârtika.

Q. There is no necessity of this vârtika, for the subsequent rules VIII. 2. 69, 68 will debar नलोप ॥ Ans. But रु and र are considered asiddha for the purposes of न elision. The रु and र would have debarred न elision, had they otherwise found no scope. But they have their scope. Q. Where have they their scope? Ans. In the penultimate अ i.e. in the अ preceding the न् ॥ Q. The very fact that the author has used the word अहन् in the sûtra VIII. 2 68, shows that रु does not replace अ but न् ॥ Ans. If so, then र will find scope in the Vocative, हे अहन् where न् is retained by VIII. 2. 8, and it will be this न् which will be replaced by र्, as ह अहर् and so also हे दीर्घाहो निदाघ!

The word दीर्घाहन् is a Bahuvrihi (II. 2. 24), the Vocative affix is elided (VI. 1. 68), and the न् changed to र् by VIII. 2. 68, and it is changed to उ (VI. 1. 114). In हे अहन्! the न् is not elided by the option of the Vârtika under VIII. 2. 8.

To remove these objections, they say, the word अहन् which is used in VIII. 2. 68 is in nominative singular without the elision of न्, and it is to be repeated as अहन् अहन् ॥ The one indicates the exact *form*, showing that the न् is not elided; and by the second word the रु is ordained for this final न् ॥

न ङिसंबुद्ध्योः ॥ ८ ॥ पदानि ॥ न, ङि, सम्बुद्ध्योः ॥

वृत्तिः ॥ ङौ परतः संबुद्धौ च नकारलोपो न भवति ॥

वार्त्तिकम् ॥ ङावुत्तरपदे प्रतिषेधस्य प्रतिषेधो वक्तव्यः ॥ वा० ॥ वा नपुंसकानामिति वक्तव्यम् ॥

8. (But such न्) is not elided in the Locative and Vocative Singular.

This debars the elision of न्, which otherwise would have taken place by the preceding sûtra. The examples of non-elision of न् in the Locative singular are to be found in the Vedas. As परमे व्योमन् (Rig. I. 164. 39), आर्द्रे चर्मन्, लोहिते चर्मन् ॥ Here the sign of the Locative, namely, इ (ङि) is elided by VII. 1. 39. In the Vocative Singular, the न् is not elided as हे राजन्, हे तक्षन् ॥

Q. When ङि or the Vocative is elided, the preceding stem is no longer a Prâtipadika, and the stem does not get the designation of पद before the affix but is भ, hence where is the necessity of making the present prohibitory rule, when the elision of न् would not have taken place in the Locative and Vocative singular, by any rule?

Ans. The very fact of the prohibition of the elision of न्, as contained in this aphorism, indicates by implication (jñâpaka), that a word retains the designation of prâtipadika, though an affix has been elided after it and though such elided affix may produce its effect (I. 2. 45 read with I. 1. 62). Nor will such elided affix give the designation of Bha (भ) to such a stem. Thus राज्ञः पुरुषः = राजपुरुषः, here the न् is elided by considering the word राजन् as a prâtipadika, even after the elision of the Genitive affix in the compound, and it is not a Bha, which would have required the elision of अ by VI. 4. 134.

Vârt:—Prohibition of the prohibition must be stated, when the Locative word is followed by another word in a compound. That is, when a compound is a Locative Tatpurusha, the न् is elided: as, चर्मणि तिला अस्य = चर्मतिलः ॥

In हे राजवृन्दारक! the first member राजन् does not retain its न् by the present sûtra, because the *whole* compound, as such, is in the Vocative case, and not the word राजन् ॥ In fact, there can be no compound, which in its analysis, will give the first member as a Vocative word.

Vârt:—Optionally so in the neuter nouns. As हे चर्मन्, हे चर्म!

मादुपधायाश्च मतोर्वो ऽयवादिभ्यः ॥ ९ ॥ पदानि ॥ म, आत्, उपधायाः, च, मतोः, वः, अ यवादिभ्यः ॥

वृत्तिः ॥ मकारान्ताद् मकारोपधादवर्णान्तादवर्णोपधाश्चोत्तरस्य मतोर्व इत्ययमादेशो भवति यवादिभ्यस्तु परतो न भवति ॥

9. For the म् of the affix मत् is substituted व, if the stem ends in म or अ (and आ) or if these are in the penultimate position; but not after यव and the rest.

After a stem ending in म् or having म् as its penultimate letter, and after a stem ending in अ or आ, or having these letters as its penultimate, there is substituted व् for the म् of मतुप् ॥ First after stems ending in म्, as किंवत् (किंवान्), शंवत् (शंवान्). Secondly म् penultimate: as शमीवान्, दाडिमीवान् ॥ Thirdly a stem ending in अ or आ, as वृक्षवान्, प्लक्षवान्, खट्वावान्, मालावान् ॥ Fourthly अ or आ in the penultimate: as—पयस्वान्, यशस्वान्, भास्वान् ॥

Why do we say "म or अ ending or म or अ penultimate"? Observe अग्निमान्, वायुमान् ॥ Why do we say "with the exception of यव &c"? Observe यवमान्, दल्मिमान्, ऊर्म्मिमान् ॥

The following is the list of यवादि words.

1. यव, 2. दल्मि, 3. ऊर्म्मि, 4. भूमि, 5. कृमि, 6. कुञ्चा, 7. वशा, 8. द्राक्षा, 9. ध्राक्षा ॥ These words either end in म and अ or have these as their penultimate. 10. ध्रजि, 11. ध्वजि, 12. सञ्जि· These are exceptions to VIII. 2. 15. 13. हरित्, 14. ककुत्, 15 गरुत् ॥ These are exceptions to VIII. 2. 10. 16. इक्षु, 17. मधु, 18. द्रुम, 19. मण्ड, 20. धूम ॥ These are exceptions to VIII. 2. 11.

This is an âkritigaṇa. Wherever in a word, the म् of मतुप् is not changed to व्, though the rules require it, that word should be classified under यवादि class. In the secondary word नार्मतं (=नृमत इदं), the व् change has not taken place, because the अ is here a Bahiranga, the real vowel being ऋ ॥

The word मात् in the sûtra is the Ablative of म, i. e. of म्+अ; it is a Samâhâra Dvandva of these two letters.

झयः ॥ १० ॥ पदानि ॥ झयः ॥

वृत्तिः ॥ झयन्तादुत्तरस्य मतोर्व इत्ययमादेशो भवति ॥

10. The व् is substituted for the म् of मत् after a stem ending in a mute consonant.

As अग्निचित्वान् ग्रामः, उदश्वित्वान् घोषः, विद्युत्वान् वलाहकः, इन्द्रो मरुत्वान्, दृषद्वान् देशः ॥

संज्ञायाम् ॥ ११ ॥ पदानि ॥ संज्ञायाम् ॥

वृत्तिः ॥ संज्ञायां विषये मतोर्व इत्ययमादेशो भवति ॥

11. The व् is substituted for म् of मत्, when the word so formed is a Name.

As अहीवती, कपीवती, ऋषीवती, मुनीवती ॥ For long vowel, see VI. 3. 120.

आसन्दीवदष्ठीवच्चक्रीवत्कक्षीवद्रुमण्वच्चर्मण्वती ॥ १२ ॥ पदानि ॥ आसन्दीवत्, अष्ठीवत्, चक्रीवत्, कक्षीवत्, रुमण्वत्, चर्मण्वती ॥

वृत्तिः ॥ आसन्दीवद् अष्ठीवत् चक्रीवत् कक्षीवद् रुमण्वत् चर्म्मण्वती इत्येतानि संज्ञायां निपात्यन्ते ॥

12. The following Names are irregularly formed: âsandîvat, ashṭhîvat, chakrîvat, kakshîvat, rumaṇvat, charmanvatî.

The change of म् to व् in these was obtained from the last sûtra. The irregularity consists in the substitutions of stems. आसन्दीवत्, is from the stem आसन which is here changed to आसन्दी ॥ As आसन्दीवान् ग्रामः, आसन्दीवद् अहिस्थलम् ॥ As in the following śloka:

आसन्दीवति धान्यादं रुक्मिणं हरितस्रजम् ।
अश्वं बबन्ध सारङ्गं देवेभ्यो जनमेजयः ॥

When not a name, we have आसनवान् ॥ Others say, that there is a separate and distinct stem आसन्दी, as in the sentence औदुम्बरी राजासन्दी भवति ॥ The change of म् to व् after this word would take place regularly by the last sûtra: its mention here, according to these authors, is merely explanatory. 2. अष्ठीवत् is from

अस्थि which is changed to अष्ठी ॥ As अष्ठीवान् the name of a particular portion of body; the knee-joints. Otherwise अस्थिवान् ॥ 3. चक्रीवत् is from चक्र which is changed to चक्री, as चक्रीवान् राजा ॥ Otherwise we have चक्रवान् ॥ चक्रीवन्ति सदोहविर्धानानि भवन्ति is a Vedic example. It means सारस्वते सत्रे जङ्गमानि सदो हविर्धानानि, न स्वेकत्रावस्थितानि, तानि तत्र तत्र कर्मणाय चक्रयुक्तानि भवन्ति ॥ 4. कक्षीवत् is from कक्ष्या, there is vocalisation of य and the lengthening is by VI, 4. 2. कक्षीवान् is the name of a Rishi. Otherwise we have, कक्ष्यावान् ॥ 5. रुमण्वत् is from लवण which is changed to रुमण् ॥ Otherwise we have लवणवान् ॥ Others say, that there is a distinct word रुमन्, and the न् is not elided, but changed to ण् ॥ Or that the affix मत् takes the augment नुट् ॥ 6. चर्मण्वती is from चर्मन्, there is non-elision of न् and its change to ण् ॥ Or मत् has taken नुट् augment. The Charmanvati is the name of a river. Otherwise we have चर्मवती ॥

उदन्वानुदधौ च ॥ १३ ॥ पदानि ॥ उदन्वान्, उदधौ, च ॥

वृत्तिः ॥ उदन्वानित्युदकशब्दस्य मतावुदन्भावो निपात्यते उदधावर्थे संज्ञायां विषये ॥

13. The word उदन्वान् is irregularly formed, in the sense of "a sea".

It is derived from उदक 'water' with the affix मत् ॥ उदन्वान् is the name of a Rishi, because he controlled the rains, it rained at his command. It also means ocean or that in which water is held, like तटाक &c. The affix कि is added by III. 3 93, and उदक changed to उद् by VI. 3. 58, and thus we have उदधिः ॥ Why do we say "when meaning a sea"? Observe उदकवान् घटः 'a pot having water'. Here the main idea is not that of "holding or containing", but simply the general fact of possessing water: a human being may also possess water in the same way.

राजन्वान्सौराज्ये ॥ १४ ॥ पदानि ॥ राजन्वान्, सौराज्ये ॥

वृत्तिः ॥ राजन्वानिति निपात्यते, सौराज्ये गम्यमाने ॥

14. Also राजन्वान्, when the sense is of a good government.

The kingdom whose king is good is called राजन्वान् देशः, राजन्वती पृथ्वी ॥ The affix मतुप् is used here in the sense of प्रशंसा or praise. Otherwise राजवान् ॥

छन्दसीरः ॥ १५ ॥ पदानि ॥ छन्दसि, इ, रः ॥

वृत्तिः ॥ छन्दसि विषये इवर्णान्ताद्रेफान्ताच्चोत्तरस्य मतोर्वत्वं भवति ॥

15. In the Chhandas व् is substituted for the म् of मत्, when the stem ends in इ (or ई) or र् ॥

To take some examples of a stem ending in इ, as त्रिवती याज्यानुवाक्या भवति ; हरिवो मे दनं त्वा ; अधिपति वती जुहोति ; चतुरग्निवानिव ; आरेवानेतु मा विशत् (आरेवान् from रयि with vocalisation). सरस्वतीवान्, भारतीवान्, दधीवांश्चरः ॥ As all rules have optional force in the Chhandas, we have no change here सप्तर्षिमन्तम्, ऋषिमान्, ऋतीमान् सूर्यं ते द्यावापृथिवीमन्त ॥ Of stems ending in र we have गीर्वाण्, धूर्वान्, आशीर्वान् ॥

अनो नुट् ॥ १६ ॥ पदानि ॥ अनः, नुट् ॥

वृत्तिः ॥ छन्दसीति वर्तते ऽनन्तादुत्तरस्य मतोर्नुडागमो भवति छन्दसि विषये ॥

16. The affix मत् gets the augment नुट्, in the Chhandas, after a stem ending in अन् ॥

As अक्षण्वन्तः कर्णवन्तः सखायः; अस्थन्वन्तं यदनस्था बिभर्ति (Rig. I. 164. 4), अक्षण्वता लाङ्गलेन; शीर्षण्वती, मूर्द्धन्वती ॥

The word अक्षण्वत् is thus formed: अक्षि + मतुप् = अक्ष् + अन् + मत् (अनङ् is substituted for the final of akshi by VII. 1. 76) = अक्षमत् (the न् is elided by VIII. 2. 7). Now we add the augment नुट्॥ If this augment is added to मतुप्, as नमतुप् then it becomes a *portion* of मतुप्, and this न् would be changed to व by VIII. 3. 9 read with I. 1. 54, and not the letter म्, because न् intervenes. If we add this augment to the end of the stem, then in अक्षण्वता &c. we cannot change it to ण because of the prohibition in VIII. 4. 37, and the augment being नुक्, the न् would be changed to रु by VIII. 3. 7 in सुपथिन्तरः &c (VIII. 2. 17). The first view, however, is the correct one and the difficulty in its acceptance is obviated by नुटोऽसिद्धत्वात् तस्य च वत्वं न भवति; ततः परस्य च भवति; as shown above.

The नुट् augment being considered as asiddha, is not changed to व, but the letter following it, is so changed. Thus अक्षन् (VII. 1. 76) + मत् = अक्ष + मत् (the न् of the stem is elided by VIII. 2. 7). Add the augment नुट् now, and we have अक्ष + न्मत् ॥ The augment according to VIII. 2. 1, is asiddha, so that according to VIII. 2. 9, व् is substituted for म्, and not for न्, as would have been required by I. 1. 54.

नाद् घस्य ॥ १७ ॥ पदानि ॥ नात्, घस्य ॥

वृत्तिः ॥ नकारान्तादुत्तरस्य घसंज्ञकस्य नुडागमो भवति छन्दसि विषये ॥

वार्त्तिकम् ॥ भूरिदाव्नस्तुड् वक्तव्यः ॥ वा० ॥ रथिन ईकारान्तादेशो घे परतः ॥

17. In the Chhandas, the affixes तर and तम receive the augment नुट् after a stem in न् ॥

The affixes तरप् and तमप् are called घ ॥ Thus सुपथिन् + तर = सुपथि + तर (VIII. 2. 7) = सुपथि + न्तर (VIII. 2. 17) = सुपथिन्तरः ॥ So also दस्युहन्तमः ॥

Vârt:—The augment तुट् is added to these affixes after भूरिदावन्; as भूरिदावत्तरः (III. 2. 74, the affix is वनिप्).

Vârt:—Long ई is the substitute of the final of रथिन् before तर and तम ॥ The word रथिन् is formed by the affix इनि in the sense of मतुप् ॥ The final न् is first elided by VIII. 2. 7, and then for the short इ of रथि the long ई is substituted by the present vârtika. If the long ई were substituted for the final न् of रथिन् as रथिई + तर, then this long ई being asiddha, it could not be compounded by ekâdeśa with the preceding इ into ई, and the form would always remain रथिईतरः ॥ As रथीतरः, and रथीतमं रथीनाम् ॥ Or this ई may be considered to have come after रथ in the sense of मतुप् ॥

कृपो रो लः ॥ १८ ॥ पदानि ॥ कृपः, रः, लः ॥

वृत्तिः ॥ कृपेर्धातो रेफस्य लकारादेशो भवति ॥

वार्त्तिकम् ॥ कृपणकृपाणकृपीटकर्पूरादयोऽपि क्रपेरेव द्रष्टव्याः ॥

वा० ॥ बालमूललघ्वसुरालमङ्गुलीनां वा रो लमापद्यतइति वक्तव्यम् ॥

वा० ॥ कपिलकादीनां संज्ञाछन्दसोर्वा रो लमापद्यतइति वक्तव्यम् ॥

18. For the र of the root कृप्, there is substituted ल् ॥

The र् here merely indicates the sound, and includes both the single consonant र् and the same consonant of the vowel ऋ ॥ So also with ऌ ॥ So that for the single र् there is substituted ल्; and for र् when a portion of ऋ, the ऌ is substituted, i.e. ऋ becomes ऌ ॥ Thus कृप्=क्लृप्, as in the sûtra लुटि च क्लृपः (I. 3. 93). कल्प्ता, कल्प्तारौ, कल्प्तारः ॥ क्लृप्तः, क्लृप्तवान् ॥

The word कृपा is derived from the root क्रप् by vocalisation, as it has been enumerated in Bhidâdi class (क्रपेः संप्रसारणं च III. 3. 104). The vocalised root-form कृप is not to be taken here, as it is a lâkshanika form.

Vârt:—The words कृपण, कृपाण, कृपीट, कर्पूर &c, are also from क्रप् ॥ Or by the Uṇâdi diversity, the ल् change does not take place.

Vârt:—Optionally so of बाल &c. As, बालः or बारः, मूलम् or मूरम्, लघु or रघु, असुरः or असुलः, अलम् or अरम्, अङ्गुलिः or अङ्गुरिः ॥

Vârt:—Optionally so in the Vedas, or when names, of कपिलका &c, as कपिरकः or कपिलकः, तिल्पिलीकम् or तिर्पिरीकम्, लोमाणि or रोमाणि, पांशुरं or पांशुलं, कर्म or कल्म, शुक्रः or शुक्लः, कल्मषं, कर्मषं ॥

Some say 'र and ल are one': and operations regarding र may be performed with regard to ल ॥

उपसर्गस्यायतौ ॥ १९ ॥ पदानि ॥ उपसर्गस्य, अयतौ ॥

वृत्तिः ॥ अयतौ परत उपसर्गस्य यो रेफस्तस्य लकारादेशो भवति ॥

19. ल is substituted for the र of a Preposition, when अयते follows.

Thus पलायते, प्लायते ॥ Here arises the queston, does the word अयति qualify the word र्, or does it qualify the word Preposition. In the first view, the sûtra would mean, "the र् *immediately* followed by अयति is changed to ल" ॥ But as a matter of fact, र् is never immediately followed by अयति ॥ Thus in प्र+अयति or परा+अयति, the letter अ and आ intervene respectively. The ekâdeśa sandhi of these, will make र् immediately followed by अयति; but the ekâdeśa, being sthânivat will prevent it. This difficulty however, is overcome by the maxim येन नाव्यवधानं तेन व्यवहितेऽपि वचनप्रामाण्यात्, for otherwise the rule will be useless. For the same reasons, परि+अयते=पल्ययते, though here य् intervenes between र् and अयते ॥ In short, the intervention of one letter is considered as no intervention.

In the second view, the sûtra would mean when a Preposition is followed by ayat then its र् is changed to ल, and none of these difficulties will arise with regard to the above forms. But then would arise a fresh difficulty, for the र् of प्रति would also require to be changed into ल्॥ Some say, that प्रति is never followed by अयति; while others hold that the form प्लयते (प्रति + अयते) is valid. According to the first view, the valid form is प्रत्ययते ॥ The स् of the Prepositions दुस् and निस् is changed to र्, but this र् is not changed to ल्, because it is asiddha: thus we have the forms निरयणम्, दुरयणम् ॥ But there is a preposition निर् also the र् of which is changed to ल्, as निलयनम् ॥ See VII. 2. 46. According to the Siddhânta Kaumudi, there is a Preposition दुर् also, which gives दुलयते ॥

ग्रो यङि ॥ २० ॥ पदानि ॥ ग्रः, यङि ॥

वृत्तिः ॥ गॄ इत्येतस्य धातो रेफस्य लकार आदेशो भवति यङि परतः ॥

20. ल is substituted for the र of गॄ in the Intensive.

Thus निजेगिल्यते, निजेगिल्येते, निजेगिल्यन्ते ॥ The root गॄ takes यङ्, when the sense of contempt is conveyed, with regard to the action denoted by the root, (III. 1. 24). गर्हितं गिलति = जेगिल्यते ॥

Some say that ग्र of the sûtra includes the two roots गॄ (गिरति Tud. 117) and गॄ (गृणाति Kry. 28). Others hold that the Tudâdi gṛî is only taken and not the Kryâdi. The Kṛyâdi gṛî never takes the Intensive form, no example of which is to be met in literature.

Why do we say in the Intensive? Observe निगीर्यते with the Passive affix यक् ॥

अचि विभाषा ॥ २१ ॥ पदानि ॥ अचि, विभाषा ॥

वृत्तिः ॥ अजादौ प्रत्यये परतो ग्रो रेफस्य विभाषा लकारादेशो भवति ॥

21. The र of gṛî is optionally changed to ल् before an affix beginning with a vowel.

As निगिरति or निगिलति, निगरणम् or निगलनम्, निगारकः or निगालकः ॥

This is a vyavasthita-vibhâshâ, the optional forms have particular meanings. Thus गलः meaning 'neck' is always with ल; while गरः 'poison' is always with र.

In निगार्यते or निगाल्यते, the elision of णि is considered sthânivad, and hence this option, though the actual affix begins with य ॥ Obj.—The sthânivad-bhâva rule is invalid here by VIII. 2. 1. Ans. The rule पूर्वत्रासिद्धं does not hold good with regard to the rules of संयोगादिलोप, लत्व and णत्व on the maxim "तस्य दोषः संयोगादिलोपलत्वणत्वेषु" ॥

Or the र् will be *first* changed to ल्, as being antaranga, and then the णि will be elided.

The forms गिरौ, गिरः are either from the Kryâdi root gṛî, or *l*-change has not taken place on the maxim धातोः स्वरूपग्रहणे तत्प्रत्यये विज्ञानम् and as the affixes औ and अः are not affixes which are ordained after a verb, but are affixes added to nouns, hence the ल change has not taken place. In fact the words 'an affix beginning with a vowel' in the sûtra, means "a verbal affix beginning with a vowel," and not a noun affix. These are the Dual and Plural of the Nominative case of गॄ formed with the affix क्विप् ॥

परेश्च घाङ्कयोः ॥ २२ ॥ पदानि ॥ परेः, च, घ-अङ्कयोः ॥

वृत्तिः ॥ परि इत्येतस्य यो रेफस्तस्य घशब्दे ऽङ्कशब्दे च परतो विभाषा लकार आदेशो भवति ॥

वार्त्तिकम् ॥ योगे चेति वक्तव्यम् ॥

22. The र् of परि is changed to ल्, before gha and anka.

As परिघः or पलिघः, पर्यङ्कः or पल्यङ्कः ॥ The word घ here means the word-form घ, and not the technical घ of तरप् and तमप् ॥ See III. 3. 84 by which हन् is replaced by घ ॥

Vârt:—So also, it must be stated, before the word योगः ॥ As, परियोगः or पलियोगः ॥

संयोगान्तस्य लोपः ॥ २३ ॥ पदानि ॥ संयोगान्तस्य, लोपः ॥

वृत्तिः ॥ संयोगान्तस्य पदस्य लोपो भवति ॥

23. When a word ends in a double consonant, the last consonant is dropped.

As गोमान्, यवमान्, कृतवान् and हतवान् ॥ In श्रेयान्, भूयान्, the रु though subsequent in order, does not prevent the operation of this rule, because it is asiddha (VIII. 2. 66). Thus श्रेयस् + सु = श्रेयन्स् + स् (VII. 1. 70), = श्रेयान्स् (VI. 1. 68) = श्रेयान्रु (VIII. 2. 66) = श्रेयन् (VIII. 2. 23) = श्रेयान् (VI. 4. 8). But though the रुत्व does not debar lopa, it debars the जश् change. By VIII. 2. 39, the final स् required to be changed to a letter of जश् class; रु prevents it. As यशः, पयः ॥

For रुत्व is ordained even where the present संयोगान्तलोप applies and where it does not apply. Thus it is ordained in श्रेयान्र् where the present sûtra applies, as well as in पयर् where this sûtra does not apply. But the जश्त्व rule (VIII. 2. 39) covers the *whole* ground of रुत्व, hence if जश्त्व rule were not debarred by रुत्व, the latter would find *no* scope. Therefore रुत्व debars जश्त्व to justify its existence, but it does not debar संयोगान्तलोपः for it still has scope left to it else where.

In दध्यत्र and मध्वत्र formed from दधि + अत्र and मधु + अत्र, by changing इ and उ to य् and व्, we have दध्य् + अत्र and मध्व् + अत्र, where य् and व् are final in a pada, and so they require to be elided. It is, however, not done, because यण् substitution is a Bahiranga operation, as it depends upon two words and consequently, is considered asiddha for the purposes of this rule, which depends on one word only.

Why do we say 'of a Pada'? Observe गोमन्तौ, गोमन्तः ॥

रात्सस्य ॥ २४ ॥ पदानि ॥ रात्, सस्य ॥

वृत्तिः ॥ संयोगान्तपदस्य यो रेफस्तस्मादुत्तरस्यान्त्यस्य सकारस्य लोपो भवति ॥

24. Of a word ending in a conjunct consonant, only स् is elided, if it comes after र्; (but any other consonant coming after र is not elided).

Thus अक्षाः and अत्साः for अक्षार्स् and अत्सार्स् the Aorist of क्षर् and त्सर् in the following passages: गोभिरक्षाः, प्रत्यञ्चमत्साः ॥ The ईट् is not added as a Vedic diversity. See VII. 3. 97.

So also मातुः, पितुः for मातुर्स् and पितुर्स् ॥ Here by VI. 1. 111, the ऋ+अ of मातृ+अस् is changed to उ, which is followed by र् by I. 1. 51.

Though the final स् would have been elided even after र् by VIII. 2. 23, the special mention of स् after र् shows, that this is a niyama rule. So that any other letter than स् following after र् will not be dropped. Thus ऊर्क् from ऊर्ज्+क्विप् (III. 2. 177), here ज् is not elided, though final in a pada, but is changed to a guttural by VIII. 2. 30, and to क् by VIII. 4. 56. Also अमार्ट् from मृज् in लङ् the तिप् (त्) is elided by VI. 1. 18; there is vṛiddhi by VII. 2. 114, the ज् is changed to ष् by VIII. 2. 36, which is changed to ड् VIII. 4. 53 and finally to ट् (चर्) ॥

धि च ॥ २५ ॥ पदानि ॥ धि, च ॥

वृत्तिः ॥ धकारादौ प्रत्यये परतः सकारस्य लोपो भवति ॥

Kârikâ:—धि सकारे सिचो लोपश्चकाद्धीति प्रयोजनम् ।
आशाध्वं तु कथं जश्त्वं सकारस्य भविष्यति ॥
सर्वमेवं प्रसिद्धं स्याच्छ्रुतिश्चापि न विद्यते ।
लुङश्चापि न मूर्द्धन्ये ग्रहणं सेटि दुष्यति ॥
धसिभसोर्न सिध्येत तस्मात्सिज्ग्रहणं न तत् ।
छान्दसो वर्णलोपो वा यथेष्कर्त्तारमध्वरे ॥

25. The स् is dropped before an affix beginning with ध ॥

As अलविध्वम्, अलविढ्ढम्, अपविध्वम्, अपविढ्ढम् for अलविस्ध्वम् and अपविस्ध्वम् ॥ Had this स् (of सिच्) not been elided; then स् would be first changed to ष्, and then to a letter of जश् class (VIII. 4. 53), ध् would never be heard even optionally, though so required by VIII, 3. 79, but the forms would be always with ढ, as अलविड्ढ्म् &c. ॥

From an *ishti*, the elision of स् is confined to the स् of the Aorist सिच्, and not to any other स् ॥ Thus स् is not elided in चकाद्धि in चकाद्धि पलितं शिरः (हे शिरः पलितं सच् चकाद्धि शोभस्वेत्यर्थः). It is the Imperative of चकास् the सिप् is changed to हि, and हि to धि (VI. 4. 101), and स् to द् by VIII. 4. 53. Similarly it does not apply to पयस् धावति, where स is changed to रु and then to उ (VI. 1. 114)

=पयो धावति ॥ The elision of स् in सग्धिः from घस् with क्तिन्, and in बब्धाम् from भस् in the Imperative with ताम्, is a Vedic diversity. But according to Patanjali चकाधि is the proper form; while in पयो धावति the antaranga रु debars this bahiranga स् elision.

Obj.—If so, how do you form आशाध्वं, by the elision of स् of शास्; for स् would not be elided? Ans.—The स् is not here elided but changed to जश् letter, by VIII. 2. 39. Obj. If so, स् may always be changed to जश् letter, and there is no need of eliding it; in pronouncing, it will make no difference, whether you pronounce with one consonant or two, e.g. आशाद्ध्वम् or आशाध्वं ॥ Moreover by so doing, you will shorten the sûtra VIII. 3. 78, by omitting the word लुङ् from it. For the forms like अच्योड्ढ्वम्, अप्लोड्ढ्वम्, will be evolved regularly by changing स् of सिच् to ष्; and the ध after it will be changed to ढ, and then ष् changed to ड् by जश्त्व (VIII. 4. 53). Ans.—So far it will be all right, but in सेट् Aorist we shall never get the alternative forms अलविध्वम् &c, though we may get the form अलविड्ढ्वम् (VIII. 3. 79). Therefore, the word सिच् should be taken.

Obj. – If सिच् is to be taken here, then the स् of घस् and भस् will not be dropped, and we shall not get the forms सग्धिः and बब्धां in the passages सग्धिश्च मे सपीतिश्च मे, and बब्धां ते हरीधानाः ॥ Therefore, the present sûtra should not be confined to सिच् only. Ans.—We shall explain सग्धिः by saying, that it is a word derived from सघ्, and so also बब्धां from the root बन्ध ॥

[*N. B.*—The word सग्धिः is generally thus derived; अद् + क्तिन् = घस् + ति (II. 4. 39) = घ्स् + ति (VI. 4. 100) = घ् + ति (VIII. 2. 26). Had the present rule been confined to सिच्, the स् could not have been elided by VIII. 2. 26. See VI. 4. 100, where these two forms are developed]. Or we may explain these forms as Vedic irregularity, by which letters are sometimes dropped, and so घस् and भस् have lost their स् ॥ That letters are sometimes dropped in the Chhandas, we see in passages like the following इष्कर्त्तारमध्वरे for निष्कर्त्तारमध्वरे; तुभ्येदमग्ने for तुभ्यमिदमग्ने; आम्बानां चरुः for नाम्बानां चरुः; अव्याधिनी रुगणः or अव्याधिनीः सुगणाः ॥

The above discussion is summarised in the following

Kârikâ:—भिसकारे सिचोलोपश्चकाद्धीति प्रयोजनम्, "This rule is confined to the elision of the स् of सिच् only, for the sake of preserving the स् in चकाद्धि" ॥

आशाध्वं तु कथं? जश्त्वं सकारस्य भविष्यति ॥ "How then do you form आशाध्वं by the elision of स्? The स is not elided but changed to a जश् letter".

सर्वमेवं प्रसिद्धं स्याच्, श्रुति श्चापि न विद्यते। लुङश्चापि न मूर्धन्ये ग्रहणं सेटि दुष्यति ॥ "If this be so, then let जश् come every where, for there is no difference in sound, moreover this will shorten VIII. 3. 78 by omitting the word लुङ् from it. The जश् cannot come every where, as the difficulty will be in सेट् Aorist". घसि भसोर्न सिध्येत, तस्मात् सिज् ग्रहणं न तत्। "The forms सग्धिः and बब्धां could not be formed from घस् and भस् if the elision of स् were confined to सिच्. Hence सिच् should not be read into this sûtra."

छान्दसो वर्णलोपो वा यथेष्कर्त्तारमध्वरे " The elision of स् in सग्धिः and बब्धां will be explained as a Vedic anomaly, for letters are often dropped in Vedic forms, as in इष्कर्त्तारमध्वरे instead of निष्कर्त्तारमध्वरे ॥"

झलो झलि ॥ २६ ॥ पदानि ॥ झलो, झलि ॥

वृत्तिः ॥ झल उत्तरस्य सकारस्य झलि परतो लोपो भवति ॥

26. The स् is elided when it is preceded by a *jhal* consonant (any consonant except semi-vowels and nasals), and is followed by an affix beginning with a *jhal* consonant.

Thus अभित्त for अभित्स्त, अभित्थाः for अभित्स्थाः ॥ So also अच्छित्त, अच्छित्थाः, अवात्ताम्, अवात्त ॥ The last example may also be explained by VII. 4. 49; the elision of the स of सिच् being considered as asiddha, the स् of the root is changed to त् ॥

Why do we say 'of a jhal consonant'? Observe अमंस्त and अमंस्थाः ॥ Why do we say followed by a *jhal* consonant ? Observe आभित्साताम्, अभित्सत ॥

The स of this sûtra refers also to the स of सिच्; no other स is elided. As सोमसुत् स्तोता; दृषत् स्थानम् ॥ Here the स of स्तोता and स्थानं, though preceded by a jhal letter त्, could never be elided as they do not form portion of *one* word.

ह्रस्वादङ्गात् ॥ २७ ॥ पदानि ॥ ह्रस्वात्, अङ्गात् ॥

वृत्तिः ॥ ह्रस्वान्तादङ्गादुत्तरस्य सकारस्यलोपो भवति झलि परतः ॥

27. The स् is elided, before an affix beginning with a *jhal* consonant, when it is preceded by a stem ending in a short vowel.

As अकृत; अहृथाः ॥ Why do we say after a short vowel stem ? Observe अच्योष्ट, अप्लोष्ट ॥ Why do we say 'after a stem'? Observe अकृथाः, अलाविष्टाम्, अलाविषुः अपाविष्टाम् and अपाविषुः ॥ Why do we say "before an affix beginning with a jhal". Observe अकृषाताम्, अकृषत ॥

This lopa is also of the सिच्, therefore not here द्विष्टरां, द्विष्टमाम् ॥ Here to the word द्वि is added the affix सुच् (V. 4. 18), and then the comparative affixes तर and तम with आम् (V. 4. 11). This स् is not dropped.

इट ईटि ॥ २८ ॥ पदानि ॥ इटः, ईटि ॥

वृत्तिः ॥ इट उत्तरस्य सकारस्य लोपो भवति ईटि परतः ॥

28. The स् is dropped after the augment इट्, if after this स् the augment ईट् follows.

Thus the Aorist-stem of लू is अलाविस् (III. 1. 44; VII. 2. 35), the Personal ending त gets the augment ईट् by VII. 3. 96; and by the present sûtra, this स् between इ and ई is dropped, and we have अलावीत्; so also, अरावीत्, असेवीत्, अकोषीत्, अमोषीत् ॥

Why do we say 'after the augment इट्'? Observe अकार्षीत्, अहार्षीत् ॥ Why when the augment ईट् follows? Observe अलाविष्टाम्, अलाविषुः ॥

स्कोः संयोगाद्योरन्ते च ॥ २९ ॥ पदानि ॥ स्कोः, संयोग-आद्योः, अन्ते, च ॥

वृत्तिः ॥ पदस्यान्ते यः संयोगः झलि परतो वा संयोगस्तदाद्योः सकारककारयोर्लोपो भवति ॥

वार्त्तिकम् ॥ झलि सङीति वक्तव्यम् ॥

29. The स् or क्, when initial in a conjunct consonant, is dropped, before a jhal affix, and at the end of a word.

A conjunct consonant, having स or क as its first member, when coming at the end of a Pada, or when followed by a jhal beginning affix, loses its स् or क् ॥ Thus from the root लस्ज् we have लग्नः and लग्नवान् before the jhal affix त and तवत्; the substitution of न् for त् is considered asiddha for this purpose (VIII. 2. 1). So also साधुलक् at the end of a Pada. Similarly मग्नः मग्नवान्, साधुमक् from मस्ज् ॥ So also with initial क्, as तट् from तक्ष्; so also तष्टः, तष्टवान्, काष्ठतट् ॥

Vârt:— It should be rather stated that "before a jhal affix included in the pratyahâra सङ्" ॥ The सङ् is a pratyâhâra formed with the स of सन् (III.1.5) and the ङ् of महिङ् (III. 4. 78). It thus includes all the kṛit affixes, and dhâtu affixes i. e. affixes which come after a *verb* and not the Taddhita or the Feminine affixes. This Vârtika applies to all the preceding sûtras of this sub-division and is of use in the following places.

गिरोऽ भोधिर्ह्विष्टरां च इषत्स्थः काष्ठशक्स्थिरः । कुञ्चाधुर्येति मा स्मैषु सस्वारीनि भवास्विति ॥

So that in गिरः there should not be the optional ल by VIII. 2. 21. In अभोर्भिः, the स् of अभस् is not elided before भि as required by VIII. 2. 25. In ह्विष्टरां the rule VIII. 2. 27 does not apply. In इषत्स्थः the rule VIII. 2. 26 does not apply. In काष्ठशक्स्थिरः the rule VIII. 2. 29 is non-applicable. In कुञ्चा the rule VIII. 2. 30 does not apply. In धुर्यः (धुरं वहति) there is not lengthening by VIII. 2. 77. Thus काष्ठशक्स्थाता ॥ Here क् would require to be elided as initial in a consonant, followed by a jhal consonant थ ॥ काष्ठशक् is formed by adding क्विप् to शक् ॥ But according to Patanjali, there can be formed no valid word from शक् with क्विप्, *a fortiori*, no such word can be formed as काष्ठशक्स्थाता (काष्ठशकि तिष्ठति).

In वास्यर्थम्, काक्यर्थम्, the स् and क् are not elided, because य् is a Bahiranga substitute and asiddha, and the word वास्य् काक्य् are not considered as Pada, ending in a conjunct consonant.

Why do we say "of स् and क्"? Observe नर्नर्त्ति, वर्वर्त्ति ॥

Why do we say 'initial in a conjunct consonant'? Observe पयः शक् ॥

Why do we say 'at the end of a word'? Observe तक्षिता, तक्षकः ॥

चोः कुः ॥ ३० ॥ पदानि ॥ चोः, कुः ॥

वृत्तिः ॥ चवर्गस्य कवर्गादेशो भवति झलि परतः पदान्ते च ॥

30. A Guttural is substituted for a Palatal, before a *jhal* affix, or at the end of a word.

Thus पक्ता, पक्तुम्, पक्तव्यम् and ओदनपक् from पच् ॥ Similarly वक्ता, वक्तुम्, वक्तव्यम् and वाक् ॥

In क्रुञ्चा the feminine in टाप् of क्रुञ्च (क्रुङ्) by IV. 1. 4 list, the ञ् a palatal is followed by च् a jhal letter, and therefore, it should be changed to a guttural. It is not so, because Pâṇini himself uses this word, in this form, in sûtra III. 2. 59. Or because the rule is confined to सड् affixes only. Or the root is क्रुञ्च् without इ and with a penultimate न्, and not ञ् as we find in Dhâtupâṭha क्रुञ्च कौटिल्याल्पी भावयोः (Bhu. 200). With the elision of न we have निकुचितिः before the क्तिन् affix (VI. 4. 24) कुचितः in Past Part. and अचोकुन् ॥ In निकुचितम् we cannot have the optional कित् of the Nishṭhâ by I. 2. 21, because the elision of the penultimate न् by VI. 4. 24 preceded on the basis of the affix being कित्, thus कुन्च्+क्त=कुच्+त ॥ This elision of न्, will not make the root उदुपधा for the purposes of the application of rule I. 2. 21, on the maxim सन्निपातलक्षणो विधिरनिमित्तं तद्विघातस्य ॥ In fact, one of the reasons on which this maxim is based, is this very fact, that the elision of न् does not make the root उदपधा for the purposes of making the affix non-कित् ॥ The affix क्तिन् takes the augment इट् under VII. 2. 9 (vârt). The word क्रुङ् is formed from this root by क्विन् affix (III. 2. 59): the final च् is first elided by VIII. 2. 23, and then ञ् is changed to ङ् by VIII. 2. 62. The rule VI. 4. 24 thus finds no scope here.

In this view of the case we say क्रुञ्च is an irregular form of this root kunch, because it is so exhibited in III. 2. 59. There the anusvâra and parasavarṇa change of this न् to ञ् by VIII. 3. 24 being considered asiddha, there is no palatal ञ्, and hence there is no guttural change.

हो ढः ॥ ३१ ॥ पदानि ॥ हः, ढः ॥

वृत्तिः ॥ हकारस्य ढकारादेशो भवति झलि परतः पदान्ते च ॥

31. ढ is substituted for ह before a jhal letter and at the end of a word.

Thus सोढा, सोढुम्, सोढव्यम् ॥ The इट् is not added by VII. 2. 48, जलाषाट्, तुराषाट् by ण्वि (III. 2. 63, VI. 3.137 and VIII. 3. 56) वोढा, वोढुम्, वोढव्यं, प्रष्ठवाट्, दित्यवाट् (III. 2. 64) from सह् and वह्, with the affixes तृ, तुम्, तव्य and ण्वि ॥ For the त् of these affixes there is substituted ध by VIII. 2. 40, and this ध is changed to ढ by VIII. 4. 41, before which is dropped the first ढ by VIII. 3. 13. For the ढ in प्रष्ठवाट् either ड् is substituted by VIII. 2. 39, or ट् by VIII. 4. 56.

दादेर्धातोर्घः ॥ ३२ ॥ पदानि ॥ द्-आदेः, धातोः, घः ॥

वृत्तिः ॥ दकारादेर्धातोर्हकारस्य घकारादेशो भवति झलि परतः पदान्ते ॥

32. Of a root beginning with द्, the घ is substituted for ह, before a jhal letter or when final in a Pada.

For the final ह् of a द-beginning root, घ is substituted under similar circumstances. As दग्धा, दग्धुम्, दग्धव्यम्, काष्ठधक्, दोग्धा, दोग्धुम्, दोग्धव्यम्, गोधुक्, from दह् and दुह् ॥ For the त् of the affixes तृ &c. ध is substituted by VIII. 2. 40, before which, the घ becomes ग by VIII. 4. 53. For the घ in काष्ठदघ् is substituted ग by VIII. 2. 39, or क् by VIII. 4. 56, and द becomes ध by VIII. 2. 37.

Why do we say "of a root beginning with द"? Observe लेढा, लेढुम्, लेढव्यम्, मधुलिट् ॥

The force of the genitive case in धातोः is not to make it in apposition with the word दादेः, but it has the force of denoting a part as related to the whole: so that it means "the word which begins with द and forms part of a root, for the ह of such a part is substituted घ." What does follow from it? The letter घ is substituted in अधोग् also, which begins with अ ॥ For without the above explanation (धातोरवयवो यो दादिशब्दस्तदवयवस्य हकारस्य &c), the घ would have come in examples like मास्म धोक्, without the augment अ, but not where there was the augment अ ॥ Moreover, that it is an अवयवयोगा षष्ठी will appear necessary in sûtra VIII. 2. 37.

If it has the force of denoting a 'portion or member', how do you explain the forms दोग्धा, दोग्धुम्, for here no *portion* is taken but the *whole* word? This will be explained on the maxim of व्यपदेशिवद् भावः "An operation which affects something on account of some special designation, which for certain reasons attaches to the latter, affects likewise that which stands alone, and to which therefore, just because the reasons for it do not exist, that special designation does not attach". (व्यपदेशिवद् एकस्मिन्) ॥ Or we may explain the sûtra, by saying 'that root which begins with द in its original enunciation in Dhâtupâṭha'? Thus in original enunciation the root is लिह् not beginning with द ॥ If a Derivative root be formed from it like दामलिह्य (दामलिहामिच्छति = दामलिह्यति), it is a root which begins with द; the ह of this Denominative root, however, will not be changed to घ, for it is not a root of upadeśa. Therefore, when we add क्विप् to this root, we get दामलिट् by VIII. 2. 31, and not दामलिक् ॥

वा द्रुहमुहष्णुहष्णिहाम् ॥ ३३ ॥ पदानि ॥ वा, द्रुह, मुह, ष्णुह, ष्णिहाम् ॥

वृत्तिः ॥ द्रुह मुह ष्णुह ष्णिह इत्येतेषां धातूनां हकारस्य वा घकारादेशो भवति झलि परतः पदान्ते च ॥

33. The ह of druh, muh, shṇuh, and shṇih is optionally changed to घ, before a jhal letter or at the end of a word.

Thus द्रुहः, द्रोढा or द्रोग्धा, मित्रधुक्, मित्रधुट्, मुह, उन्मोग्धा, उन्मोढा, उन्मुक्, उन्मुट्, ष्णुह, उत्स्नोग्धा, उत्स्नोढा, उत्स्नुक्, उत्स्नुट्, ष्णिह, स्नेग्धा, स्नेढा, स्निक्, स्निट् ॥

The root द्रुह would have taken always घ by the last sûtra, this makes it optional. The others would not have got घ but for this sûtra.

These roots belong to Radhâdi sub-class of Divâdi gaṇa: and are taught there in this very order (Div. 89-91). By belonging to Radhâdi sub-division, the इट् is optional (VII. 2. 45). Instead of making the sûtra वा द्रुहादीनाम्, this longer formation of the aphorism indicates that the rule applies to यङ्लुक् also; as दोध्रुक् or दोध्रुट् ॥ See VII. 1. 6, for if the roots were taught not specifically but by गण, then the rule would not apply to yaṅ luk.

नहो धः ॥ ३४ ॥ पदानि ॥ नहः, धः ॥

वृत्तिः ॥ नहो हकारस्य धकारादेशो भवति झलि परे पदान्ते च ॥

34. The ह of नह् is changed to ध before a *jhal* letter or at the end of a word.

As नद्धा, नद्धुम्, नद्धव्यम्, उपानत्, परीणत् ॥ The त् of the affixes तृ &c, is changed to ध by VIII. 2. 40; and for the preceding ध is substituted द् by VIII. 4. 53. उपानत् is formed by VIII. 2. 39, read with VIII. 4. 56. परीणत् is formed by क्विप् as it belongs to सम्पदादि class, the lengthening is by VI. 3. 116, and ण-change by VIII. 4. 14. It would have shortened the processes of transformation, had only द् been ordained in the sûtra, instead of ध; but the ordaining of ध is for the purposes of VIII. 2. 40, by which there should be ध for the participial त &c, in नद्धम्, and that there should not be the change of this Nishṭhâ त into न by VIII. 2. 42. Thus नध्+त=नध्+ध (VIII. 2. 40)=नद्-धम् (VIII. 4. 53). But had the substitute been द्, we should have नद्+त=नन्नं by VIII. 2. 42.

आहस्थः ॥ ३५ ॥ पदानि ॥ आहः, थः ॥

वृत्तिः ॥ आहो हकारस्य थकारादेशो भवति झलि परतः ॥

वार्त्तिकम् ॥ हग्रहो र्भश्छन्दसि हस्येति वक्तव्यम् ॥

35. For the ह of the root आह्, there is substituted थ before a jhal letter.

As इदमात्थ, किमात्थ ॥ The word आथ्थ becomes आत्थ by VIII. 4. 55. Why has the last mentioned substitute ध not been ordained here, for this ध would also have given the form आत्थ by चर् change, as the थ is also changed to त; and by so doing there would have been only one sûtra, instead of two i. e. आहनहो र्धः would have been enough? Making this separate substitute, is for the sake of indicating that the rule VIII. 2. 40, does not apply here. For had VIII. 2. 40, still applied, the substitute ध of the last sûtra would have been enough. The त substitute, however, would have been the best.

The word झलि is understood here. Hence there is no change before vowel affixes, as आह, आहतुः, आहुः ॥

Vârt:— In the Chhandas, भ is substituted for the ह of ह and मह ॥ Thus गर्दभेन संभरति; मरुत्स्य गृभ्णाति; सामिधेन्यो जभ्रिरे, उदग्राभञ्च निग्राभञ्च ब्रह्म देवा अवीवृधन् ॥

व्रश्चभ्रस्जसृजमृजयजराजभ्राजच्छशां षः ॥ ३६ ॥ पदानि ॥ व्रश्च, भ्रस्ज, सृज, मृज, यज, राज, भ्राज, छ, शाम्, षः ॥

वृत्तिः ॥ व्रश्च भ्रस्ज सृज मृज यज राज भ्राज इत्येतेषां छकारान्तानां शकारान्तानां च षकार आदेशो भवति झलि परतः पदान्ते च ॥

36. For the final consonants of vrasch, bhrasj, sṛij mṛij, yaj, râj, and bhrâj, and for the final छ and श, there is substituted ष् before a *jhal* letter, or at the end of a word.

Thus व्रश्च् :—व्रष्टा, व्रष्टुम्, व्रष्टव्यम् मूलवृट् ॥ भ्रष्टा । भ्रष्टुम् । भ्रष्टव्यम् । धानाभृट् । सृज् । स्रष्टा । स्रष्टुम् । स्रष्टव्यम् । रज्जुसृट् । मृज । मार्ष्टा । मार्ष्टुम् । मार्ष्टव्यम् । कंसपरिमृट् । यज । यष्टा । यष्टुम् । यष्टव्यम् । उपयट् । राज् । सम्राट् । स्वराट्, विराट्, विभ्राट् ॥ The श ending words would have been changed to जश्-letters and the others to Gutturals; this sûtra debars that by ordaining ष ॥ In मूलवृट् and धानाभृट् there is vocalisation by VI. 1. 16, the स् is elided by VIII. 2. 19, and ष becomes जश्-letter ड्, which becomes ट् by VIII. 4. 56. The word शब्दप्राट् is formed by क्विप्, there is lengthening and no vocalisation.

The roots राज् and भ्राज् are never followed by a *jhal* beginning affix, because such affixes will always take इट् augment. These roots are, therefore, mentioned here, for the sake of the change of their ज् to ष्, when at the end of a word. Some, however, form nouns like राष्टिः, भ्राष्टिः with क्तिन् affix from these roots by III. 3. 94, vârt., and इट् augment is prevented by VII. 2. 9.

Of roots ending in छ we have प्रच्छ :—प्रष्टा, प्रष्टुम्, प्रष्टव्यम्, शब्दप्राट् ॥ According to one view, the letter छ should not be mentioned in this sûtra: for by VI. 4. 19, छ is always changed to श, and this श will be changed to ष by the present sûtra. Others hold, that the change of छ to श by VI. 4. 19 is confined before कित् or ङित् affixes, and therefore the mention of छ is necessary in this sûtra; moreover the ष् substitution here, and the श् substitution in VI. 4. 19. refer to the conjunct letter च्छ (with the augment तुक्). For if it were not so, then छ alone being changed to ष्, the त् of तुक् would be changed to ट्, and we should have पृट्टः instead of पृष्टः ॥

Of roots ending in श् we have लिश्:—लेष्टा, लेष्टुम्, लेष्टव्यम्, लिट्; विश् :—वेष्टा, वेष्टुम्, वेष्टव्यम्, विट् ॥

एकाचो बशो भष् झषन्तस्य स्ध्वोः ॥ ३७ ॥ पदानि ॥ एक-अचः, बशः, भष्, झष-अन्तस्य, स्, ध्वोः ॥

वृत्तिः ॥ धातोरवयवो य एकाच् झषन्तः तदवयवस्य बशः स्थाने भष् आदेशो भवति झलि सकारे ध्वशब्दे च परतः पदान्ते च ॥

37. For the letters ब, ग, ड or द in the beginning of a monosyllable, and belonging to a root, and which ends in झ, भ, घ, ढ or ध, there is substituted भ, घ, ढ or ध respectively, before स or ध्व, or at the end of a pada (word).

Thus from बुध्—भोत्स्यन्ते, अभुध्वम् and अर्थभुत्; from गुह्—नि घोक्ष्यते न्यघुढ्वम्, पर्णघुट् ॥ गुह् becomes गुढ् by VIII. 2. 31, and thus it is a root ending in jhash.

From दुह्—(which becomes दुघ् by VIII. 2. 32, and thus is a jhash ending root) धोक्ष्यते अदुग्ध्वम्, गोधुक् ॥

So also from गृध् we have अजर्घाः the 2nd Person. Sing. Imperfect (लङ्) Intensive (yañ luk). There is guṇa of ऋ, the स् (of सिप् 2nd Pers. Sing.) is elided (VI. 1. 68), and we have अजगर्ध्, and for the letter ग of the monosyllabic root, घ is substituted by the present aphorism. अजर्घर्ध् ॥ Then the final ध् is changed to द्, अजर्घर्द् (VIII. 2. 39). Then द् is changed to र् by VIII. 2. 75, अजर्घर् ॥ Then the first र् is elided अजर्घर् (VIII. 3. 14). Then there is lengthening by VI. 3. 111, and we have अजर्घाः ॥

The monosyllable should be such that it should begin with a बश् and end with a झष् letter, and should be a full root or the portion (अवयव) of a root. In fact, this word which we found necessary in VIII. 2. 32, is absolutely necessary here, in order to explain forms like गर्धप् from the Denominative root गर्दभय, by क्विप् ॥

Why do we say "a monosyllable beginning with बश् and ending with झष्?" Observe दामलिट् from the Denominative root दामलिह ॥ For had एकाचः not been employed in the sûtra, the word धातोः (VIII. 2. 32) would have qualified बशः and the sûtra would have meant "in a root which ended in a jhash, and which contained a बश् letter as its member; there is jhash substitution for such बश्", and the द of दामलिह would be changed then.

Why do we say "for a बश् letter"? Observe क्रुध्—क्रोत्स्यति here क is not changed to घ ॥ Why do we say ending in jhash? Observe दास्यति ॥ Why before स and ध्व? Observe बोद्धा, बोद्धुम्, बोद्धव्यम् ॥

Why have we taken भष् and not merely भ? Observe दादद्धि from दध् in the यङ् लुक्, Imperative 2nd Per. singular, the हि being changed to धि (VI. 4. 101). The substitutes are four भ, घ, ढ and ध, and their respective sthânins are also four, i. e. ब, ग, ड and द; so that ढ is the substitite of ड; but, as a matter of fact, ड never so stands at the beginning of a monosyllable, and so there is no ढ substitition.

दधस्तथोश्च ॥ ३८ ॥ पदानि ॥ दधः, त, थोः, च ॥

वृत्तिः ॥ दध इति दधातिः कृतद्विर्वचनो निर्दिश्यते। तस्य झलन्तस्य बशः स्थाने भष् आदेशो भवति तकारथकारयोः परतश्चकारात् स्ध्वोश्च परतः ॥

38. For the द of दध (the reduplicated form of धा) is substituted ध, before the affixes beginning with त, थ, स and before ध्वम् ॥

The word दध is taken in the sûtra as the reduplicated form of धा दधाति and not the root दध धारणे of Bhuâdi class, as शप् intervenes there. By the word च we draw in the words स and ध्व ॥ Thus धत्तः, धत्थः, धत्से, धत्स्व, धध्वम् ॥ By the express injunction of this sûtra, the elided अ is not considered as sthânivat. The last sûtra could not have applied to दध for two reasons. 1st. It does not begin with a बश् letter, for the real reduplicate is धध, and द is merely a substitute, and is considered asiddha. 2ndly. The form दध does not end in a jhash consonant, but in a vowel अ, and though this अ is elided before these affixes, yet the lopa would be sthânivat. Hence the necessity of च in this sûtra. See coutra, the vârtika in Mahâbhâshya.

The word झलि is understood here, and so also झषन्तस्य; and there can be no affix, but begins with त or थ, that can come after दध् ॥ Why do we employ then the words 'before त and थ'? Had we not used these, the sûtra would have referred to स and ध्व only, as being in immediate proximity, and the च draws them in. According to Padamanjari the words तथोश्च could have been dispensed with: for before स् and ध्व, the भ change would have taken place by the last sûtra, whilst by this sûtra, the same change would have taken place before all other झल्-beginning affixes, and such affixes that can come after दध् are त or थ-beginning affixes.

The word jhash is understood here also, therefore the rule applies to दध then only, when it assumes the form of दध्, by the elision of आ; and hence not here दधाति ॥

झलां जशोन्ते ॥ ३९ ॥ पदानि ॥ झलां, जशः, अन्ते ॥

वृत्तिः ॥ झलां जश आदेशा भवन्ति पदस्यान्ते वर्त्तमानानाम् ॥

39. A corresponding ज, ब, ग, ड or द is substituted for all consonants (with the exception of semivowels and nasals) at the end of a word.

As वाग् अत्र, श्वलिड् अत्र, अग्निचिद् अत्र, त्रिष्टुब् अत्र ॥ The word श्वलिड् is formed by changing the ह् of लिह् to ढ *first*, and *then* changing this ढ to ड, a jaś-letter.

The word अन्त 'at the end' is used in the sûtra to indicate that the anuvṛitti of झलि ceases. Thus वस्ता, वस्तुम्, वस्तव्यम् ॥

The exceptions to this have been given in VIII. 2. 30 &c, and VIII. 2. 66. At an avasâna or Pause, a चर् consonant may be substituted for a झल् by VIII. 4. 56.

झषस्तथोर्धोऽधः ॥ ४० ॥ पदानि ॥ झषः, त-थोः, धः, अधः ॥

वृत्तिः ॥ झष उत्तरयोस्तकारथकारयो स्थाने धकार आदेशो भवति ॥

40. ध is substituted for त or थ coming after झ, भ, घ, ढ or ध (jhash), but not after the root धा (दध) ॥

Thus from लभ् we have लब्धा, लब्धुम्, लब्धव्यम्, अलब्ध, अलब्धाः ॥,

The भ् of लभ् is changed to ब by VIII. 4. 53. From दुह्:—दोग्धा, दोग्धुम्, दोग्धव्यम्, अदुग्ध, अदुग्धाः ॥ The ह is changed to घ by VIII. 2. 32, and then it is changed to ग by VIII. 4. 53.

From लिह् :—लेढा, लेढुम, लेढव्यम्, अलीढ, अलीढाः ॥ In लेढ्धृ &c, the ह् is changed to ढ by VIII. 2. 31, and ध changed to ढ by VIII. 4. 41, before which the preceding ढ is elided by VIII. 3. 13.

From बुध् :—बोद्धा, बोद्धुम्, बोद्धव्यम्, अबुद्ध, अबुद्धाः ॥ For the ध of बुध् there is substituted द् by VIII. 4. 53.

Why do we say "but not after the root धा"? Observe धत्तः, धत्थः ॥

षढोः कः सि ॥ ४१ ॥ पदानि ॥ षढोः, कः, सि ॥

वृत्तिः ॥ षकारढकारयोः ककारादेशो भवति सकारे परतः ॥

41. क is substituted for ष or ढ before स ॥

Thus for ष of विष् we have विवेक्ष्यते, अवेक्ष्यत्, विविक्षति ॥ For ढ of लिह् (लिढ VIII. 2. 31) we have लेक्ष्यति, अलेक्ष्यत्, लिलिक्षति ॥

For the स of the affix स्य &c, is substituted ष by VIII. 3. 59.

Why do we say "before स"? Observe पिनष्टि, लेढि ॥

रदाभ्यां निष्ठातो नः पूर्वस्य च दः ॥ ४२ ॥ पदानि ॥ रदाभ्याम्, निष्ठातः, नः, पूर्वस्य, च, दः ॥

वृत्तिः ॥ रेफदकाराभ्यामुत्तरस्य निष्ठातकारस्य नकार आदेशो भवति । पूर्वस्य चदकारस्य ॥

42. After र and द, for the त of the Participial suffix त and तवत्, there is substituted न, and the same substitution takes place also for the preceding द ॥

After र :—आस्तीर्णम्, विस्तीर्णम्, विशीर्णम्, निगीर्णम्, अवगूर्णम् ॥

After द :—भिन्नः, भिन्नवान्, छिन्नः, छिन्नवान् from भिद् and छिद् ॥

Why do we say "after र and द"? Observe कृतः, कृतवान् ॥ The word र here does not denote the common *sound* र, which would include ऋ also, but the consonant र ॥ But even if र् be taken a common sound-name including र् and ऋ, yet the न् change does not take place in कृत &c, because betneeen त and the र्-sound, there intervenes vowel-sound इ, for ऋ is sounded not like pure र्, but र्+a vowel sound.

Why do we say "of the Participial suffix"? Observe कर्त्ता, हर्त्ता ॥

Why do we say "for the त"? Observe चरितम्, हरितम् ॥ Here the त of the Nishṭhâ does not follow *immediately* after र, the augment इट् intervenes.

Why do we say "of the preceding"? The succeeding द will not be changed. As भिन्नवद्भ्याम्, भिन्नवाद्भिः ॥

In the word कार्त्तिः the descendant of कृतः the त of Nishṭhâ is immediately preceded by र्, but no change has taken place, because the Vṛiddhi, by which कृ is changed to कार्, is Bahiranga and consequently asiddha, and for the purposes of न change, the र् so obtained is invalid.

संयोगादेरातो धातोर्यण्वतः ॥ ४३ ॥ पदानि ॥ संयोग-आदेः, आतः, धातोः, यण्वतः ॥

वृत्तिः ॥ संयोगादिर्यो धातुराकारान्तो यण्वान् तस्मादुत्तरस्य निष्ठातकारस्य नकारादेशो भवति ॥

43. For the त of the Nishṭhâ there is substituted न, after a root ending in आ and commencing with a conjunct consonant, if the latter contain a semi-vowel.

Thus from द्रा we have प्रद्राणः, प्रद्राणवान् ॥ ग्लानः, ग्लानवान् from ग्ला ॥ These roots द्रा and ग्ला end in आ, have a conjunct consonant in the beginning, one of which is a semi-vowel र and ल ॥

Why do we say "beginning with a double-consonant"? Observe यातः, यातवान् ॥

Why do we say "ending in आ"? Observe च्युतः, च्युतवान्; प्लुतः, प्लुतवान् ॥

Why do we say "after a root"? Observe निर्यातः, निर्वातः ॥ For the roots here या and वा do not begin with a conjunct consonont, and that which is a conjunct i. e. र्या and र्वा is not a root, hence the rule does not apply.

Why do we say "having a यण् or semi-vowel"? Observe स्नातः, स्नातवान् ॥

ल्वादिभ्यः ॥ ४४ ॥ पदानि ॥ लू-आदिभ्यः ॥

वृत्तिः ॥ लूञ् छेदने इत्येतत्प्रभृति वॄ वरण इति यावत् वृत्करणेन समापिता ल्वादयो गृह्यन्ते । तेभ्य उत्तरस्य निष्ठातकारस्य नकारादेशो भवति ॥

वार्त्तिकम् ॥ ॠकारल्वादिभ्यः क्तिन्निष्ठावद्भवतीति वक्तव्यम् ॥ वा० ॥ दुग्वोर्दीर्घश्चेति वक्तव्यम् ॥ वा० ॥ पूञो विनाश इति वक्तव्यम् ॥ वा० ॥ सिनोतेर्ग्रासकर्म्मकर्तृकस्येति वक्तव्यम् ॥

44. The त of Nishṭhâ is changed to न, after the roots लू and those that follow it.

These roots belong to Kryâdi class, and commence from लूञ् छेदने (IX. 13) and end with वॄ वरणे (IX. 32).

Thus लूनः, लूनवान्, धूनः, धूनवान्, जीनः, जीनवान् from ज्या the vocalisation is by VI. 1. 16.

Vârt:—After a root ending in ॠ or ॠ and after a root of Luâdi class, the त of the affix क्तिन् is changed to न्, like as in Nishṭhâ. Thus कीर्णिः, गीर्णिः, शीर्णिः, लूनिः, पूनिः ॥ These are from कॄ (IX. 26), गॄ (IX. 28), शॄ (IX. 18), लू and पूञ् ॥

Vârt:—The vowel of the roots दु गतौ (Bhu. 991) and गु (Bhu. 997), are lengthened before the Nishṭhâ which is changed to न ॥ As आदूनः, विगूनः ॥

Vârt:—The न change takes place after पूञ् 'to destroy' (Bhu. 1015). As पूना यवाः = विनष्टाः ॥ But पूतं धान्यं from पूञ् 'to purify' (IX. 12).

Vârt:—The same change takes place after the root सि बन्धने of Svâdi class (2) when used in a Reflexive sense of becoming a morsel fit for swallowing. As सिनो ग्रासः स्वयमेव i.e. where a morsel by being mixed with curd, condiments &c, becomes rounded of itself, there this form is used. बध्यमानः पिण्डीक्रियमाणो ग्रासो, यदा दध्यादिव्यञ्जन वशेन तत्रानुकूल्यं प्रतिपद्यते तदाऽयम् प्रयोगः ॥ But when not used in this sense, we have सिता पाशेन सूकरी ॥ Moreover, the मास must be the object and not the subject of the verb. Therefore not here: सितो मासो देवदत्तेन ॥

ओदितश्च ॥ ४५ ॥ पदानि ॥ ओदितः, च ॥

वृत्तिः ॥ ओकारेतो धातोः उत्तरस्य निष्ठातकारस्य नकारादेशो भवति ॥

45. The त of Nishṭhâ is changed to न, after a root, which has an indicatory ओ in the Dhâtupâṭha.

Thus ओलस्जी—लग्नः, लग्नवान्, ओविजी—उद्विग्नः, उद्विग्नवान ॥ ओप्यायी वृद्धौ :—आपीनः, आ पीनवान्॥

The roots सूङ् प्राणिप्रसवे (Div. 24) &c. are considered as ओदित् ॥ Thus, सूनः, सूनवान्; दूङ्—दूनः, दूनवान्; दीङ्—दीनः, दीनवान्; डीङ्—डीनः, डीनवान्; धीङ्—धीनः, धीनवान्; मीङ्—मीनः, मीनवान्; रीङ्—रीणः, रीणवान्, लीङ्—लीनः, लीनवान्, व्रीङ्—व्रीणः, व्रीणवान् ॥

क्षियो दीर्घात् ॥ ४६ ॥ पदानि ॥ क्षियः, दीर्घात् ॥

वृत्तिः ॥ क्षियो धातोर्दीर्घादुत्तरस्य निष्ठातकारस्य नकारादेशो भवति ॥

46. The त of Nishṭhâ is changed to न, after क्षि, when the root-vowel is lengthened.

Thus क्षीणाः क्लेशाः; क्षीणो जाल्मः; क्षीणस्तपस्वी ॥ The vowel of क्षि is lengthened by VI. 4. 60 and 61.

Why do we say 'when the vowel is lengthened'? Observe अक्षितमसि मामेक्षेष्ठाः ॥ The word अक्षितं is formed with क्त in the sense of भाव and means 'imperishable'. The Nishṭhâ being added in the sense of ण्यत्, there is no lengthening of the vowel by VI. 4. 60.

The root क्षि includes the two roots क्षि क्षये and क्षि निवासगत्योः ॥ As क्षितः कामो मया ॥ See also the commentary of Sâyana on अक्षितोतिः सनेदिमं वाजमिन्द्रः सहस्रिणं ॥ (Rig I. 5. 9).

Obj:—The form क्षियः in the sûtra is the Genitive singular of the root-noun क्षी ending in long ई, and will denote the root क्षी ending in long ई according to the maxim प्रकृतिवदनुकरणं भवति "an imitative name (as क्षी here) is like its original (the root क्षी)". What is then the necessity of employing the word दीर्घात् in the sûtra? For had the root क्षि with short इ been meant, the form would have been क्षेः ॥

Ans.—The dhâtu imitative noun though taking इयङ् (VI. 4. 77) as in क्षियः, includes the dhâtu ending in short इ also, as in sûtra VI. 4. 59, 60 where क्षि ending in short इ is taken.

Q. If a root ending in short vowel may also be indicated by an imitative name, declined with इयङ् augment, then why is the root ञि exhibited in sûtra I. 3. 19 as जेः instead of जियः i. e. the sûtra ought to have been वि पराभ्यां जियः and not वि पराभ्यां जेः?

Ans. Here the word जि is not used as a dhâtu-imitative word, there is no intention here to denote the verbal idea of the particular act connoted by the root जि; on the contrary, it simply expresses the *mere form* जि ॥

श्यो ऽस्पर्शे ॥ ४७ ॥ पदानि ॥ श्यः, अ-स्पर्शे ॥

वृत्तिः ॥ श्याधातेरुत्तरस्य निष्ठातकारस्यास्पर्शे नकार आदेशो भवति ॥

47. The Nishṭhâ त is changed to न after श्यै, but not when the Participle denotes 'cold'.

Thus शीनं घृतम्, शीनो मेदः, शीना वसा; but शीतं वर्तते, शीतो वायुः, शीतमुदकम् ॥ The य् of श्या is vocalised to ई by VI. 1. 24.

The prohibition applies when the noun is an adjective and means 'cold'; and not when it means a disease. Therefore we have प्रतिशीनः with न change.

The word स्पर्श is a guna word formed by घञ्, and denotes the particular guna or sensation to be sensed through the organ of touch. In this sense it is derived from the root स्पृश संस्पर्शने ॥ It also denotes a disease, derived from स्पृश उपतापे ॥ There is nothing to show, what स्पर्श is meant in the sûtra. Explanation is the only refuge here.

अञ्चो ऽनपादाने ॥ ४८ ॥ पदानि ॥ अंचः, अन्-अपादाने ॥

वृत्तिः ॥ अञ्चतेरुत्तरपदस्य निष्ठातकारस्य नकारादेशो भवति न चेदपादानं तत्र भवति ॥

48. The Nishṭhâ त is changed to न, after अञ्च्, but not when it is in connection with an Ablative case.

Thus समक्नौ शकुनेः पादौ = सङ्गतौ; तस्मात् पशवो न्यक्ताः ॥

Why do we say 'when not in construction with an Ablative case'? Observe उदक्तमुदकं कूपात् = उद्धृतं 'drawn out'.

The word व्यक्तम् is from the root अञ्जू व्यक्तिम्रक्षण कान्तिगतिषु, and not from the root अञ्च्; and hence the Nishṭhâ is not changed.

दिवो ऽविजिगीषायाम् ॥ ४९ ॥ पदानि ॥ दिवः, अ-विजिगीषायाम् ॥

वृत्तिः ॥ दिव उत्तरस्य निष्ठातकारस्य नकारादेशो भवति अविजिगीषायामर्थे ॥

49. The Nishṭhâ त is changed to न, after दिव्, when the sense is not that of 'play'.

The word विजिगीषा means "desire of conquest or gain", but here it means "gambling".

Thus आद्यूनः, = औदरिकः, परिद्यूनः = क्षीणः ॥ Why do we say "when it does not mean to play"? Observe द्यूतं वर्तते ॥ Here the throwing of dice is with the desire of winning or gaining victory (vijigîshâ) over the opponent.

निर्वाणो ऽवाते ॥ ५० ॥ पदानि ॥ निर्वाणः, अ-वाते ॥

वृत्तिः ॥ निर्वाण इति निस्पूर्वाद्वातेरुत्तरस्य निष्ठातकारस्य नकारो निपात्यते । न चेद्वाताधिकरणो वात्यर्थो भवति ॥

50. The word निर्वाण is irregularly formed by changing the Nishṭhâ त to न, when the sense is not that of 'wind'.

The word निर्वाण is formed from the root वा, with the preposition निर् and the Participial affix त ॥ Thus निर्वाणो ऽग्निः,=उपशान्तः, निर्वाणः प्रदीपः, निर्वाणो भिक्षुः =उपरतः ॥

Why do we say when not meaning "the wind"? Observe निर्वातो वातः, निर्वातं वातेन ॥

In the sentences निर्वाणः प्रदीपो वातेन, निर्वाणोऽग्निर्वातेन, the न change has taken place, because the location of the verb वा is in the प्रदीप and अग्नि, and not in the वात, which is merely an Instrument. Hence the above vṛitti uses the words "if the sense of the verb वा does not govern वात in the locative case".

शुषः कः ॥ ५१ ॥ पदानि ॥ शुषः, कः ॥

वृत्तिः ॥ शुषेर्धातोरुत्तरस्य निष्ठातकारस्य ककारादेशो भवति ॥

51. क is substituted for the Nishṭhâ त after the root शुष् ॥

As शुष्कः, शुष्कवान् ॥

पचो वः ॥ ५२ ॥ पदानि ॥ पचः वः ॥

वृत्तिः ॥ पचेर्धातोरुत्तरस्य निष्ठातकारस्य वकारादेशो भवति ॥

52. व is substituted for the Nishṭhâ त after the root पच् ॥

As पक्वः, पक्ववान् ॥

क्षायो मः ॥ ५३ ॥ पदानि ॥ क्षायः, मः ॥

वृत्तिः ॥ क्षैधातोरुत्तरस्य निष्ठातकारस्य मकारादेशो भवति ॥

53. म is substituted for the Nishṭhâ त after the root क्षै ॥

Thus क्षामः, क्षामवान् ॥

प्रस्त्योन्यतरस्याम् ॥ ५४ ॥ पदानि ॥ प्रस्त्यः, अन्यतरस्याम् ॥

वृत्तिः ॥ प्रपूर्वात् स्त्यायतेरुत्तरस्य निष्ठातकारस्यान्यतरस्यां मकारादेशो भवति ॥

54. म is optionally substituted for the Nishṭhâ त, after the root स्त्यै preceded by प्र ॥

Thus प्रस्तीमः or प्रस्तीतः, प्रस्तीमवान् or प्रस्तीतवान् ॥ In the second alternative when म does not come, we first vocalise the root स्त्या into स्ती, and then add त ॥ Had Samprasâraṇa not taken place first, then the Nishṭhâ त would have been changed to न after स्त्या by VIII. 2. 43. But when samprasâraṇa is once made, the root no longer has a semi-vowel and so there remains no occasion for the application of VIII. 2. 43. See VI. 1. 23 for vocalisation.

अनुपसर्गात्फुल्लक्षीबकृशोल्लाघाः ॥ ५५ ॥ पदानि ॥ अनुपसर्गात्, फुल्ल-क्षीब-कृश-उल्लाघाः ॥

वृत्तिः ॥ फुल्ल क्षीब कृश उल्लाघ इत्येते निपात्यन्ते न चेदुपसर्गादुत्तरा भवन्ति ॥

वार्त्तिकम् ॥ उत्फुल्लसंफुल्लयोरिति वक्तव्यम् ॥

55. The irregular Participles फुल्ल, क्षीब, कृश and उल्लाघ are formed then only, when no Preposition precedes them.

The word फुल्ल is derived from the root ञिफला विशरणे the त is changed to ल ॥ The change of अ to उ (VII. 4. 88) and the want of इट् augment (VII. 2. 16) are regular. The same change takes place before क्तवतु also, as फुल्लवान् ॥

The affix त् is elided after the roots क्षीव्, कृश् and उत्—लाघ्, and the augment इट् is prohibited ; this is the irregularity in क्षीबः, कृशः and उल्लाघः ॥

Why do we say when not preceded by a Preposition ? Observe प्रफुल्ताः सुमनसः, प्रक्षीबितः, प्रकृशितः, प्रोल्लाघितः ॥ In the case of लाघ्, prepositions other than उत् are prohibited.

Or the augment इट् is added, and then इत् is elided from क्षीवितः &c. See VIII. 2. 3 *vârt.*

Vârt :—The forms उत्फुल्लः and संफुल्लः should be enumerated. Here त is changed to ल, though the root has taken a Preposition.

In the word परिकृशः, the word परि is not a Preposition with regard to the verb कृश्; परिगतः कृशः = परिकृशः ॥ So that परि is upasarga of the verb गतः understood, hence we have the form कृशः ॥

नुदविदोन्दत्राघ्राह्रीभ्यो ऽन्यतरस्याम् ॥ ५६ ॥ पदानि ॥ नुद, विद, उन्द, त्रा, घ्रा, ह्रीभ्यः, अन्यतरस्याम् ॥

वृत्तिः ॥ नुद विद उन्द त्रा घ्रा ह्री इत्येतेभ्य उत्तरस्य निष्ठातकारस्य नकार आदेशो भवति अन्यतरस्याम् ॥

Kârikâ :—वेत्तेस्तु विदितो निष्ठा विद्यतेर्विन्न इष्यते ।
विन्तेर्विन्नश्च वित्तश्च भोगे वित्तश्च विन्दतेः ॥

56. The Nishṭhâ त may optionally be changed to न, after नुद, विद, उन्द, त्रा, घ्रा, ह्री ॥

Thus नुन्नः or नुत्तः, विन्नः or वित्तः, समुन्नः or समुत्तः, त्राणः or त्रातः, घ्राणः or घ्रातः, ह्रीणः or ह्रीतः ॥

With regard to ह्री, the न change was not ordained by any rule, and so it is an aprâpta-vibhâshâ. With regards to others, the न change would have *always* taken place by VIII. 2. 42 and 43, this makes it optional.

The root विद विचारणे of Rudhâdi is to be taken here, and not the other विद roots. Thus the following : *Kârikâ*

The Nishṭhâ of विद्–वेत्ति of Adâdi-class is विदितः ; (2) of विद्–विद्यते of Divâdi class is विन्नः only ; (3) of विद् of Tudâdi is विन्नः ; (4) of विद् of Rudhâdi are both वित्तः and विन्नः ॥ The Tudâdi विद् has also the form वित्तः in the sense of भोग by VIII. 2. 58.

न ध्याख्यापॄमूर्च्छिमदाम् ॥ ५७ ॥ पदानि ॥ न, ध्या, ख्या, पॄ, मूर्छि, मदाम् ॥

वृत्तिः ॥ ध्या ख्या पॄ मूर्छि मद इत्येतेषां निष्ठातकारस्य नकारादेशो न भवति ॥

57. The Nishṭhâ त is not changed to न after ध्या, ख्या, पॄ, मूर्च्छि and मद ॥

Thus ध्यातः, ध्यातवान्, ख्यातः, ख्यातवान्, पूर्त्तः, पूर्त्तवान्, मूर्त्तः, मूर्त्तवान्, मत्तः, मत्तवान् ॥

This debars the न change prescribed by VIII. 2. 42, 43.

The root मूर्छि is exhibited in the sûtra in its lengthened form ; the root मुर्च्छ is lengthened by VIII. 2. 78, and the च्छ is elided before त by VI. 4. 21.

वित्तो भोगप्रत्यययोः ॥ ५८ ॥ पदानि ॥ वित्तः, भोग, प्रत्यययोः ॥

वृत्तिः ॥ वित्त इति विदेर्लाभार्थादुत्तरस्य क्तस्य नत्वाभावो निपात्यते भोगे प्रत्यये चाभिधेये ॥

58. The irregularly formed Participle वित्त denotes 'possessions' and 'renowned'.

This is derived from विदॢ लाभे of Tudâdi class, the त is not changed to न though so required by VIII. 2. 42.

Thus वित्तमस्य बहु = धनमस्य बहु 'he has much riches'. Because riches are enjoyed (भुज्यते), so they are called भोग or 'enjoyments' *par excellence.*

In the sense of 'renowned', we have वित्तोऽयं मनुष्यः "this man is renowned or famous". Here वित्तः = प्रतीतः ॥ प्रतायते = प्रत्ययः ॥

Why do we say when having the sense of 'possessions' and 'famous'? Observe विन्नः ॥

भित्तं शकलम् ॥ ५९ ॥ पदानि ॥ भित्तम्, शकलम् ॥

वृत्तिः ॥ भित्तमिति निपात्यते शकलं चेत्तद्भवति ॥

59. The word भित्त is irregularly formed in the sense of 'a fragment, a portion'.

Thus भित्तं तिष्ठति, भित्तं प्रपतति ॥ This is synonymous with शकल ॥ The root-meaning of भिद् is not very manifest in this word, it may be taken as a *rudhi* word. The regular form is भिन्नं under VIII. 2. 42.

ऋणमाधमर्ण्ये ॥ ६० ॥ पदानि ॥ ऋणम्, आधमर्ण्ये ॥

वृत्तिः ॥ ऋणमिति ऋइत्येतस्माद्धातोरुत्तरस्य निष्ठातकारस्य नकारो निपात्यते आधमर्ण्यविषये ॥

60. The word ऋण is irregularly formed in the sense of 'debt.'

It is derived from ऋ, the त is changed to न ॥ The word अधमर्ण is compounded from अधम ऋणे "he who in a debt transaction holds a lower position"—

i.e. a debtor. This nipâtana shows that such irregular Locative compounds may be formed; for here the first member is *not* in the Locative case, but the second member. The condition of being a debtor is आधमर्ण्यम् or "indebtedness:"

If this is so, then the word उत्तमर्णः 'creditor' cannot be formed? This is no valid objection. For अधमर्ण is illustrative only of something to be paid hereafter, in consideration of something formely received; and thus includes उत्तमर्ण also; which also has been so employed by the author himself in धारेरुत्तमर्णः (I. 4. 35).

The word ऋण we use in sentences like ऋणं ददाति, ऋणं धारयति ॥

Why do we say when meaning 'debt'? Observe ऋतं वक्ष्यामि, नानृतम् ॥

नसत्तनिषत्तानुत्तप्रतूर्त्तसूर्त्तगूर्त्तानि छन्दसि ॥ ६१ ॥ पदानि ॥ नसत्त, निषत्त, अनुत्त, प्रतूर्त्त, सूर्त्त, गूर्त्तानि, छन्दसि ॥

वृत्तिः ॥ नसत्त निषत्त अनुत्त प्रतूर्त्त सूर्त्त गूर्त्त इत्येतानि छन्दसि विषये निपात्यन्ते ॥

61. In the Chhandas we have the following irregular Participles:—nasatta, nishatta, anutta, pratûrtta, sûrtta, gûrtta.

The words नसत्त and निषत्त are derived from the root सद् preceded by न and नि, and there is not the न change of VIII. 2. 42. Thus नसत्तमञ्जसा ॥ In secular literature we have नसन्नम् ॥ So also निषत्तः in the Vedas, but निषण्णः in secular literature. The word अनुत्तः is from उन्द् with the negative अन् ॥ The option of VIII. 2. 56 does not apply here. As अनुत्तमा ते मघवन् (= अनुन्नम्) ॥ प्रतूर्त्तम् is from त्वर् or तूर्व्, as प्रतूर्त्तं वाजिनम् (= प्रतूर्णम्) ॥ When it is derived from त्वर् then ऊठ् is added by VI. 4. 20; and when from तूर्व् then VI. 4. 21 is applied. सूर्त्तं is from सृ, the ऋ is changed to उ irregularly, as सूर्त्तागावः = सृतागावः ॥ गूर्त्तं is from गुर्, as गूर्त्ता अमृतस्य (= गूर्णं) ॥

क्विन्प्रत्ययस्य कुः ॥ ६२ ॥ पदानि ॥ क्विन्, प्रत्ययस्य, कुः ॥

वृत्तिः ॥ पदस्यति वर्त्तते । क्विन्प्रत्ययस्य सर्वत्र पदान्ते कुत्वमिष्यते । क्विन्प्रत्ययो यस्माद्धातोः स क्विन्प्रत्ययः, तस्य पदस्यान्त्यस्य कवर्गादेशो भवति ॥

62. A stem formed with the affix क्विन् under III. 2. 58 &c, substitutes, at the end of a word, a guttural for the final consonant.

The word पदस्य is understood here. The word क्विन्प्रत्यय is a Bahuvrihi meaning 'that stem which has kvin as its affix.' For the final consonant of such a stem, a guttural is substituted. As घृतस्पृक् (III. 2. 58), हलस्पृक्, मन्त्रस्पृक् ॥

The sûtra could have been क्विनः कुः; the word प्रत्यय is used in the sûtra to show the Bahuvrihi compound; so that the न् of क्विन् may not be changed to a guttural. Moreover this Bahuvrihi also indicates that the roots which take the क्विन् affix, change their final to a guttural before other affixes than क्विन् ॥

Thus the roots सृज् and दृश् take क्विन् to form स्रक् and दृक् nouns by III. 2. 59, 60. The guttural change will take place even when these roots are declined as verbs: as, मानो अस्राक् मानो अद्राक्, where अस्राक् and अद्राक् are the Aorist of सृज् and दृश् ॥ The augment अट् is not elided, though the मा is added (VI. 4. 75) as a Vedic diversity. The ईट् augment also does not take place as a Vedic irregularity. The augment अम् is added by VI. 1. 58, and the vowel is lengthened by Vṛiddhi by VII. 2. 3. Thus अट्+सृज्+सिच्+तिप्=अस्रज् (VI. 1. 58)=अस्राक् (VII. 2. 3 and VIII. 2. 62). Other wise it would have been ष् by VIII. 2. 36. So also in दृग्भ्यां, दृग्भिः, the श् is changed to a guttural, though the noun दृश् is a क्विप् formed noun and not formed by क्विन्; and this is so, because the verb दृश् does take क्विन् also.

Obj. If this be so, there ought to be guttural change in रज्जुसृड्भ्यां from the root सृज् with क्विप्? Ans. The guttural change however in not desired here.

In gutturalisation, ज is changed to ग, and श to ख, which both become क by वावसाने (VIII. 4. 56)

नशेर्वा ॥ ६३ ॥ पदानि ॥ नशेः, वा ॥

वृत्तिः ॥ पदस्येति वर्त्तते ॥ नशेः पदस्य वा कवर्गादेशो भवति ॥

63. The final of नश् at the end of a word is optionally changed to a guttural.

The word पदस्य is understood here also. As सा वै जीवनगाहुतिः (Maitr. S. I. 4. 13): or सा वै जीवनगाहुतिः ॥ According to Pro. Bohtlingk this latter form is not found in the Samhitâ.

Here the root नश् has taken क्विप् in denoting 'condition or state'; by considering it as belonging to संपदादि class.

जीवस्य नाशः = जीवनक् or जीवनट् ॥ The gutturalisation optionally debars the ष change of VIII. 2. 36. When the ष change takes place, this ष is changed to ट् by VIII. 2. 39 and VIII. 4. 56.

मोनो धातोः ॥ ६४ ॥ पदानि ॥ मः, नः, धातोः ॥

वृत्तिः ॥ मकारान्तस्य धातोः पदस्य नकारादेशो भवति ॥

वार्त्तिकम् ॥ अनुनासिकस्य क्विझलोः क्ङितीति दीर्घत्वम् ॥

64. न is substituted, at the end of a word, for the final म of a root.

As प्रशान्, प्रतान्, प्रदान् ॥ These are formed by adding क्विप् to the roots शम्, तम् and दम् ॥ The lengthening takes place by VI. 4. 15. The न् being considered as asiddha is not elided.

Why do we say "of म-ending roots"? Observe भित्, छित् ॥

Why do we say "of a root"? Observe इदम्, किम् ॥

The word पदस्य is understood here also. So we have प्रशामौ, प्रशामः where म is not at the end of a word.

म्वोश्च ॥ ६५ ॥ पदानि ॥ म्, वोः, च ॥

वृत्तिः ॥ मकारवकारयोश्च परतः मकारान्तस्य धातोर्नकारादेशो भवति ॥

65. न is substituted for the म of a root before the affixes beginning with म and व ॥

As अगन्म, अगन्व the Imperfect of गम्, as in the sentence अगन्म तमसः पारम ॥ The शप् is elided as a Vedic diversity. So also जगन्वान् with क्वसु, the augment इट् is not added by the option allowed, owing to VII. 1. 68. This sûtra applies to those cases where the म is not at the end of a word, as it was in the last sûtra.

ससजुषो रुः ॥ ६६ ॥ पदानि ॥ स, सजुषोः, रुः ॥

वृत्तिः ॥ सकारान्तस्य पदस्य सजुष् इत्येतस्य च रुर्भवति ॥

66. For the final स् and for the ष् of सजुष् is substituted रु, at the end of a word.

Thus अग्निरत्र, वायुरत्र ॥ So also सजूर्ऋषिभिः, सजूर्देवेभिः ॥ सजुष् is derived from जुष् with the affix क्विप् and the preposition सह which is changed to स in Bahuvrihi. The lengthening takes place by VIII. 2. 76. and the word means सप्रीतिः ॥ The रु is र्, but it should be distinguished from it. This secondary र् (or रु) undergoes a distinct and separate Sandhi change from that of the primary र् ॥

अवयाः श्वेतवाः पुरोडाश्च ॥ ६७ ॥ पदानि ॥ अवयाः, श्वेतवाः, पुरोडाः, च ॥

वृत्तिः ॥ अवयाः श्वेतवाः पुरोडाः इत्येते निपात्यन्ते ॥

67. The same substitution takes place for the final of the Nominatives of अवयाः, श्वेतवाः and पुरोडाः ॥

The word अवयाः is from अव + यज्; श्वेतवाः from श्वेत + वह् and पुरोडाः from पुरस् + दाश् ॥ The affix ण्विन् is added to the two latter by III. 2. 71. The word अवयाज् is also formed by ण्विन् (III. 2. 72). Thus the three words श्वेतवाह्, पुरोडाश् and अवयाज् are formed. These words take the affix डस् before the Pada-terminations (See Vârtika to III. 2. 71). After having taken डस्, the above forms अवयाः &c., are made in Nominative singular irregularly.

Why is this nipâtana, when रु would have come by the last sûtra and the lengthening would have taken place by VI. 4. 14, of the words अवयस्, श्वेतवस् and पुरोडस्? They are so exhibited here, for making them long in the Vocative singular also. For they could not have been lengthened in the Vocative singular, because VI. 4. 14 does not apply to it. Thus हे अवयाः, हे श्वेतवाः, हे पुरोडाः ॥

The word च shows that other forms, not enumerated, may also be included here under. As हे उकथशाः ॥

अहन् ॥ ६८ ॥ पदानि ॥ अहन् ॥

वृत्तिः ॥ अहन्नित्येतस्य पदस्य रुर्भवति ॥

वार्त्तिकम् ॥ अह्नो रुविधौ रूपरात्रिरथन्तरेषूपसंख्यानं कर्त्तव्यम् ॥

68. रु is also substituted for the न् of अहन् at the end of a Pada.

Thus अहोभ्याम्, अहोभिः ॥ The sûtra exhibits the form अहन् without the elision of न्, in order to indicate that there is not elision of न् ॥ As दीर्घाहो, निदाघः, हे दीर्घाहोऽत्रोति ॥ See Vârtika to VIII. 2. 7. The न् of अहन् is not changed to र् in the sûtra by VIII. 2. 69, because it is intended to show the word-form अहन् ॥ The Nominal stem is Pada in the above examples by I. 4. 17.

Vârt:—Before the words रूप, रात्रि and रथन्तर, the न् of अहन् is changed to र् ॥ As अहोरूपम्, अहोरात्र, अहोरथन्तरं साम ॥ This is an exception to VIII. 2. 69. Others say, that this र् change takes place *universally* before all words beginning with र; as अहो रम्यम्, अहो रत्नानि ॥

रोऽसुपि ॥ ६९ ॥ पदानि ॥ रः, अ-सुपि ॥

वृत्तिः ॥ अहन्नित्येतस्य रेफादेशो भवत्यसुपि परतः ॥

69. When no case-ending follows (i. e. at the end of a Pada in the narrower sense), र् is substituted for the न् of अहन् ॥

Thus अहर्ददाति, अहर्भुङ्क्ते ॥ Why do we say 'when no case-ending follows'? Observe अहोभ्याम्, अहोभिः ॥ Here रु-called र् replaced the final न् of अहन् ॥ The difference between this रु-called र and the ordinary र is illustrated in the above set of examples. The रु-called र is changed to उ by VI. 1. 113, the ordinary र is not so changed.

Obj. In अहर्ददाति and अहर्भुङ्क्ते the case-ending is elided after अहन्, and so by Pratyaya - lakshaṇa, we may say that there is a case - ending here also? Ans. This is not so, because of the following maxim अह्नो रविधौ लुमता लुप्ते प्रत्यय लक्षणं न भवति ॥ The rule of pratya lakshana does not apply to the substitution of र for the final of अहन् when the affix has been elided by लुक् or लुप्. Therefore, this अहन् is not considered to be followed by सुप् or case-affix. But where an affix is elided by using the word लोप, there the rule of Pratyaya - lakshaṇa does apply to अहन् ॥ As हे दीर्घाहोऽत्र, हे दीर्घाहो निदाघ. (VIII. 2. 7). Here the affix is elided by using the word 'lopa' by VI. 1. 68.

अम्नरूधरवरित्युभयथा छन्दसि ॥ ७० ॥ पदानि ॥ अम्नस्, ऊधस्, अवस्, इति उभयथा, छन्दसि ॥

वृत्तिः ॥ अम्नस् ऊधस् अवस् इत्येतेषां छन्दसि विषये उभयथा भवति ॥

वार्त्तिकम् ॥ छन्दसि भाषायां च विभाषा प्रचेतसो राजन्युपसंख्यानं कर्त्तव्यम् ॥
वा० ॥ अहरादीनां पत्यादिषूपसंख्यानं कर्त्तव्यम् ॥

70. In the Chhandas, both रु and र are substituted for the final of amnas, ûdhas, and avas.

Thus अम्न एव or अम्नरेव, ऊध एव or ऊधरेव; अव एव or अवरेव ॥ When रु is substituted for the finals, this रु is replaced by य् by VIII. 3. 17, which is elided by VIII. 3. 19. The word अम्नस् means 'a little', and अवस् 'protection'.

Vârt.:—रु and र both replace the final of प्रचेतस् before राजन्, in the Vedic as well as in the secular language. As प्रचेता राजन् (VIII. 3. 14, VI. 3. 111) प्रचेतो राजन् ॥

Vârt.:—The words अहर् &c before पति &c should be enumerated. That is, the finals of अहर् &c are replaced by रु or र before पति &c. As. अहर्पतिः or अहः पतिः or अहः पतिः; अहर्पुत्रः, अह× पुत्रः, अहः पुत्रः, गीर्पतिः, गीः पति, गी × पतिः; धूर्पति, धूः पतिः, धू × पतिः ॥ Here र् is substituted for the final र् of अहर् &c, which at first sight may appear superfluous. But it is so ordained, in order to prevent the visarga change of this र ॥

भुवश्च महाव्याहृतेः ॥ ७१ ॥ पदानि ॥ भुवः, चः, महाव्याहृतेः ॥
वृत्तिः ॥ भुवस् इत्येतस्य महाव्याहृतेश्छन्दसि विषये उभयथा भवति ॥

71. In the Chhandas, रु and र may replace the final of the word भुवस् when used as a mahâ-vyâhṛiti.

Thus भुवरित्यन्तरिक्षम् or भुव इत्यन्तरिक्षम् ॥ The mahâ-vyâhṛitis are three, used generally before the famous Gâyatri mantra. They denote respectively the earth, the firmament and the heaven. भुवस् is an Indeclinable and a Vyâhriti denoting the firmament. The other two are भूः and स्वः ॥

Why do we say when it is a mahâ-vyâhṛiti? Observe भुवो विश्वेषु भुवनेषु यज्ञियः ॥ Here भुवः is a verb, 2nd Pers. Singular, Imperfect (लङ्) of the root भू, without guṇa of the root, and the अट् augment is not added as a Vedic diversity.

वसुस्रंसुध्वंस्वनडुहां दः ॥ ७२ ॥ पदानि ॥ वसु, स्रंसु, ध्वंसु, अनडुहाम्, दः ॥
वृत्तिः ॥ ससजुषोरुरित्यतः स इति वर्त्तते । वस्वन्तस्य पदस्य सकारान्तस्य स्रंसु ध्वंसु अनडुह् इत्येतेषां च दकारादेशो भवति ॥

72. द् is substituted for the final स् of a word ending in the affix वस्, and for the final of स्रंस्, ध्वंस् and अनडुह् at the end of a Pada (in the wider sense I. 4. 14, 17).

The anuvṛitti of स् is understood here from VIII. 2. 66. It qualifies वस् only, and not the rest. That is, when the word formed by the affix वस् ends with स्, such स् is replaced by द ॥ For a word formed by वस् does not sometimes end in स्, and in those cases the rule will not apply. As स्रंस् and ध्वंस् *always* end in स्, there is no necessity of qualifying these by the स् of VIII. 2. 66. अनडुह् ends in ह् and so स् cannot qualify it.

Thus विद्वद्भ्याम्, विद्वद्भिः, पपिवद्भ्याम्, पपिवद्भिः with वस् affix. स्रंस्:—उखास्रद्भ्याम्, उखास्रद्भिः ॥ (VII. 1.70 and III. 2. 36). ध्वंस्—पर्णध्वद्भ्याम्, पर्णध्वद्भिः ॥ अनडुह्—अनडुद्भ्याम्, अनडुद्भिः ॥

But when a वस् formed word does not end in स्, the rule does not apply. As विद्वान्, पपिवान् ॥ Here स् is not changed to द् ॥

In the case of वस्, the द is ordained, before any other rule manifests itself; thus in विद्वद्भ्यां this द debars रु; so why should it not debar the rule relating to the elision of the final in विद्वान् also? This rule sets aside रु, but it does not, however, over-rule the elision-rule, because it is not directly connected with this change.

Why in अनड्वान् the न् is not changed to द्? By the very fact, that नुम् is ordained (विधान-सामर्थ्यात्), this न् will not be changed to द्: otherwise नुम् rule would become superfluous; for it would be easier to say let ह् be changed to द्, and we should get the form अनड्वाद् by this rule without नुम् ॥

Obj:—If this be so, that the नुम् is not changed to द, because of giving it a scope, then in अनड्वान् अत्र, this नुम् should not be changed into रु by VIII. 3. 9?

Ans:—No; the maxim is that that rule is set aside, with regard to which a particular rule would become useless, if not so over-ruled: but that rule is not set aside which is only an occasion for the application of another rule (यं विधिं प्रति उपदेशोऽनर्थकः, सविधिर्बाध्यते, यस्य तु विधे र्निमित्तमेव नासौ बाध्यते) ॥ With regard to द change, the नुम् vidhi is *useless* (anarthaka), with regard to रु change, it is merely an occasion.

The word पदस्य is understood here also, so the change does not take place in विद्वांसौ and विद्वांसः ॥

तिप्यनस्तेः ॥ ७३ ॥ पदानि ॥ तिपि, अन्-अस्तेः ॥

वृत्तिः ॥ तिपि परतः सकारान्तस्य पदस्य अनस्तेर्दकार आदेशो भवति ॥

73. द is substituted for the final स् of a root, with the exception of अस्, before the Personal ending ति (त्), when it stands at the end of a word.

The स् of a root can stand at the end of a word when the Personal-ending is dropped. Thus अचकाद् भवान्, अन्वशाद् भवान्, from the roots चकास् and शास् ॥ The Personal affix is elided by VI. 1. 68, and thereby स् comes to stand at the end of a Pada.

Why do we say 'before तिप्'? Observe चकास् formed by क्विप् affix added to the root.

Why do we say 'with the exception of अस्'? See आप एवेदं सलिलं सर्वम् आः ॥ Here आः is the Imperfect 3rd Person singular of अस् ॥ The ईट् is not added as a Vedic irregularity. See VII. 3. 93, 97.

सिपि धातो रुर्वा ॥ ७४ ॥ पदानि ॥ सिपि, धातोः, रुः, वाः ॥

वृत्तिः ॥ सिपि परतः सकारान्तस्य पदस्य धातो रुः इत्ययमादेशो भवति दकारो वा ॥

74. द् or रु may optionally be substituted for the स् of a root, before the Personal ending सि (स्), when such स् stands at the end of a Pada.

Thus अचकास् त्वम् or अचकात् त्वम्, अन्वशास् त्वम् or अन्वशात् त्वम् ॥ For the रु is first substituted visarjanîya, which is then changed to स् ॥

The word धातुः is employed in the sûtra for the sake of the subsequent sûtras : so also the word रु ॥

दश्च ॥ ७५ ॥ पदानि ॥ दः, च ॥

वृत्तिः ॥ दकारान्तस्य धातोः पदस्य सिपि परतो रुर्भवति दकारो वा ॥

75. द् or रु may optionally be substituted for the final द् of a root, before the Personal-affix सि, when such द् stands at the end of a Pada.

Thus अभिनत् त्वम् or अभिनस् त्वम्, अच्छिनत् त्वम् or अच्छिनस् त्वम् ॥

र्वोरुपधाया दीर्घ इकः ॥ ७६ ॥ पदानि ॥ र्वोः, उपधायाः, दीर्घः, इकः ॥

वृत्तिः ॥ रेफवकारान्तस्य धातोः पदस्य उपधाया इको दीर्घो भवति ॥

76. A penultimate इ or उ is lengthened, when the final र् or व् of a root can stand at the end of a Pada.

Thus गीः, धूः, पूः, आशीः ॥ These are all examples of roots ending in र् ॥ Of roots ending in व्, examples will be given in the next sûtra.

Why have we used the word 'penultimate'? Observe अबिभर् भवान्, here the इ of the reduplicative syllable is not to be lengthened.

Why do we say 'of इक् vowels'? So that the अ of भ in the above example अबिभर् may not be lengthened.

The word धातोः 'of a root' is understood here also. Therefore इ and उ are not lengthened in अग्निः, वायुः ॥

The word पदस्य is understood here also, therefore, not here, गिरौ, गिरः ॥

हलि च ॥ ७७ ॥ पदानि ॥ हलि, च ॥

वृत्तिः ॥ हलि च परतः रेफवकारान्तस्य धातोरुपधाया इको दीर्घो भवति ॥

77. Of a root ending in र् or व्, the penultimate इ or उ is lengthened, before a consonantal beginning affix.

Thus आस्तीर्णम्, विस्तीर्णम्, विशीर्णम्, अवगूर्णम्, all ending in र् ॥ So also, दीव्यति, सीव्यति ending in व् ॥

The phrase "of the *root*", is understood here also. Therefore not here, दिव्यति and चतुर्यति, which are derived from the *nouns* दिव and चतुर i. e. दिवमिच्छति = दिव्यति, and चतुर इच्छति = चतुर्यति ॥

The phrase इकः "of the vowels इ or उ" is understood here also. Therefore not here, स्मर्यते, भव्यम् ॥

This rule applies to cases which are not final in a pada: but to cases where र् or व् are in the middle of a pada or word.

उपधायां च ॥ ७८ ॥ पदानि ॥ उपधायाम्, च ॥

वृत्तिः ॥ धातोरुपधाभूतौ यौ रेफवकारौ हल्परौ तयोरुपधाया इकः दीर्घो भवति ॥

78. The short इ or उ of a root is lengthened, when the verb has र् or व् as its penultimate letter, and is followed by a consonant.

The anuvṛitti of हलि is current. The root must end in a consonant, and must have a र् or व् as preceding such consonant, for the application of this rule. Thus हूर्छा, हूर्छिता, मूर्छा, मूर्छिता. तूर्वी, तूर्विता. धूर्वी, धूर्विता ॥

The र् or व् must be followed by a consonant. Therefore not here: as, चिरि, जिरि are roots having a penultimate र, which however is followed by a vowel. Therefore we have चिरिणोति, जिरिणोति ॥

Q.—Why there is not lengthening in रिर्यतुः, रिर्युः or विव्यतुः, विव्युः Perfect, forms derived from the roots रि गतौ and वी गतौ &c? Here the इ of the abhyâsa required lengthening, and it would not be shortened, as it is asiddha.

Ans.—The यण् substitute of इ here by VI. 4. 82, is treated as sthânivat, to इ, and therefore, the र् or व् is considered as *not* to be followed by a *consonant*, and hence there is no lengthening. Another reason is, that the यण् substitute is taught in angâdhikâra (VI. 4. 82), and depends upon the affix, and is consequently Bahiranga, with regard to this rule of lengthening which is antaranga. Hence यणादेशः is considered as asiddha. Therefore र् and व् are not followed by a consonant (for य् is not considered as such for the above reasons).

Similarly in चतुर्यितृ formed with तृच् affix from the Denominative (क्यच्) root चतुर्य ॥ Here इट् is added before तृच् as चतुर्य + इ + तृ and then अ is elided, चतुर्य् + इ + तृ ॥ Here the elision of अ is a Bahiranga process, and therefore, र् is not here really penultimate, and so there is no lengthening of the vowel.

In प्रतिदीव्ना (Instrumental singular) there is lengthening by VIII. 2. 77. To the root प्रति-दिव् is added कनिन् by Uṇ I. 156, and we have प्रतिदिवन् ॥ To this is added टा (Instrumental affix), as प्रतिदिवन् + आ, and अ is elided by VI. 4. 134, and we get प्रतिदीव्ना ॥ The lengthening takes place here, the elision of अ is not considered here as sthânivat, and so व् becomes penultimate. In fact, here we apply the maxim that a lopa substitute of a vowel is not to be considered as sthânivat when a rule of lengthening is to be applied (See I. 1. 58).

Q.—Well, let it not be sthânivat, but the elision by VI. 4. 134, depends upon a case-affix, and is Bahiranga, and therefore asiddha for the purposes of this rule which is antaranga: and so therefore, there would be no lengthening?

Ans.—The maxim of असिद्धं बहिरङ्गमन्तरङ्गे should not be applied here: because it is an *anitya* rule.

The word जिव्रिः is formed by the Uṇâdi affix क्विन् added to the root जृ (जिर्), the र् being changed to व (Uṇ V. 49). So also किरिः and गिरिः are formed by the Uṇâdi affix कि added to कृ and गृ (Uṇ IV. 143). The Genitive Dual of which is किर्योः and गिर्योः ॥ There is no lengthening in जिव्रिः, किर्योः and गिर्योः, on the maxim that the Uṇâdi formed words are primitive words and not Derivative; and so the rules of etymological changes do not apply to them (उणादयोऽव्युत्पन्नानि प्रातिपदिकानि) ॥

न भकुर्छुराम् ॥ ७९ ॥ पदानि ॥ न, भ, कुर्, छुराम् ॥

वृत्तिः ॥ रेफवकारान्तस्य भस्य कुर् छुर् इत्येतयोश्च दीर्घो न भवति ॥

79. The lengthening of vowel does not take place under VIII. 2. 77, when the Nominal stem ending in र् or व् is called Bha (i. e. when a य् follows), and also not in कुर् and छुर् ॥

Thus धुर्यः (धुरं वहति IV. 4. 77 or धुरि साधुः) ॥ Similarly कुर्यात्, छुर्यात् ॥ The latter is Benedictive of छुर् छेदने ॥

Why have we qualified the word भ by saying that it must end in र् or व्? Observe प्रतिदीव्ना, प्रतिदीव्ने ॥ For here the stem which ends in व् is not Bha, and the stem which is Bha does not end in व् but in न् ॥

अदसो ऽसेर्दादु दो मः ॥ ८० ॥ पदानि ॥ अदसः, अ-सेः, दात्, उ, दः, मः ॥

वृत्तिः ॥ अदसो ऽसकारान्तस्य वर्णस्य दात्परस्य उवर्णादेशो भवति दकारस्य च मकारः ॥

वार्त्तिकम् ॥ अदसो ऽनोम्न इति वक्तव्यम् ॥

Kârikâ:—अदसोद्रे पृथङ् ' ' ' केचिदिच्छन्ति लत्ववत् ।
के चिदन्त्यसदाशः । नेत्येके ऽसेर्हि दृश्यते ॥

80. When the pronoun अदस् does not end in स्, then there is substituted उ or ऊ for the vowel after द्, and म् for द् ॥

Thus अमुम्, अमू, अमून्, अमुना, अमूभ्याम्, ॥ अद is substituted for अदस् before a case-ending by VII. 2. 102, which in Feminine becomes अदा ॥ By the present sûtra read with I. 1. 50, अमु is substituted for अद and अमू for अदा ॥ The उ which replaces one-mâtrâ vowel will be one-mâtrâ उ i. e. short उ, and the उ which replaces a two-mâtrâ vowel will be a two-mâtrâ उ i. e. long ऊ ॥ See I. 1. 50.

Why do we say, "not ending in स"? Observe अद इच्छति = अदस्यति ॥ Obj. How can this be a valid example, as the word पदस्य is understood here, and अदस् before the affix क्य is not a pada (I. 4. 15)? Ans. This indicates that the मु change takes place, even when अदस् is not a pada. As अमुमुस ॥

Vârt:—It should rather be stated that the rule applies to that अदस् which has no ओ, or स् or र् ॥ So that the prohibition may apply to अदोऽत्र, अदः कुलम् ॥ The visarjanîya being considered as asiddha, this word is considered as ending in र् ॥

In order to apply the prohibition to ओ and र् also, some explain the sûtra thus:—अः सेर्यस्य सोयमासिः, यत्र सकारस्य अकारः क्रियते ॥ "The word असिः in the sûtra is a Bahuvrihi, and means that in which अ is substituted for स" ॥ The sûtra is thus confined to the form अद derived by changing the स् into अ by VII 2. 102: and not to any other अद ॥

When अदस् takes the final-substitute अद्रि by VI. 3. 92, how is this rule to be applied? Thus by III. 2. 59, the root अञ्च् takes क्विन् ॥ We compound it with अदस्, as अदाऽञ्चति ॥ अदस् + अञ्च + क्विन् = अद् + अद्रि + अञ्च् + क्विन् (VI. 3. 92) = अदद्र्यच् (VI. 4. 24). Now there are three views, (1) the द of अद, and द्र of अद्रि are both changed to मु by the present sûtra; (2), the first द is not changed, but only द्र; (3) none is changed. Thus we have (1) अमुमुयङ् (VII. 1. 70, VI. 1. 68, VIII. 2. 23 and 62), अमुमुयञ्चौ, अमुमुयञ्चः ॥ (2) Secondly, अदमुयङ् अदमुयञ्चौ, अदमुयञ्चः ॥ (3) Lastly अदद्र्यङ्, अदद्र्यञ्चौ, अदद्र्यञ्चः ॥ The above verse summarises this:

" Some ordain that मु should come separately for both adas and adri, as there is double ल (in चलीक्लृप्यते); others would have मु only for the last portion which stands in proximity to the final, (i. e. for द्र); while a third class would have nowhere, because they explain असेः of the sûtra, by confining it to: VII. 2. 102. " The first class interpret असेः by "that form of अदस् which has no स्"; and they do not apply the maxim अनन्त्यविकारेऽन्त्यसदेशस्य कार्यं भवति "when a modification is ordained with regard to some thing which is not final, the operation takes place on that only which is in proximity to the final." The second class apply this maxim and make मु change only for द्र which stands in proximity to the final; while the last class interpret the word असेः in a different way altogether (अः अस्य सकारस्य सोऽयम् असिः) ॥

Why do we say दात् 'for the vowel after द'? Observe अमुया, अमुयोः, the final य as not changed to उ ॥

एत ईद्बहुवचने ॥ ८१ ॥ पदानि ॥ एतः ईत्, बहुवचने ॥

वृत्तिः ॥ अदसो दकारादुत्तरस्य एकारस्य ईकारादेशो भवति दकारस्य च मकारः बहुवचने बहूनामर्थानामुक्तौ ॥

81. For the ए coming after the द of अदस्, there is substituted ई, and द् is changed to म, when plurality is to be expressed.

Thus अमी for अदे (or अते) अमीभिः for अदेभिः, अमीभ्यः for अदेभ्यः, अमीषाम् for अदेषाम्, अमीषु for अदेषु ॥ द is changed to त in अते &c.

The word बहुवचने in the sûtra does not mean the technical बहुवचन; for that would have made the sûtra have this sense "when the affixes of the Plural number follow". In that case, we could not get the form अमी where no plural affix follows. Hence we have translated it, by saying when plurality is to be denoted.

वाक्यस्य टेः प्लुत उदात्तः ॥ ८२ ॥ पदानि ॥ वाक्यस्य, टेः, प्लुतः, उदात्तः ॥

वृत्तिः ॥ वाक्यस्य टेरिति प्लुत इति च उदात्त इति च एतत्त्रयमप्यधिकृतं वेदितव्यमापादपरिसमाप्तेः, यदित ऊर्ध्वमनुक्रमिष्यामो वाक्यस्य टेः प्लुत उदात्त इत्येवं तद्वेदितव्यम् ॥

82. Upto the close of this chapter (Pâda), is always to be supplied : "the last vowel of a sentence is pluta and has the acute".

This is an adhikâra sûtra. All the three words i. e. "the last vowel (टि) of a sentence", "pluta" and "acute"—are to be supplied in the subsequent aphorisms to complete the sense, upto the end of this Pâda. Whatever we shall treat hereafter will refer to the final vowel (टि) in a sentence, and it will get the pluta lengthening and acute accent. Thus VIII. 2. 83, says "In answer to a salutation, but not when it is addressed to a Śûdra". We must supply the present aphorism to complete the meaning :—"In answer to a salutation, the last vowel of a sentence becomes pluta and gets the acute accent, but not when it is addressed to a Śûdra". As अभिवादये देवदत्तोऽहं । भो आयुष्मानेधि देवदत्ता ३ ॥

One adhikâra sets aside another adhikâra, this is the general maxim. Will therefore the adhikâra of the present aphorism set aside the adhikâra of the word पदस्य (VIII. 1. 16)? No, the adhikâra of पदस्य has not ceased, though latent. Otherwise in भवन्तौ &c. the न् would be required to be changed to रु by VIII. 3. 7. But it does not become so, because पदस्य manifests itself there.

The employment of the word "vâkya" would not debar the anuvritti of पद, for the final vowel of a sentence, will *a fortiori* be the final vowel of a word (pada), then what is the use of employing the word वाक्यस्य in this sûtra?

The word वाक्य is employed in the sûtra, so that a word which is not the last word of a sentence, will not get the pluta and acute. Had the sûtra been पदस्य टेः &c. then *all* the words of a sentence would become pluta and acute in the final.

The word टि is employed to indicate that the final *vowel* becomes pluta and acute, though the word may end in a consonant. As अग्निचि३त् ॥ Had टि not been used, the rule would have applied to words *ending* in vowels only, and not to words ending in consonants.

प्रत्यभिवादेऽशूद्रे ॥ ८३ ॥ पदानि ॥ प्रत्यभिवादे, अ-शूद्रे ॥

वृत्तिः ॥ प्रत्यभिवादो नाम यदभिवाद्यमानो गुरुराशिषं प्रयुङ्क्ते। तत्राशूद्रविषये यद्वाक्यं वर्त्तते तस्य टेः प्लुत उदात्तो भवति ॥

वार्त्तिकम् ॥ स्त्रियामपि प्रतिषेधो वक्तव्यः ॥ वा० ॥ असूयकेऽपि केचित् प्रतिषेधमिच्छन्ति ॥

इष्टिः ॥ अभिवादवाक्ये यत संकीर्त्तितं नाम गोत्रं वा तद् यत्र प्रत्यभिवाद वाक्यान्ते प्रयुज्यते तत्र प्लुत इष्यते ॥ वा० ॥ भोराजन्य विशां वेति वक्तव्यम् ॥

83. In answer to a salutation, but not when it refers to a Sûdra, the last vowel of a sentence becomes pluta and gets the acute accent.

The word अभिवादन means "respectful salutation of a superior or elder by an inferior or junior for the sake of obtaining his blessing. It consists of three acts 1. rising from the seat, 2. touching of the feet, 3. the uttering of the formula of salutation". The word प्रत्यभिवादन means, the blessing given by the superior or elder in answer to such salutation. In giving utterance to such blessing, the last vowel of the final word gets udâtta and acute, provided that, such blessing is not pronounced on a Śûdra.

Thus अभिवादये देवदत्तोऽहं is said by Devadatta to his Guru. The latter says भो आयुष्मान् एधि देवदत्ता३ ॥ "O Devadatta! be thou long-lived".

Why do we say when not referring to a Śûdra? Observe अभिवादये तुषजकोऽहं is said by a Śûdra. In reply to this the Guru replies भो आयुष्मान् एधि तुषजक!

Vârt:—Prohibition must be stated with regard to women also. As अभिवादये गार्ग्यहं is said by Gârgî. To this the Guru replies:—भो आयुष्मती भवगार्गि!॥

Vârt:—Some would have this prohibition where a detractor or an arrogant person is addressed. So long as one's arrogance or ridicule does not become manifest, there is prolation. But when one comes to know that he is my detractor, and is really ridiculing me by a show of respect; then the reply is not a blessing, but is, in fact, a curse. Thus अभिवादये स्थाल्यहं भोः, is uttered by the detractor; and the Guru understanding the word Sthâlin to be the Proper Name of the person, replies आयुष्मान् एधि स्थालिन्३ ॥ Then the detractor says, Sthâlin is not my Proper Name, but an adjective, like daṇḍin, viz. he who has a स्थाल or cooking pot. The Guru, believing this to be true, again replies, आयुष्मान् एधि स्थालिन् but without prolation, because the word is not a Proper Noun. The other then says "O Sir, it is not my epithet, it is my Proper Name". The Guru now comes to learn that he is being laughed at, and so gets angry and says : असूयकस्त्वं जाल्म,! न त्वं प्रत्यभिवादनमर्हसि ; भिद्यस्व वृषल स्थालिन् ! ॥ Here it is a curse, as well as a pun : i. e. "burst thou, O sinner! like unto a cooking pot (sthâlin = sthalî-vat).

Ishti :—This prolation takes place there only, where the Proper Noun Gotra &c. with which the salutation was made, is employed by the Guru at the end of the sentence ; and not where the position of the Proper Name &c is different. Therefore not here, देवदत्त कुशल्यसि ; देवदत्त आयुष्मान् एधि, for here the word Devadatta is not used at the end of a sentence.

Vârt :—The prolation is optional, when भोः follows such Proper Name, or when the Person addressed is a Kshatriya or a Vaishya. As भो अभिवादये देवदत्तोऽहं ॥ Reply (1) आयुष्मान् एधि देवदत्त भोः ३ or (2) आयुष्मान् एधि देवदत्त भो ॥ So also when a Kshatriya is addressed, as अभिवादये इन्द्रवर्म्माहं भोः, Reply (1) आयुष्मान् एधि इन्द्रवर्म्मन् ३ or (2) आयुष्मान् एधि इन्द्रवर्म्मन् ॥ Vaishya : अभिवादये इन्द्रपालितोऽहं भोः ॥ Guru : आयुष्मानेधि इन्द्रपालित ३ or आयुष्मानेधि इन्द्रपालित ! ॥

दूराद्धूते च ॥ ८४ ॥ पदानि ॥ दूरात्, हूते, च ॥

वृत्तिः ॥ दूराद्धूते यद्वाक्यं वर्त्तते तस्य टेः प्लुतो भवति स चोदात्तः ॥

इष्टिः ॥ वाक्यस्यान्ते यत्र सम्बोधनपदं भवति, तत्र अयं प्लुत इष्यते ॥

84. The final vowel of a sentence becomes pluta and acute, when used in calling a person from a distance.

The word दूरात् is in the Fifth case by II. 3. 35; the word हूतं means 'calling', 'addressing'. Thus आगच्छ भो माणवक देवदत्ता३ ॥ आगच्छ भो माणवक यज्ञदत्ता३ ॥ The word 'distance' is a relative term, and is not fixed at what distance there should be prolation. The prolation however takes place, when a voice is to be raised, in order that the sound may reach the person. That distance upto which the voice can be heard without raising its pitch and without any special effort, need not be considered as "distance" for the purposes of this sûtra.

The word हूत here includes, 'addressing in general', and not only 'calling'. Thus there is prolation here also सक्तून् पिब देवदत्ता३, पलायस्व देवदत्ता३ ॥ This pluta sentence becomes eka-śruti by I. 2. 33.

Why do we say "from a distance"? Observe आगच्छ भो माणवक देवदत्त !

Ishti :—This prolation takes place only then, when the noun in the vocative case stands at the end of the sentence. Therefore, there is no prolation here: देवदत्त आगच्छ ॥

हैहेप्रयोगे हैहयोः ॥ ८५ ॥ पदानि ॥ है, हे, प्रयोगे, है, हयोः ॥

वृत्तिः ॥ हैहेंप्रयोगे दूराद्धूते यद्वाक्यं वर्त्तते तत्र हैहयोरेव प्लुतो भवति ॥

85. When the words है and हे are employed, in addressing a person from a distance, there the है and हे alone get the pluta and the accent.

As है ३ देवदत्त, देवदत्त है ३ ॥ हे ३ देवदत्त, देवदत्त हे ३ ॥

The repetition of the words है and हे in the sûtra, is for the sake of indicating, that the prolation takes place even when है and हे do not stand at the end of a sentence.

गुरोरनृतोनन्त्यस्याप्येकैकस्य प्राचाम् ॥ ८६ ॥ पदानि ॥ गुरोः, अनृ-ऋतः, अनन्त्यस्य, अपि, एक, एकस्य, प्राचाम् ॥

वृत्तिः ॥ ऋकारवर्जितस्य गुरोरनन्त्यस्यापिशब्दादन्त्यस्यापि टेरेकैकस्य सम्बोधने वर्त्तमानस्य प्लुतो भवति प्राचामाचार्याणां मतेन ॥

86. In the room of a prosodially long vowel, (with the exception of ऋ) though it may not stand at the end, there is substituted a pluta for one at a time, under the above circumstances (VIII. 2.83-84), in the opinion of Eastern Grammarians.

This sûtra indicates a special sthânin for the pluta vowel taught by VIII. 2. 83 to 84. With the exception of ऋ, for every heavy vowel, though it may not be the final vowel of the vocative word, and for the final vowel also, but only one at a time, there is pluta substitution, in the opinion of Eastern Grammarians. Thus दे३वदत्त or देवदँ३त्त or देवदत्तँ३ ॥ Similarly with यँ३ज्ञदत्त, यज्ञदँ३त्त or यज्ञदत्तँ ३ ॥

Why do we say गुरोः "of a prosodially long vowel"? So that the अ of व and ज्ञ in Devadatta and Yajñadatta may not be prolated, for this अ is short.

Why do we say अनृतः "with the exception of ऋ"? Observe कृष्णमिँ३त्र, कृष्णमित्रँ३, but never कृँ३ष्णमित्र ॥

The word एकैकस्य shows that the prolation should not be simultaneous, but of one at a time; not दे३वद३त्त३ ॥

The word प्राचाम् "in the opinion of Eastern Grammarians" is used for the sake of creating option. So in one alternative, there is no prolation *at all*.

As आयुष्मान् एधि देवदत्त ॥ Thus the present sûtra, makes VIII. 2. 83 and 84, optional sûtras. This also is an authority for the following dictum of Patanjali " सर्व एव प्लुतः साहसमनिच्छता विभाषा कर्त्तव्यः " (Mahabhâshya VIII. 2. 92. Commentary). Thus *all* rules relating to Prolation become optional. In short, the word प्राचाम् should be read in all rules regarding prolation, and thus without doing violence (sâhasa) to grammatical authority, one may have optional pluta everywhere.

ओमभ्यादाने ॥ ८७ ॥ पदानि ॥ ओम्, अभ्यादाने ॥

वृत्तिः ॥ अभ्यादानं प्रारम्भः तत्र य ओम्शब्दः तस्य प्लुतो भवति ॥

87. The vowel in ओम् is pluta in the beginning of a sacred text.

The word अभ्यादानं means the commencement of a sacred mantra or Vedic text. Thus ओ३म् अग्निमीळे पुरोहितं यज्ञस्य देवमृत्विजं ॥ (Rig I. 1. 1).

Why do we say "in the beginning"? Observe ओमित्येतदक्षरमुद्गीथमुपासीत (Chhândogya Upanishad. I. 1. 1). Here ओम् is not used to indicate the commencement of a Text or Mantra, but is itself the subject of comment.

ये यज्ञकर्मणि ॥ ८८ ॥ पदानि ॥ ये, यज्ञ, कर्मणि ॥

वृत्तिः ॥ ये इत्येतस्य यज्ञकर्मणि प्लुतो भवति ॥

इष्टिः ॥ ये यजामह इत्यत्रैवायंप्लुत इष्यते ॥

88. The vowel of ये becomes pluta in a sacred text, when it is employed in a sacrificial work.

Thus ये३यजामहे ॥ Why do we say when employed in sacrificial work? Observe ये यजामह इति पञ्चाक्षरम् "Ye yajamahe consists of five syllables". Here it is simple recitation.

Ishti:—The word ये is pluta before यजामहे only. Therefore not so here: ये देवासो दिव्येकादशस्थ (Rig. I. 139. 11).

प्रणवष्टेः ॥ ८९ ॥ पदानि ॥ प्रणवः, टेः ॥

वृत्तिः ॥ यज्ञकर्मणि टेः प्रणव आदेशो भवति ॥

89. In a sacrificial work, ओ३म् is substituted for the final vowel, with the consonant, if any, that may follow it, of a sentence.

The word यज्ञकर्मणि is understood here also. The word प्रणव means ओम् ॥ It is the name given to this syllable. This ओम् is substituted for the final letter (टि) of that word which stands either at the end of a Pâda of a sacred hymns or at the end of a hemistich of such Rik. Thus for अपां रेतांसि जिन्वति (Rig. VIII. 44. 16), we may have अपां रेतांसि जिन्वतो३म् ॥ So also for देवान् जिगाति सुम्नयुः (Rig. III. 27. 1), we may have देवान् जिगाति सुम्नयो३म् ॥

The word टि is repeated in this aphorism in spite of its anuvṛitti from VIII. 2. 82, to indicate that ओम् replaces the *whole* last syllable, with its vowel and consonant. Had टि not been repeated, then by the rule of अलोऽन्त्यस्य the final *letter* only of the टि portion of a sentence would have been replaced. Thus in सुम्नयुः, the visarjaniya alone would have been replaced.

When not employed in connection with sacrificial works, there is no such substitution. Thus in simple reading of the Vedas, we should always recite अपां रेतांसि जिन्वति ॥

याज्यान्तः ॥ ९० ॥ पदानि ॥ याज्या, अन्तः ॥

वृत्तिः ॥ याज्या नाम ये याज्याकाण्डे पठ्यन्ते मन्त्रास्तेषामन्त्यो यष्टिः स प्लवते यज्ञकर्मणि ॥

90. The last vowel at the end of Mantras called Yâjya, when employed in sacrificial works, is pluta and has the Acute.

Thus स्तोमैर्विधेमाग्नये३ (Rig. VIII. 43. 11), जिह्वामग्ने चकृषे हव्यवाहा३म् (Rig. X. 8. 6).

Why do we say 'at the end'? There are some Yâjya hymns, consisting of several sentences. The final vowel (टि) of every sentence would have become pluta, in such a hymn. To prevent it, the word "anta" is used, so that the final vowel of the hymn at the end of all, becomes pluta.

ब्रूहिप्रेष्यश्रौषड्वौषडावहानामादेः ॥ ९१ ॥ पदानि ॥ ब्रूहि, प्रेष्य, श्रौषट्, वौषट्, आवहानाम्, आदेः ॥

वृत्तिः ॥ ब्रूहि प्रेष्य श्रौषट् वौषट् आवह इत्येतेषामादेः प्लुतो भवति यज्ञकर्मणि ॥

91. In a sacrificial work, the first syllable of ब्रूहि, प्रेष्य, श्रौषट्, वौषट् and आवह is pluta.

Thus अग्नयेऽनुब्रू३हि (Maitr S. I. 4. 11), अग्नये गोमयानि (or °न्) प्रे३ष्य, अस्तु श्रौ३षट्; सोमस्याग्ने वीही३ वौ३षट्, अग्निर्मा३वह ॥

So also in पित्र्यायामनुस्व३धा on the analogy of ब्रूहि, so also अस्तुस्व३धा ॥ The word वौषट् is illustrative of the six forms वषट्, वौषट्, वाषट्, वौक्षट्, वाक्षट्, वक्षाट् ॥

But there is no prolation in आवह देवान् यजमानाय ; आवह जात वेदः ॥

अग्नीत्प्रेषणे परस्य च ॥ ९२ ॥ पदानि ॥ अग्नीध्, प्रेषणे, परस्य, च ॥

वृत्तिः ॥ अग्नीधः प्रेषणमग्नीत्प्रेषणम् तत्रादेः प्लुतो भवति परस्य च ॥

92. In an order given to Âgnîdhra priest, the first syllable as well as the succeeding syllable is pluta.

In a Yajña, the principal priests (ṛtvij) are four Adhvaryu, Udgâtâ, Hotâ, Brahmâ. Every one of these has three subordinate priests (ṛtvij) under them : as shown below.

NAMES OF PRINCIPAL.	SUBORDINATE.		
I.	½.	⅓.	¼.
Adhvaryu : (Yajur)	Pratiprasthâtâ	Nesthâ (VI.4.11)	Unnetâ.
Udgâtâ (Sâman)	Prastotâ	Pratihartâ	Subrahmanya.
Hotâ (Rig) VI. 4. 11.	Maitrâ varuṇa	Achchhâvâk	Potâ (VI.4.11).
Brahmâ (Atharvan)	Brâhmanâchhansî	Âgnîdhra	Grâvastuta.

III. 2. 177.

The duty of Ágnîdhra is to kindle the sacrificial fire. In a summons or call (प्रेषण) made by the Adhvaryu, who is the Director of ceremonies, to the Ágnîdhra to perform the functions of Ágnîdh, both syllable become pluta.

The word अग्नीत् प्रेषण is a compound = अग्नीध: प्रेषणम् " a call or summon relating to Agnîdhduty."

Thus आ ३ श्रा ३ वय, ओ ३ श्रा ३ वय ॥ The pluta takes place only in these examples; therefore, not here, as अग्नीदग्नीन् विहर ; बर्हि स्तृणीहि ॥ Some, therefore, read the aunvṛitti of the word विभाषा from the next sûtra, into this, and would have it an optional rule, of fixed jurisdiction (viyavasthita vibhâshâ). Others say " all pluta rules are optional " (सर्व एव प्लुतः साहसमनिच्छता विभाषा विज्ञेयः) ॥ In उद्धर ३ उद्धर, अभिहर ३ अभिहर, there is Vedic diversity.

The words 'relating to sacrificial work' (यज्ञकर्मणि) are understood here also. Therefore not in ओ श्रावय ॥

विभाषा पृष्टप्रतिवचने हेः ॥ ९३ ॥ पदानि ॥ विभाषा, पृष्ट-प्रतिवचने:, हेः ॥

वृत्तिः ॥ पृष्टप्रतिवचने विभाषा हेः प्लुतो भवति ॥

93. हि at the end of an answer to a question may optionally be pluta.

Thus Q. अकार्षीः कटं देवदत्त ? Ans. अकार्षं ही३ or अकार्षं हि ॥ Q. अलावीः केदारं देवदत्त ? Ans. अलाविषं ही३ or हि ॥

Why do we say " in answer to a question " ? Observe कटं करिष्यति हि ॥

Why do we say हे: " of हि " ? Observe करोषि ननु ॥

निगृह्यानुयोगे च ॥ ९४ ॥ पदानि ॥ नि गृह्य, अनु योगे, च ॥

वृत्तिः ॥ स्वमतात्प्रच्यावनं निग्रहः ॥ अनुयोगस्तस्य मतस्याविष्करणम् ॥ तत्र निगृह्यानुयोगे यद्वाक्यं वर्त्तते तस्य टेः प्लुतो भवति विभाषा ॥

94. The end syllable of that sentence is optionally pluta, when it asserts something which has been refuted, and is employed by the victor by way of censure.

The word निग्रहः means the refutation of anothers opinion. निगृह्य is a gerund, and means 'having refuted'. अनुयोगः is the expression of the same proposition which has been refuted. When a person has demonstrated the untenableness of anothers assertion, and then employs the said assertion by way of taunt, reproach or reprimand, then the final syllable of such a sentence becomes pluta. The sûtra literally means "Having refuted (it) when asserting (the same by way of censure)."

Thus an opponent asserts that " The word is not eternal." (अनित्यः शब्दः). Proving by arguments the untenableness of this position, and after refuting it, the victor says by way of reprimand:—अनित्यः शब्द इत्यात्थाँ३ or अनित्य शब्द इत्यात्थ ॥ 'This is then your assertion—that the word is not eternal'. Similarly अद्य श्राद्धमित्यात्थाँ३ or अद्य श्राद्धमित्यात्थ ॥ अद्यामावास्येत्यात्थाँ३ or अद्यामावास्येत्यात्थ ॥

In some texts of Kâsikâ, according to Padamanjari, only the last example is given.

आम्रेडितं भर्त्सने ॥ ९५ ॥ पदानि ॥ आम्रेडितम्, भर्त्सने ॥

वृत्तिः ॥ वाक्यादेरामन्त्रितस्येति भर्त्सने द्विर्वचनमुक्तं तस्याम्रेडितं प्लवते ॥

वार्त्तिकम् ॥ भर्त्सने पर्यायेणेति वक्तव्यम् ॥

95. The end syllable of an âmreḍita Vocative is pluta, when threat is expressed.

A Vocative is reiterated when threat is meant (VIII. 1. 8). Its final syllable becomes pluta. Thus चौर चौरा३ घातिष्यामि त्वा ॥ So also वृषल वृषला३ बन्धयिष्यामि त्वा, दस्य दस्यो३ &c.

Though the anuvṛitti of the sûtra VIII. 2. 82, is current here, yet the final of the *sentence* is not pluta, but of the âmreḍita.

Vârt :—It should be rather stated that any one of the repeated words may be pluta by alternation. Thus चौरा३ चौर or चौर चौरा३ ॥ The word âmṛeḍita is employed in the sûtra as illustrative of the doubling, for threat is expressed by *both* words, so pluta may be of *both* words in turn: and not of the second word only,, though that is called technically âmredita.

अङ्गयुक्तं तिङाकाङ्क्षम् ॥ ९६ ॥ पदानि ॥ अङ्ग, युक्तम्, तिङाकाङ्क्षम् ॥

वृत्तिः ॥ अङ्गइत्यनेन युक्तं तिङन्तमाकाङ्क्षं भर्त्सने प्लवते ॥

96. The final syllable of a finite verb, used as a threat becomes pluta, when the word अङ्ग is joined with it, and it demands another sentence to complete the conclusion.

Thus अङ्ग कूजाँ३ इदानीं ज्ञास्यसि जाल्म ॥ अङ्ग व्याहराँ३, इदानीं ज्ञास्यसि जाल्म ॥

Why do we say 'a verb'? Observe अङ्ग देवदत्त मिथ्या वदसि ॥

Why do we say "when this calls for a conclusion"? Observe अङ्ग पच ॥ Here it is a complete sentence and does not demand another to complete the sense.

The word भर्त्सने of the last sûtra is understood here also. Therefore not here, अङ्ग अधीष्व, ओदनं ते दास्यामि ॥ Here अङ्ग has the force of solicitation. (VIII. 1. 33).

विचार्यमाणानाम् ॥ ९७ ॥ पदानि ॥ विचार्य-माणानाम् ॥

वृत्तिः ॥ प्रमाणेन वस्तुपरीक्षणं विचारः । तस्य विषये विचार्यमाणानां वाक्यानां टेः प्लुतो भवति ॥

97. The end-syllable of those sentences is pluta, which denote acts of reflection (or balancing between two alternatives).

To determine a thing by weighing all arguments *pro* and *con* is called vichâra or judgment. Thus होतव्यं दीक्षितस्य गृहा ३ इ न होतव्याँ३म् "should one perform sacrifice in the house of an initiated person". Similarly तिष्ठेद्यूपा३इ, अनुप्रहृरे

यूपाँ३इ ॥ Here also it is being reflected upon whether यूपे तिष्ठेत् or यूपे अनुप्रहेरत् ॥ i. e. should the stáke remain upright or should it be put flat by the yajamâna. किं यूपस्तिष्ठेत्, किं वा यूपं यजमानः शाययेत् ॥

पूर्वं तु भाषायाम् ॥ ९८ ॥ पदानि ॥ पूर्वम्, तु, भाषायाम् ॥

वृत्तिः ॥ भाषायां विषये विचार्यमाणानां पूर्वमेव प्लवते ॥

98. In the common speech, the end-vowel of the first alternative is only pluta.

This makes a niyama or restriction. The previous sûtra, is thus confined to Vedic literature, and not to the vernacular. तु here has the force of 'only'. Thus अहि र्नु३ रज्जुर्नु 'Is it a snake or a rope'? लोष्टो र्नु३ कपोतोनु 'Is it a clod of earth or a pigeon?'

The priority, of course, depends upon employment. The order of words depends upon one's choice.

प्रतिश्रवणे च ॥ ९९ ॥ पदानि ॥ प्रतिश्रवणे, च ॥

वृत्तिः ॥ प्रतिश्रवणमभ्युपगमः प्रतिज्ञानम् ॥ श्रवणाभिमुख्यं च तत्राविशेषात्सर्वस्य ग्रहणम् ॥ प्रतिश्रवण यद्वाक्यं वर्त्तते तस्य टेः प्लुतो भवति ॥

99. The end-syllable of the sentence which expresses assent or promise or listening to, is pluta.

The word प्रतिश्रवण means "agreement, assent or promise". It also means "listening to". All these senses are to be taken here, as there is nothing in the sûtra to restrict its scope. Thus it has three senses, 1. to promise something to a petitioner, 2. to acknowledge the truth of some proposition, 3. to listen to another's words. Thus गां मे देहि भोः, 1. हन्त ते ददामि३ ॥ 2. नित्यः शब्दो भवितुमर्हति३ ॥ 3. देवदत्त भोः, किमात्थ३ ॥

अनुदात्तं प्रश्नान्ताभिपूजितयोः ॥ १०० ॥ पदानि ॥ अनुदात्तम्, प्रश्न-अन्त, अभि पूजितयोः ॥

वृत्तिः ॥ अनुदात्तः प्लुतो भवति प्रश्नान्ते अभिपूजिते च ॥

100. The end-vowel at the end of a question or of a praise is pluta, but unaccented.

That which is employed at the end of an interrogative sentence is called प्रश्नान्तः ॥ According to some, this rule does not ordain pluta, but only ordains the anudâtta-ness of those syllables which become pluta by the previous rules VIII. 2. 84 &c. The meaning of the sûtra then is:—That pluta which comes at the end of an Interrogative sentence or a sentence denoting admiration, is anudâtta.

Thus अगमा३ः पूर्वा३न् ग्रामा३न् अग्निभूता३इ or अगम३ः पूर्वा३न् ग्रामा३न् पटा३उ (i. e. अगमः पूर्वान् ग्रामान् अग्निभूते or पटो) ॥ The words अग्निभूते, and पटो being finals in a question, become anudâtta as well as pluta. The other words अगम: &c become svarita and pluta by VIII. 2. 105. See VIII. 2. 107.

As regards अभिपूजिते we have शोभनः खल्वसि माणवका३ ॥ Here the final of माणवक becomes anudâtta and pluta.

चिदिति चोपमार्थे प्रयुज्यमाने ॥ १०१ ॥ पदानि ॥ चित्, इति, च, उपमा-अर्थे, प्रयुज्यमाने ॥

वृत्तिः ॥ अनुदात्तमिति वर्त्तते चिदित्येतस्मिन्निपाते उपमार्थे प्रयुज्यमाने वाक्यस्य टेरनुदात्तः प्लुतो भवति ॥

101. The end-vowel at the end of a sentence becomes anudâtta and pluta, when the particle चित् is employed, denoting comparison.

The word अनुदात्तं is understood here. This sûtra ordains pluta as well and not merely accent.

Thus अग्निचिद् भाया३त् 'may he shine as fire'. So also राजचिद् भाया३त् 'may be shine as a King'.

Why do we say 'when the sense is that of comparison'? Observe कथं चिद् आहुः ॥ Here चिद् has the force of 'littleness or difficulty'.

Why do we say प्रयुज्यमाने 'when expressly employed'? Observe अग्नि र्माणवको भायात् 'Let the boy shine like fire'. Here चित् is understood, hence the rule does not apply.

उपरिस्विदासीदिति च ॥ १०२ ॥ पदानि ॥ उपरि-स्वित्-आसीत्, इति, च ॥

वृत्तिः ॥ अनुदात्तमिति वर्त्तते ॥ उपरिस्विदासीदित्येतस्य टेरनुदात्तः प्लुतो भवति ॥

102. In उपरि स्विद् आसीद् the end vowel is anudâtta and pluta.

The word anudâtta is understood here also. The end-vowel would have been pluta here by VIII. 2. 97: the present sûtra really ordains accentlessness of this pluta.

Thus अधः स्विदासी३त्, उपरि स्विदासी३त् (Rig X, 129. 5). In the first portion आसीत् is pluta and udâtta by VIII. 2. 97, in the second it is anudâtta by the present sûtra.

स्वरितमाम्रेडितेसूयासंमतिकोपकुत्सनेषु ॥ १०३ ॥ पदानि ॥ स्वरितम्, आम्रेडिते, असूया, सम्मति, कोप, कुत्सनेषु ॥

वृत्तिः ॥ स्वरितः प्लुतो भवति आम्रेडिते परतः असूयायां सम्मतौ कोपे कुत्सने च गम्यमान ॥

वा० ॥ असूयादिषु वा वचनं कर्त्तव्यम् ॥

103. Of the two Vocatives of the same form standing at the beginning of a sentence, the end-vowel of the first becomes pluta and svarita, when envy, praise, anger, or blame is expressed.

The vocative is doubled by VIII. 1. 8. This sûtra ordains pluta there. Thus Envy:—माणवका३ माणवक, अभिरूपका३ अभिरूपक, रिक्तं त अभिरूप्यम् ॥ Praise:—

माणवकां३ माणवक, अँभिरूपकां३ अभिरूपक शोभनः खल्वसि ॥ Anger :—माणवकां३ माणवक, अँविनीतकां३ अविनीतक इदानीं ज्ञास्यसि जाल्म ॥ Blame :—शाक्तीकां३ शाक्तीक, याष्टीका३ याष्टीक रिक्ता ते शक्तिः ॥

Vârt:—The word "optionally" should be read into this sûtra. Thus there is no pluta and svarita in one alternative As माणवक माणवक &c.

क्षियाशीः प्रैषेषु तिङाकाङ्क्षम् ॥ १०४ ॥ पदानि ॥ क्षिया, आशी, प्रैषेषु, तिङ्-आकाङ्क्षम् ॥

वृत्तिः ॥ स्वरित इति वर्त्तते । क्षिया आचारभेदः । आशीः प्रार्थनाविशेषः । शब्देन व्यापारणं प्रैषः । एतेषु गम्यमानेषु तिङन्तामकाङ्क्षं यत्तस्य स्वरितः प्लुतो भवति ॥

104. When an error against polite usage is censured, or when a benediction or a bidding is intended, the end syllable of a finite verb becomes pluta and svarita, if this requires another sentence to complete the sense.

The word 'svarita" is understood here. The word क्षिया means 'the error in usage' or 'want of good breeding'. (VIII.1.60) आशीः means 'benediction'. प्रैषः means 'order' or 'commanding by words'.

Thus (1) स्वयं रथेन यांतिं३, उपाध्यायं पदातिं गमयति ॥ स्वयं ओदनं भुङ्क्ते३, उपाध्यायं सक्तून् पाययति ॥ In both these, the first sentence requires the second as its complement, and hence there is साकाङ्क्षा ॥

Benediction :—सुतांश्च लप्सीष्टा३ धनं च तात ; छन्दोध्येषीष्टां३ व्याकरणं च, भद्र ॥

Order :—कटं कुरु३ ग्रामं च गच्छ ; यवान् लुनीहिं३, सक्तूंश्च पिब ॥

Why do we say "when it requires another sentence as its complement"? Observe दीर्घं ते आयुरस्तु ; अग्नीन् विहर ॥ There cannot be any counter-example of क्षिया, for there two sentences are absolutely necessary to express the sense of censure.

अनन्त्यस्यापि प्रश्नाख्यानयोः ॥ १०५ ॥ पदानि ॥ अनन्त्यस्य, अपि, प्रश्न, आख्यानयोः ॥

वृत्तिः ॥ अनन्त्यस्यापि अन्त्यस्यापि पदस्य टेः प्लुतो भवति प्रश्ने आख्याने च ॥

105. In a question or narration, the end-vowel of a word, though not final in a sentence, becomes svarita and pluta, as well as of the word which is final in a sentence.

The word 'padasya' is understood here: and so also the word 'svarita'. The end-vowel of a word which is not the last word in a sentence, as well as of the last word, becomes svarita and pluta, when a question is asked, or a fact is narrated. - In fact, *all* the words of a sentence become svarita and pluta hereby.

Thus in questioning we have :—आगमां३ः पूर्वां३न् ग्रामां३न् अग्नि भूतां३इ or पटा३उ ॥ Thus all words have become svarita and pluta. The final word would, in one alternative, become anudatta also, by VIII. 2. 100, as shown under that sûtra. The force of the word अपि in the sûtra, is to make the final word also svarita, and thus this sûtra makes VIII. 2. 100 an *optional* sûtra with regard to question.

In *âkhyâna* or narration, there is no other rule, which is debarred by this. Therefore there, *all* words become svarita and pluta *necessarily*, by the force of this sûtra. Thus अगमा३म् पूर्वा३न् ग्रामा३न् भो३: ॥

Another view of this sûtra is that the word अपि applies only to âkhyâna, so that in âkhyâna *all* words become svarita. But in prasna, the final word will not become svarita, but anudâtta *necessarily* by VIII. 2. 100. According to this view, this sûtra does not ordain *option*. This view is not adopted by Kâsikâ, or Padamanjari or Siddhanta Kaumudi.

प्लुतावैच इदुतौ ॥ १०६ ॥ पदानि ॥ प्लुतौ, ऐचः, इदुतौ ॥

वृत्तिः ॥ दूराद्धूतादिषु प्लुतो विहितः तत्र ऐचः प्लुतप्रसङ्गे तदवयवभूताविदुतौ प्लुतौ ॥

106. In forming the pluta of the diphthongs ऐ and औ, their last element इ and उ get the pluta.

The pluta ordained by VIII. 2. 84 &c. when applied to ऐ or औ, cause the prolation of the last element of these diphthongs namely of इ or उ ॥ The word प्लुतौ in the sûtra is Nominative dual of प्लुत, and the aphorism literally means "इ and उ are pluta of the diphthongs ऐ and औ" ॥

Thus ऐ३तिकायन, औ३पगव ॥

The letters ऐ and औ are compound letters or diphthongs consisting of अ+इ and अ+उ ॥ In making the pluta of these, the question arises, should both अ and इ (or उ) be prolated, or only the last element, or the first only. The present sûtra answers that doubt. If in the analysis of these letters, अ be taken as having one mâtra (or *moras*), and इ and उ one mâtrâ, then the pluta इ and उ will have two mâtrâs, so that the whole pluta ऐ and औ will have *three* mâtrâs. In fact, the word प्लुत is used here as a Past Participle of प्लु, having the force of a verb ; and इदुतौ प्लुतौ means इदुतौ प्लवेते i. e. वृद्धिं गच्छतः, i. e. इ and उ are lengthened. And इ and उ are lengthened to that extent, so as to make ऐ and औ *three* mâtrâs. Thus when अ+इ and अ+उ each has one mâtrâ, then the pluta of इ and उ will have *two* mâtrâs as we have said before. But when अ+इ (ए) and अ+उ (ओ) are considered to have अ *half* mâtra, and इ and उ one mâtrâ and a half, then इ and उ are made pluta, so as to have two and a half (2½) mâtrâs each, thus the whole of ऐ and औ, has still *three* mâtrâs. In fact, the definition of *pluta* is, that it is a vowel which has *three* mâtrâs : so that we should so prolate the vowel as to make it have *three* mâtrâs.

But according to Patanjali, this pluta of ऐ and औ has *four* mâtrâs. Thus अ+इ and अ+उ each has *one* mâtrâ. The pluta of इ and उ will have *three* mâtrâs. Thus अ+इ३ and अ+उ३. or the *whole* has *four* mâtrâs. According to this view a vowel may have *four* mâtrâs also.

एचोऽप्रगृह्यस्यादूराद्धूते पूर्वस्यार्द्धस्यादुत्तरस्येदुतौ॥ १०७ ॥ पदानि ॥ एचो, अ-प्रगृह्यस्य, अदूराद्धूते, पूर्वस्य अर्धस्य, आत्, उत्तरस्य ईत्, उतौ ॥

वृत्तिः ॥ एचो ऽप्रगृह्यस्यादूराद्धूते प्लुतविषयस्यार्द्धस्याकार आदेशो भवति स च प्लुतः उत्तरस्येकारोकारावादेशो भवतः ॥

वार्त्तिकम् ॥विषयपरिगणं कर्तव्यं ॥ वा०॥ प्रश्नान्ताभिपूजितविचार्यमाणप्रत्यभिवादयाज्यान्तेष्विति वक्तव्यम् ॥ वा० ॥ आमन्त्रिते छन्दसि प्लुतविकारोयं वक्तव्यः ॥

107. In the diphthongs, which are not Pragṛhya (I. 1. 11 &c) and which become pluta under the circumstances mentioned in VIII. 2. 83 &c., but not when that circumstance is a call from a distance (VIII. 2. 84); for the first half, there is substituted the prolated आ, aud for the second portion इ or उ ॥

The diphthongs or एच् are ए, ऐ, ओ and औ ॥ Their elements are अ+इ, and अ+उ ॥ When these diphthongs are to be prolated, *at the end of a word*, the diphthong is resolved into its elements, the *first* portion अ is prolated, and इ or उ added, as the case may be. This इ and उ, in fact, are the substitutes of the second portion, which may be इ or उ, or ए or ओ ॥

This rule is not of universal application, but applies to Rules VIII. 2. 100, VIII. 2. 97, VIII. 2. 83, and VIII. 2. 90 only, according to the

Vârt:—The scope of this sûtra should be determined by enumerating the rules to which it applies.

Vârt:—It should be stated that it applies to sûtras VIII. 2. 100, 97, 83 and 90.

Thus VIII. 2. 100: As अगमा३: पूर्वा३न् ग्रामा३न् अग्निभूता३इ ॥ or पटा३उ ॥ भद्रं करोषि माणवका३ अग्निभूता३इ or पटा३उ ॥ So also VIII. 2. 97: हौतव्यं दीक्षितस्य गृहा३इ ॥ So also VIII. 2. 83, as:—आयुष्मान् एधि अग्निभूता३इ or पटा३उ ॥ So also VIII. 2. 90:—as.

उक्षान्नाय वशान्नाय सोमपृष्ठाय वेधसे ।
स्तोमै र्विधेमाग्नया३इ ॥ (Tait. S. I. 3. 14. 7).

This pluta आ is udâtta, anudâtta or svarita, according to the particular rule which has been applied, i. e. at the end of a question it is anudâtta or svarita, and every where else, udâtta. The इ and उ are of course, always udâtta: because the anuvṛitti of udâtta is current here.

Why do we restrict this sûtra to the above-mentioned four rules? Observe विष्णुभूते विष्णुभूते३ घातयिष्यामि त्वा आगच्छ भो माणवक विष्णुभूते ॥

In fact, the present sûtra being confined to the above-mentioned four rules, the words अदूराद्धूते in the sûtra, are redundant: and should not have been used. Moreover the word पदान्त should have been used in the sûtra, for it applies to diphthongs at the *end* of a pada. Therefore, not here, भद्रं करोषि गौरिति ॥ Here गौ before the sarvanâmasthâna affix सु is not a Pada (I. 4. 17).

Why do we say 'when it is not a Pragṛhya'? Observe शोभने खलु स्थः खट्वे३ ॥

Vârt :—This peculiar modification of pluta vowel takes place in the Vocative case in the Vedas. As अग्ना३इ पत्नीवा३ः सजूर्देवेन त्वष्ट्रा सोमं पिब ॥ Here by no other rule, the Vocative would have become prolated

तयोर्य्वावचि संहितायाम् ॥ १०८ ॥ पदानि ॥ तयोः य, वौ, अचि, संहितायाम् ॥

वृत्तिः ॥ तयोरिदुतोर्यकारवकारादेशौ भवतो ऽचि संहितायां विषये ॥

Kârikâ:—किं तु यणा भवतीह न सिद्धं प्लाविदुतोर्यदयं विदधाति ।
तौ च मम स्वरसन्धिषु सिद्धौ शाकलदीर्घविधी तु निवर्त्यौ ॥
इक तु यदा भवति प्लुतपूर्वस्तस्य यणं विदधात्यपवादम् ।
तेन तयोश्च न शाकलदीर्घौ यण्स्वरबाधनमेव तु हेतुः ॥

108. For these vowels इ and उ are substituted य् and व् when a vowel follows them in a samhita (in an unbroken flow of speech).

The word संहितायाम् is an adhikâra and exerts its influence upto the end of the Book. Whatever we shall teach hereafter, upto the end of the Book, will apply to words which are in Sanhitâ.

Thus अग्ना३याशा, पटा३वाशा, अग्ना३यिन्द्रम्, पटा३वुदकम् ॥

Why do we say "when a vowel follows"? Observe अग्ना३इ, पटा३उ ॥

Why do we say संहितायाम् 'in an uninterrupted flow of speech'? Observe अग्ना३ इ इन्द्रम्, पटा३उ उदकम् in Pada Pâṭha.

This sûtra is made, because इ and उ being Pluta-modifications are considered as asiddha (VIII. 2. 1) for the purposes of इको यणचि (VI. 1. 77). But supposing that some how or other, these इ and उ be considered siddha, still the present rule is necessary to prevent their lengthening before a homogeneous vowel (VI. 1. 101), or their retaining their form unchanged by VI. 1. 127. If it be said, that these rules VI. 1. 101, and VI. 1. 127, would not apply, because of the Vârtika इकः प्लुतपूर्वस्य सवर्णदीर्घ बाधनार्थं यणादेशो वक्तव्यः (Vârtika to VI. 1. 77); still the present sûtra ought to be made, in order to prevent यण् accent (VIII. 2. 4).

Kârikâ :—Q. Could not this have been accomplished by the यणादेश of VI. 1. 77, that the Âchârya has taught this separate य् and व् substitution?

Ans.—If you say that pluta is siddha in the vowel sandhi rules, because of the jñâpaka in sûtra VI. 1. 125, then still this rule is necessary in order to prevent the lengthening of VI. 1. 101, and the Sâkala rule VI. 1. 127.

Q.—But those two rules VI. 1. 101, and VI. 1. 127, have already been debarred by the Vârtika which ordains that यणादेश takes place of such a vowel following a pluta (See vârtika to VI. 1. 77), what is then the necessity of the present sûtra?

Ans.—The necessity of the present sûtra is to prevent the यण-accent of VIII. 2. 4.

According to one view, the vârtika under VI. 1. 77, refers to those vowels which are not pluta-elements, like the present इ and उ, but which are *independent* vowels following after a pluta vowel. As भो३ इ इन्द्र = भो३ यिन्द्र ॥ Here इ is a Nipâta.

ओ३म् ।

अथ अष्टमाध्यायस्य तृतीयः पादः ।

BOOK EIGHTH.

CHAPTER THIRD.

मतुवसो रु सम्बुद्धौ छन्दसि ॥ १ ॥ पदानि ॥ मतु, वसोः, रु, सबुद्धौ, छन्दसि ॥

वृत्तिः ॥ मत्वन्तस्य वस्वन्तस्य च पदस्य रुरित्ययमादेशो भवति सम्बुद्धौ परतः छन्दसि विषये ॥

वार्त्तिकम् ॥ वन उपसंख्यानं कर्त्तव्यम् ॥ वा० ॥ भवद्भगवदघवतामोच्चावस्य ॥

1. For the final of the affixes **मत्** and **वस्**, there is substituted **रु**, in the Vocative singular, in the Chhandas.

The word संहितायां is understood here. A word ending in the affix मत् or वस्, changes its final त् or स् into र्, in the Chhandas, in the Vocative singular. Thus मत् :—इन्द्रं मरुत्व इह पाहि सोमम् (Rig. III. 51. 7) हरिवो मेदिनं त्वा ॥ Here मरुत्वः is Vocative Sg. of मरुत्वत् and हरिवः of हरिवत्, meaning "he who is possessed of Maruts or Hari horses". The म of मत् is changed to व by VIII. 2. 10; 15. The base मरुत् before this termination is Bha by I. 4. 19. The affix सु (nom. sg.) is elided by VI. 1. 68; the त् is elided by VIII. 2. 23, and the न् (of नुम् VII. 1. 70) is changed to र् by this sûtra. So also इन्द्रायाहि तूतुजानः उपब्रह्माणि हरिवः (Rig. I. 3. 6).

With वस् :—मीढ्वस्तोकाय तनयाय मृळ (Rig. II. 33. 14), इन्द्रसाह्वः ॥ See VI. 1. 12, for the formation of मीढ्वान्, साह्वान् with क्वसु ॥

Why do we say 'of मत् and वस्'? Observe ब्रह्मन् स्तोष्यामः ॥ Why do we say in the Vocative Singular? Observe य एवं विद्वानग्निमाधत्ते ॥ Why do we say in the Chhandas? Observe हे गोमन्, हे पयिवन् ॥

Vârt :—The affix वन् should also be enumerated. The affixes क्वनिप् and वनिप् are both meant here. Its final is also changed to रु in the Vocative Sg. As यस्त्वायन्तं वसुना प्रातरित्वः ॥ The word प्रातरित्वन् is formed by adding क्वनिप् to the root इ (इण्) preceded by प्रातः ॥ See III. 2. 75. The तुक् is added by VI. 1. 71.

Vârt:—The finals of भवत्, भगवत् and अघवत् are changed to रु, optionally in the secular as well as the sacred literature, and the syllable अव् of these words is changed to ओ ॥ This is a general rule, applying both in the Vedas and the Bhâshâ. Thus भवत्—हे भोः or हे भवन् ॥ भगवत्—हे भगोः or हे भगवन् ॥ अघवत्—हे अघोः or हे अघवन् ॥ Or these words भोः भगोः and अघोः are so irregularly formed by the âchârya himself in VIII. 3. 17. These are found in other numbers than the Vocative Singular, as भो देवदत्तयज्ञदत्तौ, भो देवदत्तयज्ञदत्त विष्णुमित्राः ॥ It is found in connection with Feminine nouns also, as भो ब्राह्मणि ॥

The adhikâra of the word संहितायां does not exert any apparent influence in this sûtra. It however has influence in those subsequent sûtras, where the change in one word is occasioned by another word on account of sanhita or juxta-position, as in VIII. 3. 7.

See VIII. 2. 3 (Vârtika 2) by which the lopa is considered siddha in हरिवः, otherwise there would have been no उ change in हरिवो मे &c.

अत्रानुनासिकः पूर्वस्य तु वा ॥ २ ॥ पदानि ॥ अत्र, अनुनासिकः, पूर्वस्य तु वा॥

वृत्तिः ॥ अधिकारोयम् । इत उत्तरं यस्य स्थाने रुर्विधीयते ततः पूर्वस्य तु वर्णस्य वाऽनुनासिको भवतीत्येतदधिकृतं वेदितव्यम् ॥

2. In the following sûtras upto VIII. 3. 12, this is always to be supplied :—"But here a nasal vowel may optionally be substituted for the preceding vowel after which रु has been ordained".

This is an adhikâra sûtra. For the letter which stands before that letter for which रु has been substituted, there is substituted a nasal vowel, in this division of Grammar, where रु is the subject of discussion.

Thus sûtra VIII. 3. 5 says "In the place of the final of सम्, there is रु when सुट् augment follows". The vowel अ of सम् becomes nasal; as सँस्कर्त्ता, सँस्कर्त्तुम्, सँस्कर्त्तव्यम् ॥

Why have we used the word अत्र in the sûtra? It means "*here* i. e. in this division where रु is the subject of discussion". Obj. This object would have been gained, without using the word अत्रं; since it is an adhikâra sûtra and would apply to रु ॥ Ans. No. Here रु is taught in connection with nasal, therefore, the rule would not apply to any other context. For had अत्र not been used, we could not have known the extent of the jurisdiction (adhikâ rà) of this nasal; and we might have applied the rule of nasality to those *beyond* the jurisdiction of रु, such as VIII. 3. 13. The employment of अत्र prevents this doubt and shows that रु and nasality are co-extensive.

आतोटि नित्यम् ॥ ३ ॥ पदानि ॥ आतः, अटि, नित्यम् ॥

वृत्तिः ॥ अटि परतो रोः पूर्वस्याकारस्य स्थाने नित्यमनुनासिकादेशो भवति ॥

3. A nasal vowel is *always* substituted for आ before रु, when it is followed by a letter of अट् pratyâhâra (i. e. when it is followed by a vowel or ह, य, व, or र).

Thus VIII. 3. 9 teaches रु substitution of न्, the long आ preceding it, would have been optionally nasal by the last sûtra. The present sûtra makes it necessarily so. Thus महाँ असि (Rig. III. 46. 2) महाँ इन्द्रो य ओजसा (Rig. VIII. 6. 1). देवाँ अच्छादीध्यत् ॥

Some (i. e. the Taittariyas) read it as anusvâra. This is a Vedic diversity.

Why do we say "for a long आ"? Observe ये वा वनस्पतीरनु ॥ Why do we say "when a vowel or ह, य, व, or र follows"? Observe भवांश्चरति, भवाञ्छादयति ॥

The word नित्य 'always' is employed for the sake of distinctness only. The very fact of making a separate sûtra, would give it a compulsory force, even without the word nitya.

अनुनासिकात्परो ऽनुस्वारः ॥ ४ ॥ पदानि ॥ अनुनासिकात्, परः, अनुस्वारः ॥

वृत्तिः ॥ अनुनासिकादन्यो यो वर्णः रोः पूर्वः यस्यानुनासिको न विहितस्ततः परो ऽनुस्वार आगमो भवति ॥

4. After what precedes रु, if we omit to substitute the nasal, then anusvâra shall be the augment.

The substitution of nasal is *optional* by VIII. 3. 2. When nasal is not substituted, we add an anusvâra to such vowel. The word अन्य should be read into the sûtra to complete the sense, i. e. अनुनासिकात् अन्यो यो वर्णः "a letter *other than* a nasal", i. e. a letter for which nasal has not been ordained, and which stands before रु ॥

Thus VIII. 3. 5, teaches रु substitution of the म् of सम् an anusvâra would be added. As संस्कर्त्ता, संस्कर्त्तव्यम् ॥ Similarly VIII. 3. 6, teaches रु substitution of the म् of पुम् ॥ An anusvâra will be added here also, as, पुंस्कामा ॥ Similarly VIII. 3. 7, teaches रु substitution of final न् ॥ Here also an anusvâra will be added, as भवांश्चरति ॥

Some say "the word परः in the sûtra means अन्यः, and so we need not supply the word अन्यः from outside". They say अनुनासिकात् परः = अनुनासिकादन्यः ; i. e. the anusvâra takes place in that alternative when there is no nasal. That anusvâra is an *augment* and not a *substitute*. It is an augment to the vowel which precedes रु ॥

समः सुटि ॥ ५ ॥ पदानि ॥ समः, सुटि ॥

वृत्तिः ॥ सम इत्येतस्य रुर्भवति सुटि परतः संहितायां विषये ॥

वार्त्तिकम् ॥ संपुंकानां सो वक्तव्यः ॥ वा० ॥ समो वा लोपमेके ॥

5. रु is substituted for the म् of सम् (and thereby अँ or अं is substituted for अ) when the augment स् follows, in a samhitâ.

The augment सुट् is added by VI. 1. 137 &c. Thus सँस्स्कर्त्ता or संस्स्कर्त्ता, सँस्स्कर्तुम् or संस्स्कर्तुम्, सँस्स्कर्त्तव्यम् or संस्स्कर्त्तव्यम् ॥ The word is thus evolved: सम्+स+कर्ता=सर्+स+कर्ता (VIII. 3. 5). Here rule VIII. 3. 15 appears and requires र् to be changed to visarjannya. This visarga may optionally be retained unchanged by VIII. 3. 36. This, however, is not done in the present instance: but the visarga is *always* and *necessarily* changed to स् by VIII. 3. 34. In fact, the option of VIII. 3. 36 is a determinate option (vyavasthita vibhâshâ) and does not apply to the present case.

Or even this sûtra may be so read as to teach the स् substitution as well. Thus, the sûtra is समः स्सुटि with two स्, and the sûtra will mean, "रु is substituted for the म् of सम् before सुट्, and this रु is always changed to स्" ॥

Why do we say "for the म् of सम्"? Observe उपस्कर्त्ता ॥ Why do we say "before सुट्"? Observe संकृति ॥

Vârt:—For the finals of सम्, पुम् and कान् there is always substituted स ॥ There would arise anomalies, if रु be substituted. Thus संस्कर्त्ता, पुंस्स्कामा, कांस्कान् ॥ In fact, according to this vârtika, रु is never substituted for सम् (VIII. 3. 5), पुम् (VIII. 3. 6) and कान् (VIII. 3. 12).

Vârt:— समो वा लोपमेके ॥ Some would have the elision of the स् after सम् ॥ This *Vârtika* is not given in the Kâsikâ, but the Padamanjari gives it, and so also the Mahâbhâshya.

According to Bhattoji Dikshita there will be 108 forms of this word संस्कर्त्ता ॥ Thus सँस्कर्त्ता and संस्कर्त्ता with the elision of स् ॥ Then with two स्, as सँस्स्कर्त्ता, संस्स्कर्ता ॥ Then we apply VIII. 4. 47 to this latter, and have three स, as सँस्स्स्कर्ता or संस्स्स्कर्ता ॥ The anusvâra is considered to be a vowel (अच्) for this purpose. From the three nasal forms सँस्कर्ता, सँस्स्कर्ता and सँस्स्स्कर्ता, we get three more by doubling the क् by the vârtika शरः खयः ॥ The three forms having anusvâra, will also double their anusvâra in addition to क् doubling. Thus we have 12 forms in anusvâra: and six in nasal, altogether 18 forms. Then the त will be doubled and trebled: and thus with one त, two त and three त, we have $3 \times 18 = 54$ forms. This will be doubled $(2 \times 54 = 108)$ when मण् is nasalised.

पुमः खय्यम्परे ॥ ६ ॥ पदानि ॥ पुमः, खयि, अम-परे ॥

वृत्तिः ॥ पुमित्येतस्य रुर्भवति अम्परे खयि परतः ॥

6. रु is substituted for the म् of पुम्, (whereby the

उ is changed to उँ or उं) before a surd mute (खय्) which is followed by a vowel, semivowel or a nasal (अम् pratyâhâra).

Thus पुँस्कामा or पुंस्कामा; पुँस्पुत्रः or पुंस्पुत्रः; पुँस्फलं or पुंस्फलम्; पुँश्चली or पुंश्चली ॥ The visarga in पुंस्कामा required to be changed optionally to ✕ jihvâmûlîya by VIII. 3. 37, but it is not so done. It is changed *always* to स् here by VIII. 3. 34, also. The स् of पुंस् is dropped by VIII. 2. 23, and the preceding sound is म, which comes to light in forms like पुमान् &c. For the sake of distinctness, Pâṇini has elected to exhibit the shorter form पुम् when in the beginning of a composition: because this shorter form पुम् is the real stem in composition. खय् pratyâhâra includes the ten hard consonants, and अम् pratyâhâra includes all vowels, semivowels and nasals. पुंस्कामा is formed by the affix ण = पुमांसं कामयते ॥

In that alternative when we read the preceding sûtra as समःसुटि, then the anuvṛitti of this स् will be current in the present sûtra also, and so there will be no scope for the operation of VIII. 3. 37. And though the anuvṛitti of रु is also current, yet it will not apply here, because of its non-appropriateness in that alternative.

Why do we say 'before a surd mute'? Observe पुंदासः, पुंगवः (V. 4. 92). Why do we say 'followed by a vowel or semivowel or nasal'? Observe पुंक्षीरं, पुंक्षुरः ॥ Why do we use the word परे in the sûtra? Had we not used it, the sûtra might have been open to this construction also. The म of पुम् is so changed before a खय् letter which has an अम् letter, (whether *preceding* it or *following* it). So that the rule would have applied to पुमाख्यः, पुमाचारः ॥

नश्छव्यप्रशान् ॥ ७ ॥ पदानि ॥ नः, छवि, अप्रशान् ॥

वृत्तिः ॥ नकारान्तस्य पदस्य प्रशान्वर्जितस्य रुर्भवत्यम्परे छवि परतः ॥

7. रु is substituted for the final न् of a word, with the exception of the न् of प्रशान्, before a छव् letter (छ, ठ, थ, च, ट, त), which is followed by an अम् letter (vowel, semivowel and nasal).

The word अम्परे is to be read into this sûtra. The word अप्रशान् in the sûtra is in the Nominative case, but it has the force of Genitive.

Thus भवाँश्छादयति or भवांश्छादयति; भवाँश्चिनोति or भवांश्चिनोति; भवाँष्टीकते or भवांष्टीकते, (from the root टीकृ 'to go'), भवाँस्तरति or भवांस्तरति ॥

Why do we say 'before a छव् letter'? Observe भवान् करोति ॥ Why do we say 'with the exception of the न् of प्रशान्'? Observe प्रशाम् छादयति, प्रशान् चिनोति ॥ Why do we say 'when अम follows छव्'? See भवान् त्सरुकः ॥ त्सरु is sword, he who is dexterous in it, is called त्सरुकः (कन् V. 2. 64).

उभयथर्क्षु ॥ ८ ॥ पदानि ॥ उभयथा, ऋक्षु ॥

वृत्तिः ॥ नकारान्तस्य पदस्य छविपरतः अम्परे उभयथा ऋक्षु भवति ॥

8. In both ways, in the Rig verses.

This ordains an option to the last sûtra, by which the रु substitution was compulsory. A word ending in न् followed by a letter of छव् class, which itself is followed by अम्, changes its final न् to र् *optionally* in the Rig Veda. Sometimes there is र् and sometimes न् ॥ Thus तस्मिन् त्वा दधाति or तस्मिँस् त्वा दधाति ; पशूँस्ताँश्चक्रे ॥

Why do we say "in the Rig verses". No option is allowed here तांस्त्व खाद सुखादितान् ॥

दीर्घादटि समानपादे ॥ ९ ॥ पदानि ॥ दीर्घात्, अटि, समानपादे ॥

वृत्तिः ॥ दीर्घादुत्तरस्य पदान्तस्य नकारस्य रुर्भवत्यटि परतस्तौ चेन्निमित्तनिमित्तिनौ समानपादे भवतः ॥

9 रु is optionally substituted for that final न् of a word which is preceded by a long vowel, and is followed by an अट् letter (vowels and semi-vowels with the exception of ल्), when these (न् and अट्) come in contact with each other in the same stanza of the Rig Veda.

The नः of VIII. 3. 7 is understood here: and so also ऋक्षु ॥ The word समानपाद means एकपाद, i. e. when both words are in one and the same Pâda of the verse. Thus परिधीँ रति (Rig. IX. 107. 19) स देवाँ एहवक्षति (Rig. I. 1. 2) देवाँ अच्छादीव्यत्; महाँ इन्द्रो य ओजसा ॥

Why do we say 'preceded by a long vowel'? Observe अहन्नहिम् ॥ Why do we say "when followed by a vowel or य, व or र'? Observe भ्यान् क्षियान् ॥ Why do we say 'when both words are in the same Pâda of a verse'? Observe यातुधानान् उपस्पृशः ॥

The word उभयथा of the preceding sûtra is understood here also: so that it is an optional rule: and न् remains unchanged also, as आदित्यान् हवामहे आदित्यान् याचिषामहे ॥ See VIII. 3. 3.

नॄन्पे ॥ १० ॥ पदानि ॥ नॄन्, पे ॥

वृत्तिः ॥ नॄनित्येतस्य नकारस्य रुर्भवति पशब्दे परतः ॥

10. रु is optionally substituted for the न् of नॄन् before प् ॥

The अ in प is for the sake of pronunciation only. Thus नॄँः पाहि or नॄंः पाहि ; नॄँः प्रीणीहि or नॄंः प्रीणीहि ॥

Why do we say 'before प्'? Observe नॄन् भोजयति ॥ Some read the anuvṛitti of उभयथा into this sûtra, so that it is an optional one. Thus we have नॄन् पाहि also. The nominative case in नॄन् has the force of Genitive.

स्वतवान्पायौ ॥ ११ ॥ पदानि ॥ स्वतवान्, पायौ ॥

वृत्तिः ॥ स्वतवानित्येतस्य नकारस्य रुर्भवति पायुशब्द परतः ॥

11. The न् of स्वतवान् is changed to रु before पायु ॥

As स्वत वः पायुरग्ने (Rig. IV. 2. 6). The word is स्वतवस्, the नुम् is added by VII. 1. 83. The word is derived from तु वृद्धौ with the affix असुन् (स्वन्तवो यस्यऽसौ स्वतवान्) ॥

कानाम्रेडिते ॥ १२ ॥ पदानि ॥ कान्, आम्रेडिते ॥

वृत्ति ॥ कानित्येतस्य नकारस्य रुर्भवति आम्रेडिते परतः ॥

12. रु is substituted for the न् of कान् when it is followed by another कान् which is an âmreḍita.

The sûtra might have been कान् कानि; but the use of the longer form आम्रेडिते shows, that where there is 'doubling', and the word gets the designation of âmreḍita, then the rule applies. Thus काँस्कान् आमन्त्रयते, काँस्कान् भोजयति; or कांस्कान् &c. When the second कान् is not an âmreḍita, we have कान् कान् पश्यति? Here one is किं asking question, and the other is used in the sense of contempt. This word is read in the list of कस्कादि (VIII. 3. 48), and hence sûtra VIII. 3. 37, does not apply. Or the स् of समः सुटि (VIII. 3. 5), is understood here, and that स् is enjoined here and not रु ॥ It should not be objected that in the preceding sûtras also स् should be enjoined and not रु; because in those sûtras रु is appropriate but not so here.

Why do we say 'when an âmreḍita कान् follows'? Observe कान् कान् पश्यति where one is interrogatory and the other denotes contempt (II. 1. 64).

ढो ढे लोपः ॥ १३ ॥ पदानि ॥ ढः, ढे, लोपः ॥

वृत्तिः ॥ ढकारस्य ढकारे लोपो भवति ॥

13. There is elision of ढ् when ढ् follows.

Though this sûtra is read in the division of Grammar which is governed by पदाधिकार, yet this elision takes place only then when the ढ is not at the end of a pada. Thus लीढ from लिह्+त ॥ The ह is changed to ढ by VIII. 2. 31, and the त is first changed to ध by VIII. 2. 40, and then to ढ by VIII. 4. 41. Thus लिढ्+ढ ॥ The first ढ् is elided by this sûtra. Similarly मीढम्, उपगूढम् ॥ The change of ध into ढ by VIII. 4. 41, should be considered as valid and siddha for the purposes of this rule, otherwise this rule will find no scope.

Obj:—It will find scope before that ढ which is primary, as in अलिढ्+ढौकते, where ढ of ढौकते is primary.

Ans.—No. Here the first ढ will be changed to ड् by जश् rule (VIII. 2. 39) and so there will be no occasion to elide it. The form will be अलिड् ढौकते ॥ Nor is this ढ लोपः rule an apavâda to जश्त्व rule, because it has its scope in लीढ &c. For the जश् rule depends upon one pada, and is antaranga, or being prior to this the lopa is asiddha with regard to it. Therefore जश्त्व will take place first. Moreover in लिह्+ढ there is similarity of *sounds* (श्रुतिकृतं आनन्तर्यम्); though there may not be theoretical similarity (शास्त्रकृतं आनन्तर्यम्) when the change of ध into ढ by VIII. 4. 41, is considered asiddha. But this theoretical technical dissimilarity will be removed by the express text of the present sûtra. But in श्वलिड् ढौकते there is neither similarity of sounds (śruti kṛtamânantaryam) between ड् and ढ्, nor similarity created by any technical rule; therefore ढ लोप has no scope here. It is Bahiranga as well as subsequent to जश् rule (VIII. 2. 39), and therefore *doubly* asiddha; and consequently it does not debar the जश् rule. So when ढ् is changed to ड् by जश् rule (VIII. 2. 39) in श्वलिड्, then there remains no sort of ânantarya—neither of śruti nor of śâstra.

रो रि ॥ १४ ॥ पदानि ॥ रः, रि ॥

वृत्तिः ॥ रेफस्य रेफे परतो लोपो भवति ॥

14. र् is elided before a र्॥

The sûtra is रः रि, and not रोः रि ॥ That is रो रि is the form which रः रि and रोः रि will both assume. रः is the Genitive of र्, and रोः would be the Genitive of रु ॥ The sûtra is not confined to रु only, but to every र् in general including रु ॥ Thus नीरक्तम्, दूरक्तम्, where it is simple र् of निर् and दुर्; and अग्नी रथः, and इन्दू रथः where it is रु (अग्निः रथः, इन्दुः रथः). The lengthening is by VI. 3. 111. The word पदस्य is understood here, and the Genitive here has the force of विशेषण i. e. a quality, or avayava-shashṭhi; i. e. when रेफ is a *portion* of the pada. Thus a रेफ which is not at the end of a pada is also elided. Had the Genitive been construed as sthâna-shashṭhî, then रेफ would qualify पद, and the rule would mean "र् should be elided before a र् when at the *end* of a word." ॥ See VIII. 1. 16. But we have the elision of the *penultimate* र् in अजर्घर्द् the second person singular of the Imperfect of the Intensive, and we get the form अजर्घाः ॥ See VIII. 2. 37. So also अपास्पाः from स्पर्ध in Intensive, Imperfect. The reduplicate is lengthened by VII. 4. 83, the शप् is elided, and सिप् is elided by VI. 1. 68, the final ध् is changed to द् by VIII. 2. 39, and this द् changed to र् by VIII. 2. 75.

खरवसानयोर्विसर्जनीयः ॥ १५ ॥ पदानि ॥ खर, अवसानयोः, विसर्जनीयः ॥

वृत्तिः ॥ रेफान्तस्य पदस्य खरि परतो ऽवसाने च विसर्जनीयादेशो भवति ॥

15. The Visarjanîya is substituted for र्, before a खर् consonant or when there is a Pause.

Tha word रः is understood. The visarga is the substitute of र् final in a Pada, before surd consonants and sibilants, or at a Pause,

Thus वृक्षश्छादयति (VIII. 3. 34, VIII. 4. 40), प्लक्षश्छादयति, वृक्षस्तरति, प्लक्षस्तरति वृक्षष्ठकारः, प्लक्षष्ठकारः, वृक्षष्टीकते, प्लक्षष्टीकते, वृक्षश्चिनोति, प्लक्षश्चिनोति ॥ Pause:—वृक्षः; प्लक्षः ॥

Who do we say "before a खर् consonant or at a Pause"? Observe अग्निर्नयति, वायुर्नयति, नार्कुटः (नृ कुड्यां भवः), नार्पत्यः (नृपतेरपत्यं) ॥ In these two latter, the Vṛiddhi being considered as Bahiranga, and the र् being the result of such Bahiranga Vṛiddhi, is asiddha, and is consequently not changed to visarga.

The word पदस्य is understood here, and the genitive should be construed here as sthâna-sashṭhî, so that for the final र् of a Pada there is visarga, and not for that र् which is not final.

रोः सुपि ॥ पदानि ॥ रोः, सुपि ॥

वृत्तिः ॥ रु इत्येतस्य रेफस्य सुपि परतो विसर्जनीयादेशो भवति ॥

16. Visarjaniya is substituted for the रु called र (and not any other र), before the Locative Plural case-affix सु ॥

Thus पयःसु, सर्पिःषु, यशःसु ॥ The word सुप् is here the Locative Plural affix. Though the र् would have been changed to visarga by the last sûtra also; the making of this a special sûtra is for the sake of niyama. That is, only रु becomes visarga, and not any other र् ॥ Thus गीर्षु, धूर्षु, when the र् is not रु ॥ In पयस् &c, the स् becomes रु by VIII. 2. 66.

भोभगोअघोअपूर्वस्य योऽशि ॥ १७ ॥ पदानि ॥ भो, भगो, अघो, अपूर्वस्य, यः, अशि ॥

वृत्तिः ॥ भो भगो अघो इत्येवंपूर्वस्य अवर्णपूर्वस्य च रो रेफस्य यकारादेशो भवति अशि परतः ॥

17. य् is substituted for the रु called र, when it is preceded by भो, भगो, अघो, अ or आ, before an अश् letter (vowels and soft consonants).

Thus भो अत्र, भगो अत्र, अघो अत्र, भो ददाति, भगो ददाति, अघो ददाति ॥ क आस्ते, कय् आस्ते, ब्राह्मणा ददाति, पुरुषा ददाति ॥ The य् is elided by VIII. 3. 19, 20, 22 &c. With य, the forms will be भोयत्र, भगोयत्र, अघोयत्र ॥

Why do we say 'when preceded by भो &c'? Observe अग्निरत्र, वायुरत्र ॥ Why do we say 'when followed by a letter of अश् pratyâhâra'? Observe वृक्षः, प्लक्षः ॥ No, this is no valid counter-example, because no other word follows the visarga; while some word must follow it because the word sanhitâ (VIII. 2. 108) is understood here.

Ans.—If this be so, then अश् is employed in this sûtra for the sake of subsequent sûtras. Its employment here is superfluous. For letters other than अश् are खर् ॥ Before a खर् letter, the र् will be changed to visarga by VIII. 3. 15; and the यत्व of this rule will be considered as asiddha for the purposes of VIII. 3. 15, so there will necessarily be visarga. Thus अश् serves no purpose in this sûtra, but is for the sake of subsequent ones. Thus in VIII. 3. 22, the word हलि must be qualified by the word अश्, namely those consonants only which are in the class अश् ॥ Before any other consonant there will be no elision of य ॥ Thus वृक्षं वृश्चति = वृक्षवृट् ॥ The denominative verb from this will be वृक्षवयति ॥ A secondary derivative from this root, with the affix

विच् will be वृक्षव् as in वृक्षव् करोति ॥ Here व् would require elision by VIII. 3. 22, before क्, but it is not so because अशि qualifies हलि ॥

Obj.—If so, why is the word हल् used in that sutra VIII. 3. 22, it would have been better to say हशि सर्वेषाम् instead of हलि सर्वेषाम् ॥

Ans.—The word हल् is used in that sutra for the sake of the subsequent sutra VIII. 3. 23, which applies to *all* consonants. Had हशि been used in VIII. 3. 22, then in VIII. 3. 23, हलि ought to have been used.

Moreover अशि is used in this sutra, so that rules VIII. 3. 18, 19 may not apply to वृक्षव् करोति ॥

This sutra applies to रु called र्, therefore not here प्रातरत्र, पुनरत्र ॥

व्योर्लघुप्रयत्नतरः शाकटायनस्य ॥ १८ ॥ पदानि ॥ व्योः, लघुप्रयत्नतरः, शाकटायनस्य ॥

वृत्तिः ॥ वकारयकारयोर्भोभगोअघोअवर्णपूर्वयोः पदान्तयोर्लघुप्रयत्नतर आदेशो भवति, अशि परतः, शाकटायनस्याचार्यस्य मतेन ॥

18. व् and य् (in भगोय् &c and after अ or आ, at the end of a Pada) are pronounced with a lighter articulation before an अश् letter, according to the opinion of Sâkaṭâyana.

That the effort in pronouncing which is very light is called laghu-prayatna-tara. Effort or articulation is a quality of the person who utters and which is the cause of the utterance of a letter. व् and य् of lighter articulation are substituted for the final व् and य् in भोय्, भगोय्, अघोय्, or after an अ or आ ॥ The lighter व् will replace the heavy व्, and so the lighter य् the heavy य ॥

Thus भोयत्र, भगोयत्र, अघोयत्र, कयास्ते or क आस्ते, अस्मायुद्धर or अस्मा उद्धर, असावादित्यः or असा आदित्यः, द्वावत्र or द्वा अत्र, द्वावानय or द्वा आनय ॥

The lighter articulation results from the relaxation of the muscles and the organs employed in speech. The places of pronunciation are palate &c, the organs are the root, the middle and the tip of the tongue. When the contact of the tongue with the various places is very light, the articulation is laghu prayatna-tara. In fact, य् and व् are to be slurred over.

लोपः शाकल्यस्य ॥ १९ ॥ पदानि ॥ लोपः, शाकल्यस्य ॥

वृत्तिः ॥ वकारयकारयोः पदान्तयोरवर्णपूर्वयोर्लोपो भवति शाकल्यस्याचार्यस्य मतेनाशि परतः ॥

19. व् and य् preceded by अ or आ and at the end of a pada, are elided before an अश् letter, according to the opinion of Śâkalya.

As क आस्ते or कयास्ते, काक आस्ते or काकयास्ते, अस्मा उद्धर or अस्मायुद्धर, द्वावत्र or द्वा अत्र, असावादित्यः or असा आदित्यः ॥

The name of Śâkalya is used to make it an optional rule. Therefore, where there is not the lighter articulation of व् and य् by the last sûtra, there also in the other alternative the fuller sounds of व् and य् are heard. Thus there are three forms, *heavy* व् and य्, *light* व् and य् and *elision* of व् and य्॥

When व् and य् are preceded by ओ, then there is elision by the next sûtra compulsorily.

ओतो गार्ग्यस्य ॥ २० ॥ पदानि ॥ ओतः, गार्ग्यस्य ॥

वृत्तिः ॥ ओकारादुत्तरस्य यकारस्य लोपो भवति गार्ग्यस्याचार्यस्य मतेन अशि परतः ॥

20. य् preceded by ओ is elided, according to the opinion of Gârgya, before an अश् letter.

There can be no व् preceded by ओ, so only य् is taken in explaining the sutra. Thus भो अत्र, भगो अत्र, भो इदम्, भगो इदम् ॥

The making of it a separate sutra, is for the sake of indicating that this is a necessary (*nitya*) rule and not a vibhâshâ rule. The name of Gârgya is used simply *honoris causa* (pujârtha). The elision of laghu-prayatna य्, which VIII. 3. 19 would have otherwise caused, is hereby prohibited. So that laghu pratyatnatara य् does come also. As भो अत्र or भोयत्र, भगो अत्र or भगोयत्र, अघो अत्र and अघोयत्र ॥

According to others every kind of य् (whether heavy or light) is to be elided: and भोयत्र is not valid in their opinion.

उञि च पदे ॥ २१ ॥ पदानि ॥ उञि, च पदे ॥

वृत्तिः ॥ अवर्णपूर्वयोः य्वोः पादान्तयोर्लोपो भवति उञि च पदे परतः ॥

21. व् and य् (preceded by अ or आ, at the end of a pada), and followed by उ, when it is a word, are elided necessarily.

The *particle* उ is a full pada or word. That Particle is meant here by the word उञ्, and not the उञ्, which is a root obtained by the samprasâraṇa of वेञ्॥ Thus स उ एकविंशतिः, स उ एकाग्निः ॥

Why do we use the word पदे "उ when it is a pada"? So that the rule may not apply to उञ् the form assumed by वेञ् by samprasâraṇa as तन्वे उतं = तन्वयुतम् ॥ Obj. उञ् could never have meant the form assumed by वेञ्, for the samprasâraṇa of वेञ् is उ, the ञ् is merely indicatory. Moreover the maxim of lakshaṇa-pratipadokta &c, will prevent the inclusion of this उञ् resulting from vocalisation, when there is a separate Particle उञ् ॥

Ans:—The word पदे is used here for the sake of the subsequent sûtras like VIII. 3. 32. So that ङमुट् may come before a *word* beginning with a vowel, and not before a vowel which is an affix. Thus there is no double ङ् in परमदण्डिना॥ This is also a *nitya* rule, and not optional. Had it been optional, there would have been no necessity of this aphorism, because VIII. 3. 19, would have been enough.

हलि सर्वेषाम् ॥ २२ ॥ पदानि ॥ हलि, सर्वेषाम् ॥

वृत्तिः ॥ हलि परतो भोभगोअघोअपूर्वस्य यकारस्य पदान्तस्य लोपो भवति सर्वेषामाचार्याणां मतेन ॥

22. (The य् preceded by भो, भगो, अघो, or by अ or आ, being final in a pada, is elided) before a consonant, according to the opinion of all Âchâryas.

Thus भो हसति, भगो हसति, अघो हसति; भो याति, भगो याति अघो, याति, वृक्षा हसन्ति ॥ Though the anuvṛitti of व् and य् both is present here, yet we have taken य only to the exclusion of व् ॥ Because after भो, भगो and अघो there is य् only, and never व्; and व् can come only when preceded by अ or आ: the only example of which given by Grammarians is वृक्षव् करोति (VIII. 3. 17). Here व् is not elided, because the word अशि qualifies the word हलि of this sûtra.

Q.—But व् should be elided in वृक्षव् हसति, because ह is an अश् letter.

Ans.—There is no such example to be found in any standard author. Moreover Patanjali in his commentary on the Pratyâhâra sûtra लण् says that no *words* can end in ह्, य्, र्, व् or ल् ॥ So that the existence of the very word वृक्षव् is doubtful.

The word sarveshâm indicates that VIII. 3. 18, even does not apply, and there is no light articulation, but lopa there too.

मोऽनुस्वारः ॥ २३॥ पदानि ॥ मः, अनुस्वारः, ॥

वृत्तिः ॥ मकारस्य पदान्तस्यानुस्वार आदेशो भवति हलि परतः ॥

23. The Anusvâra is substituted for म्, at the end of a word, before a consonant.

Thus कुण्डं हसति, वनं हसतिं, कुण्डं याति, वनं याति ॥ The word हलि is understood in this sûtra. Therefore not here, त्वमत्र, किमत्र ॥ The म् must be at the end of pada; therefore not here; गम्यते, रम्यते ॥

नश्चापदान्तस्य झलि ॥ २४ ॥ पदानि ॥ नः, च, अपदान्तस्य, झलि ॥

वृत्तिः ॥ नाकारस्य मकारस्य चापदान्तस्यानुस्वारादेशो भवति झलि परतः ॥

24. The Anusvâra is substituted for the न् and म्, not final in a pada, before all consonants, with the exception of Nasals and semi-vowels.

Thus पयांसि, यशांसि, सर्पींषि, धनूंषि with न् (VII. 1. 72); and आक्रंस्यते, आचिक्रंस्यते, अधिजिगांसते with म् ॥

Why do we say 'not final in a Pada'? Observe राजन् भुङ्क्ष्व ॥ Why do we say 'before a झल् consonant'? See रम्यते, गम्यते ॥

मो राजि समः क्वौ ॥ २५ ॥ पदानि ॥ मः, राजि, समः, क्वौ ॥

वृत्तिः ॥ समो मकारस्य मकार आदेशो भवति राजतौ क्विप्प्रत्ययान्ते परतः ॥

25. म् is substituted for the म of सम्, before the word राज् ending with the affix क्विप् ॥

Thus सम्राट्, साम्राज्यम् ॥ The substitution of म for म is for the sake of preventing the anusvâra change (cf VII. 1. 40). Why do we say 'before राज्'? See संयत् (VI. 4. 40 Vârt). Why do we say 'of सम्'? Observe किं राट् (V. 4. 70). Why do we say 'ending with क्विप्'? Observe संराजिता, संराजितुम्, संराजितव्यम् ॥

The क्विप् is added by III. 2. 61, the ज् is changed to ष् by VIII. 2. 36, which is changed to ट् at the end of a word, in संम्राट् ॥ साम्राज्यम् is formed by ष्यञ् affix, as it belongs to Brâhmanâdi class.

हे मपरे वा ॥ २६ ॥ पदानि ॥ हे, मपरे, वा ॥

वृत्तिः ॥ हकारे मकारपरे परतो मकारस्य वा मकार आदेशो भवति ॥

वार्त्तिकम् ॥ यवलपरे यवला वा ॥

26. म is optionally substituted for म्, before ह, which itself is followed by a म ॥

The म् may be changed to anusvâra or remain unchanged before a word beginning with ह्म ॥ Thus किं or किम् ह्मलयति,. 'what does be cause to shake'? कथं ह्मलयति or कथम्ह्मलयति ॥

Vart:—Before ह्य, ह्व, and ह्ल, the preceding म् may be changed to य, व or ल respectively. Thus किं ह्यः or कियँह्यः, 'what does it matter about yesterday'? किं ह्वलयति or किवँ ह्वलयति 'what does he cause to shake'? किं ह्लादयति or किलँ ह्लादयति 'what gladdens'.

नपरे नः ॥ २७ ॥ पदानि ॥ नपरे, नः, ॥

वृत्तिः ॥ नकारपरे हे परतःमकारस्य वा नकारादेशो भवति ॥

27. न् is optionally substituted for म्, when it is followed by ह which has a न् after it.

म् becomes न् before a word beginning with ह्न; as किन् ह्नुते or किं ह्नुते 'what withholds'. कथन्ह्नुते or कथं ह्नुते ॥

ङ्णोः कुक्टुक् शरि ॥ २८ ॥ पदानि ॥ ङ्णोः, कुक्, टुक्, शरि ॥

वृत्तिः ॥ ङकारणकारयोः पदान्तयोः कुक् टुग् इत्येतावागमौ वा भवतः ॥

28. The augment क् is added to a final ङ्, and the augment ट् to a final ण्, before a śibilant, optionally.

Thus प्राङ्क् शेते, or प्राङ् शेते; प्राङ्क् षष्ठः or प्राङ् षष्ठः, प्राङ्क् साये or प्राङ् साये ॥ वण्ट् शेते or वण् शेते ॥

The augments are कुक् and टुक् with an indicatory क्, showing that they are to be added to the end of the prior word (I. 1. 46), and not to the *beginning* of the second word. In sanhita reading, it would have made no difference *practically*, whether these augments were added to the *end* of the first, or the *beginning* of the second. But they are added to the end of the *first*, in order to indicate that VIII. 4. 63, will take effect. Thus we have प्राङ्क् छेते also. This छ change of श would not have taken place had the augment क् been added to

शं of शेते; because in शश्छोऽटि (VIII. 4. 63) the झय् letter must be at the end of a pada. So that if क् were added to श of शेते, as क्शेते, here too श follows a झय् letter, but this झय् letter (क्) is not at the *end* of a pada, so श will not be changed to छ (VIII. 4. 63). Thus श is not changed to छ in the body of a word, like विरप्शिन् though प् is a झय् letter. पुरा क्रूरस्य विसृपो विरप्शिन्॥ विरप्शिन्=महत्, formed with the Preposition वि added to the root रप्, with the Uṇâdi affix शिनि॥

Moreover in प्राङ् साये, the स is not changed to ष by VIII. 3. 59. Had the augment क् been added to साये, as क्साये, the स would have been changed to ष, as प्राङ् क्षाये, for then VIII. 3. 111, would not have applied, as स was no longer at the beginning of a pada.

Moreover in वण्ट् साये, the स् is not changed to ष because of the prohibition of VIII. 4. 42. Had ट् been the augment of साये, as ट्साये, then there would have been the change of स् to ष् by VIII. 4. 41.

डः सि धुट्॥ २६॥ पदानि॥ डः, सि धुट्॥

वृत्तिः॥ डकारान्तात्पदादुत्तरस्य सकारादेः पदस्य वा धुडागमो भवति॥

29. After a word ending in ड्, there may optionally be added the augment धु् to a word beginning with स्॥

Thus श्वलिड् त्साये or श्वलिड् साये, मधुलिड् त्साये or मधुलिड् साये॥

The word डः is to be construed as Ablative singular, and not Genitive singular of ड्, because of the maxim उभयनिर्देशे पञ्चमी निर्देशो बलीयान्॥

Q.—Why it is धुट् and not धुक्, in other words, why is this augment added to the beginning of the second word and not to the end of the first?

Ans.—This is done in order to prevent the ष्टु change by VIII. 4. 41. But being at the beginning of the second word, VIII. 4. 42 would prevent this change. श्वलिड्त्+साये=श्वलिड्ट्साये, (VIII. 4. 41) but the correct form is श्वलिड् त्साये॥ For the ह of श्वलिह् is ढ substituted by VIII. 2. 31, which becomes ड् by VIII. 2. 39, for the ध् of the augment, त is substituted by VIII. 4. 55, and for ड् there is ट् by the same rule.

नश्च॥ ३०॥ पदानि॥ नः, च॥

वृत्तिः॥ नकारान्तात्पदादुत्तरस्य सकारस्य वा धुडागमो भवति॥

30. After a word ending in न्, धुट् is optionally the augment to a word beginning with स्॥

Thus भवान् त्साये, महान् त्साये or भवान् साये, महान् साये॥ The ध् of the augment becomes त् by VIII. 4. 55. This त् is asiddha (VIII. 2. 1), and therefore न् is not changed to रु by VIII. 3. 7. This is the reason why the augment is exhibited as धुट् and not तुट्॥ In sûtra VIII. 3. 29 तुट् would have done as well but not so here. This view of the Kâśikâ, however, is not approved by Padamanjari. The न् can never be changed to रु here, because न् is followed by स् which is not an अम् letter. The word अम्परे is understood in VIII. 3. 7. In fact, तुट् would have been a better augment.

शि तुक् ॥ ३१ ॥ पदानि ॥ शि, तुक् ॥

वृत्तिः ॥ नकारस्य पदान्तस्य शकारे परतो वा तुगागमो भवति ॥

31. The augment त् may optionally be added to a word ending in न्, when a word beginning with श follows.

Thus भवाञ्च्छेते ॥ The augment is added to the end of the preceding word, and not to the beginning of the second word, in order to change श into छ ॥ In fact, the augment धुट् added to the second would have been as good as तुक्, namely both are त ; but then छ change would not have taken place.

Obj.—If this be so, then why न् is not changed to ण्, since it is no longer final in a pada, when तुक् is added to it, in कुर्वञ्च्छेते ॥

Ans.—This is to be thus explained. The sûtra स्तोः श्चुना श्चुः (VIII. 4. 40) should be divided into two parts, in order to prevent ण change. Thus the first part will be स्तोः श्चुना, which will mean that स and तु followed by श and चु will not cause the change of न to ण ॥ The next sûtra will be श्चुः, which will mean that the preceding स and तु are changed to श and चु respectively.

ङमो ह्रस्वादचि ङमुण्नित्यम् ॥ ३२ ॥ पदानि ॥ ङमः, ह्रस्वात्, अचि, ङमुंट्, नित्यम् ॥

वृत्तिः ॥ ह्रस्वात्परो यो ङम् तदन्तात्पदादुत्तरस्याचो ङमुडागमो भवति नित्यम् ॥ ङणनेभ्यो यथासंख्यं ङणना भवति ॥

32. After a word ending in ङ्, ण् or न् which is preceded by a light vowel, the same consonant ङ्, ण् or न् is added invariably at the beginning of the next word, which commences with a vowel.

The word ङमः is in the Ablative singular here ; and ह्रस्वात् qualifies ङमः ; and ङम् itself qualifies the word पदस्य understood, and thus there is tadanta-viddhi. Though the word पदस्य (VIII. 1. 16) is in the Genitive singular, yet it should be converted here into Ablative singular, because of its connection with ङमः ॥ अचि is in the Locative singular, but should be construed as Genitive singular here : it is exhibited in the 7th case for the sake of brevity, and of the subsequent sûtras. ङम् is a pratyâhâra meaning ङ, ण and न ; and so also ङमुट् is a pratyâhâra containing the three augments ङुट्, णुट् and नुट् ॥

In other words ङ् is augment after ङ्, ण् after ण् and न् after न् ; or that these letters are doubled practically. Thus ङुट् is the augment after a word ending in ङ्, as प्रत्यङ्ङास्ते ॥ णुट् is the augment after a word ending in ण्, as

वणणास्ते ॥ नुट् is the augment after a word ending in न्, as कुर्वन्नास्ते, कुर्वन्नवोचत्, कृषन्नास्ते, कृषन्नवोचत् ॥

Why do we say 'ending in ङ, ण or न'? See त्वमास्ते ॥ Why do we say 'preceded by a light vowel'? Observe प्राङास्ते, भवानास्ते ॥ Why do we say "followed by a vowel"? Observe प्रत्यङ्करोति ॥

The Mahabhâshya thus comments on this aphorism :—

Vârt:—ङमुटि पदादिग्रहणम् "The ङमुट् augment is added to a vowel which stands at the beginning of a word". So that in दण्डिन्+आ (Ins. Sing.), नुट् is not added to आ, because it is not the beginning of a Pada. Then should this vârtika be held to be necessary? No, because the word पदात् is understood here: so नुट् will not come in दण्डिना ॥ But then it will come in परमदण्डिन्+आ ॥ Because it is a compound of two nouns, and though the case-affixes have been elided, yet दण्डिन् is here a Pada by reason of pratyaya lakshaṇa; and hence there should be नुट् here added to आ ॥ Ans. This is no valid objection. दण्डिन् is not here a Pada, on the maxim उत्तरपदत्वे चापदादिविधौलुमता लुप्ते प्रत्ययलक्षणं न भवति "When an affix has been elided by लुक् or लुप्, the pratyaya-lakshaṇa rule will not apply, when the object of it is to give the designation of Pada to the second member of a compound, with the exception of the rule applying to the beginning of a Pada". Thus in परमदण्डिन् the word दण्डिन् is not treated as a पद, because the rule to be applied is to the *end* here. But the second member of a compound is treated like a pada, when a rule is to be applied to the beginning of a Pada. Thus in दधिसेचौ, the second member सेच् is considered as a Pada for the purposes of the rule सात् पदाद्योः (VIII. 3. 111), and the स is not changed to ष ॥ This view proceeds upon the supposition that the word पदात् governs this sûtra. But the anuvṛitti of पदात् ceased with VIII. 1. 27, as we stated before. How are we then to get out of this difficulty? Are we to make the above vârtika necessary? No: because the anuvṛitti of पदे from VIII. 3. 21 runs into this sûtra. So that the sûtra means अजादौ पदे ङमुड् भवति ॥ "The augment ङमुट् is added to a vowel with which a Pada commences". Not therefore to the case-affix आ in दण्डिना ॥

मय उञो वो वा ॥ ३३ ॥ पदानि ॥ मयः, उञः, वः, वा ॥

वृत्तिः ॥ मय उत्तरस्य उञो वा वकारादेशो भवति अचि परतः ॥

33. व् is optionally the substitute of the Particle उ, when it is preceded by a मय् consonant (all consonants with the exception of semivowels, sibilants, ह and ञ), and is followed by a vowel.

Thus शमु अस्तु वेदिः or शम्वस्तु वेदिः, तद् उ अस्य रेतः or तद्वस्य रेतः, किम् उ आवपनम् or किम्वावपनम् ॥ The उ is a Pragṛihya by I. 1. 14, and therefore would have remained unchanged, this ordains व् optionally. This व being considered asiddha, the म is not changed to anusvâra in किम्वावपनम, शम्वस्तु &c, by VIII.3. 23.

When this उ is followed by इति, and preceded by a मय् consonant, then by I. 1. 17, it is optionally प्रगृह्य, and it may be replaced by ऊँ ॥ When it is not a pragrihya, then it is changed to व् by यणादेश (VI. 1. 77), or to व् by the present sûtra. In the case of यणादेश व्, there is anusvâra by VIII. 3. 23, as किंविति ॥ When it is a Pragrihya, then it is changed to व् by the present sûtra as किम्विति or किमु इति ॥ So also with ऊँ substitute, where the वँ will be nasal: as किम्वँति, or ऊँ will remain unchanged, as किम ऊँ इति ॥ Thus we have five forms with इति ॥

विसर्जनीयस्य सः ॥ ३४ ॥ पदानि ॥ विसर्ज्जनीयस्य, सः ॥

वृत्तिः ॥ विसर्जनीयस्य सकार आदेशो भवति खरि परतः ॥

34. स् is the substitute of a visarga, when a hard consonant (खर्) follows.

The word खरि is understood here. Thus वृक्षश्छादयति, प्लक्षश्छादयति, वृक्षष्ठकारः, प्लक्षष्ठकारः, वृक्षस्थकारः, प्लक्षस्थकारः, वृक्षश्चिनोति, प्लक्षश्चिनोति, वृक्षष्टीकते, प्लक्षष्टीकते, वृक्षस्तरति, प्लक्षस्तरति ॥

By VIII. 3. 15, the र् was changed to visarga before a hard consonant, or at the end of a Pause. In the present sûtra, no special cause being mentioned, the स् change would take place, not only before a hard consonant, but at the Pause also, i. e. in वृक्षः, प्लक्षः also. This however, is not the case, because the word संहितायाम् governs this sûtra; so the स् change will be in Sanhitâ only, and not in Pause, moreover we read the anuvṛitti of खरि here and so prevent the स् change in Pause.

शर्प्परे विसर्जनीयः ॥ ३५ ॥ पदानी ॥ शर्प्परे, विसर्जनीयः ॥

वृत्तिः ॥ शर्परे खरि परतो विसर्जनीयस्य विसर्जनीयादेशो भवति ॥

35. The visarga is the substitute of visarga, when it is followed by a hard consonant (खर्) which itself is followed by a sibilant (शर्) ॥

The word शर्परे is a Bahuvrihi, meaning that which is followed by शर् ॥ In other words, when a sibilant follows a hard consonant, the preceding visarga remains unchanged. Thus वासाः क्षुरम्, पुरुषः क्षुरम्, अद्भिः प्सातम्, वासः क्षौमम्, पुरुषः त्सरुः, घनाघनः क्षोभणश्चर्षणीनाम् ॥

Though the sûtra could have been shortened by saying शर्परे न; yet the longer form is used, in order to indicate that the jihvâmulîya and upadhmâniya changes also do not take place, in cases like अद्भिः प्सातम्, वासः क्षौमम् ॥

वा शरि ॥ ३६ ॥ पदानि ॥ वा, शरि ॥

वृत्तिः ॥ विसर्जनीयस्य विसर्जनीयादेशो वा भवति शरि परे ॥

वार्त्तिकम् ॥ खर्परेशरि वा लोपो वक्तव्यः ॥

36. The visarga is optionally the substitute of visarga, when a sibilant follows.

As वृक्षः शेते or वृक्षश्शेते, प्लक्षः शेते or प्लक्षश्शेते, वृक्षः षण्डे or वृक्षष्षण्डे, वृक्षः साये or वृक्षस्साये ॥ Cf. VIII. 4. 40, 41, for श् and ष् ॥

Vârt:—When the sibilant is followed by a hard consonant, there is optionally the elision of the preceding visarga. As वृक्षा स्थातारः or वृक्षाः स्थातारः or वृक्षास्स्थातारः ॥

कुप्वोः ≍क≍पौ च ॥ ३७ ॥ पदानि ॥ कुप्वोः, ≍क≍पौ, च ॥

वृत्तिः ॥ कवर्गपवर्गयोः परतो विसर्जनीयस्य यथासंख्यं ≍क≍प इत्येतावादेशौ भवतः ॥

37. ×क and ×प are optionally substituted for the visarga, when followed by a hard guttural or a hard labial.

Thus वृक्ष × करोति or वृक्षः करोति, वृक्ष × खनति or वृक्षः खनति, वृक्ष × पचति or वृक्षः पचति, वृक्ष × फलति or वृक्षः फलति ॥ The क and प in × क and × प are for the sake of pronunciation only. The substitutes are the Jihvamûlîya and the Upadhmâniya : two lost sibilants belonging to the class of क and प respectively.

When the rule VIII. 3. 34. does not apply, then this sûtra will apply; and will debar that. But VIII. 3. 35. will not be debarred. As वासः क्षौमम्, अद्भिः प्सातम् ॥ There is no vipratishedha between VIII. 3. 35. and 37, because of the asiddhahood of one with regard to the other. (VIII. 2. 1). In fact, every rule in these three chapters stands by itself, and ignores the *existence* of the subsequent rule. Hence VIII. 3. 35 would not have been debarred by VIII. 3. 37.

To get this, some divide this sûtra into two :—(1) कुप्वोः "The visarga is the substitute of visarga before a guttural or labial which is followed by a sibilant." (2) ×क ×पौ च The jihvâmûlîya and upadhmânîya are substitutes of a visarga before a guttural and a labial in every other case."

सोपदादौ ॥ ३८ ॥ पदानि ॥ सः, अ-पदादौ ॥

वृत्तिः ॥ सकार आदेशो भवति विसर्जनीयस्य कुप्वोरपदाद्योः परतः पाशकल्पककाम्येषु ॥

वार्त्तिकम् ॥ सोपदादावित्यनव्ययस्येति वक्तव्यम् ॥ रोरेव काम्ये नान्यस्येति नियमार्थं वक्तव्यम् ॥

वार्त्तिकम् ॥ उपध्मानीयस्य कवर्गे परतः सकार आदेशो भवतीति वक्तव्यम् ॥

38. स is the substitute of a visarga before an affix beginning with a hard guttural or labial.

The word अपदादौ means "when the guttural and labial are not at the beginning of a *word*," in other words, when they stand at the beginning of an affix. This is possible only before the affixes पाश, कल्प, क, and काम्य ॥ Thus पयस्पाशम् (V. 3. 47); पयस्कल्पम्, यशस्कल्पम्, (V. 3. 67), पयस्कं, यशस्कम्, (V. 3. 70); पयस्काम्यति, यशस्काम्यति (III. 1. 9).

Why do we say 'when not at the beginning of a word'? Observe पय× कामयते, पय×पिबति ॥

Vârt:—Prohibition must be stated, when the visarga belongs to an Indeclinable : as, प्रातः कल्पम्, पुनः कल्पम् ॥

Vârt :—The visarga which comes from र is only changed to स before काम्य, and not any other visarga. As पयस्काम्यात, and यशस्काम्यति ; but not here, गीःकाम्यति धूःकाम्यति ॥

Vârt :—स is the substitute of the Upadhmânîya when followed by a guttural. The root उ×ज् (आर्जवे Tud 20) has Upadhmâniya as its penultimate : though it is written in the Dhâtupâṭha as उब्ज the ब् only represents the प् of ×प, and is not to be pronounced. This ×प is changed to स, when the final ज् is changed to a guttural, as उं स ग, and then this स् is changed to द्, as in अभ्युद्गः, समुद्गः ॥

These words, however, may be derived from the root गम with the Prepositions अभि, उत्, and सम् उत्, by adding the affix ड ॥

इणः षः ॥ ३९ ॥ पदानि ॥ इणः, षः ॥

वृत्तिः ॥ अपदान्ताविति वर्त्तते । इण उत्तरस्य विसर्जनीयस्य षकारादेशो भवति कुप्वोरपदाद्योः परतः पाशकल्पककाम्येषु ॥

39. ष् is the substitute of that visarga, which is preceded by इ or उ and is followed by an affix beginning with a hard guttural or a labial.

The word अपदान्तौ is understood here also. The affixes meant are the same पाश, कल्प, क, and काम्य ॥ Thus सर्पिष्पाशम्, यजुष्पाशम्, सर्पिष्कल्पम्, यजुष्कल्पम्, सर्पिष्कम्, यजुष्कम् ; सर्पिष्काम्यति, यजुष्काम्यति ॥

Why do we say 'by an *affix*'? Observe अग्निः करोति, वायुः करोति, अग्निः पचति, वायुः पचति ॥

The affix should begin with a guttural or a labial. Therefore not here, सर्पिस्ते, यजुस्ते ॥

In the succeeding sûtras, the anuvṛitti of स from VIII. 3. 39 and of इणः षः from this, are both current. The visarga will be changed to ष if preceded by इ or उ, otherwise it will be स ॥

According to some, this sûtra ordains ष् in the room of the स् taught in the preceding sûtra, and not of visarga : and so also in the following sûtras.

नमस्पुरसोर्गत्योः ॥ ४० ॥ पदानि ॥ नमस्-पुरसोः, गत्योः ॥

वृत्तिः ॥ नमस्पुरस् इत्येतयोर्गतिसंज्ञकयो विसर्जनीयस्य सकारादेशो भवति कुप्वोः परतः ॥

40. For the visarga of नमस् and पुरस् there is substituted स् before a hard guttural or a labial, when these words are Gati (I. 4. 67 and 74).

Thus नमस्कर्त्ता, नमस्कर्तुम्, नमस्कर्त्तव्यम् ; पुरस्कर्त्ता पुरस्कर्तुम्, पुरस्कर्त्तव्यम् ॥

Why do we say "when they are Gati"? Observe पूःकरोति, पुरौ करोति, पुरः करोति ॥ Here पुरः is a noun, Accusative Plural of पूः ॥

नमस् is Gati by I. 4. 74, and पुरस् is Gati by I. 4. 67. The anuvṛitti of अपदान्तौ ceases.

इदुदुपधस्य चाप्रत्ययस्य ॥ ४१ ॥ पदानि ॥ इद्-उद्-उपधस्य, च, अ-प्रत्यस्य॥

वृत्तिः ॥ इकारोपधस्य उकारोपधस्य चाप्रत्यस्य विसर्जनीयस्य षकार आदेशो भवति कुप्वोः परतः ॥

वार्त्तिकम् ॥ पुम्मुहुसोःप्रतिषेधो वक्तव्यः ॥

41. ष् is substituted, before a hard guttural or a labial, for the visarga which is preceded by इ or उ, and is not part of an affix.

This applies to the visarga of निर्, दुर्, बहिर्, आविस्, चतुर् and प्रादुस् ॥ Thus निष्कृतम्, निष्पीतम्, दुष्कृतम्, दुष्पीतम्, बहिस्, बहिष्कृतम्, बहिष्पीतम्, आविस्, आविष्कृतम्, आविष्पीतम्, चतुष्कृतम्, चतुष्कपालम्, चतुष्कन्दलम्, चतुष्कलम्, प्रादुष्कृतम्, प्रादुष्पीतम् ॥

Why do we say 'when not belonging to an affix'? Observe अग्निः करोति, वायुः करोति ॥ How do you explain मातुः करोति, पितुः करोति? For here in पितुः &c, the स् of the affix is elided by VIII. 2. 24, and the र् of पितुर्+स् is changed to visarga; this is not the visarga of an affix, and ought to be changed to ष् ॥

Ans.—The inclusion of the word भ्रातुष्पुत्रः in Kaskâdi class (VIII. 3. 48) indicates by implication, that ष change does not take place of this visarga in पितुः, मातुः &c: the only exception being भ्रातुः ॥ The reason of this may be that the visarga here does not follow a simple उ, but an ekâdeśa उ (VI. 1. 111).

Vârt:—Prohibition must be stated in the case of पुम् and मुहुस्; as पुंस्कामा, मुहुस्कामा ॥

Vârt:—वृद्धिभूतानां षत्वं वक्तव्यम्। The visarga is changed to ष even when इ or उ are vṛiddhied; as नैष्कुल्यम्, दौष्कुल्यम् ॥

Vârt:—प्लुतानां तादौ च ॥ The visarga is changed to ष even when इ or उ are pluta, and then before dentals as well as gutturals and labials. Thus नि३ष्कुलम्, दु३ष्कुलम् (VIII. 2. 86 for pluta). दु३ष्पुरुषः, वही३ष्टरः ॥

These last two vârtikas may be dispensed with, because Vṛiddhi and Pluta are Bahiranga change, and so the visarga will be changed to ष in these cases also by the sûtra itself; except so far as त is concerned.

तिरसोन्यतरस्याम् ॥४२ ॥ पदानि ॥ तिरसः, अन्यरस्याम् ॥

वृत्तिः ॥ तिरसो विसर्जनीयस्यान्यतरस्यां सकारादेशो भवति कुप्वोः परतः ॥

42. The visarga of the Gati तिरस् is optionally changed to स् before a hard guttural or a labial.

Thus तिरस्कर्त्ता, तिरस्कर्त्तुम्, तिरस्कर्त्तव्यम्, or तिरः कर्त्ता, तिरः कर्त्तुम्, तिरः कर्त्तव्यम् ॥ The word गतेः is understood here also. Therefore no option is allowed here, तिरः कृत्वा काण्डं गतः, where तिरस् does not mean 'disappearance'. (I. 4. 72).

द्विस्त्रिश्चतुरिति कृत्वोर्थे ॥ ४३ ॥ पदानि ॥ द्विः-त्रिः-चतुर्, इति, कृत्वोर्थे ॥

वृत्तिः ॥ ष इति संबध्यते । द्विस् त्रिस् चतुर् इत्येतेषां कृत्वोर्थे वर्त्तमानानां विसर्जनीयस्य षकार आदेशो भवति अन्यतरस्यां कुप्वोः परतः ॥

43. **ष्** is optionally the substitute of the visargas of **द्विस्, त्रिस्** and **चतुर्** when they are used as Numeral adverbs, (before a hard guttural and labial).

The affix सुच् (स्) is added to the three words dvi, tri and chatur in the sense of kṛtvasuch by V. 4. 18.

As द्विः करोति or द्विष्करोति, त्रिः करोति or त्रिष्करोति, चतुः करोति or चतुष्करोति, द्विः पचति or द्विष्पचति, त्रिः पचति or त्रिष्पचति, चतुः पचति or चतुष्पचति ॥

Why do we say 'when used in the sense of kṛitvasuch or Numeral adverbs'? Observe चतुष्कपालम्, चतुष्कण्टकम्, where ष is compulsory by VIII. 3. 41. चतुर्षु कपालेषु संस्कृतः (IV. 2. 16 and IV. 1. 88). This sûtra is an example of ubhayatra-vibhâshâ. With regard to चतुर् the visarga is a non-affix visarga, and hence VIII. 3. 41, would have made ष compulsory, this makes it optional. With regard to द्विस् and त्रिस् the visarga is that of an affix (सुच् or स् V. 4. 18), and hence VIII. 3. 41, would not have applied. Thus with regard to चतुर् it is a Prâpta-vibhâshâ, and with regard to द्विस् and त्रिस् it is an Aprâpta-vibhâshâ.

Why have we used the words 'dvis, tris and chatur'? Objector's answer: so that the rule may not apply to पंचकृत्वः करोति, the visarga of kritvasuch (V. 4. 17) is not changed to ष् ॥

The anuvṛitti of उ and इ is understood here from VIII. 3. 41: so that the visarga must be preceded by इ and उ for the application of this rule. In पञ्चकृत्वः the visarga is preceded by अ, and so there is no applicability of this rule.

In fact, by reading the anuvṛitti of इदुदुपधा into this sûtra, and qualifying the visarga by the further epithet of 'belonging to a *word* that has the sense of kṛitvasuch'; we may dispense with the words द्विस्त्रिश्चतुरिति from the sûtra. The simple sûtra कृत्वोर्थे would have been enough. For there are no other Numerals that have a penultimate इ or उ, except these three. The chief objection to this view is, that in चतुर् the visarga is not the *affix* सुच्, but a portion of the word (See V. 4. 18): so the rule would not apply to chatur, if this word were not expressly mentioned.

The various objections and their solutions are given in the following verses.

कृत्वसुजर्थे षत्वं ब्रवीति कस्माच्चतुष्कपाले मा
षत्वं विभाषया भून्ननु सिद्धं तत्र पूर्वेण ॥
सिद्धे ह्ययं विधत्ते चतुरः षत्वं यदापि कृत्वोर्थे ॥
लुप्ते कृत्वोर्थीये रेफस्य विसर्जनीयो हि ॥
एवं सति त्विदानीं द्विस्त्रिश्चतुरित्यनेन किं कार्यम् ॥
अन्यो हि नेदुदुपधः कृत्वोर्थः कश्चिदप्यास्ति ॥
अक्रियमाणे ग्रहणे विसर्जनीयस्तदा विशेष्येत ॥

चतुरो न सिध्यति तथा रेफस्य विसर्जनीयो हि ॥
तस्मिंस्तु क्रियमाणे युक्तं चतुरो विशेषणं भवति ॥
प्रकृतं पदं तदन्तं तस्यापि विशेषणं न्याय्यम् ॥

Kârikâ :—कृत्वसुजर्थे षत्वं ब्रवीति कस्मात्? Why does the author teach षत्व when these words have the sense of Numeral-adverbs? In other words, why the word कृत्वोर्थे is used at all in the sûtra? There is no necessity of using it at all, because द्विस्, त्रिस् are clearly adverbs as they are formed by the affix सुच् (V. 4. 18) and चतुर् being read in their company will also denote the *adverb* chatur, in which सुच् has been elided (V. 4. 18). So that all these three words are सुच्-formed, and all सुच्-formed words have the sense of Kṛtvasuch. One answer to this is that the rule of साहचर्य does not always hold good, as in दीधीवेवीटाम् (I. 1.6), the words दीधी and वेवी are verbs, while इट् is an augment. Though therefore द्विस् and त्रिस् are kṛtvortha words, yet चतुर् need not be so: and may be a simple Numeral. *Ans.* चतुष्कपाले मा षत्वं विभाषया भूत् ॥ The word कृत्वोऽर्थे is employed to indicate that there should be no optional षत्व in चतुष्कपालं ॥ The षत्व here is compulsory by VIII. 3. 41. *Q.* ननु सिद्धं तत्र पूर्वेण ॥ Well this would be valid by the previous sûtra (VIII. 3. 41). That is, let in चतुष्कपाल also there be optional षत्व, as चतुःकपाल and चतुष्कपाल ॥ Now rule VIII. 3. 41 will apply to चतुःकपाल and will change this visarga to ष, so that with regard to चतुष्कपाल, we shall have *always* ष ॥ *Ans.* सिद्धे ह्ययं विधत्ते चतुरः षत्वं यदापि कृत्वोर्थे, लुप्ते कृत्वोर्थीये रेफस्य विसर्जनीयो हि । If VIII. 3. 41 be considered as applying here (siddha), then when the affix सुच् is elided after चतुर्, and the र is changed to visarga, then the adverb चतुः also ends with a non-affix visarga, and will come under the compulsory षत्व rule of VIII. 3. 41; for though we may have optionally two forms as चतुः करोति and चतुष्करोति, by the present sûtra, yet in the former the visarga would be changed to ष by VIII. 3. 41. Hence the necessity of employing the word कृत्वोऽर्थे ॥ *Q.* But we say that the र् in the adverb चतुर् is that of सुच्, thus चतुर्+स्=चतुर्+र् (VIII. 2. 66)=चतु+र् (the first र् is elided by VIII. 3. 14)=चतुर्; and that this र् when changed to visarga, will be an affix-visarga and so VIII. 3. 41 will not apply to the *adverb* चतुर् ॥ *Ans.* No. For उ would require to be lengthened by VI. 3. 111. and the form would be चतूर् ॥

एवं सति त्विदानीं द्विस्त्रिश्चतुरित्यनेन किं कार्यम् ॥ If this be so, then what is the purpose served by using the words द्विस् त्रिश्चतुरिति in the aphorism? The simple sûtra कृत्वोऽर्थे would have been enough. Because (अन्योहि नेदुदुपधः कृत्वोर्थः कश्चिदप्यस्ति) there are no other numeral adverbs than these three which have a penultimate इ or उ ॥

अक्रियमाणे ग्रहणे विसर्जनीयस्तदा विशेष्येत । If we do not use the words dvis, tris, chaturiti in the sûtra, then the word kṛtvorthe would qualify the word visarga, and the sûtra would mean "the visarga of an affix which has the sense of kṛitvasuch is changed optionally to ष" ॥ The result of this will be that (चतुरो न सिध्यति तथारंफस्य विसर्जनयोहि) it will not apply to चतुः where the visarga is that of र् and not of the affix सुच् ॥

Therefore by using dvis &c, the word कृत्वोर्थे would qualify चतुर् (तस्मिन् तु क्रियमाणे युक्तं चतुरो विशेषणं भवति) ॥

Ans.—प्रकृतं पदं तदन्तं तस्यापि, विशेषणं नाध्यम् ॥ Though we may not use dvis &c, the word kṛtvortha will not qualify visarga, but will qualify the word पद whose context runs here; and the rule of तदन्त will apply; so that the sûtra कृत्वोऽर्थे will mean, पदस्य कृत्वोर्थे वर्त्तमानस्य यो विसर्जनीयः, तस्य सकारः षकारो वा ॥ "The visarga of that word which is employed in the sense of a Numeral adverb, is optionally changed to स् or ष् before a guttural or a labial, provided that such visarga is preceded by इ or उ".

The above is the opinion of Patanjali, who considers the words dvis &c, as redundant. The Kâśikâ however controverts this opinion. According to him, if these words were not used in the sûtra, then the mere sûtra कृत्वोऽर्थे would be insufficient for the visarga of चतुः though used as an adverb, the षत्व will be compulsory by VIII.3.41; for the present sûtra will be considered as asiddha or non-existent for the purposes of VIII. 3. 41, (See VIII. 2. 1). But this however may be answered by saying that the rule of पूर्वत्रासिद्धम् applies in these chapters, with this modification, one subject-matter is considered as asiddha with regard to another subject-matter gone before; but one aphorism is not considered asiddha with regard to a previous aphorism, when belonging to the same subject matter. (प्रकरणे प्रकरणमसिद्धं न योगे योगः) ॥ Therefore the present sûtra VIII. 3. 43, would not be considered asiddha with regard to VIII. 3. 41. Or the present sûtra may be considered as an apavâda to VIII. 3. 41: and an apavâda is never asiddha with regard to an utsarga.

इसुसोः सामर्थ्ये ॥ ४४ ॥ पदानि ॥ इस्-उसोः, सामर्थ्ये ॥

वृत्तिः ॥ इस् उस् इत्येतयोर्विसर्जनीयस्यान्यतरस्यां षकारादेशो भवति सामर्थ्ये कुप्वोः परतः ॥

44. For the visarga of words ending in इस् and उस्, before a hard guttural or labial, there is optionally substituted ष, when the two words stand in correlation with one another.

The ष is understood here. Thus सर्पिष्करोति or सर्पिः करोति, यजुः करोति or यजुष्करोति ॥

Why do we say 'when the two words are correlated'? Observe तिष्ठतु सर्पिः, पिब त्वमुदकम्, where सर्पिः is not in construction with पिब, but with तिष्ठतु ॥

The word सामर्थ्य here means व्यपेक्षा or mutual relation of two words; and not "having the same meaning", or it may mean both. In fact सामर्थ्य is equivalent to आकाङ्क्षा i. e. the syntactical want of another word to complete the sense. It does not here mean 'compound'. For it being a पदविधिः the word समर्थः is understood here (समर्थः पदविधिः II. 1. 1). The employment of the word सामर्थ्य here indicates that it is a different sâmarthya from that of II. 1. 1. It does not denote एकार्थीभावः or ऐकार्थ्य which is the sâmarthya of compounds where *two* or *more* words denote *one* object. The sâmarthya here means vyapekshâ, which is thus defined नानाभूतयोः, पदार्थयो यौ शब्दौ वर्त्तेते, तयो र्यो योगः "the syntactical union of two words expressing two different ideas".

नित्यं समासे ऽनुत्तरपदस्थस्य ॥ ४५ ॥ पदानि ॥ नित्यम्, समासे, अनुत्तर पदस्थस्य ॥

वृत्तिः ॥ इसुसोरिति वर्त्तते । समासविषये इसुसोर्विसर्जनीयस्यानुत्तरपदस्थस्य नित्यं षत्वं भवति कुप्वेः परतः ॥

45. The visarga of an इस् or उस्-ending word, which is not preceded by any other word, is invariably changed to ष् in a compound, when followed by a hard guttural or labial.

The words इस् and उस् are understood here. Thus सर्पिष्कुण्डिका, धनुष्कपालम्, सर्पिष्पानम्, धनुष्फलम् ॥

Why do we say when it is not preceded by another word? Observe परमसर्पिः कुण्डिका, परमधनुः कपालम् ॥ The option even of the last sûtra does not apply to these examples.

Q.—The word सर्पिस् is derived from the root सृप् by adding the Uṇâdi affix इसि (Uṇ II. 109), and यजुस् by the Uṇâdi affix उसि (Uṇ II. 117), therefore on the maxim प्रत्ययग्रहणे &c, the word इसुसोः would denote the mere forms सर्पिस् and यजुस् and not forms like परमसर्पिस् &c. then what is the necessity of employing the word अनुत्तरपदस्थस्य in the sûtra?

The very employment of the word anuttara-pada-sthasya in this sûtra, is an indicator (jñâpaka), that the restriction of the following maxim does not apply with regard to the affixes इस् and उस् : प्रत्ययग्रहणे यस्मात् स विहित स्तदादे-स्तदन्तस्य ग्रहणम् "an affix denotes, whenever it is employed in Grammar, a word-form which begins with that to which that affix has been added and ends with the affix itself". This maxim not applying, we have परमसर्पिष्करोति or परमसर्पिः करोति by the previous sûtra VIII. 3. 44.

Q.—Why is not there option in the case of compounds also by the previous sûtra?

Ans :—Because the word सामर्थ्य there means व्यपेक्षा, and therefore does not apply to compounds.

अतः कृकमिकंसकुम्भपात्रकुशाकर्णीष्वनव्ययस्य ॥ ४६ ॥ पदानि ॥ अतः, कृ-कमि-कंस-कुम्भ-पात्र-कुशा-कर्णीषु, अन्-अव्ययस्य ॥

वृत्तिः ॥ अकारादुत्तरस्य अनव्ययविसर्जनीयस्य समासेऽनुत्तरपदस्थस्य नित्यं सकारादेशो भवति कृ कमि कंस कुम्भ पात्र कुशा कर्णी इत्येतेषुपरतः ॥

46. For the visarga of a word ending in अस, with the exception of an Indeclinable, स् is substituted in a compound, when a form of कृ and कम, or the words कंस कुम्भ, पात्र, कुशा and कर्णी follow, and the first word is not preceded by another word.

Thus कृः—अयस्कारः, पयस्कारः (III. 2. 1) कम्ः—अयस्कामः, पयस्कामः, कंसः—अयस्कंसः, पयस्कंसः, कुम्भः,-अयस्कुम्भः पयस्कुम्भः ॥ So also अयस्कुम्भी पयस्कुम्भी, on the maxim प्रातिपदिकग्रहणे लिङ्गविशिष्टस्यापि ग्रहण भवति ॥ पात्रः—अयस्पात्रम्, पयस्पात्रम्, अयस्पात्री, पयस्पात्री ॥ कुशाः—अयस्कुशा, पयस्कुशा ॥ कर्णीः—अयस्कर्णी, पयस्कर्णी ॥ The form शुनस्कर्णः belongs to Kaskâdi class (VIII. 3. 48).

Why do we say अतः "a visarga preceded by short अ, or the visarga of the word ending in अः"? See गीःकारः. धूःकारः ॥ Why do we say 'preceded by *short* अ'? Observe भाःकरणम् ॥ The form भास्करः belongs to Kaskâdi class (VIII. 3. 48). See also III. 2. 2.

Why do we say "with the exception of an Indeclinable"? Observe श्वःकारः, पुनःकारः॥

The word समासे is understood here also. Therefore not here; यशः करोति पयः करोति, यशः कामयते ॥

The word अनुत्तरपदस्थस्य is also to be read in this. Therefore not here, परमपयः कारः, परमपयः कामः ॥

Q. The word कंस need not have been taken, because it is a form of the root कम्, since it is derived from कम् by adding the Uṇâdi affix स (III. 62 Uṇ)?

Ans.—The employment of कंस indicates the existence of the following maxim:—उणादयोऽव्युत्पन्नानि प्रातिपदिकानि "Words which end with उण् &c. are crude-forms that do not undergo or cause such operations as would depend on their etymological formation."

अधः शिरसी पदे ॥४७॥ पदानि ॥ अधः-शिरसी, पदे ॥

वृत्तिः ॥ अधस् शिरस् इत्येतयोर्विसर्जनीयस्य समासेऽनुत्तरपदस्थस्य सकार आदेशो भवति पदशब्दे परतः ॥

47. For the visarga of अधस् or शिरस् when not preceded by another word, and followed by the word पद in composition with it, there is substituted स् ॥

Thus अधस्पदम्, शिरस्पदम् ॥ अधस्पदी, शिरस्पदी ॥

The word समासे is understood in this, therefore not here अधः पदम् ॥

The word अनुत्तरपदस्थस्य is also understood here. Therefore not in the following परमशिरः पदम् ॥

The word अधस्पदम् is a compound formed under Mayûravyansakâdi class.

कस्कादिषु च ॥ ४८ ॥ पदानि ॥ कस्कादिषु, च ॥

वृत्तिः ॥ कस्क इत्येवमादिषु च विसर्जनीयस्य सकारः षकारो वा यथायोगमादेशो भवति कुप्वोः परतः ॥

48. स or ष is substituted for the visarga, before a hard guttural and labial in the words कस्क and the rest.

This is an Apavâda to Sûtra VIII. 3. 37. ष् is substituted after इ or उ, and स् everywhere else. Thus कस्कः, 2. कौतस्कुतः (with अण् of कुत आगतः). 3. भ्रातुष्पुत्रः (VI. 3. 23) 4. शुनस्कर्णः (VI. 3. 21) 5. सद्यस्कालः; 6. सद्यस्की (from क्री 'to buy' with the affix क्विप्, because it belongs to Sampadâdi class.) 7. साद्यस्कः (from सद्यस्क्री in the sense of तत्रभवः क्रतुः). 8. कांस्कान् (the स् is by VIII. 3. 12). 9. सर्पिष्कुण्डिका, 10. चतुष्कपालम्, 11. धनुष्कपालम् 12. बर्हिष्पूलम्, 13. यजुष्पात्रम् ॥ "The words 9 to 13 are exceptions to VIII. 3. 45, so that there might be ष, even when सर्पिस् &c are preceded by another word. Thus परमसर्पि ष्कुण्डिका ॥ The counter-example then to VIII. 3. 45 will be परमसर्पिः फलम् ॥" This is the opinion of the Pârâyaṇikâs. But in the Mahâbhâshya, the counter-example under VIII. 3. 45 is परमसर्पिः कुण्डिका ॥ Another reason why these words are listed here, is that ष change will take place, even where there is no correlation or vyapekshâ. As तिष्ठतु सर्पिष्कुण्डिकां आनय ॥ So also when there is correlation, as इदं सर्पिष्कुण्डिकायाः ॥ Here सर्पिस् is an incomplete word. The ष change, will take place even where there is no compounding. Where there is no compounding, and there is complete want of correlation, even there the ष will invariably come. And where there is correlation, but no compounding there the ष would have been optional by VIII. 3. 44, but it becomes invariable here, on account of these words being so listed. Thus we have these cases: (1) Without correlation, as तिष्ठतु सर्पिष्कुण्डिकामानय ॥ (2) Where there is correlation, as इदं सर्पिष्कुण्डिकायाः ॥ (3) Where there is composition, as सर्पिष्कुण्डिका ॥ (4) Where there is no composition and no correlation even, as, in example (1). (5) Where there is correlation but no compounding as in example (2). In all these cases there is ष *invariably* in case of these words. 14. अयस्काण्डः, 15. मेदस्पिण्डः ॥ अविहितलक्षण उपचारः कस्कादिषु द्रष्टव्यः ।

Every change of visarga to स or ष, must be referred to Kaskâdi class, if not governed by any other rule. Thus this is an Akṛtigaṇa. Upachâra is the name of स् and ष् which replace the visarga.

The Pârâyaṇa is of two sorts, Dhâtu-Par, and Nâma-Par. Those who devote themselves in committing to memory and reciting these are Pârâyanikas.

छन्दसि वा ऽप्राम्रेडितयोः ॥ ४९ ॥ पदानि ॥ छन्दसि, वा, अ-प्र-आम्रेडितयोः ॥

वृत्तिः ॥ छन्दसि विषये विसर्जनीयस्य वा सकारादेशो भवति कुप्वोः परतः प्रशब्दं आम्रेडितं वर्जयित्वा ॥

49. स may optionally be substituted for the

visarga before a hard guttural and labial, in the Chhandas; but neither before प्र, nor before a doubled word.

Thus अयः पात्रम् or अयस्पात्रम् ॥ This is an example of non-compounds. In compounds, the स change is compulsory by VIII. 3. 46: because the option of the present sutra is asiddha there, and it finds its scope in cases other than compounds. If the maxim प्रकरणे प्रकरणमसिद्धं न योगे योगः be applied, then the two sutras VIII. 3. 46 and VIII. 3. 49 belong to the same प्रकरणं and one is not asiddha with regard to the other. Then we could give examples of compounds also under this sutra: but then such compounds will also be governed by VIII. 3. 46, and so the स would be compulsory.

विश्वतस्पात्रम् or विश्वतः पात्रम्, here the word विश्वतः is an Indeclinable and hence the rule VIII. 3. 46, does not apply to it. उरु णः कारः or उरु ण स्कारः ॥ Here नस् is substituted for अस्मद्, and then the न is changed to ण by VIII. 4. 27. The word कारः is a घञ् formed word.

Why do we say "not before प्र and a doubled word'? Observe अग्निः प्र विद्वान् (Av. V. 26. 1), पुरुषः पुरुषः परि ॥

In सूर्यरश्मिर्हरिकेशः पुरस्तात् (Rig. X. 139. 1), स नः पावकः (Rig. I. 12. 10), the स change has not taken place, as all rules are optional in the Vedas.

कःकरत्करतिकृधिकृतेष्वनदितेः ॥ ५० ॥ पदानि ॥ कः-करत्-करति-कृधि-कृतेषु, अन्-अदितेः ॥

वृत्तिः ॥ कः करत् करति कृधि कृत इत्येतेषु परतः अनदितेर्विसर्जनीयस्य सकारादेशो भवति छन्दसि विषये ॥

50. The visarga is changed to स् in the Chhandas, before कः, करत्, करति, कृधि and कृतः but not so the visarga of अदितिः ॥

Thus विश्वतस्कः ॥ कः is the Aorist of कृ, the च्लि has been elided by II. 4. 80: the ऋ of कृ is gunated before the affix तिप्, thus we have करत्, the त् is elided by VI. 1. 68; and the augment अट् is not added by VI. 4. 75. Similarly विश्वतस्करत् ॥ Here also करत् is the Aorist of कृ, with अङ् by III. 1. 59. पयस्करति, here करति is the लट् of कृ; शप् is added instead of उ, as a Vedic anomaly. उरणस्कृधि, here कृधि is the Imperative of कृ, the सि is changed to हि, the vikarana is elided, and हि changed to धि by VI. 4. 102. See VIII. 4. 27, for the change of न to ण ॥ सदस्कृतम्, here कृतम् is Past Participle of कृ ॥

Why do we say 'but not of अदितिः'? Observe यथा नो अदितिः करत् (Rig. I. 43. 2).

पञ्चम्याः परावध्यर्थे ॥ ५१ ॥ पदानि ॥ पञ्चम्याः, परौ, अध्यर्थे ॥

वृत्तिः ॥ छन्दसित्येव । पञ्चमीविसर्जनीयस्य सकारादेशो भवति परौ परतः अध्यर्थे ॥

51. The visarga of the Ablative case is changed to स् before परि meaning 'over'.

The word Chhandas is understood here also. Thus दिवस्परि प्रथमं जज्ञे (Rig X. 45. 1) अग्निर्हिमवतस्परि ॥ दिवस्परि, महस्परि ॥

Why do we say 'of the Ablative'? Observe अहिरिव भोगैः पर्येति बाहुम् ॥ Why do we say "before परि"? See एभ्योवा एतल्लोकेभ्यः प्रजापतिः समैरयत् ॥ Why do we say 'when परि means 'over'? See दिवः पृथिव्याः पर्योज उद्भृतम् (Rig. VI. 47. 27). Here परि has the sense of "on all sides".

पातौ च बहुलम् ॥ ५२ ॥ पदानि ॥ पातौ, च बहुलम् ॥

वृत्तिः ॥ पातौ च धातौ परतः पञ्चमीविसर्जनीयस्य बहुलं सकार आदेशो भवति छन्दसि विषये ॥

52. स may diversely be substituted for the visarga of the Ablative before the verb पातु in the Chhandas.

Thus दिवस्पातु, राज्ञस्पातु ॥ Sometimes, the change does not take place, as परिषदः पात ॥

षष्ठ्याःपतिपुत्त्रपृष्ठपारपदपयस्पोषेषु ॥ ५३ ॥ पदानि ॥ षष्ठ्याः-पति-पुत्र-पृष्ठ-पार-पद पयस्-पोषेषु ॥

वृत्तिः ॥ षष्ठीविसर्जनीयस्यसकारादेशो भवति पति पुत्र पृष्ठ पार पद पयस् पोष इत्येतेषु परतः छन्दसि विषये ॥

53. For the visarga of the Genitive, there is substituted स in the Vedas, before पति, पुत्र, पृष्ठ, पार, पद, पयस्, and पोष ॥

Thus वाचस्पतिं विश्वकर्माणमूतये, (Rig. x. 81. 7), दिवस्पुत्राय सूर्याय, दिवस्पृष्ठे धावमानं सुपर्णम्, अगन्म, तमसस्पारम्, इडस्पदे समिध्यसे, सूर्यं चक्षु र्दिवस्पयः, रायस्पोषं यजमानेषु धत्तम् ॥

Why do we say 'after a genitive case'? See मनुः पुत्रेभ्यो दायं व्यभजत् ॥

इडाया वा ॥ ५४ ॥ पदानि ॥ इडायाः, वा ॥

वृत्तिः ॥ इडायाः षष्ठीविसर्जनीयस्य वा सकार आदेशो भवति पत्यादिषु परतश्छन्दसि विषये ॥

54. स is optionally substituted for the visarga of इडायाः, before पति &c, (VIII. 3. 53.) in the Chhandas.

Thus इडायाः पतिः or इडायास्पतिः इडायास्पुत्त्रः । इडायाः पुत्त्रः । इडायास्पृष्ठम् । इडायाः पृष्ठम । इडाया स्पारम्, इडायाः पारम । इडायास्पदम् । इडायाः पदम् । इडायास्पयः । इडायाः पयः । इडायाः पोषम् । इडायास्पोषम् ॥

अपदान्तस्य मूर्द्धन्यः ॥ ५५ ॥ पदानि ॥ अ-पदान्तस्य, मूर्द्धन्यः ॥

वृत्तिः ॥ अपदान्तस्येति मूर्द्धन्य इति चैतदधिकृतं वेदितव्यम् । आपादपरिसमाप्तेः ॥

55. Upto the end of the Pâda, is throughout to be supplied the following: "A cerebral letter is substituted always in the room of ———, when this letter does not stand at the end of a word".

Here ceases the Padâdhikâra which commenced with VIII. 1. 16. The two words अपदान्तस्य 'not final in a pada', and मूर्द्धन्यः 'cerebral' exert a governing influence on all sûtras upto the end of this chapter. Thus VIII. 3. 59, teaches "of an affix and a substitute". The whole of the present sûtra should be read there to complete the sense: i. e. "a cerebral sound is substituted always in the room of the स of an affix and of the स which is a substitute, when it does not stand at the end of a word'. Thus सिषेव, सुष्वाप, अग्निषु, वायुषु ॥

Why do we say 'not final'? See अग्निस्तत्र, वायुस्तत्र ॥ Though the anuvritti of ष was understood here, yet the employment of the word 'cerebral' is for the sake of ढ; as अकृढ्वम्, चकृढ्वे (VIII. 3. 78).

सहेः साढः सः ॥ ५६ ॥ पदानि ॥ सहेः, साढः, सः ॥

वृत्तिः ॥ सहेर्धातोः साड्रूपस्य यः सकारस्तस्य मूर्द्धन्य आदेशो भवति ॥

56. ष् is substituted for the स् in साह, when this occurs in the form of साड् (साट्) ॥

Thus जलाषाट्, तुराषाट्, पृतनाषाट् ॥ साड् is derived from सह् by the affix ण्वि (III. 2. 63), there is vriddhi of the penultimate, the ह is changed to ढ (VIII. 2. 31). and the upapada is lengthened (VI. 3. 137).

साढः सः would have been enough, for there is no other form साड् except this derived from सह्; why then the word सहेः is used in the sûtra? There is another form साड् not derived from सह् ॥ Thus सह डेन वर्त्तते = सडः, सडस्य अपत्यं = साडिः ॥ He in whose name there is the letter ड is called सड; as मृड ॥

Why do we say 'in the form of साड्'? The rule will not apply when the form is साह, as जलासाहम्, तुरासाहम् ॥ Why do we say सः "for the स"? So that the आ of साड् may not be changed to cerebral: the ड् is already cerebral.

इण्कोः ॥ ५७ ॥ पदानि ॥ इण्, कोः ॥

वृत्तिः ॥ इण्कोरित्येतदधिकृतं वेदितव्यम् । इत उत्तरं यद्वक्ष्यामः इणः कवर्गाच्चेत्येवं तद्वेदितव्यम् ।

57. From this, upto the end of the chapter, should be supplied in every sûtra, the following:—"when a vowel (with the exception of अ or आ), or a र or a guttural precedes".

The word इण् is a pratyâhâra formed with the second ण् of लण् ॥ It includes all vowels and semivowels except अ and आ ॥ Of the semi-vowels र् is only efficient: so that only is taken in the translation. कु means the letters of the क class. Thus इण्कोः is supplied in VIII. 3. 59, to complete the sense. Thus सिषेव, सुष्वाप, अग्निषु, वायुषु, कर्तृषु, हर्तृषु, गीर्षु, धूर्षु, वाक्षु, त्वक्षु ॥

Why do we say "when preceded by इण् or कु"? Observe दास्यति, असौ ॥ Here the affix स of स्यति, and the substitute स in असौ (VII. 2. 106) are not changed to ष ॥

नुम्विसर्जनीयशर्व्यवायेपि ॥ ५८ ॥ पदानि ॥ नुम्, विसर्जनीय-शर्व्यवाये, अपि ॥

वृत्तिः ॥ नुम्व्यवायेपि विसर्जनीयव्यवायेपि शर्व्यवायेपि इण्कोरुत्तरस्य सकारस्य मूर्द्धन्यादेशो भवति ॥

58. The substitution of ष् for स् takes place then also, when the augment न् (नुम्), the visarjanîya or a sibilant occurs between the said इण् and कु letters or the स् ॥

The word व्यवाय 'separation, intervention' applies to every one of the words नुम्, &c. Thus (1) when नुम् intervenes, as सर्पींषि, यजूंषि, हवींषि (VII. 1. 72, VI. 4. 10). (2) When a visarjanîya intervenes, as सर्पिःषु, यजुःषु, हविःषु (VIII. 3. 36) (3) When a Sibilant intervenes, as सर्पिष्षु, यजुष्षु हविष्षु ॥

The षत्व takes place, when नुम् &c intervene *singly* and not when they intervene collectively. Therefore not here, निंस्से, निंस्स्व from the root निंस् 'to kiss.' Here there is the intervention of *two*, namely, नुम and स् (III. 4. 91).

The word इण्कोः is in the Ablative case, and it required that the स् should follow *immediately* after it. Hence the necessity of the present sûtra for the intervention of certain letters.

आदेशप्रत्यययोः ॥ ५९ ॥ पदानि ॥ आदेश, प्रत्यययोः ॥

वृत्तिः ॥ आदेशो यः सकारः प्रत्ययस्य च यः सकार इण्कोरुत्तरस्तस्य मूर्द्धन्यो भवति ॥

59. ष् is substituted for that स् which is a substitute (of the ष् of a root in Dhâtupâṭha by VI. 1. 64), or which is (the portion of) an affix, under the above mentioned conditions (VIII. 3. 57, 58), of being preceded by an इण् vowel or a guttural.

The word cerebral is understood here from VIII. 3. 55, as well as स ॥ The sûtra âdeśa-pratyayoḥ is in the Genitive case. The force of the Genitive however is different in the word âdeśa, from what it is in pratyaya. In the first it is samânâdhikaraṇa-shashṭhî, in the latter avayava-yogâshashthî. That is that स् which is an âdeśa, and that स् which belongs to an affix. If we took it as avayavayogâ shashṭhî in both places, then the sûtra would mean "of that स् which is a portion of a substitute, or of an affix," and there would arise the following anomaly. In doubling a word by VIII. 1. 1, one view is that two are *substituted* in the room of one (See VIII. 1. 1). Thus बिसंबिसं, मुसलंमुसलं ॥ Here the स् in these words, is a *portion* of a substitute, and would be changed to ष्, if we translate the sûtra as above.

If we take the other view, and translate the sûtra as "of that स which is a substitute or an affix", we land on the following anomaly. We must have forms like कारस्यति and हरिस्यति, and not the correct forms कारिष्यति, हरिष्यति;

for here स is not an affix, but a *portion* of an affix. In fact, with regard to affixes, the sûtra would be confined to those affixes only which consist of a single स्, such as सिप् in the Vedic subjunctive लेट् ॥ That this is the proper interpretation of the sûtra is indicated by the sûtra VIII. 3. 60, (the next aphorism). The substitute घस् is taken in this sûtra. If therefore, the force of Genitive in आदेशस्य was = आदेशस्य यः सकारः and not = आदेशः यः सकारः, then there would have been no necessity of including the substitute घस् in the sûtra, for then the present sûtra would have covered the case of घस् also. Similarly, if the force of the Genitive in प्रत्ययस्य was = प्रत्ययः यः सकारः, and not = प्रत्ययस्यः यः सकारः; then there would have been no necessity of excluding the affix सात् (V. 4. 52) from the operation of the present rule by VIII. 3. 111, because it is not an affix consisting of a single letter स् ॥

Having surmised this, we shall now give illustrations. First of that स् which is a substitute. It can only be the स् which replaces the ष् of a root in Dhâtupâṭha. Thus सिषेव, सुष्वाप ॥ Of an affix, we have अग्निषु, वायुषु, कर्तृषु, हर्तृषु; वक्षत् in इन्द्रो मा वक्षत्; and यक्षत् in स देवान् यक्षत् ॥

Q.—In the case of वक्षत् and यक्षत्, the स् is not the *portion* of an affix, but the *whole* affix itself: the present sûtra should therefore not apply to this स् ॥

Ans.—Here we apply the maxim व्यपदेशिवद् एकस्मिन् ॥

These words (वक्षत् and यक्षत्) are from the roots वच् and यज्, in लेट् with तिप्, the इ is elided by III. 4. 97, the augment अट् (III. 4. 94), the affix सिप् by III. 1. 34; the च् of वच् is changed to a guttural, and the ज् of यज् to ष् and then to a guttural.

The Uṇâdi word अक्षरं (अक्ष् + सर Uṇ III. 70) complies with this rule, but not so the word कृसरं and धूसरं (Uṇ III. 73) formed with the same affix सर ॥

शासिवसिघसीनांच ॥६०॥ पदानि ॥ शासि-वासि- घसीनाम, च ॥

वृत्तिः ॥ शासि वसि घसि इत्येतेषां च इण्कोरुत्तरस्य सकारस्य मूर्द्धन्यो भवति ॥

60. ष is substituted for the स् of शास्, वस् and घस् when it is preceded by an इण् vowel or a guttural.

Thus अन्वशिषत्, अन्वशिषताम्, अन्वशिषन्, the Aorist of शास्; the च्लि is replaced by अङ् (III. 1. 56), and the आ changed to इ by VI. 4. 34. So also शिष्टः, शिष्टवान् ॥ From वस् we have उषितः, उषितवान्, उषित्वा ॥ The Samprasâraṇa takes place by VI. 1. 15 as it belongs to yajâdi class. From घस् we have जक्षतुः, जक्षुः in the Perfect. घस् is the substitute of अद् (II. 4. 40), the penultimate अ is elided by VI. 4. 98. So also अक्षन् in अक्षन्नमीमदन्त पितरः (Rig. I. 82. 2). This is the Aorist form of अद्, the घस् is substituted for अद् (II. 4. 37): the Aorist sign is elided by II. 4. 80.

This sûtra is made to cover cases not governed by the last sûtra, namely, where the स् is not an âdeśa. Though the स् in घस् is the स् of a substitute, yet it is not governed by the preceding aphorism, because the word आदेशस्य there means 'the स् which is a substitute'. Here स् is not a substitute, but a portion of a substitute. The non-substitute घस् is not to be taken here: as it seldom occurs.

The word इण्कोः is understood here also. Therefore the rule would not apply to शास्ति, वसति and जघास ॥

स्तौतिण्योरेव षण्यभ्यासात् ॥ ६१ ॥ पदानि ॥ स्तौति-ण्योः, एव, षणि, अभ्यासात् ॥

वृत्ति ॥ स्तौतेर्ण्यन्तानां च षण्भूते सनि परतः अभ्यासादिण उत्तरस्य आदेशसकारस्य मूर्द्धन्यादेशो भवति ॥

61. ष् is substituted for स after इ or उ in the reduplication of a Desiderative, if the स of सन् is changed to ष् ; but only in स्तु and in Causative of roots which in Dhâtupâṭha begin with a ष् ॥

This rule is confined to the Desideratives of स्तु and of स् beginning roots in the Causative, provided that the Desiderative sign स् is changed to ष् ॥ The rule applies to the स् of the substitute, and not to the affix स् as there can be no such स् after a reduplicate syllable. Therefore स् means that स which replaces the ष् of the roots.

Thus from स्तु we have तुष्टूषति ॥ Here the स of सन् is changed to ष by the last sûtra, and therefore so also after the reduplicate उ, the स of स्तु is changed to ष ॥

Of the Causatives of roots beginning with ष् in Dhâtupâṭha, we have सिषेवयिषति, सिषिञ्जयिषति, सुष्वापयिषति ॥ In this last, the व् is changed to उ by VII. 4. 67.

Though this ष change would have taken place by the previous sûtra (VIII. 3. 59), yet the separate enunciation of this rule indicates that this is a niyama aphorism—the ष change takes place only in these cases of स्तु and Causatives of Desideratives under the conditions mentioned in this sûtra, and *no where else.* Thus सिसिक्षति from the root षिच क्षरणे (Tud. 140). This is a root, which is exhibited in the Dhâtupâṭha with a ष, therefore the form ought to have been सिषिक्षति by VIII. 3. 59, but it is not so, because of the niyama of the present sûtra. So also सुसूषते from षूङ् प्राणिप्रसवे (Div. 24): and सुसूषति from षू प्रेरणे (Tud 115).

If this is a niyama rule by the very fact of its separate enunciation, what is then the necessity of using the word एव in the aphorism? Ans. इष्टतोऽवधारणार्थम्; so that, the sûtra may mean "if स्तु and Causatives *only*, when षण् follows"? and not "if स्तु and Causatives when षण् only follows". In the latter view, we could not get the form सुष्टाव ; and the rule would have applied to सिसिक्षति also.

Why do we say "in the Desiderative ष"? So that the niyama may not be any where else. Had षणि not been used in the sûtra, the restriction would have been with regard to every affix, and the sûtra would have meant "if there is occasion of षत्व change after a reduplicate, it should take place only in the case of स्तु and the Causatives". Therefore ष change would not have taken place in सिषेच, as it is not a Causative.

Q.—कौ विनतेऽनुरोधः? Why have we used the word षण् with ष्, and not the word सन्? That is, what compulsion was there to exhibit the Desiderative affix सन्, in this changed form? The word विनत is the name given in the Prâtisâkhyas to ष and ण change.

Ans.—So that the restrictive rule may not apply to the अविनत form of सन् ॥ As सुषुप्सति ॥ The सन् is here कित् by I. 2. 8, and there is vocalisation by VI. 1. 15. For had सनि been used in the sûtra, then the restriction would have been with regard to *all* Desideratives in *general*, whether the सन् was changed to ष or not. Therefore as there is restriction of VIII. 3. 59, in the case of सिसिक्षति where स is not changed to ष; so there would have been restriction in सुषुप्सते, the स् could not have been changed to ष् by VIII. 3. 59. Similarly in सिष्टासति ॥

Q.—What is the necessity of exhibiting षण् with the anubandha ण्? So that the rule should not apply to ष in general, but to the Desiderative affix ष only. As सुषुपिष इन्द्रम् ॥ This सुषुपिषे is the Perfect of स्वप्, the affix थास् is added as Chhandas irregularity instead of थल्; for थास् there is से, the affix is कित् by I. 2. 5, and so there is vocalisation by VI. 1. 15, and reduplication, and the augment इट् is added by VII. 2. 13, the ए is changed to अय्, as सुषुपिषय् इन्द्रं, the य् is elided by VIII. 3. 19. Here after the reduplicate सु, the स् is changed to ष, in षु by the *general* rule VIII. 3. 59, as the restriction of this sûtra does not apply in this case. But had ष in general been taken, then सुषुपिष has an affix ष, and therefore sûtra VIII. 3. 59, would have been restricted, and there would have been no change of सु to षु after the reduplicate, as it is not a causative. Hence षण् has been employed with an anubandha.

Why do we say 'after a reduplicate'?

Ans.—So that this restriction may apply to that ष which would have been caused by the इ or उ of an abhyâsa, and not to that which would have been caused by an upasarga. As अभिषिषिक्षति, though without the Preposition, the form is सिसिक्षते ॥

Q.—No, this cannot be the reason, because the ष caused by the upasarga is considered as asiddha, and hence there would be no restriction.

Ans.—Then we say, the abhyâsa is taken to be qualified by सन्, namely that abhyâsa which is *caused* by सन्, would give occasion to this rule and not any other abhyâsa. Therefore if a reduplication has been caused by यङ्, and then षण् is added to it, then the restriction of the present sûtra will not apply, and षत्व change will take place though the root may not be a Causative &c. Thus the यङ् of स्वप् is सोषुप्य (VI. 1. 19), the Desiderative of this root is सोषुपिषते, with इट् augment, the elision of अ (VI. 4. 48) of य, the elision of य् by VI. 4. 49.

Q.—No this also cannot be the reason: because the षत्व change is antaranga, while the restriction niyama is Bahiranga. Therefore, the word abhyâsa is employed superfluously in the sûtra.

Ans.—The word abhyâsa is taken in the sûtra, so that the restriction may be with regard to that ष which might have been caused by the इ or उ of the abhyâsa; and not to that ष which might be occasioned by the इ or उ of a *dhâtu* or verbal root. Thus प्रतिषिषति, अधीषिषति ॥ Here the root इ in the sense of बोधन, is turned to Desiderative with सन्; and by VI. 1. 2, the स is reduplicated, then by VII. 4. 79, the अ is changed to इ ॥ Thus इसिस; here by the force of the इ of the abhyâsa सि, the स is changed to ष as इसिष; (VIII. 3. 59) then as the restriction of this sûtra does not apply, the root इ causes the षत्व of the abhyâsa, as इषिष ॥ Had the word अभ्यासात् not been used in the sûtra, the स of abhyâsa could not have been changed to ष, for then the sûtra would have meant "ष is substituted for स, only in the case of स्तु and Causatives in the Desiderative षण्"; and as इसिष is not a Causative-Desiderative, the restriction would have applied.

सः स्विदिस्वदिसहीनां च ॥ ६२ ॥ पदानि ॥ सः, स्विदि-स्वदि-सहीनाम्,च ॥

वृत्ति ॥ स्विदि स्वदि सहि इत्येतेषां ण्यन्तानां सनि षभूते परतो ऽभ्यासादुत्तरस्य सकारस्य सकारादेशो भवति ॥

62. स is substituted for the स् after the reduplicate of the षण् Desiderative of the Causatives of स्विद्, स्वद्, and सह् ॥

The स substitute of स् debars the cerebral change. In other words, the स of these roots remains unchanged. As सिस्वेदयिषति, सिस्वादयिषति and सिसाहयिषति ॥

प्राक्सितादड्व्यवाये ऽपि ॥ ६३ ॥ पदानि ॥ प्राक्,सितात्, अट्, व्यवाये,अपि ॥

वृत्ति ॥ सेवसितेति वक्ष्यति प्राक्सितसंशब्दनाद्यादित ऊर्ध्वमनुक्रमिष्यामस्तत्प्राड्व्यवायेपि मूर्द्धन्यो भवतीत्येवं तद्वेदितव्यमपिशब्दाश्रनड्व्यवायेपि ॥

63. (The substitution of ष् for स्, to be taught hereafter, will take place) for all roots upto सित् exclusive in

VIII. 3. 70, even when the augment अट् intervenes (between the स and the efficient letter).

The root सित् occurs in sûtra VIII. 3. 70. Thus VIII. 3. 65 teaches ष change: as अभिषुणोति, परिषुणोति, विषुणोति, निषुणोति ॥ So also when अट् intervenes; as अभ्यषुणोत्, पर्यषुणोत्, व्यषुणोत्, न्यषुणोत् ॥ The force of अपि is that the change takes place even when the augment अट् does not come, i. e. in cases other than the augment.

स्थादिष्वभ्यासेन चाभ्यासस्य ॥ ६४ ॥ पदानि ॥ स्थादिषु, अभ्यासेन, च, अभ्यासस्य ॥

वृत्तिः ॥ प्राक् सितादिति वर्त्तते ॥ उपसर्गात्सुनोतीत्यत्र स्थासेनयसेधेति स्थादयस्तेषु स्थादिषु प्राक् सितसंशब्दनाद् अभ्यासेन व्यवाये मूर्द्धन्यो भवत्यभ्याससकारस्य च भवतीत्येवं वेदितव्यम् ॥

64. In स्था &c upto सित् exclusive (VIII. 3. 65 to VIII. 3. 70), this ष substitution takes place then also, when the reduplicate intervenes, and the स of the reduplicate is also changed to ष ॥

The words प्राक् सितात् are understood here also. The स्थादि roots are, स्था, सेनय &c in VIII. 3. 65 and ending with सेव् in VIII. 3. 70. The sûtra consists of two sentences: (1) The षत्व takes place in स्था &c. even when a reduplicate intervenes; (2) The स of the reduplicates of स्था &c. is changed to ष ॥ The first is a *vidhi* rule, and the second is a *niyama* rule.

Thus परितष्ठौ where the abhyâsa त intervenes. This applies even to roots other than those which have been taught with a ष in the Dhâtupâṭha. As अभिषिषेणयिषति, परिषिषेणयिषति (सेनया अभियातुमिच्छन्ति). This applies moreover to reduplicates which end in अ, as अभितष्ठौ; here the स would not have been changed to ष (by VIII. 3. 59) as it is not preceded by इ or उ ॥ Another *raison d'etre* of this sûtra is that it prohibits षत्व (VIII. 3. 61). As अभिषिषिक्षति, परिषिषिक्षति ॥

The word अभ्यासस्य is for the sake of niyama, as we have said above. स of स्था &c. and of no other roots is changed to ष ॥ As अभिसुसूषति from षू प्रेरणे with सन्, the augment is debarred by VII. 2. 12: the root स is unchanged by the niyama prohibition of VIII. 3. 61; the reduplicate सु remains unchanged by the restriction of the present sûtra.

उपसर्गात्सुनोतिसुवतिस्यतिस्तौतिस्तोभतिस्थासेनयसेधसिचसञ्जस्वञ्जाम् ॥ ६५ ॥ पदानि ॥ उपसर्गात्, सुनोति-सुवति-स्यति-स्तौति-स्तोभति-स्था-सेनय-सेध-सिच-सञ्ज-स्वञ्जाम् ॥

वृत्तिः ॥ उपसर्गस्थान्निमित्तादुत्तरस्य सुनोति सुवति स्यति स्तौति स्तोभति स्था सेनय सेध सिच सञ्ज स्वञ्ज इत्येतेषां सकारस्य मूर्द्धन्यादेशो भवति ॥

65. ष् is substituted for स, after an इ and उ of an upasarga in the following verbs: सु (सुनोति), सू (सुवति), सो

(स्यति VII. 3. 71), स्तु (स्तौति VII. 3. 89), स्तुभ (स्तोभते), स्था, सेनय (Denominative), सिध् (सेधति), सिच्, सञ्ज् and स्वञ्ज् ॥

Thus अभिषुणोति, परिषुणोति, अभ्यषुणोत्, पर्यषुणोत् ॥ सुवति, अभिषुवति, परिषुवति, अभ्यषुवत्, पर्यषुवत् ॥ स्यति, अभिष्यति, परिष्यति, अभ्यष्यत्, पर्यष्यत् ॥ स्तौति, अभिष्टौति, परिष्टौति, अभ्यष्टौत् ॥ स्तोभति, अभिष्टोभते, परिष्टोभते, अभ्यष्टोभत, पर्यष्टोभत ॥ स्था, अभिष्ठास्यति, परिष्ठास्यति, अभ्यष्ठात्, पर्यष्ठात्, अभितष्ठौ, परितष्ठौ ॥ सेनय, अभिषेणयति, परिषेणयति, अभ्यषेणयत्, पर्यषेणयत् ॥ अभिषिषेणयिषति, परिषिषेणयिषति ॥ सेध, अभिषेधति, परिषेधति, अभ्यषेधत्, पर्यषेधत् ॥ सिच, अभिषिञ्चति, परिषिञ्चति, अभ्यषिञ्चत्, पर्यषिञ्चत्, अभिषिषिक्षति, परिषिषिक्षति ॥ सञ्ज, अभिषजति, परिषजति, अभ्यषजत्, पर्यषजत्, अभिषिषङ्क्षति, परिषिषङ्क्षति ॥ ष्वञ्ज, अभिष्वजते, परिष्वजते, अभ्यष्वजत, पर्यष्वजत, अभिषिष्वङ्क्षते, परिषिष्वङ्क्षते ॥ सेध इति शब्विकरणनिर्देशः सिध्यतिनिवृत्त्यर्थः ॥ उपसर्गादिति, किम्? दधि सिञ्चति, मधु सिञ्चति, निगताः ॥ सेचका अस्माद्देशान्निः सेचको देश इति ॥ नायं सिचेरुपसर्गः ॥ अभिसावकीयतीत्यत्रापि न सुनोतिं प्रति क्रियायोगः किं तर्हि सावकीयं प्रति ॥ अभिषावयतीत्यत्र तु सुनोतिमेव प्रति क्रियायोगो न सावयतिमिति षत्वं भवति ॥

The root सिध् is exhibited in the sûtra as सेध with शप् vikaraṇa, thus debarring सिध्-सिध्यति ॥

Why do we say "after an upasarga"? Observe दधि सिञ्चति, मधु सिञ्चति (VIII. 3. 111). So निःसेचको देशः=निर्गता सेचका अस्माद् देशात् ॥ Here निः is not an Upasarga to सिच्, but to the noun सेचक ॥ Similarly in अभिसावकीयति, the upasarga अभि is not added to the root सु (सुनोति), but to the *third* derivative of सु (सुनोति). Namely, from सु we derive सावक with ण्वुल्, and from सावक we form the Denominative root सावकीय with क्यच् ; and to this Denominative root अभि is added. The upasarga, however may be added to the root first, and then ण्वुल् and क्यच् added. In that case, the rule will apply. As अभिषावकीयति ॥ So also with the Causative, as अभिषावयति, for here the upasarga is added to the root सु and not to the causative form सावय ॥

The roots षुञ् अभिषवे belongs to Svâdi class, षु प्रेरणे to Tudadi class, षोऽन्तकर्मणि to Divâdi class, ष्टुञ् स्तुतौ to Adâdi class and ष्टुभ स्तंभे, to Bhuâdi Class. These have been shown in the sûtra in their declined form in order to indicate that the rule does not apply to their यङ् लुक्, as अभिसोषवीति ॥ See VII. 1. 6 for this rule of श्तिप् exhibited roots. On the other hand, the roots सिच् &c. being not so exhibited, change their स in यङ् लुक् also, as अभिषेषिचीति ॥

The upasarga need not *end* with इ and उ for the purposes of this rule. Thus निष्षुणोति, दुष्षुणोति, where the upasarga is निस् and दुस् ॥

सदिरप्रतेः ॥ ६६ ॥ पदानि ॥ सदिः, अप्रतेः ॥

वृत्तिः ॥ सदेः सकारस्य उपसर्गस्थान्निमित्तादप्रतेरुत्तरस्य मूर्द्धन्य आदेशो भवति ॥

66. The स of सद् is changed to ष after an Upasarga having an इ or उ, but not after प्रति ॥

The word सदिः is in the first case, but has the force of genitive. Thus निषीदति विषीदति, न्यषीदत्, व्यषीदत् ॥ निषसाद, विषसाद ॥ The second स remains unchanged in the Perfect by VIII. 3. 118.

Why do we say 'but not after प्रति'? Observe प्रातिसदिति ॥ Prof. Bohtlingk points out that the sûtra is सेदेरप्रतेः as given by Sayânâchârya in his commentary on Rig Veda VI. 13. 1. Pâṇini, however, often uses the first case with the force of the Genitive, as in VIII. 3. 80.

स्तन्भेः ॥ ६७ ॥ पदानि ॥ स्तन्भेः ॥

वृत्तिः ॥ स्तन्भेः सकारस्य उपसर्गस्थान्निमित्तादुत्तरस्य मूर्द्धन्य आदेशो भवति ॥

67. The स of स्तन्भ is changed into ष after an upasarga, having an इ or उ ॥

Thus अभिष्टभ्नाति । परिष्टभ्नाति । अभ्यष्टभ्नात् । पर्यष्टभ्नात् । अभितष्टम्भ । परितष्टम्भ । The word अप्रतेः of the last sûtra is not to be read here. Hence we have forms like:—प्रतिष्टभ्नाति । प्रत्यष्टभ्नात्, प्रत्यतितष्टम्भ ॥

अवाच्चालम्बनाविदूर्ययोः ॥ ६८ ॥ पदानि ॥ अवात्, च, आलम्बन-आविदूर्य्ययो ॥

वृत्तिः ॥ अवशब्दादुपसर्गादुत्तरस्य स्तन्भेः सकारस्य मूर्द्धन्यादेशो भवति । आलम्बनेर्थे आविदूर्ये च ॥

68. The स् of स्तन्भ is changed into ष after the preposition अव in the sense of 'support' and 'contiguity'.

The word आलम्बनं means "support, refuge, that upon which any thing depends or leans". आविदूर्य means "the state of not being विदूर or far off, i. e. to be contiguous'.

Thus अवष्टभ्यास्ते "He remains leaning upon a staff" &c, अवष्टभ्य तिष्टति ॥. So also in the sense of to be near, as अवष्टब्धा सेना 'the army near at hand'. अवष्टब्धा शरत् ॥ See V. 2. 13.

Why do we say "when having the sense of support or contiguity"? Thus अवस्तब्धो वृषलः शीतेन 'the Śûdra is afflicted with cold'.

The present sûtra is commenced in order to make the ष change even while the preceding letter is not इ or उ ॥

वेश्च स्वनो भोजने ॥ ६९ ॥ पदानि ॥ वेः, च, स्वनः, भोजने ॥

वृत्तिः ॥ वेरुपसर्गादवाच्चोत्तरस्य भोजनार्थे स्वनतेः सकारस्य मूर्द्धन्यादेशो भवति ॥

69. The ष् is substituted for the स् of स्वन्, after वि and अव, when the sense is "to smack while eating".

Thus विष्वणति, व्यष्वणत्, विषष्वाण, अवष्वणति, अवाष्वणत्, अवषष्वाण ॥ That is, he makes sound while eating, he eats with a smack.

Why do we say 'when making a smacking sound in eating"? Observe विस्वनति मृदङ्गः "the drum sounds".

परिनिविभ्यः सेवसितसयसिवुसहसुट्स्तुस्वञ्जाम् ॥ ७० ॥ पदानि ॥ परि-नि-वि-भ्यः, सेव-सित-सय-सिबु-सह-सुट्-स्तु-स्वञ्जाम् ॥

वृत्तिः ॥ परि नि वि इत्येतेभ्य उपसर्गेभ्य उत्तरेषां सेव सित सय सिवु सह सुट् स्तु स्वञ्ज इत्येतेभ्यः सकारस्य मूर्द्धन्य आदेशो भवति ॥

70. ष is substituted for the स् of सेव्, सित, सय, सिव्, सह, the augment सुट्, स्तु, and स्वञ्ज, after the prepositions परि, नि, and वि ॥

The root सेव belongs to Bhuâdi class. The word सित is the Past Participle of षिञ् बन्धने, and सय is the noun derived from the same root with the affix अच्; सिव् is a Divâdi root.

Thus परिषेवते । निषेवते । विषेवते । पर्यषेवते । व्यषेवते । न्यषेवते । परिषिषेविषते । विषिषेविषते । निषिषेविषते । सित । परिषितो, विषितो, निषितः । सय । परिषयो, निषयो, विषयः । सिव् । परिषीव्यति । निषीव्यति । विषीव्यति । पर्यषीव्यत् । न्यषीव्यत् । व्यषीव्यत् । पर्यसीव्यत् । न्यसीव्यत् । व्यसीव्यत् । सह परिषहते । निषहते । विषहते । पर्यषहत । न्यषहत । व्यषहत । पर्यसहत । न्यसहत । व्यसहत । सुट् । परिष्करोति । पर्यस्करोत् । स्तु । परिष्टौति । निष्टौति । विष्टौति । पर्यष्टौत् । न्यष्टौत् । व्यष्टौत् । पर्यस्तौत् । न्यस्तौत् । व्यस्तौत् । स्वञ्ज । दंशसञ्जस्वञ्जामिति नलोपः । परिष्वजते । निष्वजते । विष्वजते । पर्यष्वजत । पर्यस्वजत । पूर्वेणैव सिद्धे स्तुस्वञ्जिग्रहणमुत्तरार्थम् । अड्व्यवाये विभाषा यथा स्यात् ॥

The nasal is elided in स्वज् by VI. 4. 25. The स of स्तु and स्वञ्ज् would have been changed to ष by VIII. 3. 65 also. Their inclusion here is for the sake of subsequent sûtra, by which the ष change is *optional* when the augment अट् intervenes.

सिवादीनां वाड्व्यवायेपि ॥ ७१ ॥ पदानि ॥ सिवादीनाम्, वा-अट्-व्यवाये, अपि ॥

वृत्तिः ॥ अनन्तरसूत्रे सिव्सहसुट्स्तुस्वञ्जामिति सिवादयः । सिवादीनामड्व्यवायेपि परिनिविभ्य उत्तरस्य सकारस्य वा मूर्द्धन्यो भवति ॥

71. The ष्-change may take place optionally in the सिव् and the rest (of the last sûtra), even when the augment अ intervenes between the prepositions परि, नि or वि and the verb.

The सिवादि are the four roots सिव् सह, स्तु and स्वञ्ज, as well as the augment सुट् ॥ This is an example of ubhayatra-vibhâshâ. In the case of स्तु and स्वञ्ज् it is prâpta-vibhâshâ, in the case of others it is aprâpta. The examples have already been given under the preceding sûtra, and so need not be repeated here.

अनुविपर्यभिनिभ्यः स्यन्दतेरप्राणिषु ॥ ७२ ॥ पदानि ॥ अनु-वि-परि-आभि निभ्यः, स्यन्दतेः, अप्राणिषु ॥

वृत्तिः ॥ अनु वि परि आभि नि इत्येतेभ्य उत्तरस्य स्यन्देतरप्राणिषु सकारस्य वा मूर्द्धन्यादेशो भवति ॥

72. ष् is optionally the substitute of the स् of स्यन्दू, after the prepositions अनु, वि, परि, अभि and नि, when the subject is not a living being.

The root स्यन्दू प्रस्रवणे is anudâtta. Thus अनुष्यन्दते । विष्यन्दते । परिष्यन्दते । अभिष्यन्दत तैलम् । निष्यन्दते । अनुस्यन्दते । विस्यन्दते । परिस्यन्दते ।

Why do we say 'when the subject is not a living being'? Observe अनुस्यन्दते मत्स्य उदके ॥ The option of this sûtra will apply, when the subject is a compound of living and non-living beings. Thus अनुस्यन्देते or अनुष्यन्देते मत्स्योदके ॥ The subject here is a Dvandva compound, and it is not in the singular number because of II. 4. 6. The word अप्राणिषु is a Paryudâsa and not a Prasajya-pratishedha. If it be the latter sort of prohibition, then the force will be on the word *living*, and in a compound like मत्स्योदके, consisting of *living* and *non-living* beings, the prohibition will apply because it has a *living* being in it, and so there will be no षत्व ॥ In the other view, the force is on the word *non-living*, and because the compound contains a non-living being, therefore the option will be applied, and the presence of the living being along with it will be ignored.

The anuvritti of परि, नि and वि is understood here from VIII. 3. 70. So these words could well have been omitted from the sûtra, which might have then been अन्वभिभ्यांच स्यन्दतेरप्राणिषु, and by the force of च we would draw in the anuvritti of परि &c.

वेः स्कन्देरनिष्ठायाम् ॥ ७३ ॥ पदानि ॥ वेः, स्कन्देः,अनिष्ठायाम् ॥

वृत्तिः ॥ वेरुपसर्गादुत्तरस्य स्कन्देः सकारस्य मुर्द्धन्यो वा भवति अनिष्ठायाम् ॥

73. ष् is optionally substituted for the स् of स्कन्द्, after the preposition वि, but not in the participles in त and तवत् ॥

The root is स्कन्दिर् गति शोषणयोः ॥ Thus विष्कन्ता or विस्कन्ता, विष्कन्तुम् or विस्कन्तुम्, विष्कन्तव्यम् or विस्कन्तव्यम् ॥

Why do we say 'but not in the Nishṭhâ'? Observe विस्कन्नः

परेश्च ॥ ७४ ॥ पदानि ॥ परेः, च ॥

वृत्तिः ॥ परिशब्दाचोत्तरस्य स्कन्देः सकारस्य वा मुर्द्धन्यो भवति ॥

74. ष् is optionally substituted for the स् of स्कन्द् after the preposition परि every where.

Thus परिष्कन्ता or परिस्कन्ता, परिष्कन्तुम् or परिस्कन्तुम्, परिष्कन्तव्यम् or परिस्कन्तव्यम् ॥

The word परि could well have been included in the last sûtra as विपरिभ्यां स्कन्देर् &c. The very fact that it has not been so included, indicates that the prohibition of अनिष्ठायाम् does not apply to it. Thus परिष्कण्णः or परिस्कन्नः ॥

परिस्कन्दः प्राच्यभरतेषु ॥ ७५ ॥ पदानि ॥ परिस्कन्दः, प्राच्यभरतेषु ॥

वृत्तिः ॥ परिस्कन्द इति मुर्द्धन्याभावो निपात्यते प्राच्यभरतेषु प्रयोगविषयेषु ॥

75. The word परिस्कन्द is used without the cerebral change in the country of Eastern Bharata.

This is an anomaly. The ष required by the last sûtra is prohibited. The other form is परिष्कन्दः ॥ The word परिस्कन्द is formed by the affix अच् or it is a Nishṭhâ, the त being elided. The word भरत qualifies the word प्राच्य ॥

Prof. Bohtlingk translates it "परिस्कन्द is seen in the usage of the Eastern People and the Bharata". He bases his construction on the sûtras II. 4. 66, and IV. 2. 113, where प्राच्यभरतेषु means "the Eastern People and Bharata".

स्फुरतिस्फुलत्योर्निर्निविभ्यः ॥ ७६ ॥ पदानि ॥ स्फुरति, स्फुलत्योः, निस्, नि, विभ्यः ॥

वृत्तिः ॥ स्फुरतिस्फुलत्योः सकारस्य निस् नि वि इत्येतेभ्य उत्तरस्य वा मूर्द्धन्यादेशो भवति ॥

76. ष् is optionally substituted for the स् of स्फुर् and स्फुल् after the prepositions निस्, नि, and वि ॥

Thus निष्फुरति or निस्स्फुरति, निस्फुरति or निष्फुरति, विस्फुरति, विष्फुरति ॥ स्फुलति, निष्ष्फुलति, निस्स्फुलति, निस्फुलति, निष्फुलति, विस्फुलति, विष्फुलति ॥

वेः स्कभ्नातेर्नित्यम् ॥ ७७ ॥ पदानि ॥ वेः, स्कभ्नातेः, नित्यं ॥

वृत्तिः ॥ वेरुत्तरस्य स्कभ्नातेः सकारस्य नित्यं मूर्द्धन्यादेशो भवति ॥

77. ष् is always substituted for the स् of स्कम्भ, after the preposition वि ॥

Thus विष्कभ्नाति, विष्कम्भिता, विष्कम्भितुम्, विष्कम्भितव्यम् ॥

इणः षीध्वंलुङ्लिटां धोऽङ्गात् ॥ ७८ ॥ पदानि ॥ इणः, षीध्वं, लुङ्लिटाम्, धः, अङ्गात् ॥

वृत्तिः ॥ मूर्द्धन्य इति वर्त्तते । इणन्तादङ्गात्परेषां षीध्वंलुङ्लिटां यो धकारस्तस्य मूर्द्धन्यादेशो भवति ॥

78. The cerebral sound is substituted in the room of the ध् of षीध्वम्, and of the Personal-endings of the Aorist and the Perfect, after a stem ending in इण् (a vowel other than अ).

The word 'cerebral' is understood here from VIII. 3. 55. Thus च्योषीढ्वम्, ह्रोषीढ्वम् ॥ Aorist :—अच्योढ्वम्, अह्रोढ्वम् (VIII. 2. 25). Perfect : चकृढ्वे ॥

Though the anuvṛitti of इण्कोः was current here from VIII. 3. 57, yet the repetition of the word इण् here indicates that the anuvṛitti of कु or the guttural ceases. As पक्षीध्वम्, यक्षीध्वम् ॥

Why do we say "the ध of षीध्वं, लुङ् and लिट्"? Observe स्तुध्वे, अस्तुध्वम्, where the ध is of लट् and लङ् ॥

Why do we say अङ्गात् 'after a *stem*'? Observe परिवेविषीध्वम्, from विष्लृ-व्याप्तौ of the Juhotyâdi class. There is Guṇa of the reduplicate by VII. 4. 75, the सु of सीयुट् is elided by VII. 2. 79, and षीध्वम् here is made up of the ष् of the root विष्, and ईध्वम् the affix ; therefore षीध्वं here is not after the *anga* परिवे वि, for the anga here is परिवे विष्, and ईध्वम् is the affix. This result could have been obtained, without using the word अङ्गात् in the sûtra, by the maxim अर्थवद् ग्रहणे नानर्थकस्य "a combination of letters capable of expressing a meaning, denotes that combination of letters in so far as it possesses that meaning, but it does not denote a combination void of meaning".

विभाषेटः ॥ ७९ ॥ पदानि ॥ विभाषा, इटः ॥

वृत्तिः ॥ इणः परस्मादिट उत्तरेषां षीध्वंलुङ्लिटां या धकारस्तस्य मूर्द्धन्यादेशो भवति विभाषा ॥

79. The cerebral sound is optionally substituted for the ध् of षीध्वम् and of the Aorist and the Perfect after the augment इट्, when the stem ends in इण् ॥

Thus लू+इट्+षीध्वम्=लविषीध्वम् or लविषीढ्वम् so also पविषीध्वम् or पविषीढ्वम् from पू ॥ Aorist:—अलविध्वम् or अलविढ्वम् ॥ Perfect:—लुलुविध्वे or लुलुविढ्वे ॥

The word इण is understood here and it qualifies the word इट्, so that the stem should end in an इण् vowel which should be followed by the इट् augment and this letter should be followed by षीध्वम् and the ध beginning affixes of the Aorist and the Perfect. If the stem does not end in an इण् vowel, the rule will not apply; as आसिषीध्वम् from the root आस उपवेशने ॥

Then in the word उपदिदीयिढ्वे, will the cerebral change not take place by the option of this sutra or otherwise? This is from the root दीङ् क्षये in the Perfect with the augment इट् (VII. 2. 13.), and युट् (by VI. 4. 63). Some say that as the augment युट् intervenes between the stem ending in ई (इण् vowel), and the augment इट्, therefore this rule will not apply and there will not be the optional ढ ॥ Others hold that the anuvṛitti of अङ्गात् has ceased, and the anuvṛitti of इण् is only current, in this sutra, and there is no intervention and so there will be the optional change into ढ ॥

समासेऽङ्गुलेः सङ्गः ॥ ८० ॥ पदानि ॥ समासे, अङ्गुलेः, सङ्गः ॥

वृत्तिः ॥ सङ्गसकारस्याङ्गुलेरुत्तरस्य मूर्द्धन्यादेशो भवति समासे ॥

80. ष् is substituted for the स् of सङ्ग after the word अङ्गुलि in a compound.

Thus अङ्गुलिषङ्गः । अङ्गुलिषङ्गो यवागूः । अङ्गुलिषङ्गो गाः सादयति ॥ Why do we say in a compound? Observe अङ्गुले सङ्गं पश्य ॥

The word सङ्गः is exhibited in the sûtra in the nominative case. The force is here that of Genitive i. e. सङ्गस्य ॥

भीरोः स्थानम् ॥ ८१ ॥ पदानि ॥ भीरोः, स्थानम् ॥

वृत्तिः ॥ स्थानसकारस्य भीरोरुत्तरस्य मूर्द्धन्यादेशो भवति ॥

81. ष् is substituted for the स् of स्थानं when preceded by भीरु in a compound.

Thus भीरुष्ठानम् ॥ The word compound is understood here also; otherwise भीरो स्थानं पश्य ॥

अग्नेः स्तुत्स्तोमसोमाः ॥ ८२ ॥ पदानि ॥ अग्नेः, स्तुत, स्तोम, सोमाः ॥

वृत्तिः ॥ अग्नेरुत्तरस्य स्तुत् स्तोम सोम इत्येतेषां सकारस्य मूर्द्धन्यादेशो भवति समासे ॥

इष्टिः ॥ अग्नेर्दीर्घात् सोमस्येष्यते ॥

82. ष् is substituted for the स् of स्तुत्, स्तोम and सोम when preceded by अग्नि in a compound.

Thus अग्निष्टुत्, अग्निष्टोमः, अग्नीषोमः ॥

Ishti:—The इ of अग्नि is lengthened before सोम and it is after such lengthened ई, that the स of सोम is changed to ष, otherwise not. As अग्निसोमौ माणवकौ ॥ So also अग्निसोमौ तिष्ठतः (where 'agni' means fire, and 'soma' a kind of herb) "the fire and the soma plant are here."

When there is no compounding we have अग्ने सोमः ॥

The word अग्निष्टुत् is formed by क्विप्, the *sacrifice* in which Agni is praised (स्तूयते) is so called. अग्निष्टोमः is also the name of a sacrifice: the first division (संस्था) of the Soma-yâga. अग्नीषोमः is a देवता-द्वन्द्वः so where there is no Devatâ-Dvandva, the ष change will not take place. Thus where Agni and Soma are names of two boys, or where they refer to physical fire and herb. According to Âśvalâyana there is lengthening and ष change in the last case also, as अग्नीषोमौ प्रणेष्यामि ॥

ज्योतिरायुषः स्तोमः ॥ ८३ ॥ पदानि ॥ ज्योतिः, आयुषः, स्तोमः ॥

वृत्तिः ॥ ज्योतिस् आयुस् इत्येताभ्यामुत्तरस्य स्तोमसकारस्य मूर्द्धन्यादेशो भवति समासे ॥

83. The स् of स्तोमः is changed to ष् after ज्योतिस् and आयुस् in a compound.

As ज्योतिष्टोमः, आयुष्टोमः, but ज्योतिः स्तोमं दर्शयति where there is no compounding.

मातृपितृभ्यां स्वसा ॥ ८४ ॥ पदानि ॥ मातृ, पितृभ्याम, स्वसा ॥

वृत्तिः ॥ मातृ पितृ इत्येताभ्यामुत्तरस्य स्वसृसकारस्य समासे मूर्द्धन्यादेशो भवति ॥

84. The स् of स्वसृ is changed to ष् after मातृ and पितृ in a compound.

As मातृष्वसा, पितृष्वसा ॥ See VI. 3. 24.

मातुःपितुर्भ्यामन्यतरस्याम् ॥ ८५ ॥ पदानि ॥ मातुः, पितुर्भ्याम, अन्यतरस्याम् ॥

वृत्तिः ॥ मातुर् पितुर् इत्येताभ्यामुत्तरस्य स्वसृशब्दस्यान्यतरस्यां मूर्द्धन्यादेशो भवति समासे ॥

85. The स् of स्वसृ is optionally changed to ष्, after मातुर् and पितुर् in a compound.

Thus मातुःस्वसा, or मातुःष्वसा ; पितुःस्वसा or पितुःष्वसा ॥ The word मातुर् and पितुर् end in र्, which is changed to visarga (See VIII. 2. 24). In fact, the word पितुर् is so exhibited in the sûtra itself, with a र्, the word मातुः therefore, by the rule of साहचर्य is also to be understood as a र् ending word.

Q.—Well, if this be so, when this र् is changed to a visarga, and the visarga changed to स् by VIII. 3. 36, then there would be no ष change?

Ans.—The ष change would take place both after the visarga-ending or स-ending words, on the maxim एकदेशविकृतस्यानन्यत्वात् "That which has undergone a change in regard to one of its parts, is by no means, in consequence of this change, something else than what it was before the change had taken place". Therefore, these words are taken to end in र्॥ For if they were taken to end in स्, then the rule would not apply when they ended in a visarga. If they be supposed to end in a visarga, then the form पितुर्भ्याम with a र् before भ्याम् in the sûtra is hard to explain.

The word समासे is understood here also. Therefore not here मातुः स्वसा when the words are used separately in a sentence.

अभिनिसस्तनः शब्दसंज्ञायाम् ॥ ८६ ॥ पदानि ॥ अभि-निसः, स्तनः, शब्द-संज्ञायाम् ॥

वृत्तिः ॥ अभि निस् इत्येतस्मादुत्तरस्य स्तनतिसकारस्य मूर्द्धन्यादेशो भवति अन्यतरस्यां शब्दसंज्ञायां गम्यमानायाम् ॥

86. The स् of स्तन् is optionally changed to ष् after the double preposition अभि निस्, when the word so formed is the name of a particular letter (i. e. visarga).

As अभिनिष्टानो वर्णः, अभिनिष्टानो विसर्जनीयः or अभिनिस्तानो वर्णः or विसर्जनीयः ॥ The compound preposition अभि-निस् causes this change, and not any one of them separately. Thus Ápastamba:—द्व्यक्षरं चतुरक्षरं वा नामपूर्वमाख्यातोत्तरं दीर्घाभिनिष्टान्तं, घोषवदाद्यन्तरन्तस्थम् "a name (nâma) should be such that it should consist of two-syllables or four-syllables, that its first portion should be a noun (nama-pûrva), and its second portion a verb (âkhyâta), that it should end in a long vowel (dirgha) or a visarga (abhinishtâna), that the first letter of such a noun should be a ghosha or sonant letter (ghosha-vad-âdi), and a semi-vowel (antastha) should be in the body of it." Thus the names द्रविणोदा, वरिवोदा fulfill these conditions and are good names.

Why do we say "when it is the name of a particular letter.'? Observe अभिनिस्तनति मृदङ्गः ॥ The anuvṛitti of समासे ceases from this place.

उपसर्गप्रादुर्भ्यामस्तिर्यच्परः ॥ ८७ ॥ पदानि ॥ उपसर्ग, प्रादुर्भ्याम, अस्तिः, यच्परः ॥

वृत्तिः ॥ उपसर्गस्थान्निमित्तात्प्रादुसश्चोत्तरस्य यकारपरस्याच्परस्य चास्तिसकारस्य मूर्द्धन्यो भवति ॥

87. The स् of the verb अस् is changed to ष्, when it is followed by a vowel or य् and is preceded by प्रादुः, or an upasarga having इ or उ in it.

The word यच् परः means 'followed by य् or अच्' ॥ The word प्रादुः is an Indeclinable, meaning 'evidently'.

Thus अभिषन्ति, निषन्ति, विषन्ति, प्रादुःषन्ति; अभिष्यात्, निष्यात्, विष्यात्, प्रादुःष्यात् ॥

Why do we say "when preceded by an *Upasarga* having an इ or उ?" Observe दधिस्यात्, मधुस्यात् ॥ Why do we say 'of the verb अस्'? Observe अनुसृतम्, विसृतम् ॥

Q.—How is there any occasion for the application of the rule here? The context here relates to स, and the word "upasarga" qualifies that स, but here the upasarga is not applied to स् but to the *whole verb* सृ, therefore this is no counter-example. In fact, what is the necessity of using the word अस् at all in the sûtra: for even without it, the word 'upasarga' would qualify that verb which consists of स् only, and such a verb is अस्, with its अ elided and no other verb? Nor is the employment of अस् necessary for प्रादुः, for it comes only in connection with the verbs कृ, भू and अस् ॥

Ans.—All that you urge, is true, yet the following counter-example should be given, as अनुसू, the son of Anusû will be आनुसेयः with ढक् as it belongs to Subhrâdi class. Thus अनुसू + ढक् = आनुसू + एय = आनुस् + एय ॥ Here the ऊ is elided by VI. 4. 147. Now when ऊ is elided, the स् is the only verb-element that remains, अनु is upasarga, and एय is affix; so that had अस् not been taken in the sûtra, the rule would apply to this स् also.

Why do we say "when it is followed by a vowel or य्"? Observe निस्तः, विस्तः, प्रादुस्तः ॥

सुविनिर्दुर्भ्यः सुपिसूतिसमाः ॥ ८८ ॥ पदानि ॥ सु, वि, निर्, दुर्भ्यः, सुपि, सूति, समाः ॥

वृत्तिः ॥ सु वि निर् दुर् इत्येतेभ्य उत्तरस्य सुपि सूति सम इत्येतेषां सकारस्य मूर्द्धन्यादेशो भवति ॥

Kârikâ:—सुपेः षत्वं स्वपेर्मा भूद्विसुष्वापेति केन न ।
हलादिशेषान्न सुपिरिष्टं पूर्वं प्रसारणम् ॥
स्यादीनां नियमो नात्र प्राक्सितादुत्तरः सुपि ।
अनर्थके विषुषुपः सुपिभूतो द्विरुच्यते ॥

88. The स् of स्वप्, सूति, and सम is changed to ष् after सु, वि, निर् and दुर् ॥

The word सुपि is exhibited in the sûtra as the form of स्वप् with vocalisation. Thus सुषुप्तः, निः षुप्तः दुः षुप्तः ॥ The word सूति is the क्तिन् ending form of सू; the rule applies to this form only, as सुषूतिः, विषूतिः, नि षूति and दुःषूतिः ॥ The word सम also means the *noun* सम and not the verb सम स्तम वैक्लव्ये ॥ Thus सुषमम्, विषमम्, निःषमम्, दुःषमम् ॥

Kârikâ—Why is षत्व taught with regard to the सुप् form of स्वप्? *Ans.* सुपेः षत्वं स्वपेर्मा भूत्, so that the षत्व change should not take place in स्वप् form, as विस्वमः and विस्वप्नक् (III. 2. 172) ॥ Q. विसुष्वापेति केन न? 'For what reason the षत्व change has not taken place in the reduplicate विसुष्वाप, for here also in the reduplicate, is the form सुप्, as विसुष्स्वप्, and then by applying हलादिशेष rule, the प् is elided, and एकदेशविकृतस्यानन्यत्वात् applies? *Ans.* हलादि शेषान् न सुपिः, we reduplicate the form स्वप्, as विस्वप्स्वप् and then elide प्, as विस्वस्वप्, and then vocalise, as विसुस्वप् so that there being no form सुप्, there is no षत्व ॥इष्टं पूर्वं प्रसारणं, in fact, the vocalisation takes place first, and then elision according to an ishṭi. See VI 1. 17. Otherwise, in स्वप स्वप्, as प् is elided, व् would also have been elided. Why is the स of विसुष्वाप not changed to ष by VIII. 3. 64? स्थादीनां नियमो नात्र प्राक् सितादुत्तरः सुपि, the rule VIII. 3. 64 does not apply, because that rule is confined only to verbs up to सित in VIII. 3. 70, while सुप् is *after* that verb. Moreover the प् of सुप् being elided, the mere सु is अनर्थक, and the maxim is अर्थवद् ग्रहणे नानर्थकस्य ॥ *Q.* If this maxim is applied, how do you form विषुषुपु? *Ans.* अनर्थके विषुषुपुः सुपिभूतोद्विरुच्यते, here the form सुप् is doubled, and not सुप् ॥ The root is first joined with the affix वि+स्वप्, then there is vocalisation विसुप्, then there is ष change, as विषुप्, then reduplication, as विषुप्षुप् ॥ Now षत्व being considered asiddha, the doubling should take place first? No, for we have already shown that for the purposes of doubling, the षत्व change is not asiddha (VIII. 2. 3 Vârt.)

निनदीभ्यां स्नातेः कौशले ॥ ८९ ॥ पदानि ॥ नि, नदीभ्याम्, स्नातेः, कौशले ॥

वृत्तिः ॥ नि नदी इत्येताभ्यामुत्तरस्य स्नातिसकारस्य मूर्द्धन्यादेशो भवति कौशले गम्यमाने ॥

89. The ष् is substituted for स् of स्ना after नि and नदी when the word so formed denotes "dexterous."

Thus निष्णातः कटकरणे। निष्णातो रज्जुवर्त्तने। नद्यां स्नातीति नदीष्णः ॥ This last word is formed by the affix क added to स्ना preceded by the upapada नदी under sûtra III. 2. 4.

Why do we say when meaning dexterous? Observe निस्नातः, नदीस्नातः (नद्यां स्नातः)

सूत्रं प्रतिष्णातम् ॥ ९० ॥ पदानि ॥ सूत्रम्, प्रतिष्णातम् ॥

वृत्तिः ॥ प्रतिष्णातमिति निपात्यते। सूत्रं चेद्भवति। प्रतिष्णातं सूत्रम् ॥

90. The word प्रतिष्णातः is irregularly formed when meaning a sûtra.

Thus प्रतिष्णातः सूत्रम् *i. e.* शुद्धम् 'pure'. When it has not this meaning we have प्रतिस्नातं = 'bathed'

कपिष्ठलो गोत्रे ॥ ९१ ॥ पदानि ॥ कपिष्ठलः, गोत्रे ॥

वृत्तिः ॥ कपिष्ठल इति निपात्यते गोत्रविषये ॥

91. The word कपिष्ठल is irregularly formed denoting the founder of a gotra of that name.

Thus the son of Kapishṭhala will be कापिष्ठलिः ॥ The word gotra" here does not mean the grammatical "gotra," but the popular term 'gotra' denoting 'clans,' as described in the list of pravaras. Why do we say "when denoting the founder of a gotra"? Observe कपिस्थलम् The land of the monkeys.

प्रष्ठोऽग्रगामिनि ॥ ॥ ९२ ॥ पदानि ॥ प्रष्ठः, अग्रगामिनि ॥
वृत्तिः ॥ प्रष्ठ इति निपात्यते अग्रगामिन्यभिधेये ॥

92. The word प्रष्ठ is irregularly formed when denoting 'a chief' or 'one who goes in front'.

Thus प्रष्ठोऽश्वः meaning a 'best horse'. Why do we say when meaning 'going in front'? Observe प्रस्थे हिमवतः पुण्ये "On the sacred peak of the Himalaya". प्रस्थो व्रीहीणाम् 'a measure of barley'.

वृक्षासनयोर्विष्टरः ॥ ९३ ॥ पदानि ॥ वृक्ष, आसनयोः, विष्टरः ॥
वृत्तिः ॥ विष्टरं इति निपात्यते वृक्षे आसने च वाच्ये । विपूर्वस्य स्तृणातेः षत्वं निपात्यते ॥

93. The word विष्टर is irregularly formed in the sense of "tree" and "seat."

This word is formed by adding the affix अप् to the root स्तृ preceded by the preposition वि ॥ Thus विष्टरो वृक्षः ॥ विष्टरमासनम् ॥

Why do we say when meaning a 'tree' or a 'seat'? Observe वाक्यस्य विस्तरः ॥ See sûtra III. 3. 33. by which अप् is added here instead of घञ् ॥

छन्दोनाम्नि च ॥ ९४ ॥ पदानि ॥ छन्दोनाम्नि, च ॥
वृत्तिः ॥ विष्टर इतिं निपात्यते । विपूर्वात्स्तृ इत्येतस्माद्धातोः छन्दोनाम्नि चेत्येवं विहित इति विष्टर इत्यपि प्रकृते विष्टार इत्यत्र विज्ञायते ॥

94. Also when it is the name of a metre, the irregular form विष्टार is used.

By Sûtra III. 3. 34 the word विष्टार is formed denoting a sort of metre called विष्टारपंक्तिः ॥

Why do we say when denoting 'the name of a chhandas'? Observe पटस्य विस्तारः ॥

In fact this sûtra makes unnecessary the sutra III. 3. 34. To avoid this difficulty, some say that the sútra III. 3. 34 is not confined to the preposition वि, so that we can form प्रस्तारपङ्क्तिः संस्तारपङ्क्ति ॥

गवियुधिभ्यां स्थिरः ॥ ९५ ॥ पदानि ॥ गवि, युधिभ्याम्, स्थिरः ॥
वृत्तिः ॥ गवियुधिभ्यामुत्तरस्य स्थिरसकारस्य मूर्द्धन्यादेशो भवति ॥

95. The स् of स्थिरः is changed to ष् after the words गवि and युधि ॥

Thus गविष्ठिर, युधिष्ठिर ॥ The compounding takes place by II. 1. 44. and the 7th case affix is not elided by VI. 3. 9. though the word गो does not end in a consonant, yet it retains its Locative ending by virtue of this sûtra.

विकुशमिपरिभ्यः स्थलम् ॥ ९६ ॥ पदानि ॥ वि, कु, शमि, परिभ्यः, स्थलम् ॥
वृत्तिः ॥ वि कु शमिं परि इत्येतेभ्य उत्तरस्य स्थलसकारस्य मूर्द्धन्यादेशो भवति ॥

96. ष् is substituted for स् in स्थल after वि, कु, शमि, and परि ॥

Thus विष्ठलम्, कुष्ठलम्, शमिष्ठलम् and परिष्ठलम् ॥ The word वि, कु and परि are compounded under II. 2. 18.; the word शमी forms a genitive by VI. 3. 63. In the aphorism the word शमि is shown with a short इ, indicating thereby that when the इ is not shortened, the cerebral change does not take place; as शमी-स्थलम्

अम्बाम्बगोभूमिसव्यापद्वित्रिकुशेकुशङ्क्वङ्गुमञ्जिपुञ्जिपरमेबर्हिर्दिव्यग्निभ्यः स्थः ॥ ९७ ॥ पदानि ॥ अम्ब, आम्ब, गो, भूमि, सव्या, अप, द्वि, त्रि, कु, शेकु, शङ्कु, अङ्गु, मञ्जि, पुञ्जि, परमे, बर्हिस्, दिवि, अग्निभ्यः, स्थः ॥

वृत्तिः ॥ अम्ब आम्ब गो भूमि अप द्वि त्रि कु शेकु शङ्कु अङ्गु मञ्जि पुञ्जि परमे बर्हिस् दिवि अग्नि इत्येतेभ्य उत्तरस्य स्थशब्दसकारस्य मूर्द्धन्यादेशो भवति ॥ वार्त्तिकम् ॥ स्थस्थिन्स्थॄणामिति वक्तव्यम् ॥

97. The स् of स्थ is changed to ष् after अम्ब, आम्ब, गो, भूमि, सव्य, अप, द्वि, त्रि, कु, शेकु शङ्कु, अङ्गु, मञ्जि, पुञ्जि, परमे, बर्हिस्, दिवि and अग्नि ॥

Thus अम्बष्ठः, आम्बष्ठः, गोष्ठः, भूमिष्ठः, सव्येष्ठः, अपष्ठः, द्विष्ठः, त्रिष्ठ, कुष्ठः, शेकुष्ठः, शङ्कुष्ठः, अङ्गुष्ठ, मञ्जिष्ठः, पुञ्जिष्ठः, परमेष्ठः, बर्हिष्ठः, दिविष्ठः, अग्निष्ठः ॥

The word स्थ is shown in the sûtra in the first case, and means the word-form स्थ, and it is not the genitive case of स्था, for then the rule would apply to गोस्थानम्, भूमिस्थानम् &c.

Vârt:—The same change takes place in स्था, स्थिन्, and स्थॄ ॥ As सव्येष्ठाः । परमेष्ठी । सव्येष्ठा सारथिः ॥

सुषामादिषु च ॥ ९८ ॥ पदानि ॥ सुषामादि षु, च ॥

वृत्तिः ॥ सुषामादिषु शब्देषु सकारस्य मूर्द्धन्यादेशो भवति ॥

98, The स is changed to ष् in the words सुषामन् and the rest.

Thus सुषामा ब्राह्मणः = शोभनम् साम यस्य असौ ॥

1 सुषामा, 2 निःषामा, 3 दुःषामा, 4 सुषेधः, 5 निषेधः (निःषेधः), 6 दुःषेधः, 7 सुषंधिः, 8 निःषंधिः (निषंधिः), 9 दुःषंधिः, 10 सुष्टु (सुष्ठु), 11 दुष्टु (दुष्ठु), 12 गौरिषक्थः संज्ञायाम्, 13 प्रतिष्णिका, 14 जलाषाहम्, 15 नौषेचनम् (नौषेवनम्), 16 दुन्दुभिषेवणम् (दुन्दुभिषेचनम्; °षेवनम्) 17 एति संज्ञायामगात्, 18 हरिषेणः, 19 नक्षत्राद्वा, रोहिणीषेणः ॥ आकृतिगण ॥

Some of the above words would have been governed by the prohibition in VIII. 3. 111, others would never have taken ष, hence their inclusion in this list. The word सु is here a karmapravachanîya (I. 4. 94) and निर् and दुर् also are not upasargas, because they are so only in connection with the verbs गम and क्री; so VIII. 3. 65 does not apply to सेध preceded by निर् and दुर् ॥ The words निःषेधः and दुःषेधः = निर्गतः सेधः or दुर्गतः सेधः ॥ The word सेध here is a घञ् formed word, from षिधू हिंसा संराद्धोः; if it be derived from

षिध गत्याम्, then also, the word is included here in order to prevent the application of VIII. 3. 113. The words सुषन्धिः, दुःषन्धिः &c are derived from धा with the prepositions सु and सम्, and the affix कि (III. 3. 92); and the स of सम् is changed to ष्॥ The words सुष्डु, दुष्डु are Uṇâdi formed words (Un. I. 25). The word गौरिषक्थः is a Bahuvrîhi, the स of सक्थि is changed to ष and the Samâsânta षच् is added (V. 4. 113). The long ई of the first member is shortened by VI. 3. 63. The word प्रतिष्णिका is formed by adding the Preposition प्रति to the root स्ना, and the affix अङ् (III. 3. 106), and we have प्रतिष्णा with टाप्; then क is added by V. 3. 73, and आ shortened (VII. 4. 13), and इ added by VII. 3. 44. The word नैषेचव is formed by adding ल्युट् to सिच् ॥ दुन्दुभिषेवणं is also a ल्युट् formed word from सेवति or सीव्यति ॥

एति संज्ञायामगात् ॥ ९९ ॥ पदानि ॥ एति, संज्ञायाम्, अगात् ॥

वृत्तिः ॥ एकारपरस्य सकारस्य मूर्द्धन्यादेशो भवति इण्कोरुत्तरस्यागकारात्परस्य संज्ञायां विषये ॥

99 The स् followed by ए and preceded by इण् or कु is changed to ष्, when the word is a name, and when the स is not preceded by ग् ॥

Thus हरवः सेना अस्य = हरिषेणः, परितः सेना अस्य = परिषेणः, so also वारिषेणः, जानुषेणी ॥ Why do we say 'followed by ए'? Observe हरिसक्थम् ॥ Why do we say 'when a Name'? Observe पृथ्वी सेना यस्य स = पृथुसेनो राजा (VI. 3. 34). Why do we say 'when the स is not preceded by ग्'? Observe विष्वक् सेनः ॥ The phrase इण्कोः is understood here also, so the rule does not apply to सर्वसेनः ॥

नक्षत्राद्वा ॥ १०० ॥ पदानि ॥ नक्षत्रात्, वा ॥

वृत्तिः ॥ नक्षत्रवाचिनः शब्दादुत्तरस्य सकारस्य वा एति संज्ञायामगकारात् मूर्द्धन्यो भवति ॥

100 When the preceding word is the name of a Lunar mansion, the ष् substitution for स् under the above mentioned circumstances is optional.

Thus रोहिणिषेणः or रोहिणिसेनः, भरणिषेणः or भरणिसेनः ॥ But not here शतभिषक् सेनः were the preceded letter is ग् ॥ These two sûtras 99 and 100 are realy Gaṇa-sûtras, being read in the सुषामादि Gaṇa. The author of Kâsikâ has raised them to the rank of full sûtras.

All cerebral ष changes, when not referable to any specific rule, should be classified under this Sushâmâdi gaṇa.

ह्रस्वात्तादौ तद्धिते ॥ १०१ ॥ पदानि ॥ ह्रस्वात्, तादौ, तद्धिते ॥

वृत्तिः ॥ ह्रस्वादुत्तरस्य सकारस्य मूर्द्धन्यादेशो भवति तादौ तद्धिते परतः ॥

वार्त्तिकः ॥ तिङन्तस्य प्रतिषेधो वक्तव्यः ॥

101. ष् is substituted for a final स् preceded by a short इ or उ before a Taddhita affix beginning with त ॥

The following are the affixes before which this change takes place, namely, तर, तम, तय, त्व, तल्, तस्, त्यप् ॥ As तर—सर्पिष्टरम् यजुष्टरम् । तम । सर्पिष्टमम । यजुष्टमम । तय । चतुष्टये ब्राह्मणानां निकेताः । त्व । सर्पिष्ट्वम् । यजुष्ट्वम् । तल् । सार्पिष्टा । यजुष्टा । तस् । सर्पिष्टो, यजुष्टः । त्यप् । आविष्ट्यो बर्द्धते । ह्रस्वादिति किम् । गीस्तरा । धूस्तरा । तादाविति किम् । सर्पिस्साद्भवति । प्रत्ययसकारस्य स्यात्पदाद्योरिति सत्यपि प्रतिषेधे प्रकृतिसकारस्य स्यात् । तद्धितइति किम् । सर्पिस्तराति ॥

Why do we say before affixes beginning with त ॥ Observe सर्पिस्साद्भवति ॥

Q.—But this स would, never have been changed to ष because of the prohibition in VIII. 3. 111, how can you then give this counter-example?

Ans.—Though the स of the affix सात् is prohibited by VIII. 3. 111, yet the counter-example is valid, because the स् of the base सर्पिस् is also not changed. Why do we say 'of a Taddhita'? Observe सर्पिस्तरति ॥

Vârt:—Prohibition must be stated of finite verbs before Taddhita affixes. As भिन्द्युस्तराम् । छिन्द्युस्तराम् ॥ These are the Potential third person plural of भिन्द् and छिन्द् with the augment यासुट्; the Taddhita affix तरप् is added by V. 3. 56, and आम् is added by V. 4. 11.

Vart:—Prohibition must be stated with regard to पुंस् as पुंस्त्वम् पुंस्ता ॥

निसस्तपतावनासेवने ॥ १०२ ॥ पदानि ॥ निसः, तपतौ, अनासेवने ॥

वृत्तिः ॥ निसः सकारस्य मूर्द्धन्यादेशोभवति तपतौ परतोनासेवनेर्थे ॥

102. ष् is substituted for the स् of निस् before the verb तप् when the meaning is not that of 'repeatedly making red hot'.

The word आसेवन means doing a thing repeatedly and here it means making it red-hot repeatedly. Thus निष्टपतिः सुवर्णम्=सकृत् अग्निम् स्पर्शयति i. e. he puts the gold into fire only once.

Why do we say when not meaning repeatedly. Observe निस्तपति सुवर्ण सुवर्णकारः=पुनः पुनरग्नि स्पर्शयति ॥

In the sentences निष्टप्तं रक्षः, निष्टप्ता अरातयः the change has taken place either as a Vedic irregularity or because the sense of repeatedness is not implied here.

युष्मत्तत्ततक्षुःष्वन्तःपादम् ॥ १०३ ॥ पदानि ॥ युष्मत्, तत्, ततक्षुः षु, अन्तः पादम् ॥

वृत्तिः ॥ युष्मत् तत् ततक्षुस् इत्येतेषु तकारादिषु परतः सकारस्य मूर्द्धन्यादेशो भवति स चेत्सकारोन्तः पादं भवति ॥

103. The स standing in the inner half of a stanza is changed to ष before the त of त्वम् &c. and तद् and ततक्षुस् ॥

The word युष्मद् here means the substitutes त्वम्, त्वाम्, ते, तव. As अग्निष्टं, नामासीत् ॥ त्वा, अग्निष्ट्वा वर्द्धयामसि ॥ ते' अग्निष्टे विश्वमानय ॥ तव, अप्स्वग्ने सधिष्टव, (Rig VIII. 43. 9) ॥ तत्, अग्निष्टद्विश्वमापृणाति, (Rig X. 2. 4) ततक्षुस्, द्यावापृथिवी निष्टतक्षुः षु ॥ अन्तः-पादमिति किम्, नित्यमात्मनो विदाभूरग्निस्तत्पुनराह जातवेदा विचर्षणिः ॥

Why do we say in the inner half of a stanza? Observe यन्मआत्मनो मिन्दाभूदग्नि स्तत्पुनराह जातवेदा विचर्षणिः ॥ Here the word अग्निः is at the *end* of the first stanza while तत् is at the *beginning* of the second stanza, therefore the स् of अग्निस् is not in the middle of a stanza.

यजुष्येकेषाम् ॥ १०४ ॥ पदानि ॥ यजुषि, एकेषाम् ॥

वृत्तिः ॥ यजुषि विषये युष्मत्तत्तक्षुः षु परत एकेषामाचार्याणां मतेन सकारस्य मूर्द्धन्यादेशो भवति ॥

107. In the opinion of some, the above change takes place in Yajurveda also.

Thus अर्चिर्भिष्ट्वम् or अर्चिर्भिस्त्वम्। अग्निष्टेमम् or अग्निस्तेमम्। अग्निष्टत् or अग्निस्तत्। अर्चिर्भिष्टतक्षुः or अर्चिर्भिस्ततक्षुः ॥

स्तुतस्तोमयोश्छन्दसि ॥ १०५ ॥ पदानि ॥ स्तुतस्तोमयोः, छन्दसि ।

वृत्तिः ॥ एकेषामिति वर्त्तते । स्तुत स्तोम इत्येतयोः सकारस्य छन्दसि विषये मूर्द्धन्यादेशो भवति एकेषामाचार्याणां मतेन छन्दसिविषये ।

105. The स् of स्तुत and स्तोम, in the Chhandas, is changed to ष् in the opinion of some.

Thus त्रिभिष्टुतस्य or त्रिभिस्तुतस्य, गोष्टोमं षोडशिनम् or गोस्तोमं षोडशिनम् ॥ This change would have taken place by the general rule contained in the next sûtra VIII. 3. 106, the special mention of स्तुत and स्तोम here is a mere amplification. The word छन्दसि of this sûtra governs the subsequent sutra also.

पूर्वपदात् ॥ १०६ ॥ पदानि ॥ पूर्वपदात् ॥

वृत्तिः ॥ पूर्वपदस्थान्निमित्तादुत्तरस्य सकारस्य मूर्द्धन्यादेशो भवति छन्दसि विषये एकेषामाचार्याणां मतेन ।

106. In the Chhandas, according to some, स् is changed to ष्, when it stands in the beginning of a second word, preceded by a word ending in इ &c.

The words छन्दसि and एकेषां are both understood here. Thus द्विषन्धिः or द्विसन्धिः, त्रिषन्धिः or त्रिसन्धिः; मधुष्ठानम् or मधुस्थानम्, द्विसाहस्रं चिन्वीत or द्विषाहस्रं चिन्वीत ॥

The word पूर्वपद here means the first member of a compound word as well as the prior word other than that in a compound. Thus निःषमृद्धत्वाय or निःसमृद्धत्वाय ॥

सुञः ॥ १०७ ॥ पदानि ॥ सुञः ।

वृत्तिः ॥ सुञिति निपात इह गृह्यते तस्य पूर्वपदस्थान्निमित्तादुत्तरस्य मूर्द्धन्यादेशो भवति छन्दसि विषये ।

107. The स of the Particle सु is changed to ष in the Chhandas, when preceded by another word having in it the change-effecting letter इ &c.

Thus अभी षु णः सखीनाम् (Rig. IV. 31. 3) ऊर्ध्व ऊ षु णः (Rig. I. 36. 13). The lengthening takes place by VI. 3. 134, and न changed to ण by VIII. 4. 27.

सनोतेरनः ॥ १०८ ॥ पदानि ॥ सनोतेः, अनः ।

वृत्तिः ॥ सनोतिरनकारान्तस्य सकारस्य मूर्द्धन्यादेशो भवति ।

108. The स of the verb सन्, when it loses its न्, is changed to ष, under the same circumstances.

Thus गोषाः (Rig. IX. 2. 10), formed by the affix विट (III. 2. 67), the न् is elided by VI. 4. 41. So also नृषाः ॥

Why do we say 'when it loses its न्'? Observe गोसनिं वाचमुदीरयन् (Atharv. III. 20. 10). Here the affix is इन् (III. 2. 27). See however गोषणि in Rig. VI. 53. 10.

Though this ष change would have taken place by VIII. 3. 106 also, the separate enumeration is for the sake of niyama or restriction. Some however read the word गोसनिः in the list of सवनादि words (VIII. 3. 110), and they hold that the proper counter-example is सिसानयिषति ॥ So also सिसनीः formed by adding क्विप् to the Derivative root सिसनिस, thus सिसनिस + क्विप् = सिसनिस् (the अ is elided by VI. 4. 48) + ०. add सु, सिसनिस् + स् = सिसनिस् + ० [स् is elided by VI. 1. 68. Now the final स् (of the Desiderative affix सन्) is liable to be changed either to ष् or to र् (रु). The ष being asiddha, the रु change takes place.] = सिसनिर् = सिसनीः (the lengthening is by VIII. 2. 76). Here the Desiderative affix सन् is not changed to ष, hence this word is not governed by VIII. 3. 61. This being the object of this sûtra, there will be ष change in सिषाणयिषति in the Causative.

सहेः पृतनर्त्ताभ्यां च ॥ १०९ ॥ पदानि ॥ सहेः पृतना-ऋताभ्याम्, च ।

वृत्तिः ॥ पृतना ऋत इत्येताभ्यामुत्तरस्य सहिसकारस्य मूर्द्धन्यादेशो भवति ।

109. The स of सह is changed to ष, after पृतना and ऋत ॥

Thus पृतनाषाहम्, ऋताषाहम् ॥ Some divide this sûtra into two; as (1) सहेः; (2) पृतनार्त्ताभ्यांच ॥ So that the rule may apply to ऋतीषहः also. The word ऋति is lengthened by VI. 3. 116, in sanhitâ: and the ष change takes place in sanhitâ only. Otherwise the form is ऋतिसहम् ॥ The word च 'and' in the sûtra includes words other than those not mentioned in it. The word ऋतीषहं would be valid by this also.

न रपरसृपिसृजिस्पृशिस्पृहिसवनादीनाम् ॥ ११० ॥ पदानि ॥ न, र-पर, सृपि, सृजि, स्पृशि, स्पृहि-सवनादीनाम् ।

वृत्तिः ॥ रेफपरस्य सकारस्य सृपि सृजि स्पृशि स्पृहि सवनादीनां च मूर्द्धन्यो न भवति ।

110. The ष substitution does not take place if र follows the स, as well as in सृप, सृज, स्पृश स्पृह, and in सवन and the rest.

Thus विस्रंसिकायाः काण्डं जुहोति ॥ The word विस्रंसिक is formed by the affix ण्वुल् (III. 3. 109), विस्रब्धः कथयति ॥ This word is from the root स्रम्भु विश्वासे, the इट् is not added by VII. 2. 15 and the nasal is elided by VI. 4. 24. before the nisṭhhâ त ॥ सृप :—पुरा क्रूरस्य विसृपः ॥ The word विसृपः is formed by the affix कसुन् (III. 4. 17), सृज :—वाचो विसर्जनात् ॥ स्पृश :—दिविस्पृशम् ॥ स्पृहि :—निस्पृहं कथयति ॥

The following is a list of सवनादि words :—

1 सवने सवने, 2 सूते सूते, 3 सोमे सोमे, 4 सवनमुखे सवनमुखे, 5 किंसः किंसः (किंस्यतीति किंसः), 6 अनुसवनमनुसवनम्, 7 गोसनिं गोसनिम्, 8 अश्वसनिमश्वसनिम् ॥ In some books this is the list 9 सवने सवने, 10 सवनमुखे सवनमुखे, 11 अनुसवनमनुसवनम् (अनुसवने २), 12 संज्ञायां बृहस्पतिसवः, 13 शकुनिसवनम्, 14 सोमे, सोमे, 15 सुते सुते (सूते २), 16 संवत्सरे सवत्सरे, 17 बिसं बिसम्, 18 किसं किसम् (किसं किसम्), 19 मुसलं मुसलम् 20 गोसनिम्, 21 अश्वसनिम् ॥

सात्पदाद्योः ॥ १११ ॥ पदानि ॥ सात्, पदाद्योः ।

वृत्तिः ॥ सातिति चैतस्य यङि परतो मूर्द्धन्यादेशो न भवति ।

111. The ष substitution does not take place in the affix सात् and for that स which stands at the beginning of a word.

Thus सात् here is the affix ordained by V. 4. 52, and it would have been changed to ष by VIII. 3. 59. The present sûtra prevents that. The Padâdi स refers to those verbs which in the Dhâtupâṭha are taught with a ष, and for which a स is substituted. This also is an exception to VIII. 3. 59. Thus अग्निसात् । दधिसात् । मधुसात् ॥ So also with Padâdi स as दधि सिञ्चति, मधु सिञ्चति ॥

सिचो यङि ॥ ११२ ॥ पदानि ॥ सिचः, यङि ।

वृत्तिः ॥ सिचः सकारस्य यङि परतो मूर्द्धन्यादेशो न भवति ।

112. The ष substitution does not take place in the स of सिच् of the Intensive.

Thus सेसिच्यते and अभिसेसिच्यते ॥

Q.—The स of the reduplicate should be changed into ष by VIII. 3. 65, in अभिसेसिच्यते, and the स of the root should be changed into ष by VIII. 3. 64. Because सिच् is one of the roots taught in VIII. 3. 65, and therefore, as this latter rule prevents the operation of VIII. 3. 111 i. e. पदादि स so far as it goes, so it would prevent also the operation of this rule and the form ought to be अभिषे षिच्यते?

Ans.—The ष ordained by VIII. 3. 65 prevents only the operation of पदादि स of VIII. 3. 111, and not the स of this rule. Therefore the present prohibition is of universal application.

Why do we say in the Intensive. Observe अभिषिषिक्षति ॥

सेधतेर्गतौ ॥ ११३ ॥ पदानि ॥ सेधतेः, गतौ ।

वृत्तिः ॥ गतौ वर्त्तमानस्य सेधतेः सकारस्य मूर्द्धन्यादेशो न भवति ।

113. The स् of the verb सेध is not changed to ष् when the meaning is that of moving.

Thus अभिसेधयति गाः, परिसेधयति गाः ॥ This is an exception to VIII. 3. 65.

Why do we say 'when meaning to drive'? Observe शिष्यमकार्यात्प्रतिषेधयति ॥ Here the sense is that of preventing or prohibiting.

प्रतिस्तब्धनिस्तब्धौ च ॥ ११४ ॥ पदानि ॥ प्रतिस्तब्ध-निस्तब्धौ, च ।

वृत्तिः ॥ प्रतिस्तब्ध निस्तब्ध इत्येतौ मूर्द्धन्यप्रतिषेधाय निपात्येते ।

114. The words प्रतिस्तब्ध and निस्तब्ध are anomalous.

In these words the स is not changed to ष, though so required by VIII. 3. 67.

सोढः ॥ ११५ ॥ पदानि ॥ सोढः ।

वृत्तिः ॥ सहिरयं सोढभूतो गृह्यते तस्य सकारस्य मूर्द्धन्यादेशो न भवति ।

115. The स् of सोढ form of the root सह is not changed to ष् ॥

As परिसोढः, परिसोढुम्, परिसोढव्यम् ॥ This is an exception to VIII. 3. 70.

Why do we say 'when सह assumes the form of सोढ' ॥ Observe परिषहते, विषहते ॥

स्तम्भुसिवुसहां चङि ॥ ११६ ॥ पदानि ॥ स्तम्भु-सिवु-सहाम्, चङि ।

वृत्तिः ॥ स्तम्भु सिवु सह इत्येतेषां चङि परतः सकारस्य मूर्द्धन्यादेशो न भवति ।

वार्त्तिकः ॥ स्तम्भु सिवुसहां चाङि उपसर्गादिति वक्तव्यम् ।

116. The ष change does not take place in the reduplicated Aorist of the roots स्तम्भ्, सिव् and सह् ॥

The root स्तम्भ required ष change by VIII. 3. 67, and the roots सिव and सह by VIII. 3. 70. Thus पर्यतस्तम्भत्, अभ्यतस्तम्भत् ॥ सिव :—पर्यसीषिवत्, न्यसीषिवत् ॥ सह :—पर्यसीषहत्, व्यसीषहत् ॥

Vârt:—This prohibition refers to the ष change that is caused by an Upasarga and not to the reduplicate change, as we have illustrated in the above example.

सुनोतेः स्यसनोः ॥ ११७ ॥ पदानि ॥ सुनोतेः, स्य-सनोः ।

वृत्तिः ॥ सुनोतेः सकारस्य मूर्द्धन्यादेशो न भवति । स्यसनि च परतः ।

117. स् of सु (सुनोति) is not changed to ष् in the Future, Conditional and Desiderative.

Thus:—अभिसोष्यति, परिसोष्यति, अभ्यसोष्यत्, पर्यसोष्यत् ॥

What example will you give under Desiderative? सुसूषति ॥ This is not a valid example, for by VIII. 3. 61, the reduplicate will not be changed here. Then we shall give the example अभिसुसूषते ॥ This is not also a proper example, for it is governed by the restrictive rule of VIII. 3 64. Then this is the example अभिसुसूः, निसुसू derived from the desiderative root अभिसुसूषति by the affix क्विप् ॥ Here the desiderative affix सन् is not changed to ष (VIII. 3. 61) and therefore the second स would have been changed to ष as it comes after a reduplicate.

Why do we say before स्य and सन् ॥ Observe सुषाव ॥

सदिष्वञ्जोः परस्य लिटि ॥ ११८ ॥ पदानि ॥ सदि-ष्वञ्जोः, परस्य,लिटि ।

वृत्तिः ॥ सदि ष्वञ्जि इत्येतयोर्द्धात्वोर्लिटि परतः सकारस्य परस्य मूर्द्धन्यो न भवति ।

118. The स् of सद् and ष्वंज after the reduplicate in the Perfect is not changed to ष् ॥

In the Perfect, when these words are reduplicated, there are two स's, as ससाद and सस्वंज ॥ After a preposition, the first स will be changed to ष, but not so the second. Thus अभिषसाद, परिषसाद्, निषसाद, विषसाद, परिषस्वजे:, परिषस्वजाते, परिषस्वजिरे, अभिषस्वजे ॥ The nasal of स्वंज is elided though here, the लिट् affix is not कित्, because it ends in a compound vowel (VI. 4. 24), (I. 2. 5 and 6).

The word स्वंज does not occur in the sûtra, but has been inserted in it by the auther of Kâśikâ from the following Vârtika:—सद्रो लिटि प्रतिषेधे स्वञ्जे रुपसंख्यानं कर्तव्यम् ॥

निव्यभिभ्योड्व्यवाये वा छन्दसि ॥ ११९ ॥ पदानि ॥ नि-वि-अभिभ्यः, अड्-व्यवाये, वा, छन्दसि ।

वृत्तिः ॥ नि वि अभि इत्येतेभ्य उपसर्गेभ्य उत्तरस्य सकारस्याड्व्यवाये छन्दसि विषये मूर्द्धन्यादेशो न भवति वा ।

119. The ष् is optionally substituted in the Chhandas after the prepositions नि, वि and अभि, when the augment अट् intervenes.

Thus न्यषीवत् or न्यसीवत् पिता नः; व्यषीवत्; or व्यसीवत् पिता नः, अभ्यषीवत् or अभ्यसीवत् ॥

The anuvṛitti of सद् and स्वंज is not to be read into this sûtra. It is, in fact, a general rule and applies to verbs other than these two. As व्यस्तौत्, न्यष्टौत्, अभ्यष्टौत or अभ्यस्तौत ॥

ओ३म् ।

अथ अष्टमाध्यायस्य चतुर्थः पादः ।

BOOK EIGHTH.

CHAPTER FOURTH.

रषाभ्यां नो णः समानपदे ॥ १ ॥ पदानि ॥ रषाभ्याम्, नः, णः, समानपदे ॥

वृत्तिः ॥ रेफषकाराभ्यामुत्तरस्य नकारस्य णकारादेशो भवति, समानपदस्थौ चेन्निमित्तनिमित्तिनौ भवतः ।

वार्त्तिकम् ॥ ऋवर्णाच्चेति वक्तव्यम् ॥

1. After र् and ष्, the ण् is the substitute of न्, when they occur as component letters of the same word.

These letters must be parts of the same pada or word, one being the 'occasion' for the application of the rule as regards the other. As आस्तीर्णम्, विस्तीर्णम्, अवगूर्णम् ॥ So also after ष; as, कुष्णाति, पुष्णाति, मुष्णाति ॥

The letter ष् is included in this aphorism for the sake of subsequent sûtras: for न् will be changed into ण् when preceded by ष् by rule 41 of this Chapter, as well.

Why do we say "when occurring in the same word?" Observe अग्निर्नयति, वायुर्नयति ॥

Vârt:—So also after the letter ऋ ॥ As तिसृणाम्, चतसृणाम्, मातॄणाम्, पितॄणाम्॥

This vârtika may well be dispensed with: because the र in the sûtra is the common *sound* र which we perceive both in र and ऋ; and so the र will denote both the vowel ऋ and the consonont र. See contra. VIII. 2. 42. Obj. But if even this be so, the letter ऋ has three parts, its first part is a vowel, in the middle is the र् sound of a quarter mâtrâ, and a vowel sound at the end. This vowel-sound will *intervene* between the र-sound and the subsequent न, and will prevent the application of the sûtra, hence the vârtika is valid?

Ans. This vowel-sound will be no intervention, because it will be included in the exception अट् of the next sûtra. Obj. The vowel-sound at the end of ऋ is not a *full* vowel of one mâtrâ, but is of half-mâtrâ, being only a fragment of ऋ, and hence is not included in the pratyâhâra अट्, it has no separate

स्थान or प्रयत्न or homogeneity with any vowel. Hence this vowel-sound will prevent the application of this rule. Ans. The ण change, however, does take place in spite of such intervention of a fragment of a letter, as we know from the jñâpaka of VIII. 4. 39. In the kshubhnâdi list there we find नृनमन as an *exception*, implying that न is *generally* changed to ण after such a fragmentary interposition. Or we may take नृंनमन as a jñâpaka, that after the *letter* ऋ also the ण change takes place.

अट्कुप्वाङ्नुम्व्यवायेपि ॥ २ ॥ पदानि ॥ अट्-कु-पु-आङ्-नुम-व्यवाये, अपि ॥

वृत्तिः ॥ अट् कु पु आङ् नुम इत्येतैर्व्यवायेऽपि रेफषकाराभ्यामुत्तरस्य नकारस्य णकार आदेशो भवति ।

2. The substitute ण् takes the place of न्, even when a vowel, or य्, व्, ह् or a guttural, or a labial, or the preposition आ, or the augment नुम intervenes, causing separation.

The pratyâhâra अट् stands for vowels and the letters ह य व र. Thus करणम्, हरणम्, क्रिरिणा, गिरिणा, कुरुणा, गुरुणा &c.

The कु means all the gutturals, e. g. अर्केण, मूर्खेण, गर्गेण, अर्घेण ॥

The पु means all the labials, e. g. दर्पेण, रेफेण, गर्भेण, चर्म्मणा, वर्मणा ॥

The आङ् means the particle आ: e. g. पर्याणद्धम् from नह् (VIII. 2. 34) निराणद्धम् (cf VIII. 4. 14). The particle आ is a vowel and so included in अट् pratyâhâra. Its specification in the sûtra shows that the restriction of the rule to the letters occurring in the *same word*, does not apply in the case of आङ्, in which case the rule applies to letters separated by another word.

So also when the anusvâra separates the letters e. g. बृंहणम्, बृंहणीयम् ॥

It is from the root बृहिवृद्धौ, the नुम is added, because the root is इदित (VII. 1. 58) and न् changed to anusvâra by VIII. 3. 24. Q. Well the intervention is here by Anusvâra and not नुम्, why is then नुम् taken in the sûtra?

The word नुम् in the sûtra refers to anusvâra, and must be taken co-extensive with it. Otherwise the rule would not apply to words like तृंहणं from तृंह स्तृंह हिंसार्थे ॥ Here the anusvâra is not the substitute of the augment नुम् but an original anusvâra. Even where there is an augment नुम्, but where it is not changed into anusvâra, the rule does not apply. As प्रेन्वनम्, प्रेन्वनीयम् from इवि: प्रीणनार्थः ॥

The rule will apply even when these letters are combined in any possible way, or occur singly. As अर्केण, here a guttural and a vowel i. e. 2 letters come between र and न ॥ See VIII. 3. 58 in the case of ष ॥

पूर्वपदात्संज्ञायामगः ॥ ३ ॥ पदानि ॥ पूर्वपदात्, संज्ञायाम, अगः ॥

वृत्तिः ॥ पूर्वपदस्थान्निमित्तादुत्तरस्य गकारवर्जिताद् नकारस्य णकार आदेशो भवति संज्ञायां विषये ।

3. So also, न् is replaced by ण्, when the letter occasioning the substitution, occurs in the first member of a compound, and the whole compound is a Name, provided that the first member does not end with the letter ग ॥

As द्रुणसः, वार्ध्रीणसः (a kind of antelope), खरणसः, शूर्पणखा ॥ See V. 4. 118 and IV. 1. 58.

Why do we say "when a Name"? Observe, चर्मनासिकः ॥

Why do we say when 'not ending in the letter ग'? Observe; ऋगयनम् ॥

Some say, that this sûtra is a नियम or a restrictive rule, and not a विधि or original enunciation, so that the substitution takes place, only when the word is a *Name*, and not otherwise. A compound is one word or समानपद, though composed of two or more words or पद ॥ Therefore by VIII. 4. 11 the न will always be changed into ण when preceded by र or ष. But the present sûtra restricts its scope, to those cases only, when the compound denotes a *Name*, as not in चर्मनासिका ॥ The word पूर्वपद is a relative term and connotes an उत्तरपद ॥ The present sûtra therefore applies to those cases where the र् or ष् is in the पूर्वपद, and न occurs in the उत्तरपद ॥ It therefore, does not apply to तद्धित words, nor when both the letters occur in the पूर्वपद ॥ In the case of a Taddhita, there is a पूर्वपद, but there is no properly speaking उत्तरपद ॥ Thus खरपस्यापत्यं = खारपायणः (IV.1.99). Here the affix अयन is equivalent to अपत्यं, and खरप is the Pûrvapada. But the affix अयन not being a Pada, we cannot call it an uttara pada. Hence न will be changed into ण though खारपायण is not an Appellative but a generic term. So also मातृभोगाय हितः = मातृभोगीणः with ख affix. Similarly in करणप्रियः, the words र and न both occur in the Pûrvapada and are not affected by this rule, but by the general rule VIII. 4. 1. So also the proviso relating to ग, only prohibits the change of न into ण, but does not prohibit the restrictive character of this sûtra.

According to others, this sûtra is an original enunciation or a Vidhi rule, and not a Niyama rule. They say that the word समानपद in VIII. 4. 1 is equivalent to नित्यं पदं i. e. a word integral and indivisible into component words. In other words, समानपद means, a 'simple-word'. The present sûtra therefore enunciates a new rule for a "compound-word". For in a compound or समास, there being a division of पूर्वपद and an उत्तरपद, we cannot say that a compound is a समानपद or indivisible word. Hence this sûtra is a विधि ॥

The sûtra should be thus divided:—पूर्वपदात् संज्ञायाम् one sûtra, and अगः another. So that every rule relating to ण change would be debarred with regard to ग intervention.

वनं पुरगामिश्रकासिध्रकाशारिकाकोटराग्रेभ्यः ॥ ४ ॥ पदानि ॥ वनम्, पुरगा, मिश्रका-सिध्रका-शारिका-कोटराग्रेभ्यः ॥

वृत्तिः ॥ पूर्वपदात्संज्ञायामिति वर्त्तते । पुरगा मिश्रका सिध्रका शारिका कोटरा अग्रे इत्येतेभ्यः पूर्वपदेभ्य उत्तरस्य वननकारस्य णकारादेशो भवति संज्ञायां विषये ।

4. The न of वन, is changed into ण, when preceded by the words puragâ, miśrakâ, sidhrakâ, śarikâ, koṭarâ, and

agre, as first members of the compound, and the whole compound is a name.

The words पूर्वपदात् and संज्ञायाम् of the last sûtra, are to be read into this aphorism. Thus पुरगावणम्, मिश्रकावणम्, सिध्रकावणं, कोटरावणम्, अग्रेवणम (II. 2. 31) शारिकावणम् ॥

The lengthening of the finals in the above is by VI. 3. 117. Though the word अग्रेवणं is not a Name, yet the rule VI. 3. 9, applies to it and the case-affix is not elided, because it is so read in Râjadantâdi list (II. 2. 31).

The substitution of ण for न would have taken place by the preceding rule. The separate enunciation of the rule with regard to the word वन, shows that this is a restrictive or नियम rule. The न of वन is changed into ण, when preceded by these words only and no other. Thus कुबेरवनं, शतधारवनम्, असिपत्रवनम्॥

प्रनिरन्तःशरेक्षुप्लक्षाम्रकार्ष्यखदिरपीयूक्षाभ्योसंज्ञायामपि ॥ ५ ॥ पदानि ॥ प्र-निर-अन्तर्-शर-इक्षु-प्लक्ष-आम्र-कार्ष्य-खदिर-पीयुक्षाभ्यः संज्ञायां, अपि ॥

वृत्तिः ॥ प्र निर् अन्तर् शर इक्षु प्लक्ष आम्र कार्ष्य खदिर पीयूक्षा इत्येतेभ्य उत्तरस्य वननकारस्य संज्ञायाम संज्ञायामपि णकारादेशो भवति ।

5. The न of वन is replaced by ण, even when the compound is not a Name, when it is preceded by the words pra, nir, antar, śara, ikshu, plaksha, âmra, kârshya, khadira, and pîyûkshâ.

Thus प्रवणे यष्टम ; निर्वणे प्रतिधीयते, अन्तर्वणे, शरवणम्, इक्षुवणम्, प्लक्षवणम्, आम्रवणम्, कार्ष्यवणम्, खदिरवणम् and पीयुक्षावणम् ॥

The words प्रवणं and निर्वणं are प्रादिः compounds. अन्तर्वणं is an Avyayî-bhâva in the sense of a case-affix. The rest are Genitive compounds.

विभाषौषधिवनस्पतिभ्यः ॥ ६ ॥ पदानि ॥ विभाषा ओषधि-वनस्पतिभ्यः ॥

वृत्तिः ॥ ओषधिवाचि यत्पूर्वपदं वनस्पतिवाचि तत्स्थान्निमित्तादुत्तरस्य वननकारस्य णकार आदेशो भवति विभाषा ।

वार्त्तिकः ॥ द्व्यक्षरत्र्यक्षरेभ्य इति वक्तव्यम् ॥ वा॰ ॥ इरिकादिभ्यः प्रतिषेधो वक्तव्यः ॥

Kârika फली वनस्पतिर्ज्ञेयो वृक्षाः पुष्पफलोपगाः ।
ओषधः फलपाकान्ता लता गुल्माश्च वीरुधः ॥

6. The न of वन is optionally replaced by ण, when the cause of change occurs in the first member of the compound and which denotes a perrenial herb or a forest tree.

When the pûrvapada is a word denoting ओषधि or a perenniel herb, or denoting a वनस्पति or a tree, and it has a change-producing letter, then the न of वन is replaced by ण ॥ This is an optional rule. Thus :—दूर्वावनम् or दूर्वावणम् ;

मूर्वावणम् or मूर्वावनम् ॥ Here मूर्वा and मूर्गा are names of ओषधि ॥ Similarly शिरीषवनं or शिरीषवणम्; बदरीवणं or बदरीवनं ॥

Vârt:—This rule applies when the first word is a dissyllabic or trisyllabic word. Therefore the change does not occur in देवदारुवनम्; भद्रदारुवनम् ॥

Vârt:—Prohibition should be stated with regard to the words इरिका &c. As इरिकावनम्, तिमिरकावनम् ॥

Though there is a distinction, botanically speaking, between a वृक्ष and a वनस्पति also; yet in this sûtra, the word वनस्पति includes वृक्ष also.

Kârika:-Technically speaking वनस्पति is a tree that bears fruit apparently without a flower, as a fig tree udumbara. वृक्ष is a tree that bears both flower and fruit, ओषधि is an annual herb, that dies after the ripening of the fruit, and creepers and tubercles are called वीरुधः ॥

अह्नोऽदन्तात् ॥ ७ ॥ पदानि ॥ अह्नः, अदन्तात् ॥

वृत्तिः ॥ अदन्तं यत्पूर्वपदं तत्स्थान्निमित्तादुत्तरस्याह्नो नकारस्य णकार आदेशो भवति ।

7. The ण is the substitute of न of अहन्, when it is preceded by a word ending in अ, having in it a letter capable of producing the change.

Thus पूर्वाह्णः "fore-noon"; अपराह्णः "after-noon".

Why do we say "ending in अ"? Observe, निरह्नः, दुरह्नः ॥

The word अह्न is substituted for अहन् by V. 4. 88. The word अह्न being used in the sûtra as ending' in अ, the rule does not apply to other words. Thus दीर्घाह्नी शरत् ॥ The word अह्नः in the sûtra is in the nominative case, and should not be construed as the genitive of अहन्, because all sthânins are exhibited in Nominatives as, वनं (VIII. 4. 4), वाहनं (VIII.4.8), यानं &c. The compounding takes place by II. 2. 1, then is added the samâsânta affix टच् (V. 4. 91), and अह्न substitution by V. 4. 88. The word दीर्घाह्नी is a Bahuvrihi compound and not a Tatpurusha, and hence the affix टच् does not apply to it. The feminine ङीप् is added by IV. 1. 28, there is elision of अ of अहन् by VI. 4. 134.

वाहनमाहितात् ॥ ८ ॥ पदानि ॥ वाहनम, आहितात् ॥

वृत्तिः ॥ आहितवाचि यत्पूर्वपदं तत्स्थान्निमित्तादुत्तरस्य वाहननकारस्य णकार आदेशो भवति ।

8. The न of वाहन is changed into ण, when the letter, producing the change, occurs in the first member of a compound, denoting the thing carried.

Thus इक्षुवाहणम 'a sugar-cart'. शरवाहणम् "a reed-cart". दर्भवाहणम 'a hay-cart'.

The thing which being placed on a cart is carried, is called आहित ॥

Why do we say "denoting the thing carried". Observe दाक्षिवाहनम् "a vehicle belonging to Dâkshi".

The word वाहन is formed by adding ल्युट् to वह्, and lengthening of the penultimate is valid by the nipâtana of this sûtra.

पानं देशे ॥ ९ ॥ पदानि ॥ पानम्, देशे ॥

वृत्तिः ॥ पाननकारस्य पूर्वपदस्थान्निमित्तादुत्तरस्य देशाभिधाने णकार आदेशो भवति ।

9. The न of पान is changed into ण, when it occurs as the second member of a compound, the first member of which contains a letter causing change; and the whole compound denotes a country or a people:

The word पान is formed by the affix ल्युट III. 3. 113. Thus क्षीरपाणा उशीनराः = क्षीरपाणं येषां 'the milk-drinking Usînaras'. सुरापाणाः प्राच्याः 'the wine-drinking Prâchyas'. सौवीरपाणा बाह्लीकाः "the sauvîra-drinking Bâhlîkas". कषायपाणा गान्धाराः &c.

Why do we say "when denoting a country"? Observe दाक्षिपानं the drink of the Dâkshis.

The words उशीनर and the rest are applied to persons also through the medium of being country-names.

वा भावकरणयोः ॥ १० ॥ पदानि ॥ वा, भाव-करणयोः ॥

वृत्तिः ॥ भावे करणे च यः पानशब्दस्तदीयस्य नकारस्य णकार आदेशो भवति वा पूर्वपदस्थान्निमित्तादुत्तरस्य॥

वार्त्तिकम् ॥ वाप्रकरणे गिरिनद्यादीनामुपसंख्यानम् ।

10. Optionally when the compound denotes a condition or an instrument, the न of पान is changed into ण, when it is a second member, the cause of change occurring in the first member in a compound.

Thus क्षीरपाणम् or क्षीरपानम् "drinking of milk" कषायपानम् or कषायपाणम् 'drinking of kashâya'. सुरापाणम् or सुरापानम् &c are examples of भाव or condition.

Similarly क्षीरपाणः of क्षीरपानः कंसः 'a vessel for drinking milk' This is an example of करण or instrument.

Vârt: — Optionally so in the case of गिरिनदी &c. Thus गिरिनदी or गिरिणदी; चक्रनदी or चक्रणदी, चक्रनितम्बा or चक्रणितम्बा ॥

प्रातिपदिकान्तनुम्विभक्तिषु च ॥ ११ ॥ पदानि ॥ प्रातिपदिकान्त-नुम-विभक्तिषु, च ॥

वृत्तिः ॥ वेति वर्त्तते । प्रातिपदिकान्ते नुमि विभक्तौ च यो नकारस्तस्य पूर्वपदस्थान्निमित्तादुत्तरस्य वा णकार आदेशो भवति ।

वार्त्तिकम् ॥ युवादीनां प्रतिषेधो वक्तव्यः ॥

11. Optionally ण is substituted for न when it stands at the end of a Nominal-stem (Prâtipadika) or is the augment नुम् or is न of a case-affix, (when the cause of change occurs in the first member of the compound).

Thus, to take the case a प्रातिपदिकान्त first. माषवापिणौ or माषवापिनौ from माषवापिन् 'mâsha-sowing' formed by णिनि under III. 2. 81.

To take the example of a नुम् augment माषवापाणि or माषवापानि, व्रीहिवापाणि or व्रीहिवापानि nom. pl. neut. The augment नुम् is here added by VII. 1. 72 from माषान् वपयन्ति = माषवाप with कर्मणि अण्, the plural शि is added by VII. 1. 20, and then नुम् ॥

To take the विभक्ति or case-termination, माषवापेण or माषवापेन, व्रीहिवापेण or व्रीहिवापेन ॥

The word प्रातिपदिकान्त means 'final in a Prâtipadika'. But here it means 'final in a prâtipadika which is a second member, of compound, the first member containing the cause of change'. Therefore the change does not take place in गर्गाणां भगिनी = गर्गभगिनी "the sister of Garga". But गर्गभगिणी if the word is derived from गर्गभग: 'the share of Garga', with the adjectival affix इन्, feminine इनी, meaning, "enjoying the share of Garga." In this case, like the word मातृभोगीण: 'fit to be possessed by a mother': the change will invariably take place.

The word माषवापिणी or °नी is to be understood to have a final न्, the affix being added afterwards in accordance with the following maxim:—(II. 2. 19). "It should be stated that Gatis, Kârakas, and Upapadas ars compounded with bases that end with krit-affixes, before a case termination or a feminine affix has been added to the latter" गतिकारकोपपदानां कृद्भिः सह समासवचनं प्राक् सुबुत्पत्तेः ॥

Therefore the composition takes place first with the word ending in the krit affix, as माषवापिन् (माष + वापिन्), and thus the second term वापिन् is a Prâtipadika which ends in न्, and so the rule is applied to it, when the feminine affix is added.

Similarly नुम् is not considered as the end portion of the *second* member of the compound, but as the end-portion of the *full* compound word.

Vârt:—Prohibition must be stated of the words युवा &c. As आर्ययूना (VI. 4. 133 vocalisation), क्षत्रिययूना ॥ प्रपक्वानि is a gati-samas, दीर्घाह्नी शरत् ॥

एकाजुत्तरपदे णः ॥ १२ ॥ पदानि ॥ एकाच्, उत्तरपदे, णः ॥

वृत्तिः ॥ एकाजुत्तरपदं यस्य स एकाजुत्तरपदः । तस्मिन्नेकाजुत्तरपदसमासे प्रातिपदिकान्तनुम्विभक्तिषु पूर्वपदस्थान्निमित्तादुत्तरस्य नकारस्य णकार आदेशो भवति ।

12. In a compound, the second member of which is a monosyllable, there is ण in the room of न of the second member, provided that the न is at the end of a prâtipadika, or is the augment नुम्, or occurs in a vibhakti; and when the first member contains a cause of change.

Thus वृत्रहणौ and वृत्रहण: 'the Vṛitra-killer'. क्षीरपाणि "Drinkers of milk': सुरापाणि 'drinkers of wine': being examples of नुम् VII. 3. 88, क्षीरपेण and सुरापेण are examples of case-terminations.

Why the letter ण is repeated in this sûtra, while its anuvṛitti was understood from the context? It is repeated in order to show that this is not an optional rule, but an obligatory rule. In fact, it shows that the anuvṛitti of वा 'optional' ceases, and does not extend further.

कुमति च ॥ १३ ॥ पदानि ॥ कुमति, च ॥

वृत्तिः ॥ कवर्गवति चोत्तरपदे प्रातिपदिकान्तनुम्विभक्तिषु पूर्वपदस्थान्निमित्तादुत्तरस्य नकारस्य णकारादेशो भवति ।

13. In a compound, the second member of which contains a guttural, there is ण in the room of न, that follows anything which standing in the prior member is qualified to cause the change, provided the न be at the end of a prâtipadika, or be the augment नुम्, or occur in a vibhakti.

If the second part of a compound contains a letter of the class क, the change is obligatory, even though the second part be not monosyllabic. As वस्त्रयुगिणौ, वस्त्रयुगिणः, स्वर्गकामिणौ, वृषगामिणौ ॥ नुम:—वस्त्रयुगाणि, खरयुगाणि ॥ विभक्ति:— वस्त्रयुगेण, खरयुगेण ॥

The word वस्त्रयुगिणौ is a compound of वस्त्र with युगिन् (the affix इनि is added first to युग and then the word so formed is compounded with vastra). Thus the न् becomes प्रातिपदिकान्त i.e. it becomes the final of a Nominal-stem, which stands as a second member in a compound.

उपसर्गादसमासेऽपि णोपदेशस्य ॥ १४ ॥ पदानि ॥ उपसर्गात्, अ-समासे, अपि, णोपदेशस्य ॥

वृत्तिः ॥ ण उपदेशो यस्यासौ णोपदेशः । णोपदेशस्य धातोर्यो नकारः तस्य उपसर्गस्थान्निमित्तादुत्तरस्य णकारादेशो भवति असमासेपि समासेपि ।

14. Of a root which has ण in its original enunciation, when it comes after a cause of such change standing in an upasarga, even though the word be not a samâsa, the न is changed into ण ॥

The word णोपदेश means a root which is enunciated in the Dhâtupâṭha with an initial ण ॥ Thus प्रणमति 'he bows'. परिणमति, प्रणायकः 'a leader' परिणायकः &c.

Why do we say "after an Upasarga"? Observe प्रनायकः = प्रगता नायका अस्माद् देशात् 'a country without a leader'. Here the word प्र is not an upasarga, but a mere nipâta. See I. 4. 57, 58 and 59. In fact, प्र is upasarga here with regard to गत understood, and not with regard to नी ॥

Why do we say "even when it is not a compound?" Because by context, the anuvṛitti of the word पूर्वपद, which is current throughout this subdivision, would have been understood in this sûtra also, and the rule would have applied to samâsas only, for there only we have pûrvapada. By using the word असमासे it is shown that the adhikâra of pûrvapada ceases, and the rule applies to non-compounds also where there is no पूर्वपद ॥

Why do we say "having ण in Upadeśa"? Observe प्रनर्दति, प्रनर्दितुम्, प्रनर्दकः ॥ For the root नर्द is recited in Dhâtupâṭha with न ॥ There are eight such roots नर्द्, नाद्, नाथ्, नाध्, नन्द्, नक्क्, नॄ, नृत् ॥ See VI. 1. 65.

हिनुमीना ॥ १५ ॥ पदानि ॥ हिनु-मीना, ॥

वृत्तिः ॥ हिनु मीना इत्येतयोरुपसर्गस्थान्निमित्तादुत्तरस्य नकारस्य णकारादेशो भवति ।

15. The न of हिनु and मीना is changed into ण, when coming after an upasarga containing in it a cause of change.

Thus प्रहिणोति, प्रहिणुतः, प्रमीणाति, प्रमीणीतः ॥ The root हि belongs to Svâdi class of verbs and takes the vikaraṇa नु technically श्नु; and the root मी belongs to Kryâdi class which takes the vikaraṇa श्ना ॥ In the sûtra the verbs are shown with the vikaraṇas affixed. Under certain circumstances the forms of the vikaraṇa is changed from नु to नो and ना to नी, but the rule still applies, because the substitute of an अच् or vowel is like the principal. See I. 1. 57.

आनि लोट् ॥ १६ ॥ पदानि ॥ आनि, लोट् ॥

वृत्तिः ॥ उपसर्गादिति वर्तते । आनीत्येतस्य लोडादेशस्योपसर्गस्थान्निमित्तादुत्तरस्य नकारस्य णकारादेशो भवति ।

16. The न of आनि, the affix of the Imperative, 1st Person, is changed into ण when it follows a letter competent to cause such a change standing in an Upasarga.

The word आनि is the termination of the Imperative. Thus प्रवपाणि, परिवपाणि, प्रयाणि, परियाणि ॥

Why do we say 'the Imperative'? Observe प्रवपानि मांसानि ॥ Here आनि is the neuter plural termination, and the word means प्रकृष्टा वपा येषु, तानि ॥

According to Padamanjari, the employment of the word लोट् in the sûtra is redundant. For without it also आनि would have meant the *Imperative* affix, and not the Neuter termination, on the maxim of अर्थवद् ग्रहणे &c. Moreover in the *noun* प्रवपानि, प्र is not an upasarga at all, on the maxim यत् क्रियायुक्ताः प्रादयस्तं प्रति गति-उपसर्ग-संज्ञे भवतः ॥

नेर्गदनदपतपदघुमास्यतिहन्तियातिवातिद्रातिप्सातिवपतिवहतिशाम्यतिचिनोतिदेग्धिषु च ॥ १७॥ पदानि ॥ नेः, गद-नद-पत-पद-घु-मा-स्यति-हन्ति-याति-वाति-द्राति-प्साति-वपति-वहति-शाम्यति-चिनोति-देग्धिषु, च ॥

वृत्तिः ॥ निरित्येतस्योपसर्गस्थान्निमित्तादुत्तरस्य नकारस्य णकारादेशो भवति गद नद पत पद घु मा स्यति हन्ति याति वाति द्राति प्साति वपति वहति शाम्यति चिनोति देग्धि इत्येतेषु परतः ।

17. The ण् is the substitute of न् of the prefix नि, following a cause for such change standing in an upasarga, when these verbs follow, gad 'to speak', nad 'to be happy', pat 'to fall', pad 'to go', the ghu verbs, mâ 'to measure', sho 'to destroy', han 'to kill', yâ 'to go', vâ 'to blow', drâ 'to flee', psâ 'to eat', vap 'to weave', vah 'to bear', śam 'to be tranquil', chi 'to collect', and dih 'to anoint'.

Thus

गदः,	प्रणिगदति, परिणिगदति	नदः,	प्रणिनदति, परिणिनदति
पतः,	प्रणिपतति, परिणिपतति,	पदः,	प्रणिपद्यते, परिणिपद्यते
घुः,	प्रणिददाति, परिणिददाति, प्रणिदधाति, परिणिदधाति		
माङ्ः,	प्रणिमिमीते, परिणिमिमीते	मेङ्ः,	प्रणिमयते, परिणिमयते

Ishti:—By the word मा in the sûtra, both verbs माङ् and मेङ् are to be taken and not the roots मी or मि or मा माने, for they also take the form मा by VI. 1. 50.

स्यति	प्रणिष्यति, परिणिष्यति	हन्ति	प्रणिहन्ति, परिणिहन्ति
याति	प्रणियाति, परिणियाति	वाति	प्रणिवाति, परिणिवाति
द्राति	प्रणिद्राति, परिणिद्राति	प्साति	प्रणिप्साति, परिणिप्साति

The last five roots belong to Adâdi class.

वपति	प्रणिवपति, परिणिवपति	वहति	प्रणिवहति, परिणिवहति
शाम्यति	प्रणिशाम्यति, परिणिशाम्यति (VII. 3. 74)		
चिनोति	प्रणिचिनोति, परिणिचिनोति	देग्धि	प्रणिदेग्धि, परिणिदेग्धि

Ishti:—The above change takes place even when the augment अट् intervenes.. As प्रण्यगदत्, परिण्यगदत् ॥

The roots स्यति &c, are exhibited in their declined form in the sûtra, in order to indicate that the rule does not apply to यङ् लुक् form of these roots (VII. 1. 6).

शेषे विभाषाकखादावषान्तउपदेशे ॥ १८ ॥ पदानि ॥ शेषे, विभाषा, अकखादौ, अषान्ते, उपदेशे ॥

वृत्तिः ॥ नेरिति वर्तते उपसर्गादिति च । अककारखकारादिरषकारान्तश्च उपदेशे यो धातुः शेषस्तस्मिन्परत उपसर्गस्यान्निमित्तादुत्तरस्य नेर्नकारस्य विभाषा णकार आदेशो भवति ।

18. In the remaining verbs, optionally the न of नि is replaced by ण, when it is preceded by an upasarga competent to cause the change; provided that, in the original enunciation, the verb has not an initial क or ख, nor ends with ष ॥

The words नेः and उपसर्गात् are understood in the sûtra. The word शेषे means verbs other than those mentioned last. Thus प्रणिपचति or प्रनिपचति, प्रणिभिनत्ति or प्रनिभिनत्ति ॥

Why do we say अकखादौ "not beginning with क or ख"? Observe प्रनि करोति, प्रनिखादति ॥ Here there is no change.

Why do we say अषान्तः "not ending in ष"? Observe प्रनिपिनष्टि ॥

Why do we say उपदेशे "in original enunciation"? So that the prohibition may apply to forms like प्रनिचकार, प्रनिचखाद, प्रनिपेक्ष्यति (VIII. 2. 41). Here चकार &c, do not begin with क or ख nor does पिष् end with ष but with क (VIII. 2. 41) but in the Dhâtupâṭha the verb कृ and खद् begin with क and ख and पिष् ends with ष्, and hence the rule will not apply. So also in प्रणिवेष्टा and प्रणिवेक्ष्यति from the root विश् ॥ Here though the verb now ends with ष by VIII. 2. 36, yet in the original enunciation or Dhâtupâṭha, it ends with श ॥

अनितेः ॥ १६ ॥ पदानि ॥ अनितेः ॥

वृत्तिः ॥ अनितेर्नकारस्योपसर्गस्थान्निमित्तादुत्तरस्य णकारादेशो भवति ।

19. The न of the verb अन् 'to breathe', is changed into ण, when preceded by an upasarga competent to produce the change.

Thus प्र+अनिति=प्राणिति 'he breathes'. पराणिति ॥ For इट् augment, see VII. 2. 76.

अन्तः ॥ २० ॥ पदानि ॥ अन्तः ॥

वृत्तिः ॥ उपसर्गस्थान्निमित्तादुत्तरस्यानितिनकारस्य पदान्ते वर्तमानस्य णकारादेशो भवति ।

20. The न of अन् is changed into ण, when it is preceded by an upasarga competent to produce the change, provided it occurs at the end of a pada.

As हे प्राण् ! हे पराण् ! ॥ This rule is an exception to VIII. 4. 37 *sub*, by which final न् in a pada is not changed into ण ॥ The word अन्तः in the sûtra is to be understood to be equivalent to पदान्तः, and the rule applies when the word is in the vocative case.

According to some अन्तः is taken to be a part of the last sûtra, and has the meaning of 'proximity'. That is the न is changed to ण, if the र is not separated from the न by more than one letter. Therefore there is no change in परि+अनिति=पर्यनिति ॥ In this view, another अन्त should be taken for the sake of final न्, in हे प्राण् ॥

According to others the form पर्यणिति is valid, and they do not connect अन्तः with the last sûtra.

The word प्राण् is a क्विप् formed word, and the न् final is not elided in the Vocative Singular because of the prohibition of VIII. 2. 8; in every other place, when the न् is padânta, it would be dropped; and therefore the illustration is given with Vocative singular, which alone satisfies the requirements of this sûtra.

उभौ साभ्यासस्य ॥ २१ ॥ पदानि ॥ उभौ, साभ्यासस्य ॥

वृत्तिः ॥ साभ्यासस्यानितेरुपसर्गस्थान्निमित्तादुत्तरस्योभयोर्नकारयोर्णकार आदेशो भवति ।

21. Both the न s are changed into ण in the reduplicated forms of the verb अन्, when preceded by an upasarga competent to cause the change.

Thus in the Desiderative प्राणिणिषति and Aorist of the Causative प्राणिणत्, and so also पराणिणिषति and पराणिणत् ॥

If the maxim पूर्वत्रासिद्धीयमद्विर्वचने be not applied here; then we have the following dilemma in, प्रान+स+ति ॥ Here the affix सन् requires reduplication, and the present sûtra requires ण change of न ॥ The णत्व being asiddha, the reduplication being made first, we have प्रानिनि+स+ति, and then the reduplicate ण intervenes between the cause र and the root-न् of नि, and so this न would not be changed to ण ॥ If however the above maxim be applied, we first apply the णत्व rule, as प्राणि+स+ति, and then reduplicate णि; and we get the form प्राणिणिषति even without this sûtra.

If we could get this form by the application of the above maxim, where is the necessity of the present sûtra? The sûtra is necessary in order to indicate that the above maxim is *anitya* or not of universal application. And because it is *anitya*, that the form औजढत् is evolved by reduplicating हत् (See VIII. 2. 1).

हन्तेरत्पूर्वस्य ॥ २२ ॥ पदानि ॥ हन्तेः,अत्,पूर्वस्य ॥

वृत्तिः ॥ अकारपूर्वस्य हन्तिनकारस्य उपसर्गस्थान्निमित्तादुत्तरस्य णकार आदेशो भवति ।

22. The न, when preceded by अ, in the root हन्, is changed to ण, when the verb is preceded by a preposition competent to cause the change.

Thus प्रहण्यते, परिहण्यते, प्रहणनम् परिहणनम् ॥

Why do we say अत्पूर्वस्य 'when preceded by अ'? When अ is elided, the change does not take place. As प्रघ्नन्ति, परिघ्नन्ति (VI. 4. 98, and VIII. 3. 54).

Why do we say अत् "perceded by *short* अ"? Observe पर्यघानि and प्रघानि, the Aorist of हन् by the affix चिण् (III. 1. 60) प्रहन्+चिण्=प्रघन्+चिण् (VIII. 3. 54) =प्रघान्+चिण् (VIII. 2. 116)=प्रघानि 'he killed'. Here न being preceded by the long आ is not changed.

वमोर्वा ॥ २३ ॥ पदानि ॥ वमोः, वा ॥

वृत्तिः ॥ वकारमकारयोः परतो हन्तिनकारस्योपसर्गस्थान्निमित्तादुत्तरस्य वा णकारादेशो भवति ।

23. Optionally when व or म follow, the न of *han* is changed to ण, when preceded by an upasarga competent to cause the change.

Thus प्रहण्वः, परिहण्वः, or प्रहन्वः and परिहन्वः, प्रहण्मः or प्रहन्मः परिहण्मः or परिहन्मः ॥

This sûtra enjoins an option in certain cases, where it would have been obligatory by the last rule.

अन्तरदेशे ॥ २४ ॥ पदानि ॥ अन्तर्, अदेशे ॥

वृत्तिः ॥ अन्त शब्दादुत्तरस्य हन्तिनकारस्यात्पूर्वस्य णकारादेशो भवति ।

24. The न preceded by short अ of the root हन् is changed into ण, when the root follows the upasarga अन्तर्, and the word does not mean a country.

Thus अन्तर्हण्यते and अन्तर्हणनं ॥

Why do we say "when not meaning a country अदेश?" Observe अन्तर्हननो देशः ॥

The phrase अत्पूर्वस्य "preceded by short अ" of sûtra 22 *ante*, is to be read into this sûtra also. Observe, अन्तर्घ्नन्ति ॥

Why do we say "*short* अ?" See, अन्तरघानि ॥ The word antar is an upasarga for the purposes of ण change, by the vârtika under I. 4. 65; therefore, it would have caused the ण change by VIII. 4. 22. The present sûtra is made, to show that the change takes place only then, when it does not mean a country.

अयनं च ॥ २५ ॥ पदानि ॥ अयनम्, च ॥

वृत्तिः ॥ अन्तरदेशइति वर्त्तते । अयननकारस्य चान्तः शब्दादुत्तरस्य णकारादेशो भवति ।

25. The न of अयन is changed to ण, when preceded by the word अन्तर्, and the word does not denote a country.

Thus अन्तरयणं शोभनम् ॥ Why do we say "not denoting a country"? Observe अन्तरयनो देशः ॥ This ण change would have taken place by VIII. 4. 29, this special sûtra is for अदेश purposes. The word अयन is formed by ल्युट् added to अय् or इण् ॥

छन्दस्यृदवग्रहात् ॥ २६ ॥ पदानि ॥ छन्दसि, ऋत्-अवग्रहात् ॥

वृत्तिः ॥ ऋकारान्तादवग्रहात्पूर्वपदादुत्तरस्य णकारादेशो भवति छन्दसि विषये ।

26. In the Chhandas, न of a second term is changed into ण, when the prior term ends with a short ऋ even when there is an *avagraha* or hiatus between the two terms.

In the Veda, न् becomes ण्, after a ऋ, after which in Padapâṭha, the word appertaining to it is divided. Thus in Pada-pâṭha the words नृमणाः &c, are separated, and are read as नृ, मणाः ॥ The word अवगृह्यते = विच्छिद्य पठ्यते, as in Pada-pâṭha. ऋदवग्रहात् means 'after a short ऋ which is an avagraha'. The ऋ here, of course, means 'a word *ending* in ऋ', because ऋ *alone* cannot be a pûrvapada. The णत्व took place during sanhitâ, and in Pada reading this ण would not have remained, hence this sûtra.

Why have we used the word avagraha in the sûtra? Because we have already said that the word sanhitâ governs all sûtras of this chapter. So the न is changed to ण in the Sanhitâ state in these; and the ण is retained, when in the state of avagraha. The word avagraha in the sûtra indicates the scope of the rule. The न is changed to ण after that ऋ only, which is capable of avagraha, namely that ऋ which stands at the *end* of a *word* (pada), and not that which is in the body of a word. Thus in नृमणाः, पितृयाणम्, the ऋ is capable of avagraha, as it is at the end of a word नृ or पितृ; but when it is not at the end of a word, it can never become avagraha, and will not produce the ण change.

The word पूर्वपदात् is understood here. The word अवग्रह means a hiatus or separation. Thus पितृ याणम्, नृ मणाः ॥ Here ऋ is अवगृह्य ॥ The change of न into ण is effected ordinarily then, when the terms, one containing the cause, and the other न, are in संहिता or conjunction. For the rules of Sandhi and the rules like these can apply only to words in saṅhitâ. The present rule is an exception to it, and here, even when the words are not in संहिता, but there is an actual hiatus between the two, the change still takes place. The word संहिता of VIII. 2. 108, exerts regulating influence upto the end of the Book.

नश्च धातुस्थोरुषुभ्यः ॥ २७ ॥ पदानि ॥ नः, च, धातुस्थ, उरु, षुभ्यः ॥

वृत्तिः ॥ नस् इत्येतस्य नकारस्य णकारादेशो भवति धातुस्थान्निमित्तादुत्तरस्योरुशब्दात्षुशब्दाच्च च्छन्दसि विषये ।

27. In the Chhandas, the न of (the Pronoun) नस् is changed into ण, when it comes after a root having a र or ष or after the words उरु and षु (सु) ॥

Thus अग्ने रक्षाणः (Rig VII. 15. 13) 'O Agni! protect us'. शिक्षा णो अस्मिन् (Rig. VII. 32. 26) 'Teach us this'. उरुः—उरुणस्कृधि (Rig. VIII. 75. 11) षु—अभीषुणः सखीनाम्) Rig IV. 31. 3). ऊर्ध्व ऊषुणः ऊतये (Rig. I. 36. 13).

The word नस् is here the pronoun नस्, which is the substitute, in certain cases, of अस्मद् (VIII. 1. 21) and does not mean here the नस् substitute of नासिका॥ In the next sûtra, however, both नस् are taken. धातुस्थ means 'that which exists in a dhâtu', namely र् and ष् when occurring in a root. The word उरु means the word-form उरु; and षु means सुञ्, and is exhibited with ष-change. It does not mean the affix सु of the Locative Plural. Therefore, not here इन्द्रो धता गृहेषु नः ॥ The word रक्षा is the 2rd Person singular, Imperative, the lengthening is by VI. 3. 135. The root शिक्ष् has the sense of ज्ञान in the Veda. कृधी is 2nd Person sg. Imperative of कृ (VI. 4. 102), the visarga of नः is changed to स् by VIII. 3. 50. In अभीषु there is lengthening by VI. 3. 134: so also in ऊषुणः &c.

उपसर्गाद्बहुलम् ॥ २८ ॥ पदानि ॥ उपसर्गात्, बहुलम् ॥

वृत्तिः ॥ उपसर्गस्थान्निमित्तादुत्तरस्य नसो नकारस्य णकारादेशो भवति ।

28. The न of नस् is changed diversely into ण, when it comes after an upasarga having a cause of change.

Thus प्रणः शूद्रः; प्रणसः प्रणो राजा ॥ The change does not sometime take, place, as, प्र नेा क्षुऽच्यतम् ॥

By force of the word बहुलम् the rule applies to secular literature also as distinguished from the Chhandas or sacred Vedic text. Thus प्रणसं मुखं ॥ The word छन्दसि does not govern this sûtra.

In प्रणसं मुखम्, the word नस् is the substitute for नासिका and means 'nose'. See V. 4. 119.

This is not the sûtra as given by Pâṇini. His sûtra is उपसर्गान्नोत्परः "after an Upasarga, the न of नस् when not preceded by or followed by an ओ, is changed into ण्". There being several objections to this rule, the above rule is substituted as an amendment, in the Mahâbhâshya. For ओत्परः may have two meanings:—(1) ओकारात् परः, that which comes after ओ; (2) ओकारः परोऽस्मात् that which is followed by ओ ॥ In both cases, the rule is objectionable. In the first case, the ण change would be required in प्रनो क्षुऽच्यतं; in the second case, there should be no ण change in प्रणोवनिर्वेवता ॥ In fact, we find in the Vedas प्रणः as well as प्रनः, so also प्रणो as well as प्रनो ॥ Hence the necessity of this amendment.

कृत्यचः ॥ २९ ॥ पदानि ॥ कृति, अच ॥

वृत्तिः ॥ कृत्स्थो यो नकारो ऽच उत्तरस्योपसर्गस्थान्निमित्तादुत्तरस्य णकारादेशो भवति ।
वार्त्तिकः ॥ कृत्स्थस्य णत्वे निर्विण्णस्योपसंख्यानं कर्त्तव्यम् ।

29. The न् of a Kṛit affix, preceded by a vowel, is changed into ण, when it follows an upasarga having the cause of change.

The following are the specific Kṛit affixes in which this change takes place:—अन (यु), मान (शानच् &c VII. 2. 82), अनीय, (III. 1. 96) अनि, (III. 3. 111) इनि (णिनि III. 2. 78 &c) and the substitutes of निष्ठा (VIII. 2. 42) ॥

Thus

अनः	प्रयाणम्, परिमाणम्, प्रमाणम्, परियाणम् ॥	मानः	प्रयायमाणम्, परियायमाणम् ॥
अनीय	प्रयाणीयम्, परियाणीयम् ॥	अनि	अप्रयाणि, अपरियाणि ॥
इनि	प्रयायिन्, प्रयायिणौ, परियायिन्, परियायिणौ		

निष्ठादेशः प्रहीण,: परिहीणः, प्रहीणवान् परिहीणवान् ॥ Long ई by VI. 4. 66.

Why do we say अचः 'preceded by a vowel?' Observe प्रभुग्नः, परिभुग्नः the Nishṭhâ of भुज् ॥ It is thus formed: भुज् + क्त = भुज् + त = भुज् + न (VII. 2. 45, the root भुज् is read as भुजो कौटिल्ये in the dhatûpâṭha, having an indicatory ओ, thus giving scope to the rule). भुज् + न = भुग् + न (VIII. 2. 30) = भुग्न ॥

Vârt:—The word निर्विण्णः should be enumerated in this place. As निर्विण्णोऽस्मि खलसंगेन ॥ निर्विण्णोऽहमत्रवासेन ॥

णेर्विभाषा ॥ ३० ॥ पदानि ॥ णेः, विभाषा ॥

वृत्तिः ॥ ण्यन्ताद्यो विहितः कृत्प्रत्ययः तत्स्थस्य नकारस्योपसर्गस्थान्निमित्तादुत्तरस्य विभाषा णकारादेशो भवति

30. The न् of a Krit-affix ordained after a causative verb (ण्यन्त), is optionally changed to ण्, when it comes after an upasarga having a cause of change.

Thus प्रयापणम् or प्रयापनम्, परियापणम् or परियापनम्, प्रयाप्यमाणम् or प्रयाप्यमानम्, प्रयापणीयम् or प्रयापनीयं, अप्रयापणिः or अप्रयापनिः, प्रयापिणौ or प्रयापिनौ ॥

Why have we used the word विहितं 'ordained' in explaining the sûtra? Because the change takes place, even where the कृत् affix does not follow directly after the affix णि; where a third affix such as यक् intervenes. As प्रयाप्यमाणम् ॥ The णेः being in the ablative, under the ordinary rule of interpretation (I. 1. 72), the krit-affix should come immediately after णि.

हलश्चेजुपधात् ॥ ३१ ॥ पदानि ॥ हलः, च, इच्-उपधात् ॥

वृत्तिः ॥ हलादिर्यो धातुरिजुपधस्तस्मात्परो यः कृत्प्रत्ययः तस्स्थस्य नकारस्याच उत्तरस्योपसर्गस्थान्निमित्तादुत्तरस्य विभाषा णकारादेशो भवति ।

31. A krit-affix, coming after a verb, which begins with a consonant and has a penultimate इच् vowel, changes optionally its न्, which is preceded by a vowel, into ण्, when it comes after an upasarga having a cause of change.

The phrase कृत्यचः is understood here. Thus प्रकोपणम् or प्रकोपनम्, परिकोपणम् or परिकोपनम् ॥

Why do we say हलः 'beginning with a consonant'? Observe प्रेहणम् and परीहणम् where the change is obligatory, under VIII. 4. 29. These are from ईह चेष्टायाम् and ऊह वितर्के ॥

Why do we say इजुपधात् 'having a penultimate इच् vowel'? Observe प्रवपणम् and परिवपणम्; no option.

By the rule कृत्यचः the change was obligatory, this rule makes it optional.

The न of the krit-affix must come after a vowel, otherwise there will be no change. See परिभुग्नः

The word हलः in the sûtra should be interpreted as हलादेः, and not as ordinarily "after what ends in हल्" ॥ For an इजुपधा verb implies that it ends with a consonant, and so the employment of the word हलः in the text would have been useless had it meant हलन्तात् ॥

इजादेः सनुमः ॥ ३२ ॥ पदानि ॥ इजादेः, सनुमः ॥

वृत्तिः ॥ इजादेः सनुमो हलन्ताद्धातोर्विहितो यः कृत्तस्थस्य नकारस्योपसर्गस्थान्निमित्तादुत्तरस्य णकारो भवति ।

32. A krit-affix ordained after a verb beginning with an इच् vowel, having the augment नुम् in it, and ending

with a consonant, changes its न् into ण, when preceded by an upasarga having in it the cause of change.

The word हल: of the last sûtra is understood here. But contrary to the construction put upon it in the last sûtra, here it means हलन्तात्, by the natural rule of construction as given in I. 1. 72. We must interpret it so here, because it is impossible for an इजादि root to commence with a हल्; while to have done so in the last aphorism would have been redundant.

Thus प्रेङ्खणम्, परेङ्खणम् from इखि गत्यर्थः; the नुम् is added because it is इदित् ॥ प्रेङ्गणम्, परेङ्गणम्, प्रोम्भणम् परोम्भणम् ॥ In उम्भ पूरणे the nasal is part of the root. The rule will not apply to प्रेन्वनम्, because नुम् here means the anusvâra generally (VIII. 4. 2) though the change would have been valid by the general rule, (VIII. 4. 29) this sûtra makes a नियम or restriction. That is, only in the case of इजादि सनुम् verbs the change takes place, not in other सनुम् verbs. Thus प्रमङ्गनम, परिमङ्गनम from the root मगि सर्पणे ॥

This rule does not affect rule VIII. 4. 30, relating to ण्यन्त verbs, for those verbs cannot be said to end with a consonant. Moreover, we have used the word विहित: in explaining the sûtra, in order to indicate this fact, that the kṛit-affix must be *ordained* after a consonant-ending verb. In the case of causative verbs, the kṛit-affix is *ordained* after a vowel-ending (णि) verb, and the vowel is elided *after* the adding of the affix. So that *before* the adding of the affix, the verb did not end in a consonant.

वा निंसनिक्षनिन्दाम् ॥ ३३ ॥ पदानि ॥ वा, निंस-निक्ष-निन्दाम् ॥

वृत्तिः ॥ उपसर्गादितिवर्त्तते । निंस निक्ष निन्द इत्येतेषां नकारस्योपसर्गस्थान्निमित्तादुत्तरस्य वा णकारादेशो भवति ।

33. The न् of निंस निक्ष and निन्द् is changed to ण optionally, when preceded by an upasarga having in it a cause of change.

Thus प्रणिंसनम् or प्रनिंसनम्, प्रणिक्षणम् or प्रनिक्षणम्, प्रणिन्दनम् or प्रनिन्दनम् ॥

These verbs are written with ण in the Dhâtupâṭha, and therefore by rule VIII. 4. 14 ante, the change of न into ण would have been obligatory. The present sûtra makes it optional. The root णिसि means 'to kiss', णिक्षि चुम्बने, and णिदि कुत्सायाम् ॥

न भाभूपूकमिगमिप्यायिवेपाम् ॥ ३४ ॥ पदानि ॥ न, भा-भू-पू-कमि-गमि-प्यायि-वेपाम् ॥

वृत्तिः ॥ भा दीप्तौ भू सत्तायाम् पू पवने कमि कान्तौ गमि गतौ प्यायि वृद्धौ वेप कम्पने इत्येतेषामुपसर्गस्थान्निमित्तादुत्तरस्य कृत्स्थस्य नकारस्य णकारादेशो न भवति ।

वार्त्तिकम् ॥ ण्यन्तानां भादीनामुपसंख्यानं कर्त्तव्यम् ।

34. The न of a kṛit-affix is not changed to ण, though preceded by an upasarga having in it a cause of change,

when the affix is added to the following verbs: भा 'to shine', भू 'to be', पू 'to purify', कमि 'to be brilliant', गमि 'to go', प्यायि 'to increase', वेप 'to shake'.

This rule is an exception to VIII. 4. 29. Thus :—

भा प्रभानम्, परिभानम् भू प्रभवनम्, परिभवनम् पू प्रपवनम्, परिपवनम् ॥

Ishti:—The verb पूञ् is to be taken and not the verb पूङ् ॥ In the case of the latter the change is obligatory, as, प्रपवण सामस्य ॥

कमि प्रकमनम् परिकमनम् ॥ गमि प्रगमनम् परिगमनम् ॥
प्यायि प्रप्यायनम्, परिप्यायनम् ॥ वेप् प्रवेपनम्, परिवेपनम् ॥

Vârt:—The above roots, even when in the Causative, do not change the न of their kṛit-affix. As प्रभापनम्, परिभापनम् ॥

षात्पदान्तात् ॥ ३५ ॥ पदानि ॥ षात्, पदान्तात् ॥

वृत्तिः ॥ षकारात्पदान्तादुत्तरस्य नकारस्य णकारादेशो न भवति ।

35. After a ष् final in a Pada, the न् is not changed to ण् ॥

Thus निष्पानम्, दुष्पानम् ; the visarga is changed to ष् here by VIII. 3. 41. The rule VIII. 4. 29 is debarred. सर्पिष्पानम् (is a genitive compound contra II. 2. 14). So also यजुष्पानम् (II. 1. 32). The ष is in these two by VIII. 3. 45, and VIII. 4. 10 is debarred.

Why do we say "षात् after a ष्?" Observe निर्णयः ॥

Why do we say पदान्तात् 'final in a Pada'? Observe कुष्णाति, पुष्णाति ॥ The word पदान्त is equivalent to पदे अन्त or Locative Tatpurusha ; and does not mean final of a Pada. Therefore the rule does not apply here. सुसर्पिष्केण (ins. sg.) सुयजुष्केण ॥ Here the क is added by V. 4. 154. शोभनं सर्पिरस्य = सुसर्पिष्क (a Bahuvrîhi). The ष is by VIII. 3. 39. Before the affix क, the word सुसर्पिस् is a Pada (I. 4. 17), and thus स (ष्) is final of a Pada: but it is not final of a preceding member *followed* by another Pada. The rule, in fact, applies to compounds, the ष् being final in the first term.

नशेः षान्तस्य ॥ ३६ ॥ पदानि ॥ नशेः, षान्तस्य ॥

वृत्तिः ॥ नशेः षकारान्तस्य णकारादेशो न भवति ।

36. ण् is not the substitute of the verb नश 'to destroy', when ending in ष् ॥

When the श् is changed to ष् in नश्, the न of नश् is not changed. Thus प्रनष्टः, परिनष्टः ॥ The नुम ordained by VII. 1. 60, is elided by VI. 4. 24, and श् changed ष् by VIII. 2. 36.

Why do we say षान्तस्य? Observe प्रणश्यति, परिणश्यति ॥ The word अन्त is taken in order that the prohibition may apply to words like प्रनङ्क्ष्यति, which did end with ष् though the ष has been changed by other rules, and is no longer visible. For here the श् of नश् is changed to ष् by VIII. 2. 36, and then this ष् is changed to क् by VIII. 2. 41 ; and the नुम् is added by VII. 1. 60.

पदान्तस्य ॥ ३७ ॥ पदानि ॥ पदान्तस्य ॥

वृत्तिः ॥ पदान्तो यो नकारस्तस्य णकारादेशो न भवति ।

37. Of a न final in a Pada, ण is not the substitute.

Thus वृक्षान्, प्लक्षान्, अरीन्, गिरीन् ॥

पदव्यवायेपि ॥ ३८ ॥ पदानि ॥ पदव्यवाये, अपि ॥

वृत्तिः ॥ पदेन व्यवायेपि सति निमित्तनिमित्तिनोर्नकारस्य णकारादेशो न भवति ।

वार्त्तिकम् ॥ पदव्यवाये ऽतद्धितइति वक्तव्यम् ।

38. The न् is not changed to ण् when a Pada intervenes between the cause of the change and the word containing the न ॥

The word पदव्यवाय is a compound meaning पदेन व्यवाय 'separated by a Pada'. Thus माषकुम्भवापेन, चतुरङ्गयोगेन, प्रावनद्धम्, पर्यवनद्धम्, प्रगान्नयामः, परिगान्नयामः ॥ Here the Padas कुम्भ, अङ्ग, अव &c, intervening, the change does not take place.

Vârt:—It should be stated when there is separation by a Pada, except in a Taddhita. Prohibition does not apply to words like आर्द्रगोमयेण, शुष्कगोमयेण ॥ Here गो takes the affix मयट् by IV. 3. 145, and the word गो is a Pada by I. 4. 17, and it intervenes between मय and the first word. The author of Mahâbhâshya however does not approve of this Vârtika. According to him the word पदव्यवाय means पदे व्यवाय ॥

क्षुभ्नादिषु च ॥ ३९ ॥ पदानि ॥ क्षुभ्नादिषु, च ॥

वृत्तिः ॥ क्षुभ्ना इत्येवमादिषु शब्देषु नकारस्य णकारादेशो न भवति ।

39. The ण is not the substitute of न् in the words kshubhna &c.

The 'not' of sûtra 34 is to be read into this. Thus क्षुभ्नाति, so also in क्षुभ्नीतः, क्षुभ्नन्ति, the substitutes of श्नम् being like the principal I. 1. 57.

So नृनमनः where the change was called for by VIII. 4. 3, and VIII. 4. 26.

नन्दिन्, नन्दन and नगर when second members in a compound, denoting a name, as, हरिनन्दी, हरिनन्दनः, गिरिनगरः ॥

The word नृत् when taking the Intensive affix यङ्, as, नरीनृत्यते ॥

तृप्नु, तृप्नोति also belongs to this class. नर्तन, गहन, नन्दन, निवेश, निवास, अग्नि and अनूप when used as second terms in a compound. As, परिनर्त्तनम्, परिगहनम्, which required change by VIII. 4. 3. So परिनन्दनम् contrary to VIII. 4. 14. शरनिवेशः, शरनिवास, शराग्निः, दर्भानूपः ॥ All these are Names.

After the word आचार्य there is no change, as, आचार्यभोगीनः, आचार्यानी ॥

इरिका, तिमिर, समीर, कुबेर and हरि and कर्मर followed ,by वन do not cause change in the न of वन when the compound is a Name. This is an आकृतिगणः ॥

1 क्षुभ्ना (क्षुभ्नाति), 2 नृनमन; 3 नन्दिन्, 4 नन्दन, 5 नगर, एतान्युत्तरपदानि संज्ञायां प्र योजयन्ति, 6 हरिनन्दी, 7 हरिनन्दनः, 8 गिरिनगरम्; 9 नृतिर्यङि प्रयोजयाति, नरीनृत्यते; 10 नर्तन, 11 गहन,

12 नन्दन, 13 निवेश, 14 निवास, 15 अग्नि, 16 अनूप, एतान्युत्तरपदानि प्र योजयन्ति, 17 परिनर्तनम्, 18 परिगहनम, 19 परिनन्दनम्, 20 शरनिवेश:, 21 शरनिवास:, 22 शराग्नि:, 23 दर्भानूप:, 24 आचार्यावणत्वं च आचार्यभोगीन: (आचार्यानी). क्षुभ्ना, 25 तृप्नु, नृनमन, 26 नरनगर, नन्दन- यङ् नृती, 27 गिरिनदी. 28 गृहनमन, निवेश, निवास, अग्नि, अनूप, आचार्यभोगीन, 29 चतुर्हायन, 30 इरिकादीनि वनोत्तरपदानि संज्ञायाम्। इरिका, तिमिर, समीर, कुबेर, हरि कर्मार. अकृतिगण.

स्तोः श्चुना श्चुः ॥ ४० ॥ पदानि ॥ स्तोः, श्चुना, श्चुः ॥

वृत्तिः ॥ सकारतवर्गयोः शकारचवर्गाभ्यां सन्निपाते शकारचवर्गादेशौ भवतः ।

40. The letters स and the dentals when coming in contact with श and the palatals, are changed to श and palatals respectively.

The rule of यथासंख्य does not apply here with regard to first part स्तो श्चुना ॥ The स in contact with श is changed to श but it is also so changed when in contact with letters of च class. Similarly letters of त class coming in contact with श or a letter of च class, are changed to च class. The rule of यथासंख्यं, however, applies to the substitutes, namely स is changed to श, and तु to चु ॥

1st. स in contact with शः as, वृक्षस् + शेते = वृक्षश्शेते, so also प्लक्षश्शेते ॥

2nd. स in contact with चुः—as, वृक्षस् + चिनोति = वृक्षश्चिनोति, प्लक्षश्चिनोति, वृक्षश्छादयति, प्लक्षश्छादयति ॥

3rd. तु with शः—अग्निचित् + शेते = अग्निचिच्छेते, so सोमसुच्छेते ॥

4th. तु with चुः—अग्निचित् + चिनोति = अग्निचिच् चिनोति, so also सोमसुच्चिनोति, अग्निचिच्छादयति, अग्निचिज्जयति, अग्निचिज् झकारम्, सोमसुच्छादयति, सोमसुञ्जयति, सोमसुज्झकारम्, अग्निचिज्जकारः, सोमसुज्जकारः ॥ Similarly मस्ज् gives मज्जति, the स is changed to द् by झलां जश् झशि VIII. 4. 53, and then this द् is changed to a palatal i. e. to ज् here; and द् obtained by जश् rule is not considered asiddha here. See VIII. 2. 3. So also from भ्रस्ज we have भृज्जति ॥

5th. चकार followed by नकारः as, यज + न (III. 3. 90) = यज + ञ = यज्ञः, याच् + न = याच्ञा ॥ In fact the instrumental case श्चुना shows that the mere contact of स and तु with श and चु is enough to induce the change, whether स्तु is followed by श्चु, or श्चु be followed by स्तु ॥ Other examples of mere contact are :—

5th.(a) स followed by चु is changed into शःas, भ्रस्ज् + ति = भृस्ज् + श + ति (III. 1. 77, VI. 1. 16) = भृस्ज + ति = भृश्ज + ति = (VIII. 4. 53) = भृज्जति ॥ Similarly मस्ज forms मज्जति, व्रश्च forms वृश्चति ॥

The aphorism शात् (VIII. 4. 44) which prohibits the change of तु into चु when following the letter श, indicates by implication that the rule of mutual correspondence according to the order of enumeration (I. 3. 10) does not hold good here.

Had the sûtra been स्तो श्चोः श्चुः i. e. instead of instrumental, had there been the locative case, then the rule would not have applied to cases covered by the fifth clause.

ष्टुना ष्टुः ॥ ४१ ॥ पदानि ॥ ष्टुना, ष्टुः ॥

वृत्तिः ॥ सकारतवर्गयोः षकारटवर्गाभ्यां संनिपाते षकारटवर्गावादेशौ भवतः ।

41. The letters स् and dentals in contact with ष् and cerebrals, are changed into ष and cerebrals respectively.

The word स्तोः is to be read into the sûtra. Here also there is absence of mutual correspondence according to the order of enumeration.

(1) स with ष as, वृक्षस् + षण्डे = वृक्षष्षण्डे; प्लक्षष्षण्डे ॥

(2) स with टु, as, वृक्षस + टीकते = वृक्षष्टीकते, वृक्षष्ठकारः, प्लक्षष्टीकते and प्लक्षष्ठकारः ॥

(3) तु with ष as पेष् + ता = पेष्टा, पेष्टुम्, पेष्टव्यम्, कृषीष्ट, कृषीष्ठाः (Atmane, Aorist 2nd per dual).

(4) तु with टु, as, अग्निचित् + टीकते = अग्निचिट्टीकते, सोमसुट्टीकते, अग्निचिट्ठकारः, अग्निचिड् डीनः, अग्निचिड्ढौकते, अग्निचिण्णकार, सोमसुट्ठकारः, सोमसुड्डीनः, सोमसुड्ढौकते, सोमसुण् णकारः ॥

The root अतृट अतिक्रमणाहिंसयोः, and अदृड अभियोगे, are read in the Dhâtupâṭha with त् and द् penultimate, in order that when the affix क्विप् is added to them, the final ट and ड being elided by संयोगान्त rule, the derivatives will be अत् and अद् ending in त् and द् ॥ Another reason is that the sûtra VI. 1. 3, should apply to their reduplicate. In these roots the त and द are changed, as अट्टति and अड्डति ॥

न पदान्ताट्टोरनाम् ॥ ४२ ॥ पदानि ॥ न, पदान्तात्, टोः, अनाम् ॥

वृत्तिः ॥ पदान्ताट्टवर्गादुत्तरस्य स्तोः ष्टुत्वं न भवति नामित्येतद्वर्जयित्वा ।

वार्त्तिकम् ॥ अनाम्नवतिनगरीणामिति वक्तव्यम् ।

42. After टु final in a Pada, the change of a dental (स्तु) to a cerebral (ष्टु), does not take place, except in the case of the affix नाम् ॥

Thus श्वलिट् + साये = श्वलिट्साये, मधुलिट्साये, श्वलिट्तरति, मधुलिट्तरति ॥

Why do we say पदान्तात् 'final in a Pada'? Observe ईड् + ते = ईड् + टे = ईड्टे ॥

Why do we say टोः 'after टु'? Observe सर्पिष् + तमम् = सर्पिष्टमम् ॥

Why do we say अनाम् 'except in the case of the affix nâm'? Observe षड् + नाम् = षण्णाम् ॥ This exception is very inadequate. Hence the following

Vârt:—It should be stated rather that नवति and नगरी as well as नाम् are not prevented from undergoing the cerebral change. As, षण्णाम् 'of six', षण्णवतिः ninety-six, and षण्णगरी 'six cities'.

तोः षि ॥ ४३ ॥ पदानि ॥ तोः, षि ॥

वृत्तिः ॥ तवर्गस्य षकारे यदुक्तं तन्न भवति ।

43. In the room of तु there is not a cerebral substitute, when ष follows.

The word न is to be read into the aphorism. As, अग्निचित् + षण्डे = अग्निचित्षण्डे ॥ भवान्षण्डे, महान्षण्डे ॥

शात् ॥ ४४ ॥ पदानि ॥ शात् ॥

वृत्तिः ॥ शकारादुत्तरस्य तवर्गस्य यदुक्तं तन्न भवति ।

44. In the room of तु there is not a palatal substitute, when श precedes.

The words न and श्चुः are understood here. This is an exception to VIII. 4. 40. Thus, प्रच्छ + न (III. 3. 90) = प्रश् + न (VI. 4. 19) = प्रश्नः, विश्नः &c.

यरोऽनुनासिकेऽनुनासिको वा ॥ ४५ ॥ पदानि ॥ यरः, अनुनासिके, अनुनासिकः, वा ॥

वृत्तिः ॥ यरः पदान्तस्यानुनासिके परतो वानुनासिकादेशो भवति ।

वार्त्तिकम् ॥ यरोऽनुनासिके प्रत्यये भाषायां नित्यवचनं कर्त्तव्यम् ।

45. In the room of a यर letter (every consonant except ह final) in a Pada, when a Nasal follows, there is optionally a Nasal substitute.

The word पदान्त is understood here. Thus वाक् + नयति = वाग्नयति or वाङ्नयति, अग्निचिद्नयति or अग्निचिन्नयति, विड्नयति or विण्नयति, श्वलिण्नयति or श्वलिड्नयति ॥

Why do we say 'final in a Pada'? Observe, वेद् + मि = वेद्मि ॥ Here there is no option. So also क्षुभ्नाति ॥

Vârt:—When it is a pratyaya or affix that follows, the nasalisation is obligatory in the secular language. Thus वाक् + मात्रम् = वाङ्मात्रम्, कियन्मात्रम् ॥ It is, however, only before the affixes मय and मात्र that the change is obligatory, and not before every affix beginning with a nasal.'

अचो रहाभ्यां द्वे ॥ ४६ ॥ पदानि ॥ अचः, रहाभ्यां, द्वे ॥

वृत्तिः ॥ अच उत्तरौ यौ रेफहकारौ ताभ्यामुत्तरस्य यरो द्वे भवतः ।

46. There is reduplication of यर्, i. e. all the consonants except ह, after the letters र् and ह् following a vowel.

The word यर् of last sûtra is understood here. According to others, the वा is also understood, and this is an optional rule. Thus अर्क्कः, मर्क्कः, ब्रह्म्मा, अपह्न्नुते ॥

Why do we say अचः 'following a vowel'? Observe ह्नुते, ह्मलयति ॥

अनचि च ॥ ४७ ॥ पदानि ॥ अन्, अचि, च ॥

वृत्तिः ॥ अच उत्तरस्य यरो द्वे भवतोऽनचि परतः ।

वार्त्तिकम् ॥ यणो मयो द्वे भवत इति वक्तव्यम् ।

वा० ॥ शरः खयो द्वे भवत इति वक्तव्यम् । वा० ॥ अवसाने च यरो द्वे भवतः इति वक्तव्यम् ।

47. When a vowel does not follow, there is reduplication of यर् (all the consonants except ह), after a vowel.

The words अचः and यरः are understood here.

Thus दधि + अत्र = दध्य् + अत्र (VI. 1. 77) = दध्ध्य् + अत्र दद्ध्य् + अत्र (VIII. 4. 53) = दद्ध्यत्र, so also मद्ध्वत्र ॥

Why do we say अचः "after a vowel?" Observe स्मितम्, स्मातम् ॥

Vârt:—यणो मयो द्वे भवतः ॥ This Vârtika may be interpreted in two ways. First taking यणः as ablative and मयः as genitive. "The letters of the pratyâhâra मय् are reduplicated after यण् letters." उल्क्का, वाल्म्मीकः ॥ Secondly taking यणः as genitive, and मयः as ablative. "The letters यण् are reduplicated after मय् letters". As दध्य्यत्र, मध्व्वत्र ॥

Vârt:—शरः खयो द्वे भवतः ॥ This is also similarly explained in two ways. 1st "There is reduplication of खय् letters, after a sibilant for शर् letters". as स्थ्थाल, स्थ्थात. Secondly. 'There is reduplication of a sibilant (शर् letters), after खय् letters, ss, वत्स्सरः, अप्स्सराः ॥

Vârt:—अवसाने च यरो द्वे भवतः ॥ There is reduplication of यर् when a Pause ensues. As वाक्क्, त्वक्क्, षट्ट्, तत्त् &c.

These reduplications are curiosities, rather than practicalities.

नादिन्याक्रोशे पुत्रस्य ॥ ४८ ॥ पदानि ॥ न, आदिनी, आक्रोशे, पुत्रस्य ॥

वृत्तिः ॥ आदिनी परत आक्रोशे गम्यमाने पुत्रशब्दस्य न द्वे भवतः ।

वार्त्तिकम् ॥ तत्परे चेति वक्तव्यम् । वा० ॥ वा हतजग्धपरइति वक्तव्यम् ।

वा० ॥ चयो द्वितीयाः शरि पौष्करसादेः ।

48. There is not reduplication of the letters of 'putra', when the word âdinî follows, the sense being that of reviling or cursing.

This debars the reduplication required by the last sûtra. Thus पुत्रादिनी त्वमसि पापे "O sinful one! thou art eater of thy own son". Here the word पुत्रादिनी is used simply as an abusive epithet. But when a fact is described, and the word is not used as an abuse or आक्रोश, the reduplication takes place. Thus पुत्त्रादिनी व्याघ्री 'a kind of tigress, that eats up her young ones'. = शिशुमारी व्याघ्री ॥

Vârt:—So also when पुत्र is followed by पुत्रादिनी ॥ As पुत्र पुत्रादिनी त्वमसि पापे ॥ So also पुत्रपौत्रादिनी ॥

Vârt:—Optionally so when the words हत and जग्ध follow. As पुत्रहती or पुत्त्रहती, पुत्रजग्धी or पुत्त्रजग्धी ॥

Vârt:—According to the option of Âchârya Paushkarasâdi, the letters of चय् pratyâhâra are replaced by the second letters of their class, when followed by a sibilant (a letter of शर् pratyâhâra).

As वत्सः becomes वथ्सः अक्षरम् becomes अख्षरम् and अप्सरा becomes अफ्सरा ॥

शरोऽचि ॥ ४६ ॥ पदानि ॥ शरः, अचि ॥

वृत्तिः ॥ शरोऽचि परतो न द्वे भवतः ।

49. There are not two in the room of a sibilant (शर्), when a vowel follows.

The word न is to be read into the sûtra. This debars the application of rule 46 *ante*. Thus कर्षति, वर्षति, आकर्षः, अक्षदर्शः ॥

Why do we say अचि 'when a vowel follows? Observe दर्श्यते ॥

त्रिप्रभृतिषु शाकटायनस्य ॥ ५० ॥ पदानि ॥ त्रिप्रभृतिषु, शाकटायनस्य ॥

वृत्तिः ॥ त्रिप्रभृतिषु वर्णेषु संयुक्तेषु शाकटायनस्याचार्यस्य मतेन न भवति ।

50. According to the option of Śâkaṭâyana, the doubling does not take place when the conjunct consonants are three or more in number.

As इन्द्रः, चन्द्रः, उष्ट्रः, राष्ट्रम्, भ्राष्ट्रम् ॥

सर्वत्र शाकल्यस्य ॥ ५१ ॥ पदानि ॥ सर्वत्र, शाकल्यस्य ॥

वृत्तिः ॥ शाकल्याचार्यस्य मतेन सर्वत्र द्विर्वचनं न भवति ।

51. According to the opinion of Śâkalya, there is reduplication no where.

As अर्कः, मर्कः, ब्रह्मा, अपह्नुते ॥

दीर्घादाचार्याणाम् ॥ ५२ ॥ पदानि ॥ दीर्घात्, आचार्य्याणाम् ॥

वृत्तिः ॥ दीर्घादुत्तरस्याचार्याणां मतेन न भवति ।

52. According to the opinion of all Teachers, there is no doubling after a long vowel.

As दात्रम्, पात्रम्, मूत्रम्, सूत्रम् ॥

झलां जश् झशि ॥ ५३ ॥ पदानि ॥ झलाम्, जश्, झशि ॥

वृत्तिः ॥ झलां स्थाने जशादेशो भवति झशि परतः ।

53. In the room of झल् letters, there is substitution of जश् letters, when झश् letters follow.

A mute letter is changed to a sonant non-aspirate mute, when a sonant mute follows it.

This is the well-known rule of softening the hard letters. Thus लभ्+ता=लब्धा, so also लब्धुम्, लब्धव्यम् ; दोग्धा, दोग्धुम्, दोग्धव्यम् ; बोद्धा, बोद्धुम्, बोद्धव्यम् ॥

Why do we say झशि, 'when a jhaś follows'? Observe दत्तः, दत्थः, दध्मः ॥

अभ्यासे चर्च ॥ ५४ ॥ पदानि ॥ अभ्यासे, चर्, च ॥

वृत्तिः ॥ अभ्यासे वर्त्तमानानां झलां चरादेशो भवति चकाराज्जश्च ।

54. The चर् is also the substitute of झल् letters occuring in a reduplicate syllable, as well as जश् ॥

In a reduplicate syllable, a sonant non-aspirate (जश्) as well as a surd non aspirate (चर्) is the substitute of a Mute letter. By applying the rule of 'nearest in place (I. 1. 50), we find that sonant non-aspirate (जश्) is the substitute of all sonants; and is the substitute of all surds. In other words all aspirate letters become non-aspirate. The word जश् has been drawn into the sûtra by the word च 'also'.

Thus चिखनिषति ॥ Here सन् (Desiderative), is added to the root खन्, the ख is changed to छ by VII. 4. 62, and this aspirate छ is now changed to non-aspirate by the present sûtra. चिच्छिषति, टिठकारयिषति, तिष्ठासति, पिफकारयिषति, बुभूषति, जिघत्सति, डुढौकिषते ॥

If there is चर् (non-aspirate surd) in the original, it will remain of course unchanged. As, चिचीषति, टिटीकिषते, तितनिषति ॥

The original जश् also remains unchanged. Thus जिजनिषति, बुबुधे, ददौ, डिड्ये ॥ Or to be more accurate a चर् is replaced by a चर् and a जश् by a जश् letter.

खरि च ॥ ५५ ॥ पदानि ॥ खरि, च ॥

वृत्तिः ॥ खरि च परतो झलां चरादेशो भवति ।

55. In the room of झल्, there is the substitute चर्, when खर् follows.

A sonant non-aspirate mute is the substitute of a mute, when a surd mute or a sibilant follows. The words झलां and चरः are supplied from the last sûtra. Thus भेद्+ता=भेत्ता, भेत्तुम्, भेत्तव्यम्; युयुध्+सते=युयुत्सते; आरिप्सते, आलिप्सते from रभ् and लभ्, the इस् is added by VII. 4. 54, in the room of अ of रभ् and लभ्, and we have रिम्भ्स् and लिम्भ्स् then the first स is elided by VIII. 2. 29.

वावसाने ॥ ५६ ॥ पदानि ॥ वा, अवसाने ॥

वृत्तिः ॥ झलां चरिति वर्त्तते । अवसाने वर्त्तमानानां झलां वा चरादेशो भवति ।

56. The चर् is optionally the substitute of a झल् that occurs in a Pause.

The words झलां चर् is understood in the sûtra. A sonant or a surd non-aspirate may stand as final in a Pause: but not an aspirate consonant. By VIII. 2. 39, a non-aspirate sonant can only stand in a final position. This ordains that a non-aspirate surd may also stand as the final, when there is Pause. Thus वाक् or वाग्, त्वक् or त्वग्, श्वलिट् or श्वलिड्, त्रिष्टुप् or त्रिष्टुब् ॥

अणोऽप्रगृह्यस्यानुनासिकः ॥ ५७ ॥ पदानि ॥ अणः, अप्रगृह्यस्य, अनुनासिकः ॥

वृत्तिः ॥ अणः अप्रगृह्यसंज्ञस्यावसाने वर्त्तमाने वानुनासिकादेशो भवति ।

57. The anunâsika is optionally the substitute of an अण् vowel which occurs in a Pause, and is not a Pragṛihya.

अ, इ and उ, short and long, may, when final in a Pause, be pronounced as nasals, provided that they are not Pragṛihya (I. 1. 11 &c.) The अण् here is a Pratyâhâra with the first णॣ ॥ Thus दधिँ or दधि, मधुँ or मधु, कुमारीँ or कुमारी ॥

Why do we say 'of an अण् vowel?" Observe, कर्तृ, हर्तृ ॥

Why do we say 'which is not a pragṛihya'? Observe अग्नी, वायू which are pragṛihya by I. 1. 11.

अनुस्वारस्य ययि परसवर्णः ॥ ५८ ॥ पदानि ॥ अनुस्वारस्य, ययि, परसवर्णः ॥

वृत्तिः ॥ अनुस्वारस्य ययि परतः परसवर्ण आदेशो भवति ।

58. In the room of anusvâra, when यय् follows, a letter homogeneous with the latter is substituted.

Thus शङ्किता, शङ्कितुम्, शङ्कितव्यम्, उञ्छिता, कुण्डिता, नन्दिता, कम्पिता &c. These are from roots शकि शङ्कायाम्, उछि उञ्छे, कुडि दाहे, टुनदि समृद्धौ, कपि चलने ॥ Here नुम् is is added because they are इदित्, and this न् becomes anusvâra by VIII. 3. 24, and this anusvâra is changed to ङ् when followed by a guttural क् &c, to ञ् when followed by a palatal च &c, and so on to ण्, न् and म् ॥

Why do we say when यय् follows'? Observe आक्रंस्यते, आचिक्रंस्यते ॥

In कुर्वन्ति, वृषन्ति, the न is not changed into ण, though required by VIII. 4. 2. Because the णत्व is asiddha, and therefore by the prior rule VIII. 3. 24, the न is first changed into anusvâra (VIII. 2. 1). That anusvâra is again changed into न by the present rule, न being homogeneous with त ॥ This change again being असिद्ध as if it had never taken place (VIII. 2. 1), the ण is never substituted for न ॥

वा पदान्तस्य ॥ ५९ ॥ पदानि ॥ वा, पदान्तस्य ॥

वृत्तिः ॥ पदान्तस्यानुस्वारस्य ययि परतो वा परसवर्णादेशो भवति ।

59. In the room of anusvâra final in a Pada, the substitution of a letter homogeneous with the latter is optional.

Thus तं कथं चित्रपक्षं डयमानं नभःस्थं पुरुषोऽवधीत् or तङ्कथञ्चित्रपक्षण्डयमानन्नभःस्थम्पुरुषोऽवधीत् ॥

तोर्लि ॥ ६० ॥ पदानि ॥ तोः, लि ॥

वृत्तिः ॥ तवर्गस्य लकारे परतः परसवर्णादेशो भवति ।

60. In the room of तु (a dental) when the letter ल follows, one homogeneous with the latter is substituted.

Thus अग्निचित् + लुनाति = अग्निचिल्लुनाति, सोमसुल्लुनाति; भवान् + लुनाति = भवाँल्लुनाति, महाँल्लुनाति ॥ Here त has been changed to pure ल, while the dento-nasal न् is changed to a nasal लँ ॥

उदः स्थास्तम्भोः पूर्वस्य ॥ ६१ ॥ पदानि ॥ उदः, स्था स्तम्भोः, पूर्वस्य ॥

वृत्तिः ॥ उद उत्तरयोः स्था स्तम्भ इत्येतयोः पूर्वसवर्णादेशो भवति ।

वार्त्तिकम् ॥ उदः पूर्वसवर्णत्वे स्कन्देश्छन्दस्युपसंख्यानम् । वा० ॥ रोगे चेति वक्तव्यम् ।

61. After उद्, in the room of the स of sthâ and stambha, the substitute is a letter belonging to the class of the prior (i. e. a dental is substituted for this स) ॥

As उद् + स्थाता = उद् + थ्थाता = उद् + थाता (VIII. 4. 65) = उत् + थाता (VIII. 4. 55) = उत्थाता, उत्थातुम्, उत्थातव्यम् ॥ So also with स्तम्भ्, as, उत्तम्भिता, उत्तम्भितुम् &c. (See I. 1. 67 and 54).

Why do we say of स्था and स्तम्भ? Compare उत्स्नात ॥

Vârt:—In the Vedas, the above substitution takes place in the case of स्कन्द् preceded by उद् ॥ As, अग्ने दूरमुत्कन्दः ॥

Vârt:—So also when it means a disease. As उत्कन्दको नाम रोगः ॥ Or this form may have been derived from the root कन्द्, and not स्कन्द ॥

झयो होन्यतरस्याम् ॥ ६२ ॥ पदानि ॥ झयः, हः, अन्यतरस्याम् ॥

वृत्तिः ॥ झय उत्तरस्य हकारस्य पूर्वसवर्णादेशो भवति अन्यतरस्याम् ।

62. In the room of the letter ह, after (a sonant Mute) there is optionally a letter homogeneous with the prior.

The pratyâhâra झय् includes *all* Mutes. But practically sonant Mutes are only taken here.

As वाक् + हसति = वाग्घसति or वाग् हसति, श्वलिड्ढसति or हसति, अग्निचिद् धसति or हसति, त्रिष्टुब भसति or हसति, सोमसुद् धसति or सोमसुद् हसति ॥

Why do we say झयः 'after a sonant Mute?' Observe प्राङ् हसति, भवान् हसति ॥

शश्छोटि ॥ ६३ ॥ पदानि ॥ शः, छः, अटि ॥

वृत्तिः ॥ झय इति वर्त्तते । अन्यतरस्यामिति च । झय उत्तरस्य शकारस्याटि परतश्छकारादेशो भवति अन्यतरस्याम् ।

वार्त्तिकम् ॥ छत्वममीति वक्तव्यम् ।

63. In the room of श preceded by a surd Mute, there is optionally the letter छ् when a vowel or य, व or र follows such श ॥

Though झय् means all Mutes, the rule, however, applies to surd mutes. The words झय् and अन्यतरस्यां are to be read into the sûtra. Thus वाक् + शेते = वाक्छेते or °शेते ॥ अग्निचिच्छेते or अग्निचित् शेते, श्वलिट् शेते or छेते, त्रिष्टुप्छेते or शेते ॥

Vârt:—It should rather be stated when a letter of अम् pratyâhâra follows. The sûtra only gives अट् letters, the vârtika adds the letters ल, and the nasals. Thus तत् श्लोकेन = तच् छ्लोकेन, तच्छ्मश्रुणा ॥

हलो यमां यमि लोपः ॥ ६४ ॥ पदानि ॥ हलः, यमाम्, यमि, लोपः ॥

वृत्तिः ॥ हल उत्तरेषां यमां यमि परतो लोपो भवति अन्यतरस्याम् ।

64. After a consonant, the following semi-vowel or a nasal is elided optionally, when the same letters follow it.

The word अन्यतरस्याम् should be read into the sûtra. Thus शय्य्या or शय्या, the middle य् being elided. In शय्या there are two यs, one of the affix क्यप् (III. 3. 99); and the second of अयङ् (VII. 4. 22), and the third arises by doubling (VIII. 4. 47). आदित्त्य्य (formed by doubling त by the Vârtika under 47 *ante*), or आदित्य 'son of Aditi' In आदित्त्य्य there are two यs, one of ण्य (IV. 1. 85), and the second arises by doubling.

Similarly आदित्य देवता अस्य स्थाली पाकस्य=आदित्य्य ॥ Then by VIII. 4. 47, there is a third य, as आदित्त्य्य्य ॥ Here also we may elide the one middle य or both the middle य's. Thus आदित्यः or आदित्त्य्यः ॥

Why do we say हलः 'preceded by a consonant'? Observe अन्नम् when न् is preceded by a *vowel.*

Why do we say यमाम् "of यम् letters"? Observe अग्निः, अर्घ्यम् (V. 4. 25) where घ is not a यम् ॥

Why do we say यमि "when यम् follows"? Observe शार्ङ्गम् here ङ् is not followed by a यम् ॥

झरो झरि सवर्णे ॥ ६५ ॥ पदानि ॥ झरः, झरि, सवर्णे ॥

वृत्तिः ॥ हल उत्तरस्य झरो झरि सवर्णे परतो लोपो भवति अन्यतरस्याम् ।

65. A Mute or Sibilant (झर्) preceded by a consonant and followed by a homogeneous mute or sibilant, is optionally elided.

The word हलः is understood. Thus प्रत्त्तम्, अवत्त्तम् have three त, namely, one त substituted for आ by VII. 4. 47, the second त resulting from the change of द to त by चर्त्व change, the third त is that of the affix. A fourth arises by doubling (VIII. 4. 47) of these four, one or two middle ones may be dropped. मरुत्त्त्त here are four तs. A fifth may be added by doubling, and by this rule, one, two or three of them may be elided. मरुत्+दा+क्त=मरुत्+द्त्+त (VII. 4. 47) the word मरुत् being treated as an Upasarga (I. 4. 59, vârt)=मरुत्त ॥

Why do we say झरः 'of a jhar'? Compare शार्ङ्गम्, here ङ् which is not a झर् is not elided, though it is follwed by a झर् letter. Why do we say झरि 'followed by a jhar'? See प्रियपञ्च्चः ॥ This is a Bahuvṛihi compound=प्रियाः पञ्चास्य ॥ The word प्रिय stands first in the compound under II. 2. 35. (*vârt*). The full word is प्रियापञ्चन्, the अ is elided by VI. 4. 134, and we have प्रियपञ्च्न् ; and then this न् becomes a palatal ञ् ॥ Here च् is preceded by a हल् letter, and itself is a झर्, and is followed by a homogeneous letter झ्, but as ञ् is not झर्, the च् is not elided. The elided अ is not considered sthânivat, and so च is considered to be *immediately* followed by झ् ॥

Why do we say सवर्णे 'when a homogeneous jhar follows'? Observe तर्प्तुं, तर्प्तम् &c, where प् and त् are not homogeneous.

By using the word सवर्णे, the rule of mutual correspondence (I. 3. 10) is avoided. Had the rule been झरो झरि 'the rule of mutual correspondence according to order of enumeration would have applied, and the forms शिण्ढि पिण्ढि could not have been evolved by the elision of ड before ढ ॥ For the evolution of these forms see the commentary under I. 1. 58. These are the Imperative 2nd Person Singular of शिष् and पिष् ॥ The अ of श्नम् is elided by VI. 4. 111: the हि is changed to धि by VI. 4. 101, the ष् is changed to ड् by VIII. 4. 53, the न् of श्नम् is changed to anusvâra by VIII. 3. 24; this anusvâra is again changed to ण् by VIII. 4. 58; the ध is changed to ढ, and by the present rule, the preceding ड् is elided before this ढ ॥

उदात्तादनुदात्तस्य स्वरितः ॥ ६६ ॥ पदानि ॥ उदत्तात्, अनुदात्तस्य, स्वरितः ॥

वृत्तिः ॥ उदात्तादुत्तरस्यानुदात्तस्य स्वरितादेशो भवति ।

66. The Svarita is the substitute of an Anudâtta vowel which follows an Udâtta vowel.

Thus अग्निम्+ईले=अग्निमीले ॥ Here ई which was अनुदात्त by rule VIII. 1. 28, becomes svarita by the present rule, as it comes after the udâtta इ of agni.

So also गार्ग्यः, वात्स्यः ॥ Here यञ् is added by IV. 1. 105, and being ञित् the words are first acute. The final is anudâtta, which becomes svarita. So also पचति and पठति, the शप् and तिप् are anudâtta, the root is accented, the अ of शप् becomes svarita.

The rule VI. 1. 158, does not change this svarita into an Anudâtta, because for the purposes of that rule, the present rule is असिद्ध, or as if it had not taken place (VIII. 2. 1). Therefore both the udâtta and the svarita accent are heard.

नोदात्तस्वरितोदयमगार्ग्यकाश्यपगालवानाम् ॥ ६७ ॥ पदानि ॥ न, उदात्त-स्वरित-उदयम्, अ-गार्ग्य-काश्यप-गालवानाम् ॥

वृत्तिः ॥ उदात्तोदयस्य स्वरितोदयस्य चानुदात्तस्य स्वरितो न भवति अगार्ग्यकाश्यपगालवानामाचार्याणां मतेन ॥ उदात्तोदयः = उदात्तपरः ।

67 All prohibit the above substitution of svarita, except the Âchâryâs Gârgya, Kâśyapa and Gâlava; when an udâtta or a svarita follows the anudâtta.

This debars the preceding rule. That anudâtta which is *followed* by an Udâtta is उदात्तोदयः or उदात्तपरः ॥ The word उदय means पर in the terminology of ancient Grammarians. That anudâtta which is *followed* by a svarita is called स्वरितोदयः ॥ These are Bahuvrihi compounds. Thus उदात्तोदयः—गार्ग्य-

स्तैत्रं, वैात्स्यु स्तैत्रं ॥ The word तैत्र is first acute by लित् accent, before this udâtta, the य of these words does not become svarita. So with स्वरितोदयः—गार्ग्यः कुं. वात्स्युः कुं ॥ The word कु is svarita being formed by the तित् affix अत् (V. 3. 12); before this svarita the preceding य does not become svarita.

Why do we say "except in the opinion of Gârgya, Kâśyapa and Gâlava"? Observe गार्ग्यः कुं, गार्ग्यस्तत्र ॥ According to their opinion, the svarita change does take place.

The employment of the longer word उदय instead of the shorter word पर is for the sake of auspiciousness, for the Book has approached the end. The very utterance of the word उदय is auspicious. All sacred works commence with an auspicious word, have an auspicious word in the middle, and end with an auspicious word. Thus Pâṇini commences his sûtra with the auspicious word वृद्धिः 'increase' (in Sûtra I. 1. 1): has the word शिव 'the well-wisher' in the middle (IV. 4. 143), and उदय at the end.

The mention of the names of those several Âchâryas is for the sake of showing respect (pujârtham).

अ अ इति ॥ ६८ ॥ पदानि ॥ अ, अ, इति ॥

वृत्तिः ॥ एकोऽत्र विवृतो ऽपरः संवृतस्तत्र विवृतस्य संवृतः क्रियते । अकारो विवृतः संवृतो भवति ।

68. The अ which was considered to be open (विवृत) in all the preceding operations of this Grammar, is now made contracted (संवृत) ॥

The first अ is here विवृत or open; the second is संवृत or contracted. The open अ is now changed to contracted अ ॥ "In actual use the organ in the enunciation of the short अ is *contracted*; but it is considered to be *open* only, as in the case of the other vowels, when the vowel अ is in the state of taking part in some operation of Grammar. The reason for this is, that if the short अ were held to differ from the long आ in this respect, the *homogeneousness* mentioned in I. 1. 9, would not be found to exist between them, and the operation of the rules depending upon that homogeneousness would be debarred. In order to restore the short अ to its natural rights, thus infringed throughout the Ashṭâdhyâyi, Pâṇini with oracular brevity in his closing aphorism gives the injunction अ अ; which is interpreted to signify—Let short अ be held to have its organ of utterance contracted, now that we have reached the end of the work in which it was necessary to regard it as being otherwise". (Dr. Ballantyne).

Thus वृक्षः, इक्षः ॥ In this Grammar, the अ is regarded open or vivṛita, when operations are performed with it: but in actual pronunciation it is contracted. The long आ and the pluta आ ३ are not meant to be included here in the open short अ; therefore those two are not contracted by this rule. Only the *short* अ consisting of *one* mâtra, with *its* various modifications is to be taken here. In other words the *six* shorts अ are only taken here, namely अँ॒, अ॒. अं, अँ॒, अँ, अँ ॥ For these six short open अs, there are substituted six contracted corresponding अ's See I. 1. 9.

॥ शुभं भवतु ॥

10. 10. 98.

Printed by Freeman & Co., Ld., at the Tara Printing Works, Benares.

THE SIDDHANTA KAUMUDI

OF

BHATTOJI DIKSHITA,

TRANSLATED AND EDITED INTO ENGLISH

BY

ŚRĪŚA CHANDRA VASU, B. A.

VOL. III.

VAIDIC GRAMMAR.

PUBLISHED BY
THE PANINI OFFICE, BHUVANESHWARI ASHRAM,
38-40 BAHADURGANJ, ALLAHABAD.

ALLAHABAD:
PRINTED AT THE MEDICAL HALL PRESS BRANCH.

1905

CONTENTS.

FOREWORD.

We are glad to present our subscribers the third volume of the Siddhânta Kaumudi. We had hoped to send also the second volume of the same along with it, if not earlier, but the press to which we gave the work more than two years ago for printing, showed the utmost want of sense of duty and businesslike capacity, for they have not printed more than 80 pages during all this time. Now that Messrs. E. J. Lazarus & Co. have undertaken to print also the second volume, after having so quickly printed the present, we hope to publish the remaining portion of the work by the end of this year. Our thanks are specially due to the Manager, E. J. Lazarus & Co., Medical Hall Press, Allahabad Branch, for the great interest and trouble he has taken in pushing the work through the press. We trust the remaining portion of the work under his management will be out soon.

ALLAHBAD : S. N. V.
The 1st July, 1905.

THE SIDDHÂNTA KAUMUDÎ.

VOLUME III.

वैदिकी प्रक्रिया ।

प्रथमोऽध्यायः ।

THE VAIDIC GRAMMAR.

CHAPTER I.

In this volume Bhattoji Dikshita has collected together all the sûtras of Pâṇini which are peculiar to the Vedas. He has arranged them in eight Adhyâyas in the order as they are found in the Ashṭâdhyâyî. The first chapter contains all those sûtras which occur in the First Book of Pâṇini.

३३८७ । छन्दसि पुनर्वस्वोरेकवचनम् । १ । २ । ६१ ।

द्वयोरेकवचनं वा स्यात् । पुनर्वसुर्नक्षत्रं पुनर्वसू वा । लोके तु द्विवचनमेव ।

3387. In the Vedas, the two stars, Punarvasû, may optionally be singular, (and connote a dual).

In the Vedas, the star *punarvasû* which is always *dual* in form, may be in the singular form and connote a dual meaning. As पुनर्वसुर्नक्षत्रं or पुनर्वसू नक्षत्रमदितिर्देवता ॥ The option is only allowed in the Vedas and not in the secular literature. In the latter, it must be in the dual as, गां गताविव दिवः पुनर्वसू ॥ Similarly when it is not the appellation of an asterism but of a man, there is no option. As पुनर्वसू माणवकौ.

३३८८ । विशाखयोश्च । १ । २ । ६२ ।

प्राग्वत् । विशाखा नक्षत्रम् । विशाखे वा ।

3388. In the Vedas, the two stars Viśâkhâ may optionally be in the singular number.

The word विशाखा is in the dual number as a rule. In the Vedas, it is found sometimes to have the singular form, denoting duality. Thus विशाखा नक्षत्रम् or विशाखे नक्षत्रमिन्द्राग्नी देवता ॥

३३८९। षष्ठीयुक्तश्छन्दसि वा। १। ४। ९।

षष्ठ्यन्तेन युक्तः पतिशब्दश्छन्दसि घिसंज्ञो वा स्यात्। "क्षेत्रस्य पतिना वयम्"। इह वेति योगं विभज्य छन्दसीत्यनुवर्तते। तेन सर्वे विधयश्छन्दसि वैकल्पिकाः। "बहुलं छन्दसि" इत्यादिरस्यैव प्रपंचः। "यचि भम्"। नभोऽङ्गिरोमनुषां वत्युपसंख्यानम्। +। नभसा तुल्यं नभस्वत्। भत्वाद् रुत्वाभावः। अङ्गिरस्वदङ्गिरः। "मनुष्वदग्ने"। "जनेरुसि" इति विहित उसिप्रत्यये मनेरपि बाहुलकात्। वृषन् वस्वश्वयोः। +। वृषन्वर्षुकं वसु यस्य स वृषण्वसुः। वृषा अश्वो यस्यासौ वृषणश्वः। इहान्तर्वर्तिनीं विभक्तिमाश्रित्य पदत्वे सति नलोपः प्राप्तो भत्वाद्वार्यते। अतएव "पदान्तस्य" इति णत्वनिषेधोऽपि न। "अल्लोपोऽनः" इति अल्लोपो न। अनङ्गत्वात्।

3389. The word pati when used in connection with a noun ending in the sixth (or genitive) case is ghi, optionally, in the Chhandas (Veda).

The word pati is understood in this sûtra from the sûtra patiḥ samâse eva (I. 4. 8. S. 257). By that sûtra, pati would have been ghi only in composition. This sûtra makes an exception to that, when this word occurs in the Vaidic literature. Thus क्षेत्रस्य पतिना वयम् (Rig Veda. IV. 57. 1.)

This sûtra may be divided into two, (1) ṣhashṭhi yuktaśchhandasi (2) vâ. In the latter we shall read the annuvṛitti of chhandasi. The sûtra will then mean:—(1) In the Chhandas the word pati is ghi when used in connection with a word in the sixth case. (2) In the Chhandas there is option. Thus this second rule would make *all* rules optional in the Vedas. In fact, the bahulam chhandasi, which recurs so often in Pâṇini would become but a special case of this universal rule vâ chhandasi.

Note:—The word pati being treated as ghi, takes nâ in the Instrumental by VII. 3. 120. S. 214.

Note:—कुलुञ्चानां पतये or पत्ये नमः salutation to the lord of the Kuluñchas.

Why do we say 'when used in connection with a noun in the genitive case'? Observe मया पत्या जरदष्टिर्यथासः।

Why do we say 'in the Chhandas'? Observe ग्रामस्य पत्ये।

Here we repeat the sûtra यचिभम् S. 231, for the purposes of certain vârtikas which apply to the Vedas.

३३८९ क। यचि भम्। १। ४। १८।

3389A. And when an affix, with an initial य or an initial vowel, being one of the affixes, beginning with सु and ending in क, follows, not being Sarvanâmasthâna, then what precedes, is called Bha.

The word यचि is in the 7th case meaning 'when य or अच् follows,' and by the last *Vârt.* of Sûtra I. 1. 72, it means; 'when an affix beginning with ya or ach follow.'

Vârtika:—The words नभस्, अङ्गिरस् and मनुष् should be treated as Bha when the affix वत् (V. 1. 115. S. 1778) follows. Thus नभस्वत् 'like the sky.' अङ्गिरस्वत् "like the Angiras," मनुष्वत् 'like the man.' By being Bha, the स् is not changed into र् which it would have been, had it been a pada (VIII. 2. 66 S. 162.)

The word मनुस् is formed by the affix उस् of the Uṇâdi sûtra (II. 115) janerusi, by being diversely applied to √मन. The word मनुस् being treated as bha, the sûtra VIII 3. 59. S. 212 applies, and स is changed to ष।

Vârt :—The word वृषन् is treated as Bha in the Vedas when the words वसु and अश्व follow. Thus वृषण्वसुः वृषणश्वस्य मेने. Here had the word vrishan been treated as pada, the न would not have been changed into ण (VIII. 4. 37. S. 198); and this न would have been dropped before the affix vasu by VIII. 2. 7. S. 236. Nor does the sûtra VI. 4. 134. S. 234 apply, because the word is not an aṅga.

In secular language the forms are वृषवसुः and वृषाश्वः।

३३९० । अयस्मयादीनि च्छन्दसि । १ । ४ । २० ।

एतानि च्छन्दसि साधूनि । भपदसंज्ञाधिकाराद्यथायोगं संज्ञाद्वयं बोध्यम् । तथा च वार्तिकम् । उभयसंज्ञान्यपीति वक्तव्यमिति । * । "स सुष्टुभास ऋक्वता गणेन"। पदत्वात् कुत्वम् । भत्वाज्जश्त्वाभावः । जश्त्वविधानार्थाया: पदसंज्ञाया भत्वसामर्थ्येन बाधात् । "नैनं हिन्वन्त्यपि वाजिनेषु"। अत्र पदत्वाद् जश्त्वम् । भत्वात् कुत्वाभावः । "ते प्राग्धातोः"।

3390. The words like ayasmaya &c., are valid forms in the Chhandas (Veda).

These words being taught here in the topic relating to Pada and Bha show that they have been properly formed in the Chhandas by the application of the rules of Bha and Pada.

Thus we have the following Vârtika—

Vârt :—It should be stated that in some places both these Pada and Bha designations apply simultaneously. Thus in the word ऋक्वत् formed by ऋच् + वत् the च् is first changed into क् by treating the word rich as a Pada. Then the word ऋक् is treated as Bha, and therefore the क् is not changed into ग् before वत्. For had it been Pada, the form would have been ऋग्वत् 'Rigvat.' These irregularly formed words occur only in the Chhandas or Vedic literature. Thus स सुष्टुभास ऋक्वता गणेन (Rig Veda IV. 50. 5)

Similarly in the sentence नैनं हिन्वन्त्यपि वाजिनेषु (Rig Veda X. 71. 5) the word वाजिन is formed from वाच् + इन (=वाचां इनः 'lord or master of speech'). Here vâch being treated as a Pada, the ch is changed to j; and then being treated as a Bha, the j is not changed to a guttural. Similarly अयस् + मय = अयस्मय 'made of iron.' Here the word अयस् is treated as Bha and hence the स is not changed into र. Thus अयस्मयं वर्म 'iron-made coat of mail.' अयस्मयानि पात्राणि 'iron vessels.' The present form of this word is अयोमयं।

Now we repeat the sûtra I. 4. 80. S. 2230, for the purpose of showing its exception in the Vedas.

ते प्राग्धातोः । १ । ४ । ८० ।

3390A. The particles called gati and upasarga are to be employed before the verbal root: (that is to say, they are prefixes).

३३९१ । छन्दसि परेऽपि । १ । ४ । ८१ ।

3391. In the Chhandas (Veda) these gati and upasarga are employed indifferently after the verbal root, as well as before it.

As वायविन्द्रश्च सुन्वत आयातमुपनिष्कृतम् ॥ मक्ष्वित्था धिया नरा (Rig. 1. 2. 6). In this we have आयातमुप instead of उपायातम् 'Vâyu and thou Indra, ye heroes, come ye both quickly to the Soma of the worshipper by this sincere prayer.'

३३९२ । व्यवहिताश्च । १ । ४ । ८२ ।

' हरिभ्यां याह्योक आ ' ' आ मन्द्रै रिन्द्र हरिभिर्याहि ' ।

3392. In the Chhandas (Veda) these gati and upasarga are also seen separated from the verb by intervening words.

As हरिभ्यां याह्योक आ (for हरिभ्यां आयाहि ओकः).

Here आ is separated from the word याहि by the intervening word ओक. So also in the sentence आ मन्द्रैरिन्द्र हरिभिर्याहि मयूर रोमभिः (Rig Veda III. 41. 1), " O Indra ! come (आ याहि) on horses (हरि) which are spirited (मन्द्रैः=मादयितृभिः), and color of peacock's feather."

३३९३ । इन्धि-भवतिभ्यां च । १ । २ । ६ ।

आभ्यां परो ऽपित् लिट् कित् । ' समीधे दस्यु हन्तमम् ' । 'पुत्र ईधे अथर्वणः ' । बभूव । इदं प्रत्याख्यातम् । 'इन्धेश्छन्दोविषयत्वाद्भुवो वुको नित्यत्वात् ताभ्यां लिटः किद्वचनानर्थक्यम् ' इति ।

इति वैदिकप्रकरणे प्रथमोऽध्यायः ।

3393. The Lit or Perfect Tense affixes after the roots indh 'to kindle,' and bhu, 'to become,' also are kit.

After these two roots the terminations of the Perfect are कित् । These roots have been especially mentioned, because the root इन्धि ending in a compound consonant will not be governed by sútra I. 2. 5. S. 2242, and the root भू is mentioned because all the terminations of the Perfect are कित् after भू, not excepting the पित् terminations. Thus the verbs समीधे and ईधे are illustrations of Perfect Tense from the root इन्ध् as in the following examples :— समीधे दस्युहन्तमम्, (Rig Veda VI. 16. 15), and पुत्र ईधे अथर्वणः, (Rig Veda VI. 16. 14). Here the nasal of the root is dropped by regarding the affix as कित् ॥ Similarly from the root भू, we have बभूव, बभूविथ ॥

This sûtra is considered unnecessary by Patañjali the author of Mahâbhâshya, who says " we could have done without this sûtra. Because the direct application of Perfect affixes to √इन्ध् is confined only to the Vedas, while in the secular literature the Perfect will be formed by आम् as इन्धां चकार ; and so its conjugation would have been irregular, by Vaidic license (III 4. 117. S. 3435). While भू *always* takes the augment वुक् in the Perfect, for after *bhû*, the वुक् comes *invariably* whether there be guna or there be not guna. So there is no necessity of saying that the Perfect affixes are कित् after these two roots."

CHAPTER. II.

३३९४ । तृतीया च होश्छन्दसि । २ । ३ । ३ ।

जुहोतेः कर्मणि तृतीया स्याद् द्वितीया च । ' यवाग्वा अग्निहोत्रं जुहोति ' । अग्निहोत्रशब्दोऽत्र हविषि वर्तते । ' अस्याग्निहोत्रमधिश्रितममेध्यमापद्येत ' इत्यादिप्रयोगदर्शनात् । अग्नये हूयते । इति व्युत्पत्तेश्च । यवाग्वाख्यं हविर्देवताभ्यो ऽग्नेन त्यक्त्वा प्रक्षिपतीत्यर्थः ।

3394. In the Chhandas (Veda), the object of the verb हु 'to sacrifice' takes the affix of the third case, and of the second as well.

This ordains the third case-affix; and by force of the word च 'and', the second case-affix is also employed: as यवाग्वाग्निहोत्रं जुहोति ।

Here यवाग्वा is in the Instrumental case, though it is the object of sacrifice. The word अग्निहोत्र here means "the oblation," for we find it used in this sense in sentences like this:—यस्याग्निहोत्रमधिश्रितममेध्यमापद्येत । &c. The word agnihotra when in this sense, should be analysed as अग्नये हूयते "that which is sacrificed in honor of, or for the sake of Agni—*i. e.*, an oblation." The sentence यवाग्वाग्निहोत्रं जुहोति therefore means "he throws (into the fire) the oblation called yavâgû, offering it in honor of the deity."

Note:—In the above example yavâgû is in 3rd case and agnihotra in the 2nd case. In this case the latter word means हविः or oblation. The verb जुहोति in this connection means प्रक्षिपति ॥ The whole sentence means "the oblation in the shape of yavâgû, he throws (into the fire)." Though the two words yavâgû and agnihotra are in different cases, yet they are syntactically one, and refer to one and the same object.

But this sûtra is considered unnecessary by Patanjali. According to him the word agnihotra in the above example means simply "agni or fire." As we find it used in the sentence यस्याग्निहोत्रं प्रज्वलितम् ॥

The word agnihotra, when meaning fire, is analysed as हूयते ऽस्मिन् "Agni in which sacrifice is poured" or, "sacrificial fire."

Therefore, when the example is यवाग्वा अग्निहोत्रं जुहोति, then agnihotra being equivalent to Agni, juhoti means prînana or satisfaction. The whole sentence means यवाग्वा अग्निं प्रीणयति "he propitiates fire with yavâgû (barley)."

But when the sentence is यवागूं अग्निहोत्रं जुहोति, both words being in the 2nd case, then agnihotra means havis or oblation, and juhoti means prakshepana, *i. e.*, "he throws the yavâgú oblation (into the fire)" *i. e.*, he throws into the fire the materials of oblations called yavâgû.

३३९५ । द्वितीया ब्राह्मणे । २ । ३ । ६० ।

ब्राह्मणविषये प्रयोगे दिवस्तदर्थस्य कर्मणि द्वितीया स्यात् । षष्ठ्यपवादः । 'गामस्य तदहः सभायां दीव्येयुः' ।

3395. The object of the verb दिव् in the sense of 'dealing or 'staking,' takes the second case-affix, in the Brâhmaṇa literature.

This debars the Genitive case required by II. 3. 59. S. 620. Ex. गामस्य तदहः सभायां दीव्येयुः (Maitr. S. 1. 6. 11) In the Vedic literature, the simple verb दिव् takes the accusative, instead of the genitive. When, however, the root दिव् takes an upasarga, then it may optionally govern the genitive also, by II. 3. 59 S. 620.

३३९६ । चतुर्थ्यर्थे बहुलं छन्दसि । २ । ३ । ६२ ।

षष्ठी स्यात्। 'पुरुषमृगश्चन्द्रमसे'। 'गोधा कालका दार्वाघाटस्ते वनस्पतीनाम्' वनस्पतिभ्य इत्यर्थः। षष्ठ्यर्थे चतुर्थीति वाच्यम्। + । 'या खर्वेण पिबति तस्यै खर्वः'।

3396. In the Chhandas the sixth case-affix is employed diversely with the force of the fourth case-affix.

Ex. पुरुषमृगश्चन्द्रमसः or चन्द्रमसे 'to the moon, a male deer.' गोधा कालका दार्वा घाटस्ते वनस्पतीनाम् or वनस्पतिभ्यः 'to you lords of the forest, are lizard, kâlaka bird, &c.' So also वायुरस्मा उपा मन्थत् (R. Ved. X. 136. 7).

Vart:—In the Veda, the 4th case affix is employed in the sense of the sixth: as या खर्वेण पिबति तस्यै खर्वोजायते 'whosoever woman drinks with a woman in her courses, gets herself in menstrual."

३३९७। यजेश्च करणे। २। ३। ६३।

इह छन्दसि बहुलं षष्ठी। घृतस्य घृतेन वा यजते।

3397. The sixth case-affix is diversely employed in the Chhandas in denoting the instrument of the verb यज् 'to sacrifice.'

Ex. घृतस्य or घृतेन यजते 'he sacrifices with butter."

३३९८। बहुलं छन्दसि। २। ४। ३९।

अदो घस्लादेशः स्यात्। घस्तां नूनम्। लुङि "मन्त्रे घस" इति च्लेर्लुक्। अडभावः। सग्धिश्च मे'।

3398. In the Chhandas (Vedas), घस्लृ is diversely substituted for अद्।

As घस्तां नूनम्।

The words अद् and घस्लृ are to be supplied in this sûtra from II. 4. 36. S. 3080, and II. 4. 37. S. 2427. घस्ताम् is the Aorist form of अद्; the Aorist sign च्लि is elided by II. 4. 80. S. 3402. The augment अट् is not added, because of VI. 4. 74. S. 2228, read with the बहुलं of this sutra.

But the form घस्ताम् could have been obtained by II. 4. 37. S. 2427 also, for that sûtra also ordains घस् substitution for अद्। The proper example, under the present sûtra is not घस्ताम्॥ Hence the other example सग्धिः (Yajur Veda. Vaj S. XVIII. 9), which is free from this objection. The word ग्धिः = अदनं "eating." सग्धिः "companion in eating." It is formed by adding the affix क्तिन् (ति) to the √अद्; as अद् + क्तिन्; then अद् is replaced by घस by the present sûtra. Thus घस् + ति॥ Then the penultimate अ of घस् is elided by VI. 4. 100. S. 3550, as घ्स् + ति॥ Then स् is elided by VIII 2 26. S. 2281. as घ् + ति. Then त् is changed to ध् by VIII. 2. 40. S. 2280. Thus घ् + धि. Then घ् is changed to ग् by VIII. 4. 53. S. 52. The घ् is considered here as immediately in contact with ध्, though technically speaking there is an elided स् between घ् and ध्॥ But this zero is not sthânivat, because VIII. 4. 53, is a जश् rule; and the zero âdeśa is not sthânivat for the purposes of जश्त्व rule (I. 1. 58. S. 51). Thus we get ग्धिः; which with स, a shortened form of समान (VI. 3. 84. S. 1012), gives us सग्धिः॥

३३९९। हेमन्तशिशिरावहोरात्रे च च्छन्दसि। २। ४। २८।

द्वन्द्वः पूर्ववल्लिङ्गः। हेमन्तश्च शिशिरश्च हेमन्तशिशिरौ। अहोरात्रे। 'अदिप्रभृतिभ्यः शपः'

3399. Of the compounds 'hemantaśiśirau' and 'ahorâtre' the gender is like that of the first word, in the Chhandas. (Vedas).

This aphorism debars the general rule given in II. 4. 26. S. 812.

Similarly though the vikaraṇa शप् is ordained by II. 4. 72 S. 2423, to be elided after the roots of the Adâdi class, yet by Vaidic diversity it is sometimes not so elided; as taught in the next sûtra.

३४०० । बहुलं छन्दसि । २ । ४ । ७३ ।

"वृत्रं हनति वृत्रहा"। "अहिः शयत उपपृक् पृथिव्याः" अत्र लुक् न। अदादिभिन्नेऽपि क्वचिल्लुक्। "त्राध्वं नो देवाः"। "जुहोत्यादिभ्यः श्लुः"

3400. In the Chhandas (Vedas) there is diversely the luk-elision of the Vikaraṇa शप् (III. 1. 68).

There is elision in other conjugations than Adâdi: and there is sometimes even no elision in Adâdi verbs. As वृत्रं हनति वृत्रहा 'the Vṛitra-Killer kills Vṛitra.' हन् + शप् + ति = हनति instead of हन्ति। So also, अहिः शयत उपपृक् पृथिव्याः, here शयते instead of शेते (Rig. Veda I. 32. 5.) "The Dragon lies low on earth." In these cases the Vikaraṇa शप् has not been elided.

In some cases the शप् is elided even in conjugations other than Adâdi, as त्राध्वम् नो देवाः निजुरः वृकस्य (Rig Veda II. 29. 6.) "Protect us, God, let not the wolf destroy us." instead of त्रायध्वम्।

Similarly श्लु elision of the vikaraṇa is required by II. 4. 75. S. 2489, in Juhotyâdi class. But to this also, there is exception in the Vedas: as shown in the following sûtra.

३४०१ । बहुलं छन्दसि । २ । ४ । ७६ ।

"दाति प्रियाणि चिद्वसु"। अन्यत्रापि। "पूर्णां विवष्टि"।

3401. In the Chhandas there is ślu-elision of शप् diversely.

The elision does not take place where ordained, and takes place where not ordained. दाति प्रियाणि (instead of ददाति) चिद्वसु (Rig Veda IV. 8. 3) "he gives even treasures that we love." See also Rig Veda I. 65, 4; VI. 24. 2; VII. 15. 12; VII. 42. 4.

Similarly the ślu-elision with its accompanying reduplication takes place in roots other than those of the Juhotyudi class. Thus देवो वो द्रविणोदाः पूर्णां विवष्ट्यासिचम् "The God who gives your wealth demands a full libation poured to him." (Rig Veda VII 16. 11) Here विवष्टि is from the √वश् "to shine." It belongs to the Adâdi class, but takes ślu elision. Hence वश् + शप् + ति = वश् + श्लु + ति = वश् वश् + o + ति (VI. 1. 10. S. 2490) = विवश् + ति (the अ is changed to इ by VII. 4. 76. S. 2490, read with the bahulam chhandasi) = विवष् = ति (VIII. 2. 36 S. 294) = विवष्टि (VIII. 4 41. S. 26).

३४०५ । मन्त्रे घसह्वरणशवृदहाद्वृच्कृगमिजनिभ्यो लेः । २ । ४ । ८० ।

लिरिति च्लेः प्राचां संज्ञा। एभ्यो लेर्लुक् स्यात् मंत्रे। "अक्षन्नमीमदन्त हि"। घस्ला देशस्य 'गमहन' इत्युपधालोपे शासिवसीति षः। "मांहुर्मित्रस्य" "धूर्तिः प्रणङ्मर्त्यस्य"।

'नशेर्वा' इति कुत्वम्। "सुरुचो वेन आवः"। "मा न आधक्"। आत् इत्याकारान्तानां ग्रहणम्। "आप्रा द्यावापृथिवी"। "परावग् भारभृद्यथा"। "अक्रन्नुषासः"। "त्वे रयिं जागृवांसो अनुग्मन्"। मंत्रग्रहणं ब्राह्मणस्याप्युपलक्षणम्। "अजनि वा अस्य दन्ताः"। विभाषानुवृत्तेर्नेह। "न ता अगृभ्णन्नजनिष्ट हि सः"।

इति वैदिकप्रकरणे द्वितीयोऽध्यायः।

3402. In the Mantra portion of the Vedas there is luk-elision of the sign of the Aorist (and Perfect), after the verbs घस् 'to eat,' ह्वर 'to be crooked,' णश 'to destroy,' वृ 'to choose,' 'to cover,' दह 'to burn,' verbs ending in long आ, वृच् 'to avoid,' कृ 'to make,' गमि 'to go' and जनि 'to be produced.'

The word लि is the name given by ancient grammarians to the affixes of the Perfect tense as well as the Aorist, or it might be a common term for all tense-affixes. Thus from घस the substitute of अद we have अक्षन् in the sentence, अक्षन्नमीमदन्त हि "Well have they eaten and rejoiced." (Rig. I. 82. 2).

NOTE:—Thus in the Aorist of अद्, there comes घस् (II. 4. 37. S. 2427); the sign of the aorist is elided by this sutra. The penultimate अ of घस् is elided by VI. 4 98. S. 2363; and घ is changed to क by VIII. 4. 55. S. 121, and स् is changed to ष् by VIII. 3. 60. S. 2410; thus we get क्ष्, then we add the augment अट् which with the third person plural affix अन्, gives us अक्षन्॥

From the verb ह्वृ we have माह्वर्मित्रस्य त्वम्। The माह्वर् is the aorist 3rd Pers. Singular, of ह्वृ। Thus ह्वृ + च्लि + ति = ह्वृ + o + ति (S. 3402) = ह्वर् + त् (the elision of इ is by III. 4. 100. S. 2207). The guna takes place by VII. 3. 84. S. 2168; and then the त is elided by VI. 1. 68. S. 242.

From नश् we have प्रणक् in the following verse मा नः शंसो अररुषो धूर्तिः प्रणङ्मर्त्यस्य। रक्षा णो ब्रह्मणस्पते। 'Let not the foeman's curse, let not a mortal's onslaught fall on us: Preserve us Brahmanaspati." (Rig. I. 18. 3.) The श of नश् is changed to क by VIII. 2. 63. S 431.

The word वृ in the sutra includes both वृङ् and वृञ्, as the word वेन in the following ब्रह्म जज्ञानं प्रथमं पुरस्ताद्वि सीमतः सुरुचो वेन आवः। स बुध्न्या उपमा अस्य विष्ठाः सतश्च योनिमसतश्च वि वः। (Yajur veda 13. 3).

From दह we have आधक् as in सरस्वत्यभि नो नेषि वस्यो माप स्फरीः पयसा मा न आधक्। "Guide us Saraswati to glorious treasure: refuse us not thy milk, nor spurn us from thee." (Rig. VI. 61. 14).

The word आत् means verbs ending in long आ, as प्रा 'to be full." Thus, चित्रं देवानामुदगादनीकं चक्षुर्मित्रस्य वरुणस्याग्नेः। आप्रा द्यावा पृथिवी अन्तरिक्षं सूर्य आत्मा जगतस्तस्थुषश्च। (Rig I. 115. 1.) "The brilliant presence of the Gods hath risen, the eye of Mitra, Varuna and Agni. The soul of all that moveth not or moveth; the Sun hath filled the air and earth and heaven."

The root वृच् gives us वर्क्, as in the following verse:—मा नो अस्मिन्महाधने परा वर्ग् भारभृद्यथा। संवर्गं सं रयिं जय। (Rig VIII. 64. 12). "In this great battle cast us not aside as one who bears a load; snatch up the wealth and win it."

From कृ we have अक्रन् as in the following verse: अक्रन्नुषासो वयुनानि &c. (Rig Veda I. 92. 2.) "The Dawns have brought distinct perception as before."

From गम we have अग्मन् ; as in the following verse : वृतेव यन्तं बहुभिर्वसव्यैस् त्वेरयिं जागृवांसो अनुग्मन् । रुशंतमग्निं दर्शतं बृहंतं वपावन्तं विश्वहा दीदिवांसं । (Rig Veda VI. 1.3)."

From जन we have अज्ञत; as अज्ञत वा अस्य दन्ताः ॥ This is an exampie from the Brâhman literature, as the word मंत्र in the sûtra refers also to the Brâhman literature.

But sometimes, the elision does not take place, because the word "option" is understood in this sutra. Thus न ता अगृभ्रन् &c. (Rig Veda. V. 2. 4.) "These seized him not : he had been born already."

CHAPTER III.

३४०३ । अभ्युत्सादयांप्रजनयांचिकयांरमयामकः पावयांक्रियाद्विदामक्रन्निति छन्दसि । ३ । १ । ४२ ।

आद्येषु चतुर्षु लुङि 'आम्' 'अकः' इत्यनुप्रयोगश्च । अभ्युत्सादयामकः । अभ्युदसीषद-दिति लोके । प्रजनयामकः । प्राजीजनदित्यर्थः । चिकयामकः । अचैषीदित्यर्थं चिनोतेराम्द्विर्वचनं कुत्वं च । रमयामकः । अरीरमत् । पावयांक्रियात् । पाव्यादिति लोके । विदामक्रन् । अवेदिषुः ।

3403. The forms अभ्युत्सादयामकः, प्रजनयामकः, चिकयामकः, रमयामकः, पावयांक्रियाद्, विदामक्रन् are irregularly formed in the Chhandas with the augment आम्, and the auxiliary verbs अकर्, क्रियात्, and अक्रन् ।

The first two of these and the fourth are the Aorist (लुङ्) of the causatives of the roots सद् 'to sit', जन् 'to be born,' and रम् 'to sport;' to which the affix आम् is added. The third is the Aorist of the root चि 'to collect,' to which आम् has been added after the reduplication and the change of च into क of the root. The auxiliary अकः; which is the 3rd Person Singular Aorist of कृ is added to all these four. The fifth is derived from the root पू 'to blow, to purify.' by adding the causative affix णिच्, annexing the affix आम् before the terminations of the Benedictive (आशी र्लिङ्) and then using after the form so obtained, the Benedictive of कृ, क्रियात्. The last is the Aorist of विद् 'to know,' to which आम् is added and the 3rd Person Plural of the Aorist of कृ *i. e.*, the auxiliary अक्रन् is employed. These are the archaic forms ; their modern forms are as follow :—अभ्युदसीषदत्, प्राजीजनत्, अचैषीत्, अरीरमत्, पाव्याद्, अवेदिषुः ।

NOTE :—The word अभ्युत्सादयामकः is formed by adding the prepositions *abhi* and *ut* to the Causative root सादि । सादि with आम् becomes सादयां, to which is added अकः the 3rd pers. Singular Aorist of कृ "to do." Thus कृ + च्लि + तिप् = कर् + च्लि + त् = कर् + o + त् (II. 4. 80. S. 3402) = कर् + o + o (VI. 1. 68. S. 252): which with the augment अट् becomes अकर् or अकः । This auxiliary अकर् is added to all the first four words. When this periphrastic Aorist is formed with आम् and अकर्, the special mood-affix of the Aorist is elided by II. 4. 81, S. 2238. The regular Causative Aorist is अभ्युदसीषदत् (सादयामकर् = असीषदत्). The

Causative सादि is shortened to सदि by VII. 4. 1. S. 2314. This is reduplicated before the Aorist affix चङ् by VI. 1. 11. S. 2315. Thus सदसद् Then द् is elided by VII. 4. 60. S. 2179. Then applying VII. 4. 93. S. 2316, read with VII. 4. 79. S. 2317, the अ is changed to ई. Thus we have सीषद् + चङ् + त् = सीषदत् ।

The word क्रियात् is the Benedictive form of कृ 'to do.' The vikaraṇa उ is not added because of the prohibition III. 4. 116. S. 2215, and then there is रि by VII 4. 28. S. 2367.

३४०४ । गुपेश्छन्दसि । ३ । १ । ५० ।

च्लेश्चङ्वा । 'गृहानजूगुपतं युवम्' । अगोप्तमित्यर्थः ।

3404. After the verb गुप 'to protect,' चङ् is optionally the substitute of च्लि in the Chhandas.

This rule applies where the root गुप does not take the affix आय (III 2. 28). As इमान् नो मित्रावरुणौ यत् गृहान् अजूगुपतम् 'Mitra and Varuṇa protected these our houses.' The other forms are अगोप्तम्, अगोपिष्टम् or अगोपायिष्टम्. In the secular literature, the latter three forms are used, but not the first.

३४०५ । नोनयतिध्वनयत्येलयत्यर्दयतिभ्यः । ३ । १ । ५१ ।

च्लेश्चङ् न । 'मा त्वायतो जरितुः काममूनयीः' । 'मा त्वाग्निर्ध्वनयीत्' ।

3405. After the causatives of the verbs ऊन 'to decrease' ध्वन 'to sound,' इल 'to send' and अर्द 'to go or to beg' चङ् is not the substitute of च्लि in the Chhandas.

Thus मात्वायतो जरितुः काममूनयीः (Rig Veda I. 53. 3.) मात्वाग्निर्ध्वनयीत् धूमगन्धिः (Rig Veda I. 162. 15.)

Thus we have ऊनयीः in the Vedas; औनिनत् in the classical literature; so also ध्वनयीत्, ऐलयीत् and आर्दयीत्; their classical forms being अदिध्वनत्, ऐलिलत् and आर्दिदत्. See Rig Veda I. 53, 3, I. 162. 15, and Pâṇini VII. 2. 5.

३४०६ । कृमृदृरुहिभ्यश्छन्दसि । ३ । १ । ५९ ।

च्लेरङ् वा । 'इदं तेभ्यो करं नमः' । अमरत् । अदरत् । 'यत्सानोः सानुमारुहत्'

3406. After the verbs कृ 'to do,' मृ 'to die,' दृ 'to tear,' and रुह 'to rise,' अङ् is the substitute of च्लि when used in the Chhandas.

Thus अकरत् 'he did'; अमरत् 'he died'; अदरत् 'he tore'; आरुहत् 'he rose. The classical Aorist of these verbs are अकार्षीत् अमृत, अदारीत and अरुक्षत्.

Thus 'ये भूतस्य प्रचेतस इदं तेभ्यो ऽकरं नमः' (Rig. Ved. X. 85. 17). यत्सानोः सानुमारुहद्भूर्यस्पष्टकर्त्वम् (Rig, Ved. I. 10. 2).

३४०७ । छन्दसि निष्टर्क्यदेवहूयप्रणीयोन्नीयोच्छिष्यमर्यस्तर्याध्वर्यखन्यखान्यदेवयज्यापृच्छ्यप्रतिषीव्यब्रह्मवाद्यभाव्यस्ताव्योपचाय्यपृडानि । ३ । १ । १२३ ।

क्यन्तानि सूत्रेणाप्राप्ते यत् । आद्यन्तयोर्विपर्यासो निसः षत्वं च । 'निष्टर्क्यं चिन्वीत पशुकामः' । देवशब्द उ । पदे ह्वयतेर्जुहोतेर्वा क्यप्दीर्घश्च । 'स्पर्द्धन्ते वा उ देवहूये' । 'प्र' 'उत्

आभ्यां नयतेः क्यप् । प्रणीयः । उन्नीयः । उत्पूर्वाच्छिषेः क्यप् । उच्छिष्यः । 'मङ्' 'स्तृञ्' 'ध्वृ' एभ्यो यत । मर्यः । स्तर्या । स्त्रियामेवायम् । ध्वर्यः खनेर्यण्यतौ । खन्यः । खान्यः । यजेर्यः । 'शुन्धध्वं दैव्याय कर्मणे देवयज्यायै' । आङ् पूर्वात्पृच्छेः क्यप् । 'आपृच्छयं धरुणं वाज्यर्षति' । सीव्यतेः क्यप्षत्वं च प्रतिषीव्यः । ब्रह्मणि वदेर्ण्यत् । ब्रह्मवाद्यम् । लोके तु 'वदः सुपि क्यप्च' (२८५४) इति क्यब्यतौ । भवतेः स्तौतेश्च ण्यत् । भाव्यः । स्ताव्यः । उपपूर्वाच्चिनोतेर्ण्यदायादेशश्च पृड उत्तरपदे । उपचाय्यपृडम् । '* हिरण्यं इति• वक्तव्यम् *' । उपचेयपृडमेवान्यत् । 'मड' सुखने 'पृड च' इत्यस्मादिगुपधलक्षणः कः ।

3407. In the Vedas the following words are found which are formed irregularly :—निष्टर्क्य, देवहूय, प्रणीय, उन्नीय, उच्छिष्य, मर्य, स्तर्या, ध्वर्य, खन्य, खान्य, देवयज्या, आपृच्छ्य, प्रतिषीव्य, ब्रह्मवाद्य, भाव्य, स्ताव्य and उपचाय्यपृड ।

The formation of the above words is extremely irregular and they are all met with in the Vedic literature only. Thus the word निष्टर्क्य is derived from the root कृत् 'to cut,' with the preposition निस्, and the affix ण्यत्, instead of क्यप्, which is the regular affix, by III, 1. 110. S. 2859 ; निः + कृत् + ण्यत् = निः + तृक् + य (the root कृत् transformed into तृक् by transposition) = निष्टर्क्य. As निष्टर्क्यं चिन्वीत पशुकामः ।

The above is apparently a guess-work etymology of the grammarians.

So also देवहूय is formed by adding to the root ह्वयते 'to call' or हू 'to invoke,' the affix क्यप् and the upapada देव ; the vowel of the root is then lengthened and the augment त (VI. 1. 71), is not allowed, देव + ह्वे or हू + क्यप् = देवहूयः । Thus स्पर्धन्ते वा उ देवहूये (Rig. Ved. VII. 85. 2). So also प्र + नी (to lead) + क्यप् = प्रणीयः ; उत् + नी + क्यप् = उन्नीयः, उत् + शिष् (to leave) + क्य = उच्छिष्यम् ; मृ (to die) + यत् = मर्यः ; स्तृ (to cover) + यत् = स्तर्या ; it is always feminine. ध्वृ (to bend) + यत् = ध्वर्यः ; खन् (to dig) + यत् = खन्यः ; खन् + ण्यत् = खान्यः ; देव (God) + यज् (to sacrifice) + यत् = देवयज्या ; always used as feminine. Thus in शुन्धध्वं दैव्याय कर्मणे देवयज्यायै । आ + पृच्छ् (to ask) + क्यप् = आपृच्छ्यः । Thus आपृच्छ्यं धरुणं वाज्यर्षति (Rig Ved VII. 107. 5). प्रति + सीव (to sew) + क्यप् = प्रतिषीव्यः ; ब्रह्मण् + वद् (to speak) + ण्यत् = ब्रह्मवाद्यः, in secular literature both क्यप् and ण्यत् come after this word (III. 1. 106. S. 2854.). भू (to be) + ण्यत् = भाव्यः ; स्तु (to praise) + ण्यत् = स्ताव्यः ; उप + चि (to collect) + ण्यत् + पृडं = उपचाय्यपृडम्. *Vârt* :—This last word is formed then only when the word पृड follows : and when the sense is that of 'gold.' When it does not mean 'gold,' the form is उपचेयपृडम् । The root पृड is read along with मड् in the Tudâdi class and means "to please." To this root is added the affix क (III. 1. 135. S. 2897).

३४०८ । छन्दसि वनसनरक्षिमथाम् । ३ । २ । २७ ।

एभ्यः कर्मण्युपपदे इन्स्यात् । 'ब्रह्मवनिं त्वा क्षत्रवनिम्' 'उत नो गोषणिं धियम्' । 'ये पथां पथिरक्षयः' । चतुरक्षौ पथिरक्षी । 'हविर्मथीनामभि' ।

3408. In the Vedic literature, the affix इन् comes after the verbs वन् 'to honor' सन् 'to worship' रक्ष् 'to protect' and मथ् 'to agitate,' when the object is in composition.

Thus ब्रह्मवनि॑ त्वा चत्रवनिम् (Vaj. San. I. 17., V. 12., VI. 3) ; उत नो गोषणिं (Rig Ved. VI. 53. 10), यो ते श्वानौ पथिरक्षी (Rig. Ved. X. 14. 11) इन्द्रो यातूनामभवत् पराशरो हविर्मथीनाम् (Rig. Ved. VII. 104. 21).

३४०९ । छन्दसि सहः । ३ । २ । ६३ ।

ण्विः स्यात् । पृतनाषाट् ।

3409. In the Chhandas, the affix ण्वि comes after the verb सह् 'to bear' when it is in composition with a word ending in a case affix.

The words '*upasarga*' and '*supi*' are understood here. As पृतन + सह् + ण्वि = पृतनासाह्; nom. sing. पृतनाषाट् 'a name of Indra.' The dental स is changed into cerebral ष by VIII. 3. 56, and the ह् into ट by VIII. 2. 31. The final अ of पृतन is lengthened by VI. 3. 137. See Rig Veda. I. 175. 2, III. 29. 9, VI. 19. 7, IX. 88. 7, X. 103. 7.

३४१० । वहश्च । ३ । २ । ६४ ।

प्राग्वत् । दित्यवाट् । योगविभाग उत्तरार्थः ।

3410. The affix ण्वि comes after the verb वह् 'to carry,' in the Chhandas, when a word ending with a case-affix is in composition with it.

As प्रष्ठवाह् 1st sing. प्रष्ठवाट् 'carrying a *prashṭha* measure;' so, दित्यवाट् ।

The division of this sûtra from the last is for the sake of the subsequent sûtras, into which the anuvritti of वह् only is carried and not of सह्. See Yajur Veda, XIV. 10, XVIII. 26.

३४११ । कव्यपुरीषपुरीष्येषु ञ्युट् । ३ । २ । ६५ ।

एषु वहेर्ञ्युट् स्याच्छन्दसि । कव्यवाहनः । पुरीषवाहनः । पुरीष्यवाहनः ।

3411. In the Chhandas, the affix ञ्युट् comes after the verb वह् when it is in composition with the words कव्य 'oblation of food to deceased ancestors,' पुरीष 'fæces' and पुरीष्य 'water.'

As कव्यवाहनः पितॄणाम् (Yajur Ved. II. 29) 'fire that carries the oblation to the *pitṛis*;' पुरीषवाहनः 'carrier of water;' पुरीष्यवाहनः (Yaj. Ved. XI. 44). The feminine of these words is formed by adding long ई ।

३४१२ । हव्येऽनन्तःपादम् । ३ । २ । ६६ ।

अग्निर्नो हव्यवाहनः । पादमध्ये तु 'वहश्च' इति ण्विरेव 'हव्यवालग्निरजरः पिता नः'

3412. The affix ञ्युट् comes in the Chhandas, after the verb वह् 'to carry' when it is in composition with the word हव्य 'an oblation to gods,' provided that, the word so formed does not occur in the middle of a pâda (fourth part of a stanza).

As अग्निश्च हव्यवाहनः 'fire, the carrier of oblation to the gods.' (Rig Veda I. 44. 2.)

When this word occurs in the middle of a pâda, or at the beginning, the form is हव्यवट्, which is derived by adding the affix ञिव (sûtra 3410). As हव्यवाडग्निरजरः पिता नः 'the never-decaying *Agni* or fire that carries oblation to the gods, is our father.' (Rig Veda. III. 2. 2.)

३४१३ । जनसनखनक्रमगमो विट् । ३ । २ । ६७ ।

'विड्वनोः—' (२९८२) इत्यात्वम् । अब्जा गोजाः' । 'गोषा इन्द्रो नृषा असि' । 'सनोतेरनः' (३६४५) इति षत्वम् । 'इयं शुष्मेभिर्बिसखा इवारुजत्' । 'आ दधिक्राः शवसा पञ्च कृष्टीः' । अग्रेगाः ।

3413. The affix विट् (the whole of which is elided) comes in the Chhandas after the verbs जन् 'to be born,' सन् 'to bestow,' खन् 'to dig,' क्रम् 'to pace' and गम् 'to go,' when a word ending in a case-affix is in composition, and the final nasals are changed into long आ ।

The words छन्दसि, उपसर्गे and सुपि are understood in this sûtra. The verb जन् includes two verbs meaning 'to be born' and 'to happen;' so also सन् means both 'to give' and 'to worship.'

Of the affix विट् the latter ट् is indicatory, and is qualifying, as in VI. 4. 41. S 2982, by which rule the final nasal of जन्, सन् &c., is replaced by long आ when the affix विट् follows, and the whole affix is elided by VI. 1. 67. S. 375.

As अप् + जन् + विट् = अब्जाः (Rig Ved. VII. 34. 16) 'born in water' (VI. 4. 41. S. 2982); गोजाः 'born in the heaven *i. e.* God' (Rig. Veda IV. 40, 5). So also from सन्—गोषाः 'acquiring or bestowing cows' (VIII. 3, 108. S. 3645); गोषा इन्द्रो नृषा असि 'O Indra! bestower of cows! thou art lover of mankind' (Rig Veda IX. 2. 10). From खन्—बिसखाः 'digger of lotus stalk;' कूपखाः 'digger of well.' From क्रम्—दधिक्राः 'who gets milk' as, आ दधिक्राः शवसा पञ्च कृष्टीः (Rig Veda. IV. 38, 10 and 40. 5). From गम—अग्रेगाः उन्नेतॄणाम् 'the leader.'

३४१४ । मन्त्रे श्वेतवहोक्थशस्पुरोडाशो ण्विन् । ३ । २ । ७१ ।

'श्वेतवहादीनां डस्पदस्येति वक्तव्यम्' यत्र पदत्वं भावि तत्र ण्विनोऽपवादो डस्वक्तव्य इत्यर्थः । श्वेतवाः । श्वेतवाहौ । श्वेतवाहः । उक्थानि उक्थैर्वा शंसति उक्थशा यजमानः ॥ उक्थशासौ । उक्थशासः । पुरो दाश्यते पुरोडाः ।

3414. In the Mantra the affix ण्विन् comes after the words श्वेतवह, उक्थशस् and पुरोडाश् ॥

The above words contain both the verb and the upapada; the fact of their being so given indicates that there is some irregularity in the application of the affix.

Thus the affix ण्विन् comes after the verb वह् preceded by the upapada श्वेत as denoting an agent, while the force of the whole word so formed denotes an object As श्वेता एनं वहन्ति = श्वेतवाह् nom. sing. श्वेतवाः 'a name of Indra' (whom white horses carry). See VIII. 2. 67. S. 3416.

The affix ण्विन् is applied to the verb शंस् 'to praise' when preceded by the word उक्थ as object or instrument; and then the nasal is irregularly dropped. As उक्थानि उक्थैर्वा शंसति = उक्थशास्, nom. sing. उक्थशाः (Rig Veda II. 39. 1.) 'a reciter of hymns, the name of the sacrificer.'

The णिवन् is applied after the verb दाश् 'to give,' preceded by पुरो, and ट is changed into ड, the force of the whole word denoting an object. As पुरो दाशयन्ति एनं = पुरोडाश्, nom. sing. पुरोडाः (Rig Veda III. 28. 2) 'an offering.'

Vârt :—The augment डस् is added to the words श्वेतवाह् &c., when the *pada* affixes follow. Thus before *pada* terminations श्वेतवाह् becomes श्वेतवस् । Therefore its instrumental dual is श्वेतवोभ्याम्, pl. श्वेतवोभिः ।

The augment डस् is not applied before सर्वनामस्थान and भ terminations. As श्वेतवाहौ, श्वेतवाहः । The whole declension this of word is given below :—

	Sing.	Dual.	Plural.
Nom.	श्वेतवाः	श्वेतवाहौ	श्वेतवाहः
Acc.	श्वेतवाहम्	Do.	Do.
Ins.	श्वेतवाहा	श्वेतवोभ्याम्	श्वेतवोभिः
Dat.	श्वेतवाहे	Do.	श्वेतवोभ्यः
Abl.	श्वेतवाहः	Do.	Do.
Gen.	Do.	श्वेतवाहोः	श्वेतवाहाम्
Loc.	श्वेतवाहि	Do.	श्वेतवःसु
Voc.	श्वेतवाः or श्वेतवः		

३४१५ । अवे यजः । ३ । २ । ७२ ।

अवयाः । अवयाजौ । अवयाजः ।

3415. In the Mantra the affix णिवन् comes after the verb यज 'to sacrifice' when in compositon with the word अव ।

As अवयाज्, nom. sing. अवयाः (Rig Veda I. 173. 12) 'the name of a Vedic priest;' as त्वं यज्ञे वरुणस्यावया असि 'Thou art the priest of Varuna in the sacrifice.'

The division of this aphorism from the last in which it could have been included, is for the sake of the subsequent sûtras in which the *anuvritti* of यज only runs. This word is thus declined :—

	Sing.	Dual.	Plural.
1st.	अवयाः	अवयाजौ	अवयाजः
2nd.	अवयाजं	अवयाजौ	अवयाजः
3rd.	अवयाजा	अवयोभ्यां	अवयोभिः

३४१६ । अवयाः श्वेतवाः पुरोडाश्च । ८ । २ । ६७ ।

एते संबुद्धौ कृतदीर्घा निपात्यन्ते । चादवयाः ।

3416. The रु substitution of VIII. 2. 66 S. 162 takes place for the final of the Nominatives and vocatives of अवयज्, श्वेतवाह् and पुरोडाश् giving the irregular forms अवयाः, श्वेतवाः and पुरोडाः ॥

They are so exhibited here, for making them long in the Vocative singular also. For they could not have been lengthened in the Vocative singular, because VI. 4. 14 does not apply to it. Thus हे अश्वाः, हे श्वेतवाः, हे पुरोडाः ॥ By force of च in the sûtra, we form उक्थशाः also similarly.

३४१७ । त्रिवुपे छन्दसि । ३ । २ । ७३ ।

उप उपपदे यजेर्विच् । उपयट् ।

3417. The affix विच् comes after the verb यज् when उप precedes, in the Chhandas.

As उपयड्भिरूर्ध्वं वहन्ति 'they carry it up with the उपयज् formulas.' उपयज् is the name of eleven formulas at a sacrifice.

३४१८ । आतो मनिन्क्वनिब्वनिपश्च । ३ । २ । ७४ ।

सुप्युपसर्गे चोपपदे आदन्तेभ्यो धातुभ्यश्छन्दसि विषये मनिनादयस्त्रयः प्रत्ययाः स्युः । चाद्विच् सुदामा । सुधीवा । सुपीवा । भूरिदावा । घृतपावा । विच् । कीलालपाः ।

3418. The affixes मनिन् (मन्), क्वनिप् (वन्), वनिप् (वन्) and विच् come in the Chhandas, after verbs which end in long आ, when a case-inflected word or an upasarga is in composition.

The force of 'and' is to include विच्. Thus सुदा + मनिन् = सुदामन्, 1st sing. सुदामा (Rig. VI. 20. 7) 'one who gives liberally;' सुधी + क्वनिप् = सुधी + वन् (VI. 4. 66 = सुधीवन्, 1st sing. सुधीवा 'having good understanding;' सुपा + क्वनिप् = सुपीवन्, 1st sing. सुपीवा 'a good drinker,' भूरि + दा + वनिप् = भूरिदावन्, 1st sing. भूरिदावा (Rig. II. 27. 17) 'liberal;' घृतपावन् 1st sing. घृतपावा (Yaj. VI. 19) 'ghee-drinker.'

The affix विच् is also included in this aphorism. As कीलाल + पा + विच् = कीलालपाः (Rig. X. 91. 14) 'nectar-drinker.'

३४१९ । बहुलं छन्दसि । ३ । २ । ८८ ।

उपपदान्तरेऽपि हन्तेर्बहुलं क्विप्स्यात् । मातृहा । पितृहा ।

3419. In the Chhandas, the affix क्विप् diversely comes after the verb हन् 'to kill' with the sense of past time, even when the word in composition with it is other than those mentioned in III. 2. 87. S. 2998.

This aphorism ordains क्विप् in cases which are not governed by the restrictive rule contained in III. 2. 87. S. 2998. As मातृहा सप्तमं नरकं प्रविशेत् 'may the matricide enter the seventh hell;' so also पितृहा 'patricide.'

Diversely we find also मातृघातः and पितृघातः ।

The Past participle Nishṭhâ is generally formed by क्त, but in the Vedas, it is formed by the affixes of the Perfect tense also, and the Perfect itself is formed sometimes by the affixes कानच् and क्वसु as already taught in the sûtras III. 2. 105 S.3093; III. 2. 106 S. 3094; III, 2. 107 S. 3095. They are repeated here again.

३४१९ क । छन्दसि लिट् । ३ । २ । १०५ ।

भूत सामान्ये । 'अहं द्यावापृथिवी आततान' ।

3419 A. In the Chhandas, the affix लिट् comes after a verb, with the force of Past participle, and Past tense in general,

As अहं द्यावापृथिवी आततान 'I stretched the heaven and the earth.' Here the word आततान has the force of nishṭhâ.

३४१९ ख। लिटः कानज्वा । ३ । २ । १०६ ।

3419 B. In the Chhandas the affix लिट् is optionally replaced by the affix कानच् *i.e.*, the affix has the force of the Perfect.

As अग्निं चिक्यानः 'he consecrated the fire;' सोमं सुषुवाणः 'he pressed the *soma* juice.'

This affix comes after those verbs only which take Atmanepada terminations. See I.4. 100. तूतुजान (Rig Veda I. 3. 6).

३४१९ ग। क्वसुश्च । ३ । २ । १०७ ।

छन्दसि लिटः कानच्क्वसू वा स्तः । 'चक्राणा वृष्णि' । 'यो नो अग्ने अररिवाँ अघायुः' । '+ छन्दस्यघशब्दात्परेच्छायां क्यज्वक्तव्यः +' । क्याच्छन्दसि' (३१५०) । उप्रत्ययः स्यात् । अघायुः । '+ एरजधिकारे जवसवौ छन्दसि वाच्यौ +' । 'ऊर्वोस्तुमे जवः' । 'देवस्य सवितुः सवे' ।

3419 C. In the Chhandas the affix क्वसु is optionally the substitute of लिट् *i.e.*, the kvasu formed word has the force of the Perfect.

As जक्षिवस् 1st sing. जक्षिवान् 'eaten' (Yaj. VIII. 19); पपिवस् 1st sing. पपिवान् 'drunk.'

Thus चक्राणा वृष्णि पौंस्यम् (Rig Veda VIII. 7. 23).

यो नो अग्ने अररिवान् अघायुः (Rig Veda I. 147. 4).

Here the word अररिवान् is formed from the root रा 'to give,' with the affix क्वसु having the force of Perfect. The Negative Particle अ is added. Thus रा + क्वसु = रा रा + वस् = र रा+इट् + वस् (VII. 2. 67 S. 3096) = ररिवस्. The Nom. Sing. is ररिवान् "a generous man." अररिवान् "a miser, an enemy."

By S. III. 1. 8. S. 2657. the affix क्यच् is added to a noun in order to denote a *wish for one's own self*. The following vârtika makes an exception in the Vedas.

Vârt :—In the Vedas, the affix क्यच् is added after the word अघ, *even when the wish is with regard to another*. As मा त्वा वृका अघायवो विदन्. Here अघायु (pl अघायवः) is formed by *kyach*, उ being added by III. 2. 170. S. 3150, and आ is added by VII. 4. 37. See Rig Veda I. 120. 7. Thus अघ+क्यच् = अघ + य = अघ + य + उ (III. 2. 170. S. 3150) = अघा+यु (VII. 4. 37. S. 3590.)

By sûtra III. 3. 56. S. 3231. the affix अच् is added to roots ending in इ or ई, but in the Vedas this affix is added even after roots in उ or ऊ by the following Vârtika.

Vârt:—The words जव and सव are formed by the affix अच् and they occur in the Vedas. As 'ऊर्वोरस्तु मे जवः,' । देवस्य सवितुः, सवे (Rig Veda V. 82. 6.)

These roots जु and सु would have otherwise taken the affix अप्. The form would have been the same, but there would be difference of accent. See Rig. I. 112. 21, and Yaj. XI. 2.

३४२० । मन्क्तिन्व्याख्यानशयनासनस्थानयाजकादिक्रीताः — वृषेषपचमनविदभूवीरा उदात्तः । ३ । ३ । ९६ ।

वृषादिभ्यःक्तिन्स्यात् । स चोदात्तः । 'वृष्टिं दिवः' । 'सुम्नमिष्टये' । 'पचापक्तीरुत' । 'इयं ते नव्यसी मतिः' । वित्तिः । भूतिः । 'अग्ने आ याहि वीतये । 'राती स्यामोभयासः' ।

3420. In the Mantra literature, 'ktin' acutely accented comes after the following roots, forming words in the feminine gender, denoting a mere action :—'vṛish' (to rain), 'ish' (to wish), 'pach' (to cook), 'man' (to think), 'vid' (to know), 'bhû' (to be), 'vi' (to go, to consume) and 'râ' (to give).

The construction of this sûtra is anomalous. Instead of the bases being put in the ablative case, they are put in the nominative case. Thus वृष्टिः 'raining'; इष्टिः 'wishing'; पक्तिः 'cooking'; मतिः 'thinking'; वित्तिः 'knowing'; भूतिः 'being'; वीतिः 'consuming'; रातिः 'giving'.

As "स नो वृष्टिं दिवः" (Rig Veda 11. 6. 5).

सुम्नमिष्टये (Rig Veda VI. 70. 4).

पचात्पक्तीरुत (Rig Veda IV. 24. 7).

नव्यसी मतिः (Rig Veda VIII. 74. 7).

भूतिमूदिमः (Rig Veda I. 161. 1).

अग्न आयाहि वीतये (Rig Ved. VI. 16. 10).

राती स्यामोभयासः (Rig. Ved. VII. 1, 20).

३४२१। छन्दसि गत्यर्थेभ्यः। ३। ३। १२९।

ईषदादिषूपपदेषु गत्यर्थेभ्यो धातुभ्यश्छन्दसि युचस्यात्। खलोऽपवादः। सूपसदनोऽग्निः।

3421. The affix 'yuch' comes in the Chhandas, after roots having the sense of 'to go', when the word 'îshad' &c. meaning 'lightly' or 'with difficulty' are in composition with such verbs.

This debars the affix खल् of III. 3. 126, 127 S. 3305 and 3308. Thus सूपसदनोऽग्निः। सूपसदनमन्तरिक्षम्। See T. S. 7. 5. 20. 1.

३४२२। अन्येभ्योऽपि दृश्यते। ३। ३। १३०।

गत्यर्थेभ्यो येऽन्ये धातवस्तेभ्योऽपि छन्दसि युच्स्यात्। 'सुवेदनामकृणोद्ब्रह्मणे गाम्'।

3422. The affix 'yuch' is seen to come in the Vedas, after other verbs also, than those meaning 'to go'.

Thus सुदोह नाम कृणोद् ब्रह्मणे गां; so also सुवेद् नाम कृणोद् ब्रह्मणे गां॥ (Rig Veda X. 112, 8).

३४२३। छन्दसि लुङ्लङ्लिटः। ३। ४। ६।

धात्वर्थानां संबन्धे सर्वकालेष्वेते वास्युः। पक्षे यथास्वं प्रत्ययाः। लुङि। 'देवो देवेभिरागमत्'। लोडर्थे लुङ्। 'इदं तेभ्योऽकरं नमः'। लङ्। 'अग्निमद्य होतारमवृणीतायं यजमानः'। लिट्। 'अद्या ममार'। अद्य म्रियत इत्यर्थः।

3423. In the Vedas, the Aorist, Imperfect and Perfect are optionally employed in all tenses, in relation to verbs.

The words धातुसम्बन्ध and अन्यतरस्याम् are understood here also. By saying 'optionally', other tense affixes may be similarly employed.

Thus देवो देवेभिरागमत् (Rig. I. 1. 5). 'O God Agni! come hither with the gods'. Here the Aorist आगमत् has the force of the Imperative. ये भूतस्य प्रचेतस इदं तेभ्योऽकरं नमः 'I make salutation &c. &c.' (Rig. X. 85. 17). Here अकरं is Aorist (लुङ्) and has the sense of the Present.

So also अग्निमद्य होतारमवृणीतायं यजमानः। Here लङ् is used instead of लट् ।

So also अद्या ममार = अद्य म्रियते । Here लिट् is used instead of लट् ।

NOTE:—अगमत् is formed with the affix अङ् of the Aorist because the root गम्लृ has an indicatory लृ in the Dhàtupàṭha and belongs to Púshâdi class.

अकरम् here च्लि is replaced by अङ् by sûtra VII. 2. 13. S. 2293. Thus कृ + अङ् + म्. Then there is guṇa by VII. 4. 16 S. 2406. With the augment अ we get अकरम् "I did."

अवृणीत from वृञ् 'to choose'; add लङ्, and श्ना vikaraṇa because the root belongs to Kryâdi class. Then there is long ई by VI. 4. 113. S. 2497. Thus we have अवृणीत ॥

३४२४ । लिङर्थे लेट् । ३ । ४ । ७ ।

विध्यादौ हेतुहेतुमद्भावादौ च धातोर्लेट् स्याच्छन्दसि ।

3424. The affix 'Leṭ' is optionally employed in the Vedas, wherever the Potential can be used.

The formation of लेट् is shown in the subsequent sûtras. In the first place, the vikaraṇa सिप् is sometimes added between the Personal-endings and the root. Secondly, the Personal-endings themselves lose their इ thus ति becomes त्, सि becomes स् । Thirdly, the word takes the augment अट् and आट् between the Personal-endings and the root. Fourthly, the सिप् vikaraṇa sometimes causes Vriddhi also.

३४२५ । सिब्बहुलं लेटि । ३ । १ । ३४ ।

3425. सिप् is diversely the affix of a verbal root when लेट् follows.

३४२६ । इतश्च लोपः परस्मैपदेषु । ३ । ४ । ९७ ।

लेटस्तिङामितो लोपो वा स्यात्परस्मैपदेषु ।

3426. In the Parasmaipada affixes the 'i' is optionally elided in the Subjunctive.

The वा of the the preceding Ashṭâdhyâyî sûtra III. 4. 96. is understood here also.

३४२७ । लेटोऽडाटौ । ३ । ४ । ९८ ।

लेटः 'अट्' 'आट्' एतावागमौ स्तः । तौ च पितौ । '+ सिब्बहुलं णिद्वक्तव्यः +' । वृद्धिः । 'प्र ण आयूंषि तारिषत्' । 'सुपेशसस्करति जोषिषद्धि' । 'आ सविषदर्शसानाय शरुत्' । सिप इलोपस्य चाभावे । 'पताति विद्युत्' । 'प्रियः सूर्ये प्रियो अग्ना भवाति' ।

3427. The augments 'aṭ' and 'âṭ' are added to the personal endings of the Vedic Subjunctive.

The augments अट् and आट् are पित् and are not to be added at once, but by turns. Thus जुष् + सिप् + अट् + त् = जोषिषत्; तारिषत्, मान्दिषत्; similarly पत् + आट् + ति = पताति; च्यावयाति । See III. 1. 34 for the addition of सिप् in the above.

Vârt:—The vikaraṇa सिप् is treated as णित् and therefore causes Vriddhi.

Thus from the root तॄ we have तारिषत्, as तॄ + तिप् = तॄ + सिप् + तिप् – तॄ + इट् + सिप् + तिप् = तार + इ + सि + ति = तारिषत् । Thus प्र ण आयूंषि तारिषत् ।

Similarly जोषिषत् from जुषी प्रीतिसेवनयोः; as in सुपेशस्करति जोषिषद्धि ।

Similarly असाविषत् from षुप्रसवैश्वर्ययोः, as in the following—
आ साविषदर्शसानाय शरुम् (Rig Veda X. 99. 7.)

But when there is no सिप् added, and the इ of the Personal-endings is not elided, then we have forms like पताति दिद्युत् and प्रियः सूर्ये प्रियो अग्ना भवाति (Rig Veda V. 37. 5)

In fact लेट् is a composite Mood, and may be considered to have six tenses as shown below :—

I.—Present.—लेट्

I.	भवति	भवतः	भवन्ति
	भवाति	भवातः	भवान्ति
II.	भवसि	भवथः	भवथ
	भवासि	भवाथः	भवाथ
III.	भवामि	भवावः	भवामः
		भवाव	भवाम

II.—Imperfect.

I.	भवत्	भवतः	भवन्
	भवात्	भवातः	भवान्
II.	भवः	भवथः	भवथ
	भवाः	भवाथः	भवाथ
III.	भवाम्	भवावः	भवामः
		भवाव	भवाम

III.—Present Conditional.

I.	भविषति	भविषतः	भविषन्ति
	भविषाति	भविषातः	भविषान्ति
II.	भविषसि	भविषथः	भविषथ
	भविषासि	भविषाथः	भविषाथ
III.	भविषामि	भविषावः	भविषामः
		भविषाव	भविषाम

IV.—Imperfect Conditional.

I.	भविषत्	भविषतः	भविषन्
	भविषात्	भविषातः	भविषान्
II.	भविषः	भविषथः	भविषथ
	भविषाः	भविषाथः	भविषाथ
III.	भविषाम्	भविषावः	भविषामः
		भविषाव	भविषाम

V.—Strong Present Conditional.

I.	भाविषति	भाविषतः	भाविषन्ति
	भाविषाति	भाविषातः	भाविषान्ति
II.	भाविषसि	भाविषथः	भाविषथ
	भाविषासि	भाविषाथः	भाविषाथ
III.	भाविषमि	भाविषावः	भाविषामः
		भाविषाव	भाविषाम

VI.—Strong Imperfect Conditional.

I.	भाविषत्	भाविषतः	भाविषन्
	भाविषात्	भाविषातः	भाविषान्

II. भाविषः	भाविषथः	भाविषथ
भाविषाः	भाविषाथः	भाविषाथ
III. भाविषाम्	भाविषावः	भाविषामः
	भाविषाव	भाविषाम

३४२८ । स उत्तमस्य । ३ । ४ । ९८ ।

लेडुत्तमसकारस्य वा लोपः स्यात् । करवाव । करवावः । टेरेत्वम् ।

3428. The 's' of the first person is optionally elided in the Subjunctive.

As करवाव or करवावः, करवाम or करवामः । The first person is used in the sûtra to indicate that the स् is not elided in any other person.

३४२९ । आत ऐ । ३ । ४ । ९५ ।

लेट आकारस्यै स्यात् । 'सुतेभिः सुप्रयसा मादयैते' । आतामित्याकारस्यैकारः । विधि-सामर्थ्यादाट ऐत्वं न । अन्यथा हि ऐटमेव विदध्यात् । 'यो यजाति यजात इत्' ।

3429. In the Subjunctive, 'ai' is the substitute of 'â' of आताम् and आथाम् in the first and second person dual of the Atmanepada.

Thus मन्त्रयैते, मन्त्रयैथे, करवैते, करवैथे । Why is not the augment आट् changed into ऐ ? Because otherwise the rule enjoining आट् would be superfluous, and the sûtra enjoining आट् ought to have enjoined ऐट् at once.

सुतेभि : सुप्रयसा मादयैते (Rig Veda IV. 41. 3). Here the affix आताम् is changed to एते ॥ The regular form एते the आ is changed to ए by III. 4 79. S. 2233.

The आ of the augment आट् is not changed to ऐ as we have already said above, and here we have the forms यजाति &c. यो यजाति यजात इत् (Rig Veda VIII. 31. 1).

३४३० । वैतोऽन्यत्र । ३ । ४ । ९६ ।

लेट् एकारस्य 'ऐ' स्याद्वा । 'आत ऐ' (३४२९) इत्यस्य विषयं विना । 'पशूनामीशै' । 'ग्रहा गृह्यान्तै' । 'अन्यत्र' किम् । 'सुप्रयसा मादयैते' ।

3430. In the Subjunctive, 'ai' is optionally the substitute of 'e', in other places than those mentioned in the last sûtra.

Thus शयै, ईशै &c, in the following examples :—सप्ताहानि शयै, अहमेव पशूनामीशै, मदया यच्च वो यद्धा गृह्यान्तै, मळ्वत्यान्यव वः पात्राण्युच्यान्तै । And in the alternative we have simply ए, as यत्र क्व च ते मनो दक्षं दधस उत्तरम् ।

NOTE :—ईशै from the root ईश ऐश्वर्ये । It is the 1st Pers. Sing. The Atmanepada Personal ending इट् of the 1st Pers. Sing. is changed to ऐ । This इ is not elided by. III. 4. 97. S. 3426, because that sûtra is confined to Parasmaipada इ ॥ The इ is changed to ए by III. 4. 79. S. 2233, then ए changed to ऐ by this sûtra.

गृह्यान्तै from ग्रहिं in the Passive. The य of the Passive is added, and then the 3rd Pers. Plural झि or अन्ति । The Personal ending takes the augment आट् and becomes आन्ति ॥ The र of ग्रह is changed to ऋ by VI. 1. 16. S. 2412, and the इ of आन्ति is changed to ए by III. 4. 79. S. 2233, and this ए is changed to ऐ by the present sûtra.

३४३१ । उपसंवादाशङ्कयोश्च । ३ । ४ । ८ ।

पणबन्ध आशङ्कायां च लेट् स्यात् । 'अहमेव पशूनामीशै' । 'नेज्जिह्मायन्तो नरकं पताम' । हलः श्नः शानज्झौ' (२५५७) ।

3431. Where a contingent promise (a reciprocal agreement), or where apprehension is implied, the affix 'Leṭ' is employed after a root, in the Chhandas Literature.

The word उपसम्वाद means 'reciprocal agreement, contracting to do.' Thus यदि मे भवानिदं कुर्य्याद् अहमपि भवत इदं दास्यामि 'If you do this for me, I will give this to you.' Agreements like these are called उपसम्वाद ; while guessing or inferring the result from a cause is called आशङ्का 'apprehension or fear.'

Thus अहमेव पशूनामीशै ॥ This is the reply of Rûdra, when he was solicited by the Devas, to conquer Tripura. The word पशु means "bound souls, jivas treading the round of Samsâra." पताम is Leṭ the final स् is elided by III. 4. 98 S. 3428. मदग्रा एव वो ग्रहा गृह्यान्तै ॥ मद्ग्रेवत्यान्येव वः पात्राण्युच्यान्तै ॥ नेज्जिह्मायन्तो (or. नेज्जिह्मायन्त्यो) नरकं पताम ॥ (Nir. I. 11. Bohtlingk) - जिह्माचरणेन नरकपात आशंक्यते ॥ All the above examples have the sense of Potential, but the Subjunctive (Leṭ) must be employed necessarily in these senses and not optionally, which anuvṛitti was understood in the last sûtra.

By III. 1. 83, S. 2557, in the Imperative 2nd Pers. Singular, शानच् is sometimes substituted for the vikaraṇa श्ना, after the Kryâdi roots ending in consonants. By the next sûtra, शायच् is optionally the substitute in the Vedas.

३४३२ । छन्दसि शायजपि । ३ । १ । ८४ ।

अपिग्रहणाच्छानच् । '+ हृग्रहोर्भश्छन्दसि +' इति हस्य भः । 'गृभाय जिह्वया मधु' । 'बधान देव सवितः' । 'अनिदिताम्—' (४१५) इति बन्धातेर्नलोपः । 'गृभ्णामि ते' । 'मध्वा जभार' ।

3432. In the Chhandas, शायच् is also the substitute of श्ना after roots ending in consonants, when हि follows.

Thus गृभाय जिह्वया मधु. (Rig Veda VIII. 17. 5) "take up the honey with the tongue." The affix शानच् is also employed by force of the word api in the aphorism as बधान पशून् 'bind the beasts.'

Vârt :—In the Chhandas, भ is substituted for the ह of हृ and ग्रह ॥ Thus गर्दभेन संभरति ; मरुदस्य गृभ्णाति ; सामिधेन्योजभ्रिरे, उद्ग्राभञ्च निग्राभञ्च ब्रह्मदेवा अवीवृधन् ॥

NOTE :—गृभाय is derived from ग्रह् 'to seize'; the र् is vocalised by ग्रहिज्या etc. VI. 1. 16 S. 2412 ; and ह changed to भ by the vârtika above given. Thus ग्रह् + श्ना + हि = गृह् + ना = गृभ् + ना = गृभ् + आय (शायच्) = गृभाय 'take up thou.'

NOTE :—बधान is formed by शानच् ; added to the root बन्ध 'to bind' the nasal is elided by VI. 4. 24 S. 415 ; the Imperative affix हि is elided by VI. 4. 105 S. 2202. Thus बन्ध् + श्ना + हि = बध् + श्ना + हि = बध् + आन + हि = बध् + आन + ० = बधान "bind or tether."

Other examples of the change of ह into भ by the above vârtika are given below :—

गृभ्णामि ते (Rig Veda X. 85. 36). मध्वा जभार

३४३३ । व्यत्ययो बहुलम् । ३ । १ । ८५ ।

विकरणानां बहुलं व्यत्ययः स्याच्छन्दसि । 'आण्डा शुष्णस्य भेदति' । भिनत्तीति प्राप्ते । 'जरसा मरते पतिः' । म्रियत इति प्राप्ते । 'इन्द्रो वस्तेन नेषतु' । नयतेर्लोट् शप्सिपौ द्वौ विकरणौ ॥ 'इन्द्रेण युजा तरुषेम वृत्रम्' । तरेमेत्यर्थः । तरतेर्विध्यादौ लिङ् । उःशप्सिप्चेति त्रयो विकरणाः ।

सुप्तिङुपग्रहलिङ्गनराणां कालहलच्स्वरकर्तृयङां च ।
व्यत्ययमिच्छति शास्त्रकृदेषां सोऽपि च सिध्यति बाहुलकेन ।

'धुरि दक्षिणायाः' । दक्षिणस्यामिति प्राप्ते । 'चषालं ये अश्वयूपाय तक्षति' । तक्षन्तीति प्राप्ते । उपग्रहः परस्मैपदात्मनेपदे । 'ब्रह्मचारिणमिच्छते' । इच्छतीति प्राप्ते । 'प्रतीपमन्य ऊर्मिर्युध्यति' । युध्यत इति प्राप्ते । 'मधोस्तृप्ता इवासते' । मधुन इति प्राप्ते । नरः पुरुषः । 'अधा स वीरैर्दशभिर्वियूयाः' । वियूयादिति प्राप्ते । कालः कालवाची प्रत्ययः । 'श्वोऽग्नीनाधास्यमानेन' । लुटो विषये लृट् । 'तमसो गा अदुक्षत' । अधुक्षदिति प्राप्ते । 'मित्र वयं च सूरयः' । मित्रा वयमिति प्राप्ते । स्वरव्यत्ययस्तु वक्ष्यते । कर्तृशब्दः कारकमात्रपरः । तथा च तद्वाचिनां कृत्तद्धितानां व्यत्ययः । अन्नादायअण् विषयेऽच् । अवग्रहे विशेषः । यङो यशब्दादारभ्य 'लिङ्याशिष्यङ्' (३४३४) इति ङकारेण । प्रत्याहारः । तेषां व्यत्ययो भेदतीत्यादिरुक्त एव ।

3433. In the Chhandas there is diversely an interchange of the various vikaraṇas शप् and the rest, which have been ordained under special circumstances.

The word व्यत्यय means transgression of the fixed rule, or interchange; taking of two vikaraṇas at a time, and so on. Thus भेदति = भिद+शप्+ति ; in stead of भिनत्ति from the root भिद 'to split', belonging to the Rudhâdi class; *e. g.* आण्डा शुष्णस्य भेदति (Rig VIII. 40. 11) "He (Indra) breaks the eggs (children) of Shushṇa"; so also, जरसा मरते पतिः (Rig. X. 86. 11.); here there is मरते = (मृ + शप् + ते) instead of म्रियते ; the root मृ belonging to the Tudâdi class. So also there are two vikaraṇas at one and the same time, in the following. इन्द्रो वस्तेन नेषतु 'May Indra lead by this abode' ; here there is नेषतु 3rd per. sing. of the Imperative (लोट्) of the root नी 'to lead' ; there are two vikaraṇas सिप् and शप् instead of नयतु = (नी + शप् + तु); इन्द्रेण युजा तरुषेम वृत्रम् (Rig. VII. 48. 1). The word तरुषेम (तृ + उ + सिप् + शप् + अम्) is the 1st per. sing. of the Optative (लिङ्) of the root तृ and is formed by *three* vikaraṇas ; the classical form bein g तरेम 'may we cross.'

Kârikâ:—In the Vaidic literature we have many apparent irregularities with regard to the application of (1) सुप् (case-affixes), (2) तिङ् (Personal-endings), (3) उपग्रह (Parasmaipada or Atmanepada affixes), (4) rules of gender, (5) person or (6) tense (7) rules of interchange of consonants, or (8) of vowels, (9) rules of accent (10) rules relating to कृत and तद्धित affixes and (12) rules relating to the affixes included in the pratyâhâra यङ् (III. I. 22 to III. 1. 86). All these irregularities areexplained by the author by the word बहुलम् ॥ In fact, the word *bahulam* not only covers, but explains and justifies all Vaidic anomalies

NOTE :—The word शास्त्रकृत् "science-maker," in the above kârikâ refers to Pâṇini.

Thus :—

(1). Irregular application of case-affixes: धुरि दक्षिणायाः (Rig Veda I. 164. 9.)

Here दक्षिणायाः (Genitive) is used instead of the Locative दक्षिणस्याम् ॥

(2). Irregular application of Personal-endings : चषालं ये अश्वयूपाय तक्षति (Rig Veda I. 162. 6). Here तक्षति is used instead of तक्षन्ति ॥

(3). Irregular use of Parasmaipada and Atmanepadas : as, ब्रह्मचारिणमिच्छते। Here Atmanepada इच्छते is used instead of Parasmaipada इच्छति ॥ Similarly प्रतीपमन्य ऊर्मिर्युध्यति instead of युध्यते ॥

(4). Irregular use of Genders, as मधोस्तृप्ता इवासते। Here the word मधु which is Neuter gender, is declined as Masculine. The classical form is मधुनः ॥

(5). Irregular use of Person. The word नरः in the Kârikâ means Person. As अधा सवीरैः दशभिर्वियूयाः instead of वियूयात् ॥ Here 2nd Person is used for 3rd Person. This word is the Benedictive Mood of the root यु "to mix," with the prefix वि ॥

(6). Irregular use of Tenses. The word काल in the Kârikâ means the affixes denoting *time*. Thus श्वोऽग्नीन् आधास्यमानेन। Here लृट् is used instead of लुट्। It is formed from धा with the affix शानच् (III. 3. 14 S. 3107) and the Mood affix स्य (III. 1. 33. S. 2186), and the augment मुक् (VII. 2. 82. S. 3101).

(7). Irregular interchange of consonants : as, तमसो गा अदुक्षत्। Here द is not changed to ध। The proper form is अधुक्षत्।

(8) Irregular vowels : as, मित्र वयं च सूरयः instead of मित्रा वयम् ॥

(9). Irregular use of Accents. This will be illustrated later on.

(10). Irregular use of Kârakas. The word कर्तृ in the Kârikâ means Kâraka; and includes the Krit and Taddhita affixes. Thus from the root अद् 'to eat' with the upapada अन्न, a compound is formed by adding the affix अण्। Thus अन्न + अद् + अण् = अन्न + आद = अन्नादः। But in the Vedas, affix अच् is used. Thus अन्न + अद् + अच् = अन्न + अद = अन्नादः। Here though the resulting form in both cases is the same, yet in analysis they will be different. Thus in one case it would be अन्न + आदाय, in the other अन्न + अदाय ॥

(11). The यङ् in the Kârikâ is a Pratyâhâra formed with the य of III. 1. 22, and the ङ् of अङ् in III. 1. 86. There is irregular use of these affixes also in the Vedas. These affixes are :—

1. यङ् Intensive affix. 2. णिच् Causative and Churâdi class affix. 3. यक् Kandu yâdi class affix. 4. आयः 5. ईयङ् 6. णिङ् 7. स्य and तासि of the Future Tense &c. 8. सिप् of Let. 9. आम् of Perfect. 10. च्लि and सिच्, क्स, चङ्, and अङ् and चिण् of the Aorist. 11. यक् of the Passive, 12. The vikaranas शप्, श्यन्, श्नु, श, श्नम्, उ, श्ना, and the Benedictive अङ्। The irregular use of these has already been illustrated in the examples like भेदति &c.

३४३४। लिङ्याशिष्यङ्। ३। १। ८६।

आशीर्लिङि परे धातोरङ् स्याच्छन्दसि। 'वच उम्' (२४५४)। 'मंत्रं वोचेमाग्नये'। + दृशेरग्वक्तव्यः+'। 'पितरं च दृशेयं मातरं च' अङि तु 'ऋदृशोऽङि–' (२४०६) इति गुणः स्यात्।

3434. The affix अङ् is employed in the Chhandas when the affixes of the Benedictive (आशीर्लिङ्) follow.

This debars जप्. The affixes of the Benedictive are ârdhadhâtuka by III 4. 116. S. 2215; but in the Vedas they are sârvadhâtuka as well; see III. 4. 117. S 3435. The scope of the present rule is confined to the Benedictive of the verbs स्था. गा, गम, वच्, वद् शक् and रुह; as उपस्थेयम्; सत्यमुपगेयम्, गमेम जानतो गृहान्, मंत्रं वोचेमाग्नये; विदेयमेनां मनसि पविष्ठां; व्रतम् चरिष्यामि तच्छकेयम्; स्वर्गं लोकमारुहेयम्.

Várt :—The affix अक् is employed in the Chhandas after the verb दृश् in the Benedictive. Had there been अङ्, it would have caused *guṇa* by rule VII. 4. 16. S. 2406; to prevent this, अक् is ordained; as पितरंच दृशेयं मातरंच (Rig Veda I. 24. 1). 'May I see the father and the mother.'

३४३५ । छन्दस्युभयथा । ३ । ४ । ११७ ।

धात्वाधिकार उक्तः प्रत्ययः सार्वधातुकार्धधातुकोभयसंज्ञः स्यात् । 'वर्धन्तु त्वा सुष्टुतयः'। वर्धयन्त्वित्यर्थः । आर्धधातुकत्वाण्णिलोपः । 'विशृण्विरे' सार्वधातुकत्वात् श्नुः शृभावश्च । 'हुश्नुवोः–' (२३८७) इति यण् । 'आदृगमहनजनः किकिनौ लिट् च' (३१५१) । आदन्तादृवर्णान्ताद्गमादेश्च किकिनौ स्तः । तौ च लिड्वत् । 'बभ्रिर्वज्रम्' । 'पपिः सोमम्' 'ददिर्गाः । जग्मिर्युवा' । 'जघ्निर्वृत्रममित्रियम्' । जज्ञिः । लिड्वद्भावादेव सिद्धे 'ऋच्छत्यृताम्' (२३८३) इति गुणबाधनार्थं कित्त्वम् 'बहुलं छन्दसि' (३५७८) इत्युत्वम् । ततुरिः । जगुरिः ।

3435. In the Vedas this distinction of 'sârvadhâtuka' and 'ârdhadhâtuka' is not always maintained, and the affixes ordained after roots are promiscuously employed.

In the Vedas, there is no hard and fast rule about *sârvadhâtuka* and *ârdhadhâtuka* affixes. Sometimes the तिङ् and शित् are treated as if they were *ârdhadhâtuka* Thus वर्धन्तु त्वा सुष्टुतयः । Here the affixes of the लोट् are treated as *ârdhadhâtuka* and consequently there is the elision of the णिच् by rule VI. 4. 51. S. 2313; the proper form of this word would be वर्धयन्तु । Sometimes *ârdhadhâtuka* affixes are treated like *sârvadhâtuka* affixes; as शृण्विरे; here the affixes of the लिट् are treated as *sârvadhâtuka* and so there is the Vikaraṇa श्नु and the उ is changed into व । Thus, वि + शृ + श्नु + इरे = वि + शृ + नु + इरे (III. 1. 74. S. 2386.) = वि + शृ + न्व् + इरे (VI. 4. 87. S. 2387.) = विशृण्विरे । Similarly, सुन्विरे । The लिङ् is sometimes treated in the Vedas both as *ârdhadhâtuka* and *sârvadhâtuka* at one and the same time; as उपस्थेयाम् शरणं बृहन्तम् । Here, by treating the affix as *ârdhadhâtuka*, there is elision of स् in the लिङ् (VII. 2. 79. S. 2211) and by treating it again as *ârdhadhâtuka* the आ of स्था is changed into ए । So also in व्यतिन्त the affix is treated as *sârvadhâtuka* and there is no substitution of भू for अस् as required by II. 4, 52. S. 2470.

In this connection, we read here again the sûtra III. 2. 171. S. 3151.

३४३५ क । आदृगमहनजनः किकिनौ लिट् च । ३ । २ । १७१ ।

3435. A. In the Chhandas, the affixes 'ki' and 'kin' in the sense of 'the agent having such a habit &c' come after the verbs that end in long 'â' or short or long 'ṛi' and after the verbs gam 'to go,' han 'to kill,' and jan 'to be produced,' and these affixes operate like 'Lit' causing reduplication of the root.

बभ्रिर्वज्रम् (Rig Ved. VI. 23 4). From the root भृञ् + कि = बभ्रिः। Reduplication because treated as लिट्।

पपिः सोमम् (,, ,,). From पा + कि = पपिः।

ददिर्गाः (,, ,,). From दा + कि = ददिः

जग्मिर्युवा (Rig Veda VII. 20. 1.) From गम् + किन् = जग्मिः। The penultimate अ is elided by VI. 4. 98. S. 2263.

जघ्निर्वृत्रममित्रियम् (Rig Veda. IX. 61. 20). From हन् + किन् = जघ्निः। ह changed to घ by VII. 3. 54. S. 358.

जज्ञिःबीजम् (T. S. VII. 5. 20. 1.) From जन् + किन् = जज्ञिः

Q. "Now all the above roots either end in vowel or in simple consonants, and therefore by असंयोगाल्लिट् कित् (I. 2. 5. S. 2242), the affixes कि and किन् (the real affix is इ) would be कित्; why are these affixes enunciated with an indicatory क्?" Ans. They are read as कित् in order to prevent *guna* in the case of roots ending in long ॠ; for by VII. 4. 11. S. 2383, लिट् alone would not have been कित् after long ॠ॥ The usefulness of the affixes being कित् is illustrated in the next two examples.

मित्रावरुणा ततुरिम् (Rig Veda. IV. 39. 2). ततुरिम् = तारकं। दूरे अध्वाजगुरिः (Rig Veda X. 108. 1).

Here from the roots तॄ प्लवन तरणयोः and गॄ निगरणे both ending in long ॠ we get the forms ततुरिः and जगुरिः by the affix कि॥ Had the affix been merely इ without indicatory क्, it being like लिट् would have caused guṇa of ॠ by VII. 4. 11. S. 2383; but the indicatory क prevents it.

Thus तॄ + कि = तुर् + कि (the ॠ is replaced by उर् by VII. 1. 103. S. 3578.) Then there is reduplication. And we should get तुर् तुर् + इ॥ But by I. 1. 59 S. 2213, the उर् substitution does not take place first. It is after reduplication that VII. 1. 103. S. 3578. finds scope. Thus त + कि = तॄ तॄ + कि = तर्तॄ + कि (VII. 4 66. S. 2244.) = ततॄ + कि (VII. 4. 60. S. 2179) At this stage will apply sûtra VII. 4. 11, and we have ततुरिः॥

Similarly we get जगुरिः॥

३४३६ तुमर्थे सेसेनसेअसेन्क्सेकसेनध्यैअध्यैन्कध्यैकध्यैन्शध्यैशध्यैन्तवैतवेङ्-तवेनः। ३। ४। ९।

से। 'वक्षे रायः'। सेन्। 'ता वामेषे'। असे। 'शरदो जीवसे धाः'। असेसित्वादाद्युदात्तः क्से। प्रेषे। कसेन्। 'गवामिव श्रियसे'। अध्यै। अध्यैन् 'जठरं पृणध्यै'। पत्र आद्युदात्तः कध्यै। कध्यैन् आहुवध्यै। पत्रे नित्स्वरः। शध्यै। 'राधसः सह मादयध्यै'। शध्यैन्। 'वायवे पिबध्यै'। तवै। दातवाउ। तवेङ्। सूतवे। तवेन्। कर्तवे।

3436. In the Vedas the following affixes come after roots with the force of the affix 'tumun', viz:—'se', 'sen', 'ase', 'asen', 'kse', kasen', 'adhyai', 'adhyain', 'kadhyai', 'kadhyain', 'śadhyai', śadhyain', 'tavai', taveN', and 'taven.'

In the Vaidic literature, the Infinitive is formed by the above 15 affixes. These, when stripped of their indicatory letters, will be found to consist of the following five affixes:—(1) से = से, सेन् and क्से॥ (2) असे = असे, असेन् and कसेन्॥ (3) अध्यै = अध्यै, अध्यैन्, कध्यै, कध्यैन्, शध्यै and शध्यैन्॥ (4) तवै॥ (5) तवे = तवेङ् and तवेन्।

The difference in the affixes is made by four indicatory letters, viz. न्, क्, श् and ङ्। The forces of क् श् and ङ् have already been explained; the indicatory न् makes the word take the *udâtta* accent on the first syllable (VI. 1. 197. S. 3686). Thus से is acute (III. 1. 3. S. 3701); सेन् has acute on the first syllable of the word (VI. 1 197); असे has accent of the affix (III. 1. 3); असेन् throws the accent on the first syllable of the word; the indicatory श makes the numbers 11 and 12 Sârvadhâtuka, and the root takes the proper Vikaraṇa of its class before these affixes; while before तवै, the acute falls both on the first syllable and the last syllable simultaneously (VI. 1. 200. S. 3088. VI. 2. 51. S. 3785.)

Before going to give examples of these affixes, let us explain what is meant by तुमर्थ 'the sense of the affix तुम्'। The word तुमर्थ is here equivalent to भाव or 'action'; for the *pratyayas* or affixes, to which no meaning has been assigned in grammar, convey the meaning of the bases to which they are added. Thus no special meaning having been attached to तुमुन्, it will convey the meaning of the root to which it is added, *i. e.* it will denote the 'action' of the verb, or Infinitive mood. (1) से—वक्षे (from वच् + से) रायः।(2) सेन्—तावामेषे रथानाम् (Rig. V. 66. 3). from इ, एषे। (3 and 4) असे and असेन्—अस्मे शतं शरदो जीवसे धाः (Rig. III. 36. 10). So also क्रत्वे दक्षाय जीवसे' (Rig. X. 57. 4). With असेन् the word will be जीवसे। (5) क्से—प्रेषे भगाय from इ, इषे। प्र + इषे = प्रेषे (6) कसेन् गवामिव श्रियसे (Rig. V. 59. 3). It has not the नित् accent (VI. 1. 197) which would have given us श्रियसे। (7 and 8) अध्यै, अध्यैन् जठरं पृणध्यै। The accent is on the last in one case and on the first in the other. (9) कध्यै—इन्द्राग्नी आहुवध्यै (Rig VI. 60. 13). (10) कध्यैन् श्रियध्यै। (11 and 12) शध्यै, शध्यैन्—पिबध्यै (Rig VI. 27. 5); the accent however is on पि। सह मादयध्यै (Rig. VI. 60 13). (13) तवै—सोममिन्द्राय पातवै। (14) तवेङ्—तं ते गर्भं हवामहे दशमे मासि सूतवे (Rig. X. 184. 3). (15) तवेन्=गंतवे (Rig. I. 46. 7), कर्तवे (Rig. I. 85. 9); हर्तवे ॥

३४३७। प्रयै रोहिष्यै अव्यथिष्यै। ३। ४। १०।

एते तुमर्थे निपात्यन्ते। प्रयातुं रोढुमव्यथितुमित्यर्थः।

3437. The words 'prayai,' 'rohishyai,' and 'avyathishyai' are irregular Vaidic Infinitives.

Thus (1) प्रयै देवेभ्यो महीः (Rig. I. 142. 6); प्र + या + कै = प्रयै = प्रयातुम्। (2) अपामोषधीनां रोहिष्यै। रुह् + इष्यै = रोहिष्यै = रोहणाय। (3) अ + व्यथ् + इष्यै = अव्यथिष्यै = अव्यथनाय।

३४३८। दृशे विख्ये च। ३। ४। ११।

द्रष्टुं विख्यातुमित्यर्थः।

3438. The words 'dṛiśe' and 'vikhye' are anomalous Vaidic Infinitives.

Thus दृशे विश्वाय सूर्यम् (Rig. I. 50. 1) = द्रष्टुम्। विख्ये त्वा हरामि = विख्यातुम्।

३४३९। शकि णमुल्कमुलौ। ३। ४। १२।

शक्नोतावुपपदे तुमर्थे एतौ स्तः। 'विभाजं नाशकत्'। 'अपलुपं नाशकत्'। विभक्तुमपलोप्तुमित्यर्थः।

3439. The affixes 'ṇamul' and 'kamul' are added to roots in the Chhandas to form Infinitives, when they are governed by the verb 'śak' (to be able.)

Of the affix णमुल् the real affix is अम् ; the letter णू causes vṛiddhi (VII. 2. 115); and ल regulates the accent (VI. 1. 193). So also of कमुल् the letter क् prevents guṇa and vṛiddhi substitution (I. 1. 5.)

Thus अग्निं वै देवा विभाजं नाशक्नुवन् 'the Gods were not able to divide Agni.' विभज् + णमुल्=विभाजं=विभक्तुम् । So also अपलुपं नाशक्नुवन्, instead of अपलोप्तुम् ।

३४४० । ईश्वरे तोसुन्कसुनौ । ३ । ४ । १३ ।

'ईश्वरो विचरितोः' । 'ईश्वरो विलिखः' । विचरितुं विलेखितुमित्यर्थः ।

3440 The affixes 'tosun' and 'kasun' are added to roots in the Chhandas, to form Infinitives, when the word 'îśvara' is in composition.

Thus ईश्वरोऽभिचरितोः=अभिचरितुम् । ईश्वरो विलिखः=विलिखितुम । ईश्वरो वितृदः =वितर्दितुम् ।

३४४१ । कृत्यार्थे तवैकेन्केन्यत्वनः । ३ । ४ । १४ ।

'न म्लेच्छितवै' । 'अवगाहे' । 'दिदृक्षेण्यः' । 'भूर्यस्पष्ट कर्त्वम्' ।

3441. The affixes 'tavai,' 'ken,' 'kenya' and 'tvan' are added to roots in the Chhandas, in the sense of the 'Kṛitya-affixes.'

The force of *kritya* affixes is to denote 'action' (भाव) and 'object' (कर्मन्). Thus अन्वेतवै=अन्वेतव्यम ; परिधातवै=परिधातव्यम् ; नावगाहे = नावगाहितव्यम् ; दिदृक्षेण्यः (Rig. I. 106. 5)=दिदृक्षितव्य ; ; शुश्रूषेण्यः=शुश्रूषितव्यम् ; कर्त्वम् ; (Rig. I. 10. 2)=कर्तव्यम् ।

The affix तवै was mentioned in sûtra III. 4. 9, also ; there it had the force of the Infinitive, and here that of the Passive Participle. For its accent, see VI. 1. 200 ; 2. 51.

३४४२ । अवचक्षे च । ३ । ४ । १५ ।

'रिपुणा नावचक्षे' । अवख्यातव्यमित्यर्थः ।

3442. The word 'avachakshe' is an anomalous passive participle in the Vedas.

Thus रिपुणा नावचक्षे (Rig. IV. 58. 5)=नावख्यातव्यम् । अव + चक्ष् + एश्=अवचक्षे । The sûtra II. 4. 54. S. 2436, is not applied here.

३४४३ । भावलक्षणे स्थेण्कृञ्वदिचरिहुतमिजनिभ्यस्तोसुन् । ३ । ४ । १६ ।

'आसंस्थातोः सीदन्ति' । आसमाप्तेः सीदन्तीत्यर्थः । उदेतोः । अपकर्तोः । प्रवदितोः । प्रचरितोः । होतोः । आतमितोः । 'काममाविजनितोः संभवाम' ।

3443. The affix 'tosun' comes in the Vedas after the following verbs, when mere name of the action is indicated, viz :— 'sthâ' (to stand), '*in*' (to go), 'kṛiñ' (to make), 'vad' (to speak), 'char' (to walk), 'hu' (to sacrifice), 'tam' (to grow tired) and 'jan' (to produce).

These are also Infinitives. The phrase कृत्यार्थे is not to be read into this sûtra. The word भावलक्षण qualifies the sense of the root (भावो लक्ष्यते येन).

Thus, स्था—आ संस्थातोर्वेद्यां सीदन्ति=आसमाप्तेः सीदन्ति । इण्—पुरा सूर्यस्योदेतोराधेयः । कृञ्—पुरा वत्सानामपाकर्तोः । वद्—पुरा प्रवदितो रग्नो प्रहोतव्यम् । चर्—पुरा प्रचरितो-राग्नीध्रीये होतव्याः । (Gopatha Brahmaṇa II. 2. 10) । हृ—आ होतोरप्रमत्तस्तिष्ठति । तम्—आ तमितोरासीत (Taitt. Br. I. 4 4. 2) जन्—आ विजनितोः सम्भवाम (Taitt. S. II 5. 1. 5).

३४४४ । सृपितृदोः कसुन् । ३ । ४ । १७ ।

भावलक्षण इत्येव । 'पुरा क्रूरस्य विसृपो विरप्शिन्' । 'पुरा जत्रुभ्य आतृदः' ।

इति तृतीयोऽध्यायः ।

3444 In the Vedas, the affix 'kasun' comes after the verbs 'sṛip' (to creep) and 'tṛid' (to injure), in the sense of Infinitives indicating name of action.

Thus विसृपः । पुरा क्रूरस्य विसृपः (Yaj. I. 28.); आतृदः । पुरा जत्रुभ्य आतृदः (Rig. VIII. 1. 12). These words are Indeclinable by I. 1. 40. S. 450.

CHAPTER IV.

३४४५ । रात्रेश्चाजसौ । ४ । १ । ३१ ।

रात्रिशब्दान्ङीप्स्यात् अजस्विषये छन्दसि । 'रात्री व्यख्यदायती' । लोके तु कृदिकारादिति ङीषन्तोदात्तः ।

3445. The affix 'ṅîp' comes after the word 'râtri' in the Chhandas, and in denoting a Name, except when the affix 'jas' (nominative plural) is added.

Thus रात्री व्यख्यदायति, या रात्री सृष्टा, रात्रीभिः (3rd pl.) ; (Rigveda X. 127. 1. I. 35. 1.) but in the nominative plural we have रात्रयः, the regular plural of the word रात्रि, as in the sentence यास्ता रात्रयः, instead of रात्र्यः । In the classical literature. the feminine is formed by ङीष् (IV. 1. 45) with acute on the final.

NOTE:—According to Kâtyâyana, ṅîp is not added, not only when we apply the nominative plural termination जस्; but in all other terminations beginning with जस् also. Thus रात्रिं सहोषित्वा; here in the accusative singular case also the ङीप् is not employed.

But how do you explain the form रात्र्यः in the following त्रिभिष्टवं देव सवितर्वर्षिष्ठैः ... रात्र्यः? This 'râtrya' is the nominative plural of 'râtrî' which is formed by the feminine affix ṅîp ; and not by ṅish. The forms evolved by adding ङीष् or ङीप् are one and the same, except with regard to accent ; that formed by ṅish has udâtta accent on the final : the other has it on the initial. The word रात्रि is formed by the kṛit affix त्रिप् (Un. IV. 67), and therefore, it is a word which is governed by IV. 1. 45 because it is a word falling in Bahuvâdi class, by virtue of the general subrule "a word ending with the vowel इ of a kṛit affix, other than क्तिन् belongs to Bahuvâdi class ; some say that every word ending in इ, if it has not the force of the affix क्तिन् belongs to this class". Therefore it takes ङीष् in forming the feminine.

३४४६ । नित्यं छन्दसि । ४ । १ । ४६ ।

बह्वादिभ्यश्छन्दसि विषये नित्यं ङीष् । 'बह्वीषु हित्वा' । नित्यग्रहणमुत्तरार्थम् ।

3446. The affix 'Nîsh' is always employed in the Vaidic literature, in forming the feminine of the word 'bhu' and the rest.

Thus बह्वीषु हित्वा प्रपिबन् ॥ Here बह्वी is the name of a herb.

The word नित्य 'always' is used in the aphorism, more for the sake of the subsequent sûtra, which it governs than for this sûtra. For the word 'optionally' does not govern this, and the aphorism even without the word 'nitya' would have been a necessary rule and not optional: for आरम्भसामर्थ्यादेव नित्योविधिः सिद्धः, योगारम्भश्चिनत्य योजनः ॥

३४४७ । भुवश्च । ४ । १ । ४७ ।

ङीषन्यात् छन्दसि । विभ्वीं । प्रभ्वीं । विप्रसंभ्य इति डुप्रत्ययान्तं सूत्रेऽनुक्रियते । उत इत्यनुवृत्तेः । उवङादेशस्तु सौत्रः ।

'+मुद्गलाच्छन्दसि लिच्च +' ।लित्स्वरः । 'रथीरभून्मुद्गलानी' । ङीषो लित्वमानुक्चागमः ।

3447. The affix 'ṇîs' is always employed in the Chhandas in forming the feminine, after the word 'bhu.'

Thus विभ्वीं, (Rig. Ved. V. 38. 1). प्रभ्वीं (Rig Ved. I. 188. 5).

But why not so in the case of स्वयंभूः ? Because it ends in long ऊ, while विभ्वी &c. are feminine of विभु, &c. ending in short उ as these two words are formed by the affix डु (उ) of III. 2. 180. In fact the word उतः "after a word ending in short उ" of sûtra IV. 1. 44 governs this also. The word भुवः is the ablative case of भु irregularly formed by the substitution of उवङ् ; this form being confined to sûtras only.

Vârt:—In the Chhandâs, the affix ङीष् with the augment आनुक् is added to the word मुद्गल ; and the affix is treated as if it had an indicatory ल् ॥ The force of the indicatory ल् is to make the vowel preceding the affix, take the acute accent (VI 1. 193 लिति). Thus रथीरभून मुद्गलानी गविष्टौ ॥ (Rig Veda X. 120. 2.)

३४४८ । दीर्घजिह्वी च च्छन्दसि । ४ । १ । ५९ ।

संयोगोपधत्वादप्राप्तो ङीष्विधीयते । 'आसुरी वै दीर्घजिह्वी देवानां यज्ञवाट्' ।

3448. The form दीर्घजीह्वी 'long tongued' is irregularly formed in the Chhandas.

The word दीर्घजीह्वी is the feminine of दीर्घजीह्व, but as the latter has a conjunct consonant for its penultimate, the feminine affix ङीप् would not have applied to it by IV. 1. 54. The present aphorism enjoins ङीष् ॥ Thus दीर्घजीह्वी in the sentence आसुरीवै दीर्घजीह्वी देवानां यज्ञवाट् ॥

Note ;—The word च, and' in the aphorism is used in order to draw in the word संज्ञा from the last, so that the word *dîrgha-jihvî* is always a Name. Moreover by using the feminine form dîrgha-jihvî in the sûtra, it is indicated that the application of ङीष् is necessary and not optional, as was the case in the preceding Ashṭâdhyâyi sûtras.

३४४९ । कद्रुकमण्डल्वो श्छन्दसि । ४ । १ । ७१ ।

ऊङ् स्यात् । 'कद्रूश्च वै कमण्डलूः' ।

'+ गुग्गुलुमधुजतुपतयालूनामिति वक्तव्यम् +' । गुग्गुलूः । मधूः । जतूः । पतयालूः ।

'अव्ययात्त्यप् (१३०४) ।

'+ आविष्ट्यस्योपसंख्यानं छन्दसि +' । 'आविष्ट्यो वर्धते' ।

3449. The feminine affix 'ûn' comes in the Vedas after the words 'kadru' (tawny), and 'kamaṇḍalu' (a water pot).

Thus कद्रूश्च वै सुपर्णी च ॥ मास्मकमण्डलूं शूद्राय दद्यात् ॥

Why do we say "in the Vedas." Witness कद्रुः and कमण्डलुः ॥

Vârt:—So also after the words गुग्गुलु, मधु, जतु and पतयालु ॥ Thus गुग्गुलूः, मधूः, जतूः, and पतयालूः ।

Vârt:—The ष्यङ् is added to the word आविस् in the Vedas. As, आविष्ट्यो वर्धते ॥

३४५० । छन्दसि ठञ् । ४ । ३ । १९ ।

वर्षाभ्यः । ठकोऽपवादः । स्वरे भेदः । वार्षिकम् ।

3450. In the Chhandas, the word 'varshâ' takes the affix 'ṭhañ' in the remaining senses.

This debars ठक्. The form will have difference in accent. As नभश्च नभस्यश्च वार्षिकावृतू ॥ The word ऋतु here means "month," i. e. Nabha and Nabhasya are two rainy months.

३४५१ । वसन्ताच्च । ४ । ३ । २० ।

ठञ्स्याच्छन्दसि । वासन्तिकम् ।

3451. In the Chhandas, the affix 'ṭhañ' comes in the remaining senses after the word 'vasanta.'

This debars अण् (IV. 3. 16, S. 1387.) Thus मधुश्च माधवश्च वासन्तिकावृतू ॥

३४५२ । हेमन्ताच्च । ४ । ३ । २१ ।

छन्दसि ठञ् । हैमन्तिकम् । योगविभाग उत्तरार्थः । शौनकादिभ्यश्छन्दसि '(१४८६) । णिनि प्रोक्तेऽर्थे । छाणोरपवादः । शौनकेन प्रोक्तमधीयते शौनकिनः । वाजसनेयिनः । 'छन्दसि' किम् ! शौनकीया शिक्षा ।

3452. In the Chhandas, the affix 'ṭhañ' comes in the remaining senses, after the word 'hemanta.'

This debars अण् (IV. 3. 16). Thus सहश्च सहस्यश्च हैमन्तिकावृतू ॥ The making of two separate Sûtras of 20 and 21, is for the subsequent sûtra, in which, the anuvṛtti of the word हेमन्त only is taken.

Here we must refer again to IV. 3, 106. S. 1486.

३३५२ क । शौनकादिभ्यश्छन्दसि । ४ । ३ । १०६ ।

3452. A. The affix 'ṇini' comes in the sense of enounced by him, after the words 'śaunak' &c., in denoting the Chhandas enounced by them.

This debars छ and अण् ॥ Thus शौनकिनः "who study (IV. 2. 64) the Chhandas enounced by Śaunaka." Similarly वाजसनेयिनः ।

Why do we say "in denoting *chhandas* ?" Observe शौनकीया शिक्षा "the Orthography of Śaunaka." The affix here is छ (IV. 2. 114. S. 1337).

३४५३ । द्व्यचश्छन्दसि । ४ । ३ । १५० ।

विकारे मयट् स्यात् । शरमयं बर्हिः । 'यस्य पर्णमयी जुहूः' ।

3453. In the Chhandas, after a dissyllabic word, the affix 'mayaṭ' comes in the sense of 'its product or part.'

This ordains मयट् in the sacred literature in the sense dealt with in IV. 3. 143. S. 1523. Thus पर्णमयः, दर्भमयः शरमयः in the following यस्य पर्णमयी जुहूर्भवति, दर्भमयम् वासो भवति, शरमयम् बर्हिर्भवति ।

३४५४ । नोत्वद्वर्ध्रबिल्वात् । ४ । ३ । १५१ ।

उत्वानुकारवान् । मौञ्जं शिक्यम् । वर्ध्रं चर्म तस्य विकारो वार्ध्री रज्जुः । बैल्वो यूपः, सभाया यः ' (१६५७) ।

3454. The affix 'mayaṭ' does not come in the Chhandas after a dissyllabic word, having a short vowel 'u in it nor after the words 'vardhra' and 'bilwa.'

Thus मौञ्जं शिक्यम् from मुञ्ज by अण् ॥ वार्ध्री बालप्रग्रथिता भवति; बैल्वं ब्रह्मवर्चसकामेन कार्यः ॥

The word उत्वत् means 'having उत् or short u (I. 1 70).'

The word मुञ्ज is âdy-udâtta by तृणधान्यानां (Phiṭ II. 4): and therefore it takes the universal अण् (IV. 3. 134).

The word वर्ध्र meaning 'skin' is âdyudâtta by Phiṭ II. 19, and therefore takes अण्, the feminine being formed by ङीप् (IV. 1. 15), as वार्ध्री "rope made of leather." बैल्वः means the yûpa in which sacrificial victims are tied.

By the sûtra सभाया यः (IV. 4 105. S. 1657) the affix य is added to सभा in denoting excellence. But in the Chhandas, the affix ढ is added under similar conditions: as taught below.

३४५५ । ढश्छन्दसि । ४ । ४ । १०६ ।

सभेयो युवा ।

3455. The affix 'ḍh' comes in the Chhandas after the word 'sabhâ,' in the sense 'of excellent with regard thereto.'

This debars य of the preceding sûtra IV. 4. 105. S. 1657. Thus सभेयः in सभेयोऽस्य युवा यजमानस्य वीरो जायताम् 'let a refined, youthful hero be born to this sacrificer.'

३४५६ । भवे छन्दसि । ४ । ४ । ११० ।

सप्तम्यन्ताद्भवार्थे यत् । 'मेध्याय च विद्युत्याय च' । यथायथं शैषिकाणामणादीनां घापवादोऽयं यत् । पक्षे तेऽपि भवन्ति । सर्वविधीनां छन्दसि वैकल्पिकत्वात् । तद्यथा मुञ्जवान्नाम पर्वतस्तत्र भवो मौञ्जवतः । 'सोमस्येव मौञ्जवतस्य भक्षः' ॥ आचतुर्थसमाप्तेश्छन्दोऽधिकारः ।

3456. The affix 'yat' comes in the Chhandas, after a word in the locative case in construction, in the sense of 'what stays there.'

This debars अण् घ &c. (IV. 3. 53). Those affixes also are employed in the alternative, there being much latitude of grammatical rules in the Vedas. Thus the words मेध्यः and विद्युत्यः in the following hymn of the Yajur Veda (16. 38): नमो मेध्याय च विद्युत्याय च ॥ All the sûtras henceforward up to the end of the fourth chapter, are Vaidic sûtras, the word छन्दसि being understood in them all. The word भवे governs all the sûtras up to IV. 4. 118. S. 3464.

In the alternatives the affixes घ्यण् &c., will also be employed. Thus there is a mountain called मुञ्जवान् Muñjavat; from it we get the Derivative word मौञ्जवतः in the sense of तत्र भवः, as in the sentence सोमस्येव मौञ्जवतस्य भक्षः "The eater of Soma plant produced on Muñjavat Mountains."

३४५७ । पाथोनदीभ्यां ड्यण् । ४ । ४ । १११ ।

'तमु त्वा पाथ्यो वृषा' । 'चनो दधीत नाद्यो गिरो मे' । पाथसि भवः पाथ्यः । नद्यां भवो नाद्यः ।

3457. The affix 'ḍyaṇ' comes in the Chhandas, in the sense of 'what stays there,' after the words 'pâthas' and 'nadî,' wherby the last vowel, with the consonant following, is elided.

This debars यत् ॥ Thus पाथसि भवः = पाथ्यः 'watery, celestial,' so also नाद्यः "of the river, fluvial." As in the following hyms 'तमु त्वा पाथ्यो वृषा,' (Rig Ved. VI. 16. 15) 'च नो दधीत नाद्यो गिरो मे' (Rig Ved II. 35. 1). पाथः means firmament, and water.

३४५८ । वेशन्तहिमवद्भ्यामण् । ४ । ४ । ११२ ।

भवे । 'वैशन्तीभ्यः स्वाहा' । 'हैमवतीभ्यः स्वाहा' ।

3458. The affix 'aṇ' comes in the Chhandas in the sense of 'what stays there' after the words 'veśanta' and 'himavat.'

This debars यत् ॥ Thus वैशन्तीभ्यः स्वाहा हैमवतीभ्यः स्वाहा ॥

३४५९ । स्रोतसो विभाषा ड्यड्ड्यौ । ४ । ४ । ११३ ।

पक्षे यत् । ड्यड्ड्ययोस्तु स्वरे भेदः । स्रोतसि भवः स्रोत्यः – स्रोतस्यः ।

3459. The affixes 'ḍyat' and 'ḍya' come optionally in the Chhandas in the sense of 'what stays there,' after the word, 'srotas' and before these affixes the final syllable 'as' of srotas is elided.

This debars यत् which comes in the alternative. As स्रोतसि भवः = स्रोत्यः or स्रोत्यः (Rig Ved. X. 104. 8) the difference being in the accent (III. 1. 3 and VI. 1. 185). The anubandha ड causes the elision of अस् of स्रोतस् ॥ When यत् is added the form is स्रोतस्यः ॥

३४६० । सगर्भसयूथसनुताद्यन् । ४ । ४ । ११४ ।

अनुभ्राता सगर्भ्यः । अनुसखा सयूथ्यः । 'यो नः सनुत्य उत वा जिघत्नुः' । नुतिर्नुतम् । 'नपुंसके भावे क्तः' (३०९०) । सगर्भादयस्त्रयोऽपि कर्मधारयाः । 'समानस्य छन्दसि—' (१०१२) इति सः । ततो भवार्थे यन् । यतोऽपवादः ।

3460. The affix 'yan' comes in the sense of 'what stays there,' after the words 'sagarbha,' 'sayûtha' and 'sanuta.'

This debars यत् the difference being in accent (VI. 1. 197). Thus अनुभ्रातः सगर्भ्यः 'a younger brother'. अनुसखा सयूथ्यः 'a younger friend'. युता भवन्ति अस्मिन् So also यो नः सनुत्यः उत वा जिघत्नुः thief lit. 'who stays in a concealed place', sanuta meaning 'concealed' (see Rig Veda II. 31. 9). From the root नु with the Passive क्त we get नुतम् ॥ The word समान is always changed into स in the Chhandas

(VI. 3. 84). All three are karmadhâraya compounds, as समानश्चासेा गर्भश्च = सगर्भः तत्रभवः = सगर्भ्यः ।

३४६१ । तुग्राद्घन् । ४ । ४ । ११५ ।

भवेऽर्थे । पक्षे यदपि । 'आ वः शमं वृषभं तुग्र्यासु' इति बह्वृचाः । 'तुग्रियासु' इति शाखान्तरे । 'घनाकाशयज्ञवरिष्ठेषु तुग्रशब्दः' इति वृत्तिः ।

3461. The affix 'ghan' comes in the Chhandas in the sense of 'what stays there,' after the word tugra.

This debars यत्, which comes in the alternative. Thus तुग्रियः as त्वं मग्ने वृषभम् तुग्रियाणां ॥ Which assumes the form तुग्र्य tugrya also. As आवः शमम् वृषभं तुग्र्यासु (Rig Veda I. 33. 15) Tugrya meaning 'sunk in the waters'. Another reading is तुग्रियासु ॥ The word तुग्र means 'food, firmament, sacrifice and varishṭa'.

३४६२ । अग्राद्यत् । ४ । ४ । ११६ ।

3462. The affix 'yat' comes in the Chhandas in the sense of 'what stays there', after the word 'agra.'

Thus अग्रे भवं = अग्र्यम् ॥ Why this separate rule, for यत् would have come after अग्र by the general rule IV. 4. 110? The repetition is to show that यत् is not debarred by घ and छ of the next sûtra, which would have been the case, had this sûtra not existed.

३४६३ । घच्छौ च । ४ । ४ । ११७ ।

चाद्यत् । अग्रे भवोऽग्र्यः–अग्रियः – अग्रीयः ।

3463. The affixes 'ghach' and 'chha' come in the Chhandas in the sense of 'what stays there', after the word 'agra.'

Thus अग्र्यम् by (यत्), अग्रीयम् (by छ) and अग्रियम् (by घच्). And अग्रियम् (by घन्) from IV. 4. 115. See R. V. 1. 13. 10 इह त्वष्टारमग्रियम् ॥

३४६४ समुद्राभ्राद् घः । ४ । ४ । ११८ ।

'समुद्रिया अप्सरसेा मनीषिणम्' । 'नानदतेा अभ्रियस्येव घेाषाः' ।

3464. The affix 'gha' comes in the Chhandas in the senses of 'what stays there,' after the words 'samudra' and 'abhra.'

This debars यत् ॥ Thus समुद्रियः and अभ्रियः, as in समुद्रिया अप्सरसेा मनीषिणम् and नानदतेा अभ्रियस्येव घेाषाः ॥ The word 'abhra', being a word of fewer syllables than 'samudra', ought to have come first. Its coming as a second member is an irregularity, and shows that the rule of pûrva-nipâta is not of universal application.

३४६५ । बर्हिषि दत्तम् । ४ । ४ । ११९ ।

प्राग्घिताद्यदित्येव । 'बर्हिष्येषु निधिषु प्रियेषु' ।

3465. The affix 'yat' comes in the Chhandas in the sense of 'given,' after the word 'barhis' in the 7th case in construction.

The anuvṛitti of तत्र भवः ceases. Thus बर्हिष्येषु निधिषु प्रियेषु ॥ R. V. 10. 15, 5.

३३६६ । दूतस्य भागकर्मणी । ४ । ४ । १२० ।

भागेांऽशः । दूत्यम् ।

3466. The affix 'yat' comes in the Chhandas after the word 'dûta' in the genitive case in construction, in the sense of 'its share' or 'its duty.'

Thus दूत्यम् 'the share of a messenger or the work of a messenger.' As यत्ते अग्ने दूत्यम् ॥ According to VI 1. 213, the accent will be दूत्यम् but the accented Text reads दूत्यम्, ॥

३४६७ । रक्षोयातूनां हननी । ४ । ४ । १२१ ।

'या तेऽग्ने रक्षस्या तनूः' ।

3467. The affix 'yat' comes in the Chhandas in the sense of 'killer,' after the words 'raksha' and 'yâtu' in the sixth case in construction.

That by which anything is killed is called हननी ॥ Thus रक्षस्य and यातव्यं meaning 'that which kills the demons called Rakshas and Yâtus.' As या ते अग्ने रक्षस्या तनूः i. e. रक्षसां हननी ॥ 'O Agni thy bodies are killers of Rakshas.' So यातव्याः तनूः ॥ The word is in the plural as a mark of respect.

३४६८ । रेवतीजगतीहविष्याभ्यः प्रशस्ये । ४ । ४ । १२२ ।

प्रशंसने यत्स्यात् । रेवत्यादीनां प्रशंसनं रेवत्यम् । जगत्यम् । हविष्यम् ।

3468. The affix 'yat' comes in the Chhandas, in the sense of 'praising', after the words 'revatî,' 'jagatî' and 'havishya' in the sixth case in construction.

The word प्रशस्य means प्रशंसन 'praising, extolling,' formed by adding the Krit affix क्यप् to the root, with the force of भाव or 'condition.' Thus रेवत्यम्, जगत्यम् and हविष्यम् 'praising of Revatî, Jagatî or Havishya.' The word हविष्यम् is thus formed हविषे हिता = हविष्याः 'things fit for offering' i. e. butter &c. (हविष् + यत् V. I. 4) हविष्याणाम् प्रशंसनं = हविष्यम् (हविष्य + यत् IV. 4. 122 = हविष्य् + यत् the final अ being elided by VI. 4. 148 = हविष् + यत् the य् being elided by VIII. 4. 64).

३४६९ । असुरस्य स्वम् । ४ । ४ । १२३ ।

'असुर्यं देवेभिर्धायि विश्वम्' ।

3469. The affix 'yat' comes in the Chhandas in the sense of 'property,' after the word 'asura' in the 6th case in construction.

This debars अण् ॥ Thus असुर्यम् 'belonging to the Asuras.' As असुर्यं वा एतत् पात्रं यच्चक्रकृतं कुलालकृतम् 'this vessel made on a wheel by a potter belongs to the Asuras.' असुर्यं देवेभिर्धायि विश्वम् ॥ See Maitr S. I. 8. 3. So also असुर्या नाम ते लोकाः (Ishop. 3).

३४७० । मायायामण् । ४ । ४ । १२४ ।

आसुरी माया ।

3470. The affix 'aṇ' comes in the Chhandas in the sense of 'glamour,' after the word 'asura' in the 6th case in construction.

This debars यत् ॥ असुरस्य माया=आसुरः feminine आसुरी ॥ As आसुरी माया स्वधया कृतासि ॥

३४७१ । तद्वानासामुपधानो मन्त्र इतीष्टकासु लुक्च मतोः । ४ । ४ । १२५ ।

वर्चस्वानुपधानो मन्त्र आसामिष्टकानां वर्चस्याः । ऋतव्याः ।

3471. The affix 'yat' comes in the Chhandas, after a nominal stem, in the 1st case in construction, ending with the affix 'matup,' when the sense is "this is their mantra of putting up," provided that, the things put up are bricks : And the affix matup is elided by luk.

This sûtra requires analysis. तद्वान् is formed by adding मतुप् to तद् meaning 'having that,' and refers to a noun formed by the affix मतुप् ॥ The word आसाम् is genitive plural fem. of इदं meaning 'of them'; the pronoun refers to the word इष्टका ॥ The word उपधान means 'putting up,' and technically means 'used as a Mantra in the putting up of sacrificial bricks, pots &c' मन्त्र "sacred hymn" इष्टका 'bricks.' The whole sûtra means "the affix 'yat' is used with the force of a genitive (âsâm), after a word which ends with matup (tadvân), and denotes a mantra used in putting up of sacrificial objects; when such mantra refers to bricks: and when this affix yat is added, the affix matup is elided.' Thus वर्चस्वान् is a Mantra containing the word वर्चस् ॥ The bricks put up or collected (उपधीयते) with the recitation of वर्चस्वान् Mantra, will be called वर्चस्यां (वर्चस्वन् + यत् - वर्चस् + यत् the affix वत् (मतुप्) being elided = वर्चस्य, fem. वर्चस्या) ॥ Thus वर्चस्या उपदधाति 'he collects Varchasya bricks i. e. on which Varchasvân mantra has been pronounced' So तेजस्यां उपदधाति ॥ So पयस्याः, रेतस्याः ॥

NOTE :—Why do we say तद्वान् ? The affix is not to be added to the whole Mantra. Why do we say, उपधान 'putting up'? The affix is not to be added to other Mantras such as those used in praying etc. e. g वर्चस्वानुपस्थान मन्त्र आसामिष्टकानाम्, here there will be no affix. Why do we say Mantra ? Observe अंगुलिमानुपधानो हस्त आसाम् 'these bricks are collected with hand having fingers,' here there will be no affix. Why do we say इष्टकासु ? Observe वर्चस्वानुपधानो मन्त्र एषां कपालानाम्, here there will be no affix, the thing collected being potsherds and not bricks.

३४७२ । अश्विमानण् । ४ । ४ । १२६ ।

'आश्विनीरुपदधाति'।

3472. The affix 'aṇ' comes in the Chhandas, after the words aśvimân, to denote bricks put up with the Mantra containing the word Aśvin, and the affix matup is elided.

Thus अश्विमानुपधानो मन्त्र आसामिष्टकानां = आश्विनः fem, आश्विनीः ॥ The word is thus formed. अश्विमान् + अण् = अश्वि + अण् the matup being elided IV. 4 125 = अश्विन् + अण् VI. 4 164 = आश्विन् ॥ Thus आश्विनीरुपदधाति 'he collects Aśvin bricks i. e. bricks at the time of collecting which Mantras containing अश्विन् were uttered. See Yajur Veda Tait S. 5. 3. 1. 1.

३४७३ । वयस्यासु मूर्ध्नो मतुप् । ४ । ४ । १२७ ।

तद्वानासामिति सूत्रं सर्वमनुवर्तते । मतोरिति पदमावर्त्य पञ्चम्यन्तं बोध्यम् । मतुबन्तो यो मूर्धशब्दस्ततो मतुप्स्यात् । प्रथमस्य मतोर्लुक्च । वयःशब्दवन्मन्त्रोपधेयास्विष्टकासु । यस्मिन्मन्त्रे मूर्धवयःशब्दौ स्तः । तेन 'उपधेयासु मूर्धन्वतीरुपदधाति' इति प्रयोगः ।

3473. The affix 'matup' is added in the Chhandas, to the word 'mûrdhanvat,' in expressing bricks collected with the Mantra containing the word 'vayas.'

The whole of the sûtra 3471 is understood here. The word मतोः should be repeated, and is to be construed in the Ablative case. The sûtra means "After the word mûrdha ending in matup, i. e. after the word murdhavat, there is added a second matup, and there is elision of the first matup when the bricks are collected with vayas mantra." The word वयस्या means the bricks, the Upadhâna mantras of which contain the word वयस् ॥ The affix मतुप् debars यत् ॥ A mantra which contains both the word वयस् and मूर्धन्, that Mantra is both वयस्वान् and मूर्धन्वान् ॥ Now in denoting sacrificial bricks put up with such a mantra, the affix यत् would have come by IV. 4. 125 after both these words वयस्वान् and मूर्द्धन्वान् ॥ The present sûtra ordains मतुप् after मूर्द्धन्वान् ॥ Thus मूर्द्धन्वतीरुपदधाति 'he collects Mûrdhanvatî bricks.' The words वयस्याः and मूर्द्धन्वत्यः denote the same object. See VI. 1. 176.

३४७४ । मत्वर्थे मासतन्वोः । ४ । ४ । १२८ ।

नभोऽभ्रम् । तदस्मिन्नस्तीति नभस्यो मासः । ओजस्या तनूः ।

3474. The affix 'yat' comes in the Chhandas with the force of matup, after a word in the first case in construction, the word so formed meaning a month or a body.

This debars the affix मतुप् and those having the sense of मतुप् ॥ Thus नभांसि विद्यन्ते यस्मिन् मासे = नभस्यः 'the month of clouds' i. e. June-July.

Similarly ओजस्या तनूः 'the bodies full of vigor.'

३४७५ । मधोर्ञ च । ४ । ४ । १२९ ।

चाद्यत् । माधवः – मधव्यः ।

3475. The affix 'ña' as well as 'yat' comes with the force of matup, in the Chhandas, after the word 'madhu.'

Thus माधवः or मधव्यः

३४७६ । ओजसोऽहनि यत्खौ । ४ । ४ । १३० ।

ओजस्यमहः । ओजसीनं वा ।

3476. The affixes 'yat' and 'kh' come with the force of matup, after the word 'ojas,' when a day is meant.

Thus ओजस्यम् or ओजसीनं = अहः 'the day' lit. full of heat.

३४७७ । वेशोयशआदेर्भगाद्यल्खौ । ४ । ४ । १३१ ।

वेशो बलं तदेव भगः । वेशोभग्यः । यशोभग्यः । वेशोभगीनः । यशोभगीनः ।

3477. The affixes 'yal' and 'kh' come in the Chhandas, with the force of matup, after the word bhaga, having the words 'veśas' or 'yaśas' in the beginning.

The rule of yathâ-saṅkhya does not apply here.

The ल् of यल् shows that the accent falls on the vowel preceding the affix (VI. 1. 193). Thus वेशोभगो विद्यते यस्य स = वेशोभँग्यः 'strong-fortune' so also यशोभँग्यः 'famous-fortune.' The word वेश means 'strength' : भग means 'fortune, desire, effort, greatness, virility and fame.' The word वेशोभगः may be taken as a Dvandva compound of वेशस् 'force' and भग. 'fortune.' The word वेशोभग्यः would then mean 'possessed of power and fortune.' With ख, वेशोभगीनः, यशोभगीनः ।

NOTE:—Kâsikâ does not read ख into this sûtra. That is more reasonable.

३४७८ । ख च । ४ । ४ । १३२ ।

योगविभाग उत्तरार्थः । क्रमनिरासार्थश्च ।

3478. The affix 'kh' also comes after the words 'veśobhaga' and 'yaśobhaga,' in the Chhandas, with the force of matup.

Thus वेशोभगीनः and यशोभगीनः ॥

Note according to the Kâsikâ: - This sûtra has been separated from the last in order to prevent the application of the यथासंख्य rule (I. 3. 10). For had the sûtra been वेशोयश आदेर्भगाद् यल्खौ, as it occurs in the Siddhanta Kaumudi, then the affix यल् would apply to वेशोभग, and the affix ख to यशोभगः which is not what is intended. Another reason for making it a distinct aphorism is that the anuvṛitti of ख runs in the next sûtra, not so of यल् ॥

३४७९ । पूर्वैः कृतमिनयौ च । ४ । ४ । १३३ ।

'गम्भीरेभिः पथिभिः पूर्विणेभिः' । 'ये ते पन्थाः सवितः पूर्व्यासः' ।

3479. The affixes 'in' and 'ya' as well as 'kh' come in the sense of 'made by them,' after the word 'pûrva' (forefathers), in the Instrumental case in construction.

The ख is read into the sûtra by force of the word च ; the anuvṛitti of मत्वर्थ ceases. Thus पूर्वैः कृतं=पूर्विणः 'made by the ancestors' i. e. a road. So also पूर्व्यः and पूर्वीणाः ॥ The word पूर्वैः in the plural means पूर्वपुरुषैः "past generations, ancestors." These words occur generally in the plural, and mean "roads widened by the forefathers" Thus गम्भीरेभिः पथिभिः पूर्विणेभिः ॥ So also, ये ते पन्थाः सवितः पूर्व्यासः (Rig I. 35. 11). Another reading of this sûtra is पूर्वैः कृतमिनियौ च: the affixes then will be इनि (इन्), and य ; and ख will be drawn in by virtue of च ॥ The examples then will be पूर्विन् ; 3rd pl. पूर्विभिः (with इन्), as पथिभिः पूर्विभिः ; or पूर्वीणैः (ख), or पूर्व्यैः (य) ॥

३४८० । अद्भिः संस्कृतम् । ४ । ४ । १३४ ।

यस्येदमप्यं हविः ।

3480. The affix 'yat' comes in the Chhandas, in the sense of sanctified,' after the word 'apas' in the third case in construction.

Thus अप्स्य ‘offering purified with water.’ As यस्येदमप्स्यं हविः (Rig Ved. X 86. 12). The case of construction is indicated in the sûtra itself.

३४८१ । सहस्रेण संमितौ घः । ४ । ४ । १३५ ।

‘सहस्रियासोऽपां नोर्मयः’ । सहस्रेण तुल्या इत्यर्थः ।

3481. The affix ‘gha’ comes in the Chhandas, in the sense of ‘like,’ after the word ‘sahasra,’ in the third case in construction.

The case of construction is indicated by the sûtra. Thus सहस्रेण संमितः = सहस्रियः ‘like unto thousand.’ As in the following verse:—सहस्रियासोऽपां नोर्मयः (Rig Ved. I 168. 2). The word संमित means तुल्य ‘equal to.’ Some read the word समित instead of सम्मित, but the meaning will be the same.

३४८२ । मतौ च । ४ । ४ । १३६ ।

सहस्रशब्दान्मत्वर्थे घः स्यात् । सहस्रमस्यास्तीति सहस्रियः ।

3481. The affix ‘gha’ comes in the Chhandas, with the force of matup, after the word ‘sahasra.’

As सहस्रमस्य विद्यते = सहस्रियः ॥ This debars the मत्वर्थ affixes विनि and इनि and अण् of V. 2. 102 and 103.

३४८३ । सोममर्हति यः । ४ । ४ । १३७ ।

सोम्यो ब्राह्मणः । यज्ञार्ह इत्यर्थः ।

3483. The affix ‘ya’ comes in the Chhandas, after the word ‘Soma,’ in the second case in construction, when the sense is that of ‘who deserves that.’

Thus सोममर्हति = सोम्यो ब्राह्मणः “The Brâhmaṇa who deserves Soma” i. e. honorable and learned, and worthy of performing sacrifices. The difference between यत् and य is in accent.

३४८४ । मये च । ४ । ४ । १३८ ।

सोमशब्दाद्यः स्यान्मयडर्थे । सोम्यं मधु । सोममयमित्यर्थं ।

3484. The affix ‘ya’ comes in the Chhandas, after the word ‘Soma,’ with the force of the affix mayaṭ.

The force of the affix मयट् is that of ततः आगतः (IV. 3. 74 and 82). विकारावयव (IV. 3. 134 and 143) and प्रकृत (V. 4. 21). The case in construction will vary according to the sense. Thus सोम्यं मधुः पिबन्ति = सोममयः मधुः ॥

३४८५ । मधोः । ४ । ४ । १३९ ।

मधुशब्दान्मयडर्थे यत्स्यात् । मधव्यः । मधुमय इत्यर्थः ।

3485. The affix ‘yat’ comes in the Chhandas, after the word ‘madhu,’ with the force of the affix mayaṭ.

Thus मधव्यान् स्तोकान् = मधुमयान् ॥

३४८६ । वसोः समूहे च । ४ । ४ । १४० ।

चान्मयडर्थे यत् । वसव्यः । ‘+ अक्षरसमूहे छन्दस उपसंख्यानम् +’ । छन्दः शब्दादक्षरसमूहे वर्तमानात्स्वार्थे यदित्यर्थः । ‘ओश्रावय’ इति चतुरक्षरम्, ‘अस्तु श्रौषट्’ इति चतुरक्षरम्, ‘ये यजामहे’ इति पञ्चाक्षरम्, ‘यज’ इति द्व्यक्षरं द्व्यक्षरो। वषट्कार एष वै सप्तदशाक्षरश्छन्दस्यः ।

3486. The affix 'yat' comes in the Chhandas after the word 'vasu,' when a collection is meant, as well as with the force of mayat.

Thus वसव्यः = समूहः 'a collection.'

Vârt :—The affix 'yat' comes without changing the sense, after the word छन्दस् when reference is made to the collection of letters. Thus the word छन्दस्यः in the following sentence: "सप्तदशाक्षरश्छन्दस्यः प्रजापतियज्ञो मन्त्रे विहिता," The 17 letters here referred to being ओ श्रावय, four; अस्तु श्रौषट्, four; यज, two; ये यजामहे five; and वषट् two.

Vârt :—The affix यत् comes after वसु without changing the sense. As हस्तौ गृहीतस्य बहुभिर्वसव्यैः ॥ Here वसव्यैः is equal to वसुभिः ॥ Similarly अग्निरीशे वसव्यस्य = वसोः ॥

३४८७ । नक्षत्राद्घः । ४ । ४ । १४१ ।

स्वार्थे । 'नक्षत्रियेभ्यः स्वाहा' ।

3447. The affix 'gha' comes in the Chhandas after the word 'nakshatra,' without altering the meaning.

The anuvṛitti of समूह does not extend to this sûtra. Thus नक्षत्रियेभ्यः स्वाहा = नक्षत्रेभ्यः स्वाहा ॥

३४८८ । सर्वदेवात्तातिल् । ४ । ४ । १४२ ।

स्वार्थे । 'सविता नः सुवतु सर्वतातिम्' । 'प्रदक्षिणिद्देवतातिमुराणः' ।

3488. The affix 'tâtil' comes in the Chhandas after the words 'sarva' and 'deva,' without altering the meaning.

As सर्वतातिः and देवतातिः in the following hymns: "सविता नः सुवतु सर्वतातिम् (Rig Ved. X. 3 . 14), and प्रदक्षिणिद्देवतातिमुराणः (Rig Ved IV. 6. 3).

३४८९ । शिवशमरिष्टस्य करे । ४ । ४ । १४३ ।

करोतीति करः । पचाद्यच् । शिवं करोतीति शिवतातिः । 'याभिः शन्ताती भवथो ददाशुषे' । 'अथो अरिष्टतातये' ।

3489. The affix 'tâtil' comes, in the Chhandas, after the word 'śiva,' 'śam,' and 'arishṭa' in the sixth case in construction when the sense is 'he does.'

The word करः is equivalent to करोति formed by अच् (III. 1. 134).

This shows that the construction must be genitive. With a kṛit-formed word, it has accusative force, as, शिवस्य करः = शिवं करोति ॥

Thus शिवस्य करः = शिवतातिः ॥ So शंतातिः and अरिष्टतातिः ॥ As याभिः शन्ताती भवथो ददाशुषे' (Rig. I. 112 20) शंताती being dual of शन्तातिः, and meaning सुखस्य कर्तारा; so also अथो अरिष्टतातये । (Rig Ved. X. 60. 8.)

३४९० । भावे च । ४ । ४ । १४४ ।

शिवादिभ्यो भावे तातिः स्याच्छन्दसि । शिवस्य भावः शिवतातिः । शन्तातिः । अरिष्टतातिः ।

इति चतुर्थोऽध्यायः ।

3490. The affix 'tâtil' comes in the Chhandas, after the words 'śiva,' 'śam' and 'arishṭa,' being in the 6th case in construction, the sense being that of condition.

Thus शिवस्य भावः = शिवतातिः 'the condition of blissfulness.' शन्तातिः 'the state of happiness or peace,' अरिष्टतातिः ॥ Here these words have the force of Verbal nouns.

CHAPTER V.

३४९१ । सप्तनोऽञ् छन्दसि । ५ । १ । ६१ ।

'तदस्य परिमाणम्' (१७२३) इति 'वर्गे' इति च । 'सप्त साप्तान्यसृजत्' । सप्तवर्गानित्यर्थः । '+ शञ्छतोर्डिनिश्छन्दसि तदस्य परिमाणमित्यर्थे वाच्यः +' । पञ्चदशिनोऽर्धमासाः । त्रिंशिनो मासाः । '+ विंशतेश्चेति वाच्यम् +' । विंशिनोऽङ्गिरसः । '+ युष्मदस्मदोः सादृश्ये वतुब्वाच्यः +' । 'त्वावतः पुरूवसो' । 'न त्वावां अन्यः' । 'यज्ञं विप्रस्य मावतः' ।

3491. The affix añ comes after the word saptan, in the Chhandas, in the sense of "this is its measure," when the meaning is that of a Varga.

As सप्त साप्तान्यसृजत् ॥ "They created the seven seven-fold monarchies.' The phrase तदस्य परिमाणं (V. 1 57 S. 1723) and वर्गे (V. 1. 60 S. 1726) are understood here.

Thus सप्तन् + अञ् = साप्त् + अञ् (the टि portion is elided by VI. 4. 144 S. 679) = साप्त ॥ Its Plural in जस् is साप्तानि by the ordinary rules of declension of Neuter nouns.

Vârt:—The affix डिनि comes in the Chhandas, after the words ending in शत् and शन्, as पञ्चदशिनोऽर्द्धमासाः "Half-months have a measure of 15 days". त्रिंशिनो मासाः "Months are of thirty days".

Vârt:—So also after the word विंशति, as विंशिनोऽङ्गिरसः "Angirasas consist of or comprise twenty Gotras."

Vârt:—The affix वतुप् comes after युष्मद् and अस्मद् in denoting similarity. As 'त्वावतः पुरूवसो'। न त्वावां अन्यः (Rig Veda VI. 21. 10). यज्ञं विप्रस्य मावतः (Rig Veda I. 142. 2).

३४९२ । छन्दसि च । ५ । १ । ६७ ।

प्रातिपदिकमात्रात् 'तदर्हति' इत्यर्थे यत्स्याच्छन्दसि । 'सादन्यं विदथ्यम्' ।

3492. The affix yat (य) comes in the sense of 'deserving that' in the Chhandas, after every prâtipadika.

This debars ठञ् &c. Thus उदक्या वृत्तयः, यूँप्यः पलाशः, गँर्त्यो देशः ॥ See VI. I. 213.

सादन्यंविदथ्यम् (Rig. Veda. I. 91. 20).

The word सादन्य is derived from सदन "house." He who deserves a house is a सादन्यः ॥ The lengthening takes place by VI. 3. 137 S. 3539. विदथ means 'sacrifices' that which deserves a sacrifice is विदथ्यम् ॥

३४९३ । वत्सरान्ताच्छश्छन्दसि । ५ । १ । ९१ ।

निर्वृत्तादिष्वर्थेषु । इद्वत्सरीयः ।

3493. The affix chha (îya) comes in the Chhandas, in the five-fold senses taught in V. 1. 79, 80, after a stem ending with vatsara.

This debars ठञ् ॥ Thus इद्वत्सरीयः, इदावत्सरीयः ॥

३४९४ । संपरिपूर्वात् ख च । ५ । १ । ९२ ।

चाच्छः । संवत्सरीणः । संवत्सरीयः । परिवत्सरीणः । परिवत्सरीयः ।

3494. The affixes 'kha' (în) and 'chha' (îya) come in the Chhandas in the fivefold senses taught in V. 1. 79, 80, after the word vatsara, when preceded by sam and pari.

Thus संवत्सरीणः and संवत्सरीयः, परिवत्सरीणः and परिवत्सरीयः ॥

३४९५ । छन्दसि घस् । ५ । १ । १०६ ।

ऋतुशब्दात्तदस्य प्राप्तमित्यर्थे । 'भाग ऋत्वियः' ।

3495. In the Chhandas, the affix 'ghas' (iya) comes after the word 'ṛitu' in the same sense of 'season has come for it.'

This debars अण्. As भाग ऋत्वियः (Rig Ved. I. 135. 3). Here there is no Guṇa by VI. 4. 146, because by sûtra I. 4 16, ऋतु before the affix घस् gets the designation of पद, hence the guṇa rule which applies to भ (I. 4. 18) does not apply.

३४९६ । उपसर्गाच्छन्दसि धात्वर्थे । ५ । १ । ११८ ।

धात्वार्थविशिष्टे साधने वर्तमानात् उपसर्गात् उत्तरे स्वार्थे वतिः स्यात् । 'यदुद्वतो निवतः । उद्गतान्निर्गता नित्यर्थः ।

3496. In the Chhandas, the affix 'vati' is added to an Upasarga (Preposition), in the sense of a verbal root.

As the word उद्वतः and निवतः in the following Rik (X. 142. 4.)

यदुद्वतो निवतो यासि बप्सत् पृथगेषि प्रगर्धिनीव सेना ॥ "When thou O Fire! goest burning high (उद्वतः = उद्गतान्) and low (निवतः = निर्गतान्) trees &c.

३४९७ । थट् च छन्दसि । ५ । २ । ५० ।

नान्तादसंख्यादेः परस्य डटस्थट् स्यान्मट् च । पञ्चथम्-पञ्चमम् ।

3497. The 'thaṭ' is the augment of 'ḍaṭ,' in the Chhandas, after a Numeral ending in 'n' and not preceded by another numeral: as well as the augment 'maṭ.'

Thus पंचथः, सप्तथः or पञ्चमः, सप्तमः ॥ As पर्णमयानि पञ्चथानि भवन्ति and पञ्चममिन्द्रियमस्यापाक्रामत् ॥ See V. 2. 56.

३४९७ क । छन्दसि परिपन्थिपरिपरिणौ पर्यवस्थातरि । ५ । २ । ८९ ।

'पर्यवस्थाता शत्रुः' । 'अपत्यं परिपन्थिनम्' । 'मा त्वा परिपरिणो विदन्' ।

3497 A. In the Chhandas, the words paripanthin and pariparin are anomalously formed by the affix ini (in) and have the sense of "an antagonist."

अपत्यं परिपन्थिनम् (Rig Ved. I. 42. 3).

मात्वा परिपरिणो विदन् (Yaj. Ved. IV. 34). See S. 1889.

३४९८ । बहुलं छन्दसि । ५ । २ । १२२ ।

मत्वर्थे विनिः स्यात् । 'अग्निस्ते श्रोजस्वी' । '+ छन्दोविन्प्रकरणे अष्टामेखलाद्वयोभयरुजाहृदयानां दीर्घश्चेति वक्तव्यम् +' । इति दीर्घः । 'मंहिष्ठमुभयाविनम्' । 'शुनमेष्ट्राव्यचरत्' । '+ छन्दसीवनिपौ च वक्तव्यौ +' । ई । 'रथीरभूत्' 'सुमङ्गलीरियं वधूः' । 'मघवानमीमहे' ।

3498. In the Chhandas, the affix vini is added diversely in the sense of matup.

As अग्ने तेजस्विन् ॥ Sometimes it is not added, as सूर्यो वर्चस्वान् ॥

Vârt:—In the Chhandas, the final अ of द्वय, उभय and हृदय is lengthened optionally before विनि ; and it comes after अष्ट्रा, मेखला and रुजा also : as अष्ट्रावी, मेखलावी, द्वयावी, उभयावी, रुजावी, हृदयावी ॥ As मंहिष्ठमुभयाविनम् ; शुनमष्ट्रा व्यचरत् । The word "ashṭrâ" is a synonym of "dańshṭrâ" and means 'tooth.'

Vârt:—In the Chhandas, the affixes ई, and वनिप् come in the sense of मतुप् ॥ Thus ई :—रथीरभून् मुद्गलानी गविष्टौ (रथीः) Rig Ved. X. 102. 2. सुमङ्गलीरियं वधूः Rig Ved. X. 85. 33. वनिप् :—मघवानमीमहे: Rig Ved. X. 167. 2.

NOTE:—The affixes इरन् and इरच् come respectively after मेधा and रथः as मेधिर, रथिरः ॥

३४९९ । तयोर्दार्हिलौ च छन्दसि । ५ । ३ । २० ।

इदं तदोर्यथासंख्यं स्तः । 'इदा हि व उपस्तुतिम्' । तर्हि ।

3499. After these two (nominal stems idam and tad), come respectively the affixes dâ and rhil, in the Chhandas, and also the other affixes.

The affix दा comes after इदम् and र्हि after तद् ॥ Thus इदा (V. 3. 3. S. 1949), तर्हि (VII. 2. 102. S. 265) So also इदानीम् and तदानीम् ॥ As इदा हि वमुप'स्तुतिमिदा वामस्य भक्तये (Rig Veda VIII 27. 11).

NOTE:—इदम + दा = इ + दा (इदम् is replaced by इ by V. 3. 3. S. 1949).

३५०० । था हेतौ च छन्दसि । ५ । ३ । २६ ।

किमस्था स्याद्धेतौ प्रकारे च । 'कथा ग्रामं न पृच्छसि' । 'कथा दाशेम' ॥

3500. The affix 'thâ' comes in the sense of 'cause' also (as well as 'manner'). in the Chhandas, after the word kim.

The word प्रकार वचने is read into the sûtra by force of च ॥ Thus कथा wherefore? why? for what reason?', कथा 'how' The former is an example of हेतु 'reason or cause', the second of प्रकार 'manner.' As in the following sentences: कथा ग्रामं न पृच्छसि Rig Ved. X. 146. 1. केन हेतुना ग्रामं न पृच्छसि ॥ कथा दा शेम(Rig Ved. I. 77. 1).

NOTE: - किम् + था = क + था (किम् is replaced by क by VII. 2. 103. S. 342, because the affix था is a vibhakti as defined in V. 3. 1. S. 1947).

३५०१ । पश्च पश्चा च च्छन्दसि । ५ । ३ । ३३ ।

अवरस्यास्तात्यर्थे निपातौ । 'पश्च हि सः' । 'नो त पश्चा' ।

3501. The words paścha and paśchâ are anomalous in the Chhandas, having the force of astâti.

By च, the word पश्चात् is also included. As पुरा व्याघ्रो जायते, पश्च, पश्चा or पश्चात् सिंह ॥ As पश्चात् पुरस्तादधरादुदक्तात् (Rig Veda X. 87. 21) पश्चेदमन्यदभवद्यजत्रम् (Rig Veda X. 149. 3). नोत पश्चा (Rig Ved. II. 27. 11).

३५०१ क । तुश्छन्दसि । ५ । ३ । ५९ ।

तृजन्तात्तृजन्ताच्च इष्ठन्नीयसुनौ स्तः । 'आसुतिं करिष्ठः' । 'दोहीयसी धेनुः ।

3501A. The affixes ishṭan and iyasun come in the Chhandas after a Nominal stem ending in tṛi. S 2000.

आसुतिं करिष्ठः (Rig Ved. VII. 97. 7). Thus कर्तृ + इष्ठ = कर् + इष्ठ (तृ elided by VI. 4. 154. S. 2008). दोहीयसी धेनुः ॥ Thus दोग्धृ + ईयसुन् = दोग्धृ + ईयसुन् (ङीप् elided by VII. 1. 88. S. 368 = दोह् + ईयसुन् (तृ elided by VI. 4. 154. S. 2008).

३५०२ । प्रत्नपूर्वविश्वेमात् थाल् छन्दसि । ५ । ३ । १११ ।

इवार्थे । 'तं प्रत्नथा पूर्वथा विश्वथेमथा' ।

3502. In the Chhandas, the affix thâl comes in the sense of 'like this', after pratna, pûrva, viśva, and ima (idam).

Thus :—तं प्रत्नथा पूर्वथा विश्वथेमथा ज्येष्ठतातिं बर्हिषदं स्वर्विदम् ॥ (Rig Veda V. 44. 1). 'Him (Indra), as the ancients, as the predecessors, as all creatures, and as these living men have worshipped &c.'

३५०३ । अमु च छन्दसि । ५ । ४ । १२ ।

किमेत्तिङव्ययघादित्येव । 'प्रतं नय प्रतरम्' ।

3503. In the Chhandas, the affix amu (am) also is added after 'kim' &c, under similar conditions as in V. 4. 11. S. 2004.

To the word किम्, words ending in ए, finite verbs and indeclinables, when taking the comparative affixes तर and तम is added the affix अम in the Vedas, when these words are used as adverbs. By the force of the word च 'also' in the sûtra, the affix आमु is also included. Thus प्रतंनय प्रतरम् (Rig Veda X. 45. 9). प्रतरम् नयामः ॥ or प्रतराम् वस्यः । प्रतर means प्रकृष्टतर ॥

The words ending in आम् and अम् are indeclinables, as they are included in the class of Svarâdi (I. 1. 37. S. 447).

३५०४ । वृकज्येष्ठाभ्यां तिल्तातिलौ च छन्दसि । ५ । ४ । ४१ ।

स्वार्थे । 'यो नो दुरेवो वृकतिः' । 'ज्येष्ठतातिं बर्हिषदम्' ।

3504. In the Chhandas, the affix til and tâtil come after vṛik and jyeshṭha when excellence is denoted.

The word प्रशंसायाम् is to be read into this sûtra. This also debars रूपप् V. 3. 66. S. 2021. Thus वृकतिः or वृकतातिः, as, यो नो मरुतो वृकतातिमर्त्यः (Rig Veda, II. 34. 9). Similarly ज्येष्ठतातिः ॥

यो नो दुरेवो वृकतिः (Rig Ved. IV 41. 4). ज्येष्ठतातिं बर्हिषदम् (Rig Ved. V. 44. 1).

३५०५ । अनसन्तान्नपुंसकाच्छन्दसि । ५ । ४ । १०३ ।

तत्पुरुषाट्टजस्यात्समासान्तः । 'ब्रह्मसामं भवति' । देवच्छन्दसानि' ।

3505. In the Chhandas, the affix ṭach comes after a Tatpurusha compound in the Neuter Gender ending in 'an' or 'as.'

Thus हस्ति + चर्मन् = हस्तिचर्मम् as in हस्तिचर्मे जुहोति, so also ऋषभचर्मेऽभिषिच्यते ॥ So also when a word ends in अस् as, देवच्छन्दसानि (देव + छन्दस् = देव + छन्दस् + टच् = देवच्छन्दसम्) so also मनुष्य च्छन्दसानि ॥

Why do we say "when ending in अन् or अस्" ? Observe बिल्वदारु जुहोति ॥ Why do we say "in the Neuter" ? Observe सुत्रामाणं पृथिवीं द्यामनेहसम् ॥

NOTE :—The word वा "optionally" should be read into the sûtra. Therefore टच् is optionally added, as ब्रह्मसाम or ब्रह्मसामम्, देवच्छन्दः or देवच्छन्दसम् ॥

३५०६ । बहुप्रजाश्छन्दसि । ५ । ४ । १२३ ।

'बहुप्रजा निर्ऋतिमाविवेश' ।

3506. The form bahuprajas is valid in the Vedas.

Thus बहुप्रजा निर्ऋतिमाविवेश ॥ Rig Ved. I. 164. 32. In the classical literature, the form is बहुप्रजः; as बहुप्रजो ब्राह्मणः ॥

३५०७ । छन्दसि च । ५ । ४ । १४२ ।

दन्तस्य दतृ स्याद्बहुव्रीहौ । 'उभयतोदतः प्रति गृह्णाति' ।

3507. For danta is substituted dat in the Vedas, when final in a Bahuvrihi.

Thus पत्रदन्तमालभेत, उभयदत आलभेत or उभयतो दतः प्रतिगृह्णाति ॥

३५०८ । ऋतश्छन्दसि । ५ । ४ । १५८ ।

ऋदन्ताद्बहुव्रीहेर्न कप् । हता माता यस्य हतमाता ।

इति पञ्चमोऽध्यायः ।

3508. The affix 'kap' does not come after a Bahuvrîhi ending in short 'ṛi' in the Vedas.

Thus हता माताऽस्य = हतमाता, हतपिता, हतस्वसा, सुहोता ॥

CHAPTER VI.

३५०९ । क । एकाचो द्वे प्रथमस्य । ६ । १ । १ ।

'+ छन्दसि वेति वक्तव्यम् +' । 'यो जागार' । 'दाति प्रियाणि' ।

3509. A. In the room of the first portion, containing a single vowel, there are two. S. 2175.

Vârt :—In the Chhandas there is optionally reduplication of the root in the Perfect and other tenses. As दाति प्रियाणि (Rig Ved. VI. 8. 3) or ददाति प्रियाणि ॥ मघवा दातु or ददातु, मस्तुतो वीरवद् धातु or दधातु ॥

Vârt :—The root जागृ is optionally reduplicated in the Perfect. As, यो जागार (or जजागार) Rig Ved. X. 44. 14.

३५०९ । तुजादीनां दीर्घोऽभ्यासस्य । ६ । १ । ७ ।

तुजादिराकृतिगणः । 'प्रभरा तूतुजानः' 'सूर्यं मामहानम्' । 'दाधार यः पृथिवीम्' 'स तूताव' ।

3509. In the room of a short vowel of the reduplicate of the roots 'tuj' &c, a long is substituted.

There is no list of तुजादि verbs given any where. The word आदि in तुजादि therefore should be construed as "verbs *like* tuj." So that wherever we may find a word having a long vowel in the Reduplicate, we should consider it a valid form. Thus प्रभरा तूतुजानः तुज् + कानच् III. 2. 106 = तूतुजानः Rg. I. 61. 12). सूर्यं मामहानं । दाधार यः पृथिवीम् Rig Ved. III. 32. 8 स तूताव Rig Ved. I. 94. 2. This lengthening only takes place in the Vedas before some special affixes.

३५१० । बहुलं छन्दसि । ६ । १ । ३४ ।

ह्वः संप्रसारणं स्यात् । 'इन्द्रमा हुव ऊतये' ।

'+ ऋचि त्रेरुत्तरपदादिलोपश्च छन्दसि +' ऋच्शब्देपरे त्रेः संप्रसारणमुत्तरपदादेर्लोपश्चेति वक्तव्यम् । तृचं सूक्तम् । 'छन्दसि' किम् । त्र्यृचानि ।

'+ रयेर्मतौबहुलम् +' । रेवान् । रयिमान्पुष्टिवर्धनः ।

3510. In the Chhandas, the semivowel of the root hve is diversely vocalised.

Thus हुवे or हुयामि, as इन्द्रमाहुव ऊतये (Rig Ved. I. 111. 4). देवीं सरस्वतीं हुवे ॥ The form हुवे is Atmanepada, Present tense, 1st Pers. sing. the vikaraṇa शप् is elided, then there is vocalisation and substitution of उवङ् ॥ So also हुवामि मरुत. शिवान् । हुयामि विश्वान् देवान् ॥ So also हवः as श्रुधीहवम् (Rig. I. 2. 1.) 'hear the invocation.'

Vârt:—There is vocalisation of the semivowel of त्रि when followed by ऋच्, and there is elision of the ऋ of ऋच् when it refers to Metres. As तिस्र ऋच यस्मिन् = तृचं सूक्तं ॥ तृचं साम ॥ The word तृच् takes the samâsânta affix अ by V. 4. 74. Why do we say when referring to a metre? Observe त्र्यृचानि ॥

Vârt:—In the Chhandas there is diversely vocalisation of the semivowel of रयि followed by the affix मतुप्, as रयि + मत् = रइ + मत् = र + इ + मत् = र + इ + वत् (VIII. 2. 15) = रेवत्; as, आ रेवानेतु नो विशः ॥ Sometimes it does not take place, as रयिमान् पुष्टिवर्द्धनः ॥ The म here is not changed to व as required by VIII. 2. 15.

३५११ । चायः की । ६ । १ । ३५ ।

चायतेर्बहुलं कीत्ययमादेशः, स्याच्छन्दसि । 'न्य१ न्यञ्चिक्युर्न निचिक्युरन्यम्' । लिट्युसि रूपम् । बहुलग्रहणानुवृत्तेर्नेह । 'अग्निं ज्योतिर्निचाय्य' ।

3511. For chây is diversely substituted kî in the Chhandas.

Thus विधुना निचिक्युः, न्यन्यं चिक्युर्न निचिक्युरन्यम् ॥ These are forms ending in the affix उस् of the Perfect. Sometimes there is no substitution. As अग्निं-ज्योतिर्निचाय्य ॥ Thus चाय् + उस् = की + उस् = चिकी + उस् = चिक्युः । So also चाय् + क्त = चाय् + ल्यप् = चाय्य ।

३५१२ । अपस्पृधेथामानृचुरानृहुश्चिच्युषेतित्याजश्राताः श्रितमाशीराशीर्तः । ६ । १ । ३६ ।

एते छन्दसि निपात्यन्ते । 'इन्द्रश्च विष्णो यदपस्पृधेथाम्' । स्पर्धेर्लङ्याथाम् । 'अर्कमानृचुः' । 'वसून्यानृहुः' । 'अर्चैरर्हैश्च लिट्युसि' । चिच्युषे । च्युङो लिटि थासि । 'यस्तित्याज' । त्यजेर्णलि । 'श्रातास्त इन्द्र सोमाः' । 'श्रिता नो ग्रहाः' । 'श्रीञ् पाके निष्ठायाम्' । 'नाशिरं दुह्रे' । 'मध्यत आशीर्तः' । श्रीञ एव क्विपि निष्ठायां च ।

3512. In the Chhandas, the following irregular forms are met with:—अपस्पृधेयाम्, आनृचुः, आनृहुः, चिच्युषे, तित्याज, श्राताः, श्रितम्, आशीः and आशीर्तः ॥

The word छन्दसि is understood here. From the root स्पर्द्ध 'to challenge', is formed अपस्पृधेथाम् being the Imperfect (लङ्), 2nd Pers. Dual, Atmanepada: there is reduplication of the root, vocalisation of र, and the elision of अ irregularly. As, इन्द्रश्चविष्णो यदपस्पृधेथाम् (Rig Ved. VI. 69. 8). In the classical language the form is अपस्पर्धेथाम् ॥ Some say, it is derived from स्पर्द्ध with the preposition अप, the vocalisation of र, the elision of अ, and the non prefixing of the augment अट् in the Imperfect (VI. 4. 75). The counter-example of this will be अपास्पर्द्धेथाम् ॥

From अर्च and अर्ह 'to respect, to worship', are derived आनृचुः and आनृहुः in the Perfect before the 3rd per. pl. उस्, there being vocalisation of र and the elision of अ irregularly. Then there is reduplication, then ऋ changed to अ, then the lengthening of this अ, then the addition of the augment न, as : अर्च्+उस् = ऋच्+उस् = ऋ+ऋच् + उस्=अ+ऋच् + उस् (VII. 4. 66) = आ + ऋच् + उस् (VII. 4. 70) =आ+न् + ऋच्+उस् (VII. 4. 71)=आनृचुः ॥ The irregularity consists in the samprasârana with the elision of अ ॥ Thus यवया अर्कमानृचुः (Rig Ved. I. 19. 4). न यसून्यानृहुः ॥ The classical forms will be आनर्चुः, आनर्हुः ॥

The form चिच्युषे is the Perfect 2nd per. sing. of the root च्युङ् 'to go': there is vocalisation of the reduplicate, and the non-addition of the augment इट् before the affix से ॥ This is the irregularity. The regular form is चुच्युविषे ॥

The form तित्याज as in "यस्तित्याज" (Rig Ved. X. 71. 6), is the Perfect of त्यज्, the vocalisation of the reduplicate is the irregularity. The regular form is तत्याज ॥

From the root श्रीञ् 'to cook', is derived श्राता before the Nishṭhâ affix, श्री changed to श्रा irregularly. As श्रातास्त इन्द्रसोमाः ॥ The form श्रितं is also derived from the same root by shortening the vowel with the same affix. As सोमो गौरी अधिश्रितः, श्रिता नो ग्रहाः ॥ Some say the श्रा substitution of श्री takes place when the word refers to सोम, in the plural, and श्रि when it refers to other than सोम ॥ Sometimes the word श्रातः is seen in the singular, referring to objects other than सोम । Thus यदि श्रातो जुहोतन ॥ In fact, the exhibition of the word श्राताः in the plural in the sûtra is not absolutely necessary.

The words आशीर् and आशीर्त्तः are from the same root श्री, with the prefix आङ् and taking the affixes क्विप् and क्त respectively. Before these श्री is replaced by शीर्, and the non addition of न in the Nishṭhâ is irregular, As, "नाशिरं दुह्रे" (Rig Ved. III. 53. 14), क्षीरैर्मध्यत आशीर्त्तः ॥ (Rig Ved. VIII. 2. 9.)

३५१३ । खिदेश्छन्दसि । ६ । १ । ५२ ।

'खिद दैन्ये' । अस्यैच आ स्यात् । चिखाद । चिखेदेत्यर्थः ।

3513. There is optionally the substitution of â in the room of the diphthong of the verb khid 'to suffer pain,' in the Chhandas.

The word विभाषा is understood here. Thus चित्तं चिखाद or चिखेद ॥ In the classical literature we have चित्तं खेदयति ॥

३५१४ । शीर्षंश्छन्दसि । ६ । १ । ६० ।

शिरःशब्दस्य शीर्षन् स्यात् । 'शीर्ष्णो जगतः' ।

3514. The word śirshan is found in the Chhandas.

This word is another form of शिरः and means 'head.' This is not a substitute of शिर in the Vedas, for both forms are found therein. Thus शीर्ष्णो

जगतः (Rig Ved. VII. 66. 15). In the classical literature there is only one form त्रिग्रः ॥

The Sûtras VI. 1. 104 and 105 declare. "The substitution of a long vowel homogeneous with the first, does not take place when अ or आ is followed by a vowel other than अ of the case-affixes of the Nominative and the Accusative." "The substitution of a long vowel homogeneous with the first, does not take place when a long vowel is followed by a Nominative or Accusative case-affix beginning with a vowel other than अ or by the Nom. Pl. affix जस् ॥" The following sûtra makes an exception in the Vedas.

३५१५ । वा छन्दसि । ६ । १ । १०६ ।

दोर्घाज्जसीचि च पूर्वसवर्णदीर्घो वा स्यात् । वाराही । वाराह्यो । 'मानुषीरीळते विशः'। उत्तरसूत्रद्वयेऽर्योदं वाक्यभेदेन संबध्यते । तेनामिपूर्वत्वं वा स्यात् । शमीं च शम्यं च । 'सूम्यं सुषिरामिव '। सम्प्रसारणाच्च ' (३३०) इति पूर्वरूपमपि वा । इज्यमानः । यज्यमानः ।

3515. In the Vedas, the long vowel may optionally be the single substitute of both vowels, in contravention to the prohibition mentioned in VI. 1. 104 and VI. 1. 105.

Thus मारुती: or मारुत्यः, पिण्डीः or पिण्ड्यः, वाराही or वाराह्यौ; उपानही or उपानह्यौ ॥

'मानुषीरीळते विशः' (Rig Ved. V. 8. 3).

The two sûtras subsequent to this in the Ashṭâdhyâyi, namely VI. 1. 107 and VI. 1. 108 are also influenced by the present sûtra. Thus sûtra VI. 1. 107 declares. "There is the single substitution of the first vowel, when a simple vowel is followed by the अ of the Accusative singular अम् ।" But this is optional in the Vedas. Thus शमीम् or शम्यम्:, and सूम्यं सुषिरामिव (Rig Ved. VIII. 69. 12).

Similarly VI. 1. 108 declares. "There is the single substitution of the first vowel for the vocalised semi vowel and the subsequent vowel." In the Veda this rule is optional, as इज्यमानः or यज्यमानः ॥

३५१६ । शेश्छन्दसि बहुलम् । ६ । १ । ७० ।

लोपः स्यात् । 'या ते गात्राणाम्'। 'ताता पिण्डानाम्'।

'+ एमन्नादिषु छन्दसि पररूपं वक्तव्यम् +'। अपां त्वेमन् । अपां त्वोद्मन् ।

3516. In the Chhandas, the elision of case-ending i (śi) of the nominative and accusative plural neuter, is optional.

Thus या ते गात्राणाम् (Rig. Ved. I. 162. 19.) ताता पिण्डानाम् (Rig Ved I. 162. 19).

Vârt:—In the Vedas, the para-rûpa substitution takes place when एमन् &c. follow. Thus अपां त्वा एमन् = अपां त्वेमन् ॥ So also अपां त्वा ओद्मन् = अपां त्वोद्मन् ॥

३५१७ । भय्यप्रवय्ये च च्छन्दसि । ६ । १ । ८३ ।

बिभेत्यस्मादिति भय्यः । वेतेः प्रवय्या इति स्त्रियामेव निपातनम् । प्रवेयमित्यन्यत्र । 'छन्दसि' किम् । भेयम् । प्रवेयम् ।

'+हृदय्या आप उपसंख्यानम् +' हृदे भवा हृदय्या आपः । भवे छन्दसि यत् ।

3517. The forms bhayya and pravayyâ are found in the Chhandas.

The word भव्य is derived from भी+यत्, and प्रवय्या from प्र+वी+यत् ॥ The guṇa ए is changed to अय् ॥ Thus भव्यं किलासीत् ॥ वत्सतरी प्रवय्या ॥ The यत् is added to भी with the force of Ablative by virtue of the diversity allowed by कृत्यल्युटो बहुलं (III. 3. 113) ॥ Thus बिभेति अस्माद् = भय्यम् "frightening or fearable." The word प्रवय्या is always used in the feminine : in other places प्रवेय is the proper form. Why we do say 'in the Vedas'? Observe भेयम्, प्रवेयम् in the classical literature.

Vârt :—The word ह्रदय्या should also be enumerated when referring to water. As ह्रदे भवा = ह्रदय्या आपः ॥ The affix यत् is added by IV. 4. 110 (ह्रदे+य=ह्रदय्+य) ॥

३५१८ । प्रकृत्यान्तःपादमव्यपरे । ६ । १ । ११५ ।

ऋक्पादमध्यस्थ एङ् प्रकृत्या स्यादति परे न तु वकारयकारपरेऽति । 'उपप्रयन्तो अध्वरम्' । 'सुजाते अश्वसूनृते' । 'अन्तःपादम्' किम् । 'एताश्च एतेऽर्चन्ति' । 'अव्यपरे' किम् । 'तेऽवदन्' तेऽयजन् ।

3518. The final 'e' or 'o' and the following 'a' when occurring in the middle half of a foot of a Vaidic verse, retain their original forms, except when the 'a' is followed by 'v' or 'y.' ॥

The word एङः is understood here, but it should be construed here in the nominative case and not in the Ablative. The word प्रकृति means 'original nature, cause.' The word अन्तर् is an Indeclinable, used in the Locative case here and means 'in the middle.' The word पादः 'the foot of a verse' refers to the verses of the Vedas, and not to the verses of the classical poetry. The word अति is also understood here. Thus उपप्रयन्तो अध्वरम् (Rig Ved. I. 74. 1.); सुजाते अश्वसूनृते (Rig Veda. V. 79. 1).

Why do we say 'in the inner half of a foot of a verse?' Observe कया मती कुत एताश एतेऽर्चन्ति (Rig Ved. I. 165. 1) ॥ Why do we say "when व or य does not follow अ?" Observe तेऽवदन् (Rig. X. 109. 1) ॥ Why do we say ए or ओ? Observe अन्वग्निरुषसामग्रमख्यत् ॥ Some read this sûtra as नान्तः पादमव्यपरे ॥ According to them, this sûtra supersedes the whole rule of juxtaposition or संहिता (VI. 1. 72).

३५१९ । अव्यादवद्यादवक्रमुरव्रतायमवन्त्ववस्युषु च । ६ । १ । ११६ ।

एषु व्यपरेऽप्यति एङ् प्रकृत्या । 'वसुभिर्नोऽव्यात्' । 'मित्रमहो अवद्यात्' । 'मा शिवासो अवक्रमुः' । 'ते नो अव्रत' । 'शतधारो अयं मणिः' । 'ते नो अवन्तु' । 'कुशिकासो अवस्यवः' । यद्यपि । बहुचैस्तेनोऽवन्तु रथतूः' सो यमागात्' तेऽरुणेभिः' इत्यादौ प्रकृतिभावो न क्रियते तथापि बाहुलकात्समाधेयम् । प्रातिशाख्ये तु वाचनिक एवायमर्थः ।

3519. The 'e' or 'o' retain their original form in the middle of a Vaidic verse, when the following words come after them (though the 'a' in these has a 'v' and 'y' following it):—अव्यात्, अवद्यात्, अवक्रमुः, अव्रत, अयम्, अवन्तु, अवस्यु ॥

Thus अग्निः प्रथमो वसुभिर्नो अव्यात् ॥ मित्रमहो अवद्यात् (Rig IV. 4. 15), मा शिवासो अवक्रमुः (Rig VII. 32. 27); ते नो अव्रताः (Not in the Rig Veda). Prof. Bohtlingk gives the following examples from the Rig Veda :—सोचन्तोअव्रतम् (VI. 14. 3) संदहन्तो अव्रतान् (IX. 73. 5), कर्तें अव्रतान् (IX. 73. 8), शतधारो अयं मणिः, ते नो अवन्तु,

(Not in the Rig Veda according to Prof. Bohtlingk the अ of अवन्तु is generally elided in the Veda after ए or आ) कुशिकासो अवस्यवः (Rig III. 42. 9).

Though in the Rig Veda we find examples like ते नोऽवन्तु रथतूः (Rig Ved. X. 77. 8), and सोऽयमागात् and तेऽरुणेभिः (Rig Ved. I. 88. 2) &c. where there is no Prakriti-bhâva, but *sandhi*, yet these are to be explained by bahulam i. e. as a Vaidic diversity. But in the Prâtisâkhyas, there is an express rule to this effect; and not left to mere inference as here.

NOTE :—1. अव्यात् is Benedictive 3rd Per. Sing. of अव 'to protect.'

2. अवद्यात् is Ablative singular of अवद्य ॥

3. अवक्रमुः is the Perfect, 3rd Per. Plural of क्रम् preceded by the Preposition अव । There is no reduplication as a Vaidic irregularity. Some read अवचक्रमुः (with reduplication) in the text, but no such word is found in the Rig Veda.

4. अव्रत is the Aorist of वृङ् and वृञ्; the 3rd Per. Pl. झि is replaced by अत । (The Aorist sign is elided by II. 4. 80. S. 3402).

5. अयम् is from इदम् ।

6. अवन्तु is Imperative 3rd Per. Pl. of अव 'to protect.'

7. अवस्युः is a Noun, from अव्+असुन्=अवस् । Then is added क्यच् as अवस्य । Then उ is added by III. 2, 170, and we get अवस्युः ॥

३५२० । यजुष्युरः । ६ । १ । ११७ ।

उरःशब्द एङन्तोऽनि प्रकृत्या यजुषि । 'उरो अन्तरिक्षम्' । यजुषि पादाभावादनन्तःपादार्थं वचनम् ।

3520. In the Yajur Veda, the word 'uras' when changed to 'uro' retains its original form when followed by a short 'a' which is also retained.

Thus उरो अन्तरिक्षम् (Yajur Veda Vajasan. IV. 7). Some read the sûtra as यजुष्युरो: ॥ They take the word as उरु ending in उ, which in the Vocative case assumes the form उरो ॥ They give the following example उरो अन्तरिक्षं सजूः ॥ But in the Yajur Veda VI. 11, the text reads उरोरन्तरिक्षात् सजूः ॥

In the Yajur Veda, there being no stanzas, the condition of अन्तःपादं of VI. 1. 115. does not apply here, and hence the necessity of a separate sûtra; otherwise VI. 1. 115, would have covered this case also.

३५२१ । आपो जुषाणो वृष्णो वर्षिष्ठेऽम्बेऽम्बालेऽम्बिकेपूर्वे । ६ । १ । ११८ ।

यजुष्यति एङ् प्रकृत्या । 'आपो अस्मान्मातरः शुन्धयन्तु' । जुषाणो अग्निराज्यस्य' । 'वृष्णो अंशुभ्याम्' । 'वर्षिष्ठे अधि नाके' । 'अम्बे अम्बाले अम्बिके' । अस्मादेव वचनात् 'अम्बार्थ–' । (२६७) इति ह्रस्वो न ।

3521. In the Yajur Veda, the short 'a' is retained after आपो, जुषाणो, वृष्णो, वर्षिष्ठे, and also in and after 'ambe' or 'ambâle' when they stand before 'ambike.'

Thus आपो अस्मान् मातरः शुन्धयन्तु (Yaj. IV. 2). जुषाणो अप्तुराज्यस्य (Yaj. V. 35), वृष्णो अंशुभ्यां गभस्ति पूतः (Yaj. VII. 1). वर्षिष्ठे अधिनाके ॥ The Vajasaneyi Sanhita has वर्षिष्ठेऽधि (V. S. I. 22). The Taittariya Sanhita has वर्षिष्ठे अधि ॥ (I. 1. 8. 1. 4, 43, 2. 5. 5. 4) अम्बे अम्बाले, अम्बिके (V. S. 23. 18 where the reading is अम्बे अम्बिकेऽम्बालिके) but Tait. S. VII. 4. 19. 1, and Tait. Br. III. 9. 6.

3 has अम्बे अम्बाल्यम्बिके ॥ The words अम्बे &c. though in the Vocative, do not shorten their vowel by VII. 3. 107, because they have been so read here.

३५२२ । अङ्ग इत्यादौ च । ६ । १ । ११९ ।

अङ्गशब्दे य एङ् तदादौ चाकारे य एङ्पूर्वः सोऽति प्रकृत्या यजुषि । 'प्राणो अङ्गे अङ्गे अदीध्यत्' । 'अङ्गे अङ्गे अशोचिषम्' ।

3522. In the Yajur Veda, when the word 'ange' is followed by 'ange' the subsequent short *a* is retained, as well as the preceding 'e' or 'o.'

Thus ऐन्द्रः प्राणो अङ्गे अङ्गे अदाध्यत्, ऐन्द्रः प्राणो अङ्गे अङ्गे निदीध्यत्, ऐन्द्रः उदानो अङ्गे अङ्गे निधीतः, ऐन्द्रः प्राणो अङ्गे अङ्गे अशोचिषम् (Yaj. 6. 20).

३५२३ । अनुदात्ते च कुधपरे । ६ । १ । १२० ।

कवर्गधकारपरे अनुदात्तेऽति परे एङ् प्रकृत्या यजुषि । 'अयं सो अग्निः' । 'अयं सो अध्वरः' । 'अनुदात्ते' किम् । 'अधोऽग्रे रुद्रे' । अग्रशब्द आद्युदात्तः । 'कुधपरे' किम् । 'सोऽयमग्निमन्तः' ।

3523. In the Yajur Veda, when an anudâtta *a* is followed by a Guttural or a *dh*, the antecedent 'e' or 'o' retains its form, as well as this subsequent *a*.

Thus अयं सो अग्निः (Yaj. 12. 47), अयं सो अध्वरः ॥ Why do we say when अ is gravely accented? Observe अधोऽग्रे, here अग्रे has an acute accent on the first syllable. Why do we say "when followed by a Guttural (कु) or a ध"? Observe सोऽयमग्नि मन्तः ॥

३५२४ । अवपथासि च । ६ । १ । १२१ ।

अनुदात्त अकारादौ अवपथाःशब्दे परे यजुषि एङ् प्रकृत्या । 'त्रीरुद्रेभ्यो अवपथाः' । वपेस्थासि लङि 'तिङ्ङतिङः' (३९३५) इत्यनुदात्तत्वम् । 'अनुदात्ते' किम् । 'यद्रुद्रेभ्योऽवपथाः' । निपातैर्यद्यदि-' (३९३७) इति निघातो न ।

3524. In the Yajur Veda, when the gravely accented *a* of *avapathâs* follows *e* or *o* the vowels retain their original form.

Thus त्री रुद्रेभ्यो अवपथाः ॥ The word अवपथाः is 2nd per. Singular Imperfect of वप् in the Atmanepada. Thus अ+वप्+शप्+थास् ॥ The अ is grave by VIII. 1. 28. When it is not gravely accented, the अ drops. As यद्रुद्रेभ्योऽवपथाः ॥ Here अ in not grave by virtue of VIII. 1. 30.

३५२५ । आङोऽनुनासिकश्छन्दसि । ६ । १ । १२६ ।

आङोऽचि परेऽनुनासिकः स्यात् । स च प्रकृत्या । 'अभ आँ अपः' । 'गभीर आँ उग्रपुत्रे' । '+ ईषाक्षादीनां छन्दसि प्रकृतिभावो वक्तव्यः +' । 'ईषा अक्षो हिरण्ययः' । 'ज्या इयम्' । 'पूषा अविष्टु' ।

3525. For the adverb 'â' is substituted in the Chhandas the nasalised 'añ' when a vowel follows it, and it retains its original form.

Thus अभ आँ अपः (Rig Veda V. 48. 1); गभीर आँ उग्रपुत्रे जिघांसतः (Rig Veda VIII. 67. 11.)

Vârt :—In the Vedas ईवा अवः &c. are found uncombined. As, ईवा अवा, का ईमिरे पिशंगिला, यथा अङ्कदः, पथा अगमन् &c.

ज्या इयम् (Rig Ved. VI. 75. 3.) पुषा अविष्टु (Rig Ved. X. 26. 1).

३५२६ । स्यश्छन्दसि बहुलम् । ६ । १ । १३३ ।

स इत्यस्य सोर्लोपः स्याच्छन्दसि । 'एष स्य भानुः' ।

3526. In the Chhandas, the case-affix of the nominative singular is diversely elided after *sya*, when a consonant follows it.

Thus उत स्य वाजी क्षिपणिं तुरण्यति । ग्रीवायां बद्धो अपिकक्ष आसनि (Rig Veda IV. 40. 4), एष स्य ते मधुमाँ इन्द्र सोमः (Rig Veda IX. 87, 4). Sometimes it does not take place: as यत्र स्यो निपतेत् ॥ The स्य means 'he.'

३५२७ । ह्रस्वाच्चन्द्रोत्तरपदे मन्त्रे । ६ । १ । १५१ ।

ह्रस्वात्परस्य चन्द्रशब्दस्योत्तरपदस्य सुडागमः स्यान्मन्त्रे । 'हरिश्चन्द्रो मरुद्गणः' । सुश्चन्द्र स्य ।

3527. In a Mantra, the 'suṭ' is added to 'chandra,' when it is a second member in a compound and is preceded by a short vowel.

Thus हरिश्चन्द्रो मरुद्गणः (Rig Ved. IX. 66. 26). सुश्चन्द्रो युष्मान् ॥ Why do we say after a short vowel? Observe सूर्याचन्द्रमसाविव ॥ Why do we say 'in a Mantra'? Observe, सुचन्द्रा पौर्णमासी ॥ The उत्तरपद can only be in a compound (samâsa) as it is well-known to all; and it does not mean, 'the second word,' as the literal meaning might convey. Therefore the rule does not apply here सुक्रमसि चन्द्रमसि ॥

३५२८ । पितरामातरा च च्छन्दसि । ६ । ३ । ३३ ।

द्वन्द्वे निपातः । 'आ मा गन्तां पितरामातरा च' । चाद्विपरीतमपि । 'नमातरापितरा नू चिदिष्टौ' ।

'समानस्य छन्दस्यमूर्धप्रभृत्युदर्केषु' । समानस्य सः स्यान्मूर्धादिभिन्न उत्तरपदे । सगर्भ्यः ।

'+ छन्दसि स्त्रियां बहुलम् +' । विष्वग्देवयोरद्र्यादेशः । 'विश्वाची च घृताची च;' 'देवद्रीचीं नयत देवयन्तः'; 'कद्रीची' ।

3528. In the Vedas the form 'Pitarâmâtarâ' is also valid.

In the ordinary language मातापितरौ is the proper form. The Vaidic form is derived by adding अङ् to the first member, and आ is added to the second by VII. 1. 39: and then Guṇa by VII. 3. 110. Thus आ मा गन्तां पितरामातरा च ॥

By force of च: 'also', the converse is also valid. As न मातापितरा नू चिदिष्टौ ।

3528A. स is the substitute of समान in the Chhandas, but not before मूर्धन, प्रभृति and उदर्क ॥ (See VI. 3. 84. S. 1012.)

Thus सगर्भ्यः = समानो गर्भः "uterine brother."

Vârt :—In the Vedas, the finals of विश्व and देव are replaced by अद्रि diversely before the feminine nouns: thus in "विश्वाची च घृताची च"; there is no substitution in विश्वाची, but in कद्रीची there is this substitution. कद्रीची is derived from किम्+अंच = कद्रि + अंच ॥ Then is added ङीप् and then like अश्वाची ॥ This vârtika is an exception to VI. 3. 92. S. 418.

देवद्रीचीं नयत देवयन्तः (Rig Ved. III. 6. 1.) कद्रीची (Rig Ved. I. 164. 17).

३५२९ । सध मादस्थयोश्छन्दसि । ६ । ३ । ९६ ।

सहस्य सधादेशः स्यात् । 'इन्द्र त्वास्मिन्सधमादे' । सोमः सधस्थम् ।

3529. *Sadhi* is substituted for *saha* in the Chhandas when *mada* and *stha* follow.

Thus सधमादोद्युम्न्य एकास्ताः सधस्थाः ॥ Another example is आत्वा वहन्तो हरयो युजाना, अर्वागिन्द्र सधमादो वहन्तु (Rig. III. 3. 7) सहमाद्यन्ति देवा अस्मिन् = यज्ञः ॥

'इन्द्र त्वास्मिन्सधमादे' (Rig Ved. VIII. 2. 3).

३५३० । पथि च च्छन्दसि । ६ । ३ । १०८ ।

पथिशब्द उत्तरपदे कोः कवं कादेशश्च । कवपथः-कापथः-कुपथः ।

3530. The substitution of *ka*, and *kava* for *ku* takes place in the Chhandas before *patha*.

Thus कवपथः, कापथः and कुपथः ॥

३५३१ । साढ्यै साढ्वा साढेति निगमे । ६ । ३ । ११३ ।

सहेः क्त्वाप्रत्यये आद्यं द्वयं तृनि तृतीयं निपात्यते । 'मरुद्भिरुग्रः पृतनासु साह्ळा' अचोर्मध्यस्थस्य डस्य ळः ढस्य ळ्हश्च प्रातिशाख्ये विहितः । आह हि ।

'द्वयोश्चास्य स्वरयोर्मध्यमेत्य संपद्यते स डकारो ळकारः ।

ळ्हकारतामेति स एव चास्य ढकारः सन्नूष्मणा संप्रयुक्तः ॥' इति ।

3531. 'Sâḍhyai' 'sâḍhwâ' and 'sâḍhâ' are irregularly formed in the Vedas.

Thus साढ्यै समन्तात्, साढ्वा शत्रून् ॥ The words साढ्यै and साढ्वा are both formed by त्वा affix added to सह् the ओ substitution not taking place. In the first, त्वा is changed to ध्यै ॥ The third word साढा is formed by तृन् affix added to सह ॥ In the classical literature सोढा and सोढ्वा are the proper forms.

'मरुद्भिरुग्रः पृतनासु साह्ळा (Rig Ved. VII. 56. 23).

In the Prâtisâkhya it is ordained that a ड situated between two vowels is changed to ळ ; and a ढ so situated becomes ळ्ह् ॥ As says the kârikâ.

Kârikâ :—The letter ड falling between two vowels has become ळ in the pronunciation of this Professor.

So also ढ similarly situated is pronounced by him as an Ushman letter i. e., ḷḥ ळ्ह " ॥

३५३२ । छन्दसि च । ६ । ३ । १२६ ।

अष्टन आत्वं स्यादुत्तरपदे । अष्टापदी ।

3532. In the Chhandas also, the long vowel is substituted for the final of 'ashṭan' before a second member.

Thus अष्टापदी ॥ The form अष्टापदी is the feminine in ङीप् (IV. 1. 8) of अष्टपात् (V. 4. 138 the अ of पाद being elided in a Bahuvrihi), पद being substituted for पात् by VI. 4, 130.

३५३३ । मन्त्रे सोमाश्वेन्द्रियविश्वदेव्यस्य मतौ । ६ । ३ । १३१ ।

दीर्घः स्यान्मन्त्रे । 'अश्वावतीं सोमावतीम्' । इन्द्रियावान्मदिन्तमः । 'विश्वकर्मणा विश्वदेव्यावता' ।

3533. In a Mantra, the final vowels of **सोम, अश्व, इन्द्रिय** and **विश्वदेव्य** are lengthened when the affix 'matup' follows.

Thus सोमावती, अश्वावती इन्द्रियावती, विश्वदेव्यावती ॥
अश्वावतीं सोमवतीम् (Rig Ved. X 97. 7.)
विश्वकर्मणा विश्वदेव्यावता (Rig Ved. X. 170. 4).

३५३४ । ओषधेश्च विभक्तावप्रथमायाम् । ६ । ३ । १३२ ।

दीर्घः स्यान्मन्त्रे । 'यदोषधीभ्य अदधात्योषधीषु' ।

3534. In a Mantra, the final of 'oshadhi' is lengthened before the case-endings, but not in the Nominative.

Thus यद् ओषधीभ्यः अदधात्योषधीषु ॥

३५३५ । ऋचि तुनुघमक्षुतङ्कुत्रोरुष्याणाम् । ६ । ३ । १३३ ।

दीर्घः स्यात् । 'आ तू न इन्द्र' । 'नू मर्तः' । 'उत वा घा स्यालात्' । मक्षु गोमन्तमीमहे । 'भरता जातवेदसम्' । तङिति थादेशस्य ङित्त्वपक्षे ग्रहणम् । तेनेह न । 'शृणोत ग्रावाणः' । 'कूमनाः' । 'अत्रा ते भद्रा' । 'यत्रा नश्चक्रा' । 'उरुष्याणः' ।

3535. In the Rig Veda, the finals of the particles **तु, नु, घ, मक्षु**, the tense-affix **तङ्, कु**, the ending 'tra' and the word **उरुष्य** are lengthened.

Thus तु :—आ तू न इन्द्र वृत्रहन् (Rig IV. 32. 1) नु—नू मर्तः ॥ घ :—उत वा घा स्यालात् ॥ मक्षुः—मक्षू गोमन्तमीमहे ॥ तङ् :—भरता जातवेदसम् (Rig X. 176. 2). तङ् is the त substitute of था, when it is treated as ङित्, therefore it does not apply here, शृणोत ग्रावाणः (I. 2. 4.) कु—कूमनस् ; त्र—'अत्रा ते भद्रा । ' यत्रानश्चक्रा' उरुष्या णोऽग्नेः ॥

NOTE :—The घ in the sûtra is the sound घ and not the technical घ (तरप् and तमप्). स्याल means "the wife's brother." भरत is Imperative Second Person Plural. शृणोत is the Imperative Second Person Plural formed by the affix तप् (VII. 1. 46. S. 3568). Since this affix is पित् the present rule does not apply to it. उरुष्य is Imperative 2nd Per. Singular and is derived from the Kandwâdi root उरुष्य (formed by यक्). The affix हि is elided by VI. 4. 105. S. 2202. The न of the Pronoun नस् is changed to ण after उरुष्य by VIII. 4. 27. S. 3649.

३५३६ । इकः सुञि । ६ । ३ । १३४ ।

ऋचि दीर्घ इत्येव । 'अभीषुणः सखीनाम्' । 'सुञः' (३६४४) इति षः । 'नश्च धातुस्थोरुषुभ्य' (३६४९) इति णः ।

3536. In a Mantra, the finals of the preceding member ending in 'i' or 'u' are lengthened before the particle 'su.'

Thus अभी षु णः सखीनाम् (Rig. IV. 31. 3) ऊर्ध्व ऊ षुण उतये (Rig I. 36 13). The स is changed to ष by VIII. 3. 107 : S. 3644, and न changed to ण by VIII. 4. 27. S. 3649.

३५३७ । द्व्यचोऽतस्तिङः । ६ । ३ । १३५ ।

मन्त्रे दीर्घः । 'विद्मा हि चक्रा जरसम्' ।

3537. A tense affix ending in 'a' is lengthened in the Rig Veda, when the Verb consists of two syllables.

Thus विद्मा हि त्वा सत्पतिं शूर गोनाम् &c. See Rig. III. 42. 6, विद्मा हि चक्रा जरसम् । &c. But not here देवा भवत वाजिनः, as the verb consists of more than two syllables: not also here आ देवान् वक्षि यक्षि च as the verbs do not end in अ ॥

NOTE:—विद्म is Present First Person Plural. म replaces मः by III. 4. 82. चक्र is 2nd Person Plural of the Perfect of कृ ॥

३५३८ । निपातस्य च । ६ । ३ । १३६ ।

'एवा हि ते'।

3538. In the Rig Veda the final of a particle is lengthened.

Thus एवा हि ते, अच्छाते, अच्छा जरितारः (Rig Ved. I. 2. 2).

३५३९ । अन्येषामपि दृश्यते । ६ । ३ । १३७ ।

अन्येषामपि पूर्वपदस्थानां दीर्घः स्यात् । पूरुषः । दण्डादण्डि ।

3539. The elongation of the final is to be found in other words also.

Here we must follow the usage of the Śishṭhas. Where the lengthening is not ordained by any rules of Grammar, but occurs in the writing of standard authors, there we should accept such lengthening as valid. Thus पूरुषः दण्डादण्डि :।

३५४० । छन्दस्युभयथा । ६ । ४ । ५ ।

नामि दीर्घो वा । 'धाता धातॄणाम्' इति बह्वृचाः । तैत्तिरीयास्तु ह्रस्वमेव पठन्ति ।

3540. In the Chhandas, the finals are optionally lengthened before the Genitive plural 'nâm.'

In some places they are seen as lengthened, in others not. As धाता धातॄणाम् (Rig Ved. X. 128. 7). So also चतसृणाम् and चतसॄणाम् ॥

The Rig Vedins read with long ॠ, the Taittariyas read it with short ऋ ॥

३५४१ । वा षपूर्वस्य निगमे । ६ । ४ । ९ ।

षपूर्वस्याचो नोपधाया वा दीर्घोऽसंबुद्धौ सर्वनामस्थाने परे । ऋभुक्षाणम् । ऋभुक्षणम् । 'निगमे' किम् । तक्षा । तक्षाणौ ।

3541. The lengthening of the penultimate vowel of a stem ending in 'n' before the affixes of the strong-case, is optional in the Nigama, when 'sh' precedes such a vowel.

Thus ऋभुक्षाणं or ऋभुक्षणमिन्द्रम् ॥

· Why do we say 'in the Nigama'? In the classical literature we have तक्षा, तक्षाणौ, तक्षाणः always.

३५४२ । जनिता मन्त्रे । ६ । ४ । ५३ ।

इडादौ तृचि णिलोपो निपात्यते । 'यो नः पिता जनिता' ।

3542. In a Mantra, the word 'janitâ' is formed irregularly by the elision of 'ṇi' before the affix 'tṛi' with the augment 'iṭ.'

Thus यो नः पिता जनिता (Rig Veda X. 82. 3.) ॥ Otherwise जनयिता in the classical literature. It is an exception to VI. 4 51.

३३४३ । शमिता यज्ञे । ६ । ४ । ५४ ।

शमयितेत्यर्थः ।

3543. 'S'amitâ' is formed irregularly by the elision of 'ni' before an 'it' augmented affix, when meaning a sacrificial act.

Thus शृतं हविः शमितः ॥ It is formed by तृच् and is in the Vocative case. Why do we say 'when referring to a sacrificial act'? See शृतं हविः शमयितः ॥ See Satpatha Br. III. 8. 3, 4 and 5.

३५४४ । युप्लुवोर्दीर्घश्छन्दसि । ६ । ४ । ५८ ।

ल्यपीत्यनुवर्तते । वियूय । विप्लूय ।

'आडजादीनाम्' (२२५४) ।

3544. In 'yu' and 'plu,' long is substituted for 'u' before 'lyap' in the Chhandas.

Thus दान्यनुपूर्वं वियूय; यत्रा घो दक्षिणा परिप्लूय ॥ Why do we say, in the Chhandas'? Observe संयुत्य, आप्लुत्य in the classical literature.

By VI. 4. 72 the augment आट् is added to verbs beginning with a vowel, in the Aorist, the Imperfect and the Conditional. In the Vedas, it comes before verbs beginning with consonants also.

३५४५ । छन्दस्यपि दृश्यते । ६ । ४ । ७३ ।

अनजादीनामित्यर्थः । आनट् । आवः । 'न माङ्योगे' (२२२८) ।

3545. The 'âṭ' augmen is found in the Chhandas also.

It is found there before the roots beginning with a vowel as well as before consonant roots. Thus आनट्, from नश् in the Aorist. The च्लि is elided by II. 4. 80, when VIII. 2. 63 does not apply, then श् is changed to ष् by VIII. 2. 36 which becomes ड् and finally ट् ॥ आनक्, from नश् when VIII. 2. 63 applies and आयुनक् ॥ आवः is Aorist of वृञ्, the affix being elided by II 4. 80. आनक् from नश् (II. 4. 80) and आयुनक् is the Imperfect of युज् ॥

The augments अट् and आट् are elided when the Particle मा is added. See VI. 4. 74. But not necessarily so in the Vedas as taught below.

३५४६ । बहुलं छन्दस्यमाङ्योगेऽपि । ६ । ४ । ७५ ।

अडाटौ न स्तः माङ्योगेऽपि स्तः। 'जनिष्ठा उग्रः सहसे तुरायः।' 'मा वः क्षेत्रे परबीजान्यवाप्सुः'

3546. There is diversity in the Chhandas : the augment 'aṭ' or 'âṭ' is added even with 'mâ,' and sometimes not added even when there is no 'mâ'.

Thus in जनिष्ठा उग्रः (Rig. X 73. 1), काममूर्धीत् (Rig. I. 53. 3) and काममर्दयीत् the augment is not added though there is no मा ॥ In मा वः क्षेत्रे परबीजान्यवाप्सुः; मा अभित्थाः, मा आवः, the augment is not elided, though the particle मा is added.

३५४७ । इरयो रे । ६ । ४ । ७६ ।

'गर्भं प्रथमं दध्रे आपः'। रेभावस्याभीयत्वेनासिद्धत्वादालोपः । अत्र रेशब्दस्येटि कृते पुनरपि रेभावः। तदर्थं च सूत्रे द्विवचनान्तं निर्दिष्टमिरयोरिति ।

3547. 'Re' is diversely substituted for 'ire' in the Veda.

Thus कं स्विद्गर्भं प्रथमं दध्रे आपः (Rig. X. 82. 5) या स्य परिदध्रे ॥ In दध्रे, the आ of धा is elided, before the affix इरे by VI. 4. 64, the रे substitution being considered as asiddha (VI. 4. 22) for the purposes of the elision of आ ॥

Here इट् augment is first added to रे after the सेट् roots and the affix thus becomes इरे, then रे is substituted again for this इरे by this sûtra, thus the affix is brought back to its original condition. To show this repetition—रे—इरे—रे the sûtra has exhibited the word इरयोः in the dual number.

३५४८ । छन्दस्युभयथा । ६ । ४ । ८६ ।

भूसुधियोर्यणस्यादियङुवङौ च । 'वनेषु चित्रं विभ्वम्' । विभुवं वा । 'सुध्यो हव्यमग्ने;' सुधियो वा ।

'+ तन्वादीनां छन्दसि बहुलम् +' । 'तन्वं पुषेम' । तनुवं वा । त्र्यम्बकम्-त्रियम्बकं वा ।

3548. In the Chhandas, in the case of a stem in 'bhû' and 'sudhî' are found sometimes the इयङ्, उवङ्, and sometimes the semi-vowel substitution.

As विभ्वम्, विभुवम्, सुध्यः and सुधियः ॥ वनेषु चित्रं विभ्वं विशे (Rig Veda IV. 7. 1) विभुवम् ॥ सुध्यो हव्यमग्ने for सुधियो हव्यमग्ने ॥

Vârtika:—There is diversely the substitution of इयङ् and उवङ् in the Chhandas, after तनु &c. and the rest. This ordains substitution even after words which are not roots.

As, तन्वं पुषेम (Rig Ved. X. 128. 1) or तनुवं ॥ त्र्यम्बकम् or त्रियम्बकम् "Three-eyed."

तनिपत्योश्छन्दसि । ६ । ४ । ९९ ।

एतयोरुपधालोपः क्ङिति प्रत्यये । 'वितत्निरे कवयः' । 'शकुना इव पप्तिम' । भाषायां वितेनिरे । पेतिम ।

3549. In the Chhandas, the root-vowel of 'tan' 'to stretch' and 'pat' to fall, is elided before an affix beginning with a vowel, when it has an indicatory 'k' or 'N'.

As वितत्निरे कवयः ॥ It is the 3rd Person Plural Perfect of तन् ॥ The vowel अ of तन् is elided. Though the elision is *asiddha* yet the rule VI. 4. 120 requiring the substitution of ए and the elision of the reduplicate त does not apply: because then the present sûtra would be nullified. शकुना इव पप्तिमः (Rig Ved. IX. 107. 20). This is also लिट् ॥ In the classical language we have वितेनिरे, पेतिम् ॥

३५५० । घसिभसोर्हलि च । ६ । ४ । १०० ।

'सग्धिश्च मे' । 'बब्धां ते हरी धानाः' । 'हुभ्रक्ष्यां हेधिः' (२४२५) ।

3550. The root-vowel of 'ghas' and 'bhas' is elided in the Chhandas, before any affix, whether beginning with a vowel or a consonant, which has an indicatory 'k' or 'N'.

Thus सग्धिश्चमे सपीतिश्च मे, बब्धां ते हरी धानाः ॥ सग्धिः is thus derived: क्तिन् is added to the root अद् ; then by II. 4. 39, घस् is substituted for अद्; thus घस् + ति = घ्स् + ति (अ being elided by the present sûtra) = घ् + ति (स् being elided by

VIII. 2. 26), then स is changed to ध, and घ to ग and we have गिधः ॥ Then समानाः गिधः=सगिधः (समान changed to स VI. 3. 84). The word बब्धाम् is the Imperative of भस्, thus भस्+श्लु+ताम्=भ भस्+ताम्=ब भ्स्+ताम् (VI. 4. 100)=बभ्+ताम् (VIII. 2. 26)= ब ब्+धाम्=बब्धाम् ॥ This rule of elision being a nitya, and a subsequent rule, ought to have operated first, but, as a Vaidic anomaly, the reduplication takes place first. See VII. 2, 67.

Why do we read "before an affix beginning *also* with a consonant"? Because the elision takes place before a vowel affix also, as बप्सति=भस्+श्लु+झि=ब भ्स्+अति (VII. 1. 4)=बप्सति (VIII. 4. 55).

Why having an indicatory क् or ङ्? Observe अंशून् बभस्ति ॥ The च has been added into the aphorism by the Vârtikakâra.

३५५१ । श्रुशृणुपृकृवृभ्यश्छन्दसि । ६ । ४ । १०२ ।

'श्रुधी हवम्' । 'शृणुधी गिरः' । 'रायस्पूर्धि' । 'उरुणस्कृधि' । अपावृधि ।

3551. धि is substituted for हि in the Vedas, after श्रु, शृणु, पृ, कृ and वृ ॥

As श्रुधी हवम् (Rig Ved. I. 2, 1.) शृणुधि गिरः (Rig Ved. VIII. 84, 3.) रायस्पूर्धि (Rig Ved. I. 36. 12). उरुकृदुरुणस्कृधि and अवावृधि ॥

In शृणुधी, the हि is not elided after the उ or णु, as it was required by VI. 4. 106, since the present aphorism specifically mentions it. The lengthening takes place by VI. 3. 137. The forms other than शृणुधि are irregular; शप् being added *diversely* by III. 1. 85, and then elided diversely by बहुलंछन्दसि II. 4. 73.

NOTE:—पूर्धि is from पॄ 'to protect'. The शप् is elided; for the final ॠ there is उर by VII. I. 102. S. 2495 and it is lengthened by VIII. 2, 77 S. 354 उरु णस्कृधि from कृ; the न of नस् is changed to ण by VIII. 4. 27 S. 3649 and the visarjanîya is changed to स by VIII. 3. 50. S. 3635.

३५५२ । वा छन्दसि । ३ । ४ । ८८ ।

हिरपिद्वा ।

3552. In the Chhandas the substitute 'hi' is optionally treated as not having an indicatory 'p.'

The result is that in the Chhandas, the second person singular of लोट् has two forms, as प्रीणाहि or प्रीणीहि; युयुधि or युयोधि, धि being substituted for हि in the Vedas (by VI. 4. 103 S. 3553) as in the following verse:

अग्ने नय सुपथा राये अस्मान्विश्वानि देव वयुनानि विद्वान् ।
युयोध्यस्मज्जुहुराणमेनो भूयिष्ठां ते नमउक्तिं विधेम ॥

Rig Veda I. 189. 1: Yajur Veda, 40. 16.

३५५३ । अङितश्च । ६ । ४ । १०३ ।

हेर्धिः स्यात् । रारन्धि । रमेर्व्यत्ययेन परस्मैपदम् । शपः श्लुरभ्यासदीर्घश्च । 'अस्मे प्रयन्धि' 'युयोधि जातवेदः' । यमेः शपो लुक् । यौतेः शपः श्लुः । 'अङितः' किम् । प्रणीहि ।

3553. 'Dhi' is substituted for 'hi' when the tense-affix is not 'ṅit'.

Under III. 4. 88 S. 3552 हि is also पित् in the Vedas : and when it is पित्' it is not ङित् by 1. 2. 4. Thus रारन्धि, प्रयन्धि and युयोधि in the following सोमरारन्धि ; अस्मभ्य तद्धर्यश्व प्रयन्धि; युयोध्यस्मज्जुहुराणमेनः ॥

Why do we say 'when it is not ङित्' ? Observe प्रीणीहि ॥

(1) रारन्धि is irregularly formed Parasmaipada of रम ; the शप being replaced by श्लु, and the reduplicate lengthened as a Vedic form. The म is not elided, by VI. 4. 37 as the affix is not ङित् ॥ (2) प्रयन्धि is from यम the शप् is elided. (3) युयोधि from यु (यौति), the शप् being replaced by श्लु; युयोधि जातवेदः (Rig Ved. VIII. 11. 4).

३५५४ । मन्त्रेष्वाङ्यादेरात्मनः । ६ । ४ । १४१ ।

आत्मन्शब्दस्यादेर्लोपः स्यादाङि । 'त्मना देवेषु' ।

3554. In the Mantras, the beginning of 'âtman' is elided, when the affix of the Instrumental Singular follows.

आङ् is the name of the Instrumental singular affix, given by ancient Grammarians. Thus त्मना देवेषु (Rig Ved. VII. 7. 1).

३५५५ । विभाषर्जोश्छन्दसि । ६ । ४ १६२ ॥

ऋजुशब्दस्यर्तः स्थाने रः स्याद्वा इष्ठेमेयस्सु । 'त्वं रजिष्टमनुनेषि' । ऋजिष्ठं वा ।

3555. Before the affixes ishṭha, iman and îyas, the 'ṛi' of 'ṛiju' may optionally be changed to 'ra' in the Chhandas.

As रजिष्ठः and ऋजिष्ठः, in त्वं रजिष्ठमनुनेषि (Rig Ved. I. 91. 1).

३५५६ । ऋत्व्यवास्त्व्यवास्त्वमाध्वीहिरण्ययानिच्छन्दसि । ६ । ४ । १७५ ।

ऋतौ भवमृत्व्यम् । वास्तुनि भवं वास्तव्यम् । वास्त्वं च । मधुशब्दस्याणि स्त्रियां यणादेशो निपात्यते । 'माध्वीर्नः सन्त्वोषधीः' । हिरण्यशब्दात्प्रिहितस्य मयटो मशब्दस्य लोपो निपात्यते । 'हिरण्ययेन सविता रथेन' ।

इति षष्ठोऽध्यायः ।

3556. In the Chhandas the following are irregularly formed: Ṛitvya, Vâstvya, Vâstva, Mâdhvî, and Hiraṇyaya.

The word ऋत्व्य is derived from ऋतु, and वास्तव्य from वास्तु with the affix यत्, उ being changed to व ॥ ऋतौ भवम् = ऋत्व्यम्, वास्तौ भवम् = वास्त्व्यम् ॥ वास्त्व is from वस्तु, as वस्तुनि भवः = वास्त्वः with the affix अण् ॥ माध्वी from मधु with the affix अण् in the feminine as 'माध्वीर्नःसन्त्वोषधीः' Rig Ved. I. 90. 6. हिरण्यय is from हिरण्य with the affix मयट्, the म being elided, as 'हिरण्ययेन सविता रथेन' (Rig Ved. I. 35. 2.)

CHAPTER VII.

'शीङो रुट् (२४४२) ।

By VII. 1. 6 S 2442; the augment रुट् is added to the tense-affix अत the 3rd Person Plural Atmanepade. But in the Vedas the augment is added to other affixes also.

३५५७ । बहुलं छन्दसि । ७ । १ । ८ ।

रुडागमः स्यात् । 'लोपस्त आत्मनेपदेषु' (३५६३) इति पक्षे तलोपः । 'धेनवो दुह्रे' । लोपाभावे घृतं दुह्रते' । 'अदृश्रमस्य' । 'अतो भिस ऐस्' (२०३) ।

3557. The augment 'ruṭ' is diversely applied in the Chhandas.

The त of अत is elided by VII. 1. 41. S. 3563, in one alternative. Thus धेनवो दुह्रे ॥ When then there is no elision, we have घर्म दुह्रते । So also अदृश्रमस्य ॥

देवा अदुह्र ; गन्धर्वा अप्सरसो अदुह्र ॥ Here अदुह्र is the Imperfect (लङ्) plural of दुह् ॥ Thus दुह् + झ = दुह् + रत् = अदुह्र, the त् being elided by VII. 1. 41. Sometimes, the augment does not take place, as अदुहत ॥ Owing to the word बहुल, 'diversely', the augment र is added to other affixes also, than झ ॥ As अदृश्रम् in अदृश्रमस्य केतवः ॥ This is the aorist in अङ् of the root दृश by III. 1. 57. the guṇa ordained by VII. 4. 16, does not take place.

By VII. 1. 9 S. 203 ; ऐस् is substituted for भिस् in the Instrumental Plural after nouns ending in अ. But not always so, in the Vedas.

३५५८ । बहुलं छन्दसि । ७ । १ । १० ।

'अग्निर्देवेभिः' ।

3558. In the Chhandas the substitution takes place diversely.

That is ऐस् is substituted for भिस् even after stems which do not end in short अ ; as नद्यैः ; and some times the substitution does not take place even after stems ending in short अ, as, देवेभिः, in देवोदेवेभिरागमत् (Rig Veda I. 1, 4).

३५५९ । नेतराच्छन्दसि । ७ । १ । २६ ।

स्वमोरदड् न । 'वार्त्रघ्नमितरम्' । 'छन्दसि' किम् । इतरत्काष्ठम् । 'समासेऽनञ्पूर्वे क्त्वो ल्यप्' (३३३२) ।

3559. In the Chhandas, *at* (or *ad*) is not the substitute of *su* and *am* (Nom. and Acc. Sg.) endings, after *itar*.

As इतरमितरमण्डमजायत ; वार्त्रघ्नमितरम् ॥ Why in the Vedas ? See इतरत् काष्ठम्, इतरत् कुड्यम् ॥

By VII. 1. 37. S. 3332, ल्यप् is substituted for *ktvá* in a compound the first member of which is an Indeclinable but not नञ् ॥ In the Vedas, this is optional.

३५६० । क्त्वापि च्छन्दसि । ७ । १ । ३८ ।

यजमानं परिधापयित्वा ।

3560. In the Chhandas the 'ktvâ' also, as well as lyap, is substituted for ktvâ, after an Indeclinable compound, other than one preceded by the Negative 'nañ.'

Thus कृष्णं वासो यजमानं परिधापयित्वा ॥

३५६१ । सुपां सुलुक्पूर्वसवर्णाच्छेयाडाड्यायाजालः । ७ । १ । ३९ ।

'ऋजवः सन्तु पन्थाः' । पन्थान इति प्राप्ते सुः । 'परमे व्योमन्' । 'व्योमनि' इति प्राप्ते ङेर्लुक् । धीती । मती । सुष्टुती । धीत्या मत्या सुष्टुत्येति प्राप्ते पूर्वसवर्णदीर्घः । 'या सुरथा रथीतमा दिविस्पृशा अश्विना' । 'यौ सुरथौ दिविस्पृशौ' इत्यादौ प्राप्ते आ । 'नताद्ब्राह्मणम्' । नतमिति प्राप्ते आत् । 'यादेव विद्म तात्वा' । यमिति प्राप्ते । 'न युष्मे वाजबन्धवः' । 'अस्मे इन्द्राबृहस्पती' । युष्मास्वस्मभ्यमिति प्राप्ते शे । उरुया । धृष्णुया । उरुणा धृष्णुनेति प्राप्ते या ।

'नाभा पृथिव्याः' । नाभाविति प्राप्ते डा । 'ता अनुष्ठ्योच्यावयतात्' । अनुष्ठानमनुष्ठा । व्यवस्थावदङ् । आङो ड्या । साधुया । साध्विति प्राप्ते याच् । 'वसन्ता यजेत' । वसन्त इति प्राप्ते आल् । '+इयाडियाजीकाराणामुपसंख्यानम्+' । उर्विया । दार्विया । उरुणा दारुणेति प्राप्ते इया । सुक्षेत्रियेति प्राप्ते डियाच । 'दृतिं न शुष्कं सरसी शयानम्' । ङेरीकार इत्याहुः । तत्राद्युदात्ते पदे प्राप्ते व्यत्ययेनान्तोदात्तता । वस्तुतस्तु ङीषन्तान्ङेर्लुक् । ईकारादेशस्य तूदाहरणान्तरं मृग्यम् । '+आङयाजयारामुपसंख्यानम्+' । 'प्रबाहवा सिसृतम्' । बाहुनेति प्राप्ते आङादेशः । 'घेर्ङिति' (२४५) इति गुणः । स्वप्नया । स्वप्नेनेति प्राप्तेऽयाच् । 'स नः सिन्धुमिव नावया' । नावेति प्राप्तेऽयार् । रित्स्वरः ।

3561. The following irregular endings are substituted for the various case-endings in the Chhandas: (1) 's' of the Nom. Sg. for 'as' of the Plural, (2) the *luk*-elision of the case-endings, (3) the single substitution of the homogeneous long vowel for the end vowel of the stem, (4) â, (5) ât, (6) e (śe) for the ending of the Nom. Plural, (7) yâ, (8) â (ḍâ), with the elision of the last vowel and the consonant, if any, that follows it in the stem, (9) yâ (ḍyâ) with the similar shortening of the stem, (10) yâ, (yâch) and (11) 'â' (accent of 'la').

Thus (1) अनृक्षरा ऋजवः सन्तु पन्थाः (for पन्थान) Rig Veda X. 85. 23.

Vârt:—It should be stated that case-endings replace case-endings promiscuously, as धुरि दक्षिणायाः (for दक्षिणायाम् Rig I. 164. 9).

Vârt:—One personal ending replaces another personal ending in the Vedas चषालं ये अश्वयूपाय तक्षति (for तक्षन्ति) Rig. I. 162. 6.

(2) लुक्-elision :—As परमे व्योमन् (Tait-up. II. 1. 1) for व्योमनि ।. Here is elision of ङि ॥

(3) Lengthening :—धीती, मती, सुष्टुती for धीत्या, मत्या and सुष्टुत्या ॥

(4) आ substitute :—As या सुरथा रथीतमोभा देवा दिविस्पृशा । अश्विना ता हवामहे ॥ (Rig Ved. I. 22. 2). Instead of यौ, सुरथौ, दिविस्पृशौ, उभौ, &c, we have या, सुरथा, &c.

(5) आत्-नताद् ब्राह्मणम् for नतम् ॥ यादेव विद्म ता त्वा here या is for यम् ॥

(6) शे-न युष्मे (for युष्मासु) वाजबन्धवः, Rig. VIII. 68. 19. अस्मे (for अस्मभ्यम्) इन्द्राबृहस्पती; Rig. IV. 49. 4.

(7) या-उरुया, धृष्णुया for उरुणा and धृष्णुणा ॥

(8) डा-नाभा (for नाभौ) पृथिव्याः Rig. I. 143. 4.

(9) ड्या-अनुष्ठ्या उच्यावयतात् for अनुष्ठया Ait Br. II. 6. 15. अनुष्ठानेन भवान् विशसनं करोतु । The word अनुष्ठा (feminine) is derived from स्था with the affix अङ् (III. 3. 106) and the preposition अनु । In the Instrumental Singular, the टा is replaced by ड्या ॥ But is not the affix अङ् of III. 3. 106 set aside in the case of स्था by the specific affix क्तिन् of III. 3. 95 ? Not always, for Pâṇini himself has used forms like व्यवस्था (I. 1. 35) showing that स्था takes the affix अङ् also.

(10) याच्—साधुया for साधु; the elision of सु which was otherwise required does not take place.

(11) आल्-वसन्ता यजेत for वसन्ते ॥

Vârt :—The following substitutes should also be enumerated, (*a*) इया, (*b*) डियाच् with the elision of the final vowel and the consonant, if any, that follows it, and (*c*) long ई ॥ As (*a*) उर्विया परिज्मानम्, for उरुणा, so also दार्विया for दारुणा ॥ (*b*) सुक्षेत्रिया for सुक्षेत्रिणा, and सुगात्रिया for सुगात्रिणा ॥ (*c*) दृतिं न शुष्कं सरसी शयानम् (Rig Ved. VII. 103. 2) for सरसि ॥

The word सरसी however may be otherwise explained. The ordinary explanation is that ङि (Loc. Sing). is replaced by long ई of this Vârtika. The word ought to have udâtta on the first syllable, but anomalously the accent falls on the last. Thus say those who give this example. But as a matter of fact सरसी here is the feminine in ङीष् of सरस् ॥ The Loc. Sing. ङि is elided after it by clause (2) of this sûtra ; and it is not an example of the addition of long ई to सरस् ॥ Well, what is then the example of ई substitution of this vârtika ? That must be found out.

NOTE :—Sâyana also explains सरसी in this way दृतिं न ॥ दृतिमिव शुष्कं नीरसं सरसी महत्सरः ; सरसी गौरादिलक्षणो ङीष् ; सरस्यां "सुपां सुलुक्" इति सप्तम्यां लुक् । महति सरसि निर्जले घर्मकाले शयानं निवसन्तं मण्डूकगण : ॥

Vârt :—So also (*a*) आङ् (*b*) अयाच् and (*c*) अयार् : as प्रबाहवा सिसृतम् (Rig Ved. VII. 62. 5), for प्रबाहुना । The उ is gunatad to ओ by VII. 3. 111, and ओ is changed to अव् before आ (*b*) स्वप्नया सच सेवनम् for स्वप्नेन, (*c*) सिन्धुमिव नावया (Rig Ved. I, 97, 8) for नावा ॥ The र् in अयार् regulates the accent.

The word आच्छे in the sûtra is compounded of three words आ + आत् + शे, the word आत् = आ + आत् ॥

३५६२ । अमो मश् । ७ । १ । ४० ।

मिबादेशस्यामो मश् स्यात् । अकार उच्चारणार्थः । शित्वात्सर्वादेशः । 'अस्तिसिचः–' (२२२५) इति ईट् । 'वधीं वृत्रम्' । अवधिषमिति प्राप्ते ।

3562. For the Personal ending *am* of the First Person Singular (in the Aorist) *ma* (I. 1. 55) is substituted in the Chhandas.

The अम् here is the substitute of मिप्, and not the accusative singular affix. The अ in मश् is for the sake of pronunciation only. As वधीं वृत्रम् (for अवधिषम्) Rig. I. 165. 8 : ॥ The अट् augment is diversely elided (VI. 4. 75). The indicatory श् of मश् shows that the *whole* of the affix अम् is to be replaced. The long ई is added by VII. 3. 96. The substitution of म् for म् is to prevent the change of म् into anusvâra as in VIII. 3. 25.

NOTE :—Thus हन् + च्लि + मिप् = वध् + च्लि + मिप् (II. 4. 43) = वध् + सिच् + मिप् (III. 1. 44) = वध् + इ + सिच् + मिप् = वध् + इट् + सिच् + अम् (III. 4 101) = वध् + इट् + सिच् + म् (Present Sûtra) = वध् + इट् + सिच् + ईट् + म् (VII. 3. 96) = वध् + इट् + ईट् + म् (VIII. 2. 28) = वधीम् (VI. 1. 101).

३५६३ । लोपस्त आत्मनेपदेषु । ७ । १ । ४१ ।

छन्दसि । 'देवा अदुह्र' । अदुह्रतेति प्राप्ते । 'दक्षिणतः शये' । शेत इति प्राप्ते । 'आत्मने-' इति किम् । 'उत्सं दुहन्ति' ।

3563. In the Chhandas the *ta* of the Atmanepada Personal ending is elided.

As देवा अदुह्र for अदुहत (see VII. 1. 8) ; दक्षिणतः शये for शेते ॥ Owing to the anuvritti of अपि from VII. 1. 38, this substitution sometimes does not take place ; as : आत्मानमलंकुरुते ॥ Why in the Atmanepada ? Observe उत्सं दुहन्ति कलशं चतुर्बिलम् ॥

३५६४ । ध्वमो ध्वात् । ७ । १ । ४२ ।

ध्वमो ध्वादित्यादेशः स्याच्छन्दसि । 'अन्तरेवोष्माणं वारयध्वात्' । वारयध्वमिति प्राप्ते ।

3564. In the Chhandas, 'dhvât' is substituted for the Personal ending 'dhvam'.

As अन्तरेवोष्माणं वारयध्वात् for वारयध्वम् ॥ Ait Br. II. 6. 14.

३५६५ । यजध्वैनमिति च । ७ । १ । ४३ ।

एनमित्यस्मिन्परे ध्वमोऽन्त्यलोपो निपात्यते । 'यजध्वैनं प्रियमेधाः' । 'वकारस्य यकारो निपात्यते' इति वृत्तिकारोक्तिः प्रामादिकी ।

3565. यजध्वैनम् is irregularly formed in the Vedas for यजध्वमेनम् ॥

The word यजध्वम् followed by एनम् loses its final म् in the Vedas. As यजध्वैनं प्रियमेधः (Rig. VIII. 2. 37). The Kâśika adds "that व is also irregularly changed into य" : the form would then be यजध्यैनम् ॥ This is, however, a mistake.

३५६६ । तस्य तात् । ७ । १ । ४४ ।

लोटोमध्यमपुरुषबहुवचनस्यस्थाने तात् स्यात् । 'गात्रमस्यानूनं कृणुतात्' । कृणुतेति प्राप्ते । 'सूर्यं चक्षुर्गमयतात्' । गमयतेति प्राप्ते ।

3566. For the ending *ta* of the 2nd Pers. Pl. Imperative is substituted 'tât' in the Chhandas.

As गात्रं गात्रमस्या नूनं कृणुतात् (for कृणुत), and ऊवध्यं गोहं पार्थिवं खनतात् (for खनत) Ait Br. II. 6. 15, 16. अस्माच्च संसृजतात् (= संसृजत)॥ सूर्यं चक्षुर्गमयतात् (= गमयत).

३५६७ । तप्तनप्तनथनाश्च । ७ । १ । ४५ ।

तस्येत्येव । शृणोत ग्रावाणः । शृणुतेति प्राप्ते तप् । 'सुनोतन पचत ब्रह्मवाहसे' । 'दधातन द्रविणं चित्रमस्मे' । तनप् । 'मरुतस्तज्जुजुष्टन' । जुषध्वमिति प्राप्ते व्यत्ययेन परस्मैपदं श्लुश्च । 'विश्वे देवासो मरुतो यतिष्ठन' । यत्संख्याकाः स्थेत्यर्थः । यच्छब्दाच्छान्दसो डतिः । अस्तेस्तस्य थनादेशः ।

3567. Also *ta* and *tana* (before both, on account of the indicatory *p* the preceding vowel of the verbal stem is strengthened, or if weak, not shortened), *tana* and *thana* are substituted for the *ta* of the 2nd Pers. Pl. Imperative in the Chhandas.

Thus (1) शृणोत ग्रावाणः (for शृणुत),

(2) सुनोतन पचत ब्रह्मवाहसे (Rig. Ved. V. 34. 1). सुनोतन = सुनुत ॥ दधातन द्रविणं चित्रमस्मे (Rig Ved. X. 36. 13). The indicatory प् makes तप् and तनप् non-ङित् affixes (I. 2. 4).

(3) तन :—मरुतः तज्जुजुष्टन (Rig Ved. VII. 59. 9). for जुषध्वम्, the Parasmaipada and Ślu are anomalous.

(4) थन :—विश्वेदेवासो मरुतो यतिष्ठन ॥ The pronoun यत् becomes यति by taking the affix डति ; and अस् 'to be.' अस् + त = अस् + थन = स्थन ॥ Padamanjari says.

"The Rig Vedins read यत्निष्टन instead of यतिष्टन in Samhitâ Pâṭha, of कोवस्तो मरुतो यतिष्टन ; and in Pada Pâṭha they read it as यतिस्थन ॥ In this case, it is derived from अस् "to be." Kâśikâ derives it from इष् "to wish."

३५६८ । इदन्तो मसि । ७ । १ । ४६ ॥

मसीत्यविभक्तिको निर्देशः । इकार उच्चारणार्थः । मसित्ययमिकारान्तरूपचरमावयवविशिष्टः स्यात् । मस इगागमः स्यादिति यावत् । 'नमो भरन्त एमसि' । 'त्वमस्माकं तव स्मसि' । इमः स्म इति प्राप्ते ।

3568. The Personal ending *mas* becomes in the Chhandas *masi* ending with an *i*.

Thus नमो भरन्त एमसि (Rig Ved. I. 1. 7), for इमः । त्वमस्माकं तव स्मसि (Rig Ved. VIII. 92. 32) for स्मः ॥

The word मसि in the Sûtra is read without any case ending. The इ in it is for the sake of utterance only. " मस् " assumes in the Vedas a form which ends in इ । In other words the augment इक् is added to the affix मस् ॥ The sûtra might have been मस इक् ॥

३५६९ । क्त्वो यक् । ७ । १ । ४७ ।

'दिवं सुपर्णो गत्वाय' ।

3569. In the Chhandas the Absolutive affix 'ktvâ' gets at the end, the augment 'ya.'

Thus दिवं सुपर्णो गत्वाय (Rig Ved. VIII. 100. 8).

३५७० । इष्ट्वीनमिति च । ७ । १ । ४८ ।

क्त्वाप्रत्ययस्य ईनमन्तादेशो निपात्यते । 'इष्ट्वीनं देवान्' । इष्ट्वेति प्राप्ते ।

3570. In the Chhandas the Absolutive 'ishṭvînam' is irregularly used for 'ishṭvâ.'

To the root यज् is added क्त्वा, and the final आ is replaced by ईनम् ॥ As इष्ट्वीनम् देवान् for इष्ट्वा देवान ॥ The च in the sûtra indicates that there are other forms like this, as पीत्वीनम् for पीत्वा ॥

३५७१ । स्नात्व्यादयश्च । ७ । १ । ४९ ।

आदिशब्दः प्रकारार्थः । आकारस्येकारो निपात्यते । 'स्विचः स्नात्वी मलादिव' । 'पीत्वी सोमस्य वावृधे' । स्नात्वा पीत्वेति प्राप्ते ।

3571. 'Snâtvî' &c. are irregularly formed in the Chhandas.

Thus स्नात्वी मलादिव, for स्नात्वा ; पीत्वी सोमस्य वावृधे for पीत्वा ॥ The word आदि 'et cetera' means "of the form of," namely words having the form like 'स्नात्वी, as पीत्वी &c.

३५७२ । आज्जसेरसुक् । ७ । १ । ५० ।

अवर्णान्तादङ्गात्परस्य जसोऽसुक्स्यात् । देवासः । ब्राह्मणासः ।

3572. After a stem ending in *a* long or short, the affix *as* of the Nom. Pl. gets, in the Chhandas the augment *as* (*asuk*) at the end.

Thus ब्राह्मणासः पितरः सोम्यासः for ब्राह्मणाः and सोम्यः ॥ Rig VI, 75, 10. ये पूर्वासो य उपरासः (Rig X. 15. 2) for पूर्वे and उपरे ॥ So also पुतासः (R. I. 3. 4).

NOTE :—The form जसेः instead of जसः is out of respect for ancient grammarians.

३५७३ । श्रीग्रामण्योश्छन्दसि । ७ । १ । ५६ ।

आमो नुट् । 'श्रीणामुदारो धरुणो रयीणाम्' । 'सूत ग्रामणीनाम्' ।

3573. In the Chhandas after the words 'śrî' and 'grâmaṇi' Gen. Pl. 'âm' gets the augment 'n.'

As श्रीणामुदारो धरुणो रयीणाम् (Rig Ved. X. 45. 5).

NOTE :—This sûtra could be well dispensed with: by I. 4. 5. श्री is optionally a Nadi word in the Genitive plural. We make the option of that sûtra a vyavasthita-vibhâshâ, by saying श्री is *always* Nadi in the Vedas, and *optionally* every where else. As regards सूत ग्रामणीनाम्. we have सूताश्च ग्रामण्यश्च सूतग्रामण्यः, the Genitive Pl. of which by VII. 1. 54 will be सूतग्रामणीनाम्, ॥

The necessity of this sûtra will, however, arise if the compound be सूताश्च ते ग्रामण्यश्च सूतग्रामण्यः ॥

३५७४ । गोः पादान्ते । ७ । १ । ५७ ।

'विद्मा हि त्वा गोपतिं शूर गोनाम्' । 'पादान्ते' किम् । 'गवां शता पृक्षयामेषु' । पादान्तेऽपि क्वचिन्न । छन्दसि सर्वेषां वैकल्पिकत्वात् । 'विराजं गोपतिं गवाम्' ।

3574. After *go,* when standing at the end of a Rik verse, the augment *ṇa* comes before the Gen. Pl. âm.

As विद्माहि त्वा गोपतिं शूरगोनाम् (Rig Ved. X. 47. 1); but गवां गोत्रमुदसृजो यदङ्गिरः in the beginning of a Pâda. "All rules have exceptions in the Vedas" is an established maxim, so at the end of a Pâda, sometimes this rule does not apply, as हन्तारं शत्रूणां कृधि विराजं गोपतिं गवाम् । गवां शता पृक्षयामेषु (Rig Ved. I. 122. 7).

३५७५ । छन्दस्यपि दृश्यते । ७ । १ । ७६ ।

अस्थ्यादीनामनङ् । 'इन्द्रो दधीचो अस्थभिः' ।

3575. In the Chhandas also, the stems asthi, dadhi, *sakthi* and *akshi* are found to take the substitute *anaṅ* before endings other than those mentioned in VII. 1. 75 S. 322.

Thus the substitute is ordained before endings beginning with a vowel. In the Vedas it comes before affixes beginning with a consonant. As इन्द्रो दधीचो अस्थभिः (Rig Ved. I. 84. 13).

३५७६ । ई च द्विवचने । ७ । १ । ७७ ।

अस्थ्यादीनामित्येव । 'अक्षीभ्यां ते नासिकाभ्याम्' ।

3576. The acutely accented 'î' is substituted for the final of asthi, dadhi, sakthi and akshi, in the Chhandas, when the case-affixes of the dual follow.

As पद्भ्याम् ते नासिकाभ्याम् ॥ (Rig ved. X. 163. 1). In अक्षी the augment नुम् is not added to the stem before the vowel-beginning ending, because VII. 1. 73, which ordained नुम्, is superseded by the present sûtra, and being once superseded, it is superseded for good. (सकृद् गतौ विप्रतिषेधे यद्बाधितं तद्बाधितमेव) ॥

३५७७ । दृक्स्ववःस्वतवसां छन्दसि । ७ । १ । ८३ ।

एषां नुमस्यात्सौ । 'कीदृङिन्द्रः' । स्ववान् । स्वतवान् । उदोष्ठ्यपूर्वस्य' (२४९४) ।

3577. दृश्, स्ववस् and स्वतवस् take the augment *num* before the affix su (Nominative and Vocative Singular) in the Vedas.

Thus ईदृङ्, तादृङ् यादृङ्, मदृङ्, स्ववान् स्वतवान्, ॥ The श् of ईदृश् (formed by III. 2. 60), is elided by VIII. 2. 23; and ङ् substituted for न् by VIII. 2. 62. The lengthening in स्ववान् and स्वतवान् is through VI. 4. 14.

कीदृङिन्द्र (Rig. Ved. X. 108. 3).

For स्ववान् see Rig, Ved. I. 35. 10; III. 54, 12, VI. 47. 12;

For स्वतवान् see Rig Ved. IV. 2. 6.

By VII. 1. 102 S 2494 उर् is substituted for the final long ॠ of a root when it is preceded by a labial consonant belonging to the root. In the Vedas however, there is diversity.

३५७८ । बहुलं छन्दसि । ७ । १ । १०३ ।

ततुरिः । जगुरि । पपुरिः ॥

3578. In the Chhandas, the *ur* substitution for 'ṛi' of a root-stem is diverse.

That is, it takes place even when the preceding letter is not labial, and does not take place even when the letter is labial. Thus ततुरिः (Rig Ved. I. 145. 3) दूरे ह्यध्वा जगुरिः, and पपुरिः from तॄ, गॄ and पॄ ॥ All these words ततुरि, जगुरि and पपुरिः are formed by the affix किन् (III. 2. 171).

३५७९ । ह्रु ह्वरेश्छन्दसि । ७ । २ । ३१ ।

ह्वरेर्निष्ठायां, 'ह्रु'आदेशः स्यात् । 'अह्रुतमसि हविर्धानम्' ।

3579. *Hru* is substituted for *hvar* (Bhvâdi 978) in the Chhandas before the Participial-affix.

As ह्रुतस्य चाह्रुतस्य च, अह्रुतमसि हविर्धानम् (Vaj San. 1. 9). But ह्वृतम् in the classical literature.

३५८० । अपरिह्वृताश्च । ७ । २ ३२ ।

पूर्वेण प्राप्तस्य.देशस्याभावो निपात्यते । 'अपरिह्वृताः सनुयाम वाजम्' ।

3580. The word 'aparihvṛitâḥ is irregularly formed in the Chhandas.

The ह्रु substitution required by the last sûtra, does not take place here. As अपरिह्वृताः सनुयाम वाजम् (Rig I. 100. 19). The word being found in the plural number in the Vedas, it is so shown in the sûtra also.

३५८१ । सोमे ह्वरितः । ७ । २ । ३३ ।

ह्वयङ्गुणौ निपात्येते । 'मा नः सोमो ह्वरितः' ।

3581. *Hwaritah* is irregularly formed from *hvri* in the Chhandas, by guna substitution and 'iṭ' augment, when it refers to Soma.

As मा नः सोमो ह्वरितो, विह्वरितस्त्वम् ।

३५८२ । ग्रसितस्कभितस्तभितोत्तभितचत्तविकस्ता विशस्तृशंस्तृशास्तृतरुतृतरूतृवरुतृवरूतृवरूत्रीरुज्ज्वलितिक्षरितिक्षमितिवमित्यमितीति च । ७ । २ । ३४ ।

अष्टादश निपात्यन्ते । तत्र 'ग्रसु' 'स्कम्भु' 'स्तम्भु' एषामुदित्त्वान्निष्ठायामिट् प्रतिषेधे प्राप्त इण्निपात्यते । 'युवं शचीभिर्ग्रसितामुञ्चतम्' । 'विष्कभिते अजरे' । 'येन स्वः स्तभितम्' । 'सत्येनोत्तभिता भूमिः' । स्तभितेत्येव सिद्धे उत्पूर्वस्य पुनर्निपातनमन्योपसर्गपूर्वस्य मा भूदिति ।

'चते याचने' । 'कस गतौ' । आभ्यां क्त इडभावः ।'चत्ता इतश्चत्तामुतः' । 'त्रिधा ह श्यावमश्विना विकस्तम्' 'उत्तानाया हृदयं यद्विकस्तम्' । निपातनबहुत्वापेक्षया सूत्रे बहुवचनं विकस्ता इति तेनैकवचनान्तोऽपि प्रयोगः साधुरेव ।

'शसु' 'शंसु' 'शासु' एभ्यस्तृच इडभावः । 'एकस्त्वष्टुरश्वस्याविशस्ता' । ग्रावग्राभ उतशंस्ता' । 'प्रशास्ता पोता' ।

तरतेर्वृङ्वृञोश्च तृच 'उट्' ऊट्' एतावागमौ निपात्येते । 'तरुतारं रथानाम्' । तरूतारम् । वरुतारम्–वरूतारम् । 'वरूत्रीभिः सुशरणो नो अस्तु' । अत्र ङीबन्तनिपातनं प्रपंचार्थम् । वरूतृशब्दो हि निपातितः । ततो ङीपा गतार्थत्वात् ।

उज्ज्वलादिभ्यश्चतुर्भ्यः शप इकारादेशो निपात्यते । 'ज्वल दीप्तौ' । 'क्षर संचलने' । 'टुवम् उद्गिरणे' । 'अम गत्यादिषु' । इह क्षरितीत्यस्यानन्तरं क्षमितीत्यपि केचित्पठन्ति । तत्र 'क्षमूष् सहने' इति धातुर्बोध्यः । भाषायां तु 'ग्रस्तस्कब्धस्तब्धोत्तब्धचतितविकसिताः' । विशसिता–शंसिता–शासिता । तरीता–तरिता । वरीता–वरिता । उज्ज्वलति ॥ क्षरति । पाठान्तरे क्षमति । वमति । अमति ।

3582. In the Chhandas, the following irregular forms are found, some with, and some without the augment 'iṭ'—1 grasita, 2 skabhita, 3 stabhita, 4 uttabhita, 5 chatta, 6 vikastâḥ, 7 viśastṛi, 8 śanstṛi, 9 śâstṛi, 10 tarutṛi, 11 tarûtṛi, 12 varutṛi, 13 varûtṛi, 14 varûtrîḥ, 15 ujjvaliti, 16 kshariti, (17 kshamiti,) 18 vamiti and 19 amiti.

Of the above nineteen words, 1, 2, 3, and 4 are from roots ग्रसु 'to swallow' (I. 661) स्कम्भु 'to stop' (I. 414) and स्तम्भु (I. 413) all having an indicatory उ, and therefore by VII. 2 56 read with VII. 2. 15, their Nishṭhâ would not have taken इट् ॥ Thus युवशचीभिः ग्रसिता (ver. ग्रस्त) ममुञ्चतम् Rig Ved. X. 39. 13. विष्कभिते अजरे (Rig Veda VI. 70. 1) (= विष्कब्धः); येन स्वस्तभितम् (Rig Ved. X. 121 5) (= स्तब्धम्), ॥ सत्येनोत्तभिता भूमिः (= उत्तब्धः) Rig Ved. X. 85 1. the irregularity is only with the preposition उत्, with other prepositions, the form स्तभित is not employed.

Similarly (5) चत्ता (= चतिता) as in चत्तो इतश्चत्तामुतः (Rig Ved. X. 155. 2,) from चते याचने । (6) त्रिधाहश्यावमश्विना विकस्तम् (Rig Veda I. 117. 24). उत्तानाया हृदयं यद् विकस्तम् । (=विकसितम्) The word vikastâḥ generally occurs in the plural and is therefore so shown in the Sûtra. But the singular is also valid.

The forms, 7, 8, and 9 are from the roots शसु हिंसायाम and शंसु स्तुतौ, and शासु अनुशिष्टौ with the affix तृच and no augment; as एकस्त्वष्टुरश्वस्याविशस्ता (Rig

Veda I. 162. 19) (= विशसिता), उत शंस्ता सुविप्रः (Rig Veda I. 162. 5) (= शंसिता), प्रशास्ता पोता (Rig Veda I. 94. 6), (= प्रशासितम्) ॥

The forms 10, 11, 12, 13 and 14 are from the roots तॄ and वृ (वृङ् and वृञ्) with the affix तृच and the augment उट् and ऊट् ॥ As तरुतारं or तरूतारं रथानाम् Rig Veda X. 178. I. (= तरितारम् or तरीतारम्), वरुतारम् or वरूतारम् रथानाम् (= वरितारम् or वरीतारम्); वरूत्रीभिः सुशरणो नो अस्तु (Rig Veda VII. 34. 22), वरूत्रीः is exhibited in this form of Nom pl. of the feminine वरूत्री merely for the sake of showing one form in which it is found: another form is अहोरात्र णि वैवरूत्रयः । Here the plural is formed irregularly, by taking the word as वरूत्रि ॥ The feminine form could have been easily obtained from वरूतृ, by adding ङीप्, the special mention is explanatory. The rest 15, 16, 17, 18 and 19 are from उत्-ज्वल, चर्, चम्, वम् and अम्, formed with the vikaraṇa शप् and the affix of the 3rd Per. Sing तिप्, इ being substituted for अ of शप्, or शप् is elided and the augment इट् is added ॥ As अग्निरुज्ज्वलिति (= उज्ज्वलति), स्तोमं चमिति (= चमति), स्तोकं चरिति (= चरति), यः सोमं वमिति (= वमति), अभ्यमिति वरुणः (= अभ्यमति) ॥ Sometimes we have अभ्यमीति, as रावमभ्यमीति ॥

We should read here again VII. 2. 64. S. 2527.

३५८२ क ॥ बभूयाततन्यजगृभ्मववर्थेति निगमे । ७ । २ । ६४ ।

विद्मा तमुत्सं यत आबभूथ'। 'येनान्तरिक्षमुर्वाततंथ'। 'जगृभ्मा ते दक्षिणमिन्द्र हस्तम्'। त्वं ज्योतिषा वितमो ववर्थ'। भाषायां तु । बभूविथ। आतेनिथ। जगृहिम । ववरिथेति ।

3582A. In the Nigama (Veda) are found the irregular forms बभूथ, आततन्थ, जगृभ्म and ववर्थ ॥

As, विद्मा तमुत्सं यत आ बभूथ । येनान्तरिक्षमुर्वा ततन्थ (Rig Veda. III. 22. 2), जगृभ्माते दक्षिणमिन्द्र हस्तम् (Rig Veda X. 47. 1). त्वं ज्योतिषा वितमो ववर्थ ।

In the classical literature, we have बभूविथ, आतेनिथ, जगृहिम and ववरिथ respectively.

३५८३ । ससिंससनिवांसम् । ७ । २ । ६९ ।

सनिमित्येतत्पूर्वात्सनतेः सनोतेर्वा क्वसोरिट् । एत्वाभ्यासलोपाभावश्च निपात्यते ।

'+ पावकादीनां छन्दसि +' प्रत्ययस्थात्कादित्वं नेति वाच्यम् । 'हिरण्यवर्णाः शुचयः पावकाः' ।

3583. The form *sasanivānsam* with *sanin* is irregularly formed.

This is derived from सनोति or सनति root with the affix Kvasu. As अग्निं त्वाग्ने सनिं ससनिवांसम् ॥ The augment इट् is added, there is no change of अ of सन्- to ए, nor the elision of the reduplicate before वस् ॥ The other form is सेनिवांसम् when not preceded by सनिम् ॥ This form ससनिवांसम् is Vedic, in the classical literature we have सेनिवांसम् ॥

Várt:—The feminine of पावक &c. in the Vedas does not take इ for अ ॥ As हिरण्यवर्णाः शुचयः पावकाः, यासु अ लोमकाः; अलकाः &c. But पाविकाः, अलोमिकाः in the classical literature. (See VII. 3. 45. S. 464).

३५८४ । घोर्लोपो लेटि वा । ७ । ३ । ७० ।

'दधद्रत्नानि दाशुषे'। 'सोमो ददद्गन्धर्वाय'। 'यदग्निरग्नये ददात्'।

3584. The final of 'dâ' and 'dhâ' ('ghû roots) may optionally be elided in the Subjunctive 'leṭ'.

As दधद्रत्ना दाशुषे (Rig. I. 35. 8.) सोमो ददद् गन्धर्वाय (Rig. X. 85. 41.) But also यदग्निरग्नये ददात् ॥

३५८५ । मीनातेर्निगमे । ७ । ३ । ८१ ।

शिति ह्रस्वः । 'प्रमिणन्ति व्रतानि' । लोके प्रमीणाति । 'अस्तिसिचोऽपृक्ते' (२२२५) ।

3585. In the Chhandas 'mî' is shortened before a 'śit' affix.

As प्रमिनन्ति व्रतानि (Rig. X. 10. 5.) The न becomes ण (प्रमिणन्ति according to Kâśika) by VIII. 4. 15 Why in the Chhandas ? Observe प्र मीणाति ॥

By VII. 3. 96 S. 2225 a single consonantal sârvadhâtuka affix gets the augment ईट्, after अस् (अस्ति) and after the Aorist character सिच् ॥ But in the Chhandas, there is diversity.

३५८६ । बहुलं छन्दसि । ७ । ३ । ९७ ।

'सर्वमा इदम्' ।

अस्तेर्लङ् तिप् ईडभाव अपृक्तत्वाद्धल्ङ्यादिलोपः । रुत्वविसर्गौ । संहितायां तु 'भोभगो – (१६७) इति यत्वं । 'लोपः शाकल्यस्य' (६७) इति यलोपः । गोभिरक्षाः रक्षपालने' लुङ् । 'अतोल्रान्तस्य' (२३३०) इति वृद्धिः । इडभावश्छान्दसः । अट् शेषं पूर्ववत् ॥

ह्रस्वस्यगुणः' (२४२) । 'जसि च' (२४१) । '+ जसादिषु छन्दसि वा वचनं प्राङ् णौ चङ्युपधायाः +' । 'अधा शतक्रत्वो यूयम्' शतक्रतवः । 'पश्वेनृभ्यो यथा गवे' । पशवे । 'नाभ्यस्त-स्याचि-' (२५०३) इति निषेधे । '+ बहुलं छन्दसीतिवक्तव्यम् +' । 'आनुषग्जुजोषत्' ।

3586. In the Chhandas, a single consonantal Sârvadhâtuka affix gets diversely the augment 'iṭ' after *as* and *sich* ॥

As आप एवेदं सलिलं सर्वमाः ॥ Here आः is used instead of आसीत् ॥

NOTE :—आः is thus evolved. अ+अस् + लङ् + तिप् । The ई that would have come by S. 2225 does not come. So we have अ + अस्+त् = आस् (the final consonant त् is elided by VI. 1. 68 S. 252). Then the स् is changed to रु and then रु to visarga : and we have आर् । Then in sanhita, the visarga or रु is changed to य by VIII. 3. 17 S. 167. and we get आय् ॥ Then this य् is elided by VIII. 3. 19 S. 67, and so we have सर्वम् आ इदम् ॥

Similarly in गोभिरक्षाः । It is the aorist (लुङ्) of रक्ष् 'to protect.' The Vṛiddhi takes place by S. 2330. The absence of इट् is the Vaidic irregularity.

By VII. 3. 108, a guṇa is substituted for short इ and उ in the Vocative Singular, and also in the Nominative Plural by VII. 3. 109. The following Vârtika makes an exception to these as well as the other rules of the third chapter of the Seventh Book from sûtra 108 downwards.

Vârt :—All these rules up to the end of this (7th Book, 3rd) chapter are of optional application in the Vedas. As अम्बे or अम्ब, पूर्णा दर्वि or पूर्णा दर्वी, अधा शतक्रत्वः (Rig Veda X. 97. 2) or शतक्रत्वः पश्वे नृभ्यो यथागवे (Rig Veda I. 43. 2), or पशवे, नृभ्यः, किकिदीव्या, किकिदीविना ॥

By VII. 3. 87 the guṇa is not substituted for the penultimate short इ, उ ऋ in the reduplicated form of a root, before a Sârvadhâtuka affix beginning with a vowel and having an indicatory प ॥ The following Vârtika makes an exception.

Vârt:—There is diversity in the Vedas. As अनुवक्, जुजोषत् (Rig Veda III. 4. 10) the लेट् of जुष् ॥

३५८७। नित्यं छन्दसि । ७ । ४ । ८ ।

छन्दसि विषये चङ्युपधाया ऋवर्णस्य ऋनित्यम् । अवीवृधत् ।

3587. Short ऋ is invariably substituted in the Chhandas for the penultimate ऋ or ॠ of a Causative stem, in the Reduplicated Aorist.

As अवीवृधत् (Rig Veda VIII. 8. 8) अवीवृधताम्, अवीवृधन् ॥

३५८८। न च्छन्दस्यपुत्रस्य । ७ । ४ । ३५ ।

पुत्रभिन्नस्यादन्तस्य क्यचिईत्वदीर्घौ न । मित्रयुः । 'क्याच्छन्दसि' (३१५०) इति उः । 'अपुत्रस्य' किम् । 'पुत्रीयन्तः सुदानवः ।

'+ अपुत्रादीनामिति वाच्यम् +' । 'जनीयन्तोऽन्वग्रवः' । जनमिच्छन्तोऽत्यर्थः ।

3588. In the Chhandas the rules causing lengthening, or the substitution of long 'î' for the final vowel of the stem before the affix kyach, do not apply, except in the case of *putra*.

Thus मित्रयुः, संस्वेदयुः, देवाञ्जिगाति सुम्नयुः ॥ But पुत्रीयन्तः सुदानवः (Rig. VII. 96. 4.)

Vârt:—It should be rather stated पुत्र and the rest: as जनीयन्तोऽन्वग्रवः ॥ See III. 2. 170, for the affix उ ॥

३५८९। दुरस्युर्द्रविणस्युर्वृषण्यति रिषण्यति । ७ । ४ । ३६ ।

एते क्यचि निपात्यन्ते । भाषायां तु उप्रत्ययाभावाद्दुष्टीयति । द्रविणीयति । वृषीयति । रिष्टीयति ।

3589. In the Chhandas दुरस्यु, द्रविणस्यु, वृषण्यति and रिषण्यति are irregularly formed.

As अविद्येना दुरस्युः, (= दुष्टीयति with the affix क्यच् added to दुष्ट), द्रविणस्यु विपन्यया (द्रविणीयति, here द्रविणस् is substituted for द्रविण similarly). वृषण्यति = वृषीयति (वृषण् substituted for वृष) ॥ रिषण्यति = रिष्टीयति (रिषण् substituted for रिष्ट)॥

३५९०। अश्वाघस्यात् । ७ । ४ । ३७ ।

'अश्व' 'अघ' एतयोः क्यच्यात्स्याच्छन्दसि । 'अश्वायन्तो मघवन्' । 'मा त्वा वृका अघायवः' । 'न च्छन्दसि-' (३५८८) इति निषेधो नेत्त्वमात्रस्य । किंतु दीर्घस्यापीति । अत्रेदमेव सूत्रं ज्ञापकम् ।

3590. In the Chhandas, long 'â' is substituted for the final of aśva and *agha*, before the Denominative *kyach*.

As अश्वायन्तो मघवन् (Rig. VII. 32. 23), मा त्वा वृका अघायवो विदन् ॥ This also indicates that other words do not lengthen their vowel in the Vedas before क्यच्, as taught in VII. 4. 35. S. 3588. See Vârtika to III. 1. 8. The word अघायु occurs in Rig. I. 120. 7, 27; 3.

३५९१ । देवसुम्नयोर्यजुषि काठके । ७ । ४ । ३८ ।

अनयोः क्यचि आत्स्याद्यजुषि कठशाखायाम् । 'देवायन्तो यजमानाः' । 'सुम्नायन्तो हवामहे' । इह यजुःशब्दो न मन्त्रमात्रपरः किं तु वेदोपलक्षकः । तेन ऋगात्मकेऽपि मन्त्रे यजुर्वेदस्थे भवति । किं च ऋग्वेदेऽपि भवति । सचेन्मन्त्रो यजुषि कठशाखायां दृष्टः । 'यजुषि' इति किम् । 'देवाञ्जिगाति सुम्नयुः' । बह्वृचानामप्यस्ति कठशाखा ततो भवति प्रत्युदाहरणमिति हरदत्तः ।

3591. The long 'â' is substituted for the final of *deva* and *sumna* before the Denominative *kyach* in the Yajush Kâṭhaka.

As देवायन्तो यजमानः सुम्नायन्तो हवामहे । Why in the Yajus? Observe देवाञ्जिगाति सुम्नयुः । According to Haradatta the author of Padamanjari, this counter example is taken from the Kaṭha Shâkhâ of the Rig Veda, for the Rig Veda also has a Kaṭha Shâkha. Why do we say in the Kâṭhaka? Observe सुम्नयुरिदमासात् ।

In this sûtra, Yajush is not confined merely to the Mantra, but means the Veda in general. Therefore the rule will apply to a Mantra of the Rig Veda also, if it is found in the Yajur Veda. That is, the rule will apply to a Mantra of the Rig Veda also, in the Rig Veda, if it be such a Mantra which is common to the Rig and Yajur Veda Kaṭha Shâkhâ.

३५९२ । कव्यध्वरपृतनस्यर्चि लोपः । ७ । ४ । ३९ ।

'कवि' 'अध्वर' 'पृतना' एषामन्त्यस्य लोपः स्यात्क्यचि परे ऋचिविषये । 'स पूर्वया निविदा कव्यतायोः' । 'अध्वर्युं वा मधुपाणिम्' । 'दमयन्तं पृतन्यून्' । 'दधातेर्हिः' (३०७६) । जहातेश्च क्त्वि (३३३१) ।

3592. In the Rig Veda, the final of कवि, अध्वर and पृतना is dropped before the Denominative क्यच् ।

स पूर्वया निविदा कव्यतायोः (Rig. I. 96. 2). अध्वर्युं वा मधुपाणिम् (Rig Veda X. 41. 3), दमयन्तमपृतन्यून् (Rig Veda X. 74. 5).

By VII. 4. 42. S. 3076 हि is substituted for the धा of दधाति before an affix beginning with त् and having an indicatory क् । By VII. 4. 43, S. 3331 हि is substituted for the हा of जहाति before क्त्वा । But in the Vedas there is diversity

३५९३ । विभाषा छन्दसि । ७ । ४ । ४४ ।

'हित्वा शरीरम्' । हीत्वा वा ।

3593. *Hi* is optionally substituted for 'hî' before 'ktvâ' in the Chhandas.

As हित्वा शरीरं यातव्यं, or हीत्वा also. The long ई of VI. 4. 62 deos not take place also as a Vedic irregularity.

३५९४ । सुधितवसुधितनेमधितधिष्वधिषीय च । ७ । ४ । ४५ ।

'सु' 'वसु' 'नेम' एतत्पूर्वस्य दधातेः क्ते प्रत्यये इत्त्वं निपात्यते । 'गर्भं माता सुधितं वक्षणासु' । वसुधितमग्नौ । नेमधिता न पौंस्या । 'क्तिन्यपि दृश्यते' । 'उत श्वेतं वसुधितिं निरेके' । धिष्वावज्रं दक्षिण इन्द्र हस्ते' । धत्स्वेति प्राप्ते । 'सुरेता रेतो धिषीय' । आशीर्लिङ् । इट् । 'इटोऽत्' (२२५७) धासीयेति प्राप्ते । 'अपो भि' (४४२) ।

'+ मासश्छन्दसीति वक्तव्यम् +' । माद्भिः शरद्भिः । 'स्ववः स्वतवसोरुषसश्चेष्यते' । स्वतवद्भिः । अवतेरसुन् । शोभनमवो येषां ते स्ववसस्तैः । 'तु' इति सौत्रो धातुस्तस्मादसुन् । स्वं

तवेा येषां ते स्वतवद्भिः । 'समुषद्भिरजायथाः' । 'मिथुनेऽसिः । 'वसेः किच्च' इत्यसिप्रत्यय इति हरदत्तः । पञ्चपादीरीत्या तु 'उषः कित्' इति प्राग्व्याख्यातम् । 'न कवतेर्यङि' (२६४१) ।

3594. The following five Vedic forms are irregularly formed, namely सुधित, वसुधित, नेमधित, धिष्व and धिषीय ॥

Of these five, सुधित, वसुधित and नेमधित are formed from the root धा with the affix क्त, preceded by सु, वसु and नेम ॥ As गर्भं माता सुधितम् (Rig Veda X. 27. 16). (= सुहितम्), वसुधितमग्नौ जुहोति (= वसुहितं). The word वसुधितं is a Karmadhâraya compound, according to Haradatta. In the Veda-Bhâsya it is explained as वसूनां धातारं प्रदातारम् ॥ The form वसुधिति with क्तिन् is also found in the Vedas. As :—उतश्वेतं वसुधितिं निरेके (Rig Veda VII. 90. 3). नेमधिता न पौंस्या (Rig Veda X. 93. 13) (= नेमहिता) ॥ नेम means 'half.' धिष्व is Imperative 2nd Per. Sg. of धा, there is no reduplication, as धिष्व सेामम् = धत्स्व ॥ धिष्व वज्रम् हस्त आदक्षिणत्राभिः (Rig Veda VI. 18. 9) धिषीय is Benedictive Atmanepada 1st Per. Sg. of धा, the regular form being धासीय ॥ See III. 4. 106.

By VII. 4. 48. S. 442, त् is substituted for the final of the stem अप् before a case-ending beginning with भ ॥ In the Vedas this substitution takes place in the case of मास &c.

Vârtika:—The त् substitution takes place in the Chhandas for the final of मास &c. Thus माद्भिः, शरद्भिः ॥ मास becomes मास् by VI. 1. 63.

Ishti :—The त् substitution should take place, according to Patanjali, after स्ववस्, स्वतवस् and उषस् also. As स्ववद्भिः । स्ववस् is derived from अव् 'to protect,' with the affix असुन् and the prefix सु ॥ It means 'he whose protection is good.' See Rig Veda I. 35, 10; &c.

The word स्वतवस् is derived from the root तु with the affix असुन् and Prefix स्व ॥ It means धनवान् or wealthy. As स्वतवद्भिः । See S. 3633. Similarly उषद्भिः as in समुषद्भिः अजायथाः (Rig Veda I. 6. 3).

This word is formed by the affix असि which is treated as कित् after वस् (See Uṇâdi IV. 222 and 233). This is according to the opinion of Haradatta, who follows evidently the lost Uṇâdi Sûtras which consisted of Ten Padas. In the present Uṇâdi Sûtra of Five Padas we have उषः कित् and not वसेः कित् ॥ वसति सूर्येण सह इति उषा ॥

By VII. 4. 63. S. 2641, the Palatal is not substituted for the Guttural of the reduplicate of कु (कवते) in the Intensive. In the Vedas this prohibition applies to the root कृष् also.

३५९५ । कृषेश्छन्दसि । ७ । ४ । ६४ ।

यङ्यभ्यासस्य चुत्वं न । करीकृष्यते ।

3595. The Palatal is not substituted for the Guttural of the reduplicate of 'kṛish' in the Chhandas, when in the Intensive.

As करीकृष्यते यज्ञकुणपः ; otherwise चरीकृष्यते कृषीवलः ॥

३५९६ । दाधर्ति दर्धर्ति दर्धर्षि बोभूतु तेतिक्तेऽलर्ष्यापनीफणत्संसनिष्यदत्करिक्रत्कनिक्रदद्भरिभ्रद्दविध्वतोदविद्युतत्तरित्रतःसरीसृपतंवरीवृजन्मर्मृज्यागनीगन्तीति च । ७ । ४ । ६५ ।

एतेऽष्टादश निपात्यन्ते। आद्यास्त्रयो धृङो धारयतेर्वा।

भवतेर्यङ्लुगन्तस्य गुणाभावः। तेन भाषायां गुणो लभ्यते।

तिजेर्यङ्लुगन्तात्तङ्। इयर्तेर्लटि हलादिः शेषापवादो रेफस्य लत्वमित्वाभावश्च निपात्यते। 'अलर्षि युध्म खजकृत्पुरन्दरः'। सिपा निर्देशो न तन्त्रम्। 'अलर्ति दक्ष उत'।

फणतेराङ्पूर्वस्य यङ्लुगन्तस्य शतर्यभ्यासस्य नीगागमो निपात्यते। 'अन्वापनीफणत्'।

स्यन्देः संपूर्वस्य यङ्लुकि शतर्यभ्यासस्य निक्। धातुसकारस्य षत्वम्।

करोतेर्यङ्लुगन्तस्याभ्यासस्य चुत्वाभावः। 'करिक्रत्'।

क्रन्देर्लुङि च्लेरङ्द्विर्वचनमभ्यासस्य चुत्वाभावो निगागमश्च। 'कनिक्रदज्जनुषम्'। अक्रन्दीदित्यर्थः।

'बिभर्तेरभ्यासस्य जश्त्वाभावः। 'वि यो भरिभ्रदोषधीषु'।

ध्वरतेर्यङ्लुगन्तस्य शतर्यभ्यासस्य विगागमो धातोर्ऋकारलोपश्च। 'दविध्वतो रश्मयः सूर्यस्य'।

द्युतेरभ्यासस्य संप्रसारणाभावोऽत्त्वं विगागमश्च। 'दविद्युतद्दीद्यच्छोशुचानः'।

तरतेः शतरि श्लावभ्यासस्य रिगागमः। सहोर्जा तरित्रतः'। सृपेः शतरि श्लौ द्वितीयैकवचनेरीगागमोऽभ्यासस्य।

वृजेः शतरि श्लावभ्यासस्य रीक्।

मृजेर्लिटि णलभ्यासस्य रुक् धातोश्च युक्। गमेराङ्पूर्वस्य लटि श्लावभ्यासस्य चुत्वाभावो नीगागमश्च। 'वक्ष्यन्ती वेदा गनीगन्ति कर्णम्'।

3596. In the Chhandas are found the following eighteen irregularly reduplicated forms:—1 dâdharti, 2 dardharti, 3 dardharshi, 4 bobhûtu. 5 tetikte, 6 alarshi, 7 â panîphanat, 8 sam sanishyadat 9 karikrat' 10 kanikradat, 11 bharibhrat, 12 davidhvataḥ, 13 davidyutat, 14 taritrataḥ, 15 sarîsṛpatam, 16 varîvṛjat, 17 marmṛjya and 18 â ganîganti.

The word छन्दसि is drawn in to this sûtra, by force of च ॥ The from दाधर्ति, is either from the Causative of the root धृङ् अवस्थाने or from धृञ् in the श्लु or यङ् लुक्. there is lengthening of the abhyâsa and elision of णि ॥ (2) So also दर्धर्ति is the form in ślu, with रुक् augment of the abhyâsa. (3) दर्धर्षि if it be a form of यङ् लुक्. there is no irregularity. (4) बोभूतु. is from भू in the Intensive (यङ् लुक्) Imperative, irregularly without guṇa (6) अलर्षि is form the root ऋ (इयर्ति) in Present, 2nd Person, the र् of abhyâsa is not elided, though required by VII. 4. 60, and this र् is changed to ल irregularly. This form is found in the 3rd Person also as अलर्ति दक्षः ॥ अलर्षि युध्म खजकृत्पुरंदरः (Rig Veda VIII 1. 7). अलर्ति दक्ष उत (Rig Veda VIII 48. 8). (7) आ पनीफणत् is from फण् with आ augment and शतृ affix is added to यङ् लुक्, and in the reduplicate नी is added. (8) संसनिष्यदत् is from स्यन्द with the Preposition सम्, in the Intensive yaṅ luk, with शतृ affix, नि being added in the abhyâsa, the root स is changed to ष ॥ The Preposition सं is not absolutely necessary, with other Prepositions also we have this form' as आ सनिष्यदत् ॥ (9) करिक्रत is from कृ (करोति), in the Intensive yaṅ luk, with शतृ, in the abhyâsa there is no palatal change (VII. 4. 62). and रि is added to the reduplicate. (10) कनिक्रदत् from क्रन्द in the Aorist with अङ् reduplication, there is no chutva (VII. 4. 62) of the reduplicate, and the augment नि is added. In the classical literature, the form is अक्रन्दीत् ॥ कनिक्रदज्जनुषं (Rig Veda II. 4. 4). (11) भरिभ्रत् from भृ (बिभर्ति) in yaṅ luk with शतृ, without इ of VII. 4. 76, without jaśtva, and रि is added to the reduplicate. त्रियो भरिभ्रद्रोषधीषु (Rig Veda II. 4. 4). (12) दविध्वतः from ध्वृ (ध्वरते) in the yaṅ luk, śatṛi, plural number Nominative. The वि is added to the reduplicate, the ऋ is elided, दविध्वतः रश्मयः सूर्यस्य ॥ (Rig Veda IV. 13. 4.) (13) दविद्युतत् is from dyut, yaṅ luk with śatṛ, there is no vocalisation of the reduplicate, with अ change and वि augment. (14) तरित्रतः from तॄ (तरति) with ślu, śatṛ, genitive singular: and रि added to abhyâsa. सहोर्जा तरित्रतः (Rig Veda IV. 40. 3). (15) सरीसृपत् from सृप् with ślu śatṛ, Accusative with री added to abhyâsa. (16) वरीवृजत् from वृज् with ślu, śatṛ and री augment. (17) मर्मृज्य from मृज् with लिट् (Perfect) णल्, क added to abhyâsa, and य added to the root, and there is no vṛiddhi, because there is no short penultimate now. In fact VII. 2. 114 is to be qualified by the words लघूपध from VII. 3. 86. (18) आ गनीगन्ति is from गम् with the Preposition आ, in the Perfect, with ślu, there is no chutva (VII. 4. 62), and augment नी is added. वदन्ती वेदा गनीगन्ति कर्णम् ॥ (Rig Veda VI. 75. 3).

The word इति in the aphorism indicates that other forms, similar to these, are also to be included.

३५९७ । ससूवेति निगमे । ७ । ४ । ७४ ।

सूतेर्लिटि परस्मैपदं युगागमोऽभ्यासस्य चात्वं निपात्यते । 'गृष्टिः ससूव स्थविरम्' । सुषुवे इति भाषायाम् ।

3597. In the Chhandas sasûva is irregularly formed in the Perfect.

It is derived from सू । Thus गृष्टिः ससूव स्थविरं otherwise सुषुवे । Rig Veda IV. 18. 10.

३५९८ । बहुलं छन्दसि । ७ । ४ । ७८ ।

अभ्यासस्येकारः स्याच्छन्दसि । 'पूर्णां विवष्टि' । वशेरेतद्रूपम् ।

3598. 'I' is diversely substituted in the Chhandas. for the vowel of the reduplicate, in the Reduplicated Present-form.

As पूर्णां विवष्टि (from वश्).

इति सप्तमोऽध्यायः ।

CHAPTER VIII.

३५९९ । प्रसमुपोदः पादपूरणे । ८ । १ । ६ ॥

एषां द्वे स्तः पादपूरणे । 'प्रप्रायमग्निः' । संसमिद्युवसे' । 'उपोप मे परामृश' । 'किं नोदुदु हर्षसे' ।

3599. *Pra*, *sam*, *upa*, and *ut* are repeated, when by so doubling, the foot of a verse is completed.

As प्र प्रायमग्निर्भरतस्य शृण्वे (Rig. VII. 8. 4), संसमिद्युवसे वृषन् (Rig Veda X. 191. 1). उपोप मे परामृश (Rig Veda I. 126. 7), किं नोदुदु हर्षसे दातवा उ (Rig Veda IV. 21. 9).

३६०० । छन्दसीरः । ८ । २ । १५ ॥

इवर्णान्ताद्रेफान्ताच्च परस्य मतोर्मस्य वः स्यात् । 'हरिवते हर्यश्वाय' । गीर्वान् ।

3600. In the Chhandas *v* is substituted for the *m* of *mat*, when the stem ends in *i*, î or *r*.

As, हरिवते हर्यश्वाय (Rig Veda III. 52. 7). Of the stems ending in र we have गीर्वान् &c.

३६०१ । अनो नुट् । ८ । २ । १६ ॥

अन्नन्तान्मतोर्नुट् स्यात् । 'अक्षण्वन्तः कर्णवन्तः' । 'अस्थन्वन्तं यदनस्था बिभर्ति' ।

3601. The affix *mat* gets the augment 'nuṭ' in the Chhandas, after a stem ending in *an*.

As अक्षण्वन्तः कर्णवन्तः सखायः (Rig Veda X. 71. 7) अस्थन्वन्तंयदनस्था बिभर्ति (Rig Veda I. 164. 4).

३६०२ । नाद्घस्य । ८ । २ । १७ ॥

नान्तात्परस्य घस्य नुट् । 'सुपथिन्तरः' ।

'+भूरिदाव्नस्तुड्वाच्यः +' । 'भूरिदावत्तरो जनः' ।

'+ ईद्रथिनः + । 'रथीतरः' । 'रथीतमं रथीनाम्' ।

3602. In the Chhandas, the affixes *tar* and *tam* receive the augment nuṭ after a stem in *n*.

The affixes तरप् and तमप् are called घ। Thus सुपथिन् + तर = सुपथि + तर (VIII. 2. 7) = सुपथि + न्तर (VIII. 2. 17) = सुपथिन्तरः ।

Vârt:—The augment तुट् is added to these affixes after भूरिदावन्; as भूरिदावत्तरः (III. 2. 74, the affix is वनिप्) जनः (Rig Veda VIII. 5. 39).

Vârt:—Long ई is the substitute of the final of रथिन् before तर and तम । The word रथिन् is formed by the affix इनि in the sense of मतुप् । The final न् is first elided by VIII. 2. 7, and then for the short इ of रथि the long ई is substituted by the present vârtika. If the long ई were substituted for the final न् of रथिन् as रथिई + तर, then this long ई being asiddha, it could not be compounded by ekâdeśa with the preceding इ into ई and the form would always remain रथिईतरः । As रथीतरः, and रथीतमं रथीनाम् (Rig Veda I. 11. 1). Or this ई may be considered to have come after रथ in the sense of मतुप् ।

३६०३ । नसत्तनिषत्तानुत्तप्रतूर्तसूर्तगूर्तानि च्छन्दसि । ८ । २ । ६१ ॥

सदेर्नञ्पूर्वान्निपूर्वाच्च निष्ठाया नत्वाभावो निपात्यते । 'नसत्तमञ्जसा' । 'निषत्तमस्य चरतः' । असन्नं निषण्णमिति प्राप्ते । उन्देर्नञ्पूर्वस्यानुत्तम् । प्रतूर्तमिति त्वरतेः । तुर्वीत्यस्य वा । सूर्तमिति स' इत्यस्य । गूर्तमिति 'गूरी' इत्यस्य ।

3603. In the Chhandas we have the following irregular Participles: nasatta, nishatta, anutta, pratûrtta, sûrtta and gûrtta.

The words नसत्त and निषत्त are derived from the root सद् preceded by न and नि, and there is not the न change of VIII. 2. 42. Thus नसत्तमञ्जसा ॥ In the classical literature we have असन्नम् ॥ So also निषत्तः in the Vedas, as in निषत्तमस्य चरतः (Rig Ved. I. 146. 1) but निषण्णः in the classical literature. The word अनुत्तः is from उन्द with the negative अन् ॥ The option of VIII. 2. 56 does not apply here. As अनुत्तमा ते मघवन् (= अनुन्नम्) ॥ प्रतूर्तम् is from त्वर् or तुर्व, as प्रतूर्तं वाजिनम् (= प्रतूर्णम्) ॥ When it is derived from त्वर् then ऊठ् is added by VI. 4. 20; and when from

सूर्व, then VI. 4. 21 is applied. सूर्त्ते is from सृ, the ऋ is changed to उ irregularly; as सूर्त्तगावः = सृतागाव ॥ गूर्त्ते is from गूर् as गूर्त्ता अमृतस्य (=गूर्णा) ॥

३६०४ । अम्नरूधरवरित्युभयथा छन्दसि । ८ । २ । ७० ॥

रुर्वा रेफो वा । अम्न एव-अम्नः रेव । ऊध एव-ऊधरेव । अव एव-अवरेव ।

3604. In the Chhandas, both *ru* and *ra* are substituted for the final of amnas, ûdhas, and avas.

Thus अम्न एव or अम्न रेव, ऊध एव or ऊधरेव ; अव एव or अवरेव ॥ When रु is substituted for the finals, this रु is replaced by य् by VIII, 3. 17, which is elided by VIII. 3. 19. The word अम्नस् means 'a little', and अवस् 'protection.'

३६०५ । भुवश्च महाव्याहृतेः । ८ । २ । ७१ ॥

भुव इति-भुवरिति ।

3605. In the Chhandas, *ru* and *ra* may replace the final of the word 'bhuvas' when used as a mahâ-vyâhṛiti.

Thus भुवरित्यन्तरिक्षम् or भुव इत्यन्तरिक्षम् ॥ The mahâ-vyâhṛitis are three भूः, भुवः and स्वः ॥

३६०६ । ओमभ्यादाने । ८ । २ । ८७ ॥

ओंशब्दस्य प्लुतः स्यादारम्भे । 'ओ३म् अग्निमीले पुरोहितम्' । अभ्यादाने किम् । ओमित्येकाक्षरं ब्रह्म ।

3606. The vowel in *om* is pluta in the beginning of a sacred text.

The word अभ्यादानं means the commencement of a sacred mantra or vedic text. Thus ओ३म् अग्निमीले पुरोहितं यज्ञस्य देवमृत्विजं ॥ (Rig I. 1. 1.)

Why do we say "in the beginning"? Observe ओमित्येतदक्षरमुद्गीथमुपासीत (Chhândogya Upanishad I. 1. 1). Here ओम् is not used to indicate the commencement of a Text or Mantra, but is itself the subject of comment.

३६०७ । ये यज्ञकर्मणि । ८ । २ । ८८ ॥

ये३ यजामहे । 'यज्ञ-' इति किम् । ये यजामहे ।

3607. The vowel of *ye* becomes pluta in a sacred text, when it is employed in a sacrificial work.

Thus ये३यजामहे ॥ Why do we say when employed in a sacrificial work? Observe ये यजामह इति पञ्चाक्षरम् "Ye yajamahe" consists of five syllables. Here it is a simple recitation.

३६०८ । प्रणवष्टेः । ८ । २ । ८९ ॥

यज्ञकर्मणि टेरोमित्यादेशः स्यात् । 'अपां रेतांसि जिन्वतो३म्' । 'टेः' किम् । हलन्त्यस्य मा भूत् ।

3608. In a sacrificial work, ओ३म् is substituted for the final vowel, with the consonant, if any, that may follow it, of a sentence.

The word यज्ञकर्मणि is understood here also. The word प्रणव means ओम् ॥ It is the name given to this syllable. This ओम् is substituted for the final letter

(टि) of that word which stands either at the end of a Pâda of a sacred hymn or at the end of a hemistich of such Rik. Thus for अपां रेतांसि जिन्वति (Rig. VIII. 44. 16), we may have अपां रेतांसि जिन्वतो३म् ॥ So also for देवाङ् जिगाति सुम्नयुः (Rig. III. 27. 1), we may have देवाङ् जिगाति सुम्नयो३म् ॥

The word टि is repeated in this aphorism in spite of its anuvritti from VIII. 2. 82, to indicate that ओम् replaces the *whole* of the last syllable, with its vowel and consonant. Had टि not been repeated, then by the rule of अलोऽन्त्यस्य the final *letter* only of the टि portion of a sentence would have been replaced. Thus in सुम्नयुः the visarjaniya alone would have been replaced.

When not employed in connection with sacrificial works, there is no such substitution. Thus in the simple reading of the Vedas, we should always recite अपां रेतांसि जिन्वति ॥

३६०९ । याज्यान्तः । ८ । २ । ९० ॥

ये याज्यान्ता मन्त्रास्तेषामन्त्यस्य टेः प्लुतो यज्ञकर्मणि । 'जिह्वामग्ने चकृषे हव्यवाहा३म्' । 'अन्तः' किम् । 'याज्यानामृचां वाक्यसमुदायरूपाणां प्रति वाक्यं टेः स्यात् । सर्वान्त्यस्य चेष्यते ।

3609. The last vowel at the end of Mantras called Yâjya, when employed in sacrificial works, is pluta and has the Acute.

Thus स्तोमैर्विधेमाग्नये३ (Rig. VIII. 43. 11), जिह्वामग्ने चकृषे हव्यवाहा३म् (Rig. X. 8. 6).

Why do we say 'at the end'? There are some Yâjya hymns, consisting of several sentences. The final vowel (टि) of every sentence would have become pluta, in such a hymn. To prevent it, the word "anta" is used, so that the final vowel of the hymn at the end of all, becomes pluta.

३६१० । ब्रूहिप्रेष्यश्रौषड्वौषडावहानामादेः । ८ । २ । ९१ ॥

एषामादेः प्लुतो यज्ञकर्मणि । 'अग्नयेऽनुब्रू३हि' । 'अग्नये गोमयानि प्रे३ष्य' । 'अस्तु श्रौ३षट्' । 'सोमस्याग्ने वीहो वौ३षट्' । 'अग्निमा३वह' ।

3610. In a sacrificial work, the first syllable of ब्रूहि, प्रेष्य, श्रौषट् वौषट् and आवह is pluta.

Thus अग्नयेऽनुब्रू३हि (Maitr S I. 4 11), अग्नये गोमयानि (or न) प्रे३ष्य, अस्तु श्रौ३षट् ; सोमस्याग्ने वीही३ वौ३षट् अग्निमा३वह ॥

So also in पित्र्यायामनुस्व३धा on the analogy of ब्रूहि, so also अस्तुस्व३धा ॥ The word वौषट् is illustrative of the six forms वषट्, वौषट्, वाषट्, वौखट्, वाखट् वखट् ॥

But there is no prolation in आवह देवान् यजमानाय; आवह जात वेदः ॥

३६११ । अग्नीत्प्रेषणे परस्य च । ८ । २ । ९२ ॥

अग्नीधः प्रेषणे आदेः प्लुतस्तस्मात्परस्य च । 'ओ३श्रा३वय' । नेह । 'अग्नीदग्नीन्विहर । बर्हिस्तृणीहि' ।

3611. In an order given to Âgnîdhra priest, the first syllable as well as the succeeding syllable is pluta.

In a Yajña, the principal priests (ritvij) are four, Adhvaryu, Udgâtâ, Hotâ and Brahmâ. Every one of these has three subordinate priests (ritvij) under him.

The duty of Âgnidhra is to kindle the sacrificial fire. In a summons or call (प्रेषण) made by the Adhvaryu, who is the Director of ceremonies, to the Âgnidhra to perform the functions of Âgnidh, both syllables become pluta.

The word आग्नीत् प्रेषण is a compound = आग्नीधः प्रेषणम् "a call or summons relating to Agnidh duty."

Thus आ ३ श्रा ३ वय, ओ ३ श्रा ३ वय । The pluta takes place only in these examples ; therefore, not here, as आग्नीदग्नीन् विहर; बर्हि स्तृणीहि ।

३६१२ । विभाषा पृष्ट प्रतिवचने हेः । ८ । २ । ९३ ॥

प्लुतः । अकार्षीः कटम् । अकार्षं हीइ । अकार्षं हि । 'पृष्ट-'इति किम् । 'कटं करिष्यति हि' । 'हेः' किम् । करोमि ननु ।

3612. 'Hi' at the end of an answer to a question may optionally be pluta.

Thus Q. अकार्षीः कटं देवदत्त ? Ans. अकार्षं हीं ३ or अकार्षं हि ।

Why do we say "in answer to a question" ? Observe कटं करिष्यति हि ।

Why do we say हेः 'of हि" ? Observe करोमि ननु ।

३६१३ । निगृह्यानुयोगे च । ८ । २ । ९४ ॥

अत्र यद्वाक्यं तस्य टेः प्लुतो वा । 'अद्यामावास्येत्यात्थ३' । अमावास्येत्येवं वादिनं युक्त्या स्वमतात्प्रच्याव्य एवमनुयुज्यते ।

3613. The end syllable of that sentence is optionally pluta, when it asserts something which has been refuted, and is employed by the victor by the way of censure.

The word निग्रहः means the refutation of another's opinion. निगृह्य is a gerund, and means having refuted'. अनुयोगः is the expression of the same proposition which has been refuted. When a person has demonstrated the untenableness of another's assertion, and then employs the said assertion by way of taunt, reproach or reprimand, then the final syllable of such a sentence becomes pluta. The sûtra literally means "Having refuted (it) when asserting (the same by way of censure)."

Thus an opponent asserts that "The word is not eternal." (अनित्यः शब्दः) । Proving by arguments the untenableness of this position, and after refuting it, the victor says by way of reprimand:—अनित्यः शब्द इत्यात्थँ ३ or अनित्य शब्द इत्यात्थ 'This is then your assertion—that the word is not eternal'. Similarly अद्य श्राद्धमित्यात्थँ ३ or अद्य श्राद्धमित्यात्थ । अद्यामावास्येत्यात्थँ ३ or अद्यामावास्येत्यात्थ ।

३६१४ । आम्रेडितं भर्त्सने । ८ । २ । ९५ ॥

'दस्योदस्यो३ घातयिष्यामि त्वाम्' । आम्रेडितग्रहणं द्विरुक्तोपलक्षणम् । 'चौर चौर३' ।

3614. The final syllable of an âmredita vocative is pluta when a threat is expressed.

A Vocative is reiterated when a threat is meant (VIII. 1. 8, S. 2143). It's final syllable becomes pluta. Thus दस्यो दस्यो ३ घातयिष्यामि त्वा ।

Though the anuvṛitti of the sûtra VIII. 2. 82, is current here, yet the final of the *sentence* is not pluta, but of the âmreḍita.

It should be rather stated that any one of the repeated words may be pluta by alternation. Thus चौरॅ३ चौर or चौर चौरॅ३ । The word âmṛeḍita is employed in the sûtra as illustrative of the doubling, for the threat is expressed by *both* words, so that pluta may be of *both* words in turn: and not of the second word only, though that is technically called âmreḍita.

३६१५ । अङ्गयुक्तं तिङाकाङ्क्षम् । ८ । २ । ९६ ॥

अङ्गेत्यनेन युक्तं तिङन्तं प्लवते । 'अङ्गकूज३ इदानीं ज्ञास्यसि जाल्म' । 'तिङ्' किम् । 'अङ्ग देवदत्त मिथ्या वदसि' । 'आकाङ्क्षम्' किम् । 'अङ्ग पच' । नैतदपरमाकाङ्क्षति । भर्त्सन इत्येव 'अङ्गाधीष्व भक्तं तव दास्यामि' ।

3615. The final syllable of a finite verb, used as a threat becomes pluta, when the word *anga* is joined with it, and it demands another sentence to complete the conclusion.

Thus अङ्ग कूजॅ३ इदानीं ज्ञास्यसि जाल्म । अङ्ग व्याहरॅ३. इदानीं ज्ञास्यसि जाल्म ।

Why do we say 'a verb'? Observe अङ्ग देवदत्त मिथ्या वदसि ।

Why do we say 'when this calls for a conclusion'? Observe अङ्ग पच । Here it is a complete sentence and does not demand another to complete the sense.

The word भर्त्सने of the last sûtra is understood here also. Therefore not in अङ्ग अधीष्व, ओदनं ते दास्यामि । Here अङ्ग has the force of solicitation. (VIII, 1. 33. S. 3940).

३६१६ । विचार्यमाणानाम् । ८ । २ । ९७ ॥

वाक्यानां टेः प्लुतः । 'होतव्यं दीक्षितस्य गृहा३इ' । 'न होतव्य३मिति' । होतव्यं न होतव्यमिति विचार्यते । प्रमाणैर्वस्तुतत्त्वपरीक्षणं विचारः ।

3616. The final syllable of those sentences is pluta, which denote acts of reflection (or balancing between two alternatives).

To determine a thing by weighing all arguments *pro* and *con* is called vichâra or judgment. Thus होतव्यं दीक्षितस्य गृहा ३इ न होतव्यॅ३म् 'should one perform a sacrifice in the house of an initiated person.' Similarly तिष्ठेद्यूपा ३इ, अनुप्रहरेद्यॅ३इ ॥ Here also it is being reflected upon whether यूपं तिष्ठेत् or यूपे अनुप्रहरेत् ॥ i. e. should the stake remain upright or should it be put flat by the yajamâna. किं यूपस्तिष्ठेत्, किं वा यूपं यजमानः शाययेत् ॥

३६१७ । पूर्वं तु भाषायाम् । ८ । २ । ९८ ॥

विचार्यमाणानां पूर्वमेव प्लवते । 'अहिर्नु ३ रज्जुर्नु' । प्रयोगापेक्षत्वं पूर्वत्वम् । इह भाषाग्रहणात्पूर्वयोगश्छन्दसीति ज्ञायते ।

3617. In common speech, the final vowel of the first alternative is only pluta.

This makes a niyama or restriction. The previous sûtra, is thus confined to the Vedic literature, and not to the classical. तु here has the force of 'only.' Thus अहि नुँ ३ रज्जुनु, 'Is it a snake or a rope?' लोष्टो नुँ ३ कपोतो नु 'Is it a clod of earth or a pigeon?'

The priority, of course, depends upon employment. The order of words depends upon one's choice.

३६१८ । प्रतिश्रवणे च । ८ । २ । ९९ ॥

वाक्यस्य टेः प्लुतोऽभ्युपगमे प्रतिज्ञाने श्रवणाभिमुख्ये च । 'गां मे देहि भो३' । 'हन्त ते ददामि३' । 'नित्यः शब्दो भवितुमर्हति३' । 'दत्त किमात्थ३' ।

3618. The final syllable of the sentence which expresses assent or promise, or listening to, is pluta.

The word प्रतिश्रवण means 'agreement, assent or promise.' It also means 'listening to.' All these senses are to be taken here, as there is nothing in the sútra to restrict its scope. Thus it has three senses, 1. to promise something to a petitioner, 2. to acknowledge the truth of some proposition, 3. to listen to another's words Thus गां मे देहि भोः, 1. हन्त ते ददामि ३ ॥ 2. नित्यः शब्दो भवितुमर्हति ३ ॥ 3. देवदत्त भोः, किमात्थ ३ ॥

३६१९ । अनुदात्तं प्रश्नान्ताभिपूजितयोः । ८ । २ । १०० ॥

अनुदात्तः प्लुतः स्यात् । दूराद्धूतादिषु सिद्धस्य प्लुतस्यानुदात्तत्वमात्रमनेन विधीयते : अग्निभूत३ इ । पट ३ उ । 'अग्निभूते' 'पटो' एतयोः प्रश्नान्ते टेरनुदात्तः प्लुतः । शोभनः खल्वसि माणवक ३ ।

3619. The final vowel at the end of a question or of a praise is pluta, but unaccented.

That which is employed at the end of an interrogative sentence is called प्रश्नान्तः । According to some, this rule does not ordain pluta, but only ordains the anudâtta-ness of those syllables which become pluta by the previous rules VIII. 2. 84 &c. The meaning of the sútra then is:—That pluta which comes at the end of an Interrogative sentence or a sentence denoting admiration, is anudâtta.

Thus अगमा३ः पूर्वां३न् ग्रामा३न् अग्निभूता३इ or अगम३ः पूर्वां३न् ग्रामा३ पटा ३ उ (i. e. अगमः पूर्वान् ग्रामान् अग्निभूते or पटो) । The words अग्निभूते, and पटो being finals in a question, become anudâtta as well as pluta. The other words अगमः &c. become svarita and pluta by VIII. 2. 105. See VIII. 2 107.

As regards अभिपूजिते we have शोभनः खल्वसि माणवका ३ ॥ Here the final of माणवक becomes anudâtta and pluta.

३६२० । चिदिति चोपमार्थे प्रयुज्यमाने । ८ । २ । १०१ ॥

वाक्यस्य टेरनुदात्तः प्लुतः । 'अग्निचिद्भाया३त्' । अग्निरिव भायात् । 'उपमार्थे' किम् । कथंचिदाहुः । 'प्रयुज्यमाने' किम् । अग्निर्माणवको भायात् ।

3620. The end-vowel at the end of a sentence becomes anudâtta and pluta, when the particle *chit* is employed, denoting comparison.

The word अनुदात्तं is understood here. This sûtra ordains pluta as well, and not merely accent.

Thus अग्निचिद् भाया३त् 'may he shine as fire'. So also राजचिद् भाया३त् 'may he shine as a King'.

Why do we say 'when the sense is that of comparison'? Observe कथं चिद् आहुः। Here चिद् has the force of 'littleness or difficulty'.

Why do we say प्रयुज्यमाने 'when expressly employed'? Observe अग्निर्माणवको भायात् 'Let the boy shine like fire'. Here चित् is understood, hence the rule does not apply.

३६२१ । उपरिस्विदासीदिति च । ८ । २ । १०२ ॥

टेः प्लुतोऽनुदात्तः स्यात् । 'उपरिस्विदासी३त्' । 'अधःस्विदासी३त्' इत्यत्र तु 'विचार्यमाणानाम्' (३६१६) इत्युदात्तः प्लुतः ।

3621. In उपरि स्विद् आसीद् the end-vowel is anudâtta and pluta.

The word anudâtta is understood here also. The end-vowel would have been pluta here by VIII. 2. 97 : S. 3616, the present sûtra really ordains accentlessness of this pluta.

Thus अधः स्विदासी३त्, उपरि स्विदासी३त् (Rig X. 129. 5). In the first portion आसीत् is pluta and udâtta by VIII. 2. 97, in the second it is anudâtta by the present sûtra.

३६२२ । स्वरितमाम्रेडितेऽसूयासंमतिकोपकुत्सनेषु । ८ । २ । १०३ ॥

स्वरितः प्लुतः स्यादाम्रेडिते परेऽसूयादौ गम्ये । असूयायाम् । अभिरूपक३ अभिरूपक रिक्तं ते आभिरूप्यम् । संमतौ । अभिरूपक३ अभिरूपक शोभनोऽसि । कोपे । अविनीतक३ अविनीतक इदानीं ज्ञास्यसि जाल्म । कुत्सने । शाक्तीक३ शाक्तीक रिक्ता ते शक्तिः ।

3622. Of the two vocatives of the same form standing at the beginning of a sentence, the end-vowel of the first becomes pluta and svarita, when envy, praise, anger, or blame is expressed.

The Vocative is doubled by VIII. 1. 8, S 2143. This sûtra ordains pluta there. Thus Envy:—माणवका३ माणवक, अभिरूपका३ अभिरूपक, रिक्तं त अभिरूप्यम् । Praise:—माणवका३ माणवक, अभिरूपका३ अभिरूपक शोभनः खल्वसि ॥ Anger:—माणवका३ माणवक, अविनीतका३ अविनीतक इदानीं ज्ञास्यसि जाल्म ॥ Blame:—शाक्तीका३ शाक्तीक याष्टीका३ याष्टीक रिक्ता ते शक्तिः ॥

३६२३ । क्षियाशीःप्रैषेषु तिङाकाङ्क्षम् । ८ । २ । १०४ ॥

आकाङ्क्षस्य तिङन्तस्य टेः स्वरितः प्लुतः स्यात् । आचारभेदे । स्वयं ह रथेन याति३ । उपाध्यायं पदातिं गमयति । आशिषि । पुत्रांश्च लप्सीष्ट३ धनं च तात । प्रैषे । कटं कुरु३ ग्रामं गच्छ । 'आकाङ्क्षम्' किम् । दीर्घायुरसि अग्निदग्नीन्विहर ।

3623. When an error against polite usage is censured, or when a benediction or a bidding is intended, the end syllable of a finite verb becomes pluta and svarita, if this requires another sentence to complete the sense.

The word 'svarita' is understood here. The word क्षिया means 'the error in usage' or 'want of good breeding.' (VIII. 1. 60) आशीः means 'benediction.' प्रैषः means 'order' or 'commanding by words.'

Thus स्वयं रथेन याँतिं३, उपाध्यायं पदातिं गमयति ॥ स्वयं ओदनं भुङ्क्ते३, उपाध्यायं सक्तून् पाययति ॥ In both these, the first sentence requires the second as its complement, and hence there is साकाङ्क्षा ।

Benediction:—सुतांश्च लप्सीष्टा३ धनं च तात; छन्दोऽध्येषीष्टा३ व्याकरणं च, भद्र ॥

Order:—कटं कुरु३ ग्रामं च गच्छ; यवान् लुनीहि३, सक्तूंश्च पिब ॥

Why do we say 'when it requires another sentence as its complement'? Observe दीर्घायुरसि अग्नीदग्नीन् विहर । There cannot be any counter-example of क्षिया, for there two sentences are absolutely necessary to express the sense of censure.

३६२४ । अनन्त्यस्यापि प्रश्नाख्यानयोः । ८ । २ । १०५ ॥

अनन्त्यस्यान्त्यस्यापि पदस्य टेः स्वरितः प्लुत एतयोः । प्रश्ने । अगमः३: पूर्वा३न् ग्रामा३न् । सर्वपदानामयम् । आख्याने । अगमः३ म् पूर्वा३न् ग्रामा३न् ।

3624. In a question or narration, the end-vowel of a word, though not final in a sentence, becomes svarita and pluta, as well as of the word which is final in a sentence.

The word 'padasya' is understood here: and so also the word 'svarita.' The end-vowel of a word which is not the last word in a sentence, as well as of the last word, becomes svarita and pluta, when a question is asked, or a fact is narrated. In fact, *all* the words of a sentence become svarita and pluta hereby.

Thus in questioning we have:—अगमां३ः पूर्वा३न् ग्रामा३न् अग्निभूता३इ or पटा३उ ॥ Thus all words have become svarita and pluta. The final word would in one alternative, become anudâtta also, by VIII. 2. 100, as shown under that sûtra. The force of the word अपि in the sûtra, is to make the final word also svarita, and thus this sûtra makes VIII. 2. 100 an *optional* sûtra with regard to question.

In *âkhyâna* or narration, there is no other rule, which is debarred by this. Therefore there, *all* words become svarita and pluta *necessarily*, by the force of this sûtra. Thus अगमा३म् पूर्वा३न् ग्रामा३न् भो३ः ॥

३६२५ । प्लुतावैच इदुतौ । ८ । २ । १०६ ॥

दूराद्धूतादिषु प्लुतो विहितस्तत्रैचः प्लुतप्रसङ्गे तदवयवाविदुतौ प्लवेते । ऐ३ तिकायन । औ३ पगव । चतुर्मात्रावत्रैचौ संपद्येते ।

3625. In forming the pluta of the diphthongs *ai* and *au* their last element *i* and *u* get the pluta.

The pluta ordained by VIII. 2. 84 &c. when applied to ऐ or औ cause the prolation of the last element of these diphthongs namely of इ or उ । The word प्लुतौ in the sûtra is Nominative dual of प्लुत, and the aphorism literally means 'इ and उ are pluta of the diphthongs ऐ and औ' ॥

Thus ऐ३तिकायन, औ३पगव ॥

This pluta of ऐ and औ has *four* mâtrâs. Thus अ+इ and अ+उ each has *one* mâtrâ. The pluta of इ and उ will have *three* mâtrâs. Thus अ+इ३ and अ+उ३, or the *whole* has *four* mâtrâs.

३६२६ । एचोऽप्रगृह्यस्यादूराद्धूते पूर्वस्यार्धस्यादुत्तरस्येदुतौ । ८ । २ । १०७ ॥

अप्रगृह्यस्यैचोऽदूराद्धूते प्लुतविषये पूर्वस्यार्धस्याकारः प्लुतः स्यादुत्तरस्य त्विदुतौ स्तः ।

'+ प्रश्नान्ताभिपूजितविचार्यमाणप्रत्यभिवादयाज्यान्तेष्वेव +' । प्रश्नान्ते । अगमः३ पूर्वा३न् ग्रामा३न् । अग्निभूत३इ । अभिपूजिते । भद्रं करोषि पट३उ । विचार्यमाणे । होतव्यं दीक्षितस्य गृहा३इ । प्रत्यभिवादे । आयुष्मानेधि अग्निभूत३इ । याज्यान्ते । स्तोमैर्विधेमाग्नय३इ । 'परिगणनम्' किम् । विष्णुभूते३ घातयिष्यामि त्वाम्' । अदूराद्धूत इति न वक्तव्यम् । पदान्तग्रहणं तु कर्तव्यम् । इह मा भूत् । भद्रं करोषि गौरिति । 'अप्रगृह्यस्य' किम् । शोभने माले३ ।

'+ आमन्त्रिते छन्दसि प्लुतविकारोऽयं वक्तव्यः +' । अग्ना३इ पत्नी वः ।

3626. In the diphthongs, which are not Pragṛihya (I. 1. 11 &c) and which become pluta under the circumstances mentioned in VIII. 2. 83 &c., but not when that circumstance is a call from a distance (VIII. 2. 84); for the first half, there is substituted the prolated 'â', and for the second portion *e* or *u*.

The diphthongs or एच् are ए, ऐ, ओ and औ । Their elements are अ+इ, and अ+उ । When these diphthongs are to be prolated, *at the end of a word*, the diphthong is resolved into its elements, the *first* portion अ is prolated, and इ or उ added, as the case may be. This इ and उ, in fact, are the substitutes of the second portion, which may be इ or उ, or ए or ओ ।

This rule is not of universal application, but applies to Rules VIII. 2. 100. VIII. 2. 97, VIII. 2. 83, and VIII. 2. 90 only, according to the following Vârtikas.

Vârt:—The scope of this sûtra should be determined by enumerating the rules to which it applies.

Vârt:—It should be stated that it applies to sûtras VIII. 2. 100, 97, 83 and 90.

Thus VIII. 2. 100: As अगमाः पूर्वा३न् ग्रामा३न् अग्निभूता३इ or प_ट३उ । भद्रं करोषि माणवका३ अग्निभूता३इ or पटा३इ । So also VIII. 2. 97:—as होतव्यं दीक्षितस्य गृहा३इ । So also VIII. 2. 83:—as, आयुष्मान् एधि अग्निभूता३इ or पटा३उ । So also VIII. 2. 90:—as, उच्चावाय वशावाय सोमपृष्ठाय वेधसे । स्तोमैर्विधेमाग्नया३इ । (Tait. S. I. 3. 14. 7).

This pluta आ is udâtta, anudâtta or svarita, according to the particular rule which has been applied, *i. e.* at the end of a question it is anudâtta or svarita, and everywhere else, udâtta. The इ and उ are of course, always udâtta: because the anuvṛitti of udâtta is current here.

Why do we restrict this sûtra to the above mentioned four rules? Observe विष्णुभूते विष्णुभूते३ घातयिष्यामि त्वा आगच्छ भो माणवक विष्णुभूते ।

In fact, the present sûtra being confined to the above-mentioned four rules, the words अदूराद्धूते in the sûtra, are redundant: and should not have been used. Moreover the word पदान्त should have been used in the sûtra, for it applies to diphthongs at the *end* of a pada. Therefore, not in भद्रं करोषि गौरिति । Here गौ before the sarvanâmasthâna affix सु is not a pada (I. 4. 17).

Why do we say 'when it is not a Pragṛihya'? Observe शोभने माले३ ।

Vârt:—This peculiar modification of pluta vowel takes place in the Vocative case in the Vedas. As अग्ना३इ पत्नीवा३ः सजूर्देवेन त्वष्ट्रा सोमं पिब । Here by no other rule, the Vocative would have become prolated.

३६२७ । तयोर्य्वावचि संहितायाम् । ८ । २ । १०८ ॥

इदुतोर्यकारवकारौ स्तोऽचि संहितायाम् । अग्ना३याशा । पटा३वाशा । अग्ना३विन्द्रम् । पटा३-वुदकम् । 'अचि' किम् । अग्ना३वक्णौ । 'संहितायाम्' किम् । अग्ना३इ इन्द्रः । संहितायामित्यध्यायसमाप्तेरधिकारः । इदुतोरसिद्धत्वादयमारम्भः सवर्णदीर्घत्वस्य शाकलस्य च निवृत्त्यर्थः । यवयोरसिद्धत्वात् 'उदात्तस्वरितयोर्यणः स्वरितोऽनुदात्तस्य' (३६५७) इत्यस्य बाधनार्थं वा ॥

3627. For these vowels *i* and *u*, are substituted *y* and *v*, when a vowel follows them in a samhita (in an unbroken flow of speech).

The word संहितायाम् is an adhikâra and exerts its influence up to the end of the Book. Whatever we shall teach hereafter, up to the end of the Book, will apply to the words which are in the Sanhitâ.

Thus अग्ना३याशा पटा३वाशा, अग्ना३विन्द्रम, पटा३वुदकम् ॥

Why do we say 'when a vowel follows'? Observe अग्ना३वक्णौ ।

Why do we say संहितायाम् 'in an uninterrupted flow of speech'? Observe अग्ना३ इ इन्द्रम्, पटा३उ उदकम् in the Pada Pâtha.

This sûtra is made, because इ and उ being Pluta-modifications are considered as asiddha (VIII. 2. 1) for the purposes of इको यणचि (VI. 1. 77). But supposing that somehow or other, these इ and उ be considered siddha, still the present rule is necessary to prevent their lengthening before a homogeneous vowel (VI. 1. 101), or their retaining their form unchanged by VI. 1. 127. If it be said, that these rules VI. 1. 101, and VI. 1. 127, would not apply, because of the Vârtika इकः प्लुतपूर्वस्य सवर्णदीर्घबाधनार्थं यणादेशो वक्तव्यः (Vârtika to VI. 1. 77); still the present sûtra ought to be made, in order to prevent यण् accent (VII. 2. 4. S. 3657).

३६२८ । मतुवसो रु संबुद्धौ छन्दसि । ८ । ३ । १ ॥

रु इत्यविभक्तिको निर्देशः । मत्वन्तस्य वन्तस्य रुः स्यात् । 'अलोऽन्त्यस्य' (४२) इति परिभाषया नकारस्य । 'इन्द्र मरुत्व इह पाहि सोमम् । 'हरिवोमेदिनं त्वा' । 'छन्दसीरः' (३६००) इति वत्वम् ।

3628. For the final of the affixes *mat* and *vas* there is substituted *ru*, in the Vocative singular, in the Chhandas.

The word संहितायां is understood here. A word ending in the affix मत् or वस्, changes its final त् or स् (I. 1. 52. S. 42) into र्, in the Chhandas, in the Vocative singular. Thus मत् :—इन्द्र मरुत्व इह पाहि सोमम् (Rig. III. 51. 7). हरिवो मेदिनं त्वा । Here मरुत्वः is Vocative Sg. of मरुत्वत् and हरिवः of हरिवत्, meaning 'he who is possessed of Maruts or Hari horses.' The म of मत् is changed to व by VIII. 2. 10; 15. S. 3 00. The base मरुत् before this termination is Bha by I. 4 19. The affix सु (nom. sg.) is elided by VI. 1. 68; the त् is elided by VIII. 2. 23, and the न् (of नुम् VII. 1. 70) is changed to र् by this sûtra. So also इन्द्रायाहि तूतुजानः उपब्रह्माणि हरिवः (Rig. I. 3. 6).

With वस् :—मीढ्वस्तोकाय तनयाय मृळ (Rig. II. 33. 14). इन्द्र साह्वः । See VI. 1. 12, for the formation of मीढ्वान्, साह्वान् with क्वसु ॥

Why do we say 'of मत् and वस्'? Observe ब्रह्मन् स्तोष्यामः । Why do we say 'in the Vocative Singular'? Observe य एवं विद्वानग्निमाधत्ते । Why do we say 'in the Chhandas'? Observe हे गोमन्, हे यविवन् ॥

३६२९ । दाश्वान्साह्वान्मीढ्वांश्च । ६ । १ । १२ ॥

एते क्वस्वन्ता निपात्यन्ते । 'मीढ्वस्तोकाय तनयाय' ।

'+ वन उपसंख्यानम् +' । क्वनिप्वनिपोः सामान्यग्रहणम् । अनुबन्धपरिभाषा तु नोपतिष्ठते । अनुबन्धस्यैहानिर्देशात् । 'यस्त्वायन्तं वसुना प्रातरित्वः । इणः क्वनिप् ।

3629. The participles dâśvân, sâhvân and mîḍhvân are irregularly formed without reduplication.

The word दाश्वान् is from the root दाशृ 'to give' with the affix क्वसु (III. 2. 107); here the reduplication and the augment इट् are prohibited irregularly; as दाश्वांसो दाशुषः सुतम् (Rig. I. 3. 7). The word साह्वान् is derived from the root सह् 'to endure,' by adding the affix क्वसु (III. 2, 107), the irregularity being in lengthening the penultimate, not allowing the augment इट् and the reduplication Thus साह्वान् बलाहकः । So also मीढ्वान् comes from मिह् 'to sprinkle' with the affix क्वसु (III. 2. 107) the irregularity consisting in non-reduplication, non-application of इट्, the lengthening of the penultimate vowel, and the change of ह into ढ । As मीढ्वस्तोकाय तनयाय मृळ (Rig Veda II. 33. 14). It is not necessary that these words should be in the singular always; in their plural forms also they do not reduplicate.

Vârt:—The affix वन् should also be enumerated. The affixes क्वनिप् and वनिप् are both meant here. Its final is also changed to रु in the Vocative Sg. As यस्त्वायन्तं वसुना प्रातरित्वः । The word प्रातरित्वन् is formed by adding क्वनिप् to the root इ (इण) preceded by प्रातः । See III. 2. 75. The तुक् is added by VI. 1. 71.

३६३० । उभयथर्क्षु । ८ । ३ । ८ ॥

ऋक्षु उभयथा नकारस्य रुर्वा । पशूंस्तांश्चक्रे ।

3630. In both ways, in the Rig verses.

This ordains an option to the last sûtra, by which the रु substitution was compulsory. A word ending in न् followed by a letter of छव् class, which itself is followed by अम्, changes its final न् to र् *optionally* in the Rig Veda. Sometimes there is र् and sometimes न् । Thus तस्मिन् त्वा दधाति or तस्मिंस् त्वा दधाति; पशूंस्तांश्चक्रे । (Rig Veda X. 90. 8).

३६३१ । दीर्घादटि समानपादे । ८ । ३ । ९ ॥

दीर्घान्नकारस्य रुर्वा स्यादटि तौ चेन्नाटौ एकपादस्थौ स्याताम् । 'देवाँ अच्छा सुमतौ' । 'महाँ इन्द्रो य ओजसा' । उभयथेत्यनुवृत्तेर्नेह । 'आदित्यान्याचिषामहे' ।

3631. *Ru* is optionally substituted for that final *n* of a word which is preceded by a long vowel, and is followed by an 'aṭ' letter (vowels and semi-vowels with the exception of *l*), when these ('n' and 'aṭ') come in contact with each other in the same stanza of the Rig Veda.

The नः of VIII. 3. 7 is understood here: and so also रु ॥ The word समानपाद means एकपाद, i. e. when both words are in one and the same Pâda of the verse. Thus परिधीँ रति (Rig. IX. 107. 19) स देवाँ एह वक्षति (Rig. I. 1. 2) देवाँ अच्छा सुमती; (Rig Veda IV. 1. 2.) महाँ इन्द्रो य ओजसा ॥ (Rig Veda VIII. 6 1.)

The word उभयथा of the preceding sûtra is understood here also; so that is an optional rule: and न remains unchanged also, as आदित्यान् हवामहे आदित्यान् याचिषामहे (Rig Veda VIII. 67. 1). See VIII. 3. 3.

३६३२ । आतोऽटि नित्यम् । ८ । ३ । ३ ॥

अटि परतो रोः पूर्वस्यातः स्थाने नित्यमनुनासिकः । 'महाँ इन्द्रः' । तैत्तिरीयास्तु अनुस्वारमधीयते । तत्र छान्दसो व्यत्यय इति प्राञ्च । एवं च सूत्रस्य फलं चिन्त्यम् ।

3632. A nasal vowel is *always* substituted for 'â' before *ru*, when it is followed by a letter of 'aṭ' pratyâhâra (*i. e.* when it is followed by a vowel or *ha*, *ya*, *va*, or *ra*).

Thus VIII. 3. 9 teaches a substitution of न, the long आ preceding it, would have been optionally nasal by the last sûtra. The present sûtra makes it necessarily so Thus महाँ असि (Rig. III. 46. 2) महाँ इन्द्रो य ओजसा (Rig. VIII. 6. 1). देवाँ अच्छादीध्यत् ॥

Some (*i. e.* the Taittariyas) read it as anusvâra. This is a Vedic diversity according to the Easterns. In this view, the necessity of the sûtra is rather doubtful.

३६३३ । स्वतवान्पायौ । ८ । ३ । ११ ॥

रुर्वा । 'भुवस्तस्य स्वतवाँः पायुरग्ने' ।

3633. The *n* of 'svatawân' is changed to 'ru' before 'pâyu.'

As स्वत्वः पायुरग्ने (Rig. IV. 2. 6). The word is स्वतवस्, the नुम् is added by VII. 1. 83. The word is derived from तु वृद्धौ with the affix असुन् (स्वन्तवो यस्यऽसौ स्वतवान्) ॥ See S. 3594.

३६३४ । छन्दसि वाऽप्राम्रेडितयोः । ८ । ३ । ४९ ॥

विसर्गस्य सो वा स्यात्कुप्वोः प्रशब्दमाम्रेडितं च वर्जयित्वा । 'अग्ने त्रातर्ऋतस्कविः' । 'गिरिर्न विश्वतस्पृथुः' । नेह । 'वसुनः पूर्व्यः पतिः' । 'अप्र-' इत्यादि किम् । 'अग्निः प्र विद्वान्' । 'पुरुषः पुरुषः' ।

3634. *Sa* may optionally be substituted for the visarga before a hard guttural and labial, in the Chhandas; but neither before *pra*, nor before a doubled word.

Thus :—अग्ने त्रात ऋतस्कविः (Rig Ved. VIII 60 5.) गिरिर्न विश्वतस्पृथुः (Rig Veda VIII. 98. 4). But not here :—वसुनः पूर्व्यः पतिः (Rig Veda X. 48. 1).

Why do we say 'not before प्र and a doubled word'? Observe अग्निः प्र विद्वान् (Av. V. 26. 1), पुरुषः पुरुषः परि ॥

३६३५ । कःकरत्करतिकृधिकृतेष्वनदितेः । ८ । ३ । ५० ॥

विसर्गस्य सः स्यात् । 'प्रदिवो अपस्कः' । 'यथा नो वस्यसस्करत्' । 'सुपेशसस्करति' । 'उरु णस्कृधि' । 'सोमं न चारुं मघवत्सु नस्कृतम्' । 'अनदितेः' इति किम् । 'यथा नो अदितिः करत्' ।

3635. The Visarga is changed to *s* in the Chhandas, before कः, करत्, करति, कृधि and कृतः but not so the visarga of *aditi*.

Thus प्रदिवोऽअपस्कः ॥ कः is the Aorist of कृ. the च्लि has been elided by II. 4. 80: the ऋ of कृ is gunated before the affix तिप्, thus we have करत्, the त् is elided by VI. 1. 68; and the augment अट् is not added by VI. 4. 75. Similarly यथानो बन्नसस्करत् ॥ Here also करत् is the Aorist of कृ, with अङ् by III. 1. 59. सुपेशसस्करति, here करति is the लट् of कृ; शप् is added instead of उ, as a Vedic anomaly. उरुणस्कृधि, here कृधि is the Imperative of कृ, the हि is changed to धि, the vikarana is elided and हि changed to धि by VI 4. 102. See VIII. 4 27, for the change of न to ण ॥ सोमं न चारु मघवत्सु न स्कृतम्, here कृतम् is Past Participle of कृ ॥

Why do we say 'but not of अदितिः'? Observe यथा नो अदितिः करत् (Rig Veda I. 3. 42).

३६३६ । पञ्चम्याः परावध्यर्थे । ८ । ३ । ५१ ॥

पञ्चमीविसर्गस्य सः स्यादुपरिभावार्थे परिशब्दे परतः । 'दिवस्परिप्रथमं जज्ञे' । 'अध्यर्थे किम्' । 'दिवस्पृथिव्याः पर्योजः' ।

3636. The visarga of the Ablative case is changed to *s* before *pari* meaning 'over'.

The word Chhandas is understood here also. Thus दिवस्परि प्रथमं जज्ञे (Rig Ved. X. 45. 1)

Why do we say 'when परि means 'over'? See दिवः पृथिव्याः पर्योज उद्भृतम् (Rig Ved. VI. 47. 27). Here परि has the sense of 'on all sides'.

३६३७ । पातौ च बहुलम् । ८ । ३ । ५२ ॥

पञ्चम्या इत्येव । 'सूर्यो नो दिवस्पातु' ।

3637. *S* may diversely be substituted for the visarga of the Ablative before the verb 'pâtu' in the Chhandas

Thus सूर्यो नो दिवस्पातु, (Rig Veda X. 158. 1). Sometimes, the change does not take place; as परिषदः पात ॥

३६३८ । षष्ठ्याः पतिपुत्रपृष्ठपारपदपयस्पोषेषु । ८ । ३ । ५३ ॥

'वाचस्पतिं विश्वकर्माणम्' । 'दिवस्पुत्राय सूर्याय' । 'दिवस्पृष्ठं भन्दमानः' । 'तमसस्पारमस्य' । 'परिवीत इळस्पदे' । दिवस्पयो दिधिषाणाः' । 'रायस्पोषं यजमानेषु' ।

3638. For the visarga of the Genitive, there is substituted *s* in the Vedas, before पति, पुत्र, पृष्ट, पार, पद, पयस् and पोष ॥

Thus वाचस्पतिं विश्वकर्माणमूतये, (Rig Veda X. 81. 7). दिवस्पुत्राय सूर्याय, (Rig Veda X. 37. 1) दिवस्पृष्ठे भन्दमानः (Rig Veda III 2. 12) तमसस्पारम् (Rig Veda I. 92. 6). परिवीत इळस्पद (Rig Veda I 128. 1). दिवस्पयो दिधिषाणा (Rig Veda X. 114. 1). रायस्पोषं यजमानेषु (Rig. Veda X. 17. 9).

Why do we say 'after a genitive case'? See मनुः पुत्रेभ्यो दायं व्यभजत् ॥

३६३९ । इडाया वा । ८ । ३ । ५४ ॥

पतिपुत्रादिषु परेषु । इडायास्पुत्रः-इडायाः पुत्रः । इडायास्पदे-इडायाःपदे ।

3639. *Sa* is optionally substituted for the visarga of 'iḍâyâḥ' before *pati* &c., (VIII. 3. 53.) in the Chhandas.

Thus इडायाः पतिः or इडायास्पतिः इडायास्पुत्रः । इडायाः पुत्रः । इडायास्पृष्टम् । इडायाः पृष्ठम् । इडायाः स्पारम्, इडायाः पारम । इडायास्पदम् । इडायाः पदम् । इडायास्पयः । इडायाः पयः । इडायाः पोषम् । इडायास्पोषम् ॥

Here we must read again the sûtra VIII. 3. 102 S. 2403:—

३६३९ । क । निसस्तपतावनासेवने ॥

निसः सकारस्य मूर्धन्यः स्यात् । 'निष्टप्तं रक्षो निष्टप्ता अरातयः' । 'अनासेवने' किम् । निस्तपति । पुनःपुनस्तपतीत्यर्थः ॥

3639A. *Sha* is substituted for the *sa* of *nis* before the verb *tap* when the meaning is not that of 'repeatedly making red hot.'

As निष्टप्तं रक्षो निष्टप्ता अरातयः ॥

Why do we say 'when the meaning is not that of repeatedly making red hot'? Observe निस्तपति meaning 'makes repeatedly red hot.'

३६४० । युष्मत्तत्ततक्षुःष्वन्तःपादम् । ८ । ३ । १०३ ॥

पादमध्यस्थस्य सस्य मूर्धन्यः स्यात्तकारादिष्वेषु परेषु । युष्मदादेशाः त्वंत्वातेतवाः । 'त्रिभिष्ट्वं देव सवितः' 'तेभिष्ट्वा आभिष्टे' । 'अप्स्वग्ने सधिष्टव' । 'अग्निष्टद्विश्वम्' । 'द्यावापृथिवी निष्टतक्षुः' । 'अन्तःपादम्' किम् । तदग्निस्तदर्यमा' । 'यन्म आत्मनो मिन्दाभूदग्निस्तत्पुनराहार्जातवेदा विचर्षणिः' । अत्राग्निरिति पूर्वपादस्यान्तो न तु मध्यः ।

3640. The *s* standing in the inner half of a stanza is changed to *sh* before the *ta* of *twaṃ* &c. and *tad* and *tatakshus*.

The word युष्मद् here means the substitutes त्वम्, त्वाम्, ते, तव. As अग्निष्ट्वं, नामासीत् । त्वा, अग्निष्ट्वा वर्धयामसि । ते, अग्निष्टे विश्वमानय । तव, अप्स्वग्ने सधिष्टव, (Rig. VIII. 43. 9) । तत्, अग्निष्टद्विश्वमापृणाति, (Rig. X. 2. 4) ततक्षुस्, द्यावापृथिवी निष्टतक्षुः ॥

Why do we say 'in the inner half of a stanza'? Observe यन्म आत्मनो मिन्दाभूदग्निस्तत्पुनराहार्जातवेदा विचर्षणिः । Here the word अग्निः is at the *end* of the first stanza while तत् is at the *beginning* of the second stanza, therefore the स् of अग्निस् is not in the middle of a stanza.

३६४१ । यजुष्येकेषाम् । ८ । ३ । १०४ ॥

युष्मत्तत्ततक्षुषु परतः सस्य मूर्धन्यो वा । अर्चिभिष्ट्वम् । अग्निष्टे । अग्रम् । अर्चिभिष्टतक्षुः । पक्षे अर्चिभिस्त्वामित्यादि ।

3641. In the opinion of some, the above change takes place in the Yajurveda also.

Thus अर्चिभिष्ट्वम् or अर्चिभिस्त्वम् । अग्निष्टेऽग्रम् or अग्निस्तेऽग्रम् । अग्निष्टत् or अग्निस्तत् । अर्चिभिष्टतक्षुः or अर्चिभिस्ततक्षुः ॥

३६४२ । स्तुतस्तोमयोश्छन्दसि । ८ । ३ । १०५ ॥

त्रिभिष्टुतस्य-नृभिः स्तुतस्य । गोष्टोमम्-गोस्तोमम् । पूर्वपदादित्येव सिद्धे प्रपञ्चार्थमिदम् ।

3642. The *s* of *stut* and *stoma* in the Chhandas, is changed to *sh* in the opinion of some.

Thus त्रिभिष्टुतस्य or त्रिभिस्तुतस्य. गौष्टोमं षोडशिनम्, or गौस्तोमं षोडशिनम्। This change would have taken place by the general rule contained in the next sûtra VIII. 3. 106, the special mention of स्तुत and स्तोम here is a mere amplification. The word छन्दसि of this sûtra governs subsequent sûtra also.

३६४३ । पूर्वपदात् । ८ । ३ । १०६ ॥

पूर्वपदस्थाद्विमित्तात्परस्य सस्य षो वा । 'यदिन्द्राग्नी दिवि ष्ठः' । 'युवं हि स्थः स्वर्पती' ।

3643. In the Chhandas, according to some, *s* is changed to *sh*, when it stands in the beginning of a second word, preceded by a word ending in *i* &c.

The words छन्दसि and एकेषां are both understood here. Thus द्विषन्धिः or द्विसन्धिः त्रिषन्धिः or त्रिसन्धिः; मधुष्ठानम् or मधुस्थानम्, द्विषाहस्रं चिन्वीत or द्विसाहस्रं चिन्वीत ॥

The word पूर्वपद here means the first member of a compound word as well as the prior word other than that in a compound. Thus निःषमत्स्वाय or निःसमत्स्वाय ॥ यदिन्द्राग्नी दिविष्ठः (Rig Veda I. 108. 11). युवंहिस्थः स्वर्पती (Rig Veda IX. 19. 2).

३६४४ । सुञः । ८ । ३ । १०७ ॥

पूर्वपदस्थान्निमित्तात्परस्य सुञो निपातस्य सस्य षः । 'ऊर्ध्व ऊ षु णः' । 'अभी षु णः' ।

3644. The *sa* of the Particle *su* is changed to *sha* in the Chhandas, when preceded by an other word having in it the change-effecting letter *i* &c.

Thus ऊर्ध्व ऊ षु णः (Rig Veda I. 36. 13.) अभी षु णः सखीनाम् (Rig Veda IV. 31. 3). The lengthening takes place by VI. 3. 134, and न changed to ण by VIII. 4. 27.

३६४५ । सनोतेरनः । ८ । ३ । १०८ ॥

'गोषा इन्द्रो नृषा असि' । 'अनः' किम् । गोसनिः ।

3645. The *sa* of the verb *san* when it loses its *n*, is changed to *sh* under the same circumstances.

Thus गोषाः (Rig. IX. 2 10), formed by the affix विट (III. 2. 67), the न् is elided by VI. 4. 41. So also नृषाः ॥

Why do we say 'when it loses its न्'? Observe गोसनि वाचमुदीयन् (Atharv. III. 20. 10). Here the affix is इन् (III. 2. 27). See however गोषाणा in Rig. VI. 53. 10.

३६४६ । सहेः पृतनर्ताभ्यां च । ८ । ३ । १०९ ॥

पृतनाषाहम् । ऋताषाहम् । चात् । ऋतीषाहम् ।

3646. The *s* of *sha* is changed to *sh* after *pritanâ* and *rit*.

Thus पृतनाषाहम ऋताषाहम्। The word च 'and' in the sûtra includes words other than those mentioned in it. The word ऋतीषहं would be valid by this also.

३६४७ । निव्यभिभ्योऽड्व्यवाये वा छन्दसि । ८ । ३ । ११९ ॥

षस्य मूर्धन्यः । न्यषीदत्–न्यसीदत् । व्यषीदत्–व्यसीदत् । अभ्यष्टौत्–अभ्यस्तौत् ।

3647. The *sh* is optionally substituted in the Chhandas after the prepositions *ni*, *vi* and *abhi* when the augment 'aṭ' intervenes.

Thus न्यषीदत् or न्यसीदत् पिता नः; व्यषीदत्; or व्यसीदत् पिता नः; अभ्यषीदत् or अभ्यसीदत् ॥

The anuvritti of सदं and स्वंज is not to be read into this sûtra. It is, in fact a general rule and applies to verbs other than these two. As व्यस्तौत्, न्यष्टौत्, अभ्यष्टौत or अभ्यस्तौत ॥

३६४८ । छन्दस्यृदवग्रहात् । ८ । ४ । २६ ॥

ऋकारान्तादवग्रहात्परस्य नस्य णः । नृमणाः । पितृयाणम् ।

3648. In the Chhandas, *na* of a second term is changed into 'ṇa' when the prior term ends with a short 'ṛi' even when there is an *avagraha* or hiatus between the two terms.

The word पूर्वपदात् is understood here. The word अवग्रह means a hiatus or separation. Thus पितृ याणम्, नृ मणाः ॥ Here ऋ is अवग्रहं ॥ The change of न into ण is effected ordinarily then, when the terms, one containing the cause, and the other न, are in संहिता or conjunction. For the rules of Sandhi and the rules like these can apply only to words in संहिता ॥ The present rule is an exception to it, and here, even when the words are not in संहिता, but there is an actual hiatus between the two, the change still takes place. The word संहिता of VIII. 2. 108, exerts regulating influence up to the end of the Book.

३६४९ । नश्च धातुस्थोरुषुभ्यः । ८ । ४ । २७ ॥

धातुस्थात् । 'अग्ने रक्षा णः' । 'शिक्षाणो अस्मिन्' । 'उरुणस्कृधि' । 'अभीषुणः' । 'मोषु णः' ।
इत्यष्टमोऽध्यायः । इति वैदिक प्रकरणम् ॥

3649. In the Chhandas, the *na* of (the Pronoun) *nas* is changed into 'ṇa' when it comes after a root having a *ra* or *sha* or after the words *uru* and *shu*.

Thus अग्ने रक्षाणः (Rig. VII. 15. 13) 'O Agni! protect us.' शिक्षा णो अस्मिन् (Rig. VII. 32. 26) 'Teach us this.' उरुः—उरुणस्कृधि (Rig. VIII. 75. 11) षु—अभीषुणः सखीनाम् (Rig. IV. 31. 3). ऊर्ध्व ऊषुणः ऊतये (Rig. I. 36. 13).

The word नस् is here the pronoun नस्, which is the substitute, in certain cases of अस्मद् (VIII. 1. 21) and does not mean here the नस् substitute of नासिका । धातुस्थ means 'that which exists in a dhâtu,' namely र and ष when occurring in a root. The word उरु means the word form उरु; and षु means सुञ्, and is exhibited with ष-change. It does not mean the affix सु of the Locative Plural. Therefore not in इन्द्रो धाता गृहेषु नः ॥ The word रक्षा is the 2nd Person singular, Imperative the lengthening is by VI. 3. 135. The root शिक्ष has the sense of दान in the Veda. कृधि is 2nd Person Sg. Imperative of कृ (VI. 4. 102), the visarga of नः is changed to स् by VIII. 3. 50. In अभीषु there is lengthening by VI. 3. 134, so also in ऊषुणः &c.

Here ends the Book on Vedic forms.

अथ स्वर प्रकरणम् ।

ON ACCENTS.

CHAPTER I.

३६५० । अनुदात्तं पदमेकवर्जम् । ६ । १ । १५८ ॥

परिभाषेयं । स्वरविधिविषया । यस्मिन्पदे यस्योदात्तः स्वरितो वा विधीयते तमेकमचं वर्जयित्वा शेषं तत्पदमनुदात्तच्कं स्यात् । गोपायतं नः । अत्र सनाद्यन्ताः–' (२३०४) इति धातुत्वे धातुस्वरेण यकारात्कार उदात्तः शिष्टमनुदात्तम् ।

'+ सतिशिष्टस्वरबलीयस्त्वमन्यत्र विकरणेभ्य इति वाच्यम् +' । तेनोक्तोदाहरणे । गुपेर्धातुस्वर आयस्य प्रत्ययस्वरश्च न शिष्यते । 'अन्यत्र' इति किम् । 'यज्ञं यज्ञमभिवृधे गृणीतः' । अत्र सति शिष्टोऽपि 'श्ना' इत्यत्र स्वरो न शिष्यते किंतु तस एव ।

3650. A word is, with the exception of one syllable, unaccented.

That is, only one syllable in a word is accented, all the rest are anudâtta or unaccented. This is a Paribhâshâ or maxim of interpretation with regard to the laws of accent. Wherever an accent—be it acute (udâtta) or a circumflex (svarita)—is ordained with regard to a word, there this maxim must be applied, to make all the other syllables of that word unaccented. The word अनुदात्त means 'having anudâtta vowel.' What is the *one* to be excepted? That one about which any particular accent has been taught in the rules here-in-after given. Thus VI. 1. 162 teaches that a root has acute accent on the final. Therefore, with the exception of the last syllable, all the other syllables are unaccented. Thus in 'गोपायतं नः' (Rig Veda VI. 74. 4) the acute accent is on य, all the rest are unaccented.

Vârt:—The सतिशिष्ट accent is stronger than all which precede it, except when it is a Vikaraṇa accent. Thus in the above example, the root accent of गुप and the affix accent of आय do not remain, but तं accent prevails.

Why do we say 'except when it is a Vikaraṇa accent'? Observe यज्ञं यज्ञमभिवृधे गृणीतः (Rig Veda III. 6. 10). Here the vikaraṇa श्ना accent is सतिशिष्ट, but it does not prevail over तस् accent.

NOTE:—The rule is that except one special accent taught in a sûtra the other syllables take anudâtta. Therefore, where there is a conflict of rules, the accent is guided by the following maxim: "परनित्यान्तरङ्गापवादैः स्वरैर्व्यवस्था सतिशिष्टेनच" ॥ namely (1) the sequence, a succeeding rule setting aside a prior rule (2) a Nitya rule is stronger than Anitya (3) Antaranga stronger than Bahiranga, (4) the Apavâda is stronger than Utsarga. When all these are exhausted, then we apply the rule of सतिशिष्ट ॥ What is this rule? To quote the words of Kâsikâ: यो हि यस्मिन् सति शिष्यते स तस्य बाधको भवति 'that which does remain.

and must last in spite of the presence of another, debars such other.' Thus in गोपायति ; here the प्रत्ययस्वरः "the accent of the affix" (III. 1. 3) by which the acute is on the first syllable of the *affix* is an apavâda to the धातुस्वरः (VI. 1. 192) by which the final of a dhâtu is acute, and it debars the dhâtu-accent; but this affix accent is in its turn debarred in the case of derivative verbs formed with affixes by the rule of सतिशिष्ट, because even after the addition of the affix, these words *retain* the designation of dhâtu. Similarly in कार्ष्णोत्तरासङ्गपुत्रः' "The son of him whose upper garment (uttarâsanga) is of black color, the Son of Baladeva," the Bahuvrihi-accent (VI. 2. 1) being an apavâda to Samâsa-accent; (VI. I. 223), debars the samâsa-accent; but this Bahuvrihi-accent is in its turn debarred by the rule of सतिशिष्ट when a further compound is formed and the final word is a compound only and not a Bahuvrihi. Though the accent of the Vikarana is a सतिशिष्ट. yet it does not debar the Sârvadhâtuka accent (VI. 1. 186). Thus in सुनीतः, the accent of the vikarana नी does not debar the accent of तस् ॥

३६५१ । अनुदात्तस्य च यत्रोदात्तलोपः । ६ । १ । १६१ ।

यस्मिन्ननुदात्ते परे उदात्तो लुप्यते तस्योदात्तः स्यात् । 'देवीं वाचम्' । अत्र ङीबुदात्तः ।

3651. An unaccented vowel gets also the acute accent, when on account of it the preceding acute is elided.

The word udâtta is understood here. Thus कुमार + ई = कुमारी ॥ The word कुमार has acute on the last, when the unaccented (anudâtta) ङीप् is added to it; the अ is elided (VI. 1. 148); the anudâtta ई becomes udâtta. So also पथिन् + अस् = पथः (VII 1. 88); पथिन् + ए = पथे. पथिन् + आ = पथा । The पथिन् has acute on the last. So also कुमुद+ड्मतुप् = कुमुद्वान् (IV. 2. 87), नड्वान्, वेतस्वत् । The words कुमुद &c are end-acute, and the affix मत् (वत्) is anudâtta (III. 1. 4).

देवीं वाचं (Rig Veda VIII. 100. 11 and 101. 16).

३६५२ । चौ । ६ । १ । २२२ ॥

लुप्ताकारेऽञ्चतौ परे पूर्वस्यान्तोदात्तः स्यात् । उदात्तनिवृत्तिस्वरापवादः । 'देवद्रीचीं नयत देवयन्तः' ॥

'+अतद्धित इति वाच्यम्+' । दाधीचः । माधूचः । प्रत्ययस्वर एवात्र ॥

3652. In compound words ending in *anch*, the final vowel of the preceding word has the acute accent in the weak cases in which only *ch* of *anch* remains.

Thus देवद्रीचीं नयत देवयन्तः (Rig Veda III. 6. 1). This is an exception to VI. 1. 161, 170 and VI 2. 52.

Vârt:—This rule does not apply before a Taddhita affix. As दाधीचः माधूचः ॥ Here the accent is regulated by the affix (III. 1. 3).

३६५३ । आमन्त्रितस्य च । ६ । १ । १९८ ॥

आमन्त्रितविभक्त्यन्तस्यादिरुदात्तः स्यात् । 'अग्न इन्द्र वरुण मित्र देवाः' ॥

3653. The first syllable of a Vocative gets the acute accent.

Thus अग्न इन्द्र वरुण मित्र देवाः (Rig Veda V. 46. 2), This debars the final accent ordained by VI. 2. 148. Though the affix may be elided by a लुमत् word

(नक्. लुप् or श्लु), yet the effect of the affix remains behind in spite of I. 1. 63. As उ॒र्परागच्छ ! उ॒प्ता गच्छत ! ॥

३६५४ । आमन्त्रितस्य च । ८ । १ । १९ ॥

पदात्परस्यापादादिस्थितस्यामन्त्रितस्य सर्वस्यानुदात्तः स्यात् । प्रागुक्तस्य षाष्ठस्यापवादोऽयमा-ष्टमिकः । 'इमं मे गङ्गे यमुने सरस्वति' । 'अपादादौ' किम् । 'शुतुद्रि स्तोमम्' । 'आमन्त्रितं पूर्वमविद्यमानवत्' (४१२) । 'अग्न इन्द्र' । अग्नेन्द्रादीनां निघातो न । पूर्वस्याविद्यमानत्वेन पदात्परत्वाभावात् । 'नामन्त्रिते समानाधिकरणे सामान्यवचनम्' (४१३) । समानाधिकरणे आमन्त्रिते परे विशेष्यं पूर्वमविद्यमानवन्न । 'अग्ने तेजस्विन्' । 'अग्ने त्रातः' । 'सामान्यवचनम्' किम् । पर्यायेषु मा भूत् । 'अघ्न्ये देवि सरस्वति' ॥

3654. All the syllables of a Vocative are unaccented when a word precedes it, and it does not stand at the beginning of a hemistich.

The Vocative is acutely accented on the first by VI. 1. 198, the present makes it all unaccented, and is thus an exception to the last sûtra.

Thus इमं मे गङ्गे यमुने सरस्वति (Rig Veda X. 75. 5).

Why do we say 'when it does not stand at the beginning of a hemistich'? Observe शुतुद्रिस्तोमम् (Rig Veda X. 75. 5).

But rule VIII. 1. 72. S. 412 taught us that a Vocative standing before another word is considered as non-existent. Therefore in अग्न इन्द्र वरुण every Vocative gets the acute by the last sûtra, and the present sûtra does not make इन्द्र &c. accentless, for the Vocative being non-existent, इन्द्र &c. are considered as not preceded by another word.

To VIII. 1. 72. S. 412 there is however an exception made by VIII. 1. 73, S. 413. Therefore where there are two Vocatives *in apposition*, one qualifying the other, the first Vocative (or the qualified), is not considered as non-existent for the purposes of the present sûtra. Hence in अग्ने तेजस्विन् ; अग्ने त्रातः ; the words *tejasvin* and *trâtah* qualify *Agne*; and therefore they are unaccented. Why do we say 'when in apposition'? Observe अघ्न्ये देवि सरस्वति ; here the words are not in apposition, *i. e* one does not qualify the other, but they are merely synonyms: and therefore the present sûtra applies.

३६५५ । सामान्यवचनं विभाषितं विशेषवचने । ८ । १ । ७४ ॥

अत्र भाष्यकृता बहुवचनमिति पूरितम् । सामान्यवचनमिति च पूर्वसूत्रे योजितम् । आमन्त्रितान्ते विशेषणे परे पूर्वं बहुवचनान्तमविद्यमानवद्वा । 'देवीः षलुर्वीरु नः कणोत' । अत्र देवीनां विशेषणं षडिति । 'देवाः शरण्या' । इह द्वितीयस्य निघातो वैकल्पिकः ॥

3655. When the preceding Vocative is in the Plural number, it is optionally considered as non-existent, if the subsequent Vocative, in apposition with it, is a specific term.

The VIII. 1. sûtras 73 and 74 as enunciated by Pâṇini are नामन्त्रिते समानाधिकरणे, and सामान्यवचनं विभाषितं विशेषवचने । Patanjali made the amendment by adding सामान्यवचने to 73 and completed the present sûtra by adding बहुवचनम् to it.

This ordains option, where the sûtra VIII. 1. 73, S. 413 would have made the consideration of the first vocative as existent, compulsory. Thus देवीः षलुर्वीरु

नः कर्णेन (Rig Veda X. 128. 5). Here षट् is an adjective qualifying देवीः । So also देवाः शरण्याः or देवा शरण्याः ॥

३६५६ । सुबामन्त्रिते पराङ्गवत्स्वरे । २ । १ । २ ॥

सुबन्तमामन्त्रिते परे परस्याङ्गवत्स्यात्स्वरे कर्तव्ये । 'द्रवत्पाणी शुभस्पती' । शुभ इति शुभेः क्विबन्तात् षष्ठ्यन्तम् । तस्य परशरीरानुप्रवेशे षाष्ठिकमामन्त्रिताद्युदात्तत्वम् । न चाष्टमिको निघातः शङ्क्यः । पूर्वामन्त्रितस्याविद्यमानत्वेन पादादित्वात् । 'यत्ते दिवो दुहितर्मर्तभोजनम्' । इह दिवः शब्दस्याष्टमिको निघातः । 'परशुना वृश्चन्' ॥

'+ षष्ठ्यामन्त्रितकारकवचनम् +' । षष्ठ्यन्तमामन्त्रितान्तं प्रति यत्कारकं तद्वाचकं चेति परिगणनं कर्तव्यमित्यर्थः । तेनेह न । 'अयमग्ने जरिता' । 'एतेनाग्ने ब्रह्मणा'-समर्थानुवृत्त्या वा सिद्धम् ॥

'+ पूर्वाङ्गवच्चेति वक्तव्यम् +' । आ ते पितर्मरुताम् । 'प्रति त्वा दुहितर्दिवः' ॥

'+ अव्ययानां न +' । 'उच्चैरधीयान' । 'अव्ययीभावस्य त्विष्यते' । 'उपाग्न्यधीयान' ॥

3656. A word ending in a case-affix, when followed by a word in the vocative case, is regarded as if it was the añga or component part of such subsequent vocative word, when a rule relating to accent is to be applied.

In other words, the word ending in a case-affix enters, as if, into the body of the vocative (âmantrita) word. Thus sûtra VI. 1. 198 S. 3653 declares 'a word ending in a vocative case-affix, gets the udâtta accent on the beginning *i.e.*, first syllable.' Now, this rule will apply even when a word ending with a case-affix precedes such word in the vocative case. Thus the word पती 'O two lords'! has udâtta on the first syllable. Now, when this word is preceded by another inflected noun as शुभस् 'of prosperity,' the accent will fall on शु, the two words being considered as a single word; as :—अश्विना यज्वरीरिषो द्रवत्पाणी शुभस्पती । पुरुभुजा चनस्यतम् । (Rig. 1. 3. 1). 'O Asvins, riding on quick horses, lords of prosperity and bestowers of plenty of food, eat the sacrificial offerings to your satisfaction.' Here VIII. 1. 19, S. 3654 does not make the word accentless, for the preceding Vocative, 'dravatpâni' being considered as non-existent, the second is beginning of a Pâda. But in the following example यत्ते दिवो दुहितर्मर्तभोजनम् (Rig. Veda VII. 81. 5) the word दिवः is accentless because of the VIII. 1 19. S. 3654.

So also परशुना वृश्चन् 'O thou cutting with an axe'! The word परशु is formed from the root शृ with the prefix पर and the Uṇâdi affix कु which is treated as ङित् (See Uṇadi I. 34). Hence it has acute on the final. But by the present sûtra, being considered as the component part of the Vocative वृश्चन्, it becomes first-acute.

Vârt :—The rule of this sûtra should be confined to that word only that denotes the agent (kâraka) of the verb with which the Vocative is connected and to the Genitive governing the Vocative. Though the Vocative being a substantive pure and simple cannot stand in relation of a kâraka to a verb, yet the verb in the sentence has a kâraka. That is meant in the Vârtika. Therefore not so here : अयमग्ने जरिता (Rig Veda X. 142. 1) and एतेनाग्ने ब्रह्मणा (Rig Veda I. 31. 18).

Here the words अयम् and एतेन are not connected with the verb to which the Vocative refers; while in परशुना वृश्चन् the word परशुना 'with the axe' is a kâraka to the verb denoted by the root व्रश्च 'to cut' from which the Vocative वृश्चन् comes. In other words, the preceding word becomes the integral part of the Vocative under two conditions only, namely, (1), when it is a Genitive governing the Vocative as in शुभस्पती where the word शुभस् is in the sixth case (derived with the affix क्विप् from शुभ्, the base being शुभ्); or (2) when the preceding word stands in the relation of a kâraka to the action denoted by the root from which the Vocative is derived :' as in परशुना वृश्चन् 'O with axe cutting!'

Or we may dispense with this Vârtika, and get the same result by the rule of समर्थःपदविधिः ; for only that word can become the integral part of a Vocative which is syntactically connected with it, and not any word that might happen to precede it.

Vârt :—It should be rather stated : 'component part of the *preceding*.' That is, while the sûtra teaches that the preceding word becomes part of the subsequent word, Katyayana would reverse the order. Thus आ ते पितर् मरुताम् (Rig Veda II. 33. 1).

Here the subsequent word मरुताम् becomes, as an aṅga or component part of पितर् which is the preceding word. पितर् is accentless, because a Vocative, and therefore, मरुताम् also becomes accentless being considered as aṅga of पितर् । So also पति त्वा दुहितर् दिवः (Rig. VII. 81. 3).; here दिवः is accentless, because the Vocative दुहितर् is nighâta.

Vârt :—Prohibition must be stated of Indeclinables as उच्चैरधीयान ! ॥

Ishti.—But not so of the Avyayîbhâva compounds, which are also Indeclinables. As उपाग्न्यधीयान ॥

३६५७ । उदात्तस्वरितयोर्यणः स्वरितोऽनुदात्तस्य । ८ । २ । ४ ॥

उदात्तस्थाने स्वरितस्थाने च यो यणतः परस्यानुदात्तस्य स्वरितः स्यात् । अभ्यभि हि स्वरितस्य यणः । खलप्व्याशा । अस्य स्वरितस्य त्रैपादिकत्वेनासिद्धत्वाच्छेषनिघातो न ॥

3657. A svarita vowel is the substitute of an anudâtta vowel, when the latter follows after such a semi-vowel, as has replaced an udâtta or a svarita vowel.

An unaccented vowel becomes svarita, when it comes after a यण् (semi-vowel), which यण् itself has come in the room of a vowel which was acute or svarita once.

Thus अभ्यभि हि । The word अभि is finally acute (See Phiṭ Sûtras IV, 12. and I. 1). It is doubled by VIII. 1. 4. S. 2140. The second अभि gets the designation of âmredita VIII. 1. 2. and it is anudâtta by VIII. 1. 3. S. 3670. Therefore in अभि + अभि the इ of the first is udâtta, the अ of second is anudâtta, the इ is changed to य्, this य् is udâtta-yaṇ hence the अ of the second अभि after it becomes svarita by the present sûtra. अभि + अभि = अभ् य्+अभि = अभ्यभि ॥

Now to take an example of a svarita-yaṇ. The word खलपू is finally acute by krit-accent (VI. 2. 139. S. 3873). The Locative singular of this word is खलपू + इ = खलप्वि, by VI. 4. 83. S 281). This व् is a semivowel which comes in the room of the acute ऊ, therefore, it is udâtta-yaṇ. After this udâtta-yaṇ, the anudâtta इ of the Locative becomes svarita by the first part of this sûtra. Now when खलप्वि +

आर्थौ are combined by sandhi, this svarita ई is changed to यॄ; it is, therefore, a svarita-yaṇ. The unaccented आ will become svarita, after this svarita-yaṇ. As क्षिप्र व्यार्थौ The word आशा is finally acute and consequently आ is not acute (Phit. I. 18).

This svarita आे of ओंशा is evolved by the present sûtra which belongs to the Tripâdi section of the Ashṭâdhyâyî, and hence it is asiddha (VIII. 2. 1. S. 12). Therefore rule VI. 1. 158. does not cause the र्थौ to lose its accent. Cf. 3660.

३६५८ । एकादेश उदात्तेनोदात्तः । ८ । २ । ६ ॥

उदात्तेन सहैकादेश उदात्तः स्यात् । 'वोऽश्वाः'। 'क्वावरं मरुतः' ॥

3658. **The single substitute of an unaccented vowel with an udâtta vowel is udâtta.**

Thus क्व वोऽश्वाः (Rig Veda 61. 2) and क्वावरं मरुतः। The word वः is anudatta by VIII. 1. 21. S. 405. read with VIII. 1. 18. S. 403. The word अश्वः is acutely accented on the first, as it is formed by adding क्वन् to अश् (Uṇ. I. 151). The स् of वस् is changed to र् (VIII. 2. 66. S. 162), which is again changed to उ (VI. 1. 113. S. 163). Thus वो ऽश्वाः। Here अ becomes pûrva-rupa by VI. I. 109. S. 86. which is udâtta.

क्व is formed from किम् by अत् affix (V. 3. 12. S 1959. and VII. 2. 105. S. 2299) and is svarita (VI. 1. 185. S. 3729). The word अवर is acutely accented on the first by the Phiṭ II. 6. The single long substitute is udatta.

३६५९ । स्वरितो वानुदात्ते पदादौ । ८ । २ । ६ ॥

अनुदात्ते पदादौ परे उदात्तेन सहैकादेशः स्वरितो वा स्यात् । पक्षे पूर्वसूत्रेणोदात्तः । 'वीऽदं ज्योतिर्हृदये' । 'अस्य श्लोको दिवीयते' । व्यवस्थितविभाषात्वादिकारयोः स्वरितः । दीर्घप्रवेशे तूदात्तः । किञ्च 'एङः पदान्तात्-' (८६) इति पूर्वरूपे स्वरित एव । तेऽवदन् । 'सोऽयमागात्' उक्तं च प्रातिशाख्ये—'इकारयोश्च प्रश्लेषे क्षैप्राभिनिहतेषु च' इति ।

3659. **The single substitute of an unaccented vowel, standing at the beginning of a word, with an udâtta vowel, may optionally be svarita or udâtta.**

Thus वीदं ज्योतिर्हृदये। अस्य श्लोको दिवीयते। This is a vyavasthita-vibhâshâ; in this wise. There will *necessarily* be svarita (1) where a long ई is the single substitute of (इ + इ) or of two short इ's, (2) where there is pûrva rupa by the application of एङः पदान्तात् अति (VI. 1. 109. S. 86) There will be udâtta where a long vowel comes in. Thus in वि + इदम् = वीदम् in वीऽदं ज्योतिर्हृदये, the long ई is substituted for two short इ's. This substitution of a long ई for two *short* इ's is technically called प्रश्लेष। Where there is Praś lesha, the long ई is *necessarily* svarita. Similarly when there is अभिनिहतसन्धि: *i. e.*, the peculiar sandhi taught in VI. 1. 109. Thus तेऽवदन्, सोऽयमागात्। So also where there is क्षैप्र सन्धि *i. e.*, the substitution of a semi-vowel in the room of an udâtta or svarita vowel as अभ्यंभि। The above rules about svarita are thus summarised in the Prâtiśakhyas: इकारयोश्च प्रश्लेषे क्षैप्राभिनिहतेषु च। But where a long ई is substituted as a single substitute for इ + ई (one of the इ's being long), there it must *always* be acute. As अस्य श्लोको दिवीयते (Rig. 1. 190. 4). The words दिवि + ईयते are compounded into त्रिवीयते । The word दिवि (Locative singular) is finally acute by VI. 1. 171, S. 3717. दीयते is from the Divâdi root दीङ् गतौ, and has lost its accent by VIII 1. 28. S. 3935.

३६६० । उदात्तादनुदात्तस्य स्वरितः । ८ । ४ । ६६ ॥

उदात्तात्परस्यानुदात्तस्य स्वरितः स्यात् । 'अग्निमीळे' । अस्याप्यसिद्धत्वाच्छेषनिघातो न । 'तमीशानासः' ।

3660. The Svarita is the substitute of an Anudâtta vowel which follows an Udâtta vowel.

Thus अग्निम् + ईळे = अग्निमीळे । Here ई which was अनुदात्त by rule VIII. 1. 28, becomes svarita by the present rule, as it comes after the udâtta म of agni.

The rule VI. 1. 158, S. 3650, does not change this svarita into an Anudâtta because for the purposes of that rule, the present rule is असिद्ध, or as if it had not taken place (VIII. 2. 1. S. 12). Therefore both the udâtta and the svarita accent are heard.

तमीशानासः (Rig Veda I. 129. 2).

Here तम् the Accusative singular of तद् is finally acute. The word ईशानासः is the Nominative Plural of ईशान, the augment असुक् being inserted by VII. 1. 50. S. 3572. The word ईशानं is derived from ईश 'to rule' with the affix शानच्, and therefore it is finally acute because of the चित् accent. The Nom. Pl. affix जस्, being a सुप् is anudâtta. The long ई and the अ of सं are svarita.

३६६१ । नोदात्तस्वरितोदयमगार्ग्यकाश्यपगालवानाम् । ८ । ४ । ६७ ॥

उदात्तपरः स्वरितपरश्चानुदात्तः स्वरितो न स्यात् । गार्ग्यादिमते तु स्यादेव । 'प्र य आरुः' । 'वोऽश्वाः' । 'क्वाभीशवः' ।

3661. All prohibit the above substitution of svarita, except the Âchâryas Gârgya, Kâśyapa and Gâlava, when an udâtta or a svarita follows the anudâtta.

Thus प्र य आरुः (Rig Veda III. 7. 1). वोऽश्वाः; क्वाभीशवः ॥

Note :—This debars the preceding rule. That anudâtta which is *followed* by an udâtta is called उदात्तोदयः or उदात्तपरः । The word उदय means पर in the terminology of ancient Grammarians. That anudâtta which is *followed* by a svarita is called स्वरितोदयः । These are Bahuvrîhi compounds. Thus उदात्तोदयः —गार्ग्यस्तत्रं, वात्स्यस्तत्रं । The word तत्र is first acute by लित् accent, before this udâtta, the य of these words does not become svarita. So with स्वरितोदयः—गार्ग्यः क्वं; वात्स्यः क्वं । The word क्व is svarita being formed by the तित् affix अत् (V. 3 12 S. 1959); before this svarita the preceding य does not become svarita.

Why do we say 'except in the opinion of Gârgya, Kâśyapa and Gâlava'? Observe गार्ग्यः क्व, गार्ग्यस्तत्र । According to their opinion, the svarita change does take place.

The employment of the longer word उदय instead of the shorter word पर is for the sake of auspiciousness, for the Book has approached the end. The very utterance of the word उदय is auspicious. All sacred works commence with an auspicious word, have an auspicious word in the middle, and end with an auspicious word. Thus Pâṇini commences his sûtra, with the auspicious word वृद्धि: 'increase' (in Sûtra I. 1. 1), has the word शिव 'the well wisher' in the middle (IV. 4. 143), and उदय at the end.

The mention of the names of those several Achâryas is for the sake of showing respect (pujârthaṁ).

३६६२ । एकश्रुति दूरात्संबुद्धौ । १ । २ । ३३ ॥

दूरात्संबोधने वाक्यमेकश्रुतिः स्यात् । त्रैस्वर्यापवादः । 'आगच्छ भो माणवक' ।

3662. In addressing a person from a distance, the tone is called Ekaśruti or monotony.

Monotony or Ekaśruti is that tone which is perceived when a person is addressed; in it there is an absence of all the three tones mentioned above; and there is no definite pitch in it. It is, therefore, the ordinary recitative tone.

The word 'Sambuddhi' means here addressing a person from a distance; and has not its technical meaning of the singular number of the vocative case. As आगच्छ भो माणवक देवदत्ता३ 'O boy Devadatta! come.' There is vanishing of all the accents in the above case; and the final short vowel of Devadatta is changed into *pluta* by VIII. 2. 84 (दूराद्धूते च) ॥

३६६३ । यज्ञकर्मण्यजपन्यूङ्खसामसु । १ । २ । ३४ ॥

यज्ञक्रियायां मन्त्र एकश्रुतिः स्याज्जपादीन्वर्जयित्वा । 'अग्निर्मूर्धा दिवः ककुत्' । 'यज्ञ-' इति किम् । स्वाध्यायकाले त्रैस्वर्यमेव । 'अजप-' इति किम् । 'ममाग्ने वर्चो विहवेष्वस्तु' । जपो नाम उपांशुप्रयोगः । यथा जले निमग्नस्य । न्यूङ्खा नाम षोडश ओकाराः । गीतिषु सामाख्या ।

3663. In the sacrificial works, there is Monotony, except in *japa* (silent repetition of a formula), Nyûṅkha vowels (sixteen sorts of *om*) and the Sâma Vedas.

In 'sacrificial works' or on occasions of sacrifice, the mantras of the Vedas are recited in Ekaśruti or monotony. But on occasions of ordinary reading, the mantras are to be recited with their proper three-fold accents.

'Japa' is the repetition of mantras, and their recitation in a low voice or whisper as when a person immersed in a river recites them. Nyûṅkha is the name of certain hymns of the Vedas and the names of 16 sorts of 'Om.' Some of these are pronounced with udâtta and others with anudâtta accent. Sâmas are songs, or the musical cadence in which some vedic hymns are to be uttered. As :—अग्निर्मूर्धा दिवः ककुत्पतिः पृथिव्या अयम् । अपाम् रेतांसि जिन्वतो३म् । (Rig Veda VIII. 14. 16).

When a mantra is recited as a *japa*, then it must be pronounced with an accent.—As ममाग्ने वर्चो विहवेष्वस्तु (Rig Veda X. 128. 1).

When not employed on occasions of sacrifice, but are ordinarily read, the mantras must have their proper accent, and there will be no Ekaśruti.

३६६४ । उच्चैस्तरां वा वषट्कारः । १ । २ । ३५ ॥

यज्ञकर्मणि वौषट्शब्द उच्चैस्तरां वा स्यादेकश्रुतिर्वा ॥

3664. The pronunciation of the word 'vashaṭ' may optionally be by raising the voice (accutely accented), or it may be pronounced with monotony.

The phrase 'yajña karma' is understood here. Even in yajña-karmas or sacrifices the word वौषट् may optionally be pronounced in a raised tone. The word वषट् in the sûtra signifies वौषट्।

३६६५ । विभाषा छन्दसि । १ । २ । ३६ ॥

छन्दसि विभाषा एकश्रुतिः स्यात् । व्यवस्थितविभाषेयम् । संहितायां त्रैस्वर्यम् । ब्राह्मणे एकश्रुतिर्वह्वृचानाम् । अन्येषामपि यथासंप्रदायं व्यवस्था ।

3665. The monotony is optional in the recitation of the Vedas, or they may be recited with accents.

In the Chhandas or the Vedas there is option either to use the Ekaśruti tone or the three tones. Even on the occasion of ordinary reading, the Chhandas might be uttered either with the three accents or monotonously. Some say this is a limited option (vyavasthita vibhâshâ).

The option allowed by this sûtra is to be adjusted in this way. In reading the Mantra portion of the Veda, every word must be pronounced with its proper accent: but in the Brâhmaṇa portion of the Veda there might be Ekaśruti. This is the opinion of the Rig Vedins, while some say there must be Ekaśruti necessarily and not optionally in the recitation of the Brâhmaṇas.

Thus:—अग्निमीले पु रोहितं or simply अग्निमीले पुरोहितं । 'I praise Agni the purohita'.

३६६६ । न सुब्रह्मण्यायांस्वरितस्य तूदात्तः । १ । २ । ३७ ॥

सुब्रह्मण्याख्येनिगदे 'यज्ञकर्मणि —' (३६६३) इति 'विभाषा छन्दसि' (३६३५) इति च प्राप्ता एकश्रुतिर्न स्यात्स्वरितस्योदात्तश्च स्यात् । सुब्रह्मण्योम् । सुब्रह्मणि साधुरिति यत् । न च 'एकादेश उदात्तेनोदात्तः' (३६५८) इति सिद्धे पुनरत्रेदमुदात्तविधानं व्यर्थमिति वाच्यं । तत्रानुदात्त इत्यस्यानुवृत्तः ।

'+ असावित्यन्तः +'। तस्मिन्नेव निगदे प्रथमान्तस्यान्त उदात्तः स्यात् । गार्ग्यो यजते । ञित्स्वात्प्राप्त आद्युदात्तोऽनेन बाध्यते । '+अमुष्येत्यन्तः+'। षष्ठ्यन्तस्यापि प्राग्वत् । दाक्षेः पिता यजते ।

'+ स्यान्तस्योपोत्तमं च +'। चादन्तः । तेन द्वावुदात्तौ । गार्ग्यस्य पिता यजते ।

'+वानामधेयस्य+'। स्यान्तस्य नामधेयस्य उपोत्तममुदात्तं वा स्यात् । देवदत्तस्य पिता यजते ।

3666. There should be no Monotony in the recitation of the Subrahmaṇya hymns and in those hymns, the vowels, that would otherwise have taken the svarita accent, take the 'udâtta' accent instead.

The subrahmaṇya hymns are portions of the Rig Veda mentioned in Śatapatha Brâhmaṇa.

This sûtra prohibits Ekaśruti in the case of certain prayers called subrahmaṇya. By I. 2. 34 read with I. 2. 36 *ante*, prayers might be *optionally* uttered with Ekaśruti accent. This ordains an exception to that rule. In subrahmaṇya prayers there is no ekaśruti; and in these hymns, a vowel which otherwise by any rule of grammar would have taken a svarita accent, takes an udâtta accent instead.

As सुब्रह्मण्यो३मिन्द्रागच्छ हरिव आगच्छ. Here the word सुब्रह्मण्य is formed by the addition of the affix यत् (IV. 4 98) to the word सुब्रह्मण्, and this य will get *svarita* accent by VI. 1. 185, (तित्स्वरितम्) as it has an indicatory त्; by the present sûtra, this nascent *svarita* is changed into udâtta. In the phrase इन्द्र आगच्छ, the word Indra being in the vocative case, इ is udâtta, the अ of *Indra* is anudâtta VI. 1. 198. The *anudâtta* preceded by an udâtta is changed into *svarita* (VIII. 4. 66).

Thus the अ of इन्द्र must become svarita, but by the present sûtra this nascent *svarita* is changed into an udâtta. Thus in इन्द्र, both vowels become udâtta. In the word आगच्छ, the आ is *udâtta*; the next letter which was anudâtta becomes *svarita*, and from *svarita*, it is changed to *udâtta* by the present rule. Thus in the sentence इन्द्र आगच्छ, the first four syllables are all acutely accented, the fifth syllable is only *anudâtta*. So also in हरिव आगच्छ; for the reasons given above, the letters व and च्छ are anudâtta, the rest are all acutely accented. Cf. Shat Br. III. 3. 4. 17 and fgg.

Vârt:—In the Subrahmanya hymns the final vowel of a word in the Nominative case is acute.

Thus गार्ग्यो यजते। Here गार्ग्य is derived from गर्ग by the affix यञ् (IV. 1. 105), and therefore it ought to be acute on the first because of ञित् accent. But the present vârtika prevents that. Thus we have गार्ग्यः instead of गार्ग्यः॥

Vârt:—So also the final of a word in the Genitive is acute in the Subrahmanya texts. As दाक्षेः पिता यजते। Here दाक्षि is derived from दक्ष by the Patronymic affix इञ् and it would have been दाक्षेः but the vârtika makes it दाक्षेः॥

Vârt:—But the penultimate as well as the final of the Genitive ending in स्य is udâtta.

Thus गार्ग्यस्य पिता यजते। Here there are two udâttas in the same word.

Vârt:—*Optionally* the penultimate of a Genitive in स्य is udâtta, when the word is a Proper Name. As देवदत्तस्य पिता यजते or देवदत्तस्य पिता यजते।

३६६७। देवब्रह्मणोरनुदात्तः। १। २। ३८॥

अनयोः स्वरितस्यानुदात्तः स्यात्सुब्रह्मण्यायाम्। 'देवा ब्रह्माण आगच्छत'।

3667. The word 'devâ' and Brahmâṇa in those hymns have 'anudâtta' accent.

By I. 2. 37, it was declared, that in the subrahmanya hymns, *svarita* accent is replaced by *udâtta* accent. This sûtra makes an exception in favor of the words देवा and ब्रह्माण occurring in those hymns. These words have *anudâtta* accent. As देवा ब्रह्माण आगच्छत 'come ye Devâs and Brahmaṇas.' Here the word देवा gets udâtta accent on the first syllable by VI. 1. 198 (in the vocative the accent is on the beginning): वा has originally an anudâtta accent which by VIII. 4. 66 (an *anudâtta* following an *udâtta* is changed into *svarita*) would have been changed into *svarita*. This *svarita*, by the previous sûtra required to be changed into *udátta*; but by this rule, it is replaced by *anudátta*. In other words, the original *anudátta* remains unchanged.

३६६८ । स्वरितात्संहितायामनुदात्तानाम् । १ । २ । ३९ ॥

स्वरितात्परेषामनुदात्तानां संहितायामेकश्रुतिः स्यात् । 'इमं मे गङ्गे यमुने 'सरस्वति' ॥

3668. The Monotony takes the place of the *anudatta* vowels which follow the *svarita* vowels, in close proximity (*sanhita*).

Sanihtâ is the joining of two or more words in a sentence, for the purposes of reading or reciting. When words are thus glued together, then the *anudátta* accents become Ekaśruti if they are preceded by *svarita* vowels; and are pronounced monotonously. As इमं मे गङ्गे यमुने सरस्वति (Rig Veda X. 75. 5) O Ganga, Yamuna, Sarasvati ! this mine.

Here the word इमं has udâtta on the last syllable : the word मे is originally *anudátta*, but by rule VIII. 4. 66 following an *udátta*, it is changed into *svarita*; after this *svarita* all *anudátta* like गङ्गे, &c., are replaced by ekaśruti. All the vowels of the words गङ्गे यमुने &c., had anudâtta accent by rule VIII. 1. 19 (all vocative get anudâtta if standing in the middle of a sentence and not beginning a stanza.)

The word 'sanhita' has been used in the sûtra to show that when there is a hiatus between the words then there is no change of anudâtta into ekaśruti. The word sanhitâ is defined in sûtra I. 4. 109.

३६६९ । उदात्तस्वरितपरस्य सन्नतरः । १ । २ । ४० ॥

उदात्तस्वरितौ परौ यस्मात्तस्यानुदात्ततरः स्यात् । 'सरस्वि_ शुतुद्रि' । 'व्यचक्षय त्स्वः' । 'तस्य परमाम्रेडितम्' (८३) ।

3669. The accent called *Sannatara* is substituted in the room of an *anudátta* vowel, which has an *udatta* or *svarita* vowel following it.

In the previous sûtra it was said that an *anudátta* preceded by a *svarita* becomes Ekaśruti. If however such an *anudátta* is followed by an udâtta or a *svarita*, it does not become Ekaśruti but becomes *sannatara* *i.e.*, lower than *anudátta*.

The *sannatara* is therefore that accent which was originally *anudátta*, and which is preceded by a *svarita* and is followed by an udâtta or a *svarita*.

This is one explanation of the sûtra. There is another explanation which does not take the anuvritti of Ekaśruti in this sûtra. The anudâtta is replaced by *sannatara* when such anudatta immediately precedes an udatta or a *svarita*. The *sannatra* is also called anudâtta. Thus सरस्वति शुतुद्रि । व्यचक्षयत्स्व ।

As देवा मरुतः पृश्निमातरोऽपः ॥ Here the word मातरः is anudâtta. The word अपः has udâtta on the last syllable by VI. 1. 171. In the phrase मातरोऽपः (मातरः+अपः) The syllable रो is anudâtta, because anudâtta + anudâtta = anudâtta. This *anudátta* रो, preceding the *udâtta* पः, is changed into *sannatara.*

३६७० । अनुदात्तं च । ८ । १ । ३ ॥

द्विरुक्तस्य परं रूपमनुदात्तं स्यात् । 'दिवेदिवे' ।

3670. That which is called âmreḍita is gravely accented.

Thus 'दिवे दिवे' (Rig Veda I. 1. 3).

That is, all the vowels of the amreḍita become anudâtta or accentless.

Here ends the Chapter on Accents in general.

अथ धातुस्वराः ।

CHAPTER II.
ROOT-ACCENTS.

३६७१ । धातोः । ६ । १ । १६२ ॥

अन्त उदात्तः । 'गोपायतं स्यात् नः' । 'असि सत्यः' ।

3671. A root has the acute on the end-syllable.

The word अन्त is understood here. Thus 'गोपायत, उनः' 'असि सत्यः' (Rig Veda I. 87. 4).

३६७२ । स्वपादिहिंसामच्यनिटि । ६ । १ । १८८ ॥

स्वपादीनां हिंसेश्चानिडजादौ लसार्वधातुके परे आदिरुदात्तो वा स्यात् । स्वपादिरदाद्यन्तर्गणः । स्वपन्ति । श्वसन्ति । हिंसन्ति । पक्षे प्रत्ययस्वरेण मध्योदात्तता । 'ङित्येवेष्यते' । नेह । स्वपानि । हिनसानि ।

3672. The acute accent is optionally on the first syllable when a Personal-ending, being a Sârvadhâtuka tense affix beginning with a vowel, (provided that the vowel is not the augment 'iṭ') follows after 'svap' &c., or after 'hins.'

The phrase लसार्वधातुके in the locative case is understood here. Thus स्वपन्ति or स्वपन्ति, श्वसन्ति or श्वसन्ति हिंसन्ति or हिंसन्ति । The accent on the middle falls by the accent of the affix III. 1. 3. Why do we say 'before an affix beginning with a *vowel*'? Observe स्वप्यात्, हिंस्यात । Why do we say 'not taking the augment इट्?' Observe स्वपितः and श्वसितः ।

Ishti :—This rule applies to those vowel-beginning affixes which are ङित् ; it does not apply to स्वपानि, हिनसानि ।

३६७३ । अभ्यस्तानामादिः । ६ । १ । १८९ ॥

अनिडजादौ लसार्वधातुके परे अभ्यस्तानामादिरुदात्तः । 'ये ददति प्रिया वसु' । परत्वाच्चित्स्वरमयं बाधते । 'दधाना इन्द्रे' ।

3673. The acute accent falls on the first syllable of the reduplicate verbs when followed by an affix beginning with a vowel (the vowel being not 'iṭ') and being a sârvadhâtuka personal ending.

Thus ये ददति प्रिया वसु (Rig Veda VII. 32. 15). दँदति, दँदतु, दँधति, दँधतु, जँक्षति, जँक्षतु, जाँग्रति, जाँग्रतुः। Before consonant affixes: दद्याँत्। Before सेट् affixes:— जक्षितँः। Though the word अचि was understood here from the last aphorism, the repetition is for the sake of making this an *invariable* rule and not an *optional* rule as those in the foregoing. It being a subsequent sûtra, debars the चित् accent, as दधाना इन्द्रे (Rig Veda I. 4. 5).

३६७४ । अनुदात्ते च । ६ । १ । १९० ॥

अविद्यमानोदात्ते लसार्वधातुके परेऽभ्यस्तानामादिरुदात्तः। 'दधासि रत्नं द्रविणं च दाशुषे'।

3674. Also when the unaccented endings of the three persons in the singular follow, the first syllable of the reduplicate has the acute.

The endings तिप् सिप् and मिप् are anudâtta (III. 1. 4). This sûtra applies to those personal endings which do not begin with a vowel. Thus दँदाति, जँहाति, दँधाति, जिँहीते, मिँमीते। The word अनुदात्त is to be construed here as a Bahuvrihi i. e., an affix in which there is no udâtta vowel, so that the rule may apply when a portion of the affix is elided or a semivowel is substituted:- as मा हि स्म दँधात्, and दँधात्यत्र। दधासि रत्नं द्रविणं च दाशुषे (Rig Veda I. 94. 14).

३६७५ । भीह्रीभृहुमदजनधनदरिद्राजागरां प्रत्ययात्पूर्वं पिति । ६ । १ । १९२ ॥

भीप्रभृतीनामभ्यस्तानां पिति लसार्वधातुके परे प्रत्ययात्पूर्वमुदात्तं स्यात्। 'योऽग्निहोत्रं जुहोति'। ममत्तु नः परिज्मा'। 'माता यद्वीरं दधनत्'। 'जागर्षि त्वम्'।

3675. In भी, ह्री, भृ, हु, मद्, जन्, धन्, दरिद्रा and जागृ, in their reduplicates, the acute accent is, before the sârvadhâtuka unaccented endings of the three persons in singular, *pit*, on the syllable which precedes the affix.

This debars the accent on the beginning. Thus बिभेँति, जिह्रेँति, बिभँर्ति, जुहोँति ममँत्तु नः परिज्मा (Rig Veda I. 122. 3). Here the root मद has diversely taken in the Chhandas the vikaraṇa श्लु, though it belongs to Divâdi class. जजँनत्, इन्द्रम्। The verb is here लेट् or the Vedic Subjunctive, so also is the next example. दधनत् from धन धान्ये, the इ of ति being elided by III. 4. 97, and the augment अट् being added by III 4. 94. माता वीरं दधनत् (Rig Veda X. 73. 1). दधँनत्, दरिद्रॉति, जागँर्ति। In the case of other verbs we have दँदाति। Before affixes which have not the indicatory प् (i. e., all endings other than the three singular endings), the accent will be on the first syllable: as दँरिद्रति ॥

३६७६ । लिति । ६ । १ । १९३ ॥

प्रत्ययात्पूर्वमुदात्तम्। चिकीर्षकः।

3676 The acute accent falls on the syllable immediately preceding the affix that has an indicatory *l*.

Thus विकर्षकः, जिह्रीषकः with the affix वुन् (III. 1. 133), औरिकविधम् and ऐषुकारिभक्तम् with the affixes विधल् and भक्तल् (IV. 2. 54) accent on the कि and रि ॥

३६७७ । आदिर्णमुल्यन्यतरस्याम् । ६ । १ । १९४ ।

अभ्यस्तानामादिरुदात्तो वा णमुलि परे । लोलूयं लोलूयम् । पक्षे लित्स्वरः ।

3677. The first syllable may be optionally acute when the absolutive affix 'ṇamul' follows.

Thus लोलूयम् or लोलूयम् । In the reduplicate form लोलू, the second part लू is unaccented by VIII. 1. 3. The present sûtra makes लो accented, When लो is not accented, लू will get the accent by लित् accent. This rule is confined to polysyllabic the Absolutives, namely to the reduplicated Absolutives (VIII. 1. 4).

३६७८ । अचः कर्तृयकि । ६ । १ । १९५ ।

उपदेशेऽजन्तानां कर्तृयकि परे आदिरुदात्तो वा । लूयते केदारः स्वयमेव ।

3678. The roots which are exhibited in the Dhâtupâṭha with a final vowel, may optionally have the acute on the first syllable, before the affixes of the Passive 'yak' when the sense of the verb is Reflexive.

The word उपदेश is understood here. Thus लूयते or लूयते केदारः स्वयमेव स्तीर्यते or स्तीर्यते केदारः स्वयमेव । When the accent does not fall on the first syllable, it falls on य (VI. I. 186).

३६७९ । चङ्यन्यतरस्याम् । ६ । १ । २१८ ।

चङन्ते धातावुपोत्तममुदात्तं वा । 'मा हि चीकरताम्'। धात्वकार उदात्तः । पक्षान्तरेचङुदात्तः ॥

इति धातुस्वराः ।

3679. The acute accent may be optionally on the penultimate syllable of the reduplicated Aorist in 'chaṅ' the word consisting of more than two syllables.

Thus मा हि चीकरताम् or चीकरताम् । The augment अट् is elided by the addition of मा, VI. 4. 74; हि prevents the verb from becoming anudâtta VIII. 1. 34 then comes the चित् accent of चङ् ॥ The augmented form with अट् has acute always on the first syllable VI. 4. 71. When the word is of less than three syllables, the rule does not apply, as माहि दधत् ॥

Here ends the Chapter of Root-accents.

अथ प्रत्ययस्वराः ।

CHAPTER III.

AFFIX-ACCENTS.

३६८० । कर्षात्वतो घञोऽन्त उदात्तः । ६ । १ । १५९ ।

कर्षतेर्धातोराकारवतश्च घञन्तस्यान्त उदात्तः स्यात् । कर्षः । पापा निर्देशात्तुदादेराद्युदात्त एव । कर्षः । पाकः ।

3680. A stem formed with the Kṛita-affix 'ghañ' has the acute accent on the end-syllable, if it is formed from the root *krish*, (*kàr-shati*) or has a long â in it.

Thus कर्षः, पाकः, त्यागः, रागः, दायः, धायः। This is an exception to VI. 1. 197 by which affixes having an indicatory ञ् have acute accent on the first syllable. The word कर्ष formed with the Vikaraṇa शप्, is used in the aphorism instead of कृष to indicate that कृष of Bhvādi gaṇa is affected by this rule, and not कृष्–कृषति of Tudâdigaṇa. The word कर्षः derived from the Tudadi कृष् has the acute accent on the first syllable.

३६८१। उञ्छादीनां च। ६। १। १६० ॥

अन्त उदात्तः स्यात्। उञ्छादिषु युगशब्दो घञन्तोऽगुणो निपात्यते कालविशेषे रथाद्यवयवे च। 'वैश्वानरः कुशिकेभिर्युगे युगे'। अन्यत्र 'योगे योगे तवस्तरम्'। भक्षशब्दो घञन्तः। 'गावः सोमस्य प्रथमस्य भक्षः'। उत्तमशश्वत्तमावपि। 'उदुत्तमं वरुण'। 'शश्वत्तममीळते'।

3681. The words *uchchha* &c. have acute accent on the last syllable.

Thus वैश्वानरः कुशिकेभिर्युगे युगे (Rig Veda III. 26. 3).

But in other places we have योगे योगे तवस्तरम् (Rig Veda I. 30. 7).

The word भक्ष is formed by घञ् affix, as in the following गावः सोमस्य प्रथमस्य भक्षः (Rig Veda VI. 28. 5).

So also उत्तम and शश्वत as in उदुत्तमं वरुण (Rig Veda I. 24. 15). शश्वत्तममीळते (Rig Veda X. 70. 3).

Note:—1. उञ्छः, 2. म्लेच्छः, 3. जञ्जः, 4. जल्पः। These are formed by घञ्, and would have taken acute accent on the first. 5. जपः, 6. वधः are formed by अप् affix (III. 3. 61) which being grave (III. 1. 4.), these words would have taken the accent of the dhâtu (VI. 1. 162), *i. e.* acute on the first syllable. Some read व्यधः also here, 7. युगः is derived from युज् by घञ् affix, the non-causing of guṇa is irregular, and the word means 'a cycle of time', 'a part of a carriage'. In other senses, the form is योगः। 8. गरः = (दूष्ये); is formed by अप्, and has this accent when it means 'poison', in other senses, the acute is on the first syllable. 9. वेगः' वेदः, वेष्टः (चेष्टः), and बन्धः. करणे। These words are formed by घञ् by III. 3. 121. When denoting instrument (करण) they take the above accent, when denoting भाव the accent falls on the first syllable. 10. स्तुयुद्रुवश्छन्दसि, *e. g.* परिष्टुत परिद्रुत संयुत। 11. वर्तनिः स्तोत्रे, the stotra means the Sâma Veda, the word वर्तनिः occurring in the Sâma Veda has acute on the last: in other places, it has the accent on the middle. 12. श्वभ्रे दरः, the दरः has end-acute when meaning 'a cave', otherwise when formed by अप् affix it has acute on the first. 13. साम्बतापौ भावगर्हायाम्, thus साम्बः, तापः, in other senses, the acute is on the first. 14. उत्तमशश्वत्तमौ सर्वत्र, *e. g.* उत्तमः, शश्वत्तमः। Some read the limitation of भावगर्हा into this also. 15. भक्षमन्थभोगमन्थाः (भोगदेहा) । These are formed by घञ्, भक्ष though a णयन्त root is here घञन्त ॥

1 उञ्छ, 2 म्लेच्छ, 3 जञ्ज, 4 जल्प, 5 जप, 6 वध (व्यध), 7 युग, 8 गरो दूष्ये, 9 वेदवेगवेष्टबन्धाः, (चेष्ट वेष्ट) करणे, 10 स्तुयुद्रुवश्छन्दसि (परिष्टुत, संयुत, परिद्रुत), 11 वर्तनिः

स्तोत्रे, 12 षवभे दरः, 13 साम्बतापेा भावगर्हायाम्, 14 उत्तमशश्वत्तमेा (उत्तमशश्वत्तमशब्दौ) सर्वत्र, 15 भक्षमन्थ, भेागमन्थाः (भक्षमन्थभेागदेहाः) ॥

३६८२ । चतुरः शसि । ६ । १ । १६७ ॥

चतुरेाऽन्त उदात्तः शसि परे । 'चतुरः कल्पयन्तः' । 'अचि रः-' (२९९) इति रादेशस्य पूर्वविधेा स्थानिवत्त्वाचेह । चतस्रः पश्य । 'चतेरुरन्' । नित्त्वादाद्युदात्तता ॥

3682. The word *chatur*, followed by the accusative plural, has acute accent on the last syllable.

Thus चतुरः कल्पयंतः (Rig Veda X. 114. 6) the accent is on तु । The feminine of चतुर् is चतस् (VII. 2. 99), which has acute accent on the first (VII. 2. 99 Vârt.), and its accusative plural will not have accent on the last syllable. This is so, because चतुर् has acute on the first, as formed by उरन् affix (Uṇâdi V. 58). Its substitute चतस् will also be so, by the rule of स्थानिवत् । The special enunciation of आद्युदात्त with regard to चतस् in the Vârtika चतसर्याद्युदात्तनिपातनं कर्तव्यं (VII. 2. 99) indicates that the present rule does not apply to चतस् । Another reason for this is as follows : चतस + अस् = चतस्र + अस् । Now comes the present Sûtra; here, however, the र् (VII. 2. 100 S. 299) substitute of ऋ being sthânivat, will prevent the udâtta formation of the अ of त ; nor will ऋ be considered as final and take the acute, as there exists no vowel ऋ but a consonant र् which cannot take an accent. As चतस्रः पश्य । Professor Bohtlingk places the accent thus चतुरः, Pro. Max Muller चतुरः । I have followed Prof. Max Muller in interpreting this sûtra; for Bohtlingk's interpretation would make the ending अस् accented and not the final of चतुरः ॥

३६८३ । झल्युपेात्तमम् । ६ । १ । १८० ॥

षट्त्रिचतुर्भ्यो या झलादिर्विभक्तिस्तदन्ते पद उपेात्तममुदात्तं स्यात् । 'अध्वर्युभिः पञ्चभिः' 'नवभिर्वाजैर्नवती च' । 'सप्तभ्यो जायमानः' । 'आदुशभिर्विवस्वतः' । 'उपेात्तमम्' किम् । 'आ.॰ऽभिर्हूयमानः' । 'विश्वेर्देवैस्त्रिभिः' । 'झलि' किम् । 'नवानां नवतीनाम्' ॥

3683. The numerals 'shaṭ', 'tri' and 'chatur' when taking a case-affix beginning with a *bh* or *s* get the acute accent on the penultimate syllable, when the said numerals assume a form consisting of three or more syllables.

The numerals षट्, त्रि and चतुर् when ending in a case-affix beginning with a झल् consonant, form a full word (पद), in such a word the penultimate syllable gets the acute accent. The very word penultimate shows that the पद must be of three syllables at least. Thus पंचभिः, सप्तभिः, तिसृभिः, चतुर्भिः ॥ अध्वर्युभिः पञ्चभिः (Rig Veda III. 7. 7). नवभिर्वाजैर्नवतीच (Rig Veda X. 39. 10). सप्तभ्यो जायमानः (Rig Veda VIII. 96. 16). आदशभिर्विवस्वतः (Rig Veda VIII. 72. 8). Why do we say 'beginning with स् and भ्'? Observe, नवानां नवतीनाम् (Rig Veda I. 191. 13). Why do we say 'the penultimate syllable'? Observe आषड्भिर्हूयमानः (Rig Veda II. 18. 4) विश्वे देवैस्त्रिभिः (Rig Veda VIII. 35. 3).

३६८४ । विभाषा भाषायाम् । ६ । १ । १८१ ॥

उक्तविषये ।

3684. In the classical language this is optional.

The झलादि case-affixes coming after the above numerals षट्, त्रि and चतुर् may make the words so formed take the acute on the penultimate optionally, in the ordinary spoken language. Thus पंचँभिः or पंचभिँः । In the alternative, VI. 1. 179 applies. So also सप्तभिः or सप्तभिँः, तिसृँभिः or तिसृभिँः ॥

३६८५ । सर्वस्य सुपि । ६ । १ । १९१ ॥

सुपि परे सर्वशब्दस्यादिरुदात्तः स्यात् । 'सर्वे नन्दन्ति यशसा' ॥

3685. The acute is on the first syllable of *sarva* when the case-endings follow.

Thus सर्वे नन्दंति यशसा (Rig Veda X. 71. 10).

३६८६ । ञ्नित्यादिर्नित्यम् । ६ । १ । १९७ ॥

ञिदन्तस्य निदन्तस्य चाद्युदात्तः स्यात् । 'यस्मिन्विश्वानि पौंस्या' । पुंसः कर्मणि ब्राह्मणादित्वात्ष्यञ् । सुते दधिष्व नश्चनः' । चायतेरसुन् । 'चायेरन्ने ह्रस्वश्च' इति चकारादसुनो नुडागमश्च ॥

3686. Whatever is derived with an affix having an indicatory ञ् or न, has the acute invariably on the first syllable.

Thus यस्मिन् विश्वानि पौंस्या (Rig Veda I. 5. 9).

Here पौंस्य is from पुंस् with the affix ष्यञ् because it belongs to the Bráhmanâdi class. (V. 1. 124. S. 1788.)

सुते दधिष्व नश्चनः (Rig Veda I. 3. 6). Here चनः is derived from the root चायृ पूजानिशामनयोः with the affix असुन् (Uṇâdi IV. 199), which takes the augment नुट् also, by force of the word च 'and' in the sûtra above quoted (Uṇadi IV. 199), and then the य of चाय् is elided. चनस् means 'food.'

३६८७ । पथिमथोः सर्वनामस्थाने । ६ । १ । १९९ ॥

आदिरुदात्तः स्यात् । अयं पन्थाः । 'सर्वनामस्थाने' किम् । 'ज्योतिष्मतः पथो रक्ष' । उदात्तनिवृत्तिस्वरेणान्तोदात्तं पदम् ॥

3687. The acute accent is on the first syllable of *pathin* and *mathin* when followed by a strong case-ending.

The words पथिन् and मथिन् are derived by the Uṇâdi affix इनि, (IV. 12. and 13, and are oxytone by III. 1. 3. They become âdyudâtta before strong cases. Thus अयं पन्थाः (Rig Veda IV. 18. 1).

Why do we say 'when followed by a sarvanâmasthâna case-affix'? Observe 'ज्योतिष्मतः पथो रक्ष, (Rig Veda X. 53. 6). The accent is on the final by VI. 1. 162, there being elision of the udâtta इन् ॥

३६८८ । अन्तश्च तवै युगपत् । ६ । १ । २०० ॥

तवैप्रत्ययान्तस्याद्यन्तौ युगपदाद्युदात्तौ स्तः । 'हर्षसे दातवा उ' ॥

3688. The Infinitive in *tavai* has the acute on the first syllable and on the last syllable at one and the same time.

Thus हर्वे से दातवा उ (Rig Veda IV. 21. 9). This is an exception to III. 1. 3. by which त of तवे ought to have got the accent, and it also countermands rule VI. 1. 158. by which there can be only a single acute in a single word.

३६८९ । क्षयो निवासे । ६ । १ । २०१ ॥

आद्युदात्तः स्यात् । स्वे क्षये शुचिव्रत । क्षरत्यस्मिन् ॥

3689. The word *kshaya* has the acute on the first syllable in the sense of 'house, dwelling.'

Thus स्वेक्षये शुचिव्रत । (Rig Veda X. 118. 1). The word is formed by घ affix III. 1. 118. and would have had accent on the affix (III. 1. 3). When not meaning a house, we have : क्षयो वर्त्तते दस्यूनाम् । The word is formed by अच् (III. 2. 31).

३६९० । जयः करणम् । ६ । १ । २०२ ॥

करणवाची जयशब्द आद्युदात्तः स्यात् । जयत्यनेन जयोऽश्वः ॥

3690. The acute accent falls on the first syllable of *jaya*, in the sense of 'whereby one attains victory.'

Thus जयोऽश्वः, but otherwise जयो वर्त्तते ब्राह्मणानाम् । The former जय is by घ affix, (III. 1. 118), the second by अच् (III. 2. 31).

३६९१ । वृषादीनां च । ६ । १ । २०३ ॥

आदिरुदात्तः । आकृतिगणोऽयम् । 'वाजेभिर्वाजिनीवती' । 'इन्द्रं वाणीः' ॥

3691. The words *vrisha* &c., have the acute on the first syllable.

Thus वाजेभि र्वाजिनीवती (Rig. Veda I. 3. 10) इन्द्रंवाणीः (Rig Veda I. 7. 1). 1. वृषः, 2. जनः, 3. ज्वरः. 4. ग्रहः, 5. हयः, 6 गयः । These are formed by अच् (III. 1. 104). The word गय is from गै-गायते, irregularly it is treated as गे । 7. नयः, 8. तायः, 9. तयः, 10. चयः. 11. अमः. 12. वेदः, 13. सूदः, 14. वट., (formed by अच्, numbers 8 to 11 are not in Kasika). सूद is formed by क (III. 1. 135) 15. अंशः, 16. गुहा (formed by अङ् III. 3. 104). 17. शमरणौ संज्ञायां संमतौ भावकर्मणोः :—शमः and रणः, 18. मन्त्रः (formed by अच् III. 1. 134), 19. शान्तिः formed by क्तिच्, 20. कामः, 21. यामः, both formed by घञ्, 22, आरा, 23. धारा, 24. कारा, (all three formed by अङ् III. 3. 104), 25. वहः = गोचरादिषु formed by घञ्, 26, कल्प, 27. पादः formed by घञ्, which may either take the accent indicated by the affix or by VI. 1. 159, 28, पयः, 29. दवः । It is आकृतिगणः । All words which are acutely accented on the first, should be considered as belonging to this class, if their accent cannot be accounted for by any other rule.

1 वृषः, 2 जनः, 3 ज्वर, 4 ग्रहः. 5 हयः, 6 गयः. 7 नयः, 8 तायः. 9 तयः, 10 चयः*, 11 अमः*, 12 वेदः, 13 सूद *, 14 अंशः, 15 गुहा, 16 शमरणौ संज्ञायां संमतौ भावकर्मणोः, 17 मन्त्रः, 18 शान्तिः, 19 कामः, 20 यामः, 21 आरा, 22 धारा, 23 कारा, 24 वहः, 25 कल्पः, 26 पादः, 27 पयः, 28 दवः, 29 आकृतिगणः ॥

३६९२ । संज्ञायामुपमानम् । ६ । १ । २०४ ॥

उपमानशब्दः संज्ञायामाद्युदात्तः । चञ्चेव चञ्चा । कनोऽत्र लुप् । एतदेव ज्ञापयति ॥

'* क्वचित्स्वविधौ प्रत्ययलक्षणं न *' इति । 'संज्ञायाम्' किम् । अग्निर्माणवकः । 'उपमानम्' किम् । चैत्रः ॥

3692. The acute accent falls on the first syllable of that word with which something is likened, provided that it is a name.

Thus चँञ्चा, धँधिका खँरकुटी दाँसी। All these are उपमान words used as names of the उपमेय (the thing compared). The affix कन् (V. 3. 96) is elided here by V. 3. 98. It might be asked when कन् is elided, its mark, causing the first syllable to be acute (VI. 1. 197), will remain behind by virtue of I. 1. 62, where is then the necessity of this sûtra. The formation of this sûtra indicates the existence of the following maxim :—

Vârt:—The प्रत्ययलक्षण rule is not of universal application in the rules relating to accent.

When the word is not a Name, we have अग्निमाणवकः। When it is not an upamâna we have चैत्रः (VI. 2. 148).

३६९३ । निष्ठा च द्व्यजनात् । ६ । १ । २०५ ॥

निष्ठान्तस्य द्व्यचः संज्ञायामादिरुदात्तो न त्वाकारः। दत्तः। 'द्व्यचः' किम्। चिन्तितः। 'अनात्' किम्। त्रातः। 'संज्ञायाम्' इत्यनुवृत्तेर्नेह। कृतम्। हृतम् ॥

3693. A dissyllabic Participle in *ta* (Nishṭhâ), when a Name, has the acute on the first syllable, but not if the first syllable has an 'â.'

Thus गुँप्तः, बुँद्धः, दँत्तः। This debars the affix accent (III. 1. 3). In non-participles we have देवँः, भीमँः। In polysyllabic Participles we have चिन्तितँः, रचितँः। In Participles having long आ in the first syllable, we have, त्रातँः, आप्तँः। When the Participle is not a Name we have, कृतम्, हृतम् ॥

३६९४ । शुष्कधृष्टौ । ६ । १ । २०६ ॥

एतावाद्युदात्तौ स्तः। असंज्ञार्थमिदम्। 'अत्_सं न शुष्कम्'।

3694. Also शुष्क and धृष्ट have acute on the first syllable.

These are non-Names. Thus शुँष्क and धृँष्ट। अत्_सं न शुष्कम् (Rig Ve. 4. 4).

३६९५ । आशितः कर्ता । ६ । १ । २०७ ॥

कर्तृवाच्याशितशब्द आद्युदात्तः। 'कृषन्नित्फाल आशितम्' ॥

3695. The word आशित meaning 'having eaten has acute on the first syllable.

Thus 'कृषन्नित् फाल आशितम्' (Rig Veda X. 117. 7).

३६९६ । रिक्ते विभाषा । ६ । १ । २०८ ॥

रिक्तशब्दे वादिरुदात्तः। रिक्तः। संज्ञायां तु 'निष्ठा च द्व्यजनात्' (३६९३) इति नित्यमाद्युदात्तत्वं पूर्वविप्रतिषेधेन ॥

3696. The word *rikta* may have optionally the acute on the first syllable.

Thus रिँक्तः or रिक्तँः। But when it is a Name, then VI. 1. 205. S. 3693, will make it *always* first acute. No option is allowed then.

३६९७ । जुष्टार्पिते च च्छन्दसि । ६ । १ । २०९ ॥

आद्युदात्ते वा स्तः ॥

3697. In the Chhandas, the words 'Jushta' and 'arpita' have optionally the acute on the first syllable.

Thus जुष्टः or जुष्टः; अर्पितः or अर्पितः । In the classical literature the accent is always on the last syllable (III. 1. 3).

३६९८ । नित्यं मन्त्रे । ६ । १ । २१० ॥

एतत्सूत्रं शक्यमकर्तुम् । 'जुष्टो दमूनाः' । 'वलंर आहुरर्पितम्' इत्यादेः पूर्वेणैव सिद्धेः छन्दसि पाठस्य व्यवस्थिततया विपरीतापादनायोगात् । 'अर्पिताः षष्टिर्न चलाचलासः' इत्यान्तोदात्तदर्शनाच्च ॥

3698. In the Mantras, these words 'jushta' and 'arpita' have always the acute on the first syllable.

Thus जुष्टं देवानामर्पितं पितृणाम् । Some say that this rule applies only to जुष्ट and not to अर्पित ; in which option is allowed even in the Mantra : so that it has acute on the last in the Mantra even : *e. g.* तस्मिन्त्साकं त्रिशता न शंकवोऽर्पिताः ॥

This sûtra is superfluous. For in the examples जुष्टो दमूनाः (Rig Veda V. 4. 5). and वलंर आहुरर्पितम् &c., they will have acute on the first, by the preceding sûtra, for the employment of the word छन्दसि in that sûtra shows that in the Mantra the words have acute on the first, as opposed to the ordinary language. So these would never have been final acute. Moreover, in the Mantra, अर्पिताःषष्टिर्न चलाचलासः (Rig Veda I. 164. 48), we find that the word अर्पिताः is end-acute, and this also is an argument against the present sûtra. For it shows that in the Mantra, these words are not *invariably* first-acute.

३६९९ । युष्मदस्मदोर्ङसि । ६ । १ । २११ ॥

आदिरुदात्तः स्यात् । 'न हि ष स्तव नो मम' ॥

3699. The acute accent is on the first syllable of *yushmad* and *asmad* in the Genitive Singular.

This applies when the forms are मम and तव, and not मे and ते । Thus मम स्वम्, तव स्वम् । The word युष्मद् and अस्मद् are derived from युष and अस by adding the affix मदिक (Un. I. 139) युष्मद् + ङस् = युष्मद् + अश् (VII. 1. 27) = तव + अद् + अश् (VI. 2. 96) = तव + अश् (VII. 2. 90) = तव (VI. 1. 97). Here by VIII. 2. 5, व would have been udâtta, but the present sûtra makes त udâtta. So also with मम ॥

३७०० । ङयि च । ६ । १ । २१२ ॥

'तुभ्यं हिन्वानः' । 'मह्यं वातः पवताम्' ॥

3700. The acute accent is on the first syllable of *yushmad* and *asmad* in the Dative Singular.

Thus तुभ्यं हिन्वानः (Rig Veda II. 36. 1). मह्यं वातः पवताम् (Rig Veda X. 128. 2).

३७०१ । यतोऽनावः । ६ । १ । २१३ ॥

यत्प्रत्ययान्तस्य द्व्यच आदिरुदात्तः । नावं विना । 'युञ्जन्त्यस्य काम्यां' । कमेर्णिङन्तादचो यत् । 'अनावः' किम् । 'नवतिं नाव्यानाम्' ॥

3701. Whatever is formed by the affix *yat*, has, if it is a dissyllabic word, the acute on the first syllable, with the exception of 'nâvyah' from 'nau.'

The word द्व्यच is understood here from VI. 1. 205. Thus युञ्जन्त्यस्य काम्या (Rig Veda 1 6. 2). The काम्या is from कम् + णिङ + यत् । चेयम्, जेयम् (III. 1. 97); कण्ठ्यम्, ओष्ठ्यम् (V. 1. 6). This rule debars the Svarita accent required by तित् (VI. 1. 185). But नौ – नाव्यम् as नवतिं नाव्यानाम् (Rig Veda I. 121. 13). The rule does not apply to words of more than two syllables thus :—विकीर्ण्यम्, ललाट्यम् ॥

३७०२ । ईडवन्दवृशंसदुहां ण्यतः । ६ । १ । २१४ ॥

एषां ण्यदन्तानामादिरुदात्तः । 'ईड्यो नूतनैरुत' । 'आजुह्वान ईड्यो वन्द्यश्च' । 'श्रेष्ठं नो धेहि वार्यम्' । उक्थमिन्द्राय शंस्यम्' ॥

3702. The acute accent is on the first syllable of ईड्, वन्द्, वृ, शंस्, and दुह्, when they are followed by the affix 'nyat.'

Thus ईड्यम् वन्द्यम्, वार्यम्, शंस्यम्, दोह्या धेनुः ॥ The two letters ण् and त् being indicatory, the 'ṇyat' is not included in 'yat' of the last sûtra. The accent would be regulated by त् ॥ The accent of त् however is debarred by this rule. The वृ in the sûtra is वृङ् संभक्तौ of Kriyâdi class : the वृञ् of स्वादि class takes kyap affix. See III. 1. 109.

ईड्यो नूतनैरुत (Rig Veda I. 1. 2). आजुह्वान ईड्यो वन्द्यश्च (Rig Veda X. 110. 3) श्रेष्ठं नो धेहि वार्यम् (Rig Veda X. 24. 2). उक्थ मिन्द्राय शंस्य (Rig Veda I. 10. 5).

३७०३ । विभाषा वेण्विन्धानयोः । ६ । १ । २१५ ॥

आदिरुदात्तो वा । 'इन्धानो अग्निम्' ॥

3703. The acute accent is optionally on the first syllable of 'veṇu' and 'indhân.'

Thus इन्धानो अग्निम् (Rig Veda II. 25. 1), वेणुः or वेणुः, इन्धानः or इन्धानः or इन्धानः । The word वेणु is derived by the Uṇâdi affix णु (III. 38), which being a नित् would *always* have acute on the first. This allows an option. The word इन्धान, if it is formed by चानश् will have the accent on the final. If it is considered to be formed by शानच् the affix being a sârvadhâtuka is anudâtta and as it replaces udâtta final of the root, it becomes udâtta (VI. 1. 161), and thus इन्धान gets acute on the middle. It would never have acute on the first syllable, the present rule ordains that also. When वेणु is used as an upamâna वेणुरिव वेणुः, then it is *invariably* acutely accented on the first (VI. 1. 204).

३७०४ । त्यागरागहासकुहश्वठक्रथानाम् । ६ । १ । २१६ ॥

आदिरुदात्तो वा । आद्यास्रयो घञन्ताः । त्रयः पचाद्यजन्ता ॥

3704. The acute accent is optionally on the first syllables of त्याग, राग, हास, कुह, श्वठ and क्रथ ॥

Thus त्यागः, or त्यागः, रागः रागः, हासः हासः ॥ These are formed by घञ् affix and by VI. 1. 159 would take acute on the final, this ordains acute on the first syllable also. कुहः or कुहः, or श्वठः or श्वठः, क्रथः or क्रथः; formed by अच् (III. 1. 13).

३७०५ । मतोः पूर्वमात्संज्ञायां स्त्रियाम् । ६ । १ । २१९ ॥

मतोः पूर्वमाकार उदात्तः स्त्रीनाम्नि । उदुम्बरावती । शरावती ॥

3705. The 'â' before the affix 'mat' has the acute accent, when the word is a name in the Feminine Gender.

Thus उदुम्बरावती, पुष्करावती, शरावती (IV. 2. 85). The lengthening takes place by VI. 3. 120. वीरणावती ॥ Why do we say 'the आ'? Observe इक्षुमती, द्रुमवती ॥ The words इक्षु (Un. III. 157) and द्रुम (V. 2. 108) are end-acute, so the accent is on मतुप् by VI. 1. 176. Why do we say 'when a name'? Observe खट्वावती ॥ खट्वा is formed by क्वन् and has acute on the first (Un. I. 151). Why do we say 'in the Feminine Gender'? Observe शरावान् ॥ Why do we say 'when followed by मत्'? Observe गवादिनी ॥

३७०६ । अन्तोऽवत्याः । ६ । १ । २२० ॥

अवतीशब्दस्यान्त उदात्तः । वेत्रवती । ङीपः पित्त्वादनुदात्तत्वं प्राप्तम् ॥

3606. The Names ending in 'avati' have the acute accent on the last syllable.

Thus अजिरवती· खदिरवती, हंसवती, कारण्डवती ॥ These words being formed by ङीप् would have been unaccented on the final (III. 1. 4). Why do we use अवती and not वती? Then the rule would apply to राजवती also, for the word is really राजन्वती ending in अन्वत', the subsequent elision of न् is held to be non-valid for the purposes of the application of this rule (VIII. 2. 2). But the change of म into व (मत्=वत्) is considered asiddha for the purposes of this rule.

३७०७ । ईवत्याः । १ । १ । २२० ॥

ईवत्यन्तस्यापि प्राग्वत् । अहीवती । मुनीवती ॥

3707. The Names ending in îvatî have the acute on the last syllable.

Thus अहीवती ; मुनीवती ॥

अथ फिट् सूत्राणि ।

THE PHIT SUTRAS.

CHAPTER I.

१ । फिषोऽन्त उदात्तः ॥

प्रातिपदिकं फिट् । तस्यान्त उदात्तः स्यात् । उच्चैः ॥

1. A nominal stem is finally acute. As उच्चैः ॥ The word फिष् is the name of Nominal stems or Prâtipadikas, in the terminology of the ancient Grammarians.

२ । पाटलापालङ्काम्बासागरार्थानाम् ॥

एतदर्थानामन्त उदात्तः । 'पाटला' 'फलेरुहा' 'सुरूपा' 'पाकला' इति पर्यायाः । 'लघावन्ते–' इति प्राप्ते । 'अपालङ्क' 'व्याधिघात' 'आरेवत' 'आरग्वध' इति पर्यायाः । अम्बार्थाः । माता । 'उनर्वन्नन्तानाम्' इत्याद्युदात्तत्वे प्राप्ते । सागरः । समुद्रः ॥

2. The synonyms of पाटला, अपालङ्का, अम्बा and सागर are finally acute. Pâṭalâ is a kind of herb—पाटला, फलेरुहा, सुरूपा, पाकला ॥ By Phiṭ II. 19 the heavy vowel would have got the accent : this makes these end acute. So also अपालङ्क, व्याधिघात, अरिवत, and आरग्वध are synonymns meaning a kind of plant (Cassia fistula). So also अम्बा, माता । This last is an exception to Phiṭ II. 9. So also सागरः, समुद्रः ॥

३ । गेहार्थानामस्त्रियाम् ॥

गेहम् । 'नब्विषयस्य–' इति प्राप्ते । 'अस्त्रियाम्' किम् । शाला । आद्युदात्तोऽयम् । इहैव पर्युदासाज्ज्ञापकात् ॥

3. The words denoting house, are end-acute, provided they are not in the Feminine. This is an exception to Phiṭ II. 3. Thus गेहम् । Why do we say not in the Feminine ? Observe शाला which is first-acute, because of this prohibition.

४ । गुदस्य च ॥

अन्त उदात्तः स्यान्न तु स्त्रियाम् । गुदम् । 'अस्त्रियाम्' किम् । 'आन्त्रेभ्यस्ते गुदाभ्यः । स्वाङ्गशिटामदन्तानाम्' इत्यन्तरङ्गमाद्युदात्तत्वम् । ततष्टाप् ॥

4 So also the word गुद, but not in the feminine, is end-acute. As गुदम् । But in the feminine it is first-acute by Phiṭ II. 6. and then टाप् is added. As आन्त्रेभ्यस्ते गुदाभ्यः । (Rig Veda X. 136. 3).

५ । ध्यपूर्वस्य स्त्रीविषयस्य ॥

धकारयकारपूर्वो योऽन्त्योऽच स उदात्तः । अन्तर्धा । 'स्त्रीविषयवर्ण–' इति प्राप्ते । छाया माया । जाया । 'यान्तस्यान्त्यात्पूर्वम्' इत्याद्युदात्तत्वे प्राप्ते । 'स्त्री' इति किम् । बाह्यम् । यजन्तत्वादाद्युदात्तत्वम् । 'विषयग्रहणम्' किम् । इभ्या । क्षत्रिया । 'यतोऽनावः' (३७०१) इत्याद्युदात्त इभ्यशब्दः । क्षत्रियशब्दस्तु 'यान्तस्यान्त्यात्पूर्वम्' इति मध्योदात्तः ॥

5. A feminine word ending in a vowel and preceded by य् and व is end-acute; as अन्तर्वा । This is an exception to Phiṭ II. 20. So also कार्या, मार्या, जायां । This is an exception to III. 13 which would have made these first acute. Why feminine ? Observe वार्ह्यम् which is first-acute, because it ends in the affix यञ् । Why have we used the word विषय in the sûtra ? The rule is confined to those words only which are always feminine, and have no corresponding masculine form. Therefore, not here, इभ्या, क्षत्रिया । The word इभ्य is first-acute by VI. 1. 213, S. 3701. and क्षत्रिय is middle-acute by Phiṭ III. 13.

६ । खान्तस्याश्मादेः ॥

नखम् । उखा । सुखम् । दुःखम् । नखस्य 'स्वाङ्गशिटाम्–' इत्याद्युदात्तत्वे प्राप्ते । उखा नाम भाण्डविशेषः । तस्य कृत्रिमत्वात् 'खय्युवर्णं कृत्रिमाख्या चेत्' इत्युवर्णस्योदात्तत्वे प्राप्ते । सुखदुःखयोः 'नब्विषयस्य–' इति प्राप्ते । 'अश्मादेः' किम् । शिखा । मुखम् । मुखस्य 'स्वाङ्गशिटाम्–' इति 'नब्विषयस्य–' इति वा आद्युदात्तत्वम् । शिखायास्तु 'शीङः खो निद्ध्रस्वश्च' इत्युणादिषु नित्वोक्तेरन्तरङ्गत्वाट्टापः प्रागेव 'स्वाङ्गशिटाम्–' इति वा बोध्यम् ॥

6. A word ending in ख is end-acute, provided it does not begin with a श or म । Thus नखम्, सुखम्, दुःखम्, उखा । The word नख would have been first-acute by Phiṭ II. 6 ; सुख and दुःख would also have been first-acute by Phiṭ II. 3. The word उखा which means a pot would have been also first-acute by Phiṭ II. 8. because it is a manufactured article. Why do we say 'if not beginning with श or म'? Observe शिखा, मुखम्, governed by Phiṭ II. 6 or 3.

The word मुखं being the name of a part of the human body is first-acute by Phiṭ II. 6. Or because it is a Neuter noun, rule II. 3. of the Phiṭ Sûtras applies and makes it first-acute.

The word शिखा is formed by Uṇ. V. 24 with the addition of ख to the root शीङ् । The affix ख being expressly taught as नित् makes the word शिख first acute before the addition of the feminine टाप् as it is an antaraṅga operation, so the word शिखा is first acute. Or even by Phiṭ II. 6. it is first-acute.

७ । बंहिष्ठवत्सरतिशत्थान्तानाम् ॥

एषामन्त उदात्तः स्यात् । अतिशयेन बहुलो बंहिष्ठः । नित्त्वादाद्युदात्तत्वे प्राप्ते । 'बंहिष्ठैरश्वैः सुवृता रथेन' । 'यद्बंहिष्ठं नातिविधे' इत्यादौ व्यत्ययादाद्युदात्तः । संवत्सरः । अव्ययपूर्वपद प्रकृतिस्वरोऽत्रबाध्यत इत्याहुः । सप्ततिः । अशीतिः । 'लघावन्ते–' इति प्राप्ते । चत्वारिंशत् । इहापि प्राग्वत् । 'अभ्यूर्णुवाना प्रभृथस्यायोः' । अव्ययपूर्वपदप्रकृतिस्वरोऽत्र बाध्यत इत्याहुः । थाथादिसूत्रेण गतार्थमेतत् ॥

7. A word ending in ति, शत्, थ, as well as बंहिष्ठ and वत्सर are end-acute. Thus बंहिष्ठः (superlative of बहुल, the बंह is substituted by VI. 4. 157). It would have been first-acute, because of the नित् affix इष्ठन् (V. 3. 55). In बंहिष्ठैरश्वैः सुवृता रथेन ; यद्बंहिष्ठं नातिविधे, (Rig Veda V. 62. 9), the word is first-acute anomalously. In the word संवत्सरः, VI. 2. 2. is debarred, by which the first member would have retained its accent in an Indeclinable compound. With ति we have सप्ततिः, अशीतिः । This debars Phiṭ II. 19. With शत्, we have चत्वारिंशत् । Here also Phiṭ II. 19 is set aside. As regards words ending in थ

Pâṇini VI. 2. 144. would govern them; as अभ्युपर्धान । प्रभृथस्यायोः । (Rig Veda V. 41. 19). Śâkaṭâyana's sûtra, therefore, is superfluous so far.

८ । दक्षिणस्य साधौ ॥

अन्त उदात्तः स्यात् । साधुत्वाचित्वाभावे तु व्यवस्थायां सर्वनामतया 'स्वाङ्गशिटाम्–' इत्याद्युदात्तः । अर्थान्तरे तु 'लघावन्ते–' इति गुरुरुदात्तः । 'दक्षिणः सरलोदारपरच्छन्दानुवर्तिषु' इति कोशः ॥

8. The word दक्षिण is end-acute when meaning 'skilful.' As वीणायां दक्षिणः प्रवीणः । When it has not this significance, it will be first-acute, if it be a Pronoun meaning 'south,' 'right hand.' In this case Phiṭ II 6 would apply. In any other case Phiṭ II. 19 would govern it. The word dakshiṇa has other meanings, as 'sincere, courteous, submissive, &c.'

९ । स्वाङ्गाख्यायामादिर्वा ॥

इह दक्षिणस्याद्यन्तौ पर्यायेणोदात्तौ स्तः । दक्षिणो बाहुः । 'आख्याग्रहणम्' किम् । प्रत्यङ्मुखस्यासीनस्य वामपाणिर्दक्षिणो भवति ॥

9. The first-syllable of दक्षिण is optionally acute, when it is the name of a limb. When it means right hand, it may be either end-acute or first acute. As दक्षिणो बाहुः or दक्षिणो बाहु । Why is the word âkhyâ used in the sûtra? In order to prevent the application of the rule to the 'left' hand, though in one case it will be called dakshiṇa, if a person sits facing west, for then his left hand will point towards dakshiṇa or south, and may be called dakshiṇa bâhu or the arm pointing towards south.

१० । छन्दसि च ॥

अस्वाङ्गार्थमिदम् । दक्षिणः । इह पर्यायेणाद्यन्तावुदात्तौ ॥

10. In the Chhandas also the word dakshiṇa may be either first or end-acute. This is the case even when it does not mean right arm. As दक्षिणाश्वं दक्षिणा गां ददाति दक्षिणा चन्द्रमुत यद्धिरण्यं दक्षिणान्नं वनुते यो न आत्मा दक्षिणां वर्म कृणुते विजानन् । (Rig Veda X. 107. 7).

११ । कृष्णस्यामृगाख्या चेत् ॥

अन्त उदात्तः । 'वर्णानान्तण–' इत्याद्युदात्तत्वे प्राप्ते अन्तोदात्तो विधीयते । कृष्णानां व्रीहीणाम् । 'कृष्णो नो नाव वृषभः' । मृगाख्यायां तु । कृष्णो रात्र्यै ॥

11. The word कृष्ण is end-acute, if it is not the name of an animal. This is an exception to Phiṭ II. 10. As कृष्णानां व्रीहीणाम् । कृष्णो नो नाव वृषभः । But when denoting a wild animal, we have कृष्णो रात्र्यै ॥

१२ । वा नामधेयस्य ॥

कृष्णस्येत्येव । 'अयं वां कृष्णो अश्विना' । कृष्णर्षिः ॥

12. Optionally so, when Krishṇa is a Proper Name. As अयं वां कृष्णो अश्विना हवते वाजिनीवसू (Rig. VIII. 85. 3).

'The Rishi Krishṇa invokes you two, O Asvinas! O Lords of riches.'

१३ । शुक्लगौरयोरादिः ॥

नित्यमुदात्तः स्यादित्येके । वेत्यनुवर्तत इति तु युक्तम् । 'सरो गौरो यथापिब वा' इत्यत्रान्तोदात्तदर्शनात् ॥

13. The first-syllable of शुक्र and गौर is acute. Some say it is a compulsory rule and not an optional one. Others read the anuvṛitti of वा into it and make it optional. According to the first opinion, the rule is confined to Proper Names : and therefore in सरो गौरो यथापिब वा (Ṛig Veda VIII. 45. 24), it is properly end-acute, as it is not a Name.

१४ । अङ्गुष्ठोदकबकवशानां छन्दस्यन्तः ॥

अङ्गुष्ठस्य 'स्वाङ्गानामकुर्वादीनाम्' इति द्वितियस्योदात्तत्वे प्राप्तेऽन्तोदात्तार्थ आरम्भः । वशायहणं नियमार्थं छन्दस्येवेति । तेन लोक आद्युदात्तेत्याहुः ॥

14. The finals of अङ्गुष्ठ उदक, बक and वशा are acute in the Chhandas. The word अङ्गुष्ठ would have been middle-acute by Phiṭ III. 3, this ordains final-acute. So also with बकं । It would have been first-acute by Phiṭ II. 7. The word वशा is employed for the sake of niyama : it is end-acute in the Vedas only; in the classical language, it is first-acute.

१५ । पृष्ठस्य च ॥

छन्दस्यन्त उदात्तः स्याद्वा भाषायाम् । पृष्ठम् ॥

15. And the word पृष्ठ is end-acute in the Chhandas. In the classical language, it is optionally so, *i.e.*, it is first-acute also by Phiṭ II. 6. As पृष्ठम् or पृष्ठम् ॥

१६ । अर्जुनस्य तृणाख्या चेत् ॥

'उनर्वन्नन्तानाम्' इत्याद्युदात्तस्यापवादः ॥

16. अर्जुन is end-acute, if it is the name of straw. This is an exception to Phiṭ II. 9. Why do we say 'when it is the name of straw'? Observe अर्जुनो वृक्षः where it is first-acute by Phiṭ. II. 9.

१७ । अर्यस्य स्वाम्याख्या चेत् ॥

'यान्तस्यान्त्यात्पूर्वम्' इति 'यतोऽनावः' (३७०१) इति वाद्युदात्ते प्राप्ते वचनम् ॥

17. अर्य is end-acute, when it means 'master.' Otherwise it is first-acute by Phiṭ III. 13 or Pâṇini VI. 1. 213 S. 3701. See also Pâṇini III. 1. 103 for the word अर्य and its vârtika.

१८ । आशाया अदिगाख्या चेत् ॥

दिगाख्याव्यावृत्त्यर्थमिदम् । अत एव ज्ञापकाद्दिक्पर्यायस्याद्युदात्तता । 'इन्द्र आशाभ्यस्परि' ॥

18. आशा is end-acute, if it is not the name of a direction. This implies that when आशा means 'direction' then it is first-acute. As इन्द्र आशाभ्यस्परि सर्वाभ्यो अभयं करत् । जेता शत्रून् विचर्षणिः । (Rig. II. 41. 12). 'May the wise Indra, conqueror of enemies, make us free from fear from all directions or sides.' Here आशा means direction.

१९ । नक्षत्राणामाब्विषयाणाम् ॥

अन्त उदात्तः स्यात् । आश्लेषानुराधादीनां 'लघावन्ते-' इति प्राप्ते ज्येष्ठाश्रविष्ठाधनिष्ठानामिष्ठन्नन्तत्वेनाद्युदात्ते प्राप्ते वचनम् ॥

19. The names of Asterisms, which take the feminine affix आ, are end-acute. The asterisms आश्लेषा, अनुराधा, &c. would have been otherwise governed by Phiṭ II. 19; while ज्येष्ठा, धविष्ठा, धनिष्ठा, being formed by इष्ठन्, would have been first-acute by नित् accent.

२० । न कुपूर्वस्य कृत्तिकाख्या चेत् ॥

अन्त उदात्तो न । कृत्तिका नक्षत्रम् । केचित्तु कुपूर्वो य आप् तद्विषयाणामिति व्याख्याय 'आर्यिका' 'बहुलिका' इत्यत्राप्यन्तोदात्तो नेत्याहुः ॥

20. Not so, if the final letter is का and the asterism is the name of Kṛttikâ. The final of कृत्तिका is not acute; it is first-acute by Phiṭ II. 19. As कृत्तिका नक्षत्रम् । Others hold that the words ending in का in the feminine are not end-acute; and they mention आर्यिका, बहुलिका ॥

२१ । घृतादीनां च ॥

अन्त उदात्तः । 'घृतं मिमिक्षे' आकृतिगणोऽयम् ॥

21. घृत and the rest are end-acute. As घृतं मिमिक्षे घृतमस्य योनिर्घृते श्रितो घृतम्वस्य धाम (Rig. II. 3. 11). 'I sprinkle ghee on fire, ghee is its birth-place, ghee is its abode of rest, and ghee its luminosity &c.' This is an Akṛtigaṇa: all words which are end-acute, and do not fall under any other rule, should be classified under the Ghṛitâdi class.

२२ । ज्येष्ठकनिष्ठयोर्वयसि ॥

अन्त उदात्तः स्यात् । 'ज्येष्ठ आह चमसा' । 'कनिष्ठ आह चतुरः' । 'वयसि' किम् । ज्येष्ठः श्रेष्ठः । कनिष्ठोऽल्पिकः । इह नित्त्वादाद्युदात्त एव ॥

22. ज्येष्ठ and कनिष्ठ are end-acute when meaning 'age—oldest and youngest.' As ज्येष्ठ आह चमसा द्वा करेति कनीयान् त्रीन् कृणवामेत्याह । कनिष्ठ आह चतुरस्करेति त्वष्ट ऋभवस्तत् पनयद्वचो वः । (Rig. IV. 33. 5) । Here ज्येष्ठ means the 'eldest,' and refers to Ṛibhu, कनीयान् refers to his *younger* brother Bibhvâ, and कनिष्ठ refers to the youngest brother Vâja. ज्य in ज्येष्ठ here is the substitute of वृद्ध (V. 3. 62) and कन for युवन् in कनिष्ठः by V. 3. 64. Why do we say 'when meaning age'? Observe ज्येष्ठ = श्रेष्ठ derived from प्रशस्य (V. 3. 61), and कनिष्ठ from अल्प (V. 3. 64) = अल्पिकः । These are first-acute by नित् accent. The present sûtra is thus an exception to नित् accent.

२३ । बिल्वतिष्ययोः स्वरितो वा ॥

अनयोरन्तः स्वरितो वा स्यात् । पक्ष उदात्तः ॥

इति फिट्सूत्रेषु प्रथमः पादः ॥

23. The finals of बिल्व and तिष्य are optionally svarita. In the other alternative they will be acute. As बिल्व or बिल्व, तिष्य or तिष्य ॥

CHAPTER II.

१ । अथादिः प्राक् शकटेः ॥

अधिकारोऽयम् । 'शकटिशकट्योः—' इति यावत् ॥

1. From this up to the end of Chapter III, the word आदि exerts the governing influence. From this sútra up to शकटिशकट्य (IV. 1) exclusive, the accent is on the first syllable of the words taught.

२ । ह्रस्वान्तस्य स्त्रीविषयस्य ॥

आदिरुदात्तः स्यात् । बलिः । तनुः ॥

2. A word ending in a light vowel, and used always in the feminine, is first-acute. As वलिः, तनुः ॥

३ । नब्विषयस्यानिसन्तस्य ॥

'वने न वा यः' । इसन्तस्य तु सर्पिः । नबनपुंसकम् ॥

3. An invariable neuter noun, with the exception of one ending in इस्, is first-acute. The word नप् means नपुंसक or Neuter. As वने न वाय: (Rig Veda X. 29. 1). But सर्पिस्, शुचिस्, अर्चिस् &c. ending in इस् are end-acute.

४ । तृणधान्यानां च द्व्यषाम् ॥

द्व्यचामित्यर्थः । कुशाः । काशाः । माषाः । तिलाः । बह्वचां तु गोधूमाः ॥

4. Words denoting 'straw' and 'grain' are first-acute when consisting of two syllables. The word द्व्यष् = द्व्यच् । As कुशाः, काशाः, माषाः, तिलाः । But गोधूमाः is acute on the middle by Phit II. 19. The word अष् is the Name given to vowels by Ancient Grammarians.

५ । त्रः संख्यायाः ॥

पञ्च । चत्वारः ॥

5. A Numeral ending in न् or र् is first-acute. As पञ्च, चत्वारः । In चत्वारः the word is middle-acute by आम accent; see Pâṇini VII. 1. 98. The proper example is चतुष्कपालः । For चतुरः is end acute by VI. 1. 167, चतुर्भिः is middle-acute by VI. 1. 180. चतुर्णाम् is governed by VI. 1. 179. Hence example of a compound : which is first acute by VI. 2. 29.

६ । स्वाङ्गशिटामदन्तानाम् ॥

शिट् सर्वनाम । 'कर्णाभ्यां छुबुकादधि' । 'ओष्ठाविव मधु' । 'विश्वो विहायाः' ॥

6. The words denoting bodily organs and ending in अ, as well as the Pronouns are first-acute. The शिट् is the name given to Pronouns (सर्वनाम) by ancient Grammarians. As कर्णाभ्यां छुबुकादधि, (Rig Veda X. 163. 1); ओष्ठाविव मधुः, (Rig Veda II. 39. 6) विश्वो विहायाः (Rig Veda I. 28. 6).

७ । प्राणिनां कुपूर्वम् ॥

कवर्गात्पूर्व आदिरुदात्तः । काकः । वृकः । 'शुकेषु मे' । प्राणिनाम् किम् ? चीरं सर्पिर्मधूदकम् ॥

7. The syllable preceding the क is acute in the names of animate beings. Thus काकः, वृकः, शुकेषुमे (Rig Veda I. 50. 12). Why do we say 'of living beings'? Observe चीरं सर्पिर्मधूदकम । (Rig Veda IX. 67. 32). Here उदक is end-acute by Phit II. 14.

८। खय्युवर्णं कृत्रिमाख्या चेत् ॥

खयि परे उवर्णमुदात्तं स्यात्। कन्दुकः॥

8. The उ preceding a खय् (the surd letter) is acute, when the word is the name of an artificial thing. As कन्दु॑कः ॥

९। उनर्वन्नन्तानाम् ॥

उन्। 'वरु॑णं वो रिशाद॑सम्'। ऋ। 'स्वसा॑रं त्वा कृणवै'। वन्। 'पीवा॑नं मेषम्' ॥

9. The words ending in उन, ऋ, and वन् are first acute. As उनः—वरुणं वो रिशा॑सम् (Rig Veda V. 64. 1). ऋ—स्वसा॑रं त्वा कृणवै (Rig Veda X. 108. 9). वन्-पीवा॑नं मेषम् (Rig Veda X. 27 17).

१०। वर्णानां तणतिनितान्तानाम् ॥

आदिरुदात्तः। एतः। हरिणः। शितिः। पृश्निः। हरित् ॥

10. Words denoting color are first-acute, when they end in त, ण, ति, नि and त्। Thus ए॑तः, ह॑रिणः, शि॑तिः, पृ॑श्निः, ह॑रित् ॥

११। ह्रस्वान्तस्य ह्रस्वमनृत्ताच्छील्ये ॥

ऋद्वर्जं ह्रस्वान्तस्यादिभूतं ह्रस्वमुदात्तं स्यात्। मुनिः।

11. The initial short vowel is udâtta when the word ends with a short vowel, and denotes 'habit': but not so when the initial vowel is short ऋ। As मु॑निः। But not so in ऋतुः ॥

१२। अक्षस्यादेवनस्य ॥

आदिरुदात्तः। 'तस्य नाक्षः'। देवने तु। 'अक्षैर्मा दीव्यः' ॥

12. The word अक्ष is first-acute, when not meaning 'to gamble.' As तस्य नाक्षः (Rig Veda I. 164. 13). But when it means देवन् or play, we have अक्षैर्मा दी॑व्य। (Rig Veda X. 34. 13).

१३। अर्धस्यासमद्योतने ॥

अर्धो ग्रामस्य। समेंऽशके तु अर्धं पिप्पल्याः ॥

13. The word अर्ध is first-acute when meaning 'not equal.' As अ॑र्धो ग्रामस्य. But when it denotes *equal* portions, *i. e.* when it means 'half': we have अर्धं पिप्पल्याः ॥

१४। पीतद्वर्थानाम् ॥

आदिरुदात्तः। पीतद्रुः। सरलः ॥

14. The words denoting पीतद्रु or yellow-trees are first-acute. As पी॑तद्रुः। स॑रलः ॥

१५। ग्रामादीनां च ॥

ग्रामः। सोमः। यामः ॥

15. The words ग्राम and the rest are first-acute. As ग्रा॑मः, सो॑मः, या॑मः ॥

१६। लुबन्तस्योपमेयनामधेयस्य ॥

चञ्चेव चञ्चा। 'स्फिगन्तस्य' इति पाठान्तरम्। स्फिगिति लुपः प्राचां संज्ञा ॥

16. The words ending in a लुप् elided-affix denoting the name of the thing compared are first-acute. Another reading is हिफगन्तस्य । The हिफक् is the name given by Eastern Grammarians to लुप् elision. Thus चँञ्चा in which the affix कन् (V. 3. 96) is elided by V. 3. 98. Why do we say 'a लुप् ending word'? Observe अग्निर्माणवकः ॥

१७ । न वृक्षपर्वतविशेषव्याघ्रसिंहमहिषाणाम् ॥

एषामुपमेयनाम्नामादिरुदात्तो न । ताल इव तालः । मेरुरिव मेरुः । व्याघ्रः । सिंहः । महिषः ॥

17. The words denoting trees and mountains, and the words व्याघ्र, सिंह and महिष are not first-acute when objects of comparison. The word विशेष qualifies वृक्ष and पर्वत, and means *species* of trees and mountains, and not the word-forms वृक्ष and पर्वत । व्याघ्र &c., are word-forms. Thus ताल इव तालः, मेरुरिव मेरुः, व्याघ्रः, सिंहः, महिषः । But when we have वृक्ष इवायं वृक्षः, पर्वत इवायं पर्वतः, then these two words would be first-acute by the preceding sûtra.

१८ । राजविशेषस्य यमन्वा चेत् ॥

यमन्वा वृद्धः । आङ्गामुदाहरणम् । अङ्गाः प्रत्युदाहरणम् ॥

18. The name of any particular kingdom, ending with a लुप् elided comparative affix, is first-acute, provided that the word has a Vṛiddhi letter in its first syllable. The word यमन्वा = वृद्ध । Thus आँङ्गः, but अङ्गाः is counter-example, because it is not a Vṛiddham.

१९ । लघावन्ते द्वयोश्च बह्वषो गुरुः ॥

अन्ते लघौ द्वयोश्च लघ्वोः सतोर्बह्वच्कस्य गुरुरुदात्तः । कल्याणः । कोलाहलः ॥

19. A word whose final syllable is light, or a polysyllabic word whose two syllables are light, gets the acute on the heavy syllable, wherever that may be. Thus कँल्याण or कल्याँणः; कोँलाहलः or कोलाँहलः ॥

२० । स्त्रीविषयवर्णाक्षुपूर्वाणाम् ॥

एषां त्रयाणामाद्युदात्तः । स्त्रीविषयम् । मल्लिका । वर्णः । श्येनी । हरिणी । अक्षुशब्दात्पूर्वोऽस्त्येषां त अक्षुपूर्वाः । तरक्षुः ॥

20. The words which are invariably feminine, the words denoting color and words standing before the word अक्षु are first-acute. Feminine words; as—मँल्लिका; denoting color, as — श्येणी, हँरिणी ; followed by अक्षु as—तँरक्षुः ॥

२१ । शकुनीनां च लघु पूर्वम् ॥

पूर्वं लघु उदात्तं स्यात् । कुक्कुटः । तित्तिरिः ॥

21. The words denoting birds have the acute on the light syllable preceding the final. Thus कुक्कुटः, तित्तिरिः ॥

२२ । नर्तुप्राण्याख्यायाम् ॥

यथालक्षणं प्राप्तमुदात्तत्वं न । वसन्तः । कृकलासः ॥

22. The rules relating to acute accent mentioned, however, do not apply to the names of seasons and animals. As वसन्तः । कृकलासः ॥

२३ । धान्यानां च वृद्धक्षान्तानाम् ॥

आदिरुदात्तः । कान्तानाम् । श्यामाकाः । षान्तानाम् । राजमाषाः ॥

23. The words denoting the names of corns, and having a Vriddhi vowel in their first syllable and ending with a क or a ष, are first-acute. Thus श्यामाकाः, राजमाषाः ending in क and ष respectively. These are names of corns. These are the examples given by the author of the Siddhânta Kaumudi. श्यामाकाः is however governed by Phiṭ III. 18. नैवादकाः would be a better example. According to another recension, the word च does not occur in the sûtra. In the Phit-vritti the sûtra is explained as meaning 'The heavy vowel of words denoting corn is acute, &c.' Thus the accent may be नैँवादकाः or नैवाँदकाः, काँलाचाः or कालाँचाः ॥

२४ । जनपदशब्दानामषान्तानाम् ॥

आदिरुदात्तः । केकयः ॥

24. The words denoting countries and ending in a vowel, are first-acute. As केँकयः । According to some, the accent of this word is governed by Phiṭ II. 13 Their examples are अँङ्गाः, वँङ्गाः ॥

२५ । हयादीनामसंयुक्तलान्तानामन्तः पूर्वे वा ॥

हयिति हल्संज्ञा । पललम् । शललम् । 'हयादीनाम्' किम् ? एकलः । 'असंयुक्त-' इति किम् ? मल्लः ॥

25. A word beginning with a consonant, and ending with the letter ल, not being a conjunct consonant, has acute on the first syllable, or optionally on the penultimate syllable. Thus पँललम् or पलँलम्, शलँलम्, or शँललम् । The word. ह in the sûtra is equivalent to हल् । Why do we say 'beginning with a हल्'? Observe एकलः । Why do we say 'a non-conjunct ल'? See मल्लः । Some read the anuvritti of the word जनपदानां into this sûtra. They give the examples पञ्चालाः, कोशलाः and the counter-example पलालम् ॥

२६ । इगन्तानां च द्व्यषाम् ॥

आदिरुदात्तः । कृषिः ॥

इति फिट्सूत्रेषु द्वितीय पादः ॥

26. A word ending in इ, उ ऋ or ऌ long or short, is first-acute, when it consists of two syllables. Thus कृँषिः । Some read the anuvritti of the word जनपदानाम् into this sûtra: and so their examples are कुँरवः and चेदयः (कुरु and चेदि), and their counter-example is कृषिँ । Because कृषिः is found to be end-acute in अक्षै मा दीव्यः कृषिमित्कृषस्व (Rig Veda X. 34. 13).

CHAPTER III.

१ । अथ द्वितीयं प्रागीषात् ॥

'ईषान्तस्य हयादेः-' इत्यतः प्राग्द्वितीयाधिकारः ॥

1. Up to ईषान्तस्य &c, (III. 17) exclusive, the words 'second syllable' have governing force. In all rules up to sûtra 16 inclusive of this Chapter, the words 'second syllable' should be supplied.

२ । त्र्यचां प्राङ्मकरात् ॥

'मकरवरुढ–' इत्यतः प्राक् त्र्यचामित्यधिकारः ॥

2. 'Of a word consisting of three syllables' is the phrase to be supplied in the following sûtras up to मकर &c. Sûtra 8.

३ । स्वाङ्गानामकुर्वादीनाम् ॥

कवर्गरेफवकारादीनि वर्जयित्वा त्र्यचां स्वाङ्गानां द्वितीयमुदात्तम् । ललाटम् । कुर्वादीनां तु कपोलः । रसना । वदनम् ॥

3. Words consisting of three syllables and denoting limbs (or bodily organs) get the acute on their second syllable, provided that they do not begin with a guttural, a र or a व। As ललाटम् । But the guttural-beginning कपोलः is middle acute by Phiṭ II. 19 and रसना and वदनं are first-acute by Phiṭ II. 6.

४ । मादीनां च ॥

मलयः । मकरः ॥

4. A trisyllabic word beginning with म has acute on the second syllable; As मलयः । मकरः । महेन्द्रः ॥

५ । शादीनां शाकानाम् ॥

शीतन्या । शतपुष्पा ॥

5. A tri-syllabic word beginning with श and denoting vegetables, has acute on the second. As शीतन्या । शतपुष्पा । Some read the sûtra as सादीनाम् and illustrate it by सर्षपा ॥

६ । पान्तानां गुर्वादीनाम् ॥

पादपः । आतपः । लघ्वादीनां तु । अनूपम् । द्व्यचां तु । नीपम् ॥

6. A tri-syllabic word ending in प and beginning with a heavy syllable has acute on the second. As पादपः, आतपः । But अनूपम् (VI. 2. 189), because the first-syllable is light: and नीपम् (VI. 2. 192), because the word consists of two syllables.

७ । युतान्यण्यन्तानाम् ॥

युते । अयुतम् । अनि । धमनिः । अणि । विपणि ॥

7. A tri-syllabic word ending in युत, अनि and अणि has acute on the second. As अयुतम्, धमनिः, विपणी ॥

८ । मकरवरूढपारेवतवितस्तेक्ष्वार्जिद्राक्षाकलोमाकाष्ठापेष्ठाकाशीनामादिर्वा ॥

एषामादिर्द्वितीयो वोदात्तः । मकरः । वरुढ इत्यादि ॥

8. Either the first or the second syllable of these may have the acute: मकर (or मकर), वरूढ (or वरूढ), पारेवत (or पारेवत), वितस्त (or वितस्त), इक्षु (or इक्षु), आर्जि (or आर्जि), द्राक्षा (or द्राक्षा), कला (or कला), उमा (or उमा), काष्टा (or काष्ठा), पेष्ठा (or पेष्ठा), काशी (or काशी) ॥

९। छन्दसि च ॥

अमकराद्यर्थं आरम्भः। लक्ष्यानुसारादादिर्द्वितीयं वोदात्तं ज्ञेयम् ॥

9. In the Chhandas, several other words than मकर &c., have acute either on the first or on the second.

१०। कर्दमादीनां च ॥

आदिर्द्वितीयं वोदात्तम् ॥

10. The words कर्दमा &c., have acute either on the first or on the second. As कर्दमा (or कर्दमा), कुलटा (or कुलटा), उदकः or उदकः, गान्धारिः or गान्धारिः ॥

११। सुगन्धितेजनस्य ते वा ॥

आदिर्द्वितीयं तेशब्दश्चेति त्रयः पर्यायेणोदात्ताः। सुगन्धितेजनाः ॥

11. The first, second or the fourth syllable of सुगन्धितेजन may get the acute-accent. ते means the syllable ते of this word. Thus सुगन्धितेजनाः or सुगन्धि-तेजनाः or सुगन्धितेजनाः ॥

१२। नपः फलान्तानाम् ॥

आदिर्द्वितीयं वोदात्तम्। राजादनफलम् ॥

12. Of a neuter noun ending in फल, the first or the second syllable may be acute. The word नप् means नपुंसक or Neuter. Thus राजादनफलम् or राजा-दनफलम् ॥

१३। यान्तस्यान्त्यात्पूर्वम् ॥

कुलायः ॥

13. A word ending in य has acute on the syllable preceding such य। As कुलायः ॥

१४। थान्तस्य च नालघुनी ॥

नाशब्दो लघु च उदात्ते स्तः। सनाथा सभा ॥

14. A word-ending in थ has acute on the syllable ना (if any) and on the light syllable that may immediately precede it. As सनाथा सभा। Others read this sûtra as आन्तस्य च नः लघुनी 'a word ending in आ and having ना or a light syllable preceding such आ has acute on such ना and the light vowel.' They give examples of नैना, दिवा, सुधा ॥

१५। शिशुमारोदुम्बरबलीवर्दोष्ट्रारपुरूरवसां च ॥

अन्त्यात्पूर्वमुदात्तं द्वितीयं वा ॥

15. The following words have acute either on the penultimate or the second syllable:—शिशुमारः (or शिशुमारः or शिंशुमारः or शिंशुमारः), उदुम्बरः (or उदुम्बरः), बलीवर्दः (or बलीवर्दः), उष्ट्रारः (another reading is उष्टारः), पुरूरवस् (or पुरूरवस्).

१६। सांकाश्यकाम्पिल्यनासिक्यदार्वाघाटानाम् ॥

द्वितीयमुदात्तं वा ॥

16. The second syllables of the following are optionally acute. सांकाश्यः (formed by ण्य of IV. 2. 80); so also काम्पिल्यः, नासिक्यः, and दार्वाघाटः। See Vârtika दारावाहन under III. 2. 49, S. 2966.

१७ । ईषान्तस्य हयादेरादिर्वा ॥

हलीषा । लाङ्गलीषा ॥

17. A word ending in ईषा and beginning with a consonant, may optionally have acute on the first syllable. As हलीषा, लाङ्गलीषा ॥

१८ । उशीरदाशेरकपालपलालशैवालश्यामाकशरीरशरावहृदयहिरण्यारण्यापत्यदेवराणाम् ॥

एषामादिरुदात्तः स्यात् ॥

18. The following have acute on the first उशीरः, दाशेरः, कपालः, पलालः शैवाल, श्यामाक, शरीर, शराव, हृदय, हिरण्य, अरण्य, अपत्य, देवर ॥

१९ । महिष्याषाढयोर्जायेष्टकाख्या चेत् ॥

आदिरुदात्तः । महिषी जाया । आषाढा उपदधाति ॥

इति फिट्सूत्रेषु तृतीयः पादः ॥

19. The word महिषी when meaning 'queen,' and आषाढा when it is the name of a sacrifice are first acute. As महिषी जाया । आषाढा उपदधाति ॥

CHAPTER IV.

१ । शकटिशकट्योरक्षरमक्षरं पर्यायेण ॥

उदात्तम् । शकटिः । शकटी ॥

1. Every syllable of the words शकटि and शकटी is acute by turns. Thus शकटिः, शकटिः, शकटिः । शकटीः, शकटीः and शकटीः ॥

२ । गोष्ठजस्य ब्राह्मणनामधेयस्य ॥

अक्षरमक्षरं पर्यायेणोदात्तम् । गोष्ठजो ब्राह्मणः । अन्यत्र गोष्ठजः पशुः । कृदुत्तरपदप्रकृतिस्वरेणान्तोदात्तः ॥

2. So also the word गोष्ठज, when it is the name of a Brâhmaṇa. As गोष्ठजः, गोष्ठजः or गोष्ठजो ब्राह्मणः । Otherwise it will be always end-acute by कृदुत्तरपदप्रकृतिस्वर (VI. 2. 139), as गोष्ठजः पशुः ॥

३ । पारावतस्योपोत्तमवर्जम् ॥

शेषं क्रमेणोदात्तम् । पारावतः ॥

3. So also the word पारावत, with the exception of its penultimate syllable. As पारावतः, पारावतः and पारावतः । But the penultimate syllable व is never acute.

४ । धूम्रजानुमुञ्जकेशकालवालस्थालीपाकानामधूजलस्थानाम् ॥

एषां चतुर्णां धूम्रभृतींश्चतुरो वर्जयित्वा शिष्टानि क्रमेणोदात्तानि । धूम्रजानुः । मुञ्जकेशः । कालवालः । स्थालीपाकः ॥

4. So also the words धूम्रजानु with the exception of धू, मुंजकेश with the exception of ज, कालवाल with the exception of ल, and स्थालीपाक with the exception of स्था get acute in turn on every syllable. Thus धूम्रजानुः, धूम्रजानुः, धूम्रजानुः ।

मुंञ्जकेशः, मुंञ्जकेशः, मुञ्जकेशः। कालवालः, कालवालः। स्थालीपाकः, स्थालीपाकः or स्थालीपाकः॥

५। कपिकेशहरिकेशयोश्छन्दसि॥

कपिकेशः। हरिकेशः॥

5. In the Chhandas, the words कपिकेश and हरिकेश get acute on every syllable in turn. As कपिकेशः, कपिकेशः, कपिकेशः, कपिकेशः। So also with हरिकेशः॥

६। न्यङ्स्वरौ स्वरितौ॥

स्पष्टम्। न्यङ्तानः। 'व्यचक्षयत्स्वः'॥

6. The words न्यङ् and स्वर् have svarita accent. As न्यङ्तानः। व्यचक्षयत स्वः (Rig Veda II. 24. 3).

७। न्यर्बुदव्यल्कशयोरादिः॥

स्वरितः स्यात्॥

7. The first syllables of न्यर्बुद and व्यल्कश are svarita.

८। तिल्यशिक्यमर्त्यकार्म्यधान्यकन्याराजन्यमनुष्याणामन्तः॥

स्वरितः स्यात्। तिलानां भवनं क्षेत्रं तिल्यम्। वैश्वानर्यां शिक्यमादत्ते। प्रभिचायमर्त्यममृत्यास्यति। वज्रः कार्म्यैविश्व्र्य। 'यतोनावः' (३७०१) इति प्राप्ते॥

8. The finals of the following words are svarita; तिल्य, शिक्य, मर्त्य, कार्म्य धान्य, कन्या, राजन्य, मनुष्य। The word तिल्यम्=तिलानां भवनं क्षेत्रं। वैश्वानर्यां शिक्यमादत्ते, प्रभिचायमर्त्यममृत्यास्यति, वज्रः कार्म्योविश्व्र्य। Some of these are exceptions to VI. 1. 213.

९। बिल्वभक्ष्यवीर्याणि छन्दसि॥

अन्तस्वरितानि। ततो बिल्व उदतिष्ठत्॥

9. In the Chhandas the following words are finally svarita: बिल्व, भक्ष्य, वीर्य। As ततो बिल्व उदतिष्ठत्॥

१०। त्वत्त्वसमसिमेत्यनुच्चानि॥

स्तरीरुत्वत्। 'उत त्वः पश्यन्'। 'नभन्तामन्यके समे'। 'सिमस्मै'॥

10. The words त्वत्, त्व, सम, and सिम are wholly anudâtta. As स्तरीरुत्व (Rig Veda VII. 101 3), उत त्वः पश्यन् (Rig Veda X. 71. 4), नभन्ताम न्यके समे (Rig Veda VIII. 39. 1), सिमस्मै (Rig Veda I. 115. 4).

११। सिमस्याथर्वणेऽन्त उदात्तः॥

अथर्वण इति प्रायिकम्। तत्र दृष्टस्येत्येवं परं वा। तेन 'वासस्तनुते सिमस्मै' इत्यृग्वेदेऽपि भवत्येव॥

11. In the Atharva Veda the word सिम is finally acute. The rule is not confined to the Atharva Veda: it is so found in the Rig Veda also. As वासस्तनुते सिमस्मै (Rig Veda I. 115. 4).

१२। निपाता आद्युदात्ताः॥

स्वाहा।

12. The Indeclinables are first acute. As स्वाहा ॥

१३ । उपसर्गाश्चाभिवर्जम् ॥

13. The upasargas are first-acute with the exception of अभि ॥

१४ । एवादीनामन्तः ॥

एवमादीनामिति पाठान्तरम् । एव । एवम् । नूनम् । 'सह ते पुत्र सूरिभिः' । षष्ठस्य तृतीये सह । 'सहस्य सः–' (१००९) इति प्रकरणे सहशब्द आद्युदात्त इति तु प्राञ्चः । तच्चिन्त्यम् ॥

14. The words एव and the rest are finally acute. Another reading is एवमादीनाम् । As एव, एवम्, नूनम्, सह । सह ते पुत्र सूरिभिः । In VI 3. 78 S. 1009, the word सह is first-acute according to Kâśikâ. Thus there is an apparent contradiction.

१५ । वाचादीनामुभावुदात्तौ ॥

उभौ ग्रहणमनुदात्तं पदमेकवर्जमित्यस्य बाधाय ॥

15. Both syllables of the words वाच and the rest are acute. This debars the general rule by which, in one word only one syllable is accented. (VI. 1. 158).

१६ । चादयोऽनुदात्ताः ॥

स्पष्टम् ॥

16. The words च and the rest are anudâtta.

१७ । यथेति पादान्ते ॥

'तं नेमिमृभवो यथा' । 'पादान्ते' किम् । 'यथा नो अदितिः करत्' ॥

17. The word यथा is anudâtta at the end of a Pâda or verse. As तं नेमिमृभवो यथा (Rig Veda VIII. 75. 5). But यथा नो अदितिः करत् where it is not at the end of a verse (Rig Veda I 43. 2).

१८ । प्रकारादिद्विरुक्तौ ॥

परस्यान्त उदात्तः । पटुपटुः ॥

18. A double-word is finally acute when it denotes प्रकार &c. Thus पटुपटुः This would have been finally acute by Pâṇini's rule also; VIII. 1. 11 and 12.

१९ । शेषं सर्वमनुदात्तं ॥

'शेषं सर्वमनुदात्तम्' । शेषमित्यादिद्विरुक्तस्य परमित्यर्थः । प्रप्रायम् । दिवेदिवे । इति ॥

इति फिट्सूत्रेषु तुरीयः पादः ॥

19. All other double-words are anudâtta. As प्रप्रायम, (Rig Veda VII. 8. 4) दिवे दिवे (Rig Veda I. 1. 3). ॥

Here end the Phit Sutras.

अथ प्रत्ययस्वराः ।

CHAPTER III.

AFFIX-ACCENTS—(continued).

३७०८ । आद्युदात्तश्च । ३ । १ । ३ ॥

प्रत्यय आद्युदात्त एव स्यात् । अग्निः । कर्तव्यम् ॥

3708. That which is called an affix, has an acute accent on its first syllable.

This sûtra may also be treated as a Paribhâshâ or an Adhikâra sûtra. The udatta accent falls on the affix, and if it consists of more than one vowel, then on the first of the vowels. Thus the affix तव्य has udâtta on the first अ, as in कर्तव्यम् । So also अग्निः formed with the affix नि (Uṇâdi IV. 50),

३७०९ । अनुदात्तौ सुप्पितौ । ३ । १ । ४ ॥

पूर्वस्यापवादः । यज्ञस्य । न यो युच्छति । अप्तिपोरनुदात्तत्वे स्वरितप्रचयौ ॥

3709. The case-affixes (sup) and the affixes having an indicatory *pa* (pit) are anudâtta.

This is an exception (apavâda) to the last aphorism. As यज्ञस्य, so also न यो युच्छति (Rig Veda V. 54. 13).

Here the root युच्छ प्रमादे is end-acute by VI. 1. 162. To it is added शप् which becomes svarita, as it is preceded by an udâtta (VIII. 4. 66). Then is added तिप् which becomes monotone by I. 2. 39. S 3668, as it is preceded by a svarita. So the affix तिप् becomes monotone.

३७१० । चितः । ६ । १ । १६३ ॥

अन्त उदात्तः स्यात् । "चितः सप्रकृतेर्बह्वकजर्थम्"। चिति प्रत्यये सति प्रकृतिप्रत्ययसमुदायस्यान्त उदात्तो वाच्य इत्यर्थः । 'नभन्तामन्यके समे' । 'यके सरस्वतीमनु । तकत्सु ते' ॥

3710. A stem (formed by an affix or augment or substitute) having an indicatory 'ch', gets acute on the end syllable.

Várt:—In the cases of affixes having an indicatory च, the acute accent falls on the final, taking the stem and the affix in an aggregate for the sake of affixes 'bahu' and 'akach'. Thus बहुपटुः । The affix बहुच् is one of those few affixes which are really prefixes, (V. 3. 68). The accent will not, therefore, fall on हु, but on the last syllable of the whole word compounded of the prefix and the base. So also with the affix अकच् । It is added in the *middle* of the word, but the accent will fall on the *end*; as उच्चकैः (V. 3. 71).

Thus:—नभन्तामन्यके समे (Rig Veda VIII. 39. 1). यके सरस्वतीम् (Rig Veda VIII. 21. 18). तकत्सु ते (Rig Veda I. 133. 4).

३७११ । तद्धितस्य । ६ । १ । १६४ ॥

चितस्तद्धितस्यान्त उदात्तः । पूर्वेण सिद्धे ञित्स्वरबाधनार्थमिदम् । कौञ्जायनाः ॥

3711. A stem formed with a Taddhita-affix having an indicatory *ch*, has acute on the end syllable.

Thus कौञ्जायनाः formed by the affix च्फञ् (IV. 1. 98). कुञ्ज + च्फञ् + ञ्य = कौञ्जायन्यः, dual कौञ्जायन्यौ, pl. कौञ्जायनाः (ञ्य being elided by II. 4. 62, and thus giving scope to च्फञ् accent). In this affix there are two indicatory letters च and ञ् ; the च has only one function, namely, regulating the accent according to this rule, while ञ् has two functions, one to regulate the accent by VI. 1. 197, and another to cause Vṛiddhi by VII. 2. 117. Now arises the question, 'should the word get the accent of च or of ञ' । The present rule declares that it should get the accent of च and not of ञ, for the latter finds still a function left to it, while if ञ was to regulate the accent, च would have no scope.

३७१२ । कितः । ६ । १ । १६५ ॥

कितस्तद्धितस्यान्त उदात्तः । 'यदाग्नेयः' ॥

3712. A stem formed by a Taddhita affix having an indicatory *ka* has acute accent on the end syllable.

Thus यदाग्नेयः । Here the affix ढक is added to अग्नि by IV. 2. 33 S. 1236.

३७१३ । तिसृभ्यो जसः । ६ । १ । १६६ ॥

अन्त उदात्तः । 'तिस्रो द्याव॑ः सवितुः' ॥

3713. The Nominative plural *jas* of *tisri* has acute accent on the last syllable.

Thus तिस्रो द्यावः सवितुः (Rig Veda I. 35. 6).

The word त्रि is end-acute; the feminine तिसृ being its substitute would also be end-acute. Before the affix जस्, the ऋ is changed to र by VII. 2. 100. Here VIII. 2. 4 would have made the जस् svarita. This debars that svarita accent. Therefore the word तिस्रः in the above example is end-acute.

३७१४ । सावेकाचस्तृतीयादिर्विभक्तिः । ६ । १ । १६८ ॥

साविति सप्तमीबहुवचनम् । तत्र य एकाच् ततः परा तृतीयादिर्विभक्तिरुदात्ता । 'वाचा विरूपः' । सौ किम्? राज्ञेत्यादौ एकाचोऽपि राजशब्दात्परस्य मा भूत् । 'राज्ञो नु ते' । एकाच किम् ? 'विदधते राजनि त्वे' । तृतीयादिः किम् ? 'न द॑दर्श वाचम्' ॥

3714. The case-affixes of the Instrumental and of the cases that follow it have the acute accent, if the stem in the Locative Plural is monosyllabic.

The word सौ (locative of सु) refers to the सु of the Locative plural.

Thus वाचा विरूप। Why do we say 'if the stem in the Locative plural is monosyllabic'? Observe राज्ञो नु ते वरुणस्य व्रतानि बृहद्गभीरन्तव सोम धाम । (Rig Veda I. 91. 3) because the stem in the Locative Pl. of राजन् is not monosyllabic, but dissyllabic; though here it is monosyllabic. Why do wo say 'monosyllable'? Observe विदधते राजनि त्वे (Rig Veda VI. 1. 13). Why do say 'the Instrumentals and the rest'? Observe न ददर्श वाचं (Rig Veda X. 71. 4). The plural of Locative being taken in the sûtra, the rule does not apply to त्वया and त्वयि । as in the *plural* of the Locative they have more than one syllable, though in *singular* locative their stem has one syllable.

३७१५ । अन्तोदात्तादुत्तरपदादन्यतरस्यामनित्यसमासे । ६ । १ । १६९ ॥

नित्याधिकारविहितसमासादन्यत्र यदुत्तरपदमन्तोदात्तमेकाच् ततः परा तृतीयादि विभक्ति-रुदात्ता वा स्यात् । परमवाचा ॥

3715. The same case endings may optionally have the acute accent, if the monosyllabic word stands at the end of a compound, and has acute accent on the final, when the compound can be easily unloosened.

The phrases 'एकाचः' and तृतीयादिर्विभक्तिः are understood here also. The nitya or *invariable* compounds are excluded by this rule. Thus परमवाँवा, or परम-वाचाँ, परमवाँचेः or वाचे; परमवाँचः or वाँचः । So also परमत्वँचा or त्वचाँ &c.

३७१६ । अञ्चेश्छन्दस्य सर्वनामस्थानम् । ६ । १ । १७० ॥

अञ्चेः परा विभक्तिरुदात्ता । 'इन्द्रो दधीचः' । चाविति पूर्वपदान्तोदात्तत्वं प्राप्तं तृतीया-दिरित्यनुवर्तमानेऽसर्वनामस्थानग्रहणं शस्परिग्रहार्थम् । 'प्रतीचो बाहून्' ॥

3716. In the Chhandas, the case-endings other than the sarvanâmasthâna, get the acute accent when coming after añch.

In the Vedas, a stem ending in the word अञ्च्, has the acute not only on the affixes previously mentioned, but on the accusative plural affix also. Thus इन्द्रो दधीचो अस्थभिः (Rig Veda I 84. 13). Here the word दधीच् had accent on धी by VI. 1. 222, but by the present sûtra, the accent falls on the case-affix अस् ॥

Though the anuvritti of 'Instrumentals and the rest' was understood here, the word asarvanâmasthâna has been used here to include the ending शस् also. As प्रतीचो बाहून् प्रतिभङ्ध्येषाम् (Rig Veda X. 87. 4).

३७१७ । ऊडिदंपदाद्यप्पुम्रैद्युभ्यः । ६ । १ । १७१ ॥

'ऊट्' 'इदं' 'पदादि' 'अप्' 'पुम्' 'रै' 'दिव' इत्येभ्योऽसर्वनामस्थानविभक्तिरुदात्ता । ऊठ् । प्रष्ठौहः । प्रष्ठौहा ॥

'+ उठ्युपधाग्रहणं कर्तव्यम् +' । इह मा भूत् । अक्षद्युवा' । 'अक्षद्युवे' । इदम् । 'एभिर्नृभिर्नृतमः' । अन्वादेशे न । 'अन्तोदात्तात्' इत्यनुवृत्तेः । न च तत्रान्तोदात्ततास्तीति वाच्यम् । 'इदमोऽन्वादेशेऽशनुदात्तस्तृतीयादौ' (३५०) इति सूत्रेणानुदात्तस्याशोविधानात् । 'प्र ते बभ्रू' । 'माभ्यां गा अनु' । 'पद्दन्नोमास्हृन्निश्-' (२२८) इति षट् पदादयः । 'पद्भ्यां भूमिः' 'दद्भिर्न जिह्वा' । 'जायते मासिमासि' । 'मनश्चिन्मे हृद आ' । अप् । 'अपां फेनेन' । पुम् 'अभ्रातेव पुंसः' । रै । 'राया वयम्' । 'रायो धर्ता' । दिव । 'दिवेदिवे' ॥

3717. The same (asarvanâmasthâna) case-endings have the acute accent, when the stem ends in 'vâh'; also after *idam*, after *pad* &c. (upto 'nis' VI. 1. 63) after *apa*, *puns*, *rai* and *div*.

Thus: (1.) ऊट्:—प्रष्ठौहः, प्रष्ठौहा ॥

'*Vârt*:—In the case of ऊठ् the penultimate ऊ should be taken. Therefor not here: अक्षद्युवा, अक्षद्युवे ॥

(2) इदम्—एभिर्नृभिर्नृतमः (Rig Veda IV. 17. 11).

Not so in anvâdesâ (II. 4. 32 S. 350), because the anuvritti of अन्तोदात्तात् is understood in this sûtra. Nor should it be said that there is final udâtta in the case of anvâdesa इदम् also. Because in anvâdesa the अश् substitute of इदम् is expressly taught to be anudâtta by II. 4. 32, and it can never be end-acute. Thus in the following Rik verse (Rig Veda IV. 32. 22):—प्र ते बभ्रू विचक्षण शंसामि गोषणो नपात् । माभ्यां गा अनु शिश्रथः ॥

Here आभ्यां is used as अन्वादेश referring to बभ्रू of the preceding line.

(3) पद &c. These are the six words पद्, दत्, नस्, मास्, हृद् and निश् (VI. 1. 63, S. 228). Thus पद्भ्यां भूमिः । दद्भिर्न जिह्वा (Rig Veda X. 68. 6). आयते मासि मासि (Rig Veda X. 52. 3). मनश्चिचन्मे हृद आ (Rig Veda I. 24. 12).

(4) अप् :—as अपां फेनेन (Rig Veda VIII. 14. 13).

(5) पुंस् :—as अभ्रातेव पुंसः (Rig Veda I. 124. 7).

(6) रै—as राया वयम् (Rig Veda IV. 42. 10). रायो धर्ता (Rig Veda V. 15. 1).

(7) दिव्—as दिवे दिवे (Rig Veda I. 1. 3).

३७१८ । अष्टनो दीर्घात् । ६ । १ । १७२ ॥

शसादिर्विभक्तिरुदात्ता । 'अष्टाभिर्दशभिः' ॥

3718. The asarvanâmasthâna case-endings after 'ashtan' 'eight' have acute accent, when it gets the form 'ashtâ.'

The word अष्टन् has two forms in the Acc. pl. and the other cases that follow it, namely अष्टा and अष्ट । The affixes of Acc. pl. &c., are udâtta after the long form अष्टा and not after अष्ट । Thus अष्टाभिः (Rig Veda II. 18. 4) opposed to अष्टभिः, अष्टाभ्यः con. अष्टभ्यः, अष्टासु con. अष्टसु । The word अष्टन् has acute on the last syllable, as it belongs to the class of घृतादि words (Phit I. 21); and by VI. 1. 180 the accent would have been on the penultimate syllable. This rule debars it.

३७१९ । शतुरनुमो नद्यजादी । ६ । १ । १७३ ॥

अनुम् यः शतृप्रत्ययस्तदन्तादन्तोदात्तात्परा नद्यजादिश्च शसादिर्विभक्तिरुदात्ता स्यात् ' ' अच्छा रवं प्रथमा जानती' । कृण्वते । ' अन्तोदात्तात्' किम् । दधती । ' अभ्यस्तानामादिः ' (३६७३) इत्याद्युदात्तः । ' अनुमः' किम् । तुदन्ती । एकादेशोऽत्र उदात्तः । अदुपदेशात्परत्वाच्छतुः ' लसार्वधातुकम्-' (३७०३) इति निघातः ॥

3719. After an oxytone Participle in *at* the feminine suffix 'î' (nadi) and the case endings beginning with vowels (with the exception of strong cases) have acute accent, when the participa affix has not the augment *n* (*i. e* is not *ant*).

The word अन्तोदात्तात् 'after an oxytoned word' is understood here. Thus अच्छारवं प्रथमा जानती (Rig Veda III. 31. 6). So also कृण्वते (III. 2. 80 S. 2990).

If the participle is not an oxytone, the rule does not apply. As ददती, दधती । Here the accent is on the first syllable by VI. 1. 189. S. 3673. Why do we say 'not having the augment नुम् ?' Observe तुदन्ती । Here also by VI.

1. 186. S. 3730, after the root तुद् which has an indicatory अ, in the Dhâtupâṭha being written तुद, the sârvadhâtuka affix शत् (अत्) is anudâtta. This anudâtta अत्, coalescing with the udâtta अ of तुद (VI. I. 162), becomes udâtta (VIII. 2. 5); and VIII. 2. 1 not being held applicable here, the Participle gets the accent, and not the feminine affix.

३७२० । उदात्तयणो हल्पूर्वात् । ६ । १ । १७४ ॥

उदात्तस्थाने यो यण्हल्पूर्वस्तस्मात्परा नदी शसादिर्विभक्तिश्च उदात्ता स्यात् । 'चोदयित्री सूनृतानाम्' । 'एवाने त्री' । ऋतं देवाय कृण्वते सवित्रे ॥

3720. The same endings have the acute accent, when for the acutely accented final vowel of the stem, a semi-vowel is substituted, and which is preceded by a consonant.

Thus चोदयित्री सूनृतानाम् (Rig Veda I. 3. 11), एवा नेत्री (Rig Veda VII. 76. 7) ऋतं देवाय कृण्वते सवित्रे (Rig Veda II. 50. 1). All these are तृच् ending words and have consequently acute accent on the final (VI. 1. 163).

३७२१ । नोङ्धात्वोः । ६ । १ । १७५ ॥

अनयोर्यणः परे शसादय उदात्ता न स्युः । ब्रह्मबन्ध्वा । 'सेत्पृश्निः सुभ्वे' ॥

3721. But not so, when the vowel is of the feminine affix 'ऊ' (IV. 1. 66), or the final of a root.

After the semi-vowel substitutes of the udâtta ऊ (IV. 1. 66) or of the udâtta final vowels of the root, when preceded by a consonant, the weak case-endings beginning with a vowel do not take the acute accent. Thus ब्रह्मबन्ध्वा' ब्रह्मबन्ध्वे. धीरबन्ध्वा, धीरबन्ध्वे from धीरबन्धू, which has acute accent on ऊ, because ऊङ् is udâtta (III. 1. 3), and the ekâdeśa of it, when it combines with the preceding vowel is also udâtta (VIII. 2. 5). The व substituted for ऊ before the ending आ, is a semi-vowel substitute of an udâtta (उदात्तयण्); the affix after it would have become udâtta by the last sûtra, but not being so, the general rule VIII 2. 4 applies and makes it svarita. Let us take an example of a semi-vowel substitute of the vowel of a root (धातु-यण्)—सकल्ल्वा'; सकल्ल्वे' and खलप्वा, खलप्वे' from सकल्लू and खलपू' respectively formed by क्विप् affix, the second member of the compound retaining its original accent, namely, the oxytone. the semi-vowel being substituted by VI. 4. 83. before the vowel case-endings. So also सेत्पृश्निः सुभ्वे (Rig Veda VI. 66. 3).

३७२२ । ह्रस्वनुड्भ्यां मतुप् । ६ । १ । १७६ ॥

ह्रस्वान्तादन्तोदात्तान्नुटश्च परो मतुबुदात्तः । 'ये अग्निमन्तः' 'दनिमाँ इंयर्ति' । नुटः । 'अक्षण्वन्तः कर्णवन्तः सखायः' । अन्तोदात्तात् किम् ? 'मा त्व विददिषुमान्' ॥

'+ स्वरविधौ व्यञ्जनमविद्यमानवत् +' इत्येतदत्र नेष्यते । 'मरुत्वाँ इन्द्रः' । 'नियुत्वान्वा यवागहि' ॥

'+ रेशब्दाच्च +' । रेवाँ इद्रेवतः' ॥

3722. The otherwise unaccented *mat* (*vat*) takes the acute accent, when an oxytoned stem ends in a light vowel, or the affix has before it the augment *n* (VIII. 2. 16).

The word अन्तोदात्तात् is understood here also. Thus

यो अ॒ब्दिमाँ उ॒दनि॒माँ इय॑र्ति (Rig Veda V. 42. 14). So also when मतुप् takes नुट्, as अक्षण्वन्ता, अक्षण्वन्तः कर्णव॑न्तः सखायः (Rig Veda X. 71. 7). Here by VII. 1. 76, the word अक्षि takes अनङ् and becomes अक्षन्, then is added नुट् by VIII. 2. 16, and we have अक्षन् न् मतुप् । The preceding न् is elided. When the stem is not oxytone (antodâtta) this rule does not apply : as व॒सुमान् । मात्वा विद्वसुमान् (Rig Veda II. 42. 2). The word व॒सु has acute on the first syllable, as it is formed from वस् with the affix उ (Un. 1. 10) which is नित् (Un I. 9). So the मतुप् retains its anudâtta here. So also in the case of मरुत्वान्, the affix does not become acute, though the word म॒रुत् has acute on the final as the intervening त् makes the उ of रु *heavy* when the affix is added : the general maxim स्वरविधौ व्यंजनमविद्यमानवत् does not apply here, because the very fact that न् is only taken as an exception, shows this, as मरुत्वाँ इन्द्र (Rig Veda III. 47. 1) नियुत्वान्वायवागहि (Rig Veda II. 41. 2).

Vârt :—The affix मतुप् becomes acute after the heavy vowel of रै ; as आरेव॑ान = रयिरस्यास्ति । There is vocalisation of य of रयि, as र इ इ; then substitution of one, as र इ, then guna, as रे in रेवान् इद्रेवतः (Rig Veda VIII. 2. 13).

३७२३ । नामन्यतरस्याम् । ६ । १ । १७७ ॥

मतुपि योऽह्रस्वस्तदन्तादन्तोदात्तात्परो नामुदात्तो वा । 'चेतन्ती सुमतीनाम्' ॥

3723. After an oxytoned stem which ends in a light vowel the genitive ending 'nâm' has optionally the acute accent.

Thus :—चेतन्ती सुमतीनाम् (Rig Veda I. 3. 11).

So also अग्नीनाम् or अ॒ग्नीनाम्, वायूनाम्, or वायूनाम् कर्तृणाम् or कर्तृणाम् (see VII. 1. 54).

३७२४ । ङ्याश्छन्दसि बहुलम् । ६ । १ । १७८ ॥

ङ्याःपरो नामुदात्तो वा । 'देवसेनानामभिभञ्जतीनाम्' । वेत्युक्तेर्नेह । 'जयन्तीनां मरुतो यन्तु' ॥

3724. In the Chhandas, the ending 'nâm' has diversely the acute accent after the feminine affix 'î.'

Thus देवसेनानाम् अभिभञ्जतीनाम्, (Rig Veda X. 103. 8). Sometimes it does not take place, as जयन्तीनाम् मरुतः (Rig Veda X. 103. 8).

३७२५ । षट्त्रिचतुर्भ्यो हलादिः । ६ । १ । १७९ ॥

एभ्यो हलादिर्विभक्तिरुदात्ता । 'आ षड्भिर्हूयमानः' । 'त्रिभिष्ट्वं देव' ॥

3725. The case-endings beginning with a consonant, have the acute accent after the Numerals called *shat* (I. 1. 24), as well as after *tri* and *chatur*.

The anuvritti of अन्तोदात्ताद् ceases : for the present rule applies even to words like प॑ञ्चन् and न॑वन् which are acute on the initial by Phit II. 5. Thus पञ्चानाम् षड्भिः, षड्भ्यः, पञ्चानाम्, सप्तानाम्, त्रिभिः, त्रिभ्यः, त्रयाणाम्, चतुर्णाम् (See VII. 1. 55) Why do we say 'before case-affixes beginning with consonants' ? Observe चतस्रः

पश्य (VI. 1. 167 and VII. 2. 99). आ वृभिरहूयमानः (Rig Veda II. 18. 4). त्रिभिः त्वं देव सवितः (Rig Veda IX. 67. 26).

३७२६ । न गोश्वन्साववर्णराडङ्क्रुङ्कृद्भ्यः । ६ । १ । १८२ ॥

एभ्यः प्रागुक्तं न । 'गवां' शता' । 'गोभ्यो' गातुम्' । 'शुन'श्चिच्छेप'म्' । सौ प्रथमैकवचनेऽवर्णान्तात् । 'तेभ्यो' द्युम्नम्' । तेषां पाहि श्रुधी हव'म् ॥

3726. The foregoing rules from VI. 1. 168 downwards have no applicability after *go*, and 'śvan' and words ending in them; nor after a stem which before the case ending of the Nominative singuar has *a* or â, nor after 'râj,' nor after a stem ending in *anch*, nor after *krunch* and *krit*.

Thus गवा, गवे, गोभ्याम् as in गवां शता (Rig Veda I. 122. 7). Here by VI. 1. 168, the case-endings would have got otherwise the accent, which is however prohibited. So also सुगुना, सुगवे and सुगुभ्याम् । गोभ्यो गातुम् (Rig Veda VIII. 45, 30). Here VI. 1. 169 is prohibited. So also शुना, शुने, श्वभ्याम्, परमशुना, परमशुने and परमश्वभ्याम् । शुनश्चिच्छेपम् (Rig Veda V. 2. 7). The word साववर्णः (सौ अवर्णः) means 'what has अ or आ before सु (1st sing.)' Thus येभ्यः, तेभ्यः, केभ्यः । तेभ्योद्युम्नम् (Rig Veda V.79. 7). तेषां पाहि श्रुधी हवम् (Rig Veda I. 2. 1). So also राजा, राज्ञे, परमराजा । The word राज् is formed by क्विप् affix. अङ्=अञ्च+क्विन्; the prohibition applies to that form of this word wherein the nasal is not elided (VI. 4. 30). Thus प्राङ्चा, प्राङ्भ्याम् । Where the nasal is elided, there the case-ending must take the accent; as प्राचा प्राग्भ्याम् । क्रुङ् is also a क्विन् formed word. Thus क्रुञ्चा, क्रुञ्चे, परमक्रुञ्चा । कृत् is derived from कृ 'to do' or from कृत् 'to cut' by क्विप्; as कृता कृते and परमकृता । Why has the word श्वन् been especially mentioned in this sûtra, when the rule would have applied to it even without such enumeration, because in the Nominative Singular this word assumes the form श्वा and consequently it is साववर्णः? The inclusion of श्वन् indicates that the elision of न should not be considered asiddha for the purposes of this rule. Therefore, the present rule will not apply to words like नृ and पितृ which in Nom. Sing. end in आ as ना and पिता after the elision of न् of अनङ् (VII. 3. 94). Thus the Locative Singular of नृ will be नरि by VI 1. 168; this prohibition not applying, and the affix मतुप् will get udâtta after पिता by VI. 1. 176 as पितृमान् । But rule VI. I. 176 will be debarred by the present in the case of वृक्षवान्, because वृक्ष is a साववर्ण ॥

३७२७ । दिवो झल् । ६ । १ । १८३ ॥

दिवः परा झलादिर्विभक्तिर्नोदात्ता । 'द्युभिरक्तुभिः' । 'झल्' इति किम् । 'उप' त्वाग्ने दिवेदिवे' ॥

3727. After *div* a case-ending beginning with *bha* or *sa* is unaccented.

Thus द्युभ्याम्, द्युभिरक्तुभिः (Rig Veda I. 34. 8). This debars VI. 1. 168, 171. Why do we say 'beginning with a झल् consonant'? Observe उपत्वाग्ने दिवे दिवे Rig Veda I. 1. 7).

३७२८ । नृ चान्यतरस्याम् । ६ । १ । १८४ ॥

नुः परा झलादिर्विभक्तिर्वोदात्ता । 'नृभिर्यमानः' ॥

3728. After *nri*, a case ending beginning with *bha* or *sa* is optionally unaccented.

Thus नृँभिः or नृभिः, नृँभ्यः, नृभ्यः, नृँभ्याम्, नृभ्याम्, नृँषु, नृषु । नृभिर्यमानः (Rig Veda IX. 75. 3). But not so नृँा, नृे ॥

३७२९ । तित्स्वरितम् । ६ । १ । १८५ ॥

निगदव्याख्यातम् । 'क्वं नूनम्' ॥

3729. An affix having an indicatory *t*, is svarita *i. e.*, has circumflex accent.

Thus चिकीर्ष्यम्, जिहीर्ष्यम्, formed by यत् (III. 1. 97). कार्यम, हार्यम् with ण्यत् (III. 1. 124). This is an exception to III. 1. 3 which makes all affixes âdyudâtta. For exception to this rule see VI. 1, 213 &c. क्वनूनम् (Rig Veda I. 38. 2).

३७३० । तास्यनुदात्तेन्ङिद्दुपदेशाल्लसार्वधातुकमनुदात्तमह्न्विङोः । ६ । १ । १८६ ॥

अस्मात्परं लसार्वधातुकमनुदात्तं स्यात् । तासि । कर्ता । कर्तारौ । कर्तारः । प्रत्ययस्वरापवादोऽयम् । अनुदात्तेत् । य आस्ते । ङितः । 'अभि चष्टे अनृतेभिः' । अदुपदेशात् । पुरुभुजा चनस्यतम्' । चित्स्वरोऽप्यनेन बाध्यते । 'वर्धमानं स्वेदमे' । 'तास्यादिभ्यः' किम् । 'अभि वृधे गृणीतः' । उपदेशग्रहणाच्चेत्त । 'हतो वृत्राण्यार्या' । 'लसग्रहणम्' किम् । 'कतीह निघ्नाना' । 'सार्वधातुकम्' किम् । शिश्ये । 'अह्न्विङोः' किम् । ह्नुते । यदधीते । '* विदीन्धिखिदिभ्यो नेति वक्तव्यम् *' । इन्धे राजा' एतच्च 'अनुदात्तस्य च यत्र-' (३६५१) इति सूत्रे भाष्ये स्थितम् ॥

3730. The Personal-endings and their substitutes (III. 2. 124-126) are, when they are sârvadhâtuka (III. 4. 113 &c), unaccented, after the characteristic of the Periphrastic future 'tâsi' after a root which in the Dhâtupâtha has an unaccented vowel or a 'ṅ' (with the exception of 'hnuṅ' and 'iṅ') as indicatory letter, as well as after what has a final 'a' in the Grammatical system of Instruction (upadeśa).

Thus तासिः, कर्ता'—कर्तारौ, कर्तारः, this debars the affix accent (III. 1. 3). Anudâttet:—as, आस्—आस्ते, वस्—वस्ते । ङितः—षूङ्—सूते. शीङ्—शेते ; अभिचष्टे अनृतेभिः (Rig Veda VII. 104. 8). अत् उपदेशः:—as तुदतः, नुदतः, पचतः, पठतः । पुरुभुजा चनस्यतम् (Rig Veda I. 3. 1). A root taking शप् (अ) is considered as taught (upadeśa) as if ending with an अ, as the indicatory letters श् and प् are disregarded on the maxim अनुबन्धस्यानैकान्तिकत्वं (= अनवयवत्वं) । Thus पचमानः, यजमानः । The augment मुक् is added by आने मुक् VII. 2. 82 which may be explained in two ways ; *first*, the augment मुक् is added to the final अ of the base (aṅga) when आन (आसच &c.) follows ; or *secondly*, the augment मुक् is added to the base (aṅga) which ends in अ, when आन follows. In the first case मुक् becomes part and parcel of अ, and therefore अदुपदेश will mean and include an अ having such मुक्, on the maxim यदागमास्तद्गुणीभूतास्तद्ग्रहणेन गृह्यन्ते 'That to which an augment is added denotes, because the augment forms part of it not merely itself, but it denotes also whatever results from its combination with that augment.' Therefore मुक् will not prevent the verb becoming अदुपदेश । But if secondly मुक् be taken as part of the *base* which ends in अ, then the लसार्वधातुक does not follow an अदुपदेश, because म intervenes. But we get rid of this difficulty by considering मुक् augment as Bahiranga and therefore asiddha when the Antaranga operation of accent is to be performed. The augment मुक् (म) in the last two examples consequently does not prevent the application of the rule. Though the affix शानच् has an indicatory च्, yet चित accent (VI. 1. 163) is debarred by this rule, as it is *subsequent*. As वर्धमानं स्वे दमे (Rig Veda I. 1. 8).

Why do we say after तासि &c. Observe अभिवृधे गृणीतः (Rig Veda III 6. 10) चिन्वन्ति। The vikarana श्नु is ङित् (I. 2. 4) with regard to operations affecting the prior term, and not those which affect the subsequent. Therefore though श्नु is considered as ङित् for the purposes of preventing the guna of the prior term चि, it will not be considered so for the purposes of subsequent accent. Or the word ङित् in this sûtra may be taken as equal to ङिदुपदेश and not the आतिदेशिक ङित् like श्नु। Why do we use the word upadeśa ? So that the rule may apply to पचावः, पचामः, but not to हतः, हथः the dual of हन् which ends in न् in upadeśa, though before तस् and थस् it has assumed the form ह। Therefore हतः, हथः। हतोवृत्राण्यार्या (Rig Veda VI. 60. 6). Why do we use the word ल (Personal endings) ? Observe कतीह निघ्नाना formed by शानन् added to हन् (III. 2. 128), which not being a substitute of लट्, is not a personal ending like शानच्। Why do we use the word Sârvadâtuka ? Observe शिश्ये, शिश्यानो शिश्यिरे। Why do we say with the exception of हनुङ् and इङ् ? Observe हनुते, यद् अधीते॥

Vãrtika :—Prohibition must be stated of विद्, ईन्ध, and खिद्। Thus इन्धे राजा (Rig Veda VII. 8. 1).

This is explained in the Mahâbhâshya on sûtra VI. 1. 161. S. 3651.

३७३१। आदिः सिचोऽन्यतरस्याम्। ६।१।१८७॥

सिजन्तस्यादिरुदात्तो वा। 'यासिष्टं वर्तिरश्विना'॥

3731. In 'sich' Aorist, the first syllable may optionally have the acute accent.

The word उदात्त is understood here. Thus, मा हि कार्ष्टाम्, मा हि कार्ष्टाम्; मा हि लाविष्टाम or मा हि लाविष्टाम्॥ So also यासिष्टं वर्तिरश्विना (Rig Veda VII. 40. 5 and VII. 67. 10).

३७३२। थलि च सेटीडन्तो वा। ६।१।१९६॥

सेटि थलन्ते पदे इडुदात्तः अन्तो वा आदिर्वा स्यात्। यदा नैते त्रयस्तदा 'लिति' (३६७६) इति प्रत्ययात्पूर्वमुदात्तम्। लुलविथ। अत्र चत्वारोऽपि पर्यायेणोदात्ताः॥

3732 Before the ending *tha* of the Perfect, second person singular, when this ending takes the augment *i*, the acute accent falls either on the first syllable, or on this *i*, or on the personal ending.

Thus लुलविथ, लुलविथ, लुलविथ, and लुलविथ । As थल् has an indicatory ल् the syllable preceding the affix may have also the accent (VI. 1. 193). Thus we get the four forms given above. In short, with इथ termination, the accent may fall on any syllable. When the थ is not सेट्, the accent falls on the root and we have one form only by लित् accent (VI. 1. 193 S. 3676) :—यथाथ ॥

३७३३ । उपोत्तमं रिति । ६ । १ । २१७ ॥
रित्प्रत्ययान्तस्योपोत्तममुदात्तं स्यात् । 'यदाहवनीये' ॥

इति प्रत्ययस्वराः ॥

3733. What is formed by an affix having an indicatory *ra* has acute on the penultimate syllable, the full word consisting of more than two syllables.

A penultimate syllable can be only in a word consisting of three syllables or more. Thus करणीयम् and हरणीयम् formed by अनीयर् (III. 1. 96); पटुजातीयः मृदुजातीयः by जातीयर् (V. 3. 19) यदाहवनीये ॥ This debars III. 1. 3.

Here end Affix-accents.

अथ समासस्वराः ।

CHAPTER IV.

ACCENT OF COMPOUNDS.

३७३४ । समासस्य । ६ । १ । २२३ ॥
अन्त उदात्तः स्यात् । 'यज्ञश्रियम्' ॥

3734. A compound word has the acute on the last syllable.

Thus यज्ञ श्रियं (Rig Veda I. 4. 7). The consonants being held to be non-existent for the purposes of accent; the udâtta will fall on the vowel though it may not be final, the final being a consonant.

३७३५ । बहुव्रीहौ प्रकृत्या पूर्वपदम् । ६ । २ । १ ॥
उदात्तस्वरितयोगि पूर्वपदं प्रकृत्या स्यात् । 'सत्यश्चित्रश्रवस्तमः' । 'उदात्त-' इत्यादि किम् । सर्वानुदात्ते पूर्वपदे समासान्तोदात्तत्वमेव यथा स्यात् । समपादः ॥

3735. In a Bahuvrîhi, the first member preserves its own original accent.

The word पूर्वपदम् means here the accent—whether udâtta or svarita—which is in the first member : प्रकृत्या means, 'retains its own nature, does not become modified into an anudâtta accent.' By the last rule the final of a compound gets the accent, so that all the preceding members lose their accent, and become anudâtta, as in one word all syllables are unaccented except one, VI. 1. 158. Thus the first member of a Bahuvrihi would have lost its accent and become anudâtta; with the present sûtra commences the exceptions to the rule that the final of a compound is always udâtta. Thus सत्यश्चित्र श्रवस्तमः ॥

The words udâtta, and svarita are understood in this aphorism. Therefore if *all* the syllables of the pûrvapada are anudâtta, the present rule has no scope there, and such a compound will get udâtta on the final by the universal rule enunciated in VI. I. 223. Thus समभार्गः, here सम being *all* anudâtta, the accent falls on ग ॥

३७३६ । तत्पुरुषे तुल्यार्थतृतीयासप्तम्युपमानाव्ययद्वितीयाकृत्याः । ६ । २ । २ ॥

सप्तैते पूर्वपदभूतास्तत्पुरुषे प्रकृत्या । तुल्यश्वेतः । 'कृत्यतुल्याख्या अजात्या' (७४९) इति तत्पुरुषः । किरिणा काणः किरिकाणः । 'पृतन्यन्मन्दयत्सखम्' । मन्दयति मादके इन्द्रे सखेति सप्तमीतत्पुरुषः । शस्त्री श्यामा ॥

'+ अव्यये नञ्कुनिपातानाम् +' । अयज्ञो वा एषः । 'परिगणनम्' किम् । स्नात्वाकालकः । मुहूर्तसुखम् भोज्योष्णम् ॥

3736. In a Tatpurusha, the first member preserves its original accent, when it is a word (1) meaning 'a resemblance', or (2) an Instrumental or (3) a Locative or (4) a word with which the second member is compared, (5) or an Indeclinable, or (6) an Accusative, or (7) a Future Passive Participle.

Thus (1) तुल्यश्वेतः । This is a Karmadhâraya compound formed under II. 1. 68, S. 749 and तुल्य being formed by यत् is acutely accented on the first (VI. 1. 216).

(2) When the first member is in the Instrumental case, as :—किरिकाणः (II. 1. 30). किरिः is formed by the Uṇâdi affix इ to कृ (Uṇ. IV. 143), and it being treated as a कित् (Uṇ. IV. 142) has udâtta on the final.

(3) When the first member is a word in the Locative case, as पृतन्यन्मन्दयत्सखम् (Rig Veda I. 4. 7). Here मन्दयत्सखम् is a Locative Tatpurusha compound. मन्दयत् is an epithet of Indra. मन्दयति = मादके = इन्द्रे सखम् ॥

(4) When the first member is a word with which the second member is compared, as :—शस्त्रीश्यामा ॥ These compounds are formed by II. 1. 55. शस्त्री is formed by Gaurâdi ङीष् and is final-acute.

(5) When the first member is an Indeclinable as, अयज्ञोवाएषः । (Rig Veda VI. 67. 9). The Indeclinable compound has udâtta on the first, it is formed by II. 2. 5.

Vârt:—In cases of Indeclinable compounds, the rule applies only to those which are formed by the negative Particle अ, by कु, and by Particles (nipâta). Though नञ् is one of the Nipâtas, its separate mention indicates that नञ्-accent debars even the subsequent कृत्-accent as अकरणिः (III. 3. 112, S. 3389). Therefore, it does not apply to स्नात्वाकालकः which has acute on the final and belongs to Mayûravyaṅsakâdi class.

(6) When the first member is in the accusative case, as:—मुहूर्तसुखम् । They are formed by II. 1. 29. मुहूर्त belongs to पृषोदरादि class and is acutely accented on the last.

(7) When the first member is a Kritya-formed word, as, भोज्योष्णम् । The compounding is by II. 1. 68. भोज्य is formed by ण्यत् and has svarita on the final : (VI. 1. 185).

३७३७ । वर्णो वर्णेष्वनेते । ६ । २ । ३ ॥

वर्णवाचिन्युत्तरपदे एतवर्जिते वर्णवाचि पूर्वपदं प्रकृत्या तत्पुरुषे । कृष्णसारङ्गः । लोहितकल्माषः । कृष्णशब्दो नक्प्रत्ययान्तः । लोहितशब्द इतन्नन्तः । 'वर्णः' किम् । परमकृष्णः । 'वर्णेषु' किम् । कृष्णतिलाः । 'अनेते' किम् । कृष्णैतः ॥

3737. The first member of a Tatpurusha preserves its original accent, when a word denoting color is compounded with another color-denoting word, but not when it is the word *eta.*

Thus कृष्णसारङ्गः, लोहितकल्माषः । कृष्ण is formed by नक् affix (Uṇ. III. 4) and has acute on the final (III. 1. 3). लोहित is formed by the affix तन् added to रुह (Uṇ. III. 94) and has acute on the first (VI. 1. 197).

Why do we say 'color-denoting word'? Observe परमकृष्णः (VI. 1. 223). Why do we say 'with another color-denoting word'? Observe कृष्णतिलाः (VI. 1. 223). Why do we say 'but not when it is एत'? Observe कृष्णैतः । The compounding takes place by II. 1. 69.

३७३८ । गाधलवणयोः प्रमाणे । ६ । २ । ४ ॥

एतयोरुत्तरपदयोः प्रमाणवाचिनि तत्पुरुषे पूर्वपदं प्रकृत्या स्यात् । अरित्रगाधमुदकम् । तत्प्रमाणमित्यर्थः । गोलवणम् । यावद्गवे दीयते तावदित्यर्थः । अरित्रशब्द इत्रन्नन्तो मध्योदात्तः । प्रमाणमियत्तापरिच्छेदमात्रं न पुनरायाम एव । 'प्रमाणे' किम् । परमगाधम् ॥

3738. The first member of a Tatpurusha preserves its original accent, when the second term is 'gâdha' or *lavana*, and the compound expresses a 'measure or mass.'

Thus अरित्रगाधमुदकम् 'water as low or fordable as an Aritra *i. e.* of the depth of a pestle.' गोलवणम् 'so much salt as may be given to a cow.' These are Genitive Tatpurusha compounds. अरित्र is formed by the affix इत्र added to ऋ (III. 2. 184), and has acute on the middle (III. 1. 3): गो is formed by डो (Uṇ. II. 68) and has acute on the final ओ । The word प्रमाण here denotes 'quantity,' 'measure,' 'mass,' 'limit,' and not merely the length. The power of denoting measure by these words is here indicated by and is dependent upon accent.

When not denoting प्रमाण we have परमगाधम् (S. 3734).

३७३९ । दायाद्यं दायादे । ६ । २ । ५ ॥

तत्पुरुषे प्रकृत्या । धनदायादः । धनशब्दः क्युप्रत्ययान्तः प्रत्ययस्वरेणाद्युदात्तः । 'दायाद्यम्' किम् । परमदायादः ॥

3739. In a Tatpurusha compound, having the word dayada as its second member, the first member denoting inheritance preserves its original accent.

Thus विद्यादायादः, धनदायादः । The word धन is derived by adding क्यु to धाञ् (Uṇ. II. 81). Though the Uṇâdi Sútra II. 81 ordains क्यु after the root धा preceded by नि, yet by the rule of बहुल (III. 3. 1) it comes after धा, also when it is not preceded by नि, and धन has acute on the first (III. 1. 3).

Why do we say 'when meaning inheritance'? Observe परमदायादः (VI. 1. 223) taking the final acute of a compound.

३७४० । प्रतिबन्धि चिरकृच्छ्रयोः । ६ । २ । ६ ॥

प्रतिबन्धवाचि पूर्वपदं प्रकृत्या एतयोः परतस्तत्पुरुषे । गमनचिरम् । व्याहरणकृच्छ्रम् । गमने कारणविकलतया चिरकालभावि कृच्छ्रयोगि वा प्रतिबन्धि जायते । 'प्रतिबन्धि' किम् । मूत्रकृच्छ्रम् ॥

3740. In a Tatpurusha compound, having the words *chira* or *krichchhra* as its second member, the first member, when it denotes that which experiences an obstacle, preserves its original accent.

Thus गमनचिरम्, or व्याहरणकृच्छ्रम् । The words गमन and व्याहरण are formed by ल्युट् affix, and have लित् accent (VI. 1. 193). This compound belongs either to the class of Mayûra-vyaṇsakâdi (II. 1. 72), or of an attribute and the thing qualified. When *going* to a place is *delayed* owing to some defective arrangement or cause, or becomes *difficult*, there is produced an *obstacle* or hinderance, and is called गमनचिरं or गमनकृच्छ्रं । Why do we say 'which experiences a hinderance'? Observe मूत्रकृच्छ्रम् ॥

३७४१ । पदेऽपदेशे । ६ । २ । ७ ॥

व्याजवाचिनि पदशब्द उत्तरपदे पूर्वपदं प्रकृत्या तत्पुरुषे । मूत्रपदेन प्रस्थितः । उच्चारपदेन । मूत्रशब्दो घञन्तः उच्चारशब्दो घञन्तः 'थाथ–' (३८७८) आदिस्वरेणान्तोदात्तः । 'अपदेशे' किम् । विष्णुपदम् ॥

3741. In a Tatpurusha compound, the first member preserves its original accent, when the second member is the word *pada* denoting 'a pretext.'

The word अपदेश means 'a pretext,' 'a contrivance.' Thus मूत्रपदेन प्रस्थितः। उच्चारपदेन प्रस्थितः । Gone on pretext of voiding urine or excreta.

The word मूत्र is derived by adding the affix ष्ट्रन् to the root मुच्, the ऊ being substituted for उच् of मुच्, (Uṇ. IV. 163), and has acute on the first (VI. 1. 197) or it may be a word formed by घञ् to the root मूत्रयति । The word उच्चार is also formed by घञ् and by VI. 2. 144, S. 3878, has acute on the final. The compounding takes place by II. 1. 72 or it is an attributive compound.

Why do we say 'when meaning a pretext?' Observe विष्णोः पदम् = विष्णुपदम् ॥

३७४२ । निवाते वातत्राणे । ६ । २ । ८ ॥

निवातशब्दे परे वातत्राणवाचिनि तत्पुरुषे पूर्वपदं प्रकृत्या । कुटीनिवातम् । कुड्यनिवातम् । कुटीशब्दो गौरादिङीषन्तः । कुड्यशब्दो यगन्तः । यगन्तः इत्यध्ये । 'वातत्राणे' किम् । राजनिवाते वसति । निवातशब्दोऽयं रूढः पार्श्वे ॥

3742. In a Tatpurusha compound, the first member preserves its original accent, when the second member is the word 'nivâta' in the sense of 'a protection from wind.'

Thus कुट्येवं निवातं = कुटीनिवातम् 'a hut as the only shelter from the winds.' So also कुड्यनिवातम् or कुड्यनिवातम्। The word निवात is an Avyayibhâva compound = वातस्य अभावः (II. 1. 6): or a Bahuvrihi = निरुद्धो वातोऽस्मिन्। The word कुटीनिवातम् &c., are examples of compounds of two words in apposition. कुटी is formed by ङीष् (IV. 1. 41), and has acute on the last (III. 1. 3). Some say that कुड्य is derived from कु by adding यत् with the augment डक् and treating it as कित्, it has the acute on the first; others hold that it is derived by the affix ड्यक् to कु and the affix has the accent. The ड here is not indicatory but part of the affix.

Why do we say when meaning 'a shelter from wind'? Observe राजनिवाते वसति = 'he lives under the shelter of the king.' Here निवात = पार्श्वः or vicinity.

३७४३। शारदेऽनार्तवे। ६।२।९॥

ऋतौ भवमार्तवम्। तदन्यवाचिनि शारदशब्दे परे तत्पुरुषे पूर्वपदं प्रकृतिस्वरं स्यात्। रज्जुशारदमुदकम्। शारदशब्दो नूतनार्थः। तस्यास्वपदविग्रहः। 'रज्ज्वोः सद्य उद्धृतम्'। रज्जुशब्द 'सृजेरसुम्च' इत्याद्युदात्तो व्युत्पादितः। 'अनार्तवे' किम्। उत्तमशारदम्॥

3743. In a Tatpurusha compound, the first member preserves its original accent, when the second member is the word 'Sârad' having any other sense than that of 'autumnal.'

The word आर्तव means appertaining to season (ऋतु) *i. e.*, when the word शारद does not refer to the season of शरत् or autumn. Thus रज्जुशारदमुदकम् 'fresh drawn water.' The word शारद means here 'fresh,' 'new': and it forms an invariable compound. The word रज्जु is formed by उ affix added to सृज् (Un. I. 15), the स being elided. The affix उ is treated as नित् (Un. I. 9) and the accent falls on the first syllable (VI. I. 197).

Why do we say 'when not meaning autumnal'? Observe उत्तमशारदम् the best autumnal grass &c. (VI. I. 223).

३७४४। अध्वर्युकषाययोर्जातौ। ६।२।१०॥

एतयोः परतो जातिवाचिनि तत्पुरुषे पूर्वपदं प्रकृतिस्वरम्। कठाध्वर्युः। दौवारिककषायम्। कठशब्दः पचाद्यजन्तः। तस्मात्-'वैशम्पायनान्तेवासिभ्यश्च' (१४८४) इति णिनिः 'कठचरकाल्लुक्' (१४८७) इति लुक्। द्वारि नियुक्त इति ठक्यन्तोदात्तो दौवारिकशब्दः। 'जातौ' किम्। परमाध्वर्युः॥

3744. In a Tatpurusha compound denoting a genus, the first member preserves its original accent, when the second member is the word अध्वर्यु or कषाय॥

Thus कठाध्वर्युः। This is an Appositional compound denoting 'genus or kind,' with a fixed meaning. कठ is derived by अच् affix (III. I. 34), and to it is added the Taddhita affix णिनि (IV. 3. 104, S. 1484), in the sense of कठेन प्रोक्तं (IV. 3 101), and the affix is then elided by IV. 3. 107, S. 1487.

So also दौवारिककषायम्। This is a Genitive compound. The word दौवारिक is formed by ठक् affix added to द्वार and has acute on the final (VI. I. 165). Why do we say 'when meaning a genus'? Observe, परमाध्वर्युः, परमकषायः (VI. I. 223).

३७४५ । सदृशप्रतिरूपयोः सादृश्ये । ६ । २ । ११ ॥

अनयोः पूर्वं प्रकृत्या । पितृसदृशः । 'सादृश्ये' किम् । परमसदृशः । समासार्थोऽत्र पूज्यमानता न सादृश्यम् ॥

3745. In a Tatpurusha compound expressing resemblance with some one or something, the first member preserves its original accent, when the second member is 'sadṛiśa' or 'pratirûpa'

Thus पितृसदृशः The word पितृ is formed by Uṇadi affix तृच् (Uṇ II. 95) and is finally accented. Why do we say 'when meaning resemblance'? Observe परमसदृशः (VI. 1. 223): here the sense of the compound is that of 'honor' and not 'resemblance.'

३७४६ । द्विगौ प्रमाणे । ६ । २ । १२ ॥

द्विगावुत्तरपदे प्रमाणवाचिनि तत्पुरुषे पूर्वपदं प्रकृतिस्वरम् । प्राच्यसप्तसमः । सप्त समाः प्रमाणमस्य । '+प्रमाणे लो द्विगोर्नित्यम्+' इति मात्रचो लुक् । प्राच्यशब्द आद्युदात्तः । प्राच्यश्चासौ सप्तसमश्च प्राच्यसप्तसमः । 'द्विगौ' किम् । व्रीहिप्रस्थः । 'प्रमाणे' किम् परमसप्तसमम् ॥

3746. In a Tatpurusha compound denoting 'measure or quantity', the first member preserves its original accent, when the second member is a Dvigu.

Thus प्राच्यसप्तसमः । The word सप्तसमः = सप्तसमाः प्रमाणमस्य । the affix मात्रच denoting 'measure' (V. 2.37. S. 1838) is elided (See V. 2. 37. S. 1838 Vart) प्राच्यश्चासौ सप्तसमश्च = प्राच्यसप्तसमः 'an Eastern seven-years old'; प्राच्य has acute on the first. Why do we say 'before a Dvigu'? Observe व्रीहिप्रस्थः । Why do we say 'when denoting measure?' Observe परमसप्तसमम् ।

३७४७ । गन्तव्यपण्यं वाणिजे । ६ । २ । १३ ॥

वाणिजशब्दे परे तत्पुरुषे गन्तव्यवाचि पण्यवाचि च पूर्वपदं प्रकृतिस्वरम् । मद्रवाणिजः सप्तमीसमासः । मद्रशब्दो रक्प्रत्ययान्तः । 'गन्तव्य इति किम् । परमवाणिजः ॥

3747. Before the word 'vânij' 'a trader,' the first member of a Tatpurusha preserves its accent, when it is a word specifying the place whither one has to go, or the ware in which one deals.

Thus मद्रवाणिजः=मद्रादिषु गत्वा व्यवहरन्ति 'the Madra-merchants *i. e.* 'who trade by going to Madra' All these are Locative compounds. मद्र is derived by रक् affix (Uṇ II. 11) and is acutely accented on the last (VI. 1. 165). In the sense of पण्य we have : गोवाणिजः 'a dealer in cows;' गो is finally accented (Uṇ. II. 67).

Why do we say 'the place whither one goes, or the goods in which one deals?' Observe परमवाणिजः ॥

३७४८ । मात्रोपज्ञोपक्रमच्छाये नपुंसके । ६ । २ । १४ ॥

मात्रादिषु परतो नपुंसकवाचिनि तत्पुरुषे तथा । भिक्षायास्तुल्यप्रमाणं भिक्षामात्रम् । भिक्षाशब्दो 'गुरोश्च हलः (३२८) इत्यप्रत्ययान्तः । पाणिन्युपज्ञम् । पाणिनिशब्द आद्युदात्तः ।

नन्दोपक्रमम् । नन्दशब्दः । पचाद्यजन्तः । इषुच्छायम् । इषुशब्द आद्युदात्तो नित्वात् । 'नपुंसके' किम् । कुड्यच्छाया ॥

3748. The first member of a Tatpurusha preserves its accent before the words 'mâtrâ,' 'upajñâ,' 'upakrama', and 'chhâyâ' when these words appear as neuter.

Thus भिक्षामात्रं । The word मात्रा is here synonymous with तुल्य, the phrase being = भिक्षायास्तुल्यप्रमाणं, and is a Genitive compound. The word भिक्षा is derived from भिक्ष, by the feminine affix अ (III. 3. 103. S. 3280), and has acute on the final (II. 1. 3). So also with उपज्ञा, as पाणिन्युपज्ञम् (see II. 4. 21). All these are Genitive compounds. The word पाणिनि is acutely accented on the first. So also with उपक्रम, as नन्दोपक्रमाणि मानानि । The word नन्द is formed by अच् (III. 1. 144). The Tatpurusha compounds ending in उपज्ञा and उपक्रम are neuter by II. 4. 21. So also with छाया, as इषुच्छायम् । The word इषु is derived from इष् by उ affix (Un. I. 13), and it being treated as नित् (Un. I. 9) the acute falls on इ the first syllable (VI. I. 197). The compound is a Genitive Tatpurusha—इषूणां छाया; and it is Neuter by II. 4. 22. When the compound is not a Neuter we have कुड्यछाया (II. 4. 25).

३७४९ । सुखप्रिययोर्हिते । ६ । २ । १५ ॥

एतयोः परयोर्हितवाचिनि तत्पुरुषे तथा । गमनप्रियम् । गमनसुखम् । गमनशब्दे लित्स्वरः 'हिते' किम् । परमसुखम् ॥

3749. The first member of a Tatpurusha preserves its accent when the second term is *sukha* or *priya*, and the sense is 'to feel delight, or is good.'

Thus गमनसुखम् 'the pleasure of going.' गमनप्रियम् । These are appositional compounds. The word गमन is formed by ल्युट् affix and has acute on the sylla le preceding the affix (VI. I. 193). The word sukha and priya have the sen·e of हित or 'well' '*good*,' 'beneficial,' *i. e.* when the thing denoted by the first term the cause of pleasure or delight. When this is not the sense we have परमसुखम् ॥

३७५० । प्रीतौ च । ६ । २ । १६ ॥

प्रीतौ गम्यायां प्रागुक्तम् । ब्राह्मणसुखं पायसम् । छात्रप्रियोऽनध्यायः । ब्राह्मणच्छात्रशब्दौ प्रत्ययस्वरेणान्तोदात्तौ । 'प्रीतौ' किम् । राजसुखम् ॥

3750. The first member of a Tatpurusha preserves its accent, the second term being *sukha* or *priya* in the sense of 'agreeable to one, or desired.'

Thus ब्राह्मणसुखं पायसं 'the sweetmilk desired by or agreeable to the Brâhmanas,' छात्रप्रियोऽनध्यायः &c. The words ब्राह्मण and छात्र have acute on the final being formed by the affixes अण् and ण respectively (V 4. 62 and III. I. 3). When not meaning agreeable to or desired, we have राजसुखम्, ॥

३७५१ । स्वं स्वामिनि । ६ । २ । १७ ॥

स्वामिशब्दे परे स्ववाचि पूर्वपदं तथा । गोस्वामी । 'स्वम्' किम् । परमस्वामी ॥

3751. In a Tatpurusha compound, having the word 'svâmin' as its second member, the first term, when it denotes the thing possessed, retains its original accent.

Thus गो॑स्वामी । When the first member is not a word denoting possession, we have परमस्वामी ॥

३७५२ । पत्यावैश्वर्ये । ६ । २ । १८ ॥

'दमूना गृहपतिर्दमे' ॥

3752. In a Tatpurusha ending in *pati* when it means 'master' or 'lord,' the first member preserves its original accent.

Thus दमूना गृहपतिर्दमे (Rig Veda I. 60. 4). The word गृह is formed by क (III. I. 144) and has acute on the final (III I. 3).

३७५३ । न भूवाक्चिद्दिधिषु । ६ । २ । १९ ॥

पतिशब्दे परे ऐश्वर्यवाचिनि तत्पुरुषे नैतानि प्रकृत्या । भुवः पतिर्भूपतिः । वाक्पतिः । चित्पतिः । दिधिषूपतिः ॥

3753. The words भू, वाक्, चित्, and दिधिषू, however, do not preserve their original accent in a Tatpurusha, when coming before the word *pati* denoting 'lord.'

This debars the accent taught by the last aphorism. Thus भूपति॑ः, वाक्पति॑ः, चित्पति॑ः, दिधिषूपति॑ः ॥ All these are Genitive compounds and are finally accented by VI. I. 223.

३७५४ । वा भुवनम् । ६ । २ । २० ॥

उक्तविषये । भुवनपतिः । 'भूसूधूभ्रस्जिभ्यः-' इति क्युन्नन्तो भुवनशब्दः ॥

3754. The word *bhuvana* may optionally keep its accent in a Tatpurusha, before *pati* denoting 'lord.'

Thus भुवनपति॑ः or भुवनपतिः । The word भुवन is formed by क्युन् (Un. II. 80), and has acute on the first (VI. I. 197).

३७५५ । आशङ्काबाधनेदीयस्सु संभावने । ६ । २ । २१ ॥

अस्तित्वाध्यवसायः संभावनम् । गमनाशङ्कमस्ति । गमनाबाधम् । गमननेदीयः । गमनमाशङ्क्यत आबाध्यते निकटतरमिति वा संभाव्यते । 'संभावने' किम् । परमनेदीयः ॥

3755. Before आशङ्क आबाध, and नेदीयस्, the first member in a Tatpurusha compound preserves its original accent, when it treats about a supposition.

The word संभावनम् = अस्तित्वाध्यवसाय: 'the hesitation about the existence of a thing.' Thus ग॑मनाशङ्कं वर्तते 'one fears the journey'; Similarly ग॑मनाबाधम् वर्तते = गमनं बाध्यते इति संभाव्यते 'it has stepped in as an obstacle to journey.' Similarly ग॑मननेदीयो वर्तते = गमनमिति निकटतरमिति संभाव्यते 'the journey stands directly before.'

Why do we say 'when a supposition is meant'? Observe परमनेर्दायः। All the above words are formed by ल्युट् affix and have लित् accent. (VI. 1. 193).

३७५६। पूर्वे भूतपूर्वे। ६। २। २२॥

आढ्यो भूतपूर्वः : आढ्यपूर्वः। पूर्वशब्दो वृत्तिविषये भूतपूर्वे वर्तते। 'भूतपूर्वे' किम्। परमपूर्वः॥

3756. The first member of a Tatpurusha compound preserves its original accent when the word 'pûrva' is the second member, and the sense is 'this had been lately—.'

Thus आढ्यो भूतपूर्वः = आढ्यपूर्वः 'formerly had been rich.' The compound must be analysed in the above way. The compounding takes place by II. 1. 57 or it belongs to Mayûra-vyañsakâdi class.

Why do we say when meaning 'had been lately.' Observe परमपूर्वः, which should be analysed as परमश्चासौ पूर्वश्चेति। If it is analysed as परमो भूतपूर्वः then it becomes an example under the rule and not a counter-example. In order therefore, to make this rule applicable we must know the sense of the compound.

३७५७। सविधसनीडसमर्यादसवेशसदेशेषु सामीप्ये। ६। २। २३॥

एषु पूर्वं प्रकृत्या। मद्रसविधम्। गान्धारसनीडम्। काश्मीरसमर्यादम्। मद्रसवेशम् मद्रसदेशम्। 'सामीप्ये' किम्। सह मर्यादया समर्यादं क्षेत्रम्। चैत्रसमर्यादम्॥

3757. The first member of a Tatpurusha compound preserves its original accent, when the second member is सविध, सनीड, समर्याद, सवेश, and सदेश in the sense of 'what can be found in the vicinity thereof.'

Thus मद्रसविधम्, गान्धारसनीडम्, काश्मीरसमर्यादम्, मद्रसवेशम् and मद्रसदेशम्। The accents of these words have been taught before in Sûtras VI. 2. 12, 13. The words सविध &c., are derived from सह विधया &c., but they all mean 'in the vicinity': मद्रसविधं = मद्राणां सामीप्यम्। Why do we say 'when meaning in the vicinity thereof? Observe सह मर्यादया वर्तते = समर्यादं क्षेत्रम् 'a field having boundary.' चैत्रस्य समर्यादं = चैत्रसमर्यादम् 'the bounded field of Chaitra.'

३७५८। विस्पष्टादीनि गुणवचनेषु। ६। २। २४॥

विस्पष्टकटुकम्। विस्पष्टशब्दो 'गतिरनन्तरः' (३७८३) इत्याद्युदात्तः। 'विस्पष्ट-' इति किम्। परमलवणम्। 'गुण-' इति किम्। विस्पष्टब्राह्मणः। विस्पष्ट। विचित्र। व्यक्त। संपन्न। पण्डित। कुशल। चपल। निपुण॥

3758. The words 'vispashṭa' &c. preserve their accent when followed by an Adjective word in a compound.

Thus विस्पष्टकटुकम्। The compounding takes place by II. 1. 4. and it should be analysed thus विस्पष्टं कटुकम्।

The word विस्पष्ट has acute on the first by VI. 2. 49. The word (2) विचित्र is also acute on the first as it gets the accent of the Indeclinable. Some read the word as विचित्तः, which being a Bahuvrihi has also first acute. The word (3) व्यंक्त has svarita on the first by VIII. 2. 4. The remaining words of this class are (4) संपर्च, (5) पटु or कटु, (6) पण्डित, (7) कुशल (8) चपल and (9) निपुण. Of these, the word संपर्च has acute on the final by VI. 2. 144 ; पटु is formed by उ (Uṇ 1. 18), which being considered as नित् (Uṇ. 1. 9), it has acute on the first. पण्डित is formed by क्त to the root पड्, and is finally acute (VI. 2. 144). कुशल has accent on the final, being formed by a krit affix (कुशान् लाति=कुशलः, ला आदाने, or Uṇ I. 106). चपल being formed by a चित् affix (Uṇ. I. 111), has acute on the final (VI. 1. 163), for चित् is understood in the Uṇadi sûtra Uṇ. I. 111 from sûtra Uṇ. I. 106. The word निपुण has acute on the final by VI. 2. 144, being formed by क affix added to पुण् &c.

Why do we say 'of विस्पष्ट &c.,? Observe परमलवणम् having acute on the final. Why do we say 'when followed by a word expressing a quality'? Observe विस्पष्टब्राह्मणः ॥

३७५९ । श्रज्यावमकन्पापवत्सु भावे कर्मधारये । ६ । २ । २५ ॥

'श्र' 'ज्य' 'अवम' 'कन्' इत्यादेशवत्सु पापवाचिनि चोत्तरपदे भाववाचि पूर्वपदं प्रकृत्या । गमनश्रेष्ठम् । गमनज्यायः । गमनावमम् । गमनकनिष्ठम् । गमनपापिष्ठम् । 'श्र-' इत्यादि किम् । गमनशोभनम् । 'भावे' किम् । गम्यतेऽनेनेति गमनम् । गमनं श्रेयो गमनश्रेयः । कर्म-इति किम । षष्ठीसमासे मा भूत् ॥

3759. In a Karmadhâraya compound, the first member consisting of a Verbal noun 'bhâva' preserves its original accent before adjective forms built from 'śra' (V. 3. 60), 'jya' (V. 3. 61) 'avama' and 'kan' (V. 3. 64), and before a form built from the word 'pâpa.'

Thus गमनश्रेष्ठम्, गमनज्यायः, गमनावमम्, गमनकनिष्ठम् गमनपापिष्ठम् । गमन is a ल्युट् formed word and has लित् accent *i. e.*, on the first syllable, (VI. 1. 193). The words श्र, ज्य, and कन् are substitutes which certain adjectives take in the comparative and superlative degrees, and the employment of these forms in the sûtra indicates that the comparative and superlative words having these elements should be taken as second members, and so also of पाप, the comparative and superlative are taken, for this is the meaning here of the word पापवत् ॥

Why do we say 'श्र &c.'? Observe गमनशोभनम् । Why do we say 'a verbal Noun'? Observe गमनश्रेयः, गमनं श्रेयः = गमनश्रेयः a better carriage where the word गमन is = गम्यतेऽनेन 'a carriage' here ल्युट् is in the sense of करण and not भाव (III. 1. 117. S. 3293). Why do we say 'a Karmadhâraya compound'? Not so in the Genitive compound.

३७६० । कुमारश्च । ६ । २ । २६ ॥

कर्मधारये । कुमारश्रमणा । कुमारशब्दोऽन्तोदात्तः ॥

3760. The word 'kumâra' preserves its original accent, when standing as a first member in a Karmadhâraya compound.

Thus कुमारश्रमणा । The word कुमार has acute on the final, as it is derived from the root कुमार क्रीडायाम् with the affix अच् of पचादि । By II. 1. 70, S. 752 it is ordained that कुमार is compounded with श्रमणा &c.

NOTE :—Some commentators hold that the word कुमार must be followed by श्रमणा &c. (II. 1. 70) to make this rule applicable. They refer to the maxim लक्षणप्रतिपदोक्तयोः प्रतिपदोक्तस्यैव ग्रहणम् "whenever a term is employed which might denote both something original and also something else resulting from a rule of Grammar, or when a term is employed in a rule which might denote both something formed by another rule in which the same individual term has been employed, and also something else formed by a general rule, such a term should be taken to denote, in the former case, only that which is original, and in the latter case, only that which is formed by that rule in which the same individual term has been employed." Other Grammarians, however do not make any such limitation, but apply the rule to all Karmadhâraya compounds of कुमार ॥

३७६१ । आदिः प्रत्येनसि । ६ । २ । २७ ॥

कुमारस्यादिरुदात्तः प्रत्येनसि परे कर्मधारये । प्रतिगतमेनोऽस्य प्रत्येनाः । कुमारप्रत्येनाः ॥

3761. In a Karmadhâraya compound of Kumâra followed by *pratyenas*, the acute falls on the first syllable of Kumâra.

The word प्रत्येनस् = प्रतिगतमेनोऽस्य । Thus कुमारप्रत्येनाः ॥

३७६२ । पूगेष्वन्यतरस्याम् । ६ । २ । २८ ॥

पूगा गणास्तेषूक्तं वा । कुमारचातकाः । कुमारजीमूताः । आद्युदात्तत्वाभावे कुमारश्चेत्येव भवति ॥

3762. The first syllable of Kumâra is acute optionally, when the second member is a word denoting 'the name of a horde.'

The word पूग means 'a multitude, a collection &c.' Thus कुमारचातकाः or कुमारचातकाः (VI. 2. 26), or कुमारचातकाः । So also with कुमारजीमुतकाः । Here चातक &c, are horde-names ; and the affix ञ्य is added to them by V. 3. 112 : which is elided in the Plural by II. 4. 62. In the above examples when the word 'Kumâra' is not accented on the first syllable, it gets accent on the last by VI. 2. 26, when the प्रतिपदोक्त maxim is not applied : when that maxim is applied, the final of the compound takes the accent by the general rule VI. 1. 223.

३७६३ । इगन्तकालकपालभगालशरावेषु द्विगौ । ६ । २ । २९ ॥

एषु परेषु पूर्वं प्रकृत्या । पञ्चारत्नयः प्रमाणमस्य पञ्चारत्निः । दशमासान्भूतो दशमास्यः । पञ्चमासान्भूतः पञ्चमास्यः । 'तमधीष्टे –' इत्यधिकारे द्विगोर्यप् । पञ्चकपालः । पञ्चभगालः पञ्चशरावः 'त्रः संख्यायाः' इति पञ्चञ्छब्द आद्युदात्तः । 'इगन्तादिषु' किम् । पञ्चाश्वः । 'द्विगौ' किम् । परमारत्निः ॥

3763. In a Dvigu compound, the first member preserves its original accent, before a stem ending in a simple vowel, with the exception of *a* (*ik*), before a word denoting time, as well as before 'kapâla,' 'bhagâla' and 'śarâva.'

Thus पँञ्चारत्निः। The above is an example of Taddhitârtha Dvigu (II. 1. 52) equal to पंचारत्नयः प्रमाणमस्य, the प्रमाण denoting affix मात्रच् is always elided in Dvigu (V. 2. 3 Vârt). So also दँशमास्यः = दश मासान् भूतो। So also पँञ्चमास्य। This is also a Taddhitârtha Dvigu (II. 1. 52), formed by the affix यत्. (V. 1.80-82 S 1744-46). So also पँञ्चकपालः, पँञ्चभगालः, पँञ्चशरावः। These are also Taddhitârtha Dvigu formed by IV. 2. 16, the affix अण् being elided by IV. 1. 88. The word पँञ्चन् is first acute by Phit (II. 5).

Why do we say "before an इगन्त stem &c"? Observe पंचभिरश्वैः क्रीतः=पंचाश्वैः, । Why do we say "in a Dvigu Compound?" Observe परमारत्निः ॥

३७६४ । बह्वन्यतरस्याम् । ६ । २ । ३० ॥

बहुशब्दस्तथा वा । बहुरत्निः । बहुमास्यः । बहुकपालः । बहुशब्दोऽन्तोदात्तः । तस्य यणि कृते 'उदात्तस्वरितयोः –' (३६५७) इति भवति ॥

3764. In a Dvigu compound, the word *bahu* may optionally preserve its accent, when followed by an ik-ending stem, or by a time-word, or by kapâla, bhagâla and śarâva.

This allows option where the last rule required the accent necessarily. Thus बह्वँरत्निः or बहुरत्निँः, बहुँमास्यः or बहुमास्यँः, बहुँकपालः or बहुकपालँः, बहुँभगालः or बहुभगालँः, बहुँशरावः or बहुशरावँः। The word बहुँ has acute on the final being formed by the affix कु (Uṇ. I. 29). When the उ is changed to व् as in the first example, the anudâtta अ is changed into svarita by VIII. 2. 4. S. 3657, when the first member preserves its accent. In the other alternative, the accent falls on the last syllable.

३७६५ । दिष्टिवितस्त्योश्च । ६ । २ । ३१ ॥

एतयोः परतः पूर्वपदं प्रकृत्या वा द्विगौ । पञ्चदिष्टिः । पञ्चवितस्तिः ॥

3765. In a Dvigu compound, the first member may optionally preserve its accent, when followed by the words 'dishṭi' and *vitasti* as second members.

Thus पँञ्चदिष्टिः or पञ्चदिष्टिँः, पँञ्चवितस्तिः or पञ्चवितस्तिँः। The affix मात्रच् is elided after the प्रमाण denoting words dishṭi and vitasti (V. 2. 37).

३७६६ । सप्तमी सिद्धशुष्कपक्वबन्धेष्वकालात् । ६ । २ । ३२ ॥

अकालवाचि सप्तम्यन्तं प्रकृत्या सिद्धादिषु । सांकाश्यसिद्धः । सांकाश्येति ण्यान्तः । आतपशुष्कः । भ्राष्ट्रपक्वः । भ्राष्ट्रेति ष्ट्रन्नन्तः । चक्रबन्धः । चक्रशब्दोऽन्तोदात्तः । 'अकालात्' किम् । पूर्वाह्णसिद्धः । कृत्स्वरेण बाधितः सप्तमीस्वरः प्रतिप्रसूयते ॥

3766. A locative-ending word, when it does not denote time, preserves its original accent, when followed by *siddha*, 'śushka' *pakva*, and *bandha*, in a compound.

Thus सांकाश्यँसिद्धः or सांकाँश्यसिद्धः, काम्पिल्यँसिद्धः or काम्पिँल्यसिद्धः। The word सांकाश्य is formed by the affix ण्यत् added to संकाश (IV. 2. 80). The words, sâmkâśya and kâmpilya have acute on the final, and by Phiṭ Sûtra (III. 16) in the alternative the accent falls on the middle. So also आतपशुष्क। The word

भाष्ट्र is formed by ष्ट्रन् affix, and has acute on the beginning. So also चक्रंबन्धः The word chakra, has acute on the final.

Why do we say 'when not denoting time.'? Observe पूर्वाह्णसिद्धः। The compounding takes place by II. 1. 41. The accent of the Locative Tatpurusha taught in VI. 2. 1. was debarred by Krit-accent taught in VI. 2. 144. The present sûtra debars this last rule regarding Krit-accent and reordains the Locative Tatpurusha accent when the Krit-words are सिद्ध &c.

३७६७। परिप्रत्युपापा वर्ज्यमानाहोरात्रावयवेषु। ६। २। ३३॥

एते प्रकृत्या वर्ज्यमानवाचिनि अहोरात्रावयववाचिनि चोत्तरपदे। परित्रिगर्त्तं वृष्टो देवः। प्रतिपूर्वाह्णम्। प्रत्यपररात्रम्। उपपूर्वरात्रम्। अपत्रिगर्त्तम्। उपसर्गा आद्युदात्ताः। बहुव्रीहितत्पुरुषयोः सिद्धत्वादव्ययीभावार्थमिदम्। अपपर्योरेव वर्ज्यमानमुत्तरपदम् तयोरेव वर्ज्यमानार्थत्वात्। अहोरात्रावयवा अपि वर्ज्यमाना एव तयोर्भवन्ति। 'वर्ज्य-' इति किम्। अग्निं प्रति प्रत्यग्नि॥

3767. The particles *pari*, *prati*, *upa*, and *apa*, preserve their accent before that word, which specifies an exclusion, or a portion of day and night, (in an Avyayîbhâva compound also).

Thus प॑रित्रिगर्त्तं वृष्टो देवः 'It rained all round (but not in) Trigarta.' (See II. 1. 11. and 12). So also प॑रिसौवीरम् प॑रिसार्वसेनि, प॑रिपूर्वरात्रम्। So also प्र॑तिपूर्वाह्णम्, प्र॑त्यपररात्रम् उ॑पपूर्वाह्णम्, उ॑पपूर्वरात्रम्, ॥ अ॑पत्रिगर्तं वृष्टो देवः, (II. I. 11. and 12).

By Phiṭ Sûtras IV. 12, and 13 all Particles (Nipâta) have acute on the first syllable. So also upasargas with the exception of अभि। Therefore परि &c, have acute on the first. In a Tatpurusha and Bahuvrîhi compounds, these words 'pari' 'prati' &c. as first members would have retained their accent by the rules already gone before; the present sûtra, therefore, extends the principle of the preservation of the accent to Avyayîbhâva compounds also. The prepositions अप and परि alone denote the limit exclusive or वर्जन, and it is therefore with these two prepositions only that the second member can denote the thing excluded, and not with प्रति and उप। With these prepositions अप and परि, the second term if denoting a member of day or night, is also taken even as *excluded*, therefore no separate illustrations of those are given.

Why do we say 'before a word which is excluded, or is a part of a day and night'? Observe प्रत्यग्नि शलभाः पतन्ति।

३७६८। राजन्यबहुवचनद्वन्द्वेऽन्धकवृष्णिषु। ६। २। ३४॥

राजन्यवाचिनां बहुवचनान्तानामन्धकवृष्णिषु वर्तमाने द्वन्द्वे पूर्वपदं प्रकृत्या। श्वाफल्कचैत्रकाः। शिनिवासुदेवाः। शिनिराद्युदात्तो लक्षणया तदपत्ये वर्तते। 'राजन्य-' इति किम्। द्वैप्यभैमायनाः। द्वीपे भवा द्वैप्याः। भैमेरपत्यं युवा भैमायनः। अन्धकवृष्णय एते न तु राजन्याः। राजन्यग्रहणमिहाभिषिक्तवंश्यानां क्षत्रियाणां ग्रहणार्थम्। नैते तथा। 'बहुवचनम्' किम्। संकर्षणवासुदेवौ। 'द्वन्द्वे' किम्। वृष्णीनां कुमारा वृष्णिकुमाराः। 'अन्धकवृष्णिषु' किम्। कुरुपञ्चालाः॥

3768. The first member of a Dvandva compound, formed of names denoting the Kshatriya (warrior) clans in the plural number, retains its original accent when the warrior belongs to the clan of Andhaka or Vṛishṇi.

Thus श्वाफल्कचैत्रकाः, चैत्रकरोधकाः, शिनिवासुदेवाः। The word Śvâphalka is formed by अण् affix (IV. 1. 114) and has acute on the last (III. 1. 3). The word शिनि has acute on the first syllable, and does not change in denoting Patronymic.

Why do we say 'in denoting a Warrior clan'? Observe द्वैप्यहैमायनाः। Here द्वैप्य is derived from द्वीप by the affix यञ् (IV. 3. 10) = द्वीपे भवाः। हैमायनः = हेमेरपत्यं युवा। These names belong to Andhaka and Vṛishṇi clans, but are not the warrior-names. The word राजन्य here means those Kshatriyas who belong to the family of anointed kings and warriors (अभिषिक्तवंश्याः); these (Dvaipya and Haimâyana) do not belong to any such family.

Why do we say 'in the Plural number'? Observe संकर्षणवासुदेवौ॥

Why do we say 'in a Dvandva compound'? Observe वृष्णीनां कुमाराः=वृष्णिकुमाराः॥

Why do we say 'of Andhaka and Vṛishni clans'? Observe कुरुपञ्चालाः॥

३७६९। संख्या। ६। २। ३५॥

संख्यावाचि पूर्वपदं प्रकृत्या द्वन्द्वे। द्वादश। त्रयोदश। त्रेस्त्रयसादेश आद्युदात्तो निपात्यते॥

3769. The numeral word, standing as the first member of a Dvandva compound, preserves its accent.

Thus एकादश, द्वादश, त्रयोदश or त्रयोदश। The त्रयस् is the substitute of त्रि VI. 3. 48) and has acute on the final.

३७७०। आचार्योपसर्जनश्चान्तेवासी। ६। २। ३६॥

आचार्योपसर्जनान्तेवासिनां द्वन्द्वे पूर्वपदं प्रकृत्या। पाणिनीयरौढीयाः। छस्वरेण मध्योदात्तावेतौ। आचार्योपसर्जनग्रहणं द्वन्द्वविशेषणम्। सकलो द्वन्द्व आचार्योपसर्जनो यथा विज्ञायेत। तेनेह न। पाणिनीयदेवदत्तौ। 'आचार्य—' इति किम्। छान्दसवैयाकरणाः। 'अन्तेवासी' किम्। आपिशलपाणिनीये शास्त्रे॥

3770. When words denoting scholars are named after their teachers and are compounded into a Dvandva, the first member retains its accent.

The word अन्तेवासी means 'a pupil' 'a boarder; not a day scholar.' When the scholar is named by an epithet derived from the name of his teacher, that name is आचार्योपसर्जनः or teacher-derived name. Thus पाणिनीयरौढीयाः। Both words have acute on the middle as formed by छ affix. The word आचार्योपसर्जन qualifies the whole Dvandva compound and not the first member only. That is, the whole compound in all its parts should denote scholars, whose names are derived from those of their teachers. Therefore not in पाणिनीय-देवदत्तौ where though the first is a teacher-derived name, the second is not.

Why do we say "names derived from the teacher's"? Observe छान्दसवैयाकरणाः॥

Who do we say 'a scholar?' Observe आपिशलपाणिनीये शास्त्रे ॥

३७७१ । कार्तकौजपादयश्च । ६ । २ । ३७ ॥

एषां द्वन्द्वे पूर्वपदं प्रकृत्या । कार्तकौजपौ । कृतस्येदं कुजपस्येदमित्यणन्तावेतौ । सावर्णिमाण्डूकेयौ ॥

3771. Also in the Dvandvas 'kârtkaujapau' &c, the first members retain their accent.

Those words of this list which end in a dual or plural affix have been so exhibited for the sake of distinctness. The following is a list of these words. 1. कार्त–कौजपौ (formed by अण् IV. I. 114 in the sense of Patronymic, from कृत and कुजप these being Rishi names) ॥

2. सावर्णिमाण्डूकेयौ (sâvarni is formed by इञ् Patron. affix and माण्डूकेय by ढक् IV. I. 119).

3. आवन्त्यश्मकाः The word Avanti is end-acute, to which is added the Patron affix ñyaṅ by IV. I. 171, which being a Tadrâj is elided in the plural; अवन्तीनां निवासो जनपदः = अवन्ति the quadruple significant अण् being elided.

4. पैलश्यापर्णेयाः (Paila is derived from Pilâ; the son of Pilâ is Paila, the yuvan descendent of Paila will be formed by adding फिञ् IV. I. 156, which is however, elided by II. 4. 59.) The word Śyáparṇa belongs to Bidâdi class IV. I. 104, the female descendant will be Śyâparṇî the yuvan descendant of her will be Śyâparṇeya. It is not necessary that the compound should be plural always. We have पैलश्यापर्णेयौ also.

5. कपिश्यापर्णेयाः Kapi has acute on the final. The son of Kapi will be formed by यञ् IV. 1. 107, which is however elided by II. 4. 64. This compound must, therefore, be always in the plural.

6. शैतिकाक्षपांचालेयाः (Śitikâksha is the name of a Rishi, his son will be Śaitikâksha by अण्, IV. I. 114, the yuvan descendant of the latter will be formed by इञ् which is elided by II. 4. 58. Pâñchâla's female descendant is Pâñchâlî, her yuvan descendant is Pâñchâleya. The plural number here is not compulsory. We have शैतकाक्षपाञ्चालेयौ also.)

7. कटुकवार्चलेयाः or कटुकवार्चलेयाः (The son of Kaṭuka will be formed by इञ् IV. I. 59, which is elided in the Plural by II. 4. 66. The son of Varchalâ is Vârchaleya).

8. शाकलशुनकाः (The son of Śakala is Śâkalya, his pupils are Śâkalâḥ by अण् IV. 2. 111. The son of Śunaka will be Śaunaka by अञ् IV. I. 104, which will be elided in the Plural by II. 4. 64). Some read it as शकलशणकाः, where the इञ् affix after Saṇaka is elided by II. 4. 66. So also शुनकधात्रेयः ॥

9. शणकबाभ्रवाः (the son of Babhru is Bâbhrava).

10. आर्चाभिमौद्गलाः (Archâvinah are those who study the work produced by Richâva, the affix णिनि being added by IV. 3. 104. Mudgala belongs to Kaṅvâdi class IV. 2. III; Maudgalâḥ are pupils of the son of Mudgala).

11. कुन्तिसुराष्ट्राः. This a Dvandva of Kunti and Surâshṭra in the plural or of the country-names derived from them like Avanti. Kunti and Chinti have acute on the final.

12. चिन्तिसुराष्ट्राः as the last. 13. तण्डवतण्डाः (Both belong to Pachâdi class formed by अच् III. 1. 134, from तडि ताडने Bhvâdi 300, वतण्ड is formed from the same root with the prefix अव, the अ being elided, and both have acute on the final: and are enumerated in the Gargâdi list IV. 1. 105. In the plural the patronymic affix यञ् is elided by II. 4. 64.

14. गर्गवत्साः। Here also यञ् affix is elided by II. 4. 64.

15. अविमत्तकामविधाः or °विद्धाः। Avimatta has acute on the first being formed by the नञ् particle. Both the words lose इञ् patronymic by II. 4. 66.

16. बाभ्रवशालङ्कायनाः। The son of Babhru is Bâbhrava, and the son of Śalaṅku or Śalaṅka of नडादि IV. 1. 99 is Śâlaṅkâyana.

17. बाभ्रवदानच्युताः। Dânchyuta takes इञ् in the patronymic which is elided by II. 4. 66.

18. कठकालापाः, । Kaṭhâḥ are those who read the work of Kaṭha, the affix णिनि (IV. 3. 104.) being elided by IV. 3. 107. Those who study the work of Kâlâpin, are Kalâpâḥ the अण् being added by IV. 3. 108, which required the इन् of Kalâpin to be retained by VI. 4. 164 but by a Vârtika under VI. 4. 144 the इन् portion is elided before अण् ॥

19. कठकौथुमाः। Those who study the work of Kuthumin are कौथुमाः formed by अण् (IV. 1. 83) the इन् being elided before अण् by VI. 4. 144 Vârt already referred to above.

20. कौथुमलौकाक्षाः। Those who study the work of Lokâksha are Laukâkshâḥ. Or the son of Lokâksha is Laukâkshi, the pupils of latter are Laukâkshâḥ.

21. स्त्रीकुमारम्। Strî has accent on the final.

22. मौदपैप्पलादाः। The son of Muda is Maudi, the pupils of latter are Maudâḥ. So also Paippalâdâḥ.

23. मौदपैप्पलादाः। The double reading of this word indicates that Rule VI. 1. 223 also applies.

24. वत्सजरत् or वत्सजरन्तः = वत्स + जरत्। Vatsa has acute on the final.

25. So also सौश्रुतपार्थवाः, The pupils of Suśruta and Pṛithu are so called; they take अण् IV. 1. 83. 26. जरामृत्यू, 27. याज्यानुवाक्ये। Yâjya is formed by यत्, added to यज्, the ज् is not changed to a Guttural by VII. 3. 66. It has svarita on the final by तित् accent (VI. 1. 185). Anuvâkya is derived from anu + vach + ṇyat.

३७७२। महाव्रीह्यपराह्णगृष्टीष्वासजाबालभारभारतहैलिहिलरौरवप्रवृद्धेषु।
६। २। ३८॥

महच्छब्दः प्रकृत्या व्रीह्यादिषु दशसु। महाव्रीहिः। महापराह्णः। महागृष्टिः। महेष्वासः। महाहैलिहिलः। महच्छब्दोऽन्तोदात्तः। 'सन्महत्–' (७४०) इति प्रतिपदोक्तसमास एवायं स्वरः। नेह। महतो व्रीहिर्महद्व्रीहिः।

3772. The word महत् (महा) retains its accent before the following: व्रीहि, अपराह्ण, गृष्टि, इष्वास, जाबाल, भार, भारत, हैलिहिल, रौरव, and प्रवृद्ध ॥

Thus महाव्रीहिः, महापराह्णः, महागृष्टिः, महेष्वासः, महाजाबालः, महाभारः' महाभारतः, महाहैलिहिलः, महारौरवः, महाप्रवृद्धः, ॥ The महत् has acute on the final (Uṇ II. 84.) On the प्रतिपदोक्त maxim already mentioned under VI. 2. 26. S 3760, this accent will apply to that compound of महत् which it forms under rule II. 1.61. S. 740 for that is the particular rule of Karmadhâraya compounding relating to mahat (pratipadokta). This rule therefore, will not apply to Genitive Tatpurusha. Thus महतो व्रीहिः = महद्व्रीहिः which has accent on the final by VI. 1.223.

३७७३ । क्षुल्लकश्च वैश्वदेवे । ६ । २ । ३९ ॥

चान्महान् । क्षुल्लकवैश्वदेवम् । महावैश्वदेवम् । क्षुधं लातीति क्षुल्लः । तस्मादज्ञातादिषु केऽन्तोदात्तः ।

3773. The words mahat and kshullaka retain their accent before the word Vaiśvadeva.

Thus महावैश्वदेवम्, and क्षुल्लकवैश्वदेवम् ॥ The word kshullaka is derived thus क्षुधं लाति=क्षुल्लः to which the Diminutive क (V. 3. 73. &c) is added: and the word has udâtta on the final.

३७७४ । उष्ट्रः सादिवाम्योः । ६ । २ । ४० ॥

उष्ट्रसादी । उष्ट्रवामी । उषेः ष्ट्रनि उष्ट्रशब्द आद्युदात्तः ।

3774. The word 'ushṭra' retains its accent before 'sâdi' and 'vâmi'.

Thus उष्ट्रसादी and उष्ट्रवामी ॥ The word उष्ट्र is derived from उष् by ष्ट्रन् affix (Uṇ IV. 162) and has acute on the first (VI. 1. 197.)

३७७५ । गौः सादसादिसारथिषु । ६ । २ । ४१ ॥

गोसादः । गोसादिः । गोसारथिः ॥

3775. The word *go* retains its accent before 'sâda', 'sâdi', and 'sârathi'.

Thus गोसादः or गां सादयति=गोसादः, गोः सादिः=गोसादिः, and गोसारथिः ॥ साद is formed from सद् with the affix घञ् and forms a Genitive compound (गोः सादः). Or from the causative verb सादयति, we get गोसादः by adding अण् (III. 2. 1) गोसादी is formed by णिनि from the same causative root. The Kṛit-accent is debarred in the case of साद and सादिन्; the Samâsa-accent VI. 1. 223 in the case of सारथि ॥

३७७६ । कुरुगार्हपतरिक्तगुर्वसूतजरत्यश्लीलदृढरूपा पारेवडवा तैतिलकद्रूः पण्यकम्बलो दासीभाराणां च । ६ । २ । ४२ ॥

एषां सप्तानां समासानां दासीभारादेश्च पूर्वपदं प्रकृत्या । कुरूणां गार्हपतं कुरुगार्हपतम् । उप्रत्ययान्तः कुरुः ।

'+ वृजेरिति वाच्यम्+' । वृजिगार्हपतम् । वृजिराद्युदात्तः ।

रिक्तो गुरुः रिक्तगुरुः । 'रिक्ते विभाषा' (३६९६) इति रिक्तशब्द आद्युदात्तः । असूता जरती असूतजरती । अश्लीला दृढरूपा अश्लीलदृढरूपा । अश्लीलशब्दो नञ्समासत्वादाद्युदात्तः । श्रीर्यस्यास्ति तत् श्लीलम् । सिध्मादित्वाल्लच्कपिलकादित्वाल् लत्वम् । पारे वडवेव पारेवडवा । निपातनादिवार्थे समासो विभक्त्यलोपश्च । पारशब्दो घृतादित्वादन्तोदात्तः । तैतिलानां कद्रूः । तैतिलकद्रूः । तितिलिनोऽपत्यं छात्रो वेत्यणन्तः । पण्यशब्दो यदन्तत्वादाद्युदात्तः । पण्यकम्बलः ।

'+ संज्ञायामिति वक्तव्यम् +' अन्यत्र पणितव्ये कम्बले समासान्तोदात्तत्वमेव। प्रतिपदोक्ते समासे 'कृत्याः' (२८३१) इत्येव स्वरो विहितः। दास्या भारो दासीभारः। देवहूतिः। यस्य तत्पुरुषस्य पूर्वपदप्रकृतिस्वरत्वमिष्यते न विशिष्य वचनं विहितं स सर्वोऽपि दासीभारादिषु द्रष्टव्यः। 'स राये सपुरन्ध्याम्'। पुरं शरीरं धियतेऽस्यामिति 'कर्मण्यधिकरणे च' (३२७१) इति किप्रत्ययः। अलुक्छान्दसः। नब्विषयस्येत्याद्युदात्तः पुरंशब्दः॥

3776. The first member retains its accent in the following:—1. Kuru-gârhapata, 2. Riktá-guru, 3. Asûta-jaratî, 4. Aślîla-dṛiḍha-rûpâ, 5. Pâre-vaḍavâ, 6. Taitila-kadrûḥ, 7. Paṇya-kambalaḥ, and Dâsî-bhâra &c.

The first seven words are compounds, the first two of these are exhibited without any case-ending, the remaining five are in Nom. Singular. Thus कुरुगार्हपतम् (कुरूणां गार्हपत, Kuru is formed by कु affix added to कृ Uṇ. I. 24,) and has acute on the final.

Vârt:—So also वृजिगार्हपतम्, the word Vṛiji has acute accent on the first.

So also रिक्तो गुरुः=रिक्तगुरुः or रिक्तगुरुः for rikta has acute either on the first or on the second (VI. 1. 208 S. 3696). So also असूता जरती=असूतजरती, अश्लीलादृढरूपा=अश्लील दृढरूपा॥ Asûtâ and aślîlâ being formed by नञ् particle have acute on the first: VI. 2. 2. That which has श्री is called श्लील, the affix लच् being added by its belonging to Sidhmâdi class, and र changed to ल by its belonging to kapilakâdi class (VIII. 2. 18.) So also पारेवडवा, this is = पारेवडवेव॥ This is a samâsa with the force of इव, and there is irregularly no elision of the case-ending. It is not a compound under II. 1. 18, S. 672 The word पार belongs to Ghṛitâdi class, and has acute on the final. तैतिलानां कद्रूः=तैतिलकद्रूः, the son or pupil of Titilin is Taitila formed by अण् affix. पण्यकम्बलः, paṇya ends in यत् and has acute on the first (VI. 1. 213).

Vârt:—पण्यकम्बलः has acute on the first only when it is a name. Otherwise in पणितव्ये कम्बले compound, the accent will be on the final by the general rule VI. 1. 223. The word पण्य being formed by यत् affix (III. 1. 101) is acutely accented on the first (VI. 1. 213). The word पण्यकम्बलः is a Name when it means the market-blanket i. e. a blanket of a well known determinate size and fixed price, which is generally kept for sale by the blanket-sellers. But when the compound means a saleable blanket, it takes the samâsa accent (VI. 1. 223). If it be objected what is the use this Vartika, for the word पण्य being formed by a kritya affix, will retain its accent in the Tatpurusha, by VI. 2. 2, we reply that the कृत्य used in VI. 2. 2 relates to pratipadokta kritya compounds such as ordained by कृत्यतुल्याख्या अजात्या (II. 1. 68), while here the compound is by विशेषणंविशेष्येण (II. 1. 51) and is a general compound.

So also दास्याभारः=दासीभारः। The words belonging to Dàsi bhârâdi class are all those Tatpurusha compound words, not governed by any of the rules of accent, in which it is desired that the first member should retain its accent As:—स राये स पुरन्ध्याम् (Rig Veda I. 5. 3). The word पुरन्धि means 'पुरं शरीरं धीयतेऽस्याम्'। The affix is कि, and the case-ending of पुर is retained as a Vaidic anomaly. The word पुर is first acute by Phiṭ II. 3.

३७७७ । चतुर्थी तदर्थे । ६ । २ । ४३ ॥

चतुर्थ्यर्थाय यत्तद्वाचिन्युत्तरपदे चतुर्थ्यन्तं प्रकृत्या । यूपाय दारु यूपदारु ॥

3777. A word in the Dative case as the first member retains its accent, when the second member expresses that which is suited to become the former.

Thus यू॒॑पदारु । The word यूप has acute on the first syllable, as it is formed by प (Uṇ. III. 27) treated as a नित् (Uṇ. III. 26). This accent applies when the second member denoting the material is modified into the first by workmanship. The composition takes place by II. 1. 36.

३७७८ । अर्थे । ६ । २ । ४४ ॥

अर्थे परे चतुर्थ्यन्तं प्रकृत्या । देवार्थम् ॥

3778. Before the 'artha', the first member in the Dative retains its accent.

Thus दे॒व॑तार्थम्; देवता being formed by a नित् affix (V. 4. 27) has acute on the middle.

३७७९ । क्ते च । ६ । २ । ४५ ॥

क्तान्ते परे चतुर्थ्यन्तं प्रकृत्या । गोहितम् ॥

3779. The first member in the Dative case retains its accent before a Past Participle in 'kta.'

Thus गो॑हितम् । The compounding takes place by II. 1. 36.

३७८० । कर्मधारयेऽनिष्ठा । ६ । २ । ४६ ॥

क्तान्ते परे पूर्वमनिष्ठान्तं प्रकृत्या । श्रेणिकृताः । श्रेणिशब्द आद्युदात्तः । पूगकृताः । पूगशब्दोऽन्तोदात्तः । 'कर्मधारये' किम् । श्रेण्या कृतं श्रेणिकृतम् । 'अनिष्ठा' किम् । कृताऽकृतम् ॥

3780. Before a Past Participle in 'kta,' the first member, when it itself is not a Past Participle, retains its original accent in a Karmadhâraya compound.

This rule is confined to the Past Participles and the Nouns specifically mentioned in II. 1. 59, on the maxim of pratipadokta &c. Thus श्रे॑णिकृताः, पू॒ग॑कृताः । The word श्रे॑णि has acute on the first as it is formed by the affix नि which is considered नित् (Uṇ. IV. 51). The word पू॒ग॑ is end-acute as it is formed by the affix गक् (Uṇ I. 124). Why do we say 'in a Karmadhâraya compound'? Observe श्रेण्या कृतं = श्रेणिकृत॑म् । Why do we say 'when it is a non-nishṭha word'? Observe कृताऽकृतम् । Here the compounding is by II. 1. 60.

३७८१ । अहीने द्वितीया । ६ । २ । ४७ ॥

अहीनवाचिनि समासे क्तान्ते परे द्वितीयान्तं प्रकृत्या । कष्टश्रितः । ग्रामगतः । कष्टशब्दोऽन्तोदात्तः । ग्रामशब्दो नित्स्वरेण । 'अहीने' किम् । कान्तारातीतः ॥

'+ अनुपसर्ग इति वक्तव्यम् +' । नेह । सुखप्राप्तः । 'थाथ-' (३८७८) इत्यस्यापवादोऽयम् ॥

3781. Before a Past Participle in 'kta,' a word ending in the Accusative case retains its accent, when it does not mean a separation.

Thus कष्टश्रितः, ग्रामगतः। कष्ट has acute on the end; ग्राम has acute on the first, as it is formed by the नित् affix मन् added to ग्रस्, the final being replaced by आ (Uṇ. I. 143). Why do we say 'when not meaning separation'? Observe कान्तारातीतः, because one has taken himself beyond kântâra.

Vârt:—This rule does not apply when the Past Participle has an upasarga attached: as सुखप्राप्तः, (VI. 4. 144). This is an exception to rule VI. 2. 144.

३७८२। तृतीया कर्मणि। ६। २। ४८॥

कर्मवाचके क्तान्ते परे तृतीयान्तं प्रकृत्या। 'त्वोतासः'। रुद्रहतः। महाराजहतः। रुद्रो रगन्तः। 'कर्मणि' किम्। रथेन यातो रथयातः॥

3782. A word ending in an Instrumental case retains its accent before the Past Participle in 'kta', when it has a Passive meaning.

Thus त्वोतासः = त्वया ऊताः रक्षिताः 'protected by thee,' रुद्रहतः। महाराजहतः। रुद्र is formed by रक् affix (Uṇ II. 22) added to the causative रोदि; महाराज is formed by the Samâsânta affix टच्, and has acute on the final. Why do we say 'when having a Passive signification'? Observe रथेनयातः=रथयातः। The 'kta' is added to a verb of motion with an Active significance.

३७८३। गतिरनन्तरः। ६। २। ४९॥

कर्मार्थे क्तान्ते परेऽव्यवहितो गतिः प्रकृत्या। पुरोहितम्। 'अनन्तरः' किम्। अभ्युद्धृतः। कारकपूर्वपदस्य तु सतिशिष्टस्याथादिस्वर एव। दूरादागतः। 'थाथ-' (३८७८) इत्यस्यापवादः॥

3783. A word called Gati (1. 4. 60) when standing immediately before a Participle in 'kta' having a Passive significance retains its accent.

Thus पुरोहितम्। The word पुरस् is end-acute, as it is formed by the affix असि added to पूर्व by V. 3. 39. Here one of the following rules would have applied otherwise, namely, either (1) the Samâsa end-acute IV. 1. 223 (2) or the Indeclinable first member to retain its accent VI. 2. 2, (3) or the end-acute by VI. 2. 139 and 144. The present sûtra debars all these. Why do we say 'immediately?' Observe अभ्युद्धृतः। Where the distant Gati word अभि does not preserve its accent, but the immediately preceding Gati, उत् does retain its accent, though it is not the first member of the compound word. Compare also VIII. 2 70. But in दूरात् + आगतः (âgata being governed by this rule) we have दूरादागतः (II. 1. 39 and VI 3. 2), where VI 2. 144 has its scope though it had not its scope in अभि + उद्धृतः = अभ्युद्धृतः॥

NOTE:—In the former case the following maxim applies कृद्ग्रहणे गतिकारकपूर्वस्यापि ग्रहणम्। 'A Kṛit affix denotes whenever it is employed, a word-form which begins with that to which that Kṛit affix has been added, and which ends with the Kṛit affix, but moreover should a Gati or a noun such as denotes a case-relation have been prefixed to that word-form, then the Krit affix must denote the same word-form together with the Gati or the noun which may have been prefixed to it.' In the second example, this maxim is not applied, because scope should be given to the word अनन्तर in this aphorism. When the Participle has not a Passive significance, the rule does not apply because the word कर्मणि is understood here also; as प्रकृतः कटं देवदत्तः । This sûtra debars VI. 2. 144.

३७८४ । तादौ च निति कृत्यतौ । ६ । २ । ५० ॥

तकारादौ निति तुशब्दवर्जिते कृति परेऽनन्तरो गतिः प्रकृत्या । 'अग्नेरायो नृतमस्य प्रभूतौ' । 'संगतिं गोः' । कृत्स्वरापवादः । 'तादौ' किम् । प्रजल्पाकः । 'निति' किम् । प्रकर्ता । तृजन्तः । 'अतौ' किम् । आगन्तुः ॥

3784. An immediately preceding Gati retains its original accent before (a word formed by) a Krit-affix beginning with *t*, which has indicatory *n*, but not before *tu*.

Thus अग्नि रायो नृतमस्य प्रभूतौ (Rig Veda III. 19. 3). प्रकर्ता (with तृन्) प्रकर्तुम् (with तुमुन्), प्रकृतिः (with क्तिन्)। This sûtra debars the Krit-affix accent (VI. 2. 139). Why do we say 'before an affix beginning with त्'? Observe प्रजल्पाकः formed with the affix षाकन् (III. 2. 155), and the Gati प्र, the accent being governed by VI. 2. 139. Why do we say 'which is नित्'? Observe प्रकर्ता formed by तृच् affix. When a Krit-affix takes the augment इट्, it does not lose its character of beginning with त् on the Vârtika कृदुपदेशो वा ताद्यर्थमिडर्थम् । Thus प्रलविता, प्रलवितुम् । Why do we say 'but not before तु'? Observe आगन्तुः with the Unadi affix तुन् ॥

३७८५ । तवै चान्तश्च युगपत् । ६ । २ । ५१ ॥

तवैप्रत्ययान्तस्यान्त उदात्तो गतिश्चानन्तरः । प्रकृत्या युगपच्चैतदुभयं स्यात् । 'अन्वेतवा उं' । कृत्स्वरापवादः ॥

3785. An immediately preceding Gati retains its original accent before an Infinitive in *tavai* (III. 4. 14) but whereby simultaneously the final has the acute as well.

Thus अन्वेतवै । All upasargas have acute on the first except 'abhi' which therefore has acute on the final. (Phit IV. 13) which declares उपसर्गाश्चाद्युदात्ता अभिवर्जम् । This debars कृत् accent (VI. 2. 139) and is an exception to the rule that in a single word, a single syllable only has acute.

३७८६ । अनिगन्तोऽञ्चतौ वप्रत्यये । ६ । २ । ५२ ॥

अनिगन्तो गतिर्वप्रत्ययान्तेऽञ्चतौ परे प्रकृत्या । 'ये पराञ्चस्तान्' । 'अनिगन्तः' इति किम् । प्रत्यञ्चो यन्तु । कृत्स्वरात्परत्वादयमेव । 'जुहिवृष्णया नि कणुहो पराचः' । 'वप्रत्यये' किम् । उदञ्चनम् ॥

3786. An immediately preceding Gati not ending in 'i' or 'u' retains its original accent before 'añch' when an affix having a 'v' follows.

Thus पराञ्चः in ये पराञ्चस्तान् (Rig Veda I. 164. 19). The accent is acute and optionally svarita by VIII 2. 6. Why do we say 'not ending in इ or उ?' Observe प्रत्यञ्चः, here by VI. 2. 139 the second member retains its original accent. Why do we say 'before an affix व्'? Observe उदञ्चनः। When the nasal of 'añch' is elided, then rule VI. 1. 222 presents itself; but that rule is superseded when a Gati not ending in इ or उ precedes, because the present rule is subsequent. Thus पराचः in जहि वृष्ण्यानि कृणुही पराचः (Rig Veda VI. 25. 3). In some texts, the reading is अञ्चतावप्रत्यये। The affix व् is like क्विप् &c., (VI. 1. 67).

३७८७। न्यधी च। ६। २। ५३॥

वप्रत्ययान्तेऽञ्चतावगन्तावपि न्यधी प्रकृत्या। न्यङ्ङुत्तानः। 'उदात्तस्वरितयोर्यणः-' (३६५७) इति अञ्चतेरकारः स्वरितः। अध्यङ्॥

3787. The Gatis '*ni*' and '*adhi*' however, retain their original accent before 'añch' followed by a 'v' affix.

Thus न्यङ्। The अ becomes svarita by VIII. 2. 4. S. 3657. So also अध्यङ्॥

३७८८। ईषदन्यतरस्याम्। ६। २। ५४॥

ईषत्कडारः। ईषदित्ययमन्तोदात्तः। ईषद्भेद इत्यादौ कृत्स्वर एव॥

3788. The word 'îshat,' when first member of a compound, may optionally preserve its original accent.

Thus ईषत्कडारः or ईषत्कडारः। ईषत् has acute on the final. But in ईषद्भेदः &c, the Krit-accent will necessarily take place (VI. 2. 139); no option being allowed; because the compounds to which the present rule applies are, on the maxim of pratipadokta, those formed by ईषत् with non-Krit words under II. 2. 7.

३७८९। हिरण्यपरिमाणं धने। ६। २। ५५॥

सुवर्णपरिमाणवाचि पूर्वपदं वा प्रकृत्या धने। द्वे सुवर्णे परिमाणमस्येति द्विसुवर्णं। तदेव धनं द्विसुवर्णधनम्। बहुव्रीहावपि परत्वाद्विकल्प एव। 'हिरण्यम्' किम्। प्रस्थधनम्। 'परिमाणम्' किम्। काञ्चनधनम्। 'धने' किम्। निष्कमाला॥

3789. The first member, denoting the quantity of gold retains optionally its original accent, before the word धन॥

Thus द्विसुवर्णधनम् or द्विसुवर्णधनम्। This is a Karmadhâraya compound द्वे सुवर्णे परिमाणमस्य = द्विसुवर्णं, तदेव धनम्। It may also be treated as a Bahuvrîhi compound, then the accent will be of that compound, as द्विसुवर्णधनः or द्विसुवर्णधनः। Why do we say 'gold'? Observe प्रस्थधनम्। Why do we say 'quantity'? Observe कांचनधनम्। Why do we say 'धन'? Observe निष्कमाला॥

३७९०। प्रथमोऽचिरोपसंपत्तौ। ६। २। ५६॥

प्रथमशब्दो वा प्रकृत्याभिनवत्वे। प्रथमवैयाकरणः। संप्रति व्याकरणमध्येतुं प्रवृत्त इत्यर्थः। प्रथमशब्दः प्रथेरमजन्तः। 'अचिर-' इति किम्। प्रथमो वैयाकरणः॥

3790. The word 'prathama' when standing first in a compound, retains optionally its original accent, when meaning 'a novice.'

The word अचिरोपसंपत्ति = अचिरोपश्लेष or अभिनवत्वम् । Thus प्रथमवैयाकरणः or प्रथमवैयाकरणः=संप्रतिव्याकरणमध्येतुं प्रवृत्तः 'one who has recently commenced to study Grammar.' The word प्रथम is derived from प्रथ by अमच् (Uṇ V. 68) and by चित् accent the acute falls on the last. Why do we say 'when meaning a Novice?' Observe प्रथमवैयाकरणः (वैयाकरणानामाद्यो मुख्यो वा यः सः) 'the first Grammarian or a Grammarian of the first rank.' It will *always* have acute on the final.

३७९१ । कतरकतमौ कर्मधारये । ६ । २ । ५७ ॥

वा प्रकृत्या । कतरकठः । कर्मधारयग्रहणमुत्तरार्थम् । इह तु प्रतिपदोक्तत्वादेव सिद्धम् ॥

3791. The words कतर and कतम, standing as the first member of a compound, retain optionally their original accent, in a Karmadhâraya.

Thus कतरकठः or कतरकठः, कतमकठः or कतमकठः । The word Karmadhâraya is used for the sake of the next sûtra, this sûtra could have done without it, as 'katara' and 'katama' by the maxim of pratipadokta, form only Karmadhâraya compound, by II. 1. 63.

३७९२ । आर्यो ब्राह्मणकुमारयोः । ६ । २ । ५८ ॥

आर्यकुमारः । आर्यब्राह्मणः । आर्यो ण्यदन्तत्वादन्तस्वरितः । 'आर्यः' किम् । परमब्राह्मणः । 'ब्राह्मणादि–' इति किम् । आर्यक्षत्रियः । कर्मधारय इत्येव ॥

3792. The word 'ârya' optionally retains its original accent in a Karmadhâraya, before the words 'Brâhmaṇa' and 'kumâra.'

Thus आर्यब्राह्मणः or आर्यब्राह्मणः, आर्यकुमारः or आर्यकुमारः । The word आर्य is formed by ण्यत् affix and has svarita on the final. Why do we say 'Ârya' Observe परमब्राह्मणः, परमकुमारः । Why do we say before 'Brâhmaṇa' and 'Kumâra'? Observe आर्यक्षत्रियः । Why 'Karmadhâraya?' Observe आर्यस्य ब्राह्मणः =आर्यब्राह्मणः । According to the Accentuated Text the accent is आर्य (Pro. Bohtlingk).

३७९३ । राजा च । ६ । २ । ५९ ॥

ब्राह्मणकुमारयोः परतो राजा वा प्रकृत्या कर्मधारये । राजब्राह्मणः । राजकुमारः । योगविभाग उत्तरार्थः ॥

3793. The word 'râjan,' retains optionally its accent before the words 'Brâhmaṇa' and 'Kumâra', in a Karmadhâraya.

Thus राजब्राह्मणः or राजब्राह्मणः, राजकुमारः or राजकुमारः । The word राजन् is formed by the affix कनिन् added to राज् (Uṇ I. 156). But राज्ञो ब्राह्मणः=राजब्राह्मणः where the compound is not Karmadhâraya. The making of this a separate aphorism is for the sake of the subsequent sûtra into which the anuvṛitti of राजन् runs and not that of आर्य ॥

३७९४ । षष्ठी प्रत्येनसि । ६ । २ । ६० ॥

षष्ठ्यन्तो राजा प्रत्येनसि परे वा प्रकृत्या । राजप्रत्येनाः । 'षष्ठी' किम् । अन्यत्र न ॥

3794. The word 'râjan' ending in the Genitive case, optionally retains its accent, before the word 'pratyenas.'

The words राजन् and अन्यतरस्याम् are understood here also. Thus रा॑ज्ञः प्रत्येनाः or राज्ञः प्रत्येना॑ः । प्रतिगतं पुनः पापं यस्य = प्रत्येनस् । The sign of the Genitive is not elided by VI. 3. 21. When आक्रोश is not meant, we have, रा॑जप्रत्येनाः or राजप्रत्येना॑ः । Why do we say 'ending in the Genitive'? Observe राजा चासौ प्रत्येनाश्च = राजप्रत्येनाः no option.

३७९५ । क्ते नित्यार्थे । ६ । २ । ६१ ॥

क्तान्ते परे नित्यार्थे समासे पूर्वं वा प्रकृत्या । नित्यप्रहसितः । 'कालाः' (६९०) इति द्वितीयासमासोऽयम् । नित्यशब्दस्त्यबन्त आद्युदात्तः । हसित इति थाथादिस्वरेणान्तोदात्तः । 'नित्यार्थे' किम् । मुहूर्तप्रहसितः ॥

3795. A word having the sense of 'always', retains optionally its accent, before a Past Participle in 'kta.'

Thus नि॑त्यप्रहसितः or नित्यप्रहसित॑ः । These are Accusative compounds formed under Rule II. 1. 28. S. 690 ; नित्य is formed by त्यप् affix, added to the upasarga नि (IV. 2. 104 Vârt) ; and has acute on the first, the upasarga retaining its accent, the affix being anudâtta (III. 1, 4). हसित as end-acute by VI. 2. 144. S 3878. Why do we say 'when the first term means always'? Observe मुहूर्तप्रहसित॑ः ॥

NOTE:—In the case of नित्यप्रहसितः &c., the samâsa accent VI. 1. 223 was first set aside by the Accusative Tatpurusha accent VI. 2. 2 ; this in its turn was set aside by क्त accent VI. 2. 144, which is again debarred by the present.

३७९६ । ग्रामः शिल्पिनि । ६ । २ । ६२ ॥

वा प्रकृत्या । ग्रामनापितः । ग्रामशब्द आद्युदात्तः । 'ग्रामः' किम् । परमनापितः । 'शिल्पिनि' किम् । ग्रामरथ्या

3796. The word 'grâma' when first member of a compound, optionally retains its accent, before a word denoting a 'professional man or artisan.'

Thus ग्रा॑मनापितः or ग्रामनापित॑ः, ग्रा॑मकुलालः or ग्रामकुलाल॑ः । The word ग्राम was acute on the first as it is formed by the affix मनिन् (Un I. 148). Why do he say 'ग्राम'? Observe परमनापित॑ः । Why do we say 'a śilpî, a professional workman'? Observe ग्रामरथ्या ; where there is no option.

३७९७ । राजा च प्रशंसायाम् । ६ । २ । ६३ ॥

शिल्पिवाचिनि परे प्रशंसार्थे राजपदं वा प्रकृत्या । राजनापितः । राजकुलालः । 'प्रशंसायाम्' किम् । राजनापितः । 'शिल्पिनि' किम् । राजहस्ती ॥

3797. The word 'râjan' followed by a profession denoting noun, optionally retains its accent, when praise is to be expressed.

Thus राजनापितः or राजनापितः, राजकुलालः or राजकुलालः 'A royal barber i. e. a skilful barber or one fit to serve the king even' &c. It may be either a Karmadhârbya or a Genitive compound. Why do we say 'राजन्'? Observe परमनापितः। Why do we say 'when denoting praise'? Observe राजनापितः: 'king's barber.' Why do we say 'a professional man'? Observe राजहस्ती 'a royal elephant.

३७९८। आदिरुदात्तः। ६। २। ६४॥

अधिकारोऽयम्॥

3798. In the following up to VI. 2. 91 inclusive, the phrase 'the first syllable in—(the word standing in the Nominative) has the acute,' is to be always supplied.

This is an adhikâra aphorism. The first syllable of the पूर्वपद will get the acute in the following aphorisms. In short, the phrase 'âdirudâtta' should be supplied to complete the sense of the subsequent sûtras. The word आदि 'the first syllable' is understood upto VI. 2. 91, the word उदात्त has longer stretch: it governs upto VI. 2. 237.

३७९९। सप्तमीहारिणौ धर्म्येऽहरणे। ६। २। ६५॥

सप्तम्यन्तं हारिवाचि च आद्युदात्तं धर्म्ये परे। देयं यः स्वीकरोति स हारीत्युच्यते। धर्म्यमित्याचारनियतं देयम्। मुकुटेकार्षापणम्। हलेद्विपदिका। 'संज्ञायाम्' (७२१) इति सप्तमीसमासः। 'कारनाम्नि च-' (९६८) इत्यलुक्। याज्ञिकाश्वः। वैयाकरणहस्ती। क्वचिदयमाचारो मुकुटादिषु कार्षापणादि दातव्यं याज्ञिकादीनां त्वश्वादिरिति। धर्म्ये-' इति किम्। स्तम्बेरमः। 'अहरणे' किम्। वाडवाहरणम्। वडवाया अयं वाडवः। तस्य बीजनिषेकादुत्तरकालं शरीरपुष्ट्यर्थं यद्दीयते तद्धरणमित्युच्यते। परोऽपि कृत्स्वरो हारिस्वरेण बाध्यत इत्यहरण इति निषेधेन ज्ञाप्यते। तेन वाडवहार्यमिति हारिस्वरः सिध्यति॥

3799. The first member of a compound, if in the Locative case or denoting the name of the receiver of a tax, has acute on the first syllable, when the second member is a word denoting 'what is lawful', but not when it is 'harana.'

The word हारिण् means 'he who appropriates the dues or taxes': and धर्म्यम् means 'the due or tax which has been determined by the custom or usage of the country, town, sect or family, that which one is lawfully entitled to get.' The word धर्म्य is formed by यत् under IV. 4. 91 and 92, and has the sense of both. Of Locative words we have the following examples:—मुकुटे-कार्षापणम्, हले-द्विपदिका। These compounds are formed under II. 1. 44, S. 721 and the sign of the Locative is not elided by VI. 3. 9 and 10, S. 968. With the name of a due-receiver हारी we have the following:—याज्ञिकाश्वः 'the horse which is the customary due of the sacrificer.' So also वैयाकरणहस्ती। In some places the established usage is to give a kârshipana coin in a Mukuta &c or to give a horse to a sacrificer &c. Why do we say 'what is lawful'? Observe स्तम्बेरमः। Why do we say 'but not before हरण'? Observe वाडवहरणम् 'that which is given to a mare.' हरण is that customary food, which is given to a mare, after she has been covered, in order to strengthen her. The word हरण is a Krit-formed word, its exclusion here indicates that other Krit-formed words, however, are governed by this rule, when preceded by a कारक denoting word; and thus this sûtra supersedes the Krit accent enjoined by VI. 2. 139, so far. Thus वाडवभार्यः has acute on the first by this rule, the subsequent VI. 2. 139 not applying.

३८०० । युक्ते च । ६ । २ । ६६ ॥

युक्तवाचिनि समासे पूर्वमाद्युदात्तम् । गोबल्लवः । 'कर्तव्ये तत्परो युक्तः' ॥

3800. The first member of a compound has acute on the first syllable, when the second member denotes that by whom the things denoted by the first are regulated or kept in order.

The word युक्त means 'he who is prompt in the discharge of his appointed duty' *i. e.* the person appointed to look after. Thus गोबल्लवः 'a cowherd looking after cow.'

३८०१ । विभाषाध्यक्षे । ६ । २ । ६७ ॥

गवाध्यक्षः ॥

3801. The acute is optionally on the first syllable when the word अध्यक्ष follows.

Thus गवाध्यक्षः or गवाध्यक्षः 'a superintendent of cows' ॥

३८०२ । पापं च शिल्पिनि । ६ । २ । ६८ ॥

पापनापितः । 'पापाणके-' (७३३) इति प्रतिपदोक्तस्यैव ग्रहणात्षष्ठीसमासे न ॥

3802. The word 'pâpa' has optionally acute on the first syllable, when followed by a word denoting a professional man.

Thus पापनापितः or पापनापितः ॥ This rule applies to the pratipadokta samâsa of पाप, in the sense of censure, as taught in II. 1. 54. S. 733 when it is an appositional compound; and not when it forms a Genitive compound. Thus पापस्यनापितः=पापनापितः ॥

३८०३ । गोत्रान्तेवासिमाणवब्राह्मणेषु क्षेपे । ६ । २ । ६९ ॥

भार्यासौश्रुतः । सुश्रुतापत्यस्य भार्याप्रधानतया क्षेपः । अन्तेवासी । कुमारीदाक्षाः । ओदनपाणिनीयाः । कुमार्यादिलाभकामा ये दाक्ष्यादिभिः प्रोक्तानि शास्त्राण्यधीयन्ते त एव क्षिप्यन्ते । भिक्षामाणवः । भिक्षां लप्स्येऽहमिति माणवः । भयब्राह्मणः । भयेन ब्राह्मणः संपद्यते । 'गोत्रादिषु' किम् । दासीश्रोत्रियः । 'क्षेपे' किम् । परमब्राह्मणः ॥

3803 The first syllable of the first member of a compound has the acute accent before a Patronymic name or a scholar-name, as well as before 'Mâṇava' and 'Brâhmaṇa,' when a reproach is meant.

Thus भार्यासौश्रुतः 'a descendant of Suśruta, under the petticoat government of his wife.' The compounding takes place by the analogy of शाकपार्थिवः । The above is an example of a Gotra word. Now with scholar names. कुमारीदाक्षाः 'the pupils of Daksha, for the sake of marriage *i. e.* who study the work of Daksha or make themselves the pupils of Daksha, for the sake of girls.' and घोदनपाणिनीयाः &c. भिक्षामाणवः=भिक्षांलप्स्येऽहमिति माणवो भवति। भयब्राह्मणः 'he who being a Brâhmaṇa by birth, acts like a Brâhmaṇa not willingly, but through fear of punishment.'=यो भयेन ब्राह्मणः संपद्यते। The compounding is by II. 1. 4 where no other rule applies. Why do we say 'when followed by a Gotra word?' Observe दाक्षीश्रोत्रियाः। Why do we say 'when reproach is meant?' Observe परमब्राह्मणाः॥

३८०४। अङ्गानि मैरेये। ६। २। ७०॥

मद्यविशेषो मैरेयः। मधुमैरेयः। मधुविकारस्य तस्य मध्वङ्गम्। 'अङ्गानि' किम्। परम मैरेयः। 'मैरेये' किम्। पुष्पासवः॥

3804. The first syllable of the word preceding 'Maireya' gets the acute, when it denotes the ingredient of the same.

Thus मधुमैरेयः 'the maireya prepared from honey.' Why do we say when denoting 'an ingredient'? Observe परममैरेयः॥ Why do we say 'before मैरेय?' Observe पुष्पासवः॥

३८०५। भक्ताख्यास्तदर्थेषु। ६। २। ७१॥

भक्तमन्नम्। भिक्षाकंसः। भाजीकंसः। भिक्षादयोऽन्नविशेषाः। 'भक्ताख्याः' किम्। समाशशालयः। समशनं समाश इति क्रियामात्रमुच्यते। 'तदर्थेषु' किम्। भिक्षाप्रियः। बहुव्रीहिरयम्। अत्र पूर्वपदमन्तोदात्तम्॥

3805. A word denoting food, gets the acute on the first syllable, when standing before a word which denotes a repository suited to contain that.

Thus भक्तकंसः, भाजीकंसः, । The words like भिक्षा, भक्त &c. are names of food. Why do we say 'when denoting the name of food'? Observe समाशशालयः: dining halls, (the word समाश = समशन is the name of an 'action' and not of a 'substance'). Why do we say 'tadartheshu suited to contain that'? Observe भिक्षाप्रियः, which is Bahuvrîhi and the first member gets acute on the final.

३८०६। गोबिडालसिंहसैन्धवेषूपमाने। ६। २। ७२॥

धान्यगवः। गोबिडालः। तृणसिंहः। सक्तुसैन्धवः। धान्यं गौरिवेति विग्रहः। व्याघ्रादिः गवाकृत्या संनिवेशितं धान्यं धान्यगवशब्देनोच्यते। 'उपमाने' किम्। परमसिंहः॥

3806. A word denoting the object of comparison gets the acute on the first syllable when standing before गो, बिडाल, सिंह, and सैन्धव॥

Thus धान्यगवः = धान्यं गौरिव। The compounding takes place by II. 1. 56 the words गो &c, being considered to belong to Vyâghrâdi class, which is an Âkṛitigana. The meaning of the compound must be given according to usage and appropriateness. Thus धान्यगवः means गवाकृत्याऽवस्थितं धान्यं। So also गोबिडाल;

दृ॑षसिंहः, सै॑न्तुहेन्धवः, । Why do we say 'when denoting the object of comparision'? Observe परमसिंहः ॥

३८०७ । अके जीविकार्थे । ६ । २ । ७३ ॥

अकप्रत्ययान्त उत्तरपदे जीविकार्थवाचिनि समासे पूर्वपदमाद्युदात्तम् । दन्तलेखकः । यस्य दन्तलेखनेन जीविका । 'नित्यं क्रीड-' (७११) इति समासः । 'अके' किम् । रमणीयकर्ता । 'जीविकार्थे' किम् । इक्षुभक्षिकां मे धारयसि ॥

3807. The first member of a compound has the acute on the first syllable, when the second-member is a word ending in the affix 'aka,' and the compound expresses a calling by which one gets his living.

Thus द॑न्तलेखकः = दन्तलेखेन यस्य जीविका । The compounding takes place by II. 2. 17. S. 711. Why do we say when meaning 'means of living'? Observe इक्षुभक्षिकां मे धारयसि । All affixes which ultimately become अक by taking substitutes, are called अक affixes. Thus ण्वुल्, वुन्, &c. are अक affixes (VII. 1. 1). Why do we say 'ending in the affix अक'? Observe रमणीयकर्त्ता । Here the compounding takes place by II. 2. 17, and the affix तृच् is added in the sense of sport and not of livelihood.

३८०८ । प्राचां क्रीडायाम् । ६ । २ । ७४ ॥

प्राग्देशवासिनां या क्रीडा तद्वाचिनि समासे अकप्रत्ययान्ते परे पूर्वमाद्युदात्तं स्यात् । उद्दालकपुष्पभञ्जिका । 'संज्ञायाम्' (३२८६) इति ण्वुल् । 'प्राचाम्' किम् । जीवपुत्रप्रचायिका । इयमुदीचां क्रीडा । 'क्रीडायाम्' किम् । तव पुष्पप्रचायिका । पर्याये ण्वुच् ॥

3808 A compound the second member of which is a word ending in अक affix, and which denotes the sport of the Eastern people, gets the acute accent on the first syllable.

Thus उ॑द्दालकपुष्पभञ्जिका । These are formed by ण्वुल् affix (III. 3. 109, S. 3286,) and the compounding takes place by II. 2. 17. S. 711. Why do we say 'of the Eastern Folk'? Observe जीवपुत्रप्रचायिका, which is a sport of the Northern People. Why do we say 'when denoting a sport'? Observe तवपुष्पप्रचायिका 'thy turn for &c.' which is formed by ण्वुच् (III. 3. 111) and denotes 'rotation or turn.'

३८०९ । अणि नियुक्ते । ६ । २ । ७५ ॥

अणन्ते परे नियुक्तवाचिनि समासे पूर्वमाद्युदात्तम् । छत्रधारः । 'नियुक्ते' किम् । काण्डलावः ॥

3809. A compound, the second member of which is a word ending in the Krit-affix अण and which denotes a functionary, gets the acute on the first syllable.

Thus छ॑त्रधारः । Why do we say when meaning 'a functionary'? Observe काण्डलावः ॥

३८१० । शिल्पिनि चाऽकृञः । ६ । २ । ७६ ॥

शिल्पिवाचिनि समासेऽणन्ते परे पूर्वमाद्युदात्तं स चेदणकृञः परो न भवति । तन्तुवायः । 'शिल्पिनि' किम् । काण्डलावः । 'अकृञः' किम् । कुम्भकारः ॥

3810. And when such a compound ending in अण् affix denotes the name of a professional man, but not when the second term is कार (derived from कृञ्), the acute is on the first syllable of the first word.

Here also the second term ends in अण् affix. Thus तन्तुवायः ।. Why do we say when denoting 'a work-man or professional person'? Observe काण्डलावः । Why do we say 'but not when the affix अण् comes after कृ.'? Observe कुम्भकारः ॥

३८११ । संज्ञायां च । ६ । २ । ७७ ॥

अणन्ते परे । तन्तुवायो नाम कृमिः । 'अकृञः' इत्येव । रथकारो नाम ब्राह्मणः ॥

3811. Also when such an upapada compound ending in अण् affix denotes a Name, the acute falls on the first syllable: but not when the second term is कार ॥

Thus तन्तुवायः, 'a kind of insect, spider.' But not so अण् with कृ; as रथकारः 'the name of a Brâhmaṇa caste.'

३८१२ । गोतन्तियवं पाले । ६ । २ । ७८ ॥

गोपालः । तन्तिपालः । यवपालः । अनियुक्तार्थो योगः । 'गो' इति किम् । वत्सपालः । 'पाले' इति किम् । गोरक्षः ॥

3812. The words गो, तन्ति and यव get the acute on the first syllable when followed by पाल ॥

Thus गोपालः, तन्तिपालः, यवपालः । The word तन्ति is the rope with which calves are tied. (तनु विस्तारे + क्तिच्). This applies to words not denoting a functionary, which would be governed by VI. 2. 75. S. 3809. Why do we say गो &c.? Observe वत्सपालः । Why do we say 'followed by पाल'? Observe गोरक्षः ॥

३८१३ । णिनि । ६ । २ । ७९ ॥

पुष्पहारी ॥

3813. A compound ending in the Krit-affix णिनि (इन्) has the acute on the first syllable of the first member.

Thus पुष्पहारिन् ॥

३८१४ । उपमानं शब्दार्थप्रकृतावेव । ६ । २ । ८० ॥

उपमानवाचि पूर्वपदं णिन्यन्ते पर आद्युदात्तम् । उष्ट्रक्रोशी । ध्वाङ्क्षरावी । उपमानग्रहणमस्य पूर्वयोगस्य च विषयविभागार्थम् । 'शब्दार्थप्रकृतौ' किम् । वृकवञ्ची । 'प्रकृतिग्रहणम्' किम् । प्रकृतिरेव यत्रोपसर्गनिरपेक्षा शब्दार्था तत्रैव यथा स्यात् । इह मा भूत् । गर्दभोच्चारी ॥

3814. When the first member of a compound expresses that with which resemblance is denoted, then it has acute on the first syllable, before a word formed by णिनि affix, only then, when such latter word is a radical without any preposition, and means 'giving out a definite sound like so and so.'

The word उपमान means the object with which something is likened : शब्दार्थ means 'expressing a sound'; प्रकृति means 'root, without any preposition.' Thus उँष्ट्रक्रोशिन्, ध्वाँङ्क्षराविन्। The word उपमान shows the scope of this sûtra as distinguished from the last. So that; when the first term is an उपमान word, the preceding sûtra will not apply, though the second member may be a णिनि formed word.

When the second term is not a word denoting sound, the rule will not apply. At वृकवञ्चिन् which retains krit accent (VI. 2. 139).

Why do we say 'a radical word without any preposition'? Observe गर्दभोच्चारिन्। Here the second term radically (*i. e.*, chârin) does not denote sound, but it is with the help of the Preposition उत् that it means sound. The force of एव is that the उपमान words are restricted. Such words get acute on the first syllable *only then* when the second member is a radical sound name.

३८१५ । युक्तारोह्यादयश्च । ६ । २ । ८१ ॥

आद्युदात्ताः । युक्तारोही । आगतयोधी । क्षीरहोता ॥

3815. The compounds yuktârohin &c, have acute on the first syllable.

Thus 1 युँक्तारोही, 2 आँगतरोही, 3 आँगतयोधी, 4 आँगतवञ्ची, 5 आँगतनर्दी, 6 आँगतनन्दी, 7 आगतप्रहारी। These are formed by णिनि affix, and are illustrations of Rule VI. 2. 79. Some say, these declare a restrictive rule with regard to the first and second members of these terms. Thus रोहिन् &c. must be preceded by युक्त &c. and युक्त &c. followed by रोहिन् &c. to make VI. 2. 79 applicable. Thus वक्तारोहिँन् though ending in णिनि does not take acute on the first, so युक्ताध्यायिँन्। 8 आगतमत्स्या or °तस्य, 9 क्षीँरहोता, 10 भँगिनिभर्त्ता। The last two are Genitive compounds under Rule II. 2. 9. 11 ग्राँमगोधुक्, 12 अँश्वत्रिरात्रः, 13 गँर्गत्रिरात्रः, 14 व्युँष्टत्रिरात्रः, 16 शँनपादः (गणपादः), 16 सँमपादः। All these are genitive compounds. 17. एँकशितिपात्=एकः शितिः पादोऽस्य। This is a Bahuvrîhi of three terms. The word एकशितिः is a Taddhitârtha Samâsa (II. 1. 51), and being a Tatpurusha, required acute on the final, as the Tatpurusha accent is stronger. This declares acute on the first. Moreover by VI. 2. 29, this word एकशितिः would have acute on the first as it is a Dvigu ending in a simple vowel. But the very fact that this word is enumerated here, shows that other Dvigu compounds in शिति are not governed by VI. 2. 29, therefore द्विशितिँपाद् has acute on ति। The enumeration of the एकशितिपात् further proves by implication that the (एकशितिपात् स्वरवचनं ज्ञापकं निमित्त स्वरबलीयस्त्वस्य) accent for the application of which a case is present is stronger (See Mahâbhâshya II. 1. 1). The class of compounds known as पाँत्रेसमित &c, (II 1. 48) also belongs to this class.

1 युक्तारोही, 2 आगतरोही. 3 आगतयोधी, 4 आगतवञ्ची 5 आगतनन्दी (आगतनर्दी), 6 आगतप्रहारी, 7 आगतमत्स्यः (आगतमत्स्या), 8 क्षीरहोता, 9 भगिनीभर्त्ता, 10 ग्रामगोधुक्

11 अश्वत्रिरात्रः 12 गर्गत्रिरात्रः, 13 व्युष्टित्रिरात्रः, 14 गणपादः (शणपादः), 15 एकशितिपात्, 16 पात्रेसंमितादयश्च (पात्रेसमितादयश्च), 17 समपादः ॥

३८१६ । दीर्घकाशतुषभ्राष्ट्रवटंजे । ६ । २ । ८२ ॥

कुटीजः । काशजः । तुषजः । भाष्ट्रजः । वटजः ॥

3816. When the first member is a word ending in a long vowel, or is 'kâśa,' tusha, 'bhrâshṭra' or vaṭa, and is followed by 'ja' the acute falls on the first syllable.

Thus कु॑टीजः, का॑शजः, तु॑षजः, भ्रा॑ष्ट्रजः, व॑टजः। These are formed by the affix ड added to जन् (III. 2. 97).

३८१७ । अन्त्यात्पूर्वं बह्वचः । ६ । २ । ८३ ॥

बह्वचः पूर्वं स्यान्त्यात्पूर्व पदमुदात्तं जे उत्तरपदे । उपसरजः । आमलकीजः । 'बह्वचः' किम् । दग्धजानि तृणानि ॥

3817 In a word consisting of more than two syllables, followed by *ja*, the acute falls on the syllable before the last.

Thus उपस॑रजः, आमल॑कीजः, and वडे॑वाजः (though the last two words have upapadas ending in a long vowel, the accent is governed by this sûtra and not the last). Why do we say "a Polysyllabic first member"? Observe दग्धजानि तृणानि ॥

३८१८ । ग्रामेऽनिवसन्तः । ६ । २ । ८४ ॥

ग्रामे परे पूर्वपदमुदात्तम् । तच्चेन्निवसद्वाचि न । मल्लग्रामः । ग्रामशब्दोऽत्र समूहवाची देवग्रामः। देवस्वामिकः । 'अनिवसन्तः' किम् । दाक्षिग्रामः । दाक्षिनिवसः ॥

3818. Before 'grâma' the first syllable of the first member has acute, when thereby inhabitants are not meant.

Thus म॑ल्लग्रामः । Here ग्राम is equal to समूह 'an assembly'. देवग्रामः=देवस्वामिकः। Why do we say 'when not meaning inhabitants'. Observe दाक्षिग्राम, 'a village inhabited by the decendants of Daksha'.

३८१९ । घोषादिषु च । ६ । २ । ८५ ॥

दाक्षिघोषः । दाक्षिकटः । दाक्षिह्रदः ॥

3819. The first member has acute on the first syllable when followed by *ghosha* &c.

Thus दा॑क्षिघोषः, दा॑क्षिकटः, दा॑क्षिपल्वलः, दा॑क्षिबदरी, दाक्षिवल्लभः, दा॑क्षिह्रदः, दा॑क्षिपिङ्गलः, दा॑क्षिपिशङ्गः, दा॑क्षिमाला, दाक्षिरक्षा, दा॑क्षिशाला, or (°रक्षः or °शालः), दा॑क्षिशिल्पी, दा॑क्ष्यश्वत्थः, दा॑क्षिशाल्मली, कुन्दतृणम्, आ॑म्रमुनिः, दा॑क्षिपुंसा, दा॑क्षिकूटः ॥

Of the above, those which denote places of habitation, there the first members though denoting inhabitants get the acute accent. Some do not read the anuvritti of अनिवसन्तः in this aphorism, others however read it.

1 घोष, 2 कट (घट), 3 वल्लभ (पल्वल). 4 ह्रद, 5 बदरी (बदर), 6 पिङ्गल, 7 पिशङ्ग, 8 माला, 9 रक्षा (रक्षः), 10 शाला (शालः), 11 कूट, 12 शाल्मली, 13 अश्वत्थ, 14 तृण, 15, शिल्पी, 16 मुनि, 17 प्रेक्षा (प्रेक्षाकू ; पुंसा) ॥

३८२० । छात्र्यादयः शालायाम् । ६ । २ । ८६ ॥

छात्रिशाला । व्याडिशाला । यदापि शालान्तः समासो नपुंसकलिङ्गे भवति तदापि 'तत्पुरुषे शालायां नपुंसके' (३८५७) इत्येतस्मात्पूर्वं विप्रतिषेधेनायमेव स्वरः । छात्रिशालम् ॥

3820 The words 'chhâtri' &c, get acute on the first syllable when followed by the word 'śâlâ.'

Thus छात्रिशाला, पैलिशाला, भाण्डिशाला ॥

Where the Tatpurusha compound ending in शाला becomes Neuter, by the option allowed in II. 4. 25; there also in the case of these words, the acute falls on the first syllable of the first term; thus superseding VI. 2. 123 S. 3857 which specifically applies to Neuter Tatpurushas. Thus छात्रिशालम्, पैलिशालम् ॥

1 छात्रि, 2 पैलि (पेलि), 3 भाण्डि, 4 व्याडि, 5 आखण्डि, 6 आटि, 7 गामि (गोमि)॥

३८२१ । प्रस्थेऽवृद्धमकर्क्यादीनाम् । ६ । २ । ८७ ॥

प्रस्थशब्द उत्तरपदे कर्क्यादिवर्जितमवृद्धं पूर्वपदमाद्युदात्तं स्यात् । इन्द्रप्रस्थः । 'अवृद्धम्' किम् । दाक्षिप्रस्थः । 'अकर्क्यादीनाम्' इति किम् । कर्कीप्रस्थः । मकरीप्रस्थः ॥

3821. The first member, which has not a Vriddhi in the first syllable, or which is not 'karkî.' &c, gets the acute on the first syllable before 'prastha.'

Thus इन्द्रप्रस्थः । But not in दाक्षिप्रस्थः, which has Vriddhi in the first syllable; nor also in कर्कीप्रस्थः, मघीप्रस्थः &c.

1 कर्की, 2 मघी (मघो), 3 मकरी, 4 कर्कन्धु (कर्कन्धू), 5 शमी, 6 करीर, 7 कन्दुक (कटुक), 8 कवल (कुबल; कूरल), 9 बदरी (बदर)॥

३८२२ । मालादीनां च । ६ । २ । ८८ ॥

वृद्धार्थमिदम् । मालाप्रस्थः । शोणाप्रस्थः ॥

3822. The first syllable of 'mâlâ' &c, gets the acute when 'prastha' follows.

Thus मालाप्रस्थः, शालाप्रस्थः ॥ This sûtra applies even though the first syllables are Vriddhi vowels. In the word एक and शोणा the letters ए and ओ are treated as Vriddhi (I. 1. 75).

1 माला, 2 शाला, 3 शोणा (शोण), 4 द्राक्षा, 5 क्षामा, 6 क्षामा, 7 काञ्ची, 8 एक, 9 काम, 10 क्षौमा ॥

३८२३ । अमहन्नवं नगरेऽनुदीचाम् । ६ । २ । ८९ ॥

नगरे परे महन्नवन्वर्जितं पूर्वमाद्युदात्तं स्यात् तच्चेदुदीचां न । ब्रह्मनगरम् । 'अम-' इति किम् । महानगरम् । नवनगरम् । 'अनुदीचाम्' किम् । कार्तिनगरम् ॥

3823. The first member has acute on the first syllable before the word *nagara* but not when it is the word *mahat*, or *nava*, nor when it refers to a city in the lands of the Northern People.

Thus ब्रह्मनगरम् । But not in महानगरम् and नवनगरम्. Why do we say 'but not of Northern People'? Observe नान्दीनगरम् कार्तिनगरम् ॥

३८२४ । अर्मे चावर्णं द्व्यच्त्र्यच् । ६ । २ । ९० ॥

अर्मे परे द्व्यच्त्र्यच्पूर्वमवर्णान्तमाद्युदात्तम् । गुप्तार्मम् । कुक्कुटार्मम् । 'अवर्णम्' किम् । बृहदर्मम् । 'द्व्यच्त्र्यच्' किम् । कपिञ्जलार्मम् । अमहन्नवमित्येव । महार्मम् । नवार्मम् ॥

3824. A word of two or three syllables ending in 'a' or 'â' (with the exception of 'mahâ' and 'nava'), standing before the word 'arma' has acute on the first syllable.

Thus गुप्तार्मम्, कुक्कुटार्मम् । Why do we say 'ending in अ (long or short)?' Observe बृहदर्मम् । Why do we say 'consisting of two or three syllables'? Observe कपिञ्जलार्मम् । The words महा and नव are to be real here also. The rule therefore does not apply to महार्मम् and नवार्मम् ॥

३८२५ । न भूताधिकसंजीवमद्राश्मकज्जलम् । ६ । २ । ९१ ॥

अर्मे परे नैतान्याद्युदात्तानि । भूतार्मम् । अधिकार्मम् । संजीवार्मम् । मद्राश्मग्रहणं संघातविगृहीतार्थम् । मद्रार्मम् । अश्मार्मम् । मद्राश्मार्मम् । कज्जलार्मम् ॥

'+ आद्युदात्तप्रकरणे दिवोदासादीनां छन्दस्युपसंख्यानम् +' । 'दिवोदासाय दाशुषे' ॥

3825. The following words do not get acute on the first syllable, when standing before 'arma' viz. भूत, अधिक, संजीव, मद्र, अश्मन्, and कज्जल ॥

Thus भूतार्मम्, अधिकार्मम्, संजीवार्मम्, मद्रार्मम्, अश्मार्मम्, मद्राश्मार्मम् (because the sûtra shows the compounding of those words in madrâśmam) कज्जलार्मम् । All these compounds have acute on the final by VI. 1. 223.

Vârt:—In the Vedas the words दिवोदास &c, have acute on the first syllable. Thus दिवोदासाय दाशुषे (Rig Veda IV. 30. 20).

३८२६ । अन्तः । ६ । २ । ९२ ॥

अधिकारोऽयम् । प्रागुत्तरपदादिग्रहणात् ॥

3826. In the following sûtras up to VI. 2. 110 inclusive, is to be supplied the phrase 'the last syllable in a word standing in the Nominative case has the acute.'

This is an adhikâra aphorism. In the succeeding sûtras, the last syllable of the first member of a compound gets the acute accent. Thus in the next sûtra the word सर्व gets acute on the final. This adhikâra extends up to VI. 2. 110. inclusive.

३८२७ । सर्वं गुणकार्त्स्न्ये । ६ । २ । ९३ ॥

सर्वशब्दः पूर्वपदमन्तोदात्तम् । सर्वश्वेतः । सर्वमहान् । 'सर्वम्' किम् । परमश्वेतः । आश्रयव्याप्त्या परमत्वं श्वेतस्येति । गुणकार्त्स्न्ये वर्तते । 'गुण–' इति किम् । सर्वसौवर्णः । 'कार्त्स्न्ये' किम् । सर्वेषां श्वेततरः सर्वश्वेतः ॥

3827. The acute is on the final of the word 'sarva,' standing as first member before an attributive word, in the sense of 'whole, through and through.'

Thus सर्वश्वेतः सर्वमहान् ॥

Why do we say सर्व ? Observe परमश्वेतः, here the attribute of श्वेत pervades through and through the object referred to, but the accent is not on the final of परम् ॥

Why do we say 'attributive word'? Observe सर्वसौवर्णः, 'golden', सर्वराजतः 'silvery', which do not denote any attribute in their original state but modification. In fact it is not गुणकात्स्न्य here at all, but a विकारकात्स्न्य ॥

Why do we use the word 'Kârtsnya or complete pervasion.' Observe सर्वेषां श्वेततरः = सर्वश्वेतः here the compounding takes place by the elision of the affix तरप् denoting comparison, and as it shows only comparative, not absolute, whiteness, the rule does not apply. Moreover, in this example, the 'kârtsnya' is not that of 'guṇa' but of 'guṇi', not of the 'attribute', but of the 'substance'.

३८२८ । संज्ञायां गिरिनिकाययोः । ६ । २ । ९४ ॥

एतयोः परतः पूर्वमन्तोदात्तम् । अञ्जनागिरिः । मौण्डिनिकायः । 'संज्ञायाम्' किम् । परमगिरिः । ब्राह्मणनिकायः ॥

3828. The last syllable of the first member before *giri* and nikâya has the acute, when the compound is a Name.

Thus अञ्जनागिरिः । The finals of añjana is lengthened by VI. 3. 117. मौण्डिनिकायः । Why do we say 'when it is a Name'? Observe परमगिरिः, ब्राह्मणनिकायः ॥

३८२९ । कुमार्यां वयसि । ६ । २ । ९५ ॥

पूर्वपदमन्तोदात्तम् । वृद्धकुमारी । कुमारीशब्दः पुंसा सहासंप्रयोगमात्रं प्रवृत्तिनिमित्तमुपादाय प्रयुक्तो वृद्धादिभिः समानाधिकरणः । तत्र वय इह गृह्यते न कुमारत्वमेव । 'वयसि' किम् । परमकुमारी ॥

3829. The last syllable of the first member gets the acute when the word 'kumâri' follows, the compound denoting age.

Thus वृद्धकुमारी 'an old maid'. The compounding is by II. 1. 57. The word वृद्धा becomes masculine by VI. 3. 42 in the example.

Q. The word कुमारी was formed by ङीप् by IV. 1. 20 in denoting the prime of youth, how can this word be now applied to denote old age by being coupled with वृद्धा; it is a contradiction in terms. *Ans*. The word कुमारी has two senses; one denoting 'a young maiden' and second 'unmarried virgin'. It is in the latter sense, that the attribute वृद्धा is applied. Why do we say 'when the compound denotes age'? Observe परमकुमारी ॥

३८३० । उदकेऽकेवले । ६ । २ । ९६ ॥

अकेवलं मिश्रं तद्वाचिनि समासे उदके परे पूर्वमन्तोदात्तम् । गुडोदकम् । स्वरे कृतेऽत्र एकादेशः । 'स्वरितो वानुदात्ते पदादौ' (३६५९) इति पक्षे स्वरितः । 'अकेवले' किम् । शीतोदकम् ॥

3830. Before the word *udaka*, when the compound denotes a mixture, the last syllable of the first member has the acute.

Thus गु॑डोदकम् or गु॒डोदकम् । When we have already made the ड acute by this rule, then the svarita accent may result optionally, by the combination of the acute अ of guda and the subsequent grave उ of उदक, by rule VIII. 2. 6. S. 3659. The word अकेवल means mixture. When mixture is not meant, this rule does not apply. As शीतोदकम् ॥

३८३१ । द्विगौ क्रतौ । ६ । २ । ९७ ॥

द्विगावुत्तरपदे क्रतुवाचिनि समासे पूर्वमन्तोदात्तम् । गर्गत्रिरात्रः । 'द्विगौ' किम् । अतिरात्रः । 'क्रतौ' किम् । बिल्वहोमस्य सप्तरात्रो बिल्वसप्तरात्रः ॥

3831. Before a Dvigu, when the compound denotes a sacrifice, the last syllable of the first member has the acute.

Thus गर्ग॑त्रिरात्रः = गर्गाणां त्रिरात्रः Why do we say 'before a Dvigu compound'? Observe अतिरात्र॑ः (रात्रिमतिक्रान्त इति प्रादिसमासः) which being formed by the Samasânta affix अच् (V. 4. 87) has acute on the final (VI. 1. 163). Why do we say 'when denoting a sacrifice'? Observe बिल्वसप्तरात्रः=बिल्वहोमस्य सप्तरात्रः ॥

३८३२ । सभायां नपुंसके । ६ । २ । ९८ ॥

सभायां परतो नपुंसकलिङ्गे समासे पूर्वमन्तोदात्तम् । गोपालसभम् । स्त्रीसभम् । 'सभायाम्' किम् । ब्राह्मणसेनम् । 'नपुंसके' किम् । राजसभा । प्रतिपदोक्तनपुंसकग्रहणाचेह । रमणीयसभम् । ब्राह्मणकुलम् ॥

3832. Before the word sabhâ when it is exhibited as Neuter, the first member of the compound gets acute on the last syllable.

Thus गोपाल॑सभम्' स्त्री॑सभम् ॥

Why do we say 'before सभा'? Observe ब्राह्मणसेनम् ॥

Why do we say 'when in the Neuter'? Observe राजसभा ॥

The word सभा becomes Neuter under rules II. 4. 23-24 : therefore when the word सभा does not become Neuter under those rules, then by the maxim of Pratipadokta &c : the accent does not fall on the final of the preceding term, as, रमणीयसभं, here the word सभा is neuter not by the force of any particular rule, but because the thing designated (अभिधेय) is neuter.

३८३३ । पुरे प्राचाम् । ६ । २ । ९९ ॥

देवदत्तपुरम् । नान्दीपुरम् । 'प्राचाम्' किम् । शिवपुरम् ॥

3833. Before the word *pura*, when the compound denotes a city of the Eastern People, the final of the first member has the acute.

Thus देवदत्त॑पुरम्' कान्ती॑पुरम्, नान्दी॑पुरम् । Why do we say of the Eastern people'? Observe शिवपुरम् ॥

३८३४ । अरिष्टगौडपूर्वे च । ६ । २ । १०० ॥

पुरे परेऽरिष्टगौडपूर्वे समासे पूर्वमन्तोदात्तम् । अरिष्टपुरम् । गौडपुरम् । 'पूर्व' ग्रहणं किम् । इहापि यथा स्यात् । अरिष्टाश्रितपुरम् । गौडभृत्यपुरम् ॥

3834. When the words 'arishṭa' and 'gauḍa' stand first, the first member has the acute on the final before the word 'pura.'

Thus अरिष्टँपुरम्, गौडँपुरम् । By the force of the word पूर्व in the aphorism, we can apply the rule to अरिष्टश्रितँपुरम्' गौडभृत्यपुरम् ॥

३८३५ । न हास्तिनफलकमार्देयाः । ६ । २ । १०१ ॥

पुरे परे नैतान्यन्तोदात्तानि । हास्तिनपुरम् । फलकपुरम् । मार्देयपुरम् । मृदेरपत्यमिति शुभ्रादित्वात् ढक् ॥

3835. But when the word 'hâstina' 'phalaka' and 'mârdeya' precede 'pura' the acute does not fall on their final.

This is an exception to VI. 2. 99. Thus हास्तिनपुरम्, फलकपुरम्, मार्देयपुरम्. The son of मृदु is मार्देय formed by ढक्, the word belonging to Śubhrâdi class. The उ is elided by VI. 4. 147.

३८३६ । कुसूलकूपकुम्भशालं बिले । ६ । २ । १०२ ॥

एतान्यन्तोदात्तानि बिले परे । कुसूलबिलम् । कूपबिलम् । कुम्भबिलम् । शालबिलम् । 'कुसूलादि' किम् । सर्पबिलम् । 'बिल' इति किम् । कुसूलस्वामी ॥

3836, The words कुसूल, कूप, कुम्भ, and शाला have the acute on the last syllable before the word 'bila.'

Thus कुसूलँबिलम्,' कूपँबिलम्, कुम्भँबिलम्, शालाँबिलम्, । But not so in सर्पबिलम् । Why do we say 'before बिल'? Observe कुसूलस्वामी ॥

३८३७ । दिक्शब्दा ग्रामजनपदाख्यानचानराटेषु । ६ । २ । १०३ ॥

दिक्शब्दा अन्तोदात्ता भवन्त्येषु । पूर्वेषुकामशमी । अपरकृष्णमृत्तिका । जनपदः । पूर्वपञ्चालाः । आख्यानम् । पूर्वयायातम् । पूर्वचानराटम् । शब्दग्रहणं कालवाचिदिक्शब्दस्य परिग्रहार्थम् ॥

3837. Words expressing direction (in space or time) have acute on the last syllable, when followed by a word denoting a village, or a country or a narrative, and before the word 'chânarâṭa.'

Thus पूर्वेषुकामशमी or पूर्वँ (VIII. 2. 6). The compounding takes place by II. 1. 50. अपरकृष्णमृत्तिका ॥

Country name—पूर्वँ पञ्चालाः । These are Karmadhâraya compounds (II. 1. 58).

Story name :—पूर्वँयायातम् । So also पूर्वँचानराटम् । The employmen of the term शब्द in the aphorism shows that time-denoting दिक् words as in पूर्वयायात should also be included.

३८३८ । आचार्योपसर्जनश्चान्तेवासिनि । ६ । २ । १०४ ॥

आचार्योपसर्जनान्तेवासिनि परे दिक्शब्दा अन्तोदात्ता भवन्ति । पूर्वपाणिनीयाः । 'आचार्य-' इति किम् । पूर्वान्तेवासी । 'अन्तेवासिनि' किम् । पूर्वपाणिनीयं शास्त्रम् ॥

3838. The direction denoting words have acute on the final.

before the names of scholars, when such names are derived from those of their teachers.

Thus पूर्वपाणिनीयाः। Compare VI. 2. 36. Why do we say 'when derived from the names of their Teachers.'? Observe पूर्वान्तेवासी। Why do we say 'Scholar-names'? Observe पूर्वपाणिनीयं शास्त्रम्। (पाणिनीयं शास्त्रम् पूर्वं चिरन्तनम्) ॥

३८३९। उत्तरपदवृद्धौ सर्वं च। ६। २। १०५॥

उत्तरपदस्येत्यधिकृत्य या वृद्धिर्विहिता तद्वत्युत्तरपदे परे सर्वशब्दो दिक्छब्दाश्चान्तोदात्ता भवन्ति। सर्वपाञ्चालकः। अपरपाञ्चालकः। 'अधिकार' ग्रहणं किम्। सर्वमासः सर्वकारकः॥

3839. Words denoting direction and the word 'sarva' have acute on the final, before a word which takes Vṛiddhi in the first syllable of the second term by VII. 3. 12 and 13.

By the sûtra उत्तरपदस्य VII. 3. 10; 12, the Vṛiddhi of the Uttarapada is ordained when the Taddhita affixes having ञ्, ण्, or क्, follow, the Pûrvapada being सु, सर्व and अर्ध। The word उत्तरपदवृद्धिः therefore, means that word which takes Vṛiddhi, under the rule relating to uttarapada, *i. e.*, under rule VII. 3. 12 and 13 Thus अपरपाञ्चालकः, सर्वपाञ्चालकः। These are formed by वुञ् affix (IV. 2. 125)

Why do we say 'which takes Vṛiddhi in the second term under VII. 3 12 and 13?" Had the word उत्तरपदस्येति अधिकृत्य not been used by us in explaining the sûtra, then the sûtra, would have run thus वृद्धौ सर्वं च, and would have applied to cases like सर्वमासः, सर्वकारकः where मासः and कारकः are Vriddhi words not by virtue of VII. 3. 12.

३८४०। बहुव्रीहौ विश्वं संज्ञायाम्। ६। २। १०६॥

बहुव्रीहौ विश्वशब्दः पूर्वपदभूतः संज्ञायामन्तोदात्तः स्यात्। पूर्वपदप्रकृतिस्वरेण प्राप्तस्याद्युदात्तस्यापवादः। 'विश्वकर्मा विश्वदेवः'। 'आविश्वदेवं सत्पतिम्'। 'बहुव्रीहौ' किम्। विश्वे च ते देवाश्च विश्वे देवाः। 'संज्ञायाम्' किम्। विश्वदेवः। प्रागव्ययीभावद्बहुव्रीह्यधिकारः॥

3840. The word 'viśva' has acute on the final, being first member in a Bahuvrîhi when it is a Name.

This is an exception to VI. 2. 1 by which the first member in a Bahuvrîhi would have retained its original accent. Thus:—विश्वकर्मा विश्वदेव (Rig Veda. VIII. 98. 2). आविश्वदेवं सत्पतिम्॥

Why do we say in a Bahuvrihi compound? Observe विश्वे च देवाः = विश्वे देवाः॥

Why do we say when a name? Observe विश्वे देवा अस्य = विश्वदेवः। But विश्वामित्रः and विश्वाङ्गिरः have acute on the final as they are governed by the subsequent rule VI. 2. 165 which supersedes this. The word Bahuvrihi governs the succeeding sûtras up to VI. 2. 120 inclusive.

३८४१ । उदराश्वेषुषु । ६ । २ । १०७ ॥

संज्ञायामिति वर्तते । वृकोदरः । हयश्वः । महेषुः ॥

3841. The first member in a Bahuvrîhi, before the words 'udara' 'aśva' and 'ishu' gets acute on the final syllable, when the compound denotes a Name.

Thus वृकोदरः, हर्यश्वः, and महेषुः । This sûtra is also an exception to VI. 2. 1 by which the first term would have retained its original accent The word वृक has acute on the first by Phiṭ II. 7. The word हरि is also first acute as formed by इन् (Uṇ IV. 118). The word महत is end-acute by V. 2. 38. Its mention here appears redundant.

३८४२ । क्षेपे । ६ । २ । १०८ ॥

उदराश्वेषुषु पूर्वमन्तोदात्तं बहुव्रीहौ निन्दायाम् । घटोदरः । कटुकाश्वः । चलाचलेषुः अनुदर इत्यत्र नञ्सुभ्याम्–' (३९०६) इति भवति प्रतिषेधेन ॥

3842. A word before 'udar' 'aśva' and 'ishu' in a Bahuvrîhi gets acute on the final, when reproach is meant.

Thus घटोदरः कटुकाश्वः चलाचलेषुः । The word घट is formed by अच् (III. 1. 134) and has acute on the final, and so it would have retained this accent by VI. 2. 1. even without this sûtra. The word कटुक being formed by कन् (V. 3. 75) has acute on the first. In this and the last sûtra, all the acutes may optionally be changed into svarita by VIII. 2. 6. But अनुदरः and सूदरः have acute on the final by VI. 2. 172, S. 3906 which being a subsequent sûtra, supersedes this present, so far as अन् and सु are concerned.

३८४३ । नदी बन्धुनि । ६ । २ । १०९ ॥

बन्धुशब्दे परे नद्यन्तं पूर्वमन्तोदात्तं बहुव्रीहौ । गार्गीबन्धुः । 'नदी' किम् । ब्रह्मबन्धुः ब्रह्मशब्द आद्युदात्तः । 'बन्धुनि' किम् । गार्गीप्रियः ॥

3843. In a Bahuvrîhi compound, having the word 'bandhu' as its second member, the first member ending in the Feminine affix 'î' ('nadî' word) has the acute on its final syllable.

Thus गार्गीबन्धुः । The word गार्गी is formed by adding ङीप् (IV. 1. 16) to गार्ग्य ending in यञ् (IV. 1. 105), and therefore, it is first acute. By VI. 2. 1 this accent would have been retained, but for the present sûtra.

Why do we say 'a Nadî (Feminine in ई) word'? Observe ब्रह्मबन्धुः the word ब्रह्म has acute on the first syllable as it is formed by मनिन् (Uṇ IV. 146) and it retains that accent (VI. 2. 1).

Why do we say 'before बन्धु'? Observe गार्गीप्रियः ॥

३८४४ । निष्ठोपसर्गपूर्वमन्यतरस्याम् । ६ । २ । ११० ॥

निष्ठान्तं पूर्वपदमन्तोदात्तं वा । प्रधौतपादः । 'निष्ठा' किम् । प्रसेवकमुखः । 'उपसर्गपूर्वम्' किम् । शुष्कमुखः ॥

3844. In a Bahuvrîhi compound, a Participle in 'kta' preceded by a preposition, standing as the first member of the com pound, has optionally acute on the last syllable.

Thus प्रधौतपादः or प्रधौतपादः (VI 2. 169).

Why do we say 'a Nishṭhâ'? Observe प्रसेवकमुखः which is acute in the middle by the kṛit accent being retained after प्र (VI. 2. 139).

Why do we say 'preceded by a preposition'? Observe शुष्कमुखः which has acute on the first by VI. 1. 206.

३८४५ । उत्तरपदादिः । ६ । २ । १११ ॥

उत्तरपदाधिकार आपादान्तम् । आद्यधिकारस्तु 'प्रकृत्या भगालम्' (३८७६) इत्यवधिकः ॥

3845. In the following sûtras, up to VI. 2. 136 inclusive, should always be supplied the phrase 'the first syllable of the second member has the acute.'

This is an adhikâra aphorism and the word उत्तरपद exerts its influence up to the end of the chapter, while the word आदि has scope up to VI. 2. 187 exclusive.

३८४६ । कर्णो वर्णलक्षणात् । ६ । २ । ११२ ॥

वर्णवाचिनो लक्षणवाचिनश्च परः कर्णशब्द आद्युदात्तो बहुव्रीहौ । शुक्लकर्णः । शंकुकर्णः 'कर्ण' किम् । श्वेतपादः । 'वर्णलक्षणात्' किम् । शोभनकर्णः ॥

3846. In a Bahuvrîhi compound, the word 'karṇa' standing as second member, has acute on the first syllable, when it is preceded by a word denoting color or mark.

Thus with color we have शुक्लकर्णः and with mark-name, we have शङ्कूकर्णः the lengthening of शंकु takes place by VI. 3. 115. The marks of 'scythe,' 'arrow' &c., are made on the ears of cattle to mark and distinguish them. It is such a 'mark' which is meant here.

Why do we say कर्ण ? Observe श्वेतपादः, कूटशृङ्गः here श्वेत being formed by अच (II. 1. 134) is end-acute, and कूट being formed by क (III. 1. 135) is also end-acute and these accents are retained in the compound.

Why do we say 'when preceded by a word denoting color or mark'? Observe शोभनकर्णः where शोभन being formed by युच् (III. 2. 149) is end-acute and this accent is retained (VI. 2. 1).

३८४७ । संज्ञौपम्ययोश्च । ६ । २ । ११३ ॥

कर्ण आद्युदात्तः । मणिकर्णः । औपम्ये । गोकर्णः ॥

3847. In a Bahuvrîhi, the second member 'karṇa' has acute on the first syllable, when the compound denotes a Name or a Resemblance.

Thus मणिकर्णः, is a Name : गोकर्णः, denotes resemblance *i. e.*, 'persons having ears like a cow.'

३८४८ । कण्ठपृष्ठग्रीवाजङ्घं च । ६ २ । ११४ ॥

संज्ञौपम्ययोर्बहुव्रीहौ । शितिकण्ठः । काण्डपृष्ठः । सुग्रीवः । नाडीजङ्घः । औपम्ये । खरकण्ठः । गोपृष्ठः । अश्वग्रीवः । गोजङ्घः ॥

3848. In a Bahuvrihi expressing a Name or comparison, the second member कण्ठ, पृष्ठ, ग्रीवा and जङ्घा have acute on the first syllable.

Thus Name : शितिकण्ठः । Comparison खरकण्ठः । Name काण्डपृष्ठः । Resemblance गोपृष्ठ । Name सुग्रीवः । Resemblance अश्वग्रीवः । Name नाडीजङ्घः । Resemblance गोजङ्घः, ॥

The sûtra कण्ठपृष्ठग्रीवाजंघं is in Neuter gender, and जंघा is shortened, as it is a Samâhâra Dvandva. In the case of सुग्रीव, the accent would have fallen on the final व by VI. 2. 172, this ordains acute on ग्री ॥

३८४९ । शृङ्गमवस्थायां च । ६ । २ । ११५ ॥

शृङ्गशब्दोऽवस्थायां संज्ञौपम्ययोश्चाद्युदात्तो बहुव्रीहौ । उद्गतशृङ्गः । द्व्यङ्गुलशृङ्गः । अत्र शृङ्गोद्गमनादिकृतो गवां देवयोर्विशेषोऽवस्था । संज्ञायाम् । ऋष्यशृङ्गः । उपमायाम् । मेषशृङ्गः । 'अवस्था-' इति किम् । स्थूलशृङ्गः ॥

3849 In a Bahuvrihi denoting age, (as well as a Name or a Resemblance), the second member 'śringa' gets acute on the first syllable.

Thus उद्गतशृङ्गः, द्व्यंगुलशृङ्गः । Here the word शृङ्ग denotes the particular age of the cattle at which the horns come out, or become one inch long. Name : ऋष्यशृङ्गः । Comparison : मेषशृङ्गः । Why do we say when denoting 'age &c' स्थूलशृङ्गः ॥

३८५० । नञो जरमरमित्रमृताः । ६ । २ । ११६ ॥

नञः परा एते आद्युदात्ता बहुव्रीहौ । 'तां मे जरांद्वजरम्' । अमरम् । 'अमित्रमर्दय' । 'अवो देवेष्वमृतम्' । 'नञः' किम् । ब्राह्मणमित्रः । 'ज-' इति किम् । अशत्रुः ।

3850. After a Negative Particle, in a Bahuvrîhi, the acute falls on the first syllable of जर, मर, मित्र and मृत ॥

Thus अजरः अमरः, अमित्रः and अमृत । Why do we say after a Negative Particle ? Observe ब्राह्मणमित्रः । Why do we say 'जर &c.' Observe अशत्रुः when the final gets the acute by VI. 2. 172.

३८५१ । सोर्मनसी अलोमोषसी ॥ ६ । २ । ११७ ॥

सोःपरं लोमोषसी वर्जयित्वा मन्नन्तमसन्तं चाद्युदात्तं स्यात् । 'नञसुभ्याम्' (३८०८) इत्यस्यापवादः । सु कर्माणः सुरुचः । 'स नो वक्षदनिमानः सुब्रह्मा । शिवा पशुभ्यः सुमनाः सुवर्चाः' । सुपेशसस्करति' । 'सोः' किम् । कृतकर्मा । 'मनसी' किम् । सुराजा । 'अलोमोषसी' किम् । सुलोमा । सूषाः । कपि तु परत्वात् 'कपि पूर्वम्' (३८०७) इति भवति । सुकर्मकः । 'सु स्रोतस्कः' ॥

3851. After the adjective *su* in a Bahuvrîhi, a stem ending in *man* and *as* with the exception of *loman* and *ushas* has acute on the first syllable.

Thus सुकर्माणः सुरुचः (Rig Veda IV. 2. 17). सु नो वत्सदनिमानः सुब्रह्मा (Rig Veda VI. 22. 7). शिवा पशुभ्यः सुमनाः सुवर्चा (Rig Veda X. 85. 44). सु प्रेष्ठसक्तिः (Rig Veda II 35. 1). सुकर्मन्, सुधर्मन् सुप्रथिमन्, सुपयस्, सुयशस्, सुस्रोतस्, so also सुध्वत् and सुध्वस् from the root ध्वंस् and ध्वस् with the affix क्विप्। The final स् is changed to द् by VIII. 2. 72. But this substitution is considered asiddha for the purposes of accent, and these words are taken as if still ending in अस्। Why do we say 'after सु?' Observe कृतकर्मन्, कृतयशस्। Why do we say 'ending in मन् and अस्?' Observe सुराजन् and सुतक्षन् formed by the affix कनिन् (Uṇ. I. 156), and the accent is on रा and त. but with सु, the accent is thrown on the final by VI. 2, 172 S. 3906. Why do we say with the exception of लोमन and उषस्? Observe सुलोमन and सूषस (VI. 2. 127). The following maxim applies here: अनिनस्मन् ग्रहणान्यर्थवता चानर्थकेन च तदन्तविधिं प्रयोजयन्ति 'whenever अन्, or इन् or अस्, or मन्, when they are employed in Grammar, denote by I. 1. 72, something that ends with अन् or इन् or अस्, or मन्, there (अन्, इन्, अस्, and मन्) represent these combinations of letters, both in so far as they possess and also in so far as they are void of, a meaning.' Therefore the मन् and अस्, void of meaning are also included here. Thus धर्मन् is formed by मन् (Uṇ I. 140), but कर्मन् is is formed by मनिन् (Uṇ. IV. 145), and प्रथिमन is formed by इमनिच् affix (V. I. 122) in which मन् is only a part. Similarly यशस is formed by असुन् (Uṇ IV. 191), and so also स्रोतस् (Uṇ IV. 202); but in सुध्वस् (सु ध्वस्, from ध्वंस् with the affix क्विप III. 2. 76) the rule applies also, though अस् is here part of the root. But when the samâsânta affix कप् is added (V. 4. 154), then the accent falls on the syllable immediately preceding कप् for there the subsequent Rule VI. 2. 173 S, 3907 supersedes the present rule: thus सुकर्मकः, सुस्रोतस्कः॥

३८५२। क्रत्वादयश्च। ६। २। ११८॥

सोः परं आद्युदात्तः स्युः। 'साम्राज्याय सुक्रतुः'। 'सु प्रतीकः'। 'सु हव्यः'। 'सु प्रतूर्तिमनेहसम्'।

3852. After *su* in a Bahuvrîhi, the acute falls on the first syllable of *kratu* &c.

Thus साम्राज्याय सुक्रतुः (Rig Veda I. 25. 10) सुहव्यः, सुप्रतीकः। सुप्रतूर्तिमनेहसम् (Rig Veda I. 40. 4).

३८५३। आद्युदात्तं द्व्यच्छन्दसि। ६। २। ११९॥

यदाद्युदात्तं द्व्यच्तत्सोरुत्तरं बहुव्रीहावाद्युदात्तम्। 'अधा स्वश्वाः'। 'सु रथाँ आतिथिग्वे' निःस्वरेणाश्वरथावाद्युदात्तौ। 'आद्युदात्तम्' किम्। 'यासु बाहुः'। 'द्व्यच्' किम्। सु गुरसत्सु हिरण्यः। हिरण्यशब्दस्त्र्यच्॥

3853. In a Bahuvrîhi compound, in the Chhandas, a word of two syllables with acute on the first syllable, when preceded by *su*, gets acute on the first syllable.

In other words, such a word retains its accent. Thus:—अधास्वश्व सु रथाँ आतिथिग्वे (Rig Veda VIII. 68. 16). Here स्वश्वः and सुरथः have acute on श्व and र, which they had originally also, for अश्व and रथ are formed by क्विन् (Uṇ. I. 151) and क्थन् (Uṇ. II. 2) respectively and have the नित् accent (VI. 1. 197).

Why do we say 'having acute on the first syllable'? Observe या सुबाहुः स्वङ्गुरिः (Rig. II. 32. 7). Here बाहु has acute on the final (Un. I. 27 formed by उ affix and has the accent of the affix III. 1. 3).

Why do we say 'having two syllables'? Observe सुगुरसत्, सुहिरण्यः (Rig Veda I. 125. 2). This sûtra is an exception to VI. 2. 172.

३८५४ । वीरवीर्यौ च । ६ । २ । १२० ॥

सोः परौ बहुव्रीहौ छन्दस्याद्युदात्तौ । 'सुवीरेण रयिणा' । 'सुवीर्यस्य गोमतः' । वीर्यशब्दो यत्प्रत्ययान्तः । तत्र 'यतोऽनावः' (३७०१) इत्याद्युदात्तत्वं नेति वीर्यग्रहणं ज्ञापकम् । तत्र हि सति पूर्वेणैव सिद्धं स्यात् ॥

3854 In a Bahuvrîhi compound in the Chhandas, after 'su' the words 'vîra' and 'vrîya' have acute on the first syllable.

Thus सुवीरेण रयिणा (Rig Veda X. 122. 3). So also सुवीर्यस्य गोमतः (Rig Veda VIII. 95. 4). The word वीर्य is formed by यत् affix and by VI. 1. 213, S. 3701 it would have acute on the first. But its enumeration in this sûtra shows that Rule VI 1. 213, does not apply to वीर्य । The word वीर्य has svarita on the final in the Chhandas, by Phit IV. 9. In the classical literature it is âdyudâtta.

३८५५ । कूलतीरतूलमूलशालाक्षसममव्ययीभावे । ६ । २ । १२१ ॥

उपकूलम् । उपतीरम् । उपतूलम् । उपमूलम् । उपशालम् । उपाक्षम् । सुषमम् । निषःमम् । तिष्ठद्गुप्रभृतिष्वेते । 'कूलादि' ग्रहणं किम् । उपकुम्भम् । 'अव्ययीभावे' किम् । परमकूलम् ॥

3855. In an Avyayîbhâva compound, the following second terms have acute on their first syllable : कूल, तीर, तूल, मूल, शाला, अक्ष and सम ॥

Thus उपकूलम्, उपतीरम्, उपतूलम्' उपमूलम्, उपशालम्, सुषमम्, निःषमम् । These last four are to be found in Tishthadgu class of compounds (II. 1. 17).

Why do we say 'कूल &c.'? Observe उपकुम्भम् ॥

Why do we say 'in an Avyayîbhâva compound?' Observe परमकूलम्, उत्तमकूलम् । After the prepositions परि, प्रति, उप and अप, the words कूल &c. would have becomes accentless by VI. 2. 33, the present sûtra supersedes VI. 2. 33, and we have accent on कूल &c. and not on the Prepositions.

३८५६ । कंसमन्थशूर्पपाय्यकाण्डं द्विगौ । ६ । २ । १२२ ॥

द्विकंसः । द्विमन्थः । द्विशूर्पः । द्विपाय्यम् । द्विकाण्डम् । 'द्विगौ' किम् । परमकंसः ॥

3856. In a Dvigu Compound the following second members get acute on their first syllable :– कंस, मन्थ, शूर्प, पाय्य and काण्ड ॥

Thus द्विकंसः, (द्वाभ्यां कंसाभ्यां क्रीतः the affix टिठन् V. 1. 25 is elided by V. 1. 28) द्विमन्थः, (the affix ठञ् V. 1. 19 is elided by V. 1. 28) द्विशूर्पः, (the affix अञ् V. 1. 26 is elided) द्विपाय्यः, द्विकाण्डः । Why do we say in a Dvigu? Observe परमकंसः ॥

३८५७ । तत्पुरुषे शालायां नपुंसके । ६ । २ । १२३ ॥

शालाशब्दान्ते तत्पुरुषे नपुंसकलिङ्गे उत्तरपदमाद्युदात्तम् । ब्राह्मणशालम् । 'तत्पुरुषे' किम् । दृढशालं ब्राह्मणकुलम् । 'शालायाम्' किम् । ब्राह्मणशाला ॥

3857. The word 'śâlâ' at the end of a Tatpurusha compound when exhibited in the Neuter, has acute on the first syllable.

Thus ब्राह्मणशालम् । The compound becomes Neuter by II 4. 25.

Why do we say 'in a Tatpurusha'? Observe दृढशालं ब्राह्मणकुलम् which is a Bahuvrîhi compound and therefore the first member retains its accent (VI. 2. 1,) and as the first member is a Nishṭhâ word, it has acute on the final.

Why do we say 'the word शाला?' Observe ब्राह्मणसेनम् ॥

Why do we say 'in the Neuter'? Observe ब्राह्मणशाला । Compare VI. 2. 86:

३८५८ । कन्था च । ६ । २ । १२४ ॥

तत्पुरुषे नपुंसकलिङ्गे कन्थाशब्द उत्तरपदमाद्युदात्तम् । सौशमिकन्थम् । आह्वरकन्थम् । 'नपुंसके' किम् । दाक्षिकन्था ॥

3858. In a Neuter Tatpuruṣha ending in 'kanthâ' the acute falls on the first syllable of the second member.

Thus सौशमिकन्थम्, आह्वरकन्थम्, । The word सौशमि: denotes the descendant of सुशमः (शोभनः शमो यस्य) आह्वर is formed by the preposition आ with the verb ह्वृ and the affix क (III. 1. 136) The compound is Neuter by II. 4 20. These are Genitive compounds. When the word is not Neuter we have दाक्षिकन्था ॥

३८५९ । आदिश्चिहणादीनाम् । ६ । २ । १२५ ॥

कन्थान्ते तत्पुरुषे नपुंसकलिङ्गे चिहणादीनामादिरुदात्तः । चिहणकन्थम् । मन्दकन्थम् चे आदिरिति वर्तमाने पुनर्ग्रहणं पूर्वपदस्याद्युदात्तार्थम् ॥

3859. In a Neuter Tatpurushâ ending in 'kanthâ' the first syllable of 'chihaṇa' &c. have the acute.

As चिहणकन्थम्, मडरकन्थम्, मडुरकन्थम् । The repetition of the word आदि in this sûtra, though its anuvritti was present, indicates that the first syllable on the *first member* gets the acute. The word चिहण is derived from the root चिनोति with क्विप् which gives चित् and हन is formed by adding अच् (III. 1. 134) to हन् । चत्+हन = चिहण the elision of त् is irregular.

३८६० । चेलखेटकटुककाण्डं गर्हायाम् । ६ । २ । १२६ ॥

चेलादीन्युत्तरपदान्याद्युदात्तानि । पुत्रचेलम् । नगरखेटम् । दधिकटुकम् । प्रजाकाण्डम् । तादिसादृश्येन पुत्रादीनां गर्हा । व्याघ्रादित्वात्समासः । 'गर्हायाम्' किम् । परमचेलम् ॥

3860. The words चेल, खेट, कटुक and काण्ड at the end of a Tatpurusha have acute on the first syllable, when a reproach is meant.

Thus पुत्रचेलम्, नगरखेटम्, (खेट इति तृणनाम, तद्वत् दुर्बल) दधिकटुकम (कटुकम-स्वादु) प्रजाकाण्डम । The reproach is denoted of the sons &c. by comparing them to चेल &c. The analysis will be पुत्रश्चेलमिव i. e. चेलवत् तुच्छम् and the compounding takes place under II. 1. 56: the Vyaghrâdi class being an akṛtigaṇa. When reproach is not meant, we have परमचेलम् ॥

३८६१ । चीरमुपमानम् । ६ । २ । १२७ ॥

वस्त्रं चीरमिव वस्त्रचीरम् । कम्बलचीरम् । 'उपमानम्' किम् । परमचीरम् ॥

3861. The word 'chîra' at the end of a Tatpurusha, has acute on the first syllable, when something is compared with it.

Thus वस्त्रम् चीरमिव=वस्त्रचीरम्, कम्बलचीरम् । Why do we say 'when comparison is meant ?' Observe परमचीरम् ॥

३८६२ । पललसूपशाकं मिश्रे । ६ । २ । १२८ ॥

घृतपललम् । घृतसूपः । घृतशाकम् । 'भक्ष्येण मिश्रीकरणम्' (६९७) इति समासः । 'मिश्रे' किम् । परमपललम् ॥

3862. In a Tatpurusha ending in पलल, सूप and शाक the acute falls on the first syllable of these, when the compound denotes a food mixed or seasoned with something.

Thus घृतपललम्, घृतसूपः, घृतशाकम् = घृतेन मिश्रं पललं &c. The compounding takes place by II. 1. 35. S. 697. Why do we say 'when meaning mixed or seasoned ?' Observe परमपललम् ॥

३८६३ । कूलसूदस्थलकर्षाः संज्ञायाम् । ६ । २ । १२९ ॥

आद्युदात्तास्तत्पुरुषे । दाक्षिकूलम् । शाण्डिसूदम् । दाण्डायनस्थलम् । दाक्षिकर्षः । ग्रामसंज्ञा एताः । 'संज्ञायाम्' किम् । परमकूलम् ॥

3863. The words कूल, सूद, स्थल and कर्ष have acute on their first syllable, when at the end of a Tatpurusha denoting a Name.

Thus दाक्षिकूलम् शाण्डिसूदम्, दाण्डायनस्थलम्, दाक्षिकर्षः । All these are names of villages. When not a name we have परमकूलम् ॥

३८६४ । अकर्मधारये राज्यम् । ६ । २ । १३० ॥

कर्मधारयवर्जिते तत्पुरुषे राज्यमुत्तरपदमाद्युदात्तम् । ब्राह्मणराज्यम् । 'अक-' इति किम् । परमराज्यम् ॥

'+चेलराज्यादिस्वरादव्ययस्वरः पूर्वविप्रतिषेधेन+' । कुचेलम् । कुराज्यम् ॥

3864. The word 'râjyam' has acute on the first syllable, when at the end of a Tatpurusha compound, which is not a Karmadhâraya.

Thus ब्राह्मणराज्यम् । In a Karmadhâraya we have परमराज्यम् ॥

Vârt :—The accent taught in VI. 2. 126 to 130 S 3860 to 3864 is superseded by the accent of the Indeclinable taught in VI. 2. 2, though that rule stands first and this subsequent'. As कुचेलम्,' कुराज्यम् ॥

३८६५ । वर्ग्यादयश्च । ६ । २ । १३१ ॥

अर्जुनवर्ग्यः । वासुदेवपक्ष्यः । अकर्मधारय इत्येव । परमवर्ग्यः । वर्ग्यादिर्दिगाद्यन्तर्गणः ॥

3865. At the end of a non-Karmadhâraya Tatpurusha compound, the words *vargya* &c. have acute on the first syllable.

Thus अर्जुनवर्ग्यः, वासुदेवपक्ष्यः । In a Karmadhâraya we have परमवर्ग्यः । The words वर्ग्य &c. are no where exhibited as such; the primitive words वर्ग, पूग, गण &c. sub-division of दिगादि (IV. 3. 54) are here referred to, as ending with यत् affix.

३८६६ । पुत्रः पुम्भ्यः । ६ । २ । १३२ ॥

पुंशब्देभ्यः परः पुत्रशब्द आद्युदात्तस्तत्पुरुषे । दाशकिपुत्रः । माहिषपुत्रः । 'पुत्रः' किम् । कौनटिमातुलः । 'पुम्भ्यः' किम् । दासीपुत्रः ॥

3866. The word *putra* coming after a Masculine noun in a Tatpurusha has acute on the first syllable.

Thus दाशकिपुत्रः, माहिषपुत्रः । Why do we say 'a-पुत्र'? Observe कौनटिमातुलः । Why do we say 'after a masculine word'? Observe दासीपुत्रः ॥

३८६७ । नाचार्यराजर्त्विक्संयुक्तज्ञात्याख्येभ्यः । ६ । २ । १३३ ॥

एभ्यः पुत्रो नाद्युदात्तः । [आख्याग्रहणात्पर्यायाणां तद्विशेषाणां च ग्रहणम् । आचार्यपुत्रः उपाध्यायपुत्रः । शाकटायनपुत्रः । राजपुत्रः । ईश्वरपुत्रः । नन्दपुत्रः । ऋत्विक्पुत्रः । याजकपुत्रः होतुः पुत्रः । संयुक्ताः संबन्धिनः । श्यालपुत्रः । ज्ञातयो मातापितृसंबन्धेन बान्धवाः । ज्ञातिपुत्रः भ्रातुःपुत्रः ॥

3867. The word *putra* has not acute on the first syllable when preceded by a word which falls under the category of teachers, kings, priests, wife's relations, and agnates and cognates.

The word आचार्य means 'teacher,' राजा 'prince, king', ऋत्विज् 'a sacrificing priest'; संयुक्ताः 'relations through the wife's side' as श्याला 'brother-in-law' &c. ज्ञाति means 'all kinsmen related through father and mother or blood-relations.' The word आख्या shows that the rule applies to the synonyms of 'teacher' &c, as well as to particular 'teacher' &c. Thus आचार्यपुत्रः, उपाध्यायपुत्रः, शाकटायनपुत्रः राजपुत्रः, ईश्वरपुत्रः, नन्दपुत्रः, ऋत्विक्पुत्रः, याजकपुत्रः, होतुःपुत्रः, (VI. 3. 23) संयुक्तपुत्रः संबन्धिपुत्रः, श्यालकपुत्रः, ज्ञातिपुत्रः, भ्रातुष्पुत्रः, (VI. 3. 23). Here the special accent of पुत्र taught in the last sûtra being prohibited, the accent falls on the last syllable by the general rule VI. 1. 2 23.

३८६८ । चूर्णादीन्यप्राणिषष्ठ्याः । ६ । २ । १३४ ॥

एतानि प्राणिभिन्नषष्ठ्यन्तात्पराण्याद्युदात्तानि तत्पुरुषे । मुद्गचूर्णम् । 'अप्र-' इति किम् । मत्स्यचूर्णम् ॥

3868. The words 'chûrṇa' &c. in a Tatpurusha compound have acute on the first syllable, when the preceding word ends in a Genitive and does not denote a living being.

Thus मुद्गचूर्णम्, मसूरचूर्णम् but मत्स्यचूर्णम् where the first term is a living being, and परमचूर्णम् where it is not Genitive. Another reading of the sûtra is चूर्णादीन्यप्राण्युपग्रहात्, the word उपग्रह being the ancient name of षष्ठी given by old Grammarians.

1 चूर्ण, 2 करिव, 3 करिप, 4 शाकिन, 5 शाकट, 6 द्राक्षा, 7 तूस्त, 8 कुन्दुम (कुन्दम), 9 दलप, 10 चमसी, 11 चक्कन (चकन चक्यन) 12 चौल ॥

The word चूर्ण is derived from the root चूरी दाहे (Div 50) with the affix क्त; करिव and करिप are formed with the upapada करि and the verbs वा 'to go' and पा 'to protect' respectively, and the affix क (करिणं वाति = करिव) (III. 2. 3); शाक with the affix इनच् added diversely (Uṇ II. 56); शाक with अटच् (Uṇ IV. 81) gives शाकट; this with क्षा, (तद्वहति) gives शाकट; द्राक् क्षरति = द्राक्षा (Prishodarâdi); तुस्, (शब्दे) with क्त gives तूस्त the penultimate being lengthened; the word कुन्दु is formed by the affix क्विप added to the root दु with the upapada कु (कुं दुनोति कुत्सितं वा दुनोति) the augment मुम् being added to कु। कुन्दुं मिमीते = कुन्दुमः। दल with the affix कपन् gives दलपः, चम with असच् forms चमस, then is added ङीप्; चक्कन is formed by अच् (III. 1. 134) added to कन् and reduplication, चोलस्यापत्यं = चौलः ॥

३८६९। षट् च काण्डादीनि । ६ । २ । १३५ ॥

अप्राणिषष्ठ्या आद्युदात्तानि । दर्भकाण्डम् । दर्भचीरम् । तिलपललम् । मुद्गसूपः । मूलकशाकम् । नदीकूलम् । 'षट्' किम् । राजसूदः । 'अप्र-' इति किम् । दत्तकाण्डम् ॥

3869. The six words काण्ड, चीर, पलल, सूप, शाक and कूल of Sûtras VI. 2. 126-129 preceded by a non-living genitive word have acute on the first syllable.

As दर्भकाण्डम्, दर्भचीरम्। In the last example चीर is not used as a comparison, that case being governed by VI. 2. 127, तिलपललम्, मुद्गसूपः मूलकशाकम्। Here पलल, सूप and शाक do not denote mixing, which is governed by VI 2. 128. नदीकूलम्, here the compound does not denote a Name, which would be the case under VI. 2. 129. Why these 'six' only? Observe राजसूदः॥ Why 'non-living'? Observe दत्तकाण्डम् ॥

३८७०। कुण्डं वनम् । ६ । २ । १३६ ॥

कुण्डमाद्युदात्तं वनवाचिनि तत्पुरुषे। दर्भकुण्डम् । कुण्डशब्दोऽत्र सादृश्ये। 'वनम्' किम् । मृत्कुण्डम् ॥

3870. The word 'kuṇḍa' at the end of a Tatpurusha compound denoting 'a wood or forest', has acute on the first syllable.

The word कुण्ड here denotes 'a wood' by metaphor. Thus दर्भकुण्डम्। Why do we say when denoting 'a wood'? Observe मृत्कुण्डम् ॥

३८७१। प्रकृत्या भगालम् । ६ । २ । १३७ ॥

भगालवाच्युत्तरपदं तत्पुरुषे प्रकृत्या। कुम्भीभगालम्। कुम्भीनदालम्। कुम्भीकपालम्। मध्योदात्ता एते। प्रकृत्येत्यधिकृतम् 'अन्तः' (३८७७) इति यावत् ॥

3871. The word 'bhagâla' at the end of a Tatpurusha, preserves its original accent.

The synonyms of भगाल are also included. As कुम्भीभगालम्, कुम्भीकपालम्, कुम्भीनदालम्। The words भगाल &c., have acute on the middle. Phit II. 9. The word प्रकृत्या governs the subsequent sûtras up to VI. 2. 143. S. 3877.

३८७२ । शितेर्नित्याबह्वज्बहुव्रीहावभसत् । ६ । २ । १३८ ॥

शितेः परंनित्याबह्वच्कं प्रकृत्या । शितिपादः । शित्यंसः । पादशब्दो वृषादित्वादाद्युदात्तः । अंसशब्दः प्रत्ययस्य नित्त्वात् । 'शितेः' किम् । दर्शनीयपादः । 'अभसत्' किम् । शितिभसत् । शितिराद्युदात्तः । पूर्वपदप्रकृतिस्वरापवादोऽयं योगः ॥

3872. After 'śiti' a word retains in a Bahuvrîhi its original accent, when it is always of not more than two syllables, with the exception of 'bhasad.'

Thus शितिपादः, शित्यंसः । The word पाद belongs to वृषादि class (VI. 1 203) and has acute on the first, and अंसः being formed by सन् (Uṇ V. 21) affix has acute on the first (VI. 1. 197).

Why do we say 'after शिति'? Observe दर्शनीयपादः which being formed by the affix अनीयर् has acute on the penultimate syllable नी by VI. 1. 217 ॥

Why do we say 'with the exception of भसत्'? Observe शितिभसत् । The word शिति has acute on the first syllable (Phiṭ II. 10). This sûtra is an exception to VI. 2. 1.

३८७३ । गतिकारकोपपदात्कृत् । ६ । २ । १३९ ॥

एभ्य: कृदन्तं प्रकृतिस्वरं स्यात्तत्पुरुषे । प्रकारकः । प्रहरणम् । 'शोणा धृष्णू नृवाहसा' । इध्मप्रव्रश्चनः । उपपदात् । उच्चैःकारम् । ईषत्करः । 'गति' इति किम् । देवस्य कारकः । शेषे षष्ठी । कृद्ग्रहणं स्पष्टार्थम् । प्रपचतितराम्मित्यत्र तरबाद्यन्तेन समासे कृते आम् । तत्र सतिशिष्टत्वादामस्वरो भवतीत्येके । प्रपचतिदेश्यार्थं तु कृद्ग्रहणमित्यन्ये ॥

3873. In a Tatpurusha, a word ending in a Kṛit-affix preserves its original accent, when preceded by an Indeclinable called Gati (I. 4. 60), or a noun standing in intimate relation to a verb (Kâraka), or any word which gives occasion for compounding (Upapada see III. 1. 92).

Thus प्रकारकः, प्रहरणम् । शोणा धृष्णूनृवाहसा (Rig Veda I. 6. 2). The compounding is here by II 2 18. With kâraka-word we have :—इध्मप्रव्रश्चनः (III. 3. 117). With upapada words, we have :—ईषत्करः । All these are formed by लित् affixes and the accent is governed by VI. 1. 193. *i.e.*, the word प्रश्चन is formed by ल्युट् (इध्मं प्रवृश्च्यते येन)।

Why do we say 'after a Gati, Kâraka, or an Upapada word?' Observe देवस्यकारकः = देवकारकः । Here the Genitive in देव does not express a kâraka relation. The genitive is here a शेष लक्षणा षष्ठी denoting a possessor and not a कर्मलक्षणा one : for had it been the latter, there would have been no compounding at all, by II. 2. 16 see also II. 3. 65.

The word कृत् is employed in the sûtra for the sake of distinctness ; for a gati, karaka or upapada could not be followed by any other word than a kṛit-formed word, if there was to be a samâsa. For two sorts of affixes come after a root (dhâtu) namely तिङ् and कृत् । A samâsa can take place with kṛit-formed words, but not with tiṅanta words. So that without employing कृत् in the sûtra, we could have inferred that कृत् was meant. Therefore, it is said the 'Kṛit' is employed in the sûtra for the sake of distinctness. According to this view we explain the accent in प्रपचतितराम्, प्रपचतितमाम्, by saying that first compounding takes place with प्र and the words पचतितर and पचतितम ending in तरप् and तमप् and then आम्, is added and the accent of the whole word is regulated by आम् by the rule of सतिशिष्ट (see V. 3. 56. and V. 4. 11). According to others, the कृत is taken in this sutra, in order to prevent the gati accent applying to verbal compounds in words like प्र॑पचति देश्यः, or प्र॑पचति देशीयं (V. 3. 67), or प्र॑पचतिरूपम् (V. 3 66). The accent of these will be governed by the rule of the Indeclinable first term retaining its accent.

३८७४ । उभे वनस्पत्यादिषु युगपत् । ६ । २ । १४० ॥

एषु पूर्वोत्तरपदे युगपत्प्रकृत्या । 'वनस्पति॑ वन॒ आ' । 'बृ॒हस्पति॒॑ यः' । बृहच्छब्दोऽन्त्याद्युदात्तो निपात्यते । 'हवंया शचीपति॑म्' । शार्ङ्गरवादित्वादाद्युदात्तः शचीशब्दः । 'शचीभिर्न' इति दर्शनात् । 'तनू॑नपादुच्यते' । 'नरा॒शंसं॑ वा॒जिनम्' । निपातनाद्दीर्घः । 'शुन॒ःशेप॑म्' ॥

3874. In *vanaspati*, &c, both members of the compounds preserve their original accent simultaneously.

NOTE :—Thus वनस्पति॑ वन आ (Rig Veda X. 101. 11). बृहस्पति॑ यः (Rig Veda IV. 50. 7) हवंया शचीपतिम् (Rig Veda VIII. 15 13) तनूनपादुच्यते (Rig Veda III) 29. 11); नरा॑ शं॑ वाजिनम् (Rig Veda I. 106. 4) शुनःशेपम् (Rig Veda V. 2. 7 व॑नस्प॑तिः, both वन and पति have acute on the first syllable, and the सुट् augment comes by VI. 1. 157. (2) बृ॑हस्प॑तिः or बृह॑स्प॑तिः = बृहतां पतिः (VI. 1. 157). The word बृह॑त् is acutely accented on the final, some say it has acute on the first. (3) शचीं॑ प॑तिः (Śachî being formed by ङीष्) some make Śachî acute on the first श॑ची-प॑तिः, by including it in Sarangrava class (IV. 1. 73). (4) त॑नू॑नपात् (tanû being formed by ऊ Un I 80 has acute on the final, according to others it has acute on the first and napât = na pâti or na pâlayati with क्विप्, and has acute on the first). (5) न॑राश॑ंसः (नरा अस्मिन्नासीनाः शंसन्ति or नरा एव शंसन्ति) (nara is formed by अप्, and has acute on the first, Samsa is formed by घञ्, the lengthening takes place by VI. 3. 137). (6) शु॑नः शे॑पः = शुन इव शेपोऽस्य is a Bahuvrihi : the Genitive is not elided by (VI. 3. 21 Vârt), and both have acute on the first. (7) श॑ण्डाम॑र्कौ both 'Śanda' and 'Marka' being formed by घञ् have acute on the first : the lengthening takes place by VI 3. 137. (8) तृ॑ष्णावरू॑त्री । Tṛishṇa has acute on the first, वरूत्री has acute on the final. The lengthening here also is by VI. 3. 137. (9) बम्ब॑विश्व॑वयसौ । Bamba is finally acute, and viśva by VI. 2. 106 has acute on the final, as viśvavayas is a Bahuvrîhi The lengthening takes place as before by VI. 3. 137. (10) म॑र्मृ॑त्यु॑ः । मर् is formed by विच् affix and मृत्यु has acute on the final. The words governed by this sutra are those which would not be included in the next two sûtras.

३८७५ । देवताद्वन्द्वे च । ६ । २ । १४१ ॥

उभे युगपत्प्रकृत्या स्तः । 'आ य इन्द्रावरु॑णौ' । 'इन्द्राबृहस्पती॑ व॒यम्' । 'देवता' किम् । प्लक्षन्यग्रोधौ । 'द्वन्द्वे' किम् । अग्निष्टोम ॥

3875. In a Dvandva compound of names of Divinities, the both members retain their original accent.

Thus आय इन्द्रावरुणा (Rig Veda VI. 68. 1) इन्द्राबृहस्पती वयं (Rig Veda IV. 49. 5). The word इन्द्र has acute on the first (by nipâtana), वरुण is formed by उनन् (Uṇ. III. 53) and by VI. 1. 197 has acute on the first. बृहस्पति has two acutes by VI. 2. 140, and Indra-Brihaspati has three acutes. Why do we say 'names of divinities'? Observe प्लक्षन्यग्रोधौ। Why do we say 'a Dvandva'? Observe अग्निष्टोमः॥

३८७६। नोत्तरपदेऽनुदात्तादावपृथिवीरुद्रपूषमन्थिषु। ६। २। १४२॥

पृथिव्यादिवर्जितेऽनुदात्तादावुत्तरपदे प्रागुक्तं न। 'इन्द्राग्निभ्यां कं वृषणः'। 'अपृथिव्यादौ' किम्। 'द्यावापृथिवी जनयन्'। आद्युदात्तो द्यावा निपात्यते। पृथिवीत्यन्तोदात्तः। रुद्रसोमौ। रोदेर्णिलुक्च' इति रगन्तो रुद्रशब्दः। 'इन्द्रापूषणौ'। 'श्वन्नुक्षन्पूषन्—' इति पूषा अन्तोदात्तो निपात्यते। शुक्रामन्थिनौ। मन्थिन्निनन्तत्वादन्तोदात्तः। उत्तरपदग्रहणमनुदात्तादावित्युत्तरपदविशेषणं यथा स्याद्द्वन्द्वविशेषणं मा भूत्। अनुदात्तादाविति विधिप्रतिषेधयोर्विषयविभागार्थम्॥

3876. In a Dvandva compound of the names of divinities, both members of the compound simultaneously do not retain their accent, when the first syllable of the second word is anudâtta, with the exception of पृथिवी, रुद्र, पूषन् and मन्थिन्॥

Thus इन्द्राग्निभ्यां कं वृषणः (Rig Veda I. 109. 3). Agni has acute on the final.

Why do we say with the exception of 'prithivi' &c? Observe द्यावापृथिवी जनयन् (Rig Veda X. 66. 9.) dvyâvâ has acute on the first, 'prithivi' being formed by 'ṅish', has acute on the final. सोमारुद्रौ, Rudra is formed by 'rak' affix (Uṇ. II. 22.), and has acute on the final. इन्द्रापूषणा (Rig Veda VII. 35. 1) Pûshan has acute on the end. (Uṇ. I. 159) शुक्रामन्थिनौ, the words Śukra and manthin have acute on the final.

The word uttarapada is repeated in the sûtra, in order that it should be qualified by the word 'anudâttâdau', which latter would otherwise have qualified Dvandva. The word 'anudâttâdau' shows the scope of the prohibition and the injunction.

३८७७। अन्तः। ६। २। १४३॥

अधिकारोऽयम्॥

3877. In the following sûtras up to the end of the chapter should always be supplied the phrase 'the last syllable of the second member has the acute.'

३८७८। थाथघञ्क्ताजबित्रकाणाम्। ६। २। १४४॥

'थ' 'अथ' 'घञ्' 'क्त' 'अच्' 'अप्' 'इत्र' 'क' एतदन्तानां गतिकारकोपपदात्परेषामन्त उदात्तः। 'प्रभृथस्यायोः'। आवसथः। घञ्। प्रभेदः। क्त। 'धर्ता वज्री पुरुष्टुतः'। पुरुषु बहुप्रदेशेषु स्तुत इति विग्रहः। अच्। प्रक्षयः। अप्। प्रलवः। इत्र। प्रलवित्रम्। क। गोवृषः। मूलविभुजादित्वात्कः। गतिकारकोपपदादित्येव। सुस्तुतं भवता॥

3878. The last syllable of the second member has the acute in the verbal nouns ending in थ, अथ, घञ्, क्त, अच्, अप्, इत्र and क, when preceded by a Gati, a Kâraka or an Upapada (VI. 2. 139).

Thus प्रभृथस्यायोः (Rig Veda V. 41. 19), प्रभृथँ formed by क्थन् affix (Un. II. 2 and 3), and but for this sûtra, by VI. 2. 139 this word would have retained its original accent, which was acute on the first. अथः – आवसथँः formed by अथन् affix (Un. III. 116). घञ् —प्रभेदँः । क्तः—धर्ताचक्रो पुरुष्टुतः (Rig Veda I. 11. 4). The word पुरुष्टुतः should be analysed as पुरुषु बहुप्रदेशेषु स्तुतः 'praised in many lands'. अच् (III. 3 56) :—प्रचयँः, the word चय 'dwelling,' is end acute, otherwise on the first (VI. 1. 201, 202). अप्—प्रलवँः । इत्र—प्रलवित्रँम् । क-गोवृषँः= गां वर्षति, (III. 2. 5 Vârt) : (क—being added by III. 1. 135). The word वृष has acute on the first, as it belongs to वृषादि class (VI 1 203). When the preceding words are not Gati, Kâraka or Upapada, this rule does not apply : as सुस्तुतं भवता, where सु being Karmapravachanîya, the word gets the accent of the Indeclinable.

३८७९ । सूपमानात्क्तः । ६ । २ । १४५ ॥

सोऽपमानाच्च परं क्तान्तमन्तोदात्तम् । 'ऋतस्य योनौ सुकृतस्य' । शशप्लुतमः ॥

3879. The participle in *kta* has acute on the final, when it is preceded by *su* or by a word with which the second member is compared.

Thus सुकृतँम्, in the following Rik ऋतस्य योनौ सुकृतस्य (Rig Veda X. 85. 24. With Upamâna words we have—शशप्लुतँम् । This debars VI. 2. 49 and 48. When सु is not a Gati, the rule does not apply, as सुस्तुतँम् भवता ॥

३८८० । संज्ञायामनाचितादीनाम् । ६ । २ । १४६ ॥

गतिकारकोपपदात्क्तान्तमन्तोदात्तम् । चितादीन्वर्जयित्वा । उपहूतः शाकल्यः । परिजग्धः कौण्डिन्यः । 'अन-' इति किम् । आचितम् । आस्थापितम् ॥

3880. The Participle in 'kta' has acute on the last syllable when preceded by a Gati, or a Kâraka or an Upapada, if the compound denotes a Name, but not in 'âchita' &c.

Thus उपहूतँः शाकल्यः, परिजग्धँः कौण्डिन्यः । This debars VI. 2. 49. Why do we say 'when it is not आचित &c.' Observe आँचितम् &c.

1 आचित, 2 पर्याचित, 3 आस्थापित, 4 परिगृहीत, 5 निरुक्त, 6 प्रतिपन्न, 7 अपश्लिष्ट, 8 प्रश्लिष्ट, 9 उपहित (उपहत), 10 उपस्थित, 11 संहितागवि (संहिताशब्दो यदा गोरन्यस्य संज्ञा तदान्तोदात्तो न भवति । यदा तु गोः संज्ञा तदान्तोदात्त एव) ॥

The word संहिता in the above list does not take acute on the final, when it is the name of anything else than a 'cow'; but when it denotes 'a cow' it has acute on the final.

३८८१ । प्रवृद्धादीनां च । ६ । २ । १४७ ॥

एषां क्तान्तमुत्तरपदमन्तोदात्तम् । प्रवृद्धः । प्रयुक्तः । असंज्ञार्थोऽयमारम्भः । आकृतिगणोऽयम् ॥

3881. The words 'pravriddha' &c., ending in 'kta' have acute on the final.

Thus प्रवृद्धः प्रयुक्तः । The rule is applicable to compounds which do not denote a name. It is an Akritigaṇa. The words have acute on the final, even when not followed by यान &c., though in the Gaṇapâṭha they are read along with these words. Some hold it is only in connection with यान &c. that these words have acute on the final. This being an Âkritigaṇa we have पुनरुत्स्यूतं वासोदेयं, पुनर्निष्कृतो रथः &c.

1 प्रवृद्धं यानम्, 2 प्रवृद्धो वृषलः; 3 प्रयुतामूष्णवः or प्रयुक्ताः सक्तवः, 4 आकर्षेऽवहितः 5 अवहितो भोगेषु, 5 खट्वारूढः, 7 कविशस्तः, आकृतिगण ॥

३८८२ । कारकाद्दत्तश्रुतयोरेवाशिषि । ६ । २ । १४८ ॥

संज्ञायामन्त उदात्तः । देवदत्तः । विष्णुश्रुतः । 'कारकात्' किम् । संभूतो रामायणः । 'दत्तश्रुतयोः' किम् । देवपालितः । अस्मान्नियमादत्र 'संज्ञायामन-' (३८८०) इति न । 'तृतीया कर्मणि' (३७८२) इति तु भवति । 'एव' किम् । कारकावधारणं यथा स्याद्दत्तश्रुतावधारणं मा भूत् । अकारकादपि दत्तश्रुतयोरन्त उदात्तो भवति । संश्रुतः । 'आशिषि' किम् । देवैः खाता देवखाता । आशिष्येवेत्येवमत्रेष्टो नियमः । तेनानाहतो नदति देवदत्त इत्यत्र न । शङ्खविशेषस्य संज्ञेयम् । 'तृतीया कर्मणि' (३७८२) इति पूर्वपदप्रकृतिस्वरत्वमेव भवति ॥

3882. The final of Past Participles 'datta' and 'śruta' alone has acute, in a compound denoting a Name and a benediction, the preceding word being a word standing in close relation to an action (kâraka).

Thus देवा एनं देयासुः = देवदत्तः, विष्णुरेवं श्रूयात् = विष्णुश्रुतः । Why do we say 'preceded by a kâraka'? Observe संभूतो रामायणः । The word कारक indicates that the rule will not apply when a gati or upapada precedes.

Why do we say 'of दत्त and श्रुत'? Observe देवपालितः (VI. 2. 48), which, though a Name, is not governed by VI. 2. 146, and does not take acute on the final, for the present rule makes a restriction with regard to that rule even. So that where a Participle in क्त is preceded by a kâraka, and the compound denotes a benediction and a Name, the accent is not on the final, as required by VI. 2. 146, S. 3880 but such a word is governed by VI. 2. 48, S. 3782 unless the Participle be Datta and śruta, when the present rule applies.

Why do we use 'एव (*alone*)'? So that the restriction should apply to 'kâraka', and not to Datta and, Śruta. For the words Datta and Śruta will have acute on the final even after a nonkâraka word. As संश्रुतः ॥

Why do we say 'when denoting benediction'? The rule will not apply where benediction is not meant. As देवैः खाता = देवखाता । This rule applies to Datta and Śruta after a kâraka-word, only when benediction is meant. It therefore does not apply to देवदत्त 'the name of Arjuna's conch', as अनाहतो नदति देवदत्तः, which is governed by VI. 2. 48.

३८८३ । इत्थंभूतेन कृतमिति च । ६ । २ । १४९ ॥

इत्थंभूतेन कृतमित्येतस्मिन्नर्थे यः समासस्तत्र क्तान्तमुत्तरपदमन्तोदात्तं स्यात् । सुप्तप्रलपितम् । प्रमत्तगीतम् । कृतमिति क्रियासामान्ये करोतिर्नाभूतप्रादुर्भाव एव । तेन प्रलपितादपि कृतं भवति 'तृतीया कर्मणि' (३७८२) इत्यस्यापवादः ॥

3883. The Participle in *kta* has acute on the final, when the compound denotes 'done by one in such a condition.'

The word इत्थंभूत means 'being in such a condition.' Thus सुप्तप्रलपितम्, प्रमत्तगीतम्, as Adjectives and Abstract verbal nouns. This is an exception to VI. 2. 48. When the words प्रलपित &c. are used to denote Noun of Action (भाव) then by VI. 2. 144 they get of course acute on the final.

३८८४ । अनो भावकर्मवचनः । ६ । २ । १५० ॥

कारकात्परमनप्रत्ययान्तं भाववचनं कर्मवचनं चान्तोदात्तम् पयः पानं सुखम् । राजभोजनाः शालयः । 'अनः' किम् । हस्तादायः । 'भा-' इति किम् । दन्तधावनम् । करणे ल्युट् 'कारकात्' किम् । निदर्शनम् ॥

3884. After a kâraka as mentioned in VI. 2. 148, the second member ending in the affix अन, and denoting an action in the Abstract or the object (*i. e.* having the senses of a Passive Adjective), has acute on the final.

Thus पयपानं सुखम् । This is an example of भाव or Abstract Verbal Noun. राजभोजनाः शालयः, is an example of कर्मवचन or Passive Adjective. This is formed by ल्युट under III. 3. 116. For the Sútra III. 3. 116 may be explained by saying that (1) ल्युट is applied when the Upapada is in the objective case and bhâva is meant, (2) as well as when object is to be expressed. When the first explanation is taken, the above are examples of Bhâva; when the second explanation is taken they are examples of Karma. Why do we say 'ending in अन'? Observe हस्तहार्यमुदश्चित् । Why do we say 'when expressing an action in the abstract (bhâva), or an Object (karma)'? Observe दन्तधावनम्, here ल्युट is added after an Instrumental kâraka (III. 3. 117). Why do we say 'after a kâraka'? Observe निदर्शनम् । In all the counter-examples, the second members retain there original accent.

३८८५ । मन्क्तिन्व्याख्यानशयनासनस्थानयाजकादिक्रीताः । ६ । २ । १५१ ॥

कारकात्पराण्येतान्युत्तरपदान्यन्तोदात्तानि तत्पुरुषे । कृत्स्वरापवादः । रथवर्त्म । पाणिनिकृतिः छन्दोव्याख्यानम् । राजशयनम् । राजासनम् । अश्वस्थानम् । ब्राह्मणयाजकः । गोक्रीतः । 'कारकात्' किम् । 'प्रभूतौ संगतिम्' । अत्र 'तादौ च निति-' (३८८४) इति स्वरः ॥

3885. The words ending in मन् or क्तिन् affixes, and the word व्याख्यान्, शयन, आसन, स्थान and क्रीत as well as याजक &c. have acute on the final, when at the end of a compound, preceded by a kâraka word.

Thus मन्—रथवर्त्म॑। क्तिन्—पाणिनिकृति॑:। व्याख्यान—छन्दोव्याख्याने॑म्। शयन—राजशयने॑म्। आसन्—राजासने॑म्। स्थान—अश्वस्थाने॑म्। याजकादि words are those which form Genitive compounds under II. 2. 9, and those compounds only are to be taken here; as ब्राह्मणयाजक॑:, क्षत्रिययाजक॑:, ब्राह्मणपूजक॑:, क्षत्रियपूजक॑:। क्रीत—गोक्रीत॑:। This is an exception to VI. 2. 139, and in the case of क्रीत, rule VI. 2. 48 is superseded. The words व्याख्यान &c. do not denote here भाव or कर्म, had they done so, rule VI. 2. 149 would have covered them. When the first member is not a kâraka, we have प्रभूतौ संगतिम्। Here the accent is governed by VI. 2. 50, S. 3784.

1 याजक, 2 पूजक, 3 परिचारक, 4 परिषेचक परिवेषक, 5 स्नापक स्नातक, 6 अध्यापक, 7 उत्साहक (उत्सादक) 8 उद्वर्तक, 9 होतृ, 10 भर्तृ, 11 रथगणक, 12 पत्तिगणक, 13 पोतृ, 14 होतृ, 15 वर्तक ॥

३८८६। सप्तम्याः पुण्यम्। ६। २। १५२॥

अन्तोदात्तम्। अध्ययनपुण्यम्। 'तत्पुरुषे तुल्यार्थ-' (३७३६) इति प्राप्तम्। 'सप्तम्याः' किम्। वेदेन पुण्यं वेदपुण्यम्॥

3886. The word 'puṇya' has acute on the final when preceded by a noun in the Locative case.

Thus अध्ययने पुण्यम् = अध्ययनपुण्य॑म्। The compounding takes place by II. 1. 40 by the process of splitting the sûtra (yoga-vibhâga), taking सप्तमी there as a full sûtra, and शौण्डैः another. Here by VI. 2. 2, S. 3736 the first member would have preserved its accent, the present sûtra supersedes that and ordains acute on the final. The word पुण्य is derived by the Uṇâdi affix यत् (Uṇ V. 15) and would have retained its natural accent (VI. 1. 213) and thus get acute on the first syllable by kṛit-accent. (VI. 2. 139). Why do we say 'a locative case'? Observe वेदेन पुण्यं = वेदपुण्यम्॥

३८८७। ऊनार्थकलहं तृतीयायाः। ६। २। १५३॥

माषोनम्। माषविकलम्। वाक्कलहः। तृतीयापूर्वपदप्रकृतिस्वरापवादोऽयम्। अत्र केचिदर्थेति स्वरूपग्रहणमिच्छन्ति। धान्यार्थः। ऊनशब्देन स्वर्थनिर्देशार्थेन तदर्थानां ग्रहणमिति प्रतिपादोक्तत्वादेव सिद्धे तृतीयाग्रहणं स्पष्टार्थम्॥

3887. The acute falls on the final of words having the sense of 'ûṇa,' and of 'kalaha' when they are second members in a compound, preceded by a term in the instrumental case.

Thus माषोने॑म्, माषविकल॑म्, वाक्कलह॑:। The compounding takes place by II. 1. 31. This is an exception to VI. 2. 2 by which the first member being in the third case, would have retained its original accent. Some say that the word अर्थ in the sûtra means the word' form अर्थ, so that the aphorism would mean—'after an Instrumental case, the words ऊन, अर्थ, and कलह get acute on the final.' The examples will be in addition to the above:—धान्येनार्थाः = धान्यार्थ॑:। If this be so, then the word-form ऊन alone will be taken and not its synonyms like विकल &c. To this we reply, that ऊन will denote its synonyms also, by the fact of its being followed by the word अर्थ। By sûtra II. 1. 13, ऊनार्थ and कलह always take the

Instrumental case, so we could have omitted the word तृतीयायाः, from this sûtra' for by the maxim of pratipadokta &c. ऊनार्थकलहं would have referred to the compound ordained by II. 1. 31. The mention of तृतीया here is only for the sake of clearness

३८८८ । मिश्रं चानुपसर्गमसंधौ । ६ । २ । १५४ ॥

पणबन्धेनैकार्थ्यं संधिः । तिलमिश्राः । सर्पिर्मिश्राः । 'मिश्रम्' किम् । गुडधानाः । 'अनुपसर्गम्' किम् । तिलसंमिश्राः । 'मिश्रग्रहणे सोपसर्गग्रहणस्य' इदमेव ज्ञापकम् । 'असंधौ' किम् । ब्राह्मणमिश्रो राजा । ब्राह्मणैः सह संहित ऐकार्थ्यमापन्नः ॥

3888. The word 'miśra' has acute on the final after an Instrumental case, when it is not joined with any Preposition and does not mean a 'compact or alliance.'

Thus तिलमिश्राः सर्पिर्मिश्राः । Why do we say मिश्र ? Observe गुडधानाः । Why do we say 'not having a Preposition' ? Observe तिलसंमिश्राः । The employment in this sûtra of the phrase 'anupasargam' implies, that wherever else, the word miśra is used, it includes miśra with a preposition also. Therefore in II. 1. 31 where the word मिश्र is used, we can form the Instrumental compounds with मिश्र preceded by a preposition also.

Why do we say 'not denoting a compact' ? Observe ब्राह्मणमिश्रो राजा = ब्राह्मणैः सह संहित ऐकार्थ्यमापन्नः ॥

३८८९ । नञो गुणप्रतिषेधे संपाद्यर्हहितालमर्थास्तद्धिताः । ६ । २ । १५५ ॥

संपाद्याद्यर्थतद्धितान्ता नञो गुणप्रतिषेधे वर्तमानात्परेऽन्तोदात्ताः । कर्णवेष्टकाभ्यां संपादि कार्णवेष्टकिकम् । न कार्णवेष्टकिकमकार्णवेष्टकिकम् । छेदमर्हति छैदिकः । न छैदिकोऽच्छैदिकः । न वत्सेभ्यो हितोऽवात्सीयः । न संतापाय प्रभवति असंतापिकः । 'नञः' किम् । गर्दभरथमर्हति गार्दभरथिकः । विगार्दभरथिकः । 'गुणप्रतिषेधे' किम् । गार्दभरथिकादन्योऽगार्दभरथिकः । गुणो हि तद्धितार्थे प्रवृत्तिनिमित्तं संपादित्वाद्युच्यते । तत्प्रतिषेधो यत्रोच्यते तत्रायं विधिः । कर्णवेष्टकाभ्यां न संपादि मुखमिति । 'संपादि-' इति किम् । पाणिनीयमधीते पाणिनीयः । न पाणिनीय अपाणिनीयः । 'तद्धिताः' किम् । वोढुमर्हति वोढा । न वोढाऽवोढा ॥

3889. The words formed with the Taddhita affixes denoting 'fitted for that' (V. 1. 99), 'deserving that' (V. 1. 63), 'good for that' (V. 1. 5), 'capable to effect that' (V. 1. 101), have acute on the final, when preceded by the Negative Particle 'nañ' when it makes a negation with regard to the abovementioned attributes.

Thus संपादि 'suited for that' (V. 1. 99) :—अकार्णवेष्टकिकं मुखम् = न कार्णवेष्टकिकं (कर्णवेष्टकाभ्यां सम्पादि) । The affix is ठञ् । अर्ह 'deserving that' (V. 1. 63) :—अच्छैदिकः = न छैदिकः (छेदमर्हति). The affix is ठक् (V. 1. 64 and V. 1. 19). हित 'good for that' (V. 1. 5) :—अवात्सीयः = न वत्सेभ्यो हितः । The affix is छ V. 1. 1. अलमर्थः 'capable to effect that' (V. 1. 101) :—असंतापिकः = न संतापिकः । The affix is ठञ् (V. 1. 18). Why do we say 'after नञ्' ? Observe गर्दभरथमर्हति = गार्दभरथिकः, विगार्दभरथिकः, where the negative वि is used and therefore the avyaya वि retains its accent by VI. 2. 2. Why do we say 'negation of that attribute'? Observe गार्ग्यभरथिकादन्यः = अगार्ग्यभरथिकः । The word गुण here means the attribute denoted by the Taddhita affix, and not any attribute in general. Thus अकार्णवेष्टकिकं मुखं = कर्णवेष्टकाभ्याम् गुणम् । Why do we say 'in the sense of samapâdi &c'? Observe पाणिनीयमधीयते = पाणिनीयः = अपाणिनीयः । Why do we say 'Taddhita affixes'? Observe कन्यां वोढुमर्हति = कन्यावोढा, न वोढा = अवोढा । Here तृच् a krit is added in the sense of 'deserving' (III. 3. 169).

३८९० । ययतोश्चातदर्थे । ६ । २ । १५६ ॥

ययतौ यौ तद्धितौ तदन्तस्योत्तरपदस्य नञो गुणप्रतिषेधविषयात्पदस्यान्त उदात्तः स्यात् । पाशानां समूहः पाश्या अपाश्या । न पाश्या अदंत्यम् । 'अतदर्थे' किम् । अपाद्यम् । 'तद्धितः' किम् । अदेयम् । 'गुणप्रतिषेधे' किम् । दंत्यादन्यददंत्यम् ॥

'+तदनुबन्धग्रहणे नातदनुबन्धकस्य+' इति । नेह । अवामदेव्यम् ॥

3890. The words formed with the Taddhita affixes य and यत् when not denoting 'useful for that,' have acute on the last syllable, after the particle नञ् negativing the attribute.

Thus पाशानां समूहः = पाश्याः, न पाश्याः = अपाश्याः, (IV. 2. 49) दन्तेषु भवं = दन्त्यम् न दन्त्यं = अदन्त्यम्, (V. 1. 6). Why do we say 'atadartha:—not useful for that, Observe पादार्थमुदकम् = पाद्यम्, न पाद्यम् = अपाद्यम् (V. 4. 25). Why do we say 'Taddhita'? This rule does not apply when the affixes are not Taddhita, as अदेयम् formed with the krit-affix यत् । Why do we say 'negativing the attribute'? There must be negation of the attribute, otherwise दन्त्यादन्यत् = अदंत्यम् । *Paribhâshâ:*—"When a term with one or more Anubandhas is employed in Grammar, it does not denote that which in addition to those one or more anubandhas has another Anubandha attached to it." The affix य and यत्, one without any anubandha and the other with the anubandha त् being specifically mentioned, excludes all other affixes having य as their effective element, such as ड्य &c. (IV. 2. 9), thus न वामदेव्यं = अवामदेव्यम् । See IV. 2. 9.

३८९१ । अच्कावशक्तौ । ६ । २ । १५७ ॥

अजन्तं कान्तं च नञः परमन्तोदात्तमशक्तौ गम्यायाम् । अपचः पक्तुमशक्तः । अविलिखः । 'अशक्तौ' किम् । अपचो दीक्षितः । गुणप्रतिषेध इत्येव । अन्योऽयं पचादपचः ॥

3891. A word formed with the krit affix अच् and क, preceded by the particle नञ्, has acute on the final, when the meaning is 'not capable'.

Thus अपचः = य पक्तुं न शक्नोति, so also अविक्षिपः (III. 1. 134 &c). Why do we say when meaning 'not capable'? Observe अपचो दीक्षितः । A दीक्षित does not cook his food, not because he is physically incapable of cooking, but because by the vows of his particular order he is prohibited from cooking.

३८९२ । आक्रोशे च । ६ । २ । १५८ ॥

नञः परावच्कावन्तोदात्तावाक्रोशे । अपचो जाल्मः । पक्तुं न शक्नोतीत्येवमाक्रोश्यते । अविक्षिपः ॥

3892. A word formed by the kṛit-affixes अच् or क, preceded by the Negative particle, has acute on the final when one abuses somebody by that word.

Thus अपचो॑ऽयं जाल्मः 'this rogue does not cook, though he can do so.' Here avarice is indicated, the fellow wants more pay before he will cook : and not his incapacity. So also अविक्षिपः॑ ॥

३८९३ । संज्ञायाम् । ६ । २ । १५९ ॥

नञः परमन्तोदात्तं संज्ञायामाक्रोशे । अदेवदत्तः ॥

3893. When abuse is meant, a word preceded by 'nañ' has acute on the final, in denoting a Name.

Thus अदेवदत्तः॑ 'No Devadatta, not deserving of this name.'

३८९४ । कृत्योकेष्णुच्चार्वादयश्च । ६ । २ । १६० ॥

नञः परेऽन्तोदात्ताः स्युः । अकर्तव्यः । उक् । अनागामुकः । इष्णुच् । अनलंकरिष्णुः । इष्णुज्ग्रहणे खिष्णुचो द्व्यनुबन्धकस्यापि ग्रहणमिकारादेर्विधानसामर्थ्यात् । अनाढ्यंभविष्णुः । चार्वादिः । अचारुः । 'राजाह्नोश्छन्दसि' । अराजा । अनहः । 'भाषायाम्' नञः स्वर एव ॥

3894 After the Negative particle, words formed by the kṛitya affixes (III. 1. 95), by उक, and इष्णुच्, and the words चारु &c. have acute on the final.

Thus kritya:—अकर्तव्यः॑ । उक:—अनागामुकः॑ । इष्णुच् अनलंकरिष्णुः । The affix इष्णुच् includes खिष्णुच् also : though the latter contains two anubandhas. In sûtra III. 2. 57 खिष्णुच् is ordained after भू but instead of खिष्णुच् with इ, the affix might have been well exhibited as ख्ष्णुच् without इ. As भू is udâtta, भू + ख्ष्णुच् = भू + इट् + ख्ष्णुच् । So that we would have got the required form. But as a matter of fact the affix is exhibited there with an इ for the sake of the present sûtra only, so that इष्णुच् here may include खिष्णुच् also । अनाढ्यंभविष्णुः॑, चारु &c:—अचारुः॑, असाधुः॑, अयौधिकः॑, अवदान्यः, अनजमेजयः॑ (double negation). अनकस्मात् (double negation). The words वर्तमान, वर्धमान त्वरमाण, ध्रियमाण, रोचमान क्रीयमाण, and शोभमान preceded by अ (नञ्) when denoting names have acute on the final. अविकारः॑, असदृशः॑ and अविकारसदृशः॑ (विकार and सदृश taken jointly and separately). अगृहपति, अगृहपतिकः॑ । अराजा॑ and अनहः॑ in the Vedas only. In the Vernacular they have the accent of नञ्, i. e. udâtta on the first.

1. चारु, 2 साधु, 3 यौधिक (यौधिक) 4 अनङ्मेजय, 5 वदान्य, 6 अकस्मात्, 7 वर्तमानवर्धमानत्वरमाणध्रियमाणक्रीयमाणरोचमानशोभमानाः (क्रियमाण क्रीयमाण) संज्ञायाम्, 8 विकारसदृशे व्यस्ते समस्ते (अविकार, असदृश अविकारसदृश), 9 गृहपति, 10 गृहपतिक, 11 राजाह्नोश्छन्दसि ॥

३८९५ । विभाषा तृन्नन्नतीक्ष्णशुचिषु । ६ । २ । १६१ ॥

तृन् । अकर्ता । अन्न । अनन्नम् । अतीक्ष्णम् । अशुचि । पक्षेऽव्ययस्वरः ॥

3895. After the Negative particle, the final of the following is optionally acute :—a word formed with the affix 'trin,' and the words अन्न, तीक्ष्ण, and शुचि ॥

Thus तृन्-अकर्त्ता or अकर्त्ता ; अन्न &c-अनन्नम् or अनन्नम्, अतीक्ष्णम्, or अतीक्ष्णम्, अशुचिः or अशुचिः ॥ The alternative accent is that of the Indeclinable (VI. 2. 2).

३८९६ । बहुव्रीहाविदमेतत्तद्भ्यः प्रथमपूरणयोः क्रियागणने । ६ । २ । १६२ ॥

एभ्योऽनयोरन्त उदात्तः । इदं प्रथममस्य स इदंप्रथमः । एतद्द्वितीयः । तत्पञ्चमः । 'बहुव्रीहौ' किम् । अनेन प्रथम इदंप्रथमः । 'तृतीया-' (६९२) इति योगविभागात्समासः । 'इदमेतत्तद्भ्यः' किम् । यत्प्रथमः । 'प्रथमपूरणयोः' किम् । तानि बहून्यस्य तद्बहुः । 'क्रियागणने' किम् । अयं प्रथमः प्रधानं एषां त इदंप्रथमाः । द्रव्यगणनमिदम् । 'गणने' किम् । अयं प्रथम एषां त इदंप्रथमाः । इदंप्रधाना इत्यर्थः । उत्तरपदस्य कार्यित्वात्कपि पूर्वमन्तोदात्तम् । इदंप्रथमकाः । बहुव्रीहावित्यधिकारो 'वनं समासे' (३९१२) इत्यतः प्राग्बोध्यः ॥

3896. In a Bahuvrîhi, after the words इदम्, एतद् and तद् the last syllable of प्रथम and of a proper Ordinal Numeral, has the acute, when the number of times of an action is meant.

Thus इदं प्रथमं गमनं भोजनं वा=स इदम्प्रथमः 'this is the first time of going or eating.' एतद्द्वितीयः, तत्पञ्चमः । Why do we say 'in a Bahuvrîhi ?' Observe अनेन=प्रथमः इदंप्रथमः । Here the compounding takes place under S. 692 by dividing that sûtra into two parts by the method of yoga-bibhâga. Here the first member, being in the third case, retains its accent by VI. 2. 2.

Why do we say 'after idam &c.' Observe यत्प्रथमः = यःप्रथम एषाम्, here the first term retains its accent by VI. 2. 1.

Why do we say 'of prathama and the Ordinals' ? Observe तानिबहून्यस्य= तद्बहुः ॥

Why do we say 'in counting an action' ? Observe अयं प्रथम एषां = त इदं प्रथमाः । Here *substances* are counted and not *action*.

Why do we say 'in counting' ? Observe अयं प्रथम एषां=इदं प्रथमाः *i. e.* इदं प्रधानाः and the word प्रथम means here 'foremost,' and is not a numeral.

When the कप् affix is added, the acute falls on the last syllable preceding कप् । As इदं प्रथमकाः । The Bahuvrîhi governs the subsequent sûtras up to VI. 2. 178, S. 3912.

३८९७ । संख्यायाः स्तनः । ६ । २ । १६३ ॥

बहुव्रीहावन्तोदात्तः । द्विस्तना । चतुस्तना । 'संख्यायाः' किम् । दर्शनीयस्तना । 'स्तनः' किम् । द्विशिराः ॥

3897. In a Bahuvrîhi, after a Numeral, the word 'stana' has acute on the final.

Thus द्विस्तना, चतुःस्तनाः । Why do we say 'after a Numeral' ? Observe दर्शनीयस्तना । Why do we say 'स्तन' ? Observe द्विशिराः ॥

३८९८ । विभाषा छन्दसि । ६ । २ । १६४ ॥

'द्विस्तना करोति' ॥

3898. Optionally so, in the Vedas, the stana after a Numeral has acute on the final.

Thus द्विस्तना or द्विस्तना, चतुःस्तना or चतुःस्तना ॥

३८९९ । संज्ञायां मित्राजिनयोः । ६ । २ । १६५ ॥

देवमित्रः । कृष्णाजिनम् । 'संज्ञायाम्' किम् । प्रियमित्रः ॥

'+ ऋषिप्रतिषेधोऽत्र मित्रे +' विश्वामित्रऋषिः ॥

3899. In a Bahuvrîhi, ending in 'mitra' and 'ajina' the acute falls on the last syllable, when the compound denotes a Name.

As देवमित्रः, कृष्णाजिनम् । Why do we say 'a Name'? Observe प्रियमित्रः ॥

Vârt:—Prohibition must be stated in the case of मित्र when the name is that of a Rishi. As विश्वामित्रः which is governed by VI. 2. 106 ॥

३९०० । व्यवायिनोऽन्तरम् । ६ । २ । १६६ ॥

व्यवधानवाचकात्परमन्तरमन्तोदात्तम् । वस्त्रमन्तरं व्यवधायकं यस्य स वस्त्रान्तरः । 'व्यवधायिनः' किम् । आत्मान्तरः । अन्यस्वभाव इत्यर्थः ॥

3900. In a Bahuvrîhi ending in 'antara' the acute falls on the final, after a word which denotes 'that which lies between.'

Thus वस्त्रान्तरम् 'through an intervened cloth or drapery,' वस्त्रमन्तरं व्यवधायकं यस्य &c. Why do we say 'when meaning lying between.'? Observe आत्मान्तरम् = आत्मा स्वभावोऽन्तरोऽन्योयस्य ॥

३९०१ । मुखं स्वाङ्गम् । ६ । २ । १६७ ॥

गौरमुखः 'स्वाङ्गम्' किम् । दीर्घमुखा शाला ॥

3901. In a Bahuvrîhi the acute is on the final, when the second member is 'mukha' meaning mouth i. e. the actual bodily part of an animal and not used metaphorically.

Thus गौरमुखः । Why do we say 'an actual part of a body'? Observe दीर्घमुखा शाला । Here मुख means 'entrance'.

३९०२ । नाव्ययदिक्शब्दगोमहत्स्थूलमुष्टिपृथुवत्सेभ्यः । ६ । २ । १६८ ॥

उच्चैर्मुखः । प्राङ्मुखः । गोमुखः । महामुखः । स्थूलमुखः । मुष्टिमुखः । पृथुमुखः । वत्समुखः । पूर्वपदप्रकृतिस्वरोऽत्र । गोमुष्टिवत्सपूर्वपदस्योपमानलक्षणोऽपि विकल्पोऽनेन बाध्यते ॥

3902. In a Bahuvrîhi, the acute does not fall on such 'mukha' denoting a real mouth, when it comes after an Indeclinable, and a name of a direction, or after गो, महत्, स्थूल, मुष्टि, पृथु and वत्स ॥

Thus अव्ययः उच्चैर्मुखः । The word उच्चैः is finally acute and retains its accent. दिक्—प्राङ्मुखः । The word प्राङ् has acute on the first by VI. 2, 52, गो &c :—

गोमुखः, महामुखः' स्थलमुखः, मुष्टिमुखः, पृथुमुखः and वत्समुखः। In these the first members of the Bahuvrîhi preserve their respective accents, under Rule VI. 2. 1 and in the case of compounds preceded by गो, मुष्टि, and वत्स, the optional rule taught in the next sûtra is also superseded by anticipation, though the words may denote comparison.

३९०३ । निष्ठोपमानादन्यतरस्याम् । ६ । २ । १६९ ॥

निष्ठान्तादुपमानवाचिनश्च परं मुखं स्वाङ्गं वान्तोदात्तं बहुव्रीहौ । प्रक्षालितमुखः । पक्षे 'निष्ठोपसर्ग-' (३८४४) इति पूर्वपदान्तोदात्तत्वम् । पूर्वपदप्रकृतिस्वरत्वेन गतिस्वरोऽपि भवति । उपमानम् । सिंहमुखः ॥

3903. In a Bahuvrîhi, the word 'mukha' denoting 'an actual mouth,' has optionally the acute on the final, when preceded by a participle in 'ta' or by that wherewith something is compared.

Thus प्रक्षालितमुखः or प्रक्षालितमुखः or प्रक्षालितमुखः। When the final is not acute, then Rule VI. 2. 110 S. 3844 applies which makes the first member have acute on the final optionally; and when that also does not apply, then by VI. 2. 1. the first member preserves its original accent, which is that of the gati (VI. 2. 49). Thus there are three forms. So also with a word denoting comparison:— सिंहमुखः or सिंहमुखः ॥

३९०४ । जातिकालसुखादिभ्योऽनाच्छादनात्क्तोऽकृतमितप्रतिपन्नाः । ६ । २ । १७० ॥

सारङ्गजग्धः । मासजातः । सुखजातः । दुःखजातः । 'जातिकाल-' इति किम् । पुत्रजातः । 'अनाच्छादनात्' किम । वस्त्रच्छन्नः । 'अकृत-' इति किम् । कुण्डकृतः । कुण्डमितः । कुण्डप्रतिपन्नः । अस्मादेव ज्ञापकान्निष्ठान्तस्य परनिपातः ॥

3904. After a word denoting a species with the exception of a word for 'garment or covering', and after a time-denoting word, as well as after 'sukha' &c. the Participle in 'kta' has acute on the final, in a Bahuvrîhi, but not so when the participles are कृत, मित and प्रतिपन्न ॥

Thus सारङ्गजग्धः। कालः—मासजातः। सुख &c.:—सुखजातः। दुःखजातः।

Why do we say 'after a Species, a time or सुख &c. word'? Observe पुत्रजातः (II. 2. 37), the participle being placed after the word Putra.

Why do we say 'when not meaning a garment'? Observe वस्त्रच्छन्नः from the root वस् with the affixes ष्ट्रन्.

Why do we say 'when not कृत &c.'? Observe कुण्डकृतः, कुण्डमितः, कुण्डप्रतिपन्नः। कुण्ड is first acute by Phit II. 3. being neuter. These three participles do not stand first in a compound (contrary to II. 2. 36). This sûtra implies that as a special case Nishṭhâ participles may stand second in a compound. In the counter-examples, above given, the first members retain their original accent (VI. 2. 1). The words सुख &c are given under III. 1. 18.

1 सुख, 2 दुःख, 3 तृप्र, (तृप्र तीव्र) 4 कृच्छ्र, 5 अस्र, 6 आस्र, 7 अलीक, 8 प्रतीप, 9 करुण, 10 कृपण, 11 सोढ, 12 गहन.

३९०५ । वा जाते । ६ । २ । १७१ ॥

जातिकालसुखादिभ्यः परो जातशब्दो वान्तोदात्तः । दन्तजातः । मासजातः ॥

3905. After a species (with the exception of garment) or a time denoting word, or after 'sukha' &c. in a Bahuvrîhi, the word 'jâta' has optionally acute on the final.

Thus दन्तजातः or दन्तजातः, मासजातः or मासजातः, सुखजातः or सुखजातः दुःखजातः or दुःखजातः &c. The word दन्त is first-acute by Phit II. 6; मास is first-acute by Phit II. 15. The words सुख and दुःख are end-acute by Phit I. 6.

३९०६ । नञ्सुभ्याम् । ६ । २ । १७२ ॥

बहुव्रीहावुत्तरपदमन्तोदात्तम् । अव्रीहिः । सुमाषः ॥

3906. A Bahuvrîhi formed by the Negative particle 'nañ' or by 'su' has acute on the last syllable of the compound.

Thus अव्रीहिः, सुमाषः ॥

३९०७ । कपि पूर्वम् । ६ । २ । १७३ ॥

नञ्सुभ्यां परं यदुत्तरपदं तदन्तस्य समासस्य पूर्वमुदात्तं कपि परे । अब्रह्मबन्धुकः । सुकुमारीकः ॥

3907. A Bahuvrîhi, formed by 'nañ' or 'su' and ending ni the affix 'kap' (V. 4. 153) has acute on the syllable preceding the affix.

By the last sûtra, the accent would have fallen on कप्, this makes it fall on the vowel preceding it. Thus अब्रह्मबन्धुकः, सुकुमारीकः ॥

३९०८ । ह्रस्वान्तेऽन्त्यात्पूर्वम् । ६ । २ । १७४ ॥

ह्रस्वान्त उत्तरपदे समासे यान्त्यात्पूर्वमुदात्तं कपि नञ्सुभ्यां परं बहुव्रीहौ । अव्रीहिकः । सुमाषकः । पूर्वमित्यनुवर्तमाने पुनः पूर्वग्रहणं प्रवृत्तिभेदेन नियमार्थम् । ह्रस्वान्तेऽन्त्यादेव पूर्वं पदमुदात्तं न कपि पूर्वमिति । अज्ञकः । कबन्तस्य यान्तोदात्तत्वम् ॥

3908. When the compound ends in a light vowel, the acute falls on the syllable before such last, in a Bahuvrîhi preceded by 'nañ' and 'su' to which 'kap' is added.

Thus अव्रीहिकः, सुमाषकः । The repetition of पूर्व in this sûtra, though its anuvritti was present from the last, shows, that in the last aphorism, the syllable preceding कप् takes the acute, while here the syllable preceding the short-vowel-ending final syllable has the acute and not the syllable preceding कप् । This is possible with a word which is, at least, of two syllables (not counting, of course, सु and क or कप्). Therefore, in अज्ञकः and सुज्ञकः, the acute is on the syllable preceding कप् by VI. 2. 173, because it has here no antyât-purvam.

३९०९ । बहोर्नञ्वदुत्तरपदभूम्नि । ६ । २ । १७५ ॥

उत्तरपदार्थबहुत्ववाचिनो बहोः परस्य पदस्य नञः परस्येव स्वरः स्यात् । बहुव्रीहिकः । बहुमित्रकः । 'उत्तरपद-' इति किम् । बहुषु मानोऽस्य स बहुमानः ॥

3909. A Bahuvrîhi with 'bahu' has the same accent as 'nañ' when it denotes muchness of the object expressed by the second member.

In other words, a Bahuvrîhi with the word बहु in the first member, is governed by all those rules which apply to a Bahuvrîhi with a Negative Particle such as Rules VI. 2. 172 &c. when this gives the sense of multiety of the objects denoted by the second member. Thus बहुव्रीहिकः by VI. 2. 174. बहुमित्रकः ॥

Why do we say 'uttara-pada bhûmni—when multeity of the object denoted by the second member is meant'? Observe बहुषु मानोऽस्य=बहुमानः अयम् (VI. 2. 1).

३९१० । न गुणादयोऽवयवाः । ६ । २ । १७६ ॥

अवयववाचिनो बहोः परे गुणादयो नान्तोदात्ता बहुव्रीहौ । बहुगुणा रज्जुः । बह्वक्षरं पदम् । बह्वध्यायः । गुणादिराकृतिगणः । 'अवयवाः' किम् । बहुगुणो द्विजः । अध्ययनश्रुतसदाचारादयो गुणाः ॥

3910. In a Bahuvrîhi, after 'bahu,' the acute does not fall on the final of 'guṇa' &c. when they appear in the compound as ingredient of something else.

Thus बहुगुणाः रज्जुः, बह्वक्षरं पदम्, बह्वध्यायः (VI. 2. 1). गुणादि is an Akrtigaṇa. Why do we say 'when it denotes an avayava or ingredient'? Observe बहुगुणो ब्राह्मणः=अध्ययनश्रुतसदाचारादयोऽस्य गुणाः ॥

1 गुण, 2 अक्षर, 3 अध्याय, 4 सूक्त, 5 छन्दोमान, आकृतिगण ॥

३९११ । उपसर्गात्स्वाङ्गं ध्रुवमपर्शु । ६ । २ । १७७ ॥

प्रपृष्ठः । प्रललाटः । ध्रुवमेकरूपम् । 'उपसर्गात्' किम् । दर्शनीयपृष्ठः । 'स्वाङ्गम्' किम् । प्रशाखो वृक्षः । 'ध्रुवम्' किम् । उद्बाहुः 'अपर्शु' किम् । विपर्शुः ।

3911. A word denoting a part of the body, which is constant (and indispensable), with the exception of 'parśu' has, after a Preposition in a Bahuvrîhi compound, the acute on the last syllable.

Thus प्रपृष्ठः; प्रललाटः । उन्नतं यस्य प्रगतं पृष्ठं भवति स प्रपृष्ठः ॥

Why do we say 'after a Preposition'? Observe दर्शनीयपृष्ठः ॥

Why do we say 'part of the body'? Observe प्रशाखो वृक्षः ॥

Why do we say 'dhruva—constant and indispensable'? Observe उद्बाहुः क्रोशति । Here the hand is raised up only at the time of cursing and not *always* so the state of उद्बाहु is temporary and not permanent.

Why do we say with the exception of पर्शु? Observe विपर्शुः (VI. 2. 1).

३९१२ । वनं समासे । ६ । २ । १७८ ॥

समासमात्रे उपसर्गादुत्तरपदं वनमन्तोदात्तम् । तस्येदिमे प्रवणे ॥

3912. After a preposition, 'vana' has acute on the final in compounds of every kind.

Thus प्रवणे यष्टव्यम्, निर्वणे प्रणिधीयते, the न changed to ण by VIII. 4. 5. The word 'samâsa' is used in the sûtra to indicate that all sorts of compounds are meant, otherwise only Bahuvrîhi would have been meant.

३९१३ । अन्तः । ६ । २ । १७९ ॥

अस्मात्परं वनमन्तोदात्तम् । अन्तर्वणो देशः । अनुपसर्गार्थमिदम् ॥

3913. After 'antar' the acute falls on the final of 'vana.'

Thus अन्तर्वणो देशः । This sûtra is made in order to make वन oxytoned, when a preposition (upasarga) does not precede.

३९१४ । अन्तश्च । ६ । २ । १८० ॥

उपसर्गादन्तः शब्दोऽन्तोदात्तः । पर्यन्तः । समन्तः ॥

3914. The word 'antar' has acute on the final when preceded by a Preposition.

Thus पर्यन्तः, समन्तः । This is a Bahuvrîhi or a प्रादि compound.

३९१५ । न निविभ्याम् । ६ । २ । १८१ ॥

न्यन्तः । व्यन्तः । पूर्वपदप्रकृतिस्वरे यणि च कृते 'उदात्तस्वरितयोर्यणः–' (३६५७) इति स्वरितः ॥

3915. The word antar has not acute on the final, after the prepositions *ni* and *vi*.

Thus न्यन्तः, व्यन्तः, here the first member retains its acute, and semivowel is then substituted for the vowel इ then the subsequent grave is changed to svarita by VIII. 2. 4. S. 3657.

३९१६ । परेरभितोभावि मण्डलम् । ६ । २ । १८२ ॥

परेः परमभित उभयतो भावो यस्यास्ति तत्कूलादि मण्डलं चान्तोदात्तम् । परिकूलम् परिमण्डलम् ॥

3916. After 'pari' a word, which expresses something, which has both this side and that side, as well as the word 'mandala' has acute on the final.

Thus परिकूलम्, परिमण्डलम् ॥

३९१७ । प्रादस्वाङ्गं संज्ञायाम् । ६ । २ । १८३ ॥

प्रगृहम् । 'अस्वाङ्गम्' किम् । प्रपदम् ॥

3917. After *pra*, a word, which does not denote a part of body, has acute on the final, when the compound is a name.

Thus प्रगत्तृयम्। Why do we say 'not denoting a body part'? Observe प्रपदम्॥

३९१८। निरुदकादीनि च। ६। २। १८४॥

अन्तोदात्तानि। निरुदकम्। निरुपलम्॥

3918. The words *nirudaka* &c, have acute on the final.

Thus निरुदकम्, निरुपलम्, निरुपलम्, &c.

1 निरुदक, 2 निरुपल निरुलप 3 निर्मक्षिक, 4 निर्मशक, 5 निष्कालक, 6 निष्कालिक, 7 निष्पेष, 8 दुस्तरीप, 9 निस्तरीप, 10 निस्तरीक, 11 निरजिन, 12 उदजिन, 13 उपाजिन, 14 परेर्हस्तपादकेशकर्षाः आकृतिगणः॥

Note :—These may be considered either as प्रादि समास or Bahuvrihi. If they be considered as avyayî bhâva compounds then they are end-acute already by VI. I. 223. The word निष्कालकः = निष्क्रान्तः कालकात्, is a Prâdi-samâsa with the word काल ending in the affix कन्। The word दुस्तरीपः is thus formed : to the root तृ is added the affix ई and we have तरी (Un III. 158) तरीम् पाति = तरीपः ; कुत्सित स्तरीपः = दुस्तरीपः। The word निस्तरीकः is formed by adding the affix कप् to the Bahuvrihi निस्तरी। The words हस्त, पाद, केश and कर्ष have acute on the final after परि, as, परिहस्तः परिपादः, परिकेशः, and परिकर्षः॥

३९१९। अभेर्मुखम्। ६। २। १८५॥

अभिमुखम्। 'उपसर्गात्स्वाङ्गम्—' (३९११) इति सिद्धे बहुव्रीह्यर्थमध्रुवार्थमस्वाङ्गार्थं च अभिमुखा शाला॥

3919. The word *mukha* has acute on the final when preceded by *abhi*.

As, अभिमुखम्। It is a Bahuvrihi or a प्रादि samâsa. If it is an Avyayibhâva, then it would have acute on the final by VI. 1. 223 also. By VI. 2. 177, even मुख would have oxytone after an upasarga, the present sûtra makes the additional declaration that मुख is oxytone even when the compound is not a Bahuvrihi; when it does not denote an indispensable part of body, or a part of body even, as was the case in VI. 2. 177. Thus अभिमुखा शाला॥

३९२०। अपाच्च। ६। २। १८६॥

अपमुखम्। अपमुखम्, योगविभाग उत्तरार्थः॥

3920. The word 'mukha' has acute on the final, after the preposition *apa*.

Thus अपमुखम्। The separation of this from the last sûtra, is for the sake of the subsequent aphorism, in which the anuvritti of अप only goes.

३९२१। स्फिगपूतवीणाञ्जोऽध्वकुक्षिसीरनाम नाम च। ६। २। १८७॥

अपादिमान्यन्तोदात्तानि। अपस्फिगम्। अपपूतम्। अपवीणम्। अञ्जस्। अपाञ्जः। अध्वन्। अपाध्वम्। 'उपसर्गादध्वनः' (५४३) इत्यस्याभाव इदम्। एतदेव च ज्ञापकं समासान्तानित्यत्वे। अपकुक्षि। सीरनाम। अपसीरम्। अपहलम्। नाम। अपनाम। स्फिगपूतकुक्षिग्रहणमबहुव्रीह्यर्थमध्रुवार्थमस्वाङ्गार्थं च॥

3921. The words स्फिग, पूत, वीणा, अञ्जस्, अध्वन्, कुक्षि, नामन् and a word denoting 'a plough', have acute on the final, when preceded by *apa.*

Thus अपस्फिगम्, अपपूतम्, अपवीणम्, अपाञ्जः, अपाध्वा (This ordains acute on the final, where the compound apâdhwa does not take the samâsanta affix अच् by V. 4. 85, when it takes that affix, the acute will also fall on the final because अच् is a चित् affix.) This further shows that the samâsanta affixes are not compulsory. (अनित्यश्च समासान्तः), अपकुक्षिः, अपसीरः, अपहलः, अपलाङ्गलम्, अपनाम। These are प्रादि compounds or Bahuvrihi or Avyayîbhavas. Some of these viz. स्फिग, पूत and कुक्षिः will be end-acute by VI. 2. 177, also when they denote parts of body and a permanent condition and the compound is a Bahuvrihi. Here the compound must not be a Bahuvrihi, nor should these words denote parts of body and permanent condition of these parts.

३९२२ अधेरुपरिस्थम् । ६ । २ । १८८ ॥

अध्यारूढो दन्तोऽधिदन्तः । दन्तस्योपरि जातो दन्तः । 'उपरिस्थम्' किम् । अधिकरणम् ॥

3922. After अधि, that word, which denotes that thing which overlaps or stands upon, has acute on the final.

Thus अधिदन्तः=दन्तस्योपरि योऽन्योदन्तो जायते 'a tooth that grows over another tooth.'

Why do we say when meaning 'standing upon'? Observe अधिकरणम्। Here the acute is on क, the krit-formed second member retaining its accent (VI. 2. 139).

३९२३ अनोरप्रधानकनीयसी । ६ । २ । १८९ ॥

अनोःपरमप्रधानवाचि कनीयश्चान्तोदात्तम् । अनुगतो ज्येष्ठमनुज्येष्ठः । पूर्वपदार्थप्रधानः प्रादिसमासः । अनुगतः कनीयाननुकनीयान् । उत्तरपदार्थप्रधानः । प्रधानार्थं च कनीयोग्रहणम् । 'अप्र–' इति किम् । अनुगतो ज्येष्ठोऽनुज्येष्ठः ॥

3923. After 'anu' a word which is not the Principal, as well as 'kanîyas' has acute on the final.

The word अप्रधान means a word which stands in a dependant relation in a compound. Thus अनुगतो ज्येष्ठम् = अनुज्येष्ठः। These are प्रादि samâsa in which the first member is the principal or Pradhâna. अनुगतः कनीयान्=अनुकनीयान्, here the second member is the Principal : the word कनीयस् is taken as प्रधान ॥ Had it been non-pradhâna, it would be covered by the first portion of the sutra, and there would have been no necessity of its separate enumeration. Why do we say 'अप्रधान'? Observe अनुगतो ज्येष्ठः=अनुज्येष्ठः, where ज्येष्ठ is the Principal.

३९२४ । पुरुषश्चान्वादिष्टः । ६ । २ । १९० ॥

अनोः परोऽन्वादिष्टवाची पुरुषोऽन्तोदात्तः । अन्वादिष्टः पुरुषोऽनुपुरुषः । अन्वादिष्टः किम् । अनुगतः पुरुषोऽनुपुरुषः ॥

3924. After 'anu' the acute falls on the final of 'purusha,' when it means a man of whom mention was already made.

The word अन्वादिष्ट means 'of a secondary importance, inferior,' or 'mentioned again after having already been mentioned.' Thus अन्वादिष्टः पुरुषः = अनुपुरुषः; but अनुगतः पुरुषः = अनुपुरुषः ॥

३९२५ । अतेरकृत्पदे । ६ । २ । १९१ ॥

अतेः परमकृदन्तं पदशब्दश्चान्तोदात्तः । अत्यङ्कुशो नागः । अतिपदा गायत्री । 'अकृत्पदे' किम् । अतिकारकः ॥

'+ अतेर्धातुलोप इति वाच्यम् +' । इहमा भूत् । शोभनो गार्ग्योऽतिगार्ग्यः । इह च स्यात् । अतिक्रान्तः कारकमतिकारकः ॥

3925. After 'ati' a word not formed by a kṛit-affix, and the word 'pada' have acute on the last syllable.

Thus अत्यङ्कुशो नागः, अतिपदा गायत्री । Why do we say 'nonkrit-word and पद'? Observe अतिकारकः ॥

Vârt:—The rule is restricted to those compounds in which a root has been elided. That is, when in analysing the compound, a verb like क्रम् is to be employed to complete the sense. Therefore, it does not apply to शोभनो गार्ग्यः= अतिगार्ग्यः ॥ But it would apply to अतिकारकः, which when analysed becomes equal to अतिक्रान्तः कारकम् ॥

३९२६ । नेरनिधाने । ६ । २ । १९२ ॥

निधानमप्रकाशता । ततोऽन्यदनिधानं प्रकाशनमित्यर्थः । निमूलम् । न्यक्षम् । 'अनिधाने' किम् । निहितो दण्डो निदण्डः ॥

3926. After 'ni' the second member has the acute on the last syllable, when the sense is of 'not laying down.'

The word निधानं=अप्रकाशता 'not making manifest.' Thus निमूलम्, न्यक्षम् । Why do we say when meaning 'not laying down'? Observe निदण्डः=निहितो दण्डः । The force of नि is that of निधान here.

३९२७ । प्रतेरंश्वादयस्तत्पुरुषे । ६ । २ । १९३ ॥

प्रतेः परेऽश्वादयोऽन्तोदात्ताः । प्रतिगतोंऽशुः प्रत्यंशुः । प्रतिजनः । प्रतिराजा । समासान्तस्यानित्यत्वान्न टच् ॥

3927. In a Tatpurusha compound, the word 'anśu' &c. have acute on the final when preceded by 'prati.'

Thus प्रत्यंशुः; प्रतिजनः, प्रतिराजा ॥ In the case of राजन् this rule applies when the Samâsânta affix टच् is not added, when that affix is added, the acute will also be on the final by virtue of टच् which is a चित् affix.

1 अंशु, 2 जन, 3 राजन्, 4 उष्ट्र, 5 खेटक (रोटक), 6 अजिर, 7 आर्द्रा, 8 श्रवण, 9 कृत्तिका, 10 अर्ध, 11 पुर (आर्धपुर आर्धपुरः) ॥

The word अंशु is formed by the affix कु under the general class मृगय्वादि (Uṇ I. 37), राजन् is formed by the affix कनिन् (Uṇ I. 156), उष्ट्र by adding ष्ट्रन् to

उष् 'to burn'. (Uṇ IV. 162), खिट् + ण्वुल् = खेटक ; अजिर is formed by किर (Uṇ I. 53) आ + द्रा + अड् (III. 3. 106), with the augment रक् added to आ = आर्द्रा ॥ प्र + ल्युट् = प्रवण ॥ कृत + तिकन् = कृत्तिका (Uṇ III. 147) ऋधं + अच् (III. 1. 134) = ऋद्ध ; पुर् + क = पुर ॥

Why do we say 'in the Tatpurusha'? Observe प्रतिगता अंशवोऽस्य = प्रत्यंशुरयमुष्ट्रः ॥

३९२८ । उपाद्द्व्यजजिनमगौरादयः । ६ । २ । १९४ ॥

उपात्परं यद्द्व्यच्कमजिनं चान्तोदात्तं तत्पुरुषे गौरादीन्वर्जयित्वा । उपदेवः उपेन्द्रः । उपाजिनम् । 'अगौरादयः' किम् । उपगौरः । उपतैषः । 'तत्पुरुषे' किम् । उपगतः सोमोऽस्य स उपसोमः ॥

3928. In a Tatpurusha, the words of two syllables and 'ajina' have acute on the final when preceded by 'upa' but not when they are 'gaura' and the rest.

Thus उपगतो देवः=उपदेवः, उपेन्द्रः, उपाजिनम् । But not so in उपगौरः, उपतैषः &c.

1 गौर, 2 तैष (तैष) 3 तैल, 4 लेट, 5 लोट, 6 जिह्वा, 7 कृष्णा, (कृष्णा) 8 कन्या, 9 गुध (गुड) 10 कल्प, 11 पाद ।

Why 'in a Tatpurusha'? Observe उपगतः सोमोऽस्य = उपसोमः ॥

३९२९ । सोरवक्षेपणे । ६ । २ । १९५ ॥

सुप्रत्यवसितः । सूरत्र पूजायामेव । वाक्यार्थस्त्वत्र निन्दा असूयया तथाभिधानात् । 'सो' किम् । कुब्राह्मणः । 'अवक्षेपणे' किम् । सुवृषणम् ॥

3929. After 'su,' the second member has acute on the final in a Tatpurusha compound, when reproach is meant, in spite of the addition of 'su' which denotes praise.

Thus इह खल्विदानीं, सुस्थण्डिले सुमस्फिताभ्यां सुप्रत्यवसितः । The word सु here verily denotes praise, but it is the sense of the whole sentence that indicates reproach or censure. Why do we say 'after सु'? Observe सुब्राह्मणः । Why 'when reproach is meant'? Observe शोभनेषु तृणेषु = सुतृणेषु । So also सुवृषणम् ॥

३९३० । विभाषोत्पुच्छे ६ । २ । १९६ ॥

तत्पुरुषे । उत्क्रान्तः पुच्छादुत्पुच्छः । यदा तु पुच्छमुदस्यति उत्पुच्छयते । 'एरच्' (३२३१) । उत्पुच्छस्तदा थाथादिस्वरेण नित्यमन्तोदात्तत्वे प्राप्ते विकल्पोऽयम् । सेयमुभयत्र विभाषा । 'तत्पुरुषे' किम् । उदस्तं पुच्छं येन स उत्पुच्छः ॥

3930. In a Tatpurusha, the word 'utpuchha' may optionally have acute on the final.

Thus उत्क्रान्तः पुच्छात्=उत्पुच्छः or उत्पुच्छः (VI. 2. 2). When this word is derived by the affix अच् (III. 3. 56 S. 32 31) from पुच्छमुदस्यति=उत्पुच्छयति, then it would always have taken acute on the final by VI. 2. 144, the present sûtra ordains option there also. The rule does not apply to a non-Tatpursha : as, उदस्तम् पुच्छमस्य=उत्पुच्छः ॥

३९३१ । द्वित्रिभ्यां पाद्दन्मूर्धसु बहुव्रीहौ । ६ । २ । १९७ ॥

आभ्यां परेष्वेष्वन्तोदात्तो वा । 'द्विपाच्चतुष्पाच्च रथाय' । 'त्रिपादूर्ध्वः' । द्विदन् । 'त्रिमूर्धानं सप्तरश्मिम्' । मूर्धन्नित्यकृतसमासान्त एव मूर्धशब्दः । तस्येतत्प्रयोजनमसत्यपि समासान्तेऽन्तोदात्तत्वं यथा स्यात् । एतदेव ज्ञापकम् '×अनित्यः समासान्तो भवति×' इति । यद्यपि च समासान्तः क्रियते तथापि बहुव्रीहिकार्यत्वात्तदेकदेशत्वाच्च समासान्तोदात्तत्वं पक्षे भवत्येव । द्विमूर्धः । 'द्वित्रिभ्याम्' किम् । कल्याणमूर्धा । 'बहुव्रीहौ' किम् । द्वयोर्मूर्धा द्विमूर्धा ॥

3931. In a Bahuvrîhi, the words पाद्, दत् and मूर्धन् have optionally acute on the final after द्वि and त्रि ॥

Thus द्वौ पादावस्य = द्विपात् or द्विपात् as in द्विपाच्च चतुष्पाच्च रथाय (Rig Veda IV. 51. 5) त्रिपाद् or त्रिपाद् as in त्रिपादूर्ध्वः (Rig Veda X. 90. 4) द्विदन् or द्विदन् द्विमूर्धा or द्विमूर्धा as in त्रिमूर्धानम् सप्तरश्मिम् (Rig Veda I. 146, 1). The word पाद् is पाद with its अ elided, (V. 4. 140) दत् is the substitute of दन्त (V. 4. 141) and मूर्धन् retains its न् not allowing samâsanta affix. This also indicates that the samâsanta rule is not universal. When the samâsanta affix is added, then also the acute is on the final, for the कार्या is here the Bahuvrîhi compound, and this is only a part of it. Thus द्विमूर्धः, त्रिमूर्धः । Why after द्वि and त्रि ? Observe कल्याणमूर्धा here the first member is middle acute by Phiṭ II. 19 and this accent is retained (VI. 2. 1) Why 'Bahuvrîhi' ? Observe द्वयोर्मूर्धा=द्विमूर्धा ॥

३९३२ । सक्थं चाक्रान्तात् । ६ । २ । १९८ ॥

गौरसक्थः । श्लक्ष्णसक्थः । 'आक्रान्तात्' किम् । चक्रसक्थः । समासान्तस्य षचश्चित्त्वा-त्त्यमेवान्तोदात्तत्वं भवति ।

3932. The word 'saktha' has acute on the final optionally, when preceded by any word other than what ends in 'kra'

The word सक्थ is the samâsânta form of सक्थि (V. 4. 113). Thus गौरसक्थः or गौरसक्थः, श्लक्ष्णसक्थः or श्लक्ष्णसक्थः The word गौर being formed by अच् and श्लक्ष्ण by क्स्न (Uṇ. III. 19) are both end-acute. Why 'not after a word ending in क्र'? Observe चक्रसक्थः which is *always* oxytone as it is formed by षच् (V. 4. 113) a चित् affix.

३९३३ । परादिश्छन्दसि बहुलम् । ६ । २ । १९९ ॥

छन्दसि परस्य सक्थशब्दस्यादिरुदात्तो वा । 'अञ्जिसक्थमालभेत' । अत्र वार्तिकम्—

'+ परादिश्च परान्तश्च पूर्वान्तश्चापि दृश्यते ।

पूर्वादयश्च दृश्यन्ते व्यत्ययो बहुलं ततः +' ॥

इति । परादिः । 'तुविजाता उरुक्षया' । परान्तः । 'नियेन मुष्टिहत्यया' । 'चक्रिवक्षः' । पूर्वान्तः 'विश्वायुर्धेहि' ।

इति समासस्वराः ।

3933. The first syllable of the second member is diversely acute, in the Vedas.

The word पर "the second member" refers to सक्थ, as well as to any other word in general. Thus अञ्जिसक्थमालभेत, but सोमसक्थः so also ऋजुबाहुः, वाक्पतिः, चित्पतिः ।

In the non-Vedic literature these last two compounds will be final acute by VI. 1. 223, rule VI. 2. 18 not applying because of the prohibition contained in VI. 2. 19.

The rule is rather too restricted. It ought to be: "In the Vedas, the *first* syllable and the *final* syllable of the *second* member, as well as the *final* syllable and the *first* syllable of the *preceding* member are seen to have the acute accent, in supersession of all the foregoing rules."

(1) As to where the *first* syllable of the second member (परादिः) takes the accent, we have तुविजाता उरुक्षया (Rig Veda I. 2. 9.)

(2) As to where the final of all the second terms (परान्तः) takes the acute we have नियेनं मुष्टिहत्यया (Rig Veda I. 8. 2.) धस्त्रिचक्रः (Rig Veda I. 183. 1.)

(3) As to where the final of the preceding (पूर्वान्तः) takes the acute, we have विश्वायुः धेहि ॥

(4) As to where the first syllable of the preceding (पूर्वादिः) takes the acute we have as दिवोदासाय सामगाय ते ॥

Here end the Accents of Compounds.

CHAPTER V.

ACCENTS OF VERBS.

३९३४ । तिङो गोत्रादीनि कुत्सनाभीक्ष्ण्ययोः । ८ । १ । २७ ॥

तिङन्तात्पदाद्गोत्रादीन्यनुदात्तान्येतयोः । पचति गोत्रम् । पचतिपचति गोत्रम् । एवं प्रवचनप्रहसनप्रकथनप्रत्यायनादयः । कुत्सनाभीक्ष्ण्यग्रहणं पाठविशेषणम् । तेनान्यत्रापि गोत्रादिग्रहणे कुत्सनादावेव कार्यं ज्ञेयम् । 'गोत्रादि–' इति किम् । पचति पापम् । 'कुत्स–' इति किम् । खनति गोत्रं ; समेत्य कूपम् ॥

3934. The words *gotra* &c., become unaccented after a finite verb, when a contempt or a repetition is intended.

Thus पचति गोत्रम्, when contempt is meant.

Here पचति गोत्रं means 'he proclaims his Gotra &c., so that he may get food &c.' पचति is from the root पचि व्यक्तीकरणे 'to make evident' (Bhu. 184). Where contempt is not meant, it has the force of repetition, *i. e.* he repeatedly utters his Gotra as one is bound to do, in marriage-rites &c. And पचति पचति गोत्रम्, when repetition or intensity is denoted. Similarly पचति ब्रुवम्, पचति पचति ब्रुवम् । The word ब्रुवं is a noun derived from the root ब्रू by the affix कन्, the वच substitution for ब्रू has not taken place, as an anomaly.

1 गोत्र, २ ब्रुव, 3 प्रवचन, 4 प्रहसन, 5 प्रकथन, 6 प्रत्ययन, 7 प्रपञ्च, 8 प्राय, 9 न्याय 10 प्रचक्षण, 11 विचक्षण, 12 अवचक्षण, 13 स्वाध्याय, 14 भूयिष्ठ, 15 वा नाम (नाम वा) 16 प्रवचन, 17 प्रवञ्चन ॥

The word नाम optionally becomes anudâtta : in the alternative, it is first acute. Thus पचति नाम or पचति नाम ॥

The words 'contempt and repetition' in the text qualify the whole sentence or sûtra, and not the word गोत्रादि nor the word अनुदात्त understood. For we find that wherever the word गोत्रादि is used in this Chapter, it always implies the sense of 'contempt or repetition.' Thus the word गोत्रादि is used in VIII. 1. 57 and there also the sense is of contempt and repetition.

Why do we say 'Gotra and the rest'? Observe पचति पापम् । Here पापं is an adverb.

Why do we say 'when contempt or repetition is meant'? Observe खनति गोत्रं समेत्य कूपं । 'He digs a well, having assembled the Gotra.'

३९३५ । तिङ्ङतिङः । ८ । १ । २८ ॥

अतिङन्तात्पदात्परं तिङन्तं निहन्यते । 'अग्निमीळे' ॥

3935. A finite verb is unaccented, when a word precedes it, which is not a finite verb.

Thus अग्निमीडे पुरोहितं (Rv. I. 1. 1). स इद्देवेषु गच्छति (Rv. I. 1. 4), अग्ने सूपायनो भव (Rv. V. 1. 1), यजमानस्य पशून् पाहि ॥

३९३६ । न लुट् । ८ । १ । २९ ॥

लुडन्तं न निहन्यते । श्वः कर्ता ॥

3936. But the Periphrastic Future is not unaccented, when it is preceded by a word which is not a finite verb.

This restricts the scope of the last sûtra which was rather too wide. Thus श्वः कर्ता, श्वः कर्तारौ, मासेन कर्तारः । The Sarvadhâtuka affixes डा, रौ, रस्, are anudâtta after the affix तासि by VI. 1. 186, the whole affix तास् becomes udâtta (III. 1. 3) and where the टि portion of तास् *i. e.* the syllable आस्, is elided before the affix डा, there also the आ of डा becomes udâtta, because the udâtta has been elided. See VI. 1. 161.

३९३७ । निपातैर्यद्यदिहन्तकुविन्नेच्चेच्चण्कच्चिद्यत्रयुक्तम् । ८ । १ । ३० ॥

एतैर्निपातैर्युक्तं न निहन्यते । 'यदग्ने स्यामहं त्वम्' । 'युवा यदी कथः' । 'कुविदङ्ग आसन्' । 'अविलिभिश्चकमा कच्चित्' । 'पुत्रासो यत्र पितरो भवन्ति' ॥

3937. The finite verb retains its accent in connection with the particles यत्, 'that,' 'because,' यदि, 'if', हन्त, 'also'!, 'O!' कुवित्, 'well', नेत्, 'not', चेत्, 'if', च 'if', कच्चित् (interrogative particle, implying 'I hope' or 'I hope not'), and *yatra* 'where.'

Thus यदग्नेस्यामहंत्वं (Rig Veda VIII. 44. 23). युवा यदी कथः (Rig Veda V 74. 5). कुविदङ्ग आसन् (Rig Veda VII. 91. 1). नेज्जिह्मायन्त्यो नरकं पताम (Nir. I. 11), स चेद् भुङ्क्ते, स चेद् अधीते ; पुत्रासो यत्र पितरो भवन्ति (Rig Veda I. 89. 9).

The particle चण् with the indicatory ण् has the force of चेत्। Thus अयं च मरिष्यति = अयं चेन् मरिष्यति ॥

३९३८ । नह प्रत्यारम्भे । ८ । १ । ३१ ॥

नहेत्यनेन युक्तं तिङन्तं नानुदात्तम् । प्रतिषेधयुक्त आरम्भः प्रत्यारम्भः । 'नह भोक्ष्यसे' । प्रत्यारम्भे किम् । 'नह वै तस्मिँल्लोके दक्षिणामिच्छन्ति'

3938. The finite verb retains its accent in connection with 'naha' when employed in the sense of forbidding.

When something urged by one, is rejected insultingly by another, then the reply made by the first tauntingly, with a negation, is pratyârambha. Thus A says to B: 'Eat this please.' B rejects the offer repeatedly, in anger or jest. Then A in anger or jest says 'No, you will eat'—as नह भोक्ष्यसे। Here भोक्ष्यसे retains its accent, which is acute on the middle, for से becomes accentless as it follows अदुपदेश (VI. 1. 186), and स्य becomes udâtta by the प्रत्ययस्वर (III. 1. 3).

Why do we say, 'when asseverative'? Observe नह वै तस्मिँल्लोके दक्षिणामिच्छन्ति. 'Verily in that world they do not wish for fee.' Here it is pure negation. तस्मिन् is first acute by फिट् accent, लोके is final acute because it is formed by अच् of पचादि (III. 1. 134), दक्षिणा is first acute, because it is a Pronoun ending in अ (स्वाङ्गशिटामदन्तानाम् Phit II. 6) and इच्छन्ति is anudâtta by VIII. 1. 28.

३९३९ । सत्यं प्रश्ने । ८ । १ । ३२ ॥

सत्ययुक्तं तिङन्तं नानुदात्तं प्रश्ने । सत्यं भोक्ष्यसे । 'प्रश्ने' किम् । 'सत्यमिद्वा उ तं वयमिन्द्रं स्तवाम' ॥

3939. The finite verb retains its accent in connection with 'satya' when used in asking a question.

Thus सत्यं भोक्ष्यसे 'Truly, will you eat'? सत्यमध्येष्यसे। Why do we say 'in questioning'? Observe सत्यमिद्वा उ तं वयमिन्द्रं स्तवाम ॥

३९४० । अङ्गाप्रातिलोम्ये । ८ । १ । ३३ ॥

अङ्गेत्यनेन युक्तं तिङन्तं नानुदात्तम् । अङ्ग कुरु । 'अप्रातिलोम्ये' किम् । 'अङ्ग कूजसि वृषल इदानीं ज्ञास्यसि जाल्म' । अनभिप्रेतमसौ कुर्वन्प्रतिलोमो भवति ॥

3940. The finite verb retains its accent in connection with 'aṅga' when used in a friendly assertion.

Anything done to injure another is pratiloma, opposite of this is apratiloma, or friendliness. In fact, it is equal to anuloma. Thus अङ्ग कुरु 'yes, you may do.' Here aṅga has the force of friendly permission.

But when it has the force of pratiloma, we have:—अङ्ग कूज३ वृषल । इदानीं ज्ञास्यसि जाल्म 'Well, chuckle O sinner! soon wilt thou learn, O coward.' Here अङ्ग is used in the sense of censure, for chuckling is a thing not liked by the person and is pratiloma action: for pluta-vowel see VIII. 2. 96.

३९४१ । हि च । ८ । १ । ३४ ॥

हियुक्तं तिङन्तं नानुदात्तम् । 'आ हि ष्मा याति' । 'आ हि रुहतम्' ॥

3941. The finite verb retains its accent in connection with 'hi' when used in a friendly assertion.

Thus :—आहिष्मा याति (Rig Veda IV. 29. 2). आहिरुहत (Rig Veda VIII. 22. 9).

३९४२ । छन्दस्यनेकमपि साकाङ्क्षम् । ८ । १ । ३५ ॥

हीत्यनेन युक्तं साकाङ्क्षमनेकमपि नानुदात्तम् । 'अनृतं हि मत्तो वदति' । 'पाप्मा चैनं पुनाति' । तिङन्तद्वयमपि न निहन्यते ॥

3942. In the Vedas, the finite verb retains its accent (but not always), in connection with 'hi', when it stands in correlation to another verb, even more than one.

That is, sometimes one verb, sometimes more than one verb retain their accent. Thus of more than one verb, we have the following example :—अनृतं हि मत्तो वदति । पाप्मा एनं वि पुनाति 'Because the drunkard tells falsehood, therefore sin will make him impure : i. e. he does incur sin." Here both verbs वदति and विपुनाति retain their accent : and हि has the force of यत् 'because'. According to Kaiyyata the meaning of this sentence is यस्मात् मत्तोऽनृतं वदति, तस्मादनृतवदन दोषेण न युज्यते i. e. a drunkard does not incur the sin of telling a falsehood, because he is not in his senses. See Maitra Sanhita I. 11. 6.

३९४३ । यावद्यथाभ्याम् । ८ । १ । ३६ ॥

आभ्यां योगे तिङन्तं नानुदात्तम् । 'यथा चित्कण्वमावतम्' ॥

3943. A finite verb retains its accent in connection with 'yâvat' and 'yathâ'.

The meaning is that the verb retains its accent, even when यावत् and यथा followed after it. Thus यथा चित् कण्वमावतम् । The word आवतम् is the Imperative (लोट्) Second Person Dual of the root अव् ॥

३९४४ । पूजायां नानन्तरम् । ८ । १ । ३७ ॥

यावद्यथाभ्यां युक्तमनन्तरं तिङन्तं पूजायां नानुदात्तम् । यावत्पचति शोभनम् । यथा पचति शोभनम् । पूजायाम्' किम् । यावद्भुङ्क्ते । 'अनन्तरम्' किम् । यावद्देवदत्तः पचति शोभनम् । पूर्वेणात्र निघातः प्रतिषिध्यते ॥

3944. But not so when these particles 'yâvat' and 'yathâ' immediately precede the verb and denote 'praise'.

That is, the verb loses its accent, and becomes anudâtta. Thus यावत् पचति शोभनम्, यथा पचति शोभनम् ॥

Why do we say when denoting 'praise' ? Observe यावद् भुङ्क्ते ॥

Why do we say 'immediately'? Observe यावद् देवदत्तः पचति शोभनं । Here the verb retains its accent by the last sûtra.

३९४५ । उपसर्गव्यपेतं च । ८ । १ । ३८ ॥

पूर्वयोगेऽनन्तरमित्युक्तम् । उपसर्गव्यवधानार्थं वचनम् । यावत्प्रपचति शोभनम् । अनन्तरमित्येव । यावद्देवदत्तः प्रपचति शोभनम् ॥

3945. A finite verb loses its accent, when it denotes 'praise' and is joined immediately with yâvat and yathâ, through the intervention of an upasarga (or verbal preposition).

The last sûtra taught that the verb loses its accent when *immediately* preceded by यावत् and यथा । This qualifies the word 'immediately' and teaches that the intervention of a Preposition does not debar immediateness. Thus यावत् प्रपचति शोभनम् ॥

The word 'immediately' is understood here also. Thus यावद् देवदत्तः प्रपचति शोभनं ॥ The upasarga प्र has ndâtta accent.

३९४६ । तुपश्यपश्यताहैः पूजयाम् । ८ । १ । ३९ ॥

एभिर्युक्तं तिङन्तं न निहन्यते पूजायाम् । 'आदह स्वधामनु पुनर्गर्भत्वमेरिरे' ॥

3946. A finite verb retains its accent in connection with तु, पश्य, पश्यत, and अह, when meaning 'praise'.

Thus आदह स्वधामनु पुनर्गर्भत्वमेरिरे ॥

३९४७ । अहो च । ८ । १ । ४० ॥

एतद्योगे नानुदात्तं पूजायाम् । अहो देवदत्तः पचति शोभनम् ॥

3947. A finite verb retains its accent when in connection with *aho* meaning 'praise'.

Thus अहो देवदत्तः पचति शोभनं ॥

३९४८ । शेषे विभाषा । ८ । १ । ४१ ॥

अहो इत्यनेन युक्तं तिङन्तं वानुदात्तं पूजायाम् । अहो कटं करिष्यति ॥

3948. A finite verb retains its accent optionally, when in connection with *aho* in the remaining cases (*i. e.* where it does not mean praise).

What is the शेष alluded to here? The शेष means here senses other than पूजा or 'praise.' Thus कटमहो करिष्यसि or कटमहो करिष्यसि । This is a speech uttered in anger or envy and not in praise (असूया वचन) ॥

३९४९ । पुरा च परीप्सायाम् । ८ । १ । ४२ ॥

पुरेत्यनेन युक्तं वानुदात्तं त्वरायाम् । अधीष्व माणवक पुरा विद्योतते विद्युत् । निकटागामित्यत्र पुराशब्दः । परीप्सायाम् किम् । न तं स्म पुराधीयते । चिरातीतेऽत्र पुरा ॥

3949. A finite verb retains its accent optionally in connection with 'purâ' when it means 'haste' (*i. e.* when 'purâ' means 'before').

The word परीप्सा means त्वरा or 'quick.' Thus अधीष्व माणवक पुरा विद्योतते विद्युत् । The word पुरा here expresses the future occurrance which is imminent or very near at hand. It is against the rule of Dharmasâstras to study while it thunders or lightens.

Why do we say 'when meaning *haste*'? Observe मतेन स्म पुराधीयते । Here the word पुरा expresses a past time; that is, it means 'long ago.' See III. 2. 118 and 122, for the employment of पुरा in the Past Tense, and III. 3. 4, for the Present.

३९५० । नन्वित्यनुज्ञैषणायाम् । ८ । १ । ४३ ॥

नन्वित्यनेन युक्तं तिङन्तं नानुदात्तमनुज्ञाप्रार्थनायाम् । ननु गच्छामि भोः । अनुजानीहि मां गच्छन्तमित्यर्थः । 'अनु–' इति किम् । अकार्षीः कटं त्वम् । ननु करोमि । पृष्टप्रतिवचनमेतत् ॥

3950. A finite verb retains its accent in connection with *nanu*, when with this Particle permission is asked.

The word एषणा means 'asking, praying.' The word अनुज्ञा means 'permission.' The compound अनुज्ञैषणा means 'asking of permission.' Thus ननु गच्छामि भोः 'can I go sir.' The sense is 'give me permission to go.'

Why do we say when 'asking for' permission'? Observe अकार्षीः कटं त्वम् ? ननु करोमि भोः 'hast thou made the mat? Well, I am making it.' Here ननु has the force of an answering particle, and not used in asking permission and hence the verb loses its accent.

३९५१ । किं क्रियाप्रश्नेऽनुपसर्गमप्रतिषिद्धम् । ८ । १ । ४४ ॥

क्रियाप्रश्ने वर्तमानेन किंशब्देन युक्तं तिङन्तं नानुदात्तम् । किं द्विजः पचत्याहोस्विद्गच्छति । 'क्रिया–' इति किम् । साधनप्रश्ने मा भूत् । किं भक्तं पचत्यपूपान्वा । 'प्रश्ने' किम् । किं पठसि । 'क्षेपोऽयम्' । 'अनुपसर्गम्' किम् । किं प्रपचति उत प्रकरोति । 'अप्रतिषिद्धम्' किम् । किं द्विजो न पचति ॥

3951. A finite verb retains its accent in connection with *kim*, when with this is asked a question relating to an action, and when the verb is not preceded by a Preposition or by a Negation.

Thus किं द्विजः पचति, अहो स्विद् गच्छति ॥

Why do we say when the question relates to a क्रिया or action? The rule will not apply, when the question relates to an object or साधन । Thus किं भक्तं पचति अपूपान् वा ॥

Why do we say 'when a question is asked'? Observe किम् पठति । Here किं is used to express contempt, and not to ask a question.

Why do we say 'not preceded by a Preposition' Observe किं प्र पचति उत प्रकरोति ॥

Why do we say 'not preceded by a negative particle.' Observe, किं द्विजो न पठति ॥

३९५२ । लोपे विभाषा । ८ । १ । ४५ ॥

किमोऽप्रयोग उक्तं वा । देवदत्तः पचत्याहोस्वित्पठति ॥

3952. When however *kim* is not added in asking such a question, the finite verb may optionally retain its accent.

When किम् is elided in asking a question relating to an action, the finite verb which is not preceded by a Preposition or a Negative Particle, optionally does not become anudâtta. When is there the elision of this किम् because no rule of Pâṇini has taught it? When the sense is that of an interrogation, but the word किम् is not used. In short, the word 'lopa' here does not mean the Grammatical substitute, but merely non-use. As देवदत्तः पचति (or पचति) श्वोऽस्विद् पठति (or पठति) Here the sentence is interrogative, even without the employment of किम्। The option of this sûtra, is a Prâpta-vibhâsha, as it is connected with the sense of किम् ॥

३९५३। एहिमन्ये प्रहासे लृट्। ८। १। ४६॥

एहिमन्यइत्यनेन युक्तं लृडन्तं नानुदात्तं क्रीडायाम्। एहि मन्ये भक्तं भोक्ष्यसे भुक्तं तत्त्वतिथिभिः। प्रहासे' किम्। एहि मन्यसे ओदनं भोक्ष्ये इति सुष्टु मन्यसे। 'मत्यर्थलोटा- (३९५८) लृडित्यनेनैव सिद्धे नियमार्थोऽयमारम्भः। एहिमन्येयुक्ते प्रहास एव नान्यत्र। 'एहि मन्यसे ओदनं भोक्ष्ये' ॥

3953. In connection with 'ehimanye' used derisively, the First Future, that follows it, retains its accent.

The word प्रहास means great laughter, *i. e.* derision, mockery, raillery, jeering, gibing, sneering. Thus एहि मन्ये भक्तं भोक्ष्यसे, नहि भुक्तंतत्त्वतिथिभिः। The word एहि is the Imperative, second Person of the root इण् preceded by the preposition आङ् ॥

Why do we say 'used derisively'? Observe एहि मन्यसे ओदनं भोक्ष्ये इति। सुष्टु मन्यसे ॥

By sûtra VIII. 1. 51, S. 3958 after the Imperative एहि which is a verb of 'motion' (गत्यर्थ) the following First Future (लृट्) would have retained its accent. The present sûtra makes a niyama or restriction, namely, that in connection with the Imperative एहि मन्ये, the लृट् is accented only then when 'derision' is meant and not otherwise. Thus the लृट् loses its accent here:—एहि मन्यसे ओदनं भोक्ष्ये ॥

३९५४। जात्वपूर्वम्। ८। १। ४७॥

अविद्यमानं पूर्वं यस्माज्जातु तेन युक्तं तिङन्तं नानुदात्तम्। जातु भोक्ष्यसे। 'अपूर्वम्' किम्। कटं जातु करिष्यसि ॥

3954. A finite verb retains its accent after 'jâtu' when this 'jâtu' is not preceded by any other word.

Thus जातु भोक्ष्यसे। Here से is anudâtta by VI. 1. 186, as it is a sârvadhâtuka affix coming after an अनुपदेश; the word जातु is first acute, as it is a Nipâta. Why do we say 'when not preceded by any other word'? Observe —कटं जातु करिष्यति। The word कटं is end-acute as it is a फिट् or noun.

३९५५। किंवृत्तं च चिदुत्तरम्। ८। १। ४८॥

अविद्यमानपूर्वं चिदुत्तरं यत्किं वृत्तं तेन युक्तं तिङन्तं नानुदात्तम्। विभक्त्यन्तं डतरडतमान्तं किमो रूपं किंवृत्तम्। कश्चिद्भुङ्क्ते। कतरश्चित्। कतमश्चित्। 'चिदुत्तरम्' किम्। को भुङ्क्ते। 'अपूर्वं' किम्। रामः किंचित्पठति ॥

3955. Also after a form of 'kim' when the particle 'chit' follows it, and when no other word precedes such form of 'kim', the finite verb retains its accent.

The word किमवृत्तं is a Genitive Tatpurusha meaning किमोवृत्तं। The word किमवृत्तं means any form of किम with its case-affixes, as well as the forms of किम् when it takes the affixes डतर and डतम। Thus कश्चिद् भुङ्क्ते, कतरश्चित् करोति, कतमश्चिद भुङ्क्ते ॥

Why do we say 'followed by चित्'? Observe को भुङ्क्ते ॥

The word अपूर्वं of the last sûtra qualifies this also; therefore, the verb loses its accent here :— रामः किंचित् पठति ॥

३९५६ । आहो उताहो चानन्तरम् । ८ । १ । ४९ ॥

आहो उताहो इत्याभ्यां युक्तं तिङन्तं नानुदात्तम् । आहो उताहो वा भुङ्क्ते । अनन्तरमित्येव । शेषे विभाषां वक्ष्यति । 'अपूर्व–' इति किम् । देव आहो भुङ्क्ते ॥

3956. Also after an immediately preceding 'âho' and 'utâho' when these follow after no other word, the verb retains its accent.

The prohibition of *nighâta* or want of accentuation is understood here, so also there is the anuvṛitti of अपूर्व from the last.

Thus आहो or उताहो भुङ्क्ते। Why do we say 'immediately preceding'? In the following sûtra will be taught option, when these particles do not immediately precede the verb.

Why do we say 'when no word precedes them'? Observe देव आहो or उताहो भुङ्क्ते ॥

३९५७ । शेषे विभाषा । ८ । १ । ५० ॥

आभ्यां युक्तं व्यवहितं तिङन्तं वानुदात्तम् । आहो देवः पचति ॥

3957. When the abovementioned particles 'âho' and 'utâho' do not immediately precede the verb, the verb may optionally retain its accent.

Thus आहो देवः पचति or पचति ॥

३९५८ । गत्यर्थलोटा लृण्नचेत्कारकं सर्वान्यत् । ८ । १ । ५१ ॥

गत्यार्थानां लोटा युक्तं तिङन्तं नानुदात्तम् । यत्रैव कारके लोट् तत्रैव लृडपि चेत् । आगच्छ देव ग्रामं द्रक्ष्यसि । उह्यन्तां देवदत्तेन शालयः । रामेण भोक्ष्यन्ते । 'गत्यर्थ–' किम् । पच देव ओदनं भोक्ष्यसेऽन्नम् । 'लोटा' किम् । आगच्छेर्देव ग्रामं द्रक्ष्यस्येनम् । 'लृट्' किम् । आगच्छ देव देव ग्रामं पश्यस्येनम् । 'न चेत्' इति किम् । आगच्छ देव ग्रामं पिता ते ओदनं भोक्ष्यते । 'सर्वम्'-किम् । आगच्छ देव ग्रामं त्वं चाहं च द्रक्ष्याव एनमित्यत्रापि निघातनिषेधो यथा स्यात् । यत्लोडन्तस्य कारकं तच्चान्यच्च लृडन्तेनोच्यते ॥

3958. The First Future retains its accent in connection with the Imperative of a verb denoting 'motion' ('to go' 'to come' 'to start' &c), but only in that case, when the subject and object of both the verbs are not wholly different one from another.

Those verbs which have similar meaning with the word गति 'motion' are called गत्यर्थाः ॥ The Imperative of the गत्यर्थ verbal roots, is called गत्यर्थ-लोट् । In connection with such an Imperative of verbs of 'motion', the First Future does not become anudâtta, if the kâraka is not all different. The sense is, with whatever case-relation (kâraka), whether the Subject or Object, the Imperative is employed, with the same kâraka, the First Future must be employed. In connection with the finite verb here, the word कारक denotes the Subject and Object only, and not any other kâraka, such as Instrument, &c.

Thus आगच्छ देव ग्रामं, द्रक्ष्यसि 'Come O Deva, thou shalt see the village.' Here the subjects of both verbs आगच्छ and द्रक्ष्यसि are the same, and the objects of both verbs are also the same, namely ग्रामं । आ is a Preposition and is accented. गच्छ and देव both lose their accent (VIII, 1. 19 and 28,) ग्राम is first-acute being formed by the नित् affix मन् । Similarly उह्यन्तां देवदत्तेन शालयः. रामेण भोक्ष्यन्ते "Let the rice be carried by Devadatta, they will be eaten by Râma."

Why do we say 'verbs of motion'? Observe पच देव ओदनं, भोक्ष्यसे अन्नम् ॥

Why do we say 'after the Imperative'? Observe आगच्छेर्देव ग्रामं, द्रक्ष्यस्येनम् । Here the Potential mood is used.

Why do we say the 'First Future'? Observe आगच्छ देवदत्त ग्रामं, पश्यसि एनम् ॥ Here the Present Tense is used.

Why do we say 'if the kâraka is not *wholly* different'? Observe आगच्छ देवदत्त ग्रामं, पिता ते ओदनं भोक्ष्यते ॥

Why do we use the word सर्व 'wholly'? Observe आगच्छ देवदत्त ग्रामं, त्वं च अहं च द्रक्ष्याव एनम् । Here also there is prohibition of *nighâta* and the First Future retains its accent, for the subject of the Future is not *wholly* different from that of the Imperative. For here the subject of the Imperative is the subject also of the Future, though only partly, in conjunction with another. Moreover, the object here in both is the same. Had सर्व not been used in the sûtra, where the sentence would have remained the same, there the rule would have applied, and not where the sentences became different.

३९५९ । लोट् च । ८ । १ । ५२ ॥

लोडन्तं गत्यर्थलोटा युक्तं नानुदात्तम् । आगच्छ देव ग्रामं पश्य । 'गत्यर्थ—' इति किम् । पच देवौदनं भुङ्क्ष्वैनम् । 'लोट्' किम् । आगच्छ देव ग्रामं पश्यसि । न चेत्कारकं सर्वान्यदित्येव । आगच्छ देव ग्रामं पश्यत्वेनं रामः । सर्वग्रहणात्त्विह स्यादेव । आगच्छ देव ग्रामं त्वं चाहं च पश्याव: । योगविभाग उत्तरार्थः ॥

3959. Also an Imperative, following after an Imperative of verbs of 'motion', retains its accent, when the subject or object of both the verbs, is not wholly different.

Thus आगच्छ देव ग्रामं पश्य ॥

But not here पच देवदत्तौदनं, भुङ्क्ष्वैनम् because the first Imperative is not one of गत्यर्थ verb. Nor here, आगच्छेर्देव ग्रामं पश्येनम् because the first verb is not Imperative but Potential.

If the subject and object of both Imperatives are wholly different, the rule will not apply. Thus आगच्छ देव ग्रामं, पश्यतु एनं रामः ॥

By the force of the anuvritti of सर्व the rule will apply to the following: आगच्छ देव ग्रामं, त्वं चाहं च पश्यावः ॥

The separation of this sûtra from the last, is for the sake of the subsequent sûtra, by which the 'option' is with regard to लोट् and not लृट् ॥

३९६० । विभाषितं सोपसर्गमनुत्तमम् । १ । ५३ ॥

लोडन्तं गत्यर्थलोटा युक्तं तिङन्तं वानुदात्तम् । आगच्छ देव ग्रामं प्रविश । 'सोपसर्गम्' किम् । आगच्छ देव ग्रामं पश्य । 'अनुत्तमम्' किम् । आगच्छानि देव ग्रामं प्रविशानि ॥

3960. An Imperative preceded by a Preposition, and not in the First Person, following after an Imperative of verbs of 'motion', may optionally retain its accent, when the Kâraka is not wholly different.

The whole of the preceding sûtra is understood here. This is a Prâpta-vibhâshâ. Thus आगच्छ देव ग्रामं प्रविश or प्रविश । When the verb is accented the upasarga loses its accent by VIII. 1. 71.

Why do we say सोपसर्ग 'joined with a Preposition'? When there is no Preposition, there is no *option* allowed, and the last rule will apply. As आगच्छ देव ग्रामंपश्य ॥

Why do we say अनुत्तमं 'not a First Person'? Observe आ गच्छानि देव, ग्रामं प्रविशानि ॥

३९६१ । हन्त च । ८ । १ । ५४ ॥

हन्तेत्यनेन युक्तमनुत्तमं लोडन्तं वानुदात्तम् । हन्त प्रविश । सोपसर्गमित्येव । हन्त कुरु । 'निपातैर्यद्यदि–' (३९३७) इति निघातप्रतिषेधः । 'अनुत्तमम्' किम् । हन्त प्रभुनजावहै ॥

3961. An Imperative, with a Preposition preceding it, may optionally retain its accent, in connection with 'hanta,' but not the First Person.

With the exception of गत्यर्थ लोटा &c., the whole of the preceding sûtra is understood here.

Thus हन्त प्र विश or प्रविश । But no option is allowed here हन्त कुरु, as it is not preceded by a preposition. Here rule VIII. 1. 30, S. 3937 makes the accent compulsory after हन्त । So also हन्त प्रभुनजावहै, where the 1st Person is used, the verb retains its accent compulsorily by VIII. 1. 30 S. 3937.

The word प्रभुनजावहै is Imperative First Person, Dual of the root भुज् in Atmane pada (I. 3. 66) The Personal ending वहै is anudâtta by VI. 1. 186, because the verb is anudâtta-it. The vikarana न therefore retains its accent.

३९६२ । आम एकान्तरमामन्त्रितमनन्तिके । ८ । १ । ५५ ॥

आमः परमेकपदान्तरितमामन्त्रितं नानुदात्तम् । आम् । पचसि देवदत्त३ । 'एकान्तरम्' किम् । आम प्रपचसि देवदत्त३ । 'आमन्त्रितम्' किम् । आम्पचति देवदत्तः । 'अनन्तिके' किम् आम्पचसि देवदत्त ॥

3962. After 'âm,' but separated from it by not more than one word, the Vocative retains its accent, when the person addressed is not near.

Thus आम् पचसि देवँदत्ता ३ । The *nighâta* being hereby prohibited, the vocative gets accent on the first syllable by VI. 1. 198.

Why do we say आम् ? Observe शाक पचसि दे व दत्त । Here it is anudâtta by VIII. 1. 19.

Why do we say एकान्तरम् 'separated only by one word'? Observe आम् च पचसि देवदत्ता ३ ॥

Why do we say 'the Vocative'? See आम् पचति देवदत्तः ॥

Why do we say अनन्तिके 'not near'? See आम् पचसि देवदत्त ॥

३९६३ । यद्धितुपरं छन्दसि । ८ । १ । ५६ ॥

तिङन्तं नानुदात्तम् । 'उदसृजो यदङ्गिरः, । 'उशन्ति हि' । आख्यास्यामि तु ते । 'निपातैर्यद्- (३९३७), इति 'हि च' (३९४१) इति 'तुपश्य-' (३९४८) इति च सिद्धे नियमार्थमिदम् । एतैरेव परभूतैर्योगे नान्यैरिति । जाये स्वरोहावेहि । एहीति गत्यर्थलोटा युक्तस्य लोडन्तस्य निघातो भवति ॥

3963. A finite verb followed by *yat* or *hi* or *tu* retains its accent in the Chhandas.

The anuvritti of आमन्त्रित should not be taken in this sûtra, but that of तिङ् ॥ Thus with यत्परं we have:—गवां गोत्रमुदसृजो यदङ्गिरः । The verb उदसृजः is the Imperfect (लङ्) 2nd person singular of सृज् of the Tudâdi class. With हि we have, इन्द्रवो वां उशन्ति हि (Rig Veda 1. 2. 4). The verb उशन्ति is the Present (लट्) Plural of वश् of the Adâdi class. The samprasârana takes place because it belongs to ग्रहादि class. With तु we have, आख्यास्यामि तु ते । By the previous sûtra VIII. 1. 30. S. 3937 a verb in connection with यत् would have retained its accent, so also in connection with हि by the sûtra VIII. 1. 34, S. 3941 and in connection with तु by VIII. 1. 39, S. 3946 ; the present sûtra is, therefore, a niyama rule. The verb retains its accent when these three Particles *only* follow and not any other. If any other Particle follows, the verb need not retain its accent. Thus जाये स्वा रोहावेहि । Here रोहाव is the 1st Person Dual of the Imperative of रुह् (रुह् + शप् + वस् = रोह + आट् + वस् III. 4. 92 = रोहाव the स् being elided, as लोट् is like लङ् III. 4. 85 and 99). The verb एहि is the 2nd Person Singular of the Imperative of the root इण्, preceded by the Particle आङ् । Here in एहि रोहाव (= रोहाव आ इहि), the verb रोहाव is followed by the Particle आ, and does not retain its accent But for this rule, it would have retained its accent. Because एहि is a गत्यर्थ लोट् VIII. 1. 51), रोहाव is another लोट् in connection with it, and therefore, by VIII. 1. 52 it would have retained its accent. But now it loses its accent because it is a तिङ् following after a non तिङ् word स्वः । The visarga of स्वः is elided before र् by VIII. 3. 14, then the preceding अ is lengthened and we have स्वा (VI. 3. 111). Another reading is स्वो रोहावेहि । It is a Vedic anomaly, the visarga is changed to उ ॥

३९६४ । चनचिदिवगोत्रादितद्धिताम्रेडितेष्वगतेः । ८ । १ । ५७ ॥

एषु षट्सु परतस्तिङन्तं नानुदात्तम् । देवः पचति चन । देवः पचति चित् । देवः पचतीव । देवः पचति गोत्रम् । देवः पचतिकल्पम् । देवः पचतिपचति । 'अगतेः' किम् । देवः प्रपचति चन ॥

3964. A finite verb retains its accent, when it is not preceded by a Gati Particle (I. 4. 60 &c), and when it is followed by चन, चिद्, इव, गोत्र &c., a Taddhita affix, or by its own doubled form.

Thus देवः पचति चन ; देवः पचति चित्, देवः पचतीव । The list of Gotrâdi words is given under sûtra VIII. 1. 27. Thus देवः पचति गोत्रम्, देवः पचति ब्रुवम्, देवः पचति प्रवचनम् &c. The Gotrâdi words, here also, denote censure and contempt

With a Taddhita affix, देवः पचति कल्पम् रूपम् । The examples should be given with anudâtta Taddhita affixes, like रूपप्, कल्पप् (V. 3. 66 and 67). Any other Taddhita affix added to the verb would cause the verb to lose its accent, the Taddhita accent overpowers the verb accent : as पचतिदेश्य (V. 3. 67).

With a doubled verb, as ; देवः पचति पचति ॥

Why do we say 'when not preceded by a Participle called Gati'? Observe देवः प्र पचति चन ॥

३९६५ । चादिषु च । ८ । १ । ५८ ॥

चवाहाहैवेषु परेषु तिङन्तं नानुदात्तम् । देवः पचति च खादति च । अगतेरित्येव । देवः प्रपचति च प्रखादति च । प्रथमस्य "चवायोगे-' (३९६६) इति निघातः प्रतिषिध्यते द्वितीयं तु निहन्यत एव ॥

3965. A finite verb, not preceded by a gati, retains its accent before the Particles च (वा, ह, अह and एव VIII. 1. 24).

The चादि words are those mentioned in sûtra VIII. 1. 24. Thus देवः पचति च खादति च ॥

But when preceded by a gati, we have देवदत्तः प्र पचति च प्र खादति च । Here the first verb retains its accent by virtue of the next sûtra, but the second verb loses its accent.

३९६६ । चवायोगे प्रथमा । ८ । १ । ५९ ॥

चवेत्याभ्यां योगे प्रथमा तिङ्विभक्तिर्नानुदात्ता । गाश्च चारयति वीणां वा वादयति । 'इतो वा सातिमीमहे' । उत्तरवाक्ययोरनुषज्जनीयतिङन्तापेक्षयेयं प्राथमिकी । 'योगे' किम् । पूर्वभूतयोरपि योगे निघातार्थं प्रथमाग्रहणं द्वितीयादेस्तिङन्तस्य मा भूत् ॥

3966. The first finite verb only retains its accent in connection with 'cha' and 'vâ.'

The anuvritti of अगतेः which was drawn in the last sûtra, does not run into this. Thus गाश्च चारयति, वीणां च वादयति । इतो वा सातिमीमहे ॥

The word योग in the sutra indicates that the mere *connection* with the verb is meant, whether this connection takes place by adding these words च and वा, *before* the verb, or *after* the verb, is immaterial for the purposes of this sutra, (not so in the last). The word प्रथमा shows that the *first* verb is governed by this rule and not the *second.*

३९६७ । हेति क्षियायाम् । ८ । १ । ६० ॥

हयुक्ता प्रथमा तिङ्विभक्तिर्नानुदात्ता धर्मव्यतिक्रमे । स्वयं ह रथेन याति ३ । उपाध्यायं पदातिं गमयति । 'क्षियाशीः–' (३६२३) इति प्लुतः ॥

3967. In connection with 'ha,' the first verb retains its accent, when an offence against custom is reprimanded.

The word क्षिया means an error or mistake of duty, a breach of etiquette or a fault against good breeding.

Thus स्वयं ह रथेन याँति ३, उपाध्यायं पदातिं, गमयति 'He himself goes on a car, while he causes his Preceptor to trudge behind on foot.' Here the nighâta of the first verb is prohibited. The verb becomes svarita-pluta by VIII. 2. 104 S. 3623.

३९६८ । अहेति विनियोगे च । ८ । १ । ६१ ॥

अहयुक्ता प्रथमा तिङ्विभक्तिर्नानुदात्ता नानाप्रयोजने नियोगे क्षियायां च । त्वमह ग्रामं गच्छ । त्वमह रथेनारण्यं गच्छ । क्षियायां स्वयमह रथेन याति ३ । उपाध्यायं पदातिं नयति ॥.

3968. In connection with अह, the first verb retains its accent, when it refers to various commissions, (as well as when a breach of good manners is condemned).

The word विनियोग means sending a person to perform several commissions. The word च in the sûtra draws in the anuvṛitti of क्षिया also.

Thus त्वं, अह ग्रामं, गच्छ, त्वं अह रथेन अरण्यं गच्छ । So also when क्षिया is meant, स्वयमह रथेन याति ३, उपाध्यायं पदातिं नयति ॥

३९६९ । चाहलोप एवेत्यवधारणम् । ८ । १ । ६२ ॥

'च' 'अह' एतयोर्लोपे प्रथमा तिङ्विभक्तिर्नानुदात्ता । देव एव ग्रामं गच्छतु । देव एवारण्यं गच्छतु । ग्राममरण्यं च गच्छत्वित्यर्थः । देव एव ग्रामं गच्छतु । राम एवारण्यं गच्छतु । ग्रामं केवलमरण्यं केवलं गच्छत्वित्यर्थः । इहाहलोपः स च केवलार्थः । 'अवधारणम्' किम् । देव क्वेव भोक्ष्यसे । नक्वचिदित्यर्थः । अनवक्लृप्तावेव ॥

3969. When *cha* and *aha* are elided, the first verb still retains its accent, when *eva* with the force of limitation, takes their place.

When does this लोप take place? Where the sense of च or अह is connoted by the sentence, but these words are not directly employed, there is then the elision of च and अह. There the force of च is that of aggregation (समुच्चय), and of अह is that of 'only' (केवल) The च is elided when the agent is the same; and अह is elided when the agents are several.

Thus where च is elided:—देव एव ग्रामं गच्छतु, देव एवारण्यं गच्छतु ग्रामं चारण्यं च गच्छतु ॥

So where अह is elided : as—देव एव ग्रामं गच्छतु, राम एव अरण्यं गच्छतु = ग्रामं केवलं, अरण्यं केवलं गच्छतु इति अर्थः ॥

Why do we say अवधारणं 'when limitation is meant'? See देव क्वेव भोक्ष्यसे। The word एव here has the sense of 'never' 'an impossibility.' The first sentence means न क्वचिद् भोक्ष्यसे। क्व+एव=क्वेव by पररूप (VI. 1. 94. Vârt).

३९७० । चादिलोपे विभाषा । ८ । १ । ६३ ॥

चवाहाहैवानां लोपे प्रथमा तिङ्विभक्तिर्नानुदात्ता । चलोपे। 'इन्द्र वाजेषु नोऽव'। शुक्रा व्रीहयो भवन्ति। श्वेता गा आज्याय दुहन्ति। वालोपे। व्रीहिभिर्यजेत। यवैर्यजेत ॥

3970. When च, (वा, ह, अह and एव) are elided, the first verb optionally retains its accent.

Thus with च लोपः—इन्द्र वाजेषु नोऽव। शुक्रा व्रीहयो भवन्ति or भवन्ति, श्वेता गा आज्याय दुहन्ति। Here भवन्ति optionally may either lose or retain its accent. So also when वा is elided, as :—व्रीहिभि र्यजेत or यजेत, यवै र्यजेत। So also with the remaining.

३९७१ । वैवावेति च च्छन्दसि । ८ । १ । ६४ ॥

'अहर्वै देवानामासीत्'। 'अयं वाव हस्त आसीत्' ॥

3971. Also in connection with 'vai' and 'vâva' may optionally, in the Chhandas, the first verb retain its accent.

Thus अहर्वै देवानाम् आसीत् (or आसीत्), अयं वाव हस्त आसीत् (or आसीत्) ॥

वै has the force of स्फुट and क्षमा, and वाव that of प्रसिद्ध and स्फुट ।

३९७२ । एकान्याभ्यां समर्थाभ्याम् । ८ । १ । ६५ ॥

आभ्यां युक्ता प्रथमा तिङ्विभक्तिर्नानुदात्ता छन्दसि। 'प्रजामेकां जिन्वति'। 'प्रजामेकां रक्षति'। 'तयोरन्यः पिप्पलं स्वाद्वत्ति'। 'समर्थाभ्याम्' किम्। एको देवानुपातिष्ठत्। एक इति संख्या परं नान्यार्थम् ॥

3972. Also in connection with *eka* and *anya*, optionally in the Chhandas, the first verb retains its accent, when these words have the same meaning ('the one—the other').

Thus प्रजामेकां जिन्वति (or जिन्वति), ऊर्जमेकांरक्षति। तयोरन्यः पिप्पलं स्वाद्वत्ति (or अत्ति), अनश्नन्नन्यो अभिचाकशीति (Rig Veda I. 164. 20, Mundaka Upanishad III. 1).

Why do we say समर्थाभ्यां 'having the same meaning'? See एको देवानुपातिष्ठत्. Here एक is a Numeral and has not the sense of अन्य 'the one another.' The word समर्थ is used, in fact, to restrict the meaning of एक, for it has various meanings : while there is no ambiguity about the word अन्य। एकोऽन्यार्थे प्रधाने च प्रथमे केवले तथा। साधारणे समानेऽल्पे संख्यायां च प्रयुज्यते ॥

३९७३ । यद्वृत्तान्नित्यम् । ८ । १ । ६६ ॥

यत्र पदे यच्छब्दस्ततः परं तिङन्तं नानुदात्तम् । यो भुङ्क्ते । यदद्र्यङ् वायुर्वाति । अत्र 'व्यवहिते कार्यमिष्यते' ॥

3973. In connection with *yad* in all its forms, the verb retains its accent always.

The anuvṛitti of प्रथमा and छन्दसि ceases. The prohibition of nighâta, which commenced with न लुट् (VIII. 1. 29) is present here also. In what ever sentence the word यद् occurs, that is called यद्वृत्तं । The word वृत्तं denotes here the form of यद् in all its declensions with case affixes. See also the explanation of किंवृत्तं in VIII. 1. 48.

Thus यो भुङ्क्ते, यत् कामास्ते जुहुमः (Rig Veda X. 121. 10) यदद्र्यङ् वायुर्वाति (T. S. V. 5. 1. 1.) यद् वायुः पवते । For the form यदद्र्यङ् see VI. 3. 92.

Ishti:—Though the sûtra is in the Ablative (यद्वृत्तात्) and therefore requires that the verb should *immediately* follow it, yet in यदद्र्यङ् वायु र्वाति, the intervention of वायुः does not prevent the operation of this rule, according to the opinion of Pâtanjali.

३९७४ । पूजनात्पूजितमनुदात्तं काष्ठादिभ्यः । ८ । १ । ६७ ॥

पूजनेभ्यः काष्ठादिभ्यः पूजितवचनमनुदात्तम् । काष्ठाध्यापकः ॥

'+ मलोपश्च वक्तव्यः +' । दारुणाध्यापकः । समासान्तोदात्तत्वापवादः । 'एतत्समास इष्यते नेह । दारुणमध्यापक इति वृत्तिमतम् । पूजनादित्येव पूजितग्रहणे सिद्धे पूजितग्रहणमनन्तरपूजितलाभार्थम् । एतदेव ज्ञापकमत्रप्रकरणे पञ्चमीनिर्देशेऽपि नानन्तर्यमाश्रीयत इति ॥

3974. After a word denoting praise belonging to 'kâsṭhâdi' class, the word whose praise is denoted, becomes anudâtta.

This refers to compounds, the first members of which are praise-denoting words. The word काष्ठादिभ्यः, is added to the sûtra from a Vârtika.

Thus काष्ठाध्यापकः, काष्ठाभिरूपकः, दारुणाध्यापकः, दारुणाभिरूपकः ॥

अमातापुत्र । अमातापुत्राध्यापकः । अमातापुत्राभिरूपकः । अयुताध्यापकः । अयुताभिरूपकः । अद्भुत । अद्भुताध्यापकः । अनुक्त । अनुक्ताध्यापकः । भृश । भृशाध्यापकः । घोर । घोराध्यापकः । सुखः । सुखाध्यापकः । परम । परमाध्यापकः । सु । स्वध्यापकः । अति । अत्यध्यापकः । द्यौः । द्यौरध्यापकः । द्यौरभिरूपकः । स्वध्यापकः । अपुत्र । अपुत्राध्यापकः । कल्याण । कल्याणाध्यापकः ॥

Vârt:—The final म् should be elided in forming these words. The word दारुणं is an adverb, and therefore in the accusative case, like ग्रामं गतः । In such a case, there can be no compounding: hence the elision of म् is taught. This becoming of अनुदात्त takes place in the compound, and after composition. In fact it is an exception to the general rule by which a compound is *finally* acute (VI. 1. 223). But there is no elision in दारुणमध्यापकः &c. and there is no loss of accent also of the second word. By the Vârtika 'मलोपश्च', this further fact is also denoted, where the case-affix is not employed and so the म् is not heard, there the second member becomes anudâtta. When there no compounding, there is no elision of म् as दारुणमधीते, दारुणमध्यापकः ॥

Though the word पूजनं would have implied its correlative term पूजित, the specific mention of पूजित in the aphorism indicates that the word denoting पूजित should follow *immediately* after the word denoting पूजन । In fact, this peculiar construction of the sûtra, is a jñâpaka of the existence of the following rule:—इह प्रकरणे पञ्चमी निर्देशेऽपि नानन्तर्यमाश्रीयते "In this subdivision or context, though a word may be exhibited in the Ablative case, it does not follow that there should be consecutiveness between the Ablative and the word indicated by it." This has been illustrated in the previous rule of यद्वृत्तान् नित्यम्, in explaining forms like यद्वयङ् वायुर्वाति &c.

Though the anuvritti of anudâtta was current, the express employment of this term in the sûtra indicates that the *prohibition* (of anudâtta) which also was current, now ceases.

The words काष्ठ, &c. are all synonyms of श्रद्भुत, meaning *wonderful, prodigious :* and are words denoting *praise.*

1 काष्ठ, 2 दारुणं, 3 श्रमातांपुत्र, 4 वेश, 5 श्रनांज्ञात, 6 श्रनुज्ञात, 7 श्रपुत्र, 8 श्रयुत, 9 श्रद्भुत, 10 श्रनुक्त, 11 भृश, 12 घोर, 13 सुख्य, 14 परम, 15 सु, 16 श्रति, 17 कल्याण

३९७५ । सगतिरपि तिङ् । ८ । १ । ६८ ॥

पूजनेभ्यः काष्ठादिभ्यस्तिङन्तं पूजितमनुदात्तम् । यत्कांष्ठं प्रपचति । 'तिङ्ङतिङः' (३९३५) इति निघातस्य 'निपातैर्यत्–' (३९३७) इति निषेधे प्राप्ते विधिरयम् । सगतिग्रहणाच्च गतिरपि निहन्यते । 'गतिग्रहण उपसर्गग्रहणमिष्यते' । नेह । यत्काष्ठां शुक्लीकरोति ॥

3975. (After such words denoting praise) the finite verb (which is praised) becomes anudâtta, even along with the gati, if any, that may precede it.

Whether a finite verb is compounded with a gati or stands single, both the compound and the simple verb lose their accent, when it is qualified by the adverbs काष्ठं &c. Thus यत् काष्ठं प॒च॒ति, यत् काष्ठं ' प्र॒प॒च॒ति ॥ By VIII. 1. 28, S. 3935 the finite verb would have lost its accent after the word काष्ठं, but this loss was prohibited by VIII. 1. 30 S. 3937 in connection with यत् ; the present sutra re-ordains the loss, by setting aside the prohibition of VIII. 1. 30. S. 3937.

The word सगति 'along with its Gati', indicates that the Gati even loses its accent. *Ishṭi* :—The word Gati here is restricted to Upasargas. Therefore not here यत् काष्ठां शुक्ली करोति ॥

३९७६ । कुत्सने च सुप्यगोत्रादौ । ८ । १ । ६९ ॥

कुत्सने च सुबन्ते परे सगतिरगतिरपि तिङनुदात्तः । पचति पूति । प्रपचति पूति । पचति मिथ्या । 'कुत्सने' किम् । प्रपचति शोभनम् । 'सुपि' किम् । पचति क्लिश्नाति । 'अगोत्रादौ' किम् । पचति गोत्रम् ॥

'+ क्रियाकुत्सन इति वाच्यम् +' । कर्तुः कुत्सने मा भूत् । पचतिपूतिर्देवदत्तः ॥

'+ पूतिश्चानुबन्ध इति वाच्यम् +' तेनायं चकारानुबन्धत्वादन्तोदात्तः ॥

'+ वा बहुर्थमनुदात्तमिति वाच्यम् +' पचन्तिपूति ॥

3976. A finite verb, along with its preceding Gati, if any, becomes anudâtta, when a Noun, denoting the fault of the action follows, with the exception of 'gotra' &c.

The anuvṛitti of यदात् (VIII. 1. 17) ceases. But the anuvṛitti of the last sûtra is current. Thus प॒चति॒ पूति, प्र॒प॒चति॒ पूति, प॒चति॒ मिथ्या, प्र॒प॒चति॒ मिथ्या ॥

Why do we say कुत्सने 'denoting the fault of the action'? See प॑चति शोभनम् ॥

Why do we say सुपि 'a noun'? Observe प॑चति क्लिश्नाति ॥

Why do we say with the exception of गोत्र &c. See प॑चति गोत्रम्, प॑चति ब्रुवम्, पचति प्रवचनम् ॥

Vârt :—It should be mentioned that the 'fault' mentioned in the sûtra, must be the fault relating to the mode of doing the action, denoted by the verb. The rule will not apply, if the कुत्सन refers to the agent and not to the action. Thus प॑चति पूतिर्देवदत्तः ॥

Vârt :—It should be stated that पूति has an indicatory च । The effect of this is that the word पूति is finally acute, because of the indicatory च ॥

Vârt :—A finite verb in the plural number, loses its accent optionally: when it loses its accent, then पूति is end-acute. Thus प॒चन्ति॒ पूत॑यः, or पचन्ति पू॑तयः, प्र॒प॒चन्ति पूत॑यः or प्रपचन्ति पू॑तयः ॥

३९७७ । गतिर्गतौ । ८ । १ । ७० ॥

अनुदात्तः । अभ्युद्धरति । 'गतिः' किम् । दत्तः पचति । 'गतौ' किम् । 'आम॒न्द्रैरि॑न्द्र हरि॑भिर्याहि म॒यूर॑रोमभिः' ॥

3977. A Gati becomes unaccented, when followed by another Gati.

Thus अभ्यु॑द्धरति । Why do we say गतिः 'a Gati becomes &c'? Observe दे॑वदत्तः पचति । Here देवदत्त is a Prâtipadika and does not lose its accent. Why do we say 'when followed by a Gati'? Observe आ॑ मन्द्रैरिन्द्र हरिभिर्याहि मयूररोमभिः (Rig Veda III. 45. 1.) Here आ is a Gati to the verb याहि, the complete verb is आयाहि । But as आ is not followed by a Gati, but by a Prâtipadika मन्द्र, it retains its accent. Had the word गतौ not been used in the sûtra, this आ would have lost its accent, because the rule would have been too wide, without any restriction of what followed it.

३९७८ । तिङि चोदात्तवति । ८ । १ । ७१ ॥

गतिरनुदात्तः । यत्प्रपचति । तिङ्ग्रहणमुदात्तवतः परिमाणार्थम् । अन्यथा हि यत्क्रियायुक्ताः प्रादयस्तं प्रत्येव गतिस्तत्र धातावेवोदात्तवति स्यात् प्रत्यये न स्यात् । 'उदात्तवति' किम् । प्रपचति ॥

इति तिङन्तस्वराः ।

3978. A Gati becomes anudâtta, when followed by an accented finite verb.

The word गतिः is understood here. Thus यत् प्र॒प॑चति ॥

Why have we used the word तिङि in the sûtra? In order to restrict the scope of the word उदात्तवति; so that a Gati would not become accentless before udâtta root only, but before udâtta conjugated *verbs*. The employment of the term तिङि is necessary, in order to indicate that the *verb* must be a *finite* verb and not a *verbal root*. So that though a verbal root be udâtta, yet if in its conjugated form (तिङन्त) it is not udâtta, the गति will not lose its accent. Thus in यत् प्र करोति, the root कृ is anudâtta, but the तिङन्त form करोति is udâtta, hence the rule will apply here: which would not have been the case had उदात्तवति not been qualified by तिङि। For the maxim is यत्क्रियायुक्ताः प्रादयस् तेषां तं प्रति गत्युपसर्गसंज्ञे भवतः। Therefore in a तिङन्त, the designation of गति is with regard to धातु or verbal root.

Why have we used the word उदात्तवति? Observe प्र॑ पचति। Here the verb loses its accent by VIII. 1. 28 hence the Gati retains its accent.

Here end the Accents of Verbs.

A VAIDIC ILLUSTRATION ON ACCENTS.

अथ वैदिकवाक्येषु स्वरसंचारप्रकारः कथ्यते–'अग्निमीळे' इति प्रथमर्क्। तत्राग्निशब्दोऽव्युत्पत्तिपक्षे 'फिष्–' इत्यन्तोदात्त इति माधवः। वस्तुतस्तु घृतादित्वात्। व्युत्पत्तौ तु नित्प्रत्ययस्वरेण। अस्मुप्त्वादनुदात्तः। 'अमि पूर्वः' (१८४) इत्येकादेशस्तु 'एकादेश उदात्तेन–' (३६५८) इत्युदात्तः। ईळे। 'तिङ्ङतिङः' (३९३५) इति निघातः। संहितायां तु 'उदात्तादनुदात्तस्य–' (३६६०) इतीकारः स्वरितः। 'स्वरितात्संहितायाम्–' (३६६८) इति 'ळे' इत्यस्य प्रचयापरपर्याया एकश्रुतिः। पुरःशब्दोऽन्तोदात्तः 'पूर्वाधरावराणाम्–' इत्यसिप्रत्ययस्वरात्। हितशब्दोऽपि धाञो निष्ठायां 'दधातेर्हिः' (३०७६) इति ह्यादेशे प्रत्ययस्वरेणान्तोदात्तः। 'पुरोऽव्ययम्' (७६८) इति गतिसंज्ञायां 'कुगति–' (७६१) इति समासे समासान्तोदात्ते 'तत्पुरुषे तुल्यार्थ–' (३७३६) इत्यव्ययपूर्वपदप्रकृतिस्वरे 'गतिकारकोपपदात्कृत्' (३८७३) इति कृदुत्तरपदप्रकृतिस्वरे थाथादिस्वरे च पूर्वपूर्वोपमर्देन प्राप्ते 'गतिरनन्तरः' (३७८३) इति पूर्वपदप्रकृतिस्वरः। पुरःशब्दोकारस्य संहितायां प्रचये प्राप्ते 'उदात्तस्वरितपरस्य सन्नतरः' इत्यनुदात्ततरः। यज्ञस्य। नङः प्रत्ययस्वरः। विभक्तेः सुप्त्वादनुदात्तत्वे स्वरितत्वम्। देवम्। पचाद्यच्। फिट्स्वरेण प्रत्ययस्वरेण चित्स्वरेण वान्तोदात्तः। ऋत्विक्छब्दः कृदुत्तरपदप्रकृतिस्वरेणान्तोदात्तः। होतृशब्दस्तृन्प्रत्ययान्तो नित्स्वरेणाद्युदात्तः। रत्नशब्दो नन्विषयस्येत्याद्युदात्तः। रत्नानि दधातीति रत्नधाः। समासस्वरेण कृदुत्तरपदप्रकृतिस्वरेण वान्तोदात्तः। तमपः पित्त्वादनुदात्तत्वे स्वरितप्रचयावित्यादि यथाशास्त्रमुन्नेयम्॥

इति स्वरप्रकरणम्।

इत्थं वैदिकशब्दानां दिङ्मात्रमिह दर्शितम्।
तदस्तु प्रीतये श्रीमद्भवानीविश्वनाथयोः॥

Now we shall give an illustration from the Vedas, to show the application of the rules of accent. Thus the first verse of the Rig Veda is the following:—

अग्निमीळे पुरोहितं यज्ञस्य देवमृत्विजं। होतारं रत्नधातमम्॥

1. Agni:—Here if अग्नि be considered a word without any derivation then it is finally acute by Phit I. 1. This is the opinion of Mâdhava (Sâyanâchârya). But as a matter of fact, अग्नि is end-acute because it is enumerated in the Ghritâdi list of words (see Phiṭ I. 21.)

But if अग्नि be considered a derivative word, formed by the Unâdi affix नि then it is end-acute, (III. 1. 3. S. 3708), because of the affix.

The accusative affix अम् in अग्निम् is anudâtta because it is a case-affix (III. 1. 4. S. 3709). अग्नि + अम् = अग्निम् (इ + अ = इ S. 194) The ekâdeśa इ becomes udâtta by VIII. 2. 5. S. 3658. Thus अग्निम् is end-acute even in its declined form.

2. ईळे: is a verb. It loses its accent by S. 3935 (VIII. 1. 28) as it is preceded by a noun *agnim*. When अग्निम् + ईळे are combined in the Sanhita text into अग्निमिळे, then the anudâtta इ becomes svarita by S. 3660 (VIII. 4. 66) while the anudâtta of ळे becomes ekasruti by S. 3668 (1. 2. 39). Thus we have अग्निमीळे ॥

3. पुरोहितम्:—The word पुरः is end-acute because it is formed by the affix असि (V. 3. 39. S. 1975). The word हित also is end-acute, because it is the Nishthâ of धा, the हि is substituted for धा by S. 3076 (VII. 4. 42) the affix त makes it end-acute. Then पुरः + हितः । Here पुरः is a gati by S. 768 (I. 4. 67) and it is compounded with हित by S. 761 (II. 2. 18). Then the compound पुरोहित would be end-acute by S. 3734 ; but S. 3736 (VI. 2. 2) requires the Indeclinable first member पुरः to retain its accent ; but S. 3873 (VI. 2. 139) requires the second member हित which is a krit-formed word to retain its accent also VI. 2. 144 ; but this last accent is set aside by the final rule S. 3783 (VI. 2. 49) and thus the first member retains its recent, as पुरोहित ॥

It becomes anudâttatara by I. 2. 40. S. 3669.

4. यज्ञस्य:-The word यज्ञ is derived from यज् with नङ् affix. Therefore it is end-acute. The affix स्य being a case-affix (III. 1. 4. S. 3709) is anudâtta and it becomes svarita यज्ञस्य ॥

5. देवं:—It is formed from the root दिव् with the affix अच् । It is end acute, either by Phit I. 1 ; or by the affix-accent (III. 1. 3. S. 3708) or by the चित् accent (VI. 1. 163 S. 3710) of अच् । In any view, it is end-acute.

6. ऋत्विजं:—The word ऋत्विज् is end-acute, because of the krit-accent (VI. 2. 139, S. 3873).

7. होतारम्:—The word होतृ is formed by adding the affix तृन् to हु । It has accent on ओ, because the affix has an indicatory न् (VI. 1. 197 S. 3686).

8. रत्नधातमम् । It means रत्नानि दधाति । It is finally acute, either by samâsa accent (VI. 1. 223. S. 3734) or krit-accent of the second member being retained by VI. 2. 139 S. 3873.

The affix तमप् being पित् is anudâtta, the अ of त becomes svarita, and that of म becomes ekaśruti. रत्न is first acute being Neuter (Phit II. 3.)

Here ends the Section on Accents.

Thus here has been shown a brief outline only of Vaidic words and the rules applicable to them. Let it find favor with the Lord of the Universe and Bhavâni.

अथ लिङ्गानुशासनम् ॥

—o—

ON RULES OF GENDERS

CHAPTER I.

FEMININE GENDER.

१ । 'लिङ्गम्' ॥

1. The Gender.

Note:—There are three Genders, *viz*:—Masculine, Feminine and Neuter.

२ । 'स्त्री' । अधिकारसूत्रे एते ॥

2. The Feminine (Gender).

These two are Adhikâra Sûtras. The jurisdiction of the word "gender' extends up to the end; but of "feminine" up to the end of this chapter only

३ । 'ऋकारान्ता मातृदुहितृस्वसृयातृननान्दरः' । ऋकारान्ता एते पञ्चैव स्त्रीलिङ्गाः । स्वस्रादिपञ्चकस्यैव ङीब्निषेधेन कर्त्री त्यादेर्ङीपाईकारान्तत्वात् । तिसृचतसोस्तु स्त्रियामादेशतया विधानेऽपि प्रकृत्योस्त्रिचतुरोर्ऋदन्तत्वाभावात् ॥

3. मातृ 'mother,' दुहितृ 'daughter,' स्वसृ 'sister,' यातृ 'a husband's brother's wife,' ननान्दृ 'a husband's sister,' these five nouns ending in ऋ are feminines.

These five words are the only examples of feminines that naturally end in ऋ। By IV. 1. 10, S. 308, the seven words belonging to the svasrâdi class do not form their feminine by ङीप् or टाप् like the nouns kartṛi &c. which end in long ई in the feminine. Hence they are feminine in their original form. A reference to the Svasrâdi list will show that it includes all these five words, in addition to तिसृ and चतसृ । As these two are secondary derivatives, from त्रि and चतुर् they are not originally feminine but have become so by derivation. The primitive words त्रि and चतुर् do not end in ऋ; and hence तिसृ and चतसृ are not shown in this sûtra.

४ । 'अन्यूप्रत्ययान्तो धातुः' । अनिप्रत्ययान्त ऊप्रत्ययान्तश्च धातुः स्त्रियां स्यात् । अवनिः, चमूः । 'प्रत्ययग्रहणम्' किम् । देवयतेः क्विप् । द्यूः । विशेष्यलिङ्गः ॥

4. Verbal nouns formed with the affixes अनि and ऊ are feminines.

Thus अवनि: 'the earth' (Uṇ. II. 102). चमूः 'an army.' (Uṇ. I. 80). Why do we say "formed with affixes"? Observe द्यूः which is formed by adding the affix क्विप् to the root दिव् (to shine). The word द्यूः is feminine and of special gender.

५ । 'अशनिभरण्यरणयः । पुंसि च' । इयमयं वाशनिः ॥

5. The nouns अशनि, 'Indra's thunderbolt,' भरणि 'Bharaṇi' अरणि 'a piece of wood used for kindling sacred fire,' are also masculines (in addition to being feminines).

Thus इयं or अयं अशनिः । This sûtra is an exception to the preceding. These three words though formed by the affix अनि (Uṇ. II. 102) are yet both masculine and feminine.

६ । 'मिन्यन्तः' । मिप्रत्ययान्तो निप्रत्ययान्तश्च धातुः स्त्रियां स्यात् । भूमिः । ग्लानिः ॥

6. Verbal nouns formed with the affixes मि and नि are feminines.

Thus भूमिः 'the earth' (Uṇ. IV. 45); ग्लानिः 'exhaustion'. (Uṇ. IV. 51).

७ । 'वह्निवृष्ण्यग्नयः पुंसि' । पूर्वस्यापवादः ॥

7. But the nouns वह्नि 'fire' (Uṇ. IV. 51); वृष्णि 'a cloud,' (Uṇ. IV. 49) and अग्नि 'fire' (Uṇ. IV. 50) are masculines. This is an exception to the last.

८ । 'श्रोणियोन्यूर्मयः पुंसि च' । इयमयं वा श्रोणिः ॥

8. The nouns श्रोणि 'the hip,' (Uṇ. IV. 5) योनि 'the source'. (Uṇ. IV. 51) and ऊर्मि 'the wave' (Uṇ. IV. 44) are also masculines (in addition to being feminines).

Thus इयं or अयं श्रोणिः ॥

९ । 'क्तिन्नन्तः' । स्पष्टम् । कृतिरित्यादि ॥

9. Nouns formed with the affix क्तिन् are feminines.

Thus कृतिः &c.

१० । 'ईकारान्तश्च' । ईप्रत्ययान्तः स्त्री स्यात् । लक्ष्मीः ॥

10. Nouns ending in long ई affix are feminines.

Thus लक्ष्मीः ॥

The ई here must be an affix: as in लक्ष्मी the affix ई is added by Uṇ. III. 160.

११ । 'ऊङाबन्तश्च' । कुरूः । विद्या ॥

11. Nouns formed with the affixes ऊङ्, (IV. 1. 66) and आप् are feminines.

Thus कुरूः (See IV. 1. 66. S. 521) and विद्या.* The आप् includes all the three affixes टाप्, चाप् and डाप् ॥

१२ । 'यवन्तमेकाक्षरम्' । श्रीः । भूः । 'एकाक्षरम्' किम् । पृथुश्रीः ॥

12. Monosyllabic nouns formed with the affixes ई and ऊ are feminines.

Thus श्रीः (Uṇ. II. 57) भूः ॥

Why do we say 'monosyllabic nouns'? Observe पृथुश्रीः "Prithu's luck" which is masculine.

१३ । 'विंशत्यादिरानवतेः' । इयं विंशतिः । त्रिंशत् । चत्वारिंशत् । पञ्चाशत् । षष्टिः । सप्ततिः । अशीतिः । नवति ॥

13. Numerals from "twenty" to "ninety" are feminines.

Thus इयं विंशतिः 'twenty'. So also त्रिंशत् 'thirty'. चत्वारिंशत् 'forty,' पञ्चाशत् 'fifty'; षष्टिः 'sixty', सप्ततिः 'seventy,' अशीतिः 'eighty', नवतिः 'ninety.'

The list of the words "विंशति and the rest" is given in Pâṇini's Sûtra V. 1. 59. S. 1725.

१४ । 'दुन्दुभिरक्षेषु' । इयं दुन्दुभिः । 'अक्षेषु' किम् । अयं दुन्दुभिर्वाद्यविशेषोऽसुरो वेत्यर्थः ।

14. The word दुन्दुभि when used in the sense of an axle pole is feminine.

Thus इयं दुन्दुभिः ॥

Why do we say in the sense of अक्ष 'or axle'? Observe अयं दुन्दुभिः । It is masculine when it means a musical instrument or an Asura.

१५ । 'नाभिरक्षत्रिये' । इयं नाभिः ॥

15. The word नाभि 'navel' is feminine when it does not mean a Kshatriya.

Thus इयं नाभिः 'navel'.

१६। 'उभावप्यन्यत्र पुंसि'। दुन्दुभिर्नाभिश्चोक्तविषयादन्यत्र पुंसि स्तः। नाभिः क्षत्रियः। कथं तर्हि 'समुल्लसत्पङ्कजपत्रकोमलैरुपाहितश्रीण्युपनीविनाभिभिः' इति भारविः। उच्यते। दृढं भक्तिरित्यादाविव कोमलैरिति सामान्ये नपुंसकं बोध्यम्। अस्तु तस्तु 'लिङ्गमशिष्यं लोकाश्रयत्वा-ल्लिङ्गस्य' इति भाष्यात्पुंस्त्वमपीह साधु। अत एव 'नाभिर्मुख्यनृपे चक्रमध्यक्षत्रिययोः पुमान्'। द्वयोः प्राणिप्रतीके स्यात्स्त्रियां कस्तूरिकामदे' इति मेदनी। रभसोऽप्याह- 'मुख्यराट्क्षत्रिय नाभिः पुंसि प्राण्यङ्गके द्वयोः। चक्रमध्ये प्रधाने च स्त्रियां कस्तूरिकामदे' इति। एवमेवंविधेऽन्यत्रापि बोध्यम्॥

16. Otherwise दुन्दुभि and नाभि are masculines.

Thus नाभिः क्षत्रियः 'Nâbhi—a Kshatriya.'

If the word नाभिः be feminino in all senses other than that of a Kshatriya, how do you justify its use as a masculine in the following lines of Bhâravi:—
"समुल्लसत् पङ्कजपत्रकोमलै रुपाहितश्रीण्युपनीवि नाभिभिः"? ॥

To this we say, "The words कोमलैः &c here are really Neuter, denoting indiscrete gender, or having no reference to any gender, just like दृढभक्तिः" ॥ Or we may say, as a matter of fact the gender of words need not be taught, for it is a well-known maxim of grammar as enunciated by Patanjali that "the gender depends on the usage of the people: and so need not be taught:" and there fore the masculine use of the word is also correct. Thus we find in the Medini Kosha:—"Nâbhi is masculine when meaning a paramount sovereign, or the nave of a wheel, or a Kshatriya. But when meaning 'navel' of a living being, it is of both genders. And it is feminine only when meaning 'musk.'

Rasabha also says to the same effect:—

'The word nâbhi is masculine when it means a paramount lord, or a Kshatriya: it is both masculine and feminine when meaning the navel of a living being, the nave of a wheel, and a leader or chieftain. It is purely feminine when meaning "musk".

Thus it should be understood in other cases also.

१७। 'तलन्तः'। अयं स्त्रियां स्यात्। शुक्लस्य भावः। शुक्लता। ब्राह्मणस्य कर्म ब्राह्मणता ग्रामस्य समूहो ग्रामता। देव एव देवता॥

17. Nouns formed with the affix तल् (V. 1. 119 S. 1781), are feminines.

Thus शुक्लता (whiteness), ब्राह्मणता (Brahmanical), ग्रामता (rural) देवता which has the same meaning as देव ॥

१८। 'भूमिविद्युत्सरिल्लतावनिताभिधानानि'। भूमिर्भूः। विद्युत्सौदामनी। सरिन्निम्नगा। लता वल्ली। वनिता योषित्॥

18. Nouns synonymous of भूमि (the Earth), विद्युत् (lightening), सरित् (a stream or rivulet), लता (a creeper), वनिता (wife) also are feminines.

Thus भूमिर्भूः; विद्युत् सौदामनी; सरित् निम्नगा; लतावल्ली; वनिता योषित्.

१९। 'यादो नपुंसकम्'। यादःशब्दः सरिद्वाचकोऽपि क्लीबं स्यात्॥

19. यादस् although meaning 'a stream,' is Neuter and not feminine.

२० । 'भासुस्रग्दिगुष्णिगुपानहः' । एते स्त्रियां स्युः । इयं भाः इत्यादि ॥

20. The nouns भास्, स्रुक्, दिक्, उष्णिह् and उपानह् are feminines.

Thus इयं भाः &c.

२१ । 'स्थूणोर्णे नपुंसके च' । एते स्त्रियां क्लीबे च स्तः । स्थूणा–स्थूणम् । ऊर्णा–ऊर्णम्, तत्र स्थूणा काष्ठमयी द्विकर्णिका । ऊर्णा तु मेषादिलोमम् ॥

21. The nouns स्थूणा (a post or pillar) and ऊर्णा (wool) are Neuter (in addition to being feminine).

Here sthûṇâ means a wooden forked stave or pillar and ûrṇâ means the wool of sheep &c.

२२ । 'गृहशशाभ्यां क्लीबे' । नियमार्थमिदम् । गृहशशपूर्वे स्थूणोर्णे यथासंख्यं नपुंसके स्तः । गृहस्थूणम् । 'शशोर्णं शशलोमनि' इत्यमरः ॥

22. The words स्थूणा and ऊर्णा after गृह and शश are Neuter.

Thus गृहस्थूणम् (a pillar of a house) and शशोर्णं (the hare's hair). This is a niyamà or a restrictive rule. See Amarakosha II. 9. 107.

२३ । 'प्रावृड्विप्रुट्तृड्विट्त्विषः' । एते स्त्रियां स्युः ॥

23. The words प्रावृट्, 'the rainy season', विप्रुट् 'a drop of liquid,' तृट् 'thirst,' विट् 'fœces, excrement,' and त्विट् 'light' are feminine.

२४ । 'दर्विविदिवेदिखनिशान्यश्रिवेश्मिकृष्योषधिकट्यङ्गुलयः' । एते स्त्रियां स्युः । पक्षे ङीप् । दर्वी–दर्विरित्यादि ॥

24. The words दर्वि, 'a ladle,' विदि, 'knowledge' (?) वेदि, 'altar,' खनि 'a mine,' शानि 'colocynth'; अश्रि 'a corner,' वेश्मि 'an entrance' (?) कृषि 'agriculture,' ओषधि 'herb,' कटि 'loin' and अङ्गुलि 'finger' are feminine.

These words take optionally the affix ङीप्.

Thus दर्वी or दर्विः &c.

२५ । 'तिथिनाडिरुचिवीचिनालिधूलिकिकिकेलिच्छविरात्र्यादयः' । एते प्राग्वत् । इयं तिथिरित्यादि । अमरस्त्वाह–'तिथयो द्वयोः' इति । तथा च भारविः–'तस्य भुवि बहुतिथास्तिथयः' इति । स्त्रीत्वे हि बहुतिथ्य इति स्यात् । श्रीहर्षश्च–'निखिलां निशि पौर्णिमा तिथीन्' इति ॥

25. The words तिथि 'the day of the moon,' नाडि 'a vessel or pulse,' रुचि 'taste,' वीचि 'a wave,' नालि 'a drain,' धूलि 'dust,' किकि 'the cocoanut tree,' केलि 'play,' छवि 'hue, color,' रात्रि 'night' are feminines.

As इयं तिथिः &c.

But the author of Amarakosha says 'the word तिथि is both masculine and feminine.' (Amar. I. 4. 1).

So also Bhâravi in the following line: 'तस्य भुवि बहुतिथास्तिथयः । Had it been feminine the word would have been बहुतिथ्यः in the Plural and not बहुतिथाः ॥

So also Śri Harsha in the following line: निखिलान् निशि पौर्णिमा तिथीन् uses the word tithi as a masculine.

२६। 'शष्कुलिराजिकुट्यशनिवर्तिभ्रुकुटित्रुटिवलिपङ्क्तयः'। एतेऽपि स्त्रियां स्युः। इयं शष्कुलिः॥

26. The words शष्कुलि 'auditory passage,' राजि 'a streak,' कुटि 'a cottage,' अशनि 'lightening,' वर्ति 'a pad,' भ्रुकुटि 'frown,' त्रुटि 'cutting,' वलि 'sacrificial offering,' पङ्क्ति 'a line' are feminines.

Thus इयं शष्कुलिः॥

२७। 'प्रतिपदापद्विपत्संपच्छरत्संसत्परिषदुषःसंवित्क्षुत्पुन्मुत्समिधः'। इयं प्रतिपदित्यादि। उषा उच्छन्ती। उषाः प्रातरधिष्ठात्री देवता॥

27. The words प्रतिपद् 'entrance,' आपद् 'calamity' विपद् 'misfortune,' सम्पद् 'wealth,' शरद् 'the autumn' (Un I. 129). संसद् 'an assembly,' परिषद् 'a meeting,' उषस् 'Dawn,' संवित् 'knowledge,' क्षुत् 'grinding; crushing,' पुत् 'a particular division of Hell,' मुत् 'joy; delight,' समिध् 'wood; fuel,' are feminines.

Thus इयं प्रतिपद्॥

उषा उच्छन्ती। The Ushâ is the presiding deity of the dawn.

२८। 'आशीर्धूः पूर्गीर्द्वारः'। इयमाशीरित्यादि॥

28. The words आशीस् 'blessing,' धूर् 'a yoke,' पुर् 'a city,' गीर् 'speech' and द्वार् 'door' are feminines.

As इयं आशीः॥

२९। 'अप्सुमनस्समासिकतावर्षाणां बहुत्वं च'। अबादीनां पञ्चानां स्त्रीत्वं स्याद्बहुत्वं च आप इमाः। 'स्त्रियः सुमनसः पुष्पम्'। 'सुमना मालती जातिः'। देववाची तु पुंस्येव। 'सुपर्वाणः सुमनसः'। बहुत्वं प्रायिकम्। 'एका च सिकता तैलदानेऽसमर्था' इत्यर्थवत्सूत्रे भाष्यप्रयोगात्। 'समांसमां विजायते' (१८१३) इत्यत्र 'समायां समायाम्' इति भाष्याच्च। 'विभाषा घाधेट्–(२३७६) इति सूत्रे 'अघासातां सुमनसौ' इति वृत्तव्याख्यायां हरदत्तोऽप्येवम्॥

29. The words अप् 'water,' सुमनस् 'a flower' (jasmine), समा 'a year' सिकता 'sand, gravel,' and वर्षा 'rain,' are feminines and used in the plural number only.

Thus आपः इमाः। The word sumanas in the feminine means 'a kind of flower'—namely, the flower called mâlati or jâti—jasmine, as स्त्रियः सुमनस पुष्पं। Amarakosha II. 4. 17. When it means a Deva or a divine being, it is masculine only. As सुपर्वाणः सुमनसः। See Amarakosha I. 1. 7. Here the present sûtra is debarred by sûtra 9 of the next chapter, with regards to words denoting Devas.

These words are generally found, in usage, in the plural number: but sometimes they are used in the singular also; as एका च सिकता तैलदाने असमर्था 'one grain of sand is incapable of producing oil.' This example is given by Patanjali in his Mahâbhâshya under sûtra I. 2. 45.

Similarly समां समां विजायत (V. 2. 12. S. 1813) has been explained in the Bhâshya by समायां समायां in the singular number.

29

Kâśikâ uses the word सुमनस् in the dual also, under sûtra II. 4. 78. in the example अघ्रासाताम् सुमनसौ देवदत्तेन। Haradatta in his Padamanjarî, on commenting on this justifies the use of the dual, by saying "according to Amarasinha sumanasaḥ in the plural is feminine. According to Pâṇiniya sûtra apsumanasa, &c., this word requires to be always plural. That plurality is not, however, universal : as we find the Mahâbhâshya using the word *sikatâ* in the singular."

(स्त्रियः सुमनसः पुष्पमित्यमरसिंहः। 'अप्सुमनः समासिकता वर्षाणां बहुत्वं चेति पाणिनीयं सूत्रं, तद् बहुत्वं प्रायिकं मन्यते 'एका च सिकता तैलदानेऽसमर्था' इति भाष्ये प्रयोगात् ॥)

३० । 'स्रक्त्वक्ज्योग्वाग्यवागूनौस्फिचः' । इयं स्रक्त्वक्ज्योक्वाक्यवागूः नौ स्फिक् ॥

30. The words स्रज् 'garland,' त्वक् 'skin,' ज्योक् 'long' (an Indeclinable I. 1. 37), वाच् 'speech,' यवागू 'barley gruel,' नौ 'boat' and स्फिच् 'hips' are feminines.

Thus इयं स्रक्, त्वक्, ज्योक्, वाक्, यवागूः, नौ and स्फिक् ॥

३१ । 'तृटिसीमासंबध्याः' । इयं तृटिः सीमा संबध्या ॥

31. The words तृटि, ? सीमा 'boundary' and सम्बध्या ? are feminines

Thus इयः तृटि, सीमा or संबध्या ॥

३२ । 'चुल्लिवेणिखार्यश्च' । स्पष्टम् ॥

32. The words चुल्लि 'a fire-place,' वेणि 'a braid of hair' (Un. IV. 48) खारि 'a measure of grain,' are feminines

३३ । 'ताराधाराज्योत्स्नादयश्च' । शलाका स्त्रियां नित्यम् । नित्यग्रहणमन्येषां क्वचिद्व्यभिचारं ज्ञापयति । इति स्त्र्यधिकारः ॥

33. The words तारा 'a star,' धारा 'a current,' ज्योत्स्ना 'light' &c. are feminines.

The word शलाका 'a small stick,' is ALWAYS feminine.

NOTE :—The force of the word 'always' is that the other words given above, may be of masculine or neuter gender also. In fact, the gender depends upon usage.

CHAPTER II.

THE MASCULINE GENDER.

१ 'पुमान्' । अधिकारोऽयम् ॥

1. The Masculine Gender.

This is an *adhikâra* Sûtra.

२ । 'घञबन्तः' । पाकः । त्यागः । करः । गरः । भावार्थे एवेदम् । नपुंसकत्वविशिष्टे भावे क्तल्युड्भ्यां स्त्रीत्वविशिष्टे तु क्तिन्नादिभिर्बाधेनपरिशेषात् । कमठिः तु घञाद्यन्तमपि विशेष्यलिङ्गम् । तथा च भाष्यम्– 'संबन्धमनुवर्तिष्यते' इति ॥

2. Nouns formed with the affixes घञ् and अप् are masculine.

Thus with घञ्;—पाकः 'cooking', त्यागः 'renunciation,' with अप्, we have करः 'hand,' गरः 'poison'.

The affix घञ् must have the force of भावे or condition for the purposes of this rule. In other words, the nouns so formed should be abstract nouns or nouns of action. This meaning of घञ् we infer from the analogy of the two rules, one relating to the Feminines and the other to the Neuters. Thus with regards to Neuters we have the rules भावे ल्युडन्तः । निष्ठा च ॥ "Nouns formed by the affix lyuṭ with the force of *bhâva*; and the Nisṭhâ affixes with the same force are Neuters." (Chap. III. 2 and 3). Similarly in the case of the feminines, we have the rules क्तिन्नन्तः &c. (Chapter I. 9) &c. where क्तिन् &c. are *bhâva* affixes. Analogically the घञ् here must also be a bhâva denoting affix. For the force of घञ् is generally that of भाव or Noun of action. See III. 3. 16—18. To form Neuter nouns of action we have *kta* and *lyuṭ* by III. 3. 114 and 115. To form feminine nouns of action we have *ktin*, *kyap*, &c. by III. 3. 95, 98. Therefore by elimination, to form the masculine nouns of action, to us is left the affix घञ् only. Hence we say 'the ghañ here has the force of bhâva.'

But when ghañ has the force of karma or of karaṇa &c., as it has by III 3. 116 and 117 &c., then the words so formed need not be masculine. They will have the gender of the word with which they are in construction. They will have their own specific gender. As we have in the Bhâshya, सम्बन्धमनुवर्तिष्यते । Here the word 'sambandha' though formed by ghañ is used in the Neuter gender: because the force of ghañ is here that of karma.

३ । 'घाजन्तश्च' । विस्तरः । गोचरः । चयः । जयः इत्यादि ॥

3. The nouns formed with the affixes घ and अच् are masculines.

Thus विस्तरः 'extension,' गोचरः 'pasturage,' चयः 'rampart; collection'. जय 'victory' &c.

४ । 'भयलिङ्गभगपदानि नपुंसके' । एतानि नपुंसके स्युः । भयम् । लिङ्गम् । भगम् । पदम् ॥

4. The nouns भय 'fear', लिङ्ग 'gender', भग 'the perinaeum of females', पद 'foot' are neuters.

Thus भयम्, लिङ्गम्, भगम्, पदम्.

५ । 'नङन्तः' । नङ् प्रत्ययान्तः पुंसि स्यात् । यज्ञः । यत्नः ॥

5. The nouns formed with the affix नङ् are masculines.

Thus यज्ञः 'sacrifice,' यत्नः 'effort'.

६ । 'याच्ञा स्त्रियाम्' । पूर्वस्यापवादः ।

6. The noun याच्ञा 'begging' is feminine.

This is an exception to the last aphorism.

७ । 'क्यन्तो घुः' । किप्रत्ययान्तो घुः पुंसि स्यात् । आधिः । निधिः । उदधिः । 'क्यन्तः' किम् । दानम् । 'घुः' किम् । जज्ञिर्बीजम् ॥

7. The nouns formed with the affix कि from roots belonging to the घु class are masculines.

The roots belonging to घु class are दा and धा. Thus आधिः 'agony', निधिः 'abode,' उदधिः 'water.' Why do we say "formed with the affix कि"? Observe दानम (which is Neuter).

Why do we say "roots belonging to the चु class" ? Observe पञ्चबीजम्.

८। 'इषुधिः स्त्री च। इषुधिशब्दः स्त्रियां पुंसि च। पूर्वस्यापवादः।

8. The noun इषुधिः 'a quiver' is both masculine and feminine.

Thus अयं or इयं इषुधिः।

९। 'देवासुरात्मस्वर्गगिरिसमुद्रनखकेशदन्तस्तनभुजकण्ठखड्गशरपङ्काभिधानानि'। एतानि पुंसि स्युः। देवाः सुराः। असुरा दैत्याः। आत्मा क्षेत्रज्ञः। स्वर्गो नाकः। गिरिः पर्वतः। समुद्रोऽब्धिः। नखः कररुहः। केशः शिरोरुहः। दन्तो दशनः। स्तनः कुचः। भुजो दोः। कण्ठो गलः। खड्गः करवालः। शरो मार्गणः। पङ्कः कर्दम इत्यादि॥

9. The words which are synonyms of देव 'god,' असुर 'demon,' आत्म 'self,' स्वर्ग 'the heaven,' गिरि 'the mountain,' समुद्र 'the sea,' नख 'the nail', केश the hair,' दन्त 'the tooth,' स्तन 'the breast,' भुज 'the arm,' कण्ठ 'the throat,' खड्ग 'the dagger,' शर 'the lake,' पङ्क 'the mud' &c. are masculines.

Thus देवाः सुराः ; असुराः दैत्याः ; आत्मा क्षेत्रज्ञः ; स्वर्गो नाकः ; गिरिः पर्वतः ; समुद्रोऽब्धि ; नखाः कररुहाः ; केशाः शिरोरुहाः ; दन्तो दशनः ; स्तनः कुचः ; भुजो दोः ; कण्ठो गलः- खड्गः करवालः ; शरोमार्गणः ; पङ्कः कर्दमः &c.

१०। 'त्रिविष्टपत्रिभुवने नपुंसके'। स्पष्टम्। तृतीयं विष्टपं त्रिविष्टपम्। स्वर्गाभिधानतया पुंस्त्वे प्राप्तेऽयमारम्भः॥

10. The noun त्रिविष्टप meaning 'the heaven' is neuter. This word being synonymous with स्वर्ग would have been considered masculine by the last aphorism, but this aphorism prevents that.

११। 'द्यौः स्त्रियाम्'। द्योदिवोस्तन्त्रेणोपादानमिदम्॥

11. The nouns द्यो and दिव् 'the heaven' are feminines.

By sûtra 9, these two words being synonyms of स्वर्ग would have been considered masculines, but this aphorism prevents that.

१२। 'इषुबाहू स्त्रियां च'। चात्पुंसि॥

12. The nouns इषु 'the arrow' and बाहु 'the arm' are also feminines.

By the force of the letter च in the sûtra, these words are to be considered masculines also.

१३। 'बाणकाण्डौ नपुंसके च'। चात्पुंसि। त्रिविष्टपेत्यादिचतुःसूत्री देवासुरेत्यस्यापवादः॥

13. The nouns बाण 'an arrow' and काण्ड 'a section' are also neuters.

By the force of the letter च in the sûtra, these words are to be considered masculine also.

The last four sûtras are exceptions to the sûtra 9.

१४। 'नान्तः'। अयं पुंसि। राजा। तक्षा। न च चर्म वर्मादिष्वतिव्याप्तिः। 'मन्द्व्यच्कोऽकर्तरि' इति नपुंसकप्रकरणे वक्ष्यमाणत्वात्॥

14. The nouns ending in न् are masculines.

Thus राजन्, तक्षन्। But not चर्मन् 'skin,' वर्मन् 'armour' which are neuters. The rule however should not be extended to चर्मन्, वर्मन् &c. These are Neuters because of the subsequent rule III. 33.

१५। 'क्रतुपुरुषकपोलगुल्फमेघाभिधानानि'। क्रतुरध्वरः। पुरुषो नरः। कपोलो गण्डः। गुल्फः प्रपदः। मेघो नीरदः॥

15. The nouns which are synonyms of क्रतु 'the sacrifice,' पुरुषः 'the man, कपोल 'the cheek' गुल्फ 'the ankle,' मेघ 'cloud' are masculines

Thus क्रतुरध्वरः ; पुरुषोनरः ; कपोलो गण्डः ; गुल्फः प्रपदः ; मेघो नीरदः ॥

१६ । 'अभ्रं नपुंसकम्' । पूर्वस्यापवादः ॥

16. The nouns अभ्रं 'cloud' is neuter.

This is an exception to the last.

१७ । 'उकारान्तः' । अयं पुंसि स्यात् । प्रभुः । इक्षुः ॥ 'हनुर्हट्टविलासिन्यां नृत्यारम्भे गदे स्त्रियाम् । द्वयोः कपोलावयवे' इति मेदिनिः । 'करेणुरिभ्यां स्त्री नेभे' इत्यमरः । एवं जातोयक-विशेषवचनानाक्रान्तस्तु प्रकृतसूत्रस्य विषयः । उक्तं च–'लिङ्गशेषविधिर्व्यापो विशेषैर्यद्य बाधितः' इति । एवमन्यत्रापि ॥

17. The nouns ending in उ are masculine.

Thus प्रभुः ; इक्षुः ॥

According to Medini, the noun हनु when meaning 'a wanton woman,' 'the commencement of a dance,' or 'disease' is feminine. But it is both masculine and feminine when it means 'the chin.'

According to Amara, the noun करेणु when meaning 'a she-elephant' is feminine; otherwise masculine when it means an elephant. The words which are subject to this rule are like these which are not governed by any other specific text to the contrary. As it has been said: "A rule of gender is of universal application if it is a śesha rule *i. e.*, a rule that *remains* after the application of all other rules. Provided that it is not debarred by any specific rule."

१८ । 'धेनुरज्जुकुहुसरयुतनुरेणुप्रियङ्गवः स्त्रियाम्' ॥

18. The nouns धेनु 'a cow,' रज्जु 'rope,' कुहु 'new moon-day,' सरयु 'the river Sarayu,' तनु 'body,' रेणु 'atom,' प्रियङ्गु 'name of a creeper' are feminine.

१९ । 'समासे रज्जुः पुंसि च' । कर्कटरज्ज्वा=कर्कटरज्जुना ॥

19. The noun रज्जु 'rope' in a compound is also used in the masculine. Thus कर्कटरज्ज्वा or कर्कटरज्जुना.

२० । 'श्मश्रुजानुवसुस्वाद्वश्रुजतुत्रपुतालूनि नपुंसके' ॥

20. The nouns श्मश्रु 'bared,' जानु 'the knee,' स्वादु 'sweetness; relish; taste,' अश्रु 'tear,' जतु 'wax,' त्रपु 'lead' and तालु 'the palate' are neuters.

२१ । 'वसु चार्थवाचि' । 'अर्थवाचि' इति किम् । 'वसुर्मयूखाग्निधनाधिपेषु' ॥

21. The noun वसु when meaning 'wealth' is neuter. Why do we say 'when meaning wealth'? For otherwise it is masculine when meaning मयूख 'a ray of light' अग्नि 'fire' and धनाधिप 'lord of wealth'.

२२ । 'मद्गुमधुसीधुशीधुसानुकमण्डलूनि नपुंसके च' । चात्पुंसि । अयं मद्गुः । इदं मद्गु ।

22. The nouns मद्गु 'a kind of pulse'; मधु 'honey,' शीधु 'a kind of wine,' सानु 'summit,' कमण्डलु 'water-pot' are also neuters.

By the force of the letter च in the sûtra, these words are also masculines.

Thus अयं मद्गुः or इदं मद्गु.

२३ । 'रुत्वन्तः' । मेरुः । सेतुः ॥

23. The nouns formed with the affixes रु (Uṇ. IV. 101) and तु (Uṇ I. 69) are masculines.

Thus मेरुः 'Meru,' सेतुः 'a bridge.'

२४। 'दारुकसेरुजत्रुवस्तुमस्तूनि नपुंसके'। रुत्वन्त इति पुंस्त्वस्यापवादः। इदं दारु ॥

24. The nouns दारु 'tree,' कसेरु 'a kind of fruit,' जत्रु 'collar bone,' वस्तु 'object,' मस्तु 'sour cream, whey,' are Neuters.

This is an exception to the last sûtra. Thus इदं दारु। These words are all formed by रु and तु affixes and therefore ought to have been masculines.

२५। 'सक्तुर्नपुंसके च'। चात्पुंसि, सक्तुः-सक्तु ॥

25. The noun सक्तु 'porridge' is also neuter.

By the force of the letter च in the sûtra, it is also masculine. Thus सक्तुः or सक्तु.

२६। 'प्राग्रश्मेरकारान्तः'। 'रश्मिदिवसाभिधानानि' इति वक्ष्यति प्राक् एतस्मादकारान्त इत्यधिक्रियते ॥

26. From this up to sûtra 66, the gender of nouns ending in अ will be mentioned.

This is an adhikâra sûtra. It extends up to raśmi-divasâ (II. 66) and applies to nouns ending in अ ॥

२७। 'कोपधः'। कोपधोऽकारान्तः पुंसि स्यात्। स्तवकः। कल्कः ॥

27. The nouns ending in अ with the penultimate क are masculines.

Thus स्तवकः 'a cluster'; कल्कः 'filth.' (Un. III. 40).

२८। 'चिबुकशालूकप्रातिपदिकांशुकोल्मुकानि नपुंसके'। पूर्वसूत्रापवादः ॥

28. The nouns चिबुक 'the chin'; शालूक 'the root of the water-lily,' प्रातिपदिक, 'the crude-noun' अंशुक 'a garment,' उल्मुक 'torch'; are neuters.

This is an exception to the last sûtra.

२९। कण्टकानीकसरकमोदकचषकमस्तकपुस्तकतडाकनिष्कशुष्कवर्चस्कपिनाकभाण्डकपिण्डककटकशण्डकपिटकतालकफलकपुलाकानि नपुंसके च। चात्पुंसि। अयं कण्टकः। इदं कण्टकमित्यादि।

29. The nouns कण्टक 'a thorn,' अनीक 'army' (Un. IV. 16. 17) सरक 'a road;' 'liquor'; मोदक 'a sweetmeat,' चषक 'a goblet'; मस्तक 'the head,' पुस्तक 'book,' तडाक 'tank,' निष्क 'a kind of coin,' शुष्क 'dryness,' वर्चस्क 'lustre'; पिनाक 'the bow of Shiva;' भाण्डक 'a vessel,' पिण्डक 'a ball' कटक 'an army, belt', दण्डक staff,' पिटक basket "तालक "yellow orpiment,' 'an ear ornament"; फलक 'blade,' पुलक 'a thrill of joy', are also neuters.

By the force of the letter च in the sûtra these words are also masculine. Thus अयं कण्टकः or इदं कण्टकम् &c.

३०। टोपधः। टोपधोऽकारान्तः पुंसि स्यात्। घटः पटः ॥

30. Nouns ending in अ with the penultimate ट are masculines.

Thus घटः 'a jar,' पटः 'a piece of cloth.'

३१। किरीटमुकुटललाटवटवीटशृङ्गाटकराटलोष्टानि नपुंसके। किरीटमित्यादि ॥

31. The nouns किरीट 'a crown,' मुकुट 'a crown,' ललाट 'forehead,' वट 'kind of tree,' वीट (?) शृङ्गाट 'a mountain with three peaks,' 'a place where

four roads meet.' करट 'an elephant's cheek,' (Un. IV. 81) and लोष्ट 'a clod of earth' are also neuter.

By the force of the letter च in the sûtra, these words are also masculines. Thus किरीटः or किरीटम् &c.

३२ । कुटकूटकपटकपाटकर्पटनटनिकटकीटकटानि नपुंसके च । चात्पुंसि । कुटः । कुटमित्यादि ॥

32. The nouns कुट 'a water pot; a fort,' कूट 'fraud; illusion; a house' कपट 'hypocrite; 'cheating,' कपाट 'door,' कर्पट 'patched garment,' नट 'a dancer', निकट 'near; vicinity,' कीट 'a worm,' कट 'a mat'; are also neuters.

By the force of the letter च they are also masculine. Thus कुटः or कुटम् &c.

३३ । णोपधः । णोपधोऽकारान्तः पुंसि स्यात् । गुणः । गणः । पाषाणः ॥

33. Nouns ending in अ with the penultimate ण् are masculines.

Thus गुणः 'quality,' गणः 'a host,' पाषाणः 'a stone.'

३४ । ऋणलवणपर्णतोरणरणोष्णानि नपुंसके । पूर्वसूत्रापवादः ॥

34. The nouns ऋण 'debt,' लवण 'salt,' पर्ण 'leaf,' तोरण 'a portal,' रण battle' उष्ण 'heat' are neuters.

This is an exception to the last sûtra.

३५ । कार्षापणस्वर्णसुवर्णव्रणचरणवृषणविषाणचूर्णतृणानि नपुंसके च । चात्पुंसि ॥

35. The nouns कार्षापण 'a kind of coin,' स्वर्ण 'gold,' सुवर्ण 'gold,' व्रण 'boil,' चरण 'foot,' वृषण 'the scrotum; विषाण 'a horn,' चूर्ण 'powder,' तृण 'grass,' are also neuters.

By the force of the letter च in the sûtra, these words are also masculine.

३६ । थोपधः । रथः ॥

36. Nouns ending in अ with the penultimate थ् are masculines.

Thus रथः 'chariot'.

३७ । काष्ठपृष्ठरिक्थसिक्थोक्थानि नपुंसके । इदं काष्ठमित्यादि ॥

37. The nouns काष्ठ 'wood,' पृष्ठ 'back,' रिक्थ 'inheritance,' सिक्थ 'a bee's wax,' उक्थ 'a sentence' are neuters.

Thus इदं काष्ठम् &c.

३८ । काष्ठा दिगर्था स्त्रियाम् । इमाः काष्ठाः ॥

38. The noun काष्ठा when denoting 'a quarter or region of the world' is feminine.

Thus इमाः काष्ठाः ।

३९ । तीर्थप्रोथयूथगाथानि नपुंसके च । चात्पुंसि । अयं तीर्थः । इदं तीर्थम् ॥

39. The nouns तीर्थ 'pilgrimage,' प्रोथ 'the nose of a horse; the hip,' यूथ 'a herd,' and गाथ 'a singer; a song' are also neuters.

By the force of the letter च in the sûtra, these words are masculines also.

Thus अयं तीर्थः or इदम् तीर्थम्.

४० । नोपधः । अदन्तः पुंसि । इनः । फेनः ॥

40. Nouns ending in अ with the penultimate न् are masculines.

Thus इनः 'a lord,' फेनः 'foam'.

४१ । जघनाजिनतुहिनकाननवनवृजिनविपिनवेतनशासनसोपानमिथुनश्मशानरत्ननिम्नचिह्नानि नपुंसके । पूर्वस्यापवादः ॥

41. The nouns जघन 'the hip,' (Uṇ. V. 32) अजिन 'the skin of a black antelope' (Uṇ. II. 48) तुहिन 'ice,' कानन 'forest,' वन 'forest,' वृजिन 'hair' 'sin,' विपिन 'a wood; a thicket,' (Uṇ. II. 52) वेतन 'pay,' शासन 'rule,' सोपान 'ladder,' मिथुन 'copulation,' श्मशान 'cemetry,' रत्न 'gem,' निम्न 'a low place, चिह्न 'sign' are neuters.

This is an exception to the last aphorism.

४२। मानयानाभिधाननलिनपुलिनोद्यानशयनासनस्थानचन्दनालानसंमानभवनवसनसंभावनविभावनविमानानि नपुंसके च । चात्पुंसि । अयं मानः । इदं मानम् ॥

42. The nouns मान 'pride,' यान 'carriage,' अभिधान 'vocabulary, नलिन 'a lotus; a crane,' पुलिन 'a sandbank' (Uṇ. II. 53) उद्यान 'garden,' शयन 'sleeping,' आसन 'a seat,' स्थान 'a place,' चन्दन 'sandalwood,' आलान 'the tying-post,' सन्मान 'honor.' भवन 'house,' वसन 'dress,' सम्भावन 'possibility, विभावन (?) विमान 'a baloon' are also neuters.

By the force of the letter च in the sûtra, these words are also masculines.

Thus अयं मानः or इदं मानम् &c.

४३ । पोपधः । अदन्तः पुंसि । यूपः । दीपः । सर्पः ॥

43. Nouns ending in अ with the penultimate प् are masculine.

Thus यूपः 'a sacrificial' 'post' (Un. III. 27). दीपः 'a lamp' सर्पः 'a snake.'

४४ । पापरूपोडुपतल्पशिल्पपुष्पशष्पसमीपान्तरीपाणि नपुंसके । इदं पापमित्यादि ॥

44. The nouns पाप 'sin,' रूप 'form,' उडुप 'a raft,' तल्प 'bed,' शिल्प 'art,' पुष्प 'flower,' शष्प 'young grass,' समीप 'vicinity,' अन्तरीप 'an island; a promontary (VI. 3. 93) are neuters.

Thus इदं पापम् &c.

४५ । शूर्पकुतपकुणपद्वीपविटपानि नपुंसके च । इदं शूर्पमित्यादि ॥

45. The nouns शूर्प 'a winnowing basket,' कुतप 'a Brâhmaṇa; a kind of grass,' कुणप 'a corpse, 'a spear,' द्वीप 'an island,' विटप 'a branch,' are also neuters (as well as masculines).

Thus अयं शूर्पः or इदं शूर्पम् &c.

४६ । भोपधः । स्तम्भः । कुम्भः ॥

46. Nouns ending in अ with the penultimate भ् are masculines.

Thus स्तम्भः 'a pillar,' कुम्भः 'a water jar.'

४७ । तलभं नपुंसकम् । पूर्वस्यापवादः ॥

47 The noun तलभ is neuter.

This is an exception to the last.

४८। जृम्भं नपुंसके च। जृम्भम्-जृम्भः॥

48. The noun जृम्भ 'yawning' is also neuter.

Thus जृम्भम् or जृम्भः

४९। मोपधः। सोमः। भीमः॥

49. Nouns ending in अ with the penultimate म् are masculine.

Thus सोमः 'the Soma,' भीमः 'Bhîma.'

५०। रुक्मसिध्मयुग्मेध्मगुल्माध्यात्मकुङ्कुमानि नपुंसके। इदं रुक्ममित्यादि॥

50. The nouns रुक्म, 'gold,' सिध्म 'scab,' युग्म 'couple,' इध्म 'fuel,' गुल्म 'blossom,' अध्यात्म 'spiritual,' कुंकुम 'saffron' are Neuter.

Thus इदं रुक्मम् &c.

५१। संग्रामदाडिमकुसुमाश्रमक्षेमक्षौमहोमोद्दामानि नपुंसके च। चात्पुंसि। अयं संग्रामः। इदं संग्रामम्॥

51. The nouns संग्राम 'fight,' दाड़िम 'pomegranate,' कुसुम 'flower,' आश्रम 'dwelling-house,' क्षेम 'happiness' (Uṇ. I. 138) क्षौम 'silken cloth,' होम 'homa' उद्दाम 'violently' are also Neuter.

By the force of the letter च in the sûtra, these words are also masculine.

Thus अयं संग्रामः or इदं संग्रामम्॥

५२। 'योपधः'। समयः। हयः॥

52. Nouns ending in अ with the penultimate य् are masculine.

Thus समयः 'time;' हयः 'the horse.'

५३। 'किसलयहृदयेन्द्रियोत्तरीयाणि नपुंसके'। स्पष्टम्॥

53. The nouns किसलय 'a sprout,' हृदय 'the heart,' इन्द्रिय 'the sense,' उत्तरीय 'an upper garment' are neuter.

५४। 'गोमयकषायमलयान्वयाव्ययानि नपुंसके च'। गोमयः-गोमयम्॥

54. The nouns गोमय 'cow-dung,' कषाय 'the red color,' मलय 'Malaya' अन्वय 'Association,' अव्यय 'Indeclinable' are also neuters.

Thus गोमयः or गोमयम्॥

५५। 'रोपधः'। क्षुरः। अङ्कुरः॥

55. Nouns ending in अ with the penultimate र् are masculines.

Thus क्षुरः 'the hoof,' अङ्कुरः 'the blossom.'

५६। 'द्वाराग्रस्फारतक्रवक्रवप्रक्षिप्रक्षुद्रनारतीरदूरकृच्छ्ररन्ध्राश्रश्वभ्रभीरगभीरक्रूरविचित्रकेयूरकेदारोदराजस्रशरीरकन्दरमन्दारपञ्जरजठराजिरवैरचामरपुष्करगह्वरकुहरकुटीरकुलीरचत्वरकाश्मीरनीराम्बरशिशिरतन्त्रयन्त्रनक्षत्रक्षेत्रमित्रकलत्रचित्रमूत्रसूत्रवक्त्रनेत्रगोत्राङ्गुलित्रभलत्रशस्त्रशास्त्रवस्त्रपत्रपात्रछत्राणि नपुंसके'। इदं द्वारमित्यादि॥

56. The words द्वार 'door,' अग्र 'in front,' स्फार 'swelling abundance' (Uṇ. II. 13); तक्र 'curdled milk,' वक्र 'crooked,' वप्र 'rampart,' क्षिप्र 'a measure of time,'

क्षुद्र 'small,' छिद्र 'hole,' नार 'a multitude;' तीर 'shore,' दूर 'distance,' कृच्छ्र 'difficulty,' 'misery,' रन्ध्र 'a hole,' अश्रु 'a tear; blood,' श्वभ्र 'a hole; a den,' आभीर 'a cowherd,' गभीर 'deep,' क्रूर 'cruel,' विचित्र 'beautiful,' केयूर 'an armlet,' केदार 'meadow,' उदर 'the stomach,' अजस्र 'constant,' शरीर 'the body,' कन्दर, 'the root,' मन्दार 'the coral tree,' and पञ्जर 'skeleton,' अजर 'immortal,' जठर 'the stomach,' अजिर 'a court-yard,' वैर enmity, चामर 'châmara,' पुष्कर 'the lake,' गह्वर 'the cave,' कुहर 'a cavity,' कुटीर 'a hut,' कुलीर 'a crab,' चत्वर 'a court-yard' (Uṇ. II. 121), काश्मीर 'kâśmira,' नीर 'water', अम्बर 'sky; cloth,' शिशिर 'dew,' तन्त्र 'a loom,' यन्त्र 'instrument,' क्षत्र 'dominion,' क्षेत्र 'a field,' मित्र 'a friend,' कलत्र 'a wife,' चित्र 'a picture,' छत्र 'umbrella,' मूत्र, 'urine,' सूत्र 'thread,' वक्त्र 'face,' नेत्र 'the eye,' गोत्र 'gotra,' अंगुलित्र 'a finger-protector,' भलत्र (?) अस्त्र 'an instrument,' शस्त्र 'a weapon,' शास्त्र 'Śâstra,' वस्त्र 'cloth,' पत्र 'leaf,' पात्र 'a vessel,' and नक्षत्र 'star' are neuters.

Thus इदं द्वारम् &c.

५७ । 'शुक्रमदेवतायाम्' । इदं शुक्रं रेतः ॥

57. The noun शुक्र is neuter when it is not the name of the god (Śukra).

Thus इदं शुक्रम्. Here शुक्र means 'semen.'

५८ । 'चक्रवज्रान्धकारसारावारपारक्षीरतोमरशृङ्गारभृङ्गारमन्दारोशीरतिमिरशिशिराणि नपुंसके च' । चात्पुंसि । चक्रः-चक्रमित्यादि ॥

58. The nouns चक्र 'disc,' वज्र 'a thunderbolt,' अंधकार 'darkness,' सार 'essence,' आवार (?) पार 'the further or opposite side,' क्षीर 'milk,' तोमर, 'an iron club,' शृङ्गार, 'the sentiment of love,' मन्दार 'the coral tree,' उशीर 'a kind of grass,' तिमिर 'darkness,' शिशिर 'dew' are also neuters.

By the force of the word च in the sûtra, these are also masculines. Thus चक्रः or चक्रम् &c.

५९ । 'षोपधः' । वृषः । वृक्षः ॥

59. Nouns ending in ष with the penultimate, ष are masculines.

Thus वृषः 'a bull;' वृक्षः 'a tree.'

६० । 'शिरीषर्षीर्षाम्बरीषपीयूषपुरीषकिल्बिषकल्माषाणि नपुंसके' ॥

60. The शिरीष 'the name of a tree' जोषं 'an expression of joy,' शीर्ष 'the head' अम्बरीष 'a fryingpan,' पीयूष 'nectar,' (Uṇ. IV. 76), पुरीष 'faeces,' किल्बिष 'sin,' and कल्माष 'stain' are neuters.

६१ । 'यूषकरीषमिषविषवर्षाणि नपुंसके च' । चात्पुंसि । अयं यूषः । इदं यूषमित्यादि ॥

61. The words यूष 'soup,' करीष 'dry cow-dung', मिष 'pretext,' 'emulation,' विष 'poison,' वर्ष 'a year' are also neuters.

By the force of the word च in the Sûtra, these words are also masculine.

Thus अयं यूषः or इदं यूषम्.

६२ । 'सोपधः' । वत्सः । वायसः । महानसः ॥

62. Nouns ending in स with the penultimate स are masculines.

Thus वत्सः 'a calf' (Uṇ. III. 62); वायसः 'a crow,' महानसः 'a kitchen.

६३ । 'पनसबिसबुससाहसानि नपुंसके ॥

63. The words पनस 'jack fruit,' बिस 'the fibre of a lotus,' बुस 'chaff,' and साहस 'courage,' are neuters.

६४ । 'चमसांसरसनिर्यासोपवासकार्पासवासमासकासकांसमांसानि नपुंसके च' । 'इदं चमसम् । अयं चमस इत्यादि ॥

64. The words चमस 'a vessel,' अंस, रस 'juice,' निर्यास 'gum juice,' उपवास 'fast,' कार्पास 'cotton,' वास 'perfume; 'habitation;' मास 'month,' भास, कास 'cough,' कांस bell-metal,' and मांस 'flesh' are also neuters.

Thus चमसं or चमसः &c.

६५ । कंसं चाप्राणिनि । कंसोऽस्त्री पानभाजनम्' । प्राणिनि तु । कंसो नाम कश्चि-द्राजा ॥

65. The noun कंस when not meaning a living being, is neuter. It is never feminine and means 'a drinking vesel, cup or can.'

When it means a living being, then it is the name of a king of Mathura son of Ugrasena and enemy of Krishna.

६६ । 'रश्मिदिवसाभिधानानि ।' एतानि पुंसि स्युः । रश्मिर्मयूखः । दिवसो घस्रः ॥

66. Nouns which are synonyms of रश्मि 'a ray of light,' and दिवस 'a day' are masculine.

Thus रश्मिर्मयूखः ; दिवसो घस्रः ॥

६७ । 'दीधितिः स्त्रियाम्' । पूर्वस्यापवादः ॥

67. The noun दीधितिः 'a ray of light' is feminine.

This is an exception to the last aphorism.

६८ । 'दिनाहनी नपुंसके' । अयमप्यपवादः ॥

68. The nouns दिन 'a day' and अहन् 'a day' are neuters. This is also an exception to the aphorism 66.

६९ । 'मानाभिधानानि'' । एतानि पुंसि स्युः । कुडवः । प्रस्थः ॥

69. Nouns which are synonyms of मान 'a measure, a standard' are masculines.

Thus कुडवः, प्रस्थः ॥

७० । 'द्रोणाढकौ नपुंसके च' । इदं द्रोणम् । अयं द्रोणः ॥

70. The words द्रोण 'a measure of capacity' and आढक 'a measure of grain' are neuters also.

Thus इदं द्रोणम् or अयं द्रोणः ॥

७१ । 'खारीमानिके स्त्रियाम्' । इयं खारी । इयं मानिका ॥

71. The words खारी 'a measure of grain equal to 16 *dronas*' and मानिका 'a kind of weight' are feminines.

Thus इयं खारी, इयं मानिका ॥

७२ । दाराक्षतलाजासूनां बहुत्वं च । इमे दाराः ॥

72. The nouns दारा 'wife,' अक्षत 'whole grain or unhusked rice,' लाज 'parched or fried grain,' असु 'the five vital breaths' are always plural. Thus इमे दाराः ॥

By the force of the word च in the sûtra, they are feminines.

७३। 'नाड्यपजनेापपदानि व्रणाङ्गपदानि'। यथासंख्यं नाड्याद्युपपदानि व्रणादीनि पुंसि स्युः। अयं नाडीव्रणः। अपाङ्गः। जनपदः। व्रणादीनामुभयलिङ्गत्वेऽपि क्लीबत्वनिवृत्यर्थं सूत्रम् ॥

73. The nouns व्रण 'a boil,' अंग 'a member' and पद 'a foot' compounded with नाडी, अप and जन respectively are masculines.

The words व्रण &c. are of both genders (*i. e.* Masculine and Neuter), but this Sûtra debars their use as neuters, (when compounded with the above words). Thus अयं नाडीव्रणः। अपाङ्गः। जनपदः॥

७४। 'मरुद्गरुत्तरदृत्विजः'। अयं मरुत्॥

74. The words मरुत् 'wind' (Up. I. 94) गरुत् 'the wing of a bird' तरत् 'swimming' and ऋत्विज् 'a sacrificial priest,' are masculines.

Thus अयं मरुत्॥

७५। 'ऋषिराशिदृतिग्रन्थिक्रिमिध्वनिबलिकौलिमौलिरविकविकपिमुनयः'। एते पुंसि स्युः। अयमृषिः॥

75. The words ऋषि 'a seer,' राशि 'a heap,' दृति 'a leathern bag for holding water,' ग्रन्थि 'knot,' क्रिमि 'a worm,' ध्वनि 'sound,' बलि 'offering,' कौलि (?) and मौलि 'the head,' रवि 'the sun,' कवि 'the poet,' कपि 'a monkey,' and मुनि 'sage,' are masculines.

Thus अयं ऋषिः॥

७६। 'ध्वजगजमुञ्जपुञ्जाः'। एते पुंसि॥

76. The words ध्वज 'flag,' गज 'elephant,' मुंज 'a sort of grass,' पुंज a heap' are masculines.

७७। 'हस्तकुन्तान्तव्रातवातदूतधूर्तसूतचूतमुहूर्ताः'। एते पुंसि। अमरस्तु 'मुहूर्तोऽस्त्रियाम्' इत्याह॥

77. The words हस्त 'the hand,' कुंत 'a lance,' अंत 'the end,' व्रात 'a multitude,' वात 'the wind,' दूत 'a messenger,' धूर्त 'a rogue,' सूत 'a son,' चूत 'the mango tree,' मुहूर्त 'a moment,' are masculines.

According to Amarakosha, (I. 4. 11) मुहूर्त is never feminine, (*i. e.* it is both masculine and neuter).

७८। 'षण्डमण्डकरण्डभरण्डवरण्डतुण्डगण्डमुण्डपाषण्डशिखण्डाः'। अयं षण्डः॥

78. The nouns षण्ड 'a bull,' मण्ड 'the scum of boiled rice,' करण्ड 'a small box or basket of bamboo' भरण्ड 'master,' वरण्ड 'a multitude,' तुण्ड 'mouth,' गण्ड 'the cheek,' मुण्ड 'a man with bald head,' पाषंड 'a heretic,' and शिखंड 'a crest' are masculine.

Thus अयं षण्डः॥

७९। 'वंशांशपुरोडाशाः'। अयं वंशः। पुरो दाश्यते पुरोडाशः। कर्मणि घञ्। भवव्याख्यानयोः प्रकरणे 'पौरोडाशपुरोडाशात्ष्ठन्' (१४४९) इति विकारप्रकरणे 'व्रीहेः पुरोडाशे' (१५२८) इति च निपातनात् प्रकृतसूत्र एव निपातनाद्वा दस्य डत्वम्। 'पुरोडाशभुजामिष्टम्' इति माघः॥

79. The nouns वंश 'a family,' अंश 'a share,' पुरोडाश 'an oblation' are masculines.

Thus अयं वंशः । The word puroḍâśa 'a cake-offering' is derived by adding the affix घञ् with the force of karma to the root दाश् preceded by the upapada पुरो । The द is changed to ड by no particular rule of Grammar, but we find the word so spelt in sûtras IV. 3. 70, S. 1449 ; and IV. 3. 148 S. 1528. Or the द is changed to ड by nipâtana even in the present sûtra ; and sûtra III. 2. 71. S. 3414. Thus in Mâgha also we find : पुरोडाश भुजाम् इष्टम् 'the sacrifice of puroḍâśa eaters.'

८० । 'हृदकन्दकुन्दबुद्बुदशब्दाः' । अयं हृदः ॥

80. The words हृद 'a lake,' कन्द 'root,' कुन्द 'a kind of jasmine.' बुद् बुद् 'bubble' are masculines.

Thus अयं हृदः ॥

८१ । 'अर्घपथिमथ्यृभुक्षिस्तम्बनितम्बपूगाः' । अयमर्घः ॥

81. The words अर्घ 'offering,' पथिन् 'a road,' मथिन् 'a churning stick, ऋभुक्षिन् 'a name of Indra,' स्तम्ब 'a clump of grass' नितम्ब, 'the buttocks,' and पूग 'a heap' are masculines.

Thus अयं अर्घः ॥

८२ । 'पल्लवपल्वलकफरेफकटाहनिर्व्यूहमठमणितरङ्गतुरङ्गगन्धस्कन्धमृदङ्गसङ्गसमुद्रपुङ्खाः' । अयं पल्लव इत्यादि ॥

82. The words पल्लव 'a sprout,' पल्वल 'a small pool,' कफ 'cough,' रेफ 'sound,' कटाह 'frying pan,' निर्व्यूह 'a peg,' मठ 'the hut of an ascetic,' मणि 'jewel,' तरंग 'wave,' तुरङ्ग 'horse' गंध 'smell,' मृदंग 'a musical instrument,' संग 'attachment,' समुद्र 'ocean,' and पुङ्ख 'a falcon,' are masculines. Thus अयं पल्लवः &c.

८३ । सारथ्यतिथिकुक्षिबस्तिपाण्यञ्जलयः । एते पुंसि । अयं सारथिः ।

83. The words सारथि 'charioteer,' अतिथि 'a guest,' कुक्षि 'the womb,' वस्ति 'the abdomen,' पाणि 'the hand,' अंजलि 'the hollow of the hands' are masculines.

Thus अयं सारथिः &c.

इति पुंलिङ्गाधिकारः ॥

THE NEUTER GENDER.

१ । 'नपुंसकम्' । अधिकारोऽयम् ।

1. The Neuter Gender.

This is an Adhikâra sûtra.

२ । भावे ल्युडन्तः । हसनम् । 'भावे' किम् । पचनोऽग्निः । इध्मप्रव्रश्चनः कुठारः ॥

2. Abstract nouns of action formed with the affix ल्युट् are neuters. This is a repetition of III. 3. 115, S 3290. Thus हसनम् (laughter). Why do we say 'abstract nouns of action ?' Observe पचनः 'fire'; इध्मप्रव्रश्चनः 'an axe'; these words are masculines and not neuters.

३ । 'निष्ठा च' । भावे या निष्ठा तदन्तं क्लीबं स्यात् । हसितम् । गीतम् ॥

3. Abstract nouns of action formed with the निष्ठा affix are neuters. This is also repetition of III. 3 114. S. 3090.

Thus हसितम् 'laughter,' गीतम् 'a song.'

४ । त्वष्यञौ तद्धितौ । शुक्लत्वम्-शौक्ल्यम् । ष्यञः स्त्रित्वसामर्थ्यात्पक्षे स्त्रीत्वम् । चातुर्यम्-चातुरी । सामग्र्यम्-सामग्री । औचित्यम्-औचिती ॥

4. Among *taddhitas*, words formed with the affixes त्व and ष्यञ् are Neuters ; (See V. 1. 123, S. 1787).

Thus शुक्लत्वम् 'whiteness' and शौक्ल्यम् 'whiteness.' The ष्यञ् formed nouns are optionally feminines because of the indicatory letter ष by IV. 1. 41, S. 498 in order to give scope to, the indicatory ष.

Thus चातुर्यम् or चातुरी 'cleverness.' सामग्र्यम् or सामग्री 'effects, goods.' औचित्यम् or औचिती 'aptness.'

५। 'कर्मणि च ब्राह्मणादिगुणवचनेभ्यः। ब्राह्मणस्य कर्म ब्राह्मण्यम् ॥

5. Brâhmaṇâdi words when denoting work and quality are neuters. This is repetition of V. 1. 124, S. 1788.

Thus ब्राह्मण्यम् 'Brâhmaṇical.'

६। यद्यड्ढग्यगञण्वुञ्छाश्च भावकर्मणि। एतदन्तानि क्लीबानि। 'स्तेनाद्य न्नलोपश्च (१७९०)। स्तेयम्। 'सख्युर्यः (१७९१)। सख्यम्। 'कपिज्ञात्योर्ढक् (१७९२)। कापेयम्। 'पत्यन्तपुरोहितादिभ्यो यक्' (१७९३) आधिपत्यम्। 'प्राणभृज्जातिवयोवचनोद्गात्रादिभ्योऽञ्' (१७९४) औष्ट्रम्। हायनान्तयुवादिभ्योऽण् (१७९५)। द्वैहायनम्। द्वन्द्वमनोज्ञादिभ्यो वुञ्। पितापुत्रकम्। होत्राभ्यश्छः (१८००)। अच्छावाकीयम् ॥

6. Nouns formed with the affixes यत्, य, ढक्, यक्, अञ्, अण्, वुञ् and छ in the senses of nature or action thereof are neuters.

(*a*) The affix यत् is added by virtue of V. 1. 125, S. 1790. Thus स्तेयम् 'theft.'

(*b*) The affix य is added by virtue V. 1. 126, S. 1791. Thus सख्यम् 'friendship.'

(*c*) The affix ढक् is added by virtue of V. 1. 127, S. 1792. Thus कापेयम् 'ape-like.'

(*d*) The affix यक् is added by virtue of V. 1. 128, S. 1793. Thus आधिपत्यम् 'authority.'

(*e*) The affix अञ् is added by virtue of V. 1. 129, S. 1794. Thus औष्ट्रम् 'camel-like.'

(*f*) The affix अण् is added by virtue of V. 1. 130, S. 1795. Thus द्वैहायनम् 'the action of two days.'

(*g*) The affix वुञ् is added by virtue of V. 1. 132 and 133, S. 1797 and 1798. Thus पितापुत्रकम् 'paternal and filial.'

(*h*) The affix छ is added by virtue of V. 1. 135, S. 1800. Thus अच्छावाकीयम् ॥

NOTE:—This Sûtra summarises all the affixes taught in V. 1. 124-135.

७। 'अव्ययीभावः-' (६५९)। अधिस्त्रि ॥

7. Nouns which are अव्ययीभाव compounds are neuters. (See II. 84. 18, S. 659). Thus अधिस्त्रि।

८। 'द्वन्द्वैकत्वम्'। पाणिपादम् ॥

8. Nouns which are द्वन्द्व compounds are neuter. (See II. 4. 2, S. 906). Thus पाणिपादम्।

९। 'अभाषायां हेमन्तशिशिरावहोरात्रे च'। स्पष्टम् ॥

9. The compound हेमन्तशिशिरौ is masculine, and अहोरात्रे is neuter in the non-classical literature. (See II. 4. 28. S. 3399).

१० । 'अनञ्कर्मधारयस्तत्पुरुषः' । अधिकारोऽयम् ॥

10. A Tatpurusha, compound, with the exception of that which is formed by the particle nañ, and of the Karmadhâraya compound, becomes neuter gender, in the cases explained in the following sûtras. (See II. 4. 19, S. 822).

This is an adhikâra sûtra.

११ । अनल्पे छाया । शरच्छायम् ॥

11. A Tatpurusha compound ending with the word chhâyâ 'shadow' is neuter in gender, when the sense is that of profuseness of the thing indicated by the first term. (See II. 4. 22, S. 825).

Thus शरच्छायम् ॥

१२ । 'राजामनुष्यपूर्वा सभा' । इनसभमित्यादि ॥

12. A Tatpurusha compound ending in सभा 'court' when preceded by words which are synonyms of राजा and अमनुष्य 'non-human being' is neuter. (See II. 4. 23, S. 826).

Thus इनसभम् 'the king's court' &c.

१३ । 'सुरासेनाच्छायाशालानिशा स्त्रियां च' ॥

13. Tatpurusha compounds ending in सुरा 'wine,' सेना 'army,' छाया 'shadow,' शाला 'a house' निशा 'night' are also feminines (in addition to their being also neuter). See II. 4. 15, S. 828.

१४ । 'परवत्' । अन्यस्तत्पुरुषः परवल्लिङ्गः स्यात् ॥

14. The gender of a Dvanda or a Tatpurusha compound is like that of the last word in it. (See II. 4. 26. S. 812).

१५ । 'रात्राह्नाहाः पुंसि' (८१४) ॥

15. The Dvanda or a Tatpurusha compound ending with रात्र 'night,' अह्न 'a day' and अह 'a day' is masculine. (See II. 4. 29, S. 814.)

१६ । अपथपुण्याहे नपुंसके ॥

16. The words अपथ 'bad road' and पुण्याह 'sacred day' are neuters. (See II. 4. 30, S 815 and II. 4. 17, S. 821 *Vârtika*).

१७ । 'संख्यापूर्वा रात्रिः' । त्रिरात्रम् । 'संख्यापूर्वा' इति किम् । सर्वरात्रः ॥

17. A Dvigu compound ending with the word रात्रि when preceded by a numeral is neuter. (See II. 1. 52, S. 730).

Thus त्रिरात्रम् ॥

Why do we say "when preceded by a numeral"? Observe सर्वरात्रः which is masculine.

१८ । 'द्विगुः स्त्रियां च' । व्यवस्थया । पञ्चफली । त्रिभुवनम् ॥

18. Nouns which are Dvigu compounds are feminines also. (See II. 4. 17, S. 821 Vârtikas).

Thus पञ्चमूली 'five-roots,' त्रिभुवनम् 'three worlds.'

१९ । इसुसन्तः । हविः । धनुः ॥

19. Nouns ending in इस् (Uṇ. II. 108) and उस् (Uṇ. II. 115) are neuter. Thus हविः 'oblation to fire' (see Uṇ. II. 108) धनुः 'a bow' (Uṇ. II. 115 read with II. 117).

२० । अर्चिः स्त्रियां च । इसन्तत्वेऽप्यर्चिः स्त्रियां नपुंसके च स्यात् । इयमिदं वार्चिः ॥

20. The nouns अर्चि 'ray' is feminine also (in addition to its being neuter, although it ends in इस्) ॥

Thus इयं or इदं अर्चिः

२१ । छदिः स्त्रियामेव । इयं छदिः । छाद्यतेऽनेनेति छदेश्चुरादिण्यन्तात् 'अर्चिशुचि-हुस्यादिना इस् । इस्मन् इत्यादिना ह्रस्वः । पटलं छदिः इत्यमरः । तत्र पटलसाहचर्याच्छदिषः क्लीबतां वदन्तोऽमरव्याख्यातार उपेक्ष्याः ॥

21. The word छदि 'the roof' is always feminine.

Thus इयं छदिः । It is also formed by adding the affix इस् (see Uṇ. II. 108) to the root छादि belonging to the churâdi class. The root छादि becomes छद by VI. 4. 97, S 2985. In the Amarakosha, we find the word पटलं छदिः (II. 2 14). There the commentators say that the noun छदि is neuter because it is mentioned along with पटलं which neuter. This explanation of the commentators should be rejected.

२२ । मुखनयनलोहवनमांसरुधिरकार्मुकविवरजलहलधनान्नाभिधानानि । एतेषामभिधायकानि क्लीबे स्युः । मुखमाननम् । नयनं लोचनम् । लोहं कालम् । वनं गहनम् । मांसमामिषम् रुधिरं रक्तम् । कार्मुकं शरासनम् । विवरं बिलम् । जलं वारि । हलं लाङ्गलम् । धनं द्रविणम् । अन्नमशनम् । अस्यापवादानाह त्रिसूत्र्या ॥

22. The words which are synonyms of मुख 'face,' नयन 'an eye,' लोह 'copper,' वन 'forest,' मास 'a month,' रुधिर 'blood,' कार्मुक 'a bow,' विवर 'a hole,' जल 'water,' हल 'the plough,' धन 'wealth,' and अन्न 'food' are neuters.

Thus मुखं आननम् ; नयनं लोचनम् ; लोहं कालम् ; वनं गहनम् ; मांस मामिषम् ; रुधिरं रक्तम् ; कार्मुकं शरासनम् ; विवरं बिलम् ; जलं वारि ; हलं लांगलम् ; धनं द्रविणम् ; अन्नं अशनम् ॥

In the next three sûtras exceptions to this are mentioned.

२३ । सीरार्थौदनाः पुंसि ॥

23. The words सीर 'a plough,' अर्थ 'wealth' and ओदन 'food' are masculine.

२४ । वक्त्रनेत्रारण्यगाण्डीवानि पुंसि च । वक्त्रो वक्त्रम् । नेत्रो नेत्रम् । अरण्योऽरण्यम् । गाण्डीवो गाण्डीवम् ॥

24. The words वक्त्र 'the face,' नेत्र 'the eye,' अरण्य 'the forest,' and गाण्डीव 'Arjuna's bow' are also masculines (as well as neuters.)

Thus वक्त्रः or वक्त्रम् ; नेत्रः or नेत्रम् ; अरण्यः or अरण्यम् ; गाण्डीव or गाण्डीवम् ।

२५ । अटवी स्त्रियाम् ॥

25. The word अटवी 'the forest' is feminine.

२६ । लोपधः । कुलम् । कूलम् । स्थलम् ॥

26. Nouns ending in अ with the penultimate ल are neuters.

Thus कुलम् 'a race,' कूलम् 'a shore,' स्थलम् 'place.'

२७ । तूलोपलतालकुसूलतरलकम्बलदेवलवृषलाः पुंसि । अयं तूलः ॥

27. The following are masculines :—तूल 'cotton,' उपल 'a stone,' ताल 'the Palmyra tree,' कुसूल 'a granary,' तरल 'a necklace,' कम्बल 'blanket,' देवल 'a virtuous man,' वृषल 'a sûdra.'

Thus अयं तूलः &c.

२८ । शीलमूलमङ्गलसालकमलतलमुसलकुण्डलपललमृणालवालनिगलपलालबिडाल खिल-शूलाः पुंसि च' । चात्क्लीबे । इदं शीलमित्यादि ॥

28. The following are masculines also (in addition to their being neuters):—शीलः 'conduct,' मूल 'root,' मङ्गल ; the planet Mars,' साल 'a tree,' कमल 'lotus,' तल 'bottom,' मुसल 'pestle,' कुण्डल 'ear-ornament,' पलल 'a demon,' 'flesh ;' मृणाल 'a lotus fibre,' वाल 'a child,' निगल 'swallowing,' पलाल 'strand ; husk,' बिडाल, 'a cat,' खिल 'a desert,' शूल 'a spear.'

Thus शीलः or शीलम् ।

२९ । शतादिः संख्या । शतम् । सहस्रम् । 'शतादिः' इति किम् । एको द्वौ बहवः । संख्या इति किम् । शतशृङ्गो नाम पर्वतः ॥

29. The numerals शत 'a hundred' &c. are neuters.

Thus शतम् 'a hundred,' सहस्रम् 'a thousand.'

Why do we say, शत &c. ? Observe एकः 'one,' द्वौ 'two,' बहवः 'many.'

Why do we say when meaning 'the numerals' ? Observe शतशृङ्गः (the name of a mountain). Here शत is masculine.

३० । शतायुतप्रयुताः पुंसि च । अयं शतः । इदं शतमित्यादि ॥

30. The words शत 'a hundred,' अयुत 'a myriad,' प्रयुत 'a million' are also masculines.

Thus अयं शतः or इदं शतम् &c.

३१ । लक्षा कोटिः स्त्रियाम् । इयं लक्षा । इयं कोटिः । 'वा लक्षा नियुतं च तत्' इत्य, मरात्क्लीबेऽपि लक्षम् ॥

31. The words लक्षा 'a lakh' and कोटि 'ten million' are feminine.

Thus इयं लक्षा, इयं कोटिः ॥

According to Amarakosha (III. 5. 24) the word लक्ष is also neuter. Thus लक्षम् ।

३२ । शङ्कुः पुंसि । सहस्रः क्वचित् । अयं सहस्रः । इदं सहस्रम् ॥

32. The word शंकु ten billions, and sometimes सहस्र 'a thousand' is masculine.

Thus अयं सहस्रः or इदं सहस्रम् ।

३३ । मन्द्व्यचकोऽकर्तरि । मन्प्रत्ययान्तो द्व्यचकः क्लीबः स्यान्न तु कर्तरि । वर्म । चर्म । द्व्यचकः किम् । अणिमा । महिमा । अकर्तरि किम् । ददाति इति दामा ॥

33. Nouns of two syllables formed with the affix मन् and when not denoting an agent are neuters.

Thus चर्म्मन् 'skin,' वर्म्मन् 'armor,' कर्म्मन् 'work.'

Why do we say 'of two syllables?' Observe अणिमन् 'minuteness,' महिमन् 'glory.'

Why do we say 'when not denoting an agent'? Observe दामन् 'a giver.'

३४ । ब्रह्मन्पुंसि च । अयं ब्रह्मा । इदं ब्रह्म ॥

34. The word ब्रह्मन् is also masculine.

Thus अयं ब्रह्मा or इदं ब्रह्म ।

३५ । नामरोमणी नपुंसके । 'मन्द्व्यच्कः' इत्यस्यायं प्रपञ्चः ॥

35. The words नामन् 'name' and, रोमन् 'hair,' are neuters. This is merely an amplification of sûtra 33.

३६ । 'असन्तो द्व्यच्कः' । यशः । मनः । तपः । 'द्व्यच्कः' किम् । चन्द्रमाः ॥

36. Nouns of two syllables formed with the affix अस् are neuters.

Thus यशस् 'glory,' मनस् 'mind,' तपस् 'austerity.'

Why do we say 'of two syllables'? Observe चन्द्रमस् 'the moon,' which is masculine.

३७ । अप्सराः स्त्रियाम् । एता अप्सरसः । प्रायेणायं बहुवचनान्तः ॥

37. The word अप्सरस् is feminine.

Thus एता अप्सरसः । Generally, this word is used in the Plural number only.

३८ । 'त्रान्तः' । पत्रम् । छत्रम् ॥

38. Nouns formed with the affix त्र are neuters. (Un. IV. 159).

Thus पत्रम् 'a leaf;' छत्रम् 'an umbrella.'

३९ । 'यात्रामात्राभस्त्रादंष्ट्रावरत्राः स्त्रियामेव' ॥

39. The following are always feminine:—यात्रा 'journey,' मात्रा 'a measure,' भस्त्रा 'a leathern bag,' दंष्ट्रा 'tusk,' वरत्रा 'a strap.'

४० । 'भृत्रामित्रच्छात्रपुत्रमन्त्रवृत्रमेढ्रोष्ट्राः पुंसि' । अयं भृत्रः । न मित्रममित्रः । 'तस्य मित्राण्यमित्रास्ते' इति माघः । 'स्यातामभित्रौ मित्रे च' इति च । यत्तु 'द्विषोऽमित्रे' (३१११) इति सूत्रे हरदत्तेनोक्तम्–'अमेर्द्विषदित्यौणादिक इत्रच् । अमेरमित्रं मित्रस्य व्यथयेदित्यादौ मध्योदात्तस्तु चिन्त्यः । नञ्समासेऽप्येवम् । परवल्लिङ्गतापि स्यादिति तु तत्र दोषान्तरम्' इति तत्प्रकृतसूत्रापर्यालोचनमूलकम् । स्वरदोषोद्भावनमपि 'नञो जरमरमित्रमृताः' (३८५०) इति षाष्ठसूत्रास्मरणमूलकमिति दिक् ॥

40. The following are masculines:—भृत्र 'a servant,' अमित्र 'an enemy,' छात्र 'a pupil,' पुत्र 'a son,' मन्त्र 'a mantra,' वृत्र 'name of a demon killed by Indra,' मेढ्र 'a ram,' उष्ट्र 'a camel.'

Thus अयं भृत्रः । अमित्रः is equal to न मित्रम् a non-friend *i.e.* an enemy. Thus we find in Mâgha तस्य मित्राण्यमित्रास्ते । So also स्यातामभित्रौ मित्रे च ॥

In commenting on the sûtra द्विषोऽमित्रे (III. 2. 113 S. 3111), Haradatta in his Padamanjari says: 'The word *amitra* is derived from the root *am* with the Unâdi affix इत्रच् under sûtra IV. 174, in the sense of an enemy. The word amitra is not a negative compound of अ+मित्र as it would appear at first sight. Because had it been a Tatpurusha compound of *a* + *mitra*, then by sûtra II. 4. 26,

S. 812, it would have been Neuter, because the word *mitra* is Neuter. If it be said that 'the gender of a word depends upon usage, and though *mitra* be Neuter, *amitra* will be masculine,' then there arises the difficulty as to accent. For then by VI. 2. 2, S. 3736 the अ will retain its accent in the Tatpurusha. But it is intended that the accent should be on मि; *i.e.* the चित् accent. For the Rig Vedins read it with the acute on the middle of amitra, as in the following: अमित्रस्य व्यथया मन्युमिन्द्रः (Rig Veda VI. 25. 2), अमित्रमित्र मर्दय (Rig VIII. 75. 10)'

But these two objections of Haradatta proceed on the assumption that the word amitra is a Tatpurusha compound. But as a matter of fact it is a Bahuvrihi compound and consequently the rule of gender taught in II. 4. 26 does not apply to it. Haradatta overlooked the context in applying this rule. He further forgot sûtra VI. 2. 116, S. 3850 which specifically applies to the accent of amitra, when he raises the objection as to accent.

NOTE:—Did Haradatta really misapply sûtra II. 4. 26 and forget VI. 2. 116; or is not Bhattoji floundering? Why should the word अमित्र be taken as a Bahuvrihi and not a Tatpurusha? The Bahuvrihi *amitra* would mean 'friendless,' and not 'an enemy.'

४१। 'पत्रपात्रपवित्रसूत्रच्छत्राः पुंसि च' ॥

41. The following are masculines (in addition to their being neuters):—

पत्र 'a leaf;' पात्र 'a vessel;' पवित्र 'holy;' सूत्र 'a thread;' छत्र 'a line.

Thus पत्रः or पत्रम् ॥

४२। 'बलकुसुमशुल्बयुद्धपत्तनरणाभिधानानि'। बलं वीर्यम् ॥

42. The synonyms of बल 'courage or strength,' कुसुम 'a flower,' शुल्ब 'a rope, string' पत्तनं 'a town' and रण 'fight' are neuters. Thus बलं वीर्यम् ॥

४३। 'पद्मकमलोत्पलानि पुंसि च'। पद्मादयः शब्दाः कुसुमाभिधायित्वेऽपि द्विलिङ्गाः स्युः। अमरोऽप्याह–'वा पुंसि पद्मं नलिनम्' इति। एवं च 'अर्धर्चादिसूत्रे तु जलजे पद्मं नपुंसकमेव' इति वृत्तिग्रन्थो मतान्तरेण नेयः ॥

43. The words पद्म, कमल, उत्पल 'the lotus flower,' although names of a kind of flower, are masculines also (in addition to their being neuters).

In the Amarakosha, (I. 2. 39) पद्म and नलिन are optionally masculines. In II. 4. 31, Kâsikâ says '*padma* meaning *lotus* is neuter only.' This is however one view of the case.

४४। 'आहवसंग्रामौ पुंसि' ॥

44. The words आहव and संग्राम 'fight' are masculines. By III. 42 these words being synonyms of raṇa would have been Neuters. This makes them masculines.

४५। 'आजिः स्त्रियामेव' ॥

45. The word आजि fight is always feminine. This also by sûtra 42 ant would have been Neuter.

४६। 'फलजातिः'। 'फलजातिवाची शब्दो नपुंसकं स्यात्। आमलकम्। आमम् ॥

46. Names of fruits are neuters.

Thus आमलकम् 'one of the myrobolans,' आम्रम् 'mango.' But the word आमलकी is feminine also. It however does not mean the fruit, but the tree which produces that fruit.

४७ । 'वृक्षजातिः' । स्त्रियामेव क्वचिदेवेदम् । हरीतकी ॥

47. Names of trees are feminines only. This is not a universal rule.

Thus हरीतकी 'one of the myrobolans.

४८ । 'वियज्जगत्सकृच्छकन्पृषच्छकृद्यकृदुदश्वितः' । एते क्लीबाः स्युः ॥

48. The following are neuters :—

वियत् 'the sky,' जगत् 'the universe,' सकृत् 'once,' शकन 'ordure,' पृषत् 'a drop of water,' शकृत् 'ordure,' (Un. IV. 58), यकृत् 'the liver,' उदश्वित् 'whey.'

४९ । 'नवनीतावतानृतामृतनिमित्तवित्तचित्तपित्तव्रतरजतवृत्तपलितानि' ॥

49. The following are neuters :—

नवनीत 'butter,' अवत 'a well,' अनृत 'a lie,' अमृत 'nectar,' निमित्त 'cause,' वित्त 'wealth,' चित्त 'mind,' पित्त 'bile,' व्रत 'fast,' रजत 'silver,' वृत्त 'an event,' पलित 'gray hair.

५० । 'श्राद्धकुलिशदैवपीठकुण्डाङ्गदधिसक्थ्यक्ष्यस्थ्यास्पदाकाशकण्वबीजानि' । एतानि क्लीबे स्युः ॥

50. The following are neuters :—

श्राद्ध 'a funeral rite', कुलिश 'the thunderbolt of Indra,' दैव 'fate,' पीठ 'a seat,' कुण्ड 'a bowl,' (Un. I. 112). अंग 'the body.' दधि 'curdled milk,' सक्थि 'the thigh' (Un. III. 154), अक्षि 'an eye,' अस्थि 'a bone,' आस्पद 'a place,' आकाश 'the sky ;' कण्व 'sin,' and बीज 'the seed.'

५१ । 'दैवं पुंसि च' । दैवम्-दैवः ॥

51. The word दैव 'luck' is also masculine.

Thus दैवम् or दैवः ॥

५२ । 'धान्याज्यसस्यरूप्यपण्यवर्ण्यधृष्यहव्यकव्यकाव्यसत्यापत्यमूल्यशिक्यकुड्यमद्यहर्म्यतूर्यसैन्यानि' । इदं धान्यमित्यादि ॥

52. The following are neuters :—

धान्य 'corn,' आज्य 'clarified butter,' सस्य 'crop,' रूप्य 'silver,' पण्य 'vendible,' वर्ण्य 'saffron,' धृष्य 'conquerable,' हव्यं 'clarified butter,' कव्यं 'anoblation of food to deceased ancestors,' काव्य 'a poem ;' सत्य 'truth ;' अपत्य 'offspring ;' मूल्य 'the price ;' शिक्य 'a loop or swing made of rope ;' कुड्य 'a wall,' मद्य 'wine ;' हर्म्य 'a house ;' तूर्य 'a kind of musical instrument ;' सैन्यं 'an army.'

Thus इदं धान्यम् &c.

५३ । 'द्वन्द्वबर्हदुःखबडिशपिच्छबिम्बकुटुम्बकवचवरशरवृन्दारकाणि' ॥

53. The following are neuters :—

द्वन्द्व 'couple' बर्ह 'a peacock's tail,' दुःख 'sorrow ;' बडिश 'a fish hook,' पिच्छ 'the tail of a peacock,' बिम्ब 'shadow,' कुटुम्ब 'relation,' कवच 'amulet,' वरं 'boon,' शरं 'an arrow,' वृन्दारक 'a deity.'

५४ । 'अक्षमिन्द्रिये' । इन्द्रिये किम् । रथाङ्गादौ मा भूत् ।

54. The word अक्ष when it means one of the special senses is neuter.

Why do we say 'one of the special senses ? It will not be Neuter when it means the *axle* of a chariot, &c.

इति नपुंसकाधिकारः ॥

MASCULINE AND FEMININE GENDERS.

१ । 'स्त्रीपुंसयोः' । अधिकारोऽयम् ॥

1. Masculine and Feminine Genders.

This is an adhikâra sûtra.

२ । 'गोमणियष्टिमुष्टिपाटलिवस्तिशाल्मलित्रुटिमसिमरीचयः' । इयमयं वा गौः ॥

2. The following belong to both masculine and feminine genders :—

गो 'the cow,' मणि 'a gem,' यष्टि 'a stick,' मुष्टि 'the fist;' पाटलि 'the trumpet-flower,' वस्ति 'residing,' शाल्मलि 'name of a tree,' त्रुटि 'cutting' मसि ink,' मरीचि 'pepper.'

Thus इयं or अयं गौः.

३ । 'मन्युमृत्युसीधुकर्कन्धुकिष्कुकण्डुरेणवः' । इयमयं वा मन्युः ॥

3. The following are both masculine and feminines :—

मन्यु 'anger' (Uṇ. III 20), मृत्यु 'death ;' सीधु 'rum,' कर्कन्धु 'the jujube tree' (Uṇ. I. 93) कण्डु 'scratching,' रेणु 'an atom of dust.'

Thus इयं or अयं मन्युः ।

४ । 'गुणवचनमुकारान्तं नपुंसकं च' । त्रिलिङ्गमित्यर्थः । पटु–पटुः–पट्वी ॥

4. Nouns ending in उ denoting quality or qualification are also neuters. That is they belong to all the three genders. Thus पटु, पटुः, पट्वी.

५ । 'अपत्यार्थतद्धिते' । औपगवः–औपगवी ॥

5. Those तद्धित nouns which denote an offspring are both masculine and feminine.

Thus औपगवः or औपगवी ॥

इति स्त्रीपुंसाधिकारः ॥

MASCULINE AND NEUTER GENDERS.

१ । 'पुंनपुंसकयोः' । अधिकारोऽयम् ॥

1. Masculine and Neuter Genders.

This is an adhkâra sûtra.

२ । 'घृतभूतमुस्तक्ष्वेलितैरावतपुस्तकबुस्तलोहिताः' । अयं घृतः । इदं घृतम् ॥

2. The following are both masculines and neuters :—घृत 'butter,' भूत 'any being,' मुस्त 'a kind of grass,' क्ष्वेलित 'play,' ऐरावत 'Indra's elephant,' पुस्तक 'a book,' बुस्त 'the burnt crust of roast meat,' लोहित 'redness.'

Thus अयं घृतः or इदं घृतम्.

३ । 'शृङ्गार्धनिदाघोद्यमशल्यदृढाः' । अयं शृङ्गः । इदं शृङ्गम् ॥

3. The following are both masculines and neuters :—शृङ्ग 'a horn,' अर्ध 'half,' निदाघ 'heat,' उद्यम 'effort,' शल्य 'a spear,' दृढ 'firm.'

Thus अयं शृङ्गः or इदं शृंगम् ।

४ । 'व्रजकुञ्जकुथकूर्चप्रस्थदर्पार्मार्धर्चदर्भपुच्छाः' । अयं व्रजः । इदं व्रजम् ।

4. The following are both masculines and neuters :—व्रज 'a multitude,' कुञ्ज 'a tree,' कुथ 'a carpet,' कूर्च 'a bundle,' प्रस्थ 'a level plain,' दर्प 'pride' अर्म 'a cemetry' (Uṇ. I. 137), अर्धर्च 'half a verse,' दर्भ 'a kind of grass,' and पुच्छ 'tail.'

Thus अयं व्रजः or इदं व्रजम्.

५ । 'कबन्धौषधायुधान्ताः' । स्पष्टम् ॥

5. The following are both masculine and neuter :—कबन्ध 'a headless trunk,' औषध 'medicine,' आयुध 'a weapon.'

६ । 'दण्डमण्डखण्डशवसैन्धवपार्श्वकाशकुशाङ्कुशाकाशकुलिशाः' । एते पुंनपुंसकयोः स्युः । 'कुशो रामसुते दर्भे योक्त्रे द्वीपे कुशं जले' इति विश्वः । शलाकावाची तु स्त्रियाम् । तथा च 'जानपद-' (५००) आदिसूत्रेणायोविकारे ङीषि । कुशी । दारुणि तु टापा 'कुशा वानस्पत्याः स्थ ता मा पात' इति श्रुतिः । 'अतः कृकमि-' (१६०) इति सूत्रे 'कुशाकर्णीषु' इति प्रयोगश्च । व्याससूत्रे च-'हानौ तूपायनशब्दशेषत्वात्कुशाच्छन्दः' इति । तत्र शारीरकभाष्येऽप्येवम् । एवं च श्रुतिसूत्रभाष्याणामेकवाक्यत्वे स्थिते आच्छन्द इत्यादिप्रश्लेषादिपरो भामतीग्रन्थः प्रौढिवादमात्रपर इति विभावनीयं बहुश्रुतैः ॥

6. The following are both masculines and neuters :— दण्ड 'punishment,' मण्ड 'the scum of boiled rice,' खण्ड 'a break,' शव 'the corpse,' सैन्धव 'a kind of rock-salt,' पार्श्व 'the side,' काश 'cough,' अंकुश 'a hook, a goad,' आकाश 'the sky,' कुश 'kuśa grass,' कुलिश 'thunder-bolt.'

These words are both masculines and neuters. Thus we find in the Viśva-kosha—"Kuśa is the name of the son of Râma, it means also *darbha* grass, as well as the rope of kuśa grass for connecting the yoke of a plough with the plough, and an island. Kuśam (neuter) means water' But when it means a ploughshare or a rod (śalâkâ) it is feminine. That being so, when the śalâkâ is made of iron the feminine will be formed by ङीष् as कुशी । This is by sûtra IV. 1. 42, S. 500. But when it means a śalâkâ made of wood, the feminine is formed by टाप् । As कुशा 'a piece of wood.' As we find in the śruti :—कुशा वानस्पत्याः स्थ ता मा पात 'you kuśas are the children of the tree, do you protect me.'

So also in VIII. 3. 46, S. 160, we find the word कुशा used.

So also in the Vyâsa Sûtra we find the word कुशा used. See Vedânta Sûtra III. 3. 26 where the getting rid of good and evil is mentioned; "the obtaining of this good and evil by others has to be added, because the statement about the obtaining is supplementary to the statement about the getting rid of, as in the case of the *kusas*, the metres, the praise and the singing. This (*i.e.* the reason for this) has been stated in the Pûrva Mimânsâ." (According to the commentators, small wooden rods used by the Udgâtris in counting the stotras are called kuśâs. *Thibaut's* Vedânta Sûtras Part II. p. 227).

So also in the commentary on the above sûtra by Śankarâchârya, we find 'कुशानामविशेषेण वनस्पति योनित्वश्रवणं' ॥

Thus we find that the Śruti (kuśa vânaspatyâḥ), the sûtra (VIII. 3. 46, S. 160), the śârîrika Bhâshya (kuśa nâma &c) all unanimously agree in stating that there is such a word as kuśâ ; and it is this word which is used in the Vedânta Sûtra III. 3. 26 (Kuśâ Chhandas &c). The words कुशाच्छन्दः in that sûtra are equal to कुशा plus छन्दः ; and not कुश plus आच्छन्दः । Bhâmati the commentary on the Sârîrika Bhâshya is therefore evidently wrong when it analyses the words कुशाच्छन्दः of the sutra into कुश + आ + छन्दः । So it is a mere bold assertion of the author of Bhâmati, and is not borne out by any authority. Let the learned ponder over it.

७ । 'गृहमेषदेहपट्टपटहाष्टापदाम्बुदककुदाश्च' ॥

7. The following are both masculines and feminines :—गृह 'a house,' मेष 'a ram,' देह 'the body,' पट्ट 'a slab, tablet,' पटह 'a kettle-drum,' अष्टापद (?) अंबुद 'a cloud,' ककुद 'the peak or summit of a mountain.'

इति पुंनपुंसकाधिकारः ॥

COMMON GENDER.

१ । 'अवशिष्टलिङ्गम्' ॥

1. The rest.

This is an adhikâra sûtra.

२ 'अव्ययं कतियुष्मदस्मदः' ॥

2. The avyayas (Indeclinables), कति, युष्मद् and अस्मद् can be used with words in all the three genders.

३ । 'ष्णान्ता संख्या' । शिष्टा परवत् । एकः पुरुषः । एका स्त्री । एकं कुलम् ॥

3. Numerals ending in ष and ण can be used with words in all the three genders.

Thus एकः पुरुषः । एका स्त्री । एकं कुलम् ॥

४ । 'गुणवचनं च' । शुक्लः पटः । शुक्ला पटी । शुक्लं वस्त्रम् ॥

4. So also attributive words.

Thus शुक्लः पटः । शुक्ला पटि । शुक्लं वस्त्रम् ॥

५ । 'कृत्याश्च' ॥

5. The kṛitya derivatives also.

The words formed by kṛitya affixes follow the gender of the words which they qualify. (III. 3. 171: S. 3312).

६ । 'करणाधिकरणयोर्ल्युट्' ॥

6. The words formed by the affix lyuṭ added with the force of instrument or location. (III. 3. 117 S. 3 293).

७ । 'सर्वादीनि सर्वनामानि' । स्पष्टार्थं त्रिसूत्री ॥

7. The Pronominals *sarva* 'et cetera,' (I. 1. 27 S. 213).

इति लिङ्गानुशासनप्रकरणम् ।

इति श्रीभट्टोजिदीक्षितविरचिता वैयाकरणसिद्धान्तकौमुदी समाप्ता ॥

॥ शुभमस्तु ॥

17-5-05.